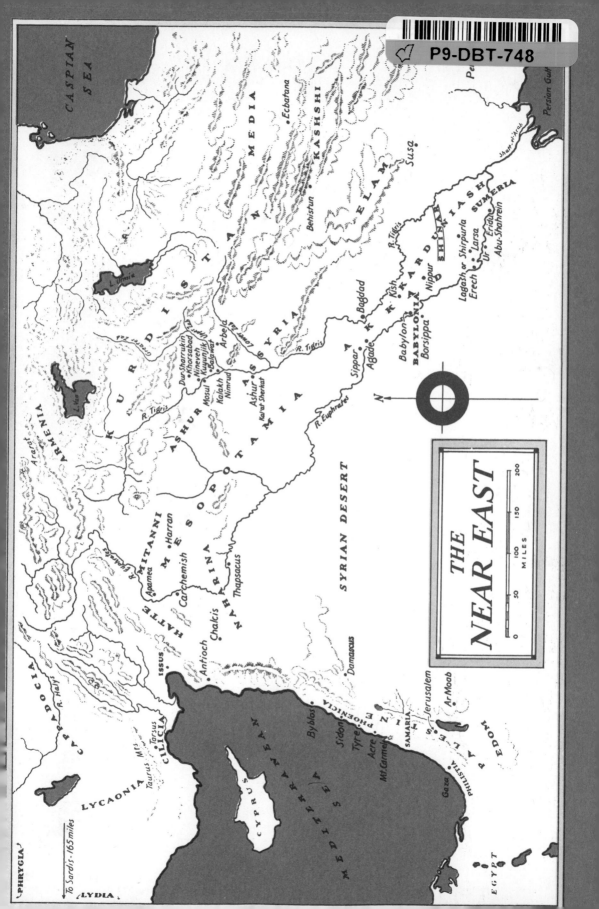

P9-DBT-748

THE
NEAR EAST

MILES
0   50   100   150   200

CASPIAN SEA

PHRYGIA

To Sardis - 165 miles

LYDIA

LYCAONIA

CAPPADOCIA

R. Halys

Taurus Mts.

CILICIA

Issus

Antioch

Chalcis

Apamea

Carchemish

MITANNI

M. Harran

HATTE

NAHARINA

Thapsacus

MESOPOTAMIA

ASHUR

Karat Sherkat

Ashur

Kalakh

Nimrud

Mosul

Kuyunjik

Balawat

Nineveh

Khorsabad

Dur-Sharrukin

Arbela

R. Tigris

Lesser Zab

Greater Zab

ARMENIA

Ararat

L. Van

KURDISTAN

L. Urmia

MEDIA

Ecbatana

Behistun

KASHSHI

ELAM

Susa

Shatt-el-Arab

Persian Gulf

SUMERIA

KARDUNIASH

SHINAR

Lagash or Shirpurla

Erech

Ur

Eridu

Larsa

Abu-Shahrein

Nippur

BABYLONIA

Borsippa

Babylon

Agade

Kish

Sippar

R. Tigris

R. Tigris

R. Euphrates

R. Euphrates

SYRIA

SYRIAN DESERT

Damascus

Byblos

Sidon

Tyre

Acre

Mt. Carmel

PHOENICIA

SAMARIA

Jerusalem

PALESTINE

Ar-Moab

EDOM

Gaza

PHILISTIA

MEDITERRANEAN

CYPRUS

EGYPT

N

Barbara Saunier

BY WILL DURANT

The Story of Philosophy
Transition
The Pleasures of Philosophy
Adventures in Genius

BY WILL AND ARIEL DURANT
THE STORY OF CIVILIZATION:

I. *Our Oriental Heritage*
II. *The Life of Greece*
III. *Caesar and Christ*
IV. *The Age of Faith*
V. *The Renaissance*
VI. *The Reformation*
VII. *The Age of Reason Begins*
VIII. *The Age of Louis XIV*
IX. *The Age of Voltaire*
X. *Rousseau and Revolution*
XI. *The Age of Napoleon*

The Lessons of History
Interpretations of Life

OUR ORIENTAL HERITAGE

*Being a history of civilization in Egypt and the Near East
to the death of Alexander, and in India, China and Japan
from the beginning to our own day; with an introduction
on the nature and foundations of civilization*

By Will Durant

SIMON AND SCHUSTER

NEW YORK : 1954

Copyright 1935 by Will Durant
Copyright renewed © 1963 by Will Durant
ALL RIGHTS RESERVED
including the right of reproduction
in whole or in part in any form
Published by Simon and Schuster
A Division of Gulf & Western Corporation
Simon & Schuster Building
Rockefeller Center
1230 Avenue of the Americas
New York, New York 10020

ISBN 0-671-54800-X
Library of Congress Catalog Card Number 35-10016

MANUFACTURED IN THE UNITED STATES OF AMERICA
BY THE HADDON CRAFTSMEN, INC., SCRANTON, PA.

30   31   32   33   34   35

TO ARIEL

Preface

I HAVE tried in this book to accomplish the first part of a pleasant assignment which I rashly laid upon myself some twenty years ago: to write a history of civilization. I wish to tell as much as I can, in as little space as I can, of the contributions that genius and labor have made to the cultural heritage of mankind—to chronicle and contemplate, in their causes, character and effects, the advances of invention, the varieties of economic organization, the experiments in government, the aspirations of religion, the mutations of morals and manners, the masterpieces of literature, the development of science, the wisdom of philosophy, and the achievements of art. I do not need to be told how absurd this enterprise is, nor how immodest is its very conception; for many years of effort have brought it to but a fifth of its completion, and have made it clear that no one mind, and no single lifetime, can adequately compass this task. Nevertheless I have dreamed that despite the many errors inevitable in this undertaking, it may be of some use to those upon whom the passion for philosophy has laid the compulsion to try to see things whole, to pursue perspective, unity and understanding through history in time, as well as to seek them through science in space.

I have long felt that our usual method of writing history in separate longitudinal sections—economic history, political history, religious history, the history of philosophy, the history of literature, the history of science, the history of music, the history of art—does injustice to the unity of human life; that history should be written collaterally as well as lineally, synthetically as well as analytically; and that the ideal historiography would seek to portray in each period the total complex of a nation's culture, institutions, adventures and ways. But the accumulation of knowledge has divided history, like science, into a thousand isolated specialties; and prudent scholars have refrained from attempting any view of the whole—whether of the material universe, or of the living past of our race. For the probability of error increases with the scope of the undertaking, and any man who sells his soul to synthesis will be a tragic target for a myriad merry darts of specialist critique. "Consider," said Ptah-hotep five thousand years ago, "how thou mayest be opposed by an expert in council. It is

vii

foolish to speak on every kind of work."* A history of civilization shares the presumptuousness of every philosophical enterprise: it offers the ridiculous spectacle of a fragment expounding the whole. Like philosophy, such a venture has no rational excuse, and is at best but a brave stupidity; but let us hope that, like philosophy, it will always lure some rash spirits into its fatal depths.

The plan of the series is to narrate the history of civilization in five independent parts:

I. *Our Oriental Heritage:* a history of civilization in Egypt and the Near East to the death of Alexander, and in India, China and Japan to the present day; with an introduction on the nature and elements of civilization.

II. *Our Classical Heritage:* a history of civilization in Greece and Rome, and of civilization in the Near East under Greek and Roman domination.

III. *Our Medieval Heritage:* Catholic and feudal Europe, Byzantine civilization, Mohammedan and Judaic culture in Asia, Africa and Spain, and the Italian Renaissance.

IV. *Our European Heritage:* the cultural history of the European states from the Protestant Reformation to the French Revolution.

V. *Our Modern Heritage:* the history of European invention and statesmanship, science and philosophy, religion and morals, literature and art from the accession of Napoleon to our own times.

Our story begins with the Orient, not merely because Asia was the scene of the oldest civilizations known to us, but because those civilizations formed the background and basis of that Greek and Roman culture which Sir Henry Maine mistakenly supposed to be the whole source of the modern mind. We shall be surprised to learn how much of our most indispensable inventions, our economic and political organization, our science and our literature, our philosophy and our religion, goes back to Egypt and the Orient.† At this historic moment—when the ascendancy of Europe is so rapidly coming to an end, when Asia is swelling with resurrected life, and the theme of the twentieth century seems destined to be an all-embrac-

* Cf. p. 193 below.
† The contributions of the Orient to our cultural heritage are summed up in the concluding pages of this volume.

ing conflict between the East and the West—the provincialism of our traditional histories, which began with Greece and summed up Asia in a line, has become no merely academic error, but a possibly fatal failure of perspective and intelligence. The future faces into the Pacific, and understanding must·follow it there.

But how shall an Occidental mind ever understand the Orient? Eight years of study and travel have only made this, too, more evident—that not even a lifetime of devoted scholarship would suffice to initiate a Western student into the subtle character and secret lore of the East. Every chapter, every paragraph in this book will offend or amuse some patriotic or esoteric soul: the orthodox Jew will need all his ancient patience to forgive the pages on Yahveh, the metaphysical Hindu will mourn this superficial scratching of Indian philosophy; and the Chinese or Japanese sage will smile indulgently at these brief and inadequate selections from the wealth of Far Eastern literature and thought. Some of the errors in the chapter on Judea have been corrected by Professor Harry Wolfson of Harvard; Dr. Ananda Coomaraswamy of the Boston Institute of Fine Arts has given the section on India a most painstaking revision, but must not be held responsible for the conclusions I have reached or the errors that remain; Professor H. H. Gowen, the learned Orientalist of the University of Washington, and Upton Close, whose knowledge of the Orient seems inexhaustible, have checked the more flagrant mistakes in the chapters on China and Japan; and Mr. George Sokolsky has given to the pages on contemporary affairs in the Far East the benefit of his first-hand information. Should the public be indulgent enough to call for a second edition of this book, the opportunity will be taken to incorporate whatever further corrections may be suggested by critics, specialists and readers. Meanwhile a weary author may sympathize with Tai T'ung, who in the thirteenth century issued his *History of Chinese Writing* with these words: "Were I to await perfection, my book would never be finished."*

Since these ear-minded times are not propitious for the popularity of expensive books on remote subjects of interest only to citizens of the world, it may be that the continuation of this series will be delayed by the prosaic necessities of economic life. But if the reception of this adventure in synthesis makes possible an uninterrupted devotion to the undertaking, Part Two should be ready by the fall of 1940, and its successors should appear,

---

* Carter, T. F., *The Invention of Printing in China, and Its Spread Westward;* New York, 1925, p. xviii.

by the grace of health, at five-year intervals thereafter. Nothing would make me happier than to be freed, for this work, from every other literary enterprise. I shall proceed as rapidly as time and circumstance will permit, hoping that a few of my contemporaries will care to grow old with me while learning, and that these volumes may help some of our children to understand and enjoy the infinite riches of their inheritance.

WILL DURANT.

Great Neck, N. Y., March, 1935

A NOTE ON THE USE OF THIS BOOK

To bring the volume into smaller compass certain technical passages, which may prove difficult for the general reader, have been printed (like this paragraph) in reduced type. Despite much compression the book is still too long, and the font of reduced type has not sufficed to indicate all the dull passages. I trust that the reader will not attempt more than a chapter at a time.

Indented passages in reduced type are quotations. The raised numbers refer to the Notes at the end of the volume; to facilitate reference to these Notes the number of the chapter is given at the head of each page. An occasional hiatus in the numbering of the Notes was caused by abbreviating the printed text. The books referred to in the Notes are more fully described in the Bibliography, whose starred titles may serve as a guide to further reading. The Glossary defines all foreign words used in the text. The Index pronounces foreign names, and gives biographical dates.

It should be added that this book has no relation to, and makes no use of, a biographical *Story of Civilization* prepared for newspaper publication in 1927-28.

ACKNOWLEDGMENTS

I am grateful to the following authors and publishers for permission to quote from their books:

Leonard, W. E., *Gilgamesh;* the Viking Press.
Giles, H. A., *A History of Chinese Literature;* D. Appleton-Century Co.
Underwood, Edna Worthley, *Tu Fu;* the Mosher Press.
Waley, Arthur, 170 *Chinese Poems;* Alfred A. Knopf.
Breasted, Jas. H., *The Development of Religion and Thought in Ancient Egypt;* Scribner's.
Obata, Shigeyoshi, *Works of Li Po;* E. P. Dutton.
Tietjens, Eunice, *Poetry of the Orient;* Alfred A. Knopf.
Van Doren, Mark, *Anthology of World Poetry;* the Literary Guild.
"Upton Close," unpublished translations of Chinese poems.

Contents

INTRODUCTION

THE ESTABLISHMENT
OF CIVILIZATION

Chapter I: THE CONDITIONS OF CIVILIZATION.. 1

Definition — Geological conditions — Geographical — Economic — Racial — Psychological — Causes of the decay of civilizations

Chapter II: THE ECONOMIC ELEMENTS OF CIVILIZATION.................. 5

I. FROM HUNTING TO TILLAGE, 5
Primitive improvidence—Beginnings of provision—Hunting and fishing—Herding—The domestication of animals—Agriculture—Food—Cooking—Cannibalism

II. THE FOUNDATIONS OF INDUSTRY, 11
Fire—Primitive Tools—Weaving and pottery—Building and transport—Trade and finance

III. ECONOMIC ORGANIZATION, 16
Primitive communism—Causes of its disappearance—Origins of pri⸱⸱ property—Slavery—Classes

Chapter III: THE POLITICAL ELEMENTS OF CIVILIZATION................ 21

I. THE ORIGINS OF GOVERNMENT, 21
The unsocial instinct—Primitive anarchism—The clan and the tribe—The king—War

II. THE STATE, 23
As the organization of force—The village community—The psychological aides of the state

III. LAW, 25
Law-lessness—Law and custom—Revenge—Fines—Courts—Ordeal—The duel—Punishment—Primitive freedom

IV. THE FAMILY, 29
Its function in civilizatⁱ⸱⸱—The clan vs. the family—Growth of parental care—Unimportance of the father—Separation of the sexes—Mother-right—Status of woman—Her occupations—Her economic achievements—The patriarchate—The subjection of woman

xi

Chapter IV: THE MORAL ELEMENTS OF CIVILIZATION.................... 36

I. MARRIAGE, 36
The meaning of marriage—Its biological origins—Sexual communism—Trial marriage
—Group marriage—Individual marriage—Polygamy—Its eugenic value—Exogamy—
Marriage by service—By capture—By purchase—Primitive love—The economic func-
tion of marriage

II. SEXUAL MORALITY, 44
Premarital relations — Prostitution — Chastity — Virginity — The double standard —
Modesty — The relativity of morals — The biological rôle of modesty — Adultery —
Divorce—Abortion—Infanticide—Childhood—The individual

III. SOCIAL MORALITY, 51
The nature of virtue and vice—Greed—Dishonesty—Violence—Homicide—Suicide—
The socialization of the individual—Altruism—Hospitality—Manners—Tribal limits of
morality—Primitive vs. modern morals—Religion and morals

IV. RELIGION, 56
Primitive atheists

1. THE SOURCES OF RELIGION
Fear—Wonder—Dreams—The soul—Animism

2. THE OBJECTS OF RELIGION
The sun — The stars — The earth — Sex — Animals — Totemism — The transition to
human gods—Ghost-worship—Ancestor-worship

3. THE METHODS OF RELIGION
Magic — Vegetation rites — Festivals of license — Myths of the resurrected god —
Magic and superstition—Magic and science—Priests

4. THE MORAL FUNCTION OF RELIGION
Religion and government—Tabu—Sexual tabus—The lag of religion—Secularization

Chapter V: THE MENTAL ELEMENTS OF CIVILIZATION.................... 72

I. LETTERS, 72
Language—Its animal background—Its human origins—Its development—Its results—
Education—Initiation—Writing—Poetry

II. SCIENCE, 78
Origins—Mathematics—Astronomy—Medicine—Surgery

III. ART, 82
The meaning of beauty—Of art—The primitive sense of beauty—The painting of the
body — Cosmetics — Tattooing — Scarification — Clothing — Ornaments — Pottery —
Painting — Sculpture — Architecture — The dance — Music — Summary of the
primitive preparation for civilization

Chronological Chart: Types and Cultures of Prehistoric Man........ 90

Chapter VI: THE PREHISTORIC BEGINNINGS OF CIVILIZATION.......... 90

I. PALEOLITHIC CULTURE, 90
The purpose of prehistory—The romances of archeology

1. MEN OF THE OLD STONE AGE
The geological background—Paleolithic types

2. ARTS OF THE OLD STONE AGE
Tools—Fire—Painting—Sculpture

II. NEOLITHIC CULTURE, 98
The Kitchen-Middens—The Lake-Dwellers—The coming of agriculture—The taming of animals—Technology—Neolithic weaving—pottery—building—transport—religion—science—Summary of the prehistoric preparation for civilization

III. THE TRANSITION TO HISTORY, 102

1. THE COMING OF METALS
Copper—Bronze—Iron

2. WRITING
Its possible ceramic origins — The "Mediterranean Signary" — Hieroglyphics — Alphabets

3. LOST CIVILIZATIONS
Polynesia—"Atlantis"

4. CRADLES OF CIVILIZATION
Central Asia—Anau—Lines of Dispersion

BOOK ONE

THE NEAR EAST

Chronological Table of Near Eastern History............................ 113

Chapter VII: SUMERIA.. 116
Orientation—Contributions of the Near East to Western civilization

I. ELAM, 117
The culture of Susa—The potter's wheel—The wagon-wheel

II. THE SUMERIANS, 118

1. THE HISTORICAL BACKGROUND
The exhuming of Sumeria—Geography—Race—Appearance—The Sumerian Flood—The kings—An ancient reformer—Sargon of Akkad—The Golden Age of Ur

2. ECONOMIC LIFE
The soil—Industry—Trade—Classes—Science

3. GOVERNMENT
The kings—Ways of war—The feudal barons—Law

4. RELIGION AND MORALITY
The Sumerian Pantheon—The food of the gods—Mythology—Education—A Sumerian prayer—Temple prostitutes—The rights of woman—Sumerian cosmetics

CONTENTS

5. LETTERS AND ARTS
   Writing – Literature – Temples and palaces – Statuary – Ceramics – Jewelry–
   Summary of Sumerian civilization

III. PASSAGE TO EGYPT, 134
   Sumerian influence in Mesopotamia – Ancient Arabia – Mesopotamian influence in
   Egypt

Chapter VIII: EGYPT.. 137

I. THE GIFT OF THE NILE, 137
   1. IN THE DELTA
      Alexandria–The Nile–The Pyramids–The Sphinx
   2. UPSTREAM
      Memphis–The masterpiece of Queen Hatshepsut–The "Colossi of Memnon"–
      Luxor and Karnak–The grandeur of Egyptian civilization

II. THE MASTER BUILDERS, 144
   1. THE DISCOVERY OF EGYPT
      Champollion and the Rosetta Stone
   2. PREHISTORIC EGYPT
      Paleolithic–Neolithic–The Badarians–Predynastic–Race
   3. THE OLD KINGDOM
      The "nomes"–The first historic individual–"Cheops"–"Chephren"–The purpose
      of the Pyramids–Art of the tombs–Mummification
   4. THE MIDDLE KINGDOM
      The Feudal Age–The Twelfth Dynasty–The Hyksos Domination
   5. THE EMPIRE
      The great queen–Thutmose III–The zenith of Egypt

III. THE CIVILIZATION OF EGYPT, 156
   1. AGRICULTURE
   2. INDUSTRY
      Miners – Manufactures – Workers – Engineers – Transport – Postal service –
      Commerce and finance – Scribes
   3. GOVERNMENT
      The bureaucrats–Law–The vizier–The pharaoh
   4. MORALS
      Royal incest–The harem–Marriage–The position of woman–The matriarchate in
      Egypt–Sexual morality
   5. MANNERS
      Character–Games–Appearance–Cosmetics–Costume–Jewelry
   6. LETTERS
      Education–Schools of government–Paper and ink–Stages in the development of
      writing–Forms of Egyptian writing
   7. LITERATURE
      Texts and libraries–The Egyptian Sinbad–The Story of Sinuhe–Fiction–An
      amorous fragment–Love poems–History–A literary revolution

8. SCIENCE
Origins of Egyptian science—Mathematics—Astronomy and the calendar—Anatomy and physiology—Medicine, surgery and hygiene

9. ART
Architecture—Old Kingdom, Middle Kingdom, Empire and Saïte sculpture—Bas-relief—Painting—Minor arts—Music—The artists

10. PHILOSOPHY
The *Instructions of Ptah-hotep*—The *Admonitions of Ipuwer*—The *Dialogue of a Misanthrope*—The Egyptian Ecclesiastes

11. RELIGION
Sky gods—The sun god—Plant gods—Animal gods—Sex gods—Human gods—Osiris —Isis and Horus—Minor deities—The priests—Immortality—The *Book of the Dead*— The "Negative Confession"—Magic—Corruption

IV. THE HERETIC KING, 205
The character of Ikhnaton—The new religion—A hymn to the sun—Monotheism—The new dogma—The new art—Reaction—Nofretete—Break-up of the Empire—Death of Ikhnaton

V. DECLINE AND FALL, 213
Tutenkhamon—The labors of Rameses II—The wealth of the clergy—The poverty of the people—The conquest of Egypt—Summary of Egyptian contributions to civilization

Chapter IX: BABYLONIA.. 218

I. FROM HAMMURABI TO NEBUCHADREZZAR, 218
Babylonian contributions to modern civilization—The Land between the Rivers— Hammurabi—His capital—The Kassite Domination—The Amarna letters—The Assyrian Conquest—Nebuchadrezzar—Babylon in the days of its glory

II. THE TOILERS, 226
Hunting — Tillage — Food — Industry — Transport — The perils of commerce — Money-lenders—Slaves

III. THE LAW, 230
The Code of Hammurabi—The powers of the king—Trial by ordeal—*Lex Talionis*— Forms of punishment—Codes of wages and prices—State restoration of stolen goods

IV. THE GODS OF BABYLON, 232
Religion and the state—The functions and powers of the clergy—The lesser gods— Marduk—Ishtar—The Babylonian stories of the Creation and the Flood—The love of Ishtar and Tammuz—The descent of Ishtar into Hell—The death and resurrection of Tammuz—Ritual and prayer—Penitential psalms—Sin—Magic—Superstition

V. THE MORALS OF BABYLON, 244
Religion divorced from morals—Sacred prostitution—Free love—Marriage—Adultery —Divorce—The position of woman—The relaxation of morals

VI. LETTERS AND LITERATURE, 248
Cuneiform—Its decipherment—Language—Literature—The epic of Gilgamesh

BOOK TWO

INDIA AND HER NEIGHBORS

Chronological Table of Indian History..................................... 389

Chapter XIV: THE FOUNDATIONS OF INDIA.................................. 391

    I. SCENE OF THE DRAMA, 391
        The rediscovery of India—A glance at the map—Climatic influences

    II. THE OLDEST CIVILIZATION?, 394
        Prehistoric India—Mohenjo-daro—Its antiquity

    III. THE INDO-ARYANS, 396
        The natives—The invaders—The village community—Caste—Warriors—Priests—Merchants—Workers—Outcastes

    IV. INDO-ARYAN SOCIETY, 399
        Herders—Tillers of the soil—Craftsmen—Traders—Coinage and credit—Morals—Marriage—Woman

    V. THE RELIGION OF THE *VEDAS*, 402
        Pre-Vedic religion—Vedic gods—Moral gods—The Vedic story of Creation—Immortality—The horse sacrifice

    VI. THE *VEDAS* AS LITERATURE, 405
        Sanskrit and English — Writing — The four *Vedas* — The *Rig-veda* — A Hymn of Creation

    VII. THE PHILOSOPHY OF THE *UPANISHADS*, 410
        The authors—Their theme—Intellect *vs.* intuition—Atman—Brahman—Their identity—A description of God—Salvation—Influence of the *Upanishads*—Emerson on Brahma

Chapter XV: BUDDHA.. 416

    I. THE HERETICS, 416
        Sceptics—Nihilists—Sophists—Atheists—Materialists—Religions without a god

    II. MAHAVIRA AND THE JAINS, 419
        The Great Hero—The Jain creed—Atheistic polytheism—Asceticism—Salvation by suicide—Later history of the Jains

    III. THE LEGEND OF BUDDHA, 422
        The background of Buddhism—The miraculous birth—Youth—The sorrows of life—Flight—Ascetic years—Enlightenment—A vision of *Nirvana*

    IV. THE TEACHING OF BUDDHA, 428
        Portrait of the Master—His methods—The Four Noble Truths—The Eightfold Way—The Five Moral Rules—Buddha and Christ—Buddha's agnosticism and anti-clericalism—His Atheism—His soul-less psychology—The meaning of *Nirvana*

    V. THE LAST DAYS OF BUDDHA, 436
        His miracles—He visits his father's house—The Buddhist monks—Death

Chapter XVI: FROM ALEXANDER TO AURANGZEB............................. 440

I. CHANDRAGUPTA, 440
Alexander in India — Chandragupta the liberator — The people — The university of Taxila—The royal palace—A day in the life of a king—An older Machiavelli—Administration—Law—Public health—Transport and roads—Municipal government

II. THE PHILOSOPHER-KING, 446
Ashoka—The Edict of Tolerance—Ashoka's missionaries—His failure—His success

III. THE GOLDEN AGE OF INDIA, 450
An epoch of invasions—The Kushan kings—The Gupta Empire—The travels of Fa-Hien—The revival of letters—The Huns in India—Harsha the generous—The travels of Yuan Chwang

IV. ANNALS OF RAJPUTANA, 454
The Samurai of India—The age of chivalry—The fall of Chitor

V. THE ZENITH OF THE SOUTH, 456
The kingdoms of the Deccan—Vijayanagar—Krishna Raya—A medieval metropolis—Laws—Arts—Religion—Tragedy

VI. THE MOSLEM CONQUEST, 459
The weakening of India—Mahmud of Ghazni—The Sultanate of Delhi—Its cultural asides—Its brutal policy—The lesson of Indian history

VII. AKBAR THE GREAT, 463
Tamerlane—Babur—Humayun—Akbar—His government—His character—His patronage of the arts—His passion for philosophy—His friendship for Hinduism and Christianity—His new religion—The last days of Akbar

VIII. THE DECLINE OF THE MOGULS, 472
The children of great men — Jehangir — Shah Jehan — His magnificence — His fall — Aurangzeb—His fanaticism—His death—The coming of the British

Chapter XVII: THE LIFE OF THE PEOPLE.. 477

I. THE MAKERS OF WEALTH, 477
The jungle background — Agriculture — Mining — Handicrafts — Commerce — Money — Taxes — Famines — Poverty and wealth

II. THE ORGANIZATION OF SOCIETY, 482
The monarchy—Law—The Code of "Manu"—Development of the caste system—Rise of the Brahmans—Their privileges and powers—Their obligations—In defense of caste

III. MORALS AND MARRIAGE, 488
Dharma — Children — Child marriage — The art of love — Prostitution — Romantic love — Marriage — The family — Woman — Her intellectual life — Her rights — *Purdah* — Suttee-The Widow

IV. MANNERS, CUSTOMS AND CHARACTER, 496
Sexual modesty—Hygiene—Dress—Appearance—The gentle art among the Hindus—Faults and virtues—Games—Festivals—Death

xix

CONTENTS

Chapter XVIII: THE PARADISE OF THE GODS...................................... 503

I. THE LATER HISTORY OF BUDDHISM, 503
The Zenith of Buddhism—The Two Vehicles—*Mahayana*—Buddhism, Stoicism and Christianity—The decay of Buddhism—Its migrations: Ceylon, Burma, Turkestan, Tibet, Cambodia, China, Japan

II. THE NEW DIVINITIES, 507
Hinduism—Brahma, Vishnu, Shiva—Krishna—Kali—Animal gods—The sacred cow—Polytheism and monotheism

III. BELIEFS, 511
The *Puranas*—The reincarnations of the universe—The migrations of the soul—*Karma*—Its philosophical aspects—Life as evil—Release

IV. CURIOSITIES OF RELIGION, 517
Superstitions — Astrology — Phallic worship — Ritual — Sacrifice — Purification — The sacred waters

V. SAINTS AND SCEPTICS, 522
Methods of sanctity—Heretics—Toleration—General view of Hindu religion

Chapter XIX: THE LIFE OF THE MIND.. 526

I. HINDU SCIENCE, 526
Its religious origins — Astronomers — Mathematicians — The "Arabic" numerals — The decimal system — Algebra — Geometry — Physics — Chemistry — Physiology — Vedic medicine — Physicians — Surgeons — Anesthetics — Vaccination — Hypnotism

II. THE SIX SYSTEMS OF BRAHMANICAL PHILOSOPHY, 533
The antiquity of Indian philosophy—Its prominent rôle—Its scholars—Forms—Conception of orthodoxy—The assumptions of Hindu philosophy

1. THE *Nyaya* SYSTEM

2. THE *Vaisheshika* SYSTEM

3. THE *Sankhya* SYSTEM
Its high repute—Metaphysics—Evolution—Atheism—Idealism—Spirit—Body, mind and soul—The goal of philosophy—Influence of the *Sankhya*

4. THE *Yoga* SYSTEM
The Holy Men—The antiquity of *Yoga*—Its meaning—The eight stages of discipline—The aim of *Yoga*—The miracles of the *Yogi*—The sincerity of *Yoga*

5. THE *Purva Mimansa*

6. THE *Vedanta* SYSTEM
Origin — Shankara — Logic — Epistemology — *Maya* — Psychology — Theology — God — Ethics — Difficulties of the system — Death of Shankara

III. THE CONCLUSIONS OF HINDU PHILOSOPHY, 552
Decadence—Summary—Criticism—Influence

CONTENTS

Chapter XX: THE LITERATURE OF INDIA... 555

    I. THE LANGUAGES OF INDIA, 555
      Sanskrit—The vernaculars—Grammar

    II. EDUCATION, 556
      Schools—Methods—Universities—Moslem education—An emperor on education

    III. THE EPICS, 561
      The *Mahabharata*—Its story—Its form—The *Bhagavad-Gita*—The metaphysics of war
      —The price of freedom—The *Ramayana*—A forest idyl—The rape of Sita—The Hindu
      epics and the Greek

    IV. DRAMA, 571
      Origins—*The Clay Cart*—Characteristics of Hindu drama—Kalidasa—The story of
      Shakuntala—Estimate of Indian drama

    V. PROSE AND POETRY, 577
      Their unity in India—Fables—History—Tales—Minor poets—Rise of the vernacular
      literature—Chandi Das—Tulsi Das—Poets of the south—Kabir

Chapter XXI: INDIAN ART... 584

    I. THE MINOR ARTS, 584
      The great age of Indian art—Its uniqueness—Its association with industry—Pottery—
      Metal—Wood—Ivory—Jewelry—Textiles

    II. MUSIC, 586
      A concert in India—Music and the dance—Musicians—Scale and forms—Themes—
      Music and philosophy

    III. PAINTING, 589
      Prehistoric—The frescoes of Ajanta—Rajput miniatures—The Mogul school—The
      painters—The theorists

    IV. SCULPTURE, 593
      Primitive—Buddhist—Gandhara—Gupta—"Colonial"—Estimate

    V. ARCHITECTURE, 596
      1. HINDU ARCHITECTURE
        Before Ashoka—Ashokan—Buddhist—Jain—The masterpieces of the north—Their
        destruction—The southern style—Monolithic temples—Structural temples
      2. "COLONIAL" ARCHITECTURE
        Ceylon — Java — Cambodia — The Khmers — Their religion — Angkor — Fall of
        the Khmers — Siam — Burma
      3. MOSLEM ARCHITECTURE IN INDIA
        The Afghan style—The Mogul style—Delhi—Agra—The Taj Mahal
      4. INDIAN ARCHITECTURE AND CIVILIZATION
        Decay of Indian art—Hindu and Moslem architecture compared—General view of
        Indian civilization

Chapter XXII: A CHRISTIAN EPILOGUE... 613

  I. THE JOLLY BUCCANEERS, 613
The arrival of the Europeans—The British Conquest—The Sepoy Mutiny—Advantages and disadvantages of British rule

  II. LATTER-DAY SAINTS, 615
Christianity in India — The *Brahma-Somaj* — Mohammedanism — Ramakrishna — Vivekananda

  III. TAGORE, 618
Science and art—A family of geniuses—Youth of Rabindranath—His poetry—His politics—His school

  IV. EAST IS WEST, 622
Changing India—Economic changes—Social—The decaying caste system—Castes and guilds—Untouchables—The emergence of woman

  V. THE NATIONALIST MOVEMENT, 625
The westernized students — The secularization of heaven — The Indian National Congress

  VI. MAHATMA GANDHI, 626
Portrait of a saint—The ascetic—The Christian—The education of Gandhi—In Africa—The Revolt of 1921—"I am the man"—Prison years—*Young India*—The revolution of the spinning-wheel—The achievements of Gandhi

  VII. FAREWELL TO INDIA, 633
The revivification of India—The gifts of India

BOOK THREE

THE FAR EAST

A. CHINA

Chronology of Chinese Civilization.. 636

Chapter XXIII: THE AGE OF THE PHILOSOPHERS............................. 639

  I. THE BEGINNINGS, 639

    1. ESTIMATES OF THE CHINESE

    2. THE MIDDLE FLOWERY KINGDOM
Geography—Race—Prehistory

    3. THE UNKNOWN CENTURIES
The Creation according to China—The coming of culture—Wine and chopsticks—The virtuous emperors—A royal atheist

    4. THE FIRST CHINESE CIVILIZATION
The Feudal Age in China—An able minister—The struggle between custom and law—Culture and anarchy—Love lyrics from the *Book of Odes*

    5. THE PRE-CONFUCIAN PHILOSOPHERS
The *Book of Changes*—The *yang* and the *yin*—The Chinese Enlightenment—Teng Shih, the Socrates of China

CONTENTS

6. THE OLD MASTER

Lao-tze—The *Tao*—On intellectuals in government—The foolishness of laws—A Rousseauian Utopia and a Christian ethic—Portrait of a wise man—The meeting of Lao-tze and Confucius

II. CONFUCIUS, 658

1. THE SAGE IN SEARCH OF A STATE

Birth and youth—Marriage and divorce—Pupils and methods—Appearance and character—The lady and the tiger—A definition of good government—Confucius in office—Wander-years—The consolations of old age

2. THE NINE CLASSICS

3. THE AGNOSTICISM OF CONFUCIUS

A fragment of logic—The philosopher and the urchins—A formula of wisdom

4. THE WAY OF THE HIGHER MAN

Another portrait of the sage—Elements of character—The Golden Rule

5. CONFUCIAN POLITICS

Popular sovereignty—Government by example—The decentralization of wealth—Music and manners—Socialism and revolution

6. THE INFLUENCE OF CONFUCIUS

The Confucian scholars—Their victory over the Legalists—Defects of Confucianism—The contemporaneity of Confucius

III. SOCIALISTS AND ANARCHISTS, 677

1. MO TI, ALTRUIST

2. YANG CHU, EGOIST

3. MENCIUS, MENTOR OF PRINCES

A model mother—A philosopher among kings—Are men by nature good?—Single tax—Mencius and the communists—The profit-motive—The right of revolution

4. HSUN-TZE, REALIST

The evil nature of man—The necessity of law

5. CHUANG-TZE, IDEALIST

The Return to Nature—Governmentless society—The Way of Nature—The limits of the intellect—The evolution of man—The Button-Moulder—The influence of Chinese philosophy in Europe

Chapter XXIV: THE AGE OF THE POETS.. 694

I. CHINA'S BISMARCK, 694

The Period of Contending States—The suicide of Ch'u P'ing—Shih Huang-ti unifies China—The Great Wall—The "Burning of the Books"—The failure of Shih Huang-ti

II. EXPERIMENTS IN SOCIALISM, 698

Chaos and poverty—The Han Dynasty—The reforms of Wu Ti—The income tax—The planned economy of Wang Mang—Its overthrow—The Tatar invasion

III. THE GLORY OF T'ANG, 701

The new dynasty—T'ai Tsung's method of reducing crime—An age of prosperity—The "Brilliant Emperor"—The romance of Yang Kwei-fei—The rebellion of An Lu-shan

IV. THE BANISHED ANGEL, 705
An anecdote of Li Po—His youth, prowess and loves—On the imperial barge—The gospel of the grape—War—The wanderings of Li Po—In prison—"Deathless Poetry"

V. SOME QUALITIES OF CHINESE POETRY, 711
"Free verse"—"Imagism"—"Every poem a picture and every picture a poem"—Sentimentality—Perfection of form

VI. TU FU, 713
T'ao Ch'ien—Po Chü-i—Poems for malaria—Tu Fu and Li Po—A vision of war—Prosperous days—Destitution—Death

VII. PROSE, 717
The abundance of Chinese literature—Romances—History—Szuma Ch'ien—Essays—Han Yü on the bone of Buddha

VIII. THE STAGE, 721
Its low repute in China—Origins—The play—The audience—The actors—Music

Chapter XXV: THE AGE OF THE ARTISTS... 724
I. THE SUNG RENAISSANCE, 724
    1. THE SOCIALISM OF WANG AN-SHIH
    The Sung Dynasty—A radical premier—His cure for unemployment—The regulation of industry—Codes of wages and prices—The nationalization of commerce—State insurance against unemployment, poverty and old age—Examinations for public office—The defeat of Wang An-shih
    2. THE REVIVAL OF LEARNING
    The growth of scholarship—Paper and ink in China—Steps in the invention of printing—The oldest book—Paper money—Movable type—Anthologies, dictionaries, encyclopedias.
    3. THE REBIRTH OF PHILOSOPHY
    Chu Hsi—Wang Yang-ming—Beyond good and evil

II. BRONZES, LACQUER AND JADE, 735
The rôle of art in China—Textiles—Furniture—Jewelry—Fans—The making of lacquer—The cutting of jade—Some masterpieces in bronze—Chinese sculpture

III. PAGODAS AND PALACES, 740
Chinese architecture—The Porcelain Tower of Nanking—The Jade Pagoda of Peking — The Temple of Confucius — The Temple and Altar of Heaven — The palaces of Kublai Khan—A Chinese home—The interior—Color and form

IV. PAINTING, 745
    1. MASTERS OF CHINESE PAINTING
    Ku K'ai-chhi, the "greatest painter, wit and fool"—Han Yü's miniature—The classic and the romantic schools—Wang Wei—Wu Tao-tze—Hui Tsung, the artist-emperor—Masters of the Sung age
    2. QUALITIES OF CHINESE PAINTING
    The rejection of perspective—Of realism—Line as nobler than color—Form as rhythm—Representation by suggestion—Conventions and restrictions—Sincerity of Chinese art

V. PORCELAIN, 754

The ceramic art—The making of porcelain—Its early history—*Céladon*—Enamels—The skill of Hao Shih-chiu—*Cloisonné*—The age of K'ang-hsi—Of Ch'ien Lung

Chapter XXVI: THE PEOPLE AND THE STATE.................................... 760

I. HISTORICAL INTERLUDE, 760

    1. MARCO POLO VISITS KUBLAI KHAN

    The incredible travelers—Adventures of a Venetian in China—The elegance and prosperity of Hangchow—The palaces of Peking—The Mongol Conquest—Jenghiz Khan—Kublai Khan—His character and policy—His harem—"Marco Millions"

    2. THE MING AND THE CH'ING

    Fall of the Mongols — The Ming Dynasty — The Manchu invasion — The Ch'ing Dynasty—An enlightened monarch—Ch'ien Lung rejects the Occident

II. THE PEOPLE AND THEIR LANGUAGE, 769

Population—Appearance—Dress—Peculiarities of Chinese speech—Of Chinese writing

III. THE PRACTICAL LIFE, 774

    1. IN THE FIELDS

    The poverty of the peasant — Methods of husbandry — Crops — Tea — Food — The stoicism of the village

    2. IN THE SHOPS

    Handicrafts — Silk — Factories — Guilds — Men of burden — Roads and canals — Merchants—Credit and coinage—Currency experiments—Printing-press inflation

    3. INVENTION AND SCIENCE

    Gunpowder, fireworks and war—The compass—Poverty of industrial invention—Geography—Mathematics—Physics—*Feng shui*—Astronomy—Medicine—Hygiene

IV. RELIGION WITHOUT A CHURCH, 783

Superstition and scepticism—Animism—The worship of Heaven—Ancestor-worship—Confucianism—Taoism—The elixir of immortality—Buddhism—Religious toleration and eclecticism—Mohammedanism—Christianity—Causes of its failure in China

V. THE RULE OF MORALS, 788

The high place of morals in Chinese society—The family—Children—Chastity—Prostitution—Premarital relations—Marriage and love—Monogamy and polygamy—Concubinage — Divorce — A Chinese empress — The patriarchal male — The subjection of woman—The Chinese character

VI. A GOVERNMENT PRAISED BY VOLTAIRE, 795

The submergence of the individual—Self-government—The village and the province—The laxity of the law—The severity of punishment—The Emperor—The Censor—Administrative boards—Education for public office—Nomination by education—The examination system—Its defects—Its virtues

Chapter XXVII: REVOLUTION AND RENEWAL.................................. 803

I. THE WHITE PERIL, 803
The conflict of Asia and Europe—The Portuguese—The Spanish—The Dutch—The English—The opium trade—The Opium Wars—The T'ai-p'ing Rebellion—The War with Japan—The attempt to dismember China—The "Open Door"—The Empress Dowager—The reforms of Kuang Hsu—His removal from power—The "Boxers"— The Indemnity

II. THE DEATH OF A CIVILIZATION, 808
The Indemnity students—Their Westernization—Their disintegrative effect in China —The rôle of the missionary—Sun Yat-sen, the Christian—His youthful adventures— His meeting with Li Hung-chang—His plans for a revolution—Their success—Yuan Shi-k'ai—The death of Sun Yat-sen—Chaos and pillage—Communism—"The north pacified"—Chiang Kai-shek—Japan in Manchuria—At Shanghai

III. BEGINNINGS OF A NEW ORDER, 814
Change in the village—In the town—The factories—Commerce—Labor unions—Wages —The new government—Nationalism vs. Westernization—The dethronement of Confucius—The reaction against religion—The new morality—Marriage in transition— Birth control—Co-education—The "New Tide" in literature and philosophy—The new language of literature—Hu Shih—Elements of destruction—Elements of renewal

B. JAPAN

Chronology of Japanese Civilization................................. 826

Chapter XXVIII: THE MAKERS OF JAPAN.................................. 829

I. THE CHILDREN OF THE GODS, 829
How Japan was created—The rôle of earthquakes

II. PRIMITIVE JAPAN, 831
Racial components—Early civilization—Religion—Shinto—Buddhism—The beginnings of art—The "Great Reform"

III. THE IMPERIAL AGE, 834
The emperors—The aristocracy—The influence of China—The Golden Age of Kyoto—Decadence

IV. THE DICTATORS, 836
The shoguns—The Kamakura Bakufu—The Hojo Regency—Kublai Khan's invasion—The Ashikaga Shogunate—The three buccaneers

V. GREAT MONKEY-FACE, 838
The rise of Hideyoshi—The attack upon Korea—The conflict with Christianity

VI. THE GREAT SHOGUN, 841
The accession of Iyeyasu—His philosophy—Iyeyasu and Christianity—Death of Iyeyasu—The Tokugawa Shogunate

CONTENTS

Chapter XXIX: THE POLITICAL AND MORAL FOUNDATIONS.............. 845

    I. THE SAMURAI, 845
    The powerless emperor—The powers of the *shogun*—The sword of the *Samurai*—
    The code of the *Samurai*—*Hara-kiri*—The Forty-seven *Ronin*—A commuted sentence

    II. THE LAW, 850
    The first code—Group responsibility—Punishments

    III. THE TOILERS, 851
    Castes—An experiment in the nationalization of land—State fixing of wages—A fam-
    ine—Handicrafts—Artisans and guilds

    IV. THE PEOPLE, 854
    Stature—Cosmetics—Costume—Diet—Etiquette—*Saki*—The tea ceremony—The flower
    ceremony—Love of nature—Gardens—Homes

    V. THE FAMILY, 860
    The paternal autocrat—The status of woman—Children—Sexual morality—The
    Geisha—Love

    VI. THE SAINTS, 863
    Religion in Japan—The transformation of Buddhism—The priests—Sceptics

    VII. THE THINKERS, 866
    Confucius reaches Japan—A critic of religion—The religion of scholarship—Kaibara
    Ekken—On education—On pleasure—The rival schools—A Japanese Spinoza—Ito
    Jinsai—Ito Togai—Ogyu Sorai—The war of the scholars—Mabuchi—Moto-ori

Chapter XXX: THE MIND AND ART OF OLD JAPAN........................ 876

    I. LANGUAGE AND EDUCATION, 876
    The language—Writing—Education

    II. POETRY, 878
    The *Manyoshu*—The *Kokinshu*—Characteristics of Japanese poetry—Examples—The
    game of poetry—The *hokka*-gamblers

    III. PROSE, 881
      1. FICTION
      Lady Muraski—The *Tale of Genji*—Its excellence—Later Japanese fiction—A
      humorist
      2. HISTORY
      The historians—Arai Hakuseki
      3. THE ESSAY
      The Lady Sei Shonagon—Kamo no-Chomei

    IV. THE DRAMA, 889
    The *No* plays—Their character—The popular stage—The Japanese Shakespeare—
    Summary judgment

    V. THE ART OF LITTLE THINGS, 891
    Creative imitation—Music and the dance—*Inro* and *netsuke*—Hidari Jingaro—Lacquer

CONTENTS

VI. ARCHITECTURE, 894
Temples—Palaces—The shrine of Iyeyasu—Homes

VII. METALS AND STATUES, 896
Swords—Mirrors—The Trinity of Horiuji—Colossi—Religion and sculpture

VIII. POTTERY, 899
The Chinese stimulus—The potters of Hizen—Pottery and tea—How Goto Saijiro brought the art of porcelain from Hizen to Kaga—The nineteenth century

IX. PAINTING, 901
Difficulties of the subject—Methods and materials—Forms and ideals—Korean origins and Buddhist inspiration—The Tosa School—The return to China—Sesshiu—The Kano School—Koyetsu and Korin—The Realistic School

X. PRINTS, 907
The *Ukiyoye* School—Its founders—Its masters—Hokusai—Hiroshige

XI. JAPANESE ART AND CIVILIZATION, 910
A retrospect—Contrasts—An estimate—The doom of the old Japan

Chapter XXXI: THE NEW JAPAN.. 914

I. THE POLITICAL REVOLUTION, 914
The decay of the Shogunate—America knocks at the door—The Restoration—The Westernization of Japan—Political reconstruction—The new constitution—Law—The army—The war with Russia—Its political results

II. THE INDUSTRIAL REVOLUTION, 919
Industrialization—Factories—Wages—Strikes—Poverty—The Japanese point of view

III. THE CULTURAL REVOLUTION, 922
Changes in dress—In manners—The Japanese character—Morals and marriage in transition—Religion—Science—Japanese medicine—Art and taste—Language and education—Naturalistic fiction—New forms of poetry

IV. THE NEW EMPIRE, 927
The precarious bases of the new civilization—Causes of Japanese imperialism—The Twenty-one Demands—The Washington Conference—The Immigration Act of 1924—The invasion of Manchuria—The new kingdom—Japan and Russia—Japan and Europe—Must America fight Japan?

Envoi: Our Oriental Heritage... 934

Glossary of Foreign Terms.. 939

Bibliography of Books Referred to in the Text............................. 945

Notes 956

Pronouncing and Biographical Index....................................... 1001

List of Illustrations

(Illustration Section follows page xxxii)

Cover Design: The god Shamash transmits a code of laws to Hammurabi
From a cylinder in The Louvre

FIG.   1. Granite statue of Rameses II
    Turin Museum, Italy

FIG.   2. Bison painted in paleolithic cave at Altamira, Spain
    Photo by American Museum of Natural History

FIG.   3. Hypothetical reconstruction of a neolithic lake dwelling
    American Museum of Natural History

FIG.   4. Development of the alphabet

FIG.   5. Stele of Naram-sin
    Louvre; photo by Archives Photographiques d'Art et d'Histoire

FIG.   6. The "little" Gudea
    Louvre; photo by Metropolitan Museum of Art

FIG.   7. Temple of Der-el-Bahri
    Photo by Lindsley F. Hall

FIG.   8. Colonnade and court of the temple at Luxor
    Photo by Metropolitan Museum of Art

FIG.   9. Hypothetical reconstruction of the Hypostyle Hall at Karnak
    From a model in the Metropolitan Museum of Art

FIG. 10. Colonnade of the Hypostyle Hall at Karnak
    Underwood & Underwood

FIG. 11. The Rosetta Stone
    British Museum

FIG. 12. Diorite head of the Pharaoh Khafre
    Cairo Museum; photo by Metropolitan Museum of Art

FIG. 13. The seated Scribe
    Louvre; photo by Metropolitan Museum of Art

FIG. 14. Wooden figure of the "Sheik-el-Beled"
    Cairo Museum; photo by Metropolitan Museum of Art

FIG. 15. Sandstone head from the workshop of the sculptor Thutmose at Amarna
    State Museum, Berlin; photo by Metropolitan Museum of Art

FIG. 16. Head of a king, probably Senusret III.
    Metropolitan Museum of Art

FIG. 17. The royal falcon and serpent. Limestone relief from First Dynasty
    Louvre; photo by Metropolitan Museum of Art

FIG. 18. Head of Thutmose III
    Cairo Museum; photo by Metropolitan Museum of Art

FIG. 19. Rameses II presenting an offering
    Cairo Museum; photo by Metropolitan Museum of Art

FIG. 20. Bronze figure of the Lady Tekoschet
    Athens Museum; photo by Metropolitan Museum of Art

LIST OF ILLUSTRATIONS

FIG. 21. Seated figure of Montumihait
State Museum, Berlin
FIG. 22. Colossi of Rameses II, with life-size figures of Queen Nofretete at his feet, at the cave temple of Abu Simbel
Ewing Galloway, N. Y.
FIG. 23. The dancing girl. Design on an ostracon
Turin Museum, Italy
FIG. 24. Cat watching his prey. A wall-painting in the grave of Khnumhotep at Beni-Hasan
Copy by Howard Carter; courtesy of Egypt Exploration Society
FIG. 25. Chair of Tutenkhamon
Cairo Museum; photo by Metropolitan Museum of Art
FIG. 26. Painted limestone head of Ikhnaton's Queen Nofretete
Metropolitan Museum of Art facsimile of original in State Museum, Berlin
FIG. 27. The god Shamash transmits a code of laws to Hammurabi
Louvre; photo copyright by W. A. Mansell & Co., London
FIG. 28. The "Lion of Babylon." Painted tile-relief
State Museum, Berlin; Courtesy of the Metropolitan Museum of Art
FIG. 29. Head of Esarhaddon
State Museum, Berlin
FIG. 30. The Prism of Sennacherib
Iraq Museum; courtesy of the Oriental Institute, University of Chicago
FIG. 31. The Dying Lioness of Nineveh
British Museum; photo by Metropolitan Museum of Art
FIG. 32. The Lion Hunt; relief on alabaster, from Nineveh
British Museum; photo by Metropolitan Museum of Art
FIG. 33. Assyrian relief of Marduk fighting Tiamat, from Kalakh
British Museum; photo copyright by W. A. Mansell, London
FIG. 34. Winged Bull from the palace of Ashurnasirpal II at Kalakh
Metropolitan Museum of Art
FIG. 35. A street in Jerusalem
FIG. 36. Hypothetical restoration of Solomon's Temple
Underwood & Underwood
FIG. 37. The ruins of Persepolis
Courtesy of the Oriental Institute, University of Chicago
FIG. 38. "Frieze of the Archers." Painted tile-relief from Susa
Louvre; photo by Archives Photographiques d'Art et d'Histoire
FIG. 39. Burning Ghat at Calcutta
Bronson de Cou, from Ewing Galloway, N. Y.
FIG. 40. "Holy Men" at Benares
FIG. 41. A fresco at Ajanta
FIG. 42. Mogul painting of Durbar of Akbar at Akbarabad. Ca. 1620
Boston Museum of Fine Arts
FIG. 43. Torso of a youth, from Sanchi
Victoria and Albert Museum, London
FIG. 44. Seated statue of Brahma, 10th century
Metropolitan Museum of Art

Fig. 1—*Granite statue of Rameses II*
Turin Museum, Italy

(See pages 188, 213)

Fig. 45. The Buddha of Sarnath, 5th century
Photo by A. K. Coomaraswamy
Fig. 46. The Naga-King. Façade relief on Ajanta Cave-temple XIX
Courtesy of A. K. Coomaraswamy
Fig. 47. The Dancing Shiva. South India, 17th century
Minneapolis Institute of Arts
Fig. 48. The Three-faced Shiva, or Trimurti, Elephanta
Underwood & Underwood
Fig. 49. The Buddha of Anuradhapura, Ceylon
Ewing Galloway, N. Y.
Fig. 50. Lion capital of Ashoka column
Sarnath Museum, Benares; copyright Archaeological Survey of India
Fig. 51. Sanchi Tope, north gate
Underwood & Underwood
Fig. 52. Façade of the Gautami-Putra Monastery at Nasik
India Office, London
Fig. 53. *Chaitya* hall interior, Cave XXVI, Ajanta.
Fig. 54. Interior of dome of the Tejahpala Temple at Mt. Abu
Johnston & Hoffman, Calcutta
Fig. 55. Temple of Vimala Sah at Mt. Abu
Underwood & Underwood
Fig. 56. Cave XIX, Ajanta
Indian State Railways
Fig. 57. Elephanta Caves, near Bombay
By Cowling, from Ewing Galloway, N. Y.
Fig. 58. The rock-cut Temple of Kailasha
Indian State Railways
Fig. 59. Guardian deities, Temple of Elura
Indian State Railways
Fig. 60. Façade, Angkor Wat, Indo-China
Publishers' Photo Service
Fig. 61. Northeast end of Angkor Wat, Indo-China
Publishers' Photo Service
Fig. 62. Rabindranath Tagore
Underwood & Underwood
Fig. 63. Ananda Palace at Pagan, Burma
Underwood & Underwood
Fig. 64. The Taj Mahal, Agra
Ewing Galloway, N. Y.
Fig. 65. Imperial jewel casket of blue lacquer
Underwood & Underwood
Fig. 66. The lacquered screen of K'ang-hsi
Victoria and Albert Museum, London
Fig. 67. A bronze Kuan-yin of the Sui period
Metropolitan Museum of Art
Fig. 68. Summer Palace, Peiping
Fig. 69. Temple of Heaven, Peiping
Publishers' Photo Service

Fɪɢ. 70. Portraits of Thirteen Emperors. Attributed to Yen Li-pen, 7th century·
Boston Museum of Fine Arts

Fɪɢ. 71. The Silk-beaters. By the Emperor Hui Tsung (1101-26)
Boston Museum of Fine Arts

Fɪɢ. 72. Landscape with Bridge and Willows. Ma Yuan, 12th century
Boston Museum of Fine Arts

Fɪɢ. 73. A hawthorn vase from the K'ang-hsi period
Metropolitan Museum of Art

Fɪɢ. 74. *Geisha* girls
Ewing Galloway, N. Y.

Fɪɢ. 75. Kiyomizu Temple, Kyoto, once a favorite resort of Japanese suicides
Underwood & Underwood

Fɪɢ. 76. Yo-mei-mon Gate, Nikko

Fɪɢ. 77. The Monkeys of Nikko. "Hear no evil, speak no evil, see no evil"
Ewing Galloway, N. Y.

Fɪɢ. 78. Image of Amida-Buddha at Horiuji
Photo by Metropolitan Museum of Art

Fɪɢ. 79. The bronze halo and background of the Amida at Horiuji.
Photo by Metropolitan Museum of Art

Fɪɢ. 80. The Vairochana Buddha of Japan. Carved and lacquered wood. Ca. 950 A.D.
Metropolitan Museum of Art

Fɪɢ. 81. The Daibutsu, or Great Buddha, at Kamakura

Fɪɢ. 82. Monkeys and Birds. By Sesshiu, 15th century

Fɪɢ. 83. A wave screen by Korin
Metropolitan Museum of Art

Fɪɢ. 84. The Falls of Yoro. By Hokusai
Metropolitan Museum of Art

Fɪɢ. 85. Foxes. By Hiroshige
Metropolitan Museum of Art

Maps of Egypt, the ancient Near East, India, and the Far East
will be found on the inside covers

Illustration Section

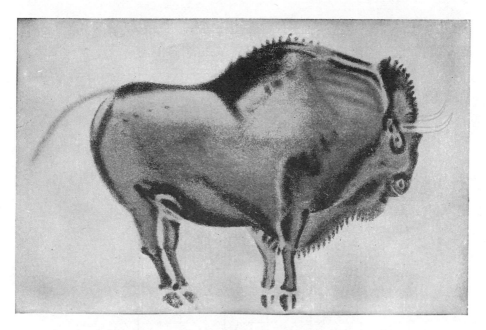

FIG. 2—*Bison painted in paleolithic cave at Altamira, Spain*
Photo by American Museum of Natural History

(See page 96)

FIG. 3—*Hypothetical reconstruction of a neolithic lake dwelling*
American Museum of Natural History

(See page 98)

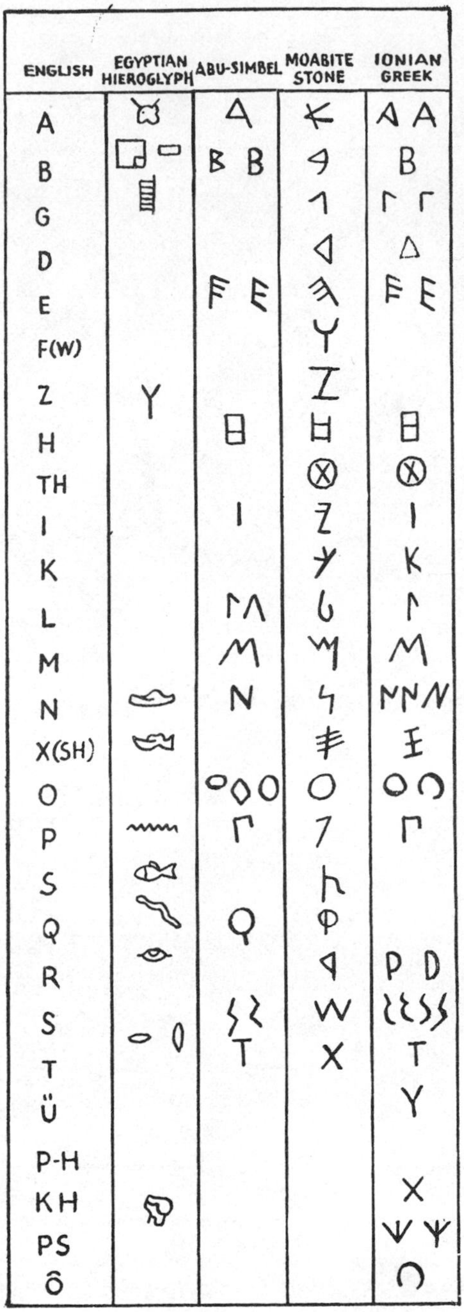

ENGLISH	EGYPTIAN HIEROGLYPH	ABU-SIMBEL	MOABITE STONE	IONIAN GREEK
A				
B				
G				
D				
E				
F(W)				
Z				
H				
TH				
I				
K				
L				
M				
N				
X(SH)				
O				
P				
S				
Q				
R				
S				
T				
Ü				
P-H				
KH				
PS				
ô				

FIG. 4—*Development of the alphabet*

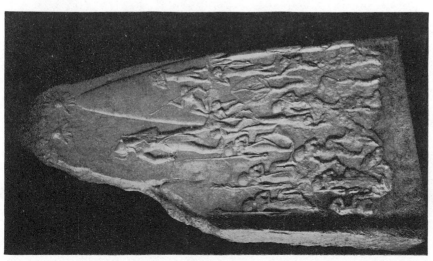

Fig. 5—*Stele of*
Naram-sin
Louvre; photo
by Archives
Photographiques
d'Art et
d'Histoire

(See page 122)

Fig. 6 –*The*
"little" Gudea
Louvre; photo
by Metropolitan
Museum of Art

(See page 122)

FIG. 7—*Temple of Der-el-Bahri*
Photo by Lindsley F. Hall

(See page 154)

FIG. 8—*Colonnade and court of the temple at Luxor*
Photo by Metropolitan Museum of Art

(See page 142)

FIG. 9—*Hypothetical reconstruction of the Hypostyle Hall at Karnak*
From a model in the Metropolitan Museum of Art

FIG. 10—*Colonnade of the Hypostyle Hall at Karnak*
Underwood & Underwood

(See page 143)

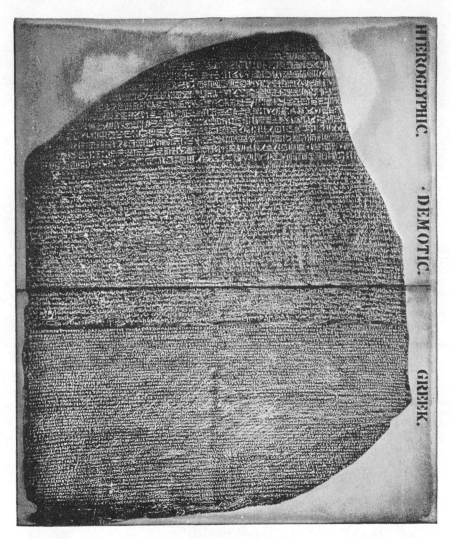

HIEROGLYPHIC. · DEMOTIC. GREEK.

FIG. 11—*The Rosetta Stone*
British Museum

(See page 145)

FIG. 12—*Diorite head of the Pharaoh Khafre*
Cairo Museum; photo by Metropolitan Museum of Art

(See pages 148, 186)

FIG. 13—*The seated Scribe*
Louvre; photo by Metropolitan Museum of Art

(See pages 161, 186)

FIG. 14—
*Wooden figure
of the
"Sheik-el-Beled"*
Cairo Museum;
photo by Metro-
politan Museum
of Art

(See pages 168, 186)

FIG. 22—*Colossi of Rameses II, with life-size figures of Queen Nefretere at his feet, at the cave temple of Abu Simbel*
Ewing Galloway, N. Y.

(*See page 188*)

FIG. 23—*The dancing girl. Design on an ostracon*
Turin Museum, Italy

(*See page 191*)

FIG. 24—*Cat watching his prey. A wall-painting in the grave of Khnumhotep
at Beni-Hasan*
Copy by Howard Carter; courtesy of Egypt Exploration Society

(*See page 190*)

FIG. 25—*Chair of Tutenkhamon*
Cairo Museum; photo by Metropolitan Museum of Art

(See page 191)

FIG. 26—*Painted limestone head of Ikhnaton's Queen Nofretete*
Metropolitan Museum of Art facsimile of original in State Museum, Berlin

(See page 188)

FIG. 27—*The god Shamash transmits a code of laws to Hammurabi*
Louvre; photo copyright W. A. Mansell & Co., London

(See page 219)

FIG. 28—*The "Lion of Babylon." Painted tile-relief*
State Museum, Berlin; courtesy of the Metropolitan Museum of Art

(See pages 254-5)

FIG. 29—*Head of Esarhaddon*
State Museum, Berlin

(See page 281)

FIG. 30—*The Prism of Sennacherib*
Iraq Museum; courtesy of the Oriental Institute, University of Chicago

(See Chapter X)

FIG. 31—*The Dying Lioness of Nineveh*
British Museum; photo by Metropolitan Museum of Art

(*See page 279*)

FIG. 32—*The Lion Hunt; relief on alabaster, from Nineveh*
British Museum; Metropolitan Museum of Art

(See page 279)

FIG. 33—*Assyrian relief of Marduk fighting Tiamat, from Kalakh*
British Museum; photo copyright by W. A. Mansell, London

(See page 278)

FIG. 37—*The ruins of Persepolis*
Courtesy of the Oriental Institute, University of Chicago

(*See page 379*)

FIG. 38—*"Frieze of the Archers." Painted tile-relief from Susa*
Louvre; photo by Archives Photographiques d'Art et d'Histoire

(See page 380)

FIG. 39—*Burning Ghat at Calcutta*
Bronson de Cou, from Ewing Galloway, N. Y.

(See page 521)

FIG. 40—*"Holy Men" at Benares*

(See page 521)

FIG. 41—*A fresco at Ajanta*

(*See pages 589-90*)

FIG. 42—*Mogul painting of Durbar of Akbar at Akbarabad. Ca. 1620*
Boston Museum of Fine Arts

(See page 591)

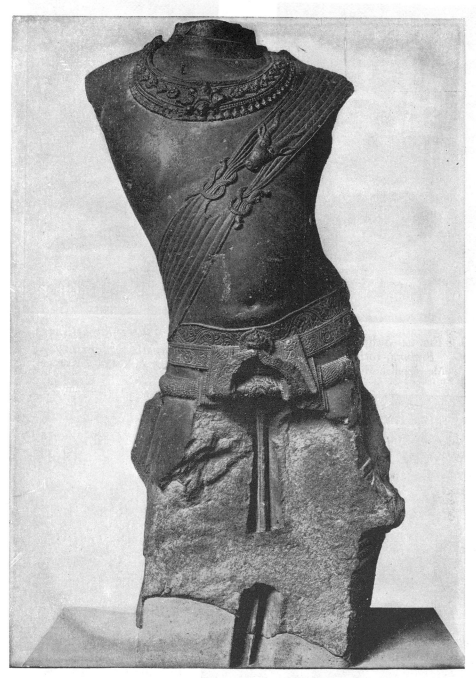

FIG. 43—*Torso of a youth, from Sanchi*
Victoria and Albert Museum, London

(See pages 593-6)

FIG. 48—*The Three-faced Shiva, or Trimurti, Elephanta*
Underwood & Underwood

(See page 594)

FIG. 49.—*The Buddha of Anuradhapura, Ceylon*
Ewing Galloway, N. Y.

(*See page 595*)

FIG. 50—*Lion capital of Ashoka column*
Sarnath Museum, Benares; copyright Archaeological Survey of India

(See page 596)

FIG. 51—*Sanchi Tope, north gate*
Underwood & Underwood

(See page 597)

FIG. 52—*Façade of the Gautami-Putra Monastery at Nasik*
India Office, London

(See page 597)

FIG. 53—*Chaitya hall interior, Cave XXVI, Ajanta*

(See page 598)

FIG. 54—*Interior of dome of the Tejahpala Temple at Mt. Abu*
Johnston & Hoffman, Calcutta

(See page 598)

FIG. 55—*Temple of Vimala Sah at Mt. Abu*
Underwood & Underwood

(See page 598)

FIG. 56—*Cave XIX, Ajanta*
Indian State Railways

(See page 598)

FIG. 57—*Elephanta Caves, near Bombay*
By Cowling, from Ewing Galloway, N. Y.

(*See page 596*)

FIG. 58—*The rock-cut Temple of Kailasha*
Indian State Railways

(*See page 601*)

FIG. 59—*Guardian deities, Temple of Elura*
Indian State Railways

(See page 601)

FIG. 60—*Façade, Angkor Wat, Indo-China*
Publishers' Photo Service

(See pages 604-5)

FIG. 61—*Northeast end of Angkor Wat, Indo-China*
Publishers' Photo Service

(*See pages 604-5*)

FIG. 62—*Rabindranath
Tagore*
Underwood & Underwood

(See page 619)

FIG. 63—*Ananda Palace at
Pagan, Burma*
Underwood & Underwood

(See page 606)

FIG. 64—*The Taj Mahal, Agra*
Ewing Galloway, N. Y.

(See page 609)

FIG. 65—*Imperial jewel casket of blue lacquer*
Underwood & Underwood

(See page 736)

FIG. 66—*The lacquered screen of K'ang-hsi*
Victoria and Albert Museum, London

(*See page 736*)

FIG. 67—*A bronze Kuan-yin of the Sui period*
Metropolitan Museum of Art

(See page 738)

FIG. 68—*Summer Palace, Peiping*

(See page 742)

FIG. 69—*Temple of Heaven, Peiping*
Publishers' Photo Service

(See page 742)

FIG. 70—
Portraits of
Thirteen
Emperors.
Attributed to
Yen Li-pen,
7th century
Boston Museum
of Fine Arts

(See pages 745-52)

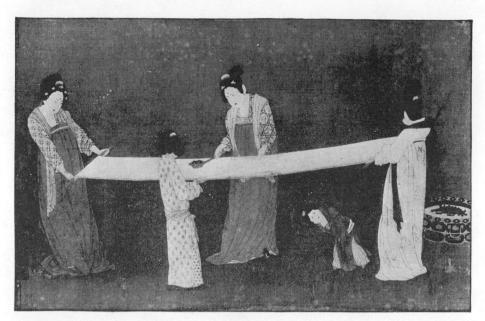

FIG. 71—*The*
Silk-beaters.
By the Emperor
Hui Tsung
(1101-26)
Boston Museum
of Fine Arts

(See page 750)

FIG. 72—*Land-*
scape with
Bridge and
Willows.
Ma Yuan,
12th century
Boston Museum
of Fine Arts

(See page 751)

FIG. 73—*A hawthorn vase from the K'ang-hsi period*
Metropolitan Museum of Art

(See page 758)

Fig. 74—*Geisha girls*
Ewing Galloway, N. Y.

(See page 862)

FIG. 75—*Kiyomizu Temple, Kyoto, once a favorite resort of Japanese suicides*
Underwood & Underwood

(See page 895)

FIG. 76—*Yo-mei-mon Gate, Nikko*

(See page 895)

FIG. 77—*The Monkeys of Nikko. "Hear no evil, speak no evil, see no evil"*
Ewing Galloway, N. Y.

(See page 895)

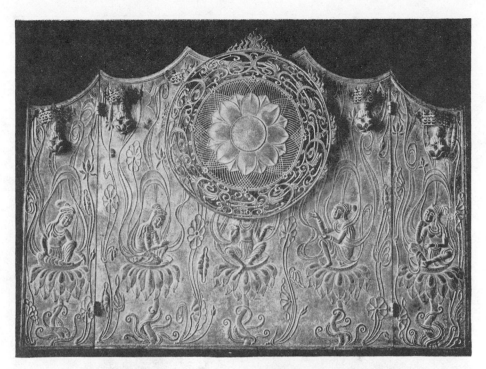

FIG. 79—*The bronze halo
and background of the
Amida at Horiuji*
Photo by
Metropolitan Museum of Art

(See page 897)

FIG. 78—*Image of Amida-
Buddha at Horiuji*
Photo by
Metropolitan Museum of Art

(See page 897)

FIG. 80—*The Vairochana Buddha of Japan. Carved and lacquered wood.*
Ca. 950 A.D.
Metropolitan Museum of Art

(See pages 896-8)

FIG. 81—*The Daibutsu, or Great Buddha, at Kamakura*

(See page 898)

FIG. 82—*Monkeys and Birds. By Sesshiu, 15th century*

(*See pages 904-5*)

FIG. 83—*A wave screen
by Korin*
Metropolitan Museum
of Art

(*See page 906*)

Fig. 85—*Foxes. By Hiroshige*
Metropolitan Museum of Art

Fig. 84—*The Falls of Yoro. By Hokusai*
Metropolitan Museum of Art

(*See pages 907–10*)

INTRODUCTION

THE ESTABLISHMENT OF CIVILIZATION

"I want to know what were the steps by which men passed from barbarism to civilization."

—VOLTAIRE.[1]

The Conditions of Civilization*

Definition—Geological conditions—Geographical—Economic—Racial—Psychological—Causes of the decay of civilizations

CIVILIZATION is social order promoting cultural creation. Four elements constitute it: economic provision, political organization, moral traditions, and the pursuit of knowledge and the arts. It begins where chaos and insecurity end. For when fear is overcome, curiosity and constructiveness are free, and man passes by natural impulse towards the understanding and embellishment of life.

Certain factors condition civilization, and may encourage or impede it. First, geological conditions. Civilization is an interlude between ice ages: at any time the current of glaciation may rise again, cover with ice and stone the works of man, and reduce life to some narrow segment of the earth. Or the demon of earthquake, by whose leave we build our cities, may shrug his shoulders and consume us indifferently.

Second, geographical conditions. The heat of the tropics, and the innumerable parasites that infest them, are hostile to civilization; lethargy and disease, and a precocious maturity and decay, divert the energies from those inessentials of life that make civilization, and absorb them in hunger and reproduction; nothing is left for the play of the arts and the mind. Rain is necessary; for water is the medium of life, more important even than the light of the sun; the unintelligible whim of the elements may condemn to desiccation regions that once flourished with empire and industry, like Nineveh or Babylon, or may help to swift strength and wealth cities apparently off the main line of transport and communication, like those of Great Britain or Puget Sound. If the soil is fertile in food or minerals, if rivers offer an easy avenue of exchange, if the coast-line is indented with natural harbors for a commercial fleet, if, above all, a nation lies on the highroad of the world's trade, like Athens or Carthage, Flor-

---

* The reader will find, at the end of this volume, a glossary defining foreign terms, a bibliography with guidance for further reading, a pronouncing index, and a body of references corresponding to the superior figures in the text.

ence or Venice—then geography, though it can never create it, smiles upon civilization, and nourishes it.

Economic conditions are more important. A people may possess ordered institutions, a lofty moral code, and even a flair for the minor forms of art, like the American Indians; and yet if it remains in the hunting stage, if it depends for its existence upon the precarious fortunes of the chase, it will never quite pass from barbarism to civilization. A nomad stock, like the Bedouins of Arabia, may be exceptionally intelligent and vigorous, it may display high qualities of character like courage, generosity and nobility; but without that simple *sine qua non* of culture, a continuity of food, its intelligence will be lavished on the perils of the hunt and the tricks of trade, and nothing will remain for the laces and frills, the curtsies and amenities, the arts and comforts, of civilization. The first form of culture is agriculture. It is when man settles down to till the soil and lay up provisions for the uncertain future that he finds time and reason to be civilized. Within that little circle of security—a reliable supply of water and food— he builds his huts, his temples and his schools; he invents productive tools, and domesticates the dog, the ass, the pig, at last himself. He learns to work with regularity and order, maintains a longer tenure of life, and transmits more completely than before the mental and moral heritage of his race.

Culture suggests agriculture, but civilization suggests the city. In one aspect civilization is the habit of civility; and civility is the refinement which townsmen, who made the word, thought possible only in the *civitas* or city.* For in the city are gathered, rightly or wrongly, the wealth and brains produced in the countryside; in the city invention and industry multiply comforts, luxuries and leisure; in the city traders meet, and barter goods and ideas; in that cross-fertilization of minds at the cross-roads of trade intelligence is sharpened and stimulated to creative power. In the city some men are set aside from the making of material things, and produce science and philosophy, literature and art. Civilization begins in the peasant's hut, but it comes to flower only in the towns.

There are no racial conditions to civilization. It may appear on any continent and in any color: at Pekin or Delhi, at Memphis or Babylon, at Ravenna or London, in Peru or Yucatan. It is not the great race that makes

---

* The word civilization (Latin *civilis*—pertaining to the *civis*, citizen) is comparatively young. Despite Boswell's suggestion Johnson refused to admit it to his Dictionary in 1772; he preferred to use the word *civility.*

the civilization, it is the great civilization that makes the people; circumstances geographical and economic create a culture, and the culture creates a type. The Englishman does not make British civilization, it makes him; if he carries it with him wherever he goes, and dresses for dinner in Timbuktu, it is not that he is creating his civilization there anew, but that he acknowledges even there its mastery over his soul. Given like material conditions, and another race would beget like results; Japan reproduces in the twentieth century the history of England in the nineteenth. Civilization is related to race only in the sense that it is often preceded by the slow intermarriage of different stocks, and their gradual assimilation into a relatively homogeneous people.*

These physical and biological conditions are only prerequisites to civilization; they do not constitute or generate it. Subtle psychological factors must enter into play. There must be political order, even if it be so near to chaos as in Renaissance Florence or Rome; men must feel, by and large, that they need not look for death or taxes at every turn. There must be some unity of language to serve as a medium of mental exchange. Through church, or family, or school, or otherwise, there must be a unifying moral code, some rules of the game of life acknowledged even by those who violate them, and giving to conduct some order and regularity, some direction and stimulus. Perhaps there must also be some unity of basic belief, some faith, supernatural or utopian, that lifts morality from calculation to devotion, and gives life nobility and significance despite our mortal brevity. And finally there must be education—some technique, however primitive, for the transmission of culture. Whether through imitation, initiation or instruction, whether through father or mother, teacher or priest, the lore and heritage of the tribe—its language and knowledge, its morals and manners, its technology and arts—must be handed down to the young, as the very instrument through which they are turned from animals into men.

The disappearance of these conditions—sometimes of even one of them —may destroy a civilization. A geological cataclysm or a profound climatic change; an uncontrolled epidemic like that which wiped out half the population of the Roman Empire under the Antonines, or the Black Death that helped to end the Feudal Age; the exhaustion of the land, or the ruin

---

* Blood, as distinct from race, may affect a civilization in the sense that a nation may be retarded or advanced by breeding from the biologically (not racially) worse or better strains among the people.

of agriculture through the exploitation of the country by the town, resulting in a precarious dependence upon foreign food supplies; the failure of
natural resources, either of fuels or of raw materials; a change in trade
routes, leaving a nation off the main line of the world's commerce; mental
or moral decay from the strains, stimuli and contacts of urban life, from
the breakdown of traditional sources of social discipline and the inability
to replace them; the weakening of the stock by a disorderly sexual life, or
by an epicurean, pessimist, or quietist philosophy; the decay of leadership
through the infertility of the able, and the relative smallness of the families that might bequeath most fully the cultural inheritance of the race; a
pathological concentration of wealth, leading to class wars, disruptive
revolutions, and financial exhaustion: these are some of the ways in which
a civilization may die. For civilization is not something inborn or imperishable; it must be acquired anew by every generation, and any serious
interruption in its financing or its transmission may bring it to an end. Man
differs from the beast only by education, which may be defined as the
technique of transmitting civilization.

Civilizations are the generations of the racial soul. As family-rearing,
and then writing, bound the generations together, handing down the lore
of the dying to the young, so print and commerce and a thousand ways
of communication may bind the civilizations together, and preserve for
future cultures all that is of value for them in our own. Let us, before
we die, gather up our heritage, and offer it to our children.

CHAPTER II

The Economic Elements
of Civilization*

IN one important sense the "savage," too, is civilized, for he carefully transmits to his children the heritage of the tribe—that complex of economic, political, mental and moral habits and institutions which it has developed in its efforts to maintain and enjoy itself on the earth. It is impossible to be scientific here; for in calling other human beings "savage" or "barbarous" we may be expressing no objective fact, but only our fierce fondness for ourselves, and our timid shyness in the presence of alien ways. Doubtless we underestimate these simple peoples, who have so much to teach us in hospitality and morals; if we list the bases and constituents of civilization we shall find that the naked nations invented or arrived at all but one of them, and left nothing for us to add except embellishments and writing. Perhaps they, too, were once civilized, and desisted from it as a nuisance. We must make sparing use of such terms as "savage" and "barbarous" in referring to our "contemporaneous ancestry." Preferably we shall call "primitive" all tribes that make little or no provision for unproductive days, and little or no use of writing. In contrast, the civilized may be defined as literate providers.

I. FROM HUNTING TO TILLAGE

Primitive improvidence—Beginnings of provision—Hunting and fishing—Herding—The domestication of animals—Agriculture—Food—Cooking—Cannibalism

"Three meals a day are a highly advanced institution. Savages gorge themselves or fast."[2] The wilder tribes among the American Indians con-

---

* Despite recent high example to the contrary,[1] the word *civilization* will be used in this volume to mean social organization, moral order, and cultural activity; while *culture* will mean, according to the context, either the practice of manners and the arts, or the sum-total of a people's institutions, customs and arts. It is in the latter sense that the word *culture* will be used in reference to primitive or prehistoric societies.

5

sidered it weak-kneed and unseemly to preserve food for the next day.³ The natives of Australia are incapable of any labor whose reward is not immediate; every Hottentot is a gentleman of leisure; and with the Bushmen of Africa it is always "either a feast or a famine."⁴ There is a mute wisdom in this improvidence, as in many "savage" ways. The moment man begins to take thought of the morrow he passes out of the Garden of Eden into the vale of anxiety; the pale cast of worry settles down upon him, greed is sharpened, property begins, and the good cheer of the "thoughtless" native disappears. The American Negro is making this transition today. "Of what are you thinking?" Peary asked one of his Eskimo guides. "I do not have to think," was the answer; "I have plenty of meat." Not to think unless we have to—there is much to be said for this as the summation of wisdom.

Nevertheless, there were difficulties in this care-lessness, and those organisms that outgrew it came to possess a serious advantage in the struggle for survival. The dog that buried the bone which even a canine appetite could not manage, the squirrel that gathered nuts for a later feast, the bees that filled the comb with honey, the ants that laid up stores for a rainy day—these were among the first creators of civilization. It was they, or other subtle creatures like them, who taught our ancestors the art of providing for tomorrow out of the surplus of today, or of preparing for winter in summer's time of plenty.

With what skill those ancestors ferreted out, from land and sea, the food that was the basis of their simple societies! They grubbed edible things from the earth with bare hands; they imitated or used the claws and tusks of the animals, and fashioned tools out of ivory, bone or stone; they made nets and traps and snares of rushes or fibre, and devised innumerable artifices for fishing and hunting their prey. The Polynesians had nets a thousand ells long, which could be handled only by a hundred men; in such ways economic provision grew hand in hand with political organization, and the united quest for food helped to generate the state. The Tlingit fisherman put upon his head a cap like the head of a seal, and hiding his body among the rocks, made a noise like a seal; seals came toward him, and he speared them with the clear conscience of primitive war. Many tribes threw narcotics into the streams to stupefy the fish into coöperation with the fishermen; the Tahitians, for example, put into the water an intoxicating mixture prepared from the *huteo* nut or the *hora* plant; the fish, drunk with it, floated leisurely on the surface, and were caught at the anglers' will. Australian natives, swimming under water while breathing through a reed, pulled ducks beneath the surface by the legs, and gently held them there till they were pacified. The Tarahumaras caught birds by stringing kernels on tough fibres half buried under the ground; the birds ate the kernels, and the Tarahumaras ate the birds.[5]

Hunting is now to most of us a game, whose relish seems based upon some mystic remembrance, in the blood, of ancient days when to hunter as well as hunted it was a matter of life and death. For hunting was not merely a quest for food, it was a war for security and mastery, a war beside which all the wars of recorded history are but a little noise. In the jungle man still fights for his life, for though there is hardly an animal that will attack him unless it is desperate for food or cornered in the chase, yet there is not always food for all, and sometimes only the fighter, or the breeder of fighters, is allowed to eat. We see in our museums the relics of that war of the species in the knives, clubs, spears, arrows, lassos, bolas, lures, traps, boomerangs and slings with which primitive men won possession of the land, and prepared to transmit to an ungrateful posterity the gift of security from every beast except man. Even today, after all these wars of elimination, how many different populations move over the earth! Sometimes, during a walk in the woods, one is awed by the variety of languages spoken there, by the myriad species of insects, reptiles, carnivores and birds; one feels that man is an interloper on this crowded scene, that he is the object of universal dread and endless hostility. Some day, perhaps, these chattering quadrupeds, these ingratiating centipedes, these insinuating bacilli, will devour man and all his works, and free the planet from this marauding biped, these mysterious and unnatural weapons, these careless feet!

Hunting and fishing were not stages in economic development, they were modes of activity destined to survive into the highest forms of civilized society. Once the center of life, they are still its hidden foundations; behind our literature and philosophy, our ritual and art, stand the stout killers of Packingtown. We do our hunting by proxy, not having the stomach for honest killing in the fields; but our memories of the chase linger in our joyful pursuit of anything weak or fugitive, and in the games of our children—even in the word *game*. In the last analysis civilization is based upon the food supply. The cathedral and the capitol, the museum and the concert chamber, the library and the university are the façade; in the rear are the shambles.

To live by hunting was not original; if man had confined himself to that he would have been just another carnivore. He began to be human when out of the uncertain hunt he developed the greater security and continuity of the pastoral life. For this involved advantages of high importance: the domestication of animals, the breeding of cattle, and the use of milk. We do not know when or how domestication began—perhaps when the helpless young of slain beasts were spared and brought to the camp as playthings for the children.[6] The animal continued to be eaten, but not so soon; it acted as a beast of burden, but it was accepted almost democratically into the society of man; it became his comrade, and formed with him a community of labor and residence. The miracle of reproduction was brought under control, and two captives were multiplied into a herd. Animal milk released women from prolonged nursing, lowered infantile mortality, and provided a new and dependable food. Population increased, life became more stable and orderly, and the mastery of that timid *parvenu*, man, became more secure on the earth.

Meanwhile woman was making the greatest economic discovery of all—the bounty of the soil. While man hunted she grubbed about the tent or hut for whatever edible things lay ready to her hand on the ground. In Australia it was understood that during the absence of her mate on the chase the wife would dig for roots, pluck fruit and nuts from the trees, and collect honey, mushrooms, seeds and natural grains.[7] Even today, in certain tribes of Australia, the grains that grow spontaneously out of the earth are harvested without any attempt to separate and sow the seed; the Indians of the Sacramento River Valley never advanced beyond this stage.[8] We shall never discover when men first noted the function of the seed, and turned collecting into sowing; such beginnings are the mysteries of history, about which we may believe and guess, but cannot know. It is possible that when men began to collect unplanted grains, seeds fell along the way between field and camp, and suggested at last the great secret of growth. The Juangs threw the seeds together into the ground, leaving them to find their own way up. The natives of Borneo put the seed into holes which they dug with a pointed stick as they walked the fields.[9] The simplest known culture of the earth is with this stick or "digger." In Madagascar fifty years ago the traveler could still see women armed with pointed sticks, standing in a row like soldiers, and then, at a signal, digging their sticks into the ground, turning over the soil, throwing in the seed, stamping the earth flat, and passing on to another furrow.[10] The second stage in complexity was culture with the hoe: the digging stick was tipped with bone, and fitted with a crosspiece to receive the pressure of the foot. When the Conquistadores arrived in Mexico they found that the Aztecs knew no other tool of tillage than the hoe. With the domestication of animals and the forging of metals a heavier implement could be used; the hoe was enlarged into a plough, and the deeper turning of the soil revealed a fertility in the earth that changed the whole career of man. Wild plants were domesticated, new varieties were developed, old varieties were improved.

Finally nature taught man the art of provision, the virtue of prudence,* the concept of time. Watching woodpeckers storing acorns in the trees, and the bees storing honey in hives, man conceived—perhaps after millenniums of improvident savagery—the notion of laying up food for the future. He found ways of preserving meat by smoking it, salting it, freezing it; better still, he built granaries secure from rain and damp, vermin and thieves, and gathered food into them for the leaner months of the year. Slowly it became apparent that agriculture could provide a better and steadier food supply than hunting. With that realization man took one of the three steps that led from the beast to civilization—speech, agriculture, and writing.

It is not to be supposed that man passed suddenly from hunting to tillage. Many tribes, like the American Indians, remained permanently becalmed in the transition—the men given to the chase, the women tilling the soil. Not only was the change presumably gradual, but it was never complete. Man merely added a new way of securing food to an old way; and for the most part, throughout his history, he has preferred the old food to the new. We picture early man experimenting with a thousand products of the earth to find, at much cost to his inward comfort, which of them could be eaten safely; mingling these more and more with the fruits and nuts, the flesh and fish he was accustomed to, but always yearning for the booty of the chase. Primitive peoples are ravenously fond of meat, even when they live mainly on cereals, vegetables and milk.[11] If they come upon the carcass of a recently dead animal the result is likely to be a wild debauch. Very often no time is wasted on cooking; the prey is eaten raw, as fast as good teeth can tear and devour it; soon nothing is left but the bones. Whole tribes have been known to feast for a week on a

---

* Note the ultimate identity of the words *provision, providence* and *prudence.*

whale thrown up on the shore.[12] Though the Fuegians can cook, they prefer their meat raw; when they catch a fish they kill it by biting it behind the gills, and then consume it from head ·to tail without further ritual.[13] The uncertainty of the food supply made these nature peoples almost literally omnivorous: shellfish, sea urchins, frogs, toads, snails, mice, rats, spiders, earthworms, scorpions, moths, centipedes, locusts, caterpillars, lizards, snakes, boas, dogs, horses, roots, lice, insects, larvæ, the eggs of reptiles and birds—there is not one of these but was somewhere a delicacy, or even a *pièce de résistance*, to primitive men.[14] Some tribes are expert hunters of ants; others dry insects in the sun and then store them for a feast; others pick the lice out of one another's hair, and eat them with relish; if a great number of lice can be gathered to make a *petite marmite*, they are devoured with shouts of joy, as enemies of the human race.[15] The menu of the lower hunting tribes hardly differs from that of the higher apes.[16]

The discovery of fire limited this indiscriminate voracity, and coöperated with agriculture to free man from the chase. Cooking broke down the cellulose and starch of a thousand plants indigestible in their raw state, and man turned more and more to cereals and vegetables as his chief reliance. At the same time cooking, by softening tough foods, reduced the need of chewing, and began that decay of the teeth which is one of the insignia of civilization.

To all the varied articles of diet that we have enumerated, man added the greatest delicacy of all—his fellowman. Cannibalism was at one time practically universal; it has been found in nearly all primitive tribes, and among such later peoples as the Irish, the Iberians, the Picts, and the eleventh-century Danes.[17] Among many tribes human flesh was a staple of trade, and funerals were unknown. In the Upper Congo living men, women and children were bought and sold frankly as articles of food;[18] on the island of New Britain human meat was sold in shops as butcher's meat is sold among ourselves; and in some of the Solomon Islands human victims, preferably women, were fattened for a feast like pigs.[19] The Fuegians ranked women above dogs because, they said, "dogs taste of otter." In Tahiti an old Polynesian chief explained his diet to Pierre Loti: "The white man, when well roasted, tastes like a ripe banana." The Fijians, however, complained that the flesh of the whites was too salty and tough, and that a European sailor was hardly fit to eat; a Polynesian tasted better.[20]

What was the origin of this practice? There is no surety that the custom arose, as formerly supposed, out of a shortage of other food; if it did, the taste once formed survived the shortage, and became a passionate predilection.[21] Everywhere among nature peoples blood is regarded as a delicacy—never with horror; even primitive vegetarians take to it with gusto. Human blood is constantly drunk by tribes otherwise kindly and generous; sometimes as medicine, sometimes as a rite or covenant, often in the belief that it will add to the drinker the vital force of the victim.[22] No shame was felt in preferring human flesh; primitive man seems to have recognized no distinction in morals between eating men and eating other animals. In Melanesia the chief who could treat his friends to a dish of roast man soared in social esteem. "When I have slain an enemy," explained a Brazilian philosopher-chief, "it is surely better to eat him than to let him waste. . . . The worst is not to be eaten, but to die; if I am killed it is all the same whether my tribal enemy eats me or not. But I could not think of any game that would taste better than he would. . . . You whites are really too dainty."[23]

Doubtless the custom had certain social advantages. It anticipated Dean Swift's plan for the utilization of superfluous children, and it gave the old an opportunity to die usefully. There is a point of view from which funerals seem an unnecessary extravagance. To Montaigne it appeared more barbarous to torture a man to death under the cover of piety, as was the mode of his time, than to roast and eat him after he was dead. We must respect one another's delusions.

II. THE FOUNDATIONS OF INDUSTRY

Fire—Primitive Tools—Weaving and pottery—Building and transport—Trade and finance

If man began with speech, and civilization with agriculture, industry began with fire. Man did not invent it; probably nature produced the marvel for him by the friction of leaves or twigs, a stroke of lightning, or a chance union of chemicals; man merely had the saving wit to imitate nature, and to improve upon her. He put the wonder to a thousand uses. First, perhaps, he made it serve as a torch to conquer his fearsome enemy, the dark; then he used it for warmth, and moved more freely from his native tropics to less enervating zones, slowly making the planet human; then he applied it to metals, softening them, tempering them, and combining them into forms stronger and suppler than those in which they had come to his hand. So beneficent and strange was it that fire always remained a miracle to primitive man, fit to be worshiped as a god; he offered it countless ceremonies of devotion, and made it the center or focus (which is Latin for hearth) of his life and home; he carried it carefully with him as he moved from place to place in his wanderings, and would not willingly let it die. Even the Romans punished with death the careless vestal virgin who allowed the sacred fire to be extinguished.

Meanwhile, in the midst of hunting, herding and agriculture, invention was busy, and the primitive brain was racking itself to find mechanical answers to the economic puzzles of life. At first man was content, apparently, to accept what nature offered him—the fruits of the earth as his food, the skins and furs of the animals as his clothing, the caves in the hillsides as his home. Then, *perhaps* (for most history is guessing, and the rest is prejudice), he imitated the tools and industry of the animal: he saw the monkey flinging rocks and fruit upon his enemies, or breaking open nuts and oysters with a stone; he saw the beaver building a dam, the birds making nests and bowers, the chimpanzees raising something very like a hut. He envied the power of their claws, teeth, tusks and horns, and the toughness of their hides; and he set to work to fashion tools and weapons that would resemble and rival these. Man, said Franklin, is a tool-using animal;[24] but this, too, like the other distinctions on which we plume ourselves, is only a difference of degree.

Many tools lay potential in the plant world that surrounded primitive man. From the bamboo he made shafts, knives, needles and bottles; out of branches he made tongs, pincers and vices; from bark and fibres he wove cord and clothing of a hundred kinds. Above all, he made himself a stick. It was a modest invention, but its uses were so varied that man always looked upon it as a symbol of power and authority, from the wand of the fairies and the staff of the shepherd to the rod of Moses or Aaron, the ivory cane of the Roman consul, the *lituus* of the augurs, and the mace of the magistrate or the king. In agriculture the stick became the hoe; in war it became the lance or javelin or spear, the sword or bayonet.[25] Again, man used the mineral world, and shaped stones into a museum of arms and implements: hammers, anvils, kettles, scrapers, arrow-heads, saws, planes, wedges, levers, axes and drills. From the animal world he made ladles, spoons, vases, gourds, plates, cups, razors and hooks out of the shells of the shore, and tough or dainty tools out of the horn or ivory, the teeth and bones, the hair and hide of the beasts. Most of these fashioned articles had handles of wood, attached to them in cunning ways, bound with braids of fibre or cords of animal sinew, and occasionally glued with strange mixtures of blood. The ingenuity of primitive men probably equaled—perhaps it surpassed—that of the average modern man; we differ from them through the social accumulation of knowledge, materials and tools, rather than through innate superiority of brains. Indeed, nature men delight in mastering the necessities of a situation with inventive wit. It was a favorite game among the Eskimos to go off into difficult and deserted places, and rival one another in devising means for meeting the needs of a life unequipped and unadorned.[26]

* This primitive skill displayed itself proudly in the art of weaving. Here, too, the animal showed man the way. The web of the spider, the nest of the bird, the crossing and texture of fibres and leaves in the natural embroidery of the woods, set an example so obvious that in all probability weaving was one of the earliest arts of the human race. Bark, leaves and grass fibres were woven into clothing, carpets and tapestry, sometimes so excellent that it could not be rivaled today, even with the resources of contemporary machinery. Aleutian women may spend a year in weaving one robe. The blankets and garments made by the North American Indians were richly ornamented with fringes and embroideries of hairs and tendon-threads dyed in brilliant colors with berry juice; colors "so alive," says Father Théodut, "that ours do not seem even to approach them."[27] Again art began where nature left off; the bones of birds and fishes, and the slim shoots of the bamboo tree, were polished into needles, and the tendons of animals were drawn into threads delicate enough to pass through the eye of the finest needle today. Bark was beaten into mats and cloths, skins were dried for clothing and shoes, fibres were twisted into the strongest yarn, and supple branches and colored filaments were woven into baskets more beautiful than any modern forms.[28]

Akin to basketry, perhaps born of it, was the art of pottery. Clay placed upon wickerwork to keep the latter from being burned, hardened into a fireproof shell which kept its form when the wickerwork was taken away;[29] this *may have been* the first stage of a development that was to culminate in the perfect porcelains of China. Or perhaps some lumps of clay, baked and hardened by the sun, suggested the ceramic art; it was but a step from this to substitute fire for the sun, and to form from the earth myriad shapes of vessels for every use—for cooking, storing and transporting, at last for

---

* Reduced type, unindented, will be used occasionally for technical or dispensable matter.

luxury and ornament. Designs imprinted by finger-nail or tool upon the wet clay were one of the first forms of art, and perhaps one of the origins of writing.

Out of sun-dried clay primitive tribes made bricks and adobe, and dwelt, so to speak, in pottery. But that was a late stage of the building art, binding the mud hut of the "savage" in a chain of continuous development with the brilliant tiles of Nineveh and Babylon. Some primitive peoples, like the Veddahs of Ceylon, had no dwellings at all, and were content with the earth and the sky; some, like the Tasmanians, slept in hollow trees; some, like the natives of New South Wales, lived in caves; others, like the Bushmen, built here and there a wind-shelter of branches, or, more rarely, drove piles into the soil and covered their tops with moss and twigs. From such wind-shelters, when sides were added, evolved the hut, which is found among the natives of Australia in all its stages from a tiny cottage of branches, grass and earth large enough to cover two or three persons, to great huts housing thirty or more. The nomad hunter or herdsman preferred a tent, which he could carry wherever the chase might lead him. The higher type of nature peoples, like the American Indian, built with wood; the Iroquois, for example, raised, out of timber still bearing the bark, sprawling edifices five hundred feet long, which sheltered many families. Finally, the natives of Oceania made real houses of carefully cut boards, and the evolution of the wooden dwelling was complete.[30]

Only three further developments were needed for primitive man to create all the essentials of economic civilization: the mechanisms of transport, the processes of trade, and the medium of exchange. The porter carrying his load from a modern plane pictures the earliest and latest stages in the history of transportation. In the beginning, doubtless, man was his own beast of burden, unless he was married; to this day, for the most part, in southern and eastern Asia, man is wagon and donkey and all. Then he invented ropes, levers, and pulleys; he conquered and loaded the animal; he made the first sledge by having his cattle draw along the ground long branches bearing his goods;* he put logs as rollers under the sledge; he cut cross-sections of the log, and made the greatest of all mechanical inventions, the wheel; he put wheels under the sledge and made a cart. Other logs he bound together as rafts, or dug into canoes; and the streams became his most convenient avenues of transport. By land he went first through trackless fields and hills, then by trails, at last by roads. He studied the stars, and guided his caravans across mountains and deserts by tracing

---

* The American Indians, content with this device, never used the wheel.

his route in the sky. He paddled, rowed or sailed his way bravely from island to island, and at last spanned oceans to spread his modest culture from continent to continent. Here, too, the main problems were solved before written history began.

Since human skills and natural resources are diversely and unequally distributed, a people may be enabled, by the development of specific talents, or by its proximity to needed materials, to produce certain articles more cheaply than its neighbors. Of such articles it makes more than it consumes, and offers its surplus to other peoples in exchange for their own; this is the origin of trade. The Chibcha Indians of Colombia exported the rock salt that abounded in their territory, and received in return the cereals that could not be raised on their barren soil. Certain American Indian villages were almost entirely devoted to making arrow-heads; some in New Guinea to making pottery; some in Africa to blacksmithing, or to making boats or lances. Such specializing tribes or villages sometimes acquired the names of their industry (Smith, Fisher, Potter . . .), and these names were in time attached to specializing families.[30a] Trade in surpluses was at first by an interchange of gifts; even in our calculating days a present (if only a meal) sometimes precedes or seals a trade. The exchange was facilitated by war, robbery, tribute, fines, and compensation; goods had to be kept moving! Gradually an orderly system of barter grew up, and trading posts, markets and bazaars were established—occasionally, then periodically, then permanently—where those who had some article in excess might offer it for some article of need.[31]

For a long time commerce was purely such exchange, and centuries passed before a circulating medium of value was invented to quicken trade. A Dyak might be seen wandering for days through a bazaar, with a ball of beeswax in his hand, seeking a customer who could offer him in return something that he might more profitably use.[32] The earliest mediums of exchange were articles universally in demand, which anyone would take in payment: dates, salt, skins, furs, ornaments, implements, weapons; in such traffic two knives equaled one pair of stockings, all three equaled a blanket, all four equaled a gun, all five equaled a horse; two elk-teeth equaled one pony, and eight ponies equaled a wife.[33] There is hardly any thing that has not been employed as money by some people at some time: beans, fish-hooks, shells, pearls, beads, cocoa seeds, tea, pepper, at last sheep, pigs, cows, and slaves. Cattle were a convenient standard of value and medium of exchange among hunters and herders; they bore interest through breeding, and they were easy to carry, since they transported themselves. Even in Homer's days men and things were valued in terms of cattle: the armor of Diomedes was worth nine head of cattle, a skilful slave was worth four. The Romans used kindred words—*pecus* and *pecunia*—for cattle and money, and placed the image of an ox upon their early coins. Our own words *capital, chattel* and *cattle* go back through the French to the Latin *capitale,* meaning property: and this in turn derives from *caput,* meaning head—i.e., of cattle. When metals were mined they slowly replaced other articles as standards of value; copper, bronze, iron, finally—because of their convenient representation of great worth in little space and weight—silver and gold, became the money of mankind. The advance from token goods to a metallic currency does not seem to have been made by primitive men; it was left for the historic civilizations to invent coinage and credit, and so, by further facilitating the exchange of surpluses, to increase again the wealth and comfort of man.[34]

III. ECONOMIC ORGANIZATION

Primitive communism—Causes of its disappearance—Origins of private property—Slavery—Classes

Trade was the great disturber of the primitive world, for until it came, bringing money and profit in its wake, there was no property, and therefore little government. In the early stages of economic development property was limited for the most part to things personally used; the property sense applied so strongly to such articles that they (even the wife) were often buried with their owner; it applied so weakly to things not personally used that in their case the sense of property, far from being innate, required perpetual reinforcement and inculcation.

Almost everywhere, among primitive peoples, land was owned by the community. The North American Indians, the natives of Peru, the Chittagong Hill tribes of India, the Borneans and South Sea Islanders seem to have owned and tilled the soil in common, and to have shared the fruits together. "The land," said the Omaha Indians, "is like water and wind— what cannot be sold." In Samoa the idea of selling land was unknown prior to the coming of the white man. Professor Rivers found communism in land still existing in Melanesia and Polynesia; and in inner Liberia it may be observed today.[35]

Only less widespread was communism in food. It was usual among "savages" for the man who had food to share it with the man who had none, for travelers to be fed at any home they chose to stop at on their way, and for communities harassed with drought to be maintained by their neighbors.[36] If a man sat down to his meal in the woods he was expected to call loudly for some one to come and share it with him, before he might justly eat alone.[37] When Turner told a Samoan about the poor in London the "savage" asked in astonishment: "How is it? No food? No friends? No house to live in? Where did he grow? Are there no houses belonging to his friends?"[38] The hungry Indian had but to ask to receive; no matter how small the supply was, food was given him if he needed it; "no one can want food while there is corn anywhere in the town."[39] Among the Hottentots it was the custom for one who had more than others to share his surplus till all were equal. White travelers in Africa before the advent of civilization noted that a present of food or other valuables to a "black man" was at once distributed; so that when a suit of clothes was given to one of them the donor soon found the recipient wearing the hat, a friend the trousers, another friend the coat. The Eskimo hunter had no personal right to his catch; it had to be divided among the inhabitants of the village, and tools and provisions were the common property of all. The North American Indians were described by Captain Carver as "strangers to all distinctions of property, except in the articles of domestic use. . . . They are extremely liberal to each other, and supply the deficiencies of their friends with any superfluity of their own." "What is extremely surprising," reports a missionary, "is to see them treat one another with a gentleness and consideration which one does not find among common people in the most civilized nations. This, doubt-less, arises from the fact that the words 'mine' and 'thine,' which St. Chrysostom says extinguish in our hearts the fire of charity and kindle that of greed, are unknown to these savages." "I have seen them," says another observer, "divide game among themselves when they sometimes had many shares to make; and cannot recollect a single instance of their falling into a dispute or finding fault with the distribution as being unequal or otherwise objectionable. They would rather lie down themselves on an empty stomach than have it laid to their charge that they neglected to satisfy the needy. . . . They look upon themselves as but one great family."[40]

Why did this primitive communism disappear as men rose to what we, with some partiality, call civilization? Sumner believed that communism proved unbiological, a handicap in the struggle for existence; that it gave insufficient stimulus to inventiveness, industry and thrift; and that the failure to reward the more able, and punish the less able, made for a leveling of capacity which was hostile to growth or to successful competition with other groups.⁴¹ Loskiel reported some Indian tribes of the northeast as "so lazy that they plant nothing themselves, but rely entirely upon the expectation that others will not refuse to share their produce with them. Since the industrious thus enjoy no more of the fruits of their labor than the idle, they plant less every year."⁴² Darwin thought that the perfect equality among the Fuegians was fatal to any hope of their becoming civilized;⁴³ or, as the Fuegians might have put it, civilization would have been fatal to their equality. Communism brought a certain security to all who survived the diseases and accidents due to the poverty and ignorance of primitive society; but it did not lift them out of that poverty. Individualism brought wealth, but it brought, also, insecurity and slavery; it stimulated the latent powers of superior men, but it intensified the competition of life, and made men feel bitterly a poverty which, when all shared it alike, had seemed to oppress none.*

Communism could survive more easily in societies where men were always on the move, and danger and want were ever present. Hunters and herders had no need of private property in land; but when agriculture became the settled life of men it soon appeared that the land was most fruitfully tilled when the rewards of careful husbandry accrued to the family that had provided it. Consequently—since there is a natural selection of institutions and ideas as well as of organisms and groups—the passage from hunting to agriculture brought a change from tribal property to family property; the most economical unit of production became the

---

* Perhaps one reason why communism tends to appear chiefly at the beginning of civilizations is that it flourishes most readily in times of dearth, when the common danger of starvation fuses the individual into the group. When abundance comes, and the danger subsides, social cohesion is lessened, and individualism increases; communism ends where luxury begins. As the life of a society becomes more complex, and the division of labor differentiates men into diverse occupations and trades, it becomes more and more unlikely that all these services will be equally valuable to the group; inevitably those whose greater ability enables them to perform the more vital functions will take more than their equal share of the rising wealth of the group. Every growing civilization is a scene of multiplying inequalities; the natural differences of human endowment unite with differences of opportunity to produce artificial differences of wealth and power; and where no laws or despots suppress these artificial inequalities they reach at last a bursting point where the poor have nothing to lose by violence, and the chaos of revolution levels men again into a community of destitution.

Hence the dream of communism lurks in every modern society as a racial memory of a

unit of ownership. As the family took on more and more a patriarchal form, with authority centralized in the oldest male, property became increasingly individualized, and personal bequest arose. Frequently an enterprising individual would leave the family haven, adventure beyond the traditional boundaries, and by hard labor reclaim land from the forest, the jungle or the marsh; such land he guarded jealously as his own, and in the end society recognized his right, and another form of individual property began.[43a] As the pressure of population increased, and older lands were exhausted, such reclamation went on in a widening circle, until, in the more complex societies, individual ownership became the order of the day. The invention of money coöperated with these factors by facilitating the accumulation, transport and transmission of property. The old tribal rights and traditions reasserted themselves in the technical ownership of the soil by the village community or the king, and in periodical redistributions of the land; but after an epoch of natural oscillation between the old and the new, private property established itself definitely as the basic economic institution of historical society.

Agriculture, while generating civilization, led not only to private property but to slavery. In purely hunting communities slavery had been unknown; the hunter's wives and children sufficed to do the menial work. The men alternated between the excited activity of hunting or war, and the exhausted lassitude of satiety or peace. The characteristic laziness of primitive peoples had its origin, presumably, in this habit of slowly recuperating from the fatigue of battle or the chase; it was not so much laziness as rest. To transform this spasmodic activity into regular work two things were needed: the routine of tillage, and the organization of labor.

Such organization remains loose and spontaneous where men are working for themselves; where they work for others, the organization of labor

---

simpler and more equal life; and where inequality or insecurity rises beyond sufferance, men welcome a return to a condition which they idealize by recalling its equality and forgetting its poverty. Periodically the land gets itself redistributed, legally or not, whether by the Gracchi in Rome, the Jacobins in France, or the Communists in Russia; periodically wealth is redistributed, whether by the violent confiscation of property, or by confiscatory taxation of incomes and bequests. Then the race for wealth, goods and power begins again, and the pyramid of ability takes form once more; under whatever laws may be enacted the abler man manages somehow to get the richer soil, the better place, the lion's share; soon he is strong enough to dominate the state and rewrite or interpret the laws; and in time the inequality is as great as before. In this aspect all economic history is the slow heart-beat of the social organism, a vast systole and diastole of naturally concentrating wealth and naturally explosive revolution.

depends in the last analysis upon force. The rise of agriculture and the inequality of men led to the employment of the socially weak by the socially strong; not till then did it occur to the victor in war that the only good prisoner is a live one. Butchery and cannibalism lessened, slavery grew." It was a great moral improvement when men ceased to kill or eat their fellowmen, and merely made them slaves. A similar development on a larger scale may be seen today, when a nation victorious in war no longer exterminates the enemy, but enslaves it with indemnities. Once slavery had been established and had proved profitable, it was extended by condemning to it defaulting debtors and obstinate criminals, and by raids undertaken specifically to capture slaves. War helped to make slavery, and slavery helped to make war.

Probably it was through centuries of slavery that our race acquired its traditions and habits of toil. No one would do any hard or persistent work if he could avoid it without physical, economic or social penalty. Slavery became part of the discipline by which man was prepared for industry. Indirectly it furthered civilization, in so far as it increased wealth and—for a minority—created leisure. After some centuries men took it for granted; Aristotle argued for slavery as natural and inevitable, and St. Paul gave his benediction to what must have seemed, by his time, a divinely ordained institution.

Gradually, through agriculture and slavery, through the division of labor and the inherent diversity of men, the comparative equality of natural society was replaced by inequality and class divisions. "In the primitive group we find as a rule no distinction between slave and free, no serfdom, no caste, and little if any distinction between chief and followers."[45] Slowly the increasing complexity of tools and trades subjected the unskilled or weak to the skilled or strong; every invention was a new weapon in the hands of the strong, and further strengthened them in their mastery and use of the weak.* Inheritance added superior opportunity to superior possessions, and stratified once homogeneous societies into a maze of classes and castes. Rich and poor became disruptively conscious of wealth and poverty; the class war began to run as a red thread through all history; and the state arose as an indispensable instrument for the regulation of classes, the protection of property, the waging of war, and the organization of peace.

---

* So in our time that Mississippi of inventions which we call the Industrial Revolution has enormously intensified the natural inequality of men.

CHAPTER III

The Political Elements of Civilization

I. THE ORIGINS OF GOVERNMENT

*The unsocial instinct—Primitive anarchism—The clan and the
tribe—The king—War*

MAN is not willingly a political animal. The human male associates
with his fellows less by desire than by habit, imitation, and the
compulsion of circumstance; he does not love society so much as he
fears solitude. He combines with other men because isolation endangers
him, and because there are many things that can be done better together
than alone; in his heart he is a solitary individual, pitted heroically against
the world. If the average man had had his way there would probably
never have been any state. Even today he resents it, classes death with
taxes, and yearns for that government which governs least. If he asks
for many laws it is only because he is sure that his neighbor needs them;
privately he is an unphilosophical anarchist, and thinks laws in his own
case superfluous.

In the simplest societies there is hardly any government. Primitive
hunters tend to accept regulation only when they join the hunting pack
and prepare for action. The Bushmen usually live in solitary families;
the Pygmies of Africa and the simplest natives of Australia admit only
temporarily of political organization, and then scatter away to their
family groups; the Tasmanians had no chiefs, no laws, no regular government; the Veddahs of Ceylon formed small circles according to family
relationship, but had no government; the Kubus of Sumatra "live without
men in authority," every family governing itself; the Fuegians are seldom
more than twelve together; the Tungus associate sparingly in groups of
ten tents or so; the Australian "horde" is seldom larger than sixty souls.[1]
In such cases association and coöperation are for special purposes, like
hunting; they do not rise to any permanent political order.

The earliest form of continuous social organization was the clan—a group
of related families occupying a common tract of land, having the same

21

totem, and governed by the same customs or laws. When a group of clans united under the same chief the tribe was formed, and became the second step on the way to the state. But this was a slow development; many groups had no chiefs at all,[2] and many more seem to have tolerated them only in time of war.[3] Instead of democracy being a wilted feather in the cap of our own age, it appears at its best in several primitive groups where such government as exists is merely the rule of the family-heads of the clan, and no arbitrary authority is allowed.[4] The Iroquois and Delaware Indians recognized no laws or restraints beyond the natural order of the family and the clan; their chiefs had modest powers, which might at any time be ended by the elders of the tribe. The Omaha Indians were ruled by a Council of Seven, who deliberated until they came to a unanimous agreement; add this to the famous League of the Iroquois, by which many tribes bound themselves—and honored their pledge—to keep the peace, and one sees no great gap between these "savages" and the modern states that bind themselves revocably to peace in the League of Nations.

It is war that makes the chief, the king and the state, just as it is these that make war. In Samoa the chief had power during war, but at other times no one paid much attention to him. The Dyaks had no other government than that of each family by its head; in case of strife they chose their bravest warrior to lead them, and obeyed him strictly; but once the conflict was ended they literally sent him about his business.[5] In the intervals of peace it was the priest, or head magician, who had most authority and influence; and when at last a permanent kingship developed as the usual mode of government among a majority of tribes, it combined— and derived from—the offices of warrior, father and priest. Societies are ruled by two powers: in peace by the word, in crises by the sword; force is used only when indoctrination fails. Law and myth have gone hand in hand throughout the centuries, coöperating or taking turns in the management of mankind; until our own day no state dared separate them, and perhaps tomorrow they will be united again.

How did war lead to the state? It is not that men were naturally inclined to war. Some lowly peoples are quite peaceful; and the Eskimos could not understand why Europeans of the same pacific faith should hunt one another like seals and steal one another's land. "How well it is"— they apostrophized their soil—"that you are covered with ice and snow! How well it is that if in your rocks there are gold and silver, for which the Christians are so greedy, it is covered with so much snow that they cannot get at it! Your unfruitfulness makes us happy, and saves us from molestation."[6] Nevertheless, primitive life was incarnadined with intermittent war. Hunters fought for happy hunting grounds still rich in prey, herders fought for new pastures for their flocks, tillers fought for virgin soil; all of them, at times, fought to avenge a murder, or to harden and discipline their youth, or to interrupt the monotony of life, or for simple plunder and rape; very rarely for religion. There were institutions and customs for the limitation of slaughter, as among ourselves—certain hours, days, weeks or months during which no gentleman savage would kill; certain functionaries who were inviolable, certain roads neutralized, certain markets and asylums set aside for peace; and the League of the Iroquois maintained the "Great Peace" for three hundred years.[7] But for the most part war was the favorite instrument of natural selection among primitive nations and groups.

Its results were endless. It acted as a ruthless eliminator of weak peoples, and raised the level of the race in courage, violence, cruelty, intelligence and skill. It stimulated invention, made weapons that became useful tools, and arts of war that became arts of peace. (How many railroads today begin in strategy and end in trade!) Above all, war dissolved primitive communism and anarchism, introduced organization and discipline, and led to the enslavement of prisoners, the subordination of classes, and the growth of government. Property was the mother, war was the father, of the state.

II. THE STATE

As the organization of force—The village community—The psychological aides of the state

"A herd of blonde beasts of prey," says Nietzsche, "a race of conquerors and masters, which with all its warlike organization and all its organizing power pounces with its terrible claws upon a population, in numbers possibly tremendously superior, but as yet formless, . . . such is the origin of the state."[8] "The state as distinct from tribal organization," says Lester Ward, "begins with the conquest of one race by another."[9] "Everywhere," says Oppenheimer, "we find some warlike tribe breaking through the boundaries of some less warlike people, settling down as nobility, and founding its state."[10] "Violence," says Ratzenhofer, "is the agent which has created the state."[11] The state, says Gumplowicz, is the result of conquest, the establishment of the victors as a ruling caste over the vanquished.¹² "The state," says Sumner, "is the product of force, and exists by force."¹³

This violent subjection is usually of a settled agricultural group by a tribe of hunters and herders.¹⁴ For agriculture teaches men pacific ways, inures them to a prosaic routine, and exhausts them with the long day's toil; such men accumulate wealth, but they forget the arts and sentiments of war. The hunter and the herder, accustomed to danger and skilled in killing, look upon war as but another form of the chase, and hardly more perilous; when the woods cease to give them abundant game, or flocks decrease through a thinning pasture, they look with envy upon the ripe fields of the village, they invent with modern ease some plausible reason for attack, they invade, conquer, enslave and rule.*

The state is a late development, and hardly appears before the time of written history. For it presupposes a change in the very principle of social organization—from kinship to domination; and in primitive societies the former is the rule. Domination succeeds best where it binds diverse natural groups into an advantageous unity of order and trade. Even such conquest is seldom lasting except where the progress of invention has strengthened the strong by putting into their hands new tools and weapons for suppressing revolt. In permanent conquest the principle of domination tends to become concealed and almost unconscious; the French who rebelled in 1789 hardly realized, until Camille Desmoulins reminded them, that the aristocracy that had ruled them for a thousand years had come from Germany and had subjugated them by force. Time sanctifies everything; even the most arrant theft, in the hands of the robber's grandchildren, becomes sacred and inviolable property. Every state begins in compulsion; but the habits of obedience become the content of conscience, and soon every citizen thrills with loyalty to the flag.

The citizen is right; for however the state begins, it soon becomes an indispensable prop to order. As trade unites clans and tribes, relations spring up that depend not on kinship but on contiguity, and therefore require an artificial principle of regulation. The village community may serve as an example: it displaced tribe and clan as the mode of local organization, and

---

* It is a law that holds only for early societies, since under more complex conditions a variety of other factors—greater wealth, better weapons, higher intelligence—contribute to determine the issue. So Egypt was conquered not only by Hyksos, Ethiopian, Arab and Turkish nomads, but also by the settled civilizations of Assyria, Persia, Greece, Rome and England—though not until these nations had become hunters and nomads on an imperialistic scale.

achieved a simple, almost democratic government of small areas through a concourse of family-heads; but the very existence and number of such communities created a need for some external force that could regulate their interrelations and weave them into a larger economic web. The state, ogre though it was in its origin, supplied this need; it became not merely an organized force, but an instrument for adjusting the interests of the thousand conflicting groups that constitute a complex society. It spread the tentacles of its power and law over wider and wider areas, and though it made external war more destructive than before, it extended and maintained internal peace; the state may be defined as internal peace for external war. Men decided that it was better to pay taxes than to fight among themselves; better to pay tribute to one magnificent robber than to bribe them all. What an interregnum meant to a society accustomed to government may be judged from the behavior of the Baganda, among whom, when the king died, every man had to arm himself; for the lawless ran riot, killing and plundering everywhere.[15] "Without autocratic rule," as Spencer said, "the evolution of society could not have commenced."[16]

A state which should rely upon force alone would soon fall, for though men are naturally gullible they are also naturally obstinate, and power, like taxes, succeeds best when it is invisible and indirect. Hence the state, in order to maintain itself, used and forged many instruments of indoctrination—the family, the church, the school—to build in the soul of the citizen a habit of patriotic loyalty and pride. This saved a thousand policemen, and prepared the public mind for that docile coherence which is indispensable in war. Above all, the ruling minority sought more and more to transform its forcible mastery into a body of law which, while consolidating that mastery, would afford a welcome security and order to the people, and would recognize the rights of the "subject"* sufficiently to win his acceptance of the law and his adherence to the State.

III. LAW

*Law-lessness—Law and custom—Revenge—Fines—Courts—Ordeal
—The duel—Punishment—Primitive freedom*

Law comes with property, marriage and government; the lowest societies manage to get along without it. "I have lived with communities of savages in South America and in the East," said Alfred Russel Wallace, "who

---

* Note how this word betrays the origin of the state.

have no law or law-courts but the public opinion of the village freely expressed. Each man scrupulously respects the rights of his fellows, and any infraction of those rights rarely or never takes place. In such a community all are nearly equal."[17] Herman Melville writes similarly of the Marquesas Islanders: "During the time I have lived among the Typees no one was ever put upon his trial for any violence to the public. Everything went on in the valley with a harmony and smoothness unparalleled, I will venture to assert, in the most select, refined, and pious associations of mortals in Christendom."[18] The old Russian Government established courts of law in the Aleutian Islands, but in fifty years those courts found no employment. "Crime and offenses," reports Brinton, "were so infrequent under the social system of the Iroquois that they can scarcely be said to have had a penal code."[19] Such are the ideal—perhaps the idealized—conditions for whose return the anarchist perennially pines.

Certain amendments must be made to these descriptions. Natural societies are comparatively free from law first because they are ruled by customs as rigid and inviolable as any law; and secondly because crimes of violence, in the beginning, are considered to be private matters, and are left to bloody personal revenge.

Underneath all the phenomena of society is the great *terra firma* of custom, that bedrock of time-hallowed modes of thought and action which provides a society with some measure of steadiness and order through all absence, changes, and interruptions of law. Custom gives the same stability to the group that heredity and instinct give to the species, and habit to the individual. It is the routine that keeps men sane; for if there were no grooves along which thought and action might move with unconscious ease, the mind would be perpetually hesitant, and would soon take refuge in lunacy. A law of economy works in instinct and habit, in custom and convention: the most convenient mode of response to repeated stimuli or traditional situations is automatic response. Thought and innovation are disturbances of regularity, and are tolerated only for indispensable readaptations, or promised gold.

When to this natural basis of custom a supernatural sanction is added by religion, and the ways of one's ancestors are also the will of the gods, then custom becomes stronger than law, and subtracts substantially from primitive freedom. To violate law is to win the admiration of half the populace, who secretly envy anyone who can outwit this ancient enemy; to violate custom is to incur almost universal hostility. For custom rises out of the people, whereas law is forced upon them from above; law is usually a decree of the master, but custom is the natural selection of those modes of action that have been found most convenient in the experience of the group. Law partly replaces custom when the state replaces the natural order of the family, the clan, the tribe, and the village community; it more fully replaces custom when writing appears, and laws graduate from a code carried down in the memory of elders and priests into a system of legislation proclaimed in written tables. But the replacement is never complete; in the determination and judgment of human conduct custom remains to the end the force behind the law, the power behind the throne, the last "magistrate of men's lives."

The first stage in the evolution of law is personal revenge. "Vengeance is mine," says the primitive individual; "I will repay." Among the Indian tribes of Lower California every man was his own policeman, and administered justice in the form of such vengeance as he was strong enough to take. So in many early societies the murder of A by B led to the murder of B by A's son or friend C, the murder of C by B's son or friend D, and so on perhaps to the end of the alphabet; we may find examples among the purest-blooded American families of today. This principle of revenge persists throughout the history of law: it appears in the *Lex Talionis**—or Law of Retaliation—embodied in Roman Law; it plays a large rôle in the Code of Hammurabi, and in the "Mosaic" demand of "an eye for an eye and a tooth for a tooth"; and it lurks behind most legal punishments even in our day.

The second step toward law and civilization in the treatment of crime was the substitution of damages for revenge. Very often the chief, to maintain internal harmony, used his power or influence to have the revengeful family content itself with gold or goods instead of blood. Soon a regular tariff arose, determining how much must be paid for an eye, a tooth, an arm, or a life; Hammurabi legislated extensively in such terms. The Abyssinians were so meticulous in this regard that when a boy fell from a tree upon his companion and killed him, the judges decided that the bereaved mother should send another of her sons into the tree to fall upon the culprit's neck.[20] The penalties assessed in cases of composition might vary with the sex, age and rank of the offender and the injured; among the Fijians, for example, petty larceny by a common man was considered a more heinous crime than murder by a chief.[21] Throughout the

---

* A phrase apparently invented by Cicero.

history of law the magnitude of the crime has been lessened by the magnitude of the criminal.* Since these fines or compositions, paid to avert revenge, required some adjudication of offenses and damages, a third step towards law was taken by the formation of courts; the chief or the elders or the priests sat in judgment to settle the conflicts of their people. Such courts were not always judgment seats; often they were boards of voluntary conciliation, which arranged some amicable settlement of the dispute.† For many centuries, and among many peoples, resort to courts remained optional; and where the offended party was dissatisfied with the judgment rendered, he was still free to seek personal revenge.[22]

In many cases disputes were settled by a public contest between the parties, varying in bloodiness from a harmless boxing-match—as among the wise Eskimos—to a duel to the death. Frequently the primitive mind resorted to an ordeal not so much on the medieval theory that a deity would reveal the culprit as in the hope that the ordeal, however unjust, would end a feud that might otherwise embroil the tribe for generations. Sometimes accuser and accused were asked to choose between two bowls of food of which one was poisoned; the wrong party might be poisoned (usually not beyond redemption), but then the dispute was ended, since both parties ordinarily believed in the righteousness of the ordeal. Among some tribes it was the custom for a native who acknowledged his guilt to hold out his leg and permit the injured party to pierce it with a spear. Or the accused submitted to having spears thrown at him by his accusers; if they all missed him he was declared innocent; if he was hit, even by one, he was adjudged guilty, and the affair was closed.[23] From such early forms the ordeal persisted through the laws of Moses and Hammurabi and down into the Middle Ages; the duel, which is one form of the ordeal, and which historians thought dead, is being revived in our own day. So brief and narrow, in some respects, is the span between primitive and modern man; so short is the history of civilization.

The fourth advance in the growth of law was the assumption, by the chief or the state, of the obligation to prevent and punish wrongs. It is but a step from settling disputes and punishing offenses to making some

---

* Perhaps an exception should be made in the case of the Brahmans, who, by the Code of Manu (VIII, 336-8), were called upon to bear greater punishments for the same crime than members of lower castes; but this regulation was well honored in the breach.

† Some of our most modern cities are trying to revive this ancient time-saving institution.

effort to prevent them.   So the chief becomes not merely a judge but a lawgiver; and to the general body of "common law" derived from the customs of the group is added a body of "positive law," derived from the decrees of the government; in the one case the laws grow up, in the other they are handed down.   In either case the laws carry with them the mark of their ancestry, and reek with the vengeance which they tried to replace. Primitive punishments are cruel,[24] because primitive society feels insecure; as social organization becomes more stable, punishments become less severe.

In general the individual has fewer "rights" in natural society than under civilization.   Everywhere man is born in chains: the chains of heredity, of environment, of custom, and of law.   The primitive individual moves always within a web of regulations incredibly stringent and detailed; a thousand tabus restrict his action, a thousand terrors limit his will.   The natives of New Zealand were apparently without laws, but in actual fact rigid custom ruled every aspect of their lives. Unchangeable and unquestionable conventions determined the sitting and the rising, the standing and the walking, the eating, drinking and sleeping of the natives of Bengal.   The individual was hardly recognized as a separate entity in natural society; what existed was the family and the clan, the tribe and the village community; it was these that owned land and exercised power. Only with the coming of private property, which gave him economic authority, and of the state, which gave him a legal status and defined rights, did the individual begin to stand out as a distinct reality.[25]   Rights do not come to us from nature, which knows no rights except cunning and strength; they are privileges assured to individuals by the community as advantageous to the common good.   Liberty is a luxury of security; the free individual is a product and a mark of civilization.

IV.   THE FAMILY

Its function in civilization—The clan vs. the family—Growth of parental care—Unimportance of the father—Separation of the sexes—Mother-right—Status of woman—Her occupations—Her economic achievements—The patriarchate—The subjection of woman

As the basic needs of man are hunger and love, so the fundamental functions of social organization are economic provision and biological maintenance; a stream of children is as vital as a continuity of food.   To institutions which seek material welfare and political order, society always adds institutions for the perpetuation of the race. Until the state—towards the dawn of the historic civilizations—becomes the central and permanent source of social ·order, the clan undertakes the delicate task of regulating the relations between the sexes and between the generations; and even after the state has been established, the essential government of mankind remains in that most deep-rooted of all historic institutions, the family.

It is highly improbable that the first human beings lived in isolated families, even in the hunting stage; for the inferiority of man in physiological organs of defense would have left such families a prey to marauding beasts. Usually, in nature, those organisms that are poorly equipped for individual defense live in groups, and find in united action a means of survival in a world bristling with tusks and claws and impenetrable hides. Presumably it was so with man; he saved himself by solidarity in the hunting-pack and the clan. When economic relations and political mastery replaced kinship as the principle of social organization, the clan lost its position as the substructure of society; at the bottom it was supplanted by the family, at the top it was superseded by the state. Government took over the problem of maintaining order, while the family assumed the tasks of reorganizing industry and carrying on the race.

Among the lower animals there is no care of progeny; consequently eggs are spawned in great number, and some survive and develop while the great majority are eaten or destroyed. Most fish lay a million eggs per year; a few species of fish show a modest solicitude for their offspring, and find half a hundred eggs per year sufficient for their purposes. Birds care better for their young, and hatch from five to twelve eggs yearly; mammals, whose very name suggests parental care, master the earth with an average of three young per female per year.[26] Throughout the animal world fertility and destruction decrease as parental care increases; throughout the human world the birth rate and the death rate fall together as civilization rises. Better family care makes possible a longer adolescence, in which the young receive fuller training and·development before they are flung upon their own resources; and the lowered birth rate releases human energy for other activities than reproduction.

Since it was the mother who fulfilled most of the parental functions, the family was at first (so far as we can pierce the mists of history) organized on the assumption that the position of the man in the family was superficial and incidental, while that of the woman was fundamental and supreme. In some existing tribes, and probably in the earliest human groups the physiological rôle of the male in reproduction appears to have escaped notice quite as completely as among animals, who rut and mate and breed with happy unconsciousness of cause and effect. The Trobriand Islanders attribute pregnancy not to any commerce of the sexes, but to the entrance of a *baloma*, or ghost, into the woman. Usually the ghost enters while the woman is bathing; "a fish has bitten me," the girl reports. "When," says Malinowski, "I asked who was the father of an illegitimate child, there was only one answer—that there was no father, since the girl was unmarried. If, then, I asked, in quite plain terms, who was the physiological father, the question was not understood. . . . The answer would be: 'It is a *baloma* who gave her this child.' " These islanders had a strange belief that the *baloma* would more readily enter a girl given to loose relations with men; nevertheless, in choosing precautions against pregnancy, the girls preferred to avoid bathing at high tide rather than to forego relations with men.[27] It is a delightful story, which must have proved a great convenience in the embarrassing aftermath of generosity; it would be still more delightful if it had been invented for anthropologists as well as for husbands.

In Melanesia intercourse was recognized as the cause of pregnancy, but unmarried girls insisted on blaming some article in their diet.[28] Even where the function of the male was understood, sex relationships were so irregular that it was never a simple matter to determine the father. Consequently the quite primitive mother seldom bothered to inquire into the paternity of her child; it belonged to her, and she belonged not to a husband but to her father—or her brother—and the clan; it was with these that she remained, and these were the only male relatives whom her child would know.[29] The bonds of affection between brother and sister were usually stronger than between husband and wife. The husband, in many cases, remained in the family and clan of his mother, and saw his wife only as a clandestine visitor. Even in classical civilization the brother was dearer than the husband: it was her brother, not her husband, that the wife of Intaphernes saved from the wrath of Darius; it was for her brother, not for her husband, that Antigone sacrificed herself.[30] "The notion that a man's wife is the nearest person in the world to him is a relatively modern notion, and one which is restricted to a comparatively small part of the human race."[31]

So slight is the relation between father and children in primitive society that in a great number of tribes the sexes live apart. In Australia and British New Guinea, in Africa and Micronesia, in Assam and Burma, among the Aleuts, Eskimos and Samoyeds, and here and there over the earth, tribes may still be found in which there is no visible family life; the men live apart from the women, and visit them only now and then; even the meals are taken separately. In northern Papua it is not considered right for a man to be seen associating socially with a woman, even if she is the mother of his children. In Tahiti "family life is quite unknown." Out of this segregation of the sexes come those secret fraternities—usually of males—which appear everywhere among primitive races, and serve most often as a refuge against women.[32] They resemble our modern fraternities in another point—their hierarchical organization.

The simplest form of the family, then, was the woman and her children, living with her mother or her brother in the clan; such an arrangement was a natural outgrowth of the animal family of the mother and her litter, and of the biological ignorance of primitive man. An alternative early form was "matrilocal marriage": the husband left his clan and went to live with the clan and family of his wife, laboring for her or with her in the service of her parents. Descent, in such cases, was traced through the female line, and inheritance was through the mother; sometimes even the kingship passed down through her rather than through the male.[33] This "mother-right" was not a "matriarchate"—it did not imply the rule of women over men.[34] Even when property was transmitted through the woman she had little power over it; she was used as a means of tracing relationships which, through primitive laxity or freedom, were otherwise obscure.[35] It is true that in any system of society the woman exercises a certain authority, rising naturally out of her importance in the home, out of her function as the dispenser of food, and out of the need that the male has of her, and her power to refuse him. It is also true that there have been, occasionally, women rulers among some South African tribes; that in the Pelew Islands the chief did nothing of consequence without the advice of a council of elder women; that among the Iroquois the squaws had an equal right, with the men, of speaking and voting in the tribal council;[36] and that among the Seneca Indians women held great power, even to the selection of the chief. But these are rare and exceptional cases. All in all the position of woman in early societies was one of subjection verging upon slavery. Her periodic disability, her unfamiliarity with weapons, the biological absorption of her strength in carrying, nursing and rearing children, handicapped her in the war of the sexes, and doomed her to a subordinate status in all but the very lowest and the very highest societies. Nor was her position necessarily to rise with the development of civilization; it was destined to be lower in Periclean Greece than among the North American Indians; it was to rise and fall with her strategic importance rather than with the culture and morals of men.

In the hunting stage she did almost all the work except the actual capture of the game. In return for exposing himself to the hardships and risks of the chase, the male rested magnificently for the greater part of the year. The woman bore her children abundantly, reared them, kept the hut or home in repair, gathered food in woods and fields, cooked, cleaned, and made the clothing and the boots.[37] Because the men, when the tribe moved, had to be ready at any moment to fight off attack, they carried nothing but their weapons; the women carried all the rest. Bushwomen were used as servants and beasts of burden; if they proved too weak to keep up with the march, they were abandoned.[38] When the natives of the Lower Murray saw pack oxen they thought that these were the wives of the whites.[39] The differences in strength which now divide the sexes hardly existed in those days, and are now environmental rather than innate: woman, apart from her biological disabilities, was almost the equal of man in stature, endurance, resourcefulness and courage; she was not yet an ornament, a thing of beauty, or a sexual toy; she was a robust animal, able to perform arduous work for long hours, and, if necessary, to fight to the death for her children or her clan. "Women," said a chieftain of the Chippewas, "are created for work. One of them can draw or carry as much as two men. They also pitch our tents, make our clothes, mend them, and keep us warm at night. . . . We absolutely cannot get along without them on a journey. They do everything and cost only a little; for since they must be forever cooking, they can be satisfied in lean times by licking their fingers."[40]

Most economic advances, in early society, were made by the woman rather than the man. While for centuries he clung to his ancient ways of hunting and herding, she developed agriculture near the camp, and those busy arts of the home which were to become the most important industries of later days. From the "wool-bearing tree," as the Greeks called the cotton plant, the primitive woman rolled thread and made cotton cloth.[41] It was she, apparently, who developed sewing, weaving, basketry, pottery, woodworking, and building; and in many cases it was she who carried on primitive trade.[42] It was she who developed the home, slowly adding man to the list of her domesticated animals, and training him in those social dispositions and amenities which are the psychological basis and cement of civilization.

But as agriculture became more complex and brought larger rewards, the stronger sex took more and more of it into its own hands.[43] The growth of cattle-breeding gave the man a new source of wealth, stability and power; even agriculture, which must have seemed so prosaic to the mighty Nimrods of antiquity, was at last accepted by the wandering male, and the economic leadership which tillage had for a time given to women was wrested from them by the men. The application to agriculture of those very animals that woman had first domesticated led to her replacement by the male in the control of the fields; the advance from the hoe to the plough put a premium upon physical strength, and enabled the man to assert his supremacy. The growth of transmissible property in cattle and in the products of the soil led to the sexual subordination of woman, for the male now demanded from her that fidelity which he thought would enable him to pass on his accumulations to children presumably his own. Gradually the man had his way: fatherhood became recognized, and property began to descend through the male; mother-right yielded to father-right; and the patriarchal family, with the oldest male at its head, became the economic, legal, political and moral unit of society. The gods, who had been mostly feminine, became great bearded patriarchs, with such harems as ambitious men dreamed of in their solitude.

This passage to the patriarchal—father-ruled—family was fatal to the position of woman. In all essential aspects she and her children became the property first of her father or oldest brother, then of her husband. She was bought in marriage precisely as a slave was bought in the market. She was bequeathed as property when her husband died; and in some places (New Guinea, the New Hebrides, the Solomon Islands, Fiji, India, etc.) she was strangled and buried with her dead husband, or was expected to commit suicide, in order to attend upon him in the other world.[44] The father had now the right to treat, give, sell or lend his wives and daughters very much as he pleased, subject only to the social condemnation of other fathers exercising the same rights. While the male reserved the privilege of extending his sexual favors beyond his home, the woman—under patriarchal institutions—was vowed to complete chastity before marriage, and complete fidelity after it. The double standard was born.

The general subjection of woman which had existed in the hunting stage, and had persisted, in diminished form, through the period of mother-right, became now more pronounced and merciless than before. In ancient Russia, on the marriage of a daughter, the father struck her gently with a whip, and then presented the whip to the bridegroom,[45] as a sign that her beatings were now to come from a rejuvenated hand. Even the American Indians, among whom mother-right survived indefinitely, treated their women harshly, consigned to them all drudgery, and often called them dogs.[46] Everywhere the life of a woman was considered cheaper than that of a man; and when girls were born there was none of the rejoicing that marked the coming of a male. Mothers sometimes destroyed their female children to keep them from misery. In Fiji wives might be sold at pleasure, and the usual price was a musket.[47] Among some tribes man and wife did not sleep together, lest the breath of the woman should enfeeble the man; in Fiji it was not thought proper for a man to sleep regularly at home; in New Caledonia the wife slept in a shed, while the man slept in the house. In Fiji dogs were allowed in some of the temples, but women were excluded from all;[48] such exclusion of women from religious services survives in Islam to this day. Doubtless woman enjoyed at all times the mastery that comes of long-continued speech; the men might be rebuffed, harangued, even—now and then—beaten.[49] But all in all the man was lord, the woman was servant. The Kaffir bought women like slaves, as a form of life-income insurance; when he had a sufficient number of wives he could rest for the remainder of his days; they would do all the work for him. Some tribes of ancient India reckoned the women of a family as part of the property inheritance, along with the domestic animals;[50] nor did the last commandment of Moses distinguish very clearly in this matter. Throughout negro Africa women hardly differed from slaves, except that they were expected to provide sexual as well as economic satisfaction. Marriage began as a form of the law of property, as a part of the institution of slavery.[51]

CHAPTER IV

The Moral Elements of Civilization

SINCE no society can exist without order, and no order without regulation, we may take it as a rule of history that the power of custom varies inversely as the multiplicity of laws, much as the power of instinct varies inversely as the multiplicity of thoughts. Some rules are necessary for the game of life; they may differ in different groups, but within the group they must be essentially the same. These rules may be conventions, customs, morals, or laws. Conventions are forms of behavior found expedient by a people; customs are conventions accepted by successive generations, after natural selection through trial and error and elimination; morals are such customs as the group considers vital to its welfare and development. In primitive societies, where there is no written law, these vital customs or morals regulate every sphere of human existence, and give stability and continuity to the social order. Through the slow magic of time such customs, by long repetition, become a second nature in the individual; if he violates them he feels a certain fear, discomfort or shame; this is the origin of that conscience, or moral sense, which Darwin chose as the most impressive distinction between animals and men.[1] In its higher development conscience is social consciousness—the feeling of the individual that he belongs to a group, and owes it some measure of loyalty and consideration. Morality is the coöperation of the part with the whole, and of each group with some larger whole. Civilization, of course, would be impossible without it.

I. MARRIAGE

The meaning of marriage—Its biological origins—Sexual communism—Trial marriage—Group marriage—Individual marriage—Polygamy—Its eugenic value—Exogamy—Marriage by service—By capture—By purchase—Primitive love—The economic function of marriage

The first task of those customs that constitute the moral code of a group is to regulate the relations of the sexes, for these are a perennial source of discord, violence, and possible degeneration. The basic form of this sexual regulation is marriage, which may be defined as the association of mates for the care of offspring. It is a variable and fluctuating institution, which has passed through almost every conceivable form and experiment in the course of its history, from the primitive care of offspring without the association of mates to the modern association of mates without the care of offspring.

Our animal forefathers invented it. Some birds seem to live as reproducing mates in a divorceless monogamy. Among gorillas and orangutans the association of the parents continues to the end of the breeding season, and has many human features. Any approach to loose behavior on the part of the female is severely punished by the male.[2] The orangs of Borneo, says De Crespigny, "live in families: the male, the female, and a young one"; and Dr. Savage reports of the gorillas that "it is not unusual to see the 'old folks' sitting under a tree regaling themselves with fruit and friendly chat, while their children are leaping around them and swinging from branch to branch in boisterous merriment."[3] Marriage is older than man.

Societies without marriage are rare, but the sedulous inquirer can find enough of them to form a respectable transition from the promiscuity of the lower mammals to the marriages of primitive men. In Futuna and Hawaii the majority of the people did not marry at all;[4] the Lubus mated freely and indiscriminately, and had no conception of marriage; certain tribes of Borneo lived in marriageless association, freer than the birds; and among some peoples of primitive Russia "the men utilized the women without distinction, so that no woman had her appointed husband." African pygmies have been described as having no marriage institutions, but as following "their animal instincts wholly without restraint."[5] This primitive "nationalization of women," corresponding to primitive communism in land and food, passed away at so early a stage that few traces of it remain. Some memory of it, however, lingered on in divers forms: in the feeling of many nature peoples that monogamy—which they would define as the monopoly of a woman by one man—is unnatural and immoral;[6] in periodic festivals of license (still surviving faintly in our *Mardi Gras*), when sexual restraints were temporarily abandoned; in the demand that a woman should give herself—as at the Temple of Mylitta in Babylon—to any man that solicited her, before she would be allowed to marry;* in

---

* Cf. below, p. 245.

the custom of wife-lending, so essential to many primitive codes of hospitality; and in the *jus primæ noctis*, or right of the first night, by which,
in early feudal Europe, the lord of the manor, perhaps representing the
ancient rights of the tribe, occasionally deflowered the bride before the
bridegroom was allowed to consummate the marriage.[6a]

A variety of tentative unions gradually took the place of indiscriminate
relations. Among the Orang Sakai of Malacca a girl remained for a time
with each man of the tribe, passing from one to another until she had
made the rounds; then she began again.[7] Among the Yakuts of Siberia,
the Botocudos of South Africa, the lower classes of Tibet, and many other
peoples, marriage was quite experimental, and could be ended at the will
of either party, with no reasons given or required. Among the Bushmen
"any disagreement sufficed to end a union, and new connections could
immediately be found for both." Among the Damaras, according to Sir
Francis Galton, "the spouse was changed almost weekly, and I seldom
knew without inquiry who the *pro tempore* husband of each lady was at
any particular time." Among the Baila "women are bandied about from
man to man, and of their own accord leave one husband for another.
Young women scarcely out of their teens often have had four or five
husbands, all still living."[8] The original word for marriage, in Hawaii,
meant to try.[9] Among the Tahitians, a century ago, unions were free and
dissoluble at will, so long as there were no children; if a child came the
parents might destroy it without social reproach, or the couple might
rear the child and enter into a more permanent relation; the man pledged
his support to the woman in return for the burden of parental care that
she now assumed.[10]

Marco Polo writes of a Central Asiatic tribe, inhabiting Peyn (now
Keriya) in the thirteenth century: "If a married man goes to a distance
from home to be absent twenty days, his wife has a right, if she is so
inclined, to take another husband; and the men, on the same principle,
marry wherever they happen to reside."[11] So old are the latest innovations
in marriage and morals.

Letourneau said of marriage that "every possible experiment compatible
with the duration of savage or barbarian societies has been tried, or is still
practised, amongst various races, without the least thought of the moral
ideas generally prevailing in Europe."[12] In addition to experiments in permanence there were experiments in relationship. In a few cases we find "group

marriage," by which a number of men belonging to one group married collectively a number of women belonging to another group.[13] In Tibet, for example, it was the custom for a group of brothers to marry a group of sisters, and for the two groups to practise sexual communism between them, each of the men cohabiting with each of the women.[14] Caesar reported a similar custom in ancient Britain.[15] Survivals of it appear in the "levirate," a custom existing among the early Jews and other ancient peoples, by which a man was obligated to marry his brother's widow;[16] this was the rule that so irked Onan.

What was it that led men to replace the semi-promiscuity of primitive society with individual marriage? Since, in a great majority of nature peoples, there are few, if any, restraints on premarital relations, it is obvious that physical desire does not give rise to the institution of marriage. For marriage, with its restrictions and psychological irritations, could not possibly compete with sexual communism as a mode of satisfying the erotic propensities of men. Nor could the individual establishment offer at the outset any mode of rearing children that would be obviously superior to their rearing by the mother, her family, and the clan. Some powerful economic motives must have favored the evolution of marriage. In all probability (for again we must remind ourselves how little we really know of origins) these motives were connected with the rising institution of property.

Individual marriage came through the desire of the male to have cheap slaves, and to avoid bequeathing his property to other men's children. Polygamy, or the marriage of one person to several mates, appears here and there in the form of polyandry—the marriage of one woman to several men—as among the Todas and some tribes of Tibet;[17] the custom may still be found where males outnumber females considerably.[18] But this custom soon falls prey to the conquering male, and polygamy has come to mean for us, usually, what would more strictly be called polygyny—the possession of several wives by one man. Medieval theologians thought that Mohammed had invented polygamy, but it antedated Islam by some years, being the prevailing mode of marriage in the primitive world.[19] Many causes conspired to make it general. In early society, because of hunting and war, the life of the male is more violent and dangerous, and the death rate of men is higher, than that of women. The consequent excess of women compels a choice between polygamy and the barren celibacy of a minority of women; but such celibacy is intolerable to peoples who require a high birth rate to make up for a high death rate, and who therefore scorn the mateless and childless woman. Again, men like variety; as the Negroes of Angola expressed it, they were "not able to eat always of the same dish." Also, men like youth in their mates, and women age rapidly in primitive communities. The women themselves often favored polygamy; it permitted them to nurse their children longer, and therefore to reduce the frequency of motherhood without interfering with the erotic and philoprogenitive inclinations of the male. Sometimes the first wife, burdened with toil, helped her husband to secure an additional wife, so that her burden might be shared, and additional children might raise the productive power and the wealth of the family.[20] Children were economic assets, and men invested in wives in order to draw children from them like interest. In the patriarchal system wives and children were in effect the slaves of the man; the more a man had of them, the richer he was. The poor man practised monogamy, but he looked upon it as a shameful condition, from which some day he would rise to the respected position of a polygamous male.[21]

Doubtless polygamy was well adapted to the marital needs of a primitive society in which women outnumbered men. It had a eugenic value superior to that of contemporary monogamy; for whereas in modern society the most able and prudent men marry latest and have least children, under polygamy the most able men, presumably, secured the bests mates and had most children. Hence polygamy has survived among practically all nature peoples, even among the majority of civilized mankind; only in our day has it begun to die in the Orient. Certain conditions, however, militated against it. The decrease in danger and violence, consequent upon a settled agricultural life, brought the sexes towards an approximate numerical equality; and under these circumstances open polygamy, even in primitive societies, became the privilege of the prosperous minority.[22] The mass of the people practised a monogamy tempered with adultery, while another minority, of willing or regretful celibates, balanced the polygamy of the rich. Jealousy in the male, and possessiveness in the female, entered into the situation more effectively as the sexes approximated in number; for where the strong could not have a multiplicity of wives except by taking the actual or potential wives of other men, and by (in some cases) offending their own, polygamy became a difficult matter, which only the cleverest could manage. As property accumulated, and men were loath to scatter it in small bequests, it became desirable to differentiate wives into "chief wife" and concubines, so that only the children of the former should share the legacy; this remained the status of marriage in Asia until our own generation. Gradually the chief wife became the only wife, the concubines became kept women in secret and apart, or they disappeared; and as Christianity entered upon the scene, monogamy, in Europe, took the place of polygamy as the lawful and outward form of sexual association. But monogamy, like letters and the state, is artificial, and belongs to the history, not to the origins, of civilization.

Whatever form the union might take, marriage was obligatory among nearly all primitive peoples. The unmarried male had no standing in the community, or was considered only half a man.[23] Exogamy, too, was compulsory: that is to say, a man was expected to secure his wife from another clan than his own. Whether this custom arose because the primitive mind suspected the evil effects of close inbreeding, or because such intergroup marriages created or cemented useful political alliances, promoted social organization, and lessened the danger of war, or because the capture of a wife from another tribe had become a fashionable mark of male maturity, or because familiarity breeds contempt and distance lends enchantment to the view—we do not know. In any case the restriction was well-nigh universal in early society; and though it was successfully violated by the Pharaohs, the Ptolemies and the Incas, who all favored the marriage of brother and sister, it survived into Roman and modern law and consciously or unconsciously moulds our behavior to this day.

How did the male secure his wife from another tribe? Where the matriarchal organization was strong he was often required to go and live with the clan of the girl whom he sought. As the patriarchal system developed, the suitor was allowed, after a term of service to the father, to take his bride back to his own clan; so Jacob served Laban for Leah and Rachel.[24] Sometimes the suitor shortened the matter with plain, blunt force. It was an advantage as well as a distinction to have stolen a wife; not only would she be a cheap slave, but new slaves could be begotten of her, and these children would chain her to her slavery. Such marriage by capture, though not the rule, occurred sporadically in the primitive world. Among the North American Indians the women were included in the spoils of war, and this happened so frequently that in some tribes the husbands and their wives spoke mutually unintelligible languages. The Slavs of Russia and Serbia practised occasional marriage by capture until the last century.*[25] Vestiges of it remain in the custom of simulating the capture of the bride by the groom in certain wedding ceremonies.[27] All in all it was a logical aspect of the almost incessant war of the tribes, and a logical starting-point for that eternal war of the sexes whose only truces are brief nocturnes and dreamless sleep.

As wealth grew it became more convenient to offer the father a substantial present—or a sum of money—for his daughter, rather than serve for her in an alien clan, or risk the violence and feuds that might come of marriage by capture. Consequently marriage by purchase and parental arrangement was the rule in early societies.[28] Transition forms occur; the Melanesians sometimes stole their wives, but made the theft legal by a later payment to her family. Among some natives of New Guinea the man abducted the girl, and then, while he and she were in hiding, commissioned his friends to bargain with her father over a purchase price.[29] The ease with which moral indignation in these matters might be financially appeased is illuminating. A Maori mother, wailing loudly, bitterly cursed the youth who had eloped with her daughter, until he presented her with a blanket. "That was all I wanted," she said; "I only wanted to get a blanket, and therefore made this noise."[30] Usually the bride cost more than a blanket: among the Hottentots her price was an ox or a cow; among the Croo three cows and a sheep; among the Kaffirs six to thirty head of cattle, depending upon the rank of the girl's family; and among the Togos sixteen dollars cash and six dollars in goods.[31]

Marriage by purchase prevails throughout primitive Africa, and is still a normal institution in China and Japan; it flourished in ancient India and Judea, and in pre-Columbian Central America and Peru; instances of it occur in Europe today.[32] It is a natural development of patriarchal institutions; the father owns the daughter, and may dispose of her, within broad limits, as he sees fit. The Orinoco Indians expressed the matter by saying that the suitor should pay the father for rearing the girl for his use.[33] Sometimes the girl was exhibited to potential suitors in a bride-show; so among the Somalis the bride, richly caparisoned, was led about on horseback or on

---

* Briffault thinks that marriage by capture was a transition from matrilocal to patriarchal marriage: the male, refusing to go and live with the tribe or family of his wife, forced her to come to his.[26] Lippert believed that exogamy arose as a peaceable substitute for capture;[26a] theft again graduated into trade.

foot, in an atmosphere heavily perfumed to stir the suitors to a handsome price.[34]   There is no record of women objecting to marriage by purchase; on the contrary, they took keen pride in the sums paid for them, and scorned the woman who gave herself in marriage without a price;[35] they believed that in a "love-match" the villainous male was getting too much for nothing.[36] On the other hand, it was usual for the father to acknowledge the bridegroom's payment with a return gift which, as time went on, approximated more and more in value to the sum offered for the bride.[37]   Rich fathers, anxious to smooth the way for their daughters, gradually enlarged these gifts until the institution of the dowry took form; and the purchase of the husband by the father replaced, or accompanied, the purchase of the wife by the suitor.[38]

In all these forms and varieties of marriage there is hardly a trace of romantic love. We find a few cases of love-marriages among the Papuans of New Guinea; among other primitive peoples we come upon instances of love (in the sense of mutual devotion rather than mutual need), but usually these attachments have nothing to do with marriage. In simple days men married for cheap labor, profitable parentage, and regular meals. "In Yariba," says Lander, "marriage is celebrated by the natives as unconcernedly as possible; a man thinks as little of taking a wife as of cutting an ear of corn—affection is altogether out of the question."[39] Since premarital relations are abundant in primitive society, passion is not dammed up by denial, and seldom affects the choice of a wife. For the same reason—the absence of delay between desire and fulfilment—no time is given for that brooding introversion of frustrated, and therefore idealizing, passion which is usually the source of youthful romantic love. Such love is reserved for developed civilizations, in which morals have raised barriers against desire, and the growth of wealth has enabled some men to afford, and some women to provide, the luxuries and delicacies of romance; primitive peoples are too poor to be romantic. One rarely finds love poetry in their songs. When the missionaries translated the Bible into the language of the Algonquins they could discover no native equivalent for the word *love*. The Hottentots are described as "cold and indifferent to one another" in marriage. On the Gold Coast "not even the appearance of affection exists between husband and wife"; and it is the same in primitive Australia. "I asked Baba," said Caillié, speaking of a Senegal Negro, "why he did not sometimes make merry with his wives. He replied that if he did he should not be able to manage them." An Australian native, asked why he wished to marry, answered honestly that he wanted a wife to secure food, water and wood for him, and to carry his belongings on the march.⁴⁰ The kiss, which seems so indispensable to America, is quite unknown to primitive peoples, or known only to be scorned.⁴¹

In general the "savage" takes his sex philosophically, with hardly more of metaphysical or theological misgiving than the animal; he does not brood over it, or fly into a passion with it; it is as much a matter of course with him as his food. He makes no pretense to idealistic motives. Marriage is never a sacrament with him, and seldom an affair of lavish ceremony; it is frankly a commercial transaction. It never occurs to him to be ashamed that he subordinates emotional to practical considerations in choosing his mate; he would rather be ashamed of the opposite, and would demand of us, if he were as immodest as we are, some explanation of our custom of binding a man and a woman together almost for life because sexual desire has chained them for a moment with its lightning. The primitive male looked upon marriage in terms not of sexual license but of economic coöperation. He expected the woman—and the woman expected herself—to be not so much gracious and beautiful (though he appreciated these qualities in her) as useful and industrious; she was to be an economic asset rather than a total loss; otherwise the matter-of-fact "savage" would never have thought of marriage at all. Marriage was a profitable partnership, not a private debauch; it was a way whereby a man and a woman, working together, might be more prosperous than if each worked alone. Wherever, in the history of civilization, woman has ceased to be an economic asset in marriage, marriage has decayed; and sometimes civilization has decayed with it.

II. SEXUAL MORALITY

Premarital relations — Prostitution — Chastity — Virginity — The double standard—Modesty—The relativity of morals—The biological rôle of modesty—Adultery—Divorce—Abortion—Infanticide—Childhood—The individual

The greatest task of morals is always sexual regulation; for the reproductive instinct creates problems not only within marriage, but before and after it, and threatens at any moment to disturb social order with its persistence, its intensity, its scorn of law, and its perversions. The first problem concerns premarital relations—shall they be restricted, or free? Even among animals sex is not quite unrestrained; the rejection of the male by the female except in periods of rut reduces sex to a much more modest rôle in the animal world than it occupies in our own lecherous species. As Beaumarchais put it, man differs from the animal in eating without being hungry, drinking without being thirsty, and making love at all seasons. Among primitive peoples we find some analogue, or converse, of animal restrictions, in the tabu placed upon relations with a woman in her menstrual period. With this general exception premarital intercourse is left for the most part free in the simplest societies. Among the North American Indians the young men and women mated freely; and these relations were not held an impediment to marriage. Among the Papuans of New Guinea sex life began at an extremely early age, and premarital promiscuity was the rule.[43] Similar premarital liberty obtained among the Soyots of Siberia, the Igorots of the Philippines, the natives of Upper Burma, the Kaffirs and Bushmen of Africa, the tribes of the Niger and the Uganda, of New Georgia, the Murray Islands, the Andaman Islands, Tahiti, Polynesia, Assam, etc.[44]

Under such conditions we must not expect to find much prostitution in primitive society. The "oldest profession" is comparatively young; it arises only with civilization, with the appearance of property and the disappearance of premarital freedom. Here and there we find girls selling themselves for a while to raise a dowry, or to provide funds for the temples; but this occurs only where the local moral code approves of it as a pious sacrifice to help thrifty parents or hungry gods.[45]

Chastity is a correspondingly late development. What the primitive maiden dreaded was not the loss of virginity, but a reputation for sterility;[46] premarital pregnancy was, more often than not, an aid rather than a handicap in finding a husband, for it settled all doubts of sterility, and promised profitable children. The simpler tribes, before the coming of property, seem to have held virginity in contempt, as indicating unpopularity. The Kamchadal bridegroom who found his bride to be a virgin was much put out, and "roundly abused her mother for the negligent way in which she had brought up her daughter."[47] In many places virginity was considered a barrier to marriage, because it laid upon the husband the unpleasant task of violating the tabu that forbade him to shed the blood of any member of his tribe. Sometimes girls offered themselves to a stranger in order to break this tabu against their marriage. In Tibet mothers anxiously sought men who would deflower their daughters; in Malabar the girls themselves begged the services of passers-by to the same end, "for while they were virgins they could not find a husband." In some tribes the bride was obliged to give herself to the wedding guests before going in to her husband; in others the bridegroom hired a man to end the virginity of his bride; among certain Philippine tribes a special official was appointed, at a high salary, to perform this function for prospective husbands.[48]

What was it that changed virginity from a fault into a virtue, and made it an element in the moral codes of all the higher civilizations? Doubtless it was the institution of property. Premarital chastity came as an extension, to the daughters, of the proprietary feeling with which the patriarchal male looked upon his wife. The valuation of virginity rose when, under marriage by purchase, the virgin bride was found to bring a higher price than her weak sister; the virgin gave promise, by her past, of that marital fidelity which now seemed so precious to men beset by worry lest they should leave their property to surreptitious children.[49]

The men never thought of applying the same restrictions to themselves; no society in history has ever insisted on the premarital chastity of the male; no language has ever had a word for a virgin man.[50] The aura of virginity was kept exclusively for daughters, and pressed upon them in a thousands ways. The Tuaregs punished the irregularity of a daughter or a sister with death; the Negroes of Nubia, Abyssinia, Somaliland, etc., practised upon their daughters the cruel art of infibulation—i.e., the attachment of a ring or lock to the genitals to prevent copulation; in Burma and Siam a similar practice survived to our own day.[51] Forms of seclusion arose by which girls were kept from providing or receiving temptation. In New Britain the richer parents confined their daughters, through five dangerous years, in huts guarded by virtuous old crones; the girls were never allowed to come out, and only their relatives could see them. Some tribes in Borneo kept their unmarried girls in solitary confinement.[52] From these primitive customs to the *purdah* of the Moslems and the Hindus is but a step, and indicates again how nearly "civilization" touches "savagery."

Modesty came with virginity and the patriarchate. There are many tribes which to this day show no shame in exposing the body;[52a] indeed, some are ashamed to wear clothing. All Africa rocked with laughter when Livingstone begged his black hosts to put on some clothing before the arrival of his wife. The Queen of the Balonda was quite naked when she held court for Livingstone.[53] A small minority of tribes practise sex relations publicly, without any thought of shame.[54] At first modesty is the feeling of the woman that she is tabu in her periods. When marriage by purchase takes form, and virginity in the daughter brings a profit to her father, seclusion and the compulsion to virginity beget in the girl a sense of obligation to chastity. Again, modesty is the feeling of the wife who, under purchase marriage, feels a financial obligation to her husband to refrain from such external sexual relations as cannot bring him any recompense. Clothing appears at this point, if motives of adornment and protection have not already engendered it; in many tribes women wore clothing only after marriage,[55] as a sign of their exclusive possession by a husband, and as a deterrent to gallantry; primitive man did not agree with the author of *Penguin Isle* that clothing encouraged lechery. Chastity, however, bears no necessary relation to clothing; some travelers report that morals in Africa vary inversely as the amount of dress.[56] It is clear that what men are ashamed of depends entirely upon the local tabus and customs of their group. Until recently a Chinese woman was ashamed to show her foot, an Arab woman her face, a Tuareg woman her mouth; but the women of ancient Egypt, of nineteenth-century India and of twentieth-century Bali (before prurient tourists came) never thought of shame at the exposure of their breasts.

We must not conclude that morals are worthless because they differ according to time and place, and that it would be wise to show our historic learning by at once discarding the moral customs of our group. A little anthropology is a dangerous thing. It is substantially true that—as Anatole France ironically expressed the matter—"morality is the sum of the prejudices of a community";[57] and that, as Anacharsis put it among the Greeks, if one were to bring together all customs considered sacred by some group, and were then to take away all customs considered immoral by some group, nothing would remain. But this does not prove the worthlessness of morals; it only shows in what varied ways social order has been preserved. Social order is none the less necessary; the game must still have rules in order to be played; men must know what to expect of one another in the ordinary circumstances of life. Hence the unanimity with which the members of a society practise its moral code is quite as important as the contents of that code. Our heroic rejection of the customs and morals of our tribe, upon our adolescent discovery of their relativity, betrays the immaturity of our minds; given another decade and we begin to understand that there may be more wisdom in the moral code of the group— the formulated experience of generations of the race—than can be explained in a college course. Sooner or later the disturbing realization comes to us that even that which we cannot understand may be true. The institutions, conventions, customs and laws that make up the complex structure of a society are the work of a hundred centuries and a billion minds; and one mind must not expect to comprehend them in one lifetime, much less in twenty years. We are warranted in concluding that morals are relative, and indispensable.

Since old and basic customs represent a natural selection of group ways after centuries of trial and error, we must expect to find some social utility, or survival value, in virginity and modesty, despite their historical relativity, their association with marriage by purchase, and their contributions to neurosis. Modesty was a strategic retreat which enabled the girl, where she had any choice, to select her mate more deliberately, or compel him to show finer qualities before winning her; and the very obstructions it raised against desire generated those sentiments of romantic love which heightened her value in his eyes. The inculcation of virginity destroyed the naturalness and ease of primitive sexual life; but, by discouraging early sex development and premature motherhood, it lessened the gap —which tends to widen disruptively as civilization develops—between economic and sexual maturity. Probably it served in this way to strengthen the individual physically and mentally, to lengthen adolescence and training, and so to lift the level of the race.

As the institution of property developed, adultery graduated from a venial into a mortal sin. Half of the primitive peoples known to us attach no great importance to it.[58] The rise of property not only led to the exaction of complete fidelity from the woman, but generated in the male a proprietary attitude towards her; even when he lent her to a guest it was because she belonged to him in body and soul. *Suttee* was the completion of this conception; the woman must go down into the master's grave along with his other belongings. Under the patriarchate adultery was classed with theft;[59] it was, so to speak, an infringement of patent. Punishment for it varied through all degrees of severity from the indifference of the simpler tribes to the disembowelment of adulteresses among certain California Indians.[60] After centuries of punishment the new virtue of wifely fidelity was firmly established, and had generated an appropriate conscience in the feminine heart. Many Indian tribes surprised their conquerors by the unapproachable virtue of their squaws; and certain male travelers have hoped that the women of Europe and America might some day equal in marital faithfulness the wives of the Zulus and the Papuans.[61]

It was easier for the Papuans, since among them, as among most primitive peoples, there were few impediments to the divorce of the woman by the man. Unions seldom lasted more than a few years among the American Indians. "A large proportion of the old and middle-aged men," says Schoolcraft, "have had many different wives, and their children, scattered around the country, are unknown to them."[62] They "laugh at Europeans for having only one wife, and that for life; they consider that the Good Spirit formed them to be happy, and not to continue together unless their tempers and dispositions were congenial."[63] The Cherokees changed wives three or four times a year; the conservative Samoans kept them as long as three years.[64] With the coming of a settled agricultural life, unions became more permanent. Under the patriarchal system the man found it uneconomical to divorce a wife, for this meant, in effect, to lose a profitable slave.[65] As the family became the productive unit of society, tilling the soil together, it prospered—other things equal—according to its size and cohesion; it was found to some advantage that the union of the mates should continue until the last child was reared. By that time no energy remained for a new romance, and the lives of the parents had been forged into one by common work and trials. Only with the passage to urban industry, and the consequent reduction of the family in size and economic importance, has divorce become widespread again.

In general, throughout history, men have wanted many children, and therefore have called motherhood sacred; while women, who know more about reproduction, have secretly rebelled against this heavy assignment, and have used an endless variety of means to reduce the burdens of maternity. Primitive men do not usually care to restrict population; under normal conditions children are profitable, and the male regrets only that they cannot all be sons. It is the woman who invents abortion, infanticide and contraception—for even the last occurs, sporadically, among primitive peoples.[66] It is astonishing to find how similar are the motives of the "savage" to the "civilized" woman in preventing birth: to escape the burden of rearing offspring, to preserve a youthful figure, to avert the disgrace of extramarital motherhood, to avoid death, etc. The simplest means of reducing maternity was the refusal of the man by the woman during the period of nursing, which might be prolonged for many years. Sometimes, as among the Cheyenne Indians, the women developed the custom of refusing to bear a second child until the first was ten years old. In New Britain the women had no children till two or four years after marriage.

The Guaycurus of Brazil were constantly diminishing because the women would bear no children till the age of thirty. Among the Papuans abortion was frequent; "children are burdensome," said the women; "we are weary of them; we go dead." Some Maori tribes used herbs or induced artificial malposition of the uterus, to prevent conception[67]

When abortion failed, infanticide remained. Most nature peoples permitted the killing of the newborn child if it was deformed, or diseased, or a bastard, or if its mother had died in giving it birth. As if any reason would be good in the task of limiting population to the available means of subsistence, many tribes killed infants whom they considered to have been born under unlucky circumstances: so the Bondei natives strangled all children who entered the world headfirst; the Kamchadals killed babes born in stormy weather; Madagascar tribes exposed, drowned, or buried alive children who made their *début* in March or April, or on a Wednesday or a Friday, or in the last week of the month. If a woman gave birth to twins it was, in some tribes, held proof of adultery, since no man could be the father of two children at the same time; and therefore one or both of the children suffered death. The practice of infanticide was particularly prevalent among nomads, who found children a problem on their long marches. The Bangerang tribe of Victoria killed half their children at birth; the Lenguas of the Paraguayan Chaco allowed only one child per family per seven years to survive; the Abipones achieved a French economy in population by rearing a boy and a girl in each household, killing off other offspring as fast as they appeared. Where famine conditions existed or threatened, most tribes strangled the newborn, and some tribes ate them. Usually it was the girl that was most subject to infanticide; occasionally she was tortured to death with a view to inducing the soul to appear, in its next incarnation, in the form of a boy.[68] Infanticide was practised without cruelty and without remorse; for in the first moments after delivery, apparently, the mother felt no instinctive love for the child.

Once the child had been permitted to live a few days, it was safe against infanticide; soon parental love was evoked by its helpless simplicity, and in most cases it was treated more affectionately by its primitive parents than the average child of the higher races.[69] For lack of milk or soft food the mother nursed the child from two to four years, sometimes for twelve;[70] one traveler describes a boy who had learned to smoke before he was weaned;[71] and often a youngster running about with other children would interrupt his play—or his work—to go and be nursed by his mother.[72] The Negro mother at work carried her infant on her back, and sometimes fed it by slinging her breasts over her shoulder.[73] Primitive discipline was indulgent but not ruinous; at an early age the child was left to face for itself the consequences of its stupidity, its insolence, or its pugnacity; and learning went on apace. Filial, as well as parental, love was highly developed in natural society.[74]

Dangers and disease were frequent in primitive childhood, and mortality was high. Youth was brief, for at an early age marital and martial responsibility began, and soon the individual was lost in the heavy tasks of replenishing and defending the group. The women were consumed in caring for children, the men in providing for them. When the youngest child had been reared the parents were worn out; as little space remained for individual life at the end as at the beginning. Individualism, like liberty, is a luxury of civilization. Only with the dawn of history were a sufficient number of men and women freed from the burdens of hunger, reproduction and war to create the intangible values of leisure, culture and art.

III. SOCIAL MORALITY

The nature of virtue and vice—Greed—Dishonesty—Violence—
Homicide — Suicide — The socialization of the individual —
Altruism—Hospitality—Manners—Tribal limits of moral-
ity—Primitive vs. modern morals—Religion and morals

Part of the function of parentage is the transmission of a moral code. For the child is more animal than human; it has humanity thrust upon it day by day as it receives the moral and mental heritage of the race. Biologically it is badly equipped for civilization, since its instincts provide only for traditional and basic situations, and include impulses more adapted to the jungle than to the town. Every vice was once a virtue, necessary in the struggle for existence; it became a vice only when it survived the conditions that made it indispensable; a vice, therefore, is not an advanced form of behavior, but usually an atavistic throwback to ancient and superseded ways. It is one purpose of a moral code to adjust the unchanged—or slowly changing—impulses of human nature to the changing needs and circumstances of social life.

Greed, acquisitiveness, dishonesty, cruelty and violence were for so many generations useful to animals and men that not all our laws, our education, our morals and our religions can quite stamp them out; some of them, doubtless, have a certain survival value even today. The animal gorges himself because he does not know when he may find food again; this uncertainty is the origin of greed. The Yakuts have been known to eat forty pounds of meat in one day; and similar stories, only less heroic, are told of the Eskimos and the natives of Australia.[75] Economic security is too recent an achievement of civilization to have eliminated this natural greed; it still appears in the insatiable acquisitiveness whereby the fretful modern man or woman stores up gold, or other goods, that may in emergency be turned into food. Greed for drink is not as widespread as greed for food, for most human aggregations have centered around some water supply. Nevertheless, the drinking of intoxicants is almost universal; not so much because men are greedy as because they are cold and wish to be warmed, or unhappy and wish to forget—or simply because the water available to them is not fit to drink.

Dishonesty is not so ancient as greed, for hunger is older than property. The simplest "savages" seem to be the most honest.[76] "Their word is sacred," said Kolben of the Hottentots; they know "nothing of the corruptness and faithless arts of Europe."[77] As international communications improved, this naïve honesty disappeared; Europe has taught the gentle art to the Hottentots. In general, dishonesty rises with civilization, because under civilization the stakes of diplomacy are larger, there are more things to be stolen, and education makes men clever. When property develops among primitive men, lying and stealing come in its train.[78]

Crimes of violence are as old as greed; the struggle for food, land and mates has in every generation fed the earth with blood,.and has offered a dark background for the fitful light of civilization. Primitive man was cruel because he had to be; life taught him that he must have an arm always ready to strike, and a heart apt for "natural killing." The blackest page in anthropology is the story of primitive torture, and of the joy that many primitive men and women seem to have taken in the infliction of pain.[79] Much of this cruelty was associated with war; within the tribe manners were less ferocious, and primitive men treated one another—and even their slaves—with a quite civilized kindliness.[80] But since men had to kill vigorously in war, they learned to kill also in time of peace; for to many a primitive mind no argument is settled until one of the disputants is dead. Among many tribes murder, even of another member of the same

clan, aroused far less horror than it used to do with us. The Fuegians punished a murderer merely by exiling him until his fellows had forgotten
his crime. The Kaffirs considered a murderer unclean, and required that
he should blacken his face with charcoal; but after a while, if he washed
himself, rinsed his mouth, and dyed himself brown, he was received into
society again. The savages of Futuna, like our own, looked upon a murderer as a hero.[81] In several tribes no woman would marry a man who had
not killed some one, in fair fight or foul; hence the practice of head-
hunting, which survives in the Philippines today. The Dyak who brought
back most heads from such a man-hunt had the choice of all the girls in
his village; these were eager for his favors, feeling that through him they
might become the mothers of brave and potent men.*[82]

Where food is dear life is cheap. Eskimo sons must kill their parents
when these have become so old as to be helpless and useless; failure to
kill them in such cases would be considered a breach of filial duty.[83] Even
his own life seems cheap to primitive man, for he kills himself with a readiness rivaled only by the Japanese. If an offended person commits suicide,
or mutilates himself, the offender must imitate him or become a pariah;[84] so
old is hara-kiri. Any reason may suffice for suicide: some Indian women
of North America killed themselves because their men had assumed the
privilege of scolding them; and a young Trobriand Islander committed
suicide because his wife had smoked all his tobacco.[85]

To transmute greed into thrift, violence into argument, murder into
litigation, and suicide into philosophy has been part of the task of civilization. It was a great advance when the strong consented to eat the weak
by due process of law. No society can survive if it allows its members to
behave toward one another in the same way in which it encourages them
to behave as a group toward other groups; internal coöperation is the first
law of external competition. The struggle for existence is not ended by
mutual aid, it is incorporated, or transferred to the group. Other things
equal, the ability to compete with rival groups will be proportionate to
the ability of the individual members and families to combine with one
another. Hence every society inculcates a moral code, and builds up in the
heart of the individual, as its secret allies and aides, social dispositions that
mitigate the natural war of life; it encourages—by calling them virtues—

---

* This is half the theme of Synge's drama, The Playboy of the Western World.

those qualities or habits in the individual which redound to the advantage of the group, and discourages contrary qualities by calling them vices. In this way the individual is in some outward measure socialized, and the animal becomes a citizen.

It was hardly more difficult to generate social sentiments in the soul of the "savage" than it is to raise them now in the heart of modern man. The struggle for life encouraged communalism, but the struggle for property intensifies individualism. Primitive man was perhaps readier than contemporary man to coöperate with his fellows; social solidarity came more easily to him since he had more perils and interests in common with his group, and less possessions to separate him from the rest.[86] The natural man was violent and greedy; but he was also kindly and generous, ready to share even with strangers, and to make presents to his guests.[87] Every schoolboy knows that primitive hospitality, in many tribes, went to the extent of offering to the traveler the wife or daughter of the host.[88] To decline such an offer was a serious offense, not only to the host but to the woman; these are among the perils faced by missionaries. Often the later treatment of the guest was determined by the manner in which he had acquitted himself of these responsibilities.[89] Uncivilized man appears to have felt proprietary, but not sexual, jealousy; it did not disturb him that his wife had "known" men before marrying him, or now slept with his guest; but as her owner, rather than her lover, he would have been incensed to find her cohabiting with another man without his consent. Some African husbands lent their wives to strangers for a consideration.[90]

The rules of courtesy were as complex in most simple peoples as in advanced nations.[91] Each group had formal modes of salutation and farewell. Two individuals, on meeting, rubbed noses, or smelled each other, or gently bit each other;[92] as we have seen, they never kissed. Some crude tribes were more polite than the modern average; the Dyak head-hunters, we are told, were "gentle and peaceful" in their home life, and the Indians of Central America considered the loud talking and brusque behavior of the white man as signs of poor breeding and a primitive culture.[93]

Almost all groups agree in holding other groups to be inferior to themselves. The American Indians looked upon themselves as the chosen people, specially created by the Great Spirit as an uplifting example for mankind. One Indian tribe called itself "The Only Men"; another called itself "Men of Men"; the Caribs said, "We alone are people." The Eskimos believed that the Europeans had come to Greenland to learn manners and virtues.[94] Consequently it seldom occurred to primitive man to extend to other tribes the moral restraints which he acknowledged in dealing with his own; he

frankly conceived it to be the function of morals to give strength and coherence to his group against other groups. Commandments and tabus applied only to the people of his tribe; with others, except when they were his
guests, he might go as far as he dared.[95]

Moral progress in history lies not so much in the improvement of the
moral code as in the enlargement of the area within which it is applied.
The morals of modern man are not unquestionably superior to those of
primitive man, though the two groups of codes may differ considerably in
content, practice and profession; but modern morals are, in normal times,
extended—though with decreasing intensity—to a greater number of people
than before.*   As tribes were gathered up into those larger units called
states, morality overflowed its tribal bounds; and as communication—or a
common danger—united and assimilated states, morals seeped through frontiers, and some men began to apply their commandments to all Europeans,
to all whites, at last to all men. Perhaps there have always been idealists
who wished to love all men as their neighbors, and perhaps in every generation they have been futile voices crying in a wilderness of nationalism
and war. But probably the number—even the relative number—of such men
has increased. There are no morals in diplomacy, and *la politique n'a pas
d'entrailles;* but there are morals in international trade, merely because such
trade cannot go on without some degree of restraint, regulation, and confidence. Trade began in piracy; it culminates in morality.

Few societies have been content to rest their moral codes upon so
frankly rational a basis as economic and political utility. For the individual is not endowed by nature with any disposition to subordinate his personal interests to those of the group, or to obey irksome regulations
for which there are no visible means of enforcement. To provide, so
to speak, an invisible watchman, to strengthen the social impulses against
the individualistic by powerful hopes and fears, societies have not invented but made use of, religion. The ancient geographer Strabo expressed
the most advanced views on this subject nineteen hundred years ago:

> For in dealing with a crowd of women, at least, or with any
> promiscuous mob, a philosopher cannot influence them by reason
> or exhort them to reverence, piety and faith; nay, there is need of
> religious fear also, and this cannot be aroused without myths and
> marvels. For thunderbolt, aegis, trident, torches, snakes, thyrsus-

---

* However, the range within which the moral code is applied has narrowed since the
Middle Ages, as the result of the rise of nationalism.

lances—arms of the gods—are myths, and so is the entire ancient theology. But the founders of states gave their sanction to these things as bugbears wherewith to scare the simple-minded. Now since this is the nature of mythology, and since it has come to have its place in the social and civil scheme of life as well as in the history of actual facts, the ancients clung to their system of education for children and applied it up to the age of maturity; and by means of poetry they believed that they could satisfactorily discipline every period of life. But now, after a long time, the writing of history and the present-day philosophy have come to the front. Philosophy, however, is for the few, whereas poetry is more useful to the people at large.[96]

Morals, then, are soon endowed with religious sanctions, because mystery and supernaturalism lend a weight which can never attach to things empirically known and genetically understood; men are more easily ruled by imagination than by science. But was this moral utility the source or origin of religion?

IV. RELIGION

Primitive atheists

If we define religion as the worship of supernatural forces, we must observe at the outset that some peoples have apparently no religion at all. Certain Pygmy tribes of Africa had no observable cult or rites; they had no totem, no fetishes, and no gods; they buried their dead without ceremony, and seem to have paid no further attention to them; they lacked even superstitions, if we may believe otherwise incredible travelers.[96a] The dwarfs of the Cameroon recognized only malevolent deities, and did nothing to placate them, on the ground that it was useless to try. The Veddahs of Ceylon went no further than to admit the possibility of gods and immortal souls; but they offered no prayers or sacrifices. Asked about God they answered, as puzzled as the latest philosopher: "Is he on a rock? On a white-ant hill? On a tree? I never saw a god!"[96b] The North American Indians conceived a god, but did not worship him; like Epicurus they thought him too remote to be concerned in their affairs.[96c] An Abipone Indian rebuffed a metaphysical inquirer in a manner quite Confucian: "Our grandfathers and our great-grandfathers were wont to contemplate the earth alone, solicitous only to see whether the plain afford grass and water for their horses. They never troubled themselves about what went on in the heavens, and who was the creator and governor of the stars." The Eskimos, when asked who had made the heavens and the earth, always replied, "We do not know."[96d] A Zulu was asked: "When you see the sun rising and setting, and the trees growing, do you know who made them and governs them?" He answered, simply: "No, we see them, but cannot tell how they came; we suppose that they came by themselves."[96e]

Such cases are exceptional, and the old belief that religion is universal is substantially correct. To the philosopher this is one of the outstanding facts of history and psychology; he is not content to know that all religions contain much nonsense, but rather he is fascinated by the problem of the antiquity and persistence of belief. What are the sources of the indestructible piety of mankind?

1. The Sources of Religion
Fear—Wonder—Dreams—The soul—Animism

Fear, as Lucretius said, was the first mother of the gods. Fear, above all, of death. Primitive life was beset with a thousand dangers, and seldom ended with natural decay; long before old age could come, violence or some strange disease carried off the great majority of men. Hence early man did not believe that death was ever natural;[97] he attributed it to the operation of supernatural agencies. In the mythology of the natives of New Britain death came to men by an error of the gods. The good god Kambinana told his foolish brother Korvouva, "Go down to men and tell them to cast their skins; so shall they avoid death. But tell the serpents that they must henceforth die." Korvouva mixed the messages; he delivered the secret of immortality to the snakes, and the doom of death to men.[98] Many tribes thought that death was due to the shrinkage of the skin, and that man would be immortal if only he could moult.[99]

Fear of death, wonder at the causes of chance events or unintelligible happenings, hope for divine aid and gratitude for good fortune, coöperated to generate religious belief. Wonder and mystery adhered particularly to sex and dreams, and the mysterious influence of heavenly bodies upon the earth and man. Primitive man marveled at the phantoms that he saw in sleep, and was struck with terror when he beheld, in his dreams, the figures of those whom he knew to be dead. He buried his dead in the earth to prevent their return; he buried victuals and goods with the corpse lest it should come back to curse him; sometimes he left to the dead the house in which death had come, while he himself moved on to another shelter; in some places he carried the body out of the house not through a door but through a hole in the wall, and bore it rapidly three times around the dwelling, so that the spirit might forget the entrance and never haunt the home.[100]

Such experiences convinced early man that every living thing had a soul, or secret life, within it, which could be separated from the body in illness, sleep or death. "Let no one wake a man brusquely," said one of the Upanishads of ancient India, "for it is a matter difficult of cure if the soul find not its way back to him."[101] Not man alone but all things had souls; the external world was not insensitive or dead, it was intensely alive;[102] if this were not so, thought primitive philosophy, nature would be full of inexplicable occurrences, like the motion of the sun, or the death-dealing lightning, or the whispering of the trees. The personal way of conceiving objects and events preceded the impersonal or abstract; religion preceded philosophy. Such animism is the poetry of religion, and the religion of poetry. We may see it at its lowest in the wonder-struck eyes of a dog that watches a paper blown before him by the wind, and perhaps believes that a spirit moves the paper from within; and we find the same feeling at its highest in the language of the poet. To the primitive mind— and to the poet in all ages—mountains, rivers, rocks, trees, stars, sun, moon and sky are sacramentally holy things, because they are the outward and visible signs of inward and invisible souls. To the early Greeks the sky was the god Ouranos, the moon was Selene, the earth was Gæa, the sea was Poseidon, and everywhere in the woods was Pan. To the ancient Germans the forest primeval was peopled with genii, elves, trolls, giants, dwarfs and fairies; these sylvan creatures survive in the music of Wagner and the poetic dramas of Ibsen. The simpler peasants of Ireland still believe in fairies, and no poet or playwright can belong to the Irish literary revival unless he employs them. There is wisdom as well as beauty in this animism; it is good and nourishing to treat all things as alive. To the sensitive spirit, says the most sensitive of contemporary writers,

> Nature begins to present herself as a vast congeries of separate living entities, some visible, some invisible, but all possessed of

mind-stuff, all possessed of matter-stuff, and all blending mind and matter together in the basic mystery of being. . . . The world is full of gods! From every planet and from every stone there emanates a presence that disturbs us with a sense of the multitudinousness of god-like powers, strong and feeble, great and little, moving between heaven and earth upon their secret purposes.[103]

2. *The Objects of Religion*

The sun—The stars—The earth—Sex—Animals—Totemism—The transition to human gods—Ghost-worship—Ancestor-worship

Since all things have souls, or contain hidden gods, the objects of religious worship are numberless. They fall into six classes: celestial, terrestrial, sexual, animal, human, and divine. Of course we shall never know which of our universe of objects was worshiped first. *One* of the first was probably the moon. Just as our own folk-lore speaks of the *"man in the moon,"* so primitive legend conceived the moon as a bold male who caused women to menstruate by seducing them. He was a favorite god with women, who worshiped him as their protecting deity. The pale orb was also the measure of time; it was believed to control the weather, and to make both rain and snow; even the frogs prayed to it for rain.[104]

We do not know when the sun replaced the moon as the lord of the sky in primitive religion. Perhaps it was when vegetation replaced hunting, and the transit of the sun determined the seasons of sowing and reaping, and its heat was recognized as the main cause of the bounty of the soil. Then the earth became a goddess fertilized by the hot rays, and men worshiped the great orb as the father of all things living.[105] From this simple beginning sun-worship passed down into the pagan faiths of antiquity, and many a later god was only a personification of the sun. Anaxagoras was exiled by the learned Greeks because he ventured the guess that the sun was not a god, but merely a ball of fire, about the size of the Peloponnesus. The Middle Ages kept a relic of sun-worship in the halo pictured around the heads of saints,[106] and in our own day the Emperor of Japan is regarded by most of his people as an incarnation of the sun-god.[107] There is hardly any superstition so old but it can be found flourishing somewhere today. Civilization is the precarious labor and luxury of a minority; the basic masses of mankind hardly change from millennium to millennium.

Like the sun and the moon, every star contained or was a god, and moved at the command of its indwelling spirit. Under Christianity these spirits became guiding angels, star-pilots, so to speak; and Kepler was not too scientific to believe in them. The sky itself was a great god, worshiped devotedly as giver and withholder of rain. Among many primitive peoples the word for god meant sky; among the Lubari and the Dinkas it meant rain. Among the Mongols the supreme god was *Tengri*—the sky; in China it was *Ti*—the sky; in Vedic India it was *Dyaus pitar*—the "father sky"; among the Greeks it was *Zeus*—the sky, the "cloud-compeller"; among the Persians it was *Ahura*—the "azure sky";[108] and among ourselves men still ask "Heaven" to protect them. The central point in most primitive mythology is the fertile mating of earth and sky.

For the earth, too, was a god, and every main aspect of it was presided over by some deity. Trees had souls quite as much as men, and it was plain murder to cut them down; the North American Indians sometimes attributed their defeat and decay to the fact that the whites had leveled the trees whose spirits had protected the Red Men. In the Molucca Islands blossoming trees were treated as pregnant; no noise, fire, or other disturbance was permitted to mar their peace; else, like a frightened woman, they might drop their fruit before time. In Amboyna no loud sounds were allowed near the rice in bloom lest it should abort into straw.[109] The ancient Gauls worshiped the trees of certain sacred forests; and the Druid priests of England reverenced as holy that mistletoe of the oak which still suggests a pleasant ritual. The veneration of trees, springs, rivers and mountains is the oldest traceable religion of Asia.[110] Many mountains were holy places, homes of thundering gods. Earthquakes were the shoulder-shrugging of irked or irate deities: the Fijians ascribed such agitations to the earth-god's turning over in his sleep; and the Samoans, when the soil trembled, gnawed the ground and prayed to the god Mafuie to stop, lest he should shake the planet to pieces.[111] Almost everywhere the earth was the Great Mother; our language, which is often the precipitate of primitive or unconscious beliefs, suggests to this day a kinship between matter (*materia*) and mother (*mater*).[112] Ishtar and Cybele, Demeter and Ceres, Aphrodite and Venus and Freya—these are comparatively late forms of the ancient goddesses of the earth, whose fertility constituted the bounty of the fields; their birth and marriage, their death and triumphant resurrection were conceived as the symbols or causes of the sprouting, the decay, and the vernal renewal of all vegetation. These deities reveal by their gender the primitive association of agriculture with woman. When agriculture became the dominant mode of human life, the vegetation goddesses reigned supreme. Most early gods were of the gentler sex; they were superseded by male deities presumably as a heavenly reflex of the victorious patriarchal family.[113]

Just as the profound poetry of the primitive mind sees a secret divinity in the growth of a tree, so it sees a supernatural agency in the conception or birth of a child. The "savage" does not know anything about the ovum or the sperm; he sees only the external structures involved, and deifies them; they, too, have spirits in them, and must be worshiped, for are not these mysteriously creative powers the most marvelous of all? In them, even more than in the soil, the miracle of fertility and growth appears; therefore they must be the most direct embodiments of the divine potency. Nearly all ancient peoples worshiped sex in some form and ritual, and not the lowest people but the highest expressed their worship most completely; we shall find such worship in Egypt and India, Babylonia and Assyria, Greece and Rome. The sexual character and functions of primitive deities were held in high regard,[114] not through any obscenity of mind, but through a passion for fertility in women and in the earth. Certain animals, like the bull and the snake, were worshiped as apparently possessing or symbolizing in a high degree the divine power of reproduction. The snake in the story of Eden is doubtless a phallic symbol, representing sex as the origin of evil, suggesting sexual awakening as the beginning of the knowledge of good and evil, and perhaps insinuating a certain proverbial connection between mental innocence and bliss.*

There is hardly an animal in nature, from the Egyptian scarab to the Hindu elephant, that has not somewhere been worshiped as a god. The Ojibwa Indians gave the name of *totem* to their special sacred animal, to the clan that worshiped it, and to any member of the clan; and this confused word has stumbled into anthropology as *totemism*, denoting vaguely any worship of a particular object—usually an animal or a plant—as especially sacred to a group. Varieties of totemism have been found scattered over apparently unconnected regions of the earth, from the Indian tribes of North America to the natives of Africa, the Dravidians

* Cf. Chap. xii, § vi below.

of India, and the tribes of Australia.[115] The totem as a religious object helped to unify the tribe, whose members thought themselves bound up with it or descended from it; the Iroquois, in semi-Darwinian fashion, believed that they were sprung from the primeval mating of women with bears, wolves and deer. The totem—as object or as symbol—became a useful sign of relationship and distinction for primitive peoples, and lapsed, in the course of secularization, into a mascot or emblem, like the lion or eagle of nations, the elk or moose of our fraternal orders, and those dumb animals that are used to represent the elephantine immobility and mulish obstreperousness of our political parties. The dove, the fish and the lamb, in the symbolism of nascent Christianity, were relics of totemic adoration; even the lowly pig was once a totem of prehistoric Jews.[116] In most cases the totem animal was tabu—i.e., forbidden, not to be touched; under certain circumstances it might be eaten, but only as a religious act, amounting to the ritual eating of the god.* The Gallas of Abyssinia ate in solemn ceremony the fish that they worshiped, and said, "We feel the spirit moving within us as we eat." The good missionaries who preached the Gospel to the Gallas were shocked to find among these simple folk a ritual so strangely similar to the central ceremony of the Mass.[119]

Probably fear was the origin of totemism, as of so many cults; men prayed to animals because the animals were powerful, and had to be appeased. As hunting cleared the woods of the beasts, and gave way to the comparative security of agricultural life, the worship of animals declined, though it never quite disappeared; and the ferocity of the first human gods was probably carried over from the animal deities whom they replaced. The transition is visible in those famous stories of metamorphoses, or changes of form, that are found in the Ovids of all languages, and tell how gods had been, or had become, animals. Later the animal qualities adhered to them obstinately, as the odor of the stable might loyally attend some rural Casanova; even in the complex mind of Homer *glaucopis Athene* had the eyes of an owl, and *Here boöpis* had the eyes of a cow. Egyptian and Babylonian gods or ogres with the face of a human being

---

* Freud, with characteristic imaginativeness, believes that the totem was a transfigured symbol of the father, revered and hated for his omnipotence, and rebelliously murdered and eaten by his sons.[117] Durkheim thought that the totem was a symbol of the clan, revered and hated (hence held "sacred" and "unclean") by the individual for its omnipotence and irksome dictatorship; and that the religious attitude was originally the feeling of the individual toward the authoritarian group.[118]

and the body of a beast reveal the same transition and make the same confession—that many human gods were once animal deities.[120]

Most human gods, however, seem to have been, in the beginning, merely idealized dead men. The appearance of the dead in dreams was enough to establish the worship of the dead, for worship, if not the child, is at least the brother, of fear. Men who had been powerful during life, and therefore had been feared, were especially likely to be worshiped after their death.[121] Among several primitive peoples the word for god actually meant "a dead man"; even today the English word *spirit* and the German word *Geist* mean both ghost and soul. The Greeks invoked their dead precisely as the Christians were to invoke the saints.[122] So strong was the belief—first generated in dreams—in the continued life of the dead, that primitive men sometimes sent messages to them in the most literal way; in one tribe the chief, to convey such a letter, recited it verbally to a slave, and then cut off his head for special delivery; if the chief forgot something he sent another decapitated slave as a postscript.[123]

Gradually the cult of the ghost became the worship of ancestors. All the dead were feared, and had to be propitiated, lest they should curse and blight the lives of the living. This ancestor-worship was so well adapted to promote social authority and continuity, conservatism and order, that it soon spread to every region of the earth. It flourished in Egypt, Greece and Rome, and survives vigorously in China and Japan today; many peoples worship ancestors but no god.[124]* The institution held the family powerfully together despite the hostility of successive generations, and provided an invisible structure for many early societies. And just as compulsion grew into conscience, so fear graduated into love; the ritual of ancestor-worship, probably generated by terror, later aroused the sentiment of awe, and finally developed piety and devotion. It is the tendency of gods to begin as ogres and to end as loving fathers; the idol passes into an ideal as the growing security, peacefulness and moral sense of the worshipers pacify and transform the features of their once ferocious deities. The slow progress of civilization is reflected in the tardy amiability of the gods.

The idea of a human god was a late step in a long development; it was slowly differentiated, through many stages, out of the conception of an ocean or multitude of spirits and ghosts surrounding and inhabiting every-

---

* Relics of ancestor-worship may be found among ourselves in our care and visitation of graves, and our masses and prayers for the dead.

thing. From the fear and worship of vague and formless spirits men seem to have passed to adoration of celestial, vegetative and sexual powers, then to reverence for animals, and worship of ancestors. The notion of God as Father was probably derived from ancestor-worship; it meant originally that men had been physically begotten by the gods.[125] In primitive theology there is no sharp or generic distinction between gods and men; to the early Greeks, for example, their gods were ancestors, and their ancestors were gods. A further development came when, out of the medley of ancestors, certain men and women who had been especially distinguished were singled out for clearer deification; so the greater kings became gods, sometimes even before their death. But with this development we reach the historic civilizations.

3. The Methods of Religion

Magic—Vegetation rites—Festivals of license—Myths of the resurrected god — Magic and superstition — Magic and science—Priests

Having conceived a world of spirits, whose nature and intent were unknown to him, primitive man sought to propitiate them and to enlist them in his aid. Hence to animism, which is the essence of primitive religion, was added magic, which is the soul of primitive ritual. The Polynesians recognized a very ocean of magic power, which they called *mana*; the magician, they thought, merely tapped this infinite supply of miraculous capacity. The methods by which the spirits, and later the gods, were suborned to human purposes were for the most part "sympathetic magic"—a desired action was suggested to the deities by a partial or imitative performance of the action by men. To make rain fall some primitive magicians poured water out upon the ground, preferably from a tree. The Kaffirs, threatened by drought, asked a missionary to go into the fields with an opened umbrella.[126] In Sumatra a barren woman made an image of a child and held it in her lap, hoping thereby to become pregnant. In the Babar Archipelago the would-be mother fashioned a doll out of red cotton, pretended to suckle it, and repeated a magic formula; then she sent word through the village that she was pregnant, and her friends came to congratulate her; only a very obstinate reality could refuse to emulate this imagination. Among the Dyaks of Borneo the magician, to ease the pains of a woman about to deliver, would go through the contortions of childbirth himself, as a magic suggestion to the foetus to come forth; sometimes the magician slowly rolled a stone down his belly and dropped it to the ground, in the hope that the backward child would imitate it. In the Middle Ages a spell was cast upon an enemy by sticking pins into a waxen image of him;[127] the Peruvian Indians burned people in effigy, and called it burning the soul.[128] Even the modern mob is not above such primitive magic.

These methods of suggestion by example were applied especially to the fertilization of the soil. Zulu medicine-men fried the genitals of a man who had died in full vigor, ground the mixture into a powder, and strewed it over the fields.[129] Some peoples chose a King and Queen of the May, or a Whitsun bridegroom and bride, and married them publicly, so that the soil might take heed and flower forth. In certain localities the rite included the public consummation of the marriage, so that Nature, though she might be nothing but a dull clod, would have no excuse for misunderstanding her duty. In Java the peasants and their wives, to ensure the fertility of the rice-fields, mated in the midst of them.[130] For primitive men did not conceive the growth of the soil in terms of nitrogen; they thought of it—apparently without knowing of sex in plants—in the same terms as those whereby they interpreted the fruitfulness of woman; our very terms recall their poetic faith.

Festivals of promiscuity, coming in nearly all cases at the season of sowing, served partly as a moratorium on morals (recalling the comparative freedom of sex relations in earlier days), partly as a means of fertilizing the wives of sterile men, and partly as a ceremony of suggestion to the earth in spring to abandon her wintry reserve, accept the proffered seed, and prepare to deliver herself of a generous litter of food. Such festivals appear among a great number of nature peoples, but particularly among the Cameroons of the Congo, the Kaffirs, the Hottentots and the Bantus. "Their harvest festivals," says the Reverend H. Rowley of the Bantus,

> are akin in character to the feasts of Bacchus. . . . It is impossible to witness them without being ashamed. . . . Not only is full sexual license permitted to the neophytes, and indeed in most cases enjoined, but any visitor attending the festival is encouraged to indulge in licentiousness. Prostitution is freely indulged in, and adultery is not viewed with any sense of heinousness, on account of the surroundings. No man attending the festival is allowed to have intercourse with his wife.[131]

Similar festivals appear in the historic civilizations: in the Bacchic celebrations of Greece, the *Saturnalia* of Rome, the *Fête des Fous* in medieval France, May Day in England, and the Carnival or *Mardi Gras* of contemporary ways.

Here and there, as among the Pawnees and the Indians of Guayaquil, vegetation rites took on a less attractive form. A man—or, in later and milder days, an animal—was sacrificed to the earth at sowing time, so that it might be fertilized by his blood. When the harvest came it was interpreted as the resurrection of the dead man; the victim was given, before and after his death, the honors of a god; and from this origin arose, in a thousand forms, the almost universal myth of a god dying for his people, and then returning triumphantly to life.[132] Poetry embroidered magic, and transformed it into theology. Solar myths mingled harmoniously with vegetation rites, and the legend of a god dying and reborn came to apply not only to the winter death and spring revival of the earth but to the autumnal and vernal equinoxes, and the waning and waxing of the day. For the coming of night was merely a part of this tragic drama; daily the sun-god was born and died; every sunset was a crucifixion, and every sunrise was a resurrection.

Human sacrifice, of which we have here but one of many varieties, seems to have been honored at some time or another by almost every people. On the island of Carolina in the Gulf of Mexico a great hollow metal statue of an old Mexican deity has been found, within which still lay the remains of human beings apparently burned to death as an offering to the god.[133] Every one knows of the Moloch to whom the Phoenicians, the Carthaginians, and occasionally other Semites, offered human victims. In our own time the custom has been practised in Rhodesia.[134] Probably it was bound up with cannibalism; men thought that the gods had tastes like their own. As religious beliefs change more slowly than other creeds, and rites change more slowly than beliefs, this divine cannibalism survived after human cannibalism disappeared.[135] Slowly, however, evolving morals changed even religious rites; the gods imitated the increasing gentleness of their worshipers, and resigned themselves to accepting animal instead of human meat; a hind took the place of Iphigenia, and a ram was substituted for Abraham's son. In time the gods did not receive even the animal; the priests liked savory food, ate all the edible parts of the sacrificial victim themselves, and offered upon the altar only the entrails and the bones.[136]

Since early man believed that he acquired the powers of whatever organism he consumed, he came naturally to the conception of eating the god. In many cases he ate the flesh and drank the blood of the human god whom he had deified and fattened for the sacrifice. When, through increased continuity in the food-supply, he became more humane, he substituted images for the victim, and was content to eat these. In ancient Mexico an image of the god was made of grain, seeds and vegetables, was kneaded with the blood of boys sacrificed for the purpose, and was then consumed as a religious ceremony of eating the god. Similar ceremonies have been found in many primitive tribes. Usually the participant was required to fast before eating the sacred image; and the priest turned the image into the god by the power of magic formulas.[137]

Magic begins in superstition, and ends in science. A wilderness of weird beliefs came out of animism, and resulted in many strange formulas and rites. The Kukis encouraged themselves in war by the notion that all the enemies they slew would attend them as slaves in the after life. On the other hand a Bantu, when he had slain his foe, shaved his own head and anointed himself with goat-dung, to prevent the spirit of the dead man from returning to pester him. Almost all primitive peoples believed in the efficacy of curses, and the destructiveness of the "evil eye."[138] Australian natives were sure that the curse of a potent magician could kill at a hundred miles. The belief in witchcraft began early in human history, and has never quite disappeared. Fetishism*—the worship of idols or other objects as having magic power—is still more ancient and indestructible. Since many amulets are limited to a special power, some peoples are heavily laden with a variety of them, so that they may be ready for any emergency.[139] Relics are a later and contemporary example of fetishes possessing magic powers; half the population of Europe wear some pendant or amulet which gives them supernatural protection or aid. At every step the history of civilization teaches us how slight and superficial a structure civilization is, and how precariously it is poised upon the apex of a never-extinct volcano of poor and oppressed barbarism, superstition and ignorance. Modernity is a cap superimposed upon the Middle Ages, which always remain.

The philosopher accepts gracefully this human need of supernatural

---

* From the Portuguese *feitico*, fabricated or factitious.

aid and comfort, and consoles himself by observing that just as animism generates poetry, so magic begets drama and science. Frazer has shown, with the exaggeration natural to a brilliant innovator, that the glories of science have their roots in the absurdities of magic. For since magic often failed, it became of advantage to the magician to discover natural operations by which he might help supernatural forces to produce the desired event. Slowly the natural means came to predominate, even though the magician, to preserve his standing with the people, concealed these natural means as well as he could, and gave the credit to supernatural magic— much as our own people often credit natural cures to magical prescriptions and pills. In this way magic gave birth to the physician, the chemist, the metallurgist, and the astronomer.[140]

More immediately, however, magic made the priest. Gradually, as religious rites became more numerous and complex, they outgrew the knowledge and competence of the ordinary man, and generated a special class which gave most of its time to the functions and ceremonies of religion. The priest as magician had access, through trance, inspiration or esoteric prayer, to the will of the spirits or gods, and could change that will for human purposes. Since such knowledge and skill seemed to primitive men the most valuable of all, and supernatural forces were conceived to affect man's fate at every turn, the power of the clergy became as great as that of the state; and from the latest societies to modern times the priest has vied and alternated with the warrior in dominating and disciplining men. Let Egypt, Judea and medieval Europe suffice as instances.

The priest did not create religion, he merely used it, as a statesman uses the impulses and customs of mankind; religion arises not out of sacerdotal invention or chicanery, but out of the persistent wonder, fear, insecurity, hopefulness and loneliness of men. The priest did harm by tolerating superstition and monopolizing certain forms of knowledge; but he limited and often discouraged superstition, he gave the people the rudiments of education, he acted as a repository and vehicle for the growing cultural heritage of the race, he consoled the weak in their inevitable exploitation by the strong, and he became the agent through which religion nourished art and propped up with supernatural aid the precarious structure of human morality. If he had not existed the people would have invented him.

4. The Moral Function of Religion

Religion and government — Tabu—Sexual tabus — The lag of religion—Secularization

Religion supports morality by two means chiefly: myth and tabu Myth creates the supernatural creed through which celestial sanctions may be given to forms of conduct socially (or sacerdotally) desirable; heavenly hopes and terrors inspire the individual to put up with restraints placed upon him by his masters and his group. Man is not naturally obedient, gentle, or chaste; and next to that ancient compulsion which finally generates conscience, nothing so quietly and continuously conduces to these uncongenial virtues as the fear of the gods. The institutions of property and marriage rest in some measure upon religious sanctions, and tend to lose their vigor in ages of unbelief. Government itself, which is the most unnatural and necessary of social mechanisms, has usually required the support of piety and the priest, as clever heretics like Napoleon and Mussolini soon discovered; and hence "a tendency to theocracy is incidental to all constitutions."[141] The power of the primitive chief is increased by the aid of magic and sorcery; and even our own government derives some sanctity from its annual recognition of the Pilgrims' God.

The Polynesians gave the word *tabu* to prohibitions sanctioned by religion. In the more highly developed of primitive societies such tabus took the place of what under civilization became laws. Their form was usually negative: certain acts and objects were declared "sacred" or "unclean"; and the two words meant in effect one warning: *untouchable.* So the Ark of the Covenant was tabu, and Uzzah was struck dead, we are told, for touching it to save it from falling.[142] Diodorus would have us believe that the ancient Egyptians ate one another in famine, rather than violate the tabu against eating the animal totem of the tribe.[143] In most primitive societies countless things were tabu; certain words and names were never to be pronounced, and certain days and seasons were tabu in the sense that work was forbidden at such times. All the knowledge, and some of the ignorance, of primitive men about food were expressed in dietetic tabus; and hygiene was inculcated by religion rather than by science or secular medicine.

The favorite object of primitive tabu was woman. A thousand superstitions made her, every now and then, untouchable, perilous, and "unclean." The moulders of the world's myths were unsuccessful husbands, for they agreed that woman was the root of all evil; this was a view sacred not only to Hebraic and Christian tradition, but to a hundred pagan mythologies. The strictest of primitive tabus was laid upon the menstruating woman; any man or thing that touched her at such times lost virtue or usefulness.¹⁴⁴ The Macusi of British Guiana forbade women to bathe at their periods lest they should poison the waters; and they forbade them to go into the forests on these occasions, lest they be bitten by enamored snakes.¹⁴⁵ Even childbirth was unclean, and after it the mother was to purify herself with laborious religious rites. Sexual relations, in most primitive peoples, were tabu not only in the menstrual period but whenever the woman was pregnant or nursing. Probably these prohibitions were originated by women themselves, out of their own good sense and for their own protection and convenience; but origins are easily forgotten, and soon woman found herself "impure" and "unclean." In the end she accepted man's point of view, and felt shame in her periods, even in her pregnancy. Out of such tabus as a partial source came modesty, the sense of sin, the view of sex as unclean, asceticism, priestly celibacy, and the subjection of woman.

Religion is not the basis of morals, but an aid to them; conceivably they could exist without it, and not infrequently they have progressed against its indifference or its obstinate resistance. In the earliest societies, and in some later ones, morals appear at times to be quite independent of religion; religion then concerns itself not with the ethics of conduct but with magic, ritual and sacrifice, and the good man is defined in terms of ceremonies dutifully performed and faithfully financed. As a rule religion sanctions not any absolute good (since there is none), but those norms of conduct which have established themselves by force of economic and social circumstance; like law it looks to the past for its judgments, and is apt to be left behind as conditions change and morals alter with them. So the Greeks learned to abhor incest while their mythologies still honored incestuous gods; the Christians practised monogamy while their Bible legalized polygamy; slavery was abolished while dominies sanctified it with unimpeachable Biblical authority; and in our own day the Church fights heroically for a moral code that the Industrial Revolution has obviously doomed. In the end terrestrial forces prevail; morals slowly adjust themselves to

economic invention, and religion reluctantly adjusts itself to moral change.*
The moral function of religion is to conserve established values, rather
than to create new ones.

Hence a certain tension between religion and society marks the higher
stages of every civilization. Religion begins by offering magical aid to
harassed and bewildered men; it culminates by giving to a people that unity
of morals and belief which seems so favorable to statesmanship and art;
it ends by fighting suicidally in the lost cause of the past. For as knowledge
grows or alters continually, it clashes with mythology and theology, which
change with geological leisureliness. Priestly control of arts and letters is
then felt as a galling shackle or hateful barrier, and intellectual history
takes on the character of a "conflict between science and religion." Institutions which were at first in the hands of the clergy, like law and
punishment, education and morals, marriage and divorce, tend to escape
from ecclesiastical control, and become secular, perhaps profane. The
intellectual classes abandon the ancient theology and—after some hesitation—the moral code allied with it; literature and philosophy become anti-
clerical. The movement of liberation rises to an exuberant worship of
reason, and falls to a paralyzing disillusionment with every dogma and
every idea. Conduct, deprived of its religious supports, deteriorates into
epicurean chaos; and life itself, shorn of consoling faith, becomes a burden
alike to conscious poverty and to weary wealth. In the end a society and
its religion tend to fall together, like body and soul, in a harmonious death.
Meanwhile among the oppressed another myth arises, gives new form to
human hope, new courage to human effort, and after centuries of chaos
builds another civilization.

---

* Cf. the contemporary causation of birth control by urban industrialism, and the
gradual acceptance of such control by the Church.

CHAPTER V

The Mental Elements of Civilization

I. LETTERS

Language—Its animal background—Its human origins—Its development—Its results—Education—Initiation—Writing—Poetry

IN the beginning was the word, for with it man became man. Without those strange noises called common nouns, thought was limited to individual objects or experiences sensorily—for the most part visually—remembered or conceived; presumably it could not think of classes as distinct from individual things, nor of qualities as distinct from objects, nor of objects as distinct from their qualities. Without words as class names one might think of this man, or that man, or that man; one could not think of Man, for the eye sees not Man but only men, not classes but particular things. The beginning of humanity came when some freak or crank, half animal and half man, squatted in a cave or in a tree, cracking his brain to invent the first common noun, the first sound-sign that would signify a *group* of like objects: *house* that would mean all houses, *man* that would mean all men, *light* that would mean every light that ever shone on land or sea. From that moment the mental development of the race opened upon a new and endless road. For words are to thought what tools are to work; the product depends largely on the growth of the tools.[1]

Since all origins are guesses, and *de fontibus non disputandum*, the imagination has free play in picturing the beginnings of speech. Perhaps the first form of language—which may be defined as communication through signs—was the love-call of one animal to another. In this sense the jungle, the woods and the prairie are alive with speech. Cries of warning or of terror, the call of the mother to the brood, the cluck and cackle of euphoric or reproductive ecstasy, the parliament of chatter from tree to tree, indicate the busy preparations made by the animal kingdom for the august speech of man. A wild girl found living among the animals in a forest near Châlons, France, had no other speech than hideous screeches and howls. These living noises of the woods seem meaningless to our provincial ear; we are like the philosophical poodle Riquet, who says of M. Bergeret: "Everything uttered by my voice means something; but from my master's mouth comes much nonsense." Whitman and Craig discovered a strange correlation between the actions and the exclamations of pigeons; Dupont learned to distinguish twelve specific sounds used by fowl and doves, fifteen by dogs, and twenty-two by horned cattle; Garner found that the apes carried on their endless gossip with at least twenty different sounds, plus a repertory of gestures; and from these modest vocabularies a few steps bring us to the three hundred words that suffice some unpretentious men.[2]

Gesture seems primary, speech secondary, in the earlier transmission of thought; and when speech fails, gesture comes again to the fore. Among the North American Indians, who had countless dialects, married couples were often derived from different tribes, and maintained communication and accord by gestures rather than speech; one couple known to Lewis Morgan used silent signs for three years. Gesture was so prominent in some Indian languages that the Arapahos, like some modern peoples, could hardly converse in the dark.[3] Perhaps the first human words were interjections, expressions of emotion as among animals; then demonstrative words accompanying gestures of direction; and imitative sounds that came in time to be the names of the objects or actions that they simulated. Even after indefinite millenniums of linguistic changes and complications every language still contains hundreds of imitative words—*roar, rush, murmur, tremor, giggle, groan, hiss, heave, hum, cackle*, etc.* The Tecuna tribe, of ancient Brazil, had a perfect verb for sneeze: *haitschu*.[5] Out of such beginnings, *perhaps*, came the root-words of every language. Renan reduced all Hebrew words to five hundred roots, and Skeat nearly all European words to some four hundred stems.†

---

* Such onomatopœia still remains a refuge in linguistic emergencies. The Englishman eating his first meal in China, and wishing to know the character of the meat he was eating, inquired, with Anglo-Saxon dignity and reserve, "Quack, quack?" To which the Chinaman, shaking his head, answered cheerfully, "Bow-wow."[4]

† E.g., *divine* is from Latin *divus*, which is from *deus*, Greek *theos*, Sanskrit *deva*, meaning god; in the Gypsy tongue the word for god, by a strange prank, becomes *devel*. *Historically* goes back to the Sanskrit root *vid*, to know; Greek *oida*, Latin *video* (see), French *voir* (see), German *wissen* (know), English *to wit*; plus the suffixes *tor* (as in *author, praetor, rhetor*), *ic, al,* and *ly* (= *like*). Again, the Sanskrit root *ar*, to plough, gives the Latin *arare*, Russian *orati*, English *to ear* the land, *arable, art, oar,* and perhaps the word *Aryan*—the ploughers.[6]

The languages of nature peoples are not necessarily primitive in any sense of simplicity; many of them are simple in vocabulary and structure, but some of them are as complex and wordy as our own, and more highly organized than Chinese.[7] Nearly all primitive tongues, however, limit themselves to the sensual and particular, and are uniformly poor in general or abstract terms. So the Australian natives had a name for a dog's tail, and another name for a cow's tail; but they had no name for tail in general.[8] The Tasmanians had separate names for specific trees, but no general name for tree; the Choctaw Indians had names for the black oak, the white oak and the red oak, but no name for oak, much less for tree. Doubtless many generations passed before the proper noun ended in the common noun. In many tribes there are no separate words for the color as distinct from the colored object; no words for such abstractions as tone, sex, species, space, spirit, instinct, reason, quantity, hope, fear, matter, consciousness, etc.[9] Such abstract terms seem to grow in a reciprocal relation of cause and effect with the development of thought; they become the tools of subtlety and the symbols of civilization.

Bearing so many gifts to men, words seemed to them a divine boon and a sacred thing; they became the matter of magic formulas, most reverenced when most meaningless; and they still survive as sacred in mysteries where, e.g., the Word becomes Flesh. They made not only for clearer thinking, but for better social organization; they cemented the generations mentally, by providing a better medium for education and the transmission of knowledge and the arts; they created a new organ of communication, by which one doctrine or belief could mold a people into homogeneous unity. They opened new roads for the transport and traffic of ideas, and immensely accelerated the tempo, and enlarged the range and content, of life. Has any other invention ever equaled, in power and glory, the common noun?

Next to the enlargement of thought the greatest of these gifts of speech was education. Civilization is an accumulation, a treasure-house of arts and wisdom, manners and morals, from which the individual, in his development, draws nourishment for his mental life; without that periodical reacquisition of the racial heritage by each generation, civilization would die a sudden death. It owes its life to education.

Education had few frills among primitive peoples; to them, as to the animals, education was chiefly the transmission of skills and the training of character; it was a wholesome relation of apprentice to master in the ways of life. This direct and practical tutelage encouraged a rapid growth in the primitive child. In the Omaha tribes the boy of ten had already learned nearly all the arts of his father, and was ready for life; among the Aleuts the boy of ten often set up his own establishment, and sometimes took a wife; in Nigeria children of six or eight would leave the parental house, build a hut, and provide for themselves by hunting and fishing.[10] Usually this educational process came to an end with the beginning of sexual life; the precocious maturity was followed by an early stagnation. The boy, under such conditions, was adult at twelve and old at twenty-five.[11] This does not mean that the "savage" had the mind of a child; it only means that he had neither the needs nor the opportunities of the modern child; he did not enjoy that long and protected adolescence which allows a more nearly complete transmission of the cultural heritage, and a greater variety and flexibility of adaptive reactions to an artificial and unstable environment.

The environment of the natural man was comparatively permanent; it called not for mental agility but for courage and character. The primitive father put his trust in character, as modern education has put its trust in intellect; he was concerned to make not scholars but men. Hence the initiation rites which, among nature peoples, ordinarily marked the arrival of the youth at maturity and membership in the tribe, were designed to test courage rather than knowledge; their function was to prepare the young for the hardships of war and the responsibilities of marriage, while at the same time they indulged the old in the delights of inflicting pain. Some of these initiation tests are "too terrible and too revolting to be seen or told."[12] Among the Kaffirs (to take a mild example) the boys who were candidates for maturity were given arduous work by day, and were prevented from sleeping by night, until they dropped from exhaustion; and to make the matter more certain they were scourged "frequently and mercilessly until blood spurted from them." A considerable proportion of the boys died as a result; but this seems to have been looked upon philosophically by the elders, perhaps as an auxiliary anticipation of natural selection.[13] Usually these initiation ceremonies marked the end of adolescence and the preparation for marriage; and the bride insisted that the bridegroom should prove his capacity for suffering. In many tribes of the Congo the initiation rite centered about circumcision; if the youth winced or cried aloud his relatives were thrashed, and his promised bride, who had watched the ceremony carefully, rejected him scornfully, on the ground that she did not want a girl for her husband.[14]

Little or no use was made of writing in primitive education. Nothing surprises the natural man so much as the ability of Europeans to communicate with one another, over great distances, by making black scratches

upon a piece of paper.¹⁵ Many tribes have learned to write by imitating
their civilized exploiters; but some, as in northern Africa, have remained
letterless despite five thousand years of intermittent contact with literate
nations. Simple tribes living for the most part in comparative isolation,
and knowing the happiness of having no history, felt little need for writing.
Their memories were all the stronger for having no written aids; they
learned and retained, and passed on to their children by recitation, whatever seemed necessary in the way of historical record and cultural transmission. It was probably by committing such oral traditions and folk-lore
to writing that literature began. Doubtless the invention of writing was
met with a long and holy opposition, as something calculated to undermine
morals and the race. An Egyptian legend relates that when the god Thoth
revealed his discovery of the art of writing to King Thamos, the good
King denounced it as an enemy of civilization. "Children and young
people," protested the monarch, "who had hitherto been forced to apply
themselves diligently to learn and retain whatever was taught them, would
cease to apply themselves, and would neglect to exercise their memories."¹⁶

Of course we can only guess at the origins of this wonderful toy. Perhaps, as we shall see, it was a by-product of pottery, and began as identifying "trade-marks" on vessels of clay. Probably a system of written signs
was made necessary by the increase of trade among the tribes, and its first
forms were rough and conventional pictures of commercial objects and
accounts. As trade connected tribes of diverse languages, some mutually
intelligible mode of record and communication became desirable. Presumably the numerals were among the earliest written symbols, usually
taking the form of parallel marks representing the fingers; we still call
them fingers when we speak of them as digits. Such words as *five*, the
German *fünf* and the Greek *pente* go back to a root meaning hand;¹⁷ so
the Roman numerals indicated fingers, "V" represented an expanded
hand, and "X" was merely two "V's" connected at their points. Writing
was in its beginnings—as it still is in China and Japan—a form of drawing,
an art. As men used gestures when they could not use words, so they
used pictures to transmit their thoughts across time and space; every word
and every letter known to us was once a picture, even as trade-marks and
the signs of the zodiac are to this day. The primeval Chinese pictures that
preceded writing were called *ku-wan*—literally, "gesture-pictures." Totem
poles were pictograph writing; they were, as Mason suggests, tribal

autographs. Some tribes used notched sticks to help the memory or to convey a message; others, like the Algonquin Indians, not only notched the sticks but painted figures upon them, making them into miniature totem poles; or perhaps these poles were notched sticks on a grandiose scale. The Peruvian Indians kept complex records, both of numbers and ideas, by knots and loops made in diversely colored cords; perhaps some light is shed upon the origins of the South American Indians by the fact that a similar custom existed among the natives of the Eastern Archipelago and Polynesia. Lao-tse, calling upon the Chinese to return to the simple life, proposed that they should go back to their primeval use of knotted cords.[18]

More highly developed forms of writing appear sporadically among nature men. Hieroglyphics have been found on Easter Island, in the South Seas; and on one of the Caroline Islands a script has been discovered which consists of fifty-one syllabic signs, picturing figures and ideas.[19] Tradition tells how the priests and chiefs of Easter Island tried to keep to themselves all knowledge of writing, and how the people assembled annually to hear the tablets read; writing was obviously, in its earlier stages, a mysterious and holy thing, a *hieroglyph* or sacred carving. We cannot be sure that these Polynesian scripts were not derived from some of the historic civilizations. In general, writing is a sign of civilization, the least uncertain of the precarious distinctions between civilized and primitive men.

Literature is at first words rather than letters, despite its name; it arises as clerical chants or magic charms, recited usually by the priests, and transmitted orally from memory to memory. *Carmina*, as the Romans named poetry, meant both verses and *charms; ode*, among the Greeks, meant originally a magic spell; so did the English *rune* and *lay*, and the German *Lied*. Rhythm and meter, suggested, perhaps, by the rhythms of nature and bodily life, were apparently developed by magicians or *shamans* to preserve, transmit, and enhance the "magic incantations of their verse."[20] The Greeks attributed the first hexameters to the Delphic priests, who were believed to have invented the meter for use in oracles.[21] Gradually, out of these sacerdotal origins, the poet, the orator and the historian were differentiated and secularized: the orator as the official lauder of the king or solicitor of the deity; the historian as the recorder of the royal deeds; the poet as the singer of originally sacred chants, the formulator and preserver of heroic legends, and the musician who put his tales to music for the instruction of populace and kings. So the Fijians, the Tahitians and the New Caledonians had official orators and narrators to make addresses on occasions of ceremony, and to incite the warriors of the tribe by recounting the deeds of their forefathers and exalting the unequaled glories of the nation's past: how little do some recent historians differ from these! The Somali had professional poets who went from village to village singing songs, like medieval minnesingers and troubadours. Only exceptionally were these poems of love; usually they dealt with physical heroism, or battle, or the relations of parents and children. Here, from the Easter Island tablets, is the lament of a father separated from his daughter by the fortunes of war:

> The sail of my daughter,
> Never broken by the force of foreign clans;
> The sail of my daughter,
> Unbroken by the conspiracy of Honiti!
> Ever victorious in all her fights,
> She could not be enticed to drink poisoned waters
> In the obsidian glass.
> Can my sorrow ever be appeased
> While we are divided by the mighty seas?
> O my daughter, O my daughter!
> It is a vast and watery road
> Over which I look toward the horizon,
> My daughter, O my daughter![22]

II. SCIENCE

Origins—Mathematics—Astronomy—Medicine—Surgery

In the opinion of Herbert Spencer, that supreme expert in the collection of evidence *post judicium*, science, like letters, began with the priests, originated in astronomic observations, governing religious festivals, and was preserved in the temples and transmitted across the generations as part of the clerical heritage.[23] We cannot say, for here again beginnings elude us, and we may only surmise. Perhaps science, like civilization in general, began with agriculture; geometry, as its name indicates, was the measurement of the soil; and the calculation of crops and seasons, necessitating the observation of the stars and the construction of a calendar, may have generated astronomy. Navigation advanced astronomy, trade developed mathematics, and the industrial arts laid the bases of physics and chemistry.

Counting was probably one of the earliest forms of speech, and in many tribes it still presents a relieving simplicity. The Tasmanians counted up to two: "Parmery, calabawa, cardia"—i.e., "one, two, plenty"; the Guaranis of Brazil adventured further and said: "One, two, three, four, innumerable." The New Hollanders had no words for *three* or *four; three* they called "two-one"; *four* was "two-two." Damara natives would not exchange two sheep for four sticks, but willingly exchanged, twice in succession, one sheep for two sticks. Counting was by the fingers; hence the decimal system. When—apparently after some time—the idea of twelve was reached, the number became a favorite because it was so pleasantly divisible by five of the first six digits; and that duodecimal system was born which obstinately survives in English measurements today: twelve months in a year, twelve pence in a shilling, twelve units in a dozen, twelve dozen in a gross, twelve inches in a foot. Thirteen, on the other hand, refused to be divided, and became disreputable and unlucky forever. Toes added to fingers created the idea of twenty or a score; the use of this unit in reckoning lingers in the French *quatre-vingt* (four twenties) for *eighty*.[24] Other parts of the body served as standards of measurement: a hand for a "span," a thumb for an inch (in French the two words are the same), an elbow for a "cubit," an arm for an "ell," a foot for a foot. At an early date pebbles were added to fingers as an aid in counting; the survival of the *abacus*, and of the "little stone" *(calculus)* concealed in the word *calculate*, reveal to us how small, again, is the gap between the simplest and the latest men. Thoreau longed for this primitive simplicity, and well expressed a universally recurrent mood: "An honest man has hardly need to count more than his ten fingers, or, in extreme cases he may add his toes, and lump the rest. I say, let our affairs be as two or three, and not as a hundred or a thousand; instead of a million count half a dozen, and keep your accounts on your thumb-nail."[25]

The measurement of time by the movements of the heavenly bodies was probably the beginning of astronomy; the very word *measure*, like the word *month* (and perhaps the word *man*—the measurer), goes back apparently to a root denoting the moon.[26] Men measured time by moons long before they counted it by years; the sun, like the father, was a comparatively late discovery; even today Easter is reckoned according to the phases of the moon. The Polynesians had a calendar of thirteen months, regulated by the moon; when their lunar year diverged too flagrantly from the procession of the seasons they dropped a moon, and the balance was restored." But such sane uses of the heavens were exceptional; astrology antedated—and perhaps will survive—astronomy; simple souls are more interested in telling futures than in telling time. A myriad of superstitions grew up anent the influence of the stars upon human character and fate; and many of these superstitions flourish in our own day.* Perhaps they are not superstitions, but only another kind of error than science.

Natural man formulates no physics, but merely practises it; he cannot plot the path of a projectile, but he can aim an arrow well; he has no chemical symbols, but he knows at a glance which plants are poison and, which are food, and uses subtle herbs to heal the ills of the flesh. Perhaps we should employ another gender here, for probably the first doctors were women; not only because they were the natural nurses of the men, nor merely because they made midwifery, rather than venality, the oldest profession, but because their closer connection with the soil gave them a superior knowledge of plants, and enabled them to develop the art of medicine as distinct from the magic-mongering of the priests. From the earliest days to a time yet within our memory, it was the woman who healed. Only when the woman failed did the primitive sick resort to the medicine-man and the *shaman*.[28]

It is astonishing how many cures primitive doctors effected despite their theories of disease.[29] To these simple people disease seemed to be possession of the body by an alien power or spirit—a conception not essentially different from the germ theory which pervades medicine today. The most popular method of cure was by some magic incantation that would propitiate the evil spirit or drive it away. How perennial this form of therapy is may be seen in the story of the Gadarene swine.[29a] Even now epilepsy is regarded by many as a possession; some contemporary religions prescribe forms of exorcism for banishing disease, and prayer is recognized by most living people as an aid to pills and drugs. Perhaps the primitive practice was based, as much as the most modern, on the healing power of suggestion. The tricks of these early doctors were more dramatic than those of their more civilized successors: they tried to scare off the possessing demon by assuming terrifying masks, covering themselves with the skins

---

* Extract from an advertisement in the Town Hall (New York) program of March 5, 1934: "Horoscopes, by ———— ———————, Astrologer to New York's most distinguished social and professional clientele. Ten dollars an hour."

of animals, shouting, raving, slapping their hands, shaking rattles, and sucking the demon out through a hollow tube; as an old adage put it, "Nature cures the disease while the remedy amuses the patient." The Brazilian Bororos carried the science to a higher stage by having the father take the medicine in order to cure the sick child; almost invariably the child got well.[30]

Along with medicative herbs we find in the vast pharmacopœia of primitive man an assortment of soporific drugs calculated to ease pain or to facilitate operations. Poisons like curare (used so frequently on the tips of arrows), and drugs like hemp, opium and eucalyptus are older than history; one of our most popular anesthetics goes back to the Peruvian use of coca for this purpose. Cartier tells how the Iroquois cured scurvy with the bark and leaves of the hemlock spruce.[31] Primitive surgery knew a variety of operations and instruments. Childbirth was well managed; fractures and wounds were ably set and dressed.[32] By means of obsidian knives, or sharpened flints, or fishes' teeth, blood was let, abscesses were drained, and tissues were scarified. Trephining of the skull was practised by primitive medicine-men from the ancient Peruvian Indians to the modern Melanesians; the latter averaged nine successes out of every ten operations, while in 1786 the same operation was invariably fatal at the Hôtel-Dieu in Paris.[33]

We smile at primitive ignorance while we submit anxiously to the expensive therapeutics of our own day. As Dr. Oliver Wendell Holmes wrote, after a lifetime of healing:

> There is nothing men will not do, there is nothing they have not done, to recover their health and save their lives. They have submitted to be half-drowned in water and half-choked with gases, to be buried up to their chins in earth, to be seared with hot irons like galley-slaves, to be crimped with knives like codfish, to have needles thrust into their flesh, and bonfires kindled on their skin, to swallow all sorts of abominations, and to pay for all this as if to be singed and scalded were a costly privilege, as if blisters were a blessing and leeches a luxury.[34]

III. ART

*The meaning of beauty—Of art—The primitive sense of beauty—
The painting of the body—Cosmetics—Tattooing—Scarifica-
tion — Clothing — Ornaments — Pottery — Painting —
Sculpture — Architecture — The dance — Music —
Summary of the primitive preparation for
civilization*

After fifty thousand years of art men still dispute as to its sources in instinct and in history. What is beauty?—why do we admire it?—why do we endeavor to create it? Since this is no place for psychological discourse we shall answer, briefly and precariously, that beauty is any quality by which an object or a form pleases a beholder. Primarily and originally the object does not please the beholder because it is beautiful, but rather he calls it beautiful because it pleases him. Any object that satisfies desire will seem beautiful: food is beautiful—Thaïs is not beautiful—to a starving man. The pleasing object may as like as not be the beholder himself; in our secret hearts no other form is quite so fair as ours, and art begins with the adornment of one's own exquisite body. Or the pleasing object may be the desired mate; and then the esthetic—beauty-feeling—sense takes on the intensity and creativeness of sex, and spreads the aura of beauty to everything that concerns the beloved one—to all forms that resemble her, all colors that adorn her, please her or speak of her, all ornaments and garments that become her, all shapes and motions that recall her symmetry and grace. Or the pleasing form may be a desired male; and out of the attraction that here draws frailty to worship strength comes that sense of sublimity—satisfaction in the presence of power—which creates the loftiest art of all. Finally nature herself—with our coöperation —may become both sublime and beautiful; not only because it simulates and suggests all the tenderness of women and all the strength of men, but because we project into it our own feelings and fortunes, our love of others and of ourselves—relishing in it the scenes of our youth, enjoying its quiet solitude as an escape from the storm of life, living with it through its almost human seasons of green youth, hot maturity, "mellow fruitfulness" and cold decay, and recognizing it vaguely as the mother that lent us life and will receive us in our death.

Art is the creation of beauty; it is the expression of thought or feeling in a form that seems beautiful or sublime, and therefore arouses in us some reverberation of that primordial delight which woman gives to man, or man to woman. The thought may be any capture of life's significance, the feeling may be any arousal or release of life's tensions. The form may satisfy us through rhythm, which falls in pleasantly with the alternations of our breath, the pulsation of our blood, and the majestic oscillations of winter and summer, ebb and flow, night and day; or the form may please us through symmetry, which is a static rhythm, standing for strength and recalling to us the ordered proportions of plants and animals, of women and men; or it may please us through color, which brightens the spirit or intensifies life; or finally the form may please us through veracity—because its lucid and transparent imitation of nature or reality catches some mortal loveliness of plant or animal, or some transient meaning of circumstance, and holds it still for our lingering enjoyment or leisurely understanding. From these many sources come those noble superfluities of life —song and dance, music and drama, pottery and painting, sculpture and architecture, literature and philosophy. For what is philosophy but an art —one more attempt to give "significant form" to the chaos of experience?

If the sense of beauty is not strong in primitive society it may be because the lack of delay between sexual desire and fulfilment gives no time for that imaginative enhancement of the object which makes so much of the object's beauty. Primitive man seldom thinks of selecting women because of what we should call their beauty; he thinks rather of their usefulness, and never dreams of rejecting a strong-armed bride because of her ugliness. The Indian chief, being asked which of his wives was loveliest, apologized for never having thought of the matter. "Their faces," he said, with the mature wisdom of a Franklin, "might be more or less handsome, but in other respects women are all the same." Where a sense of beauty is present in primitive man it sometimes eludes us by being so different from our own. "All Negro races that I know," says Reichard, "account a woman beautiful who is not constricted at the waist, and when the body from the arm-pits to the hips is the same breadth—'like a ladder,' says the Coast Negro." Elephantine ears and an overhanging stomach are feminine charms to some African males; and throughout Africa it is the fat woman who is accounted loveliest. In Nigeria, says Mungo Park, "corpulence and beauty seem to be terms nearly synonymous. A woman of even moderate pretensions must be one who cannot walk without a slave under each arm to support her; and a perfect beauty is a load for a camel." "Most savages," says Briffault, "have a preference for what we should regard as one of the most unsightly features in a woman's form, namely, long, hanging breasts."[35] "It is well known," says Darwin, "that with many Hottentot women the posterior part of the body projects in a wonderful manner . . .; and Sir Andrew Smith is certain that this peculiarity is greatly admired by the men. He once saw a woman who was considered a beauty, and she was so immensely developed behind that when seated on level ground she could not rise, and had to push herself along until she came to a slope. . . . According to Burton the Somali men are said to choose their wives by ranging them in a line, and by picking her out who projects furthest *a tergo*. Nothing can be more hateful to a Negro than the opposite form."[36]

Indeed it is highly probable that the natural male thinks of beauty in terms of himself rather than in terms of woman; art begins at home. Primitive men equaled modern men in vanity, incredible as this will seem to women. Among simple peoples, as among animals, it is the male rather than the female that puts on ornament and mutilates his body for beauty's sake. In Australia, says Bonwick, "adornments are almost entirely monopolized by men"; so too in Melanesia, New Guinea, New Caledonia, New Britain, New Hanover, and among the North American Indians.[37] In some tribes more time is given to the adornment of the body than to any other business of the day.[38] Apparently the first form of art is the artificial coloring of the body—sometimes to attract women, sometimes to frighten foes. The Australian native, like the latest American belle, always carried with him a provision of white, red, and yellow paint for touching up his beauty now and then; and when the supply threatened to run out he undertook expeditions of some distance and danger to renew it. On ordinary days he contented himself with a few spots of color on his cheeks, his shoulders and his breast; but on festive occasions he felt shamefully nude unless his entire body was painted.[39]

In some tribes the men reserved to themselves the right to paint the body; in others the married women were forbidden to paint their necks.[40] But women were not long in acquiring the oldest of the arts—cosmetics. When Captain Cook dallied in New Zealand he noticed that his sailors, when they returned from their adventures on shore, had artificially red or yellow noses; the paint of the native Helens had stuck to them.[41] The

Fellatah ladies of Central Africa spent several hours a day over their toilette: they made their fingers and toes purple by keeping them wrapped all night in henna leaves; they stained their teeth alternately with blue, yellow, and purple dyes; they colored their hair with indigo, and penciled their eyelids with sulphuret of antimony.[42] Every Bongo lady carried in her dressing-case tweezers for pulling out eyelashes and eyebrows, lancet-shaped hair-pins, rings and bells, buttons and clasps.[43]

The primitive soul, like the Periclean Greek, fretted over the transitoriness of painting, and invented tattooing, scarification and clothing as more permanent adornments. The women as well as the men, in many tribes, submitted to the coloring needle, and bore without flinching even the tattooing of their lips. In Greenland the mothers tattooed their daughters early, the sooner to get them married off.[44] Most often, however, tattooing itself was considered insufficiently visible or impressive, and a number of tribes on every continent produced deep scars on their flesh to make themselves lovelier to their fellows, or more discouraging to their enemies. As Théophile Gautier put it, "having no clothes to embroider, they embroidered their skins."[45] Flints or mussel shells cut the flesh, and often a ball of earth was placed within the wound to enlarge the scar. The Torres Straits natives wore huge scars like epaulets; the Abeokuta cut themselves to produce scars imitative of lizards, alligators or tortoises.[46] "There is," says Georg, "no part of the body that has not been perfected, decorated, disfigured, painted, bleached, tattooed, reformed, stretched or squeezed, out of vanity or desire for ornament."[47] The Botocudos derived their name from a plug (*botoque*) which they inserted into the lower lip and the ears in the eighth year of life, and repeatedly replaced with a larger plug until the opening was as much as four inches in diameter.[48] Hottentot women trained the *labia minora* to assume enoromous lengths, so producing at last the "Hottentot apron" so greatly admired by their men.[49] Ear-rings and nose-rings were *de rigueur;* the natives of Gippsland believed that one who died without a nose-ring would suffer horrible torments in the next life.[50] It is all very barbarous, says the modern lady, as she bores her ears for rings, paints her lips and her cheeks, tweezes her eyebrows, reforms her eyelashes, powders her face, her neck and her arms, and compresses her feet. The tattooed sailor speaks with superior sympathy of the "savages" he has known; and the Continental student, horrified by primitive mutilations, sports his honorific scars.

Clothing was apparently, in its origins, a form of ornament, a sexual deterrent or charm rather than an article of use against cold or shame.[51]

The Cimbri were in the habit of tobogganing naked over the snow.[52] When Darwin, pitying the nakedness of the Fuegians, gave one of them a red cloth as a protection against the cold, the native tore it into strips, which he and his companions then used as ornaments; as Cook had said of them, timelessly, they were "content to be naked, but ambitious to be fine."[53] In like manner the ladies of the Orinoco cut into shreds the materials given them by the Jesuit Fathers for clothing; they wore the ribbons so made around their necks, but insisted that "they would be ashamed to wear clothing."[54] An old author describes the Brazilian natives as usually naked, and adds: "Now alreadie some doe weare apparell, but esteem it so little that they weare it rather for fashion than for honesties sake, and because they are commanded to weare it; . . . as is well seene by some that sometimes come abroad with certaine garments no further than the navell, without any other thing, or others onely a cap on their heads, and leave the other garments at home."[55] When clothing became something more than an adornment it served partly to indicate the married status of a loyal wife, partly to accentuate the form and beauty of woman. For the most part primitive women asked of clothing precisely what later women have asked—not that it should quite cover their nakedness, but that it should enhance or suggest their charms. Everything changes, except woman and man.

From the beginning both sexes preferred ornaments to clothing. Primitive trade seldom deals in necessities; it is usually confined to articles of adornment or play.[56] Jewelry is one of the most ancient elements of civilization; in tombs twenty thousand years old, shells and teeth have been found strung into necklaces.[57] From simple beginnings such embellishments soon reached impressive proportions, and played a lofty rôle in life. The Galla women wore rings to the weight of six pounds, and some Dinka women carried half a hundredweight of decoration. One African belle wore copper rings which became hot under the sun, so that she had to employ an attendant to shade or fan her. The Queen of the Wabunias on the Congo wore a brass collar weighing twenty pounds; she had to lie down every now and then to rest. Poor women who were so unfortunate as to have only light jewelry imitated carefully the steps of those who carried great burdens of bedizenment.[58]

The first source of art, then, is akin to the display of colors and plumage on the male animal in mating time; it lies in the desire to adorn and beautify the body. And just as self-love and mate-love, overflowing, pour out their surplus of affection upon nature, so the impulse to beautify passes from the personal to the external world. The soul seeks to express its feeling in objective ways, through color and form; art really begins when men undertake to beautify things. Perhaps its first external medium was pottery. The potter's wheel, like writing and the state, belongs to the historic civilizations; but even without it primitive men—or rather women—lifted this ancient industry to an art, and achieved merely with clay, water and deft fingers an astonishing symmetry of form; witness the pottery fashioned by the Baronga of South Africa,[59] or by the Pueblo Indians.[60]

When the potter applied colored designs to the surface of the vessel he had formed, he was creating the art of painting. In primitive hands painting is not yet an independent art; it exists as an adjunct to pottery and statuary. Nature men made colors out of clay, and the Andamanese made oil colors by mixing ochre with oils or fats.[61] Such colors were used to ornament weapons, implements, vases, clothing, and buildings. Many hunting tribes of Africa and Oceania painted upon the walls of their caves or upon neighboring rocks vivid representations of the animals that they sought in the chase.[62]

Sculpture, like painting, probably owed its origin to pottery: the potter found that he could mold not only articles of use, but imitative figures that might serve as magic amulets, and then as things of beauty in themselves. The Eskimos carved caribou antlers and walrus ivory into figurines of animals and men.[63] Again, primitive man sought to mark his hut, or a totem-pole, or a grave with some image that would indicate the object worshiped, or the person deceased; at first he carved merely a face upon a post, then a head, then the whole post; and through this filial marking of graves sculpture became an art.[64] So the ancient dwellers on Easter Island topped with enormous monolithic statues the vaults of their dead; scores of such statues, many of them twenty feet high, have been found there; some, now prostrate in ruins, were apparently sixty feet tall.

How did architecture begin? We can hardly apply so magnificent a term to the construction of the primitive hut; for architecture is not mere building, but beautiful building. It began when for the first time a man or a woman thought of a dwelling in terms of appearance as well as of use. Probably this effort to give beauty or sublimity to a structure was directed first to graves rather than to homes; while the commemorative pillar developed into statuary, the tomb grew into a temple. For to primitive thought the dead were more important and powerful than the living; and, besides, the dead could remain settled in one place, while the living wandered too often to warrant their raising permanent homes.

Even in early days, and probably long before he thought of carving objects or building tombs, man found pleasure in rhythm, and began to develop the crying and warbling, the prancing and preening, of the animal into song and dance. Perhaps, like the animal, he sang before he learned to talk,[65] and danced as early as he sang. Indeed no art so characterized or expressed primitive man as the dance. He developed it from primordial simplicity to a complexity unrivaled in civilization, and varied it into a thousand forms. The great festivals of the tribes were celebrated chiefly with communal and individual dancing; great wars were opened with martial steps and chants; the great ceremonies of religion were a mingling of song, drama and dance. What seems to us now to be forms of play were probably serious matters to early men; they danced not merely to express themselves, but to offer suggestions to nature or the gods; for example, the periodic incitation to abundant reproduction was accomplished chiefly through the hypnotism of the dance. Spencer derived the dance from the ritual of welcoming a victorious chief home from the wars; Freud derived it from the natural expression of sensual desire, and the group technique of erotic stimulation; if one should assert, with similar narrowness, that the dance was born of sacred rites and mummeries, and then merge the three theories into one, there might result as definite a conception of the origin of the dance as can be attained by us today.

From the dance, we may believe, came instrumental music and the drama. The making of such music appears to arise out of a desire to mark and accentuate with sound the rhythm of the dance, and to intensify with shrill or rhythmic notes the excitement necessary to patriotism or procreation. The instruments were limited in range and accomplishment, but almost endless in variety: native ingenuity exhausted itself in fashioning horns, trumpets, gongs, tamtams, clappers, rattles, castanets, flutes and drums from horns, skins, shells, ivory, brass, copper, bamboo and wood; and it ornamented them with elaborate carving and coloring. The taut string of the bow became the origin of a hundred instruments from the primitive lyre to the Stradivarius violin and the modern pianoforte. Professional singers, like professional dancers, arose among the tribes; and vague scales, predominantly minor in tone, were developed.[66]

With music, song and dance combined, the "savage" created for us the drama and the opera. For the primitive dance was frequently devoted to mimicry; it imitated, most simply, the movements of animals and men, and passed to the mimetic performance of actions and events. So some Australian tribes staged a sexual dance around a pit ornamented with shrubbery to represent the vulva, and, after ecstatic and erotic gestures and prancing, cast their spears symbolically into the pit. The northwestern tribes of the same island played a drama of death and resurrection differing only in simplicity from the medieval mystery and modern Passion plays: the dancers slowly sank to the ground, hid their heads under the boughs they carried, and simulated death; then, at a sign from their leader, they rose abruptly in a wild triumphal chant and dance announcing the resurrection of the soul.[67] In like manner a thousand forms of pantomime described events significant to the history of the tribe, or actions important in the individual life. When rhythm disappeared from these performances the dance passed into the drama, and one of the greatest of art-forms was born.

In these ways precivilized men created the forms and bases of civilization. Looking backward upon this brief survey of primitive culture, we find every element of civilization except writing and the state. All the modes of economic life are invented for us here: hunting and fishing, herding and tillage, transport and building, industry and commerce and finance. All the simpler structures of political life are organized: the clan, the family, the village community, and the tribe; freedom and order—those hostile foci around which civilization revolves—find their first adjustment and reconciliation; law and justice begin. The fundamentals of morals are established: the training of children, the regulation of the sexes, the inculcation of honor and decency, of manners and loyalty. The bases of religion are laid, and its hopes and terrors are applied to the encouragement of morals and the strengthening of the group. Speech is developed into complex languages, medicine and surgery appear, and modest beginnings are made in science, literature and art. All in all it is a picture of astonishing creation, of form rising out of chaos, of one road after another being opened from the animal to the sage. Without these "savages," and their hundred thousand years of experiment and groping, civilization could not have been. We owe almost everything to them—as a fortunate, and possibly degenerate, youth inherits the means to culture, security and ease through the long toil of an unlettered ancestry.

TYPES AND CULTURES

Geological Divisions			Anthropological Divisions	Human Types
Period	Epoch	Stage		

		1st Interglacial		Peking (*Sinanthropus Pekinensis*)
				Pithecanthropus
		2nd Interglacial		Heidelberg
				Piltdown (*Eoanthropus*)
		3rd Interglacial	Paleolithic or Old (Unpolished) Stone Age	
Quaternary	Pleistocene ("Most Recent")	4th Ice-Age		Neanderthal
		Postglacial		Cro-Magnon
			Mesolithic (Transitional)	
			Neolithic or New (Polished) Stone Age	
	Holocene ("Wholly Recent")		The "Age of Bronze" (4000-1800 B.C., Orient; 2000-1000 B.C., Europe)	
			The "Age of Iron" (1800 B.C., Orient; 1000 B.C., Europe)	

Discovered	Cultures	Location of Principal Remains	Height	Cranial Capacity (c.c.)	Hypothetical Age B.C.
1929		Chou Kou Tien, China			1,000,000
1891		Near Trinil, Java	5'7"	950	475,000
1907		Heidelberg, Germany			300,000
1911	Pre-Chellean	Sussex, England; St.-Acheul, France		1300	125,000
	Chellean	Chelles (Seine-et-Marne), France			100,000
	Acheulean	St.-Acheul (Somme), France	5'3"	1600	75,000
1857	Mousterian	Germany; Le Moustier (Dordogne), France	5'3"	1600	40,000
	{ Aurignacian	Aurignac (Haute-Garonne), France	5'3"		25,000
1868	{ Solutrean	Solutré (near Mâcon), France			20,000
	{ Magdalenian	La Madeleine (Dordogne), France	6'0"	1590	16,000
	{ Azilian	Mas-d'Azil (Ariège), France			10,000
	{ Kitchen-Middens	Denmark, etc.			7,000
	Lake-Dwellers	Robenhausen, etc., Switzerland			5,000
	The First Civilizations	Mesopotamia, Egypt, etc.			4,500
		(Modern European Man)	5'3"	1450	

CHAPTER VI

The Prehistoric Beginnings
of Civilization

I. PALEOLITHIC CULTURE

The purpose of prehistory—The romances of archeology

BUT we have spoken loosely; these primitive cultures that we have sketched as a means of studying the elements of civilization were not necessarily the ancestors of our own; for all that we know they may be the degenerate remnants of higher cultures that decayed when human leadership moved in the wake of the receding ice from the tropics to the north temperate zone. We have tried to understand how civilization in general arises and takes form; we have still to trace the prehistoric* origins of our own particular civilization. We wish now to inquire briefly—for this is a field that only borders upon our purpose—by what steps man, before history, prepared for the civilizations of history: how the man of the jungle or the cave became an Egyptian architect, a Babylonian astronomer, a Hebrew prophet, a Persian governor, a Greek poet, a Roman engineer, a Hindu saint, a Japanese artist, and a Chinese sage. We must pass from anthropology through archeology to history.

All over the earth seekers are digging into the earth: some for gold, some for silver, some for iron, some for coal; many of them for knowledge. What strange busyness of men exhuming paleolithic tools from the banks of the Somme, studying with strained necks the vivid paintings on the ceilings of prehistoric caves, unearthing antique skulls at Chou Kou Tien, revealing the buried cities of Mohenjo-daro or Yucatan, carrying débris in basket-caravans out of curse-ridden Egyptian tombs, lifting out of the dust the palaces of Minos and Priam, uncovering the ruins of Persepolis, burrowing into the soil of Africa for some remnant of Carthage, recapturing from the jungle the majestic temples of Angkor! In 1839 Jacques Boucher de Perthes found the first Stone Age flints at Abbeville, in France;

---

* This word will be used as applying to all ages before historical records.

for nine years the world laughed at him as a dupe. In 1872 Schliemann, with his own money, almost with his own hands, unearthed the youngest of the many cities of Troy; but all the world smiled incredulously. Never has any century been so interested in history as that which followed the voyage of young Champollion with young Napoleon to Egypt (1796); Napoleon returned empty-handed, but Champollion came back with all Egypt, past and current, in his grasp. Every generation since has discovered new civilizations or cultures, and has pushed farther and farther back the frontier of man's knowledge of his development. There are not many things finer in our murderous species than this noble curiosity, this restless and reckless passion to understand.

1. Men of the Old Stone Age

The geological background—Paleolithic types

Immense volumes have been written to expound our knowledge, and conceal our ignorance, of primitive man. We leave to other imaginative sciences the task of describing the *men* of the Old and the New Stone Age; our concern is to trace the contributions of these "paleolithic" and "neolithic" cultures to our contemporary life.

The picture we must form as background to the story is of an earth considerably different from that which tolerates us transiently today: an earth presumably shivering with the intermittent glaciations that made our now temperate zones arctic for thousands of years, and piled up masses of rock like the Himalayas, the Alps and the Pyrenees before the plough of the advancing ice.* If we accept the precarious theories of contemporary science, the creature who became man by learning to speak was one of the adaptable species that survived from those frozen centuries. In the Interglacial Stages, while the ice was retreating (and, for all we know, long before that), this strange organism discovered fire, developed the art of fashioning stone and bone into weapons and tools, and thereby paved the way to civilization.

---

* Current geological theory places the First Ice Age about 500,000 B.C.; the First Interglacial Stage about 475,000 to 400,000 B.C.; the Second Ice Age about 400,000 B.C.; the Second Interglacial Stage about 375,000 to 175,000 B.C.; the Third Ice Age about 175,000 B.C.; the Third Interglacial Stage about 150,000 to 50,000 B.C.; the Fourth (and latest) Ice Age about 50,000 to 25,000 B.C.[2] We are now in the Postglacial Stage, whose date of termination has not been accurately calculated. These and other details have been arranged more visibly in the table at the head of this chapter.

Various remains have been found which—subject to later correction—are attributed to this prehistoric man. In 1929 a young Chinese paleontologist, W. C. Pei, discovered in a cave at Chou Kou Tien, some thirty-seven miles from Peiping, a skull adjudged to be human by such experts as the Abbé Breuil and G. Elliot Smith. Near the skull were traces of fire, and stones obviously worked into tools; but mingled with these signs of human agency were the bones of animals ascribed by common consent to the Early Pleistocene Epoch, a million years ago.[3] This Peking skull is by common opinion the oldest human fossil known to us; and the tools found with it are the first human artefacts in history. At Piltdown, in Sussex, England, Dawson and Woodward found in 1911 some possibly human fragments now known as "Piltdown Man," or *Eoanthropus* (Dawn Man); the dates assigned to it range spaciously from 1,000,000 to 125,000 B.C. Similar uncertainties attach to the skull and thigh-bones found in Java in 1891, and the jaw-bone found near Heidelberg in 1907. The earliest unmistakably human fossils were discovered at Neanderthal, near Düsseldorf, Germany, in 1857; they date apparently from 40,000 B.C., and so resemble human remains unearthed in Belgium, France and Spain, and even on the shores of the Sea of Galilee, that a whole race of "Neanderthal Men" has been pictured as possessing Europe some forty millenniums before our era. They were short, but they had a cranial capacity of 1600 cubic centimeters—which is 200 more than ours.[4]

These ancient inhabitants of Europe seem to have been displaced, some 20,000 B.C., by a new race, named Cro-Magnon, from the discovery of its relics (1868) in a grotto of that name in the Dordogne region of southern France. Abundant remains of like type and age have been exhumed at various points in France, Switzerland, Germany and Wales. They indicate a people of magnificent vigor and stature, ranging from five feet ten inches to six feet four inches in height, and having a skull capacity of 1590 to 1715 cubic centimeters.[5] Like the Neanderthals, Cro-Magnon men are known to us as "cave-men," because their remains are found in caves; but there is no proof that these were their sole dwelling-place; it may be again but a jest of time that only those of them who lived in caves, or died in them, have transmitted their bones to archeologists. According to present theory this splendid race came from central Asia through Africa into Europe by land-bridges presumed to have then connected Africa with Italy and Spain.[6] The distribution of their fossils suggests that they fought for many decades, perhaps centuries, a war with the Neanderthals for the possession of Europe; so old is the conflict between Germany and France. At all events, Neanderthal Man disappeared; Cro-Magnon Man survived, became the chief progenitor of the modern western European, and laid the bases of that civilization which we inherit today.

The cultural remains of these and other European types of the Old Stone Age have been classified into seven main groups, according to the location of the earliest or principal finds in France. All are characterized by the use of unpolished stone implements. The first three took form in the precarious interval between the third and fourth glaciations.

I.   The *Pre-Chellean Culture* or Industry, dating some 125,000 B.C.: most of the flints found in this low layer give little evidence of fashioning, and appear to have been used (if at all) as nature provided them; but the presence of many stones of a shape to fit the fist, and in some degree flaked and pointed, gives to Pre-Chellean man the presumptive honor of having made the first known tool of European man—the *coup-de-poing*, or "blow-of-the-fist" stone.

II.   The *Chellean Culture*, ca. 100,000 B.C., improved this tool by roughly flaking it on both sides, pointing it into the shape of an almond, and fitting it better to the hand.

III.   The *Acheulean Culture*, about 75,000 B.C., left an abundance of remains in Europe, Greenland, the United States, Canada, Mexico, Africa, the Near East, India, and China; it not only brought the *coup-de-poing* to greater symmetry and point, but it produced a vast variety of special tools—hammers, anvils, scrapers, planes, arrow-heads, spear-heads, and knives; already one sees a picture of busy human industry.

IV.   The *Mousterian Culture* is found on all continents, in especial association with the remains of Neanderthal Man, about 40,000 B.C. Among these flints the *coup-de-poing* is comparatively rare, as something already ancient and superseded. The implements were formed from a large single flake, lighter, sharper and shapelier than before, and by skilful hands with a long-established tradition of artisanship. Higher in the Pleistocene strata of southern France appear the remains of

V.   The *Aurignacian Culture*, ca. 25,000 B.C., the first of the postglacial industries, and the first known culture of Cro-Magnon Man. Bone tools—pins, anvils, polishers, etc.—were now added to those of stone; and art appeared in the form of crude engravings on the rocks, or simple figurines in high relief, mostly of nude women.[7] At a higher stage of Cro-Magnon development

VI. The *Solutrean Culture* appears ca. 20,000 B.C., in France, Spain, Czechoslovakia and Poland: points, planes, drills, saws, javelins and spears were added to the tools and weapons of Aurignacian days; slim, sharp needles were made of bone, many implements were carved out of reindeer horn, and the reindeer's antlers were engraved occasionally with animal figures appreciably superior to Aurignacian art. Finally, at the peak of Cro-Magnon growth,

VII. The *Magdalenian Culture* appears throughout Europe about 16,000 B.C.; in industry it was characterized by a large assortment of delicate utensils in ivory, bone and horn, culminating in humble but perfect needles and pins; in art it was the age of the Altamira drawings, the most perfect and subtle accomplishment of Cro-Magnon Man.

Through these cultures of the Old Stone Age prehistoric man laid the bases of those handicrafts which were to remain part of the European heritage until the Industrial Revolution. Their transmission to the classic and modern civilizations was made easier by the wide spread of paleolithic industries. The skull and cave-painting found in Rhodesia in 1921, the flints discovered in Egypt by De Morgan in 1896, the paleolithic finds of Seton-Karr in Somaliland, the Old Stone Age deposits in the basin of the Fayum,* and the Still Bay Culture of South Africa indicate that the Dark Continent went through approximately the same prehistoric periods of development in the art of flaking stone as those which we have outlined in Europe;[8] perhaps, indeed, the quasi-Aurignacian remains in Tunis and Algiers strengthen the hypothesis of an African origin or stopping-point for the Cro-Magnon race, and therefore for European man.[9] Paleolithic implements have been dug up in Syria, India, China, Siberia, and other sections of Asia;[10] Andrews and his Jesuit predecessors came upon them in Mongolia;[11] Neanderthal skeletons and Mousterian-Aurignacian flints have been exhumed in great abundance in Palestine; and we have seen how the oldest known human remains and implements have lately been unearthed near Peiping. Bone tools have been discovered in Nebraska which some patriotic authorities would place at 500,000 B.C.; arrowheads have been found in Oklahoma and New Mexico which their finders assure us were made in 350,000 B.C. So vast was the bridge by which prehistoric transmitted the foundations of civilization to historic man.

---

* An oasis west of the Middle Nile.

2. Arts of the Old Stone Age

Tools—Fire—Painting—Sculpture

If now we sum up the implements fashioned by paleolithic man we shall gain a clearer idea of his life than by giving loose rein to our fancy. It was natural that a stone in the fist should be the first tool; many an animal could have taught that to man. So the *coup-de-poing*—a rock sharp at one end, round at the other to fit the palm of the hand—became for primeval man hammer, axe, chisel, scraper, knife and saw; even to this day the word *hammer* means, etymologically, a stone.[12] Gradually these specific tools were differentiated out of the one homogeneous form: holes were bored to attach a handle, teeth were inserted to make a saw, branches were tipped with the *coup-de-poing* to make a pick, an arrow or a spear. The scraper-stone that had the shape of a shell became a shovel or a hoe; the rough-surfaced stone became a file; the stone in a sling became a weapon of war that would survive even classical antiquity. Given bone, wood and ivory as well as stone, and paleolithic man made himself a varied assortment of weapons and tools: polishers, mortars, axes, planes, scrapers, drills, lamps, knives, chisels, choppers, lances, anvils, etchers, daggers, fish-hooks, harpoons, wedges, awls, pins, and doubtless many more.[14] Every day he stumbled upon new knowledge, and sometimes he had the wit to develop his chance discoveries into purposeful inventions.

But his great achievement was fire. Darwin has pointed out how the hot lava of volcanoes might have taught men the art of fire; according to Æschylus, Prometheus established it by igniting a narthex stalk in the burning crater of a volcano on the isle of Lemnos.[15] Among Neanderthal remains we find bits of charcoal and charred bones; man-made fire, then, is at least 40,000 years old.[16] Cro-Magnon man ground stone bowls to hold the grease that he burned to give him light: the lamp, therefore, is also of considerable age. Presumably it was fire that enabled man to meet the threat of cold from the advancing ice; fire that left him free to sleep on the earth at night, since animals dreaded the marvel as much as primitive men worshiped it; fire that conquered the dark and began that lessening of fear which is one of the golden threads in the not quite golden web of history; fire that created the old and honorable art of cooking, extending the diet of man to a thousand foods inedible before; fire that led at last to the fusing of metals, and the only real advance in technology from Cro-Magnon days to the Industrial Revolution.[17]

Strange to relate—and as if to illustrate Gautier's lines on robust art outlasting emperors and states—our clearest relics of paleolithic man are fragments of his art. Sixty years ago Señor Marcelino de Sautuola came upon a large cave on his estate at Altamira, in northern Spain. For thousands of years the entrance had been hermetically sealed by fallen rocks naturally cemented with stalagmite deposits. Blasts for new construction accidentally opened the entrance. Three years later Sautuola explored the cave, and noticed some curious markings on the walls. One day his little daughter accompanied him. Not compelled, like her father, to stoop as she walked through the cave, she could look up and observe the ceiling. There she saw, in vague outline, the painting of a great bison, magnificently colored and drawn. Many other drawings were found on closer examination of the ceiling and the walls. When, in 1880, Sautuola published his report on these observations, archeologists greeted him with genial scepticism. Some did him the honor of going to inspect the drawings, only to pronounce them the forgery of a hoaxer. For thirty years this quite reasonable incredulity persisted. Then the discovery of other drawings in caves generally conceded to be prehistoric (from their contents of unpolished flint tools, and polished ivory and bone) confirmed Sautuola's judgment; but Sautuola now was dead. Geologists came to Altamira and testified, with the unanimity of hindsight, that the stalagmite coating on many of the drawings was a paleolithic deposit.[18] General opinion now places these Altamira drawings—and the greater portion of extant prehistoric art—in the Magdalenian culture, some 16,000 B.C.[19] Paintings slightly later in time, but still of the Old Stone Age, have been found in many caves of France.*

Most often the subjects of these drawings are animals—reindeers, mammoths, horses, boars, bears, etc.; these, presumably, were dietetic luxuries, and therefore favorite objects of the chase. Sometimes the animals are transfixed with arrows; these, in the view of Frazer and Reinach, were intended as magic images that would bring the animal under the power, and into the stomach, of the artist or the hunter.[20] Conceivably they were just plain art, drawn with the pure joy of esthetic creation; the crudest

---

* Combarelles, Les Eyzies, Font de Gaume, etc.

representation should have sufficed the purposes of magic, whereas these paintings are often of such delicacy, power and skill as to suggest the unhappy thought that art, in this field at least, has not advanced much in the long course of human history. Here is life, action, nobility, conveyed overwhelmingly with one brave line or two; here a single stroke (or is it that the others have faded?) creates a living, charging beast. Will Leonardo's *Last Supper*, or El Greco's *Assumption*, bear up as well as these Cro-Magnon paintings after twenty thousand years?

Painting is a sophisticated art, presuming many centuries of mental and technical development. If we may accept current theory (which it is always a perilous thing to do), painting developed from statuary, by a passage from carving in the round to bas-relief and thence to mere outline and coloring; painting is sculpture minus a dimension. The intermediate prehistoric art is well represented by an astonishingly vivid bas-relief of an archer (or a spearman) on the Aurignacian cliffs at Laussel in France.[21] In a cave in Ariège, France, Louis Begouën discovered, among other Magdalenian relics, several ornamental handles carved out of reindeer antlers; one of these is of mature and excellent workmanship, as if the art had already generations of tradition and development behind it. Throughout the prehistoric Mediterranean—Egypt, Crete, Italy, France and Spain—countless figures of fat little women are found, which indicate either a worship of motherhood or an African conception of beauty. Stone statues of a wild horse, a reindeer and a mammoth have been unearthed in Czechoslovakia, among remains uncertainly ascribed to 30,000 B.C.[22]

The whole interpretation of history as progress falters when we consider that these statues, bas-reliefs and paintings, numerous though they are, may be but an infinitesimal fraction of the art that expressed or adorned the life of primeval man. What remains is found in caves, where the elements were in some measure kept at bay; it does not follow that prehistoric men were artists only when they were in caves. They may have carved as sedulously and ubiquitously as the Japanese, and may have fashioned statuary as abundantly as the Greeks; they may have painted not only the rocks in their caverns, but textiles, wood, everything—not excepting themselves. They may have created masterpieces far superior to the fragments that survive. In one grotto a tube was discovered, made from the bones of a reindeer, and filled with pigment;[23] in another a stone palette was picked up still thick with red ochre paint despite the transit of two hundred centuries.[24] Apparently the arts were highly developed and widely practised eighteen thousand years ago. Perhaps there was a class of professional artists among paleolithic men; perhaps there were Bohemians starving in the less respectable caves, denouncing the commercial bourgeoisie, plotting the death of academies, and forging antiques.

II. NEOLITHIC CULTURE

The Kitchen-Middens — The Lake-Dwellers — The coming of agriculture — The taming of animals — Technology—Neolithic weaving—pottery—building—transport—religion— science — Summary of the prehistoric preparation for civilization

At various times in the last one hundred years great heaps of seemingly prehistoric refuse have been found, in France, Sardinia, Portugal, Brazil, Japan and Manchuria, but above all in Denmark, where they received that queer name of Kitchen-Middens *(Kjokken-möddinger)* by which such ancient messes are now generally known. These rubbish heaps are composed of shells, especially of oysters, mussels and periwinkles; of the bones of various land and marine animals; of tools and weapons of horn, bone and unpolished stone; and of mineral remains like charcoal, ashes and broken pottery. These unprepossessing relics are apparently signs of a culture formed about the eighth millennium before Christ—later than the true paleolithic, and yet not properly neolithic, because not yet arrived at the use of polished stone. We know hardly anything of the men who left these remains, except that they had a certain catholic taste. Along with the slightly older culture of the Mas-d'Azil, in France, the Middens represent a "mesolithic" (middle-stone) or transition period between the paleolithic and the neolithic age.

In the year 1854, the winter being unusually dry, the level of the Swiss lakes sank, and revealed another epoch in prehistory. At some two hundred localities on these lakes piles were found which had stood in place under the water for from thirty to seventy centuries. The piles were so arranged as to indicate that small villages had been built upon them, perhaps for isolation or defense; each was connected with the land only by a narrow bridge, whose foundations, in some cases, were still in place; here and there even the framework of the houses had survived the patient play of the waters.* Amid these ruins were tools of bone and *polished* stone which became for archeologists the distinguishing mark of the New Stone Age that flourished some 10,000 B.C. in Asia, and some 5000 B.C. in Europe.[28] Akin to these remains are the gigantic tumuli left in the valleys of the Mississippi and its tributaries by the strange race that we call the Mound-Builders, and of which we know nothing except that in these mounds, shaped in the form of altars, geometric figures, or totem animals, are found objects of stone, shell, bone and beaten metal which place these mysterious men at the end of the neolithic period.

If from such remains we attempt to patch together some picture of the New Stone Age, we find at once a startling innovation—agriculture. In one sense all human history hinges upon two revolutions: the neolithic passage from hunting to agriculture, and the modern passage from agriculture to industry; no other revolutions have been quite as real or basic as these. The remains show that the Lake-Dwellers ate wheat, millet, rye, barley and oats, besides one hundred and twenty kinds of fruit and many varieties of nut.[29] No ploughs have been found in these ruins, probably because the first ploughshares were of wood—some strong tree-trunk and branch fitted with a flint edge; but a neolithic rock-carving unmistakably shows a peasant guiding a plough drawn by two oxen.[30] This marks the appearance of one of the epochal inventions of history. Before agriculture the earth could have supported (in the rash estimate of Sir Arthur Keith) only some twenty million men, and the lives of these were shortened by the mortality of the chase and war;[31] now began that multiplication of mankind which definitely confirmed man's mastery of the planet.

Meanwhile the men of the New Stone Age were establishing another of the foundations of civilization: the domestication and breeding of animals. Doubtless this was a long process, probably antedating the neolithic period. A certain natural sociability may have contributed to the association of man and animal, as we may still see in the delight that primitive people take in taming wild beasts, and in filling their huts with monkeys, parrots and similar companions.[32] The oldest bones in the neolithic remains

---

* Remains of similar lake dwellings have been found in France, Italy, Scotland, Russia, North America, India, and elsewhere. Such villages still exist in Borneo, Sumatra, New Guinea, etc.[26] Venezuela owes its name (Little Venice) to the fact that when Alonso de Ojeda discovered it for Europe (1499) he found the natives living in pile-dwellings on Lake Maracaibo.[27]

(ca. 8000 B.C.) are those of the dog—the most ancient and honorable companion of the human race. A little later (ca. 6000 B.C.) came the goat, the sheep, the pig and the ox.[33] Finally the horse, which to paleolithic man had been, if we may judge from the cave drawings, merely a beast of prey, was taken into camp, tamed, and turned into a beloved slave;[34] in a hundred ways he was now put to work to increase the leisure, the wealth, and the power of man. The new lord of the earth began to replenish his food-supply by breeding as well as hunting; and perhaps he learned, in this same neolithic age, to use cow's milk as food.

Neolithic inventors slowly improved and extended the tool-chest and armory of man. Here among the remains are pulleys, levers, grindstones, awls, pincers, axes, hoes, ladders, chisels, spindles, looms, sickles, saws, fish-hooks, skates, needles, brooches and pins.[35] Here, above all, is the wheel, another fundamental invention of mankind, one of the modest essentials of industry and civilization; already in this New Stone Age it was developed into disc and spoked varieties. Stones of every sort—even obdurate diorite and obsidian—were ground, bored, and finished into a polished form. Flints were mined on a large scale. In the ruins of a neolithic mine at Brandon, England, eight worn picks of deerhorn were found, on whose dusty surfaces were the finger-prints of the workmen who had laid down those tools ten thousand years ago. In Belgium the skeleton of such a New Stone Age miner, who had been crushed by falling rock, was discovered with his deerhorn pick still clasped in his hands;[36] across a hundred centuries we feel him as one of us, and share in weak imagination his terror and agony. Through how many bitter millenniums men have been tearing out of the bowels of the earth the mineral bases of civilization!

Having made needles and pins man began to weave; or, beginning to weave, he was moved to make needles and pins. No longer content to clothe himself with the furs and hides of beasts, he wove the wool of his sheep and the fibres found in the plants into garments from which came the robe of the Hindu, the toga of the Greek, the skirt of the Egyptian, and all the fascinating gamut of human dress. Dyes were mixed from the juices of plants or the minerals of the earth, and garments were stained with colors into luxuries for kings. At first men seem to have plaited textiles as they plaited straw, by interlacing one fibre with another; then they pierced holes into animal skins, and bound the skins with coarse fibres passing through the holes, as with the corsets of yesterday and the shoes of today; gradually the fibres

were refined into thread, and sewing became one of the major arts of woman-
kind. The stone distaffs and spindles among the neolithic ruins reveal one of
the great origins of human industry. Even mirrors are found in these remains;[37] everything was ready for civilization.

No pottery has been discovered in the earlier paleolithic graves; fragments
of it appear in the remains of the Magdalenian culture in Belgium,[38] but it
is only in the mesolithic Age of the Kitchen-Middens that we find any developed use of earthenware. The origin of the art, of course, is unknown.
Perhaps some observant primitive noticed that the trough made by his foot
in clay held water with little seepage;[39] perhaps some accidental baking of a
piece of wet clay by an adjoining fire gave him the hint that fertilized invention, and revealed to him the possibilities of a material so abounding in quantity, so pliable to the hand, and so easy to harden with fire or the sun. Doubtless he had for thousands of years carried his food and drink in such natural
containers as gourds and coconuts and the shells of the sea; then he had made
himself cups and ladles of wood or stone, and baskets and hampers of rushes
or straw; now he made lasting vessels of baked clay, and created another of
the major industries of mankind. So far as the remains indicate, neolithic
man did not know the potter's wheel; but with his own hands he fashioned
clay into forms of beauty as well as use, decorated it with simple designs,[40]
and made pottery, almost at the outset, not only an industry but an art.

Here, too, we find the first evidences of another major industry—building.
Paleolithic man left no known trace of any other home than the cave. But
in the neolithic remains we find such building devices as the ladder, the
pulley, the lever, and the hinge.[41] The Lake-Dwellers were skilful carpenters,
fastening beam to pile with sturdy wooden pins, or mortising them head to
head, or strengthening them with crossbeams notched into their sides. The
floors were of clay, the walls of wattle-work coated with clay, the roofs of
bark, straw, rushes or reeds. With the aid of the pulley and the wheel,
building materials were carried from place to place, and great stone foundations were laid for villages. Transport, too, became an industry: canoes were
built, and must have made the lakes live with traffic; trade was carried
on over mountains and between distant continents.[42] Amber, diorite, jadeite
and obsidian were imported into Europe from afar.[43] Similar words, letters,
myths, pottery and designs betray the cultural contacts of diverse groups of
prehistoric men.[44]

Outside of pottery the New Stone Age has left us no art, nothing to compare with the painting and statuary of paleolithic man. Here and there
among the scenes of neolithic life from England to China we find circular
heaps of stone called dolmens, upright monoliths called menhirs, and gigantic

cromlechs—stone structures of unknown purpose—like those at Stonehenge or in Morbihan. Probably we shall never know the meaning or function of these megaliths; presumably they are the remains of altars and temples.[45] For neolithic man doubtless had religions, myths with which to dramatize the daily tragedy and victory of the sun, the death and resurrection of the soil, and the strange earthly influences of the moon; we cannot understand the historic faiths unless we postulate such prehistoric origins.[46] Perhaps the arrangement of the stones was determined by astronomic considerations, and suggests, as Schneider thinks, an acquaintance with the calendar.[47] Some scientific knowledge was present, for certain neolithic skulls give evidence of trephining; and a few skeletons reveal limbs apparently broken and reset.[48]

We cannot properly estimate the achievements of prehistoric men, for we must guard against describing their life with imagination that transcends the evidence, while on the other hand we suspect that time has destroyed remains that would have narrowed the gap between primeval and modern man. Even so, the surviving record of Stone Age advances is impressive enough: paleolithic tools, fire, and art; neolithic agriculture, animal breeding, weaving, pottery, building, transport, and medicine, and the definite domination and wider peopling of the earth by the human race. All the bases had been laid; everything had been prepared for the historic civilizations except (*perhaps*) metals, writing and the state. Let men find a way to record their thoughts and achievements, and thereby transmit them more securely across the generations, and civilization would begin.

III. THE TRANSITION TO HISTORY

1. *The Coming of Metals*
Copper — Bronze — Iron

When did the use of metals come to man, and how? Again we do not know; we merely surmise that it came by accident, and we presume, from the absence of earlier remains, that it began towards the end of the Neolithic Age. Dating this end about 4000 B.C., we have a perspective in which the Age of Metals (and of writing and civilization) is a mere six thousand years appended to an Age of Stone lasting at least forty thousand years, and an Age of Man lasting* a million years. So young is the subject of our history.

The oldest known metal to be adapted to human use was copper. We find it in a Lake-Dwelling at Robenhausen, Switzerland, ca. 6000 B.C.;[49] in pre-

---

* If we accept "Peking Man" as early Pleistocene.

historic Mesopotamia ca. 4500 B.C.; in the Badarian graves of Egypt towards 4000 B.C.; in the ruins of Ur ca. 3100 B.C.; and in the relics of the North American Mound-Builders at an unknown age.[50] The Age of Metals began not with their discovery, but with their transformation to human purpose by fire and working. Metallurgists believe that the first fusing of copper out of its stony ore came by haphazard when a primeval camp fire melted the copper lurking in the rocks that enclosed the flames; such an event has often been seen at primitive camp fires in our own day. *Possibly* this was the hint which, many times repeated, led early man, so long content with refractory stone, to seek in this malleable metal a substance more easily fashioned into durable weapons and tools.[51] Presumably the metal was first used as it came from the profuse but careless hand of nature—sometimes nearly pure, most often grossly alloyed. Much later, doubtless—apparently about 3500 B.C. in the region around the Eastern Mediterranean—men discovered the art of smelting, of extracting metals from their ores. Then, towards 1500 B.C. (as we may judge from bas-reliefs on the tomb of Rekh-mara in Egypt), they proceeded to cast metal: dropping the molten copper into a clay or sand receptacle, they let it cool into some desired form like a spear-head or an axe.[52] That process, once discovered, was applied to a great variety of metals, and provided man with those doughty elements that were to build his greatest industries, and give him his conquest of the earth, the sea, and the air. Perhaps it was because the Eastern Mediterranean lands were rich in copper that vigorous new cultures arose, in the fourth millennium B.C., in Elam, Mesopotamia and Egypt, and spread thence in all directions to transform the world.[53]

But copper by itself was soft, admirably pliable for some purposes (what would our electrified age do without it?), but too weak for the heavier tasks of peace and war; an alloy was needed to harden it. Though nature suggested many, and often gave man copper already mixed and hardened with tin or zinc—forming, therefore, ready-made bronze or brass—he may have dallied for centuries before taking the next step: the deliberate fusing of metal with metal to make compounds more suited to his needs. The discovery is at least five thousand years old, for bronze is found in Cretan remains of 3000 B.C., in Egyptian remains of 2800 B.C., and in the second city of Troy 2000 B.C.[54] We can no longer speak strictly of an "Age of Bronze," for the metal came to different peoples at diverse epochs, and the term would therefore be without chronological meaning;[55] furthermore, some cultures—like those of Finland, northern Russia, Polynesia, central Africa, southern India, North America, Australia and Japan—passed over the Bronze Age directly from stone to iron;[56] and in those cultures where bronze appears it seems to have had a subordinate place as a luxury of priests, aristocrats and kings, while commoners had still to be content with stone.[57] Even the terms "Old Stone Age" and "New Stone Age" are precariously relative, and describe conditions rather than times; to this day many primitive peoples (e.g., the Eskimos and the Polynesian Islanders) remain in the Age of Stone, knowing iron only as a delicacy brought to them by explorers. Captain Cook bought several pigs for a sixpenny nail when he landed in New Zealand in 1778; and another traveler described the inhabitants of Dog Island as "covetous chiefly of iron, so as to want to take the nails out of the ship."[58]

Bronze is strong and durable, but the copper and tin which were needed to make it were not available in such convenient quantities and locations as to provide man with the best material for industry and war. Sooner or later iron had to come; and it is one of the anomalies of history that, being so abundant, it did not appear at least as early as copper and bronze. Men may have begun the art by making weapons out of meteoric iron as the Mound-Builders seem to have done, and as some primitive peoples do to this day; then, perhaps, they melted it from the ore by fire, and hammered it into wrought iron. Fragments of apparently meteoric iron have been found in predynastic Egyptian tombs; and Babylonian inscriptions mention iron as a costly rarity in Hammurabi's capital (2100 B.C.). An iron foundry perhaps four thousand years old has been discovered in Northern Rhodesia; mining in South Africa is no modern invention. The oldest *wrought* iron known is a group of knives found at Gerar, in Palestine, and dated by Petrie about 1350 B.C. A century later the metal appears in Egypt, in the reign of the great Rameses II; still another century and it is found in the Ægean. In Western Europe it turns up first at Hallstatt, Austria, ca. 900 B.C., and in the La Tène industry in Switzerland ca. 500 B.C. It entered India with Alexander, America with Columbus, Oceania with Cook.[59] In this leisurely way, century by century, iron has gone about its rough conquest of the earth.

2. *Writing*

Its possible ceramic origins — The "Mediterranean Signary" — Hieroglyphics — Alphabets

But by far the most important step in the passage to civilization was writing. Bits of pottery from neolithic remains show, in some cases, painted lines which several students have interpreted as signs.[60] This is doubtful enough; but it is possible that writing, in the broad sense of graphic symbols of specific thoughts, began with marks impressed by nails or fingers upon the still soft clay to adorn or identify pottery. In the earliest Sumerian hieroglyphics the pictograph for bird bears a suggestive resemblance to the bird decorations on the oldest pottery at Susa, in Elam; and the earliest pictograph for grain is taken directly from the geometrical grain-decoration of Susan and Sumerian vases. The linear script of Sumeria, on its first appearance (ca. 3600 B.C.), is apparently an abbreviated form of the signs and pictures painted or impressed upon the primitive pottery of lower Mesopotamia and Elam.[60a] Writing, like painting and sculpture, is probably in its origin a ceramic art; it began as a form of etching and drawing, and the same clay that gave vases to the potter, figures to the sculptor and bricks to the builder, supplied writing materials to the scribe. From such a beginning to the cuneiform writing of Mesopotamia would be an intelligible and logical development.

The oldest graphic symbols known to us are those found by Flinders Petrie on shards, vases and stones discovered in the prehistoric tombs of Egypt, Spain and the Near East, to which, with his usual generosity, he attributes an age of seven thousand years. This "Mediterranean Signary" numbered some three hundred signs; most of them were the same in all localities, indicating commercial bonds from one end of the Mediterranean to the other as far back as 5000 B.C. They were not pictures but chiefly mercantile symbols—marks of property, quantity, or other business memoranda; the berated bourgeoisie may take consolation in the thought that literature originated in bills of lading. The signs were not letters, since they represented entire words or ideas; but many of them were astonishingly like letters of the "Phœnician" alphabet. Petrie concludes that "a wide body of signs had been gradually brought into use in primitive times for various purposes. These were interchanged by trade, and spread from land to land, . . . until a couple of dozen signs triumphed and became common property to a group of trading communities, while the local survivals of other forms were gradually extinguished in isolated seclusion."[61] That this signary was the source of the alphabet is an interesting theory, which Professor Petrie has the distinction of holding alone.[62]

Whatever may have been the development of these early commercial symbols, there grew up alongside them a form of writing which was a branch of drawing and painting, and conveyed connected thought by pictures. Rocks near Lake Superior still bear remains of the crude pictures with which the American Indians proudly narrated for posterity, or more probably for their associates, the story of their crossing the mighty lake.[63] A similar evolution of drawing into writing seems to have taken place throughout the Mediterranean world at the end of the Neolithic Age.

Certainly by 3600 B.C., and probably long before that, Elam, Sumeria and Egypt had developed a system of thought-pictures, called *hieroglyphics* because practised chiefly by the priests.[64] A similar system appeared in Crete ca. 2500 B.C. We shall see later how these hieroglyphics, representing thoughts, were, by the corruption of use, schematized and conventionalized into syllabaries—i.e., collections of signs indicating syllables; and how at last signs were used to indicate not the whole syllable but its initial sound, and therefore became letters. Such alphabetic writing probably dates back to 3000 B.C. in Egypt; in Crete it appears ca. 1600 B.C.[65] The Phœnicians did not create the alphabet, they marketed it; taking it apparently from Egypt and Crete,[66] they imported it piecemeal to Tyre, Sidon and Byblos, and exported it to every city on the Mediterranean; they were the middlemen, not the producers, of the alphabet. By the time of Homer the Greeks were taking over this Phœnician—or the allied Aramaic—alphabet, and were calling it by the Semitic names of the first two letters (*Alpha, Beta;* Hebrew *Aleph, Beth*).[67]

Writing seems to be a product and convenience of commerce; here again culture may see how much it owes to trade. When the priests devised a system of pictures with which to write their magical, ceremonial and medical formulas, the secular and clerical strains in history, usually in conflict, merged for a moment to produce the greatest human invention since the coming of speech. The development of writing almost created civilization by providing a means for the recording and transmission of knowledge, the accumulation of science, the growth of literature, and the spread of peace and order among varied but communicating tribes brought by one language under a single state. The earliest appearance of writing marks that ever-receding point at which history begins.

3. Lost Civilizations

Polynesia — "Atlantis"

In approaching now the history of civilized nations we must note that not only shall we be selecting a mere fraction of each culture for our study, but we shall be describing perhaps a minority of the civilizations that have probably existed on the earth. We cannot entirely ignore the legends, current throughout history, of civilizations once great and cultured, destroyed by some catastrophe of nature or war, and leaving not a wrack behind; our recent exhuming of the civilizations of Crete, Sumeria and Yucatan indicates how true such tales may be.

The Pacific contains the ruins of at least one of these lost civilizations. The gigantic statuary of Easter Island, the Polynesian tradition of powerful nations and heroic warriors once ennobling Samoa and Tahiti, the artistic ability and poetic sensitivity of their present inhabitants, indicate a glory departed, a people not rising to civilization but fallen from a high estate. And in the Atlantic, from Iceland to the South Pole, the raised central bed of the oceans* lends some support to the legend so fascinatingly transmitted to us by Plato,[68] of a civilization that once flourished on an island continent between Europe and Asia, and was suddenly lost when a geological convulsion swallowed that continent into the sea. Schliemann, the resurrector of Troy, believed that Atlantis had served as a mediating link between the cultures of Europe and Yucatan, and that Egyptian civilization had been brought from Atlantis.[69] Perhaps America itself was Atlantis, and some pre-Mayan culture may have been in touch with Africa and Europe in neolithic times. Possibly every discovery is a rediscovery.

Certainly it is probable, as Aristotle thought, that many civilizations came, made great inventions and luxuries, were destroyed, and lapsed from human memory. History, said Bacon, is the planks of a shipwreck; more of the past is lost than has been saved. We console ourselves with the thought that as the individual memory must forget the greater part of experience in order to be sane, so the race has preserved in its heritage only the most vivid and impressive—or is it only the best-recorded?—of its cultural experiments. Even if that racial heritage were but one tenth as rich as it is, no one could possibly absorb it all. We shall find the story full enough.

4. Cradles of Civilization

Central Asia — Anau — Lines of Dispersion

It is fitting that this chapter of unanswerable questions should end with the query, "Where did civilization begin?"—which is also unanswerable. If we may trust the geologists, who deal with prehistoric mists as airy as

---

* A submarine plateau, from 2000 to 3000 metres below the surface, runs north and south through the mid-Atlantic, surrounded on both sides by "deeps" of 5000 to 6000 metres.

any metaphysics, the arid regions of central Asia were once moist and temperate, nourished with great lakes and abundant streams.[70] The recession of the last ice wave slowly dried up this area, until the rainfall was insufficient to support towns and states. City after city was abandoned as men fled west and east, north and south, in search of water; half buried in the desert lie ruined cities like Bactra, which must have held a teeming population within its twenty-two miles of circumference. As late as 1868 some 80,000 inhabitants of western Turkestan were forced to migrate because their district was being inundated by the moving sand.[71] There are many who believe that these now dying regions saw the first substantial development of that vague complex of order and provision, manners and morals, comfort and culture, which constitutes civilization.[72]

In 1907 Pumpelly unearthed at Anau, in southern Turkestan, pottery and other remains of a culture which he has ascribed to 9000 B.C., with a possible exaggeration of four thousand years.[73] Here we find the cultivation of wheat, barley and millet, the use of copper, the domestication of animals, and the ornamentation of pottery in styles so conventionalized as to suggest an artistic background and tradition of many centuries.[74] Apparently the culture of Turkestan was already very old in 5000 B.C. Perhaps it had historians who delved into its past in a vain search for the origins of civilization, and philosophers who eloquently mourned the degeneration of a dying race.

From this center, if we may imagine where we cannot know, a people driven by a rainless sky and betrayed by a desiccated earth migrated in three directions, bringing their arts and civilization with them. The arts, if not the race, reached eastward to China, Manchuria and North America; southward to northern India; westward to Elam, Sumeria, Egypt, even to Italy and Spain.[75] At Susa, in ancient Elam (modern Persia), remains have been found so similar in type to those at Anau that the re-creative imagination is almost justified in presuming cultural communication between Susa and Anau at the dawn of civilization (ca. 4000 B.C.).[76] A like kinship of early arts and products suggests a like relationship and continuity between prehistoric Mesopotamia and Egypt.

We cannot be sure which of these cultures came first, and it does not much matter; they were in essence of one family and one type. If we violate honored precedents here and place Elam and Sumeria before Egypt, it is from no vainglory of unconventional innovation, but rather because the age of these Asiatic civilizations, compared with those of Africa and Europe, grows as our knowledge of them deepens. As the spades of archeology, after a century of victorious inquiry along the Nile, pass across Suez into Arabia, Palestine, Mesopotamia and Persia, it becomes more probable with every year of accumulating research that it was the rich delta of Mesopotamia's rivers that saw the earliest known scenes in the historic drama of civilization.

BOOK ONE

THE NEAR EAST

"At that time the gods called me, Hammurabi, the servant whose deeds are pleasing, ... who helped his people in time of need, who brought about plenty and abundance, ... to prevent the strong from oppressing the weak, ... to enlighten the land and further the welfare of the people."

Code of Hammurabi, Prologue.

CHRONOLOGICAL TABLE OF NEAR EASTERN HISTORY*

B.C.	EGYPT	B.C.	WESTERN ASIA
18000:	Nile Paleolithic Culture	40000:	Paleolithic Culture in Palestine
10000:	Nile Neolithic Culture	9000:	Bronze Culture in Turkestan
5000:	Nile Bronze Culture	4500:	Civilization in Susa and Kish
4241:	Egyptian Calendar appears (?)	3800:	Civilization in Crete
4000:	Badarian Culture	3638:	III Dynasty of Kish
3500-2631:	A. THE OLD KINGDOM	3600:	Civilization in Sumeria
3500-3100:	I-III Dynasties	3200:	Dynasty of Akshak in Sumeria
3100-2965:	IV Dynasty: the Pyramids	3100:	Ur-nina, first (?) King of Lagash
3098-3075:	Khufu ("Cheops" of Herodotus)	3089:	IV Dynasty of Kish
3067-3011:	Khafre ("Chephren")	2903:	King Urukagina reforms Lagash
3011-2988:	Menkaure ("Mycerinus")	2897:	Lugal-zaggisi conquers Lagash
2965-2631:	V-VI Dynasties	2872-2817:	Sargon I unites Sumeria & Akkad
2738-2644:	Pepi II (longest reign known)	2795-2739:	Naram-sin, King of Sumeria & Akkad
2631-2212:	The Feudal Age	2600:	Gudea King of Lagash
2375-1800:	B. THE MIDDLE KINGDOM	2474-2398:	Golden Age of Ur; 1st code of laws
2212-2000:	XII Dynasty	2357:	Sack of Ur by the Elamites
2212-2192:	Amenemhet I	2169-1926:	I Babylonian Dynasty
2192-2157:	Senusret ("Sesostris") I	2123-2081:	Hammurabi King of Babylon
2099-2061:	Senusret III	2117-2094:	Hammurabi conquers Sumeria & Elam
2061-2013:	Amenemhet III	1926-1703:	II Babylonian Dynasty
1800-1600:	The Hyksos Domination	1900:	Hittite Civilization appears
1580-1100:	C. THE EMPIRE	1800:	Civilization in Palestine
1580-1322:	XVIII Dynasty	1746-1169:	Kassite Domination in Babylonia
1545-1514:	Thutmose I	1716:	Rise of Assyria under Shamshi-Adad II
1514-1501:	Thutmose II	1650-1220:	Jewish Bondage in Egypt (?)
1501-1479:	Queen Hatshepsut	1600-1360:	Egyptian Domination of Palestine & Syria
1479-1447:	Thutmose III	1550:	The Civilization of Mitanni
1412-1376:	Amenhotep III	1461:	Burra-Buriash I King of Babylonia
1400-1360:	Age of the Tell-el-Amarna Correspondence; Revolt of Western Asia against Egypt		
1380-1362:	Amenhotep IV (Ikhnaton)	1276:	Shalmaneser I unifies Assyria
1360-1350:	Tutenkhamon	1200:	Conquest of Canaan by the Jews
1346-1210:	XIX Dynasty	1115-1102:	Tiglath-Pileser I extends Assyria
1346-1322:	Harmhab	1025-1010:	Saul King of the Jews
1321-1300:	Seti I	1010-974:	David King of the Jews
1300-1233:	Rameses II	1000-600:	Golden Age of Phoenicia & Syria
1233-1223:	Merneptah		
1214-1210:	Seti II	974-937:	Solomon King of the Jews
1205-1100:	XX Dynasty: the Ramessid Kings	937:	Schism of the Jews: Judah & Israel
1204-1172:	Rameses III		
1100-947:	XXI Dynasty: the Libyan Kings	884-859:	Ashurnasirpal II King of Assyria

* All dates are B.C., and are approximate before 663 B.C. In the case of rulers the dates are of their reigns, not of their lives.

CHRONOLOGICAL TABLE

B.C.	EGYPT
947-720:	XXII Dynasty: the Bubastite Kings
947-925:	Sheshonk I
925-889:	Osorkon I
880-850:	Osorkon II
850-825:	Sheshonk II
821-769:	Sheshonk III
763-725:	Sheshonk IV
850-745:	XXIII Dynasty: The Theban Kings
725-663:	XXIV Dynasty: The Memphite Kings
745-663:	XXV Dynasty: The Ethiopian Kings
689-663:	Taharka
685:	Commercial Revival of Egypt
674-650:	Assyrian Occupation of Egypt
663-525:	XXVI Dynasty: the Saïte Kings
663-609:	Psamtik ("Psammetichos") I
663-525:	Saïte Revival of Egyptian Art
615:	Jews begin to colonize Egypt
609-593:	Niku ("Necho") II
605:	Niku begins the Hellenization of Egypt
593-588:	Psamtik II

B.C.	WESTERN ASIA
859-824:	Shalmaneser III King of Assyria
811-808:	Sammuramat ("Semiramis") in Assyria
785-700:	Golden Age of Armenia ("Urartu")
745-727:	Tiglath-Pileser III
732-722:	Assyria takes Damascus & Samaria
722-705:	Sargon II King of Assyria
709:	Deioces King of the Medes
705-681:	Sennacherib King of Assyria
702:	The First Isaiah
689:	Sennacherib sacks Babylon
681-669:	Esarhaddon King of Assyria
669-626:	Ashurbanipal ("Sardanapalus") King of Assyria
660-583:	Zarathustra ("Zoroaster")?
652:	Gyges King of Lydia
640-584:	Cyaxares King of the Medes
639:	Fall of Susa; end of Elam
639:	Josiah King of the Jews
625:	Nabopolassar restores independence of Babylon
621:	Beginnings of the *Pentateuch*
612:	Fall of Nineveh; end of Assyria
610-561:	Alyattes King of Lydia
605-562:	Nebuchadrezzar II King of Babylonia
600:	Jeremiah at Jerusalem; coinage in Lydia
597-586:	Nebuchadrezzar takes Jerusalem
586-538:	Jewish Captivity in Babylon

OF NEAR EASTERN HISTORY

B.C.	EGYPT
569-526:	Ahmose ("Amasis") II
568-567:	Nebuchadrezzar II invades Egypt
560:	Growing Influence of Greece in Egypt
526-525:	Psamtik III
525:	Persian Conquest of Egypt
485:	Revolt of Egypt against Persia
484:	Reconquest of Egypt by Xerxes
482:	Egypt joins with Persia in war against Greece
455:	Failure of Athenian Expedition to Egypt
332:	Greek Conquest of Egypt; foundation of Alexandria
283-30:	The Ptolemaic Kings
30:	Egypt absorbed into the Roman Empire

B.C.	WESTERN ASIA
580:	Ezekiel in Babylon
570-546:	Croesus King of Lydia
555-529:	Cyrus I King of the Medes & the Persians
546:	Cyrus takes Sardis
540:	The Second Isaiah
539:	Cyrus takes Babylon & creates the Persian Empire
529-522:	Cambyses King of Persia
521-485:	Darius I King of Persia
520:	Building of 2nd Temple at Jerusalem
490:	Battle of Marathon
485-464:	Xerxes I King of Persia
480:	Battle of Salamis
464-423:	Artaxerxes I King of Persia
450:	The *Book of Job* (?)
444:	Ezra at Jerusalem
423-404:	Darius II King of Persia
404-359:	Artaxerxes II King of Persia
401:	Cyrus the Younger defeated at Cunaxa
359-338:	Ochus King of Persia
338-330:	Darius III King of Persia
334:	Battle of the Granicus; Alexander enters Jerusalem
333:	Battle of Issus
331:	Alexander takes Babylon
330:	Battle of Arbela; the Near East becomes part of Alexander's Empire

CHAPTER VII

Sumeria

Orient-ation—Contributions of the Near East to Western
civilization

WRITTEN history is at least six thousand years old. During half of this period the center of human affairs, so far as they are now known to us, was in the Near East. By this vague term we shall mean here all southwestern Asia south of Russia and the Black Sea, and west of India and Afghanistan; still more loosely, we shall include within it Egypt, too, as anciently bound up with the Near East in one vast web and communicating complex of Oriental civilization. In this rough theatre of teeming peoples and conflicting cultures were developed the agriculture and commerce, the horse and wagon, the coinage and letters of credit, the crafts and industries, the law and government, the mathematics and medicine, the enemas and drainage systems, the geometry and astronomy, the calendar and clock and zodiac, the alphabet and writing, the paper and ink, the books and libraries and schools, the literature and music, the sculpture and architecture, the glazed pottery and fine furniture, the monotheism and monogamy, the cosmetics and jewelry, the checkers and dice, the ten-pins and income-tax, the wet-nurses and beer, from which our own European and American culture derive by a continuous succession through the mediation of Crete and Greece and Rome. The "Aryans" did not establish civilization—they took it from Babylonia and Egypt. Greece did not begin civilization—it inherited far more civilization than it began; it was the spoiled heir of three millenniums of arts and sciences brought to its cities from the Near East by the fortunes of trade and war. In studying and honoring the Near East we shall be acknowledging a debt long due to the real founders of European and American civilization.

I. ELAM

The culture of Susa—The potter's wheel—The wagon-wheel

If the reader will look at a map of Persia, and will run his finger north along the Tigris from the Persian Gulf to Amara, and then east across the Iraq border to the modern town of Shushan, he will have located the site of the ancient city of Susa, center of a region known to the Jews as Elam— the high land. In this narrow territory, protected on the west by marshes, and on the east by the mountains that shoulder the great Iranian Plateau, a people of unknown race and origin developed one of the first historic civilizations. Here, a generation ago, French archeologists found human remains dating back 20,000 years, and evidences of an advanced culture as old as 4500 B.C.*[1]

Apparently the Elamites had recently emerged from a nomad life of hunting and fishing; but already they had copper weapons and tools, cultivated grains and domesticated animals, hieroglyphic writing and business documents, mirrors and jewelry, and a trade that reached from Egypt to India.[3] In the midst of chipped flints that bring us back to the Neolithic Age we find finished vases elegantly rounded and delicately painted with geometric designs, or with picturesque representations of animals and plants; some of this pottery is ranked among the finest ever made by man.[4] Here is the oldest appearance not only of the potter's wheel but of the wagon wheel; this modest but vital vehicle of civilization is found only later in Babylonia, and still later in Egypt.[5] From these already complex beginnings the Elamites rose to troubled power, conquering Sumeria and Babylon, and being conquered by them, turn by turn. The city of Susa survived six thousand years of history, lived through the imperial zeniths of Sumeria, Babylonia, Egypt, Assyria, Persia, Greece and Rome, and flourished, under the name of Shushan, as late as the fourteenth century of our era. At various times it grew to great wealth; when Ashurbanipal captured and sacked it (646 B.C.) his historians recounted without understatement the varied booty of gold and silver, precious stones and royal ornaments, costly garments and regal furniture, cosmetics and chariots, which the conqueror brought in his train to Nineveh. History so soon began its tragic alternance of art and war.

---

* Professor Breasted believes that the antiquity of this culture, and that of Anau, has been exaggerated by De Morgan, Pumpelly and other students.[2]

II. THE SUMERIANS

1. The Historical Background

*The exhuming of Sumeria—Geography—Race—Appearance—
The Sumerian Flood—The kings—An ancient reformer—
—Sargon of Akkad—The Golden Age of Ur*

If we return to our map and follow the combined Tigris and Euphrates from the Persian Gulf to where these historic streams diverge (at modern Kurna), and then follow the Euphrates westward, we shall find, north and south of it, the buried cities of ancient Sumeria: Eridu (now Abu Shahrein), Ur (now Mukayyar), Uruk (Biblical Erech, now Warka), Larsa (Biblical Ellasar, now Senkereh), Lagash (now Shippurla), Nippur (Niffer) and Nisin. Follow the Euphrates northwest to Babylon, once the most famous city of Mesopotamia (the land "between the rivers"); observe, directly east of it, Kish, site of the oldest culture known in this region; then pass some sixty miles farther up the Euphrates to Agade, capital, in ancient days, of the Kingdom of Akkad. The early history of Mesopotamia is in one aspect the struggle of the non-Semitic peoples of Sumeria to preserve their independence against the expansion and inroads of the Semites from Kish and Agade and other centers in the north. In the midst of their struggles these varied stocks unconsciously, perhaps unwillingly, coöperated to produce the first extensive civilization known to history, and one of the most creative and unique.*

Despite much research we cannot tell of what race the Sumerians were, nor by what route they entered Sumeria. Perhaps they came from central

---

* The unearthing of this forgotten culture is one of the romances of archeology. To those whom, with a poor sense of the amplitude of time, we call "the ancients"—that is, to the Romans, the Greeks and the Jews—Sumeria was unknown. Herodotus apparently never heard of it; if he did, he ignored it, as something more ancient to him than he to us. Berosus, a Babylonian historian writing about 250 B.C., knew of Sumeria only through the veil of a legend. He described a race of monsters, led by one Oannes, coming out of the Persian Gulf, and introducing the arts of agriculture, metal-working, and writing; "all the things that make for the amelioration of life," he declares, "were bequeathed to men by Oannes, and since that time no further inventions have been made."⁸ Not till two thousand years after Berosus was Sumeria rediscovered. In 1850 Hincks recognized that cuneiform writing—made by pressing a wedge-pointed stylus upon soft clay, and used in the Semitic languages of the Near East—had been borrowed from an earlier people with a largely non-Semitic speech; and Oppert gave to this hypothetical people the name

Asia, or the Caucasus, or Armenia, and moved through northern Mesopotamia down the Euphrates and the Tigris—along which, as at Ashur, evidences
of their earliest culture have been found; perhaps, as the legend says, they
sailed in from the Persian Gulf, from Egypt or elsewhere, and slowly made
their way up the great rivers; perhaps they came from Susa, among whose
relics is an asphalt head bearing all the characteristics of the Sumerian type;
perhaps, even, they were of remote Mongolian origin, for there is much in
their language that resembles the Mongol speech.[9] We do not know.

The remains show them as a short and stocky people, with high, straight,
non-Semitic nose, slightly receding forehead and downward-sloping eyes.
Many wore beards, some were clean-shaven, most of them shaved the upper
lip. They clothed themselves in fleece and finely woven wool; the women
draped the garment from the left shoulder, the men bound it at the waist
and left the upper half of the body bare. Later the male dress crept up
towards the neck with the advance of civilization, but servants, male and
female, while indoors, continued to go naked from head to waist. The head
was usually covered with a cap, and the feet were shod with sandals; but
well-to-do women had shoes of soft leather, heel-less, and laced like our
own. Bracelets, necklaces, anklets, finger-rings and ear-rings made the women
of Sumeria, as recently in America, show-windows of their husbands' prosperity.[10]

When their civilization was already old—about 2300 B.C.—the poets and
scholars of Sumeria tried to reconstruct its ancient history. The poets wrote
legends of a creation, a primitive Paradise and a terrible flood that engulfed
and destroyed it because of the sin of an ancient king.[11] This flood passed
down into Babylonian and Hebrew tradition, and became part of the Christian creed. In 1929 Professor Woolley, digging into the ruins of Ur, discovered, at considerable depth, an eight-foot layer of silt and clay; this, if
we are to believe him, was deposited during a catastrophic overflow of the

---

"Sumerian."[7] About the same time Rawlinson and his aides found, among Babylonian ruins,
tablets containing vocabularies of this ancient tongue, with interlinear translations, in
modern college style, from the older language into Babylonian.[8] In 1854 two Englishmen
uncovered the sites of Ur, Eridu and Uruk; at the end of the nineteenth century French
explorers revealed the remains of Lagash, including tablets recording the history of the
Sumerian kings; and in our own time Professor Woolley of the University of Pennsylvania, and many others, have exhumed the primeval city of Ur, where the Sumerians
appear to have reached civilization by 4500 B.C. So the students of many nations have
worked together on this chapter of that endless mystery story in which the detectives are
archeologists and the prey is historic truth. Nevertheless, there has been as yet only a
beginning of research in Sumeria; there is no telling what vistas of civilization and history
will be opened up when the ground has been worked, and the material studied, as men
have worked and studied in Egypt during the last one hundred years.

Euphrates, which lingered in later memory as the Flood. Beneath that layer were the remains of a prediluvian culture that would later be pictured by the poets as a Golden Age.

Meanwhile the priest-historians sought to create a past spacious enough for the development of all the marvels of Sumerian civilization. They formulated lists of their ancient kings, extending the dynasties before the Flood to 432,000 years;[12] and told such impressive stories of two of these rulers, Tammuz and Gilgamesh, that the latter became the hero of the greatest poem in Babylonian literature, and Tammuz passed down into the pantheon of Babylon and became the Adonis of the Greeks. Perhaps the priests exaggerated a little the antiquity of their civilization. We may vaguely judge the age of Sumerian culture by observing that the ruins of Nippur are found to a depth of sixty-six feet, of which almost as many feet extend below the remains of Sargon of Akkad as rise above it to the topmost stratum (ca. 1 A.D.);[13] on this basis Nippur would go back to 5262 B.C. Tenacious dynasties of city-kings seem to have flourished at Kish ca. 4500 B.C., and at Ur ca. 3500 B.C. In the competition of these two primeval centers we have the first form of that opposition between Semite and non-Semite which was to be one bloody theme of Near-Eastern history from the Semitic ascendancy of Kish and the conquests of the Semitic kings Sargon I and Hammurabi, through the capture of Babylon by the "Aryan" generals Cyrus and Alexander in the sixth and fourth centuries before Christ, and the conflicts of Crusaders and Saracens for the Holy Sepulchre and the emoluments of trade, down to the efforts of the British Government to dominate and pacify the divided Semites of the Near East today.

From 3000 B.C. onward the clay-tablet records kept by the priests, and found in the ruins of Ur, present a reasonably accurate account of the accessions and coronations, uninterrupted victories and sublime deaths of the petty kings who ruled the city-states of Ur, Lagash, Uruk, and the rest; the writing of history and the partiality of historians are very ancient things. One king, Urukagina of Lagash, was a royal reformer, an enlightened despot who issued decrees aimed at the exploitation of the poor by the rich, and of everybody by the priests. The high priest, says one edict, must no longer "come into the garden of a poor mother and take wood therefrom, nor gather tax in fruit therefrom"; burial-fees were to be cut to one-fifth of what they had been; and the clergy and high officials were forbidden to share among themselves the revenues and cattle offered to the gods. It was the King's boast that he "gave liberty to his people";[14]

and surely the tablets that preserve his decrees reveal to us the oldest, briefest and justest code of laws in history.

This lucid interval was ended normally by one Lugal-zaggisi, who invaded Lagash, overthrew Urukagina, and sacked the city at the height of its prosperity. The temples were destroyed, the citizens were massacred in the streets, and the statues of the gods were led away in ignominious bondage. One of the earliest poems in existence is a clay tablet, apparently 4800 years old, on which the Sumerian poet Dingiraddamu mourns for the raped goddess of Lagash:

> For the city, alas, the treasures, my soul doth sigh,
> For my city Girsu (Lagash), alas, the treasures, my soul doth sigh.
> In holy Girsu the children are in distress.
> Into the interior of the splendid shrine he (the invader) pressed;
> The august Queen from her temple he brought forth.
> O Lady of my city, desolated, when wilt thou return?[15]

We pass by the bloody Lugal-zaggisi, and other Sumerian kings of mighty name: Lugal-shagengur, Lugal-kigub-nidudu, Ninigi-dubti, Lugal-andanukhunga. . . . Meanwhile another people, of Semitic race, had built the kingdom of Akkad under the leadership of Sargon I, and had established its capital at Agade some two hundred miles northwest of the Sumerian city-states. A monolith found at Susa portrays Sargon armed with the dignity of a majestic beard, and dressed in all the pride of long authority. His origin was not royal: history could find no father for him, and no other mother than a temple prostitute.[16] Sumerian legend composed for him an autobiography quite Mosaic in its beginning: "My humble mother conceived me; in secret she brought me forth. She placed me in a basket-boat of rushes; with pitch she closed my door."[17] Rescued by a workman, he became a cup-bearer to the king, grew in favor and influence, rebelled, displaced his master, and mounted the throne of Agade. He called himself "King of Universal Dominion," and ruled a small portion of Mesopotamia. Historians call him "the Great," for he invaded many cities, captured much booty, and killed many men. Among his victims was that same Lugal-zaggisi who had despoiled Lagash and violated its goddess; him Sargon defeated and carried off to Nippur in chains. East and west, north and south the mighty warrior marched, conquering Elam, washing his weapons in symbolic triumph in the Persian Gulf, crossing western Asia, reaching the Mediterranean,[18] and establishing the first great empire in history. For fifty-five years he held sway, while legends gathered about him and prepared to make him a god. His reign closed with all his empire in revolt.

Three sons succeeded him in turn. The third, Naram-sin, was a mighty builder, of whose works nothing remains but a lovely stele, or memorial slab, recording his victory over an obscure king. This powerful relief, found by De Morgan at Susa in 1897, and now a treasure of the Louvre, shows a muscular Naram-sin armed with bow and dart, stepping with royal dignity upon the bodies of his fallen foes, and apparently prepared to answer with quick death the appeal of the vanquished for mercy; while between them another victim, pierced through the neck with an arrow, falls dying. Behind them tower the Zagros Mountains; and on one hill is the record, in elegant cuneiform, of Naram-sin's victory. Here the art of carving is already adult and confident, already guided and strengthened with a long tradition.

To be burned to the ground is not always a lasting misfortune for a city; it is usually an advantage from the standpoint of architecture and sanitation. By the twenty-sixth century B.C. we find Lagash flourishing again, now under another enlightened monarch, Gudea, whose stocky statues are the most prominent remains of Sumerian sculpture. The diorite figure in the Louvre shows him in a pious posture, with his head crossed by a heavy band resembling a model of the Colosseum, hands folded in his lap, bare shoulders and feet, and short, chubby legs covered by a bell-like skirt embroidered with a volume of hieroglyphics. The strong but regular features reveal a man thoughtful and just, firm and yet refined. Gudea was honored by his people not as a warrior but as a Sumerian Aurelius, devoted to religion, literature and good works; he built temples, promoted the study of classical antiquities in the spirit of the expeditions that unearthed him, and tempered the strength of the strong in mercy to the weak. One of his inscriptions reveals the policy for which his people worshiped him, after his death, as a god: "During seven years the maidservant was the equal of her mistress, the slave walked beside his master, and in my town the weak rested by the side of the strong."[19]

Meanwhile "Ur of the Chaldees" was having one of the most prosperous epochs in its long career from 3,500 B.C. (the apparent age of its oldest graves) to 700 B.C. Its greatest king, Ur-engur, brought all western Asia under his pacific sway, and proclaimed for all Sumeria the first extensive code of laws in history. "By the laws of righteousness of Shamash forever I established justice."²⁰ As Ur grew rich by the trade that flowed through it on the Euphrates, Ur-engur, like Pericles, beautified his city with temples, and built lavishly in the subject cities of Larsa, Uruk and Nippur. His son Dungi continued his work through a reign of fifty-eight years, and ruled so wisely that the people deified him as the god who had brought back their ancient Paradise.

But soon that glory faded. The warlike Elamites from the East and the rising Amorites from the West swept down upon the leisure, prosperity and peace of Ur, captured its king, and sacked the city with primitive thoroughness. The poets of Ur sang sad chants about the rape of the statue of Ishtar, their beloved mother-goddess, torn from her shrine by profane invaders. The form of these poems is unexpectedly first-personal, and the style does not please the sophisticated ear; but across the four thousand years that separate us from the Sumerian singer we feel the desolation of his city and his people.

> Me the foe hath ravished, yea, with hands unwashed;
> Me his hands have ravished, made me die of terror.
> Oh, I am wretched! Naught of reverence hath he!
> Stripped me of my robes, and clothed therein his consort,
> Tore my jewels from me, therewith decked his daughter.
> (Now) I tread his courts—my very person sought he
> In the shrines. Alas, the day when to go forth I trembled.
> He pursued me in my temple; he made me quake with fear,
> There within my walls; and like a dove that fluttering percheth
> On a rafter, like a flitting owlet in a cavern hidden,
> Birdlike from my shrine he chased me,
> From my city like a bird he chased me, me sighing,
> "Far behind, behind me is my temple."²¹

So for two hundred years, which to our self-centered eyes seem but an empty moment, Elam and Amor ruled Sumeria. Then from the north came the great Hammurabi, King of Babylon; retook from the Elamites Uruk and Isin; bided his time for twenty-three years; invaded Elam and captured its king; established his sway over Amor and distant Assyria, built an empire of unprecedented power, and disciplined it with a universal law. For many centuries now, until the rise of Persia, the Semites would rule the Land between the Rivers. Of the Sumerians nothing more is heard; their little chapter in the book of history was complete.

2. Economic Life

The soil — Industry — Trade — Classes — Science

But Sumerian civilization remained. Sumer and Akkad still produced handicraftsmen, poets, artists, sages and saints; the culture of the southern cities passed north along the Euphrates and the Tigris to Babylonia and Assyria as the initial heritage of Mesopotamian civilization.

At the basis of this culture was a soil made fertile by the annual overflow of rivers swollen with the winter rains. The overflow was perilous as well as useful; the Sumerians learned to channel it safely through irrigating canals that ribbed and crossed their land; and they commemorated those early dangers by legends that told of a flood, and how at last the land had been separated from the waters, and mankind had been saved.[23] This irrigation system, dating from 4000 B.C., was one of the great achievements of Sumerian civilization, and certainly its foundation. Out of these carefully watered fields came abounding crops of corn, barley, spelt, dates, and many vegetables. The plough appeared early, drawn by oxen as even with us until yesterday, and already furnished with a tubular seed-drill. The gathered harvest was threshed by drawing over it great sledges of wood armed with flint teeth that cut the straw for the cattle and released the grain for men.[24]

It was in many ways a primitive culture. The Sumerians made some use of copper and tin, and occasionally mixed them to produce bronze; now and then they went so far as to make large implements of iron.[25] But metal was still a luxury and a rarity. Most Sumerian tools were of flint; some, like the sickles for cutting the barley, were of clay; and certain finer articles, such as needles and awls, used ivory and bone.[26] Weaving was done on a large scale under the supervision of overseers appointed by the king,[27] after the latest fashion of governmentally controlled industry. Houses were made of reeds, usually plastered with an adobe mixture of clay and straw moistened with water and hardened by the sun; such dwellings are still easy to find in what was once Sumeria. The hut had wooden doors, revolving upon socket hinges of stone. The floors were ordinarily

the beaten earth; the roofs were arched by bending the reeds together
at the top, or were made flat with mud-covered reeds stretched over
crossbeams of wood. Cows, sheep, goats and pigs roamed about the
dwelling in primeval comradeship with man. Water for drinking was
drawn from wells.[28]

Goods were carried chiefly by water. Since stone was rare in Sumeria
it was brought up the Gulf or down the rivers, and then through numerous
canals to the quays of the cities. But land transportation was developing;
at Kish the Oxford Field Expedition unearthed some of the oldest wheeled
vehicles known.[29] Here and there in the ruins are business seals bearing
indications of traffic with Egypt and India.[30] There was no coinage yet,
and trade was normally by barter; but gold and silver were already in use
as standards of value, and were often accepted in exchange for goods—
sometimes in the form of ingots and rings of definite worth, but generally
in quantities measured by weight in each transaction. Many of the clay
tablets that have brought down to us fragments of Sumerian writing are
business documents, revealing a busy commercial life. One tablet speaks,
with *fin-de-siècle* weariness, of "the city, where the tumult of man is."
Contracts had to be confirmed in writing and duly witnessed. A system
of credit existed by which goods, gold or silver might be borrowed, interest
to be paid in the same material as the loan, and at rates ranging from 15
to 33% per annum.[31] Since the stability of a society may be partly measured by inverse relation with the rate of interest, we may suspect that
Sumerian business, like ours, lived in an atmosphere of economic and political uncertainty and doubt.

Gold and silver have been found abundantly in the tombs, not only
as jewelry, but as vessels, weapons, ornaments, even as tools. Rich and
poor were stratified into many classes and gradations; slavery was highly
developed, and property rights were already sacred.[32] Between the rich
and the poor a middle class took form, composed of small-business men,
scholars, physicians and priests. Medicine flourished, and had a specific
for every disease; but it was still bound up with theology, and admitted
that sickness, being due to possession by evil spirits, could never be cured
without the exorcising of these demons. A calendar of uncertain age and
origin divided the year into lunar months, adding a month every three or
four years to reconcile the calendar with the seasons and the sun. Each
city gave its own names to the months.[33]

3. Government

The kings—Ways of war—The feudal barons—Law

Indeed each city, as long as it could, maintained a jealous independence, and indulged itself in a private king. It called him *patesi*, or priest-king, indicating by the very word that government was bound up with religion. By 2800 B.C. the growth of trade made such municipal separatism impossible, and generated "empires" in which some dominating personality subjected the cities and their *patesis* to his power, and wove them into an economic and political unity. The despot lived in a Renaissance atmosphere of violence and fear; at any moment he might be despatched by the same methods that had secured him the throne. He dwelt in an inaccessible palace, whose two entrances were so narrow as to admit only one person at a time; to the right and left were recesses from which secret guards could examine every visitor, or pounce upon him with daggers.[34] Even the king's temple was private, hidden away in his palace, so that he might perform his religious duties without exposure, or neglect them inconspicuously.

The king went to battle in a chariot, leading a motley host armed with bows, arrows and spears. The wars were waged frankly for commercial routes and goods, without catchwords as a sop for idealists. King Manishtusu of Akkad announced frankly that he was invading Elam to get control of its silver mines, and to secure diorite stone to immortalize himself with statuary—the only instance known of a war fought for the sake of art. The defeated were customarily sold into slavery; or, if this was unprofitable, they were slaughtered on the battlefield. Sometimes a tenth of the prisoners, struggling vainly in a net, were offered as living victims to the thirsty gods. As in Renaissance Italy, the chauvinistic separatism of the cities stimulated life and art, but led to civic violence and suicidal strife that weakened each petty state, and at last destroyed Sumeria.[35]

In the empires social order was maintained through a feudal system. After a successful war the ruler gave tracts of land to his valiant chieftains, and exempted such estates from taxation; these men kept order in their territories, and provided soldiers and supplies for the exploits of the king. The finances of the government were obtained by taxes in kind, stored in royal warehouses, and distributed as pay to officials and employees of the state.[36]

To this system of royal and feudal administration was added a body of law, already rich with precedents when Ur-engur and Dungi codified the statutes of Ur; this was the fountainhead of Hammurabi's famous code. It was cruder and simpler than later legislation, but less severe: where, for example, the Semitic code killed a woman for adultery, the Sumerian code merely allowed the husband to take a second wife, and reduce the first to a subordinate position.[37] The law covered commercial as well as sexual relations, and regulated all loans and contracts, all buying and selling, all adoptions and bequests. Courts of justice sat in the temples, and the judges were for the most part priests; professional judges presided over a superior court. The best element in this code was a plan for avoiding litigation: every case was first submitted to a public arbitrator whose duty it was to bring about an amicable settlement without recourse to law.[38] It is a poor civilization from which we may not learn something to improve our own.

4. Religion and Morality

The Sumerian Pantheon — The food of the gods — Mythology — Education—A Sumerian prayer—Temple prostitutes—The rights of woman—Sumerian cosmetics

King Ur-engur proclaimed his code of laws in the name of the great god Shamash, for government had so soon discovered the political utility of heaven. Having been found useful, the gods became innumerable; every city and state, every human activity, had some inspiring and disciplinary divinity. Sun-worship, doubtless already old when Sumeria began, expressed itself in the cult of Shamash, "light of the gods," who passed the night in the depths of the north, until Dawn opened its gates for him; then he mounted the sky like a flame, driving his chariot over the steeps of the firmament; the sun was merely a wheel of his fiery car.[39] Nippur built great temples to the god Enlil and his consort Ninlil; Uruk worshiped especially the virgin earth-goddess Innini, known to the Semites of Akkad as Ishtar—the loose and versatile Aphrodite-Demeter of the Near East. Kish and Lagash worshiped a *Mater Dolorosa*, the sorrowful mother-goddess Ninkarsag, who, grieved with the unhappiness of men, interceded for them with sterner deities.[40] Ningirsu was the god of irrigation, the "Lord of Floods"; Abu or Tammuz was the god of vegetation. Even Sin was a god—of the moon; he was represented in human form with a thin crescent about his head, presaging the halos of medieval saints. The air was full of spirits—beneficent angels, one each as protector to every Sumerian, and demons or devils who sought to expel the protective deity and take possession of body and soul.

Most of the gods lived in the temples, where they were provided by the faithful with revenue, food and wives. The tablets of Gudea list the objects which the gods preferred: oxen, goats, sheep, doves, chickens, ducks, fish, dates, figs, cucumbers, butter, oil and cakes;[41] we may judge from this list that the well-to-do Sumerian enjoyed a plentiful *cuisine*. Originally, it seems, the gods preferred human flesh; but as human morality improved they had to be content with animals. A liturgical tablet found in the Sumerian ruins says, with strange theological premonitions: "The lamb is the substitute for humanity; he hath given up a lamb for his life."[42] Enriched by such beneficence, the priests became the wealthiest and most powerful class in the Sumerian cities. In most matters they were the government; it is difficult to make out to what extent the *patesi* was a priest, and to what extent a king. Urukagina rose like a Luther against the exactions of the clergy, denounced them for their voracity, accused them of taking bribes in their administration of the law, and charged that they were levying such taxes upon farmers and fishermen as to rob them of the fruits of their toil. He swept the courts clear for a time of these corrupt officials, and established laws regulating the taxes and fees paid to the temples, protecting the helpless against extortion, and providing against the violent alienation of funds or property.[43] Already the world was old, and well established in its time-honored ways.

Presumably the priests recovered their power when Urukagina died, quite as they were to recover their power in Egypt after the passing of Ikhnaton; men will pay any price for mythology. Even in this early age the great myths of religion were taking form. Since food and tools were placed in the graves with the dead, we may presume that the Sumerians believed in an after-life.[44] But like the Greeks they pictured the other world as a dark abode of miserable shadows, to which all the dead descended indiscriminately. They had not yet conceived heaven and hell, eternal reward and punishment; they offered prayer and sacrifice not for "eternal life," but for tangible advantages here on the earth.[45] Later legend told how Adapa, a sage of Eridu, had been initiated into all lore by Ea, goddess of wisdom; one secret only had been refused him—the knowledge of deathless life.[46] Another legend narrated how the gods had created man happy; how man, by his free will, had sinned, and been punished with a flood, from which but one man—Tagtug the weaver—had survived. Tagtug forfeited longevity and health by eating the fruit of a forbidden tree.[47]

The priests transmitted education as well as mythology, and doubtless sought to teach, as well as to rule, by their myths. To most of the temples were attached schools wherein the clergy instructed boys and girls in writing and arithmetic, formed their habits into patriotism and piety, and prepared some of them for the high professsion of scribe. School tablets survive, encrusted with tables of multiplication and division, square and cube roots, and exercises in applied geometry.[48] That the instruction was not much more foolish than that which is given to our children appears from a tablet which is a Lucretian outline of anthropology: "Mankind when created did not know of bread for eating or garments for wearing. The people walked with limbs on the ground, they ate herbs with their mouths like sheep, they drank ditch-water."[49]

What nobility of spirit and utterance this first of the historic religions could rise to shines out in the prayer of King Gudea to the goddess Bau, the patron deity of Lagash:

O my Queen, the Mother who established Lagash,
The people on whom thou lookest is rich in power;
The worshiper on whom thou lookest, his life is prolonged.
I have no mother—thou art my mother;
I have no father—thou art my father. . . .
My goddess Bau, thou knowest what is good;
Thou hast given me the breath of life.
Under the protection of thee, my Mother,
In thy shadow I will reverently dwell.[50]

Women were attached to every temple, some as domestics, some as concubines for the gods or their duly constituted representatives on earth. To serve the temples in this way did not seem any disgrace to a Sumerian girl; her father was proud to devote her charms to the alleviation of divine monotony, and celebrated the admission of his daughter to these sacred functions with ceremonial sacrifice, and the presentation of the girl's marriage dowry to the temple.[51]

Marriage was already a complex institution regulated by many laws.

The bride kept control of the dowry given her by her father in marriage, and though she held it jointly with her husband, she alone determined its bequest. She exercised equal rights with her husband over their children; and in the absence of the husband and a grown-up son she administered the estate as well as the home. She could engage in business independently of her husband, and could keep or dispose of her own slaves. Sometimes, like Shub-ad, she could rise to the status of queen, and rule her city with luxurious and imperious grace.[52] But in all crises the man was lord and master. Under certain conditions he could sell his wife, or hand her over as a slave to pay his debts. The double standard was already in force, as a corollary of property and inheritance: adultery in the man was a forgivable whim, but in the woman it was punished with death. She was expected to give many children to her husband and the state; if barren, she could be divorced without further reason; if merely averse to continuous maternity she was drowned. Children were without legal rights; their parents, by the act of publicly disowning them, secured their banishment from the city.[53]

Nevertheless, as in most civilizations, the women of the upper classes almost balanced, by their luxury and their privileges, the toil and disabilities of their poorer sisters. Cosmetics and jewelry are prominent in the Sumerian tombs. In Queen Shub-ad's grave Professor Woolley picked up a little compact of blue-green malachite, golden pins with knobs of lapis-lazuli, and a vanity-case of filigree gold shell. This vanity-case, as large as a little finger, contained a tiny spoon, presumably for scooping up rouge from the compact; a metal stick, perhaps for training the cuticle; and a pair of tweezers probably used to train the eyebrows or to pluck out inopportune hairs. The Queen's rings were made of gold wire; one ring was inset with segments of lapis-lazuli; her necklace was of fluted lapis and gold. Surely there is nothing new under the sun; and the difference between the first woman and the last could pass through the eye of a needle.

5. Letters and Arts

Writing—Literature—Temples and palaces—Statuary—Ceramics—Jewelry—Summary of Sumerian civilization

The startling fact in the Sumerian remains is writing. The marvelous art seems already well advanced, fit to express complex thought in commerce, poetry and religion. The oldest inscriptions are on stone, and date apparently as far back as 3600 B.C.[54] Towards 3200 B.C. the clay tablet appears, and from that time on the Sumerians seem to have delighted in the great discovery. It is our good fortune that the people of Mesopotamia wrote not upon fragile, ephemeral paper in fading ink, but upon moist clay deftly impressed with the wedge-like ("cuneiform") point of a stylus. With this malleable material the scribe kept records, executed contracts, drew up official documents, recorded property, judgments and sales, and created a culture in which the stylus became as mighty as the sword. Having completed the writing, the scribe baked the clay tablet with heat or in the sun, and made it thereby a manuscript far more durable than paper, and only less lasting than stone. This development of cuneiform script was the outstanding contribution of Sumeria to the civilizing of mankind.

Sumerian writing reads from right to left; the Babylonians were, so far as we know, the first people to write from left to right. The linear script, as we have seen, was apparently a stylized and conventionalized form of the signs and pictures painted or impressed upon primitive Sumerian pottery.* Presumably from repetition and haste over centuries of time, the original pictures were gradually contracted into signs so unlike the objects which they had once represented that they became the symbols of sounds rather than of things. We should have an analogous process in English if the picture of a bee should in time be shortened and simplified, and come to mean not a bee but the sound *be*, and then serve to indicate that syllable in any combination as in *be-ing*. The Sumerians and Babylonians never advanced from such representation of syllables to the representation of letters— never dropped the vowel in the syllabic sign to make *be* mean *b;* it seems to have remained for the Egyptians to take this simple but revolutionary step.[55]

The transition from writing to literature probably required many hundreds of years. For centuries writing was a tool of commerce, a matter of contracts and bills, of shipments and receipts; and secondarily, perhaps, it was an instrument of religious record, an attempt to preserve magic formulas, ceremonial procedures, sacred legends, prayers and hymns from alteration or decay. Nevertheless, by 2700 B.C., great libraries had been formed in Sumeria; at Tello, for example, in ruins contemporary with Gudea, De Sarzac discovered a collection of over 30,000 tablets ranged one

* Cf. above, p. 104.

upon another in neat and logical array.[56] As early as 2000 B.C. Sumerian historians began to reconstruct the past and record the present for the edification of the future; portions of their work have come down to us not in the original form but as quotations in later Babylonian chronicles. Among the original fragments, however, is a tablet found at Nippur, bearing the Sumerian prototype of the epic of Gilgamesh, which we shall study later in its developed Babylonian expression.[57] Some of the shattered tablets contain dirges of no mean power, and of significant literary form. Here at the outset appears the characteristic Near-Eastern trick of chanting repetition—many lines beginning in the same way, many clauses reiterating or illustrating the meaning of the clause before. Through these salvaged relics we see the religious origin of literature in the songs and lamentations of the priests. The first poems were not madrigals, but prayers.

Behind these apparent beginnings of culture were doubtless many centuries of development, in Sumeria and other lands. Nothing has been created, it has only grown. Just as in writing Sumeria *seems* to have created cuneiform, so in architecture it seems to have created at once the fundamental shapes of home and temple, column and vault and arch.[58] The Sumerian peasant made his cottage by planting reeds in a square, a rectangle or a circle, bending the tops together, and binding them to form an arch, a vault or a dome;[59] this, we surmise, is the simple origin, or earliest known appearance, of these architectural forms. Among the ruins of Nippur is an arched drain 5000 years old; in the royal tombs of Ur there are arches that go back to 3500 B.C., and arched doors were common at Ur 2000 B.C.[60] And these were true arches: i.e., their stones were set in full voussoir fashion—each stone a wedge tapering downward tightly into place.

The richer citizens built palaces, perched on a mound sometimes forty feet above the plain, and made purposely inaccessible except by one path, so that every Sumerian's home might be his castle. Since stone was scarce, these palaces were mostly of brick. The plain red surface of the walls was relieved by *terracotta* decoration in every form—spirals, chevrons, triangles, even lozenges and diapers. The inner walls were plastered and painted in simple mural style. The house was built around a central court, which gave shade and some coolness against the Mediterranean sun; for the same reason, as well as for security, the rooms opened upon this court rather than upon the outer world. Windows were a luxury, or perhaps they were not wanted.

Water was drawn from wells; and an extensive system of drainage drew the waste from the residential districts of the towns. Furniture was not complex or abundant but neither was it without taste. Some beds were inlaid with metal or ivory, and occasionally, as in Egypt, armchairs flaunted feet like lions' claws.[61]

For the temples stone was imported, and adorned with copper entablatures and friezes inlaid with semiprecious material. The temple of Nannar at Ur set a fashion for all Mesopotamia with pale blue enameled tiles; while its interior was paneled with rare woods like cedar and cypress, inlaid with marble, alabaster, onyx, agate and gold. Usually the most important temple in the city was not only built upon an elevation, but was topped with a ziggurat—a tower of three, four or seven stories, surrounded with a winding external stairway, and set back at every stage. Here on the heights the loftiest of the city's gods might dwell, and here the government might find a last spiritual and physical citadel against invasion or revolt.*[62]

The temples were sometimes decorated with statuary of animals, heroes and gods; figures plain, blunt and powerful, but severely lacking in sculptural finish and grace. Most of the extant statues are of King Gudea, executed resolutely but crudely in resistant diorite. In the ruins of Tell-el-Ubaid, from the early Sumerian period, a copper statuette of a bull was found, much abused by the centuries, but still full of life and bovine complacency. A cow's head in silver from the grave of Queen Shub-ad at Ur is a masterpiece that suggests a developed art too much despoiled by time to permit of our giving it its due. This is almost proved by the bas-reliefs that survive. The "Stele of the Vultures" set up by King Eannatum of Lagash, the porphyry cylinder of Ibnishar,[63] the humorous caricatures (as surely they must be) of Ur-nina,[64] and above all the "Victory Stele" of Naram-sin share the crudity of Sumerian sculpture, but have in them a lusty vitality of drawing and action characteristic of a young and flourishing art.

Of the pottery one may not speak so leniently. Perhaps time misleads our judgment by having preserved the worst; perhaps there were many pieces as well carved as the alabaster vessels discovered at Eridu;[65] but for the most part Sumerian pottery, though turned on the wheel, is mere earthenware, and cannot compare with the vases of Elam. Better work was done by the goldsmiths. Vessels of gold, tasteful in design and delicate in finish, have

---

* Such ziggurats have helped American architects to mould a new form for buildings forced by law to set back their upper stories lest they impede their neighbor's light. History suddenly contracts into a brief *coup d'œil* when we contemplate in one glance the brick ziggurats of Sumeria 5000 years old, and the brick ziggurats of contemporary New York.

been found in the earliest graves at Ur, some as old as 4000 B.C.[66] The silver vase of Entemenu, now in the Louvre, is as stocky as Gudea, but is adorned with a wealth of animal imagery finely engraved.[67] Best of all is the gold sheath and lapis-lazuli dagger exhumed at Ur;[68] here, if one may judge from photographs,* the form almost touches perfection. The ruins have given us a great number of cylindrical seals, mostly made of precious metal or stone, with reliefs carefully carved upon a square inch or two of surface; these seem to have served the Sumerians in place of signatures, and indicate a refinement of life and manners disturbing to our naïve conception of progress as a continuous rise of man through the unfortunate cultures of the past to the unrivaled zenith of today.

Sumerian civilization may be summed up in this contrast between crude pottery and consummate jewelry; it was a synthesis of rough beginnings and occasional but brilliant mastery. Here, within the limits of our present knowledge, are the first states and empires, the first irrigation, the first use of gold and silver as standards of value, the first business contracts, the first credit system, the first code of law, the first extensive development of writing, the first stories of the Creation and the Flood, the first libraries and schools, the first literature and poetry, the first cosmetics and jewelry, the first sculpture and bas-relief, the first palaces and temples, the first ornamental metal and decorative themes, the first arch, column, vault and dome. Here, for the first known time on a large scale, appear some of the sins of civilization: slavery, despotism, ecclesiasticism, and imperialistic war. It was a life differentiated and subtle, abundant and complex. Already the natural inequality of men was producing a new degree of comfort and luxury for the strong, and a new routine of hard and disciplined labor for the rest. The theme was struck on which history would strum its myriad variations.

III. PASSAGE TO EGYPT

Sumerian influence in Mesopotamia—Ancient Arabia—Mesopotamian influence in Egypt

Nevertheless, we are still so near the beginning of recorded history when we speak of Sumeria that it is difficult to determine the priority or sequence of the many related civilizations that developed in the ancient Near

---

* The original is in the Iraq Museum at Baghdad.

East. The oldest written records known to us are Sumerian; this, which may be a whim of circumstance, a sport of mortality, does not prove that the first civilization was Sumerian. Statuettes and other remains akin to those of Sumeria have been found at Ashur and Samarra, in what became Assyria; we do not know whether this early culture came from Sumeria or passed to it along the Tigris. The code of Hammurabi resembles that of Ur-engur and Dungi, but we cannot be sure that it was evolved from it rather than from some predecessor ancestral to them both. It is only probable, not certain, that the civilizations of Babylonia and Assyria were derived from or fertilized by that of Sumer and Akkad.[69] The gods and myths of Babylon and Nineveh are in many cases modifications or developments of Sumerian theology; and the languages of these later cultures bear the same relationship to Sumeria that French and Italian bear to Latin.

Schweinfurth has called attention to the interesting fact that though the cultivation of barley, millet and wheat, and the domestication of cattle, goats and sheep, appear in both Egypt and Mesopotamia as far back as our records go, these cereals and animals are found in their wild and natural state not in Egypt but in western Asia—especially in Yemen or ancient Arabia. He concludes that civilization—i.e., in this context, the cultivation of cereals and the use of domesticated animals—appeared in unrecorded antiquity in Arabia, and spread thence in a "triangular culture" to Mesopotamia (Sumeria, Babylonia, Assyria) and Egypt.[70] Current knowledge of primitive Arabia is too slight to make this more than a presentable hypothesis.

More definite is the derivation of certain specific elements of Egyptian culture from Sumeria and Babylonia. We know that trade passed between Mesopotamia and Egypt—certainly via the isthmus at Suez, and probably by water from the ancient outlets of Egyptian rivers on the Red Sea.[71] A look at the map explains why Egypt, throughout its known history, has belonged to Western Asia rather than to Africa; trade and culture could pass from Asia along the Mediterranean to the Nile, but shortly beyond that it was balked by the desert which, with the cataracts of the Nile, isolated Egypt from the remainder of Africa. Hence it is natural that we should find many Mesopotamian elements in the primitive culture of Egypt.

The farther back we trace the Egyptian language the more affinities it reveals with the Semitic tongues of the Near East.[72] The pictographic writing of the predynastic Egyptians seems to have come in from Sumeria.[73] The cylindrical seal, which is of unquestionably Mesopotamian origin, appears in the earliest period of known Egyptian history, and then disappears, as if an imported custom had been displaced by a native mode.[74] The potter's wheel is not known in Egypt before the Fourth Dynasty—long after its appearance in Sumeria; presumably it came into Egypt from the Land between the Rivers along with the wheel and the chariot.[75] Early Egyptian and Babylonian mace-heads are completely identical in form.[76] A finely worked flint knife, found in predynastic Egyptian remains at Gebel-el-Arak, bears reliefs in Mesopotamian themes and style.[77] Copper was apparently developed in western Asia, and brought thence to Egypt.[78] Early Egyptian architecture resembles Mesopotamian in the use of the recessed panel as a decoration for brick walls.[79] Predynastic pottery, statuettes and decorative motives are in many cases identical, or unmistakably allied, with Mesopotamian products.[80] Among these early Egyptian remains are small figures of a goddess of evident Asiatic origin. At a time when Egyptian civilization seems to have only begun, the artists of Ur were making statuary and reliefs whose style and conventions demonstrate the antiquity of these arts in Sumeria.[81]*

Egypt could well afford to concede the priority of Sumeria. For whatever the Nile may have borrowed from the Tigris and the Euphrates, it soon flowered into a civilization specifically and uniquely its own; one of the richest and greatest, one of the most powerful and yet one of the most graceful, cultures in history. By its side Sumeria was but a crude beginning; and not even Greece or Rome would surpass it.

---

* A great scholar, Elliot Smith, has tried to offset these considerations by pointing out that although barley, millet and wheat are not known in their natural state in Egypt, it is there that we find the oldest signs of their cultivation; and he believes that it was from Egypt that agriculture and civilization came to Sumeria.[82] The greatest of American Egyptologists, Professor Breasted, is similarly unconvinced of the priority of Sumeria. Dr. Breasted believes that the wheel is at least as old in Egypt as in Sumeria, and rejects the hypothesis of Schweinfurth on the ground that cereals have been found in their native state in the highlands of Abyssinia.

CHAPTER VIII

Egypt

I. THE GIFT OF THE NILE

1. In the Delta

Alexandria—The Nile—The Pyramids—The Sphinx

THIS is a perfect harbor. Outside the long breakwater the waves topple over one another roughly; within it the sea is a silver mirror. There, on the little island of Pharos, when Egypt was very old, Sostratus built his great lighthouse of white marble, five hundred feet high, as a beacon to all ancient mariners of the Mediterranean, and as one of the seven wonders of the world. Time and the nagging waters have washed it away, but a new lighthouse has taken its place, and guides the steamer through the rocks to the quays of Alexandria. Here that astonishing boy-statesman, Alexander, founded the subtle, polyglot metropolis that was to inherit the culture of Egypt, Palestine and Greece. In this harbor Cæsar received without gladness the severed head of Pompey.

As the train glides through the city, glimpses come of unpaved alleys and streets, heat waves dancing in the air, workingmen naked to the waist, black-garbed women bearing burdens sturdily, white-robed and turbaned Moslems of regal dignity, and in the distance spacious squares and shining palaces, perhaps as fair as those that the Ptolemies built when Alexandria was the meeting-place of the world. Then suddenly it is open country, and the city recedes into the horizon of the fertile Delta—that green triangle which looks on the map like the leaves of a lofty palm-tree held up on the slender stalk of the Nile.

Once, no doubt, this Delta was a bay; patiently the broad stream filled it up, too slowly to be seen, with detritus carried down a thousand miles;* now from this little corner of mud, enclosed by the many mouths of the river, six million peasants grow enough cotton to export a hundred million dollars' worth of it every year. There, bright and calm under the

---

* Even the ancient geographers (e.g., Strabo[1]) believed that Egypt had once been under the waters of the Mediterranean, and that its deserts had been the bottom of the sea.

glaring sun, fringed with slim palms and grassy banks, is the most famous of all rivers. We cannot see the desert that lies so close beyond it, or the great empty *wadis*—river-beds—where once its fertile tributaries flowed; we cannot realize yet how precariously narrow a thing this Egypt is, owing everything to the river, and harassed on either side with hostile, shifting sand.

Now the train passes amid the alluvial plain. The land is half covered with water, and crossed everywhere with irrigation canals. In the ditches and the fields black *fellaheen** labor, knowing no garment but a cloth about the loins. The river has had one of its annual inundations, which begin at the summer solstice and last for a hundred days; through that overflow the desert became fertile, and Egypt blossomed, in Herodotus' phrase, as the "gift of the Nile." It is clear why civilization found here one of its earliest homes; nowhere else was a river so generous in irrigation, and so controllable in its rise; only Mesopotamia could rival it. For thousands of years the peasants have watched this rise with anxious eagerness; to this day public criers announce its progress each morning in the streets of Cairo.² So the past, with the quiet continuity of this river, flows into the future, lightly touching the present on its way. Only historians make divisions; time does not.

But every gift must be paid for; and the peasant, though he valued the rising waters, knew that without control they could ruin as well as irrigate his fields. So from time beyond history he built these ditches that cross and recross the land; he caught the surplus in canals, and when the river fell he raised the water with buckets pivoted on long poles, singing, as he worked, the songs that the Nile has heard for five thousand years. For as these peasants are now, sombre and laughterless even in their singing, so they have been, in all likelihood, for fifty centuries.³ This water-raising apparatus is as old as the Pyramids; and a million of these *fellaheen*, despite the conquests of Arabic, still speak the language of the ancient monuments.⁴

Here in the Delta, fifty miles southeast of Alexandria, is the site of Naucratis, once filled with industrious, scheming Greeks; thirty miles farther east, the site of Saïs, where, in the centuries before the Persian and Greek conquests, the native civilization of Egypt had its last revival; and then, a hundred and twenty-nine miles southeast of Alexandria, is Cairo. A beautiful city, but not Egyptian; the conquering Moslems

---

* Plural form of the Arabic *fellah*, peasant; from *felaha*, to plough.

founded it in A.D. 968; then the bright spirit of France overcame the gloomy Arab and built here a Paris in the desert, exotic and unreal. One must pass through it by motorcar or leisurely *fiacre* to find old Egypt at the Pyramids.

How small they appear from the long road that approaches them; did we come so far to see so little? But then they grow larger, as if they were being lifted up into the air; round a turn in the road we surprise the edge of the desert; and there suddenly the Pyramids confront us, bare and solitary in the sand, gigantic and morose against an Italian sky. A motley crowd scrambles about their base—stout business men on blinking donkeys, stouter ladies secure in carts, young men prancing on horseback, young women sitting uncomfortably on camel-back, their silk knees glistening in the sun; and everywhere grasping Arabs. We stand where Cæsar and Napoleon stood, and remember that fifty centuries look down upon us; where the Father of History came four hundred years before Cæsar, and heard the tales that were to startle Pericles. A new perspective of time comes to us; two millenniums seem to fall out of the picture, and Cæsar, Herodotus and ourselves appear for a moment contemporary and modern before these tombs that were more ancient to them than the Greeks are to us.

Nearby, the Sphinx, half lion and half philosopher, grimly claws the sand, and glares unmoved at the transient visitor and the eternal plain. It is a savage monument, as if designed to frighten old lechers and make children retire early. The lion body passes into a human head with prognathous jaws and cruel eyes; the civilization that built it (ca. 2990 B.C.) had not quite forgotten barbarism. Once the sand covered it, and Herodotus, who saw so much that is not there, says not a word of it.

Nevertheless, what wealth these old Egyptians must have had, what power and skill, even in the infancy of history, to bring these vast stones six hundred miles, to raise some of them, weighing many tons, to a height of half a thousand feet, and to pay, or even to feed, the hundred thousand slaves who toiled for twenty years on these Pyramids! Herodotus has preserved for us an inscription that he found on one pyramid, recording the quantity of radishes, garlic and onions consumed by the workmen who built it; these things, too, had to have their immortality.* Despite

---

* Diodorus Siculus, who must always be read sceptically, writes: "An inscription on the larger pyramid . . . sets forth that on vegetables and purgatives for the workmen there were paid out over 1600 talents"—i.e., $16,000,000.[5]

these familiar friends we go away disappointed; there is something barbarically primitive—or barbarically modern—in this brute hunger for
size. It is the memory and imagination of the beholder that, swollen
with history, make these monuments great; in themselves they are a little
ridiculous—vainglorious tombs in which the dead sought eternal life.
Perhaps pictures have too much ennobled them: photography can catch
everything but dirt, and enhances man-made objects with noble vistas of
land and sky. The sunset at Gizeh is greater than the Pyramids.

2. *Upstream*

*Memphis—The masterpiece of Queen Hatshepsut—The "Colossi
of Memnon"—Luxor and Karnak—The grandeur of Egyptian civilization*

From Cairo a little steamer moves up the river—i.e., southward—through
six leisurely days to Karnak and Luxor. Twenty miles below Cairo it
passes Memphis, the most ancient of Egypt's capitals. Here, where the
great Third and Fourth Dynasties lived, in a city of two million souls,
nothing now greets the eye but a row of small pyramids and a grove of
palms; for the rest there is only desert, infinite, villainous sand, slipping
under the feet, stinging the eyes, filling the pores, covering everything,
stretching from Morocco across Sinai, Arabia, Turkestan, Tibet to Mongolia: along that sandy belt across two continents civilization once built
its seats and now is gone, driven away, as the ice receded, by increasing
heat and decreasing rain. By the Nile, for a dozen miles on either side,
runs a ribbon of fertile soil; from the Mediterranean to Nubia there is
only this strip redeemed from the desert. This is the thread upon which
hung the life of Egypt. And yet how brief seems the life-span of Greece, or
the millennium of Rome, beside the long record from Menes to Cleopatra!

A week later the steamer is at Luxor. On this site, now covered with
Arab hamlets or drifting sand, once stood the greatest of Egypt's capitals,
the richest city of the very ancient world, known to the Greeks as Thebes,
and to its own people as Wesi and Ne. On the eastern slope of the Nile is
the famous Winter Palace of Luxor, aflame with bougainvillea; across the
river the sun is setting over the Tombs of the Kings into a sea of sand,
and the sky is flaked with gaudy tints of purple and gold. Far in the west
the pillars of Queen Hatshepsut's noble temple gleam, looking for all the
world like some classic colonnade.

In the morning lazy sailboats ferry the seeker across a river so quiet and unpretentious that no one would suspect that it had been flowing here for uncounted centuries. Then over mile after mile of desert, through dusty mountain passes and by historic graves, until the masterpiece of the great Queen rises still and white in the trembling heat. Here the artist decided to transform nature and her hills into a beauty greater than her own: into the very face of the granite cliff he built these columns, as stately as those that Ictinus made for Pericles; it is impossible, seeing these, to doubt that Greece took her architecture, perhaps through Crete, from this initiative race. And on the walls vast bas-reliefs, alive with motion and thought, tell the story of the first great woman in history, and not the least of queens.

On the road back sit two giants in stone, representing the most luxurious of Egypt's monarchs, Amenhotep III, but mistakenly called the "Colossi of Memnon" by the Baedekers of Greece. Each is seventy feet high, weighs seven hundred tons, and is carved out of a single rock. On the base of one of them are the inscriptions left by Greek tourists who visited these ruins two thousand years ago; again the centuries fall out of reckoning, and those Greeks seem strangely contemporary with us in the presence of these ancient things. A mile to the north lie the stone remains of Rameses II, one of the most fascinating figures in history, beside whom Alexander is an immature trifle; alive for ninety-nine years, emperor for sixty-seven, father of one hundred and fifty children; here he is a statue, once fifty-six feet high, now fifty-six feet long, prostrate and ridiculous in the sand. Napoleon's savants measured him zealously; they found his ear three and a half feet long, his foot five feet wide, his weight a thousand tons; for him Bonaparte should have used his later salutation of Goethe: *"Voilà un homme!*—behold a man!"

All around now, on the west bank of the Nile, is the City of the Dead. At every turn some burrowing Egyptologist has unearthed a royal tomb. The grave of Tutenkhamon is closed, locked even in the faces of those who thought that gold would open anything; but the tomb of Seti I is open, and there in the cool earth one may gaze at decorated ceilings and passages, and marvel at the wealth and skill that could build such sarcophagi and surround them with such art. In one of these tombs the excavators saw, on the sand, the footprints of the slaves who had carried the mummy to its place three thousand years before.[6]

But the best remains adorn the eastern side of the river. Here at Luxor the lordly Amenhotep III, with the spoils of Thutmose III's victories, began to build his most pretentious edifice; death came upon him as he built; then, after the work had been neglected for a century, Rameses II finished it in regal style. At once the quality of Egyptian architecture floods the spirit: here are scope and power, not beauty merely, but a masculine sublimity. A wide court, now waste with sand, paved of old with marble; on three sides majestic colonnades matched by Karnak alone; on every hand carved stone in bas-relief, and royal statues proud even in desolation. Imagine eight long stems of the papyrus plant—nurse of letters and here the form of art; at the base of the fresh unopened flowers bind the stems with five firm bands that will give beauty strength; then picture the whole stately stalk in stone: this is the papyriform column of Luxor. Fancy a court of such columns, upholding massive entablatures and shade-giving porticoes; see the whole as the ravages of thirty centuries have left it; then estimate the men who, in what we once thought the childhood of civilization, could conceive and execute such monuments.

Through ancient ruins and modern squalor a rough footpath leads to what Egypt keeps as its final offering—the temples of Karnak. Half a hundred Pharaohs took part in building them, from the last dynasties of the Old Kingdom to the days of the Ptolemies; generation by generation the structures grew, until sixty acres were covered with the lordliest offerings that architecture ever made to the gods. An "Avenue of Sphinxes" leads to the place where Champollion, founder of Egyptology, stood in 1828 and wrote:

> I went at last to the palace, or rather to the city of monuments— to Karnak. There all the magnificence of the Pharaohs appeared to me, all that men have imagined and executed on the grandest scale. . . . No people, ancient or modern, has conceived the art of architecture on a scale so sublime, so great, so grandiose, as the ancient Egyptians. They conceived like men a hundred feet high.[7]

To understand it would require maps and plans, and all an architect's learning. A spacious enclosure of many courts one-third of a mile on each side; a population of once 86,000 statues;[8] a main group of buildings, constituting the Temple of Amon, one thousand by three hundred feet; great pylons or gates between one court and the next; the perfect "Heraldic

Pillars" of Thutmose III, broken off rudely at the top, but still of astonishingly delicate carving and design; the Festival Hall of the same formidable
monarch, its fluted shafts here and there anticipating all the power of the
Doric column in Greece; the little Temple of Ptah, with graceful pillars
rivaling the living palms beside them; the Promenade, again the work of
Thutmose's builders, with bare and massive colonnades, symbol of Egypt's
Napoleon; above all, the Hypostyle Hall,* a very forest of one hundred
and forty gigantic columns, crowded close to keep out the exhausting
sun, flowering out at their tops into spreading palms of stone, and holding
up, with impressive strength, a roof of mammoth slabs stretched in solid
granite from capital to capital. Nearby two slender obelisks, monoliths
complete in symmetry and grace, rise like pillars of light amid the ruins
of statues and temples, and announce in their inscriptions the proud
message of Queen Hatshepsut to the world. These obelisks, the carving says,

> are of hard granite from the quarries of the South; their tops are
> of fine gold chosen from the best in all foreign lands. They can be
> seen from afar on the river; the splendor of their radiance fills the
> Two Lands, and when the solar disc appears between them it is
> truly as if he rose up into the horizon of the sky. . . . You who after
> long years shall see these monuments, who shall speak of what I
> have done, you will say, "We do not know, we do not know how
> they can have made a whole mountain of gold." . . . To guild them
> I have given gold measured by the bushel, as though it were sacks
> of grain, . . . for I knew that Karnak is the celestial horizon of the
> earth.⁹

What a queen, and what kings! Perhaps this first great civilization was
the finest of all, and we have but begun to uncover its glory? Near the
Sacred Lake at Karnak men are digging, carrying away the soil patiently
in little paired baskets slung over the shoulder on a pole; an Egyptologist
is bending absorbed over hieroglyphics on two stones just rescued from
the earth; he is one of a thousand such men, Carters and Breasteds and
Masperos, Petries and Caparts and Weigalls, living simply here in the heat
and dust, trying to read for us the riddle of the Sphinx, to snatch from the
secretive soil the art and literature, the history and wisdom of Egypt.

* A model of this can be seen at the Metropolitan Museum of Art, New York.

Every day the earth and the elements fight against them; superstition curses and hampers them; moisture and corrosion attack the very monuments they have exhumed; and the same Nile that gives food to Egypt creeps in its overflow into the ruins of Karnak, loosens the pillars, tumbles them down,* and leaves upon them, when it subsides, a deposit of saltpetre that eats like a leprosy into the stone.

Let us contemplate the glory of Egypt once more, in her history and her civilization, before her last monuments crumble into the sand.

II. THE MASTER BUILDERS

1. The Discovery of Egypt

Champollion and the Rosetta Stone

The recovery of Egypt is one of the most brilliant chapters in archeology. The Middle Ages knew of Egypt as a Roman colony and a Christian settlement; the Renaissance presumed that civilization had begun with Greece; even the Enlightenment, though it concerned itself intelligently with China and India, knew nothing of Egypt beyond the Pyramids. Egyptology was a by-product of Napoleonic imperialism. When the great Corsican led a French expedition to Egypt in 1798 he took with him a number of draughtsmen and engineers to explore and map the terrain, and made place also for certain scholars absurdly interested in Egypt for the sake of a better understanding of history. It was this corps of men who first revealed the temples of Luxor and Karnak to the modern world; and the elaborate *Description de L'Égypte* (1809-13) which they prepared for the French Academy was the first milestone in the scientific study of this forgotten civilization.[10]

For many years, however, they were unable to read the inscriptions surviving on the monuments. Typical of the scientific temperament was the patient devotion with which Champollion, one of these *savants*, applied himself to the decipherment of the hieroglyphics. He found at last an obelisk covered with such "sacred carvings" in Egyptian, but bearing at the base a Greek inscription which indicated that the writing concerned Ptolemy and Cleopatra. Guessing that two hieroglyphics often repeated, with a royal cartouche attached, were the names of these rulers, he made out tentatively (1822) eleven Egyptian letters; this was the first proof that Egypt had had

---

* On October 3, 1899, eleven columns at Karnak, loosened by the water, fell to the ground.

an alphabet. Then he applied this alphabet to a great black stone slab that Napoleon's troops had stumbled upon near the Rosetta mouth of the Nile. This "Rosetta Stone"* contained an inscription in three languages: first in hieroglyphics, second in "demotic"—the popular script of the Egyptians—and third in Greek. With his knowledge of Greek, and the eleven letters made out from the obelisk, Champollion, after more than twenty years of labor, deciphered the whole inscription, discovered the entire Egyptian alphabet, and opened the way to the recovery of a lost world. It was one of the peaks in the history of history.†[11]

2. Prehistoric Egypt

Paleolithic—Neolithic—The Badarians—Predynastic—Race

Since the radicals of one age are the reactionaries of the next, it was not to be expected that the men who created Egyptology should be the first to accept as authentic the remains of Egypt's Old Stone Age; after forty *les savants ne sont pas curieux*. When the first flints were unearthed in the valley of the Nile, Sir Flinders Petrie, not usually hesitant with figures, classed them as the work of post-dynastic generations; and Maspero, whose lordly erudition did no hurt to his urbane and polished style, ascribed neolithic Egyptian pottery to the Middle Kingdom. Nevertheless, in 1895 De Morgan revealed an almost continuous gradation of paleolithic cultures—corresponding substantially with their succession in Europe—in the flint hand-axes, harpoons, arrow-heads and hammers exhumed all along the Nile.[13] Imperceptibly the paleolithic remains graduate into neolithic at depths indicating an age 10,000-4000 B.C.[14] The stone tools become more refined, and reach indeed a level of sharpness, finish and precision unequaled by any other neolithic culture known.[15] Towards the end of the period metal work enters in the form of vases, chisels and pins of copper, and ornaments of silver and gold.[16]

Finally, as a transition to history, agriculture appears. In the year 1901, near the little town of Badari (half way between Cairo and Karnak), bodies were excavated amid implements indicating a date approximating to forty centuries before Christ. In the intestines of these bodies, preserved through six millenniums by the dry heat of the sand, were husks of unconsumed barley.[17] Since barley does not grow wild in Egypt, it is presumed that the Badarians had learned to cultivate cereals. From that early age the in-

---

* Now in the British Museum.

† The Swedish diplomat Akerblad in 1802, and the versatile English physicist Thomas Young in 1814, had helped by partly deciphering the Rosetta Stone.[12]

habitants of the Nile valley began the work of irrigation, cleared the jungles and the swamps, won the river from the crocodile and the hippopotamus, and slowly laid the groundwork of civilization.

These and other remains give us some inkling of Egyptian life before the first of the historic dynasties. It was a culture midway between hunting and agriculture, and just beginning to replace stone with metal tools. The people made boats, ground corn, wove linen and carpets, had jewels and perfumes, barbers and domesticated animals, and delighted to draw pictures, chiefly of the prey they pursued.[18] They painted upon their simple pottery figures of mourning women, representations of animals and men, and geometrical designs; and they carved such excellent products as the Gebel-el-Arak knife. They had pictographic writing, and Sumerian-like cylinder seals.[19]

No one knows whence these early Egyptians came. Learned guesses incline to the view that they were a cross between Nubian, Ethiopian and Libyan natives on one side and Semitic or Armenoid immigrants on the other;[20] even at that date there were no pure races on the earth. Probably the invaders or immigrants from Western Asia brought a higher culture with them,[21] and their intermarriage with the vigorous native stocks provided that ethnic blend which is often the prelude to a new civilization. Slowly, from 4000 to 3000 B.C., these mingling groups became a people, and created the Egypt of history.

3. The Old Kingdom

The "nomes"—The first historic individual—"Cheops"—"Chephren"—The purpose of the Pyramids—Art of the tombs—Mummification

Already, by 4000 B.C., these peoples of the Nile had forged a form of government. The population along the river was divided into "nomes,"* in each of which the inhabitants were essentially of one stock, acknowledged the same totem, obeyed the same chief, and worshiped the same gods by the same rites. Throughout the history of ancient Egypt these nomes persisted, their "nomarchs" or rulers having more or less power and autonomy according to the weakness or strength of the reigning Pharaoh. As all developing structures tend toward an increasing interdependence of the parts, so in this case the growth of trade and the rising

---

* So called by the Greeks from their word for law (*nomos*).

costliness of war forced the nomes to organize themselves into two king-doms—one in the south, one in the north; a division probably reflecting the conflict between African natives and Asiatic immigrants. This danger-ous accentuation of geographic and ethnic differences was resolved for a time when Menes, a half-legendary figure, brought the "Two Lands" under his united power, promulgated a body of laws given him by the god Thoth,[22] established the first historic dynasty, built a new capital at Memphis, "taught the people" (in the words of an ancient Greek historian) "to use tables and couches, and . . . introduced luxury and an extravagant manner of life."[23]

The first real person in known history is not a conqueror or a king but an artist and a scientist—Imhotep, physician, architect and chief adviser of King Zoser (ca. 3150 B.C.). He did so much for Egyptian medicine that later generations worshiped him as a god of knowledge, author of their sciences and their arts; and at the same time he appears to have founded the school of architecture which provided the next dynasty with the first great builders in history. It was under his administration, accord-ing to Egyptian tradition, that the first stone house was built; it was he who planned the oldest Egyptian structure extant—the Step-Pyramid of Sakkara, a terraced structure of stone which for centuries set the style in tombs; and apparently it was he who designed the funerary temple of Zoser, with its lovely lotus columns and its limestone paneled walls.[24] In these old remains at Sakkarah, at what is almost the beginning of historic Egyptian art, we find fluted shafts as fair as any that Greece would build,[25] reliefs full of realism and vitality,[26] green *faïence*—richly colored glazed earthenware—rivaling the products of medieval Italy,[27] and a power-ful stone figure of King Zoser himself, obscured in its details by the blows of time, but still revealing an astonishingly subtle and sophisticated face.[28]

We do not know what concourse of circumstance made the Fourth Dynasty the most important in Egyptian history before the Eighteenth. Perhaps it was the lucrative mining operations in the last reign of the Third, perhaps the ascendancy of Egyptian merchants in Mediterranean trade, perhaps the brutal energy of Khufu,* first Pharaoh of the new house. Herodotus has passed on to us the traditions of the Egyptian priests concerning this builder of the first of Gizeh's pyramids:

---

* The "Cheops" of Herodotus, r. 3098-75 B.C.

Now they tell me that to the reign of Rhampsinitus there was a perfect distribution of justice and that all Egypt was in a high state of prosperity; but that after him Cheops, coming to reign over them, plunged into every kind of wickedness, for that, having shut up all the temples, . . . he ordered all the Egyptians to work for himself. Some, accordingly, were appointed to draw stones from the quarries in the Arabian mountains down to the Nile, others he ordered to receive the stones when transported in vessels across the river. . . . And they worked to the number of a hundred thousand men at a time, each party during three months. The time during which the people were thus harassed by toil lasted ten years on the road which they constructed, and along which they drew the stones; a work, in my opinion, not much less than the Pyramid.[29]

Of his successor and rival builder, Khafre,* we know something almost at first hand; for the diorite portrait which is among the treasures of the Cairo Museum pictures him, if not as he looked, certainly as we might conceive this Pharaoh of the second pyramid, who ruled Egypt for fifty-six years. On his head is the falcon, symbol of the royal power; but even without that sign we should know that he was every inch a king. Proud, direct, fearless, piercing eyes; a powerful nose and a frame of reserved and quiet strength; it is evident that nature had long since learned how to make men, and art had long since learned how to represent them.

Why did these men build pyramids? Their purpose was not architectural but religious; the pyramids were tombs, lineally descended from the most primitive of burial mounds. Apparently the Pharaoh believed, like any commoner among his people, that every living body was inhabited by a double, or *ka,* which need not die with the breath; and that the *ka* would survive all the more completely if the flesh were preserved against hunger, violence and decay. The pyramid, by its height,† its form and its position, sought stability as a means to deathlessness; and except for its square corners it took the natural form that any homogeneous group of solids would take if allowed to fall unimpeded to the earth. Again, it was to have permanence and strength; therefore stones were piled up here with mad patience as if they had grown by the wayside and had not been carried from quarries hundreds of miles away. In Khufu's pyramid there

---

* The "Chephren" of Herodotus, r. 3067-11 B.C.

† The word *pyramid* is apparently derived from the Egyptian word *pi-re-mus,* altitude, rather than from the Greek *pyr,* fire.

are two and a half million blocks, some of them weighing one hundred and fifty tons,[30] all of them averaging two and a half tons; they cover half a million square feet, and rise 481 feet into the air. And the mass is solid; only a few blocks were omitted, to leave a secret passage way for the carcass of the King. A guide leads the trembling visitor on all fours into the cavernous mausoleum, up a hundred crouching steps to the very heart of the pyramid; there in the damp, still center, buried in darkness and secrecy, once rested the bones of Khufu and his queen. The marble sarcophagus of the Pharaoh is still in place, but broken and empty. Even these stones could not deter human thievery, nor all the curses of the gods.

Since the *ka* was conceived as the minute image of the body, it had to be fed, clothed and served after the death of the frame. Lavatories were provided in some royal tombs for the convenience of the departed soul; and a funerary text expresses some anxiety lest the *ka*, for want of food, should feed upon its own *excreta*.[31] One suspects that Egyptian burial customs, if traced to their source, would lead to the primitive interment of a warrior's weapons with his corpse, or to some institution like the Hindu *suttee*—the burial of a man's wives and slaves with him that they may attend to his needs. This having proved irksome to the wives and slaves, painters and sculptors were engaged to draw pictures, carve bas-reliefs, and make statuettes resembling these aides; by a magic formula, usually inscribed upon them, the carved or painted objects would be quite as effective as the real ones. A man's descendants were inclined to be lazy and economical, and even if he had left an endowment to cover the costs they were apt to neglect the rule that religion originally put upon them of supplying the dead with provender. Hence pictorial substitutes were in any case a wise precaution: they could provide the *ka* of the deceased with fertile fields, plump oxen, innumerable servants and busy artisans, at an attractively reduced rate. Having discovered this principle, the artist accomplished marvels with it. One tomb picture shows a field being ploughed, the next shows the grain being reaped or threshed, another the bread being baked; one shows the bull copulating with the cow, another the calf being born, another the grown cattle being slaughtered, another the meat served hot on the dish.[32] A fine limestone bas-relief in the tomb of Prince Rahotep portrays the dead man enjoying the varied victuals on the table before him.[33] Never since has art done so much for men

Finally the *ka* was assured long life not only by burying the cadaver in a sarcophagus of the hardest stone, but by treating it to the most painstaking mummification. So well was this done that to this day bits of hair and flesh cling to the royal skeletons. Herodotus vividly describes the Egyptian embalmer's art:

> First they draw out the brains through the nostrils with an iron hook, raking part of it out in this manner, the rest by the infusion of drugs. Then with a sharp stone they make an incision in the side, and take out all the bowels; and having cleansed the abdomen and rinsed it with palm wine, they next sprinkle it with pounded perfume. Then, having filled the belly with pure myrrh, cassia and other perfumes, they sew it up again; and when they have done this they steep it in natron,* leaving it under for seventy days; for a longer time than this it is not lawful to steep it. At the expiration of seventy days they wash the corpse, and wrap the whole body in bandages of waxen cloth, smearing it with gum, which the Egyptians commonly use instead of glue. After this the relations, having taken the body back again, make a wooden case in the shape of a man, and having made it they enclose the body; and then, having fastened it up, they store it in a sepulchral chamber, setting it upright against the wall. In this manner they prepare the bodies that are embalmed in the most expensive way.[34]

"All the world fears Time," says an Arab proverb, "but Time fears the Pyramids."[35] However, the pyramid of Khufu has lost twenty feet of its height, and all its ancient marble casing is gone; perhaps Time is only leisurely with it. Beside it stands Khafre's pyramid, a trifle smaller, but still capped with the granite casing that once covered it all. Humbly beyond this squats the pyramid of Khafre's successor Menkaure,† covered not with granite but with shamefaced brick, as if to announce that when men raised it the zenith of the Old Kingdom had passed. The statues of Menkaure that have come down to us show him as a man more refined and less forceful than Khafre.‡ Civilization, like life, destroys what it has perfected. Already, it may be, the growth of comforts and luxuries, the

---

* A silicate of sodium and aluminum: $Na_2Al_2Si_3O_{10}2H_2O$.

† The "Mycerinus" of Herodotus, r. 3011-2988 B.C.

‡ Cf. the statues of Menkaure and his consort in the Metropolitan Museum of Art, New York.

progress of manners and morals, had made men lovers of peace and haters of war. Suddenly a new figure appeared, usurped Menkaure's throne, and put an end to the pyramid-builders' dynasty.

4. The Middle Kingdom

The Feudal Age—The Twelfth Dynasty—The Hyksos Domination

Kings were never so plentiful as in Egypt. History lumps them into dynasties—monarchs of one line or family; but even then they burden the memory intolerably.* One of these early Pharaohs, Pepi II, ruled Egypt for ninety-four years (2738-2644 B.C.)—the longest reign in history. When he died anarchy and dissolution ensued, the Pharaohs lost control, and feudal barons ruled the nomes independently: this alternation between centralized and decentralized power is one of the cyclical rhythms of history, as if men tired alternately of immoderate liberty and excessive order. After a Dark Age of four chaotic centuries a strong-willed Charlemagne arose, set things severely in order, changed the capital from Memphis to Thebes, and under the title of Amenemhet I inaugurated that Twelfth Dynasty during which all the arts, excepting perhaps architecture, reached a height of excellence never equaled in known Egypt before or again. Through an old inscription Amenemhet speaks to us:

> I was one who cultivated grain and loved the harvest god;
> The Nile greeted me and every valley;
> None was hungry in my years, none thirsted then;
> Men dwelt in peace through that which I wrought, and conversed
> 　　of me.

His reward was a conspiracy among the Talleyrands and Fouchés whom he had raised to high office. He put it down with a mighty hand, but left for his son, Polonius-like, a scroll of bitter counsel—an admirable formula for despotism, but a heavy price to pay for royalty:

---

* Historians have helped themselves by further grouping the dynasties into periods: (1) The *Old Kingdom*, Dynasties I-VI (3500-2631 B.C.), followed by an interlude of chaos; (2) The *Middle Kingdom*, Dynasties XI-XIV (2375-1800 B.C.), followed by another chaotic interlude; (3) The *Empire*, Dynasties XVIII-XX (1580-1100 B.C.), followed by a period of divided rule from rival capitals; and (4) The *Saïte Age*, Dynasty XXVI, 663-525. All these dates except the last are approximate, and Egyptologists amuse themselves by moving the earlier ones up and down by centuries.

Hearken to that which I say to thee,
That thou mayest be king of the earth, . . .
That thou mayest increase good:
Harden thyself against all subordinates—
The people give heed to him who terrorizes them;
Approach them not alone.
Fill not thy heart with a brother,
Know not a friend; . . .
When thou sleepest, guard for thyself thine own heart;
For a man hath no friend in the day of evil.[36]

This stern ruler, who seems to us so human across four thousand years, established a system of administration that held for half a millennium. Wealth grew again, and then art; Senusret I built a great canal from the Nile to the Red Sea, repelled Nubian invaders, and erected great temples at Heliopolis, Abydos, and Karnak; ten colossal seated figures of him have cheated time, and litter the Cairo Museum. Another Senusret—the Third—began the subjugation of Palestine, drove back the recurrent Nubians, and raised a stele or slab at the southern frontier, "not from any desire that ye should worship it, but that ye should fight for it."[37] Amenemhet III, a great administrator, builder of canals and irrigation, put an end (perhaps too effectively) to the power of the barons, and replaced them with appointees of the king. Thirteen years after his death Egypt was plunged into disorder by a dispute among rival claimants to the throne, and the Middle Kingdom ended in two centuries of turmoil and disruption. Then the Hyksos, nomads from Asia, invaded disunited Egypt, set fire to the cities, razed the temples, squandered the accumulated wealth, destroyed much of the accumulated art, and for two hundred years subjected the Nile valley to the rule of the "Shepherd Kings." Ancient civilizations were little isles in a sea of barbarism, prosperous settlements surrounded by hungry, envious and warlike hunters and herders; at any moment the wall of defense might be broken down. So the Kassites raided Babylonia, the Gauls attacked Greece and Rome, the Huns overran Italy, the Mongols came down upon Peking.

Soon, however, the conquerors in their turn grew fat and prosperous, and lost control; the Egyptians rose in a war of liberation, expelled the Hyksos, and established that Eighteenth Dynasty which was to lift Egypt to greater wealth, power and glory than ever before.

5. The Empire

The great queen—Thutmose III—The zenith of Egypt

Perhaps the invasion had brought another rejuvenation by the infusion of fresh blood; but at the same time the new age marked the beginning of a thousand-year struggle betwen Egypt and Western Asia. Thutmose I not only consolidated the power of the new empire, but—on the ground that western Asia must be controlled to prevent further interruptions—invaded Syria, subjugated it from the coast to Carchemish, put it under guard and tribute, and returned to Thebes laden with spoils and the glory that always comes from the killing of men. At the end of his thirty-year reign he raised his daughter Hatshepsut to partnership with him on the throne. For a time her husband and step-brother ruled as Thutmose II, and dying, named as his successor Thutmose III, son of Thutmose I by a concubine.[38] But Hatshepsut set this high-destined youngster aside, assumed full royal powers, and proved herself a king in everything but gender.

Even this exception was not conceded by her. Since sacred tradition required that every Egyptian ruler should be a son of the great god Amon, Hatshepsut arranged to be made at once male and divine. A biography was invented for her by which Amon had descended upon Hatshepsut's mother Ahmasi in a flood of perfume and light; his attentions had been gratefully received; and on his departure he had announced that Ahmasi would give birth to a daughter in whom all the valor and strength of the god would be made manifest on earth.[39] To satisfy the prejudices of her people, and perhaps the secret desire of her heart, the great Queen had herself represented on the monuments as a bearded and breastless warrior; and though the inscriptions referred to her with the feminine pronoun, they did not hesitate to speak of her as "Son of the Sun" and "Lord of the Two Lands." When she appeared in public she dressed in male garb, and wore a beard.[40]

She had a right to determine her own sex, for she became one of the most successful and beneficent of Egypt's many rulers. She maintained internal order without undue tyranny, and external peace without loss. She organized a great expedition to Punt (presumably the eastern coast of Africa), giving new markets to her merchants and new delicacies to her people. She helped to beautify Karnak. raised there two majestic obelisks, built at Der-el-Bahri the stately temple which her father had designed, and repaired some of the damage that had been done to older temples by the Hyksos kings. "I have restored that which was in ruins," one of her proud inscriptions tells us; "I have raised up that which was unfinished since the Asiatics were in the midst of the Northland, overthrowing that which had been made."[41] Finally she built for herself a secret and ornate tomb among the sand-swept mountains on the western side of the Nile, in what came to be called "The Valley of the Kings' Tombs"; her successors followed her example, until some sixty royal sepulchres had been cut into the hills, and the city of the dead began to rival living Thebes in population. The "West End" in Egyptian cities was the abode of dead aristocrats; to "go west" meant to die.

For twenty-two years the Queen ruled in wisdom and peace; Thutmose III followed with a reign of many wars. Syria took advantage of Hatshepsut's death to revolt; it did not seem likely to the Syrians that Thutmose, a lad of twenty-two, would be able to maintain the empire created by his father. But Thutmose set off in the very year of his accession, marched his army through Kantara and Gaza at twenty miles a day, and confronted the rebel forces at Har-Megiddo (i.e., Mt. Megiddo), a little town so strategically placed between the rival Lebanon ranges on the road from Egypt to the Euphrates that it has been the Ar-mageddon of countless wars from that day to General Allenby's. In the same pass where in 1918 the British defeated the Turks, Thutmose III, 3397 years before, defeated the Syrians and their allies. Then Thutmose marched victorious through western Asia, subduing, taxing and levying tribute, and returned to Thebes in triumph six months after his departure.*[42]

This was the first of fifteen campaigns in which the irresistible Thutmose made Egypt master of the Mediterranean world. Not only did he conquer, but he organized; everywhere he left doughty garrisons and capable governors. The first man in known history to recognize the importance of sea power, he built a fleet that kept the Near East effectively in leash. The spoils that he seized became the foundation of Egyptian art in the period of the Empire; the tribute that he drained from Syria gave his people an epicurean ease, and created a new class of artists who filled all Egypt with

---

* Allenby took twice as long to accomplish a similar result; Napoleon, attempting it at Acre, failed.

precious things. We may vaguely estimate the wealth of the new imperial government when we learn that on one occasion the treasury was able to measure out nine thousand pounds of gold and silver alloy.[43] Trade flourished in Thebes as never before; the temples groaned with offerings; and at Karnak the lordly Promenade and Festival Hall rose to the greater glory of god and king. Then the King retired from the battlefield, designed exquisite vases, and gave himself to internal administration. His vizier or prime minister said of him, as tired secretaries were to say of Napoleon: "Lo, His Majesty was one who knew what happened; there was nothing of which he was ignorant; he was the god of knowledge in everything; there was no matter that he did not carry out."[43a] He passed away after a rule of thirty-two (some say fifty-four) years, having made Egyptian leadership in the Mediterranean world complete.

After him another conqueror, Amenhotep II, subdued again certain idolators of liberty in Syria, and returned to Thebes with seven captive kings, still alive, hanging head downward from the prow of the imperial galley; six of them he sacrificed to Amon with his own hand.[44] Then another Thutmose, who does not count; and in 1412 Amenhotep III began a long reign in which the accumulated wealth of a century of mastery brought Egypt to the acme of her splendor. A fine bust in the British Museum shows him as a man at once of refinement and of strength, able to hold firmly together the empire bequeathed to him, and yet living in an atmosphere of comfort and elegance that might have been envied by Petronius or the Medici. Only the exhuming of Tutenkhamon's relics could make us credit the traditions and records of Amenhotep's riches and luxury. In his reign Thebes was as majestic as any city in history. Her streets crowded with merchants, her markets filled with the goods of the world, her buildings "surpassing in magnificence all those of ancient or modern capitals,"[45] her imposing palaces receiving tribute from an endless chain of vassal states, her massive temples "enriched all over with gold"[46] and adorned with every art, her spacious villas and costly chateaux, her shaded promenades and artificial lakes providing the scene for sumptuous displays of fashion that anticipated Imperial Rome[47]—such was Egypt's capital in the days of her glory, in the reign before her fall.

III. THE CIVILIZATION OF EGYPT

1. Agriculture

Behind these kings and queens were pawns; behind these temples, palaces and pyramids were the workers of the cities and the peasants of the fields.* Herodotus describes them optimistically as he found them about 450 B.C.

> They gather in the fruits of the earth with less labor than any
> other people, . . . for they have not the toil of breaking up the
> furrow with the plough, nor of hoeing, nor of any other work
> which all other men must labor at to obtain a crop of corn; but
> when the river has come of its own accord and irrigated their fields,
> and having irrigated them has subsided, then each man sows his own
> land and turns his swine into it; and when the seed has been trod-
> den into it by the swine he waits for harvest time; then . . . he
> gathers it in.[49]

As the swine trod in the seed, so apes were tamed and taught to pluck fruit from the trees.[50] And the same Nile that irrigated the fields deposited upon them, in its inundation, thousands of fish in shallow pools; even the same net with which the peasant fished during the day was used around his head at night as a double protection against mosquitoes.[51] Nevertheless it was not he who profited by the bounty of the river. Every acre of the soil belonged to the Pharaoh, and other men could use it only by his kind indulgence; every tiller of the earth had to pay him an annual tax of ten[52] or twenty[53] per cent in kind. Large tracts were owned by the feudal barons or other wealthy men; the size of some of these estates may be judged from the circumstance that one of them had fifteen hundred cows.[54] Cereals, fish and meat were the chief items of diet. One fragment tells the school-boy what he is permitted to eat; it includes thirty-three forms of flesh, forty-eight baked meats, and twenty-four varieties of drink.[55] The rich washed down their meals with wine, the poor with barley beer.[56]

The lot of the peasant was hard. The "free" farmer was subject only to the middleman and the tax-collector, who dealt with him on the most time-honored of economic principles, taking "all that the traffic would

---

* The population of Egypt in the fourth century before Christ is estimated at some 7,000,000 souls.[48]

bear" out of the produce of the land. Here is how a complacent contemporary scribe conceived the life of the men who fed ancient Egypt:

> Dost thou not recall the picture of the farmer when the tenth
> of his grain is levied? Worms have destroyed half the wheat, and
> the hippopotami have eaten the rest; there are swarms of rats in the
> fields, the grasshoppers alight there, the cattle devour, the little birds
> pilfer; and if the farmer loses sight for an instant of what remains
> on the ground, it is carried off by robbers; moreover, the thongs
> which bind the iron and the hoe are worn out, and the team has died
> at the plough. It is then that the scribe steps out of the boat at the
> landing-place to levy the tithe, and there come the Keepers of the
> Doors of the (King's) Granary with cudgels, and Negroes with
> ribs of palm-leaves, crying, "Come now, come!" There is none, and
> they throw the cultivator full length upon the ground, bind him,
> drag him to the canal, and fling him in head first; his wife is bound
> with him, his children are put into chains. The neighbors in the
> meantime leave him and fly to save their grain.[57]

It is a characteristic bit of literary exaggeration; but the author might
have added that the peasant was subject at any time to the *corvée*, doing
forced labor for the King, dredging the canals, building roads, tilling the
royal lands, or dragging great stones and obelisks for pyramids, temples
and palaces. Probably a majority of the laborers in the field were moderately content, accepting their poverty patiently. Many of them were
slaves, captured in the wars or bonded for debt; sometimes slave-raids were
organized, and women and children from abroad were sold to the highest
bidder at home. An old relief in the Leyden Museum pictures a long
procession of Asiatic captives passing gloomily into the land of bondage:
one sees them still alive on that vivid stone, their hands tied behind their
backs or their heads, or thrust through rude handcuffs of wood; their
faces empty with the apathy that has known the last despair.

2. Industry

Miners — Manufactures — Workers — Engineers — Transport—
Postal service—Commerce and finance—Scribes

Slowly, as the peasants toiled, an economic surplus grew, and food was
laid aside for workers in industry and trade. Having no minerals, Egypt

sought them in Arabia and Nubia. The great distances offered no temptation to private initiative, and for many centuries mining was a government monopoly.[58] Copper was mined in small quantities,[59] iron was imported from the Hittites, gold mines were found along the eastern coast, in Nubia, and in every vassal treasury. Diodorus Siculus (56 B.C.) describes Egyptian miners following with lamp and pick the veins of gold in the earth, children carrying up the heavy ore, stone mortars pounding it to bits, old men and women washing the dirt away. We cannot tell to what extent nationalistic exaggeration distorts the famous passage:

> The kings of Egypt collect condemned prisoners, prisoners of war and others who, beset by false accusations, have been in a fit of anger thrown into prison. These—sometimes alone, sometimes with their entire family—they send to the gold mines, partly to exact a just vengeance for crimes committed by the condemned, partly to secure for themselves a big revenue through their toil. . . . As these workers can take no care of their bodies, and have not even a garment to hide their nakedness, there is no one who, seeing these luckless people, would not pity them because of the excess of their misery, for there is no forgiveness or relaxation at all for the sick, or the maimed, or the old, or for woman's weakness; but all with blows are compelled to stick to their labor until, worn out, they die in their servitude. Thus the poor wretches even account the future more dreadful than the present because of the excess of their punishment, and look to death as more desirable than life.[60]

In its earliest dynasties Egypt learned the art of fusing copper with tin to make bronze: first, bronze weapons—swords, helmets and shields; then bronze tools—wheels, rollers, levers, pulleys, windlasses, wedges, lathes, screws, drills that bored the toughest diorite stone, saws that cut the massive slabs of the sarcophagi. Egyptian workers made brick, cement and plaster of Paris; they glazed pottery, blew glass, and glorified both with color. They were masters in the carving of wood; they made everything from boats and carriages, chairs and beds, to handsome coffins that almost invited men to die. Out of animal skins they made clothing, quivers, shields and seats; all the arts of the tanner are pictured on the walls of the tombs; and the curved knives represented there in the tanner's hand are used by cobblers to this day.[61] From the papyrus plant Egyptian artisans made ropes, mats, sandals and paper. Other workmen developed the arts of enameling and varnishing, and applied chemistry to industry. Still others wove tissues of the subtlest weave in the history of the textile art; specimens of linen woven four thousand years ago show today, despite time's corrosion, "a weave so fine that it requires a magnifying glass to distinguish it from silk; the best work of the modern machine-loom is coarse in comparison with this fabric of the ancient Egyptian hand-loom."[62] "If," says Peschel, "we compare the technical inventory of the Egyptians with our own, it is evident that before the invention of the steam-engine we scarcely excelled them in anything."[63]

The workers were mostly freemen, partly slaves. In general every trade was a caste, as in modern India, and sons were expected to follow and take over the occupations of their fathers.[64]* The great wars brought in thousands of captives, making possible the large estates and the triumphs of engineering. Rameses III presented 113,000 slaves to the temples during the course of his reign.[66] The free artisans were usually organized for the specific undertaking by a "chief workman" or overseer, who sold their labor as a group and paid them individually. A chalk tablet in the British Museum contains a chief workman's record of forty-three workers, listing their absences and their causes—"ill," or "sacrificing to the god," or just plain "lazy." Strikes were frequent. Once, their pay being long overdue, the workmen besieged the overseer and threatened him. "We have been driven here by hunger and thirst," they told him; "we have no clothes, we have no oil, we have no food. Write to our lord the Pharaoh on the subject, and write to the governor" (of the nome) "who is over us, that they may give us something for our sustenance."[67] A Greek tradition reports a great revolt in Egypt, in which the slaves captured a province, and held it so long that time, which sanctions everything, gave them legal ownership of it; but of this revolt there is no record in Egyptian inscriptions.[68] It is surprising that a civilization so ruthless in its exploitation of labor should have known—or recorded—so few revolutions.

Egyptian engineering was superior to anything known to the Greeks or Romans, or to Europe before the Industrial Revolution; only our time has excelled it, and we may be mistaken. Senusret III, for example, built† a wall twenty-seven miles long to gather into Lake Moeris the waters of

---

* "If any artisan," adds Diodorus, "takes part in public affairs he is severely beaten."[65]
† This word, when used in reference to rulers, must always be understood as a euphemism.

the Fayum basin, thereby reclaiming 25,000 acres of marsh land for cultivation, and providing a vast reservoir for irrigation.[69] Great canals were constructed, some from the Nile to the Red Sea; the caisson was used for digging,[70] and obelisks weighing a thousand tons were transported over great distances. If we may credit Herodotus, or judge from later undertakings of the same kind represented in the reliefs of the Eighteenth Dynasty, these immense stones were drawn on greased beams by thousands of slaves, and raised to the desired level on inclined approaches beginning far away.[71] Machinery was rare because muscle was cheap. See, in one relief, eight hundred rowers in twenty-seven boats drawing a barge laden with two obelisks;[72] this is the Eden to which our romantic machine-wreckers would return. Ships a hundred feet long by half a hundred feet wide plied the Nile and the Red Sea, and finally sailed the Mediterranean. On land goods were transported by human muscle, later by donkeys, later by the horse, which probably the Hyksos brought to Egypt; the camel did not appear till Ptolemaic days.[73] The poor man walked, or paddled his simple boat; the rich man rode in sedan-chairs carried by slaves, or later in chariots clumsily made with the weight placed entirely in front of the axle.[74]

There was a regular postal service; an ancient papyrus says, "Write to me by the letter-carrier."[75] Communication, however, was difficult; roads were few and bad, except for the military highway through Gaza to the Euphrates;[76] and the serpentine form of the Nile, which was the main highroad of Egypt, doubled the distance from town to town. Trade was comparatively primitive; most of it was by barter in village bazaars. Foreign commerce grew slowly, restricted severely by the most up-to-date tariff walls; the various kingdoms of the Near East believed strongly in the "protective principle," for customs dues were a mainstay of their royal treasuries. Nevertheless Egypt grew rich by importing raw materials and exporting finished products; Syrian, Cretan and Cypriote merchants crowded the markets of Egypt, and Phœnician galleys sailed up the Nile to the busy wharves of Thebes.[77]

Coinage had not yet developed; payments, even of the highest salaries, were made in goods—corn, bread, yeast, beer, etc. Taxes were collected in kind, and the Pharaoh's treasuries were not a mint of money, but storehouses of a thousand products from the fields and shops. After the influx of precious metals that followed the conquests of Thutmose III, merchants began to pay for goods with rings or ingots of gold, measured by weight at every transaction; but no coins of definite value guaranteed by the state arose to facilitate exchange. Credit, however, was highly developed; written transfers frequently took the place of barter or payment; scribes were busy everywhere accelerating business with legal documents of exchange, accounting and finance.

Every visitor to the Louvre has seen the statue of the Egyptian scribe, squatting on his haunches, almost completely nude, dressed with a pen behind the ear as reserve for the one he holds in his hand. He keeps record of work done and goods paid, of prices and costs, of profits and loss; he counts the cattle as they move to the slaughter, or corn as it is measured out in sale; he draws up contracts and wills, and makes out his master's income-tax; verily there is nothing new under the sun. He is sedulously attentive and mechanically industrious; he has just enough intelligence not to be dangerous. His life is monotonous, but he consoles himself by writing essays on the hardships of the manual worker's existence, and the princely dignity of those whose food is paper and whose blood is ink.

3. Government

The bureaucrats—Law—The vizier—The pharaoh

With these scribes as a clerical bureaucracy the Pharaoh and the provincial nobles maintained law and order in the state. Ancient slabs show such clerks taking the census, and examining income-tax returns. Through Nilometers that measured the rise of the river, the scribe-officials forecast the size of the harvest, and estimated the government's future revenue; they allotted appropriations in advance to governmental departments, supervised industry and trade, and in some measure achieved, almost at the outset of history, a planned economy regulated by the state.[78]

Civil and criminal legislation were highly developed, and already in the Fifth Dynasty the law of private property and bequest was intricate and precise.[79] As in our own days, there was absolute equality before the law—whenever the contesting parties had equal resources and influence. The oldest legal document in the world is a brief, in the British Museum, presenting to the court a complex case in inheritance. Judges required cases to be pled and answered, reargued and rebutted, not in oratory but in writing—which compares favorably with our windy litigation. Perjury was punished with death.[80] There were regular courts, rising from local judgment-seats in the nomes to supreme courts at Memphis, Thebes, or Heliopolis.[81] Torture was used occasionally as a midwife to truth;[82] beating with a rod was a frequent punishment, mutilation by cutting off nose or ears, hand or tongue, was sometimes resorted to,[83] or exile to the mines, or death by strangling, empaling, beheading, or burning at the stake; the extreme penalty was to be embalmed alive, to be eaten slowly by an inescapable coating of corrosive natron.[84] Criminals of high rank were saved the shame of public execution by being permitted to kill themselves, as in *samurai* Japan.[85] We find no signs of any system of police; even the standing army—always small because of Egypt's protected isolation between deserts and seas—was seldom used for internal discipline. Security of life and property, and the continuity of law and government, rested almost entirely on the prestige of the Pharaoh, maintained by the schools and the church. No other nation except China has ever dared to depend so largely upon psychological discipline.

It was a well-organized government, with a better record of duration than any other in history. At the head of the administration was the Vizier, who served at once as prime minister, chief justice, and head of the treasury; he was the court of last resort under the Pharaoh himself. A tomb relief shows us the Vizier leaving his house early in the morning to hear the petitions of the poor, "to hear," as the inscription reads, "what the people say in their demands, and to make no distinction between small and great."[86] A remarkable papyrus roll, which comes down to us from the days of the Empire, purports to be the form of address (perhaps it is but a literary invention) with which the Pharaoh installed a new Vizier:

> Look to the office of the Vizier; be watchful over all that is done therein. Behold, it is the established support of the whole land. . . . The Vizierate is not sweet; it is bitter. . . . Behold, it is not to show respect-of-persons to princes and councillors; it is not to make for himself slaves of any people. . . . Behold, when a petitioner comes from Upper or Lower Egypt . . . see thou to it that everything is done in accordance with law, that everything is done according to the custom thereof, (giving) to (every man) his right. . . . It is an abomination of the god to show partiality. . . . Look upon him who is known to thee like him who is unknown to thee; and him who is near the King like him who is far from (his House).

Behold, a prince who does this, he shall endure here in this place. . . . The dread of a prince is that he does justice. . . . (Behold the regulation) that is laid upon thee.[87]

The Pharaoh himself was the supreme court; any case might under certain circumstances be brought to him, if the plaintiff was careless of expense. Ancient carvings show us the "Great House" from which he ruled, and in which the offices of the government were gathered; from this Great House, which the Egyptians called *Pero* and which the Jews translated *Pharaoh*, came the title of the emperor. Here he carried on an arduous routine of executive work, sometimes with a schedule as rigorous as Chandragupta's, Louis XIV's or Napoleon's.[88] When he traveled the nobles met him at the feudal frontiers, escorted and entertained him, and gave him presents proportionate to their expectations; one lord, says a proud inscription, gave to Amenhotep II "carriages of silver and gold, statues of ivory and ebony . . . jewels, weapons, and works of art," 680 shields, 140 bronze daggers, and many vases of precious metal.[89] The Pharaoh reciprocated by taking one of the baron's sons to live with him at court—a subtle way of exacting a hostage of fidelity. The oldest of the courtiers constituted a Council of Elders called *Saru*, or The Great Ones, who served as an advisory cabinet to the king.[90] Such counsel was in a sense superfluous, for the Pharaoh, with the help of the priests, assumed divine descent, powers and wisdom; this alliance with the gods was the secret of his prestige. Consequently he was greeted with forms of address always flattering, sometimes astonishing, as when, in *The Story of Sinuhe*, a good citizen hails him: "O long-living King, may the Golden One" (Hathor the goddess) "give life to thy nose."[91]

As became so godlike a person, the Pharaoh was waited upon by a variety of aides, including generals, launderers, bleachers, guardians of the imperial wardrobe, and other men of high degree. Twenty officials collaborated to take care of his toilet: barbers who were permitted only to shave him and cut his hair, hairdressers who adjusted the royal cowl and diadem to his head, manicurists who cut and polished his nails, perfumers who deodorized his body, blackened his eyelids with kohl, and reddened his cheeks and lips with rouge.[92] One tomb inscription describes its occupant as "Overseer of the Cosmetic Box, Overseer of the Cosmetic Pencil, Sandal-Bearer to the King, doing in the matter of the King's sandals to the satisfaction of his Law."[93] So pampered, he tended to degenerate, and sometimes brightened his boredom by manning the imperial barge with young women clad only in network of a large mesh. The luxury of Amenhotep III prepared for the debacle of Ikhnaton.

4. Morals

Royal incest—The harem—Marriage—The position of woman—
The matriarchate in Egypt—Sexual morality

The government of the Pharaohs resembled that of Napoleon, even to the incest. Very often the king married his own sister—occasionally his own daughter—to preserve the purity of the royal blood. It is difficult to say whether this weakened the stock. Certainly Egypt did not think so, after several thousand years of experiment; the institution of sister-marriage spread among the people, and as late as the second century after Christ two-thirds of the citizens of Arsinoë were found to be practising the custom.[94] The words *brother* and *sister*, in Egyptian poetry, have the same significance as *lover* and *beloved* among ourselves.[95] In addition to his sisters the Pharaoh had an abundant harem, recruited not only from captive women but from the daughters of the nobles and the gifts of foreign potentates; so Amenhotep III received from a prince of Naharina his eldest daughter and three hundred select maidens.[96] Some of the nobility imitated this tiresome extravagance on a small scale, adjusting their morals to their resources.

For the most part the common people, like persons of moderate income everywhere, contented themselves with monogamy. Family life was apparently as well ordered, as wholesome in moral tone and influence, as in the highest civilizations of our time. Divorce was rare until the decadent dynasties. The husband could dismiss his wife without compensation if he detected her in adultery; if he divorced her for other reasons he was required to turn over to her a substantial share of the family property. The fidelity of the husband—so far as we can fathom such *arcana*—was as painstaking as in any later culture, and the position of woman was more advanced than in most countries today. "No people, ancient or modern," said Max Müller, "has given women so high a legal status as did the inhabitants of the Nile Valley."[97] The monuments picture them eating and drinking in public, going about their affairs in the streets unattended and unharmed, and freely engaging in industry and trade. Greek travelers, accustomed to confine their Xanthippes narrowly, were amazed at this liberty; they jibed at the henpecked husbands of Egypt, and Diodorus Siculus, perhaps with a twinkle in his eye, reported that along the Nile obedience of the husband to the wife was required in the marriage bond [98]— a stipulation not necessary in America. Women held and bequeathed property in their own names; one of the most ancient documents in history is the Third Dynasty will in which the lady Neb-sent transmits her lands to her children.[99] Hatshepsut and Cleopatra rose to be queens, and ruled and ruined like kings.

Sometimes a cynical note is heard in the literature. One ancient moralist warns his readers:

> Beware of a woman from abroad, who is not known in her city. Look not upon her when she comes, and know her not. She is like the vortex of deep waters, whose whirling is unfathomable. The woman whose husband is far away, she writes to thee every day. If there is no witness with her she arises and spreads her net. Oh, deadly crime if one hearkens![100]

But the more characteristically Egyptian tone sounds in Ptah-hotep's instructions to his son:

> If thou art successful, and hast furnished thy house, and lovest the wife of thy bosom, then fill her stomach and clothe her back. . . . Make glad her heart during the time thou hast her, for she is a field profitable to its owner. . . . If thou oppose her it will mean thy ruin.[101]

And the Boulak Papyrus admonishes the child with touching wisdom:

> Thou shalt never forget thy mother. . . . For she carried thee long beneath her breast as a heavy burden; and after thy months were accomplished she bore thee. Three long years she carried thee upon her shoulder, and gave thee her breast to thy mouth. She nurtured thee, and took no offense from thy uncleanliness. And when thou didst enter school, and wast instructed in the writings, daily she stood by the master with bread and beer from the house.[102]

It is likely that this high status of woman arose from the mildly matriarchal character of Egyptian society. Not only was woman full mistress in the house, but all estates descended in the female line; "even in late times," says Petrie, "the husband made over all his property and future earnings to his wife in his marriage settlement."[103] Men married their sisters not because familiarity had bred romance, but because they wished to enjoy the family inheritance, which passed down from mother to daughter, and they did not care to see this wealth give aid and comfort to strangers.[104] The powers of the wife underwent a slow diminution in the course of time, perhaps through contact with the patriarchal customs of the Hyksos, and through the transit of Egypt from agricultural isolation and peace to imperialism and war; under the Ptolemies the influence of the Greeks was so great that freedom of divorce, claimed in earlier times by the wife, became the exclusive privilege of the husband. Even then, however, the change was accepted only by the upper classes; the Egyptian commoner adhered to matriarchal ways.[105] Possibly because of the mastery of woman over her own affairs, infanticide was rare; Diodorus thought it a peculiarity of the Egyptians that every child born to them was reared, and tells us that parents guilty of infanticide were required by law to hold the dead child in their arms for three days and nights.[106] Families were large, and children swarmed in both hovels and palaces; the well-to-do were hard put to it to keep count of their offspring.[107]

Even in courtship the woman usually took the initiative. The love poems and letters that have come down to us are generally addressed by the lady to the man; she begs for assignations, she presses her suit directly, she formally proposes marriage.[108] "Oh my beautiful friend," says one letter, "my desire is to become, as thy wife, the mistress of all thy possessions."[109] Hence modesty, as distinct from fidelity, was not prominent among the Egyptians; they spoke of sexual affairs with a directness alien to our late morality, adorned their very temples with pictures and bas-reliefs of startling anatomical candor, and supplied their dead with obscene literature to amuse them in the grave.[110] Blood ran warm along the Nile: girls were nubile at ten, and premarital morals were free and easy; one courtesan, in Ptolemaic days, was reputed to have built a pyramid with her savings; even sodomy had its clientele.[111] Dancing-girls, in the manner of Japan, were accepted into the best male society as providers of entertainment and physical edification; they dressed in diaphanous robes, or contented themselves with anklets, bracelets and rings.[112] Evidences occur of religious prostitution on a small scale; as late as the Roman occupation the most beautiful girl among the noble families of Thebes was chosen to be consecrated to Amon. When she was too old to satisfy the god she received an honorable discharge, married, and moved in the highest circles.[112] It was a civilization with different prejudices from our own.

5. Manners

Character—Games—Appearance—Cosmetics—Costume—Jewelry

If we try to visualize the Egyptian character we find it difficult to distinguish between the ethics of the literature and the actual practices of life. Very frequently noble sentiments occur; a poet, for example, counsels his countrymen:

> Give bread to him who has no field,
> And create for thyself a good name for ever more;[114]

and some of the elders give very laudable advice to their children. A papyrus in the British Museum, known to scholars as "The Wisdom of Amenemope" (ca. 950 B.C.), prepares a student for public office with admonitions that probably influenced the author or authors of the "Proverbs of Solomon."

> Be not greedy for a cubit of land,
> And trespass not on the boundary of the widow. . . .
> Plough the fields that thou mayest find thy needs,
> And receive thy bread from thine own threshing floor.
> Better is a bushel which God giveth to thee
> Than five thousand gained by transgression. . . .
> Better is poverty in the hand of God
> Than riches in the storehouse;
> And better are loaves when the heart is joyous
> Than riches in unhappiness. . . .[115]

Such pious literature did not prevent the normal operation of human greed. Plato described the Athenians as loving knowledge, the Egyptians as loving wealth; perhaps he was too patriotic. In general the Egyptians were the Americans of antiquity: enamored of size, given to gigantic engineering and majestic building, industrious and accumulative, practical even in the midst of many ultramundane superstitions. They were the arch-conservatives of history; the more they changed, the more they remained the same; through forty centuries their artists copied the old conventions religiously. They appear to us, from their monuments, to have been a matter-of-fact people, not given to non-theological nonsense. They had no sentimental regard for human life, and killed with the clear conscience of nature; Egyptian soldiers cut off the right hand, or the phallus, of a slain enemy, and brought it to the proper scribe that it might be put into the record to their credit.[116] In the later dynasties the people, long accustomed to internal peace and to none but distant wars, lost all military habits and qualities, until at last a few Roman soldiers sufficed to master all Egypt.[117]

The accident that we know them chiefly from the remains in their tombs or the inscriptions on their temples has misled us into exaggerating their solemnity. We perceive from some of their sculptures and reliefs, and from their burlesque stories of the gods,[118] that they had a jolly turn for humor. They played many public and private games, such as checkers and dice;[119] they gave many modern toys to their children, like marbles, bouncing balls, tenpins and tops; they enjoyed wrestling contests, boxing matches and bull-fights.[120] At feasts and recreations they were anointed by attendants, were wreathed with flowers, feted with wines, and presented with gifts.

From the painting and the statuary we picture them as a physically vigorous people, muscular, broad-shouldered, thin-waisted, full-lipped, and flat-footed from going unshod. The upper classes are represented as fashionably slender, imperiously tall, with oval face, sloping forehead, regular features, a long, straight nose, and magnificent eyes. Their skin was white at birth (indicating an Asiatic rather than an African origin), but rapidly darkened under the Egyptian sun;[121] their artists idealized them in painting the men red, the women yellow; perhaps these colors were merely cosmetic styles. The man of the people, however, is pictured as short and squat, like the "Sheik-el-Beled," formed by heavy toil and an unbalanced ration; his features are rough, his nose blunt and wide; he is intelligent but coarse. Perhaps, as in so many other instances, the people and their rulers were of different races: the rulers of Asiatic, the people of African, derivation. The hair was dark, sometimes curly, but never woolly. Women bobbed their hair in the most modern mode; men shaved lips and chin, but consoled themselves with magnificent wigs. Often, in order to wear these more comfortably, they shaved the head; even the queen consort (e.g., Ikhnaton's mother Tiy) cut off all her hair to wear more easily the royal wig and crown. It was a matter of rigid etiquette that the king should have the biggest wig.[122]

According to their means they repaired the handiwork of nature with subtle cosmetic art. Faces were rouged, lips were painted, nails were colored, hair and limbs were oiled; even in the sculptures the Egyptian women have painted eyes. Those who could afford it had seven creams and two kinds of rouge put into their tombs when they died. The remains abound in toilet sets, mirrors, razors, hair-curlers, hair-pins, combs, cosmetic boxes, dishes and spoons—made of wood, ivory, alabaster or bronze, and designed in delightful and appropriate forms. Eye-paint still survives in some of the tubes. The kohl that women use today for painting the eyebrows and the face is a lineal descendant of the oil used by the Egyptians; it has come down to us through the Arabs, whose word for it, *al-kohl*, has given us our word alcohol. Perfumes of all sorts were used on the body and the clothes, and homes were made fragrant with incense and myrrh.[123]

Their clothing ran through every gradation from primitive nudity to the gorgeous dress of Empire days. Children of both sexes went about, till their teens, naked except for ear-rings and necklaces; the girls, however, showed a beseeming modesty by wearing a string of beads around the middle.[124] Servants and peasants limited their everyday wardrobe to a loin-cloth. Under the Old Kingdom free men and women went naked to the navel, and covered themselves from waist to knees with a short, tight skirt of white linen.[125] Since shame is a child of custom rather than of nature, these simple garments contented the conscience as completely as Victorian petticoats and corsets, or the evening dress of the contemporary American male; "our virtues lie in the interpretation of the time." Even the priests, in the first dynasties, wore nothing but loin-cloths, as we see from the statue of Ranofer.[126] When wealth increased, clothing increased; the Middle Kingdom added a second and larger skirt over the first, and the Empire added a covering for the breast, with now and then a cape. Coachmen and grooms took on formidable costumes, and ran through the streets in full livery to clear a way for the chariots of their masters. Women, in the prosperous dynasties, abandoned the tight skirt for a loose robe that passed over the shoulder and was joined in a clasp under the right breast. Flounces, embroideries and a thousand frills appeared, and fashion entered like a serpent to disturb the paradise of primitive nudity.[127]

Both sexes loved ornament, and covered neck, breast, arms, wrists and ankles with jewelry. As the nation fattened on the tribute of Asia and the commerce of the Mediterranean world, jewelry ceased to be restricted to the aristocracy, and became a passion with all classes. Every scribe and merchant had his seal of silver or gold; every man had a ring, every woman had an ornamental chain. These chains, as we see them in the museums today, are of infinite variety: some of them two to three inches, some of them five feet, in length; some thick and heavy, some "as slight and flexible as the finest Venetian lace."[128] About the time of the Eighteenth Dynasty ear-rings became *de rigueur;* every one had to have the ears pierced for them, not only girls and women, but boys and men.[129] Men as well as women decorated their persons with bracelets and rings, pendants and beads of costly stone. The women of ancient Egypt could learn very little from us in the matter of cosmetics and jewelry if they were reincarnated among us today.

6. Letters

Education—Schools of government—Paper and ink—Stages in the development of writing—Forms of Egyptian writing

The priests imparted rudimentary instruction to the children of the well-to-do in schools attached to the temples, as in the Roman Catholic parishes of our age.[130] One high-priest, who was what we should term Minister or Secretary of Education, calls himself "Chief of the Royal Stable of Instruction."[131] In the ruins of a school which was apparently part of the Ramesseum a large number of shells has been found, still bearing the lessons of the ancient pedagogue. The teacher's function was to produce scribes for the clerical work of the state. To stimulate his pupils he wrote eloquent essays on the advantages of education. "Give thy heart to learning, and love her like a mother," says one edifying papyrus, "for there is nothing so precious as learning." "Behold," says another, "there is no profession that is not governed; it is only the learned man who rules himself." It is a misfortune to be a soldier, writes an early bookworm; it is a weariness to till the earth; the only happiness is "to turn the heart to books during the daytime and to read during the night."[132]

Copy-books survive from the days of the Empire with the corrections of the masters still adorning the margins; the abundance of errors would console the modern schoolboy.[133] The chief method of instruction was the dictation or copying of texts, which were written upon potsherds or limestone flakes.[134] The subjects were largely commercial, for the Egyptians were the first and greatest utilitarians; but the chief topic of pedagogic discourse was virtue, and the chief problem, as ever, was discipline. "Do not spend thy time in wishing, or thou wilt come to a bad end," we read in one of the copy-books. "Let thy mouth read the book in thy hand; take advice from those who know more than thou dost"—this last is probably one of the oldest phrases in any language. Discipline was vigorous, and based upon the simplest principles. "The youth has a back," says a euphemistic manuscript, "and attends when he is beaten, . . . for the ears of the young are placed on the back." A pupil writes to his former teacher: "Thou didst beat my back, and thy instructions went into my ear." That this animal-training did not always succeed appears from a papyrus in which a teacher laments that his former pupils love books much less than beer.[135]

Nevertheless, a large number of the temple students were graduated from the hands of the priest to high schools attached to the offices of the state treasury. There, in the first known School of Government, the young scribes were instructed in public administration. On graduating they were apprenticed to officials, who taught them through plenty of work. Perhaps it was a better way of securing and training public servants than our modern selection of them by popularity and subserviency, and the noise of the hustings. In this manner Egypt and Babylonia developed, more or less simultaneously, the earliest school-systems in history;[136] not till the nineteenth century of our era was the public instruction of the young to be so well organized again.

In the higher grades the student was allowed to use paper—one of the main items of Egyptian trade, and one of the permanent gifts of Egypt to the world. The stem of the papyrus plant was cut into strips, other strips were placed crosswise upon these, the sheet was pressed, and paper, the very stuff (and nonsense) of civilization, was made.[137] How well they made it may be judged from the fact that manuscripts written by them five thousand years ago are still intact and legible. Sheets were combined into books by gumming the right edge of one sheet to the left edge of the next; in this way rolls were produced which were sometimes forty yards in length; they were seldom longer, for there were no verbose historians in Egypt. Ink, black and indestructible, was made by mixing water with soot and vegetable gums on a wooden palette; the pen was a simple reed, fashioned at the tip into a tiny brush.[138]

With these modern instruments the Egyptians wrote the most ancient of literatures. Their language had probably come in from Asia; the oldest specimens of it show many Semitic affinities.[139] The earliest writing was apparently pictographic—an object was represented by drawing a picture of it: e.g., the word for house (Egyptian *per*) was indicated by a small rectangle with an opening on one of the long sides. As some ideas were too abstract to be literally pictured, pictography passed into ideography: certain pictures were by custom and convention used to represent not the objects pictured but the ideas suggested by them; so the forepart of a lion meant supremacy (as in the Sphinx), a wasp meant royalty, and a tadpole stood for thousands. As a further development along this line, abstract ideas, which had at first resisted representation, were indicated by picturing objects whose names happened to resemble the spoken words that corresponded to the ideas; so the picture of a lute came to mean not only *lute*, but *good*, because the Egyptian word-sound for lute—*nefer*—resembled the word-sound for good—*nofer*. Queer rebus combinations grew out of these homonyms—words of like sound but different meanings. Since the verb *to be* was expressed in the spoken language by the sound *khopiru*, the scribe, being puzzled to find a picture for so intangible a conception, split the word into parts, *kho-pi-ru*, expressed these by picturing in succession a sieve (called in the spoken language *khau*), a mat (*pi*), and a mouth (*ru*); use and wont, which sanctify so many absurdities, soon made this strange assortment of characters suggest the idea of being. In this way the Egyptian arrived at the syllable, the syllabic sign, and the syllabary—i.e., a collection of syllabic signs; and by dividing difficult words into syllables, finding homonyms for these, and drawing in combination the objects suggested by these syllabic sounds, he was able, in the course of time, to make the hieroglyphic signs convey almost any idea.

Only one step remained—to invent letters. The sign for a house meant at first the word for house—*per*; then it meant the sound *per*, or *p-r* with any vowel in between, as a syllable in any word. Then the picture was shortened, and used to represent the sound *po*, *pa*, *pu*, *pe* or *pi* in any word; and since vowels were never written, this was equivalent to having a character for *P*. By a like development the sign for a hand (Egyptian *dot*) came to mean *do*, *da*, etc., finally *D*; the sign for mouth (*ro* or *ru*) came to mean *R*; the sign for snake (*zt*) became *Z*; the sign for lake (*shy*) became *Sh*. . . . The result was an alphabet of twenty-four consonants, which passed with Egyptian and Phœnician trade to all quarters of the Mediterranean, and came down, via Greece and Rome, as one of the most precious parts of our Oriental heritage.[140] Hieroglyphics are as old as the earliest dynasties; alphabetic characters appear first in inscriptions left by the Egyptians in the mines of the Sinai peninsula, variously dated at 2500 and 1500 B.C.[141]*

Whether wisely or not, the Egyptians never adopted a completely alphabetic writing; like modern stenographers they mingled pictographs, ideographs and syllabic signs with their letters to the very end of their civilization. This has made it difficult for scholars to read Egyptian, but it is quite conceivable that such a medley of longhand and shorthand facilitated the business of writing for those Egyptians who could spare the time to learn it. Since English speech is no honorable guide to English spelling, it is probably as difficult for a contemporary lad to learn the devious ways of English orthography as it was for the Egyptian scribe to memorize by use the five hundred hieroglyphs, their secondary syllabic meanings, and their tertiary alphabetic uses. In the course of time a more rapid and sketchy form of writing was developed for manuscripts, as distinguished from the careful "sacred carvings" of the monuments. Since this corruption of hieroglyphic was first made by the priests and the temple scribes, it was called by the Greeks *hieratic*; but it soon passed into common use for public, commercial and private documents. A still more abbreviated and careless form of this script was developed by the common people, and therefore came to be known as *demotic*. On the monuments, however, the Egyptian insisted on having his lordly and lovely hieroglyphic—perhaps the most picturesque form of writing ever made.

7. Literature

Texts and libraries—The Egyptian Sinbad—The Story of Sinuhe— Fiction—An amorous fragment—Love poems—History—A literary revolution

Most of the literature that survives from ancient Egypt is written in hieratic script. Little of it remains, and we are forced to estimate it from the fragments that do it only the blind justice of chance; perhaps time destroyed the Shakespeares of Egypt, and preserved only the poets laureate. A great official of the Fourth Dynasty is called on his tomb "Scribe

---

* Sir Charles Marston believes, from his recent researches in Palestine, that the alphabet was a Semitic invention, and credits it, on highly imaginative grounds, to Abraham himself.[141a]

of the House of Books";[142] we cannot tell whether this primeval library was a repository of literature, or only a dusty storehouse of public records and documents. The oldest extant Egyptian literature consists of the "Pyramid Texts"—pious matter engraved on the walls in five pyramids of the Fifth and Sixth Dynasties.*[143] Libraries have come down to us from as far back as 2000 B.C.—papyri rolled and packed in jars, labeled, and ranged.on shelves;[145] in one such jar was found the oldest form of the story of Sinbad the Sailor, or, as we might rather call it, Robinson Crusoe.

"The Story of the Shipwrecked Sailor" is a simple autobiographical fragment, full of life and feeling. "How glad is he," says this ancient mariner, in a line reminiscent of Dante, "that relateth what he hath experienced when the calamity hath passed!"

> I will relate to thee something that was experienced by me myself, when I had set out for the mines of the Sovereign and had gone down to the sea in a ship of 180 feet in length and 60 feet in breadth; and therein were 120 sailors of the pick of Egypt. They scanned the sky, they scanned the earth, and their hearts were more . . . than those of lions. They foretold a storm or ever it came, and a tempest when as yet it was not.
>
> A storm burst while we were yet at sea. . . . We flew before the wind and it made . . . a wave eight cubits high. . . .
>
> Then the ship perished, and of them that were in it not one survived. And I was cast onto an island by a wave of the sea, and I spent three days alone with mine heart as my companion. I slept under the shelter of a tree, and embraced the shade. Then I stretched forth my feet in order to find out what I could put into my mouth. I found figs and vines there, and all manner of fine leeks. . . . There were fish there and fowl, and there was nothing that was not in it. . . . When I had made me a fire-drill I kindled a fire and made a burnt-offering for the gods.[146]

Another tale recounts the adventures of Sinuhe, a public official who flees from Egypt at the death of Amenemhet I, wanders from country to country of the Near East, and, despite prosperity and honors there, suffers unbearably from lonesomeness for his native land. At last he gives up riches, and makes his way through many hardships back to Egypt.

---

* A later group of funerary inscriptions, written in ink upon the inner sides of the wooden coffins used to inter certain nobles and magnates of the Middle Kingdom, have been gathered together by Breasted and others under the name of "Coffin Texts."[144]

> O God, whosoever thou art, that didst ordain this flight, bring me
> again to the House (i.e., the Pharaoh). Peradventure thou wilt suffer
> me to see the place wherein mine heart dwelleth. What is a greater
> matter than that my corpse should be buried in the land wherein I
> was born? Come to mine aid! May good befall, may God show me
> mercy!

In the sequel we find him home again, weary and dusty with many miles
of desert travel, and fearful lest the Pharaoh reprove him for his long absence from a land which, like all others, looked upon itself as the only
civilized country in the world. But the Pharaoh forgives him, and extends
to him every cosmetic courtesy:

> I was placed in the house of a king's son, in which there was noble
> equipment, and a bath was therein. . . . Years were made to pass
> away from my body; I was shaved (?) and my hair was combed (?).
> A load (of dirt?) was given over to the desert, and the (filthy)
> clothes to the sand-farers. And I was arrayed in finest linen, and
> anointed with the best oil.[147]

Short stories are diverse and plentiful in the fragments that have come
down to us of Egyptian literature. There are marvelous tales of ghosts,
miracles, and other fascinating concoctions, as credible as the detective stories
that satisfy modern statesmen; there are high-sounding romances of princes
and princesses, kings and queens, including the oldest known form of the tale
of Cinderella, her exquisite foot, her wandering slipper, and her royal-hymen-
eal dénouement;[148] there are fables of animals illustrating by their conduct the
foibles and passions of humanity, and pointing morals sagely[149]—a kind of
premonitory plagiarism from Æsop and La Fontaine. Typical of the Egyptian
mingling of natural and supernatural is the tale of Anupu and Bitiu, older and
younger brothers, who live happily on their farm until Anupu's wife falls in
love with Bitiu, is repulsed by him, and revenges herself by accusing him, to
his brother, of having offered her violence. Gods and crocodiles come to
Bitiu's aid against Anupu; but Bitiu, disgusted with mankind, mutilates himself
to prove his innocence, retires Timon-like to the woods, and places his heart
unreachably high on the topmost flower of a tree. The gods, pitying his loneliness, create for him a wife of such beauty that the Nile falls in love with
her, and steals a lock of her hair. Drifting down the stream, the lock is
found by the Pharaoh, who, intoxicated by its scent, commands his henchmen
to find the owner. She is found and brought to him, and he marries her.
Jealous of Bitiu he sends men to cut down the tree on which Bitiu has placed

his heart. The tree is cut down, and as the flower touches the earth Bitiu dies.[150] How little the taste of our ancestors differed from our own!

The early literature of the Egyptians is largely religious; and the oldest Egyptian poems are the hymns of the Pyramid Texts. Their form is also the most ancient poetic form known to us—that "parallelism of members," or repetition of the thought in different phrase, which the Hebrew poets adopted from the Egyptians and Babylonians, and immortalized in the Psalms.[151] As the Old passes into the Middle Kingdom, the literature tends to become secular and "profane." We catch some glimpse of a lost body of amorous literature in a fragment preserved to us through the laziness of a Middle Kingdom scribe who did not complete his task of wiping clear an old papyrus, but left legible some twenty-five lines that tell of a simple shepherd's encounter with a goddess. "This goddess," says the story, "met with him as he wended his way to the pool, and she had stripped off her clothes and disarrayed her hair." The shepherd reports the matter cautiously:

> "Behold ye, when I went down to the swamp. . . . I saw a woman therein, and she looked not like a mortal being. My hair stood on end when I saw her tresses, because her color was so bright. Never will I do what she said; awe of her is in my body."[152]

The love songs abound in number and beauty, but as they celebrate chiefly the amours of brothers and sisters they will shock or amuse the modern ear. One collection is called "The Beautiful Joyous Songs of thy sister whom thy heart loves, who walks in the fields." An ostracon or shell dating back to the Nineteenth or Twentieth Dynasty plays a modern theme on the ancient chords of desire:

> The love of my beloved leaps on the bank of the stream.
> A crocodile lies in the shadows;
> Yet I go down into the water, and breast the wave.
> My courage is high on the stream,
> And the water is as land to my feet.
> It is her love that makes me strong.
> She is a book of spells to me.
> When I behold my beloved coming my heart is glad,
> My arms are spread apart to embrace her;

My heart rejoices forever . . . since my beloved came.
When I embrace her I am as one who is in Incense Land,
As one who carries perfumes.
When I kiss her, her lips are opened,
And I am made merry without beer.
Would that I were her Negress slave who is in attendance on her;
So should I behold the hue of all her limbs.[153]

The lines have been arbitrarily divided here; we cannot tell from the external form of the original that it is verse. The Egyptians knew that music and feeling are the twin essences of poetry; if these were present, the outward shape did not matter. Often, however, the rhythm was accentuated, as we have seen, by "parallelism of members." Sometimes the poet used the device of beginning every sentence or stanza with the same word; sometimes he played like a punster with like sounds meaning unlike or incongruous things; and it is clear from the texts that the trick of alliteration is as old as the Pyramids.[154] These simple forms were enough; with them the Egyptian poet could express almost every shade of that "romantic" love which Nietzsche supposed was an invention of the Troubadours. The Harris Papyrus shows that such sentiments could be expressed by a woman as well as by a man:

I am thy first sister,
And thou art to me as the garden
Which I have planted with flowers
And all sweet-smelling herbs.
I directed a canal into it,
That thou mightest dip thy hand into it
When the north wind blows cool.
The beautiful place where we take a walk,
When thy hand rests within mine,
With thoughtful mind and joyous heart
Because we walk together.
It is intoxicating to me to hear thy voice,
And my life depends upon hearing thee.
Whenever I see thee
It is better to me than food or drink.[155]

All in all it is astonishing how varied the fragments are. Formal letters, legal documents, historical narratives, magic formulas, laborious hymns, books of devotion, songs of love and war, romantic novelettes, moral exhortations, philosophical treatises—everything is represented here except epic and drama, and even of these one might by stretching a point find instances. The story of Rameses II's dashing victories, engraved patiently in verse upon brick after brick of the great pylon at Luxor, is epic at least in length and dulness. In another inscription Rameses IV boasts that in a play he had defended Osiris from Set, and had recalled Osiris to life.[156] Our knowledge does not allow us to amplify this hint.

Historiography, in Egypt, is as old as history; even the kings of the pre-dynastic period kept historical records proudly.[157] Official historians accompanied the Pharaohs on their expeditions, never saw their defeats, and recorded, or invented, the details of their victories; already the writing of history had become a cosmetic art. As far back as 2500 B.C. Egyptian scholars made lists of their kings, named the years from them, and chronicled the outstanding events of each year and reign; by the time of Thutmose III these documents became full-fledged histories, eloquent with patriotic emotion.[158] Egyptian philosophers of the Middle Kingdom thought both man and history old and effete, and mourned the lusty youth of their race; Khekheperre-Sonbu, a *savant* of the reign of Senusret II, about 2150 B.C., complained that all things had long since been said, and nothing remained for literature except repetition. "Would," he cried unhappily, "that I had words that are unknown, utterances and sayings in new language, that hath not yet passed away, and without that which hath been said repeatedly—not an utterance that hath grown stale, what the ancestors have already said."[159]

Distance blurs for us the variety and changefulness of Egyptian literature, as it blurs the individual differences of unfamiliar peoples. Nevertheless, in the course of its long development Egyptian letters passed through movements and moods as varied as those that have disturbed the history of European literature. As in Europe, so in Egypt the language of everyday speech diverged gradually, at last almost completely, from that in which the books of the Old Kingdom had been written. For a long time authors continued to compose in the ancient tongue; scholars acquired it in school, and students were compelled to translate the "classics" with the help of grammars and vocabularies, and with the occasional assistance of "interlinears." In the fourteenth century B.C. Egyptian authors rebelled against this bondage to tradition, and like Dante and Chaucer dared to write in the language of the people; Ikhnaton's famous *Hymn to the Sun* is itself composed in the popular speech. The new literature was realistic, youthful, buoyant; it took delight in flouting the old forms and describing the new life. In time this language also became literary and formal, refined and precise, rigid and impeccable with conventions of word and phrase; once again the language of letters separated from the language of speech, and scholasticism flourished; the schools of Saïte Egypt spent half their time studying and translating the "classics" of Ikhnaton's day.[160] Similar transformations of the native tongue went on under the Greeks, under the Romans, under the Arabs; another is going on today. *Panta rei*—all things flow; only scholars never change.

8. Science

Origins of Egyptian science—Mathematics—Astronomy and the calendar — Anatomy and physiology — Medicine, surgery and hygiene

The scholars of Egypt were mostly priests, enjoying, far from the turmoil of life, the comfort and security of the temples; and it was these priests who, despite all their superstitions, laid the foundations of Egyptian science. According to their own legends the sciences had been invented some 18,000 B.C. by Thoth, the Egyptian god of wisdom, during his three-thousand-year-long reign on earth; and the most ancient books in each science were among the twenty thousand volumes composed by this learned deity.*[161] Our knowledge does not permit us to improve substantially upon this theory of the origins of science in Egypt.

At the very outset of recorded Egyptian history we find mathematics highly developed; the design and construction of the Pyramids involved a precision of measurement impossible without considerable mathematical lore. The dependence of Egyptian life upon the fluctuations of the Nile led to careful records and calculations of the rise and recession of the river; surveyors and scribes were continually remeasuring the land whose boundaries had been obliterated by the inundation, and this measuring of the land was evidently the origin of *geo*-metry.[163] Nearly all the ancients agreed in ascribing the invention of this science to the Egyptians.[164] Josephus, however, thought that Abraham had brought arithmetic from Chaldea (i.e., Mesopotamia) to Egypt;[165] and it is not impossible that this and other arts came to Egypt from "Ur of the Chaldees," or some other center of western Asia.

---

* So we are assured by Iamblichus (ca. 300 A.D.). Manetho, the Egyptian historian (ca. 300 B.C.), would have considered this estimate unjust to the god; the proper number of Thoth's works, in his reckoning, was 36,000. The Greeks celebrated Thoth under the name of Hermes Trismegistus—Hermes (Mercury) the Thrice-Great.[162]

The figures used were cumbersome—one stroke for 1, two strokes for 2, . . . nine strokes for 9, with a new sign for 10. Two 10 signs stood for 20, three 10 signs for 30, . . . nine for 90, with a new sign for 100. Two 100 signs stood for 200, three 100 signs for 300, . . . nine for 900, with a new sign for 1000. The sign for 1,000,000 was a picture of a man striking his hands above his head, as if to express amazement that such a number should exist.[166] The Egyptians fell just short of the decimal system; they had no zero, and never reached the idea of expressing all numbers with ten digits: e.g., they used twenty-seven signs to write 999.[167] They had fractions, but always with the numerator 1; to express ¾ they wrote ½ + ¼. Multiplication and division tables are as old as the Pyramids. The oldest mathematical treatise known is the Ahmes Papyrus, dating back to 2000-1700 B.C.; but this in turn refers to mathematical writings five hundred years more ancient than itself. It illustrates by examples the computation of the capacity of a barn or the area of a field, and passes to algebraic equations of the first degree.[168] Egyptian geometry measured not only the area of squares, circles and cubes, but also the cubic content of cylinders and spheres; and it arrived at 3.16 as the value of π.[169] We enjoy the honor of having advanced from 3.16 to 3.1416 in four thousand years.

Of Egyptian physics and chemistry we know nothing, and almost as little of Egyptian astronomy. The star-gazers of the temples seem to have conceived the earth as a rectangular box, with mountains at the corners upholding the sky.[170] They made no note of eclipses, and were in general less advanced than their Mesopotamian contemporaries. Nevertheless they knew enough to predict the day on which the Nile would rise, and to orient their temples toward that point on the horizon where the sun would appear on the morning of the summer solstice.[171] Perhaps they knew more than they cared to publish among a people whose superstitions were so precious to their rulers; the priests regarded their astronomical studies as an esoteric and mysterious science, which they were reluctant to disclose to the common world.[172] For century after century they kept track of the position and movements of the planets, until their records stretched back for thousands of years. They distinguished between planets and fixed stars, noted in their catalogues stars of the fifth magnitude (practically invisible to the unaided eye), and charted what they thought were the astral influences of the heavens on the fortunes of men. From these observations they built the calendar which was to be another of Egypt's greatest gifts to mankind.

They began by dividing the year into three seasons of four months each: first, the rise, overflow and recession of the Nile; second, the period of cultivation; and third, the period of harvesting. To each of these months they assigned thirty days, as being the most convenient approximation to the lunar month of twenty-nine and a half days; their word for month, like ours, was derived from their symbol for the moon.* At the end of the twelfth month they added five days to bring the year into harmony with the river and the sun.[174] As the beginning of their year they chose the day on which the Nile usually reached its height, and on which, originally, the great star Sirius (which they called Sothis) rose simultaneously with the sun. Since their calendar allowed only 365, instead of 365¼, days to a year, this "heliacal rising" of Sirius (i.e., its appearance just before sunrise, after having been invisible for a number of days) came a day later every four years; and in this way the Egyptian calendar diverged by six hours annually from the actual calendar of the sky. The Egyptians never corrected this error. Many years later (46 B.C.) the Greek astronomers of Alexandria, by direction of Julius Caesar, improved this calendar by adding an extra day every fourth year; this was the "Julian Calendar." Under Pope Gregory XIII (1582) a more accurate correction was made by omitting this extra day (February 29th) in century years not divisible by 400; this is the "Gregorian Calendar" that we use today. Our calendar is essentially the creation of the ancient Near East.†[175]

Despite the opportunities offered by embalming, the Egyptians made relatively poor progress in the study of the human body. They thought that the blood-vessels carried air, water, and excretory fluids, and they believed the

---

* The clepsydra, or water-clock, was so old with the Egyptians that they attributed its invention to their handy god-of-all-trades, Thoth. The oldest clock in existence dates from Thutmose III, and is now in the Berlin Museum. It consists of a bar of wood, divided into six parts or hours, upon which a crosspiece was so placed that its shadow on the bar would indicate the time of the morning or the afternoon.[173]

† Since the heliacal rising of Sirius occurred one day later, every four years, than the Egyptian calendar demanded, the error amounted to 365 days in 1460 years; on the completion of this "Sothic cycle" (as the Egyptians called it) the paper calendar and the celestial calendar again agreed. Since we know from the Latin author Censorius that the heliacal rising of Sirius coincided in 139 A.D. with the beginning of the Egyptian calendar year, we may presume that a similar coincidence occurred every 1460 years previously— i.e., in 1321 B.C., 2781 B.C., 4241 B.C., etc. And since the Egyptian calendar was apparently established in a year when the heliacal rising of Sirius took place on the first day of the first month, we conclude that that calendar came into operation in a year that opened a Sothic cycle. The earliest mention of the Egyptian calendar is in the religious texts inscribed in the pyramids of the Fourth Dynasty. Since this dynasty is unquestionably earlier than 1321 B.C., the calendar must have been established in 2781 B.C., or 4241 B.C., or still earlier. The older date, once acclaimed as the first definite date in history, has been disputed by Professor Scharff, and it is possible that we shall have to accept 2781 B.C. as the approximate birth-year of the Egyptian calendar. This would require a foreshortening, by three or four hundred years, of the dates assigned above for the early dynasties and the great Pyramids. As the matter is very much in dispute, the chronology of the *Cambridge Ancient History* has been adopted in these pages.

heart and bowels to be the seat of the mind; perhaps if we knew what they meant by these terms we should find them not so divergent from our own ephemeral certainties. They described with general accuracy the larger bones and viscera, and recognized the function of the heart as the driving power of the organism and the center of the circulatory system: "its vessels," says the Ebers Papyrus,[176] "lead to all the members; whether the doctor lays his finger on the forehead, on the back of the head, on the hands, . . . or on the feet, everywhere he meets with the heart." From this to Leonardo and Harvey was but a step—which took three thousand years.

The glory of Egyptian science was medicine. Like almost everything else in the cultural life of Egypt, it began with the priests, and dripped with evidences of its magical origins. Among the people amulets were more popular than pills as preventive or curative of disease; disease was to them a possession by devils, and was to be treated with incantations. A cold for instance, could be exorcised by such magic words as: "Depart, cold, son of a cold, thou who breakest the bones, destroyest the skull, makest ill the seven openings of the head! . . . Go out on the floor, stink, stink, stink!"[177]—a cure probably as effective as contemporary remedies for this ancient disease. From such depths we rise in Egypt to great physicians, surgeons and specialists, who acknowledged an ethical code that passed down into the famous Hippocratic oath.[178] Some of them specialized in obstetrics or gynecology, some treated only gastric disorders, some were oculists so internationally famous that Cyrus sent for one of them to come to Persia.[179] The general practitioner was left to gather the crumbs and heal the poor; in addition to which he was expected to provide cosmetics, hair-dyes, skin-culture, limb-beautification, and flea-exterminators.[180]

Several papyri devoted to medicine have come down to us. The most valuable of them, named from the Edwin Smith who discovered it, is a roll fifteen feet long, dating about 1600 B.C., and going back for its sources to much earlier works; even in its extant form it is the oldest scientific document known to history. It describes forty-eight cases in clinical surgery, from cranial fractures to injuries of the spine. Each case is treated in logical order, under the heads of provisional diagnosis, examination, semeiology, diagnosis, prognosis, treatment, and glosses on the terms used. The author notes, with a clarity unrivaled till the eighteenth century of our era, that control of the lower limbs is localized in the "brain"—a word which here appears for the first time in literature.[181]

The Egyptians enjoyed a great variety of diseases, though they had to die of them without knowing their Greek names. The mummies and papyri tell of spinal tuberculosis, arteriosclerosis, gall-stones, small-pox, infantile paralysis, anemia, rheumatic arthritis, epilepsy, gout, mastoiditis, appendicitis, and such marvelous affections as spondylitis deformans and achondroplasia. There are no signs of syphilis or cancer; but pyorrhea and dental caries, absent in the oldest mummies, become frequent in the later ones, indicating the progress of civilization. The atrophy and fusion of the bones of the small toe, often ascribed to the modern shoe, was common in ancient Egypt, where nearly all ages and ranks went barefoot.[182]

Against these diseases the Egyptian doctors were armed with an abundant pharmacopœia. The Ebers Papyrus lists seven hundred remedies for everything from snake-bite to puerperal fever. The Kahun Papyrus (ca. 1850 B.C.) prescribes suppositories apparently used for contraception.[182a] The tomb of an Eleventh Dynasty queen revealed a medicine chest containing vases, spoons, dried drugs, and roots. Prescriptions hovered between medicine and magic, and relied for their effectiveness in great part on the repulsiveness of the concoction. Lizard's blood, swine's ears and teeth, putrid meat and fat, a tortoise's brains, an old book boiled in oil, the milk of a lying-in woman, the water of a chaste woman, the *excreta* of men, donkeys, dogs, lions, cats and lice—all these are found in the prescriptions. Baldness was treated by rubbing the head with animal fat. Some of these cures passed from the Egyptians to the Greeks, from the Greeks to the Romans, and from the Romans to us; we still swallow trustfully the strange mixtures that were brewed four thousand years ago on the banks of the Nile.[183]

The Egyptians tried to promote health by public sanitation,* by circumcision of males,†[185] and by teaching the people the frequent use of the enema. Diodorus Siculus[187] tells us:

> In order to prevent sicknesses they look after the health of their body by means of drenches, fastings and emetics, sometimes every day, and sometimes at intervals of three or four days. For they say that the larger part of the food taken into the body is superfluous, and that it is from this superfluous part that diseases are engendered.‡

Pliny believed that this habit of taking enemas was learned by the Egyptians from observing the ibis, a bird that counteracts the constipating

---

* Excavations reveal arrangements for the collection of rain-water and the disposal of sewage by a system of copper pipes.[184]

† Even the earliest tombs give evidence of this practice.[186]

‡ So old is the modern saw that we live on one-fourth of what we eat, and the doctors live on the rest.

character of its food by using its long bill as a rectal syringe.[188] Herodotus reports that the Egyptians "purge themselves every month, three days successively, seeking to preserve health by emetics and enemas; for they suppose that all diseases to which men are subject proceed from the food they use." And this first historian of civilization ranks the Egyptians as, "next to the Libyans, the healthiest people in the world.[189]

9. Art

Architecture—Old Kingdom, Middle Kingdom, Empire and Saïte sculpture—Bas-relief—Painting—Minor arts—Music—The artists

The greatest element in this civilization was its art. Here, almost at the threshold of history, we find an art powerful and mature, superior to that of any modern nation, and equaled only by that of Greece. At first the luxury of isolation and peace, and then, under Thutmose III and Rameses II, the spoils of oppression and war, gave to Egypt the opportunity and the means for massive architecture, masculine statuary, and a hundred minor arts that so early touched perfection. The whole theory of progress hesitates before Egyptian art.

Architecture* was the noblest of the ancient arts, because it combined in imposing form mass and duration, beauty and use. It began humbly in the adornment of tombs and the external decoration of homes. Dwellings were mostly of mud, with here and there some pretty woodwork (a Japanese lattice, a well-carved portal), and a roof strengthened with the tough and pliable trunks of the palm. Around the house, normally, was a wall enclosing a court; from the court steps led to the roof; from this the tenants passed down into the rooms. The well-to-do had private gardens, carefully landscaped; the cities provided public gardens for the poor, and hardly a home but had its ornament of flowers. Inside the house the walls were hung with colored mattings, and the floors, if the master could afford it, were covered with rugs. People sat on these rugs rather than on chairs; the Egyptians of the Old Kingdom squatted for their meals at tables six inches high, in the fashion of the Japanese; and ate with their fingers, like Shakespeare. Under the Empire, when slaves were cheap, the upper classes sat on high cushioned chairs, and had their servants hand them course after course.[190]

Stone for building was too costly for homes; it was a luxury reserved for priests and kings. Even the nobles, ambitious though they were, left

---

* For the architecture of the Old Kingdom cf. sections I, 1 and 3 of this chapter.

the greatest wealth and the best building materials to the temples; in consequence the palaces that overlooked almost every mile of the river in the days of Amenhotep III crumbled into oblivion, while the abodes of the gods and the tombs of the dead remained. By the Twelfth Dynasty the pyramid had ceased to be the fashionable form of sepulture. Khnumhotep (ca. 2180 B.C.) chose at Beni-Hasan the quieter form of a colonnade built into the mountainside; and this theme, once established, played a thousand variations among the hills on the western slope of the Nile. From the time of the Pyramids to the Temple of Hathor at Denderah—i.e., for some three thousand years—there rose out of the sands of Egypt such a succession of architectural achievements as no civilization has ever surpassed.

At Karnak and Luxor a riot of columns raised by Thutmose I and III, Amenhotep III, Seti I, Rameses II and other monarchs from the Twelfth to the Twenty-second Dynasty; at Medinet-Habu (ca. 1300 B.C.) a vast but less distinguished edifice, on whose columns an Arab village rested for centuries; at Abydos the Temple of Seti I, dark and sombre in its massive ruins; at Elephantine the little Temple of Khnum (ca. 1400 B.C.), "positively Greek in its precision and elegance";[191] at Der-el-Bahri the stately colonnades of Queen Hatshepsut; near it the Ramesseum, another forest of colossal columns and statues reared by the architects and slaves of Rameses II; at Philæ the lovely Temple of Isis (ca. 240 B.C.) desolate and abandoned now that the damming of the Nile at Assuan has submerged the bases of its perfect columns—these are sample fragments of the many monuments that still adorn the valley of the Nile, and attest even in their ruins the strength and courage of the race that reared them. Here, perhaps, is an excess of pillars, a crowding of columns against the tyranny of the sun, a Far-Eastern aversion to symmetry, a lack of unity, a barbaric-modern adoration of size. But here, too, are grandeur, sublimity, majesty and power; here are the arch and the vault,[192] used sparingly because not needed, but ready to pass on their principles to Greece and Rome and modern Europe; here are decorative designs never surpassed;[193] here are papyriform columns, lotiform columns, "proto-Doric" columns,[194] Caryatid columns,[195] Hathor capitals, palm capitals, clerestories, and magnificent architraves full of the strength and stability that are the very soul of architecture's powerful appeal.* The Egyptians were the greatest builders in history.

---

* A clerestory is that portion of a building which, being above the roof of the surrounding parts, admits light to the edifice by a series of openings. An architrave is the lowest part of an entablature—which is a superstructure supported by a colonnade.

Some would add that they were also the greatest sculptors. Here at the outset is the Sphinx, conveying by its symbolism the leonine quality of some masterful Pharaoh—perhaps Khafre-Chephren; it has not only size, as some have thought, but character. The cannon-shot of the Mamelukes have broken the nose and shorn the beard, but nevertheless those gigantic features portray with impressive skill the force and dignity, the calm and sceptical maturity, of a natural king. Across those motionless features a subtle smile has hovered for five thousand years, as if already the unknown artist or monarch had understood all that men would ever understand about men. It is a Mona Lisa in stone.

There is nothing finer in the history of sculpture than the diorite statue of Khafre in the Cairo Museum; as ancient to Praxiteles as Praxiteles to us, it nevertheless comes down across fifty centuries almost unhurt by time's rough usages; cut in the most intractable of stones, it passes on to us completely the strength and authority, the wilfulness and courage, the sensitivity and intelligence of the (artist or the) King. Near it, and even older, Pharaoh Zoser sits pouting in limestone; farther on, the guide with lighted match reveals the transparency of an alabaster Menkaure.

Quite as perfect in artistry as these portraits of royalty are the figures of the Sheik-el-Beled and the Scribe. The Scribe has come down to us in many forms, all of uncertain antiquity; the most illustrious is the squatting Scribe of the Louvre.* The Sheik is no sheik but only an over-seer of labor, armed with the staff of authority, and stepping forward as if in supervision or command. His name, apparently, was Kaapiru; but the Arab workmen who rescued him from his tomb at Sakkara were struck with his resemblance to the Sheik-el-Beled (i.e., Mayor-of-the-Village) under whom they lived; and this title which their good humor gave him is now inseparable from his fame. He is carved only in mortal wood, but time has not seriously reduced his portly figure or his chubby legs; his waistline has all the amplitude of the comfortable *bourgeois* in every civilization; his rotund face beams with the content of a man who knows his place and glories in it. The bald head and carelessly loosened robe display the realism of an art already old enough to rebel against idealization; but here, too, is a fine simplicity, a complete humanity, expressed without bitterness, and with the ease and grace of a practised and confident hand. "If," says Maspero, "some exhibition of the world's masterpieces

---

* Cf. p. 161 above. Other scribes adorn the Cairo Museum, and the State Museum at Berlin.

were to be inaugurated, I should choose this work to uphold the honor of Egyptian art"[196]—or would that honor rest more securely on the head of Khafre?

These are the *chefs-d'œuvres* of Old Kingdom statuary. But lesser masterpieces abound: the seated portraits of Rahotep and his wife Nofrit, the powerful figure of Ranofer the priest, the copper statues of King Phiops and his son, a falcon-head in gold, the humorous figures of the Beer-Brewer and the Dwarf Knemhotep—all but one in the Cairo Museum, all without exception instinct with character. It is true that the earlier pieces are coarse and crude; that by a strange convention, running throughout Egyptian art, figures are shown with the body and eyes facing forward, but the hands and feet in profile;* that not much attention was given to the body, which was left in most cases stereotyped and unreal—all female bodies young, all royal bodies strong; and that individualization, though masterly, was generally reserved for the head. But with all the stiffness and sameness that priestly conventions and control forced upon statuary, paintings and reliefs, these works were fully redeemed by the power and depth of the conception, the vigor and precision of the execution, the character, line and finish of the product. Never was sculpture more alive: the Sheik exudes authority, the woman grinding grain gives every sense and muscle to her work, the Scribe is on the very verge of writing. And the thousand little puppets placèd in the tombs to carry on essential industries for the dead were moulded with a like vivacity, so that we can almost believe, with the pious Egyptian, that the deceased could not be unhappy while these ministrants were there.

Not for many centuries did Egyptian sculpture equal again the achievements of the early dynasties. Because most of the statuary was made for the temples or the tombs, the priests determined to a great degree what forms the artist should follow; and the natural conservatism of religion crept into art, slowly stifling sculpture into a conventional, stylistic degeneration. Under the powerful monarchs of the Twelfth Dynasty the secular spirit reasserted itself, and art recaptured something of its old vigor and more than its old skill. A head of Amenemhet III in black diorite[197] suggests at once the recovery of character and the recovery of art; here is the quiet hardness of an able king, carved with the competence of a master. A colossal statue of Senusret III is crowned with a head and face

---

* There are important exceptions to this—e.g., the Sheik-el-Beled and the Scribe; obviously the convention was not due to incapacity or ignorance.

equal in conception and execution to any portrait in the history of sculpture; and the ruined torso of Senusret I, in the Cairo Museum, ranks with the torso of Hercules in the Louvre. Animal figures abound in the Egyptian sculpture of every age, and are always full of humor and life: here is a mouse chewing a nut, an ape devotedly strumming a harp, a porcupine with every spine on the *qui vive*. Then came the Shepherd Kings, and for three hundred years Egyptian art almost ceased to be.

In the age of Hatshepsut, the Thutmoses, the Amenhoteps and the Rameses, art underwent a second resurrection along the Nile. Wealth poured in from subject Syria, passed into the temples and the courts, and trickled through them to nourish every art. Colossi of Thutmose III and Rameses II began to challenge the sky; statuary crowded every corner of the temples; masterpieces were flung forth with unprecedented abundance by a race exhilarated with what they thought was world supremacy. The fine granite bust of the great Queen in the Metropolitan Museum of Art at New York; the basalt statue of Thutmose III in the Cairo Museum; the lion sphinx of Amenhotep III in the British Museum; the limestone seated Ikhnaton in the Louvre; the granite statue of Rameses II in Turin;* the perfect crouching figure of the same incredible monarch making an offering to the gods;[199] the meditative cow of Der-el-Bahri, which Maspero considered "equal, if not superior, to the best achievements of Greece and Rome in this *genre*";[200] the two lions of Amenhotep III, which Ruskin ranked as the best animal statuary surviving from antiquity;[201] the colossi cut into the rocks at Abu Simbel by the sculptors of Rameses II; the amazing remains found among the ruins of the artist Thutmose's studio at Tell-el-Amarna—a plaster model of Ikhnaton's head, full of the mysticism and poetry of that tragic king, the lovely limestone bust of Ikhnaton's Queen, Nofretete, and the even finer sandstone head of the same fair lady:[202] these scattered examples may illustrate the sculptural accomplishments of this abounding Empire age. Amid all these lofty masterpieces humor continues to find place; Egyptian sculptors frolic with jolly caricatures of men and animals, and even the kings and queens, in Ikhnaton's iconoclastic age, are made to smile and play.

After Rameses II this magnificence passed rapidly away. For many centuries after him art contented itself with repeating traditional works and forms. Under the Saïte kings it sought to rejuvenate itself by return-

---

* One is reminded here of the remark of an Egyptian statesman, after visiting the galleries of Europe: "*Que vous avez volé mon pays!*—How you have raped my country!"[198]

ing to the simplicity and sincerity of the Old Kingdom masters. Sculptors attacked bravely the hardest stones—basalt, *breccia*, serpentine, diorite— and carved them into such realistic portraits as that of Montumihait,[203] and the green basalt head of a bald unknown, now looking out blackly upon the walls of the State Museum at Berlin. In bronze they cast the lovely figure of the lady Tekoschet.[204] Again they delighted in catching the actual features and movements of men and beasts; they moulded laughable figures of quaint animals, slaves and gods; and they formed in bronze a cat and a goat's head which are among the trophies of Berlin.[205] Then the Persians came down like a wolf on the fold, conquered Egypt, desecrated its temples, broke its spirit, and put an end to its art.

These—architecture and sculpture*—are the major Egyptian arts; but if abundance counted, bas-relief would have to be added to them. No other people so tirelessly carved its history or legends upon its walls. At first we are shocked by the dull similarity of these glyptic narratives, the crowded confusion, the absence of proportion and perspective—or the ungainly attempt to achieve this by representing the far above the near; we are surprised to see how tall the Pharaoh is, and how small are his enemies; and, as in the sculpture, we find it hard to adjust our pictorial habits to eyes and breasts that face us boldly, while noses, chins and feet turn coldly away. But then we find ourselves caught by the perfect line and grace of the falcon and serpent carved on King Wenephes' tomb,[206] by the limestone reliefs of King Zoser on the Step-Pyramid at Sakkara, by the wood-relief of Prince Hesiré from his grave in the same locality,[207] and by the wounded Libyan on a Fifth Dynasty tomb at Abusir[208]—a patient study of muscles taut in pain. At last we bear with equanimity the long reliefs that tell how Thutmose III and Rameses II carried all before them; we recognize the perfection of flowing line in the reliefs carved for Seti I at Abydos and Karnak; and we follow with interest the picturesque engravings wherein the sculptors of Hatshepsut tell on the walls of Der-el-Bahri the story of the expedition sent by her to the mysterious land of Punt (Somaliland?). We see the long ships with full-spread sail and serried oars heading south amid waters alive with octopi, crustacea and other toilers of the sea; we watch the fleet arriving on the shores of Punt, welcomed by a startled but fascinated people and king; we see the sailors

---

* Though the word *sculpture* includes all carved forms, we shall use it as meaning especially sculpture in the round; and shall segregate under the term *bas-relief* the partial carving of forms upon a background.

carrying on board a thousand loads of native delicacies; we read the jest of the Punt workman—"Be careful of your feet, you over there; look out!" Then we accompany the heavy-laden vessels as they return northward filled (the inscription tells us) "with the marvels of the land of Punt, all the odoriferous trees of the lands of the gods, incense, ebony, ivory, gold, woods of divers kinds, cosmetics for the eyes, monkeys, dogs, panther skins, . . . never have like things been brought back for any king from the beginning of the world." The ships come through the great canal between the Red Sea and the Nile; we see the expedition landing at the docks of Thebes, depositing its varied cargo at the very feet of the Queen. And lastly we are shown, as if after the lapse of time, all these imported goods beautifying Egypt: on every side ornaments of gold and ebony, boxes of perfumes and unguents, elephants' tusks and animals' hides; while the trees brought back from Punt are flourishing so well on the soil of Thebes that under their branches oxen enjoy the shade. It is one of the supreme reliefs in the history of art.[209]*

Bas-relief is a liaison between sculpture and painting. In Egypt, except during the reign of the Ptolemies and under the influence of Greece, painting never rose to the status of an independent art; it remained an accessory to architecture, sculpture and relief—the painter filled in the outlines carved by the cutting tool. But though subordinate, it was ubiquitous; most statues were painted, all surfaces were colored. It is an art perilously subject to time, and lacking the persistence of statuary and building. Very little remains to us of Old Kingdom painting beyond a remarkable picture of six geese from a tomb at Medum;[210] but from this alone we are justified in believing that already in the early dynasties this art, too, had come near to perfection. In the Middle Kingdom we find distemper painting† of a delightful decorative effect in the tombs of Ameni and Khnumhotep at Beni-Hasan, and such excellent examples of the art as the "Gazelles and the Peasants,"[211] and the "Cat Watching the Prey";[212] here again the artist has caught the main point—that his creations must move and live. Under the Empire the tombs became a riot of painting. The Egyptian artist had now developed every color in the rainbow, and was anxious to display his skill. On the walls and ceilings of homes, temples, palaces and graves he

---

* A cast of this relief may be seen in the Twelfth Egyptian Room of the Metropolitan Museum of Art at New York.

† Painting in which the pigments are mixed or tempered with egg-yolk, size (diluted glue), or egg-white.

tried to portray refreshingly the life of the sunny fields—birds in flight
through the air, fishes swimming in the sea, beasts of the jungle in their
native haunts. Floors were painted to look like transparent pools, and ceilings sought to rival the jewelry of the sky. Around these pictures were
borders of geometric or floral design, ranging from a quiet simplicity to
the most fascinating complexity.[213] The "Dancing Girl,"[214] so full of orig
inality and *esprit*, the "Bird Hunt in a Boat,"[215] the slim, naked beauty in
ochre, mingling with other musicians in the Tomb of Nakht at Thebes[216]—
these are stray samples of the painted population of the graves. Here, as
in the bas-reliefs, the line is good and the composition poor; the participants
in an action, whom we should portray as intermingled, are represented
separately in succession;[217] superposition is again preferred to perspective;
the stiff formalism and conventions of Egyptian sculpture are the order
of the day, and do not reveal that enlivening humor and realism which
distinguish the later statuary. But through these pictures runs a freshness
of conception, a flow of line and execution, a fidelity to the life and movement of natural things, and a joyous exuberance of color and ornament,
which make them a delight to the eye and the spirit. With all its shortcomings Egyptian painting would never be surpassed by any Oriental
civilization until the middle dynasties of China.

The minor arts were the major art of Egypt. The same skill and energy
that had built Karnak and the Pyramids, and had crowded the temples
with a populace of stone, devoted itself also to the internal beautification
of the home, the adornment of the body, and the development of all the
graces of life. Weavers made rugs, tapestries and cushions rich in color
and incredibly fine in texture; the designs which they created passed down
into Syria, and are used there to this day.[218] The relics of Tutenkhamon's
tomb have revealed the astonishing luxury of Egyptian furniture, the exquisite finish of every piece and part, chairs covered gaudily with silver
and gold, beds of sumptuous workmanship and design, jewel-boxes and
perfume-baskets of minute artistry, and vases that only China would excel.
Tables bore costly vessels of silver, gold and bronze, crystal goblets, and
sparkling bowls of diorite so finely ground that the light shone through
their stone walls. The alabaster vessels of Tutenkhamon, and the perfect
lotus cups and drinking bowls unearthed amid the ruins of Amenhotep
III's villa at Thebes, indicate to what a high level the ceramic art was
raised. Finally the jewelers of the Middle Kingdom and the Empire brought
forth a profusion of precious ornaments seldom surpassed in design and

workmanship. Necklaces, crowns, rings, bracelets, mirrors, pectorals, chains, medallions; gold and silver, carnelian and felspar, *lapis lazuli* and amethyst—everything is here. The rich Egyptians took the same pleasure as the Japanese in the beauty of the little things that surrounded them; every square of ivory on their jewel-boxes had to be carved in relief and refined in precise detail. They dressed simply, but they lived completely. And when their day's work was done they refreshed themselves with music softly played on lutes, harps, sistrums, flutes and lyres.* Temples and palaces had orchestras and choirs, and on the Pharaoh's staff was a "superintendent of singing" who organized players and musicians for the entertainment of the king. There is no trace of a musical notation in Egypt, but this may be merely a lacuna in the remains. Snefrunofr and Re'mery-Ptah were the Carusos and De Reszkes of their day, and across the centuries we hear their boast that they "fulfil every wish of the king by their beautiful singing."[219]

It is exceptional that their names survive, for in most cases the artists whose labors preserved the features or memory of princes, priests and kings had no means of transmitting their own names to posterity. We hear of Imhotep, the almost mythical architect of Zoser's reign; of Ineni, who designed great buildings like Der-el-Bahri for Thutmose I; of Puymre and Hapuseneb and Senmut, who carried on the architectural enterprises of Queen Hatshepsut,† of the artist Thutmose, in whose studio so many masterpieces have been found; and of Bek, the proud sculptor who tells us, in Gautier's strain, that he has saved Ikhnaton from oblivion.[221] Amenhotep III had as his chief architect another Amenhotep, son of Hapu; the Pharaoh placed almost limitless wealth at the disposal of his talents, and this favored artist became so famous that later Egypt worshiped him as a god. For the most part, however, the artist worked in obscurity and poverty, and was ranked no higher than other artisans or handicraftsmen by the priests and potentates who engaged him.

Egyptian religion coöperated with Egyptian wealth to inspire and foster art, and coöperated with Egypt's loss of empire and affluence to ruin it. Religion offered motives, ideas and the inspiration; but it imposed con-

---

* The lute was made by stretching a few strings along a narrow sounding-board; the sistrum was a group of small discs shaken on wires.

† Senmut was so honored by his sovereigns that he said of himself: "I was the greatest of the great in the whole land."[220] This is an opinion very commonly held, but not always so clearly expressed.

ventions and restraints which bound art so completely to the church that when sincere religion died among the artists, the arts that had lived on it died too. This is the tragedy of almost every civilization—that its soul is in its faith, and seldom survives philosophy.

10. Philosophy

The "Instructions of Ptah-hotep"—The "Admonitions of Ipuwer"
—The "Dialogue of a Misanthrope"—The Egyptian Ecclesiastes

Historians of philosophy have been wont to begin their story with the Greeks. The Hindus, who believe that they invented philosophy, and the Chinese, who believe that they perfected it, smile at our provincialism. It may be that we are all mistaken; for among the most ancient fragments left to us by the Egyptians are writings that belong, however loosely and untechnically, under the rubric of moral philosophy. The wisdom of the Egyptians was a proverb with the Greeks, who felt themselves children beside this ancient race.[222]

The oldest work of philosophy known to us is the "Instructions of Ptah-hotep," which apparently goes back to 2880 B.C.—2300 years before Confucius, Socrates and Buddha.[223] Ptah-hotep was Governor of Memphis, and Prime Minister to the King, under the Fifth Dynasty. Retiring from office, he decided to leave to his son a manual of everlasting wisdom. It was transcribed as an antique classic by some scholars prior to the Eighteenth Dynasty. The Vizier begins:

> O Prince my Lord, the end of life is at hand; old age descendeth upon me; feebleness cometh and childishness is renewed; he that is old lieth down in misery every day. The eyes are small, the ears are deaf. Energy is diminished, the heart hath no rest. . . . Command thy servant, therefore, to make over my princely authority to my son. Let me speak unto him the words of them that hearken to the counsel of the men of old time, those that once heard the gods. I pray thee, let this thing be done.

His Gracious Majesty grants the permission, advising him, however, to "discourse without causing weariness"—advice not yet superfluous for philosophers. Whereupon Ptah-hotep instructs his son:

> Be not proud because thou art learned; but discourse with the ig-norant man as with the sage. For no limit can be set to skill, neither

is there any craftsman that possesseth full advantages. Fair speech is more rare than the emerald that is found by slave-maidens among the pebbles. . . . Live, therefore, in the house of kindliness, and men shall come and give gifts of themselves. . . . Beware of making enmity by thy words. . . . Overstep not the truth, neither repeat that which any man, be he prince or peasant, saith in opening the heart; it is abhorrent to the soul. . . .

If thou wouldst be a wise man, beget a son for the pleasing of the god. If he make straight his course after thine example, if he arrange thine affairs in due order, do all unto him that is good. . . . If he be heedless and trespass thy rules of conduct, and is violent; if every speech that cometh from his mouth is a vile word; then beat thou him, that his talk may be fitting. . . . Precious to a man is the virtue of his son, and good character is a thing remembered. . . .

Wheresover thou goest, beware of consorting with women. . . . If thou wouldst be wise, provide for thine house, and love thy wife that is in thine arms. . . . Silence is more profitable to thee than abundance of speech. Consider how thou mayest be opposed by an expert that speaketh in council. It is a foolish thing to speak on every kind of work. . . .

If thou be powerful make thyself to be honored for knowledge and for gentleness. . . . Beware of interruption, and of answering words with heat; put it from thee; control thyself.

And Ptah-hotep concludes with Horatian pride:

Nor shall any word that hath here been set down cease out of this land forever, but shall be made a pattern whereby princes shall speak well. My words shall instruct a man how he shall speak; . . . yea, he shall become as one skilful in obeying, excellent in speaking. Good fortune shall befall him; . . . he shall be gracious until the end of his life; he shall be contented always.[224]

This note of good cheer does not persist in Egyptian thought; age comes upon it quickly, and sours it. Another sage, Ipuwer, bemoans the disorder, violence, famine and decay that attended the passing of the Old Kingdom; he tells of sceptics who "would make offerings if" they "knew where the god is"; he comments upon increasing suicide, and adds, like another Schopenhauer: "Would that there might be an end of men, that there might be no conception, no birth. If the land would but cease from noise, and strife be no more"—it is clear that Ipuwer was tired and old. In the end he dreams of a philosopher-king who will redeem men from chaos and injustice:

> He brings cooling to the flame (of the social conflagration?). It is said he is the shepherd of all men. There is no evil in his heart. When his herds are few he passes the day to gather them together, their hearts being fevered. Would that he had discerned their character in the first generation. Then would he have smitten evil. He would have stretched forth his arm against it. He would have smitten the seed thereof and their inheritance. . . . Where is he today? Doth he sleep perchance? Behold, his might is not seen.[225]

This already is the voice of the prophets; the lines are cast into strophic form, like the prophetic writings of the Jews; and Breasted properly acclaims these "Admonitions" as "the earliest emergence of a social idealism which among the Hebrews we call 'Messianism.' "[226] Another scroll from the Middle Kingdom denounces the corruption of the age in words that almost every generation hears:

> To whom do I speak today?
> Brothers are evil,
> Friends of today are not of love.
> > To whom do I speak today?
> > Hearts are thievish,
> > Every man seizes his neighbor's goods.
> To whom do I speak today?
> The gentle man perishes,
> The bold-faced goes everywhere. . . .
> > To whom do I speak today?
> > When a man should arouse wrath by his evil conduct
> > He stirs all men to mirth, although his iniquity is wicked. . . .

And then this Egyptian Swinburne pours out a lovely eulogy of death:

> Death is before me today
> Like the recovery of a sick man,
> Like going forth into a garden after sickness.
> > Death is before me today
> > Like the odor of myrrh,
> > Like sitting under the sail on a windy day.

Death is before me today
Like the odor of lotus-flowers,
Like sitting on the shore of drunkenness.
　　Death is before me today
　　Like the course of a freshet,
　　Like the return of a man from the war-galley to his house. . . .
Death is before me today
As a man longs to see his home
When he had spent years of captivity.[227]

Saddest of all is a poem engraved upon a slab now in the Leyden Museum, and dating back to 2200 B.C. *Carpe diem*, it sings—snatch the day!

I have heard the words of Imhotep and Hardedef,
Words greatly celebrated as their utterances.
Behold the places thereof!—
Their walls are dismantled,
Their places are no more,
As if they had never been.

None cometh from thence
That he may tell us how they fare; . . .
That he may content our hearts
Until we too depart
To the place whither they have gone.

Encourage thy heart to forget it,
Making it pleasant for thee to follow thy desire
While thou livest.
Put myrrh upon thy head,
And garments upon thee of fine linen,
Imbued with marvelous luxuries,
The genuine things of the gods.

Increase yet more thy delights,
And let not thy heart languish.
Follow thy desire and thy good,
Fashion thy affairs on earth
After the mandates of thine own heart,
Till that day of lamentation come to thee
When the silent-hearted (dead) hears not their lamentation,
Nor he that is in the tomb attends the mourning.

Celebrate the glad day;
Be not weary therein.
Lo, no man taketh his goods with him;
Yea, none returneth again that is gone thither.[228]

This pessimism and scepticism were the result, it may be, of the broken spirit of a nation humiliated and subjected by the Hyksos invaders; they bear the same relation to Egypt that Stoicism and Epicureanism bear to a defeated and enslaved Greece.* In part such literature represents one of those interludes, like our own moral interregnum, in which thought has for a time overcome belief, and men no longer know how or why they should live. Such periods do not endure; hope soon wins the victory over thought; the intellect is put down to its customary menial place, and religion is born again, giving to men the imaginative stimulus apparently indispensable to life and work. We need not suppose that such poems expressed the views of any large number of Egyptians; behind and around the small but vital minority that pondered the problems of life and death in secular and naturalistic terms were millions of simple men and women who remained faithful to the gods, and never doubted that right would triumph, that every earthly pain and grief would be atoned for bountifully in a haven of happiness and peace.

11. Religion

Sky gods—The sun god—Plant gods—Animal gods—Sex gods—
Human gods—Osiris—Isis and Horus—Minor deities—The
priests—Immortality—The "Book of the Dead"—The
"Negative Confession"—Magic—Corruption

For beneath and above everything in Egypt was religion. We find it there in every stage and form from totemism to theology; we see its influence in literature, in government, in art, in everything except morality. And it is not only varied, it is tropically abundant; only in Rome and India shall we find so plentiful a pantheon. We cannot understand the Egyptian—or man—until we study his gods.

In the beginning, said the Egyptian, was the sky; and to the end this and the Nile remained his chief divinities. All these marvelous heavenly bodies were not mere bodies, they were the external forms of mighty spirits,

---

* "Civil war," says Ipuwer, "pays no revenues."[229]

gods whose wills—not always concordant—ordained their complex and varied movements.[229] The sky itself was a vault, across whose vastness a great cow stood, who was the goddess Hathor; the earth lay beneath her feet, and her belly was clad in the beauty of ten thousand stars. Or (for the gods and myths differed from nome to nome) the sky was the god Sibu, lying tenderly upon the earth, which was the goddess Nuit; from their gigantic copulation all things had been born.[230] Constellations and stars might be gods: for example, Sahu and Sopdit (Orion and Sirius) were tremendous deities; Sahu ate gods three times a day regularly. Occasionally some such monster ate the moon, but only for a moment; soon the prayers of men and the anger of the other gods forced the greedy sow to vomit it up again.[231] In this manner the Egyptian populace explained an eclipse of the moon.

The moon was a god, perhaps the oldest of all that were worshiped in Egypt; but in the official theology the greatest of the gods was the sun. Sometimes it was worshiped as the supreme deity Ra or Re, the bright father who fertilized Mother Earth with rays of penetrating heat and light; sometimes it was a divine calf, born anew at every dawn, sailing the sky slowly in a celestial boat, and descending into the west, at evening, like an old man tottering to his grave. Or the sun was the god Horus, taking the graceful form of a falcon, flying majestically across the heavens day after day as if in supervision of his realm, and becoming one of the recurrent symbols of Egyptian religion and royalty. Always Ra, or the sun, was the Creator: at his first rising, seeing the earth desert and bare, he had flooded it with his energizing rays, and all living things—vegetable, animal and human— had sprung pell-mell from his eyes, and been scattered over the world. The earliest men and women, being direct children of Ra, had been perfect and happy; by degrees their descendants had taken to evil ways, and had forfeited this perfection and happiness; whereupon Ra, dissatisfied with his creatures, had destroyed a large part of the human race. Learned Egyptians questioned this popular belief, and asserted on the contrary (like certain Sumerian scholars), that the first men had been like brutes, without articulate speech or any of the arts of life.[232] All in all it was an intelligent mythology, expressing piously man's gratitude to earth and sun.

So exuberant was this piety that the Egyptians worshiped not merely the source, but almost every form, of life. Many plants were sacred to them: the palm-tree that shaded them amid the desert, the spring that gave them drink in the oasis, the grove where they could meet and rest, the sycamore flourishing miraculously in the sand; these were, with excellent reason, holy things, and to the end of his civilization the simple Egyptian brought them offerings of cucumbers, grapes and figs.[233] Even the lowly vegetable found its devotees; and Taine amused himself by showing how the onion that so displeased Bossuet had been a divinity on the banks of the Nile.[234]

More popular were the animal gods; they were so numerous that they filled the Egyptian pantheon like a chattering menagerie. In one nome or another, in one period or another, Egyptians worshiped the bull, the crocodile, the hawk, the cow, the goose, the goat, the ram, the cat, the dog, the chicken, the swallow, the jackal, the serpent, and allowed some of these creatures to roam in the temples with the same freedom that is accorded to the sacred cow in India today.[235] When the gods became human they still retained animal doubles and symbols: Amon was represented as a goose or a ram, Ra as a grasshopper or a bull, Osiris as a bull or a ram, Sebek as a crocodile, Horus as a hawk or falcon, Hathor as a cow, and Thoth, the god of wisdom, as a baboon.[236] Sometimes women were offered to certain of these animals as sexual mates; the bull in particular, as the incarnation of Osiris, received this honor; and at Mendes, says Plutarch, the most beautiful women were offered in coitus to the divine goat.[237] From beginning to end this totemism remained as an essential and native element in Egyptian religion; human gods came to Egypt much later, and probably as gifts from western Asia.[238]

The goat and the bull were especially sacred to the Egyptians as representing sexual creative power; they were not merely symbols of Osiris, but incarnations of him.[239] Often Osiris was depicted with large and prominent organs, as a mark of his supreme power; and models of him in this form, or with a triple phallus, were borne in religious processions by the Egyptians; on certain occasions the women carried such phallic images, and operated them mechanically with strings.[240]* Signs of sex worship appear not only in the many cases in which figures are depicted, on temple reliefs, with erect organs, but in the frequent appearance, in Egyptian symbolism, of the crux ansata—a cross with a handle, as a sign of sexual union and vigorous life.[241]

At last the gods became human—or rather, men became gods. Like the

---

* The curious reader will find again a similar custom in India; cf. Dubois, Hindu Manners, Customs and Ceremonies, Oxford, 1928, p. 595.

deities of Greece, the personal gods of Egypt were merely superior men
and women, made in heroic mould, but composed of bone and muscle,
flesh and blood; they hungered and ate, thirsted and drank, loved and
mated, hated and killed, grew old and died.[242] There was Osiris, for example, god of the beneficent Nile, whose death and resurrection were
celebrated yearly as symbolizing the fall and rise of the river, and perhaps
the decay and growth of the soil. Every Egyptian of the later dynasties
could tell the story of how Set (or Sit), the wicked god of desiccation,
who shriveled up harvests with his burning breath, was angered at Osiris
(the Nile) for extending (with his overflow) the fertility of the earth,
slew him, and reigned in dry majesty over Osiris' kingdom (i.e., the river
once failed to rise), until Horus, brave son of Isis, overcame Set and
banished him; whereafter Osiris, brought back to life by the warmth
of Isis' love, ruled benevolently over Egypt, suppressed cannibalism, established civilization, and then ascended to heaven to reign there endlessly
as a god.[243] It was a profound myth; for history, like Oriental religion, is
dualistic—a record of the conflict between creation and destruction, fertility and desiccation, rejuvenation and exhaustion, good and evil, life and
death.

Profound, too, was the myth of Isis, the Great Mother. She was not
only the loyal sister and wife of Osiris; in a sense she was greater than he,
for—like woman in general—she had conquered death through love. Nor
was she merely the black soil of the Delta, fertilized by the touch of
Osiris-Nile, and making all Egypt rich with her fecundity. She was, above
all, the symbol of that mysterious creative power which had produced the
earth and every living thing, and of that maternal tenderness whereby, at
whatever cost to the mother, the young new life is nurtured to maturity.
She represented in Egypt—as Kali, Ishtar and Cybele represented in
Asia, Demeter in Greece, and Ceres in Rome—the original priority and
independence of the female principle in creation and in inheritance, and
the originative leadership of woman in tilling the earth; for it was Isis
(said the myth) who had discovered wheat and barley growing wild in
Egypt, and had revealed them to Osiris (man).[244] The Egyptians worshiped her with especial fondness and piety, and raised up jeweled images
to her as the Mother of God; her tonsured priests praised her in sonorous
matins and vespers; and in midwinter of each year, coincident with the
annual rebirth of the sun towards the end of our December, the temples

of her divine child, Horus (god of the sun), showed her, in holy effigy, nursing in a stable the babe that she had miraculously conceived. These poetic-philosophic legends and symbols profoundly affected Christian ritual and theology. Early Christians sometimes worshiped before the statues of Isis suckling the infant Horus, seeing in them another form of the ancient and noble myth by which woman (i.e., the female principle), creating all things, becomes at last the Mother of God.[245]

These—Ra (or, as he was called in the South, Amon), Osiris, Isis and Horus—were the greater gods of Egypt. In later days Ra, Amon and another god, Ptah, were combined as three embodiments or aspects of one supreme and triune deity.[246] There were countless lesser divinities: Anubis the jackal, Shu, Tefnut, Nephthys, Ket, Nut; . . . but we must not make these pages a museum of dead gods. Even Pharaoh was a god, always the son of Amon-Ra, ruling not merely by divine right but by divine birth, as a deity transiently tolerating the earth as his home. On his head was the falcon, symbol of Horus and totem of the tribe; from his forehead rose the *uræus* or serpent, symbol of wisdom and life, and communicating magic virtues to the crown.[247] The king was chief-priest of the faith, and led the great processions and ceremonies that celebrated the festivals of the gods. It was through this assumption of divine lineage and powers that he was able to rule so long with so little force.

Hence the priests of Egypt were the necessary props of the throne, and the secret police of the social order. Given a faith of such complexity, a class had to arise adept in magic and ritual, whose skill would make it indispensable in approaching the gods. In effect, though not in law, the office of priest passed down from father to son, and a class grew up which, through the piety of the people and the politic generosity of the kings, became in time richer and stronger than the feudal aristocracy or the royal family itself. The sacrifices offered to the gods supplied the priests with food and drink; the temple buildings gave them spacious homes; the revenues of temple lands and services furnished them with ample incomes; and their exemption from forced labor, military service, and ordinary taxation, left them in an enviable position of prestige and power. They deserved not a little of this power, for they accumulated and preserved the learning of Egypt, educated the youth, and disciplined themselves with rigor and zeal. Herodotus describes them almost with awe:

They are of all men the most excessively attentive to the worship of the gods, and observe the following ceremonies. . . . They wear linen garments, constantly fresh-washed. . . . They are circumcised for the sake of cleanliness, thinking it better to be clean than handsome. They shave their whole body every third day, that neither lice nor any other impurity may be found upon them. . . . They wash themselves in cold water twice every day and twice every night.[248]

What distinguished this religion above everything else was its emphasis on immortality. If Osiris, the Nile, and all vegetation, might rise again, so might man. The amazing preservation of the dead body in the dry soil of Egypt lent some encouragement to this belief, which was to dominate Egyptian faith for thousands of years, and to pass from it, by its own resurrection, into Christianity.[249] The body, Egypt believed, was inhabited by a small replica of itself called the *ka*, and also by a soul that dwelt in the body like a bird flitting among trees. All of these—body, *ka* and soul—survived the appearance of death; they could escape mortality for a time in proportion as the flesh was preserved from decay; but if they came to Osiris clean of all sin they would be permitted to live forever in the "Happy Field of Food"—those heavenly gardens where there would always be abundance and security: judge the harassed penury that spoke in this consoling dream. These Elysian Fields, however, could be reached only through the services of a ferryman, an Egyptian prototype of Charon; and this old gentleman would receive into his boat only such men and women as had done no evil in their lives. Or Osiris would question the dead, weighing each candidate's heart in the scale against a feather to test his truthfulness. Those who failed in this final examination would be condemned to lie forever in their tombs, hungering and thirsting, fed upon by hideous crocodiles, and never coming forth to see the sun.

According to the priests there were clever ways of passing these tests; and they offered to reveal these ways for a consideration. One was to fit up the tomb with food, drink and servants to nourish and help the dead. Another was to fill the tomb with talismans pleasing to the gods: fish, vultures, snakes, above all, the scarab—a beetle which, because it reproduced itself apparently with fertilization, typified the resurrected soul; if these were properly blessed by a priest they would frighten away every assailant, and annihilate every evil. A still better way was to buy the

Book of the Dead,* scrolls for which the priests had written prayers, formulas and charms calculated to appease, even to deceive, Osiris. When, after a hundred vicissitudes and perils, the dead soul at last reached Osiris, it was to address the great Judge in some such manner as this:

O Thou who speedest Time's advancing wing,
Thou dweller in all mysteries of life,
Thou guardian of every word I speak—
Behold, Thou art ashamed of me, thy son;
Thy heart is full of sorrow and of shame,
For that my sins were grievous in the world,
And proud my wickedness and my transgression.
Oh, be at peace with me, oh, be at peace,
And break the barriers that loom between us!
Let all my sins be washed away and fall
Forgotten to the right and left of thee!
Yea, do away with all my wickedness,
And put away the shame that fills thy heart,
That Thou and I henceforth may be at peace.[251]

Or the soul was to declare its innocence of all major sins, in a "Negative Confession" that represents for us one of the earliest and noblest expressions of the moral sense in man:

Hail to Thee, Great God, Lord of Truth and Justice! I have come before Thee, my Master; I have been brought to see thy beauties. . . . I bring unto you Truth. . . . I have not committed iniquity against men. I have not oppressed the poor. . . . I have not laid labor upon any free man beyond that which he wrought for himself. . . . I have not defaulted, I have not committed that which is an abomination to the gods. I have not caused the slave to be ill-treated of his master. I have not starved any man, I have not made any to weep, I have not assassinated any man, . . . I have not committed treason against any. I have not in aught diminished the sup-

---

* A modern title given by Lepsius to some two thousand papyrus rolls found in various tombs, and distinguished by containing formulas to guide the dead. The Egyptian title is *Coming Forth* (from death) *by Day.* They date from the Pyramids, but some are even older. The Egyptians believed that these texts had been composed by the god of wisdom, Thoth; chapter lxiv announced that the book had been found at Heliopolis, and was "in the very handwriting of the god."[250] Josiah made a similar discovery among the Jews; cf. Chap. XII, § v below.

plies of the temple; I have not spoiled the show-bread of the gods.
. . . I have done no carnal act within the sacred enclosure of the
temple. I have not blasphemed. . . . I have not falsified the balance.
I have not taken away milk from the mouths of sucklings. I have . . .
not taken with nets the birds of the gods . . . I am pure. I am pure.
I am pure.[252]

For the most part, however, Egyptian religion had little to say about
morality; the priests were busier selling charms, mumbling incantations,
and performing magic rites than inculcating ethical precepts. Even the
Book of the Dead teaches the faithful that charms blessed by the clergy
will overcome all the obstacles that the deceased soul may encounter on
its way to salvation; and the emphasis is rather on reciting the prayers
than on living the good life. Says one roll: "If this can be known by
the deceased he shall come forth by day"—i.e., rise to eternal life. Amulets
and incantations were designed and sold to cover a multitude of sins and
secure the entrance of the Devil himself into Paradise. At every step the
pious Egyptian had to mutter strange formulas to avert evil and attract
the good. Hear, for example, an anxious mother trying to drive out
"demons" from her child:

> Run out, thou who comest in darkness, who enterest in stealth.
> . . . Comest thou to kiss this child? I will not let thee kiss him.
> . . . Comest thou to take him away? I will not let thee take him
> away from me. I have made his protection against thee out of
> Efet-herb, which makes pain; out of onions, which harm thee; out
> of honey, which is sweet to the living and bitter to the dead; out
> of the evil parts of the Ebdu fish; out of the backbone of the
> perch.[253]

The gods themselves used magic and charms against one another. The
literature of Egypt is full of magicians—of wizards who dry up lakes with
a word, or cause severed limbs to jump back into place, or raise the dead.[254]
The king had magicians to help or guide him; and he himself was believed
to have a magical power to make the rain fall, or the river rise.[255] Life was
full of talismans, spells, divinations; every door had to have a god to
frighten away evil spirits or fortuitous strokes of bad luck. Children born
on the twenty-third of the month of Thoth would surely die soon; those
born on the twentieth of Choiakh would go blind.[256] "Each day and

month," says Herodotus, "is assigned to some particular god; and according to the day on which each person is born, they determine what will befall him, how he will die, and what kind of person he will be."[257] In the end the connection between morality and religion tended to be forgotten; the road to eternal bliss led not through a good life, but through magic, ritual, and generosity to the priests. Let a great Egyptologist express the matter:

> The dangers of the hereafter were now greatly multiplied, and for every critical situation the priest was able to furnish the dead with an effective charm which would infallibly cure him. Besides many charms which enabled the dead to reach the world of the hereafter, there were those which prevented him from losing his mouth, his head, his heart; others which enabled him to remember his name, to breathe, eat, drink, avoid eating his own foulness, to prevent his drinking-water from turning into flame, to turn darkness into light, to ward off all serpents and other hostile monsters, and many others. . . . Thus the earliest moral development which we can trace in the ancient East was suddenly arrested, or at least checked, by the detestable devices of a corrupt priesthood eager for gain.[258]

Such was the state of religion in Egypt when Ikhnaton, poet and heretic, came to the throne, and inaugurated the religious revolution that destroyed the Empire of Egypt.

IV. THE HERETIC KING

The character of Ikhnaton—The new religion—A hymn to the sun — Monotheism — The new dogma — The new art — Reaction—Nofretete—Break-up of the Empire—Death of Ikhnaton

In the year 1380 B.C. Amenhotep III, who had succeeded Thutmose III, died after a life of wordly luxury and display, and was followed by his son Amenhotep IV, destined to be known as Ikhnaton. A profoundly revealing portrait-bust of him, discovered at Tell-el-Amarna, shows a profile of incredible delicacy, a face feminine in softness and poetic in its sensitivity. Large eyelids like a dreamer's, a long, misshapen skull, a frame slender and weak: here was a Shelley called to be a king.

He had hardly come to power when he began to revolt against the religion of Amon, and the practices of Amon's priests. In the great temple at Karnak there was now a large harem, supposedly the concubines of Amon, but in reality serving to amuse the clergy.[258a] The young emperor, whose private life was a model of fidelity, did not approve of this sacred harlotry; the blood of the ram slaughtered in sacrifice to Amon stank in his nostrils; and the traffic of the priests in magic and charms, and their use of the oracle of Amon to support religious obscurantism and political corruption[259] disgusted him to the point of violent protest. "More evil are the words of the priests," he said, "than those which I heard until the year IV" (of his reign); "more evil are they than those which King Amenhotep III heard."[260] His youthful spirit rebelled against the sordidness into which the religion of his people had fallen; he abominated the indecent wealth and lavish ritual of the temples, and the growing hold of a mercenary hierarchy on the nation's life. With a poet's audacity he threw compromise to the winds, and announced bravely that all these gods and ceremonies were a vulgar idolatry, that there was but one god—Aton.

Like Akbar in India thirty centuries later, Ikhnaton saw divinity above all in the sun, in the source of all earthly life and light. We cannot tell whether he had adopted his theory from Syria, and whether Aton was merely a form of Adonis. Of whatever origin, the new god filled the king's soul with delight; he changed his own name from Amenhotep, which contained the name of Amon, to Ikhnaton, meaning "Aton is satisfied"; and helping himself with old hymns, and certain monotheistic poems published in the preceding reign,* he composed passionate songs to Aton, of which this, the longest and the best, is the fairest surviving remnant of Egyptian literature:

> Thy dawning is beautiful in the horizon of the sky,
> O living Aton, Beginning of life.
> When thou risest in the eastern horizon,
> Thou fillest every land with thy beauty.
>
> Thou art beautiful, great, glittering, high above every land,
> Thy rays, they encompass the land, even all that thou hast made.

---

* Under Amenhotep III the architects Suti and Hor had inscribed a monotheistic hymn to the sun upon a stele now in the British Museum.[261] It had long been the custom in Egypt to address the sun-god, Amon-Ra, as the greatest god,[262] but only as the god of Egypt.

Thou art Re, and thou carriest them all away captive;
Thou bindest them by thy love.
Though thou art far away, thy rays are upon earth;
Though thou art on high, thy footprints are the day.

When thou settest in the western horizon of the sky,
The earth is in darkness like the dead;
They sleep in their chambers,
Their heads are wrapped up,
Their nostrils are stopped,
And none seeth the other,
All their things are stolen
Which are under their heads,
And they know it not.
Every lion cometh forth from his den,
All serpents they sting. . . .
The world is in silence,
He that made them resteth in his horizon.

Bright is the earth when thou risest in the horizon.
When thou shinest as Aton by day
Thou drivest away the darkness.
When thou sendest forth thy rays,
The Two Lands are in daily festivity,
Awake and standing upon their feet
When thou hast raised them up.
Their limbs bathed, they take their clothing,
Their arms uplifted in adoration to thy dawning.
In all the world they do their work.

All cattle rest upon their pasturage,
The trees and the plants flourish,
The birds flutter in their marshes,
Their wings uplifted in adoration to thee.
All the sheep dance upon their feet,
All winged things fly,
They live when thou hast shone upon them.

The barks sail upstream and downstream.
Every highway is open because thou dawnest.
The fish in the river leap up before thee.
Thy rays are in the midst of the great green sea.

Creator of the germ in woman,
Maker of seed in man,
Giving life to the son in the body of his mother,
Soothing him that he may not weep,
Nurse even in the womb,
Giver of breath to animate every one that he maketh!
When he cometh forth from the body . . . on the day of his birth,
Thou openest his mouth in speech,
Thou suppliest his necessities.

When the fledgling in the egg chirps in the egg,
Thou givest him breath therein to preserve him alive.
When thou hast brought him together
To the point of bursting the egg,
He cometh forth from the egg,
To chirp with all his might.
He goeth about upon his two feet
When he hath come forth therefrom.

How manifold are thy works!
They are hidden from before us,
O sole god, whose powers no other possesseth.
Thou didst create the earth according to thy heart
While thou wast alone:
Men, all cattle large and small,
All that are upon the earth,
That go about upon their feet;
All that are on high,
That fly with their wings.
The foreign countries, Syria and Kush,
The land of Egypt;
Thou settest every man into his place,
Thou suppliest their necessities. . . .

Thou makest the Nile in the nether world,
Thou bringest it as thou desirest,
To preserve alive the people. . . .

How excellent are thy designs,
O Lord of eternity!
There is a Nile in the sky for the strangers
And for the cattle of every country that go upon their feet. . . .

Thy rays nourish every garden;
When thou risest they live,
They grow by thee.
Thou makest the seasons
In order to create all thy work:
Winter to bring them coolness,
And heat that they may taste thee.
Thou didst make the distant sky to rise therein,
In order to behold all that thou hast made,
Thou alone, shining in the form as living Aton,

Dawning, glittering, going afar and returning.
Thou makest millions of forms
Through thyself alone;
Cities, towns and tribes,
Highways and rivers.
All eyes see thee before them,
For thou art Aton of the day over the earth. . . .

Thou art in my heart,
There is no other that knoweth thee
Save thy son Ikhnaton.
Thou hast made him wise
In thy designs and in thy might.
The world is in thy hand,
Even as thou hast made them.
When thou hast risen they live,
When thou settest they die;
For thou art length of life of thyself,
Men live through thee,
While their eyes are upon thy beauty
Until thou settest.
All labor is put away
When thou settest in the west. . . .

Thou didst establish the world,
And raised them up for thy son. . . .
Ikhnaton, whose life is long;
And for the chief royal wife, his beloved,
Mistress of the Two Lands,
Nefer-nefru-aton, Nofretete,
Living and flourishing for ever and ever.[263]

This is not only one of the great poems of history, it is the first out-standing expression of monotheism—seven hundred years before Isaiah.* Perhaps, as Breasted[265] suggests, this conception of one sole god was a reflex of the unification of the Mediterranean world under Egypt by Thutmose III. Ikhnaton conceives his god as belonging to all nations equally, and even names other countries before his own as in Aton's care; this was an astounding advance upon the old tribal deities. Note the vitalistic conception: Aton is to be found not in battles and victories but in flowers and trees, in all forms of life and growth; Aton is the joy that causes the young sheep to "dance upon their legs," and the birds to "flutter in their marshes." Nor is the god a person limited to human form; the real divinity is the creative and nourishing *heat* of the sun; the flaming glory of the rising or setting orb is but an emblem of that ultimate power. Nevertheless, because of its omnipresent, fertilizing beneficence, the sun becomes to Ikhnaton also the "Lord of love," the tender nurse that "creates the man-child in woman," and "fills the Two Lands of Egypt with love." So at last Aton grows by symbolism into a solicitous father, compassionate and tender; not, like Yahveh, a Lord of Hosts, but a god of gentleness and peace.[266]

It is one of the tragedies of history that Ikhnaton, having achieved his elevating vision of universal unity, was not satisfied to let the noble quality of his new religion slowly win the hearts of men. He was unable to think of his truth in relative terms; the thought came to him that other forms of belief and worship were indecent and intolerable. Suddenly he gave orders that the names of all gods but Aton should be erased and chiseled from every public inscription in Egypt; he mutilated his father's name from a hundred monuments to cut from it the word *Amon*; he declared all creeds but his own illegal, and commanded that all the old temples should be closed. He abandoned Thebes as unclean, and built for himself a beautiful new capital at Akhetaton—"City of the Horizon of Aton."

Rapidly Thebes decayed as the offices and emoluments of government were taken from it, and Akhetaton became a rich metropolis, busy with fresh building and a Renaissance of arts liberated from the priestly bondage of tradition. The joyous spirit expressed in the new religion passed over into its art. At Tell-el-Amarna, a modern village on the site of Akhetaton,

---

* The obvious similarity of this hymn to Psalm CIV leaves little doubt of Egyptian influence upon the Hebrew poet.[264]

Sir William Flinders Petrie unearthed a beautiful pavement, adorned with birds, fishes and other animals painted with the most delicate grace.[207] Ikhnaton forbade the artists to make images of Aton, on the lofty ground that the true god has no form;[208] for the rest he left art free, merely asking his favorite artists, Bek, Auta and Nutmose, to describe things as they saw them, and to forget the conventions of the priests. They took him at his word, and represented him as a youth of gentle, almost timid, face, and strangely dolichocephalic head. Taking their lead from his vitalistic conception of deity, they painted every form of plant and animal life with loving detail, and with a perfection hardly surpassed in any other place or time.[209] For a while art, which in every generation knows the pangs of hunger and obscurity, flourished in abundance and happiness.

Had Ikhnaton been a mature mind he would have realized that the change which he had proposed from a superstitious polytheism deeply rooted in the needs and habits of the people to a naturalistic monotheism that subjected imagination to intelligence, was too profound to be effected in a little time; he would have made haste slowly, and softened the transition with intermediate steps. But he was a poet rather than a philosopher; like Shelley announcing the demise of Yahveh to the bishops of Oxford, he grasped for the Absolute, and brought the whole structure of Egypt down upon his head.

At one blow he had dispossessed and alienated a wealthy and powerful priesthood, and had forbidden the worship of deities made dear by long tradition and belief. When he had *Amon* hacked out from his father's name it seemed to his people a blasphemous impiety; nothing could be more vital to them than the honoring of the ancestral dead. He had underestimated the strength and pertinacity of the priests, and he had exaggerated the capacity of the people to understand a natural religion. Behind the scenes the priests plotted and prepared; and in the seclusion of their homes the populace continued to worship their ancient and innumerable gods. A hundred crafts that had depended upon the temples muttered in secret against the heretic. Even in his palace his ministers and generals hated him, and prayed for his death, for was he not allowing the Empire to fall to pieces in his hands?

Meanwhile the young poet lived in simplicity and trust. He had seven daughters, but no son; and though by law he might have sought an heir by his secondary wives, he would not, but preferred to remain faithful to Nofretete. A little ornament has come down to us that shows him embracing the Queen; he allowed artists to depict him riding in a chariot through the streets, engaged in pleasantries with his wife and children; on ceremonial occasions the Queen sat beside him and held his hand, while their daughters frolicked at the foot of the throne. He spoke of his wife as "Mistress of his Happiness, at hearing whose voice the King rejoices"; and for an oath he used the phrase, "As my heart is happy in the Queen and her children."[270] It was a tender interlude in Egypt's epic of power.

Into this simple happiness came alarming messages from Syria.* The dependencies of Egypt in the Near East were being invaded by Hittites and other neighboring tribes; the governors appointed by Egypt pleaded for immediate reinforcements. Ikhnaton hesitated; he was not quite sure that the right of conquest warranted him in keeping these states in subjection to Egypt; and he was loath to send Egyptians to die on distant fields for so uncertain a cause. When the dependencies saw that they were dealing with a saint, they deposed their Egyptian governors, quietly stopped all payment of tribute, and became to all effects free. Almost in a moment Egypt ceased to be a vast Empire, and shrank back into a little state. Soon the Egyptian treasury, which had for a century depended upon foreign tribute as its mainstay, was empty; domestic taxation had fallen to a minimum, and the working of the gold mines had stopped. Internal administration was in chaos. Ikhnaton found himself penniless and friendless in a world that had seemed all his own. Every colony was in revolt, and every power in Egypt was arrayed against him, waiting for his fall.

He was hardly thirty when, in 1362 B.C., he died, broken with the realization of his failure as a ruler, and the unworthiness of his race.

---

* In 1893 Sir William Flinders Petrie discovered at Tell-el-Amarna over three hundred and fifty cuneiform letter-tablets, most of which were appeals for aid addressed to Ikhnaton by the East.

V. DECLINE AND FALL

Tutenkhamon—The labors of Rameses II—The wealth of the clergy — The poverty of the people — The conquest of Egypt—Summary of Egyptian contributions to civilization

Two years after his death his son-in-law, Tutenkhamon, a favorite of the priests, ascended the throne. He changed the name Tutenkhaton which his father-in-law had given him, returned the capital to Thebes, made his peace with the powers of the Church, and announced to a rejoicing people the restoration of the ancient gods. The words *Aton* and *Ikhnaton* were effaced from all the monuments, the priests forbade the name of the heretic king to pass any man's lips, and the people referred to him as "The Great Criminal." The names that Ikhnaton had removed were recarved upon the monuments, and the feast-days that he had abolished were renewed. Everything was as before.

For the rest Tutenkhamon reigned without distinction; the world would hardly have heard of him had not unprecedented treasures been found in his grave. After him a doughty general, Harmhab, marched his armies up and down the coast, restoring Egypt's external power and internal peace. Seti I wisely reaped the fruits of renewed order and wealth, built the Hypostyle Hall at Karnak,[272] began to cut a mighty temple into the cliffs at Abu Simbel, commemorated his grandeur in magnificent reliefs, and had the pleasure of lying for thousands of years in one of the most ornate of Egypt's tombs.

At this point the romantic Rameses II, last of the great Pharaohs, mounted the throne. Seldom has history known so picturesque a monarch. Handsome and brave, he added to his charms by his boyish consciousness of them; and his exploits in war, which he never tired of recording, were equaled only by his achievements in love. After brushing aside a brother who had inopportune rights to the throne, he sent an expedition to Nubia to tap the gold mines there and replenish the treasury of Egypt; and with the resultant funds he undertook the reconquest of the Asiatic provinces, which had again rebelled. Three years he gave to recovering Palestine; then he pushed on, met a great army of the Asiatic allies at Kadesh (1288 B.C.), and turned defeat into victory by his courage and leadership. It may have been as a result of these campaigns that a considerable number of Jews were brought into Egypt, as slaves or as immigrants; and Rameses II is believed by some to have been the Pharaoh of the Exodus.[273] He had his victories commemorated, without undue impartiality, on half a hundred walls, commissioned a poet to celebrate him in epic verse, and rewarded himself with several hundred wives. When he died he left one hundred sons and fifty daughters to testify to his quality by their number and their proportion. He married several of his daughters, so that they too might have splendid children. His offspring were so numerous that they constituted for four hundred years a special class in Egypt, from which, for over a century, her rulers were chosen.

He deserved these consolations, for he seems to have ruled Egypt well. He built so lavishly that half the surviving edifices of Egypt are ascribed to his reign. He completed the main hall at Karnak, added to the temple of Luxor, raised his own vast shrine, the Ramesseum, west of the river, finished the great mountain-sanctuary at Abu Simbel, and scattered colossi of himself throughout the land. Commerce flourished under him, both across the Isthmus of Suez and on the Mediterranean. He built another canal from the Nile to the Red Sea, but the shifting sands filled it up soon after his death. He yielded up his life in 1225 B.C., aged ninety, after one of the most remarkable reigns of history.

Only one human power in Egypt had excelled his, and that was the clergy: here, as everywhere in history, ran the endless struggle between church and state. Throughout his reign and those of his immediate successors, the spoils of every war, and the lion's share of taxes from the conquered provinces, went to the temples and the priests. These reached the zenith of their wealth under Rameses III. They possessed at that time 107,000 slaves—one-thirtieth of the population of Egypt; they held 750,000 acres—one-seventh of all the arable land; they owned 500,000 head of cattle; they received the revenues from 169 towns in Egypt and Syria; and all this property was exempt from taxation.[274] The generous or timorous Rameses III showered unparalleled gifts upon the priests of Amon, including 32,000 kilograms of gold and a million kilograms of silver;[275] every year he gave them 185,000 sacks of corn. When the time came to pay the workmen employed by the state he found his treasury empty.[276] More and more the people starved in order that the gods might eat.

Under such a policy it was only a matter of time before the kings would become the servants of the priests. In the reign of the last Ramessid king the High Priest of Amon usurped the throne and ruled as openly supreme; the Empire became a stagnant theocracy in which architecture and superstition flourished, and every other element in the national life decayed. Omens were manipulated to give a divine sanction to every decision of the clergy. The most vital forces of Egypt were sucked dry by the thirst of the gods at the very time when foreign invaders were preparing to sweep down upon all this concentrated wealth.

For meanwhile on every frontier trouble brewed. The prosperity of the country had come in part from its strategic place on the main line of Mediterranean trade; its metals and wealth had given it mastery over Libya on the west, and over Phœnicia, Syria and Palestine on the north and east. But now at the other end of this trade route—in Assyria, Babylon and Persia—new nations were growing to maturity and power, were strengthening themselves with invention and enterprise, and were daring to compete in commerce and industry with the self-satisfied and pious Egyptians. The Phœnicians were perfecting the trireme galley, and with it were gradually wresting from Egypt the control of the sea. The Dorians and Achæans had conquered Crete and the Ægean (ca. 1400 B.C.), and were establishing a commercial empire of their own; trade moved less and less in slow caravans over the difficult and robber-infested mountains and deserts of the Near East; it moved more and more, at less expense and with less loss, in ships that passed through the Black Sea and the Ægean to Troy, Crete and Greece, at last to Carthage, Italy and Spain. The nations along the northern shores of the Mediterranean ripened and blossomed, the nations on the southern shores faded and rotted away. Egypt lost her trade, her gold, her power, her art, at last even her pride; one by one her rivals crept down upon her soil, harassed and conquered her, and laid her waste.

In 954 B.C. the Libyans came in from the western hills, and laid about them with fury; in 722 the Ethiopians entered from the south, and avenged their ancient slavery; in 674 the Assyrians swept down from the north and subjected priest-ridden Egypt to tribute. For a time Psamtik, Prince of Saïs, repelled the invaders, and brought Egypt together again under his leadership. During his long reign, and those of his successors, came the "Saïte Revival" of Egyptian art: the architects and sculptors, poets and scientists of Egypt gathered up the technical and esthetic traditions of their schools, and prepared to lay them at the feet of the Greeks. But in 525 B.C. the Persians under Cambyses crossed Suez, and again put an end to Egyptian independence. In 332 B.C. Alexander sallied out of Asia, and

made Egypt a province of Macedon.* In 48 B.C. Cæsar arrived to capture
Egypt's new capital, Alexandria, and to give to Cleopatra the son and heir
whom they vainly hoped to crown as the unifying monarch of the greatest
empires of antiquity.[277] In 30 B.C. Egypt became a province of Rome, and
disappeared from history.

For a time it flourished again when saints peopled the desert, and Cyril
dragged Hypatia to her death in the streets (415 A.D.); and again when the
Moslems conquered it (ca. A.D. 650), built Cairo with the ruins of Memphis, and filled it with bright-domed mosques and citadels. But these were
alien cultures not really Egypt's own, and they too passed away. Today
there is a place called Egypt, but the Egyptian people are not masters
there; long since they have been broken by conquest, and merged in language and marriage with their Arab conquerors; their cities know only the
authority of Moslems and Englishmen, and the feet of weary pilgrims who
travel thousands of miles to find that the Pyramids are merely heaps of
stones. Perhaps greatness could grow there again if Asia should once more
become rich, and make Egypt the half-way house of the planet's trade.
But of the morrow, as Lorenzo sang, there is no certainty; and today the
only certainty is decay. On all sides gigantic ruins, monuments and tombs,
memorials of a savage and titanic energy; on all sides poverty and desolation, and the exhaustion of an ancient blood. And on all sides the hostile,
engulfing sands, blown about forever by hot winds, and grimly resolved
to cover everything in the end.

Nevertheless the sands have destroyed only the body of ancient Egypt;
its spirit survives in the lore and memory of our race. The improvement
of agriculture, metallurgy, industry and engineering; the apparent invention of glass and linen, of paper and ink, of the calendar and the clock, of
geometry and the alphabet; the refinement of dress and ornament, of furniture and dwellings, of society and life; the remarkable development of
orderly and peaceful government, of census and post, of primary and
secondary education, even of technical training for office and administration; the advancement of writing and literature, of science and medicine;
the first clear formulation known to us of individual and public conscience, the first cry for social justice, the first widespread monogamy, the
first monotheism, the first essays in moral philosophy; the elevation of

---

* The history of classical Egyptian civilization under the Ptolemies and the Cæsars belongs to a later volume.

architecture, sculpture and the minor arts to a degree of excellence and power never (so far as we know) reached before, and seldom equaled since: these contributions were not lost, even when their finest exemplars were buried under the desert, or overthrown by some convulsion of the globe.* Through the Phœnicians, the Syrians and the Jews, through the Cretans, the Greeks and the Romans, the civilization of Egypt passed down to become part of the cultural heritage of mankind. The effect or remembrance of what Egypt accomplished at the very dawn of history has influence in every nation and every age. "It is even possible," as Faure has said, "that Egypt, through the solidarity, the unity, and the disciplined variety of its artistic products, through the enormous duration and the sustained power of its effort, offers the spectacle of the greatest civilization that has yet appeared on the earth."[278] We shall do well to equal it.

---

* Thebes was finally destroyed by an earthquake in 27 B.C.

CHAPTER IX

Babylonia

I. FROM HAMMURABI TO NEBUCHADREZZAR

*Babylonian contributions to modern civilization—The Land be-
tween the Rivers — Hammurabi — His capital — The Kassite
Domination—The Amarna letters—The Assyrian Conquest—Nebuchadrezzar—Babylon in the days of
its glory*

CIVILIZATION, like life, is a perpetual struggle with death. And as life maintains itself only by abandoning old, and recasting itself in younger and fresher, forms, so civilization achieves a precarious survival by changing its habitat or its blood. It moved from Ur to Babylon and Judea, from Babylon to Nineveh, from these to Persepolis, Sardis and Miletus, and from these, Egypt and Crete to Greece and Rome.

No one looking at the site of ancient Babylon today would suspect that these hot and dreary wastes along the Euphrates were once the rich and powerful capital of a civilization that almost created astronomy, added richly to the progress of medicine, established the science of language, prepared the first great codes of law, taught the Greeks the rudiments of mathematics, physics and philosophy,[1] gave the Jews the mythology which they gave to the world, and passed on to the Arabs part of that scientific and architectural lore with which they aroused the dormant soul of medieval Europe. Standing before the silent Tigris and Euphrates one finds it hard to believe that they are the same rivers that watered Sumeria and Akkad, and nourished the Hanging Gardens of Babylon.

In some ways they are not the same rivers: not only because "one never steps twice into the same stream," but because these old rivers have long since remade their beds along new courses,[2] and "mow with their scythes of whiteness"[3] other shores. As in Egypt the Nile, so here the Tigris and the Euphrates provided, for thousands of miles, an avenue of commerce and—in their southern reaches—springtime inundations that helped the peasant to fertilize his soil. For rain comes to Babylonia only in the winter months; from May to November it comes not at all; and the earth, but for the overflow of the rivers, would be as arid as northern Mesopotamia was then and is today. Through the abundance of the rivers and the toil of many generations of men, Babylonia became the Eden of Semitic legend, the garden and granary of western Asia.*

Historically and ethnically Babylonia was a product of the union of the Akkadians and the Sumerians. Their mating generated the Babylonian type, in which the Akkadian Semitic strain proved dominant; their warfare ended in the triumph of Akkad, and the establishment of Babylon as the capital of all lower Mesopotamia. At the outset of this history stands the powerful figure of Hammurabi (2123-2081 B.C.) conqueror and law-giver through a reign of forty-three years. Primeval seals and inscriptions transmit him to us partially—a youth full of fire and genius, a very whirl-wind in battle, who crushes all rebels, cuts his enemies into pieces, marches over inaccessible mountains, and never loses an engagement. Under him the petty warring states of the lower valley were forced into unity and peace, and disciplined into order and security by an historic code of laws.

The Code of Hammurabi was unearthed at Susa in 1902, beautifully engraved upon a diorite cylinder that had been carried from Babylon to Elam (ca. 1100 B.C.) as a trophy of war.† Like that of Moses, this legis-lation was a gift from Heaven, for one side of the cylinder shows the King receiving the laws from Shamash, the Sun-god himself. The Prologue is almost in Heaven:

> When the lofty Anu, King of the Anunaki and Bel, Lord of Heaven and Earth, he who determines the destiny of the land, committed the rule of all mankind to Marduk; . . . when they pronounced the lofty name of Babylon; when they made it famous among the quarters of the world and in its midst established an everlasting kingdom whose foundations were firm as heaven and earth—at that time Anu and Bel called me, Hammurabi, the ex-alted prince, the worshiper of the gods, to cause justice to prevail in the land, to destroy the wicked and the evil, *to prevent the strong from oppressing the weak, . . . to enlighten the land and to further the welfare of the people.* Hammurabi, the governor named by Bel, am I, who brought about plenty and abundance; who made

---

* The Euphrates is one of the four rivers which, according to *Genesis* (ii, 14), flowed through Paradise.
† It is now in the Louvre.

everything for Nippur and Durilu complete; . . . who gave life to the city of Uruk; who supplied water in abundance to its inhabitants; . . . who made the city of Borsippa beautiful; . . . who stored up grain for the mighty Urash; . . . who helped his people in time of need; who establishes in security their property in Babylon; the governor of the people, *the servant*, whose deeds are pleasing to Anunit.[4]

The words here arbitrarily underlined have a modern ring; one would not readily attribute them to an Oriental "despot" 2100 B.C., or suspect that the laws that they introduce were based upon Sumerian prototypes now six thousand years old. This ancient origin combined with Babylonian circumstance to give the Code a composite and heterogeneous character. It begins with compliments to the gods, but takes no further notice of them in its astonishingly secular legislation. It mingles the most enlightened laws with the most barbarous punishments, and sets the primitive *lex talionis* and trial by ordeal alongside elaborate judicial procedures and a discriminating attempt to limit marital tyranny.[5] All in all, these 285 laws, arranged almost scientifically under the headings of Personal Property, Real Estate, Trade and Business, the Family, Injuries, and Labor, form a code more advanced and civilized than that of Assyria a thousand and more years later, and in many respects "as good as that of a modern European state."[6]* There are few words finer in the history of law than those with which the great Babylonian brings his legislation to a close:

The righteous laws which Hammurabi, the wise king, established, and (by which) he gave the land stable support and pure government. . . . I am the guardian governor. . . . In my bosom I carried the people of the land of Sumer and Akkad; . . . in my wisdom I restrained them, that the strong might not oppress the weak, and that they should give justice to the orphan and the widow. . . . Let any oppressed man, who has a cause, come before my image as king of righteousness! Let him read the inscription on my monument! Let him give heed to my weighty words! And may my monument enlighten him as to his cause, and may he understand his case! May he set his heart at ease, (exclaiming:) "Ham-

* The "Mosaic Code" apparently borrows from it, or derives with it from a common original. The habit of stamping a legal contract with an official seal goes back to Hammurabi.[7]

murabi indeed is a ruler who is like a real father to his people; . . . he has established prosperity for his people for all time, and given a pure government to the land." . . .

In the days that are yet to come, for all future time, may the king who is in the land observe the words of righteousness which I have written upon my monument![8]

This unifying legislation was but one of Hammurabi's accomplishments. At his command a great canal was dug between Kish and the Persian Gulf, thereby irrigating a large area of land, and protecting the cities of the south from the destructive floods which the Tigris had been wont to visit upon them. In another inscription which has found its devious way from his time to ours he tells us proudly how he gave water (that noble and unappreciated commonplace, which was once a luxury), security and government to many tribes. Even through the boasting (an honest mannerism of the Orient) we hear the voice of statesmanship.

> When Anu and Enlil (the gods of Uruk and Nippur) gave me the lands of Sumer and Akkad to rule, and they entrusted this sceptre to me, I dug the canal *Hammurabi-nukhush-nishi* (Hammurabi-the-Abundance-of-the-People), which bringeth copious water to the land of Sumer and Akkad. Its banks on both sides I turned into cultivated ground; I heaped up piles of grain, I provided unfailing water for the lands. . . . The scattered people I gathered; with pasturage and water I provided them; I pastured them with abundance, and settled them in peaceful dwellings.[9]

Despite the secular quality of his laws Hammurabi was clever enough to gild his authority with the approval of the gods. He built temples as well as forts, and coddled the clergy by constructing at Babylon a gigantic sanctuary for Marduk and his wife (the national deities), and a massive granary to store up wheat for gods and priests. These and similar gifts were an astute investment, from which he expected steady returns in the awed obedience of the people. From their taxes he financed the forces of law and order, and had enough left over to beautify his capital. Palaces and temples rose on every hand; a bridge spanned the Euphrates to let the city spread itself along both banks; ships manned with ninety men plied up and down the river. Two thousand years before Christ Babylon was already one of the richest cities that history had yet known.*

The people were of Semitic appearance, dark in hair and features, masculinely bearded for the most part, and occasionally bewigged. Both sexes wore the hair long; sometimes even the men dangled curls; frequently the men, as well as the women, disguised themselves with perfumes. The common dress for both sexes was a white linen tunic reaching to the feet; in the women it left one shoulder bare, in the men it was augmented with mantle and robe. As wealth grew, the people developed a taste for color, and dyed for themselves garments of blue on red, or red on blue, in stripes, circles, checks or dots. The bare feet of the Sumerian period gave way to shapely sandals, and the male head, in Hammurabi's time, was swathed in turbans. The women wore necklaces, bracelets and amulets, and strings of beads in their carefully coiffured hair; the men flourished walking-sticks with carved heads, and carried on their girdles the prettily designed seals with which they attested their letters and documents. The priests wore tall conical caps to conceal their humanity.[10]

It is almost a law of history that the same wealth that generates a civilization announces its decay. For wealth produces ease as well as art; it softens a people to the ways of luxury and peace, and invites invasion from stronger arms and hungrier mouths. On the eastern boundary of the new state a hardy tribe of mountaineers, the Kassites, looked with envy upon the riches of Babylon. Eight years after Hammurabi's death they inundated the land, plundered it, retreated, raided it again and again, and finally settled down in it as conquerors and rulers; this is the normal origin of aristocracies. They were of non-Semitic stock, perhaps descendants of European immigrants from neolithic days; their victory over Semitic Babylon represented one more swing of the racial pendulum in western Asia. For several centuries Babylonia lived in an ethnic and political chaos that put a stop to the development of science and art.[11] We have a kaleidoscope of this stifling disorder in the "Amarna" letters, in which the kinglets of Babylonia and Syria, having sent modest tribute to imperial Egypt after the victories of Thutmose III, beg for aid against rebels and invaders, and quarrel about the value of the gifts that they exchange

---

* "In all essentials Babylonia, in the time of Hammurabi, and even earlier, had reached a pitch of material civilization which has never since been surpassed in Asia."—Christopher Dawson, *Enquiries into Religion and Culture*, New York, 1933, p. 107. Perhaps we should except the ages of Xerxes I in Persia, Ming Huang in China, and Akbar in India.

with the disdainful Amenhotep III and the absorbed and negligent Ikhnaton.*

The Kassites were expelled after almost six centuries of rule as disruptive as the similar sway of the Hyksos in Egypt. The disorder continued for four hundred years more under obscure Babylonian rulers, whose poly-syllabic roster might serve as an *obbligato* to Gray's *Elegy*,† until the rising power of Assyria in the north stretched down its hand and brought Babylonia under the kings of Nineveh. When Babylon rebelled, Sennach-erib destroyed it almost completely; but the genial despotism of Esar-haddon restored it to prosperity and culture. The rise of the Medes weakened Assyria, and with their help Nabopolassar liberated Babylonia, set up an independent dynasty, and dying, bequeathed this second Baby-lonian kingdom to his son Nebuchadrezzar II, villain of the vengeful and legendary *Book of Daniel*.[13] Nebuchadrezzar's inaugural address to Marduk, god-in-chief of Babylon, reveals a glimpse of an Oriental mon-arch's aims and character:

> As my precious life do I love thy sublime appearance! Outside of my city Babylon, I have not selected among all settlements any dwelling. . . . At thy command, O merciful Marduk, may the house that I have built endure forever, may I be satiated with its splendor, attain old age therein, with abundant offspring, and receive therein tribute of the kings of all regions, from all mankind.[14]

He lived almost up to his hopes, for though illiterate and not unques-tionably sane, he became the most powerful ruler of his time in the Near East, and the greatest warrior, statesman and builder in all the suc-cession of Babylonian kings after Hammurabi himself. When Egypt conspired with Assyria to reduce Babylonia to vassalage again, Nebuchad-

---

* The Amarna letters are dreary reading, full of adulation, argument, entreaty and com-plaint. Hear, e.g., Burraburiash II, King of Karduniash (in Mesopotamia), writing to Amenhotep III about an exchange of royal gifts in which Burraburiash seems to have been worsted: "Ever since my mother and thy father sustained friendly relations with one another, they exchanged valuable presents; and the choicest desire, each of the other, they did not refuse. Now my brother (Amenhotep) has sent me as a present (only) two *manehs* of gold. But send me as much gold as thy father; and if it be less, let it be half of what thy father would send. Why didst thou send me only two *manehs* of gold?"[12]

† Marduk-shapik-zeri, Ninurta-nadin-sham, Enlil-nadin-apli, Itti-Marduk-balatu, Marduk-shapik-zer-mati, etc. Doubtless our own full names, linked with such hyphens, would make a like cacophony to alien ears.

rezzar met the Egyptian hosts at Carchemish (on the upper reaches of the Euphrates), and almost annihilated them. Palestine and Syria then fell easily under his sway, and Babylonian merchants controlled all the trade that flowed across western Asia from the Persian Gulf to the Mediterranean Sea.

Nebuchadrezzar spent the tolls of this trade, the tributes of these subjects, and the taxes of his people, in beautifying his capital and assuaging the hunger of the priests. "Is not this the great Babylon that I built?"[15] He resisted the temptation to be merely a conqueror; he sallied forth occasionally to teach his subjects the virtues of submission, but for the most part he stayed at home, making Babylon the unrivaled capital of the Near East, the largest and most magnificent metropolis of the ancient world.[16] Nabopolassar had laid plans for the reconstruction of the city; Nebuchadrezzar used his long reign of forty-three years to carry them to completion. Herodotus, who saw Babylon a century and a half later, described it as "standing in a spacious plain," and surrounded by a wall fifty-six miles in length,[17] so broad that a four-horse chariot could be driven along the top, and enclosing an area of some two hundred square miles.[18]* Through the center of the town ran the palm-fringed Euphrates, busy with commerce and spanned by a handsome bridge.[19]† Practically all the better buildings were of brick, for stone was rare in Mesopotamia; but the bricks were often faced with enameled tiles of brilliant blue, yellow or white, adorned with animal and other figures in glazed relief, which remain to this day supreme in their kind. Nearly all the bricks so far recovered from the site of Babylon bear the proud inscription: "I am Nebuchadrezzar, King of Babylon."[21]

Approaching the city the traveler saw first—at the crown of a very mountain of masonry—an immense and lofty *ziggurat*, rising in seven stages of gleaming enamel to a height of 650 feet, crowned with a shrine containing a massive table of solid gold, and an ornate bed on which, each night, some woman slept to await the pleasure of the god.[22] This structure, taller than the pyramids of Egypt, and surpassing in height all but the latest of modern buildings, was probably the "Tower of Babel" of Hebraic myth, the many-storied audacity of a people who did not know

---

* Probably this included not only the city proper but a large agricultural hinterland within the walls, designed to provide the teeming metropolis with sustenance in time of siege.

† If we may trust Diodorus Siculus, a tunnel fifteen feet wide and twelve feet high connected the two banks.[20]

Yahveh, and whom the God of Hosts was supposed to have confounded with a multiplicity of tongues.* South of the *ziggurat* stood the gigantic Temple of Marduk, tutelary deity of Babylon. Around and below this temple the city spread itself out in a few wide and brilliant avenues, crossed by crowded canals and narrow winding streets alive, no doubt, with traffic and bazaars, and Orientally odorous with garbage and humanity. Connecting the temples was a spacious "Sacred Way," paved with asphalt-covered bricks overlaid with flags of limestone and red *breccia*; over this the gods might pass without muddying their feet. This broad avenue was flanked with walls of colored tile, on which stood out, in low relief, one hundred and twenty brightly enameled lions, snarling to keep the impious away. At one end of the Sacred Way rose the magnificent Ishtar Gate, a massive double portal of resplendent tiles, adorned with enameled flowers and animals of admirable color, vitality, and line.†

Six hundred yards north of the "Tower of Babel" rose a mound called Kasr, on which Nebuchadrezzar built the most imposing of his palaces. At its center stood his principal dwelling-place, the walls of finely made yellow brick, the floors of white and mottled sandstone; reliefs of vivid blue glaze adorned the surfaces, and gigantic basalt lions guarded the entrance. Nearby, supported on a succession of superimposed circular colonnades, were the famous Hanging Gardens, which the Greeks included among the Seven Wonders of the World. The gallant Nebuchadrezzar had built them for one of his wives, the daughter of Cyaxares, King of the Medes; this princess, unaccustomed to the hot sun and dust of Babylon, pined for the verdure of her native hills. The topmost terrace was covered with rich soil to the depth of many feet, providing space and nourishment not merely for varied flowers and plants, but for the largest and most deep-rooted trees. Hydraulic engines concealed in the columns and manned by shifts of slaves carried water from the Euphrates to the highest tier of the gardens.[24] Here, seventy-five feet above the ground, in the cool shade of tall trees, and surrounded by exotic shrubs and fragrant flowers, the ladies of the royal harem walked unveiled, secure from the common eye; while, in the plains and streets below, the common man and woman ploughed, wove, built, carried burdens, and reproduced their kind.

---

* *Babel*, however, does not mean confusion or babble, as the legend supposes; as used in the word *Babylon* it meant the Gate of God.[23]

† A reconstruction of the Ishtar Gate can be seen in the Vorderasiatisches Museum, Berlin.

II. THE TOILERS

*Hunting — Tillage — Food — Industry — Transport — The perils
of commerce — Money-lenders — Slaves*

Part of the country was still wild and dangerous; snakes wandered in
the thick grass, and the kings of Babylonia and Assyria made it their royal
sport to hunt in hand-to-hand conflict the lions that prowled in the woods,
posed placidly for artists, but fled timidly at the nearer approach of men.
Civilization is an occasional and temporary interruption of the jungle.

Most of the soil was tilled by tenants or by slaves; some of it by peasant
proprietors.[25] In the earlier centuries the ground was broken up with stone
hoes, as in neolithic tillage; a seal dating some 1400 B.C. is our earliest
representation of the plough in Babylonia. Probaby this ancient and honorable tool had already a long history behind it in the Land between the
Rivers; and yet it was modern enough, for though it was drawn by oxen
in the manner of our fathers, it had, attached to the plough, as in Sumeria, a
tube through which the seed was sown in the manner of our children.[26]
The waters of the rising rivers were not allowed to flood the land as in
Egypt; on the contrary, every farm was protected from the inundation by
ridges of earth, some of which can still be seen today. The overflow was
guided into a complex network of canals, or stored into reservoirs, from
which it was sluiced into the fields as needed, or raised over the ridges by
shadufs—buckets lifted and lowered on a pivoted and revolving pole. Nebuchadrezzar distinguished his reign by building many canals, and gathering the surplus waters of the overflow into a reservoir, one hundred and
forty miles in circumference, which nourished by its outlets vast areas of
land.[27] Ruins of these canals can be seen in Mesopotamia today, and—as if
further to bind the quick and the dead—the primitive *shaduf* is still in use in
the valleys of the Euphrates and the Loire.[28]

So watered, the land produced a variety of cereals and pulses, great orchards
of fruits and nuts, and above all, the date; from this beneficent concoction
of sun and soil the Babylonians made bread, honey, cake and other delicacies; they mixed it with meal to make one of their most sustaining foods;
and to encourage its reproduction they shook the flowers of the male palm
over those of the female.[29] From Mesopotamia the grape and the olive
were introduced into Greece and Rome and thence into western Europe;
from nearby Persia came the peach; and from the shores of the Black Sea
Lucullus brought the cherry-tree to Rome. Milk, so rare in the distant
Orient, now became one of the staple foods of the Near East. Meat was
rare and costly, but fish from the great streams found their way into the

poorest mouths. And in the evening, when the peasant might have been disturbed by thoughts on life and death, he quieted memory and anticipation
with wine pressed from the date, or beer brewed from the corn.

Meanwhile others pried into the earth, struck oil, and mined copper, lead,
iron, silver and gold. Strabo tells how what he calls "naphtha or liquid asphalt" was taken from the soil of Mesopotamia then as now, and how Alexander, hearing that this was a kind of water that burned, tested the report
incredulously by covering a boy with the strange fluid and igniting him
with a torch.[30] Tools, which had still been of stone in the days of Hammurabi, began, at the turn of the last millennium before Christ, to be made of
bronze, then of iron; and the art of casting metal appeared. Textiles were
woven of cotton and wool; stuffs were dyed and embroidered with such
skill that these tissues became one of the most valued exports of Babylonia,
praised to the skies by the writers of Greece and Rome.[31] As far back as we
can go in Mesopotamian history we find the weaver's loom and the potter's
wheel; these were almost the only machines. Buildings were mostly of
adobe—clay mixed with straw; or bricks still soft and moist were placed one
upon the other and allowed to dry into a solid wall cemented by the sun.
It was observed that the bricks in the fireplace became harder and more
durable than those that the sun had baked; the process of hardening them in
kilns was then a natural development, and thenceforth there was no end to
the making of bricks in Babylon. Trades multiplied and became diversified
and skilled, and as early as Hammurabi industry was organized into guilds
(called "tribes") of masters and apprentices.[32]

Local transport used wheeled carts drawn by patient asses.[33] The horse
is first mentioned in Babylonian records about 2100 B.C., as "the ass from
the East"; apparently it came from the table-lands of Central Asia, conquered
Babylonia with the Kassites, and reached Egypt with the Hyksos.[34] With
this new means of locomotion and carriage, trade expanded from local to
foreign commerce; Babylon grew wealthy as the commercial hub of the
Near East, and the nations of the ancient Mediterranean world were drawn
into closer contact for good and ill. Nebuchadrezzar facilitated trade by improving the highways; "I have turned inaccessible tracks," he reminds the
historian, "into serviceable roads."[35] Countless caravans brought to the bazaars and shops of Babylon the products of half the world. From India
they came via Kabul, Herat and Ecbatana; from Egypt via Pelusium and
Palestine; from Asia Minor through Tyre, Sidon and Sardis to Carchemish,
and then down the Euphrates. As a result of all this trade Babylon became,
under Nebuchadrezzar, a thriving and noisy market-place, from which the
wealthy sought refuge in residential suburbs. Note the contemporary ring
of a rich suburbanite's letter to King Cyrus of Persia (ca. 539 B.C.): "Our

estate seemed to me the finest in the world, for it was so near to Babylon that we enjoyed all the advantages of a great city, and yet could come back home and be rid of all its rush and worry."[36]

Government in Mesopotamia never succeeded in establishing such economic order as that which the Pharaohs achieved in Egypt. Commerce was harassed with a multiplicity of dangers and tolls; the merchant did not know which to fear the more—the robbers that might beset him on the way, or the towns and baronies that exacted heavy fees from him for the privilege of using their roads. It was safer, where possible, to take the great national highway, the Euphrates, which Nebuchadrezzar had made navigable from the Persian Gulf to Thapsacus.[37] His campaigns in Arabia and his subjugation of Tyre opened up to Babylonian commerce the Indian and Mediterranean Seas, but these opportunities were only partially explored. For on the open sea, as in the mountain passes and the desert wastes, perils beset the merchant at every hour. Vessels were large, but reefs were many and treacherous; navigation was not yet a science; and at any moment pirates, or the ambitious dwellers on the shore, might board the ships, appropriate the merchandise, and enslave or kill the crew.[38] The merchants reimbursed themselves for such losses by restricting their honesty to the necessities of each situation.

These difficult transactions were made easier by a well-developed system of finance. The Babylonians had no coinage, but even before Hammurabi they used—besides barley and corn—ingots of gold and silver as standards of value and mediums of exchange. The metal was unstamped, and was weighed at each transaction. The smallest unit of currency was the *shekel*—a half-ounce of silver worth from $2.50 to $5.00 of our contemporary currency; sixty such *shekels* made a *mina*, and sixty *minas* made a talent—from $10,000 to $20,000.[38a] Loans were made in goods or currency, but at a high rate of interest, fixed by the state at 20% *per annum* for loans of money, and 33% for loans in kind; even these rates were exceeded by lenders who could hire clever scribes to circumvent the law.[39] There were no banks, but certain powerful families carried on from generation to generation the business of lending money; they dealt also in real estate, and financed industrial enterprises;[40] and persons who had funds on deposit with such men could pay their obligations by written drafts.[41] The priests also made loans, particularly to finance the sowing and reaping of the crops. The law occasionally took the side of the debtor: e.g., if a peasant mortgaged his farm, and through storm or drought or other "act of God" had no harvest from his toil, then no interest could be exacted from him in that year.[42] But for the most part the law was written with an eye to protecting property and preventing losses;

it was a principle of Babylonian law that no man had a right to borrow money unless he wished to be held completely responsible for its repayment; hence the creditor could seize the debtor's slave or son as hostage for an unpaid debt, and could hold him for not more than three years. A plague of usury was the price that Babylonian industry, like our own, paid for the fertilizing activity of a complex credit system.[43]

It was essentially a commercial civilization. Most of the documents that have come down from it are of a business character—sales, loans, contracts, partnerships, commissions, exchanges, bequests, agreements, promissory notes, and the like. We find in these tablets abundant evidence of wealth, and a certain materialistic spirit that managed, like some later civilizations, to reconcile piety with greed. We see in the literature many signs of a busy and prosperous life, but we find also, at every turn, reminders of the slavery that underlies all cultures. The most interesting contracts of sale from the age of Nebuchadrezzar are those that have to do with slaves.[44] They were recruited from captives taken in battle, from slave-raids carried out upon foreign states by marauding Bedouins, and from the reproductive enthusiasm of the slaves themselves. Their value ranged from $20 to $65 for a woman, and from $50 to $100 for a man.[45] Most of the physical work in the towns was done by them, including nearly all of the personal service. Female slaves were completely at the mercy of their purchaser, and were expected to provide him with bed as well as board; it was understood that he would breed through them a copious supply of children, and those slaves who were not so treated felt themselves neglected and dishonored.[46] The slave and all his belongings were his master's property: he might be sold or pledged for debt; he might be put to death if his master thought him less lucrative alive than dead; if he ran away no one could legally harbor him, and a reward was fixed for his capture. Like the free peasant he was subject to conscription for both the army and the *corvée*—i.e., for forced labor in such public works as cutting roads and digging canals. On the other hand the slave's master paid his doctor's fees, and kept him moderately alive through illness, slack employment and old age. He might marry a free woman, and his children by her would be free; half his property, in such a case, went on his death to his family. He might be set up in business by his master, and retain part of the profits—with which he might then buy his freedom; or his master might liberate him for exceptional or long and faithful service. But only a few slaves achieved such freedom. The rest consoled themselves with a high birth-rate, until they became more numerous than the free. A great slave-class moved like a swelling subterranean river underneath the Babylonian state.

III. THE LAW

*The Code of Hammurabi—The powers of the king—Trial by
ordeal — "Lex Talionis" — Forms of punishment — Codes of
wages and prices—State restoration of stolen goods*

Such a society, of course, never dreamed of democracy; its economic
character necessitated a monarchy supported by commercial wealth or
feudal privilege, and protected by the judicious distribution of legal violence. A landed aristocracy, gradually displaced by a commercial plutocracy, helped to maintain social control, and served as intermediary between
people and king. The latter passed his throne down to any son of his
choosing, with the result that every son considered himself heir apparent,
formed a clique of supporters, and, as like as not, raised a war of succession if his hopes were unfulfilled.[47] Within the limits of this arbitrary
rule the government was carried on by central and local lords or administrators appointed by the king. These were advised and checked by
provincial or municipal assemblies of elders or notables, who managed to
maintain, even under Assyrian domination, a proud measure of local
self-government.[48]

Every administrator, and usually the king himself, acknowledged the
guidance and authority of that great body of law which had been given
form under Hammurabi, and had maintained its substance, despite every
change of circumstance and detail, through fifteen centuries. The legal
development was from supernatural to secular sanctions, from severity to
lenience, and from physical to financial penalties. In the earlier days an
appeal to the gods was taken through trial by ordeal. A man accused of
sorcery, or a woman charged with adultery, was invited to leap into the
Euphrates; and the gods were on the side of the best swimmers. If the
woman emerged alive, she was innocent; if the "sorcerer" was drowned,
his accuser received his property; if he was not, he received the property
of his accuser.[49] The first judges were priests, and to the end of Babylonian history the courts were for the most part located in the temples;[50]
but already in the days of Hammurabi secular courts responsible only to
the government were replacing the judgment-seats presided over by the
clergy.

Penology began with the *lex talionis*, or law of equivalent retaliation.
If a man knocked out an eye or a tooth, or broke a limb, of a patrician,

precisely the same was to be done to him.[51] If a house collapsed and killed the purchaser, the architect or builder must die; if the accident killed the buyer's son, the son of the architect or builder must die; if a man struck a girl and killed her not he but his daughter must suffer the penalty of death.[52] Gradually these punishments in kind were replaced by awards of damages; a payment of money was permitted as an alternative to the physical retaliation,[53] and later the fine became the sole punishment. So the eye of a commoner might be knocked out for sixty *shekels* of silver, and the eye of a slave might be knocked out for thirty.[54] For the penalty varied not merely with the gravity of the offense, but with the rank of the offender and the victim. A member of the aristocracy was subject to severer penalties for the same crime than a man of the people, but an offense against such an aristocrat was a costly extravagance. A plebeian striking a plebeian was fined ten *shekels*, or fifty dollars; to strike a person of title or property cost six times more.[55] From such dissuasions the law passed to barbarous punishments by amputation or death. A man who struck his father had his hands cut off;[56] a physician whose patient died, or lost an eye, as the result of an operation, had his fingers cut off;[57] a nurse who knowingly substituted one child for another had to sacrifice her breasts.[58] Death was decreed for a variety of crimes: rape, kidnaping, brigandage, burglary, incest, procurement of a husband's death by his wife in order to marry another man, the opening or entering of a wine-shop by a priestess, the harboring of a fugitive slave, cowardice in the face of the enemy, malfeasance in office, careless or uneconomical housewifery,[59] or malpractice in the selling of beer.[60] In such rough ways, through thousands of years, those traditions and habits of order and self-restraint were established which became part of the unconscious basis of civilization.

Within certain limits the state regulated prices, wages and fees. What the surgeon might charge was established by law; and wages were fixed by the Code of Hammurabi for builders, brickmakers, tailors, stonemasons, carpenters, boatmen, herdsmen, and laborers.[61] The law of inheritance made the man's children, rather than his wife, his natural and direct heirs; the widow received her dowry and her wedding-gift, and remained head of the household as long as she lived. There was no right of primogeniture; the sons inherited equally, and in this way the largest estates were soon redivided, and the concentration of wealth was in some measure checked.[62] Private property in land and goods was taken for granted by the Code.

We find no evidence of lawyers in Babylonia, except for priests who might serve as notaries, and the scribe who would write for pay anything from a will to a madrigal. The plaintiff preferred his own plea, without the luxury of terminology. Litigation was discouraged; the very first law of the Code reads, with almost illegal simplicity: "If a man bring an accusation against a man, and charge him with a (capital) crime, but cannot prove it, the accuser shall be put to death."[63] There are signs of bribery, and of tampering with witnesses.[64] A court of appeals, staffed by "the King's Judges," sat at Babylon, and a final appeal might be carried to the king himself. There was nothing in the Code about the rights of the individual against the state; that was to be a European innovation. But articles 22-24 provided, if not political, at least economic, protection. "If a man practise brigandage and be captured, that man shall be put to death. If the brigand be not captured, the man who has been robbed shall, in the presence of the god, make an itemized statement of his loss, and the city and governor within whose province and jurisdiction the robbery was committed shall compensate him for whatever was lost. If it be a life (that was lost), the city and governor shall pay one *mina* ($300) to the heirs." What modern city is so well governed that it would dare to offer such reimbursements to the victims of its negligence? Has the law progressed since Hammurabi, or only increased and multiplied?

IV. THE GODS OF BABYLON

Religion and the state—The functions and powers of the clergy—The lesser gods—Marduk—Ishtar—The Babylonian stories of the Creation and the Flood—The love of Ishtar and Tammuz—The descent of Ishtar into Hell—The death and resurrection of Tammuz — Ritual and prayer — Penitential psalms — Sin — Magic—Superstition

The power of the king was limited not only by the law and the aristocracy, but by the clergy. Technically the king was merely the agent of the city god. Taxation was in the name of the god, and found its way directly or deviously into the temple treasuries. The king was not really king in the eyes of the people until he was invested with royal authority by the priests, "took the hands of Bel," and conducted the image of Marduk in solemn procession through the streets. In these ceremonies the monarch was dressed as a priest, symbolizing the union of church and state, and perhaps the priestly origin of the kingship. All the glamor of the supernatural hedged about the throne, and made rebellion a colossal impiety which risked not only the neck but the soul. Even the mighty Hammurabi received his laws from the god. From the *patesis* or priest-governors of Sumeria to the religious coronation of Nebuchad-rezzar, Babylonia remained in effect a theocratic state, always "under the thumb of the priests."[65]

The wealth of the temples grew from generation to generation, as the uneasy rich shared their dividends with the gods. The kings, feeling an especial need of divine forgiveness, built the temples, equipped them with furniture, food and slaves, deeded to them great areas of land, and assigned to them an annual income from the state. When the army won a battle, the first share of the captives and the spoils went to the temples; when any special good fortune befell the king, extraordinary gifts were dedicated to the gods. Certain lands were required to pay to the temples a yearly tribute of dates, corn, or fruit; if they failed, the temples could foreclose on them; and in this way the lands usually came into possession by the priests. Poor as well as rich turned over to the temples as much as they thought profitable of their earthly gains. Gold, silver, copper, *lapis lazuli*, gems and precious woods accumulated in the sacred treasury.

As the priests could not directly use or consume this wealth, they turned it into productive or investment capital, and became the greatest agriculturists, manufacturers and financiers of the nation. Not only did they hold vast tracts of land; they owned a great number of slaves, or controlled hundreds of laborers, who were hired out to other employers, or worked for the temples in their divers trades from the playing of music to the brewing of beer.[66] The priests were also the greatest merchants and financiers of Babylonia; they sold the varied products of the temple shops, and handled a large proportion of the country's trade; they had a reputation for wise investment, and many persons entrusted their savings to them, confident of a modest but reliable return. They made loans on more lenient terms than the private money-lenders; sometimes they lent to the sick or the poor without interest, merely asking a return of the principal when Marduk should smile upon the borrower again.[67] Finally, they performed many legal functions: they served as notaries, attesting and signing contracts, and making wills; they heard and decided suits and trials, kept official records, and recorded commercial transactions.

Occasionally the king commandeered some of the temple accumulations to meet an expensive emergency. But this was rare and dangerous, for the priests had laid terrible curses upon all who should touch, unpermitted, the smallest jot of ecclesiastical property. Besides, their influence with the people was ultimately greater than that of the king, and they might in most cases depose him if they set their combined wits and powers to this end. They had also the advantage of permanence; the king died, but the god lived on; the council of priests, free from the fortunes of elections, illnesses, assassinations and wars, had a corporate perpetuity that made possible long-term and patient policies, such as characterize great religious organizations to this day. The supremacy of the priests under these conditions was inevitable. It was fated that the merchants should make Babylon, and that the priests should enjoy it.

Who were the gods that formed the invisible constabulary of the state? They were numerous, for the imagination of the people was limitless, and there was hardly any end to the needs that deities might serve. An official census of the gods, undertaken in the ninth century before Christ, counted them as some 65,000.[68] Every town had its tutelary divinity; and as, in our own time and faith, localities and villages, after making formal acknowledgment of the Supreme Being, worship specific minor gods with a special devotion, so Larsa lavished its temples on Shamash, Uruk on Ishtar, Ur on Nannar—for the Sumerian pantheon had survived the Sumerian state. The gods were not aloof from men; most of them lived on earth in the temples, ate with a hearty appetite, and through nocturnal visits to pious women gave unexpected children to the busy citizens of Babylon.[69]

Oldest of all were the astronomic gods: Anu, the immovable firmament, Shamash, the sun, Nannar, the moon, and Bel or Baal, the earth into whose bosom all Babylonians returned after death.[70] Every family had household gods, to whom prayers were said and libations poured each morning and night; every individual had a protective divinity (or, as we should say, a guardian angel) to keep him from harm and joy; and genii of fertility hovered beneficently over the fields. It was probably out of this multitude of spirits that the Jews moulded their cherubim.

We do not find among the Babylonians such signs of monotheism as appear in Ikhnaton and the Second Isaiah. Two forces, however, brought them near to it: the enlargement of the state by conquest and growth brought local deities under the supremacy of a single god; and several of the cities patrioti- cally conferred omnipotence upon their favored divinities. "Trust in Nebo," says Nebo, "trust in no other god";[71] this is not unlike the first of the com- mandments given to the Jews. Gradually the number of the gods was less- ened by interpreting the minor ones as forms or attributes of the major dei- ties. In these ways the god of Babylon, Marduk, originally a sun god, became sovereign of all Babylonian divinities.[72] Hence his title, Bel-Marduk— that is, Marduk *the* god. To him and to Ishtar the Babylonians sent up the most eloquent of their prayers.

Ishtar (Astarte to the Greeks, Ashtoreth to the Jews) interests us not only as analogue of the Egyptian Isis and prototype of the Grecian Aphrodite and the Roman Venus, but as the formal beneficiary of one of the strangest of Babylonian customs. She was Demeter as well as Aphrodite—no mere goddess of physical beauty and love, but the gracious divinity of bounteous motherhood, the secret inspiration of the growing soil, and the creative principle everywhere. It is impossible to find much harmony, from a modern point of view, in the attributes and functions of Ishtar: she was the goddess of war as well as of love, of prostitutes as well as of mothers; she called herself "a compassionate courtesan";[73] she was represented sometimes as a bearded bisexual deity, sometimes as a nude female offering her breasts to suck;[74] and though her worshipers repeat- edly addressed her as "The Virgin," "The Holy Virgin," and "The Virgin Mother," this merely meant that her amours were free from all taint of wedlock. Gilgamesh rejected her advances on the ground that she could not be trusted; had she not once loved, seduced, and then slain, a lion?[75] It is clear that we must put our own moral code to one side if we are to understand her. Note with what fervor the Babylonians could lift up to her throne litanies of laudation only less splendid than those which a tender piety once raised to the Mother of God:

> I beseech thee, Lady of Ladies, Goddess of Goddesses, Ishtar, Queen of all cities, leader of all men.
> Thou art the light of the world, thou art the light of heaven, mighty daughter of Sin (the moon-god). . . .
> Supreme is thy might, O Lady, exalted art thou above all gods.

Thou renderest judgment, and thy decision is righteous.

Unto thee are subject the laws of the earth and the laws of heaven, the laws of the temples and the shrines, the laws of the private apartment and the secret chamber.

Where is the place where thy name is not, and where is the spot where thy commandments are not known?

At thy name the earth and the heavens shake, and the gods they tremble. . . .

Thou lookest upon the oppressed, and to the down-trodden thou bringest justice every day.

How long, Queen of Heaven and Earth, how long,

How long, Shepherdess of pale-faced men, wilt thou tarry?

How long, O Queen whose feet are not weary, and whose knees make haste?

How long, Lady of Hosts, Lady of Battles?

Glorious one whom all the spirits of heaven fear, who subduest all angry gods; mighty above all rulers; who holdest the reins of kings.

Opener of the womb of all women, great is thy light.

Shining light of heaven, light of the world, enlightener of all the places where men dwell, who gatherest together the hosts of the nations.

Goddess of men, Divinity of women, thy counsel passeth understanding.

Where thou glancest, the dead come to life, and the sick rise and walk; the mind of the diseased is healed when it looks upon thy face.

How long, O Lady, shall mine enemy triumph over me?

Command, and at thy command the angry god will turn back.

Ishtar is great! Ishtar is Queen! My Lady is exalted, my Lady is Queen, Innini, the mighty daughter of Sin.

There is none like unto her.[76]

With these gods as *dramatis personæ* the Babylonians constructed myths which have in large measure come down to us, through the Jews, as part of our own religious lore. There was first of all the myth of the creation. In the beginning was Chaos. "In the time when nothing which was called heaven existed above, and when nothing below had yet received the name of earth, Apsu, the Ocean, who first was their father, and Tiamat, Chaos, who gave birth to them all, mingled their waters in one." Things slowly began to grow and take form; but suddenly the monster-goddess Tiamat set out to destroy all the other gods, and to make her-self—Chaos—supreme. A mighty revolution ensued in which all order was destroyed. Then another god, Marduk, slew Tiamat with her own medi-cine by casting a hurricane of wind into her mouth as she opened it to swallow him; then he thrust his lance into Tiamat's wind-swollen paunch, and the goddess of Chaos blew up. Marduk, "recovering his calm," says the legend, split the dead Tiamat into two longitudinal halves, as one does a fish for drying; "then he hung up one of the halves on high, which be-came the heavens; the other half he spread out under his feet to form the earth."⁷⁷ This is as much as we yet know about creation. Perhaps the ancient poet meant to suggest that the only creation of which we can know anything is the replacement of chaos with order, for in the end this is the essence of art and civilization. We should remember, however, that the defeat of Chaos is only a myth.*

Having moved heaven and earth into place, Marduk undertook to knead earth with his blood and thereby make men for the service of the gods. Mesopotamian legends differed on the precise way in which this was done; they agreed in general that man was fashioned by the deity from a lump of clay. Usually they represented him as living at first not in a paradise but in bestial simplicity and ignorance, until a strange mon-ster called Oannes, half fish and half philosopher, taught him the arts and sciences, the rules for founding cities, and the principles of law; after which Oannes plunged into the sea, and wrote a book on the history of civilization.⁷⁹ Presently, however, the gods became dissatisfied with the men whom they had created, and sent a great flood to destroy them and all their works. The god of wisdom, Ea, took pity on mankind, and resolved to save one man at least—Shamash-napishtim—and his wife. The flood raged; men "encumbered the sea like fishes' spawn." Then sud-denly the gods wept and gnashed their teeth at their own folly, asking themselves, "Who will make the accustomed offerings now?" But Sham-ash-napishtim had built an ark, had survived the flood, had perched on the mountain of Nisir, and had sent out a reconnoitering dove; now he decided to sacrifice to the gods, who accepted his gifts with surprise and gratitude. "The gods snuffed up the odor, the gods snuffed up the ex-cellent odor, the gods gathered like flies above the offering."⁸⁰

---

* The Babylonian story of creation consists of seven tablets (one for each day of crea-tion) found in the ruins of Ashurbanipal's library at Kuyunjik (Nineveh) in 1854; they are a copy of a legend that came down to Babylonia and Assyria from Sumeria.⁷⁸

Lovelier than this vague memory of some catastrophic inundation is the vegetation myth of Ishtar and Tammuz. In the Sumerian form of the tale Tammuz is Ishtar's young brother; in the Babylonian form he is sometimes her lover, sometimes her son; both forms seem to have entered into the myths of Venus and Adonis, Demeter and Persephone, and a hundred scattered legends of death and resurrection. Tammuz, son of the great god Ea, is a shepherd pasturing his flock under the great tree Erida (which covers the whole earth with its shade) when Ishtar, always insatiable, falls in love with him, and chooses him to be the spouse of her youth. But Tammuz, like Adonis, is gored to death by a wild boar, and descends, like all the dead, into that dark subterranean Hades which the Babylonians called Aralu, and over which they set as ruler Ishtar's jealous sister, Ereshkigal. Ishtar, mourning inconsolably, resolves to go down to Aralu and restore Tammuz to life by bathing his wounds in the waters of a healing spring. Soon she appears at the gates of Hades in all her imperious beauty, and demands entrance. The tablets tell the story vigorously:

When Ereshkigal heard this,
As when one hews down a tamarisk (she trembled?).
As when one cuts a reed (she shook?).
"What has moved her heart, what has (stirred) her liver?
Ho, there, (does) this one (wish to dwell) with me?
To eat clay as food, to drink (dust?) as wine?
I weep for the men who have left their wives;
I weep for the wives torn from the embrace of their husbands;
For the little ones (cut off) before their time.
Go, gate-keeper, open thy gate for her,
Deal with her according to the ancient decree."

The ancient decree is that none but the nude shall enter Aralu. Therefore at each of the successive gates through which Ishtar must pass, the keeper divests her of some garment or ornament: first her crown, then her ear-rings, then her necklace, then the ornaments from her bosom, then her many-jeweled girdle, then the spangles from her hands and feet, and lastly her loin-cloth; and Ishtar, protesting gracefully, yields.

Now when Ishtar had gone down into the land of no return,
Ereshkigal saw her and was angered at her presence.

Ishtar without reflection threw herself at her.
Ereshkigal opened her mouth and spoke
To Namtar, her messenger. . . .
"Go, Namtar, (imprison her?) in my palace.
Send against her sixty diseases,
Eye disease against her eyes,
Disease of the side against her side,
Foot-disease against her foot,
Heart-disease against her heart,
Head-disease against her head,
Against her whole being."

While Ishtar is detained in Hades by these sisterly attentions, the earth, missing the inspiration of her presence, forgets incredibly all the arts and ways of love: plant no longer fertilizes plant, vegetation languishes, animals experience no heat, men cease to yearn.

After the lady Ishtar had gone down into the land of no return,
The bull did not mount the cow, the ass approached not the she-ass;
To the maid in the street no man drew near;
The man slept in his apartment,
The maid slept by herself.

Population begins to diminish, and the gods note with alarm a sharp decline in the number of offerings from the earth. In panic they command Ereshkigal to release Ishtar. It is done, but Ishtar refuses to return to the surface of the earth unless she is allowed to take Tammuz with her. She wins her point, passes triumphantly through the seven gates, receives her loin-cloth, her spangles, her girdle, her pectorals, her necklace, her ear-rings and her crown. As she appears plants grow and bloom again, the land swells with food, and every animal resumes the business of reproducing his kind.[81] Love, stronger than death, is restored to its rightful place as master of gods and men. To the modern scholar it is only an admirable legend, symbolizing delightfully the yearly death and rebirth of the soil, and that omnipotence of Venus which Lucretius was to celebrate in his own strong verse; to the Babylonians it was sacred history, faithfully believed and annually commemorated in a day of mourning and wailing for the dead Tammuz, followed by riotous rejoicing over his resurrection.[82]

Nevertheless the Babylonian derived no satisfaction from the idea of personal immortality. His religion was terrestrially practical; when he prayed he asked not for celestial rewards but for earthly goods;[83] he could not trust his gods beyond the grave. It is true that one text speaks of Marduk as he "who gives back life to the dead,"[84] and the story of the flood represents its two survivors as living forever. But for the most part the Babylonian conception of another life was like that of the Greeks: dead men—saints and villains, geniuses and idiots, alike—went to a dark and shadowy realm within the bowels of the earth, and none of them saw the light again. There was a heaven, but only for the gods; the Aralu to which all men descended was a place frequently of punishment, never of joy; there the dead lay bound hand and foot forever, shivering with cold, and subject to hunger and thirst unless their children placed food periodically in their graves.[85] Those who had been especially wicked on earth were subjected to horrible tortures; leprosy consumed them, or some other of the diseases which Nergal and Allat, male and female lords of Aralu, had arranged for their rectification.

Most bodies were buried in vaults; a few were cremated, and their remains were preserved in urns.[86] The dead body was not embalmed, but professional mourners washed and perfumed it, clad it presentably, painted its cheeks, darkened its eyelids, put rings upon its fingers, and provided it with a change of linen. If the corpse was that of a woman it was equipped with scent-bottles, combs, cosmetic pencils, and eye-paint to preserve its fragrance and complexion in the nether world.[87] If not properly buried the dead would torment the living; if not buried at all, the soul would prowl about sewers and gutters for food, and might afflict an entire city with pestilence.[88] It was a medley of ideas not as consistent as Euclid, but sufficing to prod the simple Babylonian to keep his gods and priests well fed.

The usual offering was food and drink, for these had the advantage that if they were not entirely consumed by the gods the surplus need not go to waste. A frequent sacrifice on Babylonian altars was the lamb; and an old Babylonian incantation strangely anticipates the symbolism of Judaism and Christianity: "The lamb as a substitute for a man, the lamb he gives for his life."[89] Sacrifice was a complex ritual, requiring the expert services of a priest; every act and word of the ceremony was settled by sacred tradition, and any amateur deviation from these forms might mean that the gods would eat without listening. In general, to the Babylonian, religion meant correct ritual rather than the good life. To do one's duty to the gods one had to offer proper sacrifice to the temples, and recite the appropriate prayers;[90] for the rest he might cut out the eyes of his fallen enemy, cut off the hands and feet of captives, and roast their remainders alive in a furnace,[91] without much offense to heaven. To participate in—or reverently to attend—long and solemn processions like those in which the priests carried from sanctuary to sanctuary the image of Marduk, and performed the sacred drama of his death and resurrection; to anoint the idols with sweet-scented oils,* to burn incense before them, clothe them with rich vestments, or adorn them with jewelry; to offer up the virginity of their daughters in the great festival of Ishtar; to put food and drink before the gods, and to be generous to the priests—these were the essential works of the devout Babylonian soul.[93]

Perhaps we misjudge him, as doubtless the future will misjudge us from the fragments that accident will rescue from our decay. Some of the finest literary relics of the Babylonians are prayers that breathe a profound and sincere piety. Hear the proud Nebuchadrezzar humbly addressing Marduk:

> Without thee, Lord, what could there be
> For the king thou lovest, and dost call his name?
> Thou shalt bless his title as thou wilt,
> And unto him vouchsafe a path direct.
> I, the prince obeying thee,
> Am what thy hands have made.
> 'Tis thou who art my creator,
> Entrusting me with the rule of hosts of men.
> According to thy mercy, Lord, . . .
> Turn into loving-kindness thy dread power,
> And make to spring up in my heart
> A reverence for thy divinity.
> Give as thou thinkest best.[94]

The surviving literature abounds in hymns full of that passionate self abasement with which the Semite tries to control and conceal his pride. Many of them take the character of "penitential psalms," and prepare us for the magnificent feeling and imagery of "David"; who knows but they served as models for that many-headed Muse?

> I, thy servant, full of sighs cry unto thee.
> Thou acceptest the fervent prayer of him who is burdened with sin.
> Thou lookest upon a man, and that man lives. . . .
> Look with true favor upon me, and accept my supplication. . . .

---

* Therefore Tammuz was called "The Anointed."[92]

And then, as if uncertain of the sex of the god—

How long, my god,
How long, my goddess, until thy face be turned to me?
How long, known and unknown god, until the anger of thy heart
  shall be appeased?
How long, known and unknown goddess, until thy unfriendly heart
  be appeased?
Mankind is perverted, and has no judgment;
Of all men who are alive, who knows anything?
They do not know whether they do good or evil.
O Lord, do not cast aside thy servant;
He is cast into the mire; take his hand!
The sin which I have sinned, turn to mercy!
The iniquity which I have committed, let the wind carry away!
My many transgressions tear off like a garment!
My god, my sins are seven times seven; forgive my sins!
My goddess, my sins are seven times seven; forgive my sins! . . .
Forgive my sins, and I will humble myself before thee.
May thy heart, as the heart of a mother who hath borne children,
  be glad;
As a mother who hath borne children, as a father who hath begotten,
  may it be glad![95]

Such psalms and hymns were sung sometimes by the priests, sometimes by the congregation, sometimes by both in strophe and antistrophe. Perhaps the strangest circumstance about them is that—like all the religious literature of Babylon—they were written in the ancient Sumerian language, which served the Babylonian and Assyrian churches precisely as Latin serves the Roman Catholic Church today. And just as a Catholic hymnal may juxtapose the Latin text to a vernacular translation, so some of the hymns that have come down to us from Mesopotamia have a Babylonian or Assyrian translation written between the lines of the "classic" Sumerian original, in the fashion of a contemporary schoolboy's "interlinear." And as the form of these hymns and rituals led to the Psalms of the Jews and the liturgy of the Roman Church, so their content presaged the pessimistic and sin-struck plaints of the Jews, the early Christians, and the modern Puritans. The sense of sin, though it did not interfere victoriously in Babylonian life, filled the Babylonian chants, and rang a note that survives in all Semitic liturgies and their anti-Semitic derivatives. "Lord," cries one hymn, "my sins are many, great are my misdeeds! . . . I sink under affliction, I can no longer raise my head; I turn to my merciful God to call upon him, and I groan! . . . Lord, reject not thy servant!"[96]

These groanings were rendered more sincere by the Babylonian conception of sin. Sin was no mere theoretical state of the soul; like sickness it was the possession of the body by a demon that might destroy it. Prayer was in the nature of an incantation against a demon that had come down upon the individual out of the ocean of magic forces in which the ancient Orient lived and moved. Everywhere, in the Babylonian view, these hostile demons lurked: they hid in strange crannies, slipped through doors or even through bolts and sockets, and pounced upon their victims in the form of illness or madness whenever some sin had withdrawn for a moment the beneficent guardianship of the gods. Giants, dwarfs, cripples, above all, women, had sometimes the power, even with a glance of the "evil eye," to infuse such a destructive spirit into the bodies of those toward whom they were ill-disposed. Partial protection against these demons was provided by the use of magic amulets, talismans and kindred charms; images of the gods, carried on the body, would usually suffice to frighten the devils away. Little stones strung on a thread or a chain and hung about the neck were especially effective, but care had to be taken that the stones were such as tradition associated with good luck, and the thread had to be of black, white or red according to the purpose in view. Thread spun from virgin kids was particularly powerful.[97] But in addition to such means it was wise also to exorcise the demon by fervent incantation and magic ritual—for example, by sprinkling the body with water taken from the sacred streams—the Tigris or the Euphrates. Or an image of the demon could be made, placed on a boat, and sent over the water with a proper formula; if the boat could be made to capsize, so much the better. The demon might be persuaded, by the appropriate incantation, to leave its human victim and enter an animal—a bird, a pig, most frequently a lamb.[98]

Magic formulas for the elimination of demons, the avoidance of evil and the prevision of the future constitute the largest category in the Babylonian writings found in the library of Ashurbanipal. Some of the tablets are manuals of astrology; others are lists of omens celestial and terrestrial, with expert advice for reading them; others are treatises on the interpretation of dreams, rivaling in their ingenious incredibility the most advanced products of modern psychology; still others offer instruction in divining the future by examining the entrails of animals, or by observing the form and position of a drop of oil let fall into a jar of water.[99] Hepatoscopy—observation of the liver of animals—was a favorite method of divination among the Babylonian priests, and passed from them into the classical world; for the liver was believed to be the seat of the mind in both animals and men. No king would undertake a campaign or advance to a battle, no Babylonian would risk a crucial decision or begin an enterprise of great moment, without employing a priest or a soothsayer to read the omens for him in one or another of these recondite ways.

Never was a civilization richer in superstitions. Every turn of chance from the anomalies of birth to the varieties of death received a popular, sometimes an official and sacerdotal, interpretation in magical or supernatural terms. Every movement of the rivers, every aspect of the stars, every dream, every unusual performance of man or beast, revealed the future to the properly instructed Babylonian. The fate of a king could be forecast by observing the movements of a dog,[100] just as we foretell the length of the winter by spying upon the groundhog. The superstitions of Babylonia seem ridiculous to us, because they differ superficially from our own. There is hardly an absurdity of the past that cannot be found flourishing somewhere in the present. Underneath all civilization, ancient or modern, moved and still moves a sea of magic, superstition and sorcery. Perhaps they will remain when the works of our reason have passed away.

V. THE MORALS OF BABYLON

Religion divorced from morals—Sacred prostitution—Free love—
Marriage — Adultery — Divorce — The position of woman —
The relaxation of morals

This religion, with all its failings, probably helped to prod the common Babylonian into some measure of decency and civic docility, else we should be hard put to explain the generosity of the kings to the priests. Apparently, however, it had no influence upon the morals of the upper classes in the later centuries, for (in the eyes and words of her prejudiced enemies) the "whore of Babylon" was a "sink of iniquity," and a scandalous example of luxurious laxity to all the ancient world. Even Alexander, who was not above dying of drinking, was shocked by the morals of Babylon.[101]

The most striking feature of Babylonian life, to an alien observer, was the custom known to us chiefly from a famous page in Herodotus:

Every native woman is obliged, once in her life, to sit in the temple of Venus, and have intercourse with some stranger. And many disdaining to mix with the rest, being proud on account of their wealth, come in covered carriages, and take up their station at the temple with a numerous train of servants attending them. But the far greater part do thus: many sit down in the temple of Venus, wearing a crown of cord round their heads; some are continually coming in, and others are going out. Passages marked out in a straight line lead in every direction through the women, along which strangers pass and make their choice. When a woman has once seated herself she must not return home till some stranger has thrown a piece of silver into her lap, and lain with her outside the temple. He who throws the silver must say thus: "I beseech the goddess Mylitta to favor thee"; for the Assyrians call Venus Mylitta.* The silver may be ever so small, for she will not reject it, inasmuch as it is not lawful for her to do so, for such silver is accounted sacred. The woman follows the first man that throws, and refuses no one. But when she has had intercourse and has absolved herself from her obligation to the goddess, she returns home; and after that time, however great a sum you may give her you will not gain possession of her. Those that are endowed with beauty and symmetry of shape are soon set free; but the deformed are detained a long time, from inability to satisfy the law, for some wait for a space of three or four years.[102]

What was the origin of this strange rite? Was it a relic of ancient sexual communism, a concession, by the future bridegroom, of the *jus primæ noctis,* or right of the first night, to the community as represented by any casual and anonymous citizen?[103] Was it due to the bridegroom's fear of harm from the violation of the tabu against shedding blood?[104] Was it a physical preparation for marriage, such as is still practised among some Australian tribes?[105] Or was it simply a sacrifice to the goddess—an offering of first fruits?[106] We do not know.

Such women, of course, were not prostitutes. But various classes of prostitutes lived within the temple precincts, plied their trade there, and amassed, some of them, great fortunes. Such temple prostitutes were common in western Asia: we find them in Israel,[107] Phrygia, Phœnicia, Syria, etc.; in Lydia and Cyprus the girls earned their marriage dowries

---

* "Assyrians" meant for the Greeks both Assyrians and Babylonians. "Mylitta" was one of the forms of Ishtar

in this way.[108] "Sacred prostitution" continued in Babylonia until abolished by Constantine (ca. 325 A.D.).[109] Alongside it, in the wine-shops kept by women, secular prostitution flourished.[110]

In general the Babylonians were allowed considerable premarital experience. It was considered permissible for men and women to form unlicensed unions, "trial marriages," terminable at the will of either party; but the woman in such cases was obliged to wear an olive—in stone or *terra cotta*—as a sign that she was a concubine.[111] Some tablets indicate that the Babylonians wrote poems, and sang songs, of love; but all that remains of these is an occasional first line, like "My love is a light," or "My heart is full of merriment and song."[112] One letter, dating from 2100 B.C., is in the tone of Napoleon's early messages to Josephine: "To Bibiya: . . . May Shamash and Marduk give thee health forever. . . . I have sent (to ask) after thy health; let me know how thou art. I have arrived in Babylon, and see thee not; I am very sad."[113]

Legal marriage was arranged by the parents, and was sanctioned by an exchange of gifts obviously descended from marriage by purchase. The suitor presented to the father of the bride a substantial present, but the father was expected to give her a dowry greater in value than the gift,[114] so that it was difficult to say who was purchasd, the woman or the man. Sometimes, however, the arrangement was unabashed purchase; Shamashnazir, for example, received ten *shekels* ($50) as the price of his daughter.[115] If we are to believe the Father of History,

> those who had marriageable daughters used to bring them once a year to a place where a great number of men gathered round them. A public crier made them stand up and sold them all, one after another. He began with the most beautiful, and having got a large sum for her he put up the second fairest. But he only sold them on condition that the buyers married them. . . . This very wise custom no longer exists.[116]

Despite these strange practices, Babylonian marriage seems to have been as monogamous and faithful as marriage in Christendom is today. Premarital freedom was followed by the rigid enforcement of marital fidelity. The adulterous wife and her paramour, according to the Code, were drowned, unless the husband, in his mercy, preferred to let his wife off by turning her almost naked into the streets.[117] Hammurabi out-Cæsared Cæsar: "If the finger have been pointed at the wife of a man because of another man, and she have not been taken in lying with another man, for her husband's sake she shall throw herself into the river"[118]—perhaps the law was intended as a discouragement to gossip. The man could divorce his wife simply by restoring her dowry to her and saying, "Thou art not my wife"; but if she said to him, "Thou art not my husband," she was to be drowned.[119] Childlessness, adultery, incompatibility, or careless management of the household might satisfy the law as ground for granting the man a divorce;[120] indeed "if she have not been a careful mistress, have gadded about, have neglected her house, and have belittled her children, they shall throw that woman into the water."[121] As against this incredible severity of the Code, we find that in practice the woman, though she might not divorce her husband, was free to leave him, if she could show cruelty on his part and fidelity on her own; in such cases she could return to her parents, and take her marriage portion with her, along with what other property she might have acquired.[122] (The women of England did not enjoy these rights till the end of the nineteenth century.) If a woman's husband was kept from her, through business or war, for any length of time, and had left no means for her maintenance, she might cohabit with another man without legal prejudice to her reunion with her husband on the latter's return.[123]

In general the position of woman in Babylonia was lower than in Egypt or Rome, and yet not worse than in classic Greece or medieval Europe. To carry out her many functions—begetting and rearing children, fetching water from the river or the public well, grinding corn, cooking, spinning, weaving, cleaning—she had to be free to go about in public very much like the man.[124] She could own property, enjoy its income, sell and buy, inherit and bequeath.[125] Some women kept shops, and carried on commerce; some even became scribes, indicating that girls as well as boys might receive an education.[126] But the Semitic practice of giving almost limitless power to the oldest male of the family won out against any matriarchal tendencies that may have existed in prehistoric Mesopotamia. Among the upper classes—by a custom that led to the *purdah* of Islam and India—the women were confined to certain quarters of the house; and when they went out they were chaperoned by eunuchs and pages.[127] Among the lower classes they were maternity machines, and if they had no dowry they were little more than slaves.[128] The worship of Ishtar suggests a certain reverence for woman and motherhood, like the worship of Mary in the Middle Ages; but we get no glimpse of chivalry in Herodotus' report that the Babylonians, when besieged, "had strangled their wives, to prevent the consumption of their provisions."[129]

With some excuse, then, the Egyptians looked down upon the Babylonians as not quite civilized. We miss here the refinement of character and feeling indicated by Egyptian literature and art. When refinement came to Babylon it was in the guise of an effeminate degeneracy: young men dyed and curled their hair, perfumed their flesh, rouged their cheeks, and adorned themselves with necklaces, bangles, ear-rings and pendants. After the Persian Conquest the death of self-respect brought an end of self-restraint; the manners of the courtesan crept into every class; women of good family came to consider it mere courtesy to reveal their charms indiscriminately for the greatest happiness of the greatest number;[130] and "every man of the people in his poverty," if we may credit Herodotus, "prostituted his daughters for money."[131] "There is nothing more extraordinary than the manners of this city," wrote Quintus Curtius (42 A.D.), "and nowhere are things better arranged with a view to voluptuous pleasures."[132] Morals grew lax when the temples grew rich; and the citizens of Babylon, wedded to delight, bore with equanimity the subjection of their city by the Kassites, the Assyrians, the Persians, and the Greeks.

VI. LETTERS AND LITERATURE

Cuneiform—Its decipherment—Language—Literature—The epic of Gilgamesh

Did this life of venery, piety and trade receive any ennobling enshrinement in literary or artistic form? It is possible; we cannot judge a civilization from such fragments as the ocean of time has thrown up from the wreckage of Babylon. These fragments are chiefly liturgical, magical and commercial. Whether through accident or through cultural poverty, Babylonia, like Assyria and Persia, has left us a very middling heritage of literature as compared with Egypt and Palestine; its gifts were in commerce and law.

Nevertheless, scribes were as numerous in cosmopolitan Babylon as in Memphis or Thebes. The art of writing was still young enough to give its master a high rank in society; it was the open sesame to governmental and sacerdotal office; its possessor never failed to mention the distinction in narrating his deeds, and usually he engraved a notice of it on his cylinder seal,[133] precisely as Christian scholars and gentlemen once listed their academic degrees on their cards. The Babylonians wrote in cuneiform upon tablets of damp clay, with a stylus or pencil cut at the end into a triangular prism or wedge; when the tablets were filled they dried and baked them into strange but durable manuscripts of brick. If the thing written was a letter it was dusted with powder and then wrapped in a clay envelope stamped with the sender's cylinder seal. Tablets in jars classified and arranged on shelves filled numerous libraries in the temples and palaces of Babylonia. These Babylonian libraries are lost; but one of the greatest of them, that of Borsippa, was copied and preserved in the library of Ashurbanipal, whose 30,000 tablets are the main source of our knowledge of Babylonian life.

The decipherment of Babylonian baffled students for centuries; their final success is an honorable chapter in the history of scholarship. In 1802 Georg Grotefend, professor of Greek at the University of Göttingen, told the Göttingen Academy how for years he had puzzled over certain cuneiform inscriptions from ancient Persia; how at last he had identified eight of the forty-two characters used, and had made out the names of three kings in the inscriptions. There, for the most part, the matter rested until 1835, when Henry Rawlinson, a British diplomatic officer stationed in Persia, quite unaware of Grotefend's work, likewise worked out the names of Hystaspes, Darius and Xerxes in an inscription couched in Old Persian, a cuneiform derivative of Babylonian script; and through these names he finally deciphered the entire document. This, however, was not Babylonian; Rawlinson had still to find, like Champollion, a Rosetta Stone—in this case some inscription bearing the same text in old Persian and Babylonian. He found it three hundred feet high on an almost inaccessible rock at Behistun, in the mountains of Media, where Darius I had caused his carvers to engrave a record of his wars and victories in three languages—old Persian, Assyrian, and Babylonian. Day after day Rawlinson risked himself on these rocks, often suspending himself by a rope, copying every character carefully, even making plastic impressions of all the engraved surfaces. *After twelve years of work* he succeeded in translating both the Babylonian and the Assyrian texts (1847). To test these and similar findings, the Royal Asiatic Society sent an unpublished cuneiform document to four Assyriologists, and asked them—working without contact or communication with one another—to make independent translations. The four reports were found to be in almost complete agreement. Through these unheralded campaigns of scholarship the perspective of history was enriched with a new civilization.[134]

The Babylonian language was a Semitic development of the old tongues of Sumeria and Akkad. It was written in characters originally Sumerian, but the vocabulary diverged in time (like French from Latin) into a language so different from Sumerian that the Babylonians had to compose dictionaries and grammars to transmit the old "classic" and sacerdotal tongue of Sumeria to young scholars and priests. Almost a fourth of the tablets found in the royal library at Nineveh is devoted to dictionaries and grammars of the Sumerian, Babylonian and Assyrian languages. According to tradition, such dictionaries had been made as far back as Sargon of Akkad—so old is scholarship. In Babylonian, as in Sumerian, the characters represented not letters but syllables; Babylon never achieved an alphabet of its own, but remained content with a "syllabary" of some three hundred signs. The memorizing of these syllabic symbols formed, with mathematics and religious instruction, the curriculum of the temple schools in which the priests imparted to the young as much as it was expedient for them to know. One excavation unearthed an ancient classroom in which the clay tablets of boys and girls who had copied virtuous maxims upon them some two thousand years before Christ still lay on the floor, as if some almost welcome disaster had suddenly interrupted the lesson.[135]

The Babylonians, like the Phœnicians, looked upon letters as a device for facilitating business; they did not spend much of their clay upon literature. We find animal fables in verse—one generation of an endless dynasty; hymns in strict meter, sharply divided lines and elaborate stanzas;[136] very little surviving secular verse; religious rituals presaging, but never becoming, drama; and tons of historiography. Official chroniclers recorded the piety and conquests of the kings, the vicissitudes of each temple, and the important events in the career of each city. Berosus, the most famous of Babylonian historians (ca. 280 B.C.) narrated with confidence full details concerning the creation of the world and the early history of man: the first king of Babylonia had been chosen by a god, and had reigned 36,000 years; from the beginning of the world to the great Flood, said Berosus, with praiseworthy exactitude and comparative moderation, there had elapsed 691,200 years.[137]

Twelve broken tablets found in Ashurbanipal's library, and now in the British Museum, form the most fascinating relic of Mesopotamian literature—the *Epic of Gilgamesh*. Like the *Iliad* it is an accretion of loosely connected stories, some of which go back to Sumeria 3000 B.C.; part of it is the Babylonian account of the Flood. Gilgamesh was a legendary ruler of Uruk or Erech, a descendant of the Shamash-napishtim who had survived the Deluge, and had never died. Gilgamesh enters upon the scene as a sort of Adonis-Samson—tall, massive, heroically powerful and troublesomely handsome.

Two thirds of him is god,
One third of him is man,
There's none can match the form of his body. . . .
All things he saw, even to the ends of the earth,
He underwent all, learned to know all;
He peered through all secrets,
Through wisdom's mantle that veileth all.
What was hidden he saw,
What was covered he undid;
Of times before the stormflood he brought report.
He went on a long far way,
Giving himself toil and distress;
Wrote then on a stone tablet the whole of his labor.[188]

Fathers complain to Ishtar that he leads their sons out to exhausting toil "building the walls through the day, through the night"; and husbands complain that "he leaves not a wife to her master, not a single virgin to her mother." Ishtar begs Gilgamesh's godmother, Aruru, to create another son equal to Gilgamesh and able to keep him busy in conflict, so that the husbands of Uruk may have peace. Aruru kneads a bit of clay, spits upon it, and moulds from it the satyr Engidu, a man with the strength of a boar, the mane of a lion, and the speed of a bird. Engidu does not care for the society of men, but turns and lives with the animals; "he browses with the gazelles, he sports with the creatures of the water, he quenches his thirst with the beasts of the field." A hunter tries to capture him with nets and traps, but fails; and going to Gilgamesh, the hunter begs for the loan of a priestess who may snare Engidu with love. "Go, my hunter," says Gilgamesh, "take a priestess; when the beasts come to the watering-place let her display her beauty; he will see her, and his beasts that troop around him will be scattered."

The hunter and the priestess go forth, and find Engidu.

"There he is, woman!
Loosen thy buckle,
Unveil thy delight,
That he may take his fill of thee!
Hang not back, take up his lust!
When he sees thee, he will draw near.
Open thy robe that he rest upon thee!

Arouse in him rapture, the work of woman.
Then will he become a stranger to his wild beasts,
Who on his own steppes grew up with him.
His bosom will press against thee."
Then the priestess loosened her buckle,
Unveiled her delight,
For him to take his fill of her.
She hung not back, she took up his lust,
She opened her robe that he rest upon her.
She aroused in him rapture, the work of woman.
His bosom pressed against her.
Engidu forgot where he was born.[139]

For six days but seven nights Engidu remains with the sacred woman. When he tires of pleasure he awakes to find his friends the animals gone, whereupon he swoons with sorrow. But the priestess chides him: "Thou who art superb as a god, why dost thou live among the beasts of the field? Come, I will conduct thee to Uruk, where is Gilgamesh, whose might is supreme." Ensnared by the vanity of praise and the conceit of his strength, Engidu follows the priestess to Uruk, saying, "Lead me to the place where is Gilgamesh. I will fight with him and manifest to him my power"; whereat the gods and husbands are well pleased. But Gilgamesh overcomes him, first with strength, then with kindness; they become devoted friends; they march forth together to protect Uruk from Elam; they return glorious with exploits and victory. Gilgamesh "put aside his war-harness, he put on his white garments, he adorned himself with the royal insignia, and bound on the diadem." Thereupon Ishtar the insatiate falls in love with him, raises her great eyes to him, and says:

"Come, Gilgamesh, be my husband, thou! Thy love, give it to me as a gift; thou shalt be my spouse, and I shall be thy wife. I shall place thee in a chariot of lapis and gold, with golden wheels and mountings of onyx; thou shalt be drawn in it by great lions, and thou shalt enter our house with the odorous incense of cedar-wood. . . . All the country by the sea shall embrace thy feet, kings shall bow down before thee, the gifts of the mountains and the plains they will bring before thee as tribute."

Gilgamesh rejects her, and reminds her of the hard fate she has inflicted upon her varied lovers, including Tammuz, a hawk, a stallion, a gardener and a lion. "Thou lovest me now," he tells her; "afterwards thou wilt strike me as thou didst these." The angry Ishtar asks of the great god Anu that he create a wild urus to kill Gilgamesh. Anu refuses, and rebukes her: "Canst thou not remain quiet now that Gilgamesh has enumerated to thee thy unfaithfulness and ignominies?" She threatens that unless he grants her request she will suspend throughout the universe all the impulses of desire and love, and so destroy every living thing. Anu yields, and creates the ferocious urus; but Gilgamesh, helped by Engidu, overcomes the beast; and when Ishtar curses the hero, Engidu throws a limb of the urus into her face. Gilgamesh rejoices and is proud, but Ishtar strikes him down in the midst of his glory by afflicting Engidu with a mortal illness.

Mourning over the corpse of his friend, whom he has loved more than any woman, Gilgamesh wonders over the mystery of death. Is there no escape from that dull fatality? One man eluded it—Shamash-napishtim; he would know the secret of deathlessness. Gilgamesh resolves to seek Shamash-napishtim, even if he must cross the world to find him. The way leads through a mountain guarded by a pair of giants whose heads touch the sky and whose breasts reach down to Hades. But they let him pass, and he picks his way for twelve miles through a dark tunnel. He emerges upon the shore of a great ocean, and sees, far over the waters, the throne of Sabitu, virgin-goddess of the seas. He calls out to her to help him cross the water; "if it cannot be done, I will lay me down on the land and die." Sabitu takes pity upon him, and allows him to cross through forty days of tempest to the Happy Island where lives Shamash-napishtim, possessor of immortal life. Gilgamesh begs of him the secret of deathlessness. Shamash-napishtim answers by telling at length the story of the Flood, and how the gods, relenting of their mad destructiveness, had made him and his wife immortal because they had preserved the human species. He offers Gilgamesh a plant whose fruit will confer renewed youth upon him who eats it; and Gilgamesh, happy, starts back on his long journey home. But on the way he stops to bathe, and while he bathes a serpent crawls by and steals the plant.*

Desolate, Gilgamesh reaches Uruk. He prays in temple after temple that Engidu may be allowed to return to life, if only to speak to him for a moment. Engidu appears, and Gilgamesh inquires of him the state of

---

* The snake was worshiped by many early peoples as a symbol of immortality, because of its apparent power to escape death by moulting its skin.

the dead. Engidu answers, "I cannot tell it thee; if I were to open the earth before thee, if I were to tell thee that which I have seen, terror would overthrow thee, thou wouldst faint away." Gilgamesh, symbol of that brave stupidity, philosophy, persists in his quest for truth: "Terror will overthrow me, I shall faint away, but tell it to me." Engidu describes the miseries of Hades, and on this gloomy note the fragmentary epic ends.[140]

VII. ARTISTS

*The lesser arts—Music—Painting—Sculpture—Bas-relief—
Architecture*

The story of Gilgamesh is almost the only example by which we may judge the literary art of Babylon. That a keen esthetic sense, if not a profound creative spirit, survived to some degree the Babylonian absorption in commercial life, epicurean recreation and compensatory piety, may be seen in the chance relics of the minor arts. Patiently glazed tiles, glittering stones, finely wrought bronze, iron, silver and gold, delicate embroideries, soft rugs and richly dyed robes, luxurious tapestries, pedestaled tables, beds and chairs[141]—these lent grace, if not dignity or final worth, to Babylonian civilization. Jewelry abounded in quantity, but missed the subtle artistry of Egypt; it went in for a display of yellow metal, and thought it artistic to make entire statues of gold.[142] There were many musical instruments—flutes, psalteries, harps, bagpipes, lyres, drums, horns, reed-pipes, trumpets, cymbals and tambourines. Orchestras played and singers sang, individually and chorally, in temples and palaces, and at the feasts of the well-to-do.[143]

Painting was purely subsidiary; it decorated walls and statuary, but made no attempt to become an independent art.[144] We do not find among Babylonian ruins the distemper paintings that glorified the Egyptian tombs, or such frescoes as adorned the palaces of Crete. Babylonian sculpture remained similarly undeveloped, and was apparently stiffened into an early death by conventions derived from Sumeria and enforced by the priests: all the faces portrayed are one face, all the kings have the same thick and muscular frame, all the captives are cast in one mould. Very little Babylonian statuary survives, and that without excuse. The bas-reliefs are better, but they too are stereotyped and crude; a great gulf separates them from the mobile vigor of the reliefs that the Egyptians had carved a thousand years before; they reach sublimity only when they depict animals possessed of the silent dignity of nature, or enraged by the cruelty of men.[145]

Babylonian architecture is safe from judgment now, for hardly any of its remains rise to more than a few feet above the sands; and there are no carved or painted representations among the relics to show us clearly the form and structure of palaces and temples. Houses were built of dried mud, or, among the rich, of brick; they seldom knew windows, and their doors opened not upon the narrow street but upon an interior court shaded from the sun. Tradition describes the better dwellings as rising to three or four stories in height.[146] The temple was raised upon foundations level with the roofs of the houses whose life it was to dominate; usually it was an enormous square of tiled masonry, built, like the houses, around a court; in this court most of the religious ceremonies were performed. Near the temple, in most cases, rose a *ziggurat* (literally "a high place")—a tower of superimposed and diminishing cubical stories surrounded by external stairs. Its uses were partly religious, as a lofty shrine for the god, partly astronomic, as an observatory from which the priests could watch the all-revealing stars. The great *ziggurat* at Borsippa was called "The Stages of the Seven Spheres"; each story was dedicated to one of the seven planets known to Babylonia, and bore a symbolic color. The lowest was black, as the color of Saturn; the next above it was white, as the color of Venus; the next was purple, for Jupiter; the fourth blue, for Mercury; the fifth scarlet, for Mars; the sixth silver, for the moon; the seventh gold, for the sun. These spheres and stars, beginning at the top, designated the days of the week.[147]

There was not much art in this architecture, so far as we can vision it now; it was a mass of straight lines seeking the glory of size. Here and there among the ruins are vaults and arches—forms derived from Sumeria, negligently used, and unconscious of their destiny. Decoration, interior and exterior, was almost confined to enameling some of the brick surfaces with bright glazes of yellow, blue, white and red, with occasional tiled figures of animals or plants. The use of vitrified glaze, not merely to beautify, but to protect the masonry from sun and rain, was at least as old as Naram-sin, and was to continue in Mesopotamia down to Moslem days. In this way ceramics, though seldom producing rememberable pottery, became the most characteristic art of the ancient Near East. Despite such aid, Babylonian architecture remained a heavy and prosaic thing, condemned to mediocrity by the material it used. The temples rose rapidly out of the earth which slave labor turned so readily into brick and cementing pitch; they did not require centuries for their erection, like the monumental structures of Egypt or medieval Europe. But they decayed almost as quickly as they rose; fifty years of neglect reduced them to the dust from which they had been made.[148]

The very cheapness of brick corrupted Babylonian design; with such materials it was easy to achieve size, difficult to compass beauty. Brick does not lend itself to sublimity, and sublimity is the soul of architecture.

VIII. BABYLONIAN SCIENCE

Mathematics—Astronomy—The calendar—Geography—Medicine

Being merchants, the Babylonians were more likely to achieve successes in science than in art. Commerce created mathematics, and united with religion to beget astronomy. In their varied functions as judges, administrators, agricultural and industrial magnates, and soothsayers skilled in examining entrails and stars, the priests of Mesopotamia unconsciously laid the foundations of those sciences which, in the profane hands of the Greeks, were for a time to depose religion from its leadership of the world.

Babylonian mathematics rested on a division of the circle into 360 degrees, and of the year into 360 days; on this basis it developed a sexagesimal system of calculation by sixties, which became the parent of later duodecimal systems of reckoning by twelves. The numeration used only three figures: a sign for 1, repeated up to 9; a sign for 10, repeated up to 90; and a sign for 100. Computation was made easier by tables which showed not only multiplication and division, but the halves, quarters, thirds, squares and cubes of the basic numbers. Geometry advanced to the measurement of complex and irregular areas. The Babylonian figure for π (the ratio of the circumference to the diameter of a circle) was 3—a very crude approximation for a nation of astronomers.

Astronomy was the special science of the Babylonians, for which they were famous throughout the ancient world. Here again magic was the mother of science: the Babylonians studied the stars not so much to chart the courses of caravans and ships, as to divine the future fates of men; they were astrologers first and astronomers afterward. Every planet was a god, interested and vital in the affairs of men: Jupiter was Marduk, Mercury was Nabu, Mars was Nergal, the sun was Shamash, the moon was Sin, Saturn was Ninib, Venus was Ishtar. Every movement of every star determined, or forecast, some terrestrial event: if, for example, the moon was low, a distant nation would submit to the king; if the moon was in crescent the king would overcome the enemy. Such efforts to wring the future out of the stars became a passion with the Babylonians; priests skilled in astrology reaped rich rewards from both people and king. Some of them were sincere students, poring zealously over astrologic tomes which, according to their traditions, had been composed in the days of Sargon of Akkad; they complained of the quacks who, without such study, went about reading horoscopes for a fee, or predicting the weather a year ahead, in the fashion of our modern almanacs.[149]

Astronomy developed slowly out of this astrologic observation and charting of the stars. As far back as 2000 B.C. the Babylonians had made accurate records of the heliacal rising and setting of the planet Venus; they had fixed the position of various stars, and were slowly mapping the sky.[150] The Kassite conquest interrupted this development for a thousand years. Then, under Nebuchadrezzar, astronomic progress was resumed; the priest-scientists plotted the orbits of sun and moon, noted their conjunctions and eclipses, calculated the courses of the planets, and made the first clear distinction between a planet and a star;*[151] they determined the dates of winter and summer solstices, of vernal and autumnal equinoxes, and, following the lead of the Sumerians, divided the ecliptic (i.e., the path of the earth around the sun) into the twelve signs of the Zodiac. Having divided the circle into 360 degrees, they divided the degree into sixty minutes, and the minute into sixty seconds.[152] They measured time by a clepsydra or water-clock, and a sun-dial, and these seem to have been not merely developed but invented by them.[153]

They divided the year into twelve lunar months, six having thirty days, six twenty-nine; and as this made but 354 days in all, they added a thirteenth month occasionally to harmonize the calendar with the seasons. The month was divided into four weeks according to the four phases of the moon. An attempt was made to establish a more convenient calendar by dividing the month into six weeks of five days; but the phases of the moon proved more effective than the conveniences of men. The day was reckoned not from midnight to midnight but from one rising of the moon to the next;[154] it was divided into twelve hours, and each of these hours was divided into thirty minutes, so that the Babylonian minute had the feminine quality of being four times as long as its name might suggest. The division of our month into four weeks, of our clock into twelve hours (instead of twenty-four), of our hour into sixty minutes, and of

---

* To the Babylonians a planet was distinguished from the "fixed" stars by its observable motion or "wandering." In modern astronomy a planet is defined as a heavenly body regularly revolving about the sun.

our minute into sixty seconds, are unsuspected Babylonian vestiges in our contemporary world.*

The dependence of Babylonian science upon religion had a more stagnant effect in medicine than in astronomy. It was not so much the obscurantism of the priests that held the science back, as the superstition of the people. Already by the time of Hammurabi the art of healing had separated itself in some measure from the domain and domination of the clergy; a regular profession of physician had been established, with fees and penalties fixed by law. A patient who called in a doctor could know in advance just how much he would have to pay for such treatment or operation; and if he belonged to the poorer classes the fee was lowered accordingly.[157] If the doctor bungled badly he had to pay damages to the patient; in extreme cases, as we have seen, his fingers were cut off so that he might not readily experiment again.[158]

But this almost secularized science found itself helpless before the demand of the people for supernatural diagnosis and magical cures. Sorcerers and necromancers were more popular than physicians, and enforced, by their influence with the populace, irrational methods of treatment. Disease was possession, and was due to sin; therefore it had to be treated mainly by incantations, magic and prayer; when drugs were used they were aimed not to cleanse the patient but to terrify and exorcise the demon. The favorite drug was a mixture deliberately compounded of disgusting elements, apparently on the theory that the sick man had a stronger stomach than the demon that possessed him; the usual ingredients were raw meat, snake-flesh and wood-shavings mixed with wine and oil; or rotten food, crushed bones, fat and dirt, mingled with animal or human urine or excrement.[159] Occasionally this *Dreckapothek* was replaced by an effort to appease the demon with milk, honey, cream, and sweet-smelling herbs.[160] If all treatment failed, the patient was in some cases carried into the market-place, so that his neighbors might indulge their ancient propensity for prescribing infallible cures.[161]

Perhaps the eight hundred medical tablets that survive to inform us

---

* From charting the skies the Babylonians turned to mapping the earth. The oldest maps of which we have any knowledge were those which the priests prepared of the roads and cities of Nebuchadrezzar's empire.[155] A clay tablet found in the ruins of Gasur (two hundred miles north of Babylon), and dated back to 1600 B.C., contains, in a space hardly an inch square, a map of the province of Shat-Azalla; it represents mountains by rounded lines, water by tilting lines, rivers by parallel lines; the names of various towns are inscribed, and the direction of north and south is indicated in the margin.[156]

of Babylonian medicine do it injustice. Reconstruction of the whole from a part is hazardous in history, and the writing of history is the reconstruction of the whole from a part. Quite possibly these magical cures were merely subtle uses of the power of suggestion; perhaps those evil concoctions were intended as emetics; and the Babylonian may have meant nothing more irrational by his theory of illness as due to invading demons and the patient's sins than we do by interpreting it as due to invading bacteria invited by culpable negligence, uncleanliness, or greed. We must not be too sure of the ignorance of our ancestors.

IX. PHILOSOPHERS

Religion and Philosophy—The Babylonian Job—The Babylonian Koheleth—An anti-clerical

A nation is born stoic, and dies epicurean. At its cradle (to repeat a thoughtful adage) religion stands, and philosophy accompanies it to the grave. In the beginning of all cultures a strong religious faith conceals and softens the nature of things, and gives men courage to bear pain and hardship patiently; at every step the gods are with them, and will not let them perish, until they do. Even then a firm faith will explain that it was the sins of the people that turned their gods to an avenging wrath; evil does not destroy faith, but strengthens it. If victory comes, if war is forgotten in security and peace, then wealth grows; the life of the body gives way, in the dominant classes, to the life of the senses and the mind; toil and suffering are replaced by pleasure and ease; science weakens faith even while thought and comfort weaken virility and fortitude. At last men begin to doubt the gods; they mourn the tragedy of knowledge, and seek refuge in every passing delight. Achilles is at the beginning, Epicurus at the end. After David comes Job, and after Job, Ecclesiastes.

Since we know the thought of Babylon mostly from the later reigns, it is natural that we should find it shot through with the weary wisdom of tired philosophers who took their pleasures like Englishmen. On one tablet Balta-atrua complains that though he has obeyed the commands of the gods more strictly than any one else, he has been laid low with a variety of misfortunes; he has lost his parents and his property, and even the little that remained to him has been stolen on the highway. His friends, like Job's, reply that his disaster must be in punishment of some secret sin—perhaps that *hybris*, or insolent pride of prosperity, which particularly arouses the jealous anger of the gods. They assure him that evil is merely good in disguise, some part of the divine plan seen too narrowly by frail minds unconscious of the whole. Let Balta-atrua keep faith and courage, and he will be rewarded in the end; better still, his enemies will be punished. Balta-atrua calls out to the gods for help—and the fragment suddenly ends.[162]

Another poem, found among the ruins of Ashurbanipal's collection of Babylonian literature, presents the same problem more definitely in the person of Tabi-utul-Enlil, who appears to have been a ruler in Nippur. He describes his difficulties:*

> (My eyeballs he obscured, bolting them as with) a lock;
> (My ears he bolted), like those of a deaf person.
> A king, I have been changed into a slave;
> As a madman (my) companions maltreat me.
> Send me help from the pit dug (for me)! . . .
> By day deep sighs, at night weeping;
> The month—cries; the year—distress. . . .

He goes on to tell what a pious fellow he has always been, the very last man in the world who should have met with so cruel a fate:

> As though I had not always set aside the portion for the god,
> And had not invoked the goddess at the meal,
> Had not bowed my face and brought my tribute;
> As though I were one in whose mouth supplication and prayer were
>   not constant! . . .
> I taught my country to guard the name of the god;
> To honor the name of the goddess I accustomed my people. . . .
> I thought that such things were pleasing to a god.

Stricken with disease despite all this formal piety, he muses on the impossibility of understanding the gods, and on the uncertainty of human affairs.

> Who is there that can grasp the will of the gods in heaven?
> The plan of a god full of mystery—who can understand it? . . .
> He who was alive yesterday is dead today;
> In an instant he is cast into grief; of a sudden he is crushed.

---

* Parenthetical passages are guesses.

For a moment he sings and plays;
In a twinkling he wails like a mourner. . . .
Like a net trouble has covered me.
My eyes look but see not;
My ears are open but they hear not. . . .
Pollution has fallen upon my genitals,
And it has assailed the glands in my bowels. . . .
With death grows dark my whole body. . . .
All day the pursuer pursues me;
During the night he gives me no breath for a moment. . . .
My limbs are dismembered, they march out of unison.
In my dung I pass the night like an ox;
Like a sheep I mix in my excrements. . . .

Like Job, he makes another act of faith:

But I know the day of the cessation of my tears,
A day of the grace of the protecting spirits; then divinity will be
　merciful.[163]

In the end everything turns out happily. A spirit appears, and cures all of Tabi's ailments; a mighty storm drives all the demons of disease out of his frame. He praises Marduk, offers rich sacrifice, and calls upon every one never to despair of the gods.*

As there is but a step from this to the *Book of Job,* so we find in late Babylonian literature unmistakable premonitions of Ecclesiastes. In the *Epic of Gilgamesh* the goddess Sabitu advises the hero to give up his longing for a life after death, and to eat, drink and be merry on the earth.

O Gilgamesh, why dost thou run in all directions?
The life that thou seekest thou wilt not find.
When the gods created mankind they determined death for mankind;
Life they kept in their own hands.
Thou, O Gilgamesh, fill thy belly;
Day and night be thou merry; . . .
Day and night be joyous and content!
Let thy garments be pure,

---

* It is probable that this composition, prototypes of which are found in Sumeria, influenced the author of the *Book of Job.*[164]

Thy head be washed; wash thyself with water!
Regard the little one who takes hold of thy hand;
Enjoy the wife in thy bosom.[165]*

In another tablet we hear a bitterer note, culminating in atheism and blasphemy. Gubarru, a Babylonian Alcibiades, interrogates an elder sceptically:

O very wise one, O possessor of intelligence, let thy heart groan!
The heart of God is as far as the inner parts of the heavens.
Wisdom is hard, and men do not understand it.

To which the old man answers with a forboding of Amos and Isaiah:

Give attention, my friend, and understand my thought.
Men exalt the work of the great man who is skilled in murder.
They disparage the poor man who has done no sin.
They justify the wicked man, whose fault is grave.
They drive away the just man who seeks the will of God.
They let the strong take the food of the poor;
They strengthen the mighty;
They destroy the weak man, the rich man drives him away.

He advises Gubarru to do the will of the gods none the less. But Gubarru will have nothing to do with gods or priests who are always on the side of the biggest fortunes:

They have offered lies and untruth without ceasing.
They say in noble words what is in favor of the rich man.
Is his wealth diminished? They come to his help.
They ill-treat the weak man like a thief,
They destroy him in a tremor, they extinguish him like a flame.[166]

We must not exaggerate the prevalence of such moods in Babylon; doubtless the people listened lovingly to their priests, and crowded the temples to seek favors of the gods. The marvel is that they were so long

---

* Cf. *Ecclesiastes*, ix, 7-9: "Go thy way, eat thy bread with joy, and drink thy wine with a merry heart; for God now accepteth thy works. Let thy garments be always white; and let thy head lack no ointment. Live joyfully with the wife whom thou lovest, all the days of the life of thy vanity."

loyal to a religion that offered them so little consolation. Nothing could be known, said the priests, except by divine revelation; and this revelation came only through the priests. The last chapter of that revelation told how the dead soul, whether good or bad, descended into Aralu, or Hades, to spend there an eternity in darkness and suffering. Is it any wonder that Babylon gave itself to revelry, while Nebuchadrezzar, having all, understanding nothing, fearing everything, went mad?

X. EPITAPH

Tradition and the *Book of Daniel,* unverified by any document known to us, tell how Nebuchadrezzar, after a long reign of uninterrupted victory and prosperity, after beautifying his city with roads and palaces, and erecting fifty-four temples to the gods, fell into a strange insanity, thought himself a beast, walked on all fours, and ate grass.[167] For four years his name disappears from the history and governmental records of Babylonia;[168] it reappears for a moment, and then, in 562 B.C., he passes away.

Within thirty years after his death his empire crumbled to pieces. Nabonidus, who held the throne for seventeen years, preferred archeology to government, and devoted himself to excavating the antiquities of Sumeria while his own realm was going to ruin.[169] The army fell into disorder; business men forgot love of country in the sublime internationalism of finance; the people, busy with trade and pleasure, unlearned the arts of war. The priests usurped more and more of the royal power, and fattened their treasuries with wealth that tempted invasion and conquest. When Cyrus and his disciplined Persians stood at the gates, the anticlericals of Babylon connived to open the city to him, and welcomed his enlightened domination.[170] For two centuries Persia ruled Babylonia as part of the greatest empire that history had yet known. Then the exuberant Alexander came, captured the unresisting capital, conquered all the Near East, and drank himself to death in the palace of Nebuchadrezzar.[171]

The civilization of Babylonia was not as fruitful for humanity as Egypt's, not as varied and profound as India's, not as subtle and mature as China's. And yet it was from Babylonia that those fascinating legends came which, through the literary artistry of the Jews, became an inseparable portion of Europe's religious lore; it was from Babylonia, rather than from Egypt, that the roving Greeks brought to their city-states and thence to Rome and ourselves, the foundations of mathematics, astronomy, medicine, grammar, lexicography, archeology, history, and philosophy. The Greek names for the metals and the constellations, for weights and measures, for musical instruments and many drugs, are translations, sometimes mere transliterations, of Babylonian names.[172] While Greek architecture derived its forms and inspiration from Egypt and Crete, Babylonian architecture, through the *ziggurat*, led to the towers of Moslem mosques, the steeples and campaniles of medieval art, and the "setback" style of contemporary architecture in America. The laws of Hammurabi became for all ancient societies a legacy comparable to Rome's gift of order and government to the modern world. Through Assyria's conquest of Babylon, her appropriation of the ancient city's culture, and her dissemination of that culture throughout her wide empire; through the long Captivity of the Jews, and the great influence upon them of Babylonian life and thought; through the Persian and Greek conquests, which opened with unprecedented fulness and freedom all the roads of communication and trade between Babylon and the rising cities of Ionia, Asia Minor and Greece—through these and many other ways the civilization of the Land between the Rivers passed down into the cultural endowment of our race. In the end nothing is lost; for good or evil every event has effects forever.

CHAPTER X

Assyria

I. CHRONICLES

Beginnings — Cities — Race — The conquerors — Sennacherib and Esarhaddon — "Sardanapalus"

MEANWHILE, three hundred miles north of Babylon, another civilization had appeared. Forced to maintain a hard military life by the mountain tribes always threatening it on every side, it had in time overcome its assailants, had conquered its parent cities in Elam, Sumeria, Akkad and Babylonia, had mastered Phœnicia and Egypt, and had for two centuries dominated the Near East with brutal power. Sumeria was to Babylonia, and Babylonia to Assyria, what Crete was to Greece, and Greece to Rome: the first created a civilization, the second developed it to its height, the third inherited it, added little to it, protected it, and transmitted it as a dying gift to the encompassing and victorious barbarians. For barbarism is always around civilization, amid it and beneath it, ready to engulf it by arms, or mass migration, or unchecked fertility. Barbarism is like the jungle; it never admits its defeat; it waits patiently for centuries to recover the territory it has lost.

The new state grew about four cities fed by the waters or tributaries of the Tigris: Ashur, which is now Kala'at-Sherghat; Arbela, which is Irbil; Kalakh, which is Nimrud; and Nineveh, which is Kuyunjik—just across the river from oily Mosul. At Ashur prehistoric obsidian flakes and knives have been found, and black pottery with geometric patterns that suggest a central Asian origin;[1] at Tepe Gawra, near the site of Nineveh, a recent expedition unearthed a town which its proud discoverers date back to 3700 B.C., despite its many temples and tombs, its well-carved cylinder seals, its combs and jewelry, and the oldest dice known to history[2]—a thought for reformers. The god Ashur gave his name to a city (and finally to all Assyria); there the earliest of the nation's kings had their residence, until its exposure to the heat of the desert and the attacks of the neighboring Babylonians led Ashur's rulers to build a secondary capital in cooler Nineveh—named also after a god, Nina, the Ishtar of Assyria. Here, in the heyday of Ashurbanipal, 300,000 people lived, and all the western Orient came to pay tribute to the Universal King.

The population was a mixture of Semites from the civilized south (Babylonia and Akkadia) with non-Semitic tribes from the west (probably of Hittite or Mitannian affinity) and Kurdish mountaineers from the Caucasus.[3] They took their common language and their arts from Sumeria, but modified them later into an almost undistinguishable similarity to the language and arts of Babylonia.[4] Their circumstances, however, forbade them to indulge in the effeminate ease of Babylon; from beginning to end they were a race of warriors, mighty in muscle and courage, abounding in proud hair and beard, standing straight, stern and stolid on their monuments, and bestriding with tremendous feet the east-Mediterranean world. Their history is one of kings and slaves, wars and conquests, bloody victories and sudden defeat. The early kings—once mere *patesis* tributary to the south—took advantage of the Kassite domination of Babylonia to establish their independence; and soon enough one of them decked himself with that title which all the monarchs of Assyria were to display: "King of Universal Reign." Out of the dull dynasties of these forgotten potentates certain figures emerge whose deeds illuminate the development of their country.*

While Babylonia was still in the darkness of the Kassite era, Shalmaneser I brought the little city-states of the north under one rule, and made Kalakh his capital. But the first great name in Assyrian history is Tiglath-Pileser I. He was a mighty hunter before the Lord: if it is wise to believe monarchs, he slew 120 lions on foot, and 800 from his chariot.[5] One of his inscriptions —written by a scribe more royalist than the King—tells how he hunted nations as well as animals: "In my fierce valor I marched against the people of Qummuh, conquered their cities, carried off their booty, their goods and their property without reckoning, and burned their cities with fire—destroyed and devastated them. . . . The people of Adansh left their mountains and embraced my feet. I imposed taxes upon them."[6] In every direction he led his armies, conquering the Hittites, the Armenians, and forty other nations, capturing Babylon, and frightening Egypt into sending him anxious gifts. (He was particularly mollified by a crocodile.) With the proceeds of his conquests he built temples to the Assyrian gods and goddesses, who, like anxious

---

* A tablet recently found in the ruins of Sargon II's library at Khorsabad contains an unbroken list of Assyrian kings from the twenty-third century B.C. to Ashurnirari (753-46 B.C.).[4a]

débutantes, asked no questions about the source of his wealth. Then Babylon revolted, defeated his armies, pillaged his temples, and carried his gods into Babylonian captivity. Tiglath-Pileser died of shame.[7]

His reign was a symbol and summary of all Assyrian history: death and taxes, first for Assyria's neighbors, then for herself. Ashurnasirpal II conquered a dozen petty states, brought much booty home from the wars, cut out with his own hand the eyes of princely captives, enjoyed his harem, and passed respectably away.[8] Shalmaneser III carried these conquests as far as Damascus; fought costly battles, killing 16,000 Syrians in one engagement; built temples, levied tribute, and was deposed by his son in a violent revolution.[9] Sammuramat ruled as queen-mother for three years, and provided a frail historical basis (for this is all that we know of her) for the Greek legend of Semiramis—half goddess and half queen, great general, great engineer and great statesman—so attractively detailed by Diodorus the Sicilian.[10] Tiglath-Pileser III gathered new armies, reconquered Armenia, overran Syria and Babylonia, made vassal cities of Damascus, Samaria and Babylon, extended the rule of Assyria from the Caucasus to Egypt, tired of war, became an excellent administrator, built many temples and palaces, held his empire together with an iron hand, and died peacefully in bed. Sargon II, an officer in the army, made himself king by a Napoleonic *coup d'état;* led his troops in person, and took in every engagement the most dangerous post;[11] defeated Elam and Egypt, reconquered Babylonia, and received the homage of the Jews, the Philistines, even of the Cypriote Greeks; ruled his empire well, encouraged arts and letters, handicrafts and trade, and died in a victorious battle that definitely preserved Assyria from invasion by the wild Cimmerian hordes.

His son Sennacherib put down revolts in the distant provinces adjoining the Persian Gulf, attacked Jerusalem and Egypt without success,* sacked eighty-nine cities and 820 villages, captured 7,200 horses, 11,000 asses, 80,000 oxen, 800,000 sheep, and 208,000 prisoners;[13] the official historian, on his life, did not understate these figures. Then, irritated by the prejudice of Babylon in favor of freedom, he besieged it, took it, and burned it to the ground; nearly all the inhabitants, young and old, male and female, were put to death, so that mountains of corpses blocked the streets; the temples and palaces were pillaged to the last *shekel*, and the once omnipotent gods of Babylon were hacked to pieces or carried in

---

* Egyptian tradition attributed the escape of Egypt to discriminating field mice who ate up the quivers, bow-strings and shield-straps of the Assyrians encamped before Pelusium, so that the Egyptians were enabled to defeat the invaders easily the next day.[12]

bondage to Nineveh: Marduk *the* god became a menial to Ashur. Such Babylonians as survived did not conclude that Marduk had been over-rated; they told themselves—as the captive Jews would tell themselves a century later in that same Babylon—that their god had condescended to be defeated in order to punish his people. With the spoils of his con-quests and pillage Sennacherib rebuilt Nineveh, changed the courses of rivers to protect it, reclaimed waste lands with the vigor of countries suffering from an agricultural surplus, and was assassinated by his sons while piously mumbling his prayers.[14]

Another son, Esarhaddon, snatched the throne from his blood-stained brothers, invaded Egypt to punish her for supporting Syrian revolts, made her an Assyrian province, amazed western Asia with his long triumphal progress from Memphis to Nineveh, dragging endless booty in his train; established Assyria in unprecedented prosperity as master of the whole Near Eastern world; delighted Babylonia by freeing and honoring its cap-tive gods, and rebuilding its shattered capital; conciliated Elam by feeding its famine-stricken people in an act of international beneficence almost without parallel in the ancient world; and died on the way to suppress a revolt in Egypt, after giving his empire the justest and kindliest rule in its half-barbarous history.

His successor, Ashurbanipal (the Sardanapalus of the Greeks), reaped the fruits of Esarhaddon's sowing. During his long reign Assyria reached the climax of its wealth and prestige; after him his country, ruined by forty years of intermittent war, fell into exhaustion and decay, and ended its career hardly a decade after Ashurbanipal's death. A scribe has pre-served to us a yearly record of this reign;[15] it is a dull and bloody mess of war after war, siege after siege, starved cities and flayed captives. The scribe represents Ashurbanipal himself as reporting his destruction of Elam:

> For a distance of one month and twenty-five days' march I devas-tated the districts of Elam. I spread salt and thorn-bush there (to injure the soil). Sons of the kings, sisters of the kings, members of Elam's royal family young and old, prefects, governors, knights, arti-sans, as many as there were, inhabitants male and female, big and little, horses, mules, asses, flocks and herds more numerous than a swarm of locusts—I carried them off as booty to Assyria. The dust of Susa, of Madaktu, of Haltemash and of their other cities, I carried it off to Assyria. In a month of days I subdued Elam in its whole

extent. The voice of man, the steps of flocks and herds, the happy
shouts of mirth—I put an end to them in its fields, which I left for
the asses, the gazelles, and all manner of wild beasts to people.[16]

The severed head of the Elamite king was brought to Ashurbanipal as he
feasted with his queen in the palace garden; he had the head raised on a
pole in the midst of his guests, and the royal revel went on; later the
head was fixed over the gate of Nineveh, and slowly rotted away. The
Elamite general, Dananu, was flayed alive, and then was bled like a lamb;
his brother had his throat cut, and his body was divided into pieces, which
were distributed over the country as souvenirs.[17]

It never occurred to Ashurbanipal that he and his men were brutal;
these clean-cut penalties were surgical necessities in his attempt to remove
rebellions and establish discipline among the heterogeneous and turbulent
peoples, from Ethiopia to Armenia, and from Syria to Media, whom his
predecessors had subjected to Assyrian rule; it was his obligation to maintain this legacy intact. He boasted of the peace that he had established in
his empire, and of the good order that prevailed in its cities; and the
boast was not without truth. That he was not merely a conqueror intoxicated with blood he proved by his munificence as a builder and as a
patron of letters and the arts. Like some Roman ruler calling to the
Greeks, he sent to all his dominions for sculptors and architects to design
and adorn new temples and palaces; he commissioned innumerable scribes
to secure and copy for him all the classics of Sumerian and Babylonian
literature, and gathered these copies in his library at Nineveh, where
modern scholarship found them almost intact after twenty-five centuries
of time had flowed over them. Like another Frederick, he was as vain
of his literary abilities as of his triumphs in war and the chase.[18] Diodorus
describes him as a dissolute and bisexual Nero,[19] but in the wealth of documents that have come down to us from this period there is little corroboration for this view. From the composition of literary tablets Ashurbanipal passed with royal confidence—armed only with knife and javelin—to
hand-to-hand encounters with lions; if we may credit the reports of his
contemporaries he did not hesitate to lead the attack in person, and often
dealt with his own hand the decisive blow.[20] Little wonder that Byron was
fascinated with him, and wove about him a drama half legend and half
history, in which all the wealth and power of Assyria came to their
height, and broke into universal ruin and royal despair.

II. ASSYRIAN GOVERNMENT

Imperialism—Assyrian war—The conscript gods—Law—Delicacies
of penology — Administration — The violence of Oriental
monarchies

If we should admit the imperial principle—that it is good, for the sake of spreading law, security, commerce and peace, that many states should be brought, by persuasion or force, under the authority of one government—then we should have to concede to Assyria the distinction of having established in western Asia a larger measure and area of order and prosperity than that region of the earth had ever, to our knowledge, enjoyed before. The government of Ashurbanipal—which ruled Assyria, Babylonia, Armenia, Media, Palestine, Syria, Phœnicia, Sumeria, Elam and Egypt—was without doubt the most extensive administrative organization yet seen in the Mediterranean or Near Eastern world; only Hammurabi and Thutmose III had approached it, and Persia alone would equal it before the coming of Alexander. In some ways it was a liberal empire; its larger cities retained considerable local autonomy, and each nation in it was left its own religion, law and ruler, provided it paid its tribute promptly.[21] In so loose an organization every weakening of the central power was bound to produce rebellions, or, at the best, a certain tributary negligence, so that the subject states had to be conquered again and again. To avoid these recurrent rebellions Tiglath-Pileser III established the characteristic Assyrian policy of deporting conquered populations to alien habitats, where, mingling with the natives, they might lose their unity and identity, and have less opportunity to rebel. Revolts came nevertheless, and Assyria had to keep herself always ready for war.

The army was therefore the most vital part of the government. Assyria recognized frankly that government is the nationalization of force, and her chief contributions to progress were in the art of war. Chariots, cavalry, infantry and sappers were organized into flexible formations, siege mechanisms were as highly developed as among the Romans, strategy and tactics were well understood.[22] Tactics centered about the idea of rapid movement making possible a piecemeal attack—so old is the secret of Napoleon. Iron-working had grown to the point of encasing the warrior with armor to a degree of stiffness rivaling a medieval knight; even the archers and pikemen wore copper or iron helmets, padded loin-cloths, enormous shields, and a leather skirt covered with metal scales. The weapons were arrows, lances, cutlasses, maces, clubs, slings and battle-axes. The nobility fought from chariots in the van of the battle, and the king, in his royal chariot, usually led them in person; generals had not yet learned to die in bed. Ashurnasirpal introduced the use of cavalry as an aid to the chariots, and this innovation proved decisive in many engagements.[23] The principal siege engine was a battering-ram tipped with iron; sometimes it was suspended from a scaffold by ropes, and was swung back to give it forward impetus; sometimes it was run forward on wheels. The besieged fought from the walls with missiles, torches, burning pitch, chains designed to entangle the ram, and gaseous "stink-pots" (as they were called) to befuddle the enemy;[24] again the novel is not new. A captured city was usually plundered and burnt to the ground, and its site was deliberately denuded by killing its trees.[25] The loyalty of the troops was secured by dividing a large part of the spoils among them; their bravery was ensured by the general rule of the Near East that all captives in war might be enslaved or slain. Soldiers were rewarded for every severed head they brought in from the field, so that the aftermath of a victory generally witnessed the wholesale decapitation of fallen foes.[26] Most often the prisoners, who would have consumed much food in a long campaign, and would have constituted a danger and nuisance in the rear, were despatched after the battle; they knelt with their backs to their captors, who beat their heads in with clubs, or cut them off with cutlasses. Scribes stood by to count the number of prisoners taken and killed by each soldier, and apportioned the booty accordingly; the king, if time permitted, presided at the slaughter. The nobles among the defeated were given more special treatment: their ears, noses, hands and feet were sliced off, or they were thrown from high towers, or they and their children were beheaded, or flayed alive, or roasted over a slow fire. No compunction seems to have been felt at this waste of human life; the birth rate would soon make up for it, and meanwhile it relieved the pressure of population upon the means of subsistence.[27] Probably it was in part by their reputation for mercy to prisoners of war that Alexander and Cæsar undermined the morale of the enemy, and conquered the Mediterranean world.

Next to the army the chief reliance of the monarch was upon the church, and he paid lavishly for the support of the priests. The formal head of the state was by concerted fiction the god Ashur; all pronouncements were in his name, all laws were edicts of his divine will, all taxes were collected for his treasury, all campaigns were fought to furnish him (or, occasionally, another deity) with spoils and glory. The king had himself described as a god, usually an incarnation of Shamash, the sun. The religion of Assyria, like its language, its science and its arts, was imported from Sumeria and Babylonia, with occasional adaptations to the needs of a military state.

The adaptation was most visible in the case of the law, which was distinguished by a martial ruthlessness. Punishment ranged from public exhibition to forced labor, twenty to a hundred lashes, the slitting of nose and ears, castration, pulling out the tongue, gouging out the eyes, impalement, and beheading.[28] The laws of Sargon II prescribe such additional delicacies as the drinking of poison, and the burning of the offender's son or daughter alive on the altar of the god;[29] but there is no evidence of these laws being carried out in the last millennium before Christ. Adultery, rape and some forms of theft were considered capital crimes.[30] Trial by ordeal was occasionally employed; the accused, sometimes bound in fetters, was flung into the river, and his guilt was left to the arbitrament of the water. In general Assyrian law was less secular and more primitive than the Babylonian Code of Hammurabi, which apparently preceded it in time.*

Local administration, originally by feudal barons, fell in the course of time into the hands of provincial prefects or governors appointed by the king; this form of imperial government was taken over by Persia, and passed on from Persia to Rome. The prefects were expected to collect taxes, to organize the *corvée* for works which, like irrigation, could not be left to personal initiative; and above all to raise regiments and lead them in the royal campaigns. Meanwhile royal spies (or, as we should say, "intelligence officers") kept watch on these prefects and their aides, and informed the king concerning the state of the nation.

All in all, the Assyrian government was primarily an instrument of war. For war was often more profitable than peace; it cemented discipline, intensified patriotism, strengthened the royal power, and brought abundant spoils and slaves for the enrichment and service of the capital. Hence Assyrian history is largely a picture of cities sacked and villages or fields laid waste. When Ashurbanipal suppressed the revolt of his brother, Shamash-shum-ukin, and captured Babylon after a long and bitter siege,

---

* The oldest extant Assyrian laws are ninety articles contained on three tablets found at Ashur and dating ca. 1300 B.C.[31]

the city presented a terrible spectacle, and shocked even the Assyrians. . . . Most of the numerous victims to pestilence or famine lay about the streets or in the public squares, a prey to the dogs and swine; such of the inhabitants and the soldiery as were comparatively strong had endeavored to escape into the country, and only those remained who had not sufficient strength to drag themselves beyond the walls. Ashurbanipal pursued the fugitives, and having captured nearly all of them, vented on them the full fury of his vengeance. He caused the tongues of the soldiers to be torn out, and then had them clubbed to death. He massacred the common folk in front of the great winged bulls which had already witnessed a similar butchery half a century before under his grandfather Sennacherib. The corpses of the victims remained long unburied, a prey to all unclean beasts and birds.[32]

The weakness of Oriental monarchies was bound up with this addiction to violence. Not only did the subject provinces repeatedly revolt, but within the royal palace or family itself violence again and again attempted to upset what violence had established and maintained. At or near the end of almost every reign some disturbance broke out over the succession to the throne; the aging monarch saw conspiracies forming around him, and in several cases he was hastened to his end by murder. The nations of the Near East preferred violent uprisings to corrupt elections, and their form of recall was assassination. Some of these wars were doubtless inevitable: barbarians prowled about every frontier, and one reign of weakness would see the Scythians, the Cimmerians, or some other horde, sweeping down upon the wealth of the Assyrian cities. And perhaps we exaggerate the frequency of war and violence in these Oriental states, through the accident that ancient monuments and modern chroniclers have preserved the dramatic record of battles, and ignored the victories of peace. Historians have been prejudiced in favor of bloodshed; they found it, or thought their readers would find it, more interesting than the quiet achievements of the mind. We think war less frequent today because we are conscious of the lucid intervals of peace, while history seems conscious only of the fevered crises of war.

III. ASSYRIAN LIFE

Industry and trade—Marriage and morals—Religion and science—
Letters and libraries—The Assyrian ideal of a gentleman

The economic life of Assyria did not differ much from that of Babylonia, for in many ways the two countries were merely the north and south of one civilization. The southern kingdom was more commercial, the northern more agricultural; rich Babylonians were usually merchants, rich Assyrians were most often landed gentry actively supervising great estates, and looking with Roman scorn upon men who made their living by buying cheap and selling dear.[33] Nevertheless the same rivers flooded and nourished the land, the same method of ridges and canals controlled the overflow, the same *shadufs* raised the water from ever deeper beds to fields sown with the same wheat and barley, millet and sesame.* The same industries supported the life of the towns; the same system of weights and measures governed the exchange of goods; and though Nineveh and her sister capitals were too far north to be great centers of commerce, the wealth brought to them by Assyria's sovereigns filled them with handicrafts and trade. Metal was mined or imported in new abundance, and towards 700 B.C. iron replaced bronze as the basic metal of industry and armament.[35] Metal was cast, glass was blown, textiles were dyed,† earthenware was enameled, and houses were as well equipped in Nineveh as in Europe before the Industrial Revolution.[36] During the reign of Sennacherib an aqueduct was built which brought water to Nineveh from thirty miles away; a thousand feet of it, recently discovered,‡ constitute the oldest aqueduct known. Industry and trade were financed in part by private bankers, who charged 25% for loans. Lead, copper, silver and gold served as currency; and about 700 B.C. Sennacherib minted silver into half-shekel pieces—one of our earliest examples of an official coinage.[37]

The people fell into five classes: patricians or nobles; craftsmen or master-artisans, organized in guilds, and including the professions as well as the trades; the unskilled but free workmen and peasants of town and village; serfs bound to the soil on great estates, in the manner of medieval Europe;

---

* Other products of Assyrian cultivation were olives, grapes, garlic, onions, lettuce, cress, beets, turnips, radishes, cucumbers, alfalfa, and licorice. Meat was rarely eaten by any but the aristocracy;[34] except for fish this war-like nation was largely vegetarian.

† A tablet of Sennacherib, ca. 700 B.C., contains the oldest known reference to cotton: "The tree that bore wool they clipped and shredded for cotton."[35a] It was probably imported from India.

‡ By the Iraq Expedition of the Oriental Institute of the University of Chicago.

and slaves captured in war or attached for debt, compelled to announce their status by pierced ears and shaven head, and performing most of the menial labor everywhere. On a bas-relief of Sennacherib we see supervisors holding the whip over slaves who, in long parallel lines, are drawing a heavy piece of statuary on a wooden sledge.[38]

Like all military states, Assyria encouraged a high birth rate by its moral code and its laws. Abortion was a capital crime; a woman who secured miscarriage, even a woman who died of attempting it, was to be impaled on a stake.[39] Though women rose to considerable power through marriage and intrigue, their position was lower than in Babylonia. Severe penalties were laid upon them for striking their husbands, wives were not allowed to go out in public unveiled, and strict fidelity was exacted of them—though their husbands might have all the concubines they could afford.[40] Prostitution was accepted as inevitable, and was regulated by the state.[40a] The king had a varied harem, whose inmates were condemned to a secluded life of dancing, singing, quarreling, needlework and conspiracy.[41] A cuckolded husband might kill his rival *in flagrante delicto*, and was held to be within his rights; this is a custom that has survived many codes. For the rest the law of matrimony was as in Babylonia, except that marriage was often by simple purchase, and in many cases the wife lived in her father's house, visited occasionally by her husband.[42]

In all departments of Assyrian life we meet with a patriarchal sternness natural to a people that lived by conquest, and in every sense on the border of barbarism. Just as the Romans took thousands of prisoners into lifelong slavery after their victories, and dragged others to the Circus Maximus to be torn to pieces by starving animals, so the Assyrians seemed to find satisfaction—or a necessary tutelage for their sons—in torturing captives, blinding children before the eyes of their parents, flaying men alive, roasting them in kilns, chaining them in cages for the amusement of the populace, and then sending the survivors off to execution.[43] Ashurnasirpal tells how "all the chiefs who had revolted I flayed, with their skins I covered the pillar, some in the midst I walled up, others on stakes I impaled, still others I arranged around the pillar on stakes. . . . As for the chieftains and royal officers who had rebelled, I cut off their members."[44] Ashurbanipal boasts that "I burned three thousand captives with fire, I left not a single one among them alive to serve as a hostage."[45] Another of his inscriptions reads: "These warriors who had sinned against

Ashur and had plotted evil against me . . . from their hostile mouths have I torn their tongues, and I have compassed their destruction. As for the others who remained alive, I offered them as a funerary sacrifice; . . . their lacerated members have I given unto the dogs, the swine, the wolves. . . . By accomplishing these deeds I have rejoiced the heart of the great gods."[46] Another monarch instructs his artisans to engrave upon the bricks these claims on the admiration of posterity: "My war chariots crush men and beasts. . . . The monuments which I erect are made of human corpses from which I have cut the head and limbs. I cut off the hands of all those whom I capture alive."[47] Reliefs at Nineveh show men being impaled or flayed, or having their tongues torn out; one shows a king gouging out the eyes of prisoners with a lance while he holds their heads conveniently in place with a cord passed through their lips.[48] As we read such pages we become reconciled to our own mediocrity.

Religion apparently did nothing to mollify this tendency to brutality and violence. It had less influence with the government than in Babylonia, and took its cue from the needs and tastes of the kings. Ashur, the national deity, was a solar god, warlike and merciless to his enemies; his people believed that he took a divine satisfaction in the execution of prisoners before his shrine.[49] The essential function of Assyrian religion was to train the future citizen to a patriotic docility, and to teach him the art of wheedling favors out of the gods by magic and sacrifice. The only religious texts that survive from Assyria are exorcisms and omens. Long lists of omens have come down to us in which the inevitable results of every manner of event are given, and methods of avoiding them are prescribed.[50] The world was pictured as crowded with demons, who had to be warded off by charms suspended about the neck, or by long and careful incantations.

In such an atmosphere the only science that flourished was that of war. Assyrian medicine was merely Babylonian medicine; Assyrian astronomy was merely Babylonian astrology—the stars were studied chiefly with a view to divination.[51] We find no evidence of philosophical speculation, no secular attempt to explain the world. Assyrian philologists made lists of plants, probably for the use of medicine, and thereby contributed moderately to establish botany; other scribes made lists of nearly all the objects they had found under the sun, and their attempts to classify these objects ministered slightly to the natural science of the Greeks. From these lists our language has taken, usually through the Greeks, such words as *hangar, gypsum, camel, plinth, shekel, rose, ammonia, jasper, cane, cherry, laudanum, naphtha, sesame, hyssop and myrrh.*[52]

The tablets recording the deeds of the kings, though they have the distinction of being at once bloody and dull, must be accorded the honor of being among the oldest extant forms of historiography. They were in the early years mere chronicles, registering royal victories, and admitting of no defeats; they became, in later days, embellished and literary accounts of the important events of the reign. The clearest title of Assyria to a place in a history of civilization was its libraries. That of Ashurbanipal contained 30,000 clay tablets, classified and catalogued, each tablet bearing an easily identifiable tag. Many of them bore the King's bookmark: "Whoso shall carry off this tablet, . . . may Ashur and Belit overthrow him in wrath . . . and destroy his name and posterity from the land."[53] A large number of the tablets are copies of undated older works, of which earlier forms are being constantly discovered; the avowed purpose of Ashurbanipal's library was to preserve the literature of Babylonia from oblivion. But only a small number of the tablets would now be classed as literature; the majority of them are official records, astrological and augural observations, oracles, medical prescriptions and reports, exorcisms, hymns, prayers, and genealogies of the kings and the gods.[54] Among the least dull of the tablets are two in which Ashurbanipal confesses, with quaint insistence, his scandalous delight in books and knowledge:

> I, Ashurbanipal, understood the wisdom of Nabu,* I acquired an understanding of all the arts of tablet-writing. I learnt to shoot the bow, to ride horses and chariots, and to hold the reins. . . . Marduk, the wise one of the gods, presented me with information and understanding as a gift. . . . Enurt and Nergal made me virile and strong, of incomparable force. I understood the craft of the wise Adapa, the hidden secrets of all the scribal art; in heavenly and earthly buildings I read and pondered; in the meetings of clerks I was present; I watched the omens, I explained the heavens with the learned priests, recited the complicated multiplications and divisions that are not immediately apparent. The beautiful writings in Sumerian that are obscure, in Akkadian that are difficult to bear in mind, it was my joy to repeat. . . . I mounted colts, rode them with prudence so that they were not violent; I drew the bow, sped the arrow, the sign of the warrior. I flung the quivering javelins like short lances. . . . I held the reins like a charioteer. . . . I directed

---

* The god of wisdom, corresponding to Thoth, Hermes and Mercury.

the weaving of reed shields and breastplates like a pioneer. I had the learning that all clerks of every kind possess when their time of maturity comes. At the same time I learnt what is proper for lord-ship, I went my royal ways.[55]

IV. ASSYRIAN ART

Minor arts — Bas-relief — Statuary — Building — A page from "Sardanapalus"

At last, in the field of art, Assyria equaled her preceptor Babylonia, and in bas-relief surpassed her. Stimulated by the influx of wealth into Ashur, Kalakh and Nineveh, artists and artisans began to produce—for nobles and their ladies, for kings and palaces, for priests and temples—jewels of every description, cast metal as skilfully designed and finely wrought as on the great gates at Balawat, and luxurious furniture of richly carved and costly woods strengthened with metal and inlaid with gold, silver, bronze, or precious stones.[56] Pottery was poorly developed, and music, like so much else, was merely imported from Babylon; but *tempera* painting in bright colors under a thin glaze became one of the characteristic arts of Assyria, from which it passed to its perfection in Persia. Painting, as always in the ancient East, was a secondary and dependent art.

In the heyday of Sargon II, Sennacherib, Esarhaddon and Ashurbanipal, and presumably through their lavish patronage, the art of bas-relief created new masterpieces for the British Museum. One of the best examples, however, dates from Ashurnasirpal II; it represents, in chaste alabaster, the good god Marduk overcoming the evil god of chaos, Tiamat.[57] The human figures in Assyrian reliefs are stiff and coarse and all alike, as if some perfect model had insisted on being reproduced forever; all the men have the same massive heads, the same brush of whiskers, the same stout bellies, the same invisible necks; even the gods are these same Assyrians in very slight disguise. Only now and then do the human figures take on vitality, as in the alabaster relief depicting spirits in adoration before a palmetto tree,[58] and the fine limestone stele of Shamsi-Adad VII found at Kalakh.[59] Usually it is the animal reliefs that stir us; never before or since has carving pictured animals so successfully. The panels monotonously repeat scenes of war and the hunt; but the eye never tires of their vigor of action, their flow of motion, and their simple directness of line. It is as if the artist, forbidden to portray his masters realistically or individually, had given all his lore and skill to the animals; he represents them in a profusion of species—lions, horses, asses, goats, dogs, deer, birds, grasshoppers—and in every attitude except rest; too often he shows them in the agony of death; but even then they are the center and life of his picture and his art. The majestic horses of Sargon II on the reliefs at Khorsabad;[60] the wounded lioness from Sennacherib's palace at Nineveh;[61] the dying lion in alabaster from the palace of Ashurbanipal;[62] the lion-hunts of Ashurnasirpal II and Ashurbanipal;[63] the resting lioness,[64] and the lion released from a trap;[65] the fragment in which a lion and his mate bask in the shade of the trees[66]—these are among the world's choicest masterpieces in this form of art. The representation of natural objects in the reliefs is stylized and crude; the forms are heavy, the outlines are hard, the muscles are exaggerated; and there is no other attempt at perspective than the placing of the distant in the upper half of the picture, on the same scale as the foreground presented below. Gradually, however, the guild of sculptors under Sennacherib learned to offset these defects with a boldly realistic portrayal, a technical finish, and above all a vivid perception of action, which, in the field of animal sculpture, have never been surpassed. Bas-relief was to the Assyrian what sculpture was to the Greek, or painting to the Italians of the Renaissance—a favorite art uniquely expressing the national ideal of form and character.

We cannot say as much for Assyrian sculpture. The carvers of Nineveh and Kalakh seem to have preferred relief to work in the round; very little full sculpture has come down to us from the ruins, and none of it is of a high order. The animals are full of power and majesty, as if conscious of not only physical but moral superiority to man—like the bulls that guarded the gateway at Khorsabad;[67] the human or divine figures are primitively coarse and heavy, adorned but undistinguished, erect but dead. An exception might be made for the massive statue of Ashurnasirpal II now in the British Museum; through all its heavy lines one sees a man every inch a king: royal sceptre firmly grasped, thick lips set with determination, eyes cruel and alert, a bull-like neck boding short shrift for enemies and falsifiers of tax-reports, and two gigantic feet full poised on the back of the world.

We must not take too seriously our judgments of this sculpture; very likely the Assyrians idolized knotted muscles and short necks, and would have looked with martial scorn upon our almost feminine slenderness, or the smooth, voluptuous grace of Praxiteles' Hermes and the Apollo Belvedere. As for Assyrian architecture, how can we estimate its excellence when nothing remains of it but ruins almost level with the sand, and serving chiefly as a hook upon which brave archeologists may hang their imaginative "restorations"? Like Babylonian and recent American architecture, the Assyrian aimed not at beauty but at grandeur, and sought it by mass design. Following the traditions of Mesopotamian art, Assyrian architecture adopted brick as its basic material, but went its own way by facing it more lavishly with stone. It inherited the arch and the vault from the south, developed them, and made some experiments in columns which led the way to the caryatids and the voluted "Ionic" capitals of the Persians and the Greeks.[68] The palaces squatted over great areas of ground, and were wisely limited to two or three stories in height;[69] ordinarily they were designed as a series of halls and chambers enclosing a quiet and shaded court. The portals of the royal residences were guarded with monstrous stone animals, the entrance hall was lined with historical reliefs and statuary, the floors were paved with alabaster slabs, the walls were hung with costly tapestries, or paneled with precious woods, and bordered with elegant mouldings; the roofs were reinforced with massive beams, sometimes covered with leaf of silver or gold, and the ceilings were often painted with representations of natural scenery.[70]

The six mightiest warriors of Assyria were also its greatest builders. Tiglath-Pileser I rebuilt in stone the temples of Ashur, and left word about one of them that he had "made its interior brilliant like the vault of heaven, decorated its walls like the splendor of the rising stars, and made it superb with shining brightness."[71] The later emperors gave generously to the temples, but, like Solomon, they preferred their palaces. Ashurnasirpal II built at Kalakh an immense edifice of stone-faced brick, ornamented with reliefs praising piety and war. Nearby, at Balawat, Rassam found the ruins of another structure, from which he rescued two bronze gates of magnificent workmanship.[72] Sargon II commemorated himself by raising a spacious palace at Dur-Sharrukin (i.e., Fort Sargon, on the site of the modern Khorsabad); its gateway was flanked by winged bulls, its walls were decorated with reliefs and shining tiles, its vast rooms were equipped with delicately carved furniture, and were adorned with imposing statuary. From every victory Sargon brought more slaves to work on this construction, and more marble, *lapis lazuli*, bronze, silver and gold to beautify it. Around it he set a group of temples, and in the rear he offered to the god a *ziggurat* of seven stories, topped with silver and gold. Sennacherib raised at Nineveh a royal mansion called "The Incomparable," surpassing in size all other palaces of antiquity;[73] its walls and floors sparkled with precious metals, woods, and stones; its tiles vied in their brilliance with the luminaries of day and night; the metal-workers cast for it gigantic lions and oxen of copper, and the sculptors carved for it winged bulls of limestone and alabaster, and lined its walls with pastoral symphonies in bas-relief. Esarhaddon continued the rebuilding and enlargement of Nineveh, and excelled all his predecessors in the grandeur of his edifices and the luxuriousness of their equipment; a dozen provinces provided him with materials and men; new ideas for columns and decorations came to him during his sojourn in Egypt; and when at last his palaces and temples were complete they were filled with the artistic booty and conceptions of the whole Near Eastern world.[74]

The worst commentary on Assyrian architecture lies in the fact that within sixty years after Esarhaddon had finished his palace it was crumbling into ruins.[75] Ashurbanipal tells us how he rebuilt it; as we read his inscription the centuries fade, and we see dimly into the heart of the King:

> At that time the harem, the resting-place of the palace . . . which Sennacherib, my grandfather, had built for his royal dwelling, had become old with joy and gladness, and its walls had fallen. I, Ashurbanipal, the Great King, the mighty King, the King of the World, the King of Assyria, . . . because I had grown up in that harem, and Ashur, Sin, Shamash, Ramman, Bel, Nabu, Ishtar, . . . Ninib, Nergal and Nusku had preserved me therein as crown prince, and had extended their good protection and shelter of prosperity over me, . . . and had constantly sent me joyful tidings therein of victory over my enemies; and because my dreams on my bed at night were pleasant, and in the morning my fancies were bright, . . . I tore down its ruins; in order to extend its area I tore it all down. I erected a building the site of whose structure was fifty *tibki* in extent. I raised a terrace; but I was afraid before the shrines of the great gods my lords, and did not raise that structure very high. In a good month, on a favorable day, I put in its foundations upon that terrace, and laid its brickwork. I emptied wine of sesame and wine of grapes upon its cellar, and poured them also upon its earthen wall. In order to build that harem the people of

my land hauled its bricks there in wagons of Elam which I had carried away as spoil by the command of the gods. I made the kings of Arabia who had violated their treaty with me, and whom I had captured alive in battle with my own hands, carry baskets and (wear) workmen's caps in order to build that harem. . . . They spent their days in moulding its bricks and performing forced service for it to the playing of music. With joy and rejoicing I built it from its foundations to its roof. I made more room in it than before, and made the work upon it splendid. I laid upon it long beams of cedar, which grew upon Sirara and Lebanon. I covered doors of *liaru*-wood, whose odor is pleasant, with a sheath of copper, and hung them in its doorways. . . . I planted around it a grove of all kinds of trees, and . . . fruits of every kind. I finished the work of its construction, offered splendid sacrifices to the gods my lords, dedicated it with joy and rejoicing, and entered therein under a splendid canopy.[76]

V. ASSYRIA PASSES

The last days of a king — Sources of Assyrian decay — The fall of Nineveh

Nevertheless the "Great King, the mighty King, the King of the World, the King of Assyria" complained in his old age of the misfortunes that had come to his lot. The last tablet bequeathed us by his wedge raises again the questions of Ecclesiastes and Job:

I did well unto god and man, to dead and living. Why have sickness and misery befallen me? I cannot do away with the strife in my country and the dissensions in my family; disturbing scandals oppress me always. Illness of mind and flesh bow me down; with cries of woe I bring my days to an end. On the day of the city god, the day of the festival, I am wretched; death is seizing hold upon me, and bears me down. With lamentation and mourning I wail day and night, I groan, "O God! grant even to one who is impious that he may see thy light!"[77]*

---

* Diodorus—how reliably we cannot say—pictures the King as rioting away his years in feminine comforts and genderless immorality, and credits him with composing his own reckless epitaph:

Knowing full well that thou wert mortal born,
Thy heart lift up, take thy delight in feasts;

We do not know how Ashurbanipal died; the story dramatized by Byron—that he set fire to his own palace and perished in the flames—rests on the authority of the marvel-loving Ctesias,[79] and may be merely legend. His death was in any case a symbol and an omen; soon Assyria too was to die, and from causes of which Ashurbanipal had been a part. For the economic vitality of Assyria had been derived too rashly from abroad; it depended upon profitable conquests bringing in riches and trade; at any moment it could be ended with a decisive defeat. Gradually the qualities of body and character that had helped to make the Assyrian armies invincible were weakened by the very victories that they won; in each victory it was the strongest and bravest who died, while the infirm and cautious survived to multiply their kind; it was a dysgenic process that perhaps made for civilization by weeding out the more brutal types, but undermined the biological basis upon which Assyria had risen to power. The extent of her conquests had helped to weaken her; not only had they depopulated her fields to feed insatiate Mars, but they had brought into Assyria, as captives, millions of destitute aliens who bred with the fertility of the hopeless, destroyed all national unity of character and blood, and became by their growing numbers a hostile and disintegrating force in the very midst of the conquerors. More and more the army itself was filled by these men of other lands, while semi-barbarous marauders harassed every border, and exhausted the resources of the country in an endless defense of its unnatural frontiers.

Ashurbanipal died in 626 B.C. Fourteen years later an army of Babylonians under Nabopolassar united with an army of Medes under Cyaxares and a horde of Scythians from the Caucasus, and with amazing ease and swiftness captured the citadels of the north. Nineveh was laid waste as ruthlessly and completely as her kings had once ravaged Susa and Babylon; the city was put to the torch, the population was slaughtered or enslaved, and the palace so recently built by Ashurbanipal was sacked and destroyed. At one blow Assyria disappeared from history. Nothing

---

When dead no pleasure more is thine. Thus I,
Who once o'er mighty Ninus ruled, am naught
But dust. Yet these are mine which gave me joy
In life—the food I ate, my wantonness,
And love's delights. But all those other things
Men deem felicities are left behind.[78]

Perhaps there is no inconsistency between this mood and that pictured in the text; the one may have been the medical preliminary to the other.

remained of her except certain tactics and weapons of war, certain voluted capitals of semi-"Ionic" columns, and certain methods of provincial administration that passed down to Persia, Macedon and Rome. The Near East remembered her for a while as a merciless unifier of a dozen lesser states; and the Jews recalled Nineveh vengefully as "the bloody city, full of lies and robbery."[80] In a little while all but the mightiest of the Great Kings were forgotten, and all their royal palaces were in ruins under the drifting sands. Two hundred years after its capture, Xenophon's Ten Thousand marched over the mounds that had been Nineveh, and never suspected that these were the site of the ancient metropolis that had ruled half the world. Not a stone remained visible of all the temples with which Assyria's pious warriors had sought to beautify their greatest capital. Even Ashur, the everlasting god, was dead.

CHAPTER XI

A Motley of Nations

I. THE INDO-EUROPEAN PEOPLES

The ethnic scene—Mitannians—Hittites—Armenians—Scythians—Phrygians — The Divine Mother — Lydians — Crœsus — Coinage—Crœsus, Solon and Cyrus

TO a distant and yet discerning eye the Near East, in the days of Nebuchadrezzar, would have seemed like an ocean in which vast swarms of human beings moved about in turmoil, forming and dissolving groups, enslaving and being enslaved, eating and being eaten, killing and getting killed, endlessly. Behind and around the great empires—Egypt, Babylonia, Assyria and Persia—flowered this medley of half nomad, half settled tribes: Cimmerians, Cilicians, Cappadocians, Bithynians, Ashkanians, Mysians, Mæonians, Carians, Lycians, Pamphylians, Pisidians, Lycaonians, Philistines, Amorites, Canaanites, Edomites, Ammonites, Moabites and a hundred other peoples each of which felt itself the center of geography and history, and would have marveled at the ignorant prejudice of an historian who would reduce them to a paragraph. Thoughout the history of the Near East such nomads were a peril to the more settled kingdoms which they almost surrounded; periodically droughts would fling them upon these richer regions, necessitating frequent wars, and perpetual readiness for war.[1] Usually the nomad tribe survived the settled kingdom, and overran it in the end. The world is dotted with areas where once civilization flourished, and where nomads roam again.

In this seething ethnic sea certain minor states took shape, which, even if only as conductors, contributed their mite to the heritage of the race. The Mitannians interest us not as the early antagonists of Egypt in the Near East, but as one of the first Indo-European peoples known to us in Asia, and as the worshipers of gods—Mithra, Indra and Varuna—whose passage to Persia and India helps us to trace the movements of what was once so conveniently called the "Aryan" race.*

The Hittites were among the most powerful and civilized of the early Indo-European peoples. Apparently they had come down across the Bosphorus, the Hellespont, the Ægean or the Caucasus, and had established themselves as a ruling military caste over the indigenous agriculturists of that mountainous peninsula, south of the Black Sea, which we know as Asia Minor. Towards 1800 B.C. we find them settled near the sources of the Tigris and the Euphrates; thence they spread their arms and influence into Syria, and gave mighty Egypt some indignant concern. We have seen how Rameses II was forced to make peace with them, and to acknowledge the Hittite king as his equal. At Boghaz Keui† they made their capital and centered their civilization: first on the iron which they mined in the mountains bordering on Armenia, then on a code of laws much influenced by Hammurabi's, and finally on a crude esthetic sense which drove them to carve vast and awkward figures in the round, or upon the living rock.‡ Their language, recently deciphered by Hronzný from the ten thousand clay tablets found at Boghaz Keui by Hugo Winckler, was largely of Indo-European affinity; its declensional and conjugational forms closely resembled those of Latin and Greek, and some of its simpler words are visibly akin to English.§ The Hittites wrote a pictographic script in their own queer way—one line from left to right, the next from right to left, and so forth alternately. They learned cuneiform from the Babylonians, taught Crete

* The word *Aryan* first appears in the Harri, one of the tribes of Mitanni. In general it was the self-given appellation of peoples living near, or coming from, the shores of the Caspian Sea. The term is properly applied today chiefly to the Mitannians, Hittites, Medes, Persians, and Vedic Hindus—i.e., only to the *eastern* branch of the Indo-European peoples, whose western branch populated Europe.[2]

† East of the Halys River. Nearby, across the river, is Angora, capital of Turkey, and lineal descendant of Ancyra, the ancient metropolis of Phrygia. We may be helped to a cultural perspective by realizing that the Turks, whom we call "terrible," note with pride the antiquity of their capital, and mourn the domination of Europe by barbaric infidels. Every point is the center of the world.

‡ Baron von Oppenheim unearthed at Tell Halaf and elsewhere many relics of Hittite art, which he has collected into his own museum, an abandoned factory in Berlin. Most of these remains are dated by their finder about 1200 B.C.; some of them he attributes precariously to the fourth millennium B.C. The collection includes a group of lions crudely but powerfully carved in stone, a bull in fine black stone, and figures of the Hittite triad of gods—the Sun-god, the Weather-god, and Hepat, the Hittite Ishtar. One of the most impressive of the figures is an ungainly Sphinx, before which is a stone vessel intended for offerings.

§ Cf., e.g., *vadar*, water; *ezza*, eat; *uga*, I (Latin *ego*); *tug*, thee; *vesh*, we; *mu*, me; *kuish*, who (Lat. *quis*); *quit*, what (Lat. *quid*), etc.[3]

the use of the clay tablet for writing, and seem to have mingled with the ancient Hebrews intimately enough to have given them their sharply aquiline nose, so that this Hebraic feature must now be considered strictly "Aryan."[4] Some of the surviving tablets are vocabularies giving Sumerian, Babylonian and Hittite equivalents; others are administrative enactments revealing a close-knit military and monarchical state; others contain two hundred fragments of a code of laws, including price-regulations for commodities.[5] The Hittites disappeared from history almost as mysteriously as they entered it; one after another their capitals decayed—perhaps because their great advantage, iron, became equally accessible to their competitors. The last of these capitals, Carchemish, fell before the Assyrians in 717 B.C.

Just north of Assyria was a comparatively stable nation, known to the Assyrians as Urartu, to the Hebrews as Ararat, and to later times as Armenia. For many centuries, beginning before the dawn of recorded history and continuing till the establishment of Persian rule over all of western Asia, the Armenians maintained their independent government, their characteristic customs and arts. Under their greatest king, Argistis II (ca. 708 B.C.), they grew rich by mining iron and selling it to Asia and Greece; they achieved a high level of prosperity and comfort, of culture and manners; they built great edifices of stone, and made excellent vases and statuettes. They lost their wealth in costly wars of offense and defense against Assyria, and passed under Persian domination in the days of the all-conquering Cyrus.

Still farther north, along the shores of the Black Sea, wandered the Scythians, a horde of warriors half Mongol and half European, ferocious bearded giants who lived in wagons, kept their women in *purdah* seclusion,[6] rode bareback on wild horses, fought to live and lived to fight, drank the blood of their enemies and used the scalps as napkins,[7] weakened Assyria with repeated raids, swept through western Asia (ca. 630-610 B.C.), destroying and killing everything and everyone in their path, advanced to the very cities of the Egyptian Delta, were suddenly decimated by a mysterious disease, and were finally overcome by the Medes and driven back to their northern haunts.[8]* We catch from such a story another glimpse of the barbaric hinterland that hedged in every ancient state.

---

* Hippocrates tells us that "their women, so long as they are virgins, ride, shoot, throw the javelin while mounted, and fight with their enemies. They do not lay aside their virginity until they have killed three of their enemies. . . . A woman who takes to herself a husband no longer rides, unless she is compelled to do so by a general expedition. They have no right breast; for while they are yet babies their mothers make red-hot a bronze instrument constructed for this very purpose and apply it to the right breast and cauterize it, so that its growth is arrested, and all its strength and bulk are diverted to the right shoulder and right arm."[9]

Towards the end of the ninth century B.C. a new power arose in Asia Minor, inheriting the remains of the Hittite civilization, and serving as a cultural bridge to Lydia and Greece. The legend by which the Phrygians tried to explain for curious historians the foundation of their kingdom was symbolical of the rise and fall of nations. Their first king, Gordios, was a simple peasant whose sole inheritance had been a pair of oxen;* their next king, his son Midas, was a spendthrift who weakened the state by that greed and extravagance which posterity represented through the legend of his plea to the gods that he might turn anything to gold by touching it. The plea was so well heard that everything Midas touched turned to gold, even the food that he put to his lips; he was on the verge of starvation when the gods allowed him to cleanse himself of the curse by bathing in the river Pactolus—which has given up grains of gold ever since.

The Phrygians made their way into Asia from Europe, built a capital at Ancyra, and for a time contended with Assyria and Egypt for mastery of the Near East. They adopted a native mother-goddess, Ma, rechristened her Cybele from the mountains (*kybela*) in which she dwelt, and worshiped her as the great spirit of the untilled earth, the personification of all the reproductive energies of nature. They took over from the aborigines the custom of serving the goddess through sacred prostitution, and accepted into their mythical lore the story of how Cybele had fallen in love with the young god Atys,† and had compelled him to emasculate himself in her honor; hence the priests of the Great Mother sacrificed their manhood to her upon entering the service of her temples.[11] These barbarous legends fascinated the imagination of the Greeks, and entered profoundly into their mythology and their literature. The Romans officially adopted Cybele into their religion, and some of the orgiastic rites that marked the Roman carnivals were derived from the wild rituals with which the Phrygians annually celebrated the death and resurrection of the handsome Atys.[12]

---

* The oracle of Zeus had commanded the Phrygians to choose as king the first man who rode up to the temple in a wagon; hence the selection of Gordios. The new king dedicated his car to the god; and a new oracle predicted that the man who should succeed in untying the intricate bark knot that bound the yoke of the wagon to the pole would rule over all Asia. Alexander, story goes, cut the "Gordian knot" with a blow of his sword.

† Atys, we are informed, was miraculously born of the virgin-goddess Nana, who conceived him by placing a pomegranate between her breasts.[10]

The ascendency of Phrygia in Asia Minor was ended with the rise of the new kingdom of Lydia. King Gyges established it with its capital at Sardis; Alyattes, in a long reign of forty-nine years, raised it to prosperity and power; Crœsus (570-546 B.C.) inherited and enjoyed it, expanded it by conquest to include nearly all of Asia Minor, and then surrendered it to Persia. By generous bribes to local politicians he brought one after another of the petty states that surrounded him into subjection to Lydia, and by pious and unprecedented hecatombs to local deities he placated these subject peoples and persuaded them that he was the darling of their gods. Crœsus further distinguished himself by issuing gold and silver coins of admirable design, minted and guaranteed at their face value by the state; and though these were not, as long supposed, the first official coins in history, much less the invention of coinage,* nevertheless they set an example that stimulated trade throughout the Mediterranean world. Men had for many centuries used various metals as standards of value and exchange; but these, whether copper, bronze, iron, silver or gold, had in most countries been measured by weight or other tests at each transaction. It was no small improvement that replaced such cumbersome tokens with a national currency; by accelerating the passage of goods from those that could best produce them to those that most effectively demanded them it added to the wealth of the world, and prepared for mercantile civilizations like those of Ionia and Greece, in which the proceeds of commerce were to finance the achievements of literature and art.

Of Lydian literature nothing remains; nor does any specimen survive of the preciously wrought vases of gold, iron and silver that Crœsus offered to the conquered gods. The vases found in Lydian tombs, and now housed in the Louvre, show how the artistic leadership of Egypt and Babylonia was yielding, in the Lydia of Crœsus' day, to the growing influence of Greece; their delicacy of execution rivals their fidelity to nature. When Herodotus visited Lydia he found its customs almost indistinguishable from those of his fellow-Greeks; all that remained to separate them, he tells us, was the way in which the daughters of the common people earned their dowries—by prostitution.[13]

The same great gossip is our chief authority for the dramatic story of Crœsus's fall. Herodotus recounts how Crœsus displayed his riches

---

* Older coins have been found at Mohenjo-daro, in India (2900 B.C.); and we have seen how Sennacherib (ca. 700 B.C.) minted half-shekel pieces.

to Solon, and then asked him whom he considered the happiest of men. Solon, after naming three individuals who were all dead, refused to call Crœsus happy, on the ground that there was no telling what misfortunes the morrow would bring him. Crœsus dismissed the great legislator as a fool, turned his hand to plotting against Persia, and suddenly found the hosts of Cyrus at his gates. According to the same historian the Persians won through the superior stench of their camels, which the horses of the Lydian cavalry could not bear; the horses fled, the Lydians were routed, and Sardis fell. Crœsus, according to ancient tradition, prepared a great funeral pyre, took his place on it with his wives, his daughters, and the noblest young men among the surviving citizens, and ordered his eunuchs to burn himself and them to death. In his last moments he remembered the words of Solon, mourned his own blindness, and reproached the gods who had taken all his hecatombs and paid him with destruction. Cyrus, if we may follow Herodotus,[14] took pity on him, ordered the flames to be extinguished, carried Crœsus with him to Persia, and made him one of his most trusted counsellors.

II. THE SEMITIC PEOPLES

The antiquity of the Arabs—Phœnicians—Their world trade—
Their circumnavigation of Africa — Colonies — Tyre and
Sidon — Deities — The dissemination of the alphabet —
Syria — Astarte — The death and resurrection of
Adoni—The sacrifice of children

If we attempt to mitigate the confusion of tongues in the Near East by distinguishing the northern peoples of the region as mostly Indo-European, and the central and southern peoples, from Assyria to Arabia, as Semitic,* we shall have to remember that reality is never so clear-cut in its differences as the rubrics under which we dismember it for neat handling. The Near East was divided by mountains and deserts into localities naturally isolated and therefore naturally diverse in language and traditions; but not only did trade tend to assimilate language, customs and arts along its main routes (as, for example, along the great rivers from Nineveh and Carchemish to the Persian Gulf), but the migrations and imperial deportations of vast communities so mingled stocks and speech

---

* The term *Semite* is derived from Shem, legendary son of Noah, on the theory that Shem was the ancestor of all the Semitic peoples.

that a certain homogeneity of culture accompanied the heterogeneity of blood. By "Indo-European," then, we shall mean *predominantly* Indo-European; by "Semitic" we shall mean *predominantly* Semitic: no strain was unmixed, no culture was left uninfluenced by its neighbors or its enemies. We are to vision the vast area as a scene of ethnic diversity and flux, in which now the Indo-European, now the Semitic, stock for a time prevailed, but only to take on the general cultural character of the whole. Hammurabi and Darius I were separated by differences of blood and religion, and by almost as many centuries as those that divide us from Christ; nevertheless, when we examine the two great kings we perceive that they are essentially and profoundly akin.

The fount and breeding-place of the Semites was Arabia. Out of that arid region, where the "man-plant" grows so vigorously and hardly any other plant will grow at all, came, in a succession of migrations, wave after wave of sturdy, reckless stoics no longer supportable by desert and oases, and bound to conquer for themselves a place in the shade. Those who remained behind created the civilization of Arabia and the Bedouin: the patriarchal family, the stern morality of obedience, the fatalism of a hard environment, and the ignorant courage to kill their own daughters as offerings to the gods. Nevertheless they did not take religion very much to heart till Mohammed came, and they neglected the arts and refinements of life as effeminate devices for degenerate men. For a time they controlled the trade with the further East: their ports at Canneh and Aden were heaped with the riches of the Indies, and their patient caravans carried these goods precariously overland to Phœnicia and Babylon. In the interior of their broad peninsula they built cities, palaces and temples, but they did not encourage foreigners to come and see them. For thousands of years they have lived their own life, kept their own customs, kept their own counsel; they are the same today as in the time of Cheops and Gudea; they have seen a hundred kingdoms rise and fall about them; and their soil is still jealously theirs, guarded from profane feet and alien eyes.

Who, now, were those Phœnicians who have so often been spoken of in these pages, whose ships sailed every sea, whose merchants bargained in every port? The historian is abashed before any question of origins: he must confess that he knows next to nothing about either the early or the late history of this ubiquitous, yet elusive, people.[15] We do not know whence they came, nor when; we are not certain that they were Semites;* and as to the date of their arrival on the Mediterranean coast, we cannot contradict the statement of the scholars of Tyre, who told Herodotus that their ancestors had come from the Persian Gulf, and had founded the city in what we should call the twenty-eighth century before Christ.[17] Even their name is problematical: the *phoinix* from which the Greeks coined it may mean the red dye that Tyrian merchants sold, or a palm-tree that flourishes along the Phœnician coast. That coast, a narrow strip a hundred miles long and only ten miles wide, between Syria and the sea, was almost all of Phœnicia; the people never thought it worth while to settle in the Lebanon hills behind them, or to bring these ranges under their rule; they were content that this beneficent barrier should protect them from the more warlike nations whose goods they carried out into all the lanes of the sea.

Those mountains compelled them to live on the water. From the Sixth Egyptian Dynasty onward they were the busiest merchants of the ancient world; and when they liberated themselves from Egypt (ca. 1200 B.C.) they became masters of the Mediterranean. They themselves manufactured various forms and objects of glass and metal; they made enameled vases, weapons, ornaments and jewelry; they had a monopoly of the purple dye which they extracted from the molluscs abounding along their shores;[18] and the women of Tyre were famous for the gorgeous colors with which they stained the products of their deft needlework. These, and the exportable surplus of India and the Near East—cereals, wines, textiles and precious stones—they shipped to every city of the Mediterranean far and near, bringing back, in return, lead, gold and iron from the south shores of the Black Sea, copper, cypress and corn from Cyprus,† ivory from Africa, silver from Spain, tin from Britain, and slaves from everywhere. They were shrewd traders; they persuaded the natives of Spain to give them, in exchange for a cargo of oil, so great a quantity of silver that the holds of their ships could not contain it—whereupon the subtle Semites replaced the iron or stones in their anchors with silver, and sailed prosperously away.[19] Not satisfied with this, they enslaved the natives, and made them work for long hours in the mines for a subsistence wage.‡ Like all early voyagers, and some old languages, they made scant

---

* Autran has argued that they were a branch of the Cretan civilization.[16]
† Copper and cypress took their names from Cyprus.
‡ Cf. Gibbon: "Spain, by a very singular fatality, was the Peru and Mexico of the old world. The discovery of the rich western continent by the Phœnicians, and the oppres-

distinction between trade and treachery, commerce and robbery; they stole from the weak, cheated the stupid, and were honest with the rest. Sometimes they captured ships on the high seas, and confiscated their cargoes and their crews; sometimes they lured curious natives into visiting the Phœnician vessels, and then sailed off with them to sell them as slaves.[21] They had much to do with giving the trading Semites of antiquity an evil reputation, especially with the early Greeks, who did the same things.*

Their low and narrow galleys, some seventy feet long, set a new style of design by abandoning the inward-curving bow of the Egyptian vessel, and turning it outward into a sharp point for cleaving wind or water, or the ships of the enemy. One large rectangular sail, hoisted on a mast fixed in the keel, helped the galley-slaves who provided most of the motive-power with their double bank of oars. On a deck above the rowers, soldiers stood on guard, ready for trade or war. These frail ships, having no compasses and drawing hardly five feet of water, kept cautiously near the shore, and for a long time dared not move during the night. Gradually the art of navigation developed to the point where the Phœnician pilots, guiding themselves by the North Star (or the Phœnician Star, as the Greeks called it), adventured into the oceans, and at last circumnavigated Africa, sailing down the east coast first, and "discovering" the Cape of Good Hope some two thousand years before Vasco da Gama. "When autumn came," says Herodotus, "they went ashore, sowed the land, and waited for harvest; then, having reaped the corn, they put to sea again. When two years had thus passed, in the third, having doubled the Pillars of Hercules (Gibraltar), they arrived in Egypt."[23] What an adventure!

At strategic points along the Mediterranean they established garrisons that grew in time into populous colonies or cities: at Cadiz, Carthage and Marseilles, in Malta, Sicily, Sardinia and Corsica, even in distant England. They occupied Cyprus, Melos and Rhodes.[24] They took the arts and sciences of Egypt, Crete and the Near East and spread them in Greece, Africa, Italy and Spain. They bound together the East and

---

sion of the simple natives, who were compelled to labor in their own mines for the benefit of the strangers, form an exact type of the more recent history of Spanish America."[20]

* The Greeks, who for half a millennium were raiders and pirates, gave the name "Phœnician" to anyone addicted to sharp practices.[22]

The oldest examples of alphabetic writing known to us, however, appear not in Phœnicia but in Sinai. At Serabit-el-khadim, a little hamlet covering a site where anciently the Egyptians mined turquoise, Sir William Flinders Petrie found inscriptions in a strange language, dating back to an uncertain age, perhaps as early as 2500 B.C. Though these inscriptions have never been deciphered, it is apparent that they were written not in hieroglyphics, nor in syllabic cuneiform, but with an alphabet.[35] At Zapouna, in southern Syria, French archeologists discovered an entire library of clay tablets—some in hieroglyphic, some in a Semitic alphabetic script. As Zapouna seems to have been permanently destroyed about 1200 B.C., these tablets go back presumably to the thirteenth century B.C.,[36] and suggest to us again how old civilization was in those centuries to which our ignorance ascribes its origins.

Syria lay behind Phœnicia, in the very lap of the Lebanon hills, gathering its tribes together loosely under the rule of that capital which still boasts that it is the oldest city of all, and still harbors Syrians hungry for liberty. For a time the kings of Damascus dominated a dozen petty nations about them, and successfully resisted the efforts of Assyria to make Syria one of her vassal states. The inhabitants of the city were Semitic merchants, who managed to garner wealth out of the caravan trade that passed through Syria's mountains and plains. Artisans and slaves worked for them, none too happily. We hear of masons organizing great unions, and inscriptions tell of a strike of bakers in Magnesia; across the centuries we sense the strife and busyness of an ancient Syrian town.[37] These artisans were skilful in shaping graceful pottery, in carving ivory and wood, in polishing gems, and in weaving stuffs of gay colors for the adornment of their women.[38]

Fashions, manners and morals in Damascus were very much as at Babylon, which was the Paris and *arbiter elegantiarum* of the ancient East. Religious prostitution flourished, for in Syria, as throughout western Asia, the fertility of the soil was symbolized in a Great Mother, or Goddess, whose sexual commerce with her lover gave the hint to all the reproductive processes and energies of nature; and the sacrifice of virginity at the temples was not only an offering to Astarte, but a participation with her in that annual self-abandonment which, it was hoped, would offer an irresistible suggestion to the earth, and insure the increase of plants, animals and men.[39] About the time of the vernal equinox the festival of the Syrian Astarte, like that of Cybele in Phrygia, was celebrated at Hierapolis with a fervor bordering upon madness. The noise of flutes and drums mingled with the wailing of the women for Astarte's dead lord, Adoni; eunuch priests danced wildly, and slashed themselves with knives; at last many men, who had come merely as spectators, were overcome with the excitement, threw off their clothing, and emasculated themselves in pledge of lifelong service to the goddess. Then, in the dark of the night, the priests brought a mystic illumination to the scene, opened the tomb of the young god, and announced triumphantly that Adoni, the Lord, had risen from the dead. Touching the lips of the worshipers with balm, the priests whispered to them the promise that they, too, would some day rise from the grave.[40]

The other gods of Syria were not less bloodthirsty than Astarte. It is true that the priests recognized a general divinity, embracing all the gods, and called El or Ilu, like the Elohim of the Jews; but this calm abstraction was hardly noticed by the people who gave their worship to the Baal. Usually they identified this city-god with the sun, as they identified Astarte with the moon; and on occasions of great moment they offered him their own children in sacrifice, after the manner of the Phœnicians; the parents came to the ceremony dressed as for a festival, and the cries of their children burning in the lap of the god were drowned by the blaring of trumpets and the piping of flutes. Normally, however, a milder sacrifice sufficed; the priests slashed themselves until the altar was covered with their blood; or the child's foreskin was offered as a commutation for his life; or the priests condescended to accept a sum of money to be presented to the god in place of the prepuce. In some way the god had to be appeased and satisfied; for his worshipers had made him in the image and dream of themselves, and he had no great regard for human life, or womanly tears.[41]

Similar customs, varying only in name and detail, were practised by the Semitic tribes south of Syria, who filled the land with their confusion of tongues. It was forbidden the Jews to "make their children pass through the fire," but occasionally they did it none the less.[42] Abraham about to sacrifice Isaac, and Agamemnon sacrificing Iphigenia, were but resorting to an ancient rite in attempting to propitiate the gods with human blood. Mesha, King of Moab, sacrificed his eldest son by fire as a means of raising a siege; his prayer having been answered, and the sacrifice of his son having been accepted, he slaughtered seven thousand Israelites in gratitude.[43] Throughout this region, from the Sumerian days when the Amorites roamed the plains of Amurru (ca. 2800 B.C.) to the time when the Jews fell with divine wrath upon the Canaanites, and Sargon of Assyria captured Samaria, and Nebuchadrezzar captured Jerusalem (597 B.C.), the valley of the Jordan was drenched periodically with fratricidal blood, and many Lords of Hosts rejoiced. These Moabites, Canaanites, Amorites, Edomites, Philistines and Aramæans hardly enter into the cultural record of mankind. It is true that the fertile Aramæans, spreading everywhere, made their language the *lingua franca* of the Near East, and that the alphabetic script which they had learned either from the Egyptians or the Phœnicians replaced the cuneiform and syllabaries of Mesopotamia, first as a mercantile, then as a literary, medium, and became at last the tongue of Christ and the alphabet of the Arabs today." But time preserves their names not so much because of their own accomplishments as because they played some part on the tragic stage of Palestine. We must study, in greater detail than their neighbors, these numerically and geographically insignificant Jews, who gave to the world one of its greatest literatures, two of its most influential religions, and so many of its profoundest men.

CHAPTER XII

Judea

I. THE PROMISED LAND

*Palestine — Climate — Prehistory — Abraham's people — The
Jews in Egypt — The Exodus — The conquest of Canaan*

A BUCKLE or a Montesquieu, eager to interpret history through
geography, might have taken a handsome leaf out of Palestine.
One hundred and fifty miles from Dan on the north to Beersheba on the
south, twenty-five to eighty miles from the Philistines on the west to
the Syrians, Aramæans, Ammonites, Moabites and Edomites on the east—
one would not expect so tiny a territory to play a major rôle in history,
or to leave behind it an influence greater than that of Babylonia, Assyria
or Persia, perhaps greater even than that of Egypt or Greece. But it
was the fortune and misfortune of Palestine that it lay midway between
the capitals of the Nile and those of the Tigris and Euphrates. This circumstance brought trade to Judea, and it brought war; time and again
the harassed Hebrews were compelled to take sides in the struggle of the
empires, to pay tribute or be overrun. Behind the Bible, behind the
plaintive cries of the psalmists and the prophets for help from the sky,
lay this imperiled place of the Jews between the upper and nether mill-
stones of Mesopotamia and Egypt.

The climatic history of the land tells us again how precarious a thing
civilization is, and how its great enemies—barbarism and desiccation—
are always waiting to destroy it. Once Palestine was "a land flowing
with milk and honey," as many a passage in the Pentateuch describes it.[1]
Josephus, in the first century after Christ, still speaks of it as "moist
enough for agriculture, and very beautiful. They have abundance of
trees, and are full of autumn fruits both wild and cultivated. . . . They
are not naturally watered by many rivers, but derive their chief moisture
from rain, of which they have no want."[2] In ancient days the spring rains
that fed the land were stored in cisterns or brought back to the surface
by a multitude of wells, and distributed over the country by a network

of canals; this was the physical basis of Jewish civilization. The soil, so nourished, produced barley, wheat and corn, the vine throve on it, and trees bore olives, figs, dates or other fruits on every slope. When war came and devastated these artifically fertile fields, or when some conqueror exiled to distant regions the families that had cared for them, the desert crept in eagerly, and in a few years undid the work of generations. We cannot judge the fruitfulness of ancient Palestine from the barren wastes and timid oases that confronted the brave Jews who in our own time returned to their old home after eighteen centuries of exile, dispersion and suffering.

History is older in Palestine than Bishop Ussher supposed. Neanderthal remains have been unearthed near the Sea of Galilee, and five Neanderthal skeletons were recently discovered in a cave near Haifa; it appears likely that the Mousterian culture which flourished in Europe about 40,000 B.C. extended to Palestine. At Jericho neolithic floors and hearths have been exhumed that carry back the history of the region down to a Middle Bronze Age (2000-1600 B.C.), in which the towns of Palestine and Syria had accumulated such wealth as to invite conquest by Egypt. In the fifteenth century before Christ Jericho was a well-walled city, ruled by kings acknowledging the suzerainty of Egypt; the tombs of these kings, excavated by the Garstang Expedition, contained hundreds of vases, funerary offerings, and other objects indicating a settled life at Jericho in the time of the Hyksos domination, and a fairly developed civilization in the days of Hatshepsut and Thutmose III.[3] It becomes apparent that the different dates at which we begin the history of divers peoples are merely the marks of our ignorance. The Tell-el-Amarna letters carry on the general picture of Palestinian and Syrian life almost to the entrance of the Jews into the valley of the Nile. It is probable, though not certain, that the "Habiru" spoken of in this correspondence were Hebrews.*[4]

The Jews believed that the people of Abraham had come from Ur in Sumeria,[5] and had settled in Palestine (ca. 2200 B.C.) a thousand years

---

* The discoveries here summarized have restored considerable credit to those chapters of Genesis that record the early traditions of the Jews. In its outlines, and barring supernatural incidents, the story of the Jews as unfolded in the Old Testament has stood the test of criticism and archeology; every year adds corroboration from documents, monuments, or excavations. E.g., potsherds unearthed at Tel Ad-Duweir in 1935 bore Hebrew inscriptions confirming part of the narrative of the Books of Kings.[4a] We must accept the Biblical account provisionally until it is disproved. Cf. Petrie, *Egypt and Israel*, London, 1925, p. 108.

or more before Moses; and that the conquest of the Canaanites was merely a capture by the Hebrews of the land promised them by their God. The Amraphael mentioned in Genesis (xiv, 1) as "King of Shinar in those days" was probably Amarpal, father of Hammurabi, and his predecessor on the throne of Babylon.[6] There are no direct references in contemporary sources to either the Exodus or the conquest of Canaan;[7] and the only indirect reference is the stele erected by Pharaoh Merneptah (ca. 1225 B.C.), part of which reads as follows:

> The kings are overthrown, saying "Salam!" . . .
> Wasted is Tehenu,
> The Hittite land is pacified,
> Plundered is Canaan, with every evil, . . .
> Israel is desolated, her seed is not;
> Palestine has become a widow for Egypt,
> All lands are united, they are pacified;
> Every one that is turbulent is bound by King Merneptah.[8]

This does not prove that Merneptah was the Pharaoh of the Exodus; it proves little except that Egyptian armies had again ravaged Palestine. We cannot tell when the Jews entered Egypt, nor whether they came to it as freemen or as slaves.* We may take it as likely that the immigrants were at first a modest number,[11] and that the many thousands of Jews in Egypt in Moses' time were the consequence of a high birth rate; as in all periods, "the more they afflicted them, the more they multiplied and grew."[12] The story of the "bondage" in Egypt, of the use of the Jews as slaves in great construction enterprises, their rebellion and escape— or emigration—to Asia, has many internal signs of essential truth, mingled, of course, with supernatural interpolations customary in all the historical writing of the ancient East. Even the story of Moses must not be rejected offhand; it is astonishing, however, that no mention is made of him by either Amos or Isaiah, whose preaching appears to have preceded by a century the composition of the Pentateuch.†

---

* Perhaps they followed in the track of the Hyksos, whose Semitic rule in Egypt might have offered them some protection.[9] Petrie, accepting the Bible figure of four hundred and thirty years for the stay of the Jews in Egypt, dates their arrival about 1650 B.C., their exit about 1220 B.C.[10]

† Manetho, an Egyptian historian of the third century B.C., as reported by Josephus, tells us that the Exodus was due to the desire of the Egyptians to protect themselves from a plague that had broken out among the destitute and enslaved Jews, and that Moses was an Egyptian priest who went as a missionary among the Jewish "lepers," and gave

When Moses led the Jews to Mt. Sinai he was merely following the route laid down by Egyptian turquoise-hunting expeditions for a thousand years before him. The account of the forty years' wandering in the desert, once looked upon as incredible, now seems reasonable enough in a traditionally nomadic people; and the conquest of Canaan was but one more instance of a hungry nomad horde falling upon a settled community. The conquerors killed as many as they could, and married the rest. Slaughter was unconfined, and (to follow the text) was divinely ordained and enjoyed;[19] Gideon, in capturing two cities, slew 120,000 men; only in the annals of the Assyrians do we meet again with such hearty killing, or easy counting. Occasionally, we are told, "the land rested from war."[20] Moses had been a patient statesman, but Joshua was only a plain, blunt warrior; Moses had ruled bloodlessly by inventing interviews with God, but Joshua ruled by the second law of nature—that the superior killer survives. In this realistic and unsentimental fashion the Jews took their Promised Land.

II. SOLOMON IN ALL HIS GLORY

Race — Appearance — Language — Organization — Judges and kings—Saul—David—Solomon—His wealth—The Temple— Rise of the social problem in Israel

Of their racial origin we can only say vaguely that they were Semites, not sharply distinct or different from the other Semites of western Asia; it was their history that made them, not they who made their history. At their very first appearance they are already a mixture of many stocks— only by the most unbelievable virtue could a "pure" race have existed

---

them laws of cleanliness modeled upon those of the Egyptian clergy.[13] Greek and Roman writers repeat this explanation of the Exodus;[14] but their anti-Semitic inclinations make them unreliable guides. One verse of the Biblical account supports Ward's interpretation of the Exodus as a labor strike: "And the king of Egypt said unto them, Wherefore do ye, Moses and Aaron, let the people from their works? Get you unto your burdens."[15]

Moses is an Egyptian rather than a Jewish name; perhaps it is a shorter form of *Ahmose*.[16] Professor Garstang, of the Marston Expedition of the University of Liverpool, claims to have discovered, in the royal tombs of Jericho, evidence that Moses was rescued (precisely in 1527 B.C.) by the then Princess, later the great Queen, Hatshepsut; that he was brought up by her as a court favorite, and fled from Egypt upon the accession of her enemy, Thutmose III.[17] He believes that the material found in these tombs confirms the story of the fall of Jericho (Joshua, vi); he dates this fall ca. 1400 B.C., and the Exodus ca. 1447 B.C.[18] As this chronology rests upon the precarious dating of scarabs and pottery, it must be received with respectful scepticism.

among the thousand ethnic cross-currents of the Near East. But the Jews were the purest, of all, for they intermarried only very reluctantly with other peoples. Hence they have maintained their type with astonishing tenacity; the Hebrew prisoners on the Egyptian and Assyrian reliefs, despite the prejudices of the artist, are recognizably like the Jews of our own time: there, too, are the long and curved Hittite nose,* the projecting cheek-bones, the curly hair and beard; though one cannot see, under the Egyptian caricature, the scrawny toughness of body, the subtlety and obstinacy of spirit, that have characterized the Semites from the "stiff-necked" followers of Moses to the inscrutable Bedouins and tradesmen of today. In the early years of their conquest they dressed in simple tunics, low-crowned hats or turban-like caps, and easy-going sandals; as wealth came they covered their feet with leather shoes, and their tunics with fringed kaftans. Their women, who were among the most beautiful of antiquity,† painted their cheeks and their eyes, wore all the jewelry they could get, and adopted to the best of their ability the newest styles from Babylon, Nineveh, Damascus or Tyre.[21]

Hebrew was among the most majestically sonorous of all the languages of the earth. Despite its gutturals, it was full of masculine music; Renan described it as "a quiver full of arrows, a trumpet of brasses crashing through the air."[22] It did not differ much from the speech of the Phœnicians or the Moabites. The Jews used an alphabet akin to the Phœnician;[23] some scholars believe it to be the oldest alphabet known.[23a] They did not bother to write vowels, leaving these for the sense to fill in; even today the Hebrew vowels are mere points adorning the consonants.

The invaders never formed a united nation, but remained for a long time as twelve more or less independent tribes, organized and ruled on the principles not of the state but of the patriarchal family. The oldest head of each family group participated in a council of elders which was the last court of law and justice in the tribe, and which coöperated with the leaders of other tribes only under the compulsion of dire emergency. The family was the most convenient economic unit in tilling the fields and tending the flocks; this was the source of its strength, its authority, and its political power. A measure of family communism softened the rigors of paternal discipline, and created memories to which the prophets harked back disconsolately in more individualistic days. For when, under

---

* Cf. p. 287 above.
† Cf. the story of Esther, and the descriptions of Rebecca, Bathsheba, etc.

Solomon, industry came to the towns, and made the individual the new economic unit of production, the authority of the family weakened, even as today, and the inherent order of Jewish life decayed.

The "judges" to whom the tribes occasionally gave a united obedience were not magistrates, but chieftains or warriors—even when they were priests.[24] "In those days there was no king in Israel, but every man did that which was right in his own eyes."[25] This incredibly Jeffersonian condition gave way under the needs of war; the threat of domination by the Philistines brought a temporary unity to the tribes, and persuaded them to appoint a king whose authority over them should be continuous. The prophet Samuel warned them against certain disadvantages in rule by one man:

> And Samuel said, This will be the manner of the king that shall reign over you: He will take your sons and appoint them for himself, for his chariots, and to be his horsemen; and some shall run before his chariots. And he will appoint them captains over thousands, and captains over fifties; and will set them to ear his ground, and to reap his harvest, and to make his instruments of war, and instruments of his chariots. And he will take your daughters to be confectionaries, and to be cooks, and to be bakers. And he will take your fields, and your vineyards, and your oliveyards, even the best of them, and give them to his servants. And he will take your menservants, and your maidservants, and your goodliest young men, and your asses, and put them to his work. He will take the tenth of your sheep, and ye shall be his servants. And ye shall cry out in that day because of your king which ye shall have chosen you; and the Lord will not hear you in that day.
>
> Nevertheless the people refused to obey the voice of Samuel; and they said, Nay, but we shall have a king over us; that we also may be like all the nations; and that our king may judge us, and go out before us, and fight our battles.[26]

Their first king, Saul, gave them good and evil instructively: fought their battles bravely, lived simply on his own estate at Gileah, pursued young David with murderous attentions, and was beheaded in flight from the Philistines. The Jews learned, then, at the first opportunity, that wars of succession are among the appanages of monarchy. Unless the little epic of Saul, Jonathan and David is merely a masterpiece of literary creation* (for there is no contemporary mention of these personalities outside the Bible), this first king, after a bloody interlude, was succeeded by David, heroic slayer of Goliath, tender lover of Jonathan and many maidens, half-naked dancer of wild dances,[28] seductive player of the harp, sweet singer of marvelous songs, and able king of the Jews for almost forty years. Here, so early in literature, is a character fully drawn, real with all the contradictory passions of a living soul: as ruthless as his time, his tribe and his god, and yet as ready to pardon his enemies as Cæsar was, or Christ; putting captives to death wholesale, like any Assyrian monarch; charging his son Solomon to "bring down to the grave with blood" the "hoar head" of old Shimei who had cursed him many years before;[29] taking Uriah's wife into his harem incontinently, and sending Uriah into the front line of battle to get rid of him;[30] accepting Nathan's rebuke humbly, but keeping the lovely Bathsheba none the less; forgiving Saul almost seventy times seven, merely taking his shield when he might have taken his life; sparing and supporting Mephibosheth, a possible pretender to his throne; pardoning his ungrateful son Absalom, who had been caught in armed rebellion, and bitterly mourning that son's death in treasonable battle against his father ("O my son Absalom! my son, my son, Absalom! would God I had died for thee, O Absalom, my son, my son!")[31]—this is an authentic man, of full and varied elements, bearing within him all the vestiges of barbarism, and all the promise of civilization.

On coming to the throne Solomon, for his peace of mind, slew all rival claimants. This did not disturb Yahveh, who, taking a liking to the young king, promised him wisdom beyond all men before or after him.[32] Perhaps Solomon deserves his reputation; for not only did he combine in his own life the epicurean enjoyment of every pleasure and luxury with a stoic fulfillment of all his obligations as a king,† but he taught his people the values of law and order, and lured them from discord and war to industry and peace. He lived up to his name,‡ for during his long reign Jerusalem, which David had made the capital, took advantage of this unwonted quiet, and increased and multiplied its wealth. Originally the city§ had been built around a well; then it had been turned into a fortress

---

* Like the jolly story of Samson, who burned the crops of the Philistines by letting loose in them three hundred foxes with torches tied to their tails, and, in the manner of some orators, slew a thousand men with the jawbone of an ass.[27]

† "He spake three thousand proverbs, and his songs were a thousand and five."[32]

‡ Taken from *Shalom*, meaning peace.

§ Mentioned in the Tell-el-Amarna tablets as Ursalimmu, or Urusalim.

because of its exalted position above the plain; now, though it was not on the main lines of trade, it became one of the busiest markets of the Near East. By maintaining the good relations that David had established with King Hiram of Tyre, Solomon encouraged Phœnician merchants to direct their caravans through Palestine, and developed a profitable exchange of agricultural products from Israel for the manufactured articles of Tyre and Sidon. He built a fleet of mercantile vessels on the Red Sea, and persuaded Hiram to use this new route, instead of Egypt, in trading with Arabia and Africa.[34] It was probably in Arabia that Solomon mined the gold and precious stones of "Ophir";[35] probably from Arabia that the Queen of "Sheba" came to seek his friendship, and perhaps his aid.[36] We are told that "the weight of gold that came to Solomon in one year was six hundred three score and six talents of gold";[37] and though this could not compare with the revenues of Babylon, Nineveh or Tyre, it lifted Solomon to a place among the richest potentates of his time.*

Some of this wealth he used for his private pleasure. He indulged particularly his hobby for collecting concubines—though historians undramatically reduce his "seven hundred wives and three hundred concubines" to sixty and eighty.[39] Perhaps by some of these marriages he wished to strengthen his friendship with Egypt and Phœnicia; perhaps, like Rameses II, he was animated with a eugenic passion for transmitting his superior abilities. But most of his revenues went to the strengthening of his government and the beautification of his capital. He repaired the citadel around which the city had been built; he raised forts and stationed garrisons at strategic points of his realm to discourage both invasion and revolt. He divided his kingdom, for administrative purposes, into twelve districts which deliberately crossed the tribal boundaries; by this plan he hoped to lessen the clannish separatism of the tribes, and to weld them into one people. He failed, and Judea failed with him. To finance his government he organized expeditions to mine precious metals, and to import luxuries and strange delicacies—e.g., "ivory, apes and peacocks"[40] —which could be sold to the growing *bourgeoisie* at high prices; he levied

---

* On the value of the talent in the ancient Near East cf. p. 228 above. The value varied from time to time; but we should not be exaggerating it if we rated the talent, in Solomon's day, as having a purchasing power of over $10,000 in our contemporary money. Probably the Hebrew writer spoke in a literary way, and we must not take his figures too seriously. On the fluctuations of Hebrew currency cf. the *Jewish Encyclopedia*, articles "Numismatics" and "Shekel." Coinage, as distinct from rings or ingots of silver or gold, does not appear in Palestine until about 650 B.C.[38]

tolls upon all caravans passing through Palestine; he put a poll tax upon all his subject peoples, required contributions from every district except his own, and reserved to the state a monopoly of the trade in yarn, horses and chariots.[41] Josephus assures us that Solomon "made silver as plentiful in Jerusalem as stones in the street."[42] Finally he resolved to adorn the city with a new temple for Yahveh and a new palace for himself.

We gather some sense of the turbulence of Jewish life from the fact that before this time there had been, apparently, no temple at all in Judea, not even in Jerusalem; the people had sacrificed to Yahveh in local sanctuaries or on crude altars in the hills.[43] Solomon called the more substantial burghers together, announced his plans for a temple, pledged to it great quantities of gold, silver, brass, iron, wood and precious stones from his own stores, and gently suggested that the temple would welcome contributions from the citizens. If we may believe the chronicler, they pledged for his use five thousand gold talents, ten thousand silver talents, and as much iron and brass as he might need; "and they with whom precious stones were found gave them to the treasure of the house of the Lord."[44] The site chosen was on a hill; the walls of the Temple rose, like the Parthenon, continuously from the rocky slopes.* The design was in the style that the Phœnicians had adopted from Egypt, with decorative ideas from Assyria and Babylon. The Temple was not a church, but a quadrangular enclosure composed of several buildings. The main structure was of modest dimensions—about one hundred and twenty-four feet in length, fifty-five in breadth, and fifty-two in height; half the length of the Parthenon, a quarter of the length of Chartres.[46] The Hebrews who came from all- Judea to contribute to the Temple, and later to worship in it, forgivably looked upon it as one of the wonders of the world; they had not seen the immensely greater temples of Thebes, Babylon and Nineveh. Before the main structure rose a "porch" some one hundred and eighty feet high, overlaid with gold. Gold was spread lavishly about, if we may credit our sole authority: on the beams of the main ceiling, on the posts, the doors and the walls, on the candelabra, the lamps, the snuffers, the spoons, the censers, and "a hundred basins of gold." Precious stones were inlaid here and there, and two gold-plated cherubim guarded the Ark of the Covenant.[47] The walls were of great square stones; the ceiling, posts and doors were of carved cedar and olive wood. Most of the

---

* It is likely that the site of the Temple was that which is now covered by the Moslem shrine El-haram-esh-sharif; but no remains of the Temple have been found.[45]

building materials were brought from Phœnicia, and most of the skilled work was done by artisans imported from Sidon and Tyre.⁴⁸ The unskilled labor was herded together by a ruthless *corvée* of 150,000 men, after the fashion of the time.⁴⁹

So for seven years the Temple rose, to provide for four centuries a lordly home for Yahveh. Then for thirteen years more the artisans and people labored to build a much larger edifice, for Solomon and his harem. Merely one wing of it—"the house of the forest of Lebanon"—was four times as large as the Temple.⁵⁰ The walls of the main building were made of immense stone blocks fifteen feet in length, and were ornamented with statuary, reliefs and paintings in the Assyrian style. The palace contained halls for the royal reception of distinguished visitors, apartments for the King, separate quarters for the more important wives, and an arsenal as the final basis of government. Not a stone of the gigantic edifice survives, and its site is unknown.⁵¹

Having established his kingdom, Solomon settled down to enjoy it. As his reign proceeded he paid less and less attention to religion and frequented his harem rather more than the Temple. The Biblical chroniclers reproach him bitterly for his gallantry in building altars to the exotic deities of his foreign wives, and cannot forgive his philosophical—or perhaps political—impartiality to the gods. The people admired his wisdom, but suspected in it a certain centripetal quality; the Temple and the palace had cost them much gold and blood, and were not more popular with them than the Pyramids had been with the workingmen of Egypt. The upkeep of these establishments required considerable taxation, and few governments have made taxation popular. When he died Israel was exhausted, and a discontented proletariat had been created whose labor found no steady employment, and whose sufferings were to transform the warlike cult of Yahveh into the almost socialistic religion of the prophets.

III. THE GOD OF HOSTS

Polytheism—Yahveh—Henotheism—Character of the Hebrew religion—The idea of sin—Sacrifice—Circumcision—The priesthood—Strange gods

Next to the promulgation of the "Book of Law," the building of the Temple was the most important event in the epic of the Jews. It not only gave Yahveh a home, but it gave Judea a spiritual center and capital, a vehicle of tradition, a memory to serve as a pillar of fire through centuries of wandering over the earth. And it played its part in lifting the Hebrew religion from a primitive polytheism to a faith intense and intolerant, but none the less one of the creative creeds of history.

As they first entered the historic scene the Jews were nomad Bedouins who feared the djinns of the air, and worshiped rocks, cattle, sheep, and the spirits of caves and hills.[52] The cult of the bull, the sheep and the lamb was not neglected; Moses could never quite win his flock from adoration of the Golden Calf, for the Egyptian worship of the bull was still fresh in their memories, and Yahveh was for a long time symbolized in that ferocious vegetarian. In Exodus (xxxii, 25-28) we read how the Jews indulged in a naked dance before the Golden Calf, and how Moses and the Levites—or priestly class—slew three thousand of them in punishment of their idolatry.* Of serpent worship there are countless traces in early Jewish history, from the serpent images found in the oldest ruins,[54] to the brazen serpent made by Moses and worshiped in the Temple until the time of Hezekiah (ca. 720 B.C.).[55] As among so many peoples, the snake seemed sacred to the Jews, partly as a phallic symbol of virility, partly as typifying wisdom, subtlety and eternity—literally because of its ability to make both ends meet.[56] Baal, symbolized in conical upright stones much like the *linga* of the Hindus, was venerated by some of the Hebrews as the male principle of reproduction, the husband of the land that he fertilized.[57] Just as primitive polytheism survived in the worship of angels and saints, and in the *teraphim*, or portable idols, that served as household gods,[58] so the magical notions rife in the early cults persisted to a late day despite the protests of prophets and priests. The people seem to have looked upon Moses and Aaron as magicians,[59] and to have patronized professional diviners and sorcerers. Divination was sought at times by shaking dice (*Urim* and *Thummim*) out of a box (*ephod*)—a ritual still used to ascertain the will of the gods. It is to the credit of the priests that they opposed these practices, and preached an exclusive reliance on the magic of sacrifice, prayer and contributions.

Slowly the conception of Yahveh as the one national god took form, and gave to Jewish faith a unity and simplicity lifted up above the chaotic

---

* Other vestiges of animal worship among the ancient Hebrews may be found in 1 Kings, xii, 28, and Ezekiel, viii, 10. Ahab, King of Israel, worshiped heifers in the century after Solomon.[53]

multiplicity of the Mesopotamian pantheons. Apparently the conquering Jews took one of the gods of Canaan, Yahu,* and re-created him in their own image as a stern, warlike, "stiff-necked" deity, with almost lovable limitations. For this god makes no claim to omniscience: he asks the Jews to identify their homes by sprinkling them with the blood of the sacrificial lamb, lest he should destroy their children inadvertently along with the first-born of the Egyptians;[61] he is not above making mistakes, of which man is his worst; he regrets, too late, that he created Adam, or allowed Saul to become king. He is, now and then, greedy, irascible, bloodthirtsy, capricious, petulant: "I will be gracious to whom I will be gracious, and will show mercy to whom I will show mercy."[62] He approves Jacob's use of deceit in revenging himself upon Laban;[63] his conscience is as flexible as that of a bishop in politics. He is talkative, and likes to make long speeches; but he is shy, and will not allow men to see anything of him but his hind parts.[64] Never was there so thoroughly human a god.

Originally he seems to have been a god of thunder, dwelling in the hills,[65] and worshiped for the same reason that the youthful Gorki was a believer when it thundered. The authors of the Pentateuch, to whom religion was an instrument of statesmanship, formed this Vulcan into Mars, so that in their energetic hands Yahveh became predominantly an imperialistic, expansionist God of Hosts, who fights for his people as fiercely as the gods of the *Iliad*. "The Lord is a man of war," says "Moses";[66] and David echoes him: "He teacheth my hands to war."[67] Yahveh promises to "destroy all the people to whom" the Jews "shall come," and to drive out the Hivite, the Canaanite and the Hittite "by little and little";[68] and he claims as his own all the territory conquered by the Jews.[69] He will have no pacifist nonsense; he knows that even a Promised Land can be won, and held, only by the sword; he is a god of war because he has to be; it will take centuries of military defeat, political subjugation, and moral development, to transform him into the gentle and loving Father of Hillel and Christ. He is as vain as a soldier; he drinks up praise with a bottomless appetite, and he is anxious to display his prowess by drowning the Egyptians: "They shall know that I am the Lord when I have gotten me honor upon Pharaoh."[70] To gain successes for his people he commits or commands brutalities as repugnant to our taste as they were acceptable to the morals of the age; he slaughters whole

---

* Among some Bronze Age (3000 B.C.) ruins found in Canaan in 1931 were pieces of pottery bearing the name of a Canaanite deity, Yah or Yahu.[60]

nations with the naïve pleasure of a Gulliver fighting for Lilliput. Because the Jews "commit whoredom" with the daughters of Moab he bids Moses: "Take all the heads of the people, and hang them up before the Lord against the sun";[71] it is the morality of Ashurbanipal and Ashur. He offers to show mercy to those who love him and keep his commandments, but, like some resolute germ, he will punish children for the sins of their fathers, their grandfathers, even their great-great-grandfathers.[72] He is so ferocious that he thinks of destroying all the Jews for worshiping the Golden Calf; and Moses has to argue with him that he should control himself. "Turn from thy fierce wrath," the man tells his god, "and repent of this evil against thy people"; and "the Lord repented of the evil which he thought to do unto his people."[73] Again Yahveh proposes to exterminate the Jews root and branch for rebelling against Moses, but Moses appeals to his better nature, and bids him think what people will say when they hear of such a thing.[74] He asks a cruel test—human sacrifice of the bitterest sort—from Abraham. Like Moses, Abraham teaches Yahveh the principles of morals, and persuades him not to destroy Sodom and Gomorrah if there shall be found fifty—forty—thirty—twenty—ten good men in those cities;[75] bit by bit he lures his god towards decency, and illustrates the manner in which the moral development of man compels the periodical re-creation of his deities. The curses with which Yahveh threatens his chosen people if they disobey him are models of vituperation, and inspired those who burned heretics in the Inquisition, or excommunicated Spinoza:

> Cursed shalt thou be in the city, and cursed shalt thou be in the field. . . . Cursed shall be the fruit of thy body, and the fruit of thy land. . . . Cursed shalt thou be when thou comest in, and cursed shalt thou be when thou goest out. . . . The Lord shall smite thee with a consumption, and with a fever, and with an inflammation. . . . The Lord will smite thee with the botch of Egypt, and with the emerods (tumors), and with the scab, and with the itch, whereof thou canst not be healed. The Lord shall smite thee with madness, and blindness, and astonishment of heart. . . . Also every sickness, and every plague, which is not written in the Book of this Law, them will the Lord bring upon thee, until thou be destroyed.[76]

Yahveh was not the only god whose existence was recognized by the Jews, or by himself; all that he asked, in the First Commandment, was that he should be placed above the rest. "I am a jealous god," he confesses, and he bids his followers "utterly overthrow" his rivals, and "quite break down their images."[77] The Jews, before Isaiah, seldom thought of Yahveh as the god of all tribes, even of all Hebrews. The Moabites had their god Chemosh, to whom Naomi thought it right that Ruth should remain loyal;[78] Baalzebub was the god of Ekron, Milcom was the god of Ammon: the economic and political separatism of these peoples naturally resulted in what we might call their theological independence. Moses sings, in his famous song, "Who is like unto thee, O Lord, among the gods?"[79] and Solomon says, "Great is our god above all gods."[80] Not only was Tammuz accepted as a real god by all but the most educated Jews, but his cult was at one time so popular in Judea that Ezekiel complained that the ritual wailing for Tammuz' death could be heard in the Temple.[81] So distinct and autonomous were the Jewish tribes that even in the time of Jeremiah many of them had their own deities: "according to the number of thy cities are thy gods, O Judah"; and the gloomy prophet goes on to protest against the worship of Baal and Moloch by his people.[82] With the growth of political unity under David and Solomon, and the centering of worship in the Temple at Jerusalem, theology reflected history and politics, and Yahveh became the sole god of the Jews. Beyond this "henotheism"* they made no further progress towards monotheism until the Prophets.† Even in the Yahvistic stage the Hebraic religion came closer to monotheism than any other pre-Prophetic faith except the ephemeral sun-worship of Ikhnaton. At least equal as sentiment and poetry to the polytheism of Babylonia and Greece, Judaism was immensely superior to the other religions of the time in majesty and power, in philosophic unity and grasp, in moral fervor and influence.

This intense and sombre religion never took on any of the ornate ritual and joyous ceremonies that marked the worship of the Egyptian and Babylonian gods. A sense of human nothingness before an arbitrary deity darkened all ancient Jewish thought. Despite the efforts of Solomon to beau-

---

* A clumsy but useful word coined by Max Müller to designate the worship of a god as supreme, combined with the explicit (as in India) or tacit (as in Judea) admission of other gods.

† Elisha, however, as far back as the ninth century B.C., announced one God: "I know that there is no God in all the earth but in Israel."[83] It should be remembered that even modern monotheism is highly relative and incomplete. As the Jews worshiped a tribal god, so we worship a European god—or an English, or a German, or an Italian, god; no moment of modesty comes to remind us that the abounding millions of India, China and Japan—not to speak of the theologians of the jungle—do not yet recognize the God of our Fathers. Not until the machine weaves all the earth into one economic web, and forces all the nations under one rule, will there be one god—for the earth.

tify the cult of Yahveh with color and sound, the worship of this awful divinity remained for many centuries a religion of fear rather than of love. One wonders, in looking back upon these faiths, whether they brought as much consolation as terror to humanity. Religions of hope and love are a luxury of security and order; the need for striking fear into a subject or rebellious people made most primitive religions cults of mystery and dread. The Ark of the Covenant, containing the sacred scrolls of the Law, symbolized by its untouchability the character of the Jewish creed. When the pious Uzzah, to prevent the Ark from falling into the dust, caught it for a moment in his hands, "the anger of the Lord was kindled against Uzzah, and God smote him there for his error; and there he died."[84]

The central idea in Judaic theology was that of sin. Never has another people been so fond of virtue—unless it was those Puritans who seemed to step out of the Old Testament with no interruption of Catholic centuries. Since the flesh was weak and the Law complex, sin was inevitable, and the Jewish spirit was often overcast with the thought of sin's consequences, from the withholding of rain to the ruin of all Israel. There was no Hell in this faith as a distinctive place of punishment; but almost as bad was the Sheol, or "land of darkness" under the earth, which received all the dead, good and wicked alike, except such divine favorites as Moses, Enoch and Elijah. The Jews, however, made little reference to a life beyond the grave; their creed said nothing of personal immortality, and confined its rewards and punishments to this mundane life. Not until the Jews had lost hope of earthly triumph did they take over, probably from Persia and perhaps also from Egypt, the notion of personal resurrection. It was out of this spiritual *dénouement* that Christianity was born.

The threat and consequence of sin might be offset by prayer or sacrifice. Semitic, like "Aryan," sacrifice began by offering human victims;[85] then it offered animals—the "first fruits of the flocks"—and food from the fields; finally it compromised by offering praise. At first no animal might be eaten unless killed and blessed by the priest, and offered for a moment to the god.[86] Circumcision partook of the nature of a sacrifice, and perhaps of a commutation: the god took a part for the whole. Menstruation and childbirth, like sin, made a person spiritually unclean, and necessitated ritual purification by priestly sacrifice and prayer. At every turn tabus hedged in the faithful; sin lay potential in almost every desire, and donations were required in atonement for almost every sin.

Only the priests could offer sacrifice properly, or explain correctly the ritual and mysteries of the faith. The priests were a closed caste, to which none but the descendants of Levi* could belong. They could not inherit property,[87] but they were exempt from all taxation, toll, or tribute;[88] they levied a tithe upon the harvests of the flocks, and turned to their own use such offerings to the Temple as were left unused by the god.[90] After the Exile, the wealth of the clergy grew with that of the renascent community; and since this sacerdotal wealth was well administered, augmented and preserved, it finally made the priests of the Second Temple, in Jerusalem as in Thebes and Babylon, more powerful than the king.

Nevertheless the growth of clerical power and religious education never quite sufficed to win the Hebrews from superstition and idolatry. The hill-tops and groves continued to harbor alien gods and to witness secret rites; a substantial minority of the people prostrated themselves before sacred stones, or worshiped Baal or Astarte, or practised divination in the Babylonian manner, or set up images and burned incense to them, or knelt before the brazen serpent or the Golden Calf, or filled the Temple with the noise of heathen feasting,[91] or made their children "pass through the fire" in sacrifice;[92] even some of the kings, like Solomon and Ahab, went "a-whoring" after foreign gods. Holy men like Elijah and Elisha arose who, without necessarily becoming priests, preached against these practices, and tried by the example of their lives to lead their people into righteousness. Out of these conditions and beginnings, and out of the rise of poverty and exploitation in Israel, came the supreme figures in Jewish religion—those passionate Prophets who purified and elevated the creed of the Jews, and prepared it for its vicarious conquest of the western world.

IV. THE FIRST RADICALS

The class war—Origin of the Prophets—Amos at Jerusalem—
Isaiah—His attacks upon the rich—His doctrine of a Messiah—
The influence of the Prophets

Since poverty is created by wealth, and never knows itself poor until riches stare it in the face, so it required the fabulous fortune of Solomon to mark the beginning of the class war in Israel. Solomon, like Peter and Lenin, tried to move too quickly from an agricultural to an industrial state. Not only did the toil and taxes involved in his enterprises impose great burdens upon his people, but when those undertakings were com-

---

* One of the sons of Jacob.

plete, after twenty years of industry, a proletariat had been created in Jerusalem which, lacking sufficient employment, became a source of political faction and corruption in Palestine, precisely as it was to become in Rome. Slums developed step by step with the rise of private wealth and the increasing luxury of the court. Exploitation and usury became recognized practises among the owners of great estates and the merchants and money-lenders who flocked about the Temple. The landlords of Ephraim, said Amos, "sold the righteous for silver and the poor for a pair of shoes."[93]

This growing gap between the needy and the affluent, and the sharpening of that conflict between the city and the country which always accompanies an industrial civilization, had something to do with the division of Palestine into two hostile kingdoms after the death of Solomon: a northern kingdom of Ephraim,* with its capital at Samaria, and a southern kingdom of Judah, with its capital at Jerusalem. From that time on the Jews were weakened by fraternal hatred and strife, breaking out occasionally into bitter war. Shortly after the death of Solomon Jerusalem was captured by Sheshonk, Pharaoh of Egypt, and surrendered, to appease the conqueror, nearly all the gold that Solomon had gathered in his long career of taxation.

It was in this atmosphere of political disruption, economic war, and religious degeneration that the Prophets appeared. The men to whom the word (in Hebrew, Nabi†) was first applied were not quite of the character that our reverence would associate with Amos and Isaiah. Some were diviners who could read the secrets of the heart and the past, and foretell the future, according to remuneration; some were fanatics who worked themselves into a frenzy by weird music, strong drink, or dervish-like dances, and spoke, in trances, words which their hearers considered inspired—i.e., breathed into them by some spirit other than their own.[94] Jeremiah speaks with professional scorn of "every man that is mad, and maketh himself a prophet."[95] Some were gloomy recluses, like Elijah; many of them lived in schools or monasteries near the temples; but most of them had private property and wives.[96] From this motley crowd of *fakirs* the Prophets developed into responsible and consistent critics of their age and their people, magnificent street-corner statesmen

---

* This kingdom often called itself "Israel"; but this word will be used, in these pages, to include all the Jews.

† Translated by the Greeks into *pro-phe-tes*, announcer.

who were all "thorough-going anti-clericals,"[97] and "the most uncompromising of anti-Semites,"[98] a cross between soothsayers and socialists. We misunderstand them if we take them as prophets in the weather sense; their predictions were hopes or threats, or pious interpolations,[99] or prognostications after the event;[100] the Prophets themselves did not pretend to foretell, so much as to speak out; they were eloquent members of the Opposition. In one phase they were Tolstoians incensed at industrial exploitation and ecclesiastical chicanery; they came up from the simple countryside, and hurled damnation at the corrupt wealth of the towns.

Amos described himself not as a prophet but as a simple village shepherd. Having left his herds to see Beth-El, he was horrified at the unnatural complexity of the life which he discovered there, the inequality of fortune, the bitterness of competition, the ruthlessness of exploitation. So he "stood in the gate," and lashed the conscienceless rich and their luxuries:

> Forasmuch, therefore, as your treading is upon the poor, and ye take from him burdens of wheat; ye have built houses of hewn stone, but ye shall not dwell in them; ye have planted pleasant vineyards, but ye shall not drink wine of them. . . . Woe to them that are at ease in Zion, . . . that lie upon beds of ivory, and stretch themselves upon their couches, and eat the lambs out of the flock, and the calves out of the midst of the stall; that chant to the sound of the viol, and invent to themselves instruments of music, like David; that drink wine in bowls, and anoint themselves with the chief ointments. . . .
>
> I despise your feast-days (saith the Lord); . . . though ye offer me burnt offerings and your meat offerings, I will not accept them. . . . Take thou away from me the noise of thy songs, for I will not hear the melody of thy viols. But let judgment run down as waters, and righteousness as a mighty stream.[101]

This is a new note in the world's literature. It is true that Amos dulls the edge of his idealism by putting into the mouth of his god a Mississippi of threats whose severity and accumulation make the reader sympathize for a moment with the drinkers of wine and the listeners to music. But here, for the first time in the literature of Asia, the social conscience takes definite form, and pours into religion a content that lifts it from ceremony and flattery to a whip of morals and a call to nobility. With Amos begins the gospel of Jesus Christ.

One of his bitterest predictions seems to have been fulfilled while Amos was still alive. "Thus saith the Lord: As the shepherd taketh out of the mouth of the lion two legs, or a piece of an ear, so shall the children of Israel be taken out that dwell in Samaria in the corner of a bed, and in Damascus in a couch. . . . And the houses of ivory shall perish, and the great houses shall have an end."[102]* About the same time another prophet threatened Samaria with destruction in one of those myriads of vivid phrases which King James's translators minted for the currency of our speech out of the wealth of the Bible: "The calf of Samaria," said Hosea, "shall be broken into pieces; for they have sown the wind, and they shall reap the whirlwind."[104] In 733 the young kingdom of Judah, threatened by Ephraim in alliance with Syria, appealed to Assyria for help. Assyria came, took Damascus, subjected Syria, Tyre and Palestine to tribute, made note of Jewish efforts to secure Egyptian aid, invaded again, captured Samaria, indulged in unprintable diplomatic exchanges with the King of Judah,[105] failed to take Jerusalem, and retired to Nineveh laden with booty and 200,000 Jewish captives doomed to Assyrian slavery.[106]

It was during this siege of Jerusalem that the prophet Isaiah became one of the great figures of Hebrew history.† Less provincial than Amos, he thought in terms of enduring statesmanship. Convinced that little Judah could not resist the imperial power of Assyria, even with the help of distant Egypt—that broken staff which would pierce the hand that should try to use it—he pled with King Ahaz, and then with King Hezekiah, to remain neutral in the war between Assyria and Ephraim, like Amos and Hosea he foresaw the fall of Samaria,[108] and the end of the northern kingdom. When, however, the Assyrians besieged Jerusalem, Isaiah counseled Hezekiah not to yield. The sudden withdrawal of Sennacherib's hosts seemed to justify him, and for a time his repute was high with the King and the people. Always his advice was to deal justly,

---

* The reference is apparently to the room, made entirely of ivory, in the palace at Samaria where King Ahab lived with his "painted queen," Jezebel (ca. 875-50 B.C.). Several fine ivories have been found by the Harvard Library Expedition in the ruins of a palace tentatively identified with Ahab's.[103]

† The book that bears his name is a collection of "prophecies" (i.e., sermons) by two or more authors ranging in time from 710 to 300 B.C.[107] Chapters i-xxxix are usually ascribed to the "First Isaiah," who is here discussed.

and then leave the issue to Yahveh, who would use Assyria as his agent for a time, but in the end would destroy her, too. Indeed, all the nations known to Isaiah were, according to him, destined to be struck down by Yahveh; in a few chapters (xvi-xxiii) Moab, Syria, Ethiopia, Egypt, Babylon and Tyre are dedicated to destruction; "every one shall howl."[109] This ardor for ruination, this litany of curses, mars Isaiah's book, as it mars all the prophetic literature of the Bible.

Nevertheless his denunciation falls where it belongs—upon economic exploitation and greed. Here his eloquence rises to the highest point reached in the Old Testament, in passages that are among the peaks of the world's prose:

> The Lord will enter into judgment with the ancients of his people and the princes thereof; for ye have eaten up the vineyard; the spoil of the poor is in your houses. What mean ye that ye beat my people to pieces, and grind the faces of the poor? . . . Woe unto them that join house to house, that lay field to field, till there be no place, that they may be placed alone in the midst of the earth! . . . Woe unto them that decree unrighteous decrees to turn aside the needy from judgment (justice), and to take away the right from the poor of my people, that widows may be their prey, and that they may rob the fatherless. And what will ye do in the day of visitation, and in the desolation which shall come from afar? to whom will ye flee for help, and where will ye leave your glory?[110]

He is filled with scorn of those who, while fleecing the poor, present a pious face to the world.

> To what purpose is the multitude of your sacrifices unto me? saith the Lord. I am full of the burnt offerings of rams, and the fat of fed beasts. . . . Your appointed feasts my soul hateth; they are a trouble unto me; I am weary to hear them. And when ye spread forth your hands I will hide mine eyes from you; yea, when ye make many prayers I will not hear; your hands are full of blood. Wash ye, make ye clean, put away the evil of your doings from before mine eyes, cease to do evil; learn to do well; seek judgment (justice), relieve the oppressed, judge the fatherless, plead for the widow.[111]

He is bitter, but he does not despair of his people; just as Amos had ended his prophecies with a prediction, strangely apt today, of the restoration of the Jews to their native land,[112] so Isaiah concludes by formulating the Messianic hope—the trust of the Jews in some Redeemer who will end their political divisions, their subjection, and their misery, and bring an era of universal brotherhood and peace:

> Behold, a virgin shall conceive, and bear a son, and shall call his name Immanuel. . . . For unto us a child is born: and the government shall be upon his shoulder: and his name shall be called Wonderful, Counsellor, The mighty God, The everlasting Father, the Prince of Peace. . . . And there shall come forth a rod out of the stem of Jesse. . . . And the spirit of the Lord shall rest upon him, the spirit of wisdom and understanding, the spirit of counsel and might, the spirit of knowledge and of the fear of the Lord. . . . With righteousness shall he judge the poor, and reprove with equity for the meek of the earth; and he shall smite the earth with the rod of his mouth, and with the breath of his lips shall he slay the wicked. And righteousness shall be the girdle of his loins, and faithfulness the girdle of his reins. The wolf also shall dwell with the lamb, and the leopard shall lie down with the kid, and the calf and the young lion and the fatling together; and a little child shall lead them. . . . And they shall beat their swords into ploughshares, and their spears into pruning-hooks: nation shall not lift up sword against nation, neither shall they learn war any more.[113]

It was an admirable aspiration, but not for many generations yet would it express the mood of the Jews. The priests of the Temple listened with a well-controlled sympathy to these useful encouragements to piety; certain sects looked back to the Prophets for part of their inspiration; and perhaps these excoriations of all sensual delight had some share in intensifying the desert-born Puritanism of the Jews. But for the most part the old life of the palace and the tent, the market-place and the field, went on as before; war took its choice of every generation, and slavery continued to be the lot of the alien; the merchant cheated with his scales,[114] and tried to atone with sacrifice and prayer.

It was upon the Judaism of post-Exilic days, and upon the world through Judaism and Christianity, that the Prophets left their deepest mark. In Amos and Isaiah is the beginning of both Christianity and socialism, the spring from which has flowed a stream of Utopias wherein no poverty or war shall disturb human brotherhood and peace; they are the source of the early Jewish conception of a Messiah who would seize the government, reëstablish the temporal power of the Jews, and inaugurate a dictatorship of the dispossessed among mankind. Isaiah and-Amos began, in a military age, the exaltation of those virtues of simplicity and gentleness, of coöperation and friendliness, which Jesus was to make a vital element in his creed. They were the first to undertake the heavy task of reforming the God of Hosts into a God of Love; they conscripted Yahveh for humanitarianism as the radicals of the nineteenth century conscripted Christ for socialism. It was they who, when the Bible was printed in Europe, fired the Germanic mind with a rejuvenated Christianity, and lighted the torch of the Reformation; it was their fierce and intolerant virtue that formed the Puritans. Their moral philosophy was based upon a theory that would bear better documentation—that the righteous man will prosper, and the wicked will be struck down; but even if that should be a delusion it is the failing of a noble mind. The prophets had no conception of freedom, but they loved justice, and called for an end to the tribal limitations of morality. They offered to the unfortunate of the earth a vision of brotherhood that became the precious and unforgotten heritage of many generations.

V. THE DEATH AND RESURRECTION OF JERUSALEM

The birth of the Bible—The destruction of Jerusalem—The Babylonian Captivity—Jeremiah—Ezekiel—The Second Isaiah—The liberation of the Jews—The Second Temple

Their greatest contemporary influence was on the writing of the Bible. As the people fell away from the worship of Yahveh to the adoration of alien gods, the priests began to wonder whether the time had not come to make a final stand against the disintegration of the national faith. Taking a leaf from the Prophets, who attributed to Yahveh the passionate convictions of their own souls, they resolved to issue to the people a communication from God himself, a code of laws that would reinvigorate the moral life of the nation, and would at the same time attract the support of the Prophets by embodying the less extreme of their ideas. They readily won King Josiah to their plan; and about the eighteenth year of his reign the priest Hilkiah announced to the King that he had "found" in the secret archives of the Temple an astonishing scroll in which the great Moses himself, at the direct dictation of Yahveh, had settled once for all those problems of history and conduct that were being so hotly debated by prophets and priests. The discovery made a great stir. Josiah called the elders of Judah to the Temple, and there read to them the "Book of the Covenant" in the presence (we are told) of thousands of people. Then he solemnly swore that he would henceforth abide by the laws of this book; and "he caused all that were present to stand to it."[115]

We do not know just what this "Book of the Covenant" was; it may have been Exodus xx-xxiii, or it may have been Deuteronomy.[116] We need not suppose that it had been invented on the spur of the situation; it merely formulated, and put into writing, decrees, demands and exhortations which for centuries had emanated from the prophets and the Temple. In any event, those who heard the reading, and even those who only heard of it, were deeply impressed. Josiah took advantage of this mood to raid the altars of Yahveh's rivals in Judah; he cast "out of the temple of the Lord all the vessels that were made for Baal," he put down the idolatrous priests, and "them also that burned incense unto Baal, to the sun, and to the moon, and to the planets"; he "defiled Topheth, ... that no man might make his son or his daughter to pass through the fire to Molech"; and he smashed the altars that Solomon had built for Chemosh, Milcom and Astarte.[117]

These reforms did not seem to propitiate Yahveh, or bring him to the aid of his people. Nineveh fell as the Prophets had foretold, but only to leave little Judah subject first to Egypt and then to Babylon. When Pharaoh Necho, bound for Syria, tried to pass through Palestine, Josiah, relying upon Yahveh, resisted him on the ancient battle-site of Megiddo—only to be defeated and slain. A few years later Nebuchadrezzar overwhelmed Necho at Carchemish, and made Judah a Babylonian dependency. Josiah's successors sought by secret diplomacy to liberate themselves from the clutch of Babylon, and thought to bring Egypt to their rescue; but the fiery Nebuchadrezzar, getting wind of it, poured his soldiery into Palestine, captured Jerusalem, took King Jehoiakim prisoner, put Zedekiah on the throne of Judah, and carried 10,000 Jews into bondage. But Zedekiah, too, loved liberty, or power, and rebelled against Babylon. Thereupon Nebuchadrezzar returned, and—resolving to settle the Jewish problem once and for all, as he thought—recaptured Jerusalem, burned it to the ground, destroyed the Temple of Solomon, slew Zedekiah's sons before his face, gouged out his eyes, and carried practically all the population of the city into captivity in Babylonia.[118] Later a Jewish poet sang one of the world's great songs about that unhappy caravan:

> By the rivers of Babylon, there we sat down, yea, we wept, when we remembered Zion.
> We hanged our harps upon the willows in the midst thereof.
> For there they that carried us away captive required of us a song; and they that wasted us required of us mirth, saying, Sing us one of the songs of Zion.
> How shall we sing the Lord's song in a strange land?
> If I forget thee, O Jerusalem, let my right hand forget her cunning.
> If I do not remember thee, let my tongue cleave to the roof of my mouth; if I prefer not Jerusalem above my chief joy.[119]

In all this crisis the bitterest and most eloquent of the Prophets defended Babylon as a scourge in the hands of God, denounced the rulers of Judah as obstinate fools, and advised such complete surrender to Nebuchadrezzar that the modern reader is tempted to wonder could Jeremiah have been a paid agent of Babylonia. "I have made the earth, the man and the beast that are upon the ground," says Jeremiah's God, . . . "and now have I given all those lands into the hand of Nebuchadrezzar, the King of Babylon, my servant. . . . And all nations shall serve him. And it shall come to pass, that the nation and kingdom which will not serve the same Nebuchadrezzar, the King of Babylon, and that will not put their neck under the yoke of the King of Babylon, that nation will I punish, saith the Lord, with the sword, and with the famine, and with the pestilence, until I have consumed them by his hand."[120]

He may have been a traitor, but the book of his prophecies, supposedly taken down by his disciple Baruch, is not only one of the most passionately eloquent writings in all literature, as rich in vivid imagery as in merciless abuse, but it is marked with a sincerity that begins as a diffident self-questioning, and ends with honest doubts about his own course and all human life. "Woe is me, my mother, that thou hast borne me, a man of strife, and a man of contention to the whole earth! I have neither lent on usury, nor men have lent to me on usury; yet every one of them doth curse me. . . . Cursed be the day wherein I was born."[121] A flame of indignation burned in him at the sight of moral depravity and political folly in his people and its leaders; he felt inwardly compelled to stand in the

gate and call Israel to repentance. All this national decay, all this weakening of the state, this obviously imminent subjection of Judah to Babylon,
were, it seemed to Jeremiah, Yahveh's hand laid upon the Jews in punishment for their sins. "Run ye to and fro through the streets of Jerusalem,
and see now, and know, and seek in the broad places thereof, if ye can
find a man, if there be any that executeth judgment, that seeketh the
truth; and I will pardon it."[122] Everywhere iniquity ruled, and sex ran
riot; men "were as fed horses in the morning; every one neighed after
his neighbor's wife."[123] When the Babylonians besieged Jerusalem the
rich men of the city, to propitiate Yahveh, released their Hebrew slaves;
but when for a time the siege was raised, and the danger seemed past,
the rich apprehended their former slaves, and forced them into their old
bondage: it was a summary of human history that Jeremiah could not
bear silently.[124] Like the other Prophets, he denounced those hypocrites
who with pious faces brought to the Temple some part of the gains they
had made from grinding the faces of the poor; the Lord, he reminded
them, in the eternal lesson of all finer religion, asked not for sacrifice but
for justice.[125] The priests and the prophets, he thinks, are almost as false
and corrupt as the merchants; they, too, like the people, need to be
morally reborn, to be (in Jeremiah's strange phrase) circumcised in the
spirit as well as in the flesh. "Circumcise yourselves to the Lord, and take
away the foreskins of your heart."[126]

Against these abuses the Prophet preached with a fury rivaled only
by the stern saints of Geneva, Scotland and England. Jeremiah cursed
the Jews savagely, and took some delight in picturing the ruin of all who
would not heed him.[127] Time and again he predicted the destruction
of Jerusalem and the captivity in Babylon, and wept over the doomed
city (whom he called the daughter of Zion) in terms anticipatory of
Christ: "Oh, that my head were waters, and mine eyes a fountain of
tears, that I might weep day and night for the slain of the daughter of
my people!"[128]

To the "princes" of Zedekiah's court all this seemed sheer treason;
it was dividing the Jews in counsel and spirit in the very hour of war.
Jeremiah tantalized them by carrying a wooden yoke around his neck, explaining that all Judah must submit—the more peaceably the better—to
the yoke of Babylon; and when Hananiah tore this yoke away Jeremiah
cried out that Yahveh would make yokes of iron for all the Jews. The
priests tried to stop him by putting his head into the stocks; but from

even that position he continued to denounce them. They arraigned him in the Temple, and wished to kill him, but through some friend among the priests he escaped. Then the princes arrested him, and lowered him by ropes into a dungeon filled with mire; but Zedekiah had him raised to milder imprisonment in the palace court. There the Babylonians found him when Jerusalem fell. On Nebuchadrezzar's orders they treated him well, and exempted him from the general exile. In his old age, says orthodox tradition,[128a] he wrote his "Lamentations," the most eloquent of all the books of the Old Testament. He mourned now the completeness of his triumph and the desolation of Jerusalem, and raised to heaven the unanswerable questions of Job:

> How doth the city sit solitary that was full of people! how she is become as a widow! she that was great among the nations, and princess among the provinces, how is she become tributary! . . . Is it nothing to you, all ye that pass by? Behold, and see if there be any sorrow like unto my sorrow. . . . Righteous art thou, O Lord, when I plead with thee: yet let us talk with thee of thy judgments: Wherefore doth the way of the wicked prosper? Wherefore are all they happy that deal very treacherously?[129]

Meanwhile, in Babylon, another preacher was taking up the burden of prophecy. Ezekiel belonged to a priestly family that had been driven to Babylon in the first deportation from Jerusalem. He began his preaching, like the First Isaiah and Jeremiah, with fierce denunciations of idolatry and corruption in Jerusalem. At great length he compared Jerusalem to a harlot, because she sold the favors of her worship to strange gods;[130] he described Samaria and Jerusalem as twin whores; this word was as popular with him as with the dramatists of the Stuart Restoration. He made long lists of the sins of Jerusalem, and then condemned her to capture and destruction. Like Isaiah, he doomed the nations impartially, and announced the sins and fall of Moab, Tyre, Egypt, Assyria, even of the mysterious kingdom of Magog.[131] But he was not as bitter as Jeremiah; in the end he relented, declared that the Lord would save "a remnant" of the Jews, and foretold the resurrection of their city;[132] he described in vision the new Temple that would be built there, and outlined a Utopia in which the priests would be supreme, and in which Yahveh would dwell among his people forever.

He hoped, with this happy ending, to keep up the spirits of the exiles, and to retard their assimilation into the Babylonian culture and blood. Then as now it seemed that this process of absorption would destroy the unity, even the identity, of the Jews. They flourished on Mesopotamia's rich soil, they enjoyed considerable freedom of custom and worship, they grew rapidly in numbers and wealth, and prospered in the unwonted tranquillity and harmony which their subjection had brought to them. An ever-rising proportion of them accepted the gods of Babylon, and the epicurean ways of the old metropolis. When the second generation of exiles grew up, Jerusalem was almost forgotten.

It was the function of the unknown author who undertook to complete the Book of Isaiah to restate the religion of Israel for this backsliding generation; and it was his distinction, in restating it, to lift it to the loftiest plane that any religion had yet reached amid all the faiths of the Near East.* While Buddha in India was preaching the death of desire, and Confucius in China was formulating wisdom for his people, this "Second Isaiah," in majestic and luminous prose, announced to the exiled Jews the first clear revelation of monotheism, and offered them a new god, infinitely richer in "lovingkindness" and tender mercy than the bitter Yahveh even of the First Isaiah. In words that a later gospel was to choose as spurring on the young Christ, this greatest of Prophets announced his mission—no longer to curse the people for their sins, but to bring them hope in their bondage. "The Spirit of the Lord God is upon me; because the Lord hath anointed me to preach good tidings únto the meek; he hath sent me to bind up the broken-hearted, to proclaim liberty to the captives, and the opening of the prison to them that are bound."[133] For he has discovered that Yahveh is not a god of war and vengeance, but a loving father; the discovery fills him with happiness, and inspires him to magnificent songs. He predicts the coming of the new god to rescue his people:

> The voice of him that crieth in the wilderness, Prepare ye the way of the Lord, make straight in the desert a highway for our God. Every valley shall be exalted, and every mountain and hill

---

* We know nothing of the history of this writer, who, by a literary device and license common to his time, chose to speak in the name of Isaiah. We merely guess that he wrote shortly before or after Cyrus liberated the Jews. Biblical scholarship assigns to him chapters xl-lv, and to another and later unknown, or unknowns, chapters lvi-lxvi.[132a]

shall be made low; and the crooked shall be made straight, and the rough places plain.* . . . Behold, the Lord God will come with strong hand, and his arm shall rule for him. . . . He shall feed his flock like a shepherd; he shall gather the lambs with his arm, and carry them in his bosom and shall gently lead those that are with young.

The prophet then lifts the Messianic hope to a place among the ruling ideas of his people, and describes the "Servant" who will redeem Israel by vicarious sacrifice:

He is despised and rejected of men; a man of sorrows, and acquainted with grief; . . . he was despised, and we esteemed him not. Surely he hath borne our griefs, and carried our sorrows; yet we did esteem him stricken, smitten of God, and afflicted. But he was wounded for our transgressions, he was bruised for our iniquities; the chastisement of our peace was upon him; and with his stripes we are healed. . . . The Lord hath laid on him the iniquity of us all.†[134]

Persia, the Second Isaiah predicts, will be the instrument of this liberation. Cyrus is invincible; he will take Babylon, and will free the Jews from their captivity. They will return to Jerusalem and build a new Temple, a new city, a very paradise: "the wolf and the lamb shall feed together, and the lion shall eat straw like a bullock; and dust shall be the serpent's meat. They shall not hurt or destroy in all my holy mountain, saith the Lord."[135] Perhaps it was the rise of Persia, and the spread of its power, subjecting all the states of the Near East in an imperial unity vaster and better governed than any social organization men had yet known, that suggested to the Prophet the conception of one universal deity. No longer does his god say, like the Yahveh of Moses, "I am the Lord thy God; . . . thou shalt not have strange gods before me"; now it is written: "I am the Lord, and there is none else, there is no god besides me."[136] The prophet-poet describes this universal deity in one of the great passages of the Bible:

Who hath measured the waters in the hollow of his hand, and meted out heaven with the span, and comprehended the dust of

---

* Referring, presumably, to the road from Babylon to Jerusalem.
† Modern research does not regard the "Servant" as the prophetic portrayal of Jesus.[134a]

the earth in a measure, and weighed the mountains in scales, and the hills in a balance? Behold, the nations are as a drop of a bucket, and are counted as the small dust of the balance; behold, he taketh up the isles as a very little thing. All nations before him are as nothing, and they are counted to him less than nothing, and vanity. To whom, then, will ye liken God, or what likeness will ye compare with him? It is he that sitteth upon the circle of the earth, and the inhabitants thereof are as grasshoppers; that stretcheth out the heavens as a curtain, and spreadeth them out as a tent to dwell in. Lift up your eyes on high, and behold who hath created these things.[137]

It was a dramatic hour in the history of Israel when at last Cyrus entered Babylon as a world-conqueror, and gave to the exiled Jews full freedom to return to Jerusalem. He disappointed some of the Prophets, and showed his superior civilization, by leaving Babylon and its population unhurt, and offering a sceptical obeisance to its gods. He restored to the Jews what remained in the Babylonian treasury of the gold and silver taken by Nebuchadrezzar from the Temple, and instructed the communities in which the exiles lived to furnish them with funds for their long journey home. The younger Jews were not enthusiastic at this liberation; many of them had sunk strong roots into Babylonian soil, and hesitated to abandon their fertile fields and their flourishing trade for the desolate ruins of the Holy City. It was not until two years after Cyrus' coming that the first detachment of zealots set out on the long three months' journey back to the land which their fathers had left half a century before.[138]

They found themselves, then as now, not entirely welcome in their ancient home. For meanwhile other Semites had settled there, and had made the soil their own by occupation and toil; and these tribes looked with hatred upon the apparent invaders of what seemed to them their native fields. The returning Jews could not possibly have established themselves had it not been for the strong and friendly empire that protected them. The prince Zerubbabel won permission from the Persian king, Darius I, to rebuild the Temple; and though the immigrants were small in number and resources, and the work was hindered at every step by the attacks and conspiracies of a hostile population, it was carried to completion within some twenty-two years after the return. Slowly Jerusalem became again a Jewish city, and the Temple resounded with the psalms of a rescued remnant resolved to make Judea strong again. It was a great triumph, surpassed only by that which we have seen in our own historic time.

VI. THE PEOPLE OF THE BOOK

The "Book of the Law"—The composition of the Pentateuch—
The myths of "Genesis"—The Mosaic Code—The Ten Com-
mandments — The idea of God — The sabbath — The
Jewish family—Estimate of the Mosaic legislation

To build a military state was impossible, Judea had neither the numbers nor the wealth for such an enterprise. Since some system of order was needed that, while recognizing the sovereignty of Persia, would give the Jews a natural discipline and a national unity, the clergy undertook to provide a theocratic rule based, like Josiah's, on priestly traditions and laws promulgated as divine commands. About the year 444 B.C. Ezra, a learned priest, called the Jews together in solemn assembly, and read to them, from morn to midday, the "Book of the Law of Moses." For seven days he and his fellow Levites read from these scrolls; at the end the priests and the leaders of the people pledged themselves to accept this body of legislation as their constitution and their conscience, and to obey it forever.[139] From those troubled times till ours that Law has been the central fact in the life of the Jews; and their loyalty to it through all wanderings and tribulations has been one of the impressive phenomena of history.

What was this "Book of the Law of Moses"? Not quite the same as that "Book of the Covenant" which Josiah had read; for the latter had admitted of being completely read twice in a day, while the other needed a week.[140] We can only guess that the larger scroll constituted a substantial part of those first five books of the Old Testament which the Jews call *Torah* or the Law, and which others call the Pentateuch.[141]* How, when, and where had these books been written? This is an innocent question which has caused the writing of fifty thousand volumes, and must here be left unanswered in a paragraph.

The consensus of scholarship is that the oldest elements in the Bible are those distinct and yet similar legends of *Genesis* which are called "J" and

---

* *Torah* is Hebrew for Direction, Guidance; *Pentateuch* is Greek for Five Rolls.

"E" respectively because one speaks of the Creator as Jehovah (Yahveh), while the other speaks of him as Elohim.* It is believed that the Yahvist narrative was written in Judah, the Elohist in Ephraim, and that the two stories fused into one after the fall of Samaria. A third element, known as "D," and embodying the Deuteronomic Code, is probably by a distinct author or group of authors. A fourth element, "P," is composed of sections later inserted by the priests; this "Priestly Code" is probably the substance of the "Book of the Law" promulgated by Ezra.[142a] The four compositions appear to have taken their present form about 300 B.C.[143]

These delightful tales of the Creation, the Temptation and the Flood were drawn from a storehouse of Mesopotamian legend as old as 3000 B.C.; we have seen some early forms of them in the course of this history. It is possible that the Jews appropriated some of these myths from Babylonian literature during the Captivity;[144] it is more likely that they had adopted them long before, from ancient Semitic and Sumerian sources common to all the Near East. The Persian and the Talmudic forms of the Creation myth represent God as first making a two-sexed being—a male and a female joined at the back like Siamese twins—and then dividing it as an afterthought. We are reminded of a strange sentence in Genesis (v, 2): "Male and female created he them, and blessed them, and called their name Adam": i.e., our first parent was originally both male and female—which seems to have escaped all theologians except Aristophanes.†

The legend of Paradise appears in almost all folklore—in Egypt, India, Tibet, Babylonia, Persia, Greece,‡ Polynesia, Mexico, etc.[145] Most of these Edens had forbidden trees, and were supplied with serpents or dragons that stole immortality from men, or otherwise poisoned Paradise.[147] Both the serpent and the fig were probably phallic symbols; behind the myth is the thought that sex and knowledge destroy innocence and happiness, and are the origin of evil; we shall find this same idea at the end of the Old Testament in *Ecclesiastes* as here at the beginning. In most of these stories

---

* A distinction first pointed out by Jean Astruc in 1753. Passages generally ascribed to the "Yahvist" account: Gen. ii, 4 to iii, 24, iv, vi-viii, xi, 1-9, xii-xiii, xviii-xix, xxiv, xxvii, 1-45, xxxii, xliii-xliv; Exod. iv-v, viii, 20 to ix, 7, x-xi, xxxiii, 12 to xxxiv, 26; Numb. x, 29-36, xi, etc. Distinctly "Elohist" passages: Gen. xi, 10-32, xx, 1-17, xxi, 8-32, xxii, 1-14, xl-xlii, xlv; Exod. xviii, 20-23, xx-xxii, xxxiii, 7-11; Numb. xii, xxii-xxiv, etc.[142]

† Cf. Plato's *Symposium*.

‡ Cf. the Greek poet Hesiod (ca. 750 B.C.), in *Works and Days:* "Men lived like gods, without vices or passions, vexations or toil. In happy companionship with divine beings they passed their days in tranquillity and joy. . . . The earth was more beautiful then than now, and spontaneously yielded an abundant variety of fruits. . . . Men were considered mere boys at one hundred years old."[146]

woman was the lovely-evil agent of the serpent or the devil, whether as Eve, or Pandora, or the Poo See of Chinese legend. "All things," says the *Shi-ching*, "were at first subject to man, but a woman threw us into slavery. Our misery came not from heaven but from woman; she lost the human race. Ah, unhappy Poo See! Thou kindled the fire that consumes us, and which is every day increasing. . . . The world is lost. Vice over-flows all things."

Even more universal was the story of the Flood; hardly an ancient people went without it, and hardly a mountain in Asia but had given perch to some water-wearied Noah or Shamash-napishtim.[148] Usually these legends were the popular vehicle or allegory of a philosophical judgment or a moral attitude summarizing long racial experience—that sex and knowledge bring more grief than joy, and that human life is periodically threatened by floods,—i.e., ruinous inundations of the great rivers whose waters made possible the earliest known civilizations. To ask whether these stories are true or false, whether they "really happened," would be to put a trivial and superficial question; their substance, of course, is not the tales they tell but the judgments they convey. Meanwhile it would be unwise not to enjoy their disarming sim-plicity, and the vivid swiftness of their narratives.

The books which Josiah and Ezra caused to be read to the people formulated that "Mosaic" Code on which all later Jewish life was to be built. Of this legislation the cautious Sarton writes: "Its importance in the history of institutions and of law cannot be overestimated."[149] It was the most thoroughgoing attempt in history to use religion as a basis of statesmanship, and as a regulator of every detail of life; the Law became, says Renan, "the tightest garment into which life was ever laced."[150] Diet,* medicine, personal, menstrual and natal hygiene, public sanitation, sexual inversion and bestiality[152]—all are made subjects of divine ordinance and guidance; again we observe how slowly the doctor was differentiated from the priest[153]—to become in time his greatest enemy. Leviticus (xiii-xv) legislates carefully for the treatment of venereal disease, even to the most definite directions for segregation, disinfection, fumigation and, if necessary, the complete burning of the house in which the disease has run

---

*Cf. Deut. xiv. Reinach, Roberston Smith and Sir James Frazer have attributed the avoidance of pork not to hygienic knowledge and precaution but to the totemic worship of the pig (or wild boar) by the ancestors of the Jews.[151] The "worship" of the wild boar, however, may have been merely a priestly means of making it tabu in the sense of "unclean." The great number of wise hygienic rules in the Mosaic Code warrant a humble scepticism of Reinach's interpretation.

its course.[154]* "The ancient Hebrews were the founders of prophylaxis,"[156] but they seem to have had no surgery beyond circumcision. This rite—common among ancient Egyptians and modern Semites—was not only a sacrifice to God and a compulsion to racial loyalty,† it was a hygienic precaution against sexual uncleanliness.[158] Perhaps it was this Code of Cleanliness that helped to preserve the Jews through their long Odyssey of dispersion and suffering.

For the rest the Code centered about those Ten Commandments (Exodus, xx, 1-17) which were destined to receive the lip-service of half the world.‡ The first laid the foundation of the new theocratic community, which was to rest not upon any civil law, but upon the idea of God; he was the Invisible King who dictated every law and meted out every penalty; and his people were to be called *Israel*, as meaning the Defenders of God. The Hebrew state was dead, but the Temple remained; the priests of Judea, like the Popes of Rome, would try to restore what the kings had failed to save. Hence the explicitness and reiteration of the First Commandment: heresy or blasphemy must be punished with death, even if the heretic should be one's closest kin.[161] The priestly authors of the Code, like the pious Inquisitors, believed that religious unity was an indispensable condition of social organization and solidarity. It was this intolerance, and their racial pride, that embroiled and preserved the Jews.

The Second Commandment elevated the national conception of God at the expense of art: no graven images were ever to be made of him. It assumed a high intellectual level among the Jews, for it rejected superstition

---

* The procedure recommended by Leviticus (xiii-xiv) in cases of leprosy was practised in Europe to the end of the Middle Ages.[155]

† By making race ultimately unconcealable. "The Jewish rite," says Briffault, "did not assume its present form until so late a period as that of the Maccabees (167 B.C.). At that date it was still performed in such a manner that the jibes of Gentile women could be evaded, little trace of the operation being perceptible. The nationalistic priesthood therefore enacted that the prepuce should be completely removed."[157]

‡ It was the usual thing for ancient law-codes to be of divine origin. We have seen how the laws of Egypt were given it by the god Thoth, and how the sun-god Shamash begot Hammurabi's code. In like manner a deity gave to King Minos on Mt. Dicta the laws that were to govern Crete; the Greeks represented Dionysus, whom they also called "The Lawgiver," with two tables of stone on which laws were inscribed; and the pious Persians tell how, one day, as Zoroaster prayed on a high mountain, Ahura-Mazda appeared to him amid thunder and lightning, and delivered to him "The Book of the Law."[159] "They did all this," says Diodorus, "because they believed that a conception which would help humanity was marvelous and wholly divine; or because they held that the common crowd would be more likely to obey the laws if their gaze were directed towards the majesty and power of those to whom their laws were ascribed."[160]

and anthropomorphism, and—despite the all-too-human quality of the Penta-teuch Yahveh—tried to conceive of God as beyond every form and image. It conscripted Hebrew devotion for religion, and left nothing, in ancient days, for science and art; even astronomy was neglected, lest corrupt diviners should multiply, or the stars be worshiped as divinities. In Solomon's Temple there had been an almost heathen abundance of imagery;[163] in the new Temple there was none. The old images had been carried off to Babylon, and ap-parently had not been returned along with utensils of silver and gold.[164] Hence we find no sculpture, painting or bas-relief after the Captivity, and very little before it except under the almost alien Solomon; architecture and music were the only arts that the priests would allow. Song and Temple ritual redeemed the life of the people from gloom; an orchestra of several instruments joined "as one to make one sound" with a great choir of voices to sing the psalms that glorified the Temple and its God.[165] "David and all the house of Israel played before the Lord on harps, psalteries, timbrels, cornets and cymbals."[166]

The Third Commandment typified the intense piety of the Jew. Not only would he not "take the name of the Lord God in vain"; he would never pro-nounce it; even when he came upon the name of Yahveh in his prayers he would substitute for it *Adonai*—Lord.* Only the Hindus would rival this piety.

The Fourth Commandment sanctified the weekly day of rest as a Sabbath, and passed it down as one of the strongest institutions of mankind. The name, —and perhaps the custom—came from Babylon; *shabattu* was applied by the Babylonians to "tabu" days of abstinence and propitiation.[168] Besides this week-ly holyday there were great festivals—once Canaanite vegetation rites remi-niscent of sowing and harvesting, and the cycles of moon and sun: *Mazzoth* originally celebrated the beginning of the barley harvest; *Shabuoth*, later called *Pentecost*, celebrated the end of the wheat harvest; *Sukkoth* com-memorated the vintage; *Pesach*, or Passover, was the feast of the first fruits of the flock; *Rosh-ha-shanah* announced the New Year; only later were these festivals adapted to commemorate vital events in the history of the Jews.[168a] On the first day of the Passover a lamb or kid was sacrificed and eaten, and its blood was sprinkled upon the doors as the portion of the god; later the priests attached this custom to the story of Yahveh's slaughter of the first-born of the Egyptians. The lamb was once a totem of a Canaanite clan; the

---

* In Hebrew *Yahveh* is written as *Jhvh;* this was erroneously translated into *Jehovah* because the vowels *a-o-a* had been placed over *Jhvh* in the original, to indicate that *Adonai* was to be pronounced in place of *Yahveh;* and the theologians of the Renaissance and the Reformation wrongly supposed that these vowels were to be placed between the consonants of *Jhvh.*[167]

Passover, among the Canaanites, was the oblation of a lamb to the local god.* As we read (Exod., xi) the story of the establishment of the Passover rite, and see the Jews celebrating that same rite steadfastly today, we feel again the venerable antiquity of their worship, and the strength and tenacity of their race.

The Fifth Commandment sanctified the family, as second only to the Temple in the structure of Jewish society; the ideals then stamped upon the institution marked it throughout medieval and modern European history until our own disintegrative Industrial Revolution. The Hebrew patriarchal family was a vast economic and political organization, composed of the oldest married male, his wives, his unmarried children, his married sons with their wives and children, and perhaps some slaves. The economic basis of the institution was its convenience for cultivating the soil; its political value lay in its providing a system of social order so strong that it made the state—except in war—almost superfluous. The father's authority was practically unlimited; the land was his, and his children could survive only by obedience to him; he was the state. If he was poor he could sell his daughter, before her puberty, as a bondservant; and though occasionally he condescended to ask her consent, he had full right to dispose of her in marriage as he wished.[169] Boys were supposed to be products of the right testicle, girls of the left—which was believed to be smaller and weaker than the right.[170] At first marriage was matrilocal; the man had to "leave his father and mother and cleave to his wife" in her clan; but this custom gradually died out after the establishment of the monarchy. Yahveh's instructions to the wife were: "Thy desire shall be to thy husband, and he shall rule over thee." Though technically subject, the woman was often a person of high authority and dignity; the history of the Jews shines with such names as Sarah, Rachel, Miriam and Esther; Deborah was one of the judges of Israel,[172] and it was the prophetess Huldah whom Josiah consulted about the Book which the priests had found in the Temple.[173] The mother of many children was certain of security and honor. For the little nation longed to increase and multiply, feeling, as in Palestine today, its dangerous numerical inferiority to the peoples surrounding it; therefore it exalted motherhood, branded celibacy as a sin and a crime, made marriage compulsory after twenty, even in

---

* Later this gentle and ancient totem became the Paschal Lamb of Christianity, identified with the dead Christ.

priests, abhorred marriageable virgins and childless women, and looked upon abortion, infanticide and other means of limiting population as heathen abominations that stank in the nostrils of the Lord.[174] "And when Rachel saw that she bare Jacob no children, Rachel envied her sister; and said unto Jacob, Give me children, or else I die."[175] The perfect wife was one who labored constantly in and about her home, and had no thought except in her husband and her children. The last chapter of Proverbs states the male ideal of woman completely:

> Who can find a virtuous woman? For her price is far above rubies. The heart of her husband doth safely trust in her, so that he shall have no need of spoil. She will do him good and not evil all the days of her life. She seeketh wool, and flax, and worketh willingly with her hands. She is like the merchants' ships; she bringeth her food from afar. She riseth also while it is yet night, and giveth meat to her household, and a portion to her maidens. She considereth a field, and buyeth it; with the fruit of her hands she planteth a vineyard. She girdeth her loins with strength, and strengtheneth her arms. She perceiveth that her merchandise is good; her candle goeth not out by night. She layeth her hands to the spindle, and her hands hold the distaff. She stretcheth out her hand to the poor; yea, she reacheth forth her hands to the needy. . . . She maketh herself coverings of tapestry; her clothing is silk and purple. Her husband is known in the gates, when he sitteth among the elders of the land. She maketh fine linen, and selleth it; and delivereth girdles unto the merchant. Strength and honor are her clothing; and she shall rejoice in time to come. She openeth her mouth with wisdom, and in her tongue is the law of kindness. She looketh well to the ways of her household, and eateth not the bread of idleness. Her children arise up and call her blessed; her husband also, and he praiseth her. . . . Give her of the fruit of her hands; and let her own works praise her in the gates.*

The Sixth Commandment was a counsel of perfection; nowhere is there so much killing as in the Old Testament; its chapters oscillate be-

---

* This, of course, was the man's ideal; if we may believe Isaiah (iii, 16-23), the real women of Jerusalem were very much of this world, loving fine raiment and ornament, and leading the men a merry chase. "The daughters of Zion are haughty, and walk with stretched forth necks and wanton eyes, . . . mincing as they go, and making a tinkling with their feet," etc. Perhaps the historians have always deceived us about women?

tween slaughter and compensatory reproduction. Tribal quarrels, internal factions and hereditary vendettas broke the monotony of intermittent peace.[176] Despite a magnificent verse about ploughshares and pruning-hooks, the Prophets were not pacifists, and the priests—if we may judge from the speeches which they put into the mouth of Yahveh—were almost as fond of war as of preaching. Among nineteen kings of Israel eight were assassinated.[177] Captured cities were usually destroyed, the males put to the sword, and the soil deliberately ruined—in the fashion of the times.[178] Perhaps the figures exaggerate the killing; it is unbelievable that, entirely without modern inventions, "the children of Israel slew of the Syrians one hundred thousand footmen in one day."[179] Belief in themselves as the chosen people[180] intensified the pride natural in a nation conscious of superior abilities; it accentuated their disposition to segregate themselves maritally and mentally from other peoples, and deprived them of the international perspective that their descendants were to attain. But they had in high degree the virtues of their qualities. Their violence came of unmanageable vitality, their separatism came of their piety, their quarrelsomeness and querulousness came of a passionate sensitivity that produced the greatest literature of the Near East; their racial pride was the indispensable prop of their courage through centuries of suffering. Men are what they have had to be.

The Seventh Commandment recognized marriage as the basis of the family, as the Fifth had recognized the family as the basis of society; and it offered to marriage all the support of religion. It said nothing about sex relations before marriage, but other regulations laid upon the bride the obligation, under pain of death by stoning, to prove her virginity on the day of her marriage.[181] Nevertheless prostitution was common and pederasty apparently survived the destruction of Sodom and Gomorrah.[182] As the Law did not seem to prohibit relations with foreign harlots, Syrian, Moabite, Midianite and other "strange women" flourished along the highways, where they lived in booths and tents, and combined the trades of peddler and prostitute. Solomon, who had no violent prejudices in these matters, relaxed the laws that had kept such women out of Jerusalem; in time they multiplied so rapidly there that in the days of the Maccabees the Temple itself was described by an indignant reformer as full of fornication and harlotry.[183]

Love affairs probably occurred, for there was much tenderness between the sexes; "Jacob served seven years for Rachel, and they seemed unto him but a few days for the love he had to her."[184] But love played a very small rôle in the choice of mates. Before the Exile marriage was completely secular, arranged by the parents, or by the suitor with the parents of the bride. Vestiges of capture-marriage are found in the Old Testament; Yahveh approves of it in war;[185] and the elders, on the occasion of a shortage of women, "commanded the children of Benjamin, saying, Go and lie in wait in the vineyards; and see and behold if the daughters of Shiloh come out to dance in dances; then come ye out of the vineyards, and catch you every man his wife of the daughters of Shiloh, and go to the land of Benjamin."[186] But this was exceptional; usually the marriage was by purchase; Jacob purchased Leah and Rachel by his toil, the gentle Ruth was quite simply bought by Boaz, and the prophet Hosea regretted exceedingly that he had given fifty shekels for his wife.[187] The word for wife, *beulah*, meant owned.[187a] The father of the bride reciprocated by giving his daughter a dowry—an institution admirably adapted to diminish the socially disruptive gap between the sexual and the economic maturity of children in an urban civilization.

If the man was well-to-do, he might practise polygamy; if the wife was barren, like Sarah, she might encourage her husband to take a concubine. The purpose of these arrangements was prolific reproduction; it was taken as a matter of course that after Rachel and Leah had given Jacob all the children they were capable of bearing, they should offer him their maids, who would also bear him children.[188] A woman was not allowed to remain idle in this matter of reproduction; if a husband died, his brother, however many wives he might already have, was obliged to marry her; or, if the husband had no brother, the obligation fell upon his nearest surviving male kin.[189] Since private property was the core of Jewish economy, the double standard prevailed: the man might have many wives, but the woman was confined to one man. Adultery meant relations with a woman who had been bought and paid for by another man; it was a violation of the law of property, and was punished with death for both parties.[190] Fornication was forbidden to women, but was looked upon as a venial offense in men.[191] Divorce was free to the man, but extremely difficult for the woman, until Talmudic days.[193] The husband does not seem to have abused his privileges unduly; he is pictured to us, all in all, as zealously devoted to his wife and his children. And though love did not determine marriage, it often flowered out of it. "Isaac took Rebecca, and she became his wife; and he loved her; and Isaac was comforted after his mother's death."[194] Probably in no other people outside of the Far East has family life reached so high a level as among the Jews.

The Eighth Commandment sanctified private property,* and bound it up with religion and the family as one of the three bases of Hebrew society. Property was almost entirely in land; until the days of Solomon there was little industry beyond that of the potter and the smith. Even agriculture was not completely developed; the bulk of the population devoted itself to rearing sheep and cattle, and tending the vine, the olive and the fig. They lived in tents rather than houses, in order to move more easily to fresh pastures. In time their growing economic surplus generated trade, and the Jewish merchants, by their tenacity and their skill, began to flourish in Damascus, Tyre and Sidon, and in the precincts of the Temple itself. There was no coinage till near the time of the Captivity, but gold and silver, weighed in each transaction, became a medium of exchange, and bankers appeared in great numbers to finance commerce and enterprise. It was nothing strange that these "money-lenders" should use the courts of the Temple; it was a custom general in the Near East, and survives there in many places to this day.[196] Yahveh beamed upon the growing power of the Hebrew financiers; "thou shalt lend unto many nations," he said, "but thou shalt not borrow"[197]—a generous philosophy that has made great fortunes, though it has not seemed, in our century, to be divinely inspired.

As in the other countries of the Near East, war captives and convicts were used as slaves, and hundreds of thousands of them toiled in cutting timber and transporting materials for such public works as Solomon's Temple and palace. But the owner had no power of life and death over his slaves, and the slave might acquire property and buy his liberty.[198] Men could be sold as bondservants for unpaid debts, or could sell their children in their place; and this continued to the days of Christ.[199] These typical institutions of the Near East were mitigated in Judea by generous charity, and a vigorous campaign, by priest and prophet, against exploitation. The Code laid it down hopefully that "ye shall not oppress one another";[200] it asked that Hebrew bondservants should be released, and debts among Jews canceled, every seventh year;[201] and when this was found too idealistic for the masters, the Law proclaimed the institution of the Jubilee, by which, every fifty years, all slaves and debtors should be freed. "And ye shall hallow the fiftieth year, and proclaim liberty

---

* Theoretically the land belonged to Yahveh.[195]

throughout all the land unto all the inhabitants thereof: it shall be a Jubilee unto you; and ye shall return every man unto his possession, and ye shall return every man unto his family."[202]

We have no evidence that this fine edict was obeyed, but we must give credit to the priests for leaving no lesson in charity untaught. "If there be among you a poor man of one of thy brethren, . . . thou shalt open thine hand wide unto him, and shalt surely lend him sufficient for his need"; and "take thou no usury" (i.e., interest) "of him."[203] The Sabbath rest was to be extended to every employee, even to animals; stray sheaves and fruits were to be left in the fields and orchards for the poor to glean.[204] And though these charities were largely for fellow Jews, "the stranger in the gates" was also to be treated with kindness; the sojourner was to be sheltered and fed, and dealt with honorably. At all times the Jews were bidden to remember that they, too, had once been homeless, even bondservants, in a foreign land.

The Ninth Commandment, by demanding absolute honesty of witnesses, put the prop of religion under the whole structure of Jewish law. An oath was to be a religious ceremony: not merely was a man, in swearing, to place his hand on the genitals of him to whom he swore, as in the old custom;[205] he was now to be taking God himself as his witness and his judge. False witnesses, according to the Code, were to receive the same punishment that their testimony had sought to bring upon their victims.[206] Religious law was the sole law of Israel; the priests and the temples were the judges and the courts; and those who refused to accept the decision of the priests were to be put to death.[207] Ordeal by the drinking of poisonous water was prescribed in certain cases of doubtful guilt.[208] There was no other than religious machinery for enforcing the law; it had to be left to personal conscience, and public opinion. Minor crimes might be atoned for by confession and compensation.[209] Capital punishment was decreed, by Yahveh's instructions, for murder, kidnaping, idolatry, adultery, striking or cursing a parent, stealing a slave, or "lying with a beast," but not for the killing of a servant;[210] and "thou shalt not suffer a witch to live."[211] Yahveh was quite satisfied to have the individual take the law into his own hands in case of murder: "The revenger of blood, himself shall slay the murderer; when he meeteth him, he shall slay him."[212] Certain cities, however, were to be set apart, to which a criminal might flee, and in which the avenger must stay his revenge.[213] In general the principle of punishment was the *lex talionis:* "life for life, eye for eye, tooth for tooth, hand for hand, foot for foot, burning for burning, stripe for stripe"[214]—we trust that this was a counsel of perfection, never quite realized. The Mosaic Code, though *written down* at least fifteen hundred years later, shows no advance, in criminal legislation, upon the Code of Hammurabi; in legal organization it shows an archaic retrogression to primitive ecclesiastical control.

The Tenth Commandment reveals how clearly woman was conceived under the rubric of property. "Thou shalt not covet thy neighbor's house, thou shalt not covet thy neighbor's wife, nor his manservant, nor his maid-servant, nor his ox, nor his ass, nor anything that is thy neighbor's."[215] Never-theless, it was an admirable precept; could men follow it, half the fever and anxiety of our life would be removed. Strange to say, the greatest of the commandments is not listed among the Ten, though it is part of the "Law." It occurs in Leviticus, xix, 18, lost amid "a repetition of sundry laws," and reads very simply: "Thou shalt love thy neighbor as thyself."

In general it was a lofty code, sharing its defects with its age, and rising to virtues characteristically its own. We must remember that it was only a law—indeed, only a "priestly Utopia"[216]—rather than a descrip-tion of Jewish life; like other codes, it was honored plentifully in the breach, and won new praise with every violation. But its influence upon the conduct of the people was at least as great as that of most legal or moral codes. It gave to the Jews, through the two thousand years of wandering which they were soon to begin, a "portable Fatherland," as Heine was to call it, an intangible and spirtual state; it kept them united despite every dispersion, proud despite every defeat, and brought them across the centuries to our own time, a strong and apparently indestructi-ble people.

VII. THE LITERATURE AND PHILOSOPHY OF THE BIBLE

History—Fiction—Poetry—The Psalms—The Song of Songs—
Proverbs—Job—The idea of immortality—The pessimism of
Ecclesiastes—The advent of Alexander

The Old Testament is not only law; it is history, poetry and philos-ophy of the highest order. After making every deduction for primitive legend and pious fraud, after admitting that the historical books are not quite as accurate or as ancient as our forefathers supposed, we find in them, nevertheless, not merely some of the oldest historical writing known to us, but some of the best. The books of Judges, Samuel and Kings may, as some scholars believe,[217] have been put together hastily during or shortly after the Exile to collect and preserve the national traditions of a scattered and broken people; nevertheless the stories of Saul, David and Solomon are immeasurably finer in structure and style than the other his-torical writing of the ancient Near East. Even Genesis, if we read it with some understanding of the function of legend, is (barring its genealogies) an admirable story, told without frill or ornament, with simplicity, vividness and force. And in a sense we have here not mere history, but philosophy of history; this is the first recorded effort of man to reduce the multiplicity of past events to a measure of unity by seeking in them some pervading purpose and significance, some law of sequence and causation, some illumination for the present and the future. The conception of history promulgated by the Prophets and the priestly authors of the Pentateuch survived a thousand years of Greece and Rome to become the world-view of European thinkers from Boëthius to Bossuet.

Midway between the history and the poetry are the fascinating romances of the Bible. There is nothing more perfect in the realm of prose than the story of Ruth; only less excellent are the tales of Isaac and Rebecca, Jacob and Rachel, Joseph and Benjamin, Samson and Delilah, Esther, Judith and Daniel. The poetical literature begins with the "Song of Moses" (Exod. xv) and the "Song of Deborah" (Judges v), and reaches finally to the heights of the Psalms. The "penitential" hymns of the Babylonians had prepared for these, and perhaps had given them material as well as form; Ikhnaton's ode to the sun seems to have contributed to Psalm CIV; and the majority of the Psalms, instead of being the impressively united work of David, are probably the compositions of several poets writing long after the Captivity, probably in the third century before Christ.[218] But all this is as irrelevant as the name or sources of Shakespeare; what matters is that the Psalms are at the head of the world's lyric poetry. They were not meant to be read at a sitting, or in a Higher Critic's mood; they are at their best as expressing moments of pious ecstasy and stimulating faith. They are marred for us by bitter imprecations, tiresome "groanings" and complaints, and endless adulation of a Yahveh who, with all his "lovingkindness," "longsuffering" and "compassion," pours "smoke out of his nostrils, and fire out of his mouth" (VIII), promises that "the wicked shall be turned into hell" (IX), laps up flattery,* and threatens to "cut off all flattering lips" (XII). The Psalms are full of military ardor, hardly Christian, but very Pilgrim. Some of them, however, are jewels of tenderness, or cameos of humility. "Verily every man at his best state is altogether vanity. . . . As for man, his days are as grass; as a flower of the field, so he flourisheth. For the wind passeth over it, and it is gone; and the place thereof shall know it no more"

---

*Psalm is a Greek word, meaning "song of praise."

(XXIX, CIII). In these songs we feel the antistrophic rhythm of ancient Oriental poetry, and almost hear the voices of majestic choirs in alternate answering. No poetry has ever excelled this in revealing metaphor or living imagery; never has religious feeling been more intensely or vividly expressed. These poems touch us more deeply than any lyric of love; they move even the sceptical soul, for they give passionate form to the final longing of the developed mind—for some perfection to which it may dedicate its striving. Here and there, in the King James' Version, are pithy phrases that have become almost words in our language—"out of the mouths of babes" (VIII), "the apple of the eye" (XVII), "put not your trust in princes" (CXLVI); and everywhere, in the original, are similes that have never been surpassed: "The rising sun is as a bridegroom coming out of his chamber, and rejoiceth as a strong man to run a race" (XIX). We can only imagine what majesty and beauty must clothe these songs in the sonorous language of their origin.*

When, beside these Psalms, we place in contrast the "Song of Solomon," we get a glimpse of that sensual and terrestrial element in Jewish life which the Old Testament, written almost entirely by prophets and priests, has perhaps concealed from us—just as Ecclesiastes reveals a scepticism not otherwise discernible in the carefully selected and edited literature of the ancient Jews. This strangely amorous composition is an open field for surmise: it may be a collection of songs of Babylonian origin, celebrating the love of Ishtar and Tammuz; it may be (since it contains words borrowed from the Greek) the work of several Hebrew Anacreons touched by the Hellenistic spirit that entered Judea with Alexander; or (since the lovers address each other as brother and sister in the Egyptian manner) it may be a flower of Alexandrian Jewry, plucked by some quite emancipated soul from the banks of the Nile. In any case its presence in the Bible is a charming mystery: by what winking—or hoodwinking—of the theologians did these songs of lusty passion find room between Isaiah and the Preacher?

> A bundle of myrrh is my well-beloved unto me; he shall lie all night betwixt my breasts.
> My beloved is unto me as a cluster of camphire in the vineyards of Engedi.

---

* A selection of the best Psalms would probably include VIII, XXIII, LI, CIV, CXXXVII and CXXXIX. The last is strangely like Whitman's pæan to evolution.[219]

> Behold, thou art fair, my love; behold, thou art fair; thou hast dove's eyes.
>
> Behold, thou art fair, my beloved, yea, pleasant; also our bed is green. . . .
>
> I am the rose of Sharon, and the lily of the valleys. . . .
>
> Stay me with flagons, comfort me with apples, for I am sick of love. . . .
>
> I charge you, O ye daughters of Jerusalem, by the roes, or by the hinds of the field, that ye stir not up, nor awake my love, till he please. . . .
>
> My beloved is mine, and I am his; he feedeth among the lilies.
>
> Until the day break, and the shadows flee away, turn, my beloved, and be thou like a roe or a young hart upon the mountains of Bether. . . .
>
> Come, my beloved, let us go forth into the field, let us lodge in the villages.
>
> Let us get up early to the vineyards; let us see if the vine flourish, whether the tender grape appear, and the pomegranates bud forth; there will I give thee my loves.[220]

This is the voice of youth, and that of the Proverbs is the voice of old age. Men look to love and life for everything; they receive a little less than that; they imagine that they have received nothing: these are the three stages of the pessimist. So this legendary Solomon* warns youth against the evil woman, "for she hath cast down many wounded; yea, many strong men have been slain by her. . . . Whoso committeth adultery with a woman lacketh understanding. . . . There be three things which are wonderful to me; yea, four which I know not: the way of an eagle in the air, the way of a serpent upon a rock, the way of a ship in the midst of the sea, and the way of a man with a maid."[221] He agrees with St. Paul that it is better to marry than to burn. "Rejoice with the wife of thy youth. Let her be as the loving hind and the pleasant roe; let her breasts satisfy thee at all times; and be thou ravished always with her love. . . . Better is a dinner of herbs where love is, than a stalled ox with hatred therewith."[222] Can these be the words of the husband of seven hundred wives?

---

* The Proverbs, of course, are not the work of Solomon, though several of them may have come from him; they owe something to Egyptian literature and Greek philosophy, and were probably put together in the third or second century B.C. by some Hellenized Alexandrian Jew.

Next to unchastity, in the way from wisdom, is sloth: "Go to the ant, thou sluggard. . . . How long wilt thou sleep, O sluggard?"[223] "Seest thou a man diligent in his business?—he shall stand before kings."[224] Yet will the Philosopher not brook crass ambition. "He that maketh haste to be rich shall not be innocent"; and "the prosperity of fools shall destroy them."[225] Work is wisdom, words are mere folly. "In all labor there is profit, but the talk of the lips tendeth only to penury. . . . A fool uttereth all his mind, but a wise man keepeth it in till afterwards; . . . even a fool, when he holdeth his peace, is counted wise."[226] The lesson which the Sage never tires of repeating is an almost Socratic identification of virtue and wisdom, redolent of those schools of Alexandria in which Hebrew theology was mating with Greek philosophy to form the intellect of Europe. "Understanding is a well-spring of life unto him that hath it; but the instruction of fools is folly. . . . Happy is the man that findeth wisdom, and the man that getteth understanding; for the merchandise of it is better than the merchandise of silver, and the gain thereof than fine gold. She is more precious than rubies; and all things thou canst desire are not to be compared with her. Length of days is in her right hand; and in her left hand riches and honor. Her ways are ways of pleasantness, and all her paths are peace."[227]

Job is earlier than Proverbs; perhaps it was written during the Exile, and described by allegory the captives of Babylon.* "I call it," says the perfervid Carlyle, "one of the grandest things ever written with a pen. . . . A noble book; all men's book! It is our first, oldest statement of the never-ending problem—man's destiny, and God's ways with him here on this earth. . . . There is nothing written, I think, in the Bible or out of it, of equal literary merit."[230a] The problem arose out of the Hebrew emphasis on this world. Since there was no Heaven in ancient Jewish theology,[231] virtue had to be rewarded here or never. But often it seemed that only the wicked prospered, and that the choicest sufferings are reserved for the good man. Why, as the Psalmist complained, did the "ungodly prosper in the world?"[232] Why did God hide himself, instead of

---

* Scholarship assigns it tentatively to the fifth century B.C.[228] Its text is corrupt beyond even the custom of sacred scriptures everywhere. Jastrow accepts only chapters iii-xxxi, considers the rest to be edifying emendations, and suspects many interpolations and mistranslations in the accepted chapters. E.g., "Though he slay me, yet will I trust in him" (xiii, 5) should be, "Yet I tremble not," or "Yet I have no hope."[229] Kallen and others have found in the book the likeness of a Greek tragedy, written on the model of Euripides.[230] Chapters iii-xli are cast in the typical antistrophic form of Hebrew poetry.

punishing the evil and rewarding the good?[233] The author of *Job* now asked the same questions more resolutely, and offered his hero, perhaps, as a symbol for his people. All Israel had worshiped Yahveh (fitfully), as Job had done; Babylon had ignored and blasphemed Yahveh; and yet Babylon flourished, and Israel ate the dust and wore the sackcloth of desolation and captivity. What could one say of such a god?

In a prologue in heaven, which some clever scribe may have inserted to take the scandal out of the book, Satan suggests to Yahveh that Job is "perfect and upright" only because he is fortunate; would he retain his piety in adversity? Yahveh permits Satan to heap a variety of calamities upon Job's head. For a time the hero is as patient as Job; but at last his fortitude breaks, he ponders suicide, and bitterly reproaches his god for forsaking him. Zophar, who has come out to enjoy the sufferings of his friend, insists that God is just, and will yet reward the good man, even on earth; but Job shuts him up sharply:

> No doubt but ye are the people, and wisdom shall die with you. But I have understanding as well as you; . . . yea, who knoweth not these things? . . . The tabernacles of robbers prosper, and they that provoke God are secure; into whose hand God bringeth abundantly. . . . . Lo, mine eye hath seen all this, mine ear hath heard and understood it. . . . But ye are forgers of lies, ye are all physicians of no value. Oh, that ye would altogether hold your peace! and it should be your wisdom.[234]

He reflects on the brevity of life, and the length of death:

> Man that is born of woman is of few days, and full of trouble. He cometh forth like a flower, and is cut down; he fleeth also as a shadow, and continueth not. . . . For there is hope of a tree, if it be cut down, that it will sprout again, and that the tender branch thereof will not cease. . . . But man dieth, and wasteth away; yea, man giveth up the ghost, and where is he? As the waters fall from the sea, and the flood decayeth and drieth up, so man lieth down, and riseth not. . . . If a man die, shall he live again?[235]

The debate continues vigorously, and Job becomes more and more sceptical of his God, until he calls him "Adversary," and wishes that this Adversary would destroy himself by writing a book[235a]—perhaps some

Leibnitzian theodicy. The concluding words of this chapter—"The words of Job are ended"—suggest that this was the original termination of a discourse which, like that of Ecclesiates, represented a strong heretical minority among the Jews.* But a fresh philosopher enters at this point—Elihu—who demonstrates, in one hundred and sixty-five verses, the justice of God's ways with men. Finally, in one of the most majestic passages in the Bible, a voice comes down out of the clouds:

> Then the Lord answered Job out of the whirlwind, and said:

> Who is this that darkeneth counsel by words without knowledge? Gird up now thy loins like a man; for I will demand of thee, and answer thou me. Where wast thou when I laid the foundations of the earth? declare, if thou hast understanding. Who hath laid the measures thereof, if thou knowest? or who hath stretched his line upon it? Whereupon are the foundations thereof fastened? or who laid the cornerstone thereof; when the morning stars sang together, and all the sons of God shouted for joy? Or who shut up the sea with doors, when it brake forth, as if it had issued out of the womb? When I made the cloud the garment thereof, and thick darkness a swaddling band for it, and brake up for it my decreed place, and set bars and doors, and said, Hitherto shalt thou come, but no further; and here shall thy proud waves be stayed? Hast thou commanded the morning since thy days; and caused the dayspring to know his place? . . . Hast thou entered into the springs of the sea? or hast thou walked in the search of the depth? Have the gates of death been opened unto thee? or hast thou seen the doors of the shadow of death? Hast thou perceived the breath of the earth? declare if thou knowest it all. . . . Hast thou entered into the treasures of the snow? or hast thou seen the treasures of the hail? . . . Canst thou bind the sweet influences of the Pleiades, or loose the bands of Orion? . . . Knowest thou the ordinances of heaven? canst thou set the dominion thereof in the earth? . . . Who hath put wisdom in the inward parts, or who hath given understanding to the heart? . . .

---

* "The sceptic," wrote that prolific sceptic, Renan, "writes little, and there are many chances that his writings will be lost. The destiny of the Jewish people having been exclusively religious, the secular part of its literature had to be sacrificed."[236] The repetition of "The fool hath said in his heart, There is no God" in the Psalms (XIV, 1; LIII, 1), indicates that such fools were sufficiently numerous to create some stir in Israel. There is apparently a reference to this minority in Zephaniah, i, 12.

Shall he that contendeth with the Almighty instruct him? He that reproveth God, let him answer it.[237]

Job humbles himself in terror before this apparition. Yahveh, appeased, forgives him, accepts his sacrifice, denounces Job's friends for their feeble arguments,[238] and gives Job fourteen thousand sheep, six thousand camels, a thousand yoke of oxen, a thousand she-asses, seven sons, three daughters, and one hundred and forty years. It is a lame but happy ending; Job receives everything but an answer to his questions. The problem remained; and it was to have profound effects upon later Jewish thought. In the days of Daniel (ca. 167 B.C.) it was to be abandoned as insoluble in terms of this world; no answer could be given—Daniel and Enoch (and Kant) would say—unless one believed in some other life, beyond the grave, in which all wrongs would be righted, the wicked would be punished, and the just would inherit infinite reward. This was one of the varied currents of thought that flowed into Christianity, and carried it to victory.

In Ecclesiastes* the problem is given a pessimistic reply; prosperity and misfortune have nothing to do with virtue and vice.

All things have I seen in the days of my vanity: there is a just man that perisheth in his righteousness, and there is a wicked man that prolongeth his life in his wickedness. . . . So I returned, and considered all the oppressions that are done under the sun: and beheld the tears of such as were oppressed, and they had no comforter; and on the side of their oppressors there was power. . . . If thou seest the oppression of the poor, and violent perverting of judgment and justice in a province, marvel not at the matter, . . . for there be higher than they.[241]

It is not virtue and vice that determine a man's lot, but blind and merciless chance. "I saw under the sun that the race is not to the swift, nor the battle to the strong, neither yet bread to the wise, nor yet riches to men of understanding, nor yet favor to men of skill; but time and chance happeneth to them all."[242] Even wealth is insecure, and does not long bring happiness. "He that loveth silver shall not be satisfied with silver; nor he that loveth abundance, with increase: this is also vanity. . . . The

---

* The authorship and date of the book are quite unknown. Sarton attributes it to the period between 250 and 168 B.C.[239] The author calls himself, by a confusing literary fiction, both "Koheleth" and "the son of David, king in Jerusalem"—i.e., Solomon.[240]

sleep of a laboring man is sweet, whether he eat little or much; but the abundance of the rich will not suffer him to sleep."[243] Remembering his relatives, he formulates Malthus in a line: "When goods are increased, they are increased that eat them."[224] Nor can he be soothed by any legend of a Golden Past, or a Utopia to come: things have always been as they are now, and so they will always be. "Say not thou, What is the cause that the former days were better than these? for thou dost not inquire wisely concerning this";[245] one must choose his historians carefully. And "the thing that hath been, it is that which shall be; and that which is done is that which shall be done; and there is nothing new under the sun. Is there anything whereof it may be said, See, this is new? It hath been already of old time, which was before us."[246] Progress, he thinks, is a delusion; civilizations have been forgotten, and will be again.[247]

In general he feels that life is a sorry business, and might well be dispensed with; it is aimless and circuitous motion without permanent result, and ends where it began; it is a futile struggle, in which nothing is certain except defeat.

> Vanity of vanities, saith the Preacher, vanity of vanities; all is vanity. What profit hath a man of all his labor which he taketh under the sun? One generation passeth away, and another generation cometh; but the earth abideth forever. The sun also ariseth, and the wind goeth toward the south, and turneth about unto the north; it whirleth about continually, and the wind returneth again according to his circuits. All the rivers run into the sea, yet the sea is not full; unto the place from whence the rivers came, thither they return again. . . . Wherefore I praised the dead which are already dead, more than the living which are yet alive. Yea, better is he, than both they, which hath not yet been, who hath not seen the evil work that is done under the sun. . . . A good name is better than precious ointment, and the day of death than the day of one's birth.[248]

For a time he seeks the answer to the riddle of life in abandonment to pleasure. "Then I commended mirth, because a man hath no better thing under the sun than to eat, and to drink, and to be merry." But "behold, this also is vanity."[250] The difficulty with pleasure is woman, from whom the Preacher seems to have received some unforgettable sting. "One man among a thousand have I found; but a woman among all those have I not found. . . . I find more bitter than death the woman whose heart is snares and nets, and her hands as bands; whoso pleaseth God shall escape her."[251] He concludes his digression into this most obscure realm of philosophy by reverting to the advice of Solomon and Voltaire, who did not practise it: "Live joyfully with the wife whom thou lovest, all the days of the life of thy vanity which God hath given thee under the sun."[252]

Even wisdom is a questionable thing; he lauds it generously, but he suspects that anything more than a little knowledge is a dangerous thing. "Of making many books," he writes, with uncanny foresight, "there is no end; and much study is a weariness of the flesh."[253] It might be wise to seek wisdom if God had given it a better income; "wisdom is good, with an inheritance"; otherwise it is a snare, and is apt to destroy its lovers.[254] (Truth is like Yahveh, who said to Moses: "Thou canst not see my face; for there shall no man see me and live."[255]) In the end the wise man dies as thoroughly as the fool, and both come to the same odor.

> And I gave my heart to seek and search out by wisdom concerning all things that are done under heaven: this sore travail hath God given to the sons of man to be exercised therewith. I have seen all the works that are done under the sun; and behold, all is vanity and a chasing after the wind. . . . I communed with mine own heart, saying, Lo, I am come to great estate, and have gotten more wisdom than all they that have been before me in Jerusalem; yea, my heart had great experience of wisdom and knowledge. And I gave my heart to know wisdom, and to know madness and folly; I perceived that this also is a chasing after the wind. For in much wisdom is much grief; and he that increaseth knowledge increaseth sorrow.[256]

All these darts of outrageous fortune might be borne with hope and courage if the just man could look forward to some happiness beyond the grave. But that, too, Ecclesiastes feels, is a myth; man is an animal, and dies like any other beast.

> For that which befalleth the sons of men befalleth beasts; even one thing befalleth them; as the one dieth, so dieth the other; yea, they have all one breath; so that a man hath no preëminence over a beast; for all is vanity. All go unto one place: all are of the dust,

and all turn to dust again. . . . Wherefore I perceive that there is nothing better than that a man should rejoice in his own works; for that is his portion; for who shall bring him to see what shall be after him? . . . Whatsoever thy hand findeth to do, do it with thy might; for there is no work, nor device, nor knowledge, nor wisdom in the grave, whither thou goest.[257]

What a commentary on the wisdom so lauded in the Proverbs! Here, evidently, civilization had for a time gone to seed. The vitality of Israel's youth had been exhausted by her struggles against the empires that surrounded her. The Yahveh in whom she had trusted had not come to her aid; and in her desolation and dispersion she raised to the skies this bitterest of all voices in literature to express the profoundest doubts that ever come to the human soul.

Jerusalem had been restored, but not as the citadel of an unconquerable god; it was a vassal city ruled now by Persia, now by Greece. In 334 B.C. the young Alexander stood at its gates, and demanded the surrender of the capital. The high-priest at first refused; but the next morning, having had a dream, he consented. He ordered the clergy to put on their most impressive vestments, and the people to garb themselves in immaculate white; then he led the population pacifically out through the gates to solicit peace. Alexander bowed to the high-priest, expressed his admiration for the people and their god, and accepted Jerusalem.[258]

It was not the end of Judea. Only the first act had been played in this strange drama that binds forty centuries. Christ would be the second, Ahasuerus the third; today another act is played, but it is not the last. Destroyed and rebuilt, destroyed and rebuilt, Jerusalem rises again, symbol of the vitality and pertinacity of an heroic race. The Jews, who are as old as history, may be as lasting as civilization.

CHAPTER XIII

Persia

I. THE RISE AND FALL OF THE MEDES

Their origins—Rulers—The blood treaty of Sardis—Degeneration

WHO were the Medes that had played so vital a rôle in the destruction of Assyria? Their origin, of course, eludes us; history is a book that one must begin in the middle. The first mention we have of them is on a tablet recording the expedition of Shalmaneser III into a country called *Parsua*, in the mountains of Kurdistan (837 B.C.); there, it seems, twenty-seven chieftain-kings ruled over twenty-seven states thinly populated by a people called Amadai, Madai, Medes. As Indo-Europeans they had probably come into western Asia about a thousand years before Christ, from the shores of the Caspian Sea. The *Zend-Avesta*, sacred scriptures of the Persians, idealized the racial memory of this ancient home-land, and described it as a paradise: the scenes of our youth, like the past, are always beautiful if we do not have to live in them again. The Medes appear to have wandered through the region of Bokhara and Samarkand, and to have migrated farther and farther south, at last reaching Persia.[1] They found copper, iron, lead, gold and silver, marble and precious stones, in the mountains in which they made their new home;[2] and being a simple and vigorous people they developed a prosperous agriculture on the plains and the slopes of the hills.

At Ecbatana*—i.e., "a meeting-place of many ways"—in a picturesque valley made fertile by the melting snows of the highlands, their first king, Deioces, founded their first capital, adorning and dominating it with a royal palace spread over an area two-thirds of a mile square. According to an uncorroborated passage in Herodotus, Deioces achieved power by acquiring a reputation for justice, and having achieved power, became a despot. He issued regulations "that no man should be admitted to the King's presence, but every one should consult him by means of messengers; and moreover, that it should be accounted indecency for any one

---

* Probably the modern Hamadan.

to laugh or spit before him. He established such ceremony about his person for this reason, . . . that he might appear to be of a different nature to them who did not see him."³ Under his leadership the Medes, strengthened by their natural and frugal life, and hardened by custom and environment to the necessities of war, became a threat to the power of Assyria—which repeatedly invaded Media, thought it most instructively defeated, and found it in fact never tired of fighting for its liberty. The greatest of the Median kings, Cyaxares, settled the matter by destroying Nineveh. Inspired by this victory, his army swept through western Asia to the very gates of Sardis, only to be turned back by an eclipse of the sun. The opposing leaders, frightened by this apparent warning from the skies, signed a treaty of peace, and sealed it by drinking each other's blood.⁴ In the next year Cyaxares died, having in the course of one reign expanded his kingdom from a subject province into an empire embracing Assyria, Media and Persia. Within a generation after his death this empire came to an end.

Its tenure was too brief to permit of any substantial contribution to civilization, except in so far as it prepared for the culture of Persia. To Persia the Medes gave their Aryan language, their alphabet of thirty-six characters, their replacement of clay with parchment and pen as writing materials,⁵ their extensive use of the column in architecture, their moral code of conscientious husbandry in time of peace and limitless bravery in time of war, their Zoroastrian religion of Ahura-Mazda and Ahriman, their patriarchal family and polygamous marriage, and a body of law sufficiently like that of the later empire to be united with it in the famous phrase of Daniel about "the law of the Medes and the Persians, which altereth not."⁶ Of their literature and their art not a stone or a letter remains.

Their degeneration was even more rapid than their rise. Astyages, who succeeded his father Cyaxares, proved again that monarchy is a gamble, in whose royal succession great wits and madness are near allied. He inherited the kingdom with equanimity, and settled down to enjoy it. Under his example the nation forgot its stern morals and stoic ways; wealth had come too suddenly to be wisely used. The upper classes became the slaves of fashion and luxury, the men wore embroidered trousers, the women covered themselves with cosmetics and jewelry, the very horses were often caparisoned in gold.⁷ These once simple and pastoral people, who had been glad to be carried in rude wagons with wheels cut roughly out of the trunks of trees,[8] now rode in expensive chariots from feast to feast. The early kings had prided themselves on justice; but Astyages, being displeased with Harpagus, served up to him the dismembered and headless body of his own son, and forced him to eat of it.[9] Harpagus ate, saying that whatever a king did was agreeable to him; but he revenged himself by helping Cyrus to depose Astyages. When Cyrus, the brilliant young ruler of the Median dependency of Anshan, in Persia, rebelled against the effeminate despot of Ecbatana, the Medes themselves welcomed Cyrus' victory, and accepted him, almost without protest, as their king. By one engagement Media ceased to be the master of Persia, Persia became the master of Media, and prepared to become master of the whole Near Eastern world.

II. THE GREAT KINGS

The romantic Cyrus—His enlightened policies—Cambyses—Darius the Great—The invasion of Greece

Cyrus was one of those natural rulers at whose coronation, as Emerson said, all men rejoice. Royal in spirit and action, capable of wise administration as well as of dramatic conquest, generous to the defeated and loved by those who had been his enemies—no wonder the Greeks made him the subject of innumerable romances, and—to their minds—the greatest hero before Alexander. It is a disappointment to us that we cannot draw a reliable picture of him from either Herodotus or Xenophon. The former has mingled many fables with his history,[10] while the other has made the *Cyropædia* an essay on the military art, with incidental lectures on education and philosophy; at times Xenophon confuses Cyrus and Socrates. These delightful stories being put aside, the figure of Cyrus becomes merely an attractive ghost. We can only say that he was handsome—since the Persians made him their model of physical beauty to the end of their ancient art;[11] that he established the Achæmenid Dynasty of "Great Kings," which ruled Persia through the most famous period of its history; that he organized the soldiery of Media and Persia into an invincible army, captured Sardis and Babylon, ended for a thousand years the rule of the Semites in western Asia, and absorbed the former realms of Assyria, Babylonia, Lydia and Asia Minor into the Persian Empire, the largest political organization of pre-Roman antiquity, and one of the best-governed in history.

So far as we can visualize him through the haze of legend, he was the most amiable of conquerors, and founded his empire upon generosity. His enemies knew that he was lenient, and they did not fight him with that desperate courage which men show when their only choice is to kill or die. We have seen how, according to Herodotus, he rescued Crœsus from the funeral pyre at Sardis, and made him one of his most honored counselors; and we have seen how magnanimously he treated the Jews. The first principle of his policy was that the various peoples of his empire should be left free in their religious worship and beliefs, for he fully understood the first principle of statesmanship—that religion is stronger than the state. Instead of sacking cities and wrecking temples he showed a courteous respect for the deities of the conquered, and con-tributed to maintain their shrines; even the Babylonians, who had resisted him so long, warmed towards him when they found him preserving their sanctuaries and honoring their pantheon. Wherever he went in his un-precedented career he offered pious sacrifice to the local divinities. Like Napoleon he accepted indifferently all religions, and—with much better grace—humored all the gods.

Like Napoleon, too, he died of excessive ambition. Having won all the Near East, he began a series of campaigns aimed to free Media and Persia from the inroads of central Asia's nomadic barbarians. He seems to have carried these excursions as far as the Jaxartes on the north and India on the east. Suddenly, at the height of his curve, he was slain in battle with the Massagetæ, an obscure tribe that peopled the southern shores of the Caspian Sea. Like Alexander he conquered an empire, but did not live to organize it.

One great defect had sullied his character—occasional and incalculable cruelty. It was inherited, unmixed with Cyrus' generosity, by his half-mad son. Cambyses began by putting to death his brother and rival, Smerdis; then, lured by the accumulated wealth of Egypt, he set forth to extend the Persian Empire to the Nile. He succeeded, but apparently at the cost of his sanity. Memphis was captured easily, but an army of fifty thousand Persians sent to annex the Oasis of Ammon perished in the desert, and an expedition to Carthage failed because the Phœnician crews of the Persian fleet refused to attack a Phœnician colony. Cambyses lost his head, and abandoned the wise clemency and tolerance of his father. He publicly scoffed at the Egyptian religion, and plunged his dagger derisively into the bull revered by the Egyptians as the god Apis;

he exhumed mummies and pried into royal tombs regardless of ancient curses; he profaned the temples and ordered their idols to be burned. He thought in this way to cure the Egyptians of superstition; but when he was stricken with illness—apparently epileptic convulsions—the Egyptians were certain that their gods had punished him, and that their theology was now confirmed beyond dispute. As if again to illustrate the inconveniences of monarchy, Cambyses, with a Napoleonic kick in the stomach, killed his sister and wife Roxana, slew his son Prexaspes with an arrow, buried twelve noble Persians alive, condemned Crœsus to death, repented, rejoiced to learn that the sentence had not been carried out, and punished the officers who had delayed in executing it.[12] On his way back to Persia he learned that a usurper had seized the throne and was being supported by widespread revolution. From that moment he disappears from history; tradition has it that he killed himself.[13]

The usurper had pretended to be Smerdis, miraculously preserved from Cambyses' fratricidal jealousy; in reality he was a religious fanatic, a devotee of the early Magian faith who was bent upon destroying Zoroastrianism, the official religion of the Persian state. Another revolution soon deposed him, and the seven aristocrats who had organized it raised one of their number, Darius, son of Hystaspes, to the throne. In this bloody way began the reign of Persia's greatest king.

Succession to the throne, in Oriental monarchies, was marked not only by palace revolutions in strife for the royal power, but by uprisings in subject colonies that grasped the chance of chaos, or an inexperienced ruler, to reclaim their liberty. The usurpation and assassination of "Smerdis" gave to Persia's vassals an excellent opportunity: the governors of Egypt and Lydia refused submission, and the provinces of Susiana, Babylonia, Media, Assyria, Armenia, Sacia and others rose in simultaneous revolt. Darius subdued them with a ruthless hand. Taking Babylon after a long siege, he crucified three thousand of its leading citizens as an inducement to obedience in the rest; and in a series of swift campaigns he "pacified" one after another of the rebellious states. Then, perceiving how easily the vast empire might in any crisis fall to pieces, he put off the armor of war, became one of the wisest administrators in history, and set himself to reëstablish his realm in a way that became a model of imperial organization till the fall of Rome. His rule gave western Asia a generation of such order and prosperity as that quarrelsome region had never known before.

He had hoped to govern in peace, but it is the fatality of empire to breed repeated war. For the conquered must be periodically reconquered, and the conquerors must keep the arts and habits of camp and battlefield; and at any moment the kaleidoscope of change may throw up a new empire to challenge the old. In such a situation wars must be invented if they do not arise of their own accord; each generation must be inured to the rigors of campaigns, and taught by practice the sweet decorum of dying for one's country.

Perhaps it was in part for this reason that Darius led his armies into southern Russia, across the Bosphorus and the Danube to the Volga, to chastise the marauding Scythians; and again across Afghanistan and a hundred mountain ranges into the valley of the Indus, adding thereby extensive regions and millions of souls and rupees to his realm. More substantial reasons must be sought for his expedition into Greece. Herodotus would have us believe that Darius entered upon this historic *faux pas* because one of his wives, Atossa, teased him into it in bed;[14] but it is more dignified to believe that the King recognized in the Greek city-states and their colonies a potential empire, or an actual confederacy, dangerous to the Persian mastery of western Asia. When Ionia revolted and received aid from Sparta and Athens, Darius reconciled himself reluctantly to war. All the world knows the story of his passage across the Ægean, the defeat of his army at Marathon, and his gloomy return to Persia. There, amid far-flung preparations for another attempt upon Greece, he suddenly grew weak, and died.

III. PERSIAN LIFE AND INDUSTRY

The empire—The people—The language—The peasants—The imperial highways—Trade and finance

At its greatest extent, under Darius, the Persian Empire included twenty provinces or "satrapies," embracing Egypt, Palestine, Syria, Phœnicia, Lydia, Phrygia, Ionia, Cappadocia, Cilicia, Armenia, Assyria, the Caucasus, Babylonia, Media, Persia, the modern Afghanistan and Baluchistan, India west of the Indus, Sogdiana, Bactria, and the regions of the Massagetæ and other central Asiatic tribes. Never before had history recorded so extensive an area brought under one government.

Persia itself, which was to rule these forty million souls for two hundred years, was not at that time the country now known to us as *Persia,* and to its inhabitants as *Iran;* it was that smaller tract, immediately east of the Persian Gulf, known to the ancient Persians as *Pars,* and to the modern Persians as *Fars* or *Farsistan.*[15] Composed almost entirely of mountains and deserts, poor in rivers, subject to severe winters and hot, arid summers,* it could support its two million inhabitants[17] only through such external contributions as trade or conquest might bring. Its race of hardy mountaineers came, like the Medes, of Indo-European stock perhaps from South Russia; and its language and early religion reveal its close kinship with those Aryans who crossed Afghanistan to become the ruling caste of northern India. Darius I, in an inscription at Naksh-i-Rustam, described himself as "a Persian, the son of a Persian, an Aryan of Aryan descent." The Zoroastrians spoke of their primitive land as *Airyana-vaejo*—"the Aryan home."† Strabo applied the name *Ariana* to what is now called by essentially the same word—*Iran.*[18]

The Persians were apparently the handsomest people of the ancient Near East. The monuments picture them as erect and vigorous, made hardy by their mountains and yet refined by their wealth, with a pleasing symmetry of features, an almost Greek straightness of nose, and a certain nobility of countenance and carriage. They adopted for the most part the Median dress, and later the Median ornaments. They considered it indecent to reveal more than the face; clothing covered them from turban, fillet or cap to sandals or leather shoes. Triple drawers, a white under-garment of linen, a double tunic, with sleeves hiding the hands, and a girdle at the waist, kept the population warm in winter and hot in summer. The king distinguished himself with embroidered trousers of a crimson hue, and saffron-buttoned shoes. The dress of the women differed from that of the men only in a slit at the breast. The men wore long beards and hung their hair in curls, or, later, covered it with wigs.[19] In the wealthier days of the empire men as well as women made much use of cosmetics; creams were employed to improve the complexion, and coloring matter was applied to the eyelids to increase the apparent size and brilliance of the eyes. A special class of "adorners," called *kosmetai* by the Greeks, arose as beauty experts to the aristocracy. The Persians were connoisseurs in scents, and were believed by the ancients to have invented cosmetic creams. The king never went to war without a case of costly unguents to ensure his fragrance in victory or defeat.[20]

Many languages have been used in the long history of Persia. The speech of the court and the nobility in the days of Darius I was Old Persian—so

---

* At Susa, says Strabo, the summer heat was so intense that snakes and lizards could not cross the streets quickly enough to escape being burned to death by the sun.[16]

† Generally identified with the district of Arran on the river Araxes.

closely related to Sanskrit that evidently both were once dialects of an older tongue, and were cousins to our own.* Old Persian developed on the one hand into Zend—the language of the *Zend-Avesta*—and on the other hand into Pahlavi, a Hindu tongue from which has come the Persian language of to-day.[22] When the Persians took to writing they adopted the Babylonian cuneiform for their inscriptions, and the Aramaic alphabetic script for their documents.[23] They simplified the unwieldly syllabary of the Babylonians from three hundred characters to thirty-six signs which gradually became letters instead of syllables, and constituted a cuneiform alphabet.[24] Writing, however, seemed to the Persians an effeminate amusement, for which they could spare little time from love, war and the chase. They did not condescend to produce literature.

The common man was contentedly illiterate, and gave himself completely to the culture of the soil. The *Zend-Avesta* exalted agriculture as the basic and noblest occupation of mankind, pleasing above all other labors to Ahura-Mazda, the supreme god. Some of the land was tilled by peasant proprietors, who occasionally joined several families in agricultural coöperatives to work extensive areas together.[25] Part of the land was owned by feudal barons, and cultivated by tenants in return for a share of the crop; part of it was tilled by foreign (never Persian) slaves. Oxen pulled a plough of wood armed with a metal point. Artificial irrigation drew water from the mountains to the fields. Barley and wheat were the staple crops and foods, but much meat was eaten and much wine drunk. Cyrus served wine to his army,[26] and Persian councils never undertook serious discussions of policy when sober†—though they took care to revise their decisions the next morning. One intoxicating drink, the *haoma*, was offered as a pleasant sacrifice to the gods, and was believed to engender in its addicts not excitement and anger, but righteousness and piety.[28]

Industry was poorly developed in Persia; she was content to let the nations of the Near East practice the handicrafts while she bought their

---

* Some examples of the correlation:

Old Persian	Sanskrit	Greek	Latin	German	English
pitar	pitar	pater	pater	Vater	father
nama	nama	onoma	nomen	Nahme	name
napat (grandson)	napat	anepsios	nepos	Neffe	nephew
bar	bhri	ferein	ferre	führen	bear
matar	matar	meter	mater	Mutter	mother
bratar	bhratar	phrater	frater	Bruder	brother
çta	stha	istemi	sto	stehen	stand [21]

† "They carry on their most important deliberations," Strabo reports, "when drinking wine; and they regard decisions then made as more lasting than those made when they are sober."[27]

products with their imperial tribute. She showed more originality in the improvement of communications and transport. Engineers under the instructions of Darius I built great roads uniting the various capitals; one of these highways, from Susa to Sardis, was fifteen hundred miles long. The roads were accurately measured by parasangs (3.4 miles); and at every fourth parasang, says Herodotus, "there are royal stations and excellent inns, and the whole road is through an inhabited and safe country."[29] At each station a fresh relay of horses stood ready to carry on the mail, so that, though the ordinary traveler required ninety days to go from Susa to Sardis, the royal mail moved over the distance as quickly as an automobile party does now—that is, in a little less than a week. The larger rivers were crossed by ferries, but the engineers could, when they wished, throw across the Euphrates, even across the Hellespont, substantial bridges over which hundreds of sceptical elephants could pass in safety. Other roads led through the Afghanistan passes to India, and made Susa a half-way house to the already fabulous riches of the East. These roads were built primarily for military and governmental purposes, to facilitate central control and administration; but they served also to stimulate commerce and the exchange of customs, ideas, and the indispensable superstitions of mankind. Along these roads, for example, angels and the Devil passed from Persian into Jewish and Christian mythology.

Navigation was not so vigorously advanced as land transportation; the Persians had no fleet of their own, but merely engaged or conscripted the vessels of the Phœnicians and the Greeks. Darius built a great canal uniting Persia with the Mediterranean through the Red Sea and the Nile, but the carelessness of his successors soon surrendered this achievement to the shifting sands. When Xerxes royally commanded part of his naval forces to circumnavigate Africa, it turned back in disgrace shortly after passing through the Pillars of Hercules.[30] Commerce was for the most part abandoned to foreigners—Babylonians, Phœnicians and Jews; the Persians despised trade, and looked upon a market place as a breeding-ground of lies. The wealthy classes took pride in supplying most of their wants directly from their own fields and shops, not contaminating their fingers with either buying or selling.[31] Payments, loans and interest were at first in the form of goods, especially cattle and grain; coinage came later from Lydia. Darius issued gold and silver "darics" stamped with his features,* and valued at a gold-to-silver ratio of 13.5 to 1. This was the origin of the bimetallic ratio in modern currencies.[33]

---

* But having no relation with his name; *daric* was from the Persian *zariq*—"a piece of gold." The gold daric had a face value of $5.00. Three thousand gold darics made one Persian talent.[32]

IV. AN EXPERIMENT IN GOVERNMENT

The king—The nobles—The army—Law—A savage punishment—
The capitals—The satrapies—An achievement in administration

The life of Persia was political and military rather than economic; its wealth was based not on industry but on power; it existed precariously as a little governing isle in an immense and unnaturally subject sea. The imperial organization that maintained this artefact was one of the most unique and competent in history. At its head was the king, or *Khshathra* —i.e., warrior;* the title indicates the military origin and character of the Persian monarchy. Since lesser kings were vassal to him, the Persian ruler entitled himself "King of Kings," and the ancient world made no protest against his claim; the Greeks called him simply *Basileus*—The King.³⁴ His power was theoretically absolute; he could kill with a word, without trial or reason given, after the manner of some very modern dictator; and occasionally he delegated to his mother or his chief wife this privilege of capricious slaughter.³⁵ Few even of the greatest nobles dared offer any criticism or rebuke, and public opinion was cautiously impotent. The father whose innocent son had been shot before his eyes by the king merely complimented the monarch on his excellent archery; offenders bastinadoed by the royal order thanked His Majesty for keeping them in mind.³⁶ The king might rule as well as reign, if, like Cyrus and the first Darius, he cared to bestir himself; but the later monarchs delegated most of the cares of government to noble subordinates or imperial eunuchs, and spent their time at love, dice or the chase.³⁷ The court was overrun with eunuchs who, from their coigns of vantage as guards of the harem and pedagogues to the princes, stewed a poisonous brew of intrigue in every reign.†³⁸ The king had the right to choose his successor from among his sons, but ordinarily the succession was determined by assassination and revolution.

The royal power was limited in practice by the strength of the aristocracy that mediated between the people and the throne. It was a matter of custom that the six families of the men who had shared with Darius I

---

* The word survives in the present title of the Persian king—*Shah.* Its stem appears also in the *Satraps* or provincial officials of Persia, and in the *Kshatriya* or warrior caste of India.

† Five hundred castrated boys came annually from Babylonia to act as "keepers of the women" in the harems of Persia.³⁹

the dangers of the revolt against false Smerdis, should have exceptional privileges and be consulted in all matters of vital interest. Many of the nobles attended court, and served as a council for whose advice the monarch usually showed the highest regard. Most members of the aristocracy were attached to the throne by receiving their estates from the king; in return they provided him with men and materials when he took the field. Within their fiefs they had almost complete authority—levying taxes, enacting laws, executing judgment, and maintaining their own armed forces.[40]

The real basis of the royal power and imperial government was the army; an empire exists only so long as it retains its superior capacity to kill. The obligation to enlist on any declaration of war fell upon every able-bodied male from fifteen to fifty years of age.[41] When the father of three sons petitioned Darius to exempt one of them from service, all three were put to death; and when another father, having sent four sons to the battlefield, begged Xerxes to permit the fifth son to stay behind and manage the family estate, the body of this fifth son was cut in two by royal order and placed on both sides of the road by which the army was to pass.[42] The troops marched off to war amid the blare of martial music and the plaudits of citizens above the military age.

The spearhead of the army was the Royal Guard—two thousand horsemen and two thousand infantry, all nobles—whose function it was to guard the king. The standing army consisted exclusively of Persians and Medes, and from this permanent force came most of the garrisons stationed as centers of persuasion at strategic points in the empire. The complete force consisted of levies from every subject nation, each group with its own distinct language, weapons and habits of war. Its equipment and retinue was as varied as its origin: bows and arrows, scimitars, javelins, daggers, pikes, slings, knives, shields, helmets, leather cuirasses, coats of mail, horses, elephants, heralds, scribes, eunuchs, prostitutes, concubines, and chariots armed on each hub with great steel scythes. The whole mass, though vast in number, and amounting in the expedition of Xerxes to 1,800,000 men, never achieved unity, and at the first sign of a reverse it became a disorderly mob. It conquered by mere force of numbers, by an elastic capacity for absorbing casualties; it was destined to be overthrown as soon as it should encounter a well-organized army speaking one speech and accepting one discipline. This was the secret of Marathon and Platæa.

In such a state the only law was the will of the king and the power of the army; no rights were sacred against these, and no precedents could

avail except an earlier decree of the king. For it was a proud boast of
Persia that its laws never changed, and that a royal promise or decree
was irrevocable. In his edicts and judgments the king was supposed to
be inspired by the god Ahura-Mazda himself; therefore the law of
the realm was the Divine Will, and any infraction of it was an offense
against the deity. The king was the supreme court, but it was his custom
to delegate this function to some learned elder in his retinue. Below him
was a High Court of Justice with seven members, and below this were
local courts scattered through the realm. The priests formulated the law,
and for a long time acted as judges; in later days laymen, even laywomen,
sat in judgment. Bail was accepted in all but the most important cases,
and a regular procedure of trial was followed. The court occasionally
decreed rewards as well as punishments, and in considering a crime
weighed against it the good record and services of the accused. The
law's delays were mitigated by fixing a time-limit for each case, and by
proposing to all disputants an arbitrator of their own choice who might
bring them to a peaceable settlement. As the law gathered precedents
and complexity a class of men arose called "speakers of the law," who
offered to explain it to litigants and help them conduct their cases.[43]
Oaths were taken, and use was occasionally made of the ordeal.[44] Bribery
was discouraged by making the tender or acceptance of it a capital
offense. Cambyses improved the integrity of the courts by causing an
unjust judge to be flayed alive, and using his skin to upholster the judicial
bench—to which he then appointed the dead judge's son.[45]

Minor punishments took the form of flogging—from five to two hundred blows with a horsewhip; the poisoning of a shepherd dog received
two hundred strokes, manslaughter ninety.[46] The administration of the
law was partly financed by commuting stripes into fines, at the rate of
six rupees to a stripe.[47] More serious crimes were punished with branding,
maiming, mutilation, blinding, imprisonment or death. The letter of the
law forbade any one, even the king, to sentence a man to death for a
simple crime; but it could be decreed for treason, rape, sodomy, murder,
"self-pollution," burning or burying the dead, intrusion upon the king's
privacy, approaching one of his concubines, accidentally sitting upon his
throne, or for any displeasure to the ruling house.[48] Death was procured
in such cases by poisoning, impaling, crucifixion, hanging (usually with
the head down), stoning, burying the body up to the head, crushing
the head between huge stones, smothering the victim in hot ashes, or by

the incredibly cruel rite called "the boats."* Some of these barbarous
punishments were bequeathed to the invading Turks of a later age, and
passed down into the heritage of mankind.⁴⁹

With these laws and this army the king sought to govern his twenty
satrapies from his many capitals—originally Pasargadæ, occasionally Persepolis, in summer Ecbatana, usually Susa; here, in the ancient capital of
Elam, the history of the ancient Near East came full circle, binding the
beginning and the end. Susa had the advantage of inaccessibility, and
the disadvantages of distance; Alexander had to come two thousand miles
to take it, but it had to send its troops fifteen hundred miles to suppress
revolts in Lydia or Egypt. Ultimately the great roads merely paved the
way for the physical conquest of western Asia by Greece and Rome,
and the theological conquest of Greece and Rome by western Asia.

The empire was divided into provinces or satrapies for convenience
of administration and taxation. Each province was governed in the name
of the King of Kings, sometimes by a vassal prince, ordinarily by a
"satrap" (ruler) royally appointed for as long a time as he could retain
favor at the court. To keep the satraps in hand Darius sent to each
province a general to control its armed forces independently of the governor; and to make matters trebly sure he appointed in each province a
secretary, independent of both satrap and general, to report their behavior
to the king. As a further precaution an intelligence service known as
"The King's Eyes and Ears" might appear at any moment to examine the
affairs, records and finances of the province. Sometimes the satrap was

* Because the soldier Mithridates, in his cups, blurted out the fact that it was he, and
not the king, who should have received credit for slaying Cyrus the Younger at the
battle of Cunaxa, Artaxerxes II, says Plutarch, "decreed that Mithridates should be put to
death in boats; which execution is after the following manner: Taking two boats framed
exactly to fit and answer each other, they lay down in one of them the malefactor that
suffers, upon his back; then, covering it with the other, and so setting them together that
the head, hands and feet of him are left outside, and the rest of his body lies shut up
within, they offer him food, and if he refuse to eat it, they force him to do it by prick-
ing his eyes; then, after he has eaten, they drench him with a mixture of milk and honey,
pouring it not only into his mouth but all over his face. They then keep his face continually turned toward the sun; and it becomes completely covered up and hidden by the
multitude of flies that settle upon it. And as within the boats he does what those that eat
and drink must do, creeping things and vermin spring out of the corruption of the excrement, and these entering into the bowels of him, his body is consumed. When the man
is manifestly dead, the uppermost boat being taken off, they find his flesh devoured, and
swarms of such noisome creatures preying upon and, as it were, growing to his inwards.
In this way Mithridates, after suffering for seventeen days, at last expired."⁵⁰

deposed without trial, sometimes he was quietly poisoned by his servants at the order of the king. Underneath the satrap and the secretary was a horde of clerks who carried on so much of the government as had no direct need of force; this body of clerks carried over from one administration to another, even from reign to reign. The king dies, but the bureaucracy is immortal.

The salaries of these provincial officials were paid not by the king but by the people whom they ruled. The remuneration was ample enough to provide the satraps with palaces, harems, and extensive hunting parks to which the Persians gave the historic name of *paradise*. In addition, each satrapy was required to send the king, annually, a fixed amount of money and goods by way of taxation. India sent 4680 talents, Assyria and Babylonia 1000, Egypt 700, the four satrapies of Asia Minor 1760, etc., making a total of some 14,560 talents—variously estimated as equivalent to from $160,000,000 to $218,000,000 a year. Furthermore, each province was expected to contribute to the king's needs in goods and supplies: Egypt had to furnish corn annually for 120,000 men; the Medes provided 100,000 sheep, the Armenians 30,000 foals, the Babylonians five hundred young eunuchs. Other sources of wealth swelled the central revenue to such a point that when Alexander captured the Persian capitals after one hundred and fifty years of Persian extravagance, after a hundred expensive revolts and wars, and after Darius III had carried off 8000 talents with him in his flight, he found 180,000 talents left in the royal treasuries— some $2,700,000,000.[51]

Despite these high charges for its services, the Persian Empire was the most successful experiment in imperial government that the Mediterranean world would know before the coming of Rome—which was destined to inherit much of the earlier empire's political structure and administrative forms. The cruelty and dissipation of the later monarchs, the occasional barbarism of the laws, and the heavy burdens of taxation were balanced, as human governments go, by such order and peace as made the provinces rich despite these levies, and by such liberty as only the most enlightened empires have accorded to subject states. Each region retained its own language, laws, customs, morals, religion and coinage, and sometimes its native dynasty of kings. Many of the tributary nations, like Babylonia, Phœnicia and Palestine, were well satisfied with the situation, and suspected that their own generals and tax-gatherers would have plucked them even more ferociously. Under Darius I the

Persian Empire was an achievement in political organization; only Trajan, Hadrian and the Antonines would equal it.

V. ZARATHUSTRA

*The coming of the Prophet—Persian religion before Zarathustra—
The Bible of Persia—Ahura-Mazda—The good and the evil
spirits—Their struggle for the possession of the world*

Persian legend tells how, many hundreds of years before the birth of Christ, a great prophet appeared in *Airyana-vaejo*, the ancient "home of the Aryans." His people called him Zarathustra; but the Greeks, who could never bear the orthography of the "barbarians" patiently, called him Zoroastres. His conception was divine: his guardian angel entered into an *haoma* plant, and passed with its juice into the body of a priest as the latter offered divine sacrifice; at the same time a ray of heaven's glory entered the bosom of a maid of noble lineage. The priest espoused the maid, the imprisoned angel mingled with the imprisoned ray, and Zarathustra began to be.[53] He laughed aloud on the very day of his birth, and the evil spirits that gather around every life fled from him in tumult and terror.[54] Out of his great love for wisdom and righteousness he withdrew from the society of men, and chose to live in a mountain wilderness on cheese and the fruits of the soil. The Devil tempted him, but to no avail. His breast was pierced with a sword, and his entrails were filled with molten lead; he did not complain, but clung to his faith in Ahura-Mazda—the Lord of Light—as supreme god. Ahura-Mazda appeared to him and gave into his hands the *Avesta*, or Book of Knowledge and Wisdom, and bade him preach it to mankind. For a long time all the world ridiculed and persecuted him; but at last a high prince of Iran—Vishtaspa or Hystaspes—heard him gladly, and promised to spread the new faith among his people. Thus was the Zoroastrian religion born. Zarathustra himself lived to a very old age, was consumed in a flash of lightning, and ascended into heaven.[55]

We cannot tell how much of his story is true; perhaps some Josiah discovered him. The Greeks accepted him as historical, and honored him with an antiquity of 5500 years before their time;[56] Berosus the Babylonian brought him down to 2000 B.C.;[57] modern historians, when they believe in his existence, assign him to any century between the tenth and the sixth before Christ.*[58] When he appeared, among the ancestors of the Medes and the Persians, he found his people worshiping animals,[59] ancestors,[60] the earth and the sun, in a religion having many elements and deities in common with the Hindus of the Vedic age. The chief divinities of this pre-Zoroastrian faith were Mithra, god of the sun, Anaita, goddess of fertility and the earth, and Haoma the bull-god who, dying, rose again, and gave mankind his blood as a drink that would confer immortality; him the early Iranians worshiped by drinking the intoxicating juice of the *haoma* herb found on their mountain slopes.[61] Zarathustra was shocked at these primitive deities and this Dionysian ritual; he rebelled against the "Magi" or priests who prayed and sacrificed to them; and with all the bravery of his contemporaries Amos and Isaiah he announced to the world one God—here Ahura-Mazda, the Lord of Light and Heaven, of whom all other gods were but manifestations and qualities. Perhaps Darius I, who accepted the new doctrine, saw in it a faith that would both inspire his people and strengthen his government. From the moment of his accession he declared war upon the old cults and the Magian priesthood, and made Zoroastrianism the religion of the state.

The Bible of the new faith was the collection of books in which the disciples of the Master had gathered his sayings and his prayers. Later followers called these books *Avesta;* by the error of a modern scholar they are known to the Occidental world as the *Zend-Avesta.*† The contemporary non-Persian reader is terrified to find that the substantial volumes that survive, though much shorter than our Bible, are but a small fraction of the revelation vouchsafed to Zarathustra by his god.‡ What remains is, to the

---

* If the Vishtaspa who promulgated him was the father of Darius I, the last of these dates seems the most probable.

† Anquetil-Duperron (ca. 1771 A.D.) introduced the prefix *Zend,* which the Persians had used to denote merely a translation and interpretation of the *Avesta.* The last is a word of uncertain origin, probably derived, like *Veda,* from the Aryan root *vid,* to know.[62]

‡ Native tradition tells of a larger *Avesta* in twenty-one books called *Nasks;* these in turn, we are told, were but part of the original Scriptures. One of the *Nasks* remains intact—the *Vendidad;* the rest survive only in scattered fragments in such later compositions as the *Dinkard* and the *Bundahish.* Arab historians speak of the complete text as having covered 12,000 cowhides. According to a sacred tradition, two copies of this were made by Prince Vishtaspa; one of them was destroyed when Alexander burned the royal palace at Persepolis; the other was taken by the victorious Greeks to their own country, and being translated, provided the Greeks (according to the Persian authorities) with all their scientific knowledge. During the third century of the Christian Era Vologesus V, a Parthian king of the Arsacid Dynasty, ordered the collection of all

foreign and provincial observer, a confused mass of prayers, songs, legends, prescriptions, ritual and morals, brightened now and then by noble language, fervent devotion, ethical elevation, or lyric piety. Like our Old Testament it is a highly eclectic composition. The student discovers here and there the gods, the ideas, sometimes the very words and phrases of the *Rig-veda*—to such an extent that some Indian scholars consider the *Avesta* to have been inspired not by Ahura-Mazda but by the *Vedas*;[65] at other times one comes upon passages of ancient Babylonian provenance, such as the creation of the world in six periods (the heavens, the waters, the earth, plants, animals, man,) the descent of all men from two first parents, the establishment of an earthly paradise,[66] the discontent of the Creator with his creation, and his resolve to destroy all but a remnant of it by a flood.[67] But the specifically Iranian elements suffice abundantly to characterize the whole: the world is conceived in dualistic terms as the stage of a conflict, lasting twelve thousand years, between the god Ahura-Mazda and the devil Ahriman; purity and honesty are the greatest of the virtues, and will lead to everlasting life; the dead must not be buried or burned, as by the obscene Greeks or Hindus, but must be thrown to the dogs or to birds of prey.[68]

The god of Zarathustra was first of all ":the whole circle of the heavens" themselves. Ahura-Mazda "clothes himself with the solid vault of the firmament as his raiment; . . . his body is the light and the sovereign glory; the sun and the moon are his eyes." In later days, when the religion passed from prophets to politicians, the great deity was pictured as a gigantic king of imposing majesty. As creator and ruler of the world he was assisted by a legion of lesser divinities, originally pictured as forms and powers of nature—fire and water, sun and moon, wind and

---

fragments surviving either in writing or in the memory of the faithful; this collection was fixed in its present form as the Zoroastrian canon in the fourth century, and became the official religion of the Persian state. The compilation so formed suffered further ravages during the Moslem conquest of Persia in the seventh century.[63]

The extant fragments may be divided into five parts:

(1) The *Yasna*—forty-five chapters of the liturgy recited by the Zoroastrian priests, and twenty-seven chapters (chs. 28-54) called *Gathas*, containing, apparently in metric form, the discourses and revelations of the Prophet;

(2) The *Vispered*—twenty-four additional chapters of liturgy;

(3) The *Vendidad*—twenty-two chapters or *fargards* expounding the theology and moral legislation of the Zoroastrians, and now forming the priestly code of the Parsees;

(4) The *Yashts*, i.e., songs of praise—twenty-one psalms to angels, interspersed with legendary history and a prophecy of the end of the world; and

(5) The *Khordah Avesta* or Small *Avesta*—prayers for various occasions of life.[64]

rain; but it was the achievement of Zarathustra that he conceived his god as supreme over all things, in terms as noble as the Book of Job:

> This I ask thee, tell me truly, O Ahura-Mazda: Who determined the paths of suns and stars—who is it by whom the moon waxes and wanes? . . . Who, from below, sustained the earth and the firmament from falling—who sustained the waters and plants—who yoked swiftness with the winds and the clouds—who, Ahura-Mazda, called forth the Good Mind?[69]

This "Good Mind" meant not any human mind, but a divine wisdom, almost a *Logos*,* used by Ahura-Mazda as an intermediate agency of creation. Zarathustra had interpreted Ahura-Mazda as having seven aspects or qualities: Light, Good Mind, Right, Dominion, Piety, Well-being, and Immortality. His followers, habituated to polytheism, interpreted these attributes as persons (called by them *amesha spenta*, or immortal holy ones) who, under the leadership of Ahura-Mazda, created and managed the world; in this way the majestic monotheism of the founder became—as in the case of Christianity—the polytheism of the people. In addition to these holy spirits were the guardian angels, of which Persian theology supplied one for every man, woman and child. But just as these angels and the immortal holy ones helped men to virtue, so, according to the pious Persian (influenced, presumably, by Babylonian demonology), seven *dævas*, or evil spirits, hovered in the air, always tempting men to crime and sin, and forever engaged in a war upon Ahura-Mazda and every form of righteousness. The leader of these devils was Angro-Mainyus or Ahriman, Prince of Darkness and ruler of the nether world, prototype of that busy Satan whom the Jews appear to have adopted from Persia and bequeathed to Christianity. It was Ahriman, for example, who had created serpents, vermin, locusts, ants, winter, darkness, crime, sin, sodomy, menstruation, and the other plagues of life; and it was these inventions of the Devil that had ruined the Paradise in which Ahura-Mazda had placed the first progenitors of the human race.[71] Zarathustra seems to have regarded these evil spirits as spurious deities, popular and superstitious incarnations of the abstract forces that resist the progress of man. His followers, however, found it easier to think of them as living

---

* Darmesteter believes the "Good Mind" to be a semi-Gnostic adaptation of Philo's *logos theios*, or Divine Word, and therefore dates the *Yasna* about the first century B.C.[70]

beings, and personified them in such abundance that in after times the devils of Persian theology were numbered in millions.[72]

As this system of belief came from Zarathustra it bordered upon monotheism. Even with the intrusion of Ahriman and the evil spirits it remained as monotheistic as Christianity was to be with its Satan, its devils and its angels; indeed, one hears, in early Christian theology, as many echoes of Persian dualism as of Hebrew Puritanism or Greek philosophy. The Zoroastrian conception of God might have satisfied as particular a spirit as Matthew Arnold: Ahura-Mazda was the sum-total of all those forces in the world that make for righteousness; and morality lay in coöperation with those forces. Furthermore there was in this dualism a certain justice to the contradictoriness and perversity of things, which monotheism never provided; and though the Zoroastrian theologians, after the manner of Hindu mystics and Scholastic philosophers, sometimes argued that evil was unreal,[73] they offered, in effect, a theology well adapted to dramatize for the average mind the moral issues of life. The last act of the play, they promised, would be—for the just man—a happy ending: after four epochs of three thousand years each, in which Ahura-Mazda and Ahriman would alternately predominate, the forces of evil would be finally destroyed; right would triumph everywhere, and evil would forever cease to be. Then all good men would join Ahura-Mazda in Paradise, and the wicked would fall into a gulf of outer darkness, where they would feed on poison eternally.[74]

VI. ZOROASTRIAN ETHICS

Man as a battlefield—The Undying Fire—Hell, Purgatory and Paradise—The cult of Mithra—The Magi—The Parsees

By picturing the world as the scene of a struggle between good and evil, the Zoroastrians established in the popular imagination a powerful supernatural stimulus and sanction for morals. The soul of man, like the universe, was represented as a battleground of beneficent and maleficent spirits; every man was a warrior, whether he liked it or not, in the army of either the Lord or the Devil; every act or omission advanced the cause of Ahura-Mazda or of Ahriman. It was an ethic even more admirable than the theology—if men must have supernatural supports for their morality; it gave to the common life a dignity and significance grander than any that could come to it from a world-view that locked upon man (in medieval phrase) as a helpless worm or (in modern terms) as a mechanical automaton. Human beings were not, to Zarathustra's thinking, mere pawns in this cosmic war; they had free will, since Ahura-Mazda wished them to be personalities in their own right; they might freely choose whether they would follow the Light or the Lie. For Ahriman was the Living Lie, and every liar was his servant.

Out of this general conception emerged a detailed but simple code of morals, centered about the Golden Rule. "That nature alone is good which shall not do unto another whatever is not good unto its own self."*[75] Man's duty, says the *Avesta*, is three-fold: "To make him who is an enemy a friend; to make him who is wicked righteous; and to make him who is ignorant learned."[76] The greatest virtue is piety; second only to that is honor and honesty in action and ·peech. Interest was not to be charged to Persians, but loans were to be looked upon as almost sacred.[77] The worst sin of all (in the Avestan as in the Mosaic code) is unbelief. We may judge from the severe punishments with which it was honored that scepticism existed among the Persians; death was to be visited upon the apostate without delay.[78] The generosity and kindliness enjoined by the Master did not apply, in practice, to infidels—i.e., foreigners; these were inferior species of men, whom Ahura-Mazda had deluded into loving their own countries only in order that they should not invade Persia. The Persians, says Herodotus, "esteem themselves to be far the most excellent of men in every respect"; they believe that other nations approach to excellence according to their geographical proximity to Persia, "but that they are the worst who live farthest from them."[79] The words have a contemporary ring, and a universal application.

Piety being the greatest virtue, the first duty of life was the worship of God with purification, sacrifice and prayer. Zoroastrian Persia tolerated neither temples nor idols; altars were erected on hill-tops, in palaces, or in the center of the city, and fires were kindled upon them in honor of Ahura-Mazda or some lesser divinity. Fire itself was worshiped as a god, Atar, the very son of the Lord of Light. Every family centered round the hearth; to keep the home fire burning, never to let it be extinguished, was part of the ritual of faith. And the Undying Fire of the skies, the Sun, was adored as the highest and most characteristic embodiment of

---

* But *Yasna* xlvi, 6 reads: "Wicked is he who is good to the wicked." Inspired works are seldom consistent.

Ahura-Mazda or Mithra, quite as Ikhnaton had worshiped it in Egypt. "The morning Sun," said the Scriptures, "must be reverenced till mid-day, and that of mid-day must be reverenced till the afternoon, and that of the afternoon must be reverenced till evening. . . . While men reverence not the Sun, the good works which they do that day are not their own."[80] To the sun, to fire, to Ahura-Mazda, sacrifice was offered of flowers, bread, fruit, perfumes, oxen, sheep, camels, horses, asses and stags; anciently, as elsewhere, human victims had been offered too.[81] The gods received only the odor; the edible portions were kept for the priests and the worshipers, for as the Magi explained, the gods required only the soul of the victim.[82] Though the Master abominated it, and there is no mention of it in the *Avesta*, the old Aryan offering of the intoxicating *haoma* juice to the gods continued far into Zoroastrian days; the priest drank part of the sacred fluid, and divided the remainder among the faithful in holy communion.[83] When people were too poor to offer such tasty sacrifices they made up for it by adulatory prayer. Ahura-Mazda, like Yahveh, liked to sip his praise, and made for the pious an imposing list of his accomplishments, which became a favorite Persian litany.[84]

Given a life of piety and truth, the Persian might face death unafraid: this, after all, is one of the secret purposes of religion. Astivihad, the god of death, finds every one, no matter where; he is the confident seeker

from whom not one of mortal men can escape. Not those who go down deep, like Afrasyab the Turk, who made himself an iron palace under the earth, a thousand times the height of a man, with a hundred columns; in that palace he made the stars, the moon and the sun go round, making the light of day; in that palace he did everything at his pleasure, and he lived the happiest life: with all his strength and witchcraft he could not escape from Astivihad. . . . Nor he who dug this wide, round earth, with extremities that lie afar, like Dahak, who went from the east to the west searching for immortality and did not find it: with all his strength and power he could not escape from Astivihad. . . . To every one comes the unseen, deceiving Astivihad, who accepts neither compliments nor bribes, who is no respecter of persons, and ruthlessly makes men perish.[85]

And yet—for it is in the nature of religion to threaten and terrify as well as to console—the Persian could not look upon death unafraid unless he had been a faithful warrior in Ahura-Mazda's cause. Beyond that most awful of all mysteries lay a hell and a purgatory as well as a paradise. All dead souls would have to pass over a Sifting Bridge: the good soul would come, on the other side, to the "Abode of Song," where it would be welcomed by a "young maiden radiant and strong, with well-developed bust," and would live in happiness with Ahura-Mazda to the end of time; but the wicked soul, failing to get across, would fall into as deep a level of hell as was adjusted to its degree of wickedness.[86] This hell was no mere Hades to which, as in earlier religions, all the dead descended, whether good or bad; it was an abyss of darkness and terror in which condemned souls suffered torments to the end of the world.[87] If a man's virtues outweighed his sins he would endure the cleansing of a temporary punishment; if he had sinned much but had done good works, he would suffer for only twelve thousand years, and then would rise into heaven.[88] Already, the good Zoroastrians tell us, the divine consummation of history approaches: the birth of Zarathustra began the last world-epoch of three thousand years; after three prophets of his seed have, at intervals, carried his doctrine throughout the world, the Last Judgment will be pronounced, the Kingdom of Ahura-Mazda will come, and Ahriman and all the forces of evil will be utterly destroyed. Then all good souls will begin life anew in a world without evil, darkness or pain.[89] "The dead shall rise, life shall return to the bodies, and they shall breathe again; . . . the whole physical world shall become free from old age and death, from corruption and decay, forever and ever."[90]

Here again, as in the Egyptian *Book of the Dead*, we hear the threat of that awful Last Judgment which seems to have passed from Persian to Jewish eschatology in the days of the Persian ascendancy in Palestine. It was an admirable formula for frightening children into obeying their parents; and since one function of religion is to ease the difficult and necessary task of disciplining the young by the old, we must grant to the Zoroastrian priests a fine professional skill in the brewing of theology. All in all it was a splendid religion, less warlike and bloody, less idolatrous and superstitious, than the other religions of its time; and it did not deserve to die so soon.

For a while, under Darius I, it became the spiritual expression of a nation at its height. But humanity loves poetry more than logic, and without a myth the people perish. Underneath the official worship of Ahura-Mazda the cult of Mithra and Anaita—god of the sun and goddess of

372 THE STORY OF CIVILIZATION (CHAP. XIII

vegetation and fertility, generation and sex—continued to find devotees; and in the days of Artaxerxes II their names began to appear again in the royal inscriptions. Thereafter Mithra grew powerfully in favor and Ahura-Mazda faded away until, in the first centuries of our era, the cult of Mithra as a divine youth of beautiful countenance—with a radiant halo over his head as a symbol of his ancient identity with the sun—spread throughout the Roman Empire, and shared in giving Christmas to Christianity.* Zarathustra, had he been immortal, would have been scandalized to find statues of Anaita, the Persian Aphrodite, set up in many cities of the empire within a few centuries after his death.[91] And surely it would not have pleased him to find so many pages of his revelation devoted to magic formulas for healing, divination and sorcery.[92] After his death the old priesthood of "Wise Men" or Magi conquered him as priesthoods conquer in the end every vigorous rebel or heretic—by adopting and absorbing him into their theology; they numbered him among the Magi and forgot him.[93] By an austere and monogamous life, by a thousand precise observances of sacred ritual and ceremonial cleanliness, by abstention from flesh food, and by a simple and unpretentious dress, the Magi acquired, even among the Greeks, a high reputation for wisdom, and among their own people an almost boundless influence. The Persian kings themselves became their pupils, and took no step of consequence without consulting them. The higher ranks among them were sages, the lower were diviners and sorcerers, readers of stars and interpreters of dreams;[94] the very word *magic* is taken from their name. Year by year the Zoroastrian elements in Persian religion faded away; they were revived for a time under the Sassanid Dynasty (226-651 A.D.), but were finally eliminated by the Moslem and Tatar invasions of Persia. Zoroastrianism survives today only among small communities in the province of Fars, and among the ninety thousand Parsees of India. These devotedly preserve and study the ancient scriptures, worship fire, earth, water and air as sacred, and expose their dead in "Towers of Silence" to birds of prey lest burning or burial should defile the holy elements. They are a people of excellent morals and character, a living tribute to the civilizing effect of Zarathustra's doctrine upon mankind.

---

* Christmas was originally a solar festival, celebrating, at the winter solstice (about December 22nd), the lengthening of the day and the triumph of the sun over his enemies. It became a Mithraic, and finally a Christian, holy day.

VII. PERSIAN MANNERS AND MORALS

*Violence and honor—The code of cleanliness—Sins of the flesh—
Virgins and bachelors—Marriage—Women—Children—
Persian ideas of education*

Nevertheless it is surprising how much brutality remained in the Medes and the Persians despite their religion. Darius I, their greatest king, writes in the Behistun inscription: "Fravartish was seized and brought to me. I cut off his nose and ears, and I cut out his tongue, and I put out his eyes. At my court he was kept in chains; all the people saw him. Later I crucified him in Ecbatana. . . . Ahura-Mazda was my strong support; under the protection of Ahura-Mazda my army utterly smote the rebellious army, and they seized Citrankakhara and brought him to me. Then I cut off his nose and ears and put out his eyes. He was kept in chains at my court; all the people saw him. Afterwards I crucified him."[95] The murders retailed in Plutarch's life of Artaxerxes II offer a sanguinary specimen of the morals of the later courts. Traitors were dealt with without sentiment: they and their leaders were crucified, their followers were sold as slaves, their towns were pillaged, their boys were castrated, their girls were sold into harems.[96] But it would be unfair to judge the people from their kings; virtue is not news, and virtuous men, like happy nations, have no history. Even the kings showed on occasion a fine generosity, and were known among the faithless Greeks for their fidelity; a treaty made with them could be relied upon, and it was their boast that they never broke their word.[97] It is a testimony to the character of the Persians that whereas any one could hire Greeks to fight Greeks, it was rare indeed that a Persian could be hired to fight Persians.*

Manners were milder than the blood and iron of history would suggest. The Persians were free and open in speech, generous, warm-hearted and hospitable.[99] Etiquette was almost as punctilious among them as with the Chinese. When equals met they embraced, and kissed each other on the lips; to persons of higher rank they made a deep obeisance; to those of lower rank they offered the cheek; to commoners they bowed.[100] They thought it unbecoming to eat or drink anything in the street, or publicly to spit or blow the nose.[101] Until the reign of Xerxes the people were abstemious in food and drink, eating only one meal per day, and drinking nothing but

---

* When the Persians fought Alexander at the Granicus practically all the "Persian" infantry were Greek mercenaries. At the battle of Issus 30,000 Greek mercenaries formed the center of the Persian line.[98]

water.[102] Cleanliness was rated as the greatest good after life itself. Good works done with dirty hands were worthless; "for while one doth not utterly destroy corruption" ("germs"?), "there is no coming of the angels to his body."[103] Severe penalties were decreed for those who spread contagious diseases. On festal occasions the people gathered together all clothed in white.[104] The Avestan code, like the Brahman and the Mosaic, heaped up ceremonial precautions and ablutions; great arid tracts of the Zoroastrian Scriptures are given over to wearisome formulas for cleansing the body and the soul.[105] Parings of nails, cuttings of hair and exhalations of the breath were marked out as unclean things, which the wise Persian would avoid unless they had been purified.[106]

The code was again Judaically stern against the sins of the flesh. Onanism was to be punished with flogging; and men and women guilty of sexual promiscuity or prostitution "ought to be slain even more than gliding serpents, than howling wolves."[107] That practice kept its usual distance from precept appears from an item in Herodotus: "To carry off women by violence the Persians think is the act of wicked men; but to trouble one's self about avenging them when so carried off is the act of foolish men; and to pay no regard to them when carried off is the act of wise men; for it is clear that if they had not been willing, they could not have been carried off."[108] He adds, elsewhere, that the Persians "have learnt from the Greeks a passion for boys";[109] and though we cannot always trust this supreme reporter, we scent some corroboration of him in the intensity with which the *Avesta* excoriates sodomy; for that deed, it says again and again, there is no forgiveness; "nothing can wash it away."[110]

Virgins and bachelors were not encouraged by the code, but polygamy and concubinage were allowed; a military society has use for many children. "The man who has a wife," says the *Avesta*, "is far above him who lives in continence; he who keeps a house is far above him who has none; he who has children is far above him who has none; he who has riches is far above him who has none";[111] these are criteria of social standing fairly common among the nations. The family is ranked as the holiest of all institutions. "O Maker of the material world," Zarathustra asks Ahura-Mazda, "thou Holy One, which is the second place where the earth feels most happy?" And Ahura-Mazda answers him: "It is the place whereon one of the faithful erects a house with a priest within, with cattle, with a wife, with children, and good herds within; and wherein afterwards the cattle continue to thrive, the wife to thrive, the child to thrive, the fire to thrive, and every blessing of life to thrive."[112] The animal—above all others the dog—was an integral part of the family, as in the last commandment given to Moses. The nearest family was enjoined to take in and care for any homeless pregnant beast.[113] Severe penalties were prescribed for those who fed unfit food to dogs, or served them their food too hot; and fourteen hundred stripes were the punishment for "smiting a bitch which has been covered by three dogs."[114] The bull was honored for his procreative powers, and prayer and sacrifice were offered to the cow.[115]

Matches were arranged by the parents on the arrival of their children at puberty. The range of choice was wide, for we hear of the marriage of brother and sister, father and daughter, mother and son.[116] Concubines were for the most part a luxury of the rich; the aristocracy never went to war without them.[117] In the later days of the empire the king's harem contained from 329 to 360 concubines, for it had become a custom that no woman might share the royal couch twice unless she was overwhelmingly beautiful.[118]

In the time of the Prophet the position of woman in Persia was high, as ancient manners went: she moved in public freely and unveiled; she owned and managed property, and could, like most modern women, direct the affairs of her husband in his name, or through his pen. After Darius her status declined, especially among the rich. The poorer women retained their freedom of movement, because they had to work; but in other cases the seclusion always enforced in the menstrual periods was extended to the whole social life of woman, and laid the foundations of the Moslem institution of *purdah*. Upper-class women could not venture out except in curtained litters, and were not permitted to mingle publicly with men; married women were forbidden to see even their nearest male relatives, such as their fathers or brothers. Women are never mentioned or represented in the public inscriptions and monuments of ancient Persia. Concubines had greater freedom, since they were employed to entertain their masters' guests. Even in the later reigns women were powerful at the court, rivaling the eunuchs in the persistence of their plotting and the kings in the refinements of their cruelty.[119]*

Children as well as marriage were indispensable to respectability. Sons were highly valued as economic assets to their parents and military assets to the king; girls were regretted, for they had to be brought up for some other man's home and profit. "Men do not pray for daughters," said the Persians, "and angels do not reckon them among their gifts to mankind."[120]

---

* Statira was a model queen to Artaxerxes II; but his mother, Parysatis, poisoned her out of jealousy, encouraged the king to marry his own daughter Atossa, played dice with him for the life of a eunuch, and, winning, had him flayed alive. When Artaxerxes ordered the execution of a Carian soldier, Parysatis bettered his instructions by having the man stretched upon the rack for ten days, his eyes torn out, and molten lead poured into his ears until he died.[119a]

The king annually sent gifts to every father of many sons, as if in advance payment for their blood.[121] Fornication, even adultery, might be forgiven if there was no abortion; abortion was a worse crime than the others, and was to be punished with death.[122] One of the ancient commentaries, the *Bundahish*, specifies means for avoiding conception, but warns the people against them. "On the nature of generation it is said in Revelation that a woman when she cometh out from menstruation, during ten days and nights, when they go near unto her, readily becometh pregnant."[123]

The child remained under the care of the women till five, and under the care of his father from five to seven; at seven he went to school. Education was mostly confined to the sons of the well-to-do, and was usually administered by priests. Classes met in the temple or the home of the priest; it was a principle never to have a school meet near a market-place, lest the atmosphere of lying, swearing and cheating that prevailed in the bazaars should corrupt the young.[124] The texts were the *Avesta* and its commentaries; the subjects were religion, medicine or law; the method of learning was by commission to memory and by the rote recitation of long passages.[125] Boys of the unpretentious classes were not spoiled with letters, but were taught only three things—to ride a horse, to use the bow, and to speak the truth.[126] Higher education extended to the age of twenty or twenty-four among the sons of the aristocracy; some were especially prepared for public office or provincial administration; all were trained in the art of war. The life in these higher schools was arduous: the students rose early, ran great distances, rode difficult horses at high speed, swam, hunted, pursued thieves, sowed farms, planted trees, made long marches under a hot sun or in bitter cold, and learned to bear every change and rigor of climate, to subsist on coarse foods, and to cross rivers while keeping their clothes and armor dry.[127] It was such a schooling as would have gladdened the heart of Friedrich Nietzsche in those moments when he could forget the bright and varied culture of ancient Greece.

VIII. SCIENCE AND ART

Medicine—Minor arts—The tombs of Cyrus and Darius—The palaces of Persepolis—The Frieze of the Archers—Estimate of Persian art

The Persians seem to have deliberately neglected to train their children in any other art than that of life. Literature was a delicacy for which they had small use; science was a commodity which they could import from Babylon. They had a certain relish for poetry and romantic fiction, but they left these arts to hirelings and inferiors, preferring the exhilaration of keen-witted conversation to the quiet and solitary pleasures of reading and research. Poetry was sung rather than read, and perished with the singers.

Medicine was at first a function of the priests, who practised it on the principle that the Devil had created 99,999 diseases, which should be treated by a combination of magic and hygiene. They resorted more frequently to spells than to drugs, on the ground that the spells, though they might not cure the illness, would not kill the patient—which was more than could be said for the drugs.[128] Nevertheless lay medicine developed along with the growing wealth of Persia, and in the time of Artaxerxes II there was a well-organized guild of physicians and surgeons, whose fees were fixed by law—as in Hammurabi's code—according to the social rank of the patient.[129] Priests were to be treated free. And just as, among ourselves, the medical novice practises for a year or two, as interne, upon the bodies of the immigrant and the poor, so among the Persians a young physician was expected to begin his career by treating infidels and foreigners. The Lord of Light himself had decreed it:

> O Maker of the material world, thou Holy One, if a worshiper of God wish to practice the art of healing, on whom shall he first prove his skill—on the worshipers of Ahura-Mazda, or on the worshipers of the *Daevas* (the evil spirits)? Ahura-Mazda made answer and said: On worshipers of the *Daevas* shall he prove himself, rather than on worshipers of God. If he treat with the knife a worshiper of the *Daevas* and he die; if he treat with the knife a second worshiper of the *Daevas* and he die; if he treat with the knife a third worshiper of the *Daevas* and he die, he is unfit forever and ever; let him never attend any worshiper of God. . . . If he treat with the knife a worshiper of the *Daevas* and he recover; if he treat with the knife a second worshiper of the *Daevas* and he recover; if he treat with the knife a third worshiper of the *Daevas* and he recover; then he is fit forever and ever; he may at his will treat worshipers of God, and heal them with the knife.[130]

Having dedicated themselves to empire, the Persians found their time and energies taken up with war, and, like the Romans, depended largely upon imports for their art. They had a taste for pretty things, but they relied upon foreign or foreign-born artists to produce them, and upon

provincial revenues to pay for them. They had beautiful homes and lux-
uriant gardens, which sometimes became hunting-parks or zoological collections; they had costly furniture—tables plated or inlaid with silver or
gold, couches spread with exotic coverlets, floors carpeted with rugs resilient in texture and rich in all the colors of earth and sky;[131] they drank
from golden goblets, and adorned their tables or their shelves with vases
turned by foreign hands;* they liked song and dance, and the playing
of the harp, the flute, the drum and the tambourine. Jewelry abounded,
from tiaras and ear-rings to golden anklets and shoes; even the men
flaunted jewels on necks and ears and arms. Pearls, rubies, emeralds and
lapis lazuli came from abroad, but turquoise came from the Persian mines,
and contributed the customary material for the aristocrat's signet-ring.
Gems of monstrous and grotesque form copied the supposed features of
favorite devils. The king sat on a golden throne covered with golden
canopies upheld with pillars of gold.[133]

Only in architecture did the Persians achieve a style of their own.
Under Cyrus, Darius I and Xerxes I they erected tombs and palaces which
archeology has very incompletely exhumed; and it may be that those
prying historians, the pick and the shovel, will in the near future raise
our estimate of Persian art.† At Pasargadæ Alexander spared for us, with
characteristic graciousness, the tomb of Cyrus I. The caravan road now
crosses the bare platform that once bore the palaces of Cyrus and his
mad son; of these nothing survives except a few broken columns here
and there, or a door-jamb bearing the features of Cyrus in bas-relief. Nearby, on the plain, is the tomb, showing the wear of twenty-four centuries:
a simple stone chapel, quite Greek in restraint and form, rising to some
thirty-five feet in height upon a terraced base. Once, surely, it was a
loftier monument, with some fitting pedestal; today it seems a little bare
and forlorn, having the shape but hardly the substance of beauty; the
cracked and ruined stones merely chasten us with the quiet permanence
of the inanimate. Far south, at Naksh-i-Rustam, near Persepolis, is the
tomb of Darius I, cut like some Hindu chapel into the face of the moun-

---

* One of these vases, shown at the International Exhibition of Persian Art in London,
1931, bears an inscription testifying that it belonged to Artaxerxes II.[132]

† An expedition of the Oriental Institute of the University of Chicago is now engaged
in excavating Persepolis under the direction of Dr. James H. Breasted. In January, 1931,
this expedition unearthed a mass of statuary equal in amount to all Persian sculptures previously known.[134]

tain rock. The entrance is carved to simulate a palace façade, with four slender columns about a modest portal; above it, as if on a roof, figures representing the subject peoples of Persia support a dais on which the King is shown worshiping Ahura-Mazda and the moon. It is conceived and executed with aristocratic refinement and simplicity.

The rest of such Persian architecture as has survived the wars, raids, thefts and weather of two millenniums is composed of palace ruins. At Ecbatana the early kings built a royal residence of cedar and cypress, plated with metal, which still stood in the days of Polybius (ca. 150 B.C.), but of which no sign remains. The most imposing relics of ancient Persia, now rising day by day out of the grasping and secretive earth, are the stone steps, platform and columns at Persepolis; for there each monarch from Darius onward built a palace to defer the oblivion of his name. The great external stairs that mounted from the plain to the elevation on which the buildings rested were unlike anything else in architectural records; derived, presumably, from the flights of steps that approached and encircled the Mesopotamian *ziggurats*, they had nevertheless a character specifically their own—so gradual in ascent and so spacious that ten horsemen could mount them abreast*[135] They must have formed a brilliant approach to the vast platform, twenty to fifty feet high, fifteen hundred feet long and one thousand feet wide, that bore the royal palaces.† Where the two flights of steps, coming from either side, met at their summit, stood a gateway, or propyleum, flanked by winged and human-headed bulls in the worst Assyrian style. At the right stood the masterpiece of Persian architecture—the Chehil Minar or Great Hall of Xerxes I, covering, with its roomy antechambers, an area of more than a hundred thousand square feet—vaster, if size mattered, than vast Karnak, or any European cathedral except Milan's.[138] Another flight of steps led to this Great Hall; these stairs were flanked with ornamental parapets, and their supporting sides were carved with the finest bas-reliefs yet discovered in Persia.[139] Thirteen of the once seventy-two columns of Xerxes' palace stand among the ruins, like palm-trees in some desolate oasis; and these marble columns, though mutilated, are among the nearly perfect works of man. They are slenderer than any columns of Egypt or Greece, and rise to the unusual height

---

* Fergusson pronounced them "the noblest example of a flight of stairs to be found in any part of the world."[136]

† Underneath the platform ran a complicated system of drainage tunnels, six feet in diameter, often drilled through the solid rock.[137]

of sixty-four feet. Their shafts are fluted with forty-eight small grooves; their bases resemble bells overlaid with inverted leaves; their capitals for the most part take the form of floral—almost "Ionic" volutes, surmounted by the forequarters of two bulls or unicorns upon whose necks, joined back to back, rested the crossbeam or architrave. This was surely of wood, for such fragile columns, so wide apart, could hardly have supported a stone entablature. The door-jambs and window-frames were of ornamented black stone that shone like ebony; the walls were of brick, but they were covered with enameled tiles painted in brilliant panels of animals and flowers; the columns, pilasters and steps were of fine white limestone or hard blue marble. Behind, or east of, this Chehil Minar rose the "Hall of a Hundred Columns"; nothing remains of it but one pillar and the outlines of the general plan. Possibly these palaces were the most beautiful ever erected in the ancient or modern world.

At Susa the Artaxerxes I and II built palaces of which only the foundations survive. They were constructed of brick, redeemed by the finest glazed tiles known; from Susa comes the famous "Frieze of the Archers"—probably the faithful "Immortals" who guarded the king. The stately bowmen seem dressed rather for court ceremony than for war; their tunics resound with bright colors, their hair and beards are wondrously curled, their hands bear proudly and stiffly their official staffs. In Susa, as in the other capitals, painting and sculpture were dependent arts serving architecture, and the statuary was mostly the work of artists imported from Assyria, Babylonia and Greece.[140]

One might say of Persian art, as perhaps of nearly every art, that all the elements of it were borrowed. The tomb of Cyrus took its form from Lydia, the slender stone columns improved upon the like pillars of Assyria, the colonnades and bas-reliefs acknowledged their inspiration from Egypt, the animal capitals were an infection from Nineveh and Babylon. It was the *ensemble* that made Persian architecture individual and different—an aristocratic taste that refined the overwhelming columns of Egypt and the heavy masses of Mesopotamia into the brilliance and elegance, the proportion and harmony of Persepolis. The Greeks would hear with wonder and admiration of these halls and palaces; their busy travelers and observant diplomats would bring them stimulating word of the art and luxury of Persia. Soon they would transform the double volutes and stiff-necked animals of these graceful pillars into the smooth lobes of the Ionic capital; and they would shorten and strengthen the shafts to make them bear any entablature, whether of wood or of stone.

Architecturally there was but a step from Persepolis to Athens. All the Near Eastern world, about to die for a thousand years, prepared to lay its heritage at the feet of Greece.

IX. DECADENCE

How a nation may die—Xerxes—A paragraph of murders—Artax-erxes II—Cyrus the Younger—Darius the Little—Causes of decay: political, military, moral — Alexander conquers Persia, and advances upon India

The empire of Darius lasted hardly a century. The moral as well as the physical backbone of Persia was broken by Marathon, Salamis and Platæa; the emperors exchanged Mars for Venus, and the nation descended into corruption and apathy. The decline of Persia anticipated almost in detail the decline of Rome: immorality and degeneration among the people accompanied violence and negligence on the throne. The Persians, like the Medes before them, passed from stoicism to epicureanism in a few generations. Eating became the principal occupation of the aristocracy: these men who had once made it a rule to eat but once a day now inter-preted the rule to allow them one meal—prolonged from noon to night; they stocked their larders with a thousand delicacies, and often served entire animals to their guests; they stuffed themselves with rich rare meats, and spent their genius upon new sauces and desserts.[140a] A corrupt and corrupting multitude of menials filled the houses of the wealthy, while drunkenness became the common vice of every class.[140b] Cyrus and Darius created Persia, Xerxes inherited it, his successors destroyed it.

Xerxes I was every inch a king—externally; tall and vigorous, he was by royal consent the handsomest man in his empire.[141] But there was never yet a handsome man who was not vain, nor any physically vain man whom some woman has not led by the nose. Xerxes was divided by many mistresses, and became for his people an exemplar of sensuality. His defeat at Salamis was in the nature of things; for he was great only in his love of magnitude, not in his capacity to rise to a crisis or to be in fact and need a king. After twenty years of sexual intrigue and administrative indolence he was murdered by a courtier, Artabanus, and was buried with regal pomp and general satisfaction.

Only the records of Rome after Tiberius could rival in bloodiness the royal annals of Persia. The murderer of Xerxes was murdered by

Artaxerxes I, who, after a long reign, was succeeded by Xerxes II, who was murdered a few weeks later by his half-brother Sogdianus, who was murdered six months later by Darius II, who suppressed the revolt of Terituchmes by having him slain, his wife cut into pieces, and his mother, brothers and sisters buried alive. Darius II was followed by his son Artaxerxes II, who at the battle of Cunaxa, had to fight to the death his own brother, the younger Cyrus, when the youth tried to seize the royal power. Artaxerxes II enjoyed a long reign, killed his son Darius for conspiracy, and died of a broken heart on finding that another son, Ochus, was planning to assassinate him. Ochus ruled for twenty years, and was poisoned by his general Bagoas. This iron-livered Warwick placed Arses, son of Ochus, on the throne, assassinated Arses' brothers to make Arses secure, then assassinated Arses and his infant children, and gave the sceptre to Codomannus, a safely effeminate friend. Codomannus reigned for eight years under the name of Darius III, and died in battle against Alexander at Arbela, in the final ruin of his country. Not even the democracies of our time have known such indiscriminate leadership.

It is in the nature of an empire to disintegrate soon, for the energy that created it disappears from those who inherit it, at the very time that its subject peoples are gathering strength to fight for their lost liberty. Nor is it natural that nations diverse in language, religion, morals and traditions should long remain united; there is nothing organic in such a union, and compulsion must repeatedly be applied to maintain the artificial bond. In its two hundred years of empire Persia did nothing to lessen this heterogeneity, these centrifugal forces; she was content to rule a mob of nations, and never thought of making them into a state. Year by year the union became more difficult to preserve. As the vigor of the emperors relaxed, the boldness and ambition of the satraps grew; they purchased or intimidated the generals and secretaries who were supposed to share and limit their power, they arbitrarily enlarged their armies and revenues, and engaged in recurrent plots against the king. The frequency of revolt and war exhausted the vitality of little Persia; the braver stocks were slaughtered in battle after battle, until none but the cautious survived; and when these were conscripted to face Alexander they proved to be cowards almost to a man. No improvements had been made in the training or equipment of the troops, or in the tactics of the generals; these blundered childishly against Alexander, while their disorderly ranks, armed mostly with darts, proved to be mere targets for the long spears and solid phalanxes of the Macedonians.[142] Alexander frolicked, but only after the battle was won; the Persian leaders brought their concubines with them, and had no ambition for war. The only real soldiers in the Persian army were the Greeks.

From the day when Xerxes turned back defeated from Salamis, it became evident that Greece would one day challenge the empire. Persia controlled one end of the great trade route that bound western Asia with the Mediterranean, Greece controlled the other; and the ancient acquisitiveness and ambition of men made such a situation provocative of war. As soon as Greece found a master who could give her unity, she would attack.

Alexander crossed the Hellespont without opposition, having what seemed to Asia a negligible force of 30,000 footmen and 5,000 cavalry.* A Persian army of 40,000 troops tried to stop him at the Granicus; the Greeks lost 115 men, the Persians 20,000.[144] Alexander marched south and east, taking cities and receiving surrenders for a year. Meanwhile Darius III gathered a horde of 600,000 soldiers and adventurers; five days were required to march them over a bridge of boats across the Euphrates; six hundred mules and three hundred camels were needed to carry the royal purse.[145] When the two armies met at Issus Alexander had no more than 30,000 followers; but Darius, with all the stupidity that destiny could require, had chosen a field in which only a small part of his multitude could fight at one time. When the slaughter was over the Macedonians had lost some 450, the Persians 110,000 men, most of these being slain in wild retreat; Alexander, in reckless pursuit, crossed a stream on a bridge of Persian corpses.[146] Darius fled ignominiously, abandoning his mother, a wife, two daughters, his chariot, and his luxuriously appointed tent. Alexander treated the Persian ladies with a chivalry that surprised the Greek historians, contenting himself with marrying one of the daughters. If we may believe Quintus Curtius, the mother of Darius became so fond of Alexander that after his death she put an end to her own life by voluntary starvation.[147]

The young conqueror turned aside now with what seemed foolhardy leisureliness to establish his control over all of western Asia; he did not wish to advance farther without organizing his conquests and building a secure line of communications. The citizens of Babylon, like those of

---

* "All those that were in Asia," says Josephus, "were persuaded that the Macedonians would not so much as come to battle with the Persians, on account of their multitude."[143]

Jerusalem, came out *en masse* to welcome him, offering him their city and their gold; he accepted these graciously, and pleased them by restoring the temples which the unwise Xerxes had destroyed. Darius sent him a proposal of peace, saying that he would give Alexander ten thousand talents* for the safe return of his mother, his wife and his children, would offer him his daughter in marriage, and would acknowledge his sovereignty over all Asia west of the Euphrates, if only Alexander would end the war and become his friend. Parmenio, second in command among the Greeks, said that if he were Alexander he would be glad to accept such happy terms, and avoid with honor the hazard of some disastrous defeat. Alexander remarked that he would do likewise—if he were Parmenio. Being Alexander, he answered Darius that his offer meant nothing, since he, Alexander, already possessed such parts of Asia as Darius proposed to cede to him, and could marry the daughter of the emperor when he pleased. Darius, despairing of peace with so reckless a logician, turned unwillingly to the task of collecting another and larger force.

Meanwhile Alexander had taken Tyre, and annexed Egypt; now he marched back across the great empire, straight to its distant capitals. In twenty days from Babylon his army reached Susa, and took it without resistance; thence it advanced so quickly to Persepolis that the guards of the royal treasury had no time to secrete its funds. There Alexander committed one of the most unworthy acts of his incredible career: against the counsel of Parmenio, and (we are told) to please the courtesan Thaïs,† he burned the palaces of Persepolis to the ground, and permitted his troops to loot the city. Then, having raised the spirits of his army with booty and gifts, he turned north to meet Darius for the last time.

Darius had gathered, chiefly from his eastern provinces, a new army of a million men[148]—Persians, Medes, Babylonians, Syrians, Armenians, Cappadocians, Bactrians, Sogdians, Arachosians, Sacæ and Hindus—and had equipped them no longer with bows and arrows, but with javelins, spears, shields, horses, elephants, and scythe-wielding chariots intended to mow down the enemy like wheat; with this vast force old Asia would make one more effort to preserve itself from adolescent Europe. Alexander, with 7,000 cavalry and 40,000 infantry, met the motley mob at

---

* Probably equivalent to $60,000,000 in contemporary currencies.

† Plutarch, Quintus Curtius and Diodorus agree on this tale, and it does not do violence to Alexander's impetuous character; but one may meet the story with a certain scepticism none the less.

Gaugamela,* and by superior weapons, generalship and courage destroyed it in a day. Darius again chose the better part of valor, but his generals, disgusted with this second flight, murdered him in his tent. Alexander put to death such of the assassins as he could find, sent the body of Darius in state to Persepolis, and ordered it to be buried in the manner of the Achæmenid kings. The Persian people flocked readily to the standard of the conquerer, charmed by his generosity and his youth. Alexander organized Persia into a province of the Macedonian Empire, left a strong garrison to guard it, and marched on to India.

*A town sixty miles from the Arbela which gave the battle its name.

BOOK TWO

INDIA AND HER NEIGHBORS

"The highest truth is this: God is present in all beings. They are His multiple forms. There is no other God to seek. . . . It is a man-making religion that we want. . . . Give up these weakening mysticisms, and be strong. . . . For the next fifty years. . . . let all other gods disappear from our minds. This is the only God that is awake, our own race, everywhere His hands, everywhere His feet, everywhere His ears; He covers everything. . . . The first of all worships is the worship of those all around us. . . . He alone serves God who serves all other beings."

—Vivekananda.[1]

CHRONOLOGICAL TABLE OF INDIAN HISTORY*

B.C.

4000: Neolithic Culture in Mysore
2900: Culture of Mohenjo-daro
1600: Aryan invasion of India
1000-500: Formation of the *Vedas*
800-500: The *Upanishads*
599-527: Mahavira, founder of Jainism
563-483: Buddha
500: Sushruta, physician
500: Kapila and the *Sankhya* Philosophy
500: The earliest *Puranas*
329: Greek invasion of India
325: Alexander leaves India
322-185: The *Maurya Dynasty*
322-298: Chandragupta Maurya
302-298: Megasthenes at Pataliputra
273-232: Ashoka
A.D. 120: Kanishka, Kushan King
120: Charaka, physician
320-530: The *Gupta Dynasty*
320-330: Chandragupta I
330-380: Samudragupta
380-413: Vikramaditya
399-414: Fa-Hien in India
100-700: Temples and frescoes of Ajanta
400: Kalidasa, poet and dramatist
455-500: Hun invasion of India
499: Aryabhata, mathematician
505-587: Varahamihira, astronomer
598-660: Brahmagupta, astronomer
606-648: King Harsha-Vardhana
608-642: Pulakeshin II, Chalukyan King
629-645: Yuan Chwang in India
629-50: Srong-tsan Gampo, King of Tibet
630-800: Golden Age of Tibet
639: Srong-tsan Gampo founds Lhasa
712: Arab conquest of Sind
750: Rise of the Pallava Kingdom
750-780: Building of Borobudur, Java
760: The Kailasha Temple
788-820: Shankara, *Vedanta* philosopher
800-1300: Golden Age of Cambodia
800-1400: Golden Age of of Rajputana
900: Rise of the Chola Kingdom
973-1048: Alberuni, Arab scholar
993: Foundation of Delhi
997-1030: Sultan Mahmud of Ghazni

A.D.

1008: Mahmud invades India
1076-1126: Vikramaditya Chalukya
1114: Bhaskara, mathematician
1150: Building of Angkor Wat
1186: Turkish invasion of India
1206-1526: The *Sultanate of Delhi*
1206-1210: Sultan Kutbu-d Din Aibak
1288-1293: Marco Polo in India
1296-1315: Sultan Alau-d-din
1303: Alau-d-din takes Chitor
1325-1351: Sultan Muhammad bin Tughlak
1336: Foundation of Vijayanagar
1336-1405: Timur (Tamerlane)
1351-1388: Sultan Firoz Shah
1398: Timur invades India
1440-1518: Kabir, poet
1469-1538: Baba Nanak, founder of the Sikhs
1483-1530: Babur founds the *Mogul Dynasty*
1483-1573: Sur Das, poet
1498: Vasco da Gama reaches India
1509-1529: Krishna deva Raya rules Vijayanagar
1510: Portugese occupy Goa
1530-1542: Humayun
1532-1624: Tulsi Das, poet
1542-1545: Sher Shah
1555-1556: Restoration and death of Humayun
1560-1605: Akbar
1565: Fall of Vijayanagar at Talikota
1600: Foundation of East India Co.
1605-1627: Jehangir
1628-1658: Shah Jehan
1631: Death of Mumtaz Mahal
1632-1653: Building of the Taj Mahal
1658-1707: Aurangzeb
1674: The French found Pondicherry
1674-1680: Raja Shivaji
1690: The English found Calcutta
1756-1763: French-English War in India
1757: Battle of Plassey
1765-1767: Robert Clive, Gov. of Bengal
1772-1774: Warren Hastings, Gov. of Bengal
1788-1795: Trial of Warren Hastings

---

* Dates before 1600 A.D. are uncertain; dates before 329 B.C. are guesswork.

CHRONOLOGICAL TABLE OF INDIAN HISTORY

A.D.

1786-1793: Lord Cornwallis, Gov. of Bengal

1798-1805: Marquess Wellesley, Gov. of Bengal

1828-1835: Lord William Cavendish-Bentinck, Governor-General of India

1828: Ram Mohun Roy founds the *Brahma-Somaj*

1829: Abolition of suttee

1836-1886: Ramakrishna

1857: The Sepoy Mutiny

A.D. 1858: India taken over by the British Crown

1861: Birth of Rabindranath Tagore

A.D.

1863-1902: Vivekananda (Narendranath Dutt)

1869: Birth of Mohandas Karamchand Gandhi

1875: Dayananda founds the *Arya-Somaj*.

1880-1884: Marquess of Ripon, Viceroy

1885: Foundation of India National Congress

1889-1905: Baron Curzon, Viceroy

1916-1921: Baron Chelmsford, Viceroy

1919: Amritsar

1921-1926: Earl of Reading, Viceroy

1926-1931: Lord Irwin, Viceroy

1931-   : Lord Willingdon, Viceroy

CHAPTER XIV

The Foundations of India

I. SCENE OF THE DRAMA

The rediscovery of India—A glance at the map—Climatic influences

NOTHING should more deeply shame the modern student than the recency and inadequacy of his acquaintance with India. Here is a vast peninsula of nearly two million square miles; two-thirds as large as the United States, and twenty times the size of its master, Great Britain; 320,000,000 souls, more than in all North and South America combined, or one-fifth of the population of the earth; an impressive continuity of development and civilization from Mohenjo-daro, 2900 B.C. or earlier, to Gandhi, Raman and Tagore; faiths compassing every stage from barbarous idolatry to the most subtle and spiritual pantheism; philosophers playing a thousand variations on one monistic theme from the *Upanishads* eight centuries before Christ to Shankara eight centuries after him; scientists developing astronomy three thousand years ago, and winning Nobel prizes in our own time; a democratic constitution of untraceable antiquity in the villages, and wise and beneficent rulers like Ashoka and Akbar in the capitals; minstrels singing great epics almost as old as Homer, and poets holding world audiences today; artists raising gigantic temples for Hindu gods from Tibet to Ceylon and from Cambodia to Java, or carving perfect palaces by the score for Mogul kings and queens—this is the India that patient scholarship is now opening up, like a new intellectual continent, to that Western mind which only yesterday thought civilization an exclusively European thing.*

---

* From the time of Megasthenes, who described India to Greece ca. 302 B.C., down to the eighteenth century, India was all a marvel and a mystery to Europe. Marco Polo (1254-1323 A.D.) pictured its western fringe vaguely, Columbus blundered upon America in trying to reach it, Vasco da Gama sailed around Africa to rediscover it, and merchants spoke rapaciously of "the wealth of the Indies." But scholars left the mine almost untapped. A Dutch missionary to India, Abraham Roger, made a beginning with his *Open Door to the Hidden Heathendom* (1651); Dryden showed his alertness by writing the play *Aurangzeb* (1675); and an Austrian monk, Fra Paolino de S. Bartolomeo, advanced

The scene of the history is a great triangle narrowing down from the everlasting snows of the Himalayas to the eternal heat of Ceylon. In a corner at the left lies Persia, close akin to Vedic India in people, language and gods. Following the northern frontier eastward we strike Afghanistan; here is Kandahar, the ancient Gandhara, where Greek and Hindu* sculpture fused for a while, and then parted never to meet again; and north of it is Kabul, from which the Moslems and the Moguls made those bloody raids that gave them India for a thousand years. Within the Indian frontier, a short day's ride from Kabul, is Peshawar, where the old northern habit of invading the south still persists. Note how near to India Russia comes at the Pamirs and the passes of the Hindu Kush; hereby will hang much politics. Directly at the northern tip of India is the province of Kashmir, whose very name recalls the ancient glory of India's textile crafts. South of it is the Punjab—i.e., "Land of the Five Rivers"—with the great city of Lahore, and Shimla, summer capital at the foot of the Himalayas ("Home of the Snow"). Through the western Punjab runs the mighty river Indus, a thousand miles in length;

---

the matter with two Sanskrit grammars and a treatise on the *Systema Brahmanicum* (1792).[1a] In 1789 Sir William Jones opened his career as one of the greatest of Indologists by translating Kalidasa's *Shakuntala;* this translation, re-rendered into German in 1791, profoundly affected Herder and Goethe, and—through the Schlegels—the entire Romantic movement, which hoped to find in the East all the mysticism and mystery that seemed to have died on the approach of science and Enlightenment in the West. Jones startled the world of scholarship by declaring that Sanskrit was cousin to all the languages of Europe, and an indication of our racial kinship with the Vedic Hindus; these announcements almost created modern philology and ethnology. In 1805 Colebrooke's essay *On the Vedas* revealed to Europe the oldest product of Indian literature; and about the same time Anquetil-Duperron's translation of a Persian translation of the *Upanishads* acquainted Schelling and Schopenhauer with what the latter called the profoundest philosophy that he had ever read.[2] Buddhism was practically unknown as a system of thought until Burnouf's *Essai sur le Pali* (1826)—i.e., on the language of the Buddhist documents. Burnouf in France, and his pupil Max Müller in England, roused scholars and philanthropists to make possible a translation of all the "Sacred Books of the East"; and Rhys Davids furthered this task by a lifetime devoted to the exposition of the literature of Buddhism. Despite and because of these labors it has become clear that we have merely begun to know India; our acquaintance with its literature is as limited as Europe's knowledge of Greek and Roman literature in the days of Charlemagne. Today, in the enthusiasm of our discovery, we exaggerate generously the value of the new revelation; a European philosopher believes that "Indian wisdom is the profoundest that exists"; and a great novelist writes: "I have not found, in Europe or America, poets, thinkers or popular leaders equal, or even comparable, to those of India today."[3]

* The word *Indian* will be used in this Book as applying to India in general; the word *Hindu,* for variety's sake, will occasionally be used in the same sense, following the custom of the Persians and the Greeks; but where any confusion might result, *Hindu* will be used in its later and stricter sense, as referring only to those inhabitants of India who (as distinct from Moslem Indians) accept one of the native faiths.

its name came from the native word for river, *sindhu,* which the Persians (changing it to *Hindu*) applied to all northern India in their word *Hindustan* —i.e., "Land of the Rivers." Out of this Persian term *Hindu* the invading Greeks made for us the word *India*.

From the Punjab the Jumna and the Ganges flow leisurely to the south-east; the Jumna waters the new capital at Delhi, and mirrors the Taj Mahal at Agra; the Ganges broadens down to the Holy City, Benares, washes ten million devotees daily, and fertilizes with its dozen mouths the province of Bengal and the old British capital at Calcutta. Still farther east is Burma, with the golden pagodas of Rangoon and the sunlit road to Mandalay. From Mandalay back across India to the western airport at Karachi is almost as long a flight as from New York to Los Angeles. South of the Indus, on such a flight, one would pass over Rajputana, land of the heroic Rajputs, with its famed cities of Gwalior and Chitor, Jaipur, Ajmer and Udaipur. South and west is the "Presidency" or province of Bombay, with teeming cities at Surat, Ahmedabad, Bombay and Poona. East and south lie the progressive native-ruled states of Hyderabad and Mysore, with picturesque capitals of the same names. On the west coast is Goa, and on the eastern coast is Pondicherry, where the conquering British have left to the Portuguese and the French respectively a few square miles of territorial consolation. Along the Bay of Bengal the Madras Presidency runs, with the well-governed city of Madras as its center, and the sublime and gloomy temples of Tanjore, Trichinopoly, Madura and Rameshvaram adorning its southern boundaries. And then "Adam's Bridge"—a reef of sunken islands—beckons us across the strait to Ceylon, where civilization flourished sixteen hundred years ago. All these are a little part of India.

We must conceive it, then, not as a nation, like Egypt, Babylonia, or England, but as a continent as populous and polyglot as Europe, and almost as varied in climate and race, in literature, philosophy and art. The north is harassed by cold blasts from the Himalayas, and by the fogs that form when these blasts meet the southern sun. In the Punjab the rivers have created great alluvial plains of unsurpassed fertility;[4] but south of the river-valleys the sun rules as an unchecked despot, the plains are dry and bare, and require for their fruitful tillage no mere husbandry but an almost stupefying slavery.[5] Englishmen do not stay in India more than five years at a time; and if a hundred thousand of them rule three thousand times their number of Hindus it is because they have not stayed there long enough.

Here and there, constituting one-fifth of the land, the primitive jungle remains, a breeding-place of tigers, leopards, wolves and snakes. In the southern third, or Deccan,* the heat is drier, or is tempered with breezes from the sea. But from Delhi to Ceylon the dominating fact in India is heat: heat that has weakened the physique, shortened the youth, and affected the quietist religion and philosophy of the inhabitants. The only relief from this heat is to sit still, to do nothing, to desire nothing; or in the summer months the monsoon wind may bring cooling moisture and fertilizing rain from the sea. When the monsoon fails to blow, India starves, and dreams of Nirvana.

II. THE OLDEST CIVILIZATION?

Prehistoric India—Mohenjo-daro—Its antiquity

In the days when historians supposed that history had begun with Greece, Europe gladly believed that India had been a hotbed of barbarism until the "Aryan" cousins of the European peoples had migrated from the shores of the Caspian to bring the arts and sciences to a savage and benighted peninsula. Recent researches have marred this comforting picture—as future researches will change the perspective of these pages. In India, as elsewhere, the beginnings of civilization are buried in the earth, and not all the spades of archeology will ever quite exhume them. Remains of an Old Stone Age fill many cases in the museums of Calcutta, Madras and Bombay; and neolithic objects have been found in nearly every state.⁶ These, however, were cultures, not yet a civilization.

In 1924 the world of scholarship was again aroused by news from India: Sir John Marshall announced that his Indian aides, R. D. Banerji in particular, had discovered at Mohenjo-daro, on the western bank of the lower Indus, remains of what seemed to be an older civilization than any yet known to historians. There, and at Harappa, a few hundred miles to the north, four or five superimposed cities were excavated, with hundreds of solidly-built brick houses and shops, ranged along wide streets as well as narrow lanes, and rising in many cases to several stories. Let Sir John estimate the age of these remains:

> These discoveries establish the existence in Sind (the northernmost province of the Bombay Presidency) and the Punjab, during the fourth and third millennium B.C., of a highly developed city life; and

---

* From *dakshina*, "right hand" (Latin *dexter*); secondarily meaning "south," since southern India is on the right hand of a worshiper facing the rising sun.

the presence, in many of the houses, of wells and bathrooms as well as an elaborate drainage-system, betoken a social condition of the citizens at least equal to that found in Sumer, and superior to that prevailing in contemporary Babylonia and Egypt. . . . Even at Ur the houses are by no means equal in point of construction to those of Mohenjo-daro.[7]

Among the finds at these sites were household utensils and toilet outfits; pottery painted and plain, hand-turned and turned on the wheel; terracottas, dice and chess-men; coins older than any previously known; over a thousand seals, most of them engraved, and inscribed in an unknown pictographic script; *faïence* work of excellent quality; stone carving superior to that of the Sumerians;[8] copper weapons and implements, and a copper model of a two-wheeled cart (one of our oldest examples of a wheeled vehicle); gold and silver bangles, ear-ornaments, necklaces, and other jewelry "so well finished and so highly polished," says Marshall, "that they might have come out of a Bond Street jeweler's of today rather than from a prehistoric house of 5,000 years ago."[9]

Strange to say, the lowest strata of these remains showed a more developed art than the upper layers—as if even the most ancient deposits were from a civilization already hundreds, perhaps thousands, of years old. Some of the implements were of stone, some of copper, some of bronze, suggesting that this Indus culture had arisen in a Chalcolithic Age —i.e., in a transition from stone to bronze as the material of tools.[10] The indications are that Mohenjo-daro was at its height when Cheops built the first great pyramid; that it had commercial, religious and artistic connections with Sumeria and Babylonia;* and that it survived over three thousand years, until the third century before Christ.†[13] We cannot tell

* These connections are suggested by similar seals found at Mohenjo-daro and in Sumeria (especially at Kish), and by the appearance of the Naga, or hooded serpent, among the early Mesopotamian seals.[11] In 1932 Dr. Henrí Frankfort unearthed, in the ruins of a Babylonian-Elamite village at the modern Tell-Asmar (near Baghdad), pottery seals and beads which in his judgment (Sir John Marshall concurring) were imported from Mohenjo-daro ca. 2000 B.C.[12]

† Macdonell believes that this amazing civilization was derived from Sumeria;[14] Hall believes that the Sumerians derived their culture from India;[15] Woolley derives both the Sumerians and the early Hindus from some common parent stock and culture in or near Baluchistan.[16] Investigators have been struck by the fact that similar seals found both in Babylonia and in India belong to the *earliest* ("pre-Sumerian") phase of the Mesopotamian culture, but to the *latest* phase of the Indus civilization[17]—which suggests the priority of India. Childe inclines to this conclusion: "By the end of the fourth millennium

yet whether, as Marshall believes, Mohenjo-daro represents the oldest of all civilizations known. But the exhuming of prehistoric India has just begun; only in our time has archeology turned from Egypt across Mesopotamia to India. When the soil of India has been turned up like that of Egypt we shall probably find there a civilization older than that which flowered out of the mud of the Nile.*

III. THE INDO-ARYANS

The natives—The invaders—The village community—Caste—Warriors—Priests—Merchants—Workers—Outcastes

Despite the continuity of the remains in Sind and Mysore, we feel that between the heyday of Mohenjo-daro and the advent of the Aryans a great gap stands in our knowledge; or rather that our knowledge of the past is an occasional gap in our ignorance. Among the Indus relics is a peculiar seal, composed of two serpent heads, which was the characteristic symbol of the oldest historic people of India—those serpent-worshiping Nagas whom the invading Aryans found in possession of the northern provinces, and whose descendants still linger in the remoter hills.[20] Farther south the land was occupied by a dark-skinned, broad-nosed people whom, without knowing the origin of the word, we call Dravidians. They were already a civilized people when the Aryans broke down upon them; their adventurous merchants sailed the sea even to Sumeria and Babylon, and their cities knew many refinements and luxuries.[21] It was from them, apparently, that the Aryans took their village community and their systems of land-tenure and taxation.[22] To this day the Deccan is still essentially Dravidian in stock and customs, in language, literature and arts.

B.C. the *material* culture of Abydos, Ur, or Mohenjo-daro would stand comparison with that of Periclean Athens or of any medieval town. . . . Judging by the domestic architecture, the seal-cutting, and the grace of the pottery, the Indus civilization was ahead of the Babylonian at the beginning of the third millennium (ca. 3000 B.C.). But that was a late phase of the Indian culture; it may have enjoyed no less lead in earlier times. Were then the innovations and discoveries that characterize proto-Sumerian civilization not native developments on Babylonian soil, but the results of Indian inspiration? If so, had the Sumerians themselves come from the Indus, or at least from regions in its immediate sphere of influence?"[18] These fascinating questions cannot yet be answered; but they serve to remind us that a history of civilization, because of our human ignorance, begins at what was probably a late point in the actual development of culture.

* Recent excavations near Chitaldrug, in Mysore, revealed six levels of buried cultures, rising from Stone Age implements and geometrically adorned pottery apparently as old as 4000 B.C., to remains as late as 1200 A.D.[19]

The invasion and conquest of these flourishing tribes by the Aryans was part of that ancient process whereby, periodically, the north has swept down violently upon the settled and pacified south; this has been one of the main streams of history, on which civilizations have risen and fallen like epochal undulations. The Aryans poured down upon the Dravidians, the Achæans and Dorians upon the Cretans and Ægeans, the Germans upon the Romans, the Lombards upon the Italians, the English upon the world. Forever the north produces rulers and warriors, the south produces artists and saints, and the meek inherit heaven.

Who were these marauding Aryans? They themselves used the term as meaning noblemen (Sanskrit *arya*, noble), but perhaps this patriotic derivation is one of those after-thoughts which cast scandalous gleams of humor into philology.* Very probably they came from that Caspian region which their Persian cousins called *Airyana-vaejo*—"The Aryan home."† About the same time that the Aryan Kassites overran Babylonia, the Vedic Aryans began to enter India.

Like the Germans invading Italy, these Aryans were rather immigrants than conquerors. But they brought with them strong physiques, a hearty appetite in both solids and liquids, a ready brutality, a skill and courage in war, which soon gave them the mastery of northern India. They fought with bows and arrows, led by armored warriors in chariots, who wielded battle-axes and hurled spears. They were too primitive to be hypocrites: they subjugated India without pretending to elevate it. They wanted land, and pasture for their cattle; their word for war said nothing about national honor, but simply meant "a desire for more cows."[28] Slowly they made their way eastward along the Indus and the Ganges, until all Hindustan‡ was under their control.

---

* Monier-Williams derives *Aryan* from the Sanskrit root *ri-ar*, to plough;[28] cf. the Latin *aratrum*, a plough, and *area*, an open space. On this theory the word *Aryan* originally meant not nobleman but peasant.

† We find such typically Vedic deities as Indra, Mitra and Varuna mentioned in a treaty concluded by the Aryan Hittites and Mitannians at the beginning of the fourteenth century B.C.;[24] and so characteristic a Vedic ritual as the drinking of the sacred *soma* juice is repeated in the Persian ceremony of drinking the sap of the *haoma* plant. (Sanskrit *s* corresponds regularly to Zend or Persian *h*: *soma* becomes *haoma*, as *sindhu* becomes Hindu.[25]) We conclude that the Mitannians, the Hittites, the Kassites, the Sogdians, the Bactrians, the Medes, the Persians, and the Aryan invaders of India were branches of an already heterogeneous "Indo-European" stock which spread out from the shores of the Caspian Sea.

‡ A word applied by the ancient Persians to India north of the Narbada River.

As they passed from armed warfare to settled tillage their tribes gradually coalesced into petty states. Each state was ruled by a king checked by a council of warriors; each tribe was led by a *raja* or chieftain limited in his power by a tribal council; each tribe was composed of comparatively independent village communities governed by assemblies of family heads. "Have you heard, Ananda," Buddha is represented as asking his St. John, "that the Vajjians foregather often, and frequent public meetings of their clans? . . . So long, Ananda, as the Vajjians foregather thus often, and frequent the public meetings of their clan, so long may they be expected not to decline, but to prosper."[27]

Like all peoples, the Aryans had rules of endogamy and exogamy—forbidding marriage outside the racial group or within near degrees of kinship. From these rules came the most characteristic of Hindu institutions. Outnumbered by a subject people whom they considered inferior to themselves, the Aryans foresaw that without restrictions on intermarriage they would soon lose their racial identity; in a century or two they would be assimilated and absorbed. The first caste division, therefore, was not by status but by color;* it divided long noses from broad noses, Aryans from Nagas and Dravidians; it was merely the marriage regulation of an endogamous group.[28] In its later profusion of hereditary, racial and occupational divisions the caste system hardly existed in Vedic times.[29] Among the Aryans themselves marriage (except of near kin) was free, and status was not defined by birth.

As Vedic India (2000-1000 B.C.) passed into the "Heroic" age (1000-500 B.C.)—i.e., as India changed from the conditions pictured in the *Vedas* into those described in the *Mahabharata* and the *Ramayana*—occupations became more specialized and hereditary, and caste divisions were more rigidly defined. At the top were the Kshatriyas, or fighters, who held it a sin to die in bed.[30] Even the religious ceremonials were in the early days performed by chieftains or kings, in the fashion of Cæsar playing *Pontifex*; the Brahmans or priests were then mere assistants at the sacrifice.[31] In the *Ramayana* a Kshatriya protests passionately against mating a "proud and peerless bride" of warrior stock to "a prating priest and Brahman";[32] the Jain books take for granted the leadership of the Kshatriyas, and the Buddhist literature goes so far as to call the Brahmans "low-born."[33] Even in India things change.

---

* The early Hindu word for caste is *varna*, color. This was translated by the Portuguese invaders as *casta*, from the Latin *castus*, pure.

But as war gradually gave way to peace—and as religion, being then largely an aide to agriculture in the face of the incalculable elements, grew in social importance and ritual complexity, and required expert intermediaries between men and gods—the Brahmans increased in number, wealth and power. As educators of the young, and oral transmitters of the race's history, literature and laws, they were able to recreate the past and form the future in their own image, moulding each generation into greater reverence for the priests, and building for their caste a prestige which would, in later centuries, give them the supreme place in Hindu society. Already in Buddha's days they had begun to challenge the supremacy of the Kshatriyas; they pronounced these warriors inferior, even as the Kshatriyas pronounced the priests inferior;[34] and Buddha felt that there was much to be said for both points of view. Even in Buddha's time, however, the Kshatriyas had not conceded intellectual leadership to the Brahmans; and the Buddhist movement itself, founded by a Kshatriya noble, contested the religious hegemony of India with the Brahmans for a thousand years.

Below these ruling minorities were the Vaisyas, merchants and freemen hardly distinct as a caste before Buddha, the Shudras, or workingmen, who comprised most of the native population; and finally the Outcastes or Pariahs—unconverted native tribes like the Chandalas, war captives, and men reduced to slavery as a punishment.[35] Out of this originally small group of casteless men grew the 40,000,000 "Untouchables" of India today.

IV. INDO-ARYAN SOCIETY

Herders—Tillers of the soil—Craftsmen—Traders—Coinage and credit—Morals—Marriage—Woman

How did these Aryan Indians live? At first by war and spoliation; then by herding, tillage and industry in a rural routine not unlike that of medieval Europe; for until the Industrial Revolution in which we live, the basic economic and political life of man had remained essentially the same since neolithic days. The Indo-Aryans raised cattle, used the cow without considering it sacred, and ate meat when they could afford it, having offered a morsel to priests or gods;[36] Buddha, after nearly starving himself in his ascetic youth, seems to have died from a hearty meal of pork.[37] They planted barley, but apparently knew nothing of rice in Vedic times. The fields were divided by each village community among its constituent families, but were irrigated in common; the land could not be sold to an outsider, and could be bequeathed only to the family heirs in direct male line. The majority of the people were yeomen owning their own soil; the Aryans held it a disgrace to work for hire. There were, we are assured, no landlords and no paupers, no millionaires and no slums.[38]

In the towns handicrafts flourished among independent artisans and apprentices, organized, half a thousand years before Christ, into powerful guilds of metal-workers, wood-workers, stone-workers, leather-workers, ivory-workers, basket-makers, house-painters, decorators, potters, dyers, fishermen, sailors, hunters, trappers, butchers, confectioners, barbers, shampooers, florists, cooks—the very list reveals the fulness and variety of Indo-Aryan life. The guilds settled intra-guild affairs, even arbitrating difficulties between members and their wives. Prices were determined, as among ourselves, not by supply and demand but by the gullibility of the purchaser; in the palace of the king, however, was an official Valuer who, like our secretive Bureau of Standards, tested goods to be bought, and dictated terms to the makers.[39]

Trade and travel had advanced to the stage of horse and two-wheeled wagon, but were still medievally difficult; caravans were held up by taxes at every petty frontier, and as like as not by highwaymen at any turn. Transport by river and sea was more developed: about 860 B.C. ships with modest sails and hundreds of oars carried to Mesopotamia, Arabia and Egypt such typical Indian products as perfumes and spices, cotton and silk, shawls and muslins, pearls and rubies, ebony and precious stones, and ornate brocades of silver and gold.[40]

Trade was stunted by clumsy methods of exchange—at first by barter, then by the use of cattle as currency; brides like Homer's "oxen-bearing maidens" were bought with cows.[41] Later a heavy copper coinage was issued, guaranteed, however, only by private individuals. There were no banks; hoarded money was hidden in the house, or buried in the ground, or deposited with a friend. Out of this, in Buddha's age, grew a credit system: merchants in different towns facilitated trade by giving one another letters of credit; loans could be obtained from such Rothschilds at eighteen per cent,[42] and there was much talk of promissory notes. The coinage was not sufficiently inconvenient to discourage gambling; already dice were essential to civilization. In many cases gambling halls were provided for his subjects by the king, in the fashion, if not quite in the style, of Monaco; and a portion of the receipts went to the royal treasury.[43] It seems a scandalous arrangement to us, who are not quite accustomed to having our gambling institutions contribute so directly to the support of our public officials.

Commercial morality stood on a high level. The kings of Vedic India, as of Homeric Greece, were not above lifting cattle from their neighbors;[44] but the Greek historian of Alexander's campaigns describes the Hindus as "remarkable for integrity, so reasonable as seldom to have recourse to lawsuits, and so honest as to require neither locks to their doors nor writings to bind their agreements; they are in the highest degree truthful."[45] The *Rig-veda* speaks of incest, seduction, prostitution, abortion and adultery,[46] and there are some signs of homosexuality;[47] but the general picture that we derive from the *Vedas* and the epics is one of high standards in the relations of the sexes and the life of the family.

Marriage might be entered into by forcible abduction of the bride, by purchase of her, or by mutual consent. Marriage by consent, however, was considered slightly disreputable; women thought it more honorable to be bought and paid for, and a great compliment to be stolen.[48] Polygamy was permitted, and was encouraged among the great; it was an act of merit to support several wives, and to transmit ability.[49] The story of Draupadi,[50] who married five brothers at once, indicates the occasional occurrence, in Epic days, of that strange polyandry—the marriage of one woman to several men, usually brothers—which survived in Ceylon till 1859, and still lingers in the mountain villages of Tibet.[51] But polygamy was usually the privilege of the male, who ruled the Aryan household with patriarchal omnipotence. He held the right of ownership over his wives and his children, and might in certain cases sell them or cast them out.[52]

Nevertheless, woman enjoyed far greater freedom in the Vedic period than in later India. She had more to say in the choice of her mate than the forms of marriage might suggest. She appeared freely at feasts and dances, and joined with men in religious sacrifice. She could study, and might, like Gargi, engage in philosophic disputation.[53] If she was left a widow there were no restrictions upon her remarriage.[54] In the Heroic Age woman seems to have lost something of this liberty. She was discouraged from mental pursuits, on the ground that "for a woman to study the *Vedas* indicates confusion in the realm;"[55] the remarriage of widows became uncommon; *purdah*—the seclusion of women—began; and the practice of suttee, almost unknown in Vedic times, increased.[56] The ideal woman was now typified in the heroine of the *Ramayana*—that faithful Sita who follows and obeys her husband humbly, through every test of fidelity and courage, until her death.

V. THE RELIGION OF THE VEDAS

Pre-Vedic religion—Vedic gods—Moral gods—The Vedic story of Creation—Immortality—The horse sacrifice

The oldest known religion of India, which the invading Aryans found among the Nagas, and which still survives in the ethnic nooks and crannies of the great peninsula, was apparently an animistic and totemic worship of multitudinous spirits dwelling in stones and animals, in trees and streams, in mountains and stars. Snakes and serpents were divinities—idols and ideals of virile reproductive power; and the sacred *Bodhi* tree of Buddha's time was a vestige of the mystic but wholesome reverence for the quiet majesty of trees.[57] Naga, the dragon-god, Hanuman the monkey-god, Nandi the divine bull, and the *Yakshas* or tree-gods passed down into the religion of historic India.[58] Since some of these spirits were good and some evil, only great skill in magic could keep the body from being possessed or tortured, in sickness or mania, by one or more of the innumerable demons that filled the air. Hence the medley of incantations in the *Atharva-veda*, or *Book of the Knowledge of Magic;* one must recite spells to obtain children, to avoid abortion, to prolong life, to ward off evil, to woo sleep, to destroy or harass enemies.*[59]

The earliest gods of the *Vedas* were the forces and elements of nature herself—sky, sun, earth, fire, light, wind, water and sex.[62] Dyaus (the Greek Zeus, the Roman Jupiter) was at first the sky itself; and the Sanskrit word *deva*, which later was to mean divine, originally meant only bright. By that poetic license which makes so many deities, these natural objects were personified; the sky, for example, became a father, Varuna; the earth became a mother, Prithivi; and vegetation was the fruit of their union through the rain.[63] The rain was the god Parjanya, fire was Agni, the wind was Vayu, the pestilential wind was Rudra, the storm was Indra,

---

* Cf. *Atharva-veda*, vi, 138, and vii, 35, 90, where incantations "bristling with hatred," and "language of unbridled wildness" are used by women seeking to oust their rivals, or to make them barren.[60] In the *Brihadaranyaka Upanishad* (6-12) formulas are given for raping a woman by incantation, and for "sinning without conceiving."[61]

the dawn was Ushas, the furrow in the field was Sita, the sun was Surya, Mitra, or Vishnu; and the sacred *soma* plant, whose juice was at once holy and intoxicating to gods and men, was itself a god, a Hindu Dionysus, inspiring man by its exhilarating essence to charity, insight and joy, and even bestowing upon him eternal life.[64] A nation, like an individual, begins with poetry, and ends with prose. And as things became persons, so qualities became objects, adjectives became nouns, epithets became deities. The life-giving sun became a new sun-god, Savitar the Life-Giver; the shining sun became Vivasvat, Shining God; the life-generating sun became the great god Prajapati, Lord of all living things.*[65]

For a time the most important of the Vedic gods was Agni—fire; he was the sacred flame that lifted the sacrifice to heaven, he was the lightning that pranced through the sky, he was the fiery life and spirit of the world. But the most popular figure in the pantheon was Indra, wielder of thunder and storm. For Indra brought to the Indo-Aryans that precious rain which seemed to them even more vital than the sun; therefore they made him the greatest of the gods, invoked the aid of his thunderbolts in their battles, and pictured him enviously as a gigantic hero feasting on bulls by the hundred, and lapping up lakes of wine.[66] His favorite enemy was Krishna, who in the *Vedas* was as yet only the local god of the Krishna tribe. Vishnu, the sun who covered the earth with his strides, was also a subordinate god, unaware that the future belonged to him and to Krishna, his avatar. This is one value of the *Vedas* to us, that through them we see religion in the making, and can follow the birth, growth and death of gods and beliefs from animism to philosophic pantheism, and from the superstition of the *Atharva-veda* to the sublime monism of the *Upanishads*.

These gods are human in figure, in motive, almost in ignorance. One of them, besieged by prayers, ponders what he should give his devotee: "This is what I will do—no, not that; I will give him a cow—or shall it be a horse? I wonder if I have really had *soma* from him?"[67] Some of them, however, rose in later Vedic days to a majestic moral significance. Varuna, who began as the encompassing heaven, whose breath was the storm and whose garment was the sky, grew with the development of his worshipers into the most ethical and ideal deity of the *Vedas*—watching

---

* An almost monotheistic devotion was accorded to Prajapati, until he was swallowed up, in later theology, by the all-consuming figure of Brahma.

over the world through his great eye, the sun, punishing evil, rewarding good, and forgiving the sins of those who petitioned him. In this aspect Varuna was the custodian and executor of an eternal law called Rita; this was at first the law that established and maintained the stars in their courses; gradually it became also the law of right, the cosmic and moral rhythm which every man must follow if he would not go astray and be destroyed.[68]

As the number of the gods increased, the question arose as to which of them had created the world. This primal rôle was assigned now to Agni, now to Indra, now to Soma, now to Prajapati. One of the *Upanishads* attributed the world to an irrepressible Pro-creator:

> Verily, he had no delight; one alone had no delight; he desired a second. He was, indeed, as large as a woman and a man closely embraced. He caused that self to fall *(v pat)* into two pieces; therefrom arose a husband *(pati)* and a wife *(patni)*. Therefore . . . one's self is like a half fragment; . . . therefore this space is filled by a wife. He copulated with her. Therefore human beings were produced. And she bethought herself: "How, now, does he copulate with me after he has produced me just from himself? Come, let me hide myself." She became a cow. He became a bull. With her he did indeed copulate. Then cattle were born. She became a mare, he a stallion. She became a female ass, he a male ass; with her he copulated of a truth. Thence were born solid hoofed animals. She became a she-goat, he a he-goat; she a ewe, he a ram. With her he did verily copulate. Therefore were born goats and sheep. Thus indeed he created all, whatever pairs there are, even down to the ants. He knew: "I, indeed, am this creation, for I emitted it all from myself." Thence arose creation.[69]

In this unique passage we have the germ of pantheism and transmigration: the Creator is one with his creation, and all things, all forms of life, are one; every form was once another form, and is distinguished from it only in the prejudice of perception and the superficial separateness of time. This view, though formulated in the *Upanishads*, was not yet in Vedic days a part of the popular creed; instead of transmigration the Indo-Aryans, like the Aryans of Persia, accepted a simple belief in personal immortality. After death the soul entered into eternal punishment or happiness; it was thrust by Varuna into a dark abyss, half Hades and half hell, or was raised by Yama into a heaven where every earthly joy was made endless and complete.[70] "Like corn decays the mortal," said the *Katha Upanishad*, "like corn is he born again."[71]

In the earlier Vedic religion there were, so far as the evidence goes, no temples and no images;[72] altars were put up anew for each sacrifice as in Zoroastrian Persia, and sacred fire lifted the offering to heaven. Vestiges of human sacrifice occur here,[73] as at the outset of almost every civilization; but they are few and uncertain. Again as in Persia, the horse was sometimes burnt as an offering to the gods.[74] The strangest ritual of all was the *Ashvamedha*, or Sacrifice of the Horse, in which the queen of the tribe seems to have copulated with the sacred horse after it had been killed.*[75] The usual offering was a libation of *soma* juice, and the pouring of liquid butter into the fire.[77] The sacrifice was conceived for the most part in magical terms; if it were properly performed it would win its reward, regardless of the moral deserts of the worshiper.[78] The priests charged heavily for helping the pious in the ever more complicated ritual of sacrifice: if no fee was at hand, the priest refused to recite the necessary formulas; his payment had to come before that of the god. Rules were laid down by the clergy as to what the remuneration should be for each service—how many cows or horses, or how much gold; gold was particularly efficacious in moving the priest or the god.[79] The *Brahmanas*, written by the Brahmans, instructed the priest how to turn the prayer or sacrifice secretly to the hurt of those who had employed him, if they had given him an inadequate fee.[80] Other regulations were issued, prescribing the proper ceremony and usage for almost every occasion of life, and usually requiring priestly aid. Slowly the Brahmans became a privileged hereditary caste, holding the mental and spiritual life of India under a control that threatened to stifle all thought and change.[81]

VI. THE VEDAS AS LITERATURE

Sanskrit and English—Writing—The four "Vedas"—The "Rig-veda"—A Hymn of Creation

The language of the Indo-Aryans should be of special interest to us, for Sanskrit is one of the oldest in that "Indo-European" group of languages to which our own speech belongs. We feel for a moment a strange sense of cultural continuity across great stretches of time and space when

---

* *Ponebatque in gremium regina genitale victimae membrum.*[76]

we observe the similarity—in Sanskrit, Greek, Latin and English—of the numerals, the family terms, and those insinuating little words that, by some oversight of the moralists, have been called the copulative verb.* It is quite unlikely that this ancient tongue, which Sir William Jones pronounced "more perfect than the Greek, more copious than the Latin, and more exquisitely refined than either,"[83] should have been the spoken language of the Aryan invaders. What that speech was we do not know; we can only presume that it was a near relative of the early Persian dialect in which the *Avesta* was composed. The Sanskrit of the *Vedas* and the epics has already the earmarks of a classic and literary tongue, used only by scholars and priests; the very word *Sanskrit* means "prepared, pure, perfect, sacred." The language of the people in the Vedic age was not one but many; each tribe had its own Aryan dialect.[84] India has never had *one* language.

The *Vedas* contain no hint that writing was known to their authors. It was not until the eighth or ninth century B.C. that Hindu—probably Dravidian—merchants brought from western Asia a Semitic script, akin to the Phœnician; and from this "Brahma script," as it came to be called, all the later alphabets of India were derived.[85] For centuries writing seems

---

* Cf. English *one, two, three, four, five* with Sanskrit *ek, dwee, tree, chatoor, panch;* Latin *unus, duo, tres, quattuor, quinque;* Greek *heis, duo, tria, tettara, pente.* (*Quattuor* becomes *four,* as Latin *quercus* becomes *fir.*) Or cf. English *am, art, is* with Sanskrit *asmi, asi, asti;* Latin *sum, es, est;* Greek *eimi, ei, esti.* For family terms cf. p. 357 above. Grimm's Law, which formulated the changes effected in the consonants of a word through the different vocal habits of separated peoples, has revealed to us more fully the surprising kinship of Sanskrit with our own tongue. The law may be roughly summarized by saying that in most cases (there are numerous exceptions):

1. Sanskrit *k* (as in *kratu,* power) corresponds to Greek *k* (*kartos,* strength), Latin *c* or *qu* (*cornu,* horn), German *h, g* or *k* (*hart*), and English *h, g* or *f* (*hard*);

2. Skt. *g* or *j* (as in *jan,* to beget), corresponds to Gk. *g* (*genos,* race), L. *g* (*genus*), Ger. *ch* or *k* (*kind,* child), E. *k* (*kin*);

3. Skt. *gh* or *h* (as in *hyas,* yesterday), corresponds to Gk. *ch* (*chthes*), L. *h, f, g,* or *v* (*heri*), Ger. *k* or *g* (*gestern*), E. *g* or *y* (*yesterday*);

4. Skt. *t* (as in *tar,* to cross) corresponds to Gk. *t* (*terma,* end), L. *t* (*ter-minus*), Ger. *d* (*durch,* through), E. *th* or *d* (*through*);

5. Skt. *d* (as in *das,* ten) corresponds to Gk. *d* (*deka*), L. *d* (*decem*), Ger. *z* (*zehn*), E. *t* (*ten*);

6. Skt. *dh* or *h* (as in *dha,* to place or put) corresponds to Gk. *th* (*ti-the-mi,* I place), L. *f, d* or *b* (*fa-cere,* do), Ger. *t* (*tun,* do), E. *d* (*do, deed*);

7. Skt. *p* (as in *patana,* feather) corresponds to Gk. *p* (*pteros,* wing), L. *p* (*penna,* feather), Ger. *f* or *v* (*feder*), E. *f* or *b* (*feather*);

8. Skt. *bh* (as in *bhri,* to bear) corresponds to Gk. *ph* (*pherein*), L. *f* or *b* (*fero*), Ger. *p, f* or *ph* (*fahren*), E. *b* or *p* (*bear, birth, brother,* etc.).[82]

to have been confined to commercial and administrative purposes, with little thought of using it for literature; "merchants, not priests, developed this basic art."[86] Even the Buddhist canon does not appear to have been written down before the third century B.C. The oldest extant inscriptions in India are those of Ashoka.[87] We who (until the air about us was filled with words and music) were for centuries made eye-minded by writing and print, find it hard to understand how contentedly India, long after she had learned to write, clung to the old ways of transmitting history and literature by recitation and memory. The *Vedas* and the epics were songs that grew with the generations of those that recited them; they were intended not for sight but for sound.* From this indifference to writing comes our dearth of knowledge about early India.

What, then, were these *Vedas* from which nearly all our understanding of primitive India is derived? The word *Veda* means knowledge;† a *Veda* is literally a Book of Knowledge. *Vedas* is applied by the Hindus to all the sacred lore of their early period; like our Bible it indicates a literature rather than a book. Nothing could be more confused than the arrangement and division of this collection. Of the many *Vedas* that once existed, only four have survived:

    I. The *Rig-veda*, or Knowledge of the Hymns of Praise;
    II. The *Sama-veda*, or Knowledge of the Melodies;
    III. The *Yajur-veda*, or Knowledge of the Sacrificial Formulas; and
    IV. The *Atharva-veda*, or Knowledge of the Magic Formulas.

Each of these four *Vedas* is divided into four sections:

    1. The *Mantras*, or Hymns;
    2. The *Brahmanas*, or manuals of ritual, prayer and incantation for the priests;
    3. The *Aranyaka*, or "forest-texts" for hermit saints; and
    4. The *Upanishads*, or confidential conferences for philosophers.‡

---

* Perhaps poetry will recover its ancient hold upon our people when it is again recited rather than silently read.

† Greek *(f)oida*, Latin *video*, German *weise*, English *wit* and *wisdom*.

‡ This is but one of many possible divisions of the material. In addition to the "inspired" commentaries contained in the *Brahmanas* and *Upanishads*, Hindu scholars usually include in the *Vedas* several collections of shorter commentaries in aphoristic form, called *Sutras* (lit., threads, from Skt. *siv*, to sew). These, while not directly inspired from heaven, have the high authority of an ancient tradition. Many of them are brief to the

Only one of the *Vedas* belongs to literature rather than to religion, philosophy or magic. The *Rig-veda* is a kind of religious anthology, composed of 1028 hymns, or psalms of praise, to the various objects of Indo-Aryan worship—sun, moon, sky, stars, wind, rain, fire, dawn, earth, etc.* Most of the hymns are matter-of-fact petitions for herds, crops, and longevity; a small minority of them rise to the level of literature; a few of them reach to the eloquence and beauty of the Psalms.[92] Some of them are simple and natural poetry, like the unaffected wonder of a child. One hymn marvels that white milk should come from red cows; another cannot understand why the sun, once it begins to descend, does not fall precipitately to the earth; another inquires how "the sparkling waters of all rivers flow into one ocean without ever filling it." One is a funeral hymn, in the style of *Thanatopsis*, over the body of a comrade fallen in battle:

> From the dead hand I take the bow he wielded
> To gain for us dominion, might and glory.
> Thou there, we here, rich in heroic offspring,
> Will vanquish all assaults of every foeman.
> Approach the bosom of the earth, the mother,
> This earth extending far and most propitious;
> Young, soft as wool to bounteous givers, may she
> Preserve thee from the lap of dissolution.
> Open wide, O earth, press not heavily upon him,
> Be easy of approach, hail him with kindly aid;
> As with a robe a mother hides
> Her son, so shroud this man, O earth.[93]

Another of the poems (*Rv. x*, 10) is a frank dialogue between the first parents of mankind, the twin brother and sister, Yama and Yami. Yami tempts her brother to cohabit with her despite the divine prohibition of incest, and alleges that all that she desires is the continuance of the race. Yama

---

point of unintelligibility; they were convenient condensations of doctrine, mnemonic devices for students who still relied upon memory rather than upon writing.

As to the authorship or date of this mass of poetry, myth, magic, ritual and philosophy, no man can say. Pious Hindus believe every word of it to be divinely inspired, and tell us that the great god Brahma wrote it with his own hand upon leaves of gold;[89] and this is a view which cannot easily be refuted. According to the fervor of their patriotism, divers native authorities assign to the oldest hymns dates ranging from 6000 to 1000 B.C.[90] The material was probably collected and arranged between 1000 and 500 B.C.[91]

* They are composed in stanzas generally of four lines each. The lines are of 5, 8, 11 or 12 syllables, indifferent as to quantity, except that the last four syllables are usually two trochees, or a trochee and a spondee.

resists her on high moral grounds. She uses every inducement, and as a last weapon, calls him a weakling. The story as we have it is left unfinished, and we may judge the issue only from circumstantial evidence. The loftiest of the poems is an astonishing Creation Hymn, in which a subtle pantheism, even a pious scepticism, appears in this oldest book of the most religious of peoples:

> Nor Aught nor Nought existed; yon bright sky
> Was not, nor heaven's broad woof outstretched above.
> What covered all? what sheltered? what concealed?
> Was it the water's fathomless abyss?
> There was not death—yet was there naught immortal,
> There was no confine betwixt day and night;
> The Only One breathed breathless by itself;
> Other than It there nothing since has been.
> Darkness there was, and all at first was veiled
> In gloom profound—an ocean without light—
> The germ that still lay covered in the husk
> Burst forth, one nature, from the fervent heat.
> Then first came love upon it, the new spring
> Of mind—yea, poets in their hearts discerned,
> Pondering, this bond between created things
> And uncreated. Comes this spark from earth
> Piercing and all-pervading, or from heaven?
> Then seeds were sown, and mighty powers arose—
> Nature below, and power and will above—
> Who knows the secret? who proclaimed it here,
> Whence, whence this manifold creation sprang?
> The gods themselves came later into being—
> Who knows from whence this great creation sprang?
> He from whom all this great creation came,
> Whether his will created or was mute,
> The Most High Seer that is in highest heaven,
> He knows it—or perchance even He knows not.[64]

It remained for the authors of the *Upanishads* to take up these problems, and elaborate these hints, in the most typical, and perhaps the greatest, product of the Hindu mind.

VII. THE PHILOSOPHY OF THE UPANISHADS

The authors—Their theme—Intellect vs. *intuition—Atman—Brah-*
man—Their identity—A description of God—Salvation—In-
fluence of the "Upanishads"—Emerson on Brahma

"In the whole world," said Schopenhauer, "there is no study so beneficial and so elevating as that of the *Upanishads*. It has been the solace
of my life—it will be the solace of my death."[95] Here, excepting the moral
fragments of Ptah-hotep, are the oldest extant philosophy and psychology
of our race; the surprisingly subtle and patient effort of man to understand the mind and the world, and their relation. The *Upanishads* are
as old as Homer, and as modern as Kant.

The word is composed of *upa*, near, and *shad*, to sit. From "sitting
near" the teacher the term came to mean the secret or esoteric doctrine
confided by the master to his best and favorite pupils.[96] There are one
hundred and eight of these discourses, composed by various saints and
sages between 800 and 500 B.C.[97] They represent not a consistent system
of philosophy, but the opinions, *aperçus* and lessons of many men, in
whom philosophy and religion were still fused in the attempt to understand—and reverently unite with—the simple and essential reality underlying the superficial multiplicity of things. They are full of absurdities
and contradictions, and occasionally they anticipate all the wind of
Hegelian verbiage;[98] sometimes they present formulas as weird as that
of Tom Sawyer for curing warts;[99] sometimes they impress us as the profoundest thinking in the history of philosophy.

We know the names of many of the authors,[100] but we know nothing
of their lives except what they occasionally reveal in their teachings.
The most vivid figures among them are Yajnavalkya, the man, and Gargi,
the woman who has the honor of being among the earliest of philosophers.
Of the two, Yajnavalkya has the sharper tongue. His fellow teachers
looked upon him as a dangerous innovator; his posterity made his doctrine the cornerstone of unchallengeable orthodoxy.[101] He tells us how he
tried to leave his two wives in order to become a hermit sage; and in the
plea of his wife Maitreyi that he should take her with him, we catch some
feeling of the intensity with which India has for thousands of years pursued religion and philosophy.

And then Yajnavalkya was about to commence another mode of life.

"Maitreyi!" said Yajnavalkya, "lo, I am about to wander forth from this state. Let me make a final settlement for you and that Katyayani."

Then spake Maitreyi: "If, now, Sir, this whole earth filled with wealth were mine, would I now thereby be immortal?"

"No, no!" said Yajnavalkya. "Of immortality there is no hope through wealth."

Then spake Maitreyi: "What should I do with that through which I may not be immortal? What you know, Sir—that, indeed, explain to me."[102]

The theme of the *Upanishads* is all the mystery of this unintelligible world. "Whence are we born, where do we live, and whither do we go? O ye who know *Brahman*, tell us at whose command we abide here. . . . Should time, or nature, or necessity, or chance, or the elements be considered the cause, or he who is called *Purusha*"—the Supreme Spirit?[103] India has had more than her share of men who wanted "not millions, but answers to their questions." In the *Maitri Upanishad* we read of a king abandoning his kingdom and going into the forest to practice austerities, clear his mind for understanding, and solve the riddle of the universe. After a thousand days of the king's penances a sage, "knower of the soul," came to him. "You are one who knows its true nature," says the king; "do you tell us." "Choose other desires," warns the sage. But the king insists; and in a passage that must have seemed Schopenhauerian to Schopenhauer, he voices that revulsion against life, that fear of being reborn, which runs darkly through all Hindu thought:

> "Sir, in this ill-smelling, unsubstantial body, which is a conglomerate of bone, skin, muscle, marrow, flesh, semen, blood, mucus, tears, rheum, feces, urine, wind, bile and phlegm, what is the good of enjoyment of desire? In this body, which is afflicted with desire, anger, covetousness, delusion, fear, despondency, envy, separation from the desirable, union with the undesirable, hunger, thirst, senility, death, disease, sorrow and the like, what is the good of enjoyment of desires? And we see that this whole world is decaying like these gnats, these mosquitoes, this grass, and these trees that arise and perish. . . . Among other things there is the drying up of great oceans, the falling-away of mountain-peaks, the deviation of the fixed pole-

star, . . . the submergence of the earth. . . . In this sort of cycle
of existence what is the good of enjoyment of desires, when, after
a man has fed upon them, there is seen repeatedly his return here to
the earth?"[104]

The first lesson that the sages of the *Upanishads* teach their selected
pupils is the inadequacy of the intellect. How can this feeble brain, that
aches at a little calculus, ever hope to understand the complex immensity
of which it is so transitory a fragment? Not that the intellect is useless;
it has its modest place, and serves us well when it deals with relations and
things; but how it falters before the eternal, the infinite, or the elementally
real! In the presence of that silent reality which supports all appearances,
and wells up in all consciousness, we need some other organ of perception
and understanding than these senses and this reason. "Not by learning
is the *Atman* (or Soul of the World) attained, not by genius and much
knowledge of books. . . . Let a Brahman renounce learning and become
as a child. . . . Let him not seek after many words, for that is mere weariness of tongue."[105] The highest understanding, as Spinoza was to say,
is direct perception, immediate insight; it is, as Bergson would say, intuition, the inward seeing of the mind that has deliberately closed, as far
as it can, the portals of external sense. "The self-evident *Brahman* pierced
the openings of the senses so that they turned outwards; therefore man
looks outward, not inward into himself; some wise man, however, with
his eyes closed and wishing for immortality, saw the self behind."[106]

If, on looking inward, a man finds nothing at all, that may only prove
the accuracy of his introspection; for no man need expect to find the
eternal in himself if he is lost in the ephemeral and particular. Before
that inner reality can be felt one has to wash away from himself all evil
doing and thinking, all turbulence of body and soul.[107] For a fortnight
one must fast, drinking only water;[108] then the mind, so to speak, is starved
into tranquillity and silence, the senses are cleansed and stilled, the spirit
is left at peace to feel itself and that great ocean of soul of which it is
a part; at last the individual ceases to be, and Unity and Reality appear.
For it is not the individual self which the seer sees in this pure inward
seeing; that individual self is but a series of brain or mental states, it is
merely the body seen from within. What the seeker seeks is *Atman*,* the

---

* The derivation of this word is uncertain. Apparently (as in *Rig.* x, 16), it originally
meant breath, like the Latin *spiritus;* then vital essence, then soul.[109]

Self of all selves, the Soul of all souls, the immaterial, formless Absolute in which we bathe ourselves when we forget ourselves.

This, then, is the first step in the Secret Doctrine: that the essence of our own self is not the body, or the mind, or the individual ego, but the silent and formless depth of being within us, *Atman*. The second step is *Brahman*,* the one pervading, neuter,† impersonal, all-embracing, underlying, intangible essence of the world, the "Real of the Real," "the unborn Soul, undecaying, undying,"[110] the Soul of all Things as *Atman* is the Soul of all Souls; the one force that stands behind, beneath and above all forces and all gods.

> Then Vidagda Sakayla questioned him. "How many gods are there, Yajnavalkya?"
>
> He answered, . . . "As many as are mentioned in the Hymn to All the Gods, namely, three hundred and three, and three thousand and three."
>
> "Yes, but just how many gods are there, Yajnavalkya?"
> "Thirty-three."
> "Yes, but just how many gods are there, Yajnavalkya?"
> "Six."
> "Yes, but just how many gods are there, Yajnavalkya?"
> "Two."
> "Yes, but just how many gods are there, Yajnavalkya?"
> "One and a half."
> "Yes, but just how many gods are there, Yajnavalkya?"
> "One."[111]

The third step is the most important of all: *Atman* and *Brahman* are one. The (non-individual) soul or force within us is identical with the impersonal Soul of the World. The *Upanishads* burn this doctrine into the pupil's mind with untiring, tiring repetition. Behind all forms and

---

* *Brahman* as here used, meaning the impersonal Soul of the World, is to be distinguished from the more personal *Brahma*, member of the Hindu triad of gods (Brahma, Vishnu, Shiva); and from *Brahman* as denoting a member of the priestly caste. The distinction, however, is not always carried out, and *Brahma* is sometimes used in the sense of *Brahman*. *Brahman* as God will be distinguished in these pages from Brahman as priest by being italicized.

† The Hindu thinkers are the least anthropomorphic of all religious philosophers. Even in the later hymns of the *Rig-veda* the Supreme Being is indifferently referred to as *he* or *it*, to show that it is above sex.[112]

veils the subjective and the objective are one; we, in our de-individualized reality, and God as the essence of all things, are one. A teacher expresses it in a famous parable:

"Bring hither a fig from there."
"Here it is, Sir."
"Divide it."
"It is divided, Sir."
"What do you see there?"
"These rather fine seeds, Sir."
"Of these please divide one."
"It is divided, Sir."
"What do you see there?"
"Nothing at all, Sir."
"Verily, my dear one, that finest essence which you do not perceive—verily from that finest essence this great tree thus arises. Believe me, my dear one, that which is the finest essence—this whole world has that as its soul. That is Reality. That is *Atman*. *Tat tvam asi*—that art thou, Shwetaketu."
"Do you, Sir, cause me to understand even more."
"So be it, my dear one."[112]

This almost Hegelian dialectic of *Atman*, *Brahman* and their synthesis is the essence of the *Upanishads*. Many other lessons are taught here, but they are subordinate. We find already, in these discourses, the belief in transmigration,* and the longing for release (*Moksha*) from this heavy chain of reincarnations. Janaka, King of the Videhas, begs Yajnavalkya to tell him how rebirth can be avoided. Yajnavalkya answers by expounding *Yoga*: through the ascetic elimination of all personal desires one may cease to be an individual fragment, unite himself in supreme bliss with the Soul of the World, and so escape rebirth. Whereupon the king, metaphysically overcome, says: "I will give you, noble Sir, the Videhas, and myself also to be your slave."[118] It is an abstruse heaven, however, that Yajnavalkya promises the devotee, for in it there will be no individual consciousness,[119] there will only be absorption into Being, the reunion of

---

* It occurs first in the *Satapatha Upanishad*, where repeated births and deaths are viewed as a punishment inflicted by the gods for evil living. Most primitive tribes believe that the soul can pass from a man to an animal and *vice versa;* probably this idea became, in the pre-Aryan inhabitants of India, the basis of the transmigration creed.[117]

the temporarily separated part with the Whole. "As flowing rivers disappear in the sea, losing their name and form, thus a wise man, freed from name and form, goes to the divine person who is beyond all."[129]

Such a theory of life and death will not please Western man, whose religion is as permeated with individualism as are his political and economic institutions. But it has satisfied the philosophical Hindu mind with astonishing continuity. We shall find this philosophy of the *Upanishads*—this monistic theology, this mystic and impersonal immortality—dominating Hindu thought from Buddha to Gandhi, from Yajnavalkya to Tagore. To our own day the *Upanishads* have remained to India what the *New Testament* has been to Christendom—a noble creed occasionally practised and generally revered. Even in Europe and America this wistful theosophy has won millions upon millions of followers, from lonely women and tired men to Schopenhauer and Emerson. Who would have thought that the great American philosopher of individualism would give perfect expression to the Hindu conviction that individuality is a delusion?

Brahma

If the red slayer thinks he slays,
    Or if the slain thinks he is slain,
They know not well the subtle ways
    I keep, and pass, and turn again.

Far or forgot to me is near;
    Shadow and sunlight are the same;
The vanished gods to me appear;
    And one to me are shame and fame.

They reckon ill who leave me out;
    When me they fly I am the wings;
I am the doubter and the doubt,
    And I the hymn the Brahman sings.

CHAPTER XV

Buddha

I. THE HERETICS

Sceptics—Nihilists—Sophists—Atheists—Materialists—Religions
without a god

THAT there were doubters, even in the days of the *Upanishads*, appears from the *Upanishads* themselves. Sometimes the sages ridiculed the priests, as when the *Chandogya Upanishad* likens the orthodox clergy of the time to a procession of dogs each holding the tail of its predecessor, and saying, piously, "Om, let us eat; Om, let us drink."[1] The *Swasanved Upanishad* announces that there is no god, no heaven, no hell, no reincarnation, no world; that the *Vedas* and *Upanishads* are the work of conceited fools; that ideas are illusions, and all words untrue; that people deluded by flowery speech cling to gods and temples and "holy men," though in reality there is no difference between Vishnu and a dog.[2] And the story is told of Virocana, who lived as a pupil for thirty-two years with the great god Prajapati Himself, received much instruction about "the Self which is free from evil, ageless, deathless, sorrowless, hungerless, thirstless, whose desire is the Real," and then suddenly returned to earth and preached this highly scandalizing doctrine: "One's self is to be made happy here on earth. One's self is to be waited upon. He who makes himself happy here on earth, who waits upon himself, obtains both worlds, this world and the next."[3] Perhaps the good Brahmans who have preserved the history of their country have deceived us a little about the unanimity of Hindu mysticism and piety.

Indeed, as scholarship unearths some of the less respectable figures in Indian philosophy before Buddha, a picture takes form in which, along with saints meditating on *Brahman*, we find a variety of persons who despised all priests, doubted all gods, and bore without trepidation the name of *Nastiks*, No-sayers, Nihilists. Sangaya, the agnostic, would neither admit nor deny life after death; he questioned the possibility of knowledge, and limited philosophy to the pursuit of peace. Purana Kashyapa refused to accept moral distinctions, and taught that the soul is a passive slave to chance. Maskarin Gosala held that fate determines everything, regardless of the merits of men. Ajita Kasakambalin reduced man to earth, water, fire and wind, and said: "Fools and wise alike, on the dissolution of the body, are cut off, annihilated, and after death they are not."' The author of the *Ramayana* draws a typical sceptic in Jabali, who ridicules Rama for rejecting a kingdom in order to keep a vow.

> Jabali, a learned Brahman and a Sophist skilled in word,
> Questioned Faith and Law and Duty, spake to young Ayodhya's lord:
> "Wherefore, Rama, idle maxims cloud thy heart and warp thy mind,
> Maxims which mislead the simple and the thoughtless human-kind? . . .
> Ah, I weep for erring mortals who, on erring duty bent,
> Sacrifice this dear enjoyment till their barren life is spent,
> Who to Gods and to the Fathers vainly still their offerings make.
> Waste of food! for God nor Father doth our pious homage take!
> And the food by one partaken, can it nourish other men?
> Food bestowed upon a Brahman, can it serve our Fathers then?
> Crafty priests have forged these maxims, and with selfish objects say,
> "Make thy gifts and do thy penance, leave thy worldly wealth, and pray!"
> There is no hereafter, Rama, vain the hope and creed of men;
> Seek the pleasures of the present, spurn illusions poor and vain.[5]

When Buddha grew to manhood he found the halls, the streets, the very woods of northern India ringing with philosophic disputation, mostly of an atheistic and materialistic trend. The later *Upanishads* and the oldest Buddhist books are full of references to these heretics.[6] A large class of traveling Sophists—the *Paribbajaka*, or Wanderers—spent the better part of every year in passing from locality to locality, seeking pupils, or antagonists, in philosophy. Some of them taught logic as the art of proving anything, and earned for themselves the titles of "Hair-splitters" and "Eel-wrigglers"; others demonstrated the non-existence of God, and the inexpediency of virtue. Large audiences gathered to hear such lectures and debates; great halls were built to accommodate them; and sometimes princes offered rewards for those who should emerge victorious from these intellectual jousts.' It was an age of amazingly free thought, and of a thousand experiments in philosophy.

Not much has come down to us from these sceptics, and their memory has been preserved almost exclusively through the diatribes of their enemies.[8] The oldest name among them is Brihaspati, but his nihilistic *Sutras* have perished, and all that remains of him is a poem denouncing the priests in language free from all metaphysical obscurity:

> No heaven exists, no final liberation,
> No soul, no other world, no rites of caste. . . .
> The triple *Veda*, triple self-command,
> And all the dust and ashes of repentance—
> These yield a means of livelihood for men
> Devoid of intellect and manliness. . . .
> How can this body when reduced to dust
> Revisit earth? And if a ghost can pass
> To other worlds, why does not strong affection
> For those he leaves behind attract him back?
> The costly rites enjoined for those who die
> Are but a means of livelihood devised
> By sacerdotal cunning—nothing more. . . .
> While life endures let life be spent in ease
> And merriment; let a man borrow money
> From all his friends, and feast on melted butter.[9]

Out of the aphorisms of Brihaspati came a whole school of Hindu materialists, named, after one of them, *Charvakas*. They laughed at the notion that the *Vedas* were divinely revealed truth; truth, they argued, can never be known, except through the senses. Even reason is not to be trusted, for every inference depends for its validity not only upon accurate observation and correct reasoning, but also upon the assumption that the future will behave like the past; and of this, as Hume was to say, there can be no certainty.[10] What is not perceived by the senses, said the *Charvakas*, does not exist; therefore the soul is a delusion, and *Atman* is humbug. We do not observe, in experience or history, any interposition of supernatural forces in the world. All phenomena are natural; only simpletons trace them to demons or gods.[11] Matter is the one reality; the body is a combination of atoms;[12] the mind is merely matter thinking; the

body, not the soul, feels, sees, hears, thinks.¹² "Who has seen the soul existing in a state separate from the body?" There is no immortality, no rebirth. Religion is an aberration, a disease, or a chicanery; the hypothesis
of a god is useless for explaining or understanding the world. Men think
religion necessary only because, being accustomed to it, they feel a sense
of loss, and an uncomfortable void, when the growth of knowledge
destroys this faith.¹⁴ Morality, too, is natural; it is a social convention and
convenience, not a divine command. Nature is indifferent to good and
bad, virtue and vice, and lets the sun shine indiscriminately upon knaves
and saints; if nature has any ethical quality at all it is that of transcendent
immorality. There is no need to control instinct and passion, for these
are the instructions of nature to men. Virtue is a mistake; the purpose of
life is living, and the only wisdom is happiness.¹⁵

This revolutionary philosophy of the *Charvakas* put an end to the age
of the *Vedas* and the *Upanishads*. It weakened the hold of the Brahmans on the mind of India, and left in Hindu society a vacuum which
almost compelled the growth of a new religion. But the materialists had
done their work so thoroughly that both of the new religions which
arose to replace the old Vedic faith were, anomalous though it may sound,
atheistic religions, devotions without a god. Both belonged to the *Nastika*
or Nihilistic movement; and both were originated not by the Brahman
priests but by members of the Kshatriya warrior caste, in a reaction
against sacerdotal ceremonialism and theology. With the coming of
Jainism and Buddhism a new epoch began in the history of India.

II. MAHAVIRA AND THE JAINS

The Great Hero—The Jain creed—Atheistic polytheism—Asceti-
cism—Salvation by suicide—Later history of the Jains

About the middle of the sixth century B.C. a boy was born to a wealthy
nobleman of the Lichchavi tribe in a suburb of the city of Vaishali, in what
is now the province of Bihar.* His parents, though wealthy, belonged to
a sect that looked upon rebirth as a curse, and upon suicide as a blessed
privilege. When their son had reached his thirty-first year they ended
their lives by voluntary starvation. The young man, moved to the depths

---

* Tradition gives Mahavira's dates as 599-527 B.C.; but Jacobi believes that 549-477 B.C.
would be nearer the fact.¹⁶

of his soul, renounced the world and its ways, divested himself of all clothing, and wandered through western Bengal as an ascetic, seeking self-purification and understanding. After thirteen years of such self-denial, he was hailed by a group of disciples as a *Jina* ("conqueror"), i.e., one of the great teachers whom fate, they believed, had ordained to appear at regular intervals to enlighten the people of India. They rechristened their leader *Mahavira*, or the Great Hero, and took to themselves, from their most characteristic belief, the name of *Jains*. Mahavira organized a celibate clergy and an order of nuns, and when he died, aged seventy-two, left behind him fourteen thousand devotees.

Gradually this sect developed one of the strangest bodies of doctrine in all the history of religion. They began with a realistic logic, in which knowledge was described as confined to the relative and temporal. Nothing is true, they taught, except from one point of view; from other points of view it would probably be false. They were fond of quoting the story of the six blind men who laid hands on different parts of an elephant; he who held the ear thought that the elephant was a great winnowing fan; he who held the leg said the animal was a big, round pillar.[17] All judgments, therefore, are limited and conditional; absolute truth comes only to the periodic Redeemers or *Jinas*. Nor can the *Vedas* help; they are not inspired by God, if only for the reason that there is no God. It is not necessary, said the Jains, to assume a Creator or First Cause; any child can refute that assumption by showing that an uncreated Creator, or a causeless Cause, is just as hard to understand as an uncaused or uncreated world. It is more logical to believe that the universe has existed from all eternity, and that its infinite changes and revolutions are due to the inherent powers of nature rather than to the intervention of a deity.[18]

But the climate of India does not lend itself to a persistently naturalistic creed. The Jains, having emptied the sky of God, soon peopled it again with the deified saints of Jain history and legend. These they worshiped with devotion and ceremony, but even them they considered subject to transmigration and decay, and not in any sense as the creators or rulers of the world.[19] Nor were the Jains materialists; they accepted a dualistic distinction of mind and matter everywhere; in all things, even in stones and metals, there were souls. Any soul that achieved a blameless life became a *Paramatman*, or supreme soul, and was spared reincarnation for a while; when its reward had equaled its merit, however, it was born into the flesh again. Only the highest and most perfect spirits could achieve complete "release"; these were the *Arhats,* or supreme lords, who lived like Epicurus' deities in some distant and shadowy realm, impotent to affect the affairs of men, but happily removed from all chances of rebirth.[20]

The road to release, said the Jains, was by ascetic penances and complete *ahimsa*—abstinence from injury to any living thing. Every Jain ascetic must take five vows: not to kill anything, not to lie, not to take what is not given, to preserve chastity, and to renounce pleasure in all external things. Sense pleasure, they thought, is always a sin; the ideal is indifference to pleasure and pain, and independence of all external objects. Agriculture is forbidden to the Jain, because it tears up the soil and crushes insects or worms. The good Jain rejects honey as the life of the bee, strains water lest he destroy creatures lurking in it when he drinks, veils his mouth for fear of inhaling and killing the organisms of the air, screens his lamp to protect insects from the flame, and sweeps the ground before him as he walks lest his naked foot should trample out some life. The Jain must never slaughter or sacrifice an animal; and if he is thoroughgoing he establishes hospitals or asylums, as at Ahmedabad, for old or injured beasts. The only life that he may kill is his own. His doctrine highly approves of suicide, especially by slow starvation, for this is the greatest victory of the spirit over the blind will to live. Many Jains have died in this way; and the leaders of the sect are said to leave the world, even today, by self-starvation.[21]

A religion based upon so profound a doubt and denial of life might have found some popular support in a country where life has always been hard; but even in India its extreme asceticism limited its appeal. From the beginning the Jains were a select minority; and though Yuan Chwang found them numerous and powerful in the seventh century,[22] it was a passing zenith in a quiet career. About 79 A.D. a great schism divided them on the question of nudity; from that time on the Jains have belonged either to the *Shwetambara*—white-robed—sect, or to the *Digambaras*—skyclad or nude. Today both sects wear the usual clothing of their place and time; only their saints go about the streets naked. These sects have further sects to divide them: the Digambaras have four, the Shwetambaras eighty-four;[23] together they number only 1,300,-000 adherents out of a population of 320,000,000 souls.[24] Gandhi has been strongly influenced by the Jain sect, has accepted *ahimsa* as the basis of his policy and his life, contents himself with a loin-cloth, and may starve himself to death. The Jains may yet name him as one of their *Jinas,* another incarnation of the great spirit that periodically is made flesh to redeem the world.

III. THE LEGEND OF BUDDHA

*The background of Buddhism—The miraculous birth—Youth—
The sorrows of life — Flight — Ascetic years — Enlightenment—A vision of "Nirvana"*

It is difficult to see, across 2,500 years, what were the economic, political and moral conditions that called forth religions so ascetic and pessimistic as Jainism and Buddhism. Doubtless much material progress had been made since the establishment of the Aryan rule in India: great cities like Pataliputra and Vaishali had been built; industry and trade had created wealth, wealth had generated leisure, leisure had devel-' oped knowledge and culture. Probably it was the riches of India that produced the epicureanism and materialism of the seventh and sixth centuries before Christ. Religion does not prosper under prosperity; the senses liberate themselves from pious restraints, and formulate philosophies that will justify their liberation. As in the China of Confucius and the Greece of Protagoras—not to speak of our own day—so in Buddha's India the intellectual decay of the old religion had begotten ethical scepticism and moral anarchy. Jainism and Buddhism, though impregnated with the melancholy atheism of a disillusioned age, were religious reactions against the hedonistic creeds of an "emancipated" and worldly leissure class.*

Hindu tradition describes Buddha's father, Shuddhodhana, as a man of the world, member of the Gautama clan of the proud Shakya tribe, and prince or king of Kapilavastu, at the foot of the Himalayan range.[25] In truth, however, we know nothing certain about Buddha; and if we give here the stories that have gathered about his name it is not because these are history, but because they are an essential part of Hindu literature and Asiatic religion. Scholarship assigns his birth to approximately 563 B.C., and can say no more; legend takes up the tale, and reveals to us in

---

* It has often been remarked that this period was distinguished by a shower of stars in the history of genius: Mahavira and Buddha in India, Lao-tze and Confucius in China, Jeremiah and the Second Isaiah in Judea, the pre-Socratic philosophers in Greece, and perhaps Zarathustra in Persia. Such a simultaneity of genius suggests more intercommunication and mutual influence among these ancient cultures than it is possible to trace definitely today.

what strange ways men may be conceived. At that time, says one of the
Jataka books,*

> in the city of Kapilavastu the festival of the full moon . . . had
> been proclaimed. Queen Maya from the seventh day before the full
> moon celebrated the festival without intoxicants, and with abundance
> of garlands and perfumes. Rising early on the seventh day she bathed
> in scented water, and bestowed a great gift of four hundred thou-
> sand pieces as alms. Fully adorned, she ate of choice food, took upon
> herself the *Uposatha* vows,† entered her adorned state bed-chamber,
> lay down on the bed, and falling asleep, dreamt this dream.
>
> Four great kings, it seemed, raised her together with the bed, and
> taking her to the Himalayas, set her on the Manosila table-land. . . .
> Then their queens came and took her to the Anotatta Lake, bathed
> her to remove human stain, robed her in heavenly clothing, anointed
> her with perfumes, and bedecked her with divine flowers. Not far
> away is a silver mountain, and thereon a golden mansion. There
> they prepared a divine bed with head to the east, and laid her upon
> it. Now the *Bodhisattwa*‡ became a white elephant. Not far from
> there is a golden mountain; and going there he descended from it,
> alighted on the silver mountain, approaching it from the direction
> of the north. In his trunk, which was like a silver rope, he held a
> white lotus. Then, trumpeting, he entered the golden mansion, made
> a rightwise circle three times around his mother's bed, smote her
> right side, and appeared to enter her womb. Thus he received . . .
> a new existence.
>
> The next day the Queen awoke and told her dream to the King.
> The King summoned sixty-four eminent Brahmans, showed them
> honor, and satisfied them with excellent food and other presents.
> Then, when they were satisfied with these pleasures, he caused the
> dream to be told, and asked what would happen. The Brahmans
> said: Be not anxious, O King; the Queen has conceived, a male not
> a female, and thou shalt have a son; and if he dwells in a house he

---

* "Birth-stories" of Buddha, written about the fifth century A.D. Another legend, the
Lalitavistara, has been paraphrased by Sir Edwin Arnold in *The Light of Asia*.

† I.e., vows appropriate to the *Uposatha*, or four holy days of the month: the full
moon, the new moon, and the eighth day after either of them.[26]

‡ I.e., one destined to be a Buddha; here meaning *the* Buddha himself. Buddha, meaning
"Enlightened," is among the many titles given to the Master, whose personal name was
Siddhartha, and whose clan name was Gautama. He was also called *Shakya-muni*, or
"Sage of the Shakyas," and *Tathagata*, "One Who Has Won the Truth." Buddha never
applied any of these titles to himself, so far as we know.[27]

will become a king, a universal monarch; if he leaves his house and goes forth from the world, he will become a Buddha, a remover, in the world, of the veil (of ignorance). . . .

Queen Maya, bearing the *Bodhisattwa* for ten months like oil in a bowl, when her time was come, desired to go to her relatives' house, and addressed King Shuddhodhana: "I wish, O King, to go to Deva-daha, the city of my family." The King approved, and caused the road from Kapilavastu to Devadaha to be made smooth and adorned with vessels filled with plantains, flags and banners; and seating her in a golden palanquin borne by a thousand courtiers, sent her with a great retinue. Between the two cities, and belonging to the inhabitants of both, is a pleasure grove of Sal trees named the Lumbini Grove. At that time, from the roots to the tips of the branches, it was one mass of flowers. . . . When the Queen saw it, a desire to sport in the grove arose. . . . She went to the foot of a great Sal tree, and desired to seize a branch. The branch, like the tip of a supple reed, bent down and came within reach of her hand. Stretching out her hand she received the branch. Thereupon she was shaken with the throes of birth. So the multitude set up a curtain for her, and retired. Holding the branch, and even while standing, she was delivered. . . . And as other beings when born come forth stained with impure matter, not so the *Bodhisattwa*. But the *Bodhisattwa*, like a preacher of the Doctrine descending from the seat of Doctrine, like a man descending stairs, stretched out his two hands and feet, and standing unsoiled and unstained by any impurity, shining like a jewel laid on Benares cloth, descended from his mother.[28]

It must further be understood that at Buddha's birth a great light appeared in the sky, the deaf heard, the dumb spoke, the lame were made straight, gods bent down from heaven to assist him, and kings came from afar to welcome him. Legend paints a colorful picture of the splendor and luxury that surrounded him in his youth. He dwelt as a happy prince in three palaces "like a god," protected by his loving father from all contact with the pain and grief of human life. Forty thousand dancing girls entertained him, and when he came of age five hundred ladies were sent to him that he might choose one as his wife. As a member of the Kshatriya caste, he received careful training in the military arts; but also he sat at the feet of sages, and made himself master of all the philosophical theories current in his time." He married, became a happy father, and lived in wealth, peace and good repute.

One day, says pious tradition, he went forth from his palace into the streets among the people, and saw an old man; and on another day he went forth and saw a sick man; and on a third day he went forth and saw a dead man. He himself, in the holy books of his disciples, tells the tale movingly:

> Then, O monks, did I, endowed with such majesty and such excessive delicacy, think thus: "An ignorant, ordinary person, who is himself subject to old age, not beyond the sphere of old age, on seeing an old man, is troubled, ashamed and disgusted, extending the thought to himself. I, too, am subject to old age, not beyond the sphere of old age; and should I, who am subject to old age, . . . on seeing an old man, be troubled, ashamed and disgusted?" This seemed to me not fitting. As I thus reflected, all the elation in youth suddenly disappeared. . . . Thus, O monks, before my enlightenment, being myself subject to birth, I sought out the nature of birth; being subject to old age I sought out the nature of old age, of sickness, of sorrow, of impurity. Then I thought: "What if I, being myself subject to birth, were to seek out the nature of birth, . . . and having seen the wretchedness of the nature of birth, were to seek out the unborn, the supreme peace of Nirvana?"[30]

Death is the origin of all religions, and perhaps if there had been no death there would have been no gods. To Buddha these sights were the beginning of "enlightenment." Like one overcome with "conversion," he suddenly resolved to leave his father,* his wife and his newborn son, and become an ascetic in the desert. During the night he stole into his wife's room, and looked for the last time upon his son, Rahula. Just then, say the Buddhist Scriptures, in a passage sacred to all followers of Gautama,

> a lamp of scented oil was burning. On the bed strewn with heaps of jessamine and other flowers, the mother of Rahula was sleeping, with her hand on her son's head. The *Bodhisattwa*, standing with his foot on the threshold, looked, and thought, "If I move aside the Queen's

---

* His mother had died in giving him birth.

hand and take my son, the Queen will awake, and this will be an obstacle to my going. When I have become a Buddha I will come back and see him." And he descended from the palace.[31]

In the dark of the morning he rode out of the city on his horse Kanthaka, with his charioteer Chauna clinging desperately to the tail. Then Mara, Prince of Evil, appeared to him and tempted him, offering him great empires. But Buddha refused, and riding on, crossed a broad river with one mighty leap. A desire to look again at his native city arose in him, but he did not turn. Then the great earth turned round, so that he might not have to look back.[32]

He stopped at a place called Uruvela. "There," he says, "I thought to myself, truly this is a pleasant spot, and a beautiful forest. Clear flows the river, and pleasant are the bathing-places; all around are meadows and villages." Here he devoted himself to the severest forms of asceticism; for six years he tried the ways of the Yogis who had already appeared on the Indian scene. He lived on seeds and grass, and for one period he fed on dung. Gradually he reduced his food to a grain of rice each day. He wore hair cloth, plucked out his hair and beard for torture's sake, stood for long hours, or lay upon thorns. He let the dust and dirt accumulate upon his body until he looked like an old tree. He frequented a place where human corpses were exposed to be eaten by birds and beasts, and slept among the rotting carcasses. And again, he tells us,

> I thought, what if now I set my teeth, press my tongue to my palate, and restrain, crush and burn out my mind with my mind. (I did so.) And sweat flowed from my arm-pits. . . . Then I thought, what if I now practice trance without breathing. So I restrained breathing in and out from mouth and nose. And as I did so there was a violent sound of winds issuing from my ears. . . . Just as if a strong man were to crush one's head with the point of a sword, even so did violent winds disturb my head. . . . Then I thought, what if I were to take food only in small amounts, as much as my hollowed palm would hold, juices of beans, vetches, chick-peas, or pulse. . . . My body became extremely lean. The mark of my seat was like a camel's foot-print through the little food. The bones of my spine, when bent and straightened, were like a row of spindles through the little food. And as, in a deep well, the deep, low-lying sparkling of the waters is seen, so in my eye-sockets was seen the deep, low-lying

sparkling of my eyes through the little food. And as a bitter gourd, cut off raw, is cracked and withered through rain and sun, so was the skin of my head withered through the little food. When I thought I would touch the skin of my stomach I actually took hold of my spine. . . . When I thought I would ease myself I thereupon fell prone through the little food. To relieve my body I stroked my limbs with my hand, and as I did so the decayed hairs fell from my body through the little food.[33]

But one day the thought came to Buddha that self-mortification was not the way. Perhaps he was unusually hungry on that day, or some memory of loveliness stirred within him. He perceived that no new enlightenment had come to him from these austerities. "By this severity I do not attain superhuman—truly noble—knowledge and insight." On the contrary, a certain pride in his self-torture had poisoned any holiness that might have grown from it. He abandoned his asceticism, went to sit under a shade-giving tree,* and remained there steadfast and motionless, resolving never to leave that seat until enlightenment came to him. What, he asked himself, was the source of human sorrow, suffering, sickness, old age and death? Suddenly a vision came to him of the infinite succession of deaths and births in the stream of life: he saw every death frustrated with new birth, every peace and joy balanced with new desire and discontent, new disappointment, new grief and pain. "Thus, with mind concentrated, purified, cleansed, . . . I directed my mind to the passing away and rebirth of beings. With divine, purified, superhuman vision I saw beings passing away and being reborn, low and high, of good and bad color, in happy or miserable existences, according to their *karma*"— according to that universal law by which every act of good or of evil will be rewarded or punished in this life, or in some later incarnation of the soul.

It was the vision of this apparently ridiculous succession of deaths and births that made Buddha scorn human life. Birth, he told himself, is the origin of all evil. And yet birth continues endlessly, forever replenishing the stream of human sorrow. If birth could be stopped. . . . Why is birth not stopped? † Because the law of *karma* demands new reincarnations in which the soul may atone for evil done in past existences.

---

* The *Bodhi*-tree of later Buddhist worship, still shown to tourists at Bodh-gaya.
† The philosophy of Schopenhauer stems from this point.

If, however, a man could live a life of perfect justice, of unvarying patience and kindness to all, if he could tie his thoughts to eternal things, not binding his heart to those that begin and pass away—then, perhaps, he would be spared rebirth, and for him the fountain of evil would run dry. If one could still all desires for one's self, and seek only to do good, then individuality, that first and worst delusion of mankind, might be overcome, and the soul would merge at last with unconscious infinity. What peace there would be in the heart that had cleansed itself of every personal desire!—and what heart that had not so cleansed itself could ever know peace? Happiness is possible neither here, as paganism thinks, nor hereafter, as many religions think. Only peace is possible, only the cool quietude of craving ended, only *Nirvana.*

And so, after seven years of meditation, the Enlightened One, having learned the cause of human suffering, went forth to the Holy City of Benares, and there, in the deer-park at Sarnath, preached *Nirvana* to men.

IV. THE TEACHING OF BUDDHA*

*Portrait of the Master—His methods—The Four Noble Truths—
The Eightfold Way—The Five Moral Rules—Buddha and
Christ—Buddha's agnosticism and anti-clericalism—His
Atheism — His soul-less psychology — The mean-
ing of "Nirvana"*

Like the other teachers of his time, Buddha taught through conversation, lectures, and parables. Since it never occurred to him, any more than to Socrates or Christ, to put his doctrine into writing, he summarized it in *sutras* ("threads") designed to prompt the memory. As preserved for us in the remembrance of his followers these discourses unconsciously portray for us the first distinct character in India's history: a

---

* The oldest extant documents purporting to be the teaching of Buddha are the *Pitakas,* or "Baskets of the Law," prepared for the Buddhist Council of 241 B.C., accepted by it as genuine, transmitted orally for four centuries from the death of Buddha, and finally put into writing, in the Pali tongue, about 80 B.C. These *Pitakas* are divided into three groups: the *Sutta,* or tales; the *Vinaya,* or discipline; and the *Abhidhamma,* or doctrine. The *Sutta-pitaka* contains the dialogues of Buddha, which Rhys Davids ranks with those of Plato.[34] Strictly speaking, however, these writings give us the teaching not necessarily of Buddha himself, but only of the Buddhist schools. "Though these narratives," says Sir Charles Eliot, "are compilations which accepted new matter during several centuries, I see no reason to doubt that the oldest stratum contains the recollections of those who had seen and heard the master."[35]

man of strong will, authoritative and proud, but of gentle manner and speech, and of infinite benevolence. He claimed "enlightenment," but not inspiration; he never pretended that a god was speaking through him. In controversy he was more patient and considerate than any other of the great teachers of mankind. His disciples, perhaps idealizing him, represented him as fully practising *ahimsa*: "putting away the killing of living things, Gautama the recluse holds aloof from the destruction of life. He" (once a Kshatriya warrior) "has laid the cudgel and the sword aside, and ashamed of roughness, and full of mercy, he dwells compassionate and kind to all creatures that have life. . . . Putting away slander, Gautama holds himself aloof from calumny. . . . Thus does he live as a binder-together of those who are divided, an encourager of those who are friends, a peacemaker, a lover of peace, impassioned for peace, a speaker of words that make for peace."[36] Like Lao-tze and Christ he wished to return good for evil, love for hate; and he remained silent under misunderstanding and abuse. "If a man foolishly does me wrong, I will return to him the protection of my ungrudging love; the more evil comes from him, the more good shall come from me." When a simpleton abused him, Buddhā listened in silence; but when the man had finished, Buddha asked him: "Son, if a man declined to accept a present made to him, to whom would it belong?" The man answered: "To him who offered it." "My son," said Buddha, "I decline to accept your abuse, and request you to keep it for yourself."[37] Unlike most saints, Buddha had a sense of humor, and knew that metaphysics without laughter is immodesty.

His method of teaching was unique, though it owed something to the Wanderers, or traveling Sophists, of his time. He walked from town to town, accompanied by his favorite disciples, and followed by as many as twelve hundred devotees. He took no thought for the morrow, but was content to be fed by some local admirer; once he scandalized his followers by eating in the home of a courtesan.[38] He stopped at the outskirts of a village, and pitched camp in some garden or wood, or on some river-bank. The afternoon he gave to meditation, the evening to instruction. His discourses took the form of Socratic questioning, moral parables, courteous controversy, or succinct formulas whereby he sought to compress his teaching into convenient brevity and order. His favorite *sutra* was the "Four Noble Truths," in which he expounded his view that life is pain, that pain is due to desire, and that wisdom lies in stilling all desire.

1. Now this, O monks, is the noble truth of pain: birth is painful, sickness is painful, old age is painful, sorrow, lamentation, dejection and despair are painful. . . .

2. Now, this, O monks, is the noble truth of the cause of pain: that craving, which leads to rebirth, combined with pleasure and lust, finding pleasure here and there, namely, the craving for passion, the craving for existence, the craving for non-existence.

3. Now this, O monks, is the noble truth of the cessation of pain: the cessation, without a remainder, of that craving; abandonment, forsaking, release, non-attachment.

4. Now this, O monks, is the noble truth of the way that leads to the cessation of pain: this is the noble Eightfold Way: namely, right views, right intention, right speech, right action, right living, right effort, right mindfulness, right concentration.[39]

Buddha was convinced that pain so overbalanced pleasure in human life that it would be better never to have been born. More tears have flowed, he tells us, than all the water that is in the four great oceans.[40] Every pleasure seemed poisoned for him by its brevity. "Is that which is impermanent, sorrow or joy?" he asks one of his disciples; and the answer is, "Sorrow, Lord."[41] The basic evil, then, is *tanha*—not all desire, but selfish desire, desire directed to the advantage of the part rather than to the good of the whole; above all, sexual desire, for that leads to reproduction, which stretches out the chain of life into new suffering aimlessly. One of his disciples concluded that Buddha would approve of suicide, but Buddha reproved him; suicide would be useless, since the soul, unpurified, would be reborn in other incarnations until it achieved complete forgetfulness of self.

When his disciples asked him to define more clearly his conception of right living, he formulated for their guidance "Five Moral Rules"—commandments simple and brief, but "perhaps more comprehensive, and harder to keep, than the Decalogue":[42]

1. Let not one kill any living being.
2. Let not one take what is not given to him.
3. Let not one speak falsely.
4. Let not one drink intoxicating drinks.
5. Let not one be unchaste.[43]

Elsewhere Buddha introduced elements into his teaching strangely anticipatory of Christ. "Let a man overcome anger by kindness, evil by good. . . . Victory breeds hatred, for the conquered is unhappy. . . . Never in the world does hatred cease by hatred; hatred ceases by love."⁴⁴ Like Jesus he was uncomfortable in the presence of women, and hesitated long before admitting them into the Buddhist order. His favorite disciple, Ananda, once asked him:

> "How are we to conduct ourselves, Lord, with regards to woman-kind?"
> "As not seeing them, Ananda."
> "But if we should see them, what are we to do?"
> "No talking, Ananda."
> "But if they should speak to us, Lord, what are we to do?"
> "Keep wide awake, Ananda."⁴⁵

His conception of religion was purely ethical; he cared everything about conduct, nothing about ritual or worship, metaphysics or theology. When a Brahman proposed to purify himself of his sins by bathing at Gaya, Buddha said to him: "Have thy bath here, even here, O Brahman. Be kind to all beings. If thou speakest not false, if thou killest not life, if thou takest not what is not given to thee, secure in self-denial—what wouldst thou gain by going to Gaya? Any water is Gaya to thee."⁴⁶ There is nothing stranger in the history of religion than the sight of Buddha founding a worldwide religion, and yet refusing to be drawn into any discussion about eternity, immortality, or God. The infinite is a myth, he says, a fiction of philosophers who have not the modesty to confess that an atom can never understand the cosmos. He smiles⁴⁷ at the debate over the finity or infinity of the universe, quite as if he foresaw the futile astromythology of physicists and mathematicians who debate the same question today. He refuses to express any opinion as to whether the world had a beginning or will have an end; whether the soul is the same as the body, or distinct from it; whether, even for the greatest saint, there is to be any reward in any heaven. He calls such questions "the jungle, the desert, the puppet-show, the writhing, the entanglement, of speculation,"⁴⁸ and will have nothing to do with them; they lead only to feverish disputation, personal resentments, and sorrow; they never lead to wisdom and peace. Saintliness and content lie not in knowledge of the universe and God, but simply in selfless and beneficent living.⁴⁹ And then, with scandalous humor, he suggests that the gods themselves, if they existed, could not answer these questions.

Once upon a time, Kevaddha, there occurred to a certain brother in this very company of the brethren a doubt on the following point: "Where now do these four great elements—earth, water, fire and wind—pass away, leaving no trace behind?" So that brother worked himself up into such a state of ecstasy that the way leading to the world of the Gods became clear to his ecstatic vision.

Then that brother, Kevaddha, went up to the realm of the Four Great Kings, and said to the gods thereof: "Where, my friends, do the four great elements—earth, water, fire and wind—cease, leaving no trace behind?"

And when he had thus spoken the gods in the Heaven of the Four Great Kings said to him: "We, brother, do not know that. But there are the Four Great Kings, more potent and more glorious than we. They will know it."

Then that brother, Kevaddha, went to the Four Great Kings (and put the same question, and was sent on, by a similar reply, to the Thirty-three, who sent him on to their king, Sakka; who sent him on to the Yama gods, who sent him on to their king, Suyama; who sent him on to the Tusita gods, who sent him on to their king, Santusita; who sent him on to the Nimmana-rati gods, who sent him on to their king, Sunimmita; who sent him on to the Para-nimmita Vasavatti gods, who sent him on to their king, Vasavatti, who sent him on to the gods of the Brahma-world).

Then that brother, Kevaddha, became so absorbed by self-concentration that the way to the Brahma-world became clear to his mind thus pacified. And he drew near to the gods of the retinue of Brahma, and said: "Where, my friends, do the four great elements—earth, water, fire and wind—cease, leaving no trace behind?"

And when he had thus spoken, the gods of the retinue of Brahma replied: "We, brother, do not know that. But there is Brahma, the great Brahma, the Supreme One, the Mighty One, the All-seeing One, the Ruler, the Lord of all, the Controller, the Creator, the Chief of all, . . . the Ancient of days, the Father of all that are and are to be! He is more potent and more glorious than we. He will know it."

"Where, then, is that great Brahma now?"

"We, brother, know not where Brahma is, nor why Brahma is,

nor whence. But, brother, when the signs of his coming appear, when the light ariseth, and the glory shineth, then will he be manifest. For that is the portent of the manifestation of Brahma when the light ariseth, and the glory shineth."

And it was not long, Kevaddha, before that great Brahma became manifest. And that brother drew near to him, and said: "Where, my friend, do the four great elements—earth, water, fire and wind—cease, leaving no trace behind?"

And when he had thus spoken that great Brahma said to him: "I, brother, am the great Brahma, the Supreme, the Mighty, the All-seeing, the Ruler, the Lord of all, the Controller, the Creator, the Chief of all, appointing to each his place, the Ancient of days, the Father of all that are and are to be!"

Then that brother answered Brahma, and said: "I did not ask you, friend, as to whether you were indeed all that you now say. But I ask you where the four great elements—earth, water, fire and wind—cease, leaving no trace behind?"

Then again, Kevaddha, Brahma gave the same reply. And that brother yet a third time put to Brahma his question as before.

Then, Kevaddha, the great Brahma took that brother and led him aside, and said: "These gods, the retinue of Brahma, hold me, brother, to be such that there is nothing I cannot see, nothing I have not understood, nothing I have not realized. Therefore I gave no answer in their presence. I do not know, brother, where those four great elements—earth, water, fire and wind—cease, leaving no trace behind."[50]

When some students remind him that the Brahmans claim to know the solutions of these problems, he laughs them off: "There are, brethren, some recluses and Brahmans who wriggle like eels; and when a question is put to them on this or that they resort to equivocation, to eel-wriggling."[51] If ever he is sharp it is against the priests of his time; he scorns their assumption that the *Vedas* were inspired by the gods,[52] and he scandalizes the caste-proud Brahmans by accepting into his order the members of any caste. He does not explicitly condemn the caste-system, but he tells his disciples, plainly enough: "Go into all lands and preach this gospel. Tell them that the poor and the lowly, the rich and the high, are all one, and that all castes unite in this religion as do the rivers in the sea."[53] He denounces the notion of sacrificing to the gods, and looks with horror upon the slaughter of animals for these rites;[54] he rejects all cult and worship of supernatural beings, all *mantras* and incantations, all asceticism and all prayer.[55] Quietly, and without controversy, he offers a religion absolutely free of dogma and priestcraft, and proclaims a way of salvation open to infidels and believers alike.

At times this most famous of Hindu saints passes from agnosticism to outright atheism.[56]* He does not go out of his way to deny deity, and occasionally he speaks as if Brahma were a reality rather than an ideal;[58] nor does he forbid the popular worship of the gods.[59] But he smiles at the notion of sending up prayers to the Unknowable; "it is foolish," he says, "to suppose that another can cause us happiness or misery"[60]—these are always the product of our own behavior and our own desires. He refuses to rest his moral code upon supernatural sanctions of any kind; he offers no heaven, no purgatory, and no hell.[61] He is too sensitive to the suffering and killing involved in the biological process to suppose that they have been consciously willed by a personal divinity; these cosmic blunders, he thinks, outweigh the evidences of design.[62] In this scene of order and confusion, of good and evil, he finds no principle of permanence, no center of everlasting reality,[63] but only a whirl and flux of obstinate life, in which the one metaphysical ultimate is change.

As he proposes a theology without a deity, so he offers a psychology without a soul; he repudiates animism in every form, even in the case of man. He agrees with Heraclitus and Bergson about the world, and with Hume about the mind. All that we know is our sensations; therefore, so far as we can see, all matter is force, all substance is motion. Life is change, a neutral stream of becoming and extinction; the "soul" is a myth which, for the convenience of our weak brains, we unwarrantably posit behind the flow of conscious states.[64] This "transcendental unity of apperception," this "mind" that weaves sensations and perceptions into thought, is a ghost; all that exists is the sensations and perceptions themselves, falling automatically into memories and ideas.[65] Even the precious "ego" is not an entity distinct from these mental states; it is merely the continuity of these states, the remembrance of earlier by later states, together with the mental and moral habits, the dispositions and tendencies, of the organism.[66] The succession of these states is caused not by a mythical "will" superadded to them, but by the determinism of heredity, habit,

---

* In Buddha, says Sir Charles Eliot, "the world is not thought of as the handiwork of a divine personality, nor the moral law as his will. The fact that religion can exist without these ideas is of capital importance."[57]

environment and circumstance.⁶⁷ This fluid mind that is only mental states, this soul or ego that is only a character or prejudice formed by helpless inheritance and transient experience, can have no immortality in any sense that implies the continuance of the individual.⁶⁸ Even the saint, even Buddha himself, will not, as a personality, survive death.⁶⁹

But if this is so, how can there be rebirth? If there is no soul, how can it pass into other existences, to be punished for the sins of this embodiment? Here is the weakest point in Buddha's philosophy; he never quite faces the contradiction between his rationalistic psychology and his uncritical acceptance of reincarnation. This belief is so universal in India that almost every Hindu accepts it as an axiom or assumption, and hardly bothers to prove it; the brevity and multiplicity of the generations there suggests irresistibly the transmigration of vital force, or—to speak theologically—of the soul. Buddha received the notion along with the air he breathed; it is the one thing that he seems never to have doubted.⁷⁰ He took the Wheel of Rebirth and the Law of *Karma* for granted; his one thought was how to escape from that Wheel, how to achieve *Nirvana* here, and annihilation hereafter.

But what is *Nirvana?* It is difficult to find an erroneous answer to this question; for the Master left the point obscure, and his followers have given the word every meaning under the sun. In general Sanskrit use it meant "extinguished"—as of a lamp or fire. The Buddhist Scriptures use it as signifying: (1) a state of happiness attainable in this life through the complete elimination of selfish desires; (2) the liberation of the individual from rebirth; (3) the annihilation of the individual consciousness; (4) the union of the individual with God; (5) a heaven of happiness after death. In the teaching of Buddha it seemed to mean the extinction of all individual desire, and the reward of such selflessness—escape from rebirth.⁷¹ In Buddhist literature the term has often a terrestrial sense, for the *Arhat*, or saint, is repeatedly described as achieving it in this life, by acquiring its seven constituent parts: self-possession, investigation into the truth, energy, calm, joy, concentration, and magnanimity.⁷³ These are its content, but hardly its productive cause: the cause and source of *Nirvana* is the extinction of selfish desire; and *Nirvana*, in most early contexts, comes to mean the painless peace that rewards the moral annihilation of the self.⁷⁴ "Now," says Buddha, "this is the noble truth as to the passing of pain. Verily, it is the passing away so that no passion remains, the giving up, the getting rid of, the emancipation from, the harboring no longer of, this craving thirst'"[75]—this fever of self-seeking desire. In the body of the Master's teaching it is almost always synonymous with bliss,[76] the quiet content of the soul that no longer worries about itself. But complete *Nirvana* includes annihilation: the reward of the highest saintliness is never to be reborn.[77]

In the end, says Buddha, we perceive the absurdity of moral and psychological individualism. Our fretting selves are not really separate beings and powers, but passing ripples on the stream of life, little knots forming and unraveling in the wind-blown mesh of fate. When we see ourselves as parts of a whole, when we reform our selves and our desires in terms of the whole, then our personal disappointments and defeats, our varied suffering and inevitable death, no longer sadden us as bitterly as before; they are lost in the amplitude of infinity. When we have learned to love not our separate life, but all men and all living things, then at last we shall find peace.

V. THE LAST DAYS OF BUDDHA

His miracles—He visits his father's house—The Buddhist monks—Death

From this exalted philosophy we pass to the simple legends which are all that we have concerning Buddha's later life and death. Despite his scorn of miracles, his disciples brewed a thousand tales of the marvels that he wrought. He wafted himself magically across the Ganges in a moment; the tooth-pick he had let fall sprouted into a tree; at the end of one of his sermons the "thousand-fold world-system shook."[80] When his enemy Devadatta sent a fierce elephant against him, Buddha "pervaded it with love," and it was quite subdued.[81] Arguing from such pleasantries Senart and others have concluded that the legend of Buddha has been formed on the basis of ancient sun myths.[82] It is unimportant; Buddha means for us the ideas attributed to Buddha in the Buddhist literature; and this Buddha exists.

The Buddhist Scriptures paint a pleasing picture of him. Many disciples gathered around him, and his fame as a sage spread through the cities of northern India. When his father heard that Buddha was near Kapilavastu he sent a messenger to him with an invitation to come and spend a day in his boyhood home. He went, and his father, who had mourned the loss of a prince, rejoiced, for a while, over the return of a saint.

Buddha's wife, who had been faithful to him during all their separation, fell down before him, clasped his ankles, placed his feet about her head, and reverenced him as a god. Then King Shuddhodhana told Buddha of her great love: "Lord, my daughter (in-law), when she heard that you were wearing yellow robes (as a monk), put on yellow robes; when she heard of your having one meal a day, herself took one meal; when she knew that you had given up a large bed, she lay on a narrow couch; and when she knew that you had given up garlands and scents, she gave them up." Buddha blessed her, and went his way.[83]

But now his son, Rahula, came to him, and also loved him. "Pleasant is your shadow, ascetic," he said. Though Rahula's mother had hoped to see the youth made king, the Master accepted him into the Buddhist order. Then another prince, Nanda, was called to be consecrated as heir-apparent to the throne; but Nanda, as if in a trance, left the ceremony unfinished, abandoned a kingdom, and going to Buddha, asked that he, too, might be permitted to join the Order. When King Shuddhodhana heard of this he was sad, and asked a boon of Buddha. "When the Lord abandoned the world," he said, "it was no small pain to me; so when Nanda went; and even more so with Rahula. The love of a son cuts through the skin, through the hide, the flesh, the sinew, the marrow. Grant, Lord, that thy noble ones may not confer the ordination on a son without the permission of his father and mother." Buddha consented, and made such permission a prerequisite to ordination.[84]

Already, it seems, this religion without priestcraft had developed an order of monks dangerously like the Hindu priests. Buddha would not be long dead before they would surround themselves with all the paraphernalia of the Brahmans. Indeed it was from the ranks of the Brahmans that the first converts came; and then from the richest youth of Benares and the neighboring towns. These *Bhikkhus*, or monks, practised in Buddha's days a simple rule. They saluted one another, and all those to whom they spoke, with an admirable phrase: "Peace to all beings."* They were not to kill any living thing; they were never to take anything save what was given them; they were to avoid falsehood and slander; they were to heal divisions and encourage concord; they were always to show compassion for all men and all animals; they were to shun all amusements of sense or flesh, all music, *nautch* dances, shows, games, luxuries,

---

* Cf. the beautiful form of greeting used by the Jews: *Shalom aleichem*—"Peace be with you." In the end men do not ask for happiness, but only for peace.

idle conversation, argument, or fortune-telling; they were to have nothing
to do with business, or with any form of buying or selling; above all, they
were to abandon incontinence, and live apart from women, in perfect
chastity.[85] Yielding to many soft entreaties, Buddha allowed women to
enter the Order as nuns, but he never completely reconciled himself to
this move. "If, Ananda," he said, "women had not received permission to
enter the Order, the pure religion would have lasted long, the good law
would have stood fast a thousand years. But since they have received that
permission, it will now stand fast for only five hundred years."[86] He was
right. The great Order, or *Sangha*, has survived to our own time; but
it has long since corrupted the Master's doctrine with magic, polytheism,
and countless superstitions.

Towards the end of his long life his followers already began to deify
him, despite his challenge to them to doubt him and to think for themselves. Now, says one of the last Dialogues,

> the venerable Sariputta came to the place where the Exalted One
> was, and having saluted him, took his seat respectfully at his side,
> and said:
>
> "Lord, such faith have I in the Exalted One that methinks there
> never has been, nor will there be, nor is there now, any other,
> whether Wanderer or Brahman, who is greater and wiser than the
> Exalted One . . . as regards the higher wisdom."
>
> "Grand and bold are the words of thy mouth, Sariputta" (an-
> swered the Master); "verily, thou hast burst forth into a song of
> ecstasy! Of course, then, thou hast known all the Exalted Ones of
> the past, . . . comprehending their minds with yours, and aware
> what their conduct was, what their wisdom, . . . and what the
> emancipation they attained to?"
>
> "Not so, O Lord!"
>
> "Of course, then, thou hast perceived all the Exalted Ones of
> the future, . . . comprehending their whole minds with yours?"
>
> "Not so, O Lord!"
>
> "But at least, then, O Sariputta, thou knowest me, . . . and hast
> penetrated my mind?" . . .
>
> "Not even that, O Lord."
>
> "You see, then, Sariputta, that you know not the hearts of the
> Able, Awakened Ones of the past and of the future. Why, there-
> fore, are your words so grand and bold? Why do you burst forth
> into such a song of ecstasy?"[87]

And to Ananda he taught his greatest and noblest lesson:

"And whosoever, Ananda, either now or after I am dead, shall be a lamp unto themselves, and a refuge unto themselves, shall betake themselves to no external refuge, but, holding fast to the Truth as their lamp, . . . shall not look for refuge to any one besides themselves—it is they . . . who shall reach the very topmost height! But they must be anxious to learn!"[88]

He died in 483 B.C., at the age of eighty. "Now then, O monks," he said to them as his last words, "I address you. Subject to decay are compound things. Strive with earnestness."[89]

CHAPTER XVI

From Alexander to Aurangzeb

I. CHANDRAGUPTA

*Alexander in India—Chandragupta the liberator—The people—
The university of Taxila—The royal palace—A day in the life
of a king — An older Machiavelli — Administration —
Law—Public health—Transport and roads—Municipal government*

IN THE year 327 B.C. Alexander the Great, pushing on from Persia,
marched over the Hindu Kush and descended upon India. For a year
he campaigned among the northwestern states that had formed one of the
Persian Empire's richest provinces, exacting supplies for his troops and
gold for his treasury. Early in 326 B.C. he crossed the Indus, fought his
way slowly through Taxila and Rawalpindi to the south and east, en-
countered the army of King Porus, defeated 30,000 infantry, 4,000 cavalry, 300 chariots and 200 elephants, and slew 12,000 men. When Porus,
having fought to the last, surrendered, Alexander, admiring his courage,
stature and fine features, bade him say what treatment he wished to receive. "Treat me, Alexander," he answered, "in a kingly way." "For my
own sake," said Alexander, "thou shalt be so treated; for thine own sake
do thou demand what is pleasing to thee." But Porus said that everything was included in what he had asked. Alexander was much pleased
with this reply; he made Porus king of all conquered India as a Mace-
donion tributary, and found him thereafter a faithful and energetic ally.[1]
Alexander wished then to advance even to the eastern sea, but his soldiers
protested. After much oratory and pouting he yielded to them, and led
them—through patriotically hostile tribes that made his wearied troops
fight almost every foot of the way—down the Hydaspes and up the coast
through Gedrosia to Baluchistan. When he arrived at Susa, twenty
months after turning back from his conquests, his army was but a miserable fragment of that which had crossed into India with him three years
before.

Seven years later all trace of Macedonian authority had already disappeared from India.² The chief agent of its removal was one of the most romantic figures in Indian history, a lesser warrior but a greater ruler than Alexander. Chandragupta was a young Kshatriya noble exiled from Magadha by the ruling Nanda family, to which he was related. Helped by his subtle Machiavellian adviser, Kautilya Chanakya, the youth organized a small army, overcame the Macedonian garrisons, and declared India free. Then he advanced upon Pataliputra,* capital of the Magadha kingdom, fomented a revolution, seized the throne, and established that Mauryan Dynasty which was to rule Hindustan and Afghanistan for one hundred and thirty-seven years. Subordinating his courage to Kautilya's unscrupulous wisdom, Chandragupta soon made his government the most powerful then existing in the world. When Megasthenes came to Pataliputra as ambassador from Seleucus Nicator, King of Syria, he was amazed to find a civilization which he described to the incredulous Greeks—still near their zenith—as entirely equal to their own.³

The Greek gave a pleasant, perhaps a lenient, account, of Hindu life in his time. It struck him as a favorable contrast with his own nation that there was no slavery in India;† and that though the population was divided into castes according to occupations, it accepted these divisions as natural and tolerable. "They live happily enough," the ambassador reported,

> being simple in their manners, and frugal. They never drink wine except at sacrifice. . . . The simplicity of their laws and their contracts is proved by the fact that they seldom go to law. They have no suits about pledges and deposits, nor do they require either seals or witnesses, but make their deposits and confide in each other. . . . Truth and virtue they hold alike in esteem. . . . The greater part of the soil is under irrigation, and consequently bears two crops in the course of the year. . . . It is accordingly affirmed that famine has never visited India, and that there has never been a general scarcity in the supply of nourishing food.⁵

The oldest of the two thousand cities⁶ of northern India in Chandragupta's time was Taxila, twenty miles northwest of the modern Rawalpindi. Arrian describes it as "a large and prosperous city"; Strabo says

---

* The modern Patna.
† "This is a great thing in India," says Arrian, "that all the inhabitants are free, not a single Indian being a slave."⁴

it "is large, and has most excellent laws."[7] It was both a military and a university town, strategically situated on the main road to Western Asia, and containing the most famous of the several universities possessed by India at that time. Students flocked to Taxila as in the Middle Ages they flocked to Paris; there all the arts and sciences could be studied under eminent professors, and the medical school especially was held in high repute throughout the Oriental world.*

Megasthenes describes Chandragupta's capital, Pataliputra, as nine miles in length and almost two miles in width.[10] The palace of the King was of timber, but the Greek ambassador ranked it as excelling the royal residences of Susa and Ecbatana, being surpassed only by those at Persepolis. Its pillars were plated with gold, and ornamented with designs of bird-life and foliage; its interior was sumptuously furnished and adorned with precious metals and stones.[11] There was a certain Oriental ostentation in this culture, as in the use of gold vessels six feet in diameter;[12] but an English historian concludes, from the testimony of the literary, pictorial and material remains, that "in the fourth and third centuries before Christ the command of the Maurya monarch over luxuries of all kinds and skilled craftsmanship in all the manual arts was not inferior to that enjoyed by the Mogul emperors eighteen centuries later."[13]

In this palace Chandragupta, having won the throne by violence, lived for twenty-four years as in a gilded jail. Occasionally he appeared in public, clad in fine muslin embroidered with purple and gold, and carried in a golden palanquin or on a gorgeously accoutred elephant. Except when he rode out to the hunt, or otherwise amused himself, he found his time crowded with the business of his growing realm. His days were divided into sixteen periods of ninety minutes each. In the first he arose, and prepared himself by meditation; in the second he studied the reports of his agents, and issued secret instructions; the third he spent with his councillors in the Hall of Private Audience; in the fourth he attended to state finances and national defense; in the fifth he heard the petitions and suits of his subjects; in the sixth he bathed and dined, and read religious literature; in the seventh he received taxes and tribute, and made official

---

* The excavations of Sir John Marshall on the site of Taxila have unearthed delicately carved stones, highly polished statuary, coins as old as 600 B.C., and glassware of a fine quality never bettered in later India.[8] "It is manifest," says Vincent Smith, "that a high degree of material civilization had been attained, and that all the arts and crafts incident to the life of a wealthy, cultured city were familiar."[9]

appointments; in the eighth he again met his Council, and heard the reports of his spies, including the courtesans whom he used for this purpose;[14] the ninth he devoted to relaxation and prayer, the tenth and eleventh to military matters, the twelfth again to secret reports, the thirteenth to the evening bath and repast, the fourteenth, fifteenth and sixteenth to sleep.[15] Perhaps the historian tells us what Chandragupta might have been, or how Kautilya wished the people to picture him, rather than what he really was. Truth does not often escape from palaces.

The actual direction of government was in the hands of the crafty vizier. Kautilya was a Brahman who knew the political value of religion, but took no moral guidance from it; like our modern dictators he believed that every means was justifiable if used in the service of the state. He was unscrupulous and treacherous, but never to his King; he served Chandragupta through exile, defeat, adventure, intrigue, murder and victory, and by his wily wisdom made the empire of his master the greatest that India had ever known. Like the author of *The Prince*, Kautilya saw fit to preserve in writing his formulas for warfare and diplomacy; tradition ascribes to him the *Arthashastra*, the oldest book in extant Sanskrit literature.[16] As an example of its delicate realism we may take its list of means for capturing a fort: "Intrigue, spies, winning over the enemy's people, siege, and assault"[17]—a wise economy of physical effort.

The government made no pretense to democracy, and was probably the most efficient that India has ever had.[18] Akbar, greatest of the Moguls, "had nothing like it, and it may be doubted if any of the ancient Greek cities were better organized."[19] It was based frankly upon military power. Chandragupta, if we may trust Megasthenes (who should be as suspect as any foreign correspondent) kept an army of 600,000 foot, 30,000 horse, 9,000 elephants, and an unnamed number of chariots.[20] The peasantry and the Brahmans were exempt from military service; and Strabo describes the farmers tilling the soil in peace and security in the midst of war.[21] The power of the King was theoretically unlimited, but in practice it was restricted by a Council which—sometimes with the King, sometimes in his absence—initiated legislation, regulated national finances and foreign affairs, and appointed all the more important officers of state. Megasthenes testifies to the "high character and wisdom" of Chandragupta's councillors, and to their effective power.[22]

The government was organized into departments with well-defined duties and a carefully graded hierarchy of officials, managing respectively revenue, customs, frontiers, passports, communications, excise, mines, agriculture, cattle, commerce, warehouses, navigation, forests, public games, prostitution, and the mint. The Superintendent of Excise controlled the sale of drugs and intoxicating drinks, restricted the number and location of taverns, and the quantity of liquors which they might sell. The Superintendent of Mines leased mining areas to private persons, who paid a fixed rent and a share of the profits to the government; a similar system applied to agriculture, for all the land was owned by the state. The Superintendent of Public Games supervised the gambling halls, supplied dice, charged a fee for their use, and gathered in for the treasury five per cent of all money taken in by the "bank." The Superintendent of Prostitution looked after public women, controlled their charges and expenditures, appropriated their earnings for two days of each month, and kept two of them in the royal palace for entertainment and intelligence service. Taxes fell upon every profession, occupation and industry; and in addition rich men were from time to time persuaded to make "benevolences" to the King. The government regulated prices and periodically assayed weights and measures; it carried on some manufactures in state factories, sold vegetables, and kept a monopoly of mines, salt, timber, fine fabrics, horses and elephants.[23]

Law was administered in the village by local headmen, or by *panchayats* —village councils of five men; in towns, districts and provinces by inferior and superior courts; at the capital by the royal council as a supreme court, and by the King as a court of last appeal. Penalties were severe, and included mutilation, torture and death, usually on the principle of *lex talionis*, or equivalent retaliation. But the government was no mere engine of repression; it attended to sanitation and public health, maintained hospitals and poor-relief stations, distributed in famine years the food kept in state warehouses for such emergencies, forced the rich to contribute to the assistance of the destitute, and organized great public works to care for the unemployed in depression years.[24]

The Department of Navigation regulated water transport, and protected travelers on rivers and seas; it maintained bridges and harbors, and provided government ferries in addition to those that were privately managed and owned[25]—an admirable arrangement whereby public competition could check private plunder, and private competition could discourage official extravagance. The Department of Communications built and repaired roads throughout the empire, from the narrow wagon-tracks of the villages to trade routes thirty-two feet, and royal roads sixty-four feet, wide. One of these imperial highways extended twelve hundred miles from Pataliputra to the northwestern frontier[26]—a distance equal to half the transcontinental spread of the United States. At approximately every mile, says Megasthenes, these roads were marked with pillars indicating directions and distances to various destinations.[27] Shade-trees, wells, police-stations and hotels were provided at regular intervals along the route.[28] Transport was by chariots, palanquins, bullock-carts, horses, camels, elephants, asses and men. Elephants were a luxury usually confined to royalty and officialdom, and so highly valued that a woman's virtue was thought a moderate price to pay for one of them.*

The same method of departmental administration was applied to the government of the cities. Pataliputra was ruled by a commission of thirty men, divided into six groups. One group regulated industry; another supervised strangers, assigning to them lodgings and attendants, and watching their movements; another kept a record of births and deaths; another licensed merchants, regulated the sale of produce, and tested measures and weights; another controlled the sale of manufactured articles; another collected a tax of ten per cent on all sales. "In short," says Havell, "Pataliputra in the fourth century B.C. seems to have been a thoroughly well-organized city, and administered according to the best principles of social science."[28a] "The perfection of the arrangements thus indicated," says Vincent Smith, "is astonishing, even when exhibited in outline. Examination of the departmental details increases our wonder that such an organization could have been planned and efficiently operated in India in 300 B.C."[28b]

The one defect of this government was autocracy, and therefore continual dependence upon force and spies. Like every autocrat, Chandragupta held his power precariously, always fearing revolt and assassination. Every night he used a different bedroom, and always he was surrounded by guards. Hindu tradition, accepted by European historians, tells how, when a long famine (*pace* Megasthenes) came upon his kingdom, Chandragupta, in despair at his helplessness, abdicated his throne, lived for twelve years thereafter as a Jain ascetic, and then starved himself to death. "All things considered," said Voltaire, "the life of a gondolier is preferable to that of a doge; but I believe the difference is so trifling that it is not worth the trouble of examining."[29]

---

* "Their women, who are very chaste, and would not go astray for any other reason, on the receipt of an elephant have communion with the donor. The Indians do not think it disgraceful to prostitute themselves for an elephant, and to the women it even seems an honor that their beauty should appear equal in value to an elephant."—Arrian, *Indica*, xvii.

II. THE PHILOSOPHER-KING

Ashoka—The Edict of Tolerance—Ashoka's missionaries—His
failure—His success

Chandragupta's successor, Bindusara, was apparently a man of some intellectual inclination. He is said to have asked Antiochos, King of Syria, to make him a present of a Greek philosopher; for a real Greek philosopher, wrote Bindusara, he would pay a high price.[30] The proposal could not be complied with, since Antiochos found no philosophers for sale; but chance atoned by giving Bindusara a philosopher for his son.

Ashoka Vardhana mounted the throne in 273 B.C. He found himself ruler of a vaster empire than any Indian monarch before him: Afghanistan, Baluchistan, and all of modern India but the extreme south—*Tamila-kam*, or Tamil Land. For a time he governed in the spirit of his grandfather Chandragupta, cruelly but well. Yuan Chwang, a Chinese traveler who spent many years in India in the seventh century A.D., tells us that the prison maintained by Ashoka north of the capital was still remembered in Hindu tradition as "Ashoka's Hell." There, said his informants, all the tortures of any orthodox Inferno had been used in the punishment of criminals; to which the King added an edict that no one who entered that dungeon should ever come out of it alive. But one day a Buddhist saint, imprisoned there without cause, and flung into a cauldron of hot water, refused to boil. The jailer sent word to Ashoka, who came, saw, and marveled. When the King turned to leave, the jailer reminded him that according to his own edict he must not leave the prison alive. The King admitted the force of the remark, and ordered the jailer to be thrown into the cauldron.

On returning to his palace Ashoka, we are told, underwent a profound conversion. He gave instructions that the prison should be demolished, and that the penal code should be made more lenient. At the same time he learned that his troops had won a great victory over the rebellious Kalinga tribe, had slaughtered thousands of the rebels, and had taken many prisoners. Ashoka was moved to remorse at the thought of all this "violence, slaughter, and separation" of captives "from those whom they love." He ordered the prisoners freed, restored their lands to the Kalingas, and sent them a message of apology which had no precedents and has had few imitations. Then he joined the Buddhist Order, wore for a time the garb of a monk, gave up hunting and the eating of meat, and entered upon the Eightfold Noble Way.[31]

It is at present impossible to say how much of this is myth, and how much is history; nor can we discern, at this distance, the motives of the King. Perhaps he saw the growth of Buddhism, and thought that its code of generosity and peace might provide a convenient regimen for his people, saving countless policemen. In the eleventh year of his reign he began to issue the most remarkable edicts in the history of government, and commanded that they should be carved upon rocks and pillars in simple phrase and local dialects, so that any literate Hindu might be able to understand them. The Rock Edicts have been found in almost every part of India; of the pillars ten remain in place, and the position of twenty others has been determined. In these edicts we find the Emperor accepting the Buddhist faith completely, and applying it resolutely throughout the last sphere of human affairs in which we should have expected to find it—statesmanship. It is as if some modern empire had suddenly announced that henceforth it would practice Christianity.

Though these edicts are Buddhist they will not seem to us entirely religious. They assume a future life, and thereby suggest how soon the scepticism of Buddha had been replaced by the faith of his followers. But they express no belief in, make no mention of, a personal God.[32] Neither is there any word in them about Buddha. The edicts are not interested in theology: the Sarnath Edict asks for harmony within the Church, and prescribes penalties for those who weaken it with schism;[33] but other edicts repeatedly enjoin religious tolerance. One must give alms to Brahmans as well as to Buddhist priests; one must not speak ill of other men's faiths. The King announces that all his subjects are his beloved children, and that he will not discriminate against any of them because of their diverse creeds.[34] Rock Edict XII speaks with almost contemporary pertinence:

> His Sacred and Gracious Majesty the King does reverence to men of all sects, whether ascetics or householders, by gifts and various forms of reverence.
> His Sacred Majesty, however, cares not so much for gifts or external reverence, as that there should be a growth of the essence of the matter in all sects. The growth of the essence of the matter assumes various forms, but the root of it is restraint of speech; to wit, a man must not do reverence to his own sect, or disparage that

of another, without reason. Depreciation should be for specific reasons only, because the sects of other people all deserve reverence for some reason or another.

By thus acting a man exalts his own sect, and at the same time does service to the sects of other people. By acting contrariwise a man hurts his own sect, and does disservice to the sects of other people. . . . Concord is meritorious.

"The essence of the matter" is explained more clearly in the Second Pillar Edict. "The Law of Piety is excellent. But wherein consists the Law of Piety? In these things: to wit, little impiety, many good deeds, compassion, liberality, truthfulness, purity." To set an example Ashoka ordered his officials everywhere to regard the people as his children, to treat them without impatience or harshness, never to torture them, and never to imprison them without good cause; and he commanded the officials to read these instructions periodically to the people.[35]

Did these moral edicts have any result in improving the conduct of the people? Perhaps they had something to do with spreading the idea of *ahimsa,* and encouraging abstinence from meat and alcoholic drinks among the upper classes of India.[36] Ashoka himself had all the confidence of a reformer in the efficacy of his petrified sermons: in Rock Edict IV he announces that marvelous results have already appeared; and his summary gives us a clearer conception of his doctrine:

Now, by reason of the practice of piety by His Sacred and Gracious Majesty the King, the reverberation of the war-drums has become the reverberation of the Law. . . . As for many years before has not happened, now, by reason of the inculcation of the Law of Piety by His Sacred and Gracious Majesty the King, (there is) increased abstention from the sacrificial slaughter of living creatures, abstention from the killing of animate beings, seemly behavior to relatives, seemly behavior to Brahmans, hearkening to father and mother, hearkening to elders. Thus, as in many other ways, the practice of the Law (of Piety) has increased, and His Sacred and Gracious Majesty the King will make such practice of the Law increase further.

The sons, grandsons and great-grandsons of His Sacred and Gracious Majesty the King will cause this practice of the Law to increase until the eon of universal destruction.

The good King exaggerated the piety of men and the loyalty of sons. He himself labored arduously for the new religion; he made himself head of the Buddhist Church, lavished gifts upon it, built 84,000 monasteries for it,[37] and in its name established throughout his kingdom hospitals for men and animals.[38] He sent Buddhist missionaries to all parts of India and Ceylon, even to Syria, Egypt and Greece,[39] where, perhaps, they helped to prepare for the ethics of Christ;[40] and shortly after his death missionaries left India to preach the gospel of Buddha in Tibet, China, Mongolia and Japan. In addition to this activity in religion, Ashoka gave himself zealously to the secular administration of his empire; his days of labor were long, and he kept himself available to his aides for public business at all hours.[41]

His outstanding fault was egotism; it is difficult to be at once modest and a reformer. His self-respect shines out in every edict, and makes him more completely the brother of Marcus Aurelius. He failed to perceive that the Brahmans hated him and only bided their time to destroy him, as the priests of Thebes had destroyed Ikhnaton a thousand years before. Not only the Brahmans, who had been given to slaughtering animals for themselves and their gods, but many thousands of hunters and fishermen resented the edicts that set such severe limitations upon the taking of animal life; even the peasants growled at the command that "chaff must not be set on fire along with the living things in it."[42] Half the empire waited hopefully for Ashoka's death.

Yuan Chwang tells us that according to Buddhist tradition Ashoka in his last years was deposed by his grandson, who acted with the aid of court officials. Gradually all power was taken from the old King, and his gifts to the Buddhist Church came to an end. Ashoka's own allowance of goods, even of food, was cut down, until one day his whole portion was half an *amalaka* fruit. The King gazed upon it sadly, and then sent it to his Buddhist brethren, as all that he had to give.[43] But in truth we know nothing of his later years, not even the year of his death. Within a generation after his passing, his empire, like Ikhnaton's, crumbled to pieces. As it became evident that the sovereignty of the Kingdom of Magadha was maintained rather by the inertia of tradition than by the organization of force, state after state renounced its adherence to the King of Kings at Pataliputra. Descendants of Ashoka continued to rule Magadha till the seventh century after Christ; but the Maurya Dynasty that Chandragupta had founded came to an end when King Brihadratha was assassinated. States are built not on the ideals but on the nature of men.

In the political sense Ashoka had failed; in another sense he had accomplished one of the greatest tasks in history. Within two hundred years after his death Buddhism had spread throughout India, and was entering upon the bloodless conquest of Asia. If to this day, from Kandy in Ceylon to Kamakura in Japan, the placid face of Gautama bids men be gentle to one another and love peace, it is partly because a dreamer, perhaps a saint, once held the throne of India.

III. THE GOLDEN AGE OF INDIA

An epoch of invasions—The Kushan kings—The Gupta Empire—
The travels of Fa-Hien—The revival of letters—The Huns
in India—Harsha the generous—The travels of Yuan
Chwang

From the death of Ashoka to the empire of the Guptas—i.e., for a period of almost six hundred years—Hindu inscriptions and documents are so few that the history of this interval is lost in obscurity." It was not necessarily a Dark Age; great universities like those at Taxila continued to function, and in the northwestern portion of India the influence of Persia in architecture, and of Greece in sculpture, produced a flourishing civilization in the wake of Alexander's invasion. In the first and second centuries before Christ, Syrians, Greeks and Scythians poured down into the Punjab, conquered it, and established there, for some three hundred years, this Greco-Bactrian culture. In the first century of what we so provincially call the Christian Era the Kushans, a central Asian tribe akin to the Turks, captured Kabul, and from that city as capital extended their power throughout northwestern India and most of Central Asia. In the reign of their greatest king, Kanishka, the arts and sciences progressed: Greco-Buddhist sculpture produced some of its fairest masterpieces, fine buildings were reared in Peshawar, Taxila and Mathura, Charaka advanced the art of medicine, and Nagarjuna and Ashvaghosha laid the bases of that *Mahayana* (Greater Vehicle) Buddhism which was to help Gautama to win China and Japan. Kanishka tolerated many religions, and experimented with various gods; finally he chose the new mythological Buddhism that had made Buddha into a deity and had filled the skies with *Bodhisattwas* and *Arhats;* he called a great council of

Buddhist theologians to formulate this creed for his realms, and became almost a second Ashoka in spreading the Buddhist faith. The Council composed 300,000 *sutras*, lowered Buddha's philosophy to the emotional needs of the common soul, and raised him to divinity.

Meanwhile Chandragupta I (quite distinct, despite his name and number, from Chandragupta Maurya) had established in Magadha the Gupta Dynasty of native kings. His successor, Samudragupta, in a reign of fifty years, made himself one of the foremost monarchs in India's long history. He changed his capital from Pataliputra to Ayodhya, ancient home of the legendary Rama; sent his conquering armies and tax-gatherers into Bengal, Assam, Nepal, and southern India; and spent the treasure brought to him from vassal states in promoting literature, science, religion and the arts. He himself, in the interludes of war, achieved distinction as a poet and a musician. His son, Vikramaditya ("Sun of Power"), extended these conquests of arms and the mind, supported the great dramatist Kalidasa, and gathered a brilliant circle of poets, philosophers, artists, scientists and scholars about him in his capital at Ujjain. Under these two kings India reached a height of development unsurpassed since Buddha, and a political unity rivaled only under Ashoka and Akbar.

We discern some outline of Gupta civilization from the account that Fa-Hien gave of his visit to India at the opening of the fifth century of our era. He was one of many Buddhists who came from China to India during this Golden Age; and these pilgrims were probably less numerous than the merchants and ambassadors who, despite her mountain barriers, now entered pacified India from East and West, even from distant Rome, and brought to her a stimulating contact with foreign customs and ideas. Fa-Hien, after risking his life in passing through western China, found himself quite safe in India, traveling everywhere without encountering molestation or thievery.[45] His journal tells how he took six years in coming, spent six years in India, and needed three years more for his return *via* Ceylon and Java to his Chinese home.[46] He describes with admiration the wealth and prosperity, the virtue and happiness, of the Hindu people, and the social and religious liberty which they enjoyed. He was astonished at the number, size and population of the great cities, at the free hospitals and other charitable institutions which dotted the land,* at the number of students in the universities and monasteries, and at the impos-

---

* These antedated by three centuries the first hospital built in Europe—*viz.*, the *Maison Dieu* erected in Paris in the seventh century A.D.[47]

ing scale and splendor of the imperial palaces.⁴⁸ His description is quite Utopian, except for the matter of right hands:

> The people are numerous and happy; they have not to register their households, or attend to any magistrates or their rules; only those who cultivate the royal land have to pay a portion of the gain from it. If they want to go they go; if they want to stay they stay. The king governs without decapitation or corporal punishments. Criminals are simply fined; . . . even in cases of repeated attempts at wicked rebellion they only have their right hands cut off. . . . Throughout the whole country the people do not kill any living creature, nor eat onions or garlic. The only exception is that of the Chandalas. . . . In that country they do not keep pigs and fowls, and do not sell live cattle; in the markets there are no butchers' shops, and no dealers in intoxicating drinks.⁴⁹

Fa-Hien hardly noted that the Brahmans, who had been in disfavor with the Mauryan dynasty since Ashoka, were growing again in wealth and power under the tolerant rule of the Gupta kings. They had revived the religious and literary traditions of pre-Buddhist days, and were developing Sanskrit into the Esperanto of scholars throughout India. It was under their influence and the patronage of the court that the great Hindu epics, the *Mahabharata* and the *Ramayana*, were written down into their present form.⁵⁰ Under this dynasty, too, Buddhist art reached its zenith in the frescoes of the Ajanta caves. In the judgment of a contemporary Hindu scholar, the "mere names of Kalidasa and Varahamihira, Gunavarman and Vashubandu, Aryabhata and Brahmagupta, are sufficient to mark this epoch as an apogee of Indian culture."⁵¹ "An impartial historian," says Havell, "might well consider that the greatest triumph of British administration would be to restore to India all that she enjoyed in the fifth century A.D."⁵²

This heyday of native culture was interrupted by a wave of those Hun invasions which now overran both Asia and Europe, ruining for a time India as well as Rome. While Attila was raiding Europe, Toramana was capturing Malwa, and the terrible Mihiragula was hurling the Gupta rulers from their throne. For a century India relapsed into bondage and chaos. Then a scion of the Gupta line, Harsha-Vardhana, recaptured northern India, built a capital at Kanauj, and for forty-two years gave peace and security to a wide realm, in which once more native arts and letters flourished. We may conjecture the size, splendor and prosperity of Kanauj from the one unbelievable item that when the Moslems sacked it (1018 A.D.) they destroyed 10,000 temples.[53] Its fine public gardens and free bathing tanks were but a small part of the beneficence of the new dynasty. Harsha himself was one of those rare kings who make monarchy appear—for a time—the most admirable of all forms of government. He was a man of personal charm and accomplishments, writing poetry and dramas that are read in India to this day; but he did not allow these foibles to interfere with the competent administration of his kingdom. "He was indefatigable," says Yuan Chwang, "and the day was too short for him; he forgot sleep in his devotion to good works."[54] Having begun as a worshiper of Shiva he was later converted to Buddhism, and became another Ashoka in his pious benefactions. He forbade the eating of animal food, established travelers' rests throughout his domain, and erected thousands of topes, or Buddhist shrines, on the banks of the Ganges.

Yuan Chwang, most famous of the Chinese Buddhists who visited India, tells us that Harsha proclaimed, every five years, a great festival of charity, to which he invited all officials of all religions, and all the poor and needy of the realm. At this gathering it was his custom to give away in public alms all the surplus brought into the state treasury since the last quinquennial feast. Yuan was surprised to see a great quantity of gold, silver, coins, jewelry, fine fabrics and delicate brocades piled up in an open square, surrounded by a hundred pavilions each seating a thousand persons. Three days were given to religious exercises; on the fourth day (if we·may believe the incredible pilgrim) the distribution began. Ten thousand Buddhist monks were fed, and each received a pearl, garments, flowers, perfumes, and one hundred pieces of gold. Then the Brahmans were given alms almost as abundant; then the Jains; then other sects; then all the poor and orphaned laity that had come from every quarter of the kingdom. Sometimes the distribution lasted three or four months. At the end Harsha divested himself of his costly robes and jewelry, and added them to the alms.[55]

The memoirs of Yuan Chwang reveal a certain theological exhilaration as the mental spirit of the age. It is a pleasant picture, and significant of India's repute in other lands—this Chinese aristocrat leaving his comforts and perquisites in far-off Ch'ang-an, passing across half-civilized western China, through Tashkent and Samarkand (then a flourishing city), over the Himalayas into India, and then studying zealously, for three years, in the monastic university at Nalanda. His fame as a scholar and a man of rank brought him many invitations from the princes of India. When Harsha heard that Yuan was at the court of Kumara, King of Assam, he summoned Kumara to come with Yuan to Kanauj. Kumara refused, saying that Harsha could have his head, but not his guest. Harsha answered: "I trouble you for your head," and Kumara came. Harsha was fascinated by Yuan's learning and fine manners, and called a convocation of Buddhist notables to hear Yuan expound the Mahayana doctrine. Yuan nailed his theses to the gateway of the pavilion in which the discourse was to be held, and added a postscript in the manner of the day: "If any one here can find a single wrong argument and can refute it, I will let him cut off my head." The discussion lasted eighteen days, but Yuan (Yuan reports) answered all objections and confounded all heretics. (Another account has it that his opponents ended the conference by setting fire to the pavilion.)[56] After many adventures Yuan found his way back to Chang-an, where an enlightened emperor enshrined in a rich temple the Buddhist relics which this holy Polo had brought with him, and gave him a corps of scholars to help translate the manuscripts that he had purchased in India.[57]

All the glory of Harsha's rule, however, was artificial and precarious, for it depended upon the ability and generosity of a mortal king. When he died a usurper seized the throne, and illustrated the nether side of monarchy. Chaos ensued, and continued for almost a thousand years. India, like Europe, now suffered her Middle Ages, was overrun by barbarians, was conquered, divided, and despoiled. Not until the great Akbar would she know peace and unity again.

IV. ANNALS OF RAJPUTANA

The Samurai of India—The age of chivalry—The fall of Chitor

This Dark Age was lighted up for a moment by the epic of Rajputana. Here, in the states of Mewar, Marwar, Amber, Bikaner and many others of melodious name, a people half native in origin and half descended from invading Scythians and Huns, had built a feudal civilization under the government of warlike rajas who cared more for the art of life than for the life of art. They began by acknowledging the suzerainty of the Mauryas and the Guptas; they ended by defending their independence, and all India, from the inroads of Moslem hordes. Their clans were distinguished by a military ardor and courage not usually associated with India;* if we may trust their admiring historian, Tod, every man of them was a dauntless Kshatriya, and every woman among them was a heroine. Their very name, *Rajputs,* meant "sons of kings"; and if sometimes they called their land *Rajasthan,* it was to designate it as "the home of royalty."

All the nonsense and glamor—all the bravery, loyalty, beauty, feuds, poisons, assassinations, wars, and subjection of woman—which our traditions attach to the Age of Chivalry can be found in the annals of these plucky states. "The Rajput chieftains," says Tod, "were imbued with all the kindred virtues of the western cavalier, and far his superior in mental attainments."[59] They had lovely women for whom they did not hesitate to die, and who thought it only a matter of courtesy to accompany their husbands to the grave by the rite of suttee. Some of these women were educated and refined; some of the rajas were poets, or scientists; and for a while a delicate *genre* of water-color painting flourished among them in the medieval Persian style. For four centuries they grew in wealth, until they could spend $20,000,000 on the coronation of Mewar's king.[60]

It was their pride and their tragedy that they enjoyed war as the highest art of all, the only one befitting a Rajput gentleman. This military spirit enabled them to defend themselves against the Moslems with historic valor,† but it kept their little states so divided and weakened with strife that not all their bravery could preserve them in the end. Tod's account of the fall of Chitor, one of the Rajput capitals, is as romantic as any legend of Arthur or Charlemagne; and indeed (since it is based solely upon native historians too faithful to their fatherland to be in love with truth) these marvelous *Annals of Rajasthan* may be as legendary as *Le Morte d'Arthur* or *Le Chanson de Roland.* In this version the Mohammedan invader, Alau-d-din, wanted not Chitor but the princess Pudmini—"a title bestowed only on the superlatively fair." The Moslem chieftain proposed to raise the siege if the regent of Chitor would surrender the princess. Being refused, Alau-d-din agreed to withdraw if he were allowed to *see*

---

* But cf. Arrian on ancient India: "In war the Indians were by far the bravest of all the races inhabiting Asia at that time."[58]

† "No place on earth," says Count Keyserling about Chitor, "has been the scene of equal heroism, knightliness, or an equally noble readiness to die."[61]

Pudmini. Finally he consented to depart if he might see Pudmini in à mirror; but this too was denied him. Instead, the women of Chitor joined in defending their city; and when the Rajputs saw their wives and daughters dying beside them they fought until every man of them was dead. When Alau-d-din entered the capital he found no sign of human life within its gates; all the males had died in battle, and their wives, in the awful rite known as the *Johur*, had burned themselves to death.[62]

V. THE ZENITH OF THE SOUTH

The kingdoms of the Deccan—Vijayanagar—Krishna Raya— A medieval metropolis—Laws—Arts—Religion—Tragedy

As the Moslems advanced into India native culture receded farther and farther south; and towards the end of these Middle Ages the finest achievements of Hindu civilization were those of the Deccan. For a time the Chalyuka tribe maintained an independent kingdom reaching across central India, and achieved, under Pulakeshin II, sufficient power and glory to defeat Harsha, to attract Yuan Chwang, and to receive a respectful embassy from Khosrou II of Persia. It was in Pulakeshin's reign and territory that the greatest of Indian paintings—the frescoes of Ajanta—were completed. Pulakeshin was overthrown by the king of the Pallavas, who for a brief period became the supreme power in central India. In the extreme south, and as early as the first century after Christ, the Pandyas established a realm comprising Madura, Tinnevelly, and parts of Travancore; they made Madura one of the finest of medieval Hindu cities, and adorned it with a gigantic temple and a thousand lesser works of architectural art. In their turn they too were overthrown, first by the Cholas, and then by the Mohammedans. The Cholas ruled the region between Madura and Madras, and thence westward to Mysore. They were of great antiquity, being mentioned in the edicts of Ashoka; but we know nothing of them until the ninth century, when they began a long career of conquest that brought them tribute from all southern India, even from Ceylon. Then their power waned, and they passed under the control of the greatest of the southern states, Vijayanagar.*

Vijayanagar—the name both of a kingdom and of its capital—is a melancholy instance of forgotten glory. In the years of its grandeur it com-

---

* In this medley of now almost forgotten kingdoms there were periods of literary and artistic—above all, architectural—creation; there were wealthy capitals, luxurious palaces, and mighty potentates; but so vast is India, and so long is its history, that in this congested paragraph we must pass by, without so much as mentioning them, men who for a

prised all the present native states of the lower peninsula, together with Mysore and the entire Presidency of Madras. We may judge of its power and resources by considering that King Krishna Raya led forth to battle at Talikota 703,000 foot, 32,600 horse, 551 elephants, and some hundred thousand merchants, prostitutes and other camp followers such as were then wont to accompany an army in its campaigns.[63] The autocracy of the king was softened by a measure of village autonomy, and by the occasional appearance of an enlightened and human monarch on the throne. Krishna Raya, who ruled Vijayanagar in the days of Henry VIII, compares favorably with that constant lover. He led a life of justice and courtesy, gave abounding alms, tolerated all Hindu faiths, enjoyed and supported literature and the arts, forgave fallen enemies and spared their cities, and devoted himself sedulously to the chores of administration. A Portuguese missionary, Domingos Paes (1522), describes him as

> the most feared and perfect king that could possibly be; cheerful of disposition, and very merry; he is one that seeks to honor foreigners, and receives them kindly. . . . He is a great ruler, and a man of much justice, but subject to sudden fits of rage. . . . He is by rank a greater lord than any, by reason of what he possesses in armies and territories; but it seems that he has in fact nothing compared to what a man like him ought to have, so gallant and perfect is he in all things.[64]*

The capital, founded in 1336, was probably the richest city that India had yet known. Nicolo Conti, visiting it about 1420, estimated its circumference at sixty miles; Paes pronounced it "as large as Rome, and very beautiful to the sight." There were, he added, "many groves of trees within it, and many conduits of water"; for its engineers had constructed a huge dam in the Tungabadra River, and had formed a reservoir from which water was conveyed to the city by an aqueduct fifteen miles long, cut for several miles out of the solid rock. Abdu-r Razzak, who saw the city in 1443, reported it as "such that eye has not seen, nor ear heard, of any place resembling it upon the whole earth." Paes considered it "the

---

time thought they dominated the earth. For example, Vikramaditya, who ruled the Chalyukans for half a century (1076-1126), was so successful in war that (like Nietzsche) he proposed to found a new chronological era, dividing all history into before him and after him. Today he is a footnote.

* Among these modest possessions were twelve thousand wives.[65]

best-provided city in tne world, . . . ror in this one everything abounds."
The houses, he tells us, numbered over a hundred thousand—implying
a population of half a million souls. He marvels at a palace in which one
room was built entirely of ivory; "it is so rich and beautiful that you
would hardly find anywhere another such."⁶⁶ When Firoz Shah, Sultan of
Delhi, married the daughter of Vijayanagar's king in the latter's capital,
the road was spread for six miles with velvet, satin, cloth of gold and other
costly stuffs.⁶⁷ However, every traveler is a liar.

Underneath this wealth a population of serfs and laborers lived in
poverty and superstition, subject to a code of laws that preserved some
commercial morality by a barbarous severity. Punishment ranged from
mutilation of hands or feet to casting a man to the elephants, cutting off
his head, impaling him alive by a stake thrust through his belly, or hanging him on a hook under his chin until he died;⁶⁸ rape as well as large-
scale theft was punished in this last way. Prostitution was permitted,
regulated, and turned into royal revenue. "Opposite the mint," says
Abdu-r Razzak, "is the office of the prefect of the city, to which it is
said twelve thousand policemen are attached; and their pay . . . is derived from the proceeds of the brothels. The splendor of these houses,
the beauty of the heart-ravishers, their blandishments and ogles, are beyond all description."⁶⁹ Women were of subject status, and were expected
to kill themselves on the death of their husbands, sometimes by allowing
themselves to be buried alive.⁷⁰

Under the Rayas or Kings of Vijayanagar literature prospered, both
in classical Sanskrit and in the Telugu dialect of the south. Krishna Raya
was himself a poet, as well as a liberal patron of letters; and his poet
laureate, Alasani-Peddana, is ranked among the highest of India's singers.
Painting and architecture flourished; enormous temples were built, and
almost every foot of their surface was carved into statuary or bas-relief.
Buddhism had lost its hold, and a form of Brahmanism that especially
honored Vishnu had become the faith of the people. The cow was holy
and was never killed; but many species of cattle and fowl were sacrificed
to the gods, and eaten by the people. Religion was brutal, and manners
were refined.

In one day all this power and luxury were destroyed. Slowly the
conquering Moslems had made their way south; now the sultans of
Bijapur, Ahmadnagar, Golkonda and Bidar united their forces to reduce
this last stronghold of the native Hindu kings. Their combined armies

met Rama Raja's half-million men at Talikota; the superior numbers of the attackers prevailed; Rama Raja was captured and beheaded in the sight of his followers, and these, losing courage, fled. Nearly a hundred thousand of them were slain in the retreat, until all the streams were colored with their blood. The conquering troops plundered the wealthy capital, and found the booty so abundant "that every private man in the allied army became rich in gold, jewels, effects, tents, arms, horses and slaves."[71] For five months the plunder continued: the victors slaughtered the help- less inhabitants in indiscriminate butchery, emptied the stores and shops, smashed the temples and palaces, and labored at great pains to destroy all the statuary and painting in the city; then they went through the streets with flaming torches, and set fire to all that would burn. When at last they retired, Vijayanagar was as completely ruined as if an earth- quake had visited it and had left not a stone upon a stone. It was a de- struction ferocious and absolute, typifying that terrible Moslem con- quest of India which had begun a thousand years before, and was now complete.

VI. THE MOSLEM CONQUEST

The weakening of India—Mahmud of Ghazni—The Sultanate of Delhi—Its cultural asides—Its brutal policy—The lessson of Indian history

The Mohammedan Conquest of India is probably the bloodiest story in history. It is a discouraging tale, for its evident moral is that civiliza- tion is a precarious thing, whose delicate complex of order and liberty, culture and peace may at any time be overthrown by barbarians invading from without or multiplying within. The Hindus had allowed their strength to be wasted in internal division and war; they had adopted re- ligions like Buddhism and Jainism, which unnerved them for the tasks of life; they had failed to organize their forces for the protection of their frontiers and their capitals, their wealth and their freedom, from the hordes of Scythians, Huns, Afghans and Turks hovering about India's boundaries and waiting for national weakness to let them in. For four hundred years (600-1000 A.D.) India invited conquest; and at last it came.

The first Moslem attack was a passing raid upon Multan, in the western Punjab (664 A.D.) Similar raids occurred at the convenience of the in- vaders during the next three centuries, with the result that the Moslems established themselves in the Indus valley about the same time that their Arab co-religionists in the West were fighting the battle of Tours (732 A.D.) for the mastery of Europe. But the real Moslem conquest of India did not come till the turn of the first millennium after Christ.

In the year 997 a Turkish chieftain by the name of Mahmud became sultan of the little state of Ghazni, in eastern Afghanistan. Mahmud knew that his throne was young and poor, and saw that India, across the border, was old and rich; the conclusion was obvious. Pretending a holy zeal for destroying Hindu idolatry, he swept across the frontier with a force inspired by a pious aspiration for booty. He met the unprepared Hindus at Bhimnagar, slaughtered them, pillaged their cities, destroyed their temples, and carried away the accumulated treasures of centuries. Returning to Ghazni he astonished the ambassadors of foreign powers by displaying "jewels and unbored pearls and rubies shining like sparks, or like wine congealed with ice, and emeralds like fresh sprigs of myrtle, and diamonds in size and weight like pomegranates."[72] Each winter Mahmud descended into India, filled his treasure chest with spoils, and amused his men with full freedom to pillage and kill; each spring he returned to his capital richer than before. At Mathura (on the Jumna) he took from the temple its statues of gold encrusted with precious stones, and emptied its coffers of a vast quantity of gold, silver and jewelry; he expressed his admiration for the architecture of the great shrine, judged that its duplication would cost one hundred million *dinars* and the labor of two hundred years, and then ordered it to be soaked with naphtha and burnt to the ground.[73] Six years later he sacked another opulent city of northern India, Somnath, killed all its fifty thousand inhabitants, and dragged its wealth to Ghazni. In the end he became, perhaps, the richest king that history has ever known. Sometimes he spared the population of the ravaged cities, and took them home to be sold as slaves; but so great was the number of such captives that after some years no one could be found to offer more than a few shillings for a slave. Before every important engagement Mahmud knelt in prayer, and asked the blessing of God upon his arms. He reigned for a third of a century; and when he died, full of years and honors, Moslem historians ranked him as the greatest monarch of his time, and one of the greatest sovereigns of any age.[74]

Seeing the canonization that success had brought to this magnificent thief, other Moslem rulers profited by his example, though none succeeded in bettering his instruction. In 1186 the Ghuri, a Turkish tribe of Afghanistan, invaded India, captured the city of Delhi, destroyed its temples, confiscated its wealth, and settled down in its palaces to establish the Sultanate ôf Delhi—an alien despotism fastened upon northern India for three centuries, and checked only by assassination and revolt. The first of these bloody sultans, Kutb-d Din Aibak, was a normal specimen of his kind—fanatical, ferocious and merciless. His gifts, as the Mohammedan historian tells us, "were bestowed by hundreds of thousands, and his slaughters likewise were by hundreds of thousands." In one victory of this warrior (who had been purchased as a slave), "fifty thousand men came under the collar of slavery, and the plain became black as pitch with Hindus."[75] Another sultan, Balban, punished rebels and brigands by casting them under the feet of elephants, or removing their skins, stuffing these with straw, and hanging them from the gates of Delhi. When some Mongol inhabitants who had settled in Delhi, and had been converted to Islam, attempted a rising, Sultan Alau-d-din (the conquerer of Chitor) had all the males—from fifteen to thirty thousand of them—slaughtered in one day. Sultan Muhammad bin Tughlak acquired the throne by murdering his father, became a great scholar and an elegant writer, dabbled in mathematics, physics and Greek philosophy, surpassed his predecessors in bloodshed and brutality, fed the flesh of a rebel nephew to the rebel's wife and children, ruined the country with reckless inflation, and laid it waste with pillage and murder till the inhabitants fled to the jungle. He killed so many Hindus that, in the words of a Moslem historian, "there was constantly in front of his royal pavilion and his Civil Court a mound of dead bodies and a heap of corpses, while the sweepers and executioners were wearied out by their work of dragging" the victims "and putting them to death in crowds."[76] In order to found a new capital at Daulatabad he drove every inhabitant from Delhi and left it a desert; and hearing that a blind man had stayed behind in Delhi, he ordered him to be dragged from the old to the new capital, so that only a leg remained of the wretch when his last journey was finished.[77] The Sultan complained that the people did not love him, or recognize his undeviating justice. He ruled India for a quarter of a century, and died in bed. His successor, Firoz Shah, invaded Bengal, offered a reward for every Hindu head, paid for 180,000 of them, raided Hindu villages for slaves, and died at the ripe age of eighty. Sultan Ahmad Shah feasted for three days whenever the number of defenseless Hindus slain in his territories in one day reached twenty thousand.[78]

These rulers were often men of ability, and their followers were gifted with fierce courage and industry; only so can we understand how they could have maintained their rule among a hostile people so overwhelmingly outnumbering them. All of them were armed with a religion militaristic in operation, but far superior in its stoical monotheism to any of the popular cults of India; they concealed its attractiveness by making the public exercise of the Hindu religions illegal, and thereby driving them more deeply into the Hindu soul. Some of these thirsty despots had culture as well as ability; they patronized the arts, and engaged artists and artisans—usually of Hindu origin—to build for them magnificent mosques and tombs; some of them were scholars, and delighted in converse with historians, poets and scientists. One of the greatest scholars of Asia, Alberuni, accompanied Mahmud of Ghazni to India, and wrote a scientific survey of India comparable to Pliny's *Natural History* and Humboldt's *Cosmos*. The Moslem historians were almost as numerous as the generals, and yielded nothing to them in the enjoyment of bloodshed and war. The Sultans drew from the people every rupee of tribute that could be exacted by the ancient art of taxation, as well as by straightforward robbery; but they stayed in India, spent their spoils in India, and thereby turned them back into India's economic life. Nevertheless, their terrorism and exploitation advanced that weakening of Hindu physique and morale which had been begun by an exhausting climate, an inadequate diet, political disunity, and pessimistic religions.

The usual policy of the Sultans was clearly sketched by Alau-d-din, who required his advisers to draw up "rules and regulations for grinding down the Hindus, and for depriving them of that wealth and property which fosters disaffection and rebellion."[80] Half of the gross produce of the soil was collected by the government; native rulers had taken one-sixth. "No Hindu," says a Moslem historian, "could hold up his head, and in their houses no sign of gold or silver . . . or of any superfluity was to be seen. . . . Blows, confinement in the stocks, imprisonment and chains, were all employed to enforce payment." When one of his own advisers protested against this policy, Alau-d-din answered: "Oh, Doctor, thou art a learned man, but thou hast no experience; I am an unlettered man, but I have a great deal. Be assured, then, that the Hindus will never become submissive and obedient till they are reduced to poverty. I have therefore given orders that just sufficient shall be left to them from year to year of corn, milk and curds, but that they shall not be allowed to accumulate hoards and property."[81]

This is the secret of the political history of modern India. Weakened by division, it succumbed to invaders; impoverished by invaders, it lost all power of resistance, and took refuge in supernatural consolations; it argued that both mastery and slavery were superficial delusions, and concluded that freedom of the body or the nation was hardly worth defending in so brief a life. The bitter lesson that may be drawn from this tragedy is that eternal vigilance is the price of civilization. A nation must love peace, but keep its powder dry.

VII. AKBAR THE GREAT

Tamerlane—Babur—Humayun—Akbar—His government—His character—His patronage of the arts—His passion for philosophy—His friendship for Hinduism and Christianity—His new religion—The last days of Akbar

It is in the nature of governments to degenerate; for power, as Shelley said, poisons every hand that touches it.[82] The excesses of the Delhi Sultans lost them the support not only of the Hindu population, but of their Moslem followers. When fresh invasions came from the north these Sultans were defeated with the same ease with which they themselves had won India.

Their first conqueror was Tamerlane himself—more properly Timur-i-lang—a Turk who had accepted Islam as an admirable weapon, and had given himself a pedigree going back to Genghis Khan, in order to win the support of his Mongol horde. Having attained the throne of Samarkand and feeling the need of more gold, it dawned upon him that India was still full of infidels. His generals, mindful of Moslem courage, demurred, pointing out that the infidels who could be reached from Samarkand were already under Mohammedan rule. *Mullahs* learned in the *Koran* decided the matter by quoting an inspiring verse: "Oh Prophet, make war upon infidels and unbelievers, and treat them with severity."[83] Thereupon Timur crossed the Indus (1398), massacred or enslaved such of the inhabitants as could not flee from him, defeated the forces of Sultan Mahmud Tughlak, occupied Delhi, slew a hundred thousand prisoners in cold blood, plundered the city of all the wealth that the Afghan dynasty had gathered there, and carried it off to Samarkand with a multitude of women and slaves, leaving anarchy, famine and pestilence in his wake.[84]

The Delhi Sultans remounted their throne, and taxed India for another century before the real conqueror came. Babur, founder of the great

Mogul* Dynasty, was a man every whit as brave and fascinating as Alexander. Descended from both Timur and Genghis Khan, he inherited all the ability of these scourges of Asia without their brutality. He suffered from a surplus of energy in body and mind; he fought, hunted and traveled insatiably; it was nothing for him, single-handed, to kill five enemies in five minutes.[87] In two days he rode one hundred and sixty miles on horseback, and swam the Ganges twice in the bargain; and in his last years he remarked that not since the age of eleven had he kept the fast of Ramadan twice in the same place.[88]

"In the twelfth year of my age," he begins his *Memoirs*, "I became the ruler in the country of Farghana."[89] At fifteen he besieged and captured Samarkand; lost it again when he could not pay his troops; nearly died of illness; hid for a time in the mountains, and then recaptured the city with two hundred and forty men; lost it again through treachery; hid for two years in obscure poverty, and thought of retiring to a peasant life in China; organized another force, and, by the contagion of his own bravery, took Kabul in his twenty-second year; overwhelmed the one hundred thousand soldiers of Sultan Ibrahim at Panipat with twelve thousand men and some fine horses, killed prisoners by the thousands, captured Delhi, established there the greatest and most beneficent of the foreign dynasties that have ruled India, enjoyed four years of peace, composed excellent poems and memoirs, and died at the age of fortyseven after living, in action and experience, a century.

His son, Humayun, was too weak and vacillating, and too addicted to opium, to carry on Babur's work. Sher Shah, an Afghan chief, defeated him in two bloody battles, and restored for a time the Afghan power in India. Sher Shah, though capable of slaughter in the best Islamic style, rebuilt Delhi in fine architectural taste, and established governmental reforms that prepared for the enlightened rule of Akbar. Two minor Shahs held the power for a decade; then Humayun, after twelve years of hardship and wandering, organized a force in Persia, reentered India, and recaptured the throne. Eight months later Humayun fell from the terrace of his library, and died.

---

* *Mogul* is another form of *Mongol*. The Moguls were really Turks; but the Hindus called—and still call—all northern Moslems (except the Afghans) Moguls.[85] "Babur" was a Mongol nickname, meaning lion; the real name of the first Mogul Emperor of India was Zahiru-d din Muhammad.[96]

During his exile and poverty his wife had borne him a son whom he had piously called Muhammad, but whom India was to call Akbar—that is, "Very Great." No effort was spared to make him great; even his ancestry had taken every precaution, for in his veins ran the blood of Babur, Timur and Genghis Khan. Tutors were supplied him in abundance, but he rejected them, and refused to learn how to read. Instead he educated himself for kingship by incessant and dangerous sport; he became a perfect horseman, played polo royally, and knew the art of controlling the most ferocious elephants; he was always ready to set out on a lion or tiger hunt, to undergo any fatigue, and to face all dangers in the first person. Like a good Turk he had no effeminate distaste for human blood; when, at the age of fourteen, he was invited to win the title of *Ghazi*—Slayer of the Infidel—by killing a Hindu prisoner, he cut off the man's head at once with one stroke of his scimitar. These were the barbarous beginnings of a man destined to become one of the wisest, most humane and most cultured of all the kings known to history.*

At the age of eighteen he took over from the Regent the full direction of affairs. His dominion then extended over an eighth of India—a belt of territory some three hundred miles broad, running from the northwest frontier at Multan to Benares in the East. He set out with the zeal and voracity of his grandfather to extend these borders; and by a series of ruthless wars he made himself ruler of all Hindustan except for the little Rajput kingdom of Mewar. Returning to Delhi he put aside his armor, and devoted himself to re-organizing the administration of his realm. His power was absolute, and all important offices, even in distant provinces, were filled by his appointment. His principal aides were four: a Prime Minister or *Vakir*; a Finance Minister, called sometimes *Vazir* (Vizier), sometimes *Diwan*; a Master of the Court, or *Bakhshi*; and a Primate or *Sadr*, who was head of the Mohammedan religion in India. As his rule acquired tradition and prestige he depended less and less upon military power, and contented himself with a standing army of some twenty-five thousand men. In time of war this modest force was augmented with troops recruited by the provincial military governors—a precarious arrangement which had something to do with the fall of the

---

* Later he came to recognize the value of books, and—being still unable to read—listened for hours while others read to him, often from abstruse and difficult volumes. In the end he became an illiterate scholar, loving letters and art, and supporting them with royal largesse.

Mogul Empire under Aurangzeb.* Bribery and embezzlement throve among these governors and their subordinates, so that much of Akbar's time was spent in checking corruption. He regulated with strict economy the expenses of his court and household, fixing the prices of food and materials bought for them, and the wages of labor engaged by the state. When he died he left the equivalent of a billion dollars in the treasury, and his empire was the most powerful on earth.⁹⁰

Both law and taxation were severe, but far less than before. From one-sixth to one-third of the gross produce of the soil was taken from the peasants, amounting to some $100,000,000 a year in land tax. The Emperor was legislator, executive and judge; as supreme court he spent many hours in giving audience to important litigants. His law forbade child marriage and compulsory suttee, sanctioned the remarriage of widows, abolished the slavery of captives and the slaughter of animals for sacrifice, gave freedom to all religions, opened career to every talent of whatever creed or race, and removed the head-tax that the Afghan rulers had placed upon all Hindus unconverted to Islam.⁹¹ At the beginning of his reign the law included such punishments as mutilation; at the end it was probably the most enlightened code of any sixteenth-century government. Every state begins with violence, and (if it becomes secure) mellows into liberty.

But the strength of a ruler is often the weakness of his government. The system depended so much upon Akbar's superior qualities of mind and character that obviously it would threaten to disintegrate at his death. He had, of course, most of the virtues, since he engaged most of the historians: he was the best athlete, the best horseman, the best swordsman, one of the greatest architects, and by all odds the handsomest man in the kingdom. Actually he had long arms, bow legs, narrow Mongoloid eyes, a head drooping leftward, and a wart on his nose.⁹² He made himself presentable by neatness, dignity, serenity, and brilliant eyes that could sparkle (says a contemporary) "like the sea in sunshine," or flare up in a way to make the offender tremble with terror, like Vandamme before Napoleon. He dressed simply, in brocaded cap, blouse and trousers, jewels and bare feet. He cared little for meat, and gave it up almost entirely

---

* The army was supplied with the best ordnance yet seen in India, but inferior to that then in use in Europe. Akbar's efforts to secure better guns failed; and this inferiority in the instruments of slaughter coöperated with the degeneration of his descendants in determining the European conquest of India.

in his later years, saying that "it is not right that a man should make his stomach the grave of animals." Nevertheless he was strong in body and will, excelled in many active sports, and thought nothing of walking thirty-six miles in a day. He liked polo so much that he invented a luminous ball in order that the game might be played at night. He inherited the violent impulses of his family, and in his youth (like his Christian contemporaries) he was capable of solving problems by assassination. Gradually he learned, in Woodrow Wilson's phrase, to sit upon his own volcano; and he rose far above his time in that spirit of fair play which does not always distinguish Oriental rulers. "His clemency," says Firishta, "was without bounds; this virtue he often carried beyond the line of prudence."[93] He was generous, expending vast sums in alms; he was affable to all, but especially to the lowly; "their little offerings," says a Jesuit missionary, "he used to accept with such a pleased look, handling them and putting them in his bosom, as he did not do with the most lavish gifts of the nobles." One of his contemporaries described him as an epileptic; many said that melancholy possessed him to a morbid degree. Perhaps to put a brighter color on reality, he drank liquor and took opium, in moderation; his father and his children had similar habits, without similar self-control.* He had a harem suitable to the size of his empire; one gossip tells us that "the King hath in Agra and Fathpur-Sikri, as they do credibly report, one thousand elephants, thirty thousand horses, fourteen hundred tame deer, eight hundred concubines." But he does not seem to have had sensual ambitions or tastes. He married widely, but politically; he pleased the Rajput princes by espousing their daughters, and thereby bound them to the support of his throne; and from that time the Mogul Dynasty was half native in blood. A Rajput became his leading general, and a raja rose to be his greatest minister. His dream was a united India.[94]

His mind was not quite as realistic and coldly accurate as Cæsar's or Napoleon's; he had a passion for metaphysics, and might, if deposed, have become a mystic recluse. He thought constantly, and was forever making inventions and suggesting improvements.[95] Like Haroun-al-Rashid he took nocturnal rambles in disguise, and came back bursting with reforms. In the midst of his complex activity he made time to collect a great library, composed entirely of manuscripts beautifully written and

* Two of his children died in youth of chronic alcoholism.[96]

engraved by those skilful penmen whom he esteemed as artists fully
equal to the painters and architects that adorned his reign. He despised
print as a mechanical and impersonal thing, and soon disposed of the
choice specimens of European typography presented to him by his Jesuit
friends. The volumes in his library numbered only twenty-four thousand,
but they were valued at $3,500,000[97] by those who thought that such
hoards of the spirit could be estimated in material terms. He patronized
poets without stint, and loved one of them—the Hindu Birbal—so much
that he made him a court favorite, and finally a general; whereupon Birbal
made a mess of a campaign, and was slaughtered in no lyric flight.*[98]
Akbar had his literary aides render into Persian—which was the language
of his court—the masterpieces of Hindu literature, history and science,
and himself supervised the translation of the interminable *Mahabharata*.[100]
Every art flourished under his patronage and stimulation. Hindu music
and poetry had now one of their greatest periods; and painting, both
Persian and Hindu, reached its second zenith through his encouragement.[101] At Agra he directed the building of the famous Fort, and within
its walls erected (by proxy) five hundred buildings that his contemporaries considered to be among the most beautiful in the world. They
were torn down by the impetuous Shah Jehan, and can be judged only
by such remnants of Akbar's architecture as the tomb of Humayun at
Delhi, and the remains at Fathpur-Sikri, where the mausoleum of Akbar's
beloved friend, the ascetic Shaik Salim Chisti, is among the fairest structures in India.

Deeper than these interests was his *penchant* for speculation. This
well-nigh omnipotent emperor secretly yearned to be a philosopher—
much as philosophers long to be emperors, and cannot comprehend the
stupidity of Providence in withholding from them their rightful thrones.
After conquering the world, Akbar was unhappy because he could not
understand it. "Although," he said, "I am the master of so vast a kingdom,
and all the appliances of government are at my hand, yet since true greatness consists in doing the will of God, my mind is not at ease in this diversity of sects and creeds; and apart from this outward pomp of circumstance, with what satisfaction, in this despondency, can I undertake the
sway of empire? I await the coming of some discreet man of principle

---

* The Moslems hated Birbal, and rejoiced at his death. One of them, the historian
Badaoni, recorded the incident with savage pleasure: "Birbal, who had fled from fear of
his life, was slain, and entered the row of the dogs in Hell."[99]

who will resolve the difficulties of my conscience. . . . Discourses in philosophy have such a charm for me that they distract me from all else, and I forcibly restrain myself from listening to them lest the necessary duties of the hour should be neglected."[102] "Crowds of learned men from all nations," says Badaoni, "and sages of various religions and sects, came to the court and were honored with private conversations. After inquiries and investigations, which were their only business and occupation day and night, they would talk about profound points of science, the subtleties of revelation, the curiosities of history, and the wonders of nature."[103] "The superiority of man," said Akbar, "rests on the jewel of reason."[104]

As became a philosopher, he was profoundly interested in religion. His careful reading of the *Mahabharata*, and his intimacy with Hindu poets and sages, lured him into the study of Indian faiths. For a time, at least, he accepted the theory of transmigration, and scandalized his Moslem followers by appearing in public with Hindu religious marks on his forehead. He had a flair for humoring all the creeds: he pleased the Zoroastrians by wearing their sacred shirt and girdle under his clothes, and allowed the Jains to persuade him to abandon hunting, and to prohibit, on certain days, the killing of animals. When he learned of the new religion called Christianity, which had come into India with the Portuguese occupation of Goa, he despatched a message to the Paulist missionaries there, inviting them to send two of their learned men to him. Later some Jesuits came to Delhi and so interested him in Christ that he ordered his scribes to translate the New Testament.[105] He gave the Jesuits full freedom to make converts, and allowed them to bring up one of his sons. While Catholics were murdering Protestants in France, and Protestants, under Elizabeth, were murdering Catholics in England, and the Inquisition was killing and robbing Jews in Spain, and Bruno was being burned at the stake in Italy, Akbar invited the representatives of all the religions in his empire to a conference, pledged them to peace, issued edicts of toleration for every cult and creed, and, as evidence of his own neutrality, married wives from the Brahman, Buddhist, and Mohammedan faiths.

His greatest pleasure, after the fires of youth had cooled, was in the free discussion of religious beliefs. He had quite discarded the dogmas of Islam, and to such an extent that his Moslem subjects fretted under his impartial rule. "This king," St. Francis Xavier reported with some exaggeration, "has destroyed the false sect of Mohammed, and wholly discredited it. In this city there is neither a mosque nor a *Koran*—the book of their law; and the mosques that were there have been made stables for horses, and storehouses." The King took no stock in revelations, and would accept nothing that could not justify itself with science and philosophy. It was not unusual for him to gather friends and prelates of various sects together, and discuss religion with them from Thursday evening to Friday noon. When the Moslem *mullahs* and the Christian priests quarreled he reproved them both, saying that God should be worshiped through the intellect, and not by a blind adherence to supposed revelations. "Each person," he said, in the spirit—and perhaps through the influence—of the *Upanishads* and Kabir, "according to his condition gives the Supreme Being a name; but in reality to name the Unknowable is vain." Certain Moslems suggested an ordeal by fire as a test of Christianity *vs.* Islam: a *mullah* holding the *Koran* and a priest holding one of the Gospels were to enter a fire, and he who should come out unhurt would be adjudged the teacher of truth. Akbar, who did not like the *mullah* who was proposed for this experiment, warmly seconded the suggestion, but the Jesuit rejected it as blasphemous and impious, not to say dangerous. Gradually the rival groups of theologians shunned these conferences, and left them to Akbar and his rationalist intimates.[106]

Harassed by the religious divisions in his kingdom, and disturbed by the thought that they might disrupt it after his death, Akbar finally decided to promulgate a new religion, containing in simple form the essentials of the warring faiths. The Jesuit missionary Bartoli records the matter thus:

> He summoned a General Council, and invited to it all the masters of learning and the military commandants of the cities round about, excluding only Father Ridolfo, whom it was vain to expect to be other than hostile to his sacrilegious purpose. When he had them all assembled in front of him, he spoke in a spirit of astute and knavish policy, saying:
>
> "For an empire ruled by one head it was a bad thing to have the members divided among themselves and at variance one with the other; . . . whence it came about that there are as many factions as religions. We ought, therefore, to bring them all into one, but in such fashion that they should be both 'one' and 'all'; with the great advantage of not losing what is good in any one religion, while gaining whatever is better in another. In that way honor would be rendered to God, peace would be given to the people, and security to the empire."[107]

The Council perforce consenting, he issued a decree proclaiming him-self the infallible head of the church; this was the chief contribution of Christianity to the new religion. The creed was a pantheistic monotheism in the best Hindu tradition, with a spark of sun and fire worship from the Zoroastrians, and a semi-Jain recommendation to abstain from meat. The slaughter of cows was made a capital offense: nothing could have pleased the Hindus more, or the Moslems less. A later edict made vege-tarianism compulsory on the entire population for at least a hundred days in the year; and in further consideration of native ideas, garlic and onions were prohibited. The building of mosques, the fast of Ramadan, the pilgrimage to Mecca, and other Mohammedan customs were banned. Many Moslems who resisted the edicts were exiled.[108] In the center of the Peace Court at Fathpur-Sikri a Temple of United Religion was built (and still stands there) as a symbol of the Emperor's fond hope that now all the inhabitants of India might be brothers, worshiping the same God.

As a religion the *Din Ilahi* never succeeded; Akbar found tradition too strong for his infallibility. A few thousand rallied to the new cult, largely as a means of securing official favor; the vast majority adhered to their in-herited gods. Politically the stroke had some beneficent results. The abolition of the head-tax and the pilgrim-tax on the Hindus, the freedom granted to all religions,* the weakening of racial and religious fanaticism, dogmatism and division, far outweighed the egotism and excesses of Akbar's novel revelation. And it won him such loyalty from even the Hindus who did not accept his creed that his. prime purpose—political unity—was largely achieved.

With his own fellow Moslems, however, the *Din Ilahi* was a source of bitter resentment, leading at one time to open revolt, and stirring Prince Jehangir into treacherous machinations against his father. The Prince complained that Akbar had reigned forty years, and had so strong a con-stitution that there was no prospect of his early death. Jehangir organized an army of thirty thousand horsemen, killed Abu-l Fazl, the King's court historian and dearest friend, and proclaimed himself emperor. Akbar per-suaded the youth to submit, and forgave him after a day; but the disloy-alty of his son, added to the death of his mother and his friend, broke his spirit, and left him an easy prey for the Great Enemy. In his last days his children ignored him, and gave their energies to quarreling for his throne. Only a few intimates were with him when he died—presumably

* With the exception of the transient persecution of Islam (1582-5).

of dysentery, perhaps of poisoning by Jehangir. *Mullahs* came to his deathbed to reconvert him to Islam, but they failed; the King "passed away without the benefit of the prayers of any church or sect."[109] No crowd followed his simple funeral; and the sons and courtiers who had worn mourning for the event discarded it the same evening, and rejoiced that they had inherited his kingdom. It was a bitter death for the justest and wisest ruler that Asia has ever known.

VIII. THE DECLINE OF THE MOGULS

The children of great men—Jehangir—Shah Jehan—His magnificence—His fall—Aurangzeb—His fanaticism—His death— The coming of the British

The children who had waited so impatiently for his death found it difficult to hold together the empire that had been created by his genius. Why is it that great men so often have mediocrities for their offspring? Is it because the gamble of the genes that produced them—the commingling of ancestral traits and biological possibilities—was but a chance, and could not be expected to recur? Or is it because the genius exhausts in thought and toil the force that might have gone to parentage, and leaves only his diluted blood to his heirs? Or is it that children decay under ease, and early good fortune deprives them of the stimulus to ambition and growth?

Jehangir was not so much a mediocrity as an able degenerate. Born of a Turkish father and a Hindu princess, he enjoyed all the opportunities of an heir apparent, indulged himself in alcohol and lechery, and gave full vent to that sadistic joy in cruelty which had been a recessive character in Babur, Humayun and Akbar, but had always lurked in the Tatar blood. He took delight in seeing men flayed alive, impaled, or torn to pieces by elephants. In his *Memoirs* he tells how, because their careless entrance upon the scene startled his quarry in a hunt, he had a groom killed, and the groom's servants hamstrung—i.e., crippled for life by severing the tendons behind the knees; having attended to this, he says, "I continued hunting."[110] When his son Khusru conspired against him he had seven hundred supporters of the rebel impaled in a line along the streets of Lahore; and he remarks with pleasure on the length of time it took these men to die.[111] His sexual life was attended to by a harem of six thousand women,[112] and graced by his later attachment to his favorite wife, Nur Jehan*—whom he acquired by murdering her husband. His administration of justice was impartial as well as severe, but the extravagance of his expenditures laid a heavy burden upon a nation which had become the most prosperous on the globe through the wise leadership of Akbar and many years of peace.

Toward the end of his reign Jehangir took more and more to his cups, and neglected the tasks of government. Inevitably conspiracies arose to replace him; already in 1622 his son Jehan had tried to seize the throne. When Jehangir died Jehan hurried up from the Deccan where he had been hiding, proclaimed himself emperor, and murdered all his brothers to ensure his peace of mind. His father passed on to him his habits of extravagance, intemperance and cruelty. The expenses of Jehan's court, and the high salaries of his innumerable officials, absorbed more and more of the revenue produced by the thriving industry and commerce of the people. The religious tolerance of Akbar and the indifference of Jehangir were replaced by a return to the Moslem faith, the persecution of Christians, and the ruthless and wholesale destruction of Hindu shrines.

Shah Jehan redeemed himself in some measure by his generosity to his friends and the poor, his artistic taste and passion in adorning India with the fairest architecture that it had ever seen, and his devotion to his wife Mumtaz Mahal—"Ornament of the Palace." He had married her in his twenty-first year, when he had already had two children by an earlier consort. Mumtaz gave her tireless husband fourteen children in eighteen years, and died, at the age of thirty-nine, in bringing forth the last. Shah Jehan built the immaculate Taj Mahal as a monument to her memory and her fertility, and relapsed into a scandalous licentiousness.[113] The most beautiful of all the world's tombs was but one of a hundred masterpieces that Jehan erected, chiefly at Agra and in that new Delhi which grew up under his planning. The costliness of these palaces, the luxuriousness of the court, the extravagant jewelry of the Peacock Throne,† would

---

* I.e., "Light of the World"; also called Nur Mahal—"Light of the Palace." *Jehangir* means "Conqueror of the World"; *Shah Jehan*, of course, was "King of the World."

† This throne, which required seven years for its completion, consisted entirely of jewels, precious metals and stones. Four legs of gold supported the seat; twelve pillars made of emeralds held up the enameled canopy; each pillar bore two peacocks encrusted with gems; and between each pair of peacocks rose a tree covered with diamonds, emeralds, rubies and pearls. The total cost was over $7,000,000. The throne was captured and carried off to Persia by Nadir Shah (1739), and was gradually dismembered to defray the expenses of Persian royalty.[114]

suggest a rate of taxation ruinous to India. Nevertheless, though one of the worst famines in India's history occurred in Shah Jehan's reign, his thirty years of government marked the zenith of India's prosperity and prestige. The lordly Shah was a capable ruler, and though he wasted many lives in foreign war he gave his own land a full generation of peace. As a great British administrator of Bombay, Mountstuart Elphinstone, wrote,

> those who look on India in its present state may be inclined to sus-
> pect the native writers of exaggerating its former prosperity; but
> the deserted cities, ruined palaces and choked-up aqueducts which
> we still see, with the great reservoirs and embankments in the midst
> of jungles, and the decayed causeways, wells and caravanserais of
> the royal roads, concur with the evidence of contemporary trav-
> elers in convincing us that those historians had good grounds for
> their commendation.[115]

Jehan had begun his reign by killing his brothers; but he had neglected to kill his sons, one of whom was destined to overthrow him. In 1657 the ablest of these, Aurangzeb, led an insurrection from the Deccan. The Shah, like David, gave instructions to his generals to defeat the rebel army, but to spare, if possible, the life of his son. Aurangzeb overcame all the forces sent against him, captured his father, and imprisoned him in the Fort of Agra. For nine bitter years the deposed king lingered there, never visited by his son, attended only by his faithful daughter Jahanara, and spending his days looking from the Jasmine Tower of his prison across the Jumna to where his once-beloved Mumtaz lay in her jeweled tomb.

The son who so ruthlessly deposed him was one of the greatest saints in the history of Islam, and perhaps the most nearly unique of the Mogul emperors. The *mullahs* who had educated him had so imbued him with religion that at one time the young prince had thought of renouncing the empire and the world, and becoming a religious recluse. Throughout his life, despite his despotism, his subtle diplomacy, and a conception of morals as applying only to his own sect, he remained a pious Moslem, reading prayers at great length, memorizing the entire *Koran*, and warring against infidelity. He spent hours in devotion, and days in fasts. For the most part he practised his religion as earnestly as he professed it. It is true that in politics he was cold and calculating, capable of lying cleverly for his country and his god. But he was the least cruel of the Moguls, and the mildest; slaughter abated in his reign, and he made hardly any use of punishment in dealing with crime. He was consistently humble in deportment, patient under provocation, and resigned in misfortune. He abstained scrupulously from all food, drink or luxury forbidden by his faith; though skilled in music, he abandoned it as a sensual pleasure; and apparently he carried out his resolve to spend nothing upon himself save what he had been able to earn by the labor of his hands.[116] He was a St. Augustine on the throne.

Shah Jehan had given half his revenues to the promotion of architecture and the other arts; Aurangzeb cared nothing for art, destroyed its "heathen" monuments with coarse bigotry, and fought, through a reign of half a century, to eradicate from India almost all religions but his own. He issued orders to the provincial governors, and to his other subordinates, to raze to the ground all the temples of either Hindus or Christians, to smash every idol, and to close every Hindu school. In one year (1679-80) sixty-six temples were broken to pieces in Amber alone, sixty-three at Chitor, one hundred and twenty-three at Udaipur;[117] and over the site of a Benares temple especially sacred to the Hindus he built, in deliberate insult, a Mohammedan mosque.[118] He forbade all public worship of the Hindu faiths, and laid upon every unconverted Hindu a heavy capitation tax.[119] As a result of his fanaticism, thousands of the temples which had represented or housed the art of India through a millennium were laid in ruins. We can never know, from looking at India today, what grandeur and beauty she once possessed.

Aurangzeb converted a handful of timid Hindus to Islam, but he wrecked his dynasty and his country. A few Moslems worshiped him as a saint, but the mute and terrorized millions of India looked upon him as a monster, fled from his tax-gatherers, and prayed for his death. During his reign the Mogul empire in India reached its height, extending into the Deccan; but it was a power that had no foundation in the affection of the people, and was doomed to fall at the first hostile and vigorous touch. The Emperor himself, in his last years, began to realize that by the very narrowness of his piety he had destroyed the heritage of his fathers. His deathbed letters are pitiful documents.

> I know not who I am, where I shall go, or what will happen to this sinner full of sins. . . . My years have gone by profitless. God has been in my heart, yet my darkened eyes have not recognized his

light. . . . There is no hope for me in the future. The fever is gone, but only the skin is left. . . . I have greatly sinned, and know not what torments await me. . . . May the peace of God be upon you.[120]

He left instructions that his funeral should be ascetically simple, and that no money should be spent on his shroud except the four rupees that he had made by sewing caps. The top of his coffin was to be covered with a plain piece of canvas. To the poor he left three hundred rupees earned by copying the *Koran*.[121] He died at the age of eighty-nine, having long outstayed his welcome on the earth.

Within seventeen years of his death his empire was broken into fragments. The support of the people, so wisely won by Akbar, had been forfeited by the cruelty of Jehangir, the wastefulness of Jehan, and the intolerance of Aurangzeb. The Moslem minority, already enervated by India's heat, had lost the military ardor and physical vigor of their prime, and no fresh recruits were coming from the north to buttress their declining power. Meanwhile, far away in the west, a little island had sent its traders to cull the riches of India. Soon it would send its guns, and take over this immense empire in which Hindu and Moslem had joined to build one of the great civilizations of history.

CHAPTER XVII

The Life of the People*

I. THE MAKERS OF WEALTH

The jungle background — Agriculture — Mining — Handicrafts —
Commerce — Money — Taxes — Famines — Poverty and wealth

THE soil of India had not lent itself willingly to civilization. A great part of it was jungle, the jealously guarded home of lions, tigers, elephants, serpents, and other individualists with a Rousseauian contempt for civilization. The biological struggle to free the land from these enemies had continued underneath all the surface dramas of economic and political strife. Akbar shot tigers near Mathura, and captured wild elephants in many places where none can be found today. In Vedic times the lion might be met with anywhere in northwest or central India; now it is almost extinct throughout the peninsula. The serpent and the insect, however, still carry on the war: in 1926 some two thousand Hindus were killed by wild animals (875 by marauding tigers); but twenty thousand Hindus met death from the fangs of snakes.[1]

Gradually, as the soil was redeemed from the beast, it was turned to the cultivation of rice, pulse, millet, vegetables and fruits. Through the greater part of Indian history the majority of the population have lived abstemiously on these natural foods, reserving flesh, fish and fowl for the Outcastes and the rich.[2]† To render their diet more exciting, and perhaps to assist Aphrodite,[3] the Hindus have grown and consumed an unusual abundance of curry, ginger, cloves, cinnamon and other spices. Europeans valued these spices so highly that they stumbled upon a hemisphere in search for them; who knows but that America was discovered for the sake of love? In Vedic times the land belonged to the people,[5] but from the days of Chandragupta Maurya it became the habit of the kings to claim royal owner-

---

* The following analysis will apply for the most part to post-Vedic and pre-British India. The reader should remember that India is now in flux, and that institutions, morals and manners once characteristic of her may be disappearing today.

† Vijayanagar was an exception; its people ate fowl and flesh (barring oxen and cows), as well as lizards, rats and cats.[4]

ship of all the soil, and to let it out to the tiller for an annual rental and tax.[6] Irrigation was usually a governmental undertaking. One of the dams raised by Chandragupta functioned till 150 A.D.; remains of the ancient canals can be seen everywhere today; and signs still survive of the artificial lake that Raj Sing, Rajput Rana of Mewar, built as an irrigation reservoir (1661), and which he surrounded with a marble wall twelve miles in length.[7]

The Hindus seem to have been the first people to mine gold.[8] Herodotus[9] and Megasthenes[10] tell of the great "gold-digging ants, in size somewhat less than dogs, but bigger than foxes," which helped the miners to find the metal by turning it up in their scratching of the sand.[*] Much of the gold used in the Persian Empire in the fifth century before Christ came from India. Silver, copper, lead, tin, zinc and iron were also mined—iron as early as 1500 B.C.[11] The art of tempering and casting iron developed in India long before its known appearance in Europe; Vikramaditya, for example, erected at Delhi (ca. 380 A.D.) an iron pillar that stands untarnished today after fifteen centuries; and the quality of metal, or manner of treatment, which has preserved it from rust or decay is still a mystery to modern metallurgical science.[12] Before the European invasion the smelting of iron in small charcoal furnaces was one of the major industries of India.[13] The Industrial Revolution taught Europe how to carry out these processes more cheaply on a larger scale, and the Indian industry died under the competition. Only in our own time are the rich mineral resources of India being again exploited and explored.[14]

The growing of cotton appears earlier in India than elsewhere; apparently it was used for cloth in Mohenjo-daro.[15] In our oldest classical reference to cotton Herodotus says, with pleasing ignorance: "Certain wild trees there bear *wool* instead of fruit, which in beauty and quality excels that of sheep; and the Indians make their clothing from these trees."[16] It was their wars in the Near East that acquainted the Romans with this tree-grown "wool."[17] Arabian travelers in ninth-century India reported that "in this country they make garments of such extraordinary perfection that nowhere else is their like to be seen—sewed and woven to such a degree of fineness, they may be drawn through a ring of moderate size."[18] The medieval Arabs took over the art from India, and their word *quttan* gave us our word *cotton*.[19] The name *muslin* was originally applied to fine cotton weaves made in Mosul from Indian models; *calico* was so called because it came (first in 1631) from Calicut, on the southwestern shores of India. "Embroidery," says Marco Polo, speaking of Gujarat in 1293 A.D., "is here performed with more

---

[*] We do not know what these "ants" were; they were more probably anteaters than ants.

delicacy than in any other part of the world."[20] The shawls of Kashmir and the rugs of India bear witness even today to the excellence of Indian weaving in texture and design.* But weaving was only one of the many handicrafts of India, and the weavers were only one of the many craft and merchant guilds that organized and regulated the industry of India. Europe looked upon the Hindus as experts in almost every line of *manu*facture— wood-work, ivory-work, metal-work, bleaching, dyeing, tanning, soap-making, glass-blowing, gunpowder, fireworks, cement, etc.[21] China imported eyeglasses from India in 1260 A.D. Bernier, traveling in India in the seventeenth century, described it as humming with industry. Fitch, in 1585, saw a fleet of one hundred and eighty boats carrying a great variety of goods down the river Jumna.

Internal trade flourished; every roadside was—and is—a bazaar. The foreign trade of India is as old as her history;[22] objects found in Sumeria and Egypt indicate a traffic between these countries and India as far back as 3000 B.C.[23] Commerce between India and Babylon by the Persian Gulf flourished from 700 to 480 B.C.; and perhaps the "ivory, apes and peacocks" of Solomon came by the same route from the same source. India's ships sailed the sea to Burma and China in Chandragupta's days; and Greek merchants, called *Yavana* (Ionians) by the Hindus, thronged the markets of Dravidian India in the centuries before and after the birth of Christ.[24] Rome, in her epicurean days, depended upon India for spices, perfumes and unguents, and paid great prices for Indian silks, brocades, muslins and cloth of gold; Pliny condemned the extravagance which sent $5,000,000 yearly from Rome to India for such luxuries. Indian cheetahs, tigers and elephants assisted in the gladiatorial games and sacrificial rites of the Colosseum.[25] The Parthian wars were fought by Rome largely to keep open the trade route to India. In the seventh century the Arabs captured Persia and Egypt, and thereafter trade between Europe and Asia passed through Moslem hands; hence the Crusades, and Columbus. Under the Moguls foreign commerce rose again; the wealth of Venice, Genoa and other Italian cities grew through their service as ports for European trade with India and the East; the Renaissance owed more to the wealth derived from this trade than to the manuscripts brought to Italy by the Greeks. Akbar had an admiralty which supervised the building of ships and the regulation of ocean traffic; the ports of Bengal and Sindh were famous for shipbuilding, and did their work so well that the Sultan of Constantinople found it cheaper to have his vessels built there than in Alexandria; even the East India Company had many of its ships built in Bengal docks.[26]

---

* Cf. the red rug, from seventeenth-century India, presented to the Metropolitan Museum of Art (Room D 3) by Mr. J. P. Morgan.

The development of coinage to facilitate this trade took many centuries. In Buddha's days rough rectangular coins were issued by various economic and political authorities; but it was not until the fourth century before Christ that India, under the influence of Persia and Greece, arrived at a coinage guaranteed by the state.[27] Sher Shah issued well-designed pieces of copper, silver and gold, and established the rupee as the basic coin of the realm.[28] Under Akbar and Jehangir the coinage of India was superior, in artistic execution and purity of metal, to that of any modern European state.[29] As in medieval Europe, so in medieval India the growth of industry and commerce was impeded by a religious antipathy to the taking of interest. "The Indians," says Megasthenes, "neither put out money at usury" (interest), "nor know how to borrow. It is contrary to established usage for an Indian either to do or to suffer wrong; and therefore they neither make contracts nor require securities."[30] When the Hindu could not invest his savings in his own economic enterprises he preferred to hide them, or to buy jewelry as conveniently hoardable wealth.[31] Perhaps this failure to develop a facile credit system aided the Industrial Revolution to establish the European domination of Asia. Slowly, however, despite the hostility of the Brahmans, money-lending grew. The rates varied, according to the caste of the borrower, from twelve to sixty per cent, usually ranging about twenty.[32] Bankruptcy was not permitted as a liquidation of debts; if a debtor died insolvent his descendants to the sixth generation continued to be responsible for his obligations.[33]

Both agriculture and trade were heavily taxed to support the government. The peasant had to surrender from one-sixth to one-half of his crop; and, as in medieval and contemporary Europe, many tolls were laid upon the flow and exchange of goods.[34] Akbar raised the land-tax to one-third, but abolished all other exactions.[35] The land-tax was a bitter levy, but it had the saving grace of rising with prosperity and falling with depression; and in famine years the poor could at least die untaxed. For famines occurred, even in Akbar's palmy days; that of 1556 seems to have led to cannibalism and widespread desolation. Roads were bad, transportation was slow, and the surplus of one region could with difficulty be used to supply the dearth of another.

As everywhere, there were extremes of poverty and wealth, but hardly so great as in India or America today. At the bottom was a small minority of slaves; above them the Shudras were not so much slaves as hired men, though their status, like that of almost all Hindus, was hereditary. The poverty described by Père Dubois (1820)[36] was the result of fifty years of political chaos; under the Moguls the condition of the people had been relatively prosperous.[37] Wages were modest, ranging for manual workers from three to nine cents a day in Akbar's reign; but prices were correspondingly low. In 1600 a rupee (normally 32.5 cents) bought 194 pounds of wheat, or 278 pounds of barley; in 1901 it bought only 29 pounds of wheat, or 44 pounds of barley.[38] An Englishman resident in India in 1616 described "the plenty of all provisions" as "very great throughout the whole monarchy," and added that "every one there may eat bread without scarceness."[39] Another Englishman, touring India in the seventeenth century, found that his expenses averaged four cents a day.[40]

The wealth of the country reached its two peaks under Chandragupta Maurya and Shah Jehan. The riches of India under the Gupta kings became a proverb throughout the world. Yuan Chwang pictured an Indian city as beautified with gardens and pools, and adorned with institutes of letters and arts; "the inhabitants were well off, and there were families with great wealth; fruit and flowers were abundant. . . . The people had a refined appearance, and dressed in glossy silk attire; they were . . . clear and suggestive in discourse; they were equally divided between orthodoxy and heterodoxy."[41] "The Hindu kingdoms overthrown by the Moslems," says Elphinstone, "were so wealthy that the historians tire of telling of the immense loot of jewels and coin captured by the invaders."[42] Nicolo Conti described the banks of the Ganges (ca. 1420) as lined with one prosperous city after another, each well designed, rich in gardens and orchards, silver and gold, commerce and industry.[43] Shah Jehan's treasury was so full that he kept two underground strong rooms, each of some 150,000 cubic feet capacity, almost filled with silver and gold.[44] "Contemporary testimonies," says Vincent Smith, "permit of no doubt that the urban population of the more important cities was well to do."[45] Travelers described Agra and Fathpur-Sikri as each greater and richer than London.[46] Anquetil-Duperron, journeying through the Mahratta districts in 1760, found himself "in the midst of the simplicity and happiness of the Golden Age. . . . The people were cheerful, vigorous, and in high health."[47] Clive, visiting Murshidabad in 1759, reckoned that ancient capital of Bengal as equal in extent, population and wealth to the London of his time, with palaces far greater than those of Europe, and men richer than any individual in London.[48] India, said Clive, was "a country of inexhaustible riches."[49] Tried by Parliament for helping himself too readily to this wealth, Clive excused himself ingeniously: he described the riches that he had found about him in India—opulent cities ready to offer him any bribe to escape indiscriminate plunder, bankers throwing open to his grasp vaults piled high with jewels and gold; and he concluded: "At this moment I stand astonished at my own moderation."[50]

II. THE ORGANIZATION OF SOCIETY

*The monarchy—Law—The Code of "Manu"—Development of
the caste system—Rise of the Brahmans—Their privileges and
powers—Their obligations—In defense of caste*

Because the roads were poor and communication difficult, it was easier to conquer than to rule India. Its topography ordained that this semi-continent would remain, until the coming of railways, a medley of divided states. Under such conditions a government could have security only through a competent army; and as the army required, in frequent crises, a dictatorial leader immune to political eloquence, the form of government which developed in India was naturally monarchical. The people enjoyed a considerable measure of liberty under the native dynasties, partly through the autonomous communities in the villages and the trade guilds in the towns, and partly through the limitations that the Brahman aristocracy placed upon the authority of the king.[51] The laws of Manu, though they were more a code of ethics than a system of practised legislation, expressed the focal ideas of India about monarchy: that it should be impartially rigorous, and paternally solicitous of the public good.[52] The Mohammedan rulers paid less attention than their Hindu predecessors to these ideals and checks; they were a conquering minority, and rested their rule frankly on the superiority of their guns. "The army," says a Moslem historian, with charming clarity, "is the source and means of government."[53] Akbar was an exception, for he relied chiefly upon the good will of a people prospering under his mild and benevolent despotism. Perhaps in the circumstances his was the best government possible. Its vital defect, as we have seen, lay in its dependence upon the character of the king; the supreme centralized authority that proved beneficent under Akbar proved ruinous under Aurangzeb. Having been raised up by violence, the Afghan and Mogul rulers were always subject to recall by assassination; and wars of succession were almost as expensive—though not as disturbing to economic life—as a modern election.*

Under the Moslems law was merely the will of the emperor or sultan; under the Hindu kings it was a confused mixture of royal commands, village traditions and caste rules. Judgment was given by the head of the family, the head of the village, the headmen of the caste, the court of the guild, the governor of the province, the minister of the king, or the king himself.[55] Litigation was brief, judgment swift; lawyers came only with the British.[56] Torture was used under every dynasty until abolished by Firoz Shah.[57] Death was the penalty for any of a great variety of crimes, such as housebreaking, damage to royal property, or theft on a scale that would now make a man a very pillar of society. Punishments were cruel, and included amputation of hands, feet, nose or ears, tearing out of eyes, pouring molten lead into the throat, crushing the bones of hands and feet with a mallet, burning the body with fire, driving nails into the hands, feet or bosom, cutting the sinews, sawing men asunder, quartering them, impaling them, roasting them alive, letting them be trampled to death by elephants, or giving them to wild and hungry dogs.[58]†

No code of laws applied to all India. In the ordinary affairs of life the place of law was taken by the *dharma-shastras*—metrical textbooks of caste regulations and duties, composed by the Brahmans from a strictly

---

* The story of how Nasiru-d-din poisoned his father Ghiyasu-d-din, Sultan of Delhi (1501), illustrates the Moslem conception of peaceable succession. Jehangir, who did his best to depose his father Akbar, tells the story:

"After this I went to the building containing the tombs of the Khalji rulers. The grave of Nasiru-d-din, whose face is blackened forever, was also there. It is well known that that wretch advanced himself by the murder of his father. Twice he gave him poison, and the father twice expelled it by means of a poison-antidote amulet he had on his arm. The third time the son mixed poison in a cup of sherbet and gave it to his father with his own hand. . . . As his father understood what efforts the son was making in this matter, he loosened the amulet from his arm and threw it before him; and then, turning his face in humility and supplication towards the throne of the Creator, said: 'O Lord, my age has arrived at eighty years, and I have passed this time in prosperity and happiness such as has been attained by no king. Now as this is my last time, I hope that thou wilt not seize Nasir for my murder, and that, reckoning my death as a thing decreed, thou wilt not avenge it.' After he had spoken these words, he drank off that poisoned cup of sherbet at a gulp, and delivered his soul to his Creator.

"When I went to his (Nasir's) tomb," adds the virtuous Jehangir, "I gave it several kicks."[54]

† Still more sadistic refinements of penology may be found in Dubois, p. 659.

ligious duties, and a Brahman not hospitably received could walk away with all the accumulated merits of the householder's good deeds.[80]* Even if a Brahman committed every crime, he was not to be killed; the king might exile him, but must allow him to keep his property.[83] He who tried to strike a Brahman would suffer in hell for a hundred years; he who actually struck a Brahman would suffer in hell for a thousand years.[85] If a Shudra debauched the wife of a Brahman, the Shudra's property was to be confiscated, and his genitals were to be cut off.[86] A Shudra who killed a Shudra might atone for his crime by giving ten cows to the Brahmans; if he killed a Vaisya, he must give the Brahmans a hundred cows; if he killed a Kshatriya, he must give the Brahmans a thousand cows; if he killed a Brahman he must die; only the murder of a Brahman was really murder.[87]

The functions and obligations that corresponded to these privileges were numerous and burdensome. The Brahman not only acted as priest,† but trained himself for the clerical, pedagogical and literary professions. He was required to study law and learn the *Vedas;* every other duty was subordinate to this;[89] even to repeat the *Vedas* entitled the Brahman to beatitude, regardless of rites or works;[90] and if he memorized the *Rig-Veda* he might destroy the world without incurring any guilt.[91] He must not marry outside his caste; if he married a Shudra his children were to be pariahs;‡ for, said Manu, "the man who is good by birth becomes low by low associations, but the man who is low by birth cannot become high by high associations."[92] The Brahman had to bathe every day, and again after being shaved by a barber of low caste; he had to purify with cow-dung the place where he intended to sleep; and he had to follow a strict hygienic ritual in attending to the duties of nature.[93] He was to abstain from all animal food, including eggs, and from onions, garlic, mushrooms and leeks. He was to drink nothing but water, and it must have been drawn and carried by a Brahman.[94] He was to abstain from unguents, perfumes, sensual pleasure, coveteousness, and wrath.[95] If he touched an unclean

---

* Certain sexual perquisites seem to have belonged to some Brahman groups. The Nambudri Brahmans exercised the jus *primæ noctis* over all brides in their territory; and the Pushtimargiya priests of Bombay maintained this privilege until recent times.[81] If we may believe Père Dubois, the priests of the Temple of Tirupati (in southeastern India) offered to cure barrenness in all women who would spend a night at the temple.[82]

† Not all priests were Brahmans, and latterly many Brahmans have not been priests. In the United Provinces a large number of them are cooks.[88]

‡ This word is from the Tamil *paraiyan,* meaning one of low caste.

thing, or the person of any foreigner (even the Governor-General of India), he was to purify himself by ceremonial ablutions. If he committed a crime he had to accept a heavier punishment than would fall upon a lower caste: if, for example, a Shudra stole he was to be fined eightfold the sum or value of his theft; if a Vaisya stole he was to be fined sixteen-fold; a Kshatriya, thirty-twofold; a Brahman, sixty-fourfold.[96] The Brahman was never to injure any living thing.[97]

Given a moderate observation of these rules, and a people too burdened with the tillage of the fields, and therefore too subject to the apparently personal whims of the elements, to rise out of superstition to education, the power of the priests grew from generation to generation, and made them the most enduring aristocracy in history. Nowhere else can we find this astonishing phenomenon—so typical of the slow rate of change in India—of an upper class maintaining its ascendancy and privileges through all conquests, dynasties and governments for 2500 years. Only the outcast Chandalas can rival them in perpetuity. The ancient Kshatriyas who had dominated the intellectual as well as the political field in the days of Buddha disappeared after the Gupta age; and though the Brahmans recognized the Rajput warriors as the later equivalent of the old fighting caste, the Kshatriyas, after the fall of Rajputana, soon became extinct. At last only two great divisions remained: the Brahmans as the social and mental rulers of India, and beneath them three thousand castes that were in reality industrial guilds.*

Much can be said in defense of what, after monogamy, must be the most abused of all social institutions. The caste system had the eugenic value of keeping the presumably finer strains from dilution and disappearance through indiscriminate mixture; it established certain habits of diet and cleanliness as a rule of honor which all might observe and emulate; it gave order to the chaotic inequalities and differences of men, and spared the soul the modern fever of climbing and gain; it gave order to every life by prescribing for each man a *dharma*, or code of conduct for his caste; it gave order to every trade and profession, elevated every occupation into a vocation not lightly to be changed, and, by making every industry a caste, provided its members with a means of united action against exploitation and tyranny. It offered an escape from the plutocracy or the military dictatorship which are apparently the only alterna-

---

* On the caste system in our time cf. Chap. XXII, Sect. iv, below.

tives to aristocracy; it gave to a country shorn of political stability by a hundred invasions and revolutions a social, moral and cultural order and continuity rivaled only by the Chinese. Amid a hundred anarchic changes in the state, the Brahmans maintained, through the system of caste, a stable society, and preserved, augmented and transmitted civilization. The nation bore with them patiently, even proudly, because every one knew that in the end they were the one indispensable government of India.

III. MORALS AND MARRIAGE

"Dharma"—Children—Child marriage—The art of love—Prostitution—Romantic love—Marriage—The family—Woman—Her intellectual life — Her rights — "Purdah" — Suttee—The Widow

When the caste system dies the moral life of India will undergo a long transition of disorder, for there the moral code has been bound up almost inseparably with caste. Morality was *dharma*—the rule of life for each man as determined by his caste. To be a Hindu meant not so much to accept a creed as to take a place in the caste system, and to accept the *dharma* or duties attaching to that place by ancient tradition and regulation. Each post had its obligations, its limitations and its rights; with them and within them the pious Hindu would lead his life, finding in them a certain contentment of routine, and never thinking of stepping into another caste. "Better thine own work is, though done with fault," said the *Bhagavad-Gita*,[98] "than doing others' work, even excellently." *Dharma* is to the individual what its normal development is to a seed—the orderly fulfilment of an inherent nature and destiny.[99] So old is this conception of morality that even today it is difficult for all, and impossible for most, Hindus to think of themselves except as members of a specific caste, guided and bound by its rule. "Without caste," says an English historian, "Hindu society is inconceivable."[100]

In addition to the *dharma* of each caste the Hindu recognized a general *dharma* or obligation affecting all castes, and embracing chiefly respect for Brahmans, and reverence for cows.[101] Next to these duties was that of bearing children. "Then only is a man a perfect man," says Manu's code,[102] "when he is three—himself, his wife, and his son." Not only would children be economic assets to their parents, and support them as a matter of course in old age, but they would carry on the household worship of their ancestors, and would offer to them periodically the food without which these ghosts would starve.[103] Consequently there was no birth control in India, and abortion was branded as a crime equal to the murder of a Brahman.[104] Infanticide occurred,[105] but it was exceptional; the father was glad to have children, and proud to have many. The tenderness of the old to the young is one of the fairest aspects of Hindu civilization.[106]

The child was hardly born when the parents began to think of its marriage. For marriage, in the Hindu system, was compulsory; an unmarried man was an outcast, without social status or consideration, and prolonged virginity was a disgrace.[107] Nor was marriage to be left to the whim of individual choice or romantic love; it was a vital concern of society and the race, and could not safely be entrusted to the myopia of passion or the accidents of proximity;[108] it must be arranged by the parents before the fever of sex should have time to precipitate a union doomed, in the Hindu view, to disillusionment and bitterness. Manu gave the name of *Gandharva* marriage to unions by mutual choice, and stigmatized them as born of desire; they were permissible, but hardly respectable.

The early maturity of the Hindu, making a girl of twelve as old as a girl of fourteen or fifteen in America, created a difficult problem of moral and social order.* Should marriage be arranged to coincide with sexual maturity, or should it be postponed, as in America, until the male arrives at economic maturity? The first solution apparently weakens the national physique,[110] unduly accelerates the growth of population, and sacrifices the woman almost completely to reproduction; the second solution leaves the problems of unnatural delay, sexual frustration, prostitution, and venereal disease. The Hindus chose child marriage as the lesser evil, and tried to mitigate its dangers by establishing, between the marriage and its consummation, a period in which the bride should remain with her parents until the coming of puberty.[111] The institution was old, and therefore holy; it had been rooted in the desire to prevent intercaste marriage through casual sexual attraction;[112] it was later encouraged by the fact that the conquering and otherwise ruthless Moslems were restrained

---

* It should be added that Gandhi denies that this precocity has any physical basis. "I loathe and detest child marriage," he writes. "I shudder to see a child widow. I have never known a grosser superstition than that the Indian climate causes sexual precocity. What does bring about untimely puberty is the mental and moral atmosphere surrounding family life."[109]

by their religion from carrying away *married* women as slaves;[113] and finally it took rigid form in the parental resolve to protect the girl from the erotic sensibilities of the male.

That these were reasonably keen, and that the male might be trusted to attend to his biological functions on the slightest provocation, appears from the Hindu literature of love. The *Kamasutra*, or "Doctrine of Desire," is the most famous in a long list of works revealing a certain preoccupation with the physical and mental technique of sex. It was composed, the author assures us, "according to the precepts of Holy Writ, for the benefit of the world, by Vatsyayana, while leading the life of a religious student at Benares, and wholly engaged in the contemplation of the Deity."[114] "He who neglects a girl, thinking she is too bashful," says this anchorite, "is despised by her as a beast ignorant of the working of the female mind."[115] Vatsyayana gives a delightful picture of a girl in love,[116] but his wisdom is lavished chiefly upon the parental art of getting her married away, and the husbandly art of keeping her physically content.

We must not presume that the sexual sensitivity of the Hindu led to any unusual license. Child marriage raised a barrier against premarital relations, and the strong religious sanctions used in the inculcation of wifely fidelity made adultery far more difficult and rare than in Europe or America. Prostitution was for the most part confined to the temples. In the south the needs of the esurient male were met by the providential institution of *devadasis*—literally "servants of the gods," actually prostitutes. Each Tamil temple had a troop of "sacred women," engaged at first to dance and sing before the idols, and perhaps to entertain the Brahmans. Some of them seem to have lived lives of almost conventual seclusion; others were allowed to extend their services to all who could pay, on condition that a part of their earnings should be contributed to the clergy. Many of these temple courtesans, or *nautch** girls, provided dancing and singing in public functions and private gatherings, in the style of the *geishas* of Japan; some of them learned to read, and, like the *hetairai* of Greece, furnished cultured conversation in homes where the married women were neither encouraged to read nor allowed to mingle with guests. In 1004 A.D., as a sacred inscription informs us, the temple of the Chola King Rajaraja at Tanjore had four hundred *devadasis*. The custom

---

* From the Hindu *nâch*, dancer.

acquired the sanctity of time, and no one seems to have considered it immoral; respectable women now and then dedicated a daughter to the profession of temple prostitute in much the same spirit in which a son might be dedicated to the priesthood.[117] Dubois, at the beginning of the nineteenth century, described the temples of the south as in some cases "converted into mere brothels"; the *devadasis*, whatever their original functions, were frankly called harlots by the public, and were used as such. If we may believe the old *abbé*, who had no reason to be prejudiced in favor of India,

> their official duties consist in dancing and singing within the temples twice a day, . . . and also at all public ceremonies. The first they execute with sufficient grace, although their attitudes are lascivious and their gestures indecorous. As regards their singing, it is almost always confined to obscene verses describing some licentious episode in the history of their gods.[118]

Under these circumstances of temple prostitution and child marriage little opportunity was given for what we call "romantic love." This idealistic devotion of one sex to the other appears in Indian literature—for example in the poems of Chandi Das and Jayadeva—but usually as a symbol of the soul surrendering to God; while in actual life it took most often the form of the complete devotion of the wife to her mate. The love poetry is sometimes of the ethereal type depicted by the Tennysons and Longfellows of our Puritan tradition; sometimes it is the full-bodied and sensuous passion of the Elizabethan stage.[119] One writer unites religion and love, and sees in either ecstasy a recognition of identity; another lists the three hundred and sixty different emotions that fill the lover's heart, and counts the patterns which his teeth have left on his beloved's flesh, or shows him decorating her breasts with painted flowers of sandal paste; and the author of the Nala and Damayanti episode in the *Mahabharata* describes the melancholy sighs and pale dyspepsia of the lovers in the best style of the French troubadours.[120]

Such whimsical passions were seldom permitted to determine marriage in India. Manu allowed eight different forms of marriage, in which marriage by capture and marriage "from affection" were ranked lowest in the moral scale, and marriage by purchase was accepted as the sensible way of arranging a union; in the long run, the Hindu legislator thought, those marriages are most soundly based that rest upon an economic foundation.[121] In the days of Dubois "to marry" and "to buy a wife" were "synonymous expressions in India."*[122] The wisest marriage was held to be one arranged by the parents with full regard for the rules of endogamy and exogamy: the youth must marry within his caste, and outside his *gotra* or group.[123] He might take several wives, but only one of his own caste—who was to have precedence over the rest; preferably, said Manu, he was to be monogamous.†[124] The woman was to love her husband with patient devotion; the husband was to give to his wife not romantic affection, but solicitous protection.[125]

The Hindu family was typically patriarchal, with the father full master of his wife, his children, and his slaves.[127] Woman was a lovely but inferior being. In the beginning, says Hindu legend, when Twashtri, the Divine Artificer, came to the creation of woman he found that he had exhausted his materials in the making of man, and had no solid elements left. In this dilemma he fashioned her eclectically out of the odds and ends of creation:

> He took the rotundity of the moon, and the curves of creepers, and the clinging of tendrils, and the trembling of grass, and the slenderness of the reed, and the bloom of flowers, and the lightness of leaves, and the tapering of the elephant's trunk, and the glances of deer, and the clustering of rows of bees, and the joyous gaiety of sunbeams, and the weeping of clouds, and the fickleness of the winds, and the timidity of the hare, and the vanity of the peacock, and the softness of the parrot's bosom, and the hardness of adamant, and the sweetness of honey, and the cruelty of the tiger, and the warm glow of fire, and the coldness of snow, and the chattering of jays, and the cooing of the *kokila*, and the hypocrisy of the crane, and the fidelity of the *chakravaka*; and compounding all these together he made woman, and gave her to man.[129]

---

* Strabo (ca. 20 A.D.), relying on Aristobulus, describes "some novel and unusual customs at Taxila: those who by reason of poverty are unable to marry off their daughters, lead them forth to the market place in the power of their age to the sound of both trumpets and drums (precisely the instruments used to signal the call to battle), thus assembling a crowd; and to any man who comes forward they first expose her rear parts up to the shoulders, and then her front parts, and if she pleases him, and at the same time allows herself to be persuaded, on approved terms, he marries her."[128]

† Among the Rajputs, if we may believe Tod, it was usual for the prince to have different wives for each day of the week.[125]

Nevertheless, despite all this equipment, woman fared poorly in India. Her high status in Vedic days was lost under priestly influence and Mohammedan example. The Code of Manu set the tone against her in phrases reminiscent of an early stage in Christian theology: "The source of dishonor is woman; the source of strife is woman; the source of earthly existence is woman; therefore avoid woman."[130] "A female," says another passage, "is able to draw from the right path in this life not a fool only but even a sage, and can lead him in subjection to desire or to wrath."[131] The law laid it down that all through her life woman should be in tutelage, first to her father, then to her husband, and finally to her son.[132] The wife addressed her husband humbly as "master," "lord," even as "my god"; in public she walked some distance behind him, and seldom received a word from him.[133] She was expected to show her devotion by the most minute service, preparing the meals, eating—after they had finished—the food left by her husband and her sons, and embracing her husband's feet at bedtime.[134] "A faithful wife," said Manu, "must serve . . . her lord as if he were a god, and never do aught to pain him, whatsoever be his state, and even though devoid of every virtue."[135] A wife who disobeyed her husband would become a jackal in her next incarnation.[136]

Like their sisters in Europe and America before our own times, the women of India received education only if they were ladies of high degree, or temple prostitutes.[137] The art of reading was considered inappropriate in a woman; her power over men could not be increased by it, and her attractiveness would be diminished. Says Chitra in Tagore's play: "When a woman is merely a woman—when she winds herself round and round men's hearts with her smiles and sobs and services and caressing endearments—then she is happy. Of what use to her are learning and great achievements?"[138] Knowledge of the *Vedas* was denied to her;[139] "for a woman to study the *Vedas*," says the *Mahabharata*, "is a sign of confusion in the realm."[140]* Megasthenes reported, in Chandragupta's days, that "the Brahmans keep their wives—and they have many wives—ignorant of all philosophy; for if women learned to look upon pleasure and pain, life and death, philosophically, they would become depraved, or else no longer remain in subjection."[141]

---

* We must compare this attitude not with our contemporary European or American views, but with the reluctance of the medieval clergy to allow a general reading of the Bible, or the intellectual education of woman.

In the Code of Manu three persons were ineligible to hold property: a wife, a son, and a slave; whatever these might earn became the property of their master.[142] A wife, however, could retain as her own the dowry and gifts that she had received at her nuptials; and the mother of a prince might govern in his stead during his minority.[143] The husband could divorce his wife for unchastity; the woman could not divorce her husband for any cause.[144] A wife who drank liquor, or was diseased, or rebellious, or wasteful, or quarrelsome, might at any time be (not divorced but) superseded by another wife. Passages of the Code advocate an enlightened gentleness to women: they are not to be struck "even with a flower"; they are not to be watched too strictly, for then their subtlety will find a way to mischief; and if they like fine raiment it is wise to indulge them, for "if the wife be not elegantly attired, she will not exhilarate her husband," whereas when "a wife is gaily adorned, the whole house is embellished."[145] Way must be made for a woman, as for the aged or a priest; and "pregnant women, brides, and damsels shall have food before all other guests."[146] Though woman could not rule as a wife, she might rule as a mother; the greatest tenderness and respect was paid to the mother of many children; and even the patriarchal code of Manu said, "The mother exceedeth a thousand fathers in the right to reverence."[147]

Doubtless the influx of Islamic ideas had something to do with the decline in the status of woman in India after Vedic days. The custom of *purdah* (curtain)—the seclusion of married women—came into India with the Persians and the Mohammedans, and has therefore been stronger in the north than in the south. Partly to protect their wives from the Moslems, Hindu husbands developed a system of *purdah* so rigid that a respectable woman could show herself only to her husband and her sons, and could move in public only under a heavy veil; even the doctor who treated her and took her pulse had to do so through a curtain.[148] In some circles it was a breach of good manners to inquire after a man's wife, or to speak, as a guest, to the ladies of the house.[149]

The custom of burning widows on their husbands' pyres was also an importation into India. Herodotus describes it as practised by the ancient Scythians and Thracians; if we may believe him, the wives of a Thracian fought for the privilege of being slain over his grave.[150] Probably the rite came down from the almost world-wide primitive usage of immolating one or more of the wives or concubines of a prince or rich man, along with slaves and other perquisites, to take care of him in the Beyond.[151] The

Atharva-veda speaks of it as an old custom, but the *Rig-veda* indicates that in Vedic days it had been softened to the requirement that the widow should lie on her husband's pyre for a moment before his cremation.[152] The *Mahabharata* shows the institution restored and unrepentant; it gives several examples of suttee,* and lays down the rule that the chaste widow does not wish to survive her husband, but enters proudly into the fire.[153] The sacrifice was effected by burning the wife in a pit, or, among the Telugus in the south, by burying her alive.[154] Strabo reports that suttee prevailed in India in the time of Alexander, and that the Kathæi, a Punjab tribe, had made suttee a law in order to prevent wives from poisoning their husbands.[155] Manu makes no mention of the practice. The Brahmans opposed it at first, then accepted it, and finally lent it a religious sanction by interpreting it as bound up with the eternity of marriage: a woman once married to a man remained his forever, and would be rejoined to him in his later lives.[156] In Rajasthan the absolute possession of the wife by the husband took the form of the *johur*, in which a Rajput, facing certain defeat, immolated his wives before advancing to his own death in battle.[157] The usage was widespread under the Moguls, despite Moslem abhorrence; and even the powerful Akbar failed to dislodge it. On one occasion Akbar himself tried to dissuade a Hindu bride who wished to be burned on the pyre of her dead betrothed; but though the Brahmans added their pleas to the king's, she insisted on the sacrifice; as the flames reached her, and Akbar's son Daniyal continued to argue with her, she replied, "Do not annoy, do not annoy." Another widow, rejecting similar pleas, held her finger in the flame of a lamp until the finger was completely burned; giving no sign of pain, she indicated in this way her scorn of those who advised her to refuse the rite.[158] In Vijayanagar suttee sometimes took a wholesale form; not one or a few but all of the many wives of a prince or a captain followed him to death. Conti reports that the Raya or King had selected three thousand of his twelve thousand wives as favorites, "on condition that at his death they should voluntarily burn themselves with him, which is considered to be a great honor for them."[159] It is difficult to say how thoroughly the medieval Hindu widow was reconciled to suttee by religious inculcation and belief, and the hope of reunion with her husband in another life.

Suttee became less and less popular as India developed contacts with

---

*More properly *sati*, pronounced *suttee*, and meaning "devoted wife."

Europe; but the Hindu widow continued to suffer many disabilities. Since marriage bound a woman eternally to her husband, her remarriage after his death was a mortal offense, and was bound to create confusion in his later existences. The widow was therefore required by Brahmanical law to remain unmarried, to shave her head, and live out her life (if she did not prefer suttee) in the care of her children and in acts of private charity.[160] She was not left destitute; on the contrary she had a first lien on her husband's estate for her maintenance.[161] These rules were followed only by the orthodox women of the middle and upper classes—i.e., by some thirty per cent of the population; they were ignored by Moslems, Sikhs, and the lower castes.[162] Hindu opinion likened this second virginity of the widow to the celibacy of nuns in Christendom; in either case some women renounced marriage, and were set aside for charitable ministrations.*

IV. MANNERS, CUSTOMS AND CHARACTER

Sexual modesty—Hygiene—Dress—Appearance—The gentle art among the Hindus—Faults and virtues—Games— Festivals—Death

It will seem incredible to the provincial mind that the same people that tolerated such institutions as child marriage, temple prostitution and suttee was also pre-eminent in gentleness, decency and courtesy. Aside from a few *devadasis*, prostitutes were rare in India, and sexual propriety was exceptionally high. "It must be admitted," says the unsympathetic Dubois, "that the laws of etiquette and social politeness are much more clearly laid down, and much better observed by all classes of Hindus, even by the lowest, than they are by people of corresponding social position in Europe."[164] The leading rôle played by sex in Occidental conversation and wit was quite alien to Hindu manners, which forbade any public intimacy between men and women, and looked upon the physical contact of the sexes in dancing as improper and obscene.[165] A Hindu woman might go anywhere in public without fear of molestation or insult;[166] indeed the

* In considering alien customs we must continually remind ourselves that foreign practices cannot be judged intelligently by our own moral code. "The superficial observer who applies his own standard to the customs of all nations," says Tod, "laments with affected philanthropy the degraded condition of the Hindu female, in which sentiment he would find her little disposed to join him."[163] On contemporary changes in these customs cf. Chapter XXII below.

risk, as the Oriental saw the matter, was all on the other side. Manu warns men: "Woman is by nature ever inclined to tempt man; hence a man should not sit in a secluded place even with his nearest female relative"; and he must never look higher than the ankles of a passing girl.[167]

Cleanliness was literally next to godliness in India; hygiene was not, as Anatole France thought it, *la seule morale*, but it was made an essential part of piety. Manu laid down, many centuries ago, an exacting code of physical refinement. "Early in the morning," one instruction reads, "let him" (the Brahman) "bathe, decorate his body, clean his teeth, apply collyrium to his eyes, and worship the gods."[168] The native schools made good manners and personal cleanliness the first courses in the curriculum. Every day the caste Hindu would bathe his body, and wash the simple robe he was to wear; it seemed to him abominable to use the same garment, unwashed, for more than a day.[169] "The Hindus," said Sir William Huber, "stand out as examples of bodily cleanliness among Asiatic races, and, we may add, among the races of the world. The ablutions of the Hindu have passed into a proverb."[170]*

Yuan Chwang, 1300 years ago, described thus the eating habits of the Hindus:

> They are pure of themselves, and not from compulsion. Before every meal they must have a wash; the fragments and remains are not served up again; the food utensils are not passed on; those which are of pottery or of wood must be thrown away after use, and those which are of gold, silver, copper or iron get another polishing. As soon as a meal is over they chew the tooth-stick and make themselves clean. Before they have finished ablutions they do not come in contact with each other.[172]

The Brahman usually washed his hands, feet and teeth before and after each meal; he ate with his fingers from food on a leaf, and thought it unclean to use twice a plate, a knife or a fork; and when finished he rinsed his mouth seven times.[173] The toothbrush was always new—a twig freshly plucked from a tree; to the Hindu it seemed disreputable to brush the teeth with the hair of an animal, or to use the same brush twice:[174] so many are the ways in which men may scorn one another. The Hindu

---

* A great Hindu, Lajpat Rai, reminded Europe that "long before the European nations knew anything of hygiene, and long before they realized the value of tooth-brush and a daily bath, the Hindus were, as a rule, given to both. Only twenty years ago London houses had no bath-tubs, and the tooth-brush was a luxury."[171]

chewed almost incessantly the leaf of the betel plant, which blackened the teeth in a manner disagreeable to Europeans, and agreeable to himself. This and the occasional use of opium consoled him for his usual abstention from tobacco and intoxicating drinks.

Hindu law books give explicit rules for menstrual hygiene,[175] and for meeting the demands of nature. Nothing could exceed in complexity or solemnity the ritual for Brahman defecation.[176] The Twice-born must use only his left hand in this rite, and must cleanse the parts with water; and he considered his house defiled by the very presence of Europeans who contented themselves with paper.[177] The Outcastes, however, and many Shudras, were less particular, and might turn any roadside into a privy.[178] In the quarters occupied by these classes public sanitation was confined to an open sewer line in the middle of the street.[179]

In so warm a climate clothing was a superfluity, and beggars and saints bridged the social scale in agreeing to do without it. One southern caste, like the Canadian Doukhobors, threatened to migrate if its members were compelled to wear clothing.[180] Until the late eighteenth century it was probably the custom in southern India (as still in Bali) for both sexes to go naked above the waist.[181] Children were dressed for the most part in beads and rings. Most of the population went barefoot; if the orthodox Hindu wore shoes they had to be of cloth, for under no circumstances would he use shoes of leather. A large number of the men contented themselves with loin cloths; when they needed more covering they bound some fabric about the waist, and threw the loose end over the left shoulder. The Rajputs wore trousers of every color and shape, with a tunic girdled by a *ceinture*, a scarf at the neck, sandals or boots on the feet, and a turban on the head. The turban had come in with the Moslems, and had been taken over by the Hindus, who wound it carefully around the head in varying manner according to caste, but always with the generosity of a magician unfurling endless silk; sometimes one turban, unraveled, reached a length of seventy feet.[182] The women wore a flowing robe—colorful silk *sari*, or homespun *khaddar*—which passed over both shoulders, clasped the waist tightly, and then fell to the feet; often a few inches of bronze flesh were left bare below the breast. Hair was oiled to guard it against the desiccating sun; men divided theirs in the center and drew it together into a tuft behind the left ear; women coiled a part of theirs upon their heads, but let the rest hang free, often decorating it with flowers, or covering it with a scarf. The men were handsome, the young women were beautiful and all presented a magnificent carriage;[183] an ordinary Hindu in a loin cloth often had more dignity than a European diplomat completely equipped. Pierre Loti thought it "incontestable that the beauty of the Aryan race reaches its highest development of perfection and refinement among the upper class" in India.[184] Both sexes were adept in cosmetics, and the women felt naked without jewelry. A ring in the left nostril denoted marriage. On the forehead, in most cases, was a painted symbol of religious faith.

It is difficult to go below these surface appearances and describe the character of the Hindus, for every people harbors all virtues and all vices, and witnesses tend to select such of these as will point their moral and adorn their tale. "I think we may take as their greatest vice," says Père Dubois, "the untrustworthiness, deceit and double-dealing . . . which are common to all Hindus. . . . Certain it is that there is no nation in the world which thinks so lightly of an oath or of perjury."[185] "Lying," says Westermarck, "has been called the national vice of the Hindus."[186] "Hindus are wily and deceitful," says Macaulay.[187] According to the laws of Manu and the practice of the world a lie told for good motives is forgivable; if, for example, the death of a priest would result from speaking the truth, falsehood is justifiable.[188] But Yuan Chwang tells us: "They do not practice deceit, and they keep their sworn obligations. . . . They will not take anything wrongfully, and they yield more than fairness requires."[189] Abu-l Fazl, not prejudiced in favor of India, reports the Hindus of the sixteenth century as "religious, affable, cheerful, lovers of justice, given to retirement, able in business, admirers of truth, grateful, and of unbounded fidelity."[190] "Their honesty," said honest Keir Hardie, "is proverbial. They borrow and lend on word of mouth, and the repudiation of a debt is almost unknown."[191] "I have had before me," says a British judge in India, "hundreds of cases in which a man's property, liberty and life depended upon his telling a lie, and he has refused to tell it."[192] How shall we reconcile these conflicting testimonies? Perhaps it is very simple: some Hindus are honest, and some are not.

Again the Hindus are very cruel and gentle. The English language has derived a short and ugly word from that strange secret society—almost a caste—of *Thugs* which in the eighteenth and nineteenth centuries committed thousands of atrocious murders in order (they said) to offer the victims as sacrifices to the goddess Kali.[193] Vincent Smith writes of these Thugs (literally, "cheats") in terms not quite irrelevant to our time:

> The gangs had little to fear, and enjoyed almost complete immunity; . . . they always had powerful protectors. The moral feeling of the people had sunk so low that there were no signs of general reprehension of the cold-blooded crimes committed by the

Thugs. They were accepted as part of the established order of things; and until the secrets of the organization were given away, . . . it was usually impossible to obtain evidence against even the most notorious Thugs.[193a]

Nevertheless there is comparatively little crime in India, and little violence. By universal admission the Hindus are gentle to the point of timidity;[194] too worshipful and good-natured, too long broken upon the wheel of conquest and alien despotisms, to be good fighters except in the sense that they can bear pain with unequaled bravery.[195] Their greatest faults are probably listlessness and laziness; but in the Hindus these are not faults but climatic necessities and adaptations, like the *dolce far niente* of the Latin peoples, and the economic fever of Americans. The Hindus are sensitive, emotional, temperamental, imaginative; therefore they are better artists and poets than rulers or executives. They can exploit their fellows with the same zest that characterizes the *entrepreneur* everywhere; yet they are given to limitless charity, and are the most hospitable hosts this side of barbarism.[196] Even their enemies admit their courtesy,[197] and a generous Britisher sums up his long experience by ascribing to the higher classes in Calcutta "polished manners, clearness and comprehensiveness of understanding, liberality of feeling, and independence of principle, that would have stamped them gentlemen in any country in the world."[198]

The Hindu genius, to an outsider, seems sombre, and doubtless the Hindus have not had much cause for laughter. The dialogues of Buddha indicate a great variety of games, including one that strangely resembles chess;[199]*

---

* Chess is so old that half the nations of antiquity claim its birthplace. The view generally accepted by archeologists of the game is that it arose in India; certainly we find there its oldest indisputable appearance (ca. 750 A.D.). The word *chess* comes from the Persian *shah*, king; and *checkmate* is originally *shah-mat*—"king dead." The Persians called it *shatranj*, and took both the word and the game, through the Arabs, from India, where it was known as *chaturanga*, or "four angles"—elephants, horses, chariots and foot-soldiers. The Arabs still call the bishop *al-fil*—i.e., elephant (from *aleph-hind*, Arabic for "ox of India").[200]

The Hindus tell a delightful legend to account for the origin of the game. At the beginning of the fifth century of our era (the story goes), a Hindu monarch offended his Brahman and Kshatriya admirers by ignoring their counsels and forgetting that the love of the people is the surest support of a throne. A Brahman, Sissa, undertook to open the eyes of the young king by devising a game in which the piece that represented the king, though highest in dignity and value (as in Oriental war), should be, alone, almost helpless; hence came chess. The ruler liked the game so well that he invited Sissa to name his reward. Sissa modestly asked for some grains of rice, the quantity to be determined by placing one grain upon the first of the sixty-four squares of the chess-board, and then doubling the number of grains with each succeeding square. The king agreed at

but neither these nor their successors exhibit the vivacity and joyousness of Western games. Akbar, in the sixteenth century, introduced into India the game of polo,* which had apparently come from Persia and was making its way across Tibet to China and Japan;[202] and it pleased him to play *pachisi* (the modern "parchesi") on squares cut in the pavement of the palace quadrangle at Agra, with pretty slave-girls as living pieces.[203]

Frequent religious festivals lent color to public life. Greatest of all was the *Durga-Puja,* in honor of the great goddess-mother Kali. For weeks before its approach the Hindus feasted and sang; but the culminating ceremonial was a procession in which every family carried an image of the goddess to the Ganges, flung it into the river, and returned homeward with all merriness spent.[204] The *Holi* festival celebrated in honor of the goddess Vasanti took on a Saturnalian character: phallic emblems were carried in parade, and were made to simulate the motions of coitus.[205] In Chota Nagpur the harvest was the signal for general license; "men set aside all conventions, women all modesty, and complete liberty was given to the girls." The Parganait, a caste of peasants in the Rajmahal Hills, held an annual agricultural festival in which the unmarried were allowed to indulge freely in promiscuous relations.[206] Doubtless we have here again relics of vegetation magic, intended to promote the fertility of families and the fields. More decorous were the wedding festivals that marked the great event in the life of every Hindu; many a father brought himself to ruin in providing a sumptuous feast for the marriage of his daughter or his son.[207]

At the other end of life was the final ceremony—cremation. In Buddha's days the Zoroastrian exposure of the corpse to birds of prey was the usual mode of departure; but persons of distinction were burned, after death, on a pyre, and their ashes were buried under a *tope* or *stupa*—i.e., a memorial shrine.[208] In later days cremation became the privilege of every man; each night one might see fagots being brought together for the burning of the dead. In Yuan Chwang's time it was not unusual for the very old to take death by the forelock and have themselves rowed by their children to the middle of the Ganges, where they threw themselves

once, but was soon surprised to find that he had promised away his kingdom. Sissa took the opportunity to point out to his master how easily a monarch may be led astray when he scorns his counsellors.[201] *Credat qui vult.*

   * From the Tibetan word *pulu,* Hindu Balti dialect *polo,* meaning ball; cf. the Latin *pila.*

into the saving stream.[209] Suicide under certain conditions has always found more approval in the East than in the West; it was permitted under the laws of Akbar to the old or the incurably diseased, and to those who wished to offer themselves as sacrifices to the gods. Thousands of Hindus have made their last oblation by starving themselves to death, or burying themselves in snow, or covering themselves with cow-dung and setting it on fire, or allowing crocodiles to devour them at the mouths of the Ganges. Among the Brahmans a form of *hara-kiri* arose, by which suicide was committed to avenge an injury or point a wrong. When one of the Rajput kings levied a subsidy upon the priestly caste, several of the wealthiest Brahmans stabbed themselves to death in his presence, laying upon him the supposedly most terrible and effective curse of all—that of a dying priest. The Brahmanical lawbooks required that he who had resolved to die by his own hand should fast for three days; and that he who attempted suicide and failed should perform the severest penances.[210] Life is a stage with one entrance, but many exits.

CHAPTER XVIII

The Paradise of the Gods

IN no other country is religion so powerful, or so important, as in India. If the Hindus have permitted alien governments to be set over them again and again it is partly because they did not care much who ruled or exploited them—natives or foreigners; the crucial matter was religion, not politics; the soul, not the body; endless later lives rather than this passing one. When Ashoka became a saint, and Akbar almost adopted Hinduism, the power of religion was revealed over even the strongest men. In our century it is a saint, rather than a statesman, who for the first time in history has unified all India.

I. THE LATER HISTORY OF BUDDHISM

The Zenith of Buddhism — The Two Vehicles — "Mahayana"— Buddhism, Stoicism and Christianity — The decay of Buddhism—Its migrations: Ceylon, Burma, Turkestan, Tibet, Cambodia, China, Japan

Two hundred years after Ashoka's death Buddhism reached the peak of its curve in India. The period of Buddhist growth from Ashoka to Harsha was in many ways the climax of Indian religion, education and art. But the Buddhism that prevailed was not that of Buddha; we might better describe it as that of his rebellious disciple Subhadda, who, on hearing of the Master's death, said to the monks: "Enough, sirs! Weep not, neither lament! We are well rid of the great *Samana*. We used to be annoyed by being told, 'This beseems you, this beseems you not.' But now we shall be able to do whatever we like; and what we do not like, that we shall not have to do!"[1]

The first thing they did with their freedom was to split into sects. Within two centuries of Buddha's death eighteen varieties of Buddhistic doctrine had divided the Master's heritage. The Buddhists of south India and Ceylon held fast for a time to the simpler and purer creed of the Founder, which came to be called *Hinayana*, or the "Lesser Vehicle":

503

they worshiped Buddha as a great teacher, but not as a god, and their Scriptures were the Pali texts of the more ancient faith. But throughout northern India, Tibet, Mongolia, China and Japan the Buddhism that prevailed was the *Mahayana,* or the "Greater Vehicle," defined and propagated by Kanishka's Council; these (politically) inspired theologians announced the divinity of Buddha, surrounded him with angels and saints, adopted the *Yoga* asceticism of Patanjali, and issued in Sanskrit a new set of Holy Writ which, though it lent itself readily to metaphysical and scholastic refinements, proclaimed and certified a more popular religion than the austere pessimism of Shakya-muni.

The *Mahayana* was Buddhism softened with Brahmanical deities, practices and myths, and adapted to the needs of the Kushan Tatars and the Mongols of Tibet, over whom Kanishka had extended his rule. A heaven was conceived in which there were many Buddhas, of whom Amida Buddha, the Redeemer, came to be the best beloved by the people; this heaven and a corresponding hell were to be the reward or punishment of good or evil done on earth, and would thereby liberate some of the King's militia for other services. The greatest of the saints, in this new theology, were the *Bodhisattwas,* or future Buddhas, who voluntarily refrained from achieving the *Nirvana* (here freedom from rebirth) that was within their merit and power, in order to be reborn into life after life, and to help others on earth to find the Way.* As in Mediterranean Christianity, these saints became so popular that they almost crowded out the head of the pantheon in worship and art. The veneration of relics, the use of holy water, candles, incense, the rosary, clerical vestments, a liturgical dead language, monks and nuns, monastic tonsure and celibacy, confession, fast days, the canonization of saints, purgatory and masses for the dead flourished in Buddhism as in medieval Christianity, and seem to have appeared in Buddhism first.† *Mahayana* became to *Hinayana* or primitive Buddhism what Catholicism was to Stoicism and primitive Christianity. Buddha, like Luther, had made

---

* In one of the *Puranas* there is a typical legend of the king who, though deserving heaven, stays in hell to comfort the sufferers, and will not leave it until all the damned are released.²

† "The Buddhists," says Fergusson, "kept five centuries in advance of the Roman Church in the invention and use of all the ceremonies and forms common to both religions."³ Edmunds has shown in detail the astonishing parallelism between the Buddhist and the Christian gospels.⁴ However, our knowledge of the beginnings of these customs and beliefs is too vague to warrant positive conclusions as to priority.

the mistake of supposing that the drama of religious ritual could be replaced with sermons and morality; and the victory of a Buddhism rich in myths, miracles, ceremonies and intermediating saints corresponds to the ancient and current triumph of a colorful and dramatic Catholicism over the austere simplicity of early Christianity and modern Protestantism.

That same popular preference for polytheism, miracles and myths which destroyed Buddha's Buddhism finally destroyed, in India, the Buddhism of the Greater Vehicle itself. For—to speak with the hindsight wisdom of the historian—if Buddhism was to take over so much of Hinduism, so many of its legends, its rites and its gods, soon very little would remain to distinguish the two religions; and the one with the deeper roots, the more popular appeal, and the richer economic resources and political support would gradually absorb the other. Rapidly superstition, which seems to be the very lifeblood of our race, poured over from the older faith to the younger one, until even the phallic enthusiasms of the *Shakti* sects found place in the ritual of Buddhism. Slowly the patient and tenacious Brahmans recaptured influence and imperial patronage; and the success of the youthful philosopher Shankara in restoring the authority of the *Vedas* as the basis of Hindu thought put an end to the intellectual leadership of the Buddhists in India.

The final blow came from without, and was in a sense invited by Buddhism itself. The prestige of the *Sangha*, or Buddhist Order, had, after Ashoka, drawn the best blood of Magadha into a celibate and pacific clergy; even in Buddha's time some patriots had complained that "the monk Gautama causes fathers to beget no sons, and families to become extinct."⁵ The growth of Buddhism and monasticism in the first year of our era sapped the manhood of India, and conspired with political division to leave India open to easy conquest. When the Arabs came, pledged to spread a simple and stoic monotheism, they looked with scorn upon the lazy, venal, miracle-mongering Buddhist monks; they smashed the monasteries, killed thousands of monks, and made monasticism unpopular with the cautious. The survivors were re-absorbed into the Hinduism that had begotten them; the ancient orthodoxy received the penitent heresy, and "Brahmanism killed Buddhism by a fraternal embrace."⁶ Brahmanism had always been tolerant; in all the history of the rise and fall of Buddhism and a hundred other sects we find much disputation, but no instance of persecution. On the contrary Brahmanism eased the return of the prodigal by proclaiming Buddha a god (as an avatar of Vishnu), ending animal sacrifice, and accepting into orthodox practice the Buddhist doctrine of the sanctity of all animal life. Quietly and peacefully, after half a thousand years of gradual decay, Buddhism disappeared from India.*

Meanwhile it was winning nearly all the remainder of the Asiatic world. Its ideas, its literature and its art spread to Ceylon and the Malay Peninsula in the south, to Tibet and Turkestan in the north, to Burma, Siam, Cambodia, China, Korea and Japan in the east; in this way all of these regions except the Far East received as much civilization as they could digest, precisely as western Europe and Russia received civilization from Roman and Byzantine monks in the Middle Ages. The cultural zenith of most of these nations came from the stimulus of Buddhism. From the time of Ashoka to its decay in the ninth century, Anuradhapura, in Ceylon, was one of the major cities of the Oriental world; the Bo-tree there has been worshiped for two thousand years, and the temple on the heights of Kandy is one of the Meccas of the 150,000,000 Buddhists of Asia.† The Buddhism of Burma is probably the purest now extant, and its monks often approach the ideal of Buddha; under their ministrations the 13,000,000 inhabitants of Burma have reached a standard of living considerably higher than that of India.[7] Sven Hedin, Aurel Stein and Pelliot have unearthed from the sands of Turkestan hundreds of Buddhist manuscripts, and other evidences of a culture which flourished there from the time of Kanishka to the thirteenth century A.D. In the seventh century of our era the enlightened warrior, Srong-tsan Gampo, established an able government in Tibet, annexed Nepal, built Lhasa as his capital, and made it rich as a halfway house in Chinese-Indian trade. Having invited Buddhist monks to come from India and spread Buddhism and education among his people, he retired from rule for four years in order to learn how to read and write, and inaugurated the Golden Age of Tibet. Thousands of monasteries were built in the mountains and on the great plateau; and a voluminous Tibetan canon of Buddhist books was published, in three hundred and thirty-three volumes, which preserved for modern scholarship many works whose Hindu originals

---

* Today there are in India proper only 3,000,000 Buddhists—one per cent of the population.

† The temple at Kandy contains the famous "eye-tooth of Buddha"—two inches long and an inch in diameter. It is enclosed in a jeweled casket, carefully guarded from the eyes of the people, and carried periodically in a solemn procession which draws Buddhists from every corner of the Orient. On the walls of the temple, frescoes show the gentle Buddha killing sinners in hell. The lives of great men all remind us how helplessly they may be transmogrified after their death.

have long been lost.[8] Here, eremitically sealed from the rest of the world, Buddhism developed into a maze of superstitions, monasticism and ecclesiasticism rivaled only by early medieval Europe; and the Dalai Lama (or "All-Embracing Priest"), hidden away in the great Potala monastery that overlooks the city of Lhasa, is still believed by the good people of Tibet to be the living incarnation of the *Bodhisattwa* Avalokiteshvara.[9] In Cambodia, or Indo-China, Buddhism conspired with Hinduism to provide the religious framework for one of the richest ages in the history of Oriental art. Buddhism, like Christianity, won its greatest triumphs outside the land of its birth; and it won them without shedding a drop of blood.

II. THE NEW DIVINITIES

Hinduism—Brahma, Vishnu, Shiva—Krishna—Kali—Animal gods
—The sacred cow—Polytheism and monotheism

The "Hinduism" that now replaced Buddhism was not one religion, nor was it only religion; it was a medley of faiths and ceremonies whose practitioners had only four qualities in common: they recognized the caste system and the leadership of the Brahmans, they reverenced the cow as especially representative of divinity, they accepted the law of *Karma* and the transmigration of souls, and they replaced with new gods the deities of the *Vedas*. These faiths had in part antedated and survived Vedic nature worship; in part they had grown from the connivance of the Brahmans at rites, divinities and beliefs unknown to the Scriptures and largely contrary to the Vedic spirit; they had boiled in the cauldron of Hindu religious thought even while Buddhism maintained a passing intellectual ascendancy.

The gods of Hinduism were characterized by a kind of anatomical superabundance vaguely symbolizing extraordinary knowledge, activity or power. The new Brahma had four faces, Kartikeya six; Shiva had three eyes, Indra a thousand; and nearly every deity had four arms.[10] At the head of this revised pantheon was Brahma, chivalrously neuter, acknowledged master of the gods, but no more noticed in actual worship than a constitutional monarch in modern Europe. Combined with him and Shiva in a triad—not a trinity—of dominant deities was Vishnu, a god of love who repeatedly became man in order to help mankind. His greatest incarnation was Krishna; as such he was born in a prison, had accomplished many marvels of heroism and romance, healed the deaf and the blind, helped lepers, championed the poor, and raised men from the grave. He had a beloved disciple, Arjuna, before whom he was trans-figured. He died, some say, by an arrow; others say by a crucifixion on a tree. He descended into hell, rose to heaven, and will return on the last day to judge the quick and the dead.[11]

To the Hindu there are three chief processes in life and the universe: creation, preservation and destruction. Hence divinity takes for him three main forms: Brahma the Creator, Vishnu the Preserver, and Shiva the Destroyer; these are the *Trimurti*, or "Three Shapes," which all Hindus but the Jains adore.* Popular devotion is divided between Vaishnavism, the religion of Vishnu, and Shivaism, the religion of Shiva. The two cults are peaceful neighbors, and sometimes hold sacrifices in the same temple;[14] and the wise Brahmans, followed by a majority of the people, pay equal honor to both these gods. Pious Vaishnavites paint upon their foreheads every morning with red clay the trident sign of Vishnu; pious Shivaites trace horizontal lines across their brows with cow-dung ashes, or wear the *linga*—symbol of the male organ—fastened on their arms or hung from their necks.[14]

The worship of Shiva is one of the oldest, most profound and most terrible elements in Hinduism. Sir John Marshall reports "unmistakable evidence" of the cult of Shiva at Mohenjo-daro, partly in the form of a three-headed Shiva, partly in the form of little stone columns which he presumes to be as phallic as their modern counterparts. "Shivaism," he concludes, "is therefore the most ancient living faith in the world."†[15] The name of the god is a euphemism; literally it means "propitious"; whereas Shiva himself is viewed chiefly as a god of cruelty and destruc-tion, the personification of that cosmic force which destroys, one after another, all the forms that reality takes—all cells, all organisms, all species, all ideas, all works, all planets and all things. Never has another people dared to face the impermanence of forms, and the impartiality of nature, so frankly, or to recognize so clearly that evil balances good, that destruc-tion goes step by step with creation, and that all birth is a capital crime, punishable with death. The Hindu, tortured with a thousand misfortunes and sufferings, sees in them the handiwork of a vivacious force that

* In the census of 1921 the religions of India divided the population as follows: Hindu-ism, 216,261,000; Sikhs, 3,239,000; Jains, 1,178,000; Buddhists, 11,571,000 (nearly all in Burma and Ceylon); Zoroastrians (Parsees), 102,000; Moslems, 68,735,000; Jews, 22,000; Christians, 4,754,000 (chiefly Europeans).[12]

† Nevertheless the name of Shiva, like that of *Brahman* itself, cannot be found in the *Rig-veda*. Patanjali the grammarian mentions Shiva images and devotees ca. 150 B.C.[16]

appears to find pleasure in breaking down everything that Brahma—the creative power in nature—has produced. Shiva dances to the tune of a perpetually forming, dissolving and re-forming world.

Just as death is the penalty of birth, so birth is the frustration of death; and the same god who symbolizes destruction represents also, for the Hindu mind, that passion and torrent of reproduction which overrides the death of the individual with the continuance of the race. In some parts of India, particularly Bengal, this creative or reproductive energy *(Shakti)* of Shiva or nature is personified in the figure of Shiva's wife, Kali (Parvati, Uma, Durga), and is worshiped in one of the many *Shakti* cults. Until the last century this worship was a bloody ritual, often involving human sacrifice; latterly the goddess has been content with goats.[17] The deity is portrayed for the populace by a black figure with gaping mouth and protruding tongue, adorned with snakes and dancing upon a corpse; her earrings are dead men, her necklace is a string of skulls, her face and breasts are smeared with blood.[18] Two of her four hands carry a sword and a severed head; the other two are extended in blessing and protection. For Kali-Parvati is the goddess of motherhood as well as the bride of destruction and death; she can be tender as well as cruel, and can smile as well as kill; once, perhaps, she was a mother-goddess in Sumeria, and was imported into India before she became so terrible.[19] Doubtless she and her lord are made as horrible as possible in order that timid worshipers may be frightened into decency, and perhaps into generosity to the priests.*

These are the greater gods of Hinduism; but they are merely five of thirty million deities in the Hindu pantheon; only to catalogue them would take a hundred volumes. Some of them are more properly angels, some are what we should call devils, some are heavenly bodies like the sun, some are mascots like *Lakshmi* (goddess of good luck), many of them are beasts of the field or fowl of the air. To the Hindu mind there was no real gap between animals and men; animals as well as men had souls, and souls were perpetually passing from men into animals, and back again; all these species were woven into one infinite web of *Karma* and reincarnation. The elephant, for example, became the god Ganesha, and was recognized as Shiva's son;[21] he personified man's animal nature, and at the same time his image served as a charm against evil fortune. Monkeys

---

* The priests of Shivaism, however, are seldom Brahmans; and the majority of the Brahmans look with scorn and regret upon the *Shakti* cult.[20]

and snakes were terrible, and therefore divine. The cobra or *naga*, whose bite causes almost immediate death, received especial veneration; annually the people of many parts of India celebrated a religious feast in honor of snakes, and made offerings of milk and plantains to the cobras at the entrance to their holes.[22] Temples have been erected in honor of snakes, as in eastern Mysore; great numbers of reptiles take up their residence in these buildings, and are fed and cared for by the priests.[23] Crocodiles, tigers, peacocks, parrots, even rats, receive their meed of worship.[24]

Most sacred of all animals to a Hindu is the cow. Images of bulls, in every material and size, appear in temples and homes, and in the city squares; the cow itself is the most popular organism in India, and has full freedom of the streets; its dung is used as fuel or a holy ointment; its urine is a sacred wine that will wash away all inner or outer uncleanness. Under no circumstances are these animals to be eaten by a Hindu, nor is their flesh to be worn as clothing—headgear or gloves or shoes; and when they die they are to be buried with the pomp of religious ritual.[25] Perhaps wise statesmanship once decreed this tabu in order to preserve agricultural draft animals for the growing population of India;[26] today, however, they number almost one-fourth as many as the population.[27] The Hindu view is that it is no more unreasonable to feel a profound affection for cows, and a profound revulsion at the thought of eating them, than it is to have similar feelings in regard to domestic cats and dogs; the cynical view of the matter is that the Brahmans believed that cows should never be slaughtered, that insects should never be injured, and that widows should be burned alive. The truth is that the worship of animals occurs in the history of every people, and that if one must deify any animal, the kind and placid cow seems entitled to her measure of devotion. We must not be too haughtily shocked by the menagerie of Hindu gods; we too have had our serpent-devil of Eden, our golden calf of the Old Testament, our sacred fish of the catacombs, and our gracious Lamb of God.

The secret of polytheism is the inability of the simple mind to think in impersonal terms; it can understand persons more readily than forces, wills more easily than laws.[28] The Hindu suspects that our human senses see only the outside of the events that they report; behind the veil of these phenomena, he thinks, there are countless superphysical beings whom, in Kant's phrase, we can only conceive but never perceive. A certain philosophical tolerance in the Brahmans has added to the teeming pantheon of India; local or tribal gods have been received into the Hindu Valhalla by adoption, usually by interpreting them as aspects or avatars of accepted deities; every faith could get its credentials if it paid its dues. In the end nearly every god became a phase, attribute or incarnation of another god, until all these divinities, to adult Hindu minds, merged into one; polytheism became pantheism, almost monotheism, almost monism. Just as a good Christian may pray to the Madonna or one of a thousand saints, and yet be a monotheist in the sense that he recognizes one God as supreme, so the Hindu prays to Kali or Rama or Krishma or Ganesha without presuming for a moment that these are supreme deities.* Some Hindus recognize Vishnu as supreme, and call Shiva merely a subordinate divinity; some call Shiva supreme, and make Vishnu an angel; if only a few worship Brahma it is because of its impersonality, its intangibility, its distance, and for the same reason that most churches in Christendom were erected to Mary or a saint, while Christianity waited for Voltaire to raise a chapel to God.

III. BELIEFS

The "Puranas" — The reincarnations of the universe — The migrations of the soul—"Karma"—Its philosophical aspects —Life as evil—Release

Mingled with this complex theology is a complex mythology at once superstitious and profound. The *Vedas* having died in the language in which they were written, and the metaphysics of the Brahman schools being beyond the comprehension of the people, Vyasa and others, over a period of a thousand years (500 B.C.–500 A.D.), composed eighteen *Puranas*—"old stories"—in 400,000 couplets, expounding to the laity the exact truth about the creation of the world, its periodical evolution and dissolution, the genealogy of the gods, and the history of the heroic age. These books made no pretense to literary form, logical order, or numerical moderation; they insisted that the lovers Urvashi and Pururavas spent 61,000 years in pleasure and delight.[30] But through the intelligibility of their language, the attractiveness of their parables, and the orthodoxy of their doctrine they became the second Bible of Hinduism, the grand repository of its superstitions, its myths, even of its philosophy. Here, for example, in the *Vishnupurana*, is the oldest and ever-recurrent theme

---

* Excerpt from the 1901 Census Report to the British Government of India: "The general result of my inquiries is that the great majority of Hindus have a firm belief in one Supreme Being."[29]

of Hindu thought—that individual separateness is an illusion, and that all life is one:

> After a thousand years came Ribhu
> To Nidagha's city, to impart further knowledge to him.
> He saw him outside the city
> Just as the King was about to enter with a great train of attendants,
> Standing afar and holding himself apart from the crowd,
> His neck wizened with fasting, returning from the wood with fuel
>   and grass.
> When Ribhu saw him, he went to him and greeted him and said:
> "O Brahman, why standest thou here alone?"
> Nidagha said: "Behold the crowd pressing about the King,
> Who is just entering the city. That is why I stand alone."
> Ribhu said: "Which of these is the King?
> And who are the others?
> Tell me that, for thou seemest informed."
> Nidagha said: "He who rides upon the fiery elephant, towering
>   like a mountain peak,
> That is the King. The others are his attendants."
> Ribhu said: "These two, the King and the elephant, are pointed out
>   by you
> Without being separated by mark of distinction;
> Give me the mark of distinction between them.
> I would know, which is here the elephant and which the King."
> Nidagha said: "The elephant is below, the King is above him;
> Who does not know the relationship of borne to bearer?"
> Ribhu said: "That I may know, teach me.
> What is that which is indicated by the word 'below', and what is
>   'above'?"
> Straight Nidagha sprang upon the *Guru*,* and said to him:
> "Hear now, I will tell thee what thou demandest of me:
> I am above like the King. You are below, like the elephant.
> For thy instruction I give thee this example."
> Ribhu said: "If you are in the position of the King, and I in that of
>   the elephant,
> So tell me this still: Which of us is you, and which is I?"
> Then swiftly Nidagha, falling down before him, clasped his feet
>   and spake:

---

* Teacher.

"Truly thou art Ribhu, my Master. . . .
By this I know that thou, my *Guru*, art come."
Ribhu said: "Yes, to give thee teaching,
Because of thy former willingness to serve me,
I, Ribhu by name, am come to thee.
And what I have just taught thee in short—
Heart of highest truth—that is complete non-duality."*
When he had thus spoken to Nidagha the *Guru* Ribhu departed
   thence.
But forthwith Nidagha, taught by this symbolic teaching, turned his
   mind completely to non-duality.
All beings from thenceforth he saw not distinct from himself.
And so he saw *Brahman*. And thus he achieved the highest sal-
   vation.[31]

In these *Puranas*, and kindred writings of medieval India, we find a very modern theory of the universe. There is no creation in the sense of Genesis; the world is perpetually evolving and dissolving, growing and decaying, through cycle after cycle, like every plant in it, and every organism. Brahma—or, as the Creator is more often called in this literature, Prajapati— is the spiritual force that upholds this endless process. We do not know how the universe began, if it did; perhaps, say the *Puranas*, Brahma laid it as an egg and then hatched it by sitting on it; perhaps it is a passing error of the Maker, or a little joke.[32] Each cycle or *Kalpa* in the history of the universe is divided into a thousand *mahayugas*, or great ages, of 4,320,000 years each; and each *mahayuga* contains four *yugas* or ages, in which the human race undergoes a gradual deterioration. In the present *mahayuga* three ages have now passed, totaling 3,888,888 years; we live in the fourth age, the *Kali-yuga*, or Age of Misery; 5035 years of this bitter era have elapsed, but 426,965 remain. Then the world will suffer one of its periodical deaths, and Brahma will begin another "day of Brahma," i.e., a *Kalpa* of 4,320,000,000 years. In each *Kalpa* cycle the universe develops by natural means and processes, and by natural means and processes decays; the destruction of the whole world is as certain as the death of a mouse, and, to the philosopher, not more important. There is no final purpose towards which the whole creation moves; there is no "progress"; there is only endless repetition.[33]

Through all these ages and great ages billions of souls have passed from species to species, from body to body, from life to life, in weary trans-

---

* *Advaitam;* this is the central word of Hindu philosophy; cf. page 549 below.

migration. An individual is not really an individual, he is a link in the chain of life, a page in the chronicle of a soul; a species is not really a separate species, for the souls in these flowers or fleas may yesterday have been, or tomorrow may be, the spirits of men; all life is one. A man is only partly a man, he is also an animal; shreds and echoes of past lower existences linger in him, and make him more akin to the brute than to the sage. Man is only a part of nature, not actually its center or master;[34] a life is only a part of a soul's career, not the entirety; every form is transitory, but every reality is continuous and one. The many reincarnations of a soul are like years or days in a single life, and may bring the soul now to growth, now to decay. How can the individual life, so brief in the tropic torrent of generations, contain all the history of a soul, or give it due punishment and reward for its evil and its good? And if the soul is immortal, how could one short life determine its fate forever?*

Life can be understood, says the Hindu, only on the assumption that each existence is bearing the penalty or enjoying the fruits of vice or virtue in some antecedent life. No deed small or great, good or bad, can be without effect; everything will out. This is the Law of *Karma*—the Law of the Deed—the law of causality in the spiritual world; and it is the highest and most terrible law of all. If a man does justice and kindness without sin his reward cannot come in one mortal span; it is stretched over other lives in which, if his virtue persists, he will be reborn into loftier place and larger good fortune; but if he lives evilly he will be reborn as an Outcaste, or a weasel, or a dog.[35]† This law of *Karma*, like the Greek *Moira* or Fate, is above both gods and men; even the gods do not change its absolute operation; or, as the theologians put it, *Karma* and the will or action of the gods are one.[38] But *Karma* is not Fate; Fate implies the helplessness of man to determine his own lot; *Karma* makes him (taking all his lives as a whole) the creator of his own destiny. Nor do heaven and hell end the work of *Karma*, or the chain of births and deaths; the soul, after the death of the body, may go to hell for special punishment, or to heaven for quick and special reward; but no soul stays in hell, and few souls stay in heaven, forever; nearly every soul that enters them must

---

* When the Hindu is asked why we have no memory of our past incarnations, he answers that likewise we have no memory of our infancy; and as we presume our infancy to explain our maturity, so he presumes past existences to explain our place and fate in our present life.

† A monk explained his appetite on the ground that in a previous existence he had been an elephant, and *Karma* had forgotten to change the appetite with the body.[36] A woman of strong odor was believed to have been formerly a fish.[37]

sooner or later return to earth, and live out its *Karma* in new incarnations.[39]*

Biologically there was much truth in this doctrine. We *are* the reincarnations of our ancestors, and will be reincarnated in our children; and the defects of the fathers are to some extent (though perhaps not as much as good conservatives suppose) visited upon the children, even through many generations. *Karma* was an excellent myth for dissuading the human beast from murder, theft, procrastination, or offertorial parsimony; furthermore, it extended the sense of moral unity and obligations to all life, and gave the moral code an extent of application far greater, and more logical, than in any other civilization. Good Hindus do not kill insects if they can possibly avoid it; "even those whose aspirations to virtue are modest treat animals as humble brethren rather than as lower creatures over whom they have dominion by divine command."[41] Philosophically, *Karma* explained for India many facts otherwise obscure in meaning or bitterly unjust. All those eternal inequalities among men which so frustrate the eternal demands for equality and justice; all the diverse forms of evil that blacken the earth and redden the stream of history; all the suffering that enters into human life with birth and accompanies it unto death, seemed intelligible to the Hindu who accepted *Karma;* these evils and injustices, these variations between idiocy and genius, poverty and wealth, were the results of past existences, the inevitable working out of a law unjust for a life or a moment, but perfectly just in the end.†

Karma is one of those many inventions by which men have sought to bear

---

* The Hindus believe in seven heavens, one of them on earth, the others rising in gradations above it; there are twenty-one hells, divided into seven sections. Punishment is not eternal, but it is diversified. Père Dubois' description of the Hindu hells rivals Dante's account of Inferno, and illustrates, like it, the many fears, and the sadistic imagination, of mankind. "Fire, steel, serpents, venomous insects, savage beasts, birds of prey, gall, poison, stenches; in a word, everything possible is employed to torment the damned. Some have a cord run through their nostrils, by which they are forever dragged over the edges of extremely sharp knives; others are condemned to pass through the eye of a needle; others are placed between two flat rocks, which meet, and crush, without killing, them; others have their eyes pecked incessantly by famished vultures; while millions of them continually swim and paddle in a pool filled with the urine of dogs or with the mucus from men's nostrils."[40] Such beliefs were probably the privilege of the lowest Hindus and the strictest theologians. We shall find it easier to forgive them if we remember that our own Hell, unlike that of India, was not only varied, but eternal.

† The belief in *Karma* and transmigration is the greatest theoretical obstacle to the removal of the caste system from India; for the orthodox Hindu presumes that caste differences are decreed by the soul's conduct in past lives, and are part of a divine plan which it would be sacrilegious to disturb.

evil patiently, and to face life with hope. To explain evil, and to find for men some scheme in which they may accept it, if not with good cheer, then with peace of mind—this is the task that most religions have attempted to fulfill. Since the real problem of life is not suffering but undeserved suffering, the religion of India mitigates the human tragedy by giving meaning and value to grief and pain. The soul, in Hindu theology, has at least this consolation, that it must bear the consequences only of its own acts; unless it questions all existence it can accept evil as a passing punishment, and look forward to tangible rewards for virtue borne.

But in truth the Hindus do question all existence. Oppressed with an enervating environment, national subjection and economic exploitation, they have tended to look upon life as more a bitter punishment than an opportunity or a reward. The *Vedas*, written by a hardy race coming in from the north, were almost as optimistic as Whitman; Buddha, representing the same stock five hundred years later, already denied the value of life; the *Puranas*, five centuries later still, represented a view more profoundly pessimistic than anything known in the West except in stray moments of philosophic doubt.* The East, until reached by the Industrial Revolution, could not understand the zest with which the Occident has taken life; it saw only superficiality and childishness in our merciless busyness, our discontented ambition, our nerve-racking labor-saving devices, our progress and speed; it could no more comprehend this profound immersion in the surface of things, this clever refusal to look ultimates in the face, than the West can fathom the quiet inertia, the "stagnation" and "hopelessness" of the traditional East. Heat cannot understand cold.

"What is the most wonderful thing in the world?" asks Yama of Yudishthira; and Yudishthira replies: "Man after man dies; seeing this, men still move about as if they were immortal."⁴⁴ "By death the world is afflicted," say the *Mahabharata*, "by age it is held in bar, and the nights

---

* Schopenhauer, like Buddha, reduced all suffering to the will to live and beget, and advocated race suicide by voluntary sterility. Heine could hardly pen a stanza without speaking of death, and could write, in Hindu strain,
> Sweet is sleep, but death is better;
> Best of all is never to be born.⁴²
Kant, scorning the optimism of Leibnitz, asked: "Would any man of sound understanding who has lived long enough, and has meditated on the worth of human existence, care to go again through life's poor play, I do not say on the same conditions, but on any conditions whatever?"⁴³

are the Unfailing Ones that are ever coming and going. When I know
that death cannot halt, what can I expect from walking in a cover of
lore?"[45] And in the *Ramayana* Sita asks, as her reward for fidelity through
every temptation and trial, only death:

> If in truth unto my husband I have proved a faithful wife,
> Mother Earth, relieve thy Sita from the burden of this life![46]

So the last word of Hindu religious thought is *moksha*, release—first
from desire, then from life. *Nirvana* may be one release or the other;
but it is fullest in both. The sage Bhartri-hari expresses the first:

> Everything on earth gives cause for fear, and the only freedom
> from fear is to be found in the renunciation of all desire. . . . Once
> upon a time the days seemed long to me when my heart was sorely
> wounded through asking favors from the rich; and yet again the
> days seemed all too short for me when I sought to carry out all my
> worldly desires and ends. But now as a philosopher I sit on a hard
> stone in a cave on the mountainside, and time and again I laugh
> when I think of my former life.[47]

Gandhi expresses the second form of release: "I do not want to be reborn," he says.[48] The highest and final aspiration of the Hindu is to escape
reincarnation, to lose that fever of ego which revives with each individual
body and birth. Salvation does not come by faith, nor yet by works; it
comes by such uninterrupted self-denial, by such selfless intuition of the
part-engulfing Whole, that at last the self is dead, and there is nothing
to be reborn. The hell of individuality passes into the haven and heaven
of unity, of complete and impersonal absorption into *Brahman*, the soul
or Force of the World.

IV. CURIOSITIES OF RELIGION

*Superstitions — Astrology — Phallic worship — Ritual — Sacrifice
—Purification—The sacred waters*

Amid all this theology of fear and suffering, superstition—first aid
from the supernatural for the minor ills of life—flourished with rank fertility. Oblations, charms, exorcisms, astrology, oracles, incantations, vows,

palmistry, divination, 2,728,812 priests, a million fortune-tellers, a hundred thousand snake-charmers, a million *fakirs, yogis* and other holy men —this is one part of the historic picture of India. For twelve hundred years the Hindus have had a great number of *Tantras* (manuals) expounding mysticism, witchcraft, divination and magic, and formulating the holy *mantras* (spells) by which almost any purpose might be magically attained. The Brahmans looked with silent contempt upon this religion of magic; they tolerated it partly because they feared that superstition among the people might be essential to their own power, partly, perhaps, because they believed that superstition is indestructible, dying in one form only to be reborn in another. No man of sense, they felt, would quarrel with a force capable of so many reincarnations.

The simple Hindu, like many cultured Americans,* accepted astrology, and took it for granted that every star exercised a special influence over those born under its ascendancy.[50] Menstruating women, like Ophelia, were to keep out of the sunshine, for this might make them pregnant.[51] The secret of material prosperity, said the *Kaushitaki Upanishad*, is the regular adoration of the new moon. Sorcerers, necromancers and soothsayers, for a pittance, expounded the past and the future by studying palms, ordure, dreams, signs in the sky, or holes eaten into cloth by mice. Chanting the charms which only they knew how to recite, they laid ghosts, bemused cobras, enthralled birds, and forced the gods themselves to come to the aid of the contributor. Magicians, for the proper fee, introduced a demon into one's enemy, or expelled it from one's self; they caused the enemy's sudden death, or brought him down with an incurable disease. Even a Brahman, when he yawned, snapped his fingers to right and left to frighten away the evil spirits that might enter his mouth.† At all times the Hindu, like many European peasants, was on his guard against the evil eye; at any time he might be visited with misfortune, or death, magically brought upon him by his enemies. Above all, the magician could restore sexual vitality, or inspire love in any one for any one, or give children to barren women.[52]

There was nothing, not even *Nirvana*, that the Hindu desired so intensely as children. Hence, in part, his longing for sexual power, and his

---

* Cf. footnote to page 80 above.

† So the good European caps each sneeze with a benediction, originally to guard against the soul being ejected by the force of the expiration.

ritual adoration of the symbols of reproduction and fertility. Phallic worship, which has prevailed in most countries at one time or another, has persisted in India from ancient times to the twentieth century. Shiva was its deity, the phallus was its ikon, the *Tantras* were its *Talmud*. The *Shakti*, or energizing power, of Shiva was conceived sometimes as his consort Kali, sometimes as a female element in Shiva's nature, which included both male and female powers; and these two powers were represented by idols called *linga* or *yoni*, representing respectively the male or the female organs of generation.[53] Everywhere in India one sees signs of this worship of sex: in the phallic figures on the Nepalese and other temples in Benares; in the gigantic *lingas* that adorn or surround the Shivaite temples of the south; in phallic processions and ceremonies, and in the phallic images worn on the arm or about the neck. *Linga* stones may be seen on the highways; Hindus break upon them the cocoanuts which they are about to offer in sacrifice.[54] At the Rameshvaram Temple the *linga* stone is daily washed with Ganges water, which is afterwards sold to the pious,[55] as holy water or mesmerized water has been sold in Europe. Usually the phallic ritual is simple and becoming; it consists in anointing the stone with consecrated water or oil, and decorating it with leaves.[56]

Doubtless the lower orders in India derive some profane amusement from phallic processions;[57] but for the most part the people appear to find no more obscene stimulus in the *linga* or the *yoni* than a Christian does in the contemplation of the Madonna nursing her child; custom lends propriety, and time lends sanctity, to anything. The sexual symbolism of the objects seems long since to have been forgotten by the people; the images are now merely the traditional and sacred ways of representing the power of Shiva.[58] Perhaps the difference between the European and the Hindu conception of this matter arose from divergence in the age of marriage; early marriage releases those impulses which, when long frustrated, turn in upon themselves and beget prurience as well as romantic love. The sexual morals and manners of India are in general higher than those of Europe and America, and far more decorous and restrained. The worship of Shiva is one of the most austere and ascetic of all the Hindu cults; and the devoutest worshipers of the *linga* are the Lingayats— the most Puritanic sect in India.[59] "It has remained for our Western visitors," says Gandhi, "to acquaint us with the obscenity of many practices which we have hitherto innocently indulged in. It was in a missionary book that I first learned that *Shivalingam* had any obscene significance at all."[60]

The use of the *linga* and the *yoni* was but one of the myriad rituals that seemed, to the passing and alien eye, not merely the form but half the essence of Indian religion. Nearly every act of life, even to washing and dressing, had its religious rite. In every pious home there were private and special gods to be worshiped, and ancestors to be honored, every day; indeed religion, to the Hindu, was a matter for domestic observances rather than for temple ceremonies, which were reserved for holydays. But the people rejoiced in the many feasts that marked the ecclesiastical year and brought them in great processions or pilgrimages to their ancient shrines. They could not understand the service there, for it was conducted in Sanskrit, but they could understand the idol. They decked it with ornaments, covered it with paint, and encrusted it with jewels; sometimes they treated it as a human being—awakened it, bathed it, dressed it, fed it, scolded it, and put it to bed at the close of the day.[61]

The great public rite was sacrifice or offering; the great private rite was purification. Sacrifice, to the Hindu, was no empty form; he believed that if no food was offered them the gods would starve to death.[62] When men were cannibals human sacrifices were offered in India as elsewhere; Kali particularly had an appetite for men, but the Brahmans explained that she would eat only men of the lower castes.[63]* As morals improved, the gods had to content themselves with animals, of which great numbers were offered them. The goat was especially favored for these ceremonies. Buddhism, Jainism and *ahimsa* put an end to animal sacrifice in Hindustan,[67] but the replacement of Buddhism with Hinduism restored the custom, which survived, in diminishing extent, to our own time. It is to the credit of the Brahmans that they refused to take part in any sacrifice that involved the shedding of blood.[68]

Purification rites took many an hour of Hindu life, for fears of pollution were as frequent in Indian religion as in modern hygiene. At any moment the Hindu might be made unclean—by improper food, by offal, by the touch of a Shudra, an Outcaste, a corpse, a menstruating woman, or in a

---

*Such human sacrifices were recorded as late as 1854.[64] It was formerly believed that devotees had offered themselves as sacrifices, as in the case of fanatics supposed to have thrown themselves under the wheels of the Juggernaut (Indian *Jagannath*) car;[65] but it is now held that the rare cases of such apparent self-sacrifice may have been accidents.[66]

hundred other ways. The woman herself, of course, was defiled by menstruation or childbirth; Brahmanical law required isolation in such cases, and complex hygienic precautions.[69] After all such pollutions—or, as we should say, possible infections—the Hindu had to undergo ritual purification: in minor cases by such simple ceremonies as being sprinkled with holy water;[70] in major cases by more complicated methods, culminating in the terrible *Panchagavia*. This purification was decreed as punishment for violating important caste laws (e.g., for leaving India), and consisted in drinking a mixture of "five substances" from the sacred cow: milk, curds, ghee, urine and dung.[71]*

A little more to our taste was the religious precept to bathe daily; here again a hygienic measure, highly desirable in a semitropical climate, was clothed in a religious form for more successful inculcation. "Sacred" pools and tanks were built, many rivers were called holy, and men were told that if they bathed in these they would be purified in body and soul. Already in the days of Yuan Chwang millions bathed in the Ganges every morning;[73] from that century to ours those waters have never seen the sun rise without hearing the prayers of the bathers seeking purity and release, lifting their arms to the holy orb, and calling out patiently, "Om, Om, Om." Benares became the Holy City of India, the goal of millions of pilgrims, the haven of old men and women come from every part of the country to bathe in the river, and so to face death sinless and clean. There is an element of awe, even of terror, in the thought that such men have come to Benares for two thousand years, and have gone down shivering into its waters in the winter dawn, and smelled with misgiving the flesh of the dead on the burning *ghats*, and uttered the same trusting prayers, century after century, to the same silent deities. The unresponsiveness of a god is no obstacle to his popularity; India believes as strongly today as ever in the gods that have so long looked down with equanimity upon her poverty and her desolation.

---

* Ghee is clarified butter. Urine, says the Abbé Dubois (1820), "is looked upon as most efficacious for purifying any kind of uncleanness. I have often seen superstitious Hindus following the cows to pasture, waiting for the moment when they could collect the precious liquid in vessels of brass, and carrying it away while still warm to their houses. I have also seen them waiting to catch it in the hollow of their hands, drinking some of it and rubbing their faces and heads with the rest."[72] *De gustibus non disputandum.*

V. SAINTS AND SCEPTICS

Methods of sanctity — Heretics — Toleration — General view of
Hindu Religion

Saints seem more abundant in India than elsewhere, so that at last the visitor feels that they are a natural product of the country, like the poppy or the snake. Hindu piety recognized three main avenues to sanctity: *Jnana-yoga*, the Way of Meditation, *Karma-yoga*, the Way of Action, and *Bhakti-yoga*, the Way of Love. The Brahmans allowed for all three by their rule of the four *Ashramas*, or stages of sanctity. The young Brahman was to begin as a *Brahmachari*, vowed to premarital chastity, to piety, study, truthfulness, and loving service of his *Guru* or teacher. After marriage, which he should not delay beyond his eighteenth year, he was to enter the second stage of Brahmanical life as *Grihastha*, or householder, and beget sons for the care and worship of himself and his ancestors. In the third stage (now seldom practiced) the aspirant to sanctity retired with his wife to live as a *Vanaprastha*, or jungle-dweller, accepting hard conditions gladly, and limiting sexual relations to the begetting of children. Finally the Brahman who wished to reach the highest stage might, in his old age, leave even his wife, and become a *Sannyasi*, or "abandoner" of the world; giving up all property, all money and all ties, he would keep only an antelope skin for his body, a staff for his hand, and a gourd of water for his thirst. He must smear his body with ashes every day, drink the Five Substances frequently, and live entirely by alms. "He must," says the Brahmanical Rule, "regard all men as equals. He must not be influenced by anything that happens, and must be able to view with perfect equanimity even revolutions that overthrow empires. His one object must be to acquire that measure of wisdom and of spirituality which shall finally reunite him to the Supreme Divinity, from which we are separated by our passions and our material surroundings."[74]*

In the midst of all this piety one comes occasionally upon a sceptical voice stridently out of tune with the solemnity of the normal Hindu note. Doubtless when India was wealthy, sceptics were numerous, for humanity doubts its gods most when it prospers, and worships them most when it is miserable. We have noted the Charvakas and other heretics of Buddha's time. Almost as old is a work called, in the sesquipedalian

---

* Dubois, sceptical of everything but his own myth, adds: "The greater number of these *sannyasin* are looked upon as utter impostors, and that by the most enlightened of their fellow-countrymen."[75]

fashion of the Hindus, *Shwasamvedyopanishad*, which simplifies theology into four propositions: (1) that there is no reincarnation, no god, no heaven, no hell, and no world; (2) that all traditional religious literature is the work of conceited fools; (3) that Nature the originator and Time the destroyer are the rulers of all things, and take no account of virtue or vice in awarding happiness or misery to men; and (4) that people, deluded by flowery speech, cling to gods, temples and priests, when in reality there is no difference between Vishnu and a dog.[76] With all the inconsistency of a Bible harboring Ecclesiastes, the Pali canon of Buddhism offers us a remarkable treatise, probably as old as Christianity, called "The Questions of King Milinda," in which the Buddhist teacher Nagasena is represented as giving very disturbing answers to the religious inquiries made of him by the Greco-Bactrian King Menander, who ruled northern India at the turn of the first century before Christ. Religion, says Nagasena, must not be made a mere way of escape for suffering men; it should be an ascetic search for sanctity and wisdom without presuming a heaven or a god; for in truth, this saint assures us, these do not exist.[77] *The Mahabharata* inveighs against doubters and atheists who, it tells us, deny the reality of souls, and despise immortality; such men, it says, "wander over the whole earth"; and it warns them of their future punishment by the horrible example of a jackal who explains his species by admitting that in a previous incarnation he had been "a rationalist, a critic of the *Vedas*, . . . a reviler and opposer of priests, . . . an unbeliever, a doubter of all."[78] The *Bhagavad-Gita* refers to heretics who deny the existence of a god and describe the world as "none other than a House of Lust."[79] The Brahmans themselves were often sceptics, but too completely so to attack the religion of the people. And though the poets of India are as a rule assiduously pious, some of them, like Kabir and Vemana, speak in defense of a very emancipated theism. Vemana, a South Indian poet of the seventeenth century, writes scornfully of ascetic hermits, pilgrimages, and caste:

> The solitariness of a dog! the meditations of a crane! the chanting of an ass! the bathing of a frog! . . . How are you the better for smearing your body with ashes? Your thoughts should be set on God alone; for the rest, an ass can wallow in dirt as well as you. . . . The books called *Vedas* are like courtesans, deluding men, and wholly unfathomable; but the hidden knowledge of God is like an

honorable wife. . . . Will the application of white ashes do away
with the smell of a wine-pot?—will a cord cast over your neck
make you twice-born? . . . Why should we constantly revile the
Pariah? Are not his flesh and blood the same as our own? And of
what caste is He who pervades the Pariah? . . . He who says, "I
know nothing" is the shrewdest of all.[80]

It is worthy of note that pronouncements of this kind could be made
with impunity in a society mentally ruled by a priestly caste. Except
for foreign repressions (and perhaps because of alien rulers indifferent
to native theologies) India has enjoyed a freedom of thought far greater
than that of the medieval Europe to which its civilization corresponds;
and the Brahmans have exercised their authority with discrimination and
lenience. They relied upon the conservatism of the poor to preserve the
orthodox religion, and they were not disappointed. When heresies or
strange gods became dangerously popular they tolerated them, and then
absorbed them into the capacious caverns of Hindu belief; one god more
or less could not make much difference in India. Hence there has been
comparatively little sectarian animosity within the Hindu community,
though much between Hindus and Moslems; and no blood has been shed
for religion in India except by its invaders.[81] Intolerance came with Islam
and Christianity; the Moslems proposed to buy Paradise with the blood of
"infidels," and the Portuguese, when they captured Goa, introduced the
Inquisition into India.[82]

If we look for common defining elements in this jungle of faiths, we
shall find them in the practical unanimity of the Hindus in worshiping
both Vishnu and Shiva, in reverencing the *Vedas*, the Brahmans, and the
cow, and in accepting the *Mahabharata* and the *Ramayana* as no mere
literary epics, but as the secondary scriptures of the race.[83] It is significant
that the deities and dogmas of India today are not those of the *Vedas*;
in a sense Hinduism represents the triumph of aboriginal Dravidic India
over the Aryans of the Vedic age. As the result of conquest, spoliation
and poverty, India has been injured in body and soul, and has sought
refuge from harsh terrestrial defeat in the easy victories of myth and
imagination. Despite its elements of nobility, Buddhism, like Stoicism,
was a slave philosophy, even if voiced by a prince; it meant that all desire
or struggle, even for personal or national freedom, should be abandoned,
and that the ideal was a desireless passivity; obviously the exhausting heat

of India spoke in this rationalization of fatigue. Hinduism continued the weakening of India by binding itself, through the caste system, in permanent servitude to a priesthood; it conceived its gods in unmoral terms, and maintained for centuries brutal customs, like human sacrifice and suttee, which many nations had long since outgrown; it depicted life as inevitably evil, and broke the courage and darkened the spirit of its devotees; it turned all earthly phenomena into illusion, and thereby destroyed the distinction between freedom and slavery, good and evil, corruption and betterment. In the words of a brave Hindu, "Hindu religion . . . has now degenerated into an idol-worship and conventional ritualism, in which the form is regarded as everything, and its substance as nothing."[84] A nation ridden with priests and infested with saints, India awaits with unformulated longing her Renaissance, her Reformation, and her Enlightenment.

We must, however, keep our historical perspective in thinking of India; we too were once in the Middle Ages, and preferred mysticism to science, priestcraft to plutocracy—and may do likewise again. We cannot judge these mystics, for our judgments in the West are usually based upon corporeal experience and material results, which seem irrelevant and superficial to the Hindu saint. What if wealth and power, war and conquest, were only surface illusions, unworthy of a mature mind? What if this science of hypothetical atoms and genes, of whimsical protons and cells, of gases generating Shakespeares and chemicals fusing into Christ, were only one more *faith*, and one of the strangest, most incredible and most transitory of all? The East, resentful of subjection and poverty, may go in for science and industry at the very time when the children of the West, sick of machines that impoverish them and of sciences that disillusion them, may destroy their cities and their machines in chaotic revolution or war, go back, beaten, weary and starving, to the soil, and forge for themselves another mystic faith to give them courage in the face of hunger, cruelty, injustice and death. There is no humorist like history.

CHAPTER XIX

The Life of the Mind

I. HINDU SCIENCE

Its religious origins—Astronomers—Mathematicism—The "Arabic" numerals—The decimal system—Algebra—Geometry— Physics — Chemistry — Physiology — Vedic medicine— Physicians—Surgeons — Anesthetics—Vaccination —Hypnotism

INDIA'S work in science is both very old and very young: young as an independent and secular pursuit, old as a subsidiary interest of her priests. Religion being the core of Hindu life, those sciences were cultivated first that contributed to religion: astronomy grew out of the worship of the heavenly bodies, and the observation of their movements aimed to fix the calendar of festival and sacrificial days; grammar and philology developed out of the insistence that every prayer and formula, though couched in a dead language, should be textually and phonetically correct.[1] As in our Middle Ages, the scientists of India, for better and for worse, were her priests.

Astronomy was an incidental offspring of astrology, and slowly emancipated itself under Greek influence. The earliest astronomical treatises, the *Siddhantas* (ca. 425 B.C.), were based on Greek science,[2] and Varahamihira, whose compendium was significantly entitled *Complete System of Natural Astrology*, frankly acknowledged his dependence upon the Greeks. The greatest of Hindu astronomers and mathematicians, Aryabhata, discussed in verse such poetic subjects as quadratic equations, sines, and the value of π; he explained eclipses, solstices and equinoxes, announced the sphericity of the earth and its diurnal revolution on its axis, and wrote, in daring anticipation of Renaissance science: "The sphere of the stars is stationary, and the earth, by its revolution, produces the daily rising and setting of planets and stars."[4] His most famous successor, Brahmagupta, systematized the astronomic knowledge of India, but obstructed its development by rejecting Aryabhata's theory of the revolution of the earth. These men and their followers adapted to Hindu usage the Babylonian division of the skies into zodiacal constellations; they made a calendar of twelve months, each of thirty days, each of thirty hours, inserting an intercalary month every five years; they calculated with remarkable accuracy the diameter of the moon, the eclipses of the moon and the sun, the position of the poles, and the position and motion of the major stars.[5] They expounded the theory, though not the law, of gravity when they wrote in the *Siddhantas*: "The earth, owing to its force of gravity, draws all things to itself."[6]

To make these complex calculations the Hindus developed a system of mathematics superior, in everything except geometry, to that of the Greeks.[7] Among the most vital parts of our Oriental heritage are the "Arabic" numerals and the decimal system, both of which came to us, through the Arabs, from India. The miscalled "Arabic" numerals are found on the Rock Edicts of Ashoka (256 B.C.), a thousand years before their occurrence in Arabic literature. Said the great and magnanimous Laplace:

> It is India that gave us the ingenious method of expressing all numbers by ten symbols, each receiving a value of position as well as an absolute value; a profound and important idea which appears so simple to us now that we ignore its true merit. But its very simplicity, the great ease which it has lent to all computations, puts our arithmetic in the first rank of useful inventions; and we shall appreciate the grandeur of this achievement the more when we remember that it escaped the genius of Archimedes and Apollonius, two of the greatest men produced by antiquity.[8]

The decimal system was known to Aryabhata and Brahmagupta long before its appearance in the writings of the Arabs and the Syrians; it was adopted by China from Buddhist missionaries; and Muhammad Ibn Musa al-Khwarazmi, the greatest mathematician of his age (d. ca. 850 A.D.), seems to have introduced it into Baghdad. The oldest known use of the zero in Asia or Europe* is in an Arabic document dated 873 A.D., three years sooner than its first known appearance in India; but by general consent the Arabs borrowed this too from India,[9] and the most modest and most valuable of all numerals is one of the subtle gifts of India to mankind.

---

* It was used by the Mayas of America in the first century A.D.[9a] Dr. Breasted attributes a knowledge of the place value of numerals to the ancient Babylonians (*Saturday Review of Literature*, New York, July 13, 1935, p. 15).

Algebra was developed in apparent independence by both the Hindus and the Greeks;* but our adoption of its Arabic name (*al-jabr*, adjustment) indicates that it came to western Europe from the Arabs—i.e., from India— rather than from Greece.[10] The great Hindu leaders in this field, as in astronomy, were Aryabhata, Brahmagupta and Bhaskara. The last (b. 1114 A.D.), appears to have invented the radical sign, and many algebraic symbols.[12] These men created the conception of a negative quantity, without which algebra would have been impossible;[13] they formulated rules for finding permutations and combinations; they found the square root of 2, and solved, in the eighth century A.D., indeterminate equations of the second degree that were unknown to Europe until the days of Euler a thousand years later.[14] They expressed their science in poetic form, and gave to mathematical problems a grace characteristic of India's Golden Age. These two may serve as examples of simpler Hindu algebra:

> Out of a swarm of bees one-fifth part settled on a Kadamba blossom; one-third on a Silindhra flower; three times the difference of those numbers flew to the bloom of a Kutaja. One bee, which remained, hovered about in the air. Tell me, charming woman, the number of bees. . . . Eight rubies, ten emeralds, and a hundred pearls, which are in thy ear-ring, my beloved, were purchased by me for thee at an equal amount; and the sum of the prices of the three sorts of gems was three less than half a hundred; tell me the price of each, auspicious woman.[15]

The Hindus were not so successful in geometry. In the measurement and construction of altars the priests formulated the Pythagorean theorem (by which the square of the hypotenuse of a right-angled triangle equals the sum of the squares of the other sides) several hundred years before the birth of Christ.[16] Aryabhata, probably influenced by the Greeks, found the area of a triangle, a trapezium and a circle, and calculated the value of π (the relation of diameter to circumference in a circle) at 3.1416—a figure not equaled in accuracy until the days of Purbach (1423-61) in Europe.[17] Bhaskara crudely anticipated the differential calculus, Aryabhata drew up a table of sines, and the *Surya Siddhanta* provided a system of trigonometry more advanced than anything known to the Greeks.[18]

Two systems of Hindu thought propound physical theories suggestively similar to those of Greece. Kanada, founder of the Vaisheshika philosophy, held that the world was composed of atoms as many in kind as the various

---

* The first algebraist known to us, the Greek Diophantus (360 A.D.), antedates Aryabhata by a century; but Cajori believes that he took his lead from India.[11]

elements. The Jains more nearly approximated to Democritus by teaching that all atoms were of the same kind, producing different effects by diverse modes of combination.[19] Kanada believed light and heat to be varieties of the same substance; Udayana taught that all heat comes from the sun; and Vachaspati, like Newton, interpreted light as composed of minute particles emitted by substances and striking the eye.[20] Musical notes and intervals were analyzed and mathematically calculated in the Hindu treatises on music;[*] and the "Pythagorean Law" was formulated by which the number of vibrations, and therefore the pitch of the note, varies inversely as the length of the string between the point of attachment and the point of touch. There is some evidence that Hindu mariners of the first centuries A.D. used a compass made by an iron fish floating in a vessel of oil and pointing north.[21]

Chemistry developed from two sources—medicine and industry. Something has been said about the chemical excellence of cast iron in ancient India, and about the high industrial development of Gupta times, when India was looked to, even by Imperial Rome, as the most skilled of the nations in such chemical industries as dyeing, tanning, soap-making, glass and cement. As early as the second century B.C. Nagarjuna devoted an entire volume to mercury. By the sixth century the Hindus were far ahead of Europe in industrial chemistry; they were masters of calcination, distillation, sublimation, steaming, fixation, the production of light without heat, the mixing of anesthetic and soporific powders, and the preparation of metallic salts, compounds and alloys. The tempering of steel was brought in ancient India to a perfection unknown in Europe till our own times; King Porus is said to have selected, as a specially valuable gift for Alexander, not gold or silver, but thirty pounds of steel.[22] The Moslems took much of this Hindu chemical science and industry to the Near East and Europe; the secret of manufacturing "Damascus" blades, for example, was taken by the Arabs from the Persians, and by the Persians from India.[22a]

Anatomy and physiology, like some aspects of chemistry, were by-products of Hindu medicine. As far back as the sixth century B.C. Hindu physicians described ligaments, sutures, lymphatics, nerve plexus, fascia, adipose and vascular tissues, mucous and synovial membranes, and many more muscles than any modern cadaver is able to show.[23] The doctors of pre-Christian India shared Aristotle's mistaken conception of the heart as the seat and organ of consciousness, and supposed that the nerves ascended to and descended from the heart. But they understood remarkably well the processes of digestion—the different functions of the gastric juices, the conversion of chyme into chyle, and of this into blood.[24] Anticipating Weismann by 2400 years,

---

[*] E.g., in *The Ocean of Music* (*Samgita-ratnakara*) of Sharamgadeva (1210-47).

Atreya (ca. 500 B.C.) held that the parental seed is independent of the parent's body, and contains in itself, in miniature, the whole parental organism.[25] Examination for virility was recommended as a prerequisite for marriage in men; and the Code of Manu warned against marrying mates affected with tuberculosis, epilepsy, leprosy, chronic dyspepsia, piles, or loquacity.[26] Birth control in the latest theological fashion was suggested by the Hindu medical schools of 500 B.C. in the theory that during twelve days of the menstrual cycle impregnation is impossible.[27] Fœtal development was described with considerable accuracy; it was noted that the sex of the fœtus remains for a time undetermined, and it was claimed that in some cases the sex of the embryo could be influenced by food or drugs.[28]

The records of Hindu medicine begin with the *Atharva-veda;* here, embedded in a mass of magic and incantations, is a list of diseases with their symptoms. Medicine arose as an adjunct to magic: the healer studied and used earthly means of cure to help his spiritual formulas; later he relied more and more upon such secular methods, continuing the magic spell, like our bedside manner, as a psychological aid. Appended to the *Atharva-veda* is the *Ajur-veda* ("The Science of Longevity"). In this oldest system of Hindu medicine illness is attributed to disorder in one of the four humors (air, water, phlegm and blood), and treatment is recommended with herbs and charms. Many of its diagnoses and cures are still used in India, with a success that is sometimes the envy of Western physicians. The *Rig-veda* names over a thousand such herbs, and advocates water as the best cure for most diseases. Even in Vedic times physicians and surgeons were being differentiated from magic doctors, and were living in houses surrounded by gardens in which they cultivated medicinal plants.[29]

The great names in Hindu medicine are those of Sushruta in the fifth century before, and Charaka in the second century after Christ. Sushruta, professor of medicine in the University of Benares, wrote down in Sanskrit a system of diagnosis and therapy whose elements had descended to him from his teacher Dhanwantari. His book dealt at length with surgery, obstetrics, diet, bathing, drugs, infant feeding and hygiene, and medical education.[30] Charaka composed a *Samhita* (or encyclopedia) of medicine, which is still used in India,[31] and gave to his followers an almost Hippocratic conception of their calling: "Not for self, not for the fulfilment of any earthly desire of gain, but solely for the good of suffering humanity should you treat your patients, and so excell all."[32] Only less illustrious than these are Vagbhata (625 A.D.), who prepared a medical compendium in prose and verse, and Bhava Misra (1550 A.D.), whose voluminous work on anatomy, physiology and medicine mentioned, a hundred years before Harvey, the circulation of the blood, and prescribed mercury for that novel disease, syphilis, which had recently been brought in by the Portuguese as part of Europe's heritage to India.[33]

Sushruta described many surgical operations—cataract, hernia, lithotomy, Cæsarian section, etc.—and 121 surgical instruments, including lancets, sounds, forceps, catheters, and rectal and vaginal speculums.[34] Despite Brahmanical prohibitions he advocated the dissection of dead bodies as indispensable in the training of surgeons. He was the first to graft upon a torn ear portions of skin taken from another part of the body; and from him and his Hindu successors rhinoplasty—the surgical reconstruction of the nose—descended into modern medicine.[35] "The ancient Hindus," says Garrison, "performed almost every major operation except ligation of the arteries."[36] Limbs were amputated, abdominal sections were performed, fractures were set, hemorrhoids and fistulas were removed. Sushruta laid down elaborate rules for preparing an operation, and his suggestion that the wound be sterilized by fumigation is one of the earliest known efforts at antiseptic surgery.[37] Both Sushruta and Charaka mention the use of medicinal liquors to produce insensibility to pain. In 927 A.D. two surgeons trepanned the skull of a Hindu king, and made him insensitive to the operation by administering a drug called *Samohini.*[*][38]

For the detection of the 1120 diseases that he enumerated, Sushruta recommended diagnosis by inspection, palpation, and auscultation.[40] Taking of the pulse was described in a treatise dating 1300 A.D.[41] Urinalysis was a favorite method of diagnosis; Tibetan physicians were reputed able to cure any patient without having seen anything more of him than his water.[42] In the time of Yuan Chwang Hindu medical treatment began with a seven-day fast; in this interval the patient often recovered; if the illness continued, drugs were at last employed.[43] Even then drugs were used very sparingly; reliance was placed largely upon diet, baths, enemas, inhalations, urethral and vaginal injections, and blood-lettings by leeches or cups.[44] Hindu physicians were especially skilled in concocting antidotes for poisons; they still excel European physicians in curing snakebites.[45] Vaccination, unknown to Europe before the eighteenth century,

---

* Hospitals were erected in Ceylon as early as 427 B.C., and in northern India as early as 226 B.C.[39]

was known in India as early as 550 A.D., if we may judge from a text attributed to Dhanwantari, one of the earliest Hindu physicians: "Take the fluid of the pock on the udder of the cow . . . upon the point of a lancet, and lance with it the arms between the shoulders and elbows until the blood appears; then, mixing the fluid with the blood, the fever of the small-pox will be produced."[46] Modern European physicians believe that caste separateness was prescribed because of the Brahman belief in invisible agents transmitting disease; many of the laws of sanitation enjoined by Sushruta and "Manu" seem to take for granted what we moderns, who love new words for old things, call the germ theory of disease.[47] Hypnotism as therapy seems to have originated among the Hindus, who often took their sick to the temples to be cured by hypnotic suggestion or "temple-sleep," as in Egypt and Greece.[48] The Englishmen who introduced hypnotherapy into England—Braid, Esdaile and Elliotson—"undoubtedly got their ideas, and some of their experience, from contact with India."[49]

The general picture of Indian medicine is one of rapid development in the Vedic and Buddhist periods, followed by centuries of slow and cautious improvement. How much Atreya, Dhanwantari and Sushruta owed to Greece, and how much Greece owed to them, we do not know. In the time of Alexander, says Garrison, "Hindu physicians and surgeons enjoyed a well-deserved reputation for superior knowledge and skill," and even Aristotle is believed by some students to have been indebted to them.[50] So too with the Persians and the Arabs: it is difficult to say how much Indian medicine owed to the physicians of Baghdad, and through them to the heritage of Babylonian medicine in the Near East; on the one hand certain remedies, like opium and mercury, and some modes of diagnosis, like feeling the pulse, appear to have entered India from Persia; on the other we find Persians and Arabs translating into their languages, in the eighth century A.D., the thousand-year-old compendia of Sushruta and Charaka.[51] The great Caliph Haroun-al-Rashid accepted the preëminence of Indian medicine and scholarship, and imported Hindu physicians to organize hospitals and medical schools in Baghdad.[52] Lord Ampthill concludes that medieval and modern Europe owes its system of medicine directly to the Arabs, and through them to India.[53] Probably this noblest and most uncertain of the sciences had an approximately equal antiquity, and developed in contemporary contact and mutual influence, in Sumeria, Egypt and India.

II. THE SIX SYSTEMS OF BRAHMANICAL PHILOSOPHY

The antiquity of Indian philosophy — Its prominent rôle — Its scholars — Forms — Conception of orthodoxy — The assumptions of Hindu philosophy

The priority of India is clearer in philosophy than in medicine, though here too origins are veiled, and every conclusion is an hypothesis. Some *Upanishads* are older than any *extant* form of Greek philosophy, and Pythagoras, Parmenides and Plato seem to have been influenced by Indian metaphysics; but the speculations of Thales, Anaximander, Anaximenes, Heraclitus, Anaxagoras and Empedocles not only antedate the secular philosophy of the Hindus, but bear a sceptical and physical stamp suggesting any other origin than India. Victor Cousin believed that "we are constrained to see in this cradle of the human race the native land of the highest philosophy."[54] It is more probable that no one of the civilizations known to us was the originator of any of the elements of civilization.

But nowhere else has the lust for philosophy been so strong as in India. It is, with the Hindus, not an ornament or a recreation, but a major interest and practice of life itself; and sages receive in India the honor bestowed in the West upon men of wealth or action. What other nation has ever thought of celebrating festivals with gladiatorial debates between the leaders of rival philosophical schools? We read in the *Upanishads* how the King of the Videhas, as part of a religious feast, set one day apart for a philosophical disputation among Yajnavalkya, Asvala, Artabhaga and Gargi (the Aspasia of India); to the victor the King promised—and gave— a reward of a thousand cows and many pieces of gold.[56] It was the usual course for a philosophical teacher in India to speak rather than to write; instead of attacking his opponents through the safe medium of print, he was expected to meet them in living debate, and to visit other schools in order to submit himself to controversy and questioning; leading philosophers like Shankara spent much of their time in such intellectual journeys.[57] Sometimes kings joined in these discussions with the modesty becoming a monarch in the presence of a philosopher—if we may credit the reports of the philosophers. The victor in a vital debate was as great a hero among his people as a general returning from the bloody triumphs of war.[58]

In a Rajput painting of the eighteenth century[59] we see a typical Indian "School of Philosophy"—the teacher sits on a mat under a tree, and his pupils squat on the grass before him. Such scenes were to be witnessed everywhere, for teachers of philosophy were as numerous in India as merchants in Babylonia. No other country has ever had so many schools of thought. In one of Buddha's dialogues we learn that there were sixty-two distinct theories of the soul among the philosophers of his time.[60] "This philosophical nation *par excellence*," says Count Keyserling, "has more Sanskrit words for philosophical and religious thought than are found in Greek, Latin and German combined."[61]

Since Indian thought was transmitted rather by oral tradition than by writing, the oldest form in which the theories of the various schools have come down to us is that of *sutras*—aphoristic "threads" which teacher or student jotted down, not as a means of explaining his thought to another, but as an aid to his own memory. These extant *sutras* are of varying age, some as old as 200 A.D., some as recent as 1400; in all cases they are much younger than the traditions of thought that they summarize, for the origin of these schools of philosophy is as old as Buddha, and some of them, like the *Sankhya*, were probably well-established when he was born.[62]

All systems of Indian philosophy are ranged by the Hindus in two categories: *Astika* systems, which affirm, and *Nastika* systems, which deny.* We have already studied the *Nastika* systems, which were chiefly those of the Charvakas, the Buddhists, and the Jains. But, strange to say, these systems were called *Nastika*, heterodox and nihilist, not because they questioned or denied the existence of God (which they did), but because they questioned, denied or ignored the authority of the *Vedas*. Many of the *Astika* systems also doubted or denied God; they were nevertheless called orthodox because they accepted the infallibility of the *Scriptures*, and the institution of caste; and no hindrance was placed against the free thought, however atheistic, of those schools that acknowledged these fundamentals of orthodox Hindu society. Since a wide latitude was allowed in interpreting the holy books, and clever dialecticians could find in the *Vedas* any doctrine which they sought, the only practical requirement for intellectual respectability was the recognition of caste; this being the real government of India, rejection of it was treason, and acceptance of it covered a multitude of sins. In effect, therefore, the philosophers of India enjoyed far more liberty than their Scholastic analogues in Europe,

---

* *Asti*, it is; *n'asti*, it is not.

though less, perhaps, than the thinkers of Christendom under the enlightened Popes of the Renaissance.

Of the "orthodox" systems or *darshanas* ("demonstrations"), six became so prominent that in time every Hindu thinker who acknowledged the authority of the Brahmans attached himself to one or another of these schools. All six make certain assumptions which are the bases of Hindu thought: that the *Vedas* are inspired; that reasoning is less reliable as a guide to reality and truth than the direct perception and feeling of an individual properly prepared for spiritual receptiveness and subtlety by ascetic practices and years of obedient tutelage; that the purpose of knowledge and philosophy is not control of the world so much as release from it; and that the goal of thought is to find freedom from the suffering of frustrated desire by achieving freedom from desire itself. These are the philosophies to which men come when they tire of ambition, struggle, wealth, "progress," and "success."

1. The Nyaya System
A Hindu logician

The first of the "Brahmanical" systems in the logical order of Indian thought (for their chronological order is uncertain, and they are in all essentials contemporary) is a body of logical theory extending over two millenniums. *Nyaya* means an argument, a way of leading the mind to a conclusion. Its most famous text is the *Nyaya Sutra* ascribed without surety to a Gautama dated variously between the third century before, and the first century after, Christ.[63] Like all Hindu thinkers, Gautama announces, as the purpose of his work, the achievement of *Nirvana*, or release from the tyranny of desire, here to be reached by clear and consistent thinking; but we suspect that his simple intent was to offer a guide to the perplexed wrestlers in India's philosophical debates. He formulates for them the principles of argument, exposes the tricks of controversy, and lists the common fallacies of thought. Like another Aristotle, he seeks the structure of reasoning in the syllogism, and finds the crux of argument in the middle term;* like another James or Dewey he looks upon knowledge and thought as pragmatic tools and organs of human need and will, to be tested by their ability to lead to successful action.[64] He is a realist, and will have nothing to do with the sublime idea that the world ceases to exist when no one takes the precaution to perceive it.

---

* The *Nyaya* syllogism, however, has five propositions: theorem, reason, major premiss, minor premiss and conclusion. E.g.: (1) Socrates is mortal, (2) for he is a man; (3) all men are mortal; (4) Socrates is a man; (5) therefore Socrates is mortal.

Gautama's predecessors in *Nyaya* were apparently atheists; his successors became epistemologists.[65] His achievement was to give India an organon of investigation and thought, and a rich vocabulary of philosophical terms.

2. The Vaisheshika System
Democritus in India

As Gautama is the Aristotle of India, so Kanada is its Democritus. His name, which means the "atom-eater," suggests that he may be a legendary construct of the historical imagination. The date at which the *Vaisheshika* system was formulated has not been fixed with excessive accuracy: we are told that it was not before 300 B.C., and not after 800 A.D. Its name came from *vishesha*, meaning particularity: the world, in Kanada's theory, is full of a number of things, but they are all, in some form, mere combinations of atoms; the forms change, but the atoms remain indestructible. Thoroughly Democritean, Kanada announces that nothing exists but "atoms and the void," and that the atoms move not according to the will of an intelligent deity, but through an impersonal force or law—*Adrishta*, "the invisible." Since there is no conservative like the child of a radical, the later exponents of *Vaisheshika*, unable to see how a blind force could give order and unity to the cosmos, placed a world of minute souls alongside the world of atoms, and supervised both worlds with an intelligent God.[66] So old is the "pre-established harmony" of Leibnitz.

3. The Sankhya System
Its high repute — Metaphysics — Evolution — Atheism — Idealism —Spirit—Body, mind and soul—The goal of philosophy —Influence of the Sankhya

This, says a Hindu historian, "is the most significant system of philosophy that India has produced."[67] Professor Garbe, who devoted a large part of his life to the study of the *Sankhya*, consoled himself with the thought that "in Kapila's doctrine, for the first time in the history of the world, the complete independence and freedom of the human mind, its full confidence in its own powers, were exhibited."[68] It is the oldest of the six systems,[69] and perhaps the oldest philosophical system of all.* Of

---

* Its earliest extant literature, the *Sankhya-karika* of the commentator Ishvara Krishna, dates back only to the fifth century A.D., and the *Sankhya-sutras* once attributed to Kapila are not older than our fifteenth century; but the origins of the system apparently antedate Buddhism itself.[70] The Buddhist texts and the *Mahabharata*[70a] repeatedly refer to it, and Winternitz finds its influence in Pythagoras.[70b]

Kapila himself nothing is known, except that Hindu tradition, which has a schoolboy's scorn for dates, credits him with founding the *Sankhya* philosophy in the sixth century B.C.[n]

Kapila is at once a realist and a scholastic. He begins almost medically by laying it down, in his first aphorism, that "the complete cessation of pain . . . is the complete goal of man." He rejects as inadequate the attempt to elude suffering by physical means; he refutes, with much logical prestidigitation, the views of all and sundry on the matter, and then proceeds to construct, in one unintelligibly abbreviated *sutra* after another, his own metaphysical system. It derives its name from his enumeration (for this is the meaning of *sankhya*) of the twenty-five Realities (*Tattwas*, "Thatnesses") which, in Kapila's judgment, make up the world. He arranges these Realities in a complex relationship that may possibly be clarified by the following scheme:

(1)　A. SUBSTANCE (*Prakriti*, "Producer"), a universal physical principle which, through its evolutionary powers (*Gunas*), produces

(2)　　I. Intellect (*Buddhi*), the power of perception; which, through its evolutionary powers (*Gunas*), produces

(3)　　　i. The Five Subtle Elements, or Sensory Powers of the Internal World:

(4)　　　　1. Sight,

(5)　　　　2. Hearing,

(6)　　　　3. Smell,

(7)　　　　4. Taste, and

(8)　　　　5. Touch; (Realities (1) to (8) coöperate to produce (10) to (24))

(9)　　　ii. Mind (*Manas*), the power of conception;

　　　　iii. The Five Organs of Sense (corresponding with Realities (4) to (8)):

(10)　　　　1. Eye,

(11)　　　　2. Ear,

(12)　　　　3. Nose,

(13)　　　　4. Tongue, and

(14)　　　　5. Skin;

　　　　iv. The Five Organs of Action:

(15)　　　　1. Larynx,

(16)　　　　2. Hands,

(17)　　　　3. Feet,

(18)　　　　4. Excretory organs, and

(19)   5. Generative organs;
                  v. The Five Gross Elements of the External World:
(20)   1. Ether,
(21)   2. Air,
(22)   3. Fire and light,
(23)   4. Water, and
(24)   5. Earth.
(25) B. SPIRIT (*Purusha*, "Person"), a universal psychical principle which,
     though unable to do anything of itself, animates and vitalizes *Prakriti*,
     and stirs its evolutionary powers to all their activities.

At its outset this seems to be a purely materialistic system: the world
of mind and self as well as of body and matter appears entirely as an
evolution by natural means, a unity and continuity of elements in perpetual development and decay from the lowest to the highest and back
again. There is a premonition of Lamarck in Kapila's thought: the need
of the organism (the "Self") generates the function (sight, hearing, smell,
taste and touch), and the function produces the organ (eye, ear, nose,
tongue and skin). There is no gap in the system, and no vital distinction
in any Hindu philosophy, between the inorganic and the organic, between
the vegetable and the animal, or between the animal and the human,
world; these are all links in one chain of life, spokes on the wheel of evolution and dissolution, birth and death and birth. The course of evolution
is determined fatalistically by the three active qualities or powers (*Gunas*)
of Substance: purity, activity, and blind ignorance. These powers are not
prejudiced in favor of development against decay; they produce the one
after the other in an endless cycle, like some stupid magician drawing an
infinity of contents from a hat, putting them back again, and repeating
the process forever. Every state of evolution contains in itself, as Herbert
Spencer was to say some time later, a tendency to lapse into dissolution as
its fated counterpart and end.

Kapila, like Laplace, saw no need of calling in a deity to explain creation or evolution;[72] in this most religious and philosophical of nations it is
nothing unusual to find religions and philosophies without a god. Many
of the *Sankhya* texts explicitly deny the existence of a personal creator;
creation is inconceivable, for "a thing is not made out of nothing";[73] creator
and created are one.[74] Kapila contents himself with writing (precisely as
if he were Immanuel Kant) that a personal creator can never be demonstrated by human reason. For whatever exists, says this subtle sceptic, must

be either bound or free, and God cannot be either. If God is perfect, he had no need to create a world; if he is imperfect he is not God. If God were good, and had divine powers, he could not possibly have created so imperfect a world, so rich in suffering, so certain in death.[75] It is instructive to see with what calmness the Hindu thinkers discuss these questions, seldom resorting to persecution or abuse, and keeping the debate upon a plane reached in our time only by the controversies of the maturest scientists. Kapila protects himself by recognizing the authority of the *Vedas*: "The *Vedas*," he says, simply, "are an authority, since the author of them knew the established truth."[76] After which he proceeds without paying any attention to the *Vedas*.

But he is no materialist; on the contrary, he is an idealist and a spiritualist, after his own unconventional fashion. He derives reality entirely from perception; our sense organs and our thought give to the world all the reality, form and significance which it can ever have for us; what the world might be independently of them is an idle question that has no meaning, and can never have an answer.[77] Again, after listing twenty-four *Tattwas* which belong, in his system, under physical evolution, he upsets all his incipient materialism by introducing, as the last Reality, the strangest and perhaps the most important of them all—*Purusha*, "Person" or Soul. It is not, like twenty-three other *Tattwas*, produced by *Prakriti* or physical force; it is an independent psychical principle, omnipresent and everlasting, incapable of acting by itself, but indispensable to every action. For *Prakriti* never develops, the *Gunas* never act, except through the inspiration of *Purusha*; the physical is animated, vitalized and stimulated to evolve by the psychical principle everywhere.[78] Here Kapila speaks like Aristotle: "There is a ruling influence of the Spirit" (over *Prakriti*, or the evolving world), "caused by their proximity, just as the loadstone (draws iron to itself). That is, the proximity of *Purusha* to *Prakriti* impels the latter to go through the steps of production. This sort of attraction between the two leads to creation, but in no other sense is Spirit an agent, or concerned in creation at all."[79]*

Spirit is plural in the sense that it exists in each organism; but in all it is alike, and does not share in individuality. Individuality is physical; we are what we are, not because of our Spirit, but because of the origin,

---

* "The evolution of *Prakriti*," says one Hindu commentator on Kapila, "has no purpose except to provide a spectacle for the soul."[80] Perhaps, as Nietzsche suggested, the wisest way to view the world is as an esthetic and dramatic spectacle.

evolution and experiences of our bodies and minds. In *Sankhya* the mind is as much a part of the body as any other organ is. The secluded and untouched Spirit within us is free, while the mind and body are bound by the laws and *Gunas* or qualities of the physical world;[81] it is not the Spirit that acts and is determined, it is the body-mind. Nor is Spirit affected by the decay and passing of the body and the personality; it is untouched by the stream of birth and death. "Mind is perishable," says Kapila, "but not Spirit";[82] only the individual self, bound up with matter and body, is born, dies, and is born again, in that tireless fluctuation of physical forms which constitutes the history of the external world.[83] Kapila, capable of doubting everything else, never doubts transmigration.

Like most Hindu thinkers, he looks upon life as a very doubtful good, if a good at all. "Few are these days of joy, few are these days of sorrow; wealth is like a swollen river, youth is like the crumbling bank of a swollen river, life is like a tree on the crumbling bank."[84] Suffering is the result of the fact that the individual self and mind are bound up with matter, caught in the blind forces of evolution. What escape is there from this suffering? Only through philosophy, answers our philosopher; only through understanding that all these pains and griefs, all this division and turbulence of striving egos, are *Maya*, illusion, the insubstantial pageantry of life and time. "Bondage arises from the error of not discriminating"[85]— between the self that suffers and the Spirit that is immune, between the surface that is disturbed and the basis that remains unvexed and unchanged. To rise above these sufferings it is only necessary to realize that the essence of us, which is Spirit, is safe beyond good and evil, joy and pain, birth and death. These acts and struggles, these successes and defeats, distress us only so long as we fail to see that they do not affect, or come from, the Spirit; the enlightened man will look upon them as from outside them, like an impartial spectator witnessing a play. Let the soul recognize its independence of things, and it will at once be free; by that very act of understanding it will escape from the prison of space and time, of pain and reincarnation.[86] "Liberation obtained through knowledge of the twenty-five Realities," says Kapila, "teaches the one only knowledge —that neither I am, nor is aught mine, nor do I exist;"[87] that is to say, personal separateness is an illusion; all that exists is the vast evolving and dissolving froth of matter and mind, of bodies and selves, on the one side, and on the other the quiet eternity of the immutable and imperturbable soul.

Such a philosophy will bring no comfort to one who may find some difficulty in separating himself from his aching flesh and his grieving memory; but it seems to have well expressed the mood of speculative India. No other body of philosophic thought, barring the *Vedanta*, has so profoundly affected the Hindu mind. In the atheism and epistemological idealism of Buddha, and his conception of *Nirvana*, we see the influence of Kapila; we see it in the *Mahabharata* and the Code of Manu, in the *Puranas** and the *Tantras*— which transform *Purusha* and *Prakriti* into the male and female principles of creation;[88] above all in the system of *Yoga*, which is merely a practical development of *Sankhya*, built upon its theories and couched in its phrases. Kapila has few explicit adherents today, since Shankara and the *Vedanta* have captured the Hindu mind; but an old proverb still raises its voice occasionally in India: "There is no knowledge equal to the *Sankhya*, and no power equal to the *Yoga*."[89]

4. The Yoga System

The Holy Men—The antiquity of "Yoga"—Its meaning—The eight stages of discipline—The aim of "Yoga"—The miracles of the "Yogi"—The sincerity of "Yoga"

> In a fair, still spot
> Having fixed his abode—not too much raised,
> Nor yet too low—let him abide, his goods
> A cloth, a deerskin, and the *Kusha*-grass.
> There, setting hard his mind upon the **One,**
> Restraining heart and senses, silent, calm,
> Let him accomplish *Yoga*, and achieve
> Pureness of soul, holding immovable
> Body and neck and head, his gaze absorbed
> Upon his nose-end, rapt from all around,
> Tranquil in spirit, free of fear, intent
> Upon his *Brahmacharya* vow, devout,
> Musing on Me, lost in the thought of Me.†

On the bathing-ghats, scattered here and there among reverent Hindus, indifferent Moslems and staring tourists, sit the Holy Men, or *Yogis*, in

---

* Cf. the poem quoted on page 512 above.

† The *Bhagavad-Gita*, translated by Sir Edwin Arnold as *The Song Celestial*, London, 1925, bk. vi, p. 35. *Brahmacaria* is the vow of chastity taken by the ascetic student. "Me" is Krishna.

whom the religion and philosophy of India find their ultimate and strangest expression. In lesser numbers one comes upon them in the woods or on the roadside, immovable and absorbed. Some are old, some are young; some wear a rag over the shoulders, some a cloth over the loins; some are clothed only in dust of ashes, sprinkled over the body and into the mottled hair. They squat cross-legged and motionless, staring at their noses or their navels. Some of them look squarely into the face of the sun hour after hour, day after day, letting themselves go slowly blind; some surround themselves with hot fires during the midday heat; some walk barefoot upon hot coals, or empty the coals upon their heads; some lie naked for thirty-five years on beds of iron spikes; some roll their bodies thousands of miles to a place of pilgrimage; some chain themselves to trees, or imprison themselves in cages, until they die; some bury themselves in the earth up to their necks, and remain that way for years or for life; some pass a wire through both cheeks, making it impossible to open the jaws, and so condemning themselves to live on liquids; some keep their fists clenched so long that their nails come through the back of the hand; some hold up an arm or a leg until it is withered and dead. Many of them sit quietly in one position, perhaps for years, eating leaves and nuts brought to them by the people, deliberately dulling every sense, and concentrating every thought, in the resolve to understand. Most of them avoid spectacular methods, and pursue truth in the quiet retreat of their homes.

We have had such men in our Middle Ages, but we should have to look for them today in the nooks and crannies of Europe and America. India has had them for 2500 years—possibly from the prehistoric days when, perhaps, they were the *shamans* of savage tribes. The system of ascetic meditation known as *Yoga* existed in the time of the *Vedas;*[90] the *Upanishads* and the *Mahabharata* accepted it; it flourished in the age of Buddha;[91] and even Alexander, attracted by the ability of these "gymnosophists" to bear pain silently, stopped to study them, and invited one of their number to come and live with him. The *Yogi* refused as firmly as Diogenes, saying that he wanted nothing from Alexander, being content with the nothing that he had. His fellow ascetics laughed at the Macedonian's boyish desire to conquer the earth when, as they told him, only a few feet of it sufficed for any man, alive or dead. Another sage, Calanus (326 B.C.), accompanied Alexander to Persia; growing ill there, he asked permission to die, saying that he preferred death to illness; and calmly mounting a funeral pyre, he allowed himself to be burned to death without uttering a sound—to the astonishment of the Greeks, who had never seen this unmurderous sort of bravery before.[93] Two centuries later (ca. 150 B.C.), Patanjali brought the practices and traditions of the system together in his famous *Yoga-sutras*, which are still used as a text in *Yoga* centers from Benares to Los Angeles.[93] Yuan Chwang, in the seventh century A.D., described the system as having thousands of devotees;[94] Marco Polo, about 1296, gave a vivid description of it;[95] today, after all these centuries, its more extreme followers, numbering from one to three million in India,[96] still torture themselves to find the peace of understanding. It is one of the most impressive and touching phenomena in the history of man.

What is *Yoga?* Literally, a yoke: not so much a yoking or union of the soul with the Supreme Being,[97] as the yoke of ascetic discipline and abstinence which the aspirant puts upon himself in order to cleanse his spirit of all material limitations, and achieve supernatural intelligence and powers.[98] Matter is the root of ignorance and suffering; therefore *Yoga* seeks to free the soul from all sense phenomena and all bodily attachment; it is an attempt to attain supreme enlightenment and salvation in one life by atoning in one existence for all the sins of the soul's past incarnations.[99]

Such enlightenment cannot be won at a stroke; the aspirant must move towards it step by step, and no stage of the process can be understood by anyone who has not passed through the stages before it; one comes to *Yoga* only by long and patient study and self-discipline. The stages of *Yoga* are eight:

I. *Yama*, or the death of desire; here the soul accepts the restraints of *ahimsa* and *Brahmacharia*, abandons all self-seeking, emancipates itself from all material interests and pursuits, and wishes well to all things.[100]

II. *Niyama*, a faithful observance of certain preliminary rules for *Yoga*: cleanliness, content, purification, study, and piety.

III. *Asana*, posture; the aim here is to still all movement as well as all sensation; the best *asana* for this purpose is to place the right foot upon the left thigh and the left foot upon the right thigh, to cross the hands and grasp the two great toes, to bend the chin upon the chest, and direct the eyes to the tip of the nose.[101]

IV. *Pranayama*, or regulation of the breath: by these exercises one may forget everything but breathing, and in this way clear his mind for the passive emptiness that must precede absorption; at the same time one may learn to live on a minimum of air, and may let himself, with impunity, be buried in the earth for many days.

V. *Pratyahara*, abstraction; now the mind controls all the senses, and withdraws itself from all sense objects.

VI. *Dharana*, or concentration—the identification or filling of the mind and the senses with one idea or object to the exclusion of everything else.* The fixation of any one object long enough will free the soul of all sensation, all specific thought, and all selfish desire; then the mind, abstracted from things, will be left free to feel the immaterial essence of reality.†

VII. *Dhyana*, or meditation: this is an almost hypnotic condition, resulting from *Dharana*; it may be produced, says Patanjali, by the persistent repetition of the sacred syllable *Om*. Finally, as the summit of *Yoga*, the ascetic arrives at

VIII. *Samadhi*, or trance contemplation; even the last thought now disappears from the mind; empty, the mind loses consciousness of itself as a separate being;[103] it is merged with totality, and achieves a blissful and godlike comprehension of all things in One. No words can describe this condition to the uninitiate; no intellect or reasoning can find or formulate it; "through *Yoga* must *Yoga* be known."[104]

Nevertheless it is not God, or union with God, that the *yogi* seeks; in the *Yoga* philosophy God (Ishvara) is not the creator or preserver of the universe, or the rewarder and punisher of men, but merely one of several objects on which the soul may meditate as a means of achieving concentration and enlightenment. The aim, frankly, is that dissociation of the mind from the body, that removal of all material obstruction from the spirit, which brings with it, in *Yoga* theory, supernatural understanding and capacity.[105] If the soul is cleansed of all bodily subjection and involvement it will not be united with *Brahman*, it will *be Brahman*; for *Brahman* is precisely that hidden spiritual base, that selfless and immaterial soul,

---

* Cf. Hobbes: *Semper idem sentire idem est ac nihil sentire*: "always to feel the same thing is the same as to feel nothing."

† Eliot compares, for the illumination of this stage, a passage from Schopenhauer, obviously inspired by his study of Hindu philosophy: "When some sudden cause or inward disposition lifts us out of the endless stream of willing, the attention is no longer directed to the motives of willing, but comprehends things free from their relation to the will, and thus observes them without subjectivity, purely objectively, gives itself entirely up to them so far as they are ideas, but not in so far as they are motives. Then all at once the peace that we were always seeking, but which always fled from us on the former path of the desires, comes to us of its own accord, and it is well with us."[102]

which remains when all sense attachments have been exercised away. To the extent to which the soul can free itself from its physical environment and prison it *becomes Brahman*, and exercises *Brahman's* intelligence and power. Here the magical basis of religion reappears, and almost threatens the essence of religion itself—the worship of powers superior to man.

In the days of the *Upanishads, Yoga* was pure mysticism—an attempt to realize the identity of the soul with God. In Hindu legend it is said that in ancient days seven Wise Men, or *Rishis*, acquired, by penance and meditation, complete knowledge of all things.[106] In the later history of India *Yoga* became corrupted with magic, and thought more of the power of miracles than of the peace of understanding. The *Yogi* trusts that by *Yoga* he will be able to anesthetize and control any part of his body by concentrating upon it;[107] he will be able at will to make himself invisible, or to prevent his body from being moved, or to pass in a moment from any part of the earth, or to live as long as he desires, or to know the past and the future, and the most distant stars.[108]

The sceptic must admit that there is nothing impossible in all this; fools can invent more hypotheses than philosophers can ever refute, and philosophers often join them in the game. Ecstasy and hallucinations can be produced by fasting and self-mortification, concentration may make one locally or generally insensitive to pain; and there is no telling what reserve energies and abilities lurk within the unknown mind. Many of the *Yogis*, however, are mere beggars who go though their penances in the supposedly Occidental hope of gold, or in the simple human hunger for notice and applause.* Asceticism is the reciprocal of sensuality, or at best an attempt to control it; but the attempt itself verges upon a masochistic sensuality in which the ascetic takes an almost erotic delight in his pain. The Brahmans have wisely abstained from such practices, and have counseled their followers to seek sanctity through the conscientious performance of the normal duties of life.[110]

5. *The Purva-Mimansa*

To step from *Yoga* to the *Purva-Mimansa* is to pass from the most renowned to the least known and least important of the six systems of Brahmanical philosophy. And as *Yoga* is magic and mysticism rather than phil-

---

* The blunt Dubois describes them as "a tribe of vagabonds."[109] The word *fakir*, sometimes applied to *Yogis*, is an Arab term, originally meaning "poor," and properly applied only to members of Moslem religious orders vowed to poverty.

osophy, so this system is less philosophy than religion; it is an orthodox re-action against the impious doctrines of the philosophers. Its author, Jaimini, protested against the disposition of Kapila and Kanada to ignore, while acknowledging, the authority of the *Vedas*. The human mind, said Jaimini, is too frail an instrument to solve the problems of metaphysics and the-ology; reason is a wanton who will serve any desire; it gives us not "science" and "truth," but merely our own rationalized sensuality and pride. The road to wisdom and peace lies not through the vain labyrinths of logic, but in the modest acceptance of tradition and the humble performance of the rituals prescribed in the Scriptures. For this, too, there is something to be said: *cela vous abêtira.*

6. The Vedanta System

Origin — Shankara — Logic — Epistemology — "Maya" — Psy-chology — Theology — God — Ethics — Difficulties of the system — Death of Shankara

The word *Vedanta* meant originally the end of the *Vedas*—that is, the *Upanishads*. Today India applies it to that system of philosophy which sought to give logical structure and support to the essential doctrine of the *Upanishads*—the organ-point that sounds throughout Indian thought—that God *(Brahman)* and the soul *(Atman)* are one. The oldest known form of this most widely accepted of all Hindu philosophies is the *Brahma-sutra* of Badarayana (ca. 200 B.C.)—555 aphorisms, of which the first announces the purpose of all: "Now, then, a desire to know *Brahman.*" Almost a thousand years later Gaudapada wrote a commentary on these *sutras,* and taught the esoteric doctrine of the system to Govinda, who taught it to Shankara, who composed the most famous of *Vedanta* commentaries, and made himself the greatest of Indian philosophers.

In his short life of thirty-two years Shankara achieved that union of sage and saint, of wisdom and kindliness, which characterizes the loftiest type of man produced in India. Born among the studious Nambudri Brahmans of Malabar, he rejected the luxuries of the world, and while still a youth became a *sannyasi,* worshiping unpretentiously the gods of the Hindu pantheon, and yet mystically absorbed in a vision of an all-embracing *Brahman.* It seemed to him that the profoundest religion and the profoundest philosophy were those of the *Upanishads.* He could pardon the polytheism of the people, but not the atheism of *Sankhya* or the agnos-ticism of Buddha. Arriving in the north as a delegate of the south, he won such popularity at the University of Benares that it crowned him with its highest honors, and sent him forth, with a retinue of disciples, to champion Brahmanism in all the debating halls of India. At Benares, probably, he wrote his famous commentaries on the *Upanishads* and the *Bhagavad-Gita*, in which he attacked with theological ardor and scholastic subtlety all the heretics of India, and restored Brahmanism to that position of intellectual leadership from which Buddha and Kapila had deposed it.

There is much metaphysical wind in these discourses, and arid deserts of textual exposition; but they may be forgiven in a man who at the age of thirty could be at once the Aquinas and the Kant of India. Like Aquinas, Shankara accepts the full authority of his country's Scriptures as a divine revelation, and then sallies forth to find proofs in experience and reason for all Scriptural teachings. Unlike Aquinas, however, he does not believe that reason can suffice for such a task; on the contrary he wonders have we not exaggerated the power and rôle, the clarity and reliability, of reason.[111] Jaimini was right: reason is a lawyer, and will prove anything we wish; for every argument it can find an equal and opposite argument, and its upshot is a scepticism that weakens all force of character and undermines all values of life. It is not logic that we need, says Shankara, it is insight, the faculty (akin to art) of grasping at once the essential out of the irrelevant, the eternal out of the temporal, the whole out of the part: this is the first prerequisite to philosophy. The second is a willingness to observe, inquire and think for understanding's sake, not for the sake of invention, wealth or power; it is a withdrawal of the spirit from all the excitement, bias and fruits of action. Thirdly, the philosopher must acquire self-restraint, patience, and tranquillity; he must learn to live above physical temptation or material concerns. Finally there must burn, deep in his soul, the desire for *moksha*, for liberation from ignorance, for an end to all consciousness of a separate self, for a blissful absorption in the *Brahman* of complete understanding and infinite unity.[112] In a word, the student needs not the logic of reason so much as a cleansing and deepening discipline of the soul. This, perhaps, has been the secret of all profound education.

Shankara establishes the source of his philosophy at a remote and subtle point never quite clearly visioned again until, a thousand years later, Immanuel Kant wrote his *Critique of Pure Reason*. How, he asks, is knowledge possible? Apparently, all our knowledge comes from the senses, and reveals not the external reality itself, but our sensory adaptation—perhaps transformation—of that reality. By sense, then, we can never quite know the "real"; we can know it only in that garb of space, time and cause which may be a web created by our organs of sense and understanding, designed or evolved to catch and hold that fluent and elusive reality whose existence we can surmise, but whose character we can never objectively describe; our way of perceiving will forever be inextricably mingled with the thing perceived.

This is not the airy subjectivism of the solipsist who thinks that he can destroy the world by going to sleep. The world exists, but it is *Maya*—not delusion, but phenomenon, an appearance created partly by our thought. Our incapacity to perceive things except through the film of space and time, or to think of them except in terms of cause and change, is an innate limitation, an *Avidya*, or ignorance, which is bound up with our very mode of perception, and to which, therefore, all flesh is heir. *Maya* and *Avidya* are the subjective and objective sides of the great illusion by which the intellect supposes that it knows the real; it is through *Maya and Avidya*, through our birthright of ignorance, that we see a multiplicity of objects and a flux of change; in truth there is only one Being, and change is "a mere name" for the superficial fluctuations of forms. Behind the *Maya* or Veil of change and things, to be reached not by sensation or intellect but only by the insight and intuition of the trained spirit, is the one universal reality, *Brahman*.

This natural obscuration of sense and intellect by the organs and forms of sensation and understanding bars us likewise from perceiving the one unchanging Soul that stands beneath all individual souls and minds. Our separate selves, visible to perception and thought, are as unreal as the phantasmagoria of space and time; individual differences and distinct personalities are bound up with body and matter, they belong to the kaleidoscopic world of change; and these merely phenomenal selves will pass away with the material conditions of which they are a part. But the underlying life which we feel in ourselves when we forget space and time, cause and change, is the very essence and reality of us, that *Atman* which we share with all selves and things, and which, undivided and omnipresent, is identical with *Brahman*, God.[113]

But what is God? Just as there are two selves—the ego and *Atman*—and two worlds—the phenomenal and the noumenal—so there are two deities: an *Ishvara* or Creator worshiped by the people through the patterns of space, cause, time and change; and a *Brahman* or Pure Being worshiped by that philosophical piety which seeks and finds, behind all separate things and selves, one universal reality, unchanging amid all changes, indivisible amid all divisions, eternal despite all vicissitudes of form, all birth and death. Polytheism, even theism, belongs to the world of *Maya* and *Avidya;* they are forms of worship that correspond to the forms of perception and thought; they are as necessary to our moral life as space, time and cause are necessary to our intellectual life, but they have no absolute validity or objective truth.[114]

To Shankara the existence of God is no problem, for he defines God as existence, and identifies all real being with God. But of the existence of a personal God, creator or redeemer, there may, he thinks, be some question; such a deity, says this pre-plagiarist of Kant, cannot be proved by reason, he can only be postulated as a practical necessity,[115] offering peace to our limited intellects, and encouragement to our fragile morality. The philosopher, though he may worship in every temple and bow to every god, will pass beyond these forgivable forms of popular faith; feeling the illusoriness of plurality, and the monistic unity of all things,* he will adore, as the Supreme Being, Being itself—indescribable, limitless, spaceless, timeless, causeless, changeless Being, the source and substance of all reality.† We may apply the adjectives "conscious," "intelligent," even "happy" to *Brahman,* since *Brahman* includes all selves, and these may have such qualities;[116] but all other adjectives would be applicable to *Brahman* equally, since It includes all qualities of all things. Essentially *Brahman* is neuter, raised above personality and gender, beyond good and evil, above all moral distinctions, all differences and attributes, all desires and ends. *Brahman* is the cause and effect, the timeless and secret essence, of the world.

The goal of philosophy is to find that secret, and to lose the seeker in the secret found. To be one with God means, for Shankara, to rise above—or to sink beneath—the separateness and brevity of the self, with all its narrow purposes and interests; to become unconscious of all parts, divisions, things; to be placidly at one, in a desireless *Nirvana,* with that great ocean of Being in which there are no warring purposes, no competing selves, no

---

* Hence the name *Advaita*—non-dualism—often given to the *Vedanta* philosophy.

† Shankara and the *Vedanta* are not quite pantheistic: things considered as distinct from one another are not *Brahman;* they are *Brahman* only in their essential, indivisible and changeless essence and reality. "*Brahman,*" says Shankara, "resembles not the world, and (yet) apart from *Brahman* there is naught; all that which seems to exist outside of It (*Brahman*) cannot exist (in such fashion) save in an illusory manner, like the semblance of water in the desert."[115a]

parts, no change, no space, and no time.* To find this blissful peace (*Ananda*) a man must renounce not merely the world but himself; he must care nothing for possessions or goods, even for good or evil; he must look upon suffering and death as *Maya*, surface incidents of body and matter, time and change; and he must not think of his own personal quality and fate; a single moment of self-interest or pride can destroy all his liberation.[119] Good works cannot give a man salvation, for good works have no validity or meaning except in the *Maya* world of space and time; only the knowledge of the saintly seer can bring that salvation which is the recognition of the identity of self and the universe, *Atman* and *Brahman*, soul and God, and the absorption of the part in the whole.[120] Only when this absorption is complete does the wheel of reincarnation stop; for then it is seen that the separate self and personality, to which reincarnation comes, is an illusion.[121] It is *Ishvara*, the *Maya* god, that gives rebirth to the self in punishment and reward; but "when the identity" of *Atman* and *Brahman* "has become known, then," says Shankara, "the soul's existence as wanderer, and *Brahman's* existence as creator" (i.e., as *Ishvara*) "have vanished away."[122] *Ishvara* and *Karma*, like things and selves, belong to the exoteric doctrine of *Vedanta* as adapted to the needs of the common man; in the esoteric or secret doctrine soul and *Brahman* are one, never wandering, never dying, never changed.[123]

It was thoughtful of Shankara to confine his esoteric doctrine to philosophers; for as Voltaire believed that only a society of philosophers could survive without laws, so only a society of supermen could live beyond good and evil. Critics have complained that if good and evil are *Maya*,

---

* Cf. Blake:
    "I will go down to self-annihilation and Eternal Death.
    Lest the Last Judgment come and find me unannihilate,
    And I be seized and given into the hands of my own Selfhood."[117]
Or Tennyson's "Ancient Sage":
    "For more than once when I
    Sat all alone, revolving in myself
    The word that is the symbol of myself,
    The mortal limit of the Self was loosed,
    And passed into the Nameless, as a cloud
    Melts into Heaven. I touched my limbs—the limbs
    Were strange, not mine—and yet not shade of doubt
    But utter clearness, and through loss of Self
    The gain of such large life as matched with ours
    Were Sun to spark—unshadowable in words,
    Themselves but shadows of a shadow-world."[118]

part of the unreal world, then all moral distinctions fall away, and devils are as good as saints. But these moral distinctions, Shankara cleverly replies, are real *within* the world of space and time, and are binding for those who live in the world. They are not binding upon the soul that has united itself with *Brahman;* such a soul can do no wrong, since wrong implies desire and action, and the liberated soul, by definition, does not move in the sphere of desire and (self-considering) action. Whoever consciously injures another lives on the plane of *Maya,* and is subject to its distinctions, its morals and its laws. Only the philosopher is free, only wisdom is liberty.*

It was a subtle and profound philosophy to be written by a lad in his twenties. Shankara not only elaborated it in writing and defended it successfully in debate, but he expressed snatches of it in some of the most sensitive religious poetry of India. When all challenges had been met he retired to a hermitage in the Himalayas, and, according to Hindu tradition, died at the age of thirty-two.[124] Ten religious orders were founded in his name, and many disciples accepted and developed his philosophy. One of them—some say Shankara himself—wrote for the people a popular exposition of the *Vedanta*—the *Mohamudgara,* or "Hammer of Folly"— in which the essentials of the system were summed up with clarity and force:

> Fool! give up thy thirst for wealth, banish all desires from thy heart. Let thy mind be satisfied with what is gained by thy *Karma.* . . . Do not be proud of wealth, of friends, or of youth; time takes all away in a moment. Leaving quickly all this, which is full of illusion, enter into the place of *Brahman.* . . . Life is tremulous, like a water-drop on a lotus-leaf. . . . Time is playing, life is waning— yet the breath of hope never ceases. The body is wrinkled, the hair grey, the mouth has become toothless, the stick in the hand shakes, yet man leaves not the anchor of hope. . . . Preserve equanimity always. . . . In thee, in me and in others there dwells Vishnu alone; it is useless to be angry with me, or impatient. See every self in Self, and give up all thought of difference.[125]

---

*We do not know how much Parmenides' insistence that the Many are unreal, and that only the One exists, owed to the *Upanishads,* or contributed to Shankara; nor can we establish any connection, of cause or suggestion, between Shankara and the astonishingly similar philosophy of Immanuel Kant.

III. THE CONCLUSIONS OF HINDU PHILOSOPHY

Decadence—Summary—Criticism—Influence

The Mohammedan invasions put an end to the great age of Hindu philosophy. The assaults of the Moslems, and later of the Christians, upon the native faith drove it, for self-defense, into a timid unity that made treason of all debate, and stifled creative heresy in a stagnant uniformity of thought. By the twelfth century the system of the *Vedanta*, which in Shankara had tried to be a religion for philosophers, was reinterpreted by such saints as Ramanuja (ca. 1050) into an orthodox worship of Vishnu, Rama and Krishna. Forbidden to think new thoughts, philosophy became not only scholastic but barren; it accepted its dogmas from the priesthood, and proved them laboriously by distinctions without difference, and logic without reason.[126]

Nevertheless the Brahmans, in the solitude of their retreats and under the protection of their unintelligibility, preserved the old systems carefully in esoteric *sutras* and commentaries, and transmitted across generations and centuries the conclusions of Hindu philosophy. In all these systems, Brahmanical or other, the categories of the intellect are represented as helpless or deceptive before a reality immediately felt or seen;* and all our eighteenth-century rationalism appears to the Indian metaphysician as a vain and superficial attempt to subject the incalculable universe to the concepts of a *salonnière.* "Into blind darkness pass they who worship ignorance; into still greater darkness they who are content with knowledge."[129] Hindu philosophy begins where European philosophy ends—with an inquiry into the nature of knowledge and the limitations of reason; it starts not with the physics of Thales and Democritus, but with the epistemology of Locke and Kant; it takes mind as that which is most immediately known, and therefore refuses to resolve it into a matter known only mediately and through mind. It accepts an external world, but does not believe that our senses can ever know it as it is. All science is a charted ignorance, and belongs to *Maya*; it formulates, in ever changing concepts and phrases, the rationale of a world in which reason is but a part—one shifting current in

---

* "No Indian saint ever had anything but contempt for the knowledge gained by the senses and the intellect."[127] "Never have the Indian sages . . . fallen into our typical error of taking any intellectual formation seriously in the metaphysical sense; these are no more substantial than any *Maya* formation."[128]

an interminable sea. Even the person that reasons is *Maya*, illusion; what is he but a temporary conjunction of events, a passing node in the curves of matter and mind through space and time?—and what are his acts or his thoughts but the fulfilment of forces far antedating his birth? Nothing is real but *Brahman*, that vast ocean of Being in which every form is a moment's wave, or a fleck of froth on the wave. Virtue is not the quiet heroism of good works, nor any pious ecstasy; it is simply the recognition of the identity of the self with every other self in *Brahman;* morality is such living as comes from a sense of union with all things.* "He who discerns all creatures in his Self, and his Self in all creatures, has no disquiet thence. What delusion, what grief can he with him?"[130]

Certain characteristic qualities which would not seem to be defects from the Hindu point of view have kept this philosophy from exercising a wider influence in other civilizations. Its method, its scholastic terminology, and its Vedic assumptions handicap it in finding sympathy among nations with other assumptions or more secularized cultures. Its doctrine of *Maya* gives little encouragement to morality or active virtue; its pessimism is a confession that it has not, despite the theory of *Karma*, explained evil; and part of the effect of these systems has been to exalt a stagnant quietism in the face of evils that might conceivably have been corrected, or of work that cried out to be done. None the less there is a depth in these meditations which by comparison casts an air of superficiality upon the activistic philosophies generated in more invigorating zones. Perhaps our Western systems, so confident that "knowledge is power," are the voices of a once lusty youth exaggerating human ability and tenure. As our energies tire in the daily struggle against impartial Nature and hostile Time, we look with more tolerance upon Oriental philosophies of surrender and peace. Hence the influence of Indian thought upon other cultures has been greatest in the days of their weakening or decay. While Greece was winning victories she paid little attention to Pythagoras or Parmenides; when Greece was declining, Plato and the Orphic priests took up the doctrine of reincarnation, while Zeno the Oriental preached an almost Hindu fatalism and resignation; and when Greece was dying, the Neo-Platonists and the Gnostics drank deep at Indian wells. The impoverishment of Europe by the

* Cf. Spinoza: "The greatest good is the knowledge of the union which the mind has with the whole of Nature."[131] "The intellectual love of God" is a summary of Hindu philosophy.

fall of Rome, and the Moslem conquest of the routes between Europe and India, seem to have obstructed, for a millennium, the direct interchange of Oriental and Occidental ideas. But hardly had the British established themselves in India before editions and translations of the *Upanishads* began to stir Western thought. Fichte conceived an idealism strangely like Shankara's;[132] Schopenhauer almost incorporated Buddhism, the *Upanishads* and the *Vedanta* into his philosophy; and Schelling, in his old age, thought the *Upanishads* the maturest wisdom of mankind. Nietzsche had dwelt too long with Bismarck and the Greeks to care for India, but in the end he valued above all other ideas his haunting notion of eternal recurrence —a variant of reincarnation.

In our time Europe borrows more and more from the philosophy of the East,* while the East borrows more and more from the science of the West. Another world war might leave Europe open again (as the break-up of Alexander's empire opened Greece, and the fall of the Roman Republic opened Rome)—to an influx of Oriental philosophies and faiths. The mounting insurrection of the Orient against the Occident, the loss of those Asiatic markets that have sustained the industry and prosperity of the West, the weakening of Europe by poverty, faction and revolution, might make that divided continent ripe for a new religion of celestial hope and earthly despair. Probably it is prejudice that makes such a dénouement seem inconceivable in America: quietism and resignation do not comport with our electric atmosphere, or with the vitality born of rich resources and a spacious terrain. Doubtless our weather will protect us in the end.

---

* Cf. Bergson, Keyserling, Christian Science, Theosophy.

CHAPTER XX

The Literature of India

I. THE LANGUAGES OF INDIA

Sanskrit—The vernaculars—Grammar

JUST as the philosophy and much of the literature of medieval Europe were composed in a dead language unintelligible to the people, so the philosophy and classic literature of India were written in a Sanskrit that had long since passed out of common parlance, but had survived as the *Esperanto* of scholars having no other common tongue. Divorced from contact with the life of the nation, this literary language became a model of scholasticism and refinement; new words were formed not by the spontaneous creations of the people, but by the needs of technical discourse in the schools; until at last the Sanskrit of philosophy lost the virile simplicity of the Vedic hymns, and became an artificial monster whose *sesquipedalia verba* crawled like monstrous tapeworms across the page.*

Meanwhile the people of northern India, about the fifth century before Christ, had transformed Sanskrit into Prakrit, very much as Italy was to change Latin into Italian. Prakrit became for a time the language of Buddhists and Jains, until it in turn was developed into Pali—the language of the oldest extant Buddhist literature.[2] By the end of the tenth century of our era these "Middle Indian" languages had given birth to various vernaculars, of which the chief was Hindi. In the twelfth century this in turn generated Hindustani as the language of the northern half of India. Finally the invading Moslems filled Hindustani with Persian words, thereby creating a new dialect, Urdu. All these were "Indo-Germanic" tongues, confined to Hindustan; the Deccan kept its old Dravidian languages—Tamil, Telugu, Kanarese and Malayalam—and Tamil became the chief literary vehicle of the south. In the nineteenth century Bengali replaced Sanskrit as the literary language of Bengal; the novelist Chatterjee was its Boccaccio, the poet Tagore was its Petrarch. Even today India has a hundred languages, and the literature of *Swaraj*† uses the speech of the conquerors.

---

* Some examples of Sanskrit agglutination: *citerapratisamkramayastadakarapattau, upada-navisvamasattakaruapattih.*[1]

† The movement for self-rule.

At a very early date India began to trace the roots, history, relations and combinations of words. By the fourth century B.C. she had created for herself* the science of grammar, and produced probably the greatest of all known grammarians, Panini. The studies of Panini, Patanjali (ca. 150 A.D.) and Bhartrihari (ca. 650) laid the foundations of philology; and that fascinating science of verbal genetics owed almost its life in modern times to the rediscovery of Sanskrit.

Writing, as we have seen, was not popular in Vedic India. About the fifth century B.C. the Kharosthi script was adapted from Semitic models, and in the epics and the Buddhist literature we begin to hear of clerks.[3] Palm-leaves and bark served as writing material, and an iron stylus as a pen; the bark was treated to make it less fragile, the pen scratched letters into it, ink was smeared over the bark, and remained in the scratches when the rest of it was wiped away.[4] Paper was brought in by the Moslems (ca. 1000 A.D.), but did not finally replace bark till the seventeenth century. The bark pages were kept in order by stringing them upon a cord, and books of such leaves were gathered in libraries which the Hindus termed "Treasure-houses of the Goddess of Speech." Immense collections of this wooden literature have survived the devastations of time and war.†

II. EDUCATION

Schools—Methods—Universities—Moslem education—An emperor on education

Writing continued, even to the nineteenth century, to play a very small part in Indian education. Perhaps it was not to the interest of the priests that the sacred or scholastic texts should become an open secret to all.[6] As far as we can trace Indian history we find a system of education,[7] always in the hands of the clergy, open at first only to the sons of Brahmans, then spreading its privileges from caste to caste until in our time it excludes only the Untouchables. Every Hindu village had its schoolmaster, supported out of the public funds; in Bengal alone, before the coming of the British, there were some eighty thousand native schools—one to every four

---

* The Babylonians had done likewise; cf. p. 250 above.

† Of printing there is no sign till the nineteenth century—possibly because, as in China, the adjustment of movable type to the native scripts was too expensive, possibly because printing was looked upon as a vulgar descent from the art of calligraphy. The printing of newspapers and books was brought by the English to the Hindus, who bettered the instruction; today there are 1,517 newspapers in India, 3,627 periodicals, and over 17,000 new books published in an average year.[5]

hundred population.[8] The percentage of literacy under Ashoka was apparently higher than in India today.[9]

Children went to the village school from September to February, entering at the age of five and leaving at the age of eight.[10] Instruction was chiefly of a religious character, no matter what the subject; rote memorizing was the usual method, and the *Vedas* were the inevitable text. The three R's were included, but were not the main business of education; character was rated above intellect, and discipline was the essence of schooling. We do not hear of flogging, or of other severe measures; but we find that stress was laid above all upon the formation of wholesome and proper habits of life.[11] At the age of eight the pupil passed to the more formal care of a *Guru*, or personal teacher and guide, with whom the student was to live, preferably till he was twenty. Services, sometimes menial, were required of him, and he was pledged to continence, modesty, cleanliness, and a meatless diet.[12] Instruction was now given him in the "Five *Shastras*" or sciences: grammar, arts and crafts, medicine, logic, and philosophy. Finally he was sent out into the world with the wise admonition that education came only one-fourth from the teacher, one-fourth from private study, one-fourth from one's fellows, and one-fourth from life.[13]

From his *Guru* the student might pass, about the age of sixteen, to one of the great universities that were the glory of ancient and medieval India: Benares, Taxila, Vidarbha, Ajanta, Ujjain, or Nalanda. Benares was the stronghold of orthodox Brahman learning in Buddha's days as in ours; Taxila, at the time of Alexander's invasion, was known to all Asia as the leading seat of Hindu scholarship, renowned above all for its medical school; Ujjain was held in high repute for astronomy, Ajanta for the teaching of art. The façade of one of the ruined buildings at Ajanta suggests the magnificence of these old universities.[14] Nalanda, most famous of Buddhist institutions for higher learning, had been founded shortly after the Master's death, and the state had assigned for its support the revenues of a hundred villages. It had ten thousand students, one hundred lecture-rooms, great libraries, and six immense blocks of dormitories four stories high; its observatories, said Yuan Chwang, "were lost in the vapors of the morning, and the upper rooms towered above the clouds."[15] The old Chinese pilgrim loved the learned monks and shady groves of Nalanda so well that he stayed there for five years. "Of those from abroad who wished to enter the schools of discussion" at Nalanda, he tells us, "the majority,

beaten by the difficulties of the problem, withdrew; and those who were deeply versed in old and modern learning were admitted, only two or three out of ten succeeding."[16] The candidates who were fortunate enough to gain admission were given free tuition, board and lodging, but they were subjected to an almost monastic discipline. Students were not permitted to talk to a woman, or to see one; even the desire to look upon a woman was held a great sin, in the fashion of the hardest saying in the New Testament. The student guilty of sex relations had to wear, for a whole year, the skin of an ass, with the tail turned upward, and had to go about begging alms and declaring his sin. Every morning the entire student body was required to bathe in the ten great swimming pools that belonged to the university. The course of study lasted for twelve years, but some students stayed thirty years, and some remained till death.[17]

The Mohammedans destroyed nearly all the monasteries, Buddhist or Brahman, in northern India. Nalanda was burned to the ground in 1197, and all its monks were slaughtered; we can never estimate the abundant life of ancient India from what these fanatics spared. Nevertheless, the destroyers were not barbarians; they had a taste for beauty, and an almost modern skill in using piety for the purposes of plunder. When the Moguls ascended the throne they brought a high but narrow standard of culture with them; they loved letters as much as the sword, and knew how to combine a successful siege with poetry. Among the Moslems education was mostly individual, through tutors engaged by prosperous fathers for their sons. It was an aristocratic conception of education as an ornament—occasionally an aid—to a man of affairs and power, but usually an irritant and a public danger in one doomed to poverty or modest place. What the methods of the tutors were we may judge from one of the great letters of history—the reply of Aurangzeb to his former teacher, who was seeking some sinecure and emolument from the King:

> What is it you would have of me, Doctor? Can you reasonably desire that I should make you one of the chief *Omrahs* of my court? Let me tell you, if you had instructed me as you should have done, nothing would be more just; for I am of this persuasion, that a child well educated and instructed is as much, at least, obliged to his master as to his father. But where are those good documents* you have given me? In the first place, you have taught me that

* I.e., instructions.

all Frangistan (so it seems they call Europe) was nothing but I
know not what little island, of which the greatest king was he of
Portugal, and next to him he of Holland, and after him he of England: and as to the other kings, as those of France and Andalusia,
you have represented them to me as our petty rajas, telling me
that the kings of Indostan were far above them altogether, that
they (the kings of Indostan) were . . . the great ones, the conquerors and kings of the world; and those of Persia and Usbec,
Kashgar, Tartary and Cathay, Pegu, China and Matchina did
tremble at the name of the kings of Indostan. Admirable geography! You should rather have taught me exactly to distinguish
all those states of the world, and well to understand their strength,
their way of fighting, their customs, religions, governments, and
interests; and by the pursual of solid history, to observe their rise,
progress, decay; and whence, how, and by what accidents and errors those great changes and revolutions of empires and kingdoms
have happened. I have scarce learned of you the name of my grand-
sires, the famous founders of this empire; so far were you from
having taught me the history of their life, and what course they
took to make such great conquest. You had a mind to teach me
the Arabian tongue, to read and to write. I am much obliged, for-
sooth, for having made me lose so much time upon a language that
requires ten or twelve years to attain to its perfection; as if the son
of a king should think it to be an honor to him to be a grammarian
or some doctor of the law, and to learn other languages than of his
neighbors when he can well be without them; he, to whom time is
so precious for so many weighty things, which he ought by times
to learn. As if there were any spirit that did not with some reluc-
tancy, and even with a kind of debasement, employ itself in so sad
and dry an exercise, so longsome and tedious, as is that of learning
words.[18]

"Thus," says the contemporary Bernier, "did Aurangzeb resent the
pedantic instructions of his tutors; to which 'tis affirmed in that court that
. . . he added the following reproof";*

Know you not that childhood well governed, being a state which
is ordinarily accompanied with an happy memory, is capable of

---

* We cannot tell how much of the following (and perhaps of the preceding) quotation
is Bernier's, and how much Aurangzeb's; we only know that it bears reprinting.

thousands of good precepts and instructions, which remain deeply impressed the whole remainder of a man's life, and keep the mind always raised for great actions? The law, prayers and sciences, may they not as well be learned in our mother-tongue as in Arabick? You told my father Shah Jehan that you would teach me philosophy. 'Tis true, I remember very well, that you have entertained me for many years with airy questions of things that afford no satisfaction at all to the mind, and are of no use in humane society, empty notions and mere fancies, that have only this in them, that they are very hard to understand and very easy to forget. . . . I still remember that after you had thus amused me, I know not how long, with your fine philosophy, all I retained of it was a multitude of barbarous and dark words, proper to bewilder, perplex and tire out the best wits, and only invented the better to cover the vanity and ignorance of men like yourself, that would make us believe that they know all, and that under those obscure and ambiguous words are hid great mysteries which they alone are capable to understand. If you had seasoned me with that philosophy which formeth the mind to ratiocination, and insensibly accustoms it to be satisfied with nothing but solid reasons, if you had given me those excellent precepts and doctrines which raise the soul above the assaults of fortune, and reduce her to an unshakable and always equal temper, and permit her not to be lifted up by prosperity nor debased by adversity; if you had taken care to give me the knowledge of what we are and what are the first principles of things, and had assisted me in forming in my mind a fit idea of the greatness of the universe, and of the admirable order and motion of the parts thereof; if, I say, you had instilled into me this kind of philosophy, I should think myself incomparably more obliged to you than Alexander was to his Aristotle, and believe it my duty to recompense you otherwise than he did him. Should you not, instead of your flattery, have taught me somewhat of that point so important to a king, which is, what the reciprocal duties are of a sovereign to his subjects and those of subjects to their sovereigns; and ought not you to have considered that one day I should be obliged with the sword to dispute my life and my crown with my brothers? . . . Have you ever taken any care to make me learn what 'tis to besiege a town, or to set an army in array? For these things I am obliged to others, not at all to you. Go, and return to the village whence you are come, and let nobody know who you are or what is become of you.[19]

III. THE EPICS

*The "Mahabharata"—Its story—Its form—The "Bhagavad-Gita"—
The metaphysics of war—The price of freedom—The "Ramayana"—A forest idyl—The rape of Sita—The Hindu
epics and the Greek*

The schools and the universities were only a part of the educational system of India. Since writing was less highly valued than in other civilizations, and oral instruction preserved and disseminated the nation's history and poetry, the habit of public recitation spread among the people the most precious portions of their cultural heritage. As nameless *raconteurs* among the Greeks transmitted and expanded the *Iliad* and the *Odyssey*, so the reciters and declaimers of India carried down from generation to generation, and from court to people, the ever-growing epics into which the Brahmans crowded their legendary lore.

A Hindu scholar has rated the *Mahabharata* as "the greatest work of imagination that Asia has produced";[20] and Sir Charles Eliot has called it "a greater poem than the *Iliad*."[21] In one sense there is no doubt about the latter judgment. Beginning (ca. 500 B.C.) as a brief narrative poem of reasonable length, the *Mahabharata* took on, with every century, additional episodes and homilies, and absorbed the *Bhagavad-Gita* as well as parts of the story of Rama, until at last it measured 107,000 octameter couplets—seven times the length of the *Iliad* and the *Odyssey* combined. The name of the author was legion; "Vyasa," to whom tradition assigns it, means "the arranger."[22] A hundred poets wrote it, a thousand singers moulded it, until, under the Gupta kings (ca. 400 A.D.), the Brahmans poured their own religious and moral ideas into a work originally Kshatriyan, and gave the poem the gigantic form in which we find it today.

The central subject was not precisely adapted to religious instruction, for it told a tale of violence, gambling and war. Book One presents the fair Shakuntala (destined to be the heroine of India's most famous drama) and her mighty son Bharata; from his loins come those "great Bharata" (*Maha-Bharata*) tribes, the Kurus and the Pandavas, whose bloody strife constitutes the oft-broken thread of the tale. Yudhishthira, King of the Pandavas, gambles away his wealth, his army, his kingdom, his brothers, at last his wife Draupadi, in a game in which his Kuru enemy plays with loaded dice. By agreement the Pandavas are to receive their kingdom back after enduring a twelve-year banishment from their native soil. The twelve years pass; the Pandavas call upon the Kurus to restore their land; they receive no answer, and declare war. Allies are brought in on either side, until almost all northern India is engaged.* The battle rages for eighteen days and five books; all the Kurus are slain, and nearly all the Pandavas; the heroic Bhishma alone slays 100,000 men in ten days; altogether, the poet-statistician reports, the fallen numbered several hundred million men.[23] Amid this bloody scene of death Gandhari, queen consort of the blind Kuru king, Dhrita-rashtra, wails with horror at the sight of vultures hovering greedily over the corpse of Prince Duryodhan, her son.

> Stainless Queen and stainless woman, ever righteous, ever good,
> Stately in her mighty sorrow on the field Gandhari stood.
> Strewn with skulls and clotted tresses, darkened by the stream of gore,
> With the limbs of countless warriors is the red field covered o'er. . . .
> And the long-drawn howl of jackals o'er the scene of carnage rings,
> And the vulture and the raven flap their dark and loathsome wings.
> Feasting on the blood of warriors foul *Pishachas* fill the air,
> Viewless forms of hungry *Rakshas* limb from limb the corpses tear.
>
> Through this scene of death and carnage was the ancient monarch led,
> Kuru dames with faltering footsteps stepped amidst the countless dead,
> And a piercing wail of anguish burst upon the echoing plain,
> As they saw their sons or fathers, brothers, lords, amidst the slain,
> As they saw the wolves of jungle feed upon the destined prey,
> Darksome wanderers of the midnight prowling in the light of day.
> Shriek of pain and wail of anguish o'er the ghastly field resound,
> And their feeble footsteps falter and they sink upon the ground,
> Sense and life desert the mourners as they faint in common grief,
> Death-like swoon succeeding sorrow yields a moment's short relief.
>
> Then a mighty sigh of anguish from Gandhari's bosom broke,
> Gazing on her anguished daughters unto Krishna thus she spoke:
> "Mark my unconsoled daughters, widowed queens of Kuru's house,

---

* References in the *Vedas* to certain characters of the *Mahabharata* indicate that the story of a great intertribal war in the second millennium B.C. is fundamentally historical.

Wailing for their dear departed, like the osprey for her spouse;
How each cold and fading feature wakes in them a woman's love,
How amidst the lifeless warriors still with restless steps they rove;
Mothers hug their slaughtered children all unconscious in their
    sleep,
Widows bend upon their husbands and in ceaseless sorrow
    weep. . . ."

Thus to Krishna Queen Gandhari strove her woeful thoughts to tell,
When, alas, her wandering vision on her son Duryodhan fell.
Sudden anguish smote her bosom, and her senses seemed to stray;
Like a tree by tempest shaken, senseless on the earth she lay.
Once again she waked in sorrow, once again she cast her eye
Where her son in blood empurpled slept beneath the open sky.
And she clasped her dear Duryodhan, held him close unto her breast,
Sobs convulsive shook her bosom as the lifeless form she prest,
And her tears like rains of summer fell and washed his noble head,
Decked with garlands still untarnished, graced with *nishkas* bright
    and red.
" 'Mother,' said my dear Duryodhan, when he went unto the war,
'Wish me joy and wish me triumph as I mount the battle-car.'
'Son,' I said to dear Duryodhan, 'Heaven avert a cruel fate,
Yato dharma stato jayah—triumph doth on virtue wait.'
But he set his heart on battle, by his valor wiped his sins;
Now he dwells in realms celestial which the faithful warrior wins.
And I weep not for Duryodhan, like a prince he fought and fell,
But my sorrow-stricken husband, who can his misfortunes tell? . . .

"Hark the loathsome cry of jackals, how the wolves their vigils
    keep—
Maidens rich in song and beauty erst were wont to watch his sleep.
Hark the foul and blood-beaked vultures flap their wings upon the
    dead—
Maidens waved their feathery *pankhas* round Duryodhan's royal
    bed. . . .
Mark Duryodhan's noble widow, mother proud of Lakshman bold,
Queenly in her youth and beauty, like an altar of bright gold,
Torn from husband's sweet embraces, from her son's entwining
    arms,
Doomed to life-long woe and anguish in her youth and in her
    charms.

Rend my hard and stony bosom crushed beneath this cruel pain,
Should Gandhari live to witness noble son and grandson slain?

Mark again Duryodhan's widow, how she hugs his gory head,
How with gentle hands and tender softly holds him on his bed;
How from dear departed husband turns she to her dearest son,
And the tear-drops of the mother choke the widow's bitter groan;
Like the fibre of the lotus tender-golden is her frame.
O my lotus, O my daughter, Bharat's pride and Kuru's fame!
If the truth resides in *Vedas*, brave Duryodhan dwells above;
Wherefore linger we in sadness severed from his cherished love?
If the truth resides in *Shastra*, dwells in sky my hero son;
Wherefore linger we in sorrow since their earthly task is done?"[23a]

Upon this theme of love and battle a thousand interpolations have been hung. The god Krishna interrupts the slaughter for a canto to discourse on the nobility of war and Krishna; the dying Bhishma postpones his death to expound the laws of caste, bequest, marriage, gifts and funeral rites, to explain the philosophy of the *Sankhya* and the *Upanishads*, to narrate a mass of legends, traditions and myths, and to lecture Yudishthira at great length on the duties of a king; dusty stretches of genealogy and geography, of theology and metaphysics, separate the oases of drama and action; fables and fairy-tales, love-stories and lives of the saints contribute to give the *Mahabharata* a formlessness worse, and a body of thought richer, than can be found in either the *Iliad* or the *Odyssey*. What was evidently a Kshatriyan enthronement of action, heroism and war becomes, in the hands of the Brahmans, a vehicle for teaching the people the laws of Manu, the principles of *Yoga*, the precepts of morality, and the beauty of *Nirvana*. The Golden Rule is expressed in many forms;* moral aphorisms of beauty and wisdom abound;† and pretty stories of marital fidelity (Nala and Damayanti, Savitri) convey to women listeners the Brahman ideal of the faithful and patient wife.

Embedded in the narrative of the great battle is the loftiest philosophical poem in the world's literature—the *Bhagavad-Gita*, or Lord's Song. This

---

* E.g.: "Do naught to others which if done to thee would cause thee pain."[24] "Even if the enemy seeks help, the good man will be ready to grant him aid."[25] "With meekness conquer wrath, and ill with ruth; by giving niggards vanquish, lies with truth."[26]

† E.g.: "As in the great ocean one piece of wood meets another, and parts from it again, such is the meeting of creatures."[27]

is the New Testament of India, revered next to the *Vedas* themselves, and used in the law-courts, like our Bible or the *Koran*, for the administration of oaths.[28] Wilhelm von Humboldt pronounced it "the most beautiful, perhaps the only true, philosophical song existing in any known tongue; . . . perhaps the deepest and loftiest thing the world has to show."[29] Sharing the anonymity that India, careless of the individual and the particular, wraps around her creations, the *Gita* comes to us without the author's name, and without date. It may be as old as 400 B.C.,[30] or as young as 200 A.D.[31]

The *mise-en-scène* of the poem is the battle between the Kurus and the Pandavas; the occasion is the reluctance of the Pandava warrior Arjuna to attack in mortal combat his own near relatives in the opposing force. To Lord Krishna, fighting by his side like some Homeric god, Arjuna speaks the philosophy of Gandhi and Christ:

> "As I behold—come here to shed
> Their common blood—yon concourse of our kin,
> My members fail, my tongue dries in my mouth. . . .
> It is not good, O Keshav! Naught of good
> Can spring from mutual slaughter! Lo, I hate
> Triumph and domination, wealth and ease
> Thus sadly won! Alas, what victory
> Can bring delight, Govinda, what rich spoils
> Could profit, what rule recompense, what span
> Of life itself seem sweet, bought with such blood? . . .
>   Thus if we slay
> Kinsfolk and friends for love of earthly power,
> *Ahovat!* what an evil fault it were!
> Better I deem it, if my kinsmen strike,
> To face them weaponless, and bare my breast
> To shaft and spear, than answer blow with blow."[32]

Thereupon Krishna, whose divinity does not detract from his joy in battle, explains, with all the authority of a son of Vishnu, that according to the Scriptures, and the best orthodox opinion, it is meet and just to kill one's relatives in war; that Arjuna's duty is to follow the rules of his Kshatriya caste, to fight and slay with a good conscience and a good will; that after all, only the body is slain, while the soul survives. And he expounds the imperishable *Purusha* of *Sankhya*, the unchanging *Atman* of the *Upanishads:*

> "Indestructible,
> Learn thou, the Life is, spreading life through all;
> It cannot anywhere, by any means,
> Be anywise diminished, stayed or changed.
> But for these fleeting frames which it informs
> With spirit deathless, endless, infinite—
> *They* perish. Let them perish, Prince, and fight!
> He who shall say, 'Lo, I have slain a man!'
> He who shall think, 'Lo, I am slain!' those both
> Know naught. Life cannot slay! Life is not slain!
> Never the spirit was born; the spirit shall cease to be never;
> Never was time it was not; End and Beginning are dreams!
> Birthless and deathless and changeless remaineth the spirit forever;
> Death hath not touched it at all, dead though the house of it
>   seems."[33]

Krishna proceeds to instruct Arjuna in metaphysics, blending *Sankhya* and *Vedanta* in the peculiar synthesis accepted by the Vaishnavite sect. All things, he says, identifying himself with the Supreme Being,

> "hang on me
> As hangs a row of pearls upon its string.
> I am the fresh taste of the water; I
> The silver of the moon, the gold o' the sun,
> The word of worship in the Veds, the thrill
> That passeth in the ether, and the strength
> Of man's shed seed. I am the good sweet smell
> Of the moistened earth, I am the fire's red light,
> The vital air moving in all which moves,
> The holiness of hallowed souls, the root
> Undying, whence hath sprung whatever is;
> The wisdom of the wise, the intellect
> Of the informed, the greatness of the great,
> The splendor of the splendid. . . .
>   To him who wisely sees,
> The Brahman with his scrolls and sanctities,
> The cow, the elephant, the unclean dog,
> The outcaste gorging dog's meat, all are one."[34]

It is a poem rich in complementary colors, in metaphysical and ethical contradictions that reflect the contrariness and complexity of life. We are a little shocked to find the man taking what might seem to be the higher moral stand, while the god argues for war and slaughter on the shifty ground that life is unkillable and individuality unreal. What the author had in mind to do, apparently, was to shake the Hindu soul out of the enervating quietism of Buddhist piety into a willingness to fight for India; it was the rebellion of a Kshatriya who felt that religion was weakening his country, and who proudly reckoned that many things were more precious than peace. All in all it was a good lesson which, if India had learned it, might have kept her free.

The second of the Indian epics is the most famous and best beloved of all Hindu books,[35] and lends itself more readily than the *Mahabharata* to Occidental understanding. The *Ramayana* is briefer, merely running to a thousand pages of forty-eight lines each; and though it, too, grew by accretion from the third century B.C. to the second century A.D., the interpolations are fewer, and do not much disturb the central theme. Tradition attributes the poem to one Valmiki, who, like the supposed author of the larger epic, appears as a character in the tale; but more probably it is the product of many wayside bards like those who still recite these epics, sometimes for ninety consecutive evenings, to fascinated audiences.[36]

As the *Mahabharata* resembles the *Iliad* in being the story of a great war fought by gods and men, and partly occasioned by the loss of a beautiful woman from one nation to another, so the *Ramayana* resembles the *Odyssey*, and tells of a hero's hardships and wanderings, and of his wife's patient waiting for reunion with him.[37] At the outset we get a picture of a Golden Age, when Dasa-ratha, from his capital Ayodhya, ruled the kingdom of Kosala (now Oudh).

> Rich in royal worth and valor, rich in holy Vedic lore,
> Dasa-ratha ruled his empire in the happy days of yore. . . .
> Peaceful lived the righteous people, rich in wealth, in merit high;
> Envy dwelt not in their bosoms, and their accents shaped no lie.
> Fathers with their happy households owned their cattle, corn and
>   gold;
> Galling penury and famine in Ayodhya had no hold.[38]

Nearby was another happy kingdom, Videha, over which King Janak ruled. He himself "held the plough and tilled the earth" like some doughty Cincinnatus; and one day, at the touch of his plough, a lovely daughter, Sita, sprang up from a furrow of the soil. Soon Sita had to be married, and Janak held a contest for her suitors: he who could unbend Janak's bow of war should win the bride. To the contest came the oldest son of Dasa-ratha—Rama "lion-chested, mighty arméd, lotus-eyed, stately as the jungle tusker, with his crown of tresses tied."[39] Only Rama bent the bow; and Janak offered him his daughter with the characteristic formula of Hindu marriage:

> This is Sita, child of Janak, dearer unto him than life;
> Henceforth sharer of thy virtue, be she, prince, thy faithful wife;
> Of thy weal and woe partaker, be she thine in every land;
> Cherish her in joy and sorrow, clasp her hand within thy hand;
> As the shadow to the substance, to her lord is faithful wife,
> And my Sita, best of women, follows thee in death or life."[40]

So Rama returns to Ayodhya with his princess-bride—"ivory brow and lip of coral, sparkling teeth of pearly sheen"—and wins the love of the Kosalas by his piety, his gentleness, and his generosity. Suddenly evil enters into this Eden in the form of Dasa-ratha's second wife, Kaikeyi. Dasa-ratha has promised her any boon she may ask; and now, jealous of the first wife, whose son Rama is heir to the throne, she requires Dasa-ratha to banish Rama from the kingdom for fourteen years. Dasa-ratha, with a sense of honor which only a poet unacquainted with politics could conceive, keeps his word, and, broken-hearted, exiles his favorite son. Rama forgives him handsomely, and prepares to go and live in the forest, alone; but Sita insists upon going with him. Her speech is part of the memory of almost every Hindu bride:

> "Car and steed and gilded palace, vain are these to woman's life;
> Dearer is her husband's shadow to the loved and loving wife. . . .
> Happier than in father's mansions, in the woods will Sita rove,
> Waste no thought on home or kindred, nestling in her husband's love. . . .
> And the wild fruit she will gather from the fresh and fragrant wood,
> And the food by Rama tasted shall be Sita's cherished food."[41]

Even his brother Lakshman begs leave to accompany Rama:

"All alone with gentle Sita thou shalt trace thy darksome way;
Grant it that thy faithful Lakshman shall protect her night and day;
Grant it with his bow and quiver Lakshman shall all forests roam,
And his axe shall fell the jungle, and his hands shall rear the
   home."[42]

The epic becomes at this point a sylvan idyl, telling how Rama, Sita and Lakshman set out for the woods; how the population of Ayodhya, mourning for them, travel with them all the first day; how the exiles steal away from their solicitous company at night, abandon all their valuables and princely raiment, dress themselves in bark and matted grass, clear a way through the forest with their swords, and live on the fruits and nuts of the trees.

Oft to Rama turned his consort, pleased and curious ever more,
Asked the name of tree or creeper, fruit oı flower unseen before. . . .
Peacocks flew around them gayly, monkeys leapt on branches
   bent. . . .
Rama plunged into the river 'neath the morning's crimson beam,
Sita softly sought the waters as the lily seeks the stream.[43]

They build a hut beside the river, and learn to love their life in the woods. But a southern princess, Surpa-nakha, wandering in the forest, meets Rama, falls in love with him, resents his virtue, and instigates her brother Ravan to come and kidnap Sita. He succeeds, snatches her away to his distant castle, and tries in vain to seduce her. Since nothing is impossible to gods and authors, Rama raises a great army, invades Ravan's realm, defeats him in battle, rescues Sita, and then (his years of exile having ended) flies with her in an airplane back to Ayodhya, where another loyal brother gladly surrenders to him the Kosala throne.

In what is probably a later epilogue, Rama gives way to the sceptics who will not believe that Sita could have been so long in Ravan's palace without being occasionally in his arms. Though she passes through the Ordeal of Fire to prove her innocence, he sends her away to a forest hermitage with that bitter trick of heredity whereby one generation repeats upon the next the sins and errors which it suffered from its elders in its youth. In the woods Sita meets Valmiki, and bears two sons to Rama.

Many years later these sons, as traveling minstrels, sing before the unhappy
Rama the epic composed about him by Valmiki from Sita's memories. He
recognizes the boys as his own, and sends a message begging Sita to return.
But Sita, broken-hearted over the suspicion to which she has been subjected, disappears into the earth that was once her mother. Rama reigns
many years in loneliness and sorrow, and under his kindly sway Ayodhya
knows again the Utopia of Dasa-ratha's days:

> And 'tis told by ancient sages, during Rama's happy reign,
> Death untimely, dire diseases, came not to his subject men;
> Widows wept not in their sorrow for their lords untimely lost,
> Mothers wailed not in their anguish for their babes by Yama crost;
> Robbers, cheats and gay deceivers tempted not with lying word,
> Neighbor loved his righteous neighbor, and the people loved their
>   lord.
> Trees their ample produce yielded as returning seasons went,
> And the earth in grateful gladness never-failing harvest lent.
> Rains descended in their season, never came the blighting gale,
> Rich in crop and rich in pasture was each soft and smiling vale.
> Loom and anvil gave their produce, and the tilled and fertile soil,
> And the nation lived rejoicing in their old ancestral toil.["](#)

It is a delightful story, which even a modern cynic can enjoy if he is
wise enough to yield himself now and then to romance and the lilt of song.
These poems, though perhaps inferior to the epics of Homer in literary
quality—in logic of structure, and splendor of language, in depth of portraiture and fidelity to the essence of things—are distinguished by fine
feeling, a lofty idealization of woman and man, and a vigorous—sometimes
realistic—representation of life. Rama and Sita are too good to be true,
but Draupadi and Yudhishthira, Dhrita-rashtra and Gandhari, are almost
as living as Achilles and Helen, Ulysses and Penelope. The Hindu would
rightly protest that no foreigner can judge these epics, or even understand
them. To him they are not mere stories, they are a gallery of ideal characters upon whom he may mould his conduct; they are a repertory of the
traditions, philosophy and theology of his people; in a sense they are sacred
scriptures to be read as a Christian reads *The Imitation of Christ* or *The
Lives of the Saints*. The pious Hindu believes that Krishna and Rama were
incarnations of divinity, and still prays to them; and when he reads their
story in these epics he feels that he derives religious merit as well as literary

delight and moral exaltation. He trusts that if he reads the *Ramayana* he will be cleansed of all sin, and will beget a son;[45] and he accepts with simple faith the proud conclusion of the *Mahabharata*:

> If a man reads the *Mahabharata* and has faith in its doctrines, he becomes free from all sin, and ascends to heaven after his death. . . . As butter is to all other food, as Brahmans are to all other men, . . . as the ocean is to a pool of water, as the cow is to all other quadrupeds—so is the *Mahabharata* to all other histories. . . . He who attentively listens to the *shlokas** of the *Mahabharata*, and has faith in them, enjoys a long life and solid reputation in this world, and an eternal abode in the heavens in the next.[46]

IV. DRAMA

Origins—"The Clay Cart"—Characteristics of Hindu drama—Kalidasa — The story of "Shakuntala" — Estimate of Indian drama

In one sense drama in India is as old as the *Vedas*, for at least the germ of drama lies in the *Upanishads*. Doubtless older than these Scriptures is a more active source of the drama—the sacrificial and festival ceremonies and processions of religion. A third origin was in the dance—no mere release of energy, much less a substitute for coitus, but a serious ritual imitating and suggesting actions and events vital to the tribe. Perhaps a fourth source lay in the public and animated recitation of epic verse. These factors coöperated to produce the Indian theatre, and gave it a religious stamp that lingered throughout the classic age† in the serious nature of the drama, the Vedic or epic source of its subjects, and the benediction that always preceded the play.

Perhaps the final stimulus to drama came from the intercourse, established by Alexander's invasion, between India and Greece. We have no evidence of Hindu dramas before Ashoka, and only uncertain evidence during his reign. The oldest extant Hindu plays are the palm-leaf manuscripts lately discovered in Chinese Turkestan. Among them were three dramas, one of which names as its author Ashvaghosha, a theological luminary at Kanishka's court. The technical form of this play, and the resemblance of its buffoon

---

* Couplets.

† I.e., the age in which literature used Sanskrit as its medium.

to the type traditionally characteristic of the Hindu theatre, suggest that drama was already old in India when Ashvaghosha was born.[47] In 1910 thirteen ancient Sanskrit plays were found in Travancore, which are dubiously ascribed to Bhasa (ca. 350 A.D.), a dramatic predecessor much honored by Kalidasa. In the prologue to his *Malavika* Kalidasa unconsciously but admirably illustrates the relativity of time and adjectives: "Shall we," he asks, "neglect the works of such renowned authors as Bhasa, Saumilla, and Kaviputra? Can the audience feel any respect for the work of a *modern* poet, a Kalidasa?"[48]

Until recently, the oldest Hindu play known to research was *The Clay Cart.* The text, which need not be believed, names as author of the play an obscure King Shudraka, who is described as an expert in the *Vedas,* in mathematics, in the management of elephants, and in the art of love.[49] In any event he was an expert in the theatre. His play is by all means the most interesting that has come to us from India—a clever combination of melodrama and humor, with excellent passages of poetic fervor and description.

A synopsis of its plot will serve better than a volume of commentary to illustrate the character of Indian drama. In Act I we meet Charu-datta, once rich, now impoverished by generosity and bad fortune. His friend Maitreya, a stupid Brahman, acts as jester in the play. Charu asks Maitreya to offer an oblation to the gods, but the Brahman refuses, saying: "What's the use, when the gods you have worshiped have done nothing for you?" Suddenly a young Hindu woman, of high family and great wealth, rushes into Charu's courtyard, seeking refuge from a pursuer who turns out to be the King's brother, Samsthanaka—as completely and incredibly evil as Charu is completely and irrevocably good. Charu protects the girl, sends Samsthanaka off, and scorns the latter's threat of vengeance. The girl, Vasanta-sena, asks Charu to keep a casket of jewels in safe custody for her, lest her enemies steal it from her, and lest she may have no excuse for revisiting her rescuer. He agrees, takes the casket, and escorts her to her palatial home.

Act II is a comic interlude. A gambler, running away from two other gamblers, takes refuge in a temple. When they enter he eludes them by posing as the idol of the shrine. The pursuing gamblers pinch him to see if he is really a stone god, but he does not move. They abandon their search, and console themselves with a game of dice at the foot of the altar. The game becomes so exciting that the "statue," unable to control himself, leaps off his pedestal, and asks leave to take part. The others beat him; he again finds help in his heels, and is saved by Vasanta-sena, who recognizes in him a former servant of Charu-datta.

Act III shows Charu and Maitreya returning from a concert. A thief, Sharvilaka, breaks in, and steals the casket. Charu, discovering the theft, feels disgraced, and sends Vasanta-sena his last string of pearls as a substitute.

In Act IV Sharvilaka is seen offering the stolen casket to Vasanta-sena's maid as a bribe for her love. Seeing that it is her mistress' casket, she berates Sharvilaka as a thief. He answers her with Schopenhauerian acerbity:

> A woman will for money smile or weep
> According to your will; she makes a man
> Put trust in her, but trusts him not herself.
> Women are as inconstant as the waves
> Of ocean, their affection is as fugitive
> As streak of sunset glow upon a cloud.
> They cling with eager fondness to the man
> Who yields them wealth, which they squeeze out like sap
> Out of a juicy plant, and then they leave him.

The maid refutes him by forgiving him, and Vasanta-sena by allowing them to marry.

At the opening of Act V Vasanta-sena comes to Charu's house to return both his jewels and her casket. While she is there a storm blows up, which she describes in excellent Sanskrit.* The storm obligingly increases its fury, and compels her, much according to her will, to spend the night under Charu's roof.

Act VI shows Vasanta leaving Charu's house the next morning. By mistake she steps not into the carriage he has summoned for her, but into one which belongs to the villainous Samsthanaka. Act VII is concerned with a subordinate plot, inessential to the theme. Act VIII finds Vasanta deposited, not in her palace as she had expected, but in the home, almost in the arms, of her enemy. When she again spurns his love he chokes her, and buries her. Then he goes to court and lodges against Charu a charge of murdering Vasanta for her jewels.

Act IX describes the trial, in which Maitreya unwittingly betrays his master by letting Vasanta's jewels fall from his pocket. Charu is condemned to death. In Act X Charu is seen on his way to execution. His child pleads with the executioners to be allowed to take his place, but they refuse. At the

---

* An exceptional instance. Usually, in Hindu plays, the women speak Prakrit, on the ground that it would be unbecoming in a lady to be familiar with a dead language.

last moment Vasanta herself appears. Sharvilaka had seen Samsthanaka bury her; he had exhumed her in time, and had revived her. Now, while Vasanta rescues Charu, Sharvilaka accuses the King's brother of murder. But Charu refuses to support the charge, Samsthanaka is released, and everybody is happy.[50]

Since time is more plentiful in the East, where nearly all work is done by human hands, than in the West, where there are so many labor-saving devices, Hindu plays are twice as long as the European dramas of our day. The acts vary from five to ten, and each act is unobtrusively divided into scenes by the exit of one character and the entrance of another. There are no unities of time or place, and no limits to imagination. Scenery is scanty, but costumes are colorful. Sometimes living animals enliven the play,[51] and for a moment redeem the artificial with the natural. The performance begins with a prologue, in which an actor or the manager discusses the play; Goethe seems to have taken from Kalidasa the idea of a prologue for *Faust*. The prologue concludes by introducing the first character, who marches into the middle of things. Coincidences are innumerable, and supernatural influences often determine the course of events. A love-story is indispensable; so is a jester. There is no tragedy in the Indian theatre; happy endings are unavoidable; faithful love must always triumph, virtue must always be rewarded, if only to balance reality. Philosophical discourse, which obtrudes so often into Hindu poetry, is excluded from Hindu drama; drama, like life, must teach only by action, never by words.* Lyric poetry alternates with prose according to the dignity of the topic, the character, and the action. Sanskrit is spoken by the upper castes in the play, Prakrit by the women and the lower castes. Descriptive passages excel, character delineation is poor. The actors—who include women—do their work well, with no Occidental haste, and with no Far-Eastern fustian. The play ends with an epilogue, in which the favorite god of the author or the locality is importuned to bring prosperity to India.

Ever since Sir William Jones translated it and Goethe praised it, the most famous of Hindu dramas has been the *Shakuntala* of Kalidasa. Nevertheless we know Kalidasa only through three plays, and through

---

* The great Hindu theorist of the drama, Dhanamjaya (ca. 1000 A.D.), writes: "As for any simple man of little intelligence who says that from dramas, which distil joy, the gain is knowledge only—homage to him, for he has averted his face from what is delightful."[52]

the legends that pious memory has hung upon his name. Apparently he was one of the "Nine Gems"—poets, artists and philosophers—who were cherished by King Vikramaditya (380-413 A.D.) in the Gupta capital at Ujjain.

Shakuntala is in seven acts, written partly in prose, partly in vivid verse. After a prologue in which the manager invites the audience to consider the beauties of nature, the play opens upon a forest glade in which a hermit dwells with his foster daughter Shakuntala. The peace of the scene is disturbed by the noise of a chariot; its occupant, King Dushyanta, appears, and falls in love with Shakuntala with literary speed. He marries her in the first act, but is suddenly called back to his capital; he leaves her with the usual promises to return at his earliest convenience. An ascetic tells the sorrowing girl that the King will remember her as long as she keeps the ring Dushyanta has given her; but she loses the ring while bathing. About to become a mother, she journeys to the court, only to discover that the King has forgotten her after the manner of men to whom women have been generous. She tries to refresh his memory.

> *Shakuntala.* Do you not remember in the jasmine-bower,
> One day, how you had poured the rain-water
> That a lotus had collected in its cup
> Into the hollow of your hand?
> *King.*   Tell on,
> I am listening.
> *Shakuntala.* Just then my adopted child,
> The little fawn, ran up with long, soft eyes,
> And you, before you quenched your own thirst, gave
> To the little creature, saying, "Drink you first,
> Gentle fawn!" But she would not from strange hands.
> And yet, immediately after, when
> I took some water in my hand, she drank,
> Absolute in her trust. Then, with a smile,
> You said: "Each creature has faith in its own kind.
> You are children both of the same wild wood, and each
> Confides in the other, knowing where its trust is."
> *King.* Sweet, fair and false! Such women entice fools. . . .
> The female gift of cunning may be marked
> In creatures of all kinds; in women most.
> The cuckoo leaves her eggs for dupes to hatch,
> Then flies away secure and triumphing.[53]

Shakuntala, spurned and despondent, is miraculously lifted into the air and carried off to another forest, where she bears her child—that great Bharata whose progeny must fight all the battles of the *Mahabharata*. Meanwhile a fisherman has found the ring, and seeing the King's seal on it, has brought it to Dushyanta. His memory of Shakuntala is restored, and he seeks her everywhere. Traveling in his airplane over the Himalayas, he alights by dramatic providence at the very hermitage where Shakuntala is pining away. He sees the boy Bharata playing before the cottage, and envies his parents:

> "Ah, happy father, happy mother, who,
>   Carrying their little son, are soiled with dust
>   Rubbed from his body; it nestles with fond faith
> Into their lap, the refuge that he craves—
>   The white buds of his teeth just visible
> When he breaks out into a causeless smile,
>   And he attempts sweet wordless sounds, . . .
> Melting the heart more than any word."[54]

Shakuntala appears, the King begs her forgiveness, receives it, and makes her his queen. The play ends with a strange but typical invocation:

> "May kings reign only for their subjects' weal!
>   May the divine Sarasvati, the source
>   Of speech, and goddess of dramatic art,
> Be ever honored by the great and wise!
>   And may the purple, self-existent god,
>   Whose vital energy pervades all space,
> From future transmigrations save my soul!"[55]

Drama did not decline after Kalidasa, but it did not again produce a *Shakuntala* or a *Clay Cart*. King Harsha, if we may believe a possibly inspired tradition, wrote three plays, which held the stage for centuries. A hundred years after him Bhavabhuti, a Brahman of Berar, wrote three romantic dramas which are ranked second only to Kalidasa's in the history of the Indian stage. His style, however, was so elaborate and obscure that he had to be—and of course protested that he was—content with a narrow audience. "How little do they know," he wrote, "who speak of us with censure. The entertainment is not for them. Possibly some one exists or will exist, of similar tastes with myself; for time is boundless, and the world is wide."[56]

We cannot rank the dramatic literature of India on a plane with that of Greece or Elizabethan England; but it compares favorably with the theatre of China or Japan. Nor need we look to India for the sophistication that marks the modern stage; that is an accident of time rather than an eternal verity, and may pass away—even into its opposite. The supernatural agencies of Indian drama are as alien to our taste as the *deus ex machina* of the enlightened Euripides; but this, too, is a fashion of history. The weaknesses of Hindu drama (if they may be listed diffidently by an alien) are artificial diction disfigured with alliteration and verbal conceits, monochromatic characterization in which each person is thoroughly good or thoroughly bad, improbable plots turning upon unbelievable coincidences, and an excess of description and discourse over that action which is, almost by definition, the specific medium by which drama conveys significance. Its virtues are its creative fancy, its tender sentiment, its sensitive poetry, and its sympathetic evocation of nature's beauty and terror. About national types of art there can be no disputation; we can judge them only from the provincial standpoint of our own, and mostly through the prism of translation. It is enough that Goethe, ablest of all Europeans to transcend provincial and national barriers, found the reading of *Shakuntala* among the profound experiences of his life, and wrote of it gratefully:

> Wouldst thou the young year's blossoms, and the fruits of its decline,
>   And all by which the soul is charmed, enraptured, feasted, fed;
> Wouldst thou the Earth and Heaven itself in one sole name combine?
> I name thee, O Shakuntala! and all at once is said.[57]

V. PROSE AND POETRY

Their unity in India—Fables—History—Tales—Minor poets—Rise of the vernacular literature—Chandi Das—Tulsi Das— Poets of the south—Kabir

Prose is largely a recent phenomenon in Indian literature, and might be termed an exotic corruption through contact with Europeans. To the naturally poetic soul of the Hindu everything worth writing about had a poetic content, and invited a poetic form. Since he felt that literature should be read aloud, and knew that his work would spread and endure, if at all, by oral rather than written dissemination, he chose to give to his compositions a metric or aphoristic form that would lend itself to recitation and memory. Consequently nearly all the literature of India is verse: scientific, medical, legal and art treatises are, more often than not, presented in metre or rhyme or both; even grammars and dictionaries have been turned into poetry. Fables and history, which in the West are content with prose, found in India a melodious poetic form.

Hindu literature is especially rich in fables; indeed, India is probably responsible for most of the fables that have passed like an international currency across the frontiers of the world.* Buddhism flourished best in the days when the Jataka legends of Buddha's birth and youth were popular among the people. The best-known book in India is the *Panchatantra*, or "Five Headings" (ca. 500 A.D.); it is the source of many of the fables that have pleased Europe as well as Asia. The *Hitopadesha*, or "Good Advice," is a selection and adaption of tales from the *Panchatantra*. Both, strange to say, are classed by the Hindus under the rubric of *Niti-shastra*—i.e., instructions in politics or morals; every tale is told to point a moral, a principle of conduct or government; usually these stories pretend to have been invented by some wise Brahman for the instruction of a king's sons. Often they turn the lowliest animals to the uses of the subtlest philosophy. The fable of the monkey who tried to warm himself by the light of a glowworm, and slew the bird who pointed out his error, is a remarkably apt illustration of the fate that awaits the scholar who exposes a popular delusion.†

Historical literature did not succeed in rising above the level of either bare chronicles or gorgeous romance. Perhaps through a scorn of the *Maya* events of space and time, perhaps through a preference of oral to written traditions, the Hindus neglected to compose works of history that could bear comparison with Herodotus or Thucydides, Plutarch or Tacitus, Gibbon or Voltaire. Details of place and date were so scantily recorded, even in the case of famous men, that Hindu scholars assigned to their greatest poet, Kalidasa, dates ranging over a millennium.[59] Living to our own time in an almost unchanging world of custom, morals and beliefs, the Hindu hardly dreamed of progress, and never bothered about antiquities. He was content

---

* Sir William Jones reported that the Hindus laid claim to three inventions: chess, the decimal system, and teaching by fables.

† A lively war rages in the fields of Oriental scholarship as to whether these fables passed from India to Europe, or turn about; we leave the dispute to men of leisure. Perhaps they passed to both India and Europe from Egypt, via Mesopotamia and Crete. The influence of the *Panchatantra* upon the *Arabian Nights*, however, is beyond question.[58]

to accept the epics as authentic history, and to let legend serve for biography. When Ashvaghosha wrote his life of Buddha (the *Buddha-charita*), it was legend rather than history; and when, five hundred years later, Bana wrote his *Harsha-charita*, it was again an idealization rather than a reliable portrait of the great king. The native chronicles of Rajputana appear to be exercises in patriotism. Only one Hindu writer seems to have grasped the function of the historian. Kalhana, author of the *Rajatarangini*, or "Stream of Kings," expressed himself as follows: "That noble-minded poet alone merits praise whose word, like the sentence of a judge, keeps free from love or hatred in recording the past." Winternitz calls him "the only great historian that India has produced."[60]

The Moslems were more acutely conscious of history, and left some admirable prose records of their doings in India. We have mentioned Alberuni's ethnographical study of India, and Babur's *Memoirs*. Contemporary with Akbar was an excellent historian, Muhammad Qazim Firishta, whose *History of India* is our most reliable guide to the events of the Moslem period. Less impartial was Akbar's prime minister or general political factotum, Abu-l Fazl, who put his master's administrative methods down for posterity in the *Ain-i Akbari*, or "Institutes of Akbar," and told his master's life with forgivable fondness in the *Akbar Nama*. The Emperor returned his affection; and when the news came that Jehangir had slain the vizier, Akbar burst into passionate grief, and cried out: "If Salim (Jehangir) wished to be emperor, he might have slain me and spared Abu-l Fazl."[61]

Midway between fables and history were the vast collections of poetic tales put together by industrious versifiers for the delectation of the romantic Indian soul. As far back as the first century A.D. one Gunadhya wrote in one hundred thousand couplets the *Brihatkatha*, or "Great Romance"; and a thousand years later Somadeva composed the *Kathasaritzagara*, or "Ocean of the Rivers of Story," a torrent 21,500 couplets long. In the same eleventh century a clever story-teller of uncertain identity built a framework for his *Vetalapanchavimchatika* ("The Twenty-five Stories of the Vampire") by representing King Vikramaditya as receiving annually from an ascetic a fruit containing a precious stone. The King inquires how he may prove his gratitude; he is asked to bring to the *yogi* the corpse of a man hanging on the gallows, but is warned not to speak if the corpse should address him. The corpse is inhabited by a vampire who, as the King stumbles along, fascinates him with a story; at the end of the story the vampire propounds a question which the King, forgetting his instructions, answers. Twenty-five times the King attempts the task of bringing a corpse to the ascetic and holding his peace; twenty-four times he is so absorbed in the story that the vampire tells him that he answers the question put to him at the end.[62] It was an excellent scaffold on which to hang a score of tales.

Meanwhile there was no dearth of poets writing what we should call poetry. Abu-l Fazl describes "thousands of poets" at Akbar's court; there were hundreds at minor capitals, and doubtless dozens in every home.* One of the earliest and greatest was Bhartrihari, monk, grammarian and lover, who, before retiring into the arms of religion, instructed his soul with amours. He has left us a record of them in his "Century of Love"—a Heine-like sequence of a hundred poems. "Erstwhile," he writes to one of his loves, "we twain deemed that thou wast I and I was thou; how comes it now that thou are thou and I am I?" He did not care for reviewers, and told them: "It is easy to satisfy one who is ignorant, even easier to satisfy a connoisseur; but not the Creator himself can please the man who has just a morsel of knowledge."[63] In Jayadeva's *Gita-Govinda*, or "Song of the Divine Cowherd," the amorousness of the Hindu turns to religion, and intones the sensuous love of Radha and Krishna. It is a poem of full-bodied passion, but India interprets it reverently as a mystic and symbolic portrayal of the soul's longing for God—an interpretation that would be intelligible to those immovable divines who composed such pious headings for the *Song of Songs*.

In the eleventh century the vernaculars made inroads upon the classical dead language as a medium of literary expression, as they were to do in Europe a century later. The first major poet to use the living speech of the people was Chand Bardai, who wrote in Hindi an immense historical poem of sixty cantos, and was only persuaded to interrupt his work by the call of death. Sur Das, the blind poet of Agra, composed 60,000 verses on the life and adventures of Krishna; we are told that he was helped by the god himself, who became his amanuensis, and wrote faster than the poet could dictate.[64] Meanwhile a poor priest, Chandi Das, was shocking Bengal by composing Dantean songs to a peasant Beatrice, idealizing her with romantic passion, exalting her as a symbol of divinity, and

---

* Poetry tended now to be less objective than in the days of the epic, and gave itself more and more to the interweaving of religion and love. Metre, which had been loose and free in the epics, varying in the length of the line, and requiring regularity only in the last four or five syllables, became at once stricter and more varied; a thousand complications of prosody were introduced, which disappear in translation; artifices of letter and phrase abounded, and rhyme appeared not only at the end but often in the middle of the line. Rigid rules were composed for the poetic art, and the form became more precise as the content thinned.

making his love an allegory of his desire for absorption in God; at the same time he inaugurated the use of Bengali as a literary language. "I have taken refuge at your feet, my beloved. When I do not see you my mind has no rest . . . . I cannot forget your grace and your charm,—and yet there is no desire in my heart." Excommunicated by his fellow Brahmans on the ground that he was scandalizing the public, he agreed to renounce his love, Rami, in a public ceremony of recantation; but when, in the course of this ritual, he saw Rami in the crowd, he withdrew his recantation, and going up to her, bowed before her with hands joined in adoration.[64a]

The supreme poet of Hindi literature is Tulsi Das, almost a contemporary of Shakespeare. His parents exposed him because he had been born under an unlucky star. He was adopted by a forest mystic, who instructed him in the legendary lore of Rama. He married; but when his son died, Tulsi Das retired to the woods to lead a life of penance and meditation. There, and in Benares, he wrote his religious epic, the *Ramacharita-manasa*, or "Lake of the Deeds of Rama," in which he told again the story of Rama, and offered him to India as the supreme and only god. "There is one God," says Tulsi Das; "it is Rama, creator of heaven and earth, and redeemer of mankind. . . . For the sake of his faithful people a very god, Lord Rama, became incarnate as a king, and for our sanctification lived, as it were, the life of any ordinary man."[65] Few Europeans have been able to read the work in the now archaic Hindi original; one of these considers that it establishes Tulsi Das as "the most important figure in the whole of Indian literature."[66] To the natives of Hindustan the poem constitutes a popular Bible of theology and ethics. "I regard the *Ramayana* of Tulsi Das," says Gandhi, "as the greatest book in all devotional literature."[67]

Meanwhile the Deccan was also producing poetry. Tukaram composed in the Mahrathi tongue 4600 religious songs which are as current in India today as the Psalms of "David" are in Judaism or Christendom. His first wife having died, he married a shrew and became a philosopher. "It is not hard to win salvation," he wrote, "for it may readily be found in the bundle on our back."[68] As early as the second century A.D. Madura became the capital of Tamil letters; a *Sangam*, or court of poets and critics, was set up there under the patronage of the Pandya kings, and, like the French Academy, regulated the development of the language, conferred titles, and gave prizes.[69] Tiruvallavar, an Outcaste weaver, wrote in the most difficult of Tamil meters a religious and philosophical work—the *Kurral*—expounding moral and political ideals. Tradition assures us that when the members of the *Sangam*, who were all Brahmans, saw the success of this Pariah's poetry, they drowned themselves to a man;[70] but this is not to be believed of any Academy.

We have kept for the last, though out of his chronological place, the greatest lyric poet of medieval India. Kabir, a simple weaver of Benares, prepared for his task of uniting Islam and Hinduism by having, we are told, a Mohammedan for his father and a Brahman virgin for his mother.[71] Fascinated by the preacher Ramananda, he became a devotee of Rama, enlarged him (as Tulsi Das would also do) into a universal deity, and began to write Hindi poems of rare beauty to explain a creed in which there should be no temples, no mosques, no idols, no caste, no circumcision, and but one god.* "Kabir," he says,

> is a child of Ram and Allah, and accepteth all *Gurus* and *Pirs*. . . . O God, whether Allah or Rama, I live by thy name. . . . Lifeless are all the images of the gods; they cannot speak; I know it, for I have called aloud to them. . . . What avails it to wash your mouth, count your beads, bathe in holy streams, and bow in temples, if, whilst you mutter your prayers or go on pilgrimages, deceitfulness is in your hearts?[72]

The Brahmans were shocked, and to refute him (the story runs) sent a courtesan to tempt him; but he converted her to his creed. This was easy, for he had no dogmas, but only profound religious feeling.

> There is an endless world, O my brother,
> And there is a nameless Being, of whom naught can be said;
> Only he knows who has reached that region.
> It is other than all that is heard or said.
> No form, no body, no length, no breadth is seen there;
> How can I tell you that which it is?
> Kabir says: "It cannot be told by the words of the mouth, it cannot be written on paper;
> It is like a dumb person who tastes a sweet thing—how shall it be explained?[73]

* Rabindranath Tagore has translated, with characteristic perfection, one hundred *Songs of Kabir*, New York, 1915.

He accepted the theory of reincarnation which was in the air about him, and prayed, like a Hindu, to be released from the chain of re-birth and redeath. But his ethic was the simplest in the world: live justly, and look for happiness at your elbow.

> I laugh when I hear that the fish in the water is thirsty;
> You do not see that the Real is in your home, and you wander from forest to forest listlessly!
> Here is the truth! Go where you will, to Benares or to Mathura, if you do not find your soul, the world is unreal to you. . . .
> To what shore would you cross, O my heart? There is no traveler before you, there is no road. . . .
> There there is neither body nor mind; and where is the place that shall still the thirst of the soul? You shall find naught in the emptiness.
> Be strong, and enter into your own body; for there your foothold is firm. Consider it well, O my heart! Go not elsewhere.
> Kabir says: Put all imaginations away, and stand fast in that which you are.[74]

After his death, runs the legend, Hindus and Mohammedans contended for his body, and disputed whether it should be buried or burned. But while they disputed some one raised the cloth that covered the corpse, and nothing could be seen but a mass of flowers. The Hindus burned a part of the flowers in Benares, and the Moslems buried the rest.[75] After his death his songs passed from mouth to mouth among the people; Nanak the Sikh was inspired by them to found his sturdy sect; others made the poor weaver into a deity.[76] Today two small sects, jealously separate, follow the doctrine and worship the name of this poet who tried to unite Moslems and Hindus. One sect is Hindu, the other is Moslem.

CHAPTER XXI

Indian Art

I. THE MINOR ARTS

The great age of Indian art—Its uniqueness—Its association with industry—Pottery—Metal—Wood—Ivory—Jewelry—
Textiles

BEFORE Indian art, as before every phase of Indian civilization, we stand in humble wonder at its age and its continuity. The ruins of Mohenjo-daro are not all utilitarian; among them are limestone bearded men (significantly like Sumerians), terra-cotta figures of women and animals, beads and other ornaments of carnelian, and jewelry of finely polished gold.[1] One seal[2] shows in bas-relief a bull so vigorously and incisively drawn that the observer almost leaps to the conclusion that art does not progress, but only changes its form.

From that time to this, through the vicissitudes of five thousand years, India has been creating its peculiar type of beauty in a hundred arts. The record is broken and incomplete, not because India ever rested, but because war and the idol-smashing ecstasies of Moslems destroyed uncounted masterpieces of building and statuary, and poverty neglected the preservation of others. We shall find it difficult to enjoy this art at first sight; its music will seem weird, its painting obscure, its architecture confused, its sculpture grotesque. We shall have to remind ourselves at every step that our tastes are the fallible product of our local and limited traditions and environments; and that we do ourselves and foreign nations injustice when we judge them, or their arts, by standards and purposes natural to our life and alien to their own.

In India the artist had not yet been separated from the artisan, making art artificial and work a drudgery; as in our Middle Ages, so, in the India that died at Plassey, every mature workman was a craftsman, giving form and personality to the product of his skill and taste. Even today, when

584

factories replace handicrafts, and craftsmen degenerate into "hands," the stalls and shops of every Hindu town show squatting artisans beating metal, moulding jewelry, drawing designs, weaving delicate shawls and embroideries, or carving ivory and wood. Probably no other nation known to us has ever had so exuberant a variety of arts.[3]

Strange to say, pottery failed to rise from an industry to an art in India; caste rules put so many limitations upon the repeated use of the same dish* that there was small incentive to adorn with beauty the frail and transient earthenware that came so rapidly from the potter's hand.[4] If the vessel was to be made of some precious metal, then artistry could spend itself upon it without stint; witness the Tanjore silver vase in the Victoria Institute at Madras, or the gold Betel Dish of Kandy.[5] Brass was hammered into an endless variety of lamps, bowls and containers; a black alloy (*bidri*) of zinc was often used for boxes, basins and trays; and one metal was inlaid or overlaid upon another, or encrusted with silver or gold.[6] Wood was carved with a profusion of plant and animal forms. Ivory was cut into everything from deities to dice; doors and other objects of wood were inlaid with it; and dainty receptacles were made of it for cosmetics and perfumes. Jewelry abounded, and was worn by rich and poor as ornament or hoard; Jaipur excelled in firing enamel colors upon a gold background; clasps, beads, pendants, knives and combs were moulded into tasteful shapes, with floral, animal, or theological, designs; one Brahman pendant harbors in its tiny space half a hundred gods.[7] Textiles were woven with an artistry never since excelled; from the days of Cæsar to our own the fabrics of India have been prized by all the world.† Sometimes, by the subtlest and most painstaking of precalculated measurements, every thread of warp and woof was dyed before being placed upon the loom; the design appeared as the weaving progressed, and was identical on either side.[9] From homespun *khaddar* to complex brocades flaming with gold, from picturesque pyjamas‡ to the invisibly-seamed shawls of Kashmir,§ every garment woven in India has a beauty that comes only of a very ancient, and now almost instinctive, art.

---

* Cf. p. 497 above.

† Perhaps the oldest printing of textiles from blocks was done in India,[8] though it never grew there into the kindred art of block-printing books.

‡ From the Hindu *paijamas*, meaning leg-clothing.

§ These fine woolen shawls are made of several strips, skilfully joined into what seems to be a single fabric.[10]

II. MUSIC

A concert in India—Music and the dance—Musicians—Scale and forms—Themes—Music and philosophy

An American traveler, permitted to intrude upon a concert in Madras, found an audience of some two hundred Hindus, apparently all Brahmans, seated some on benches, some on a carpeted floor, listening intently to a small *ensemble* beside which our orchestral mobs would have seemed designed to make themselves heard on the moon. The instruments were unfamiliar to the visitor, and to his provincial eye they looked like the strange and abnormal products of some neglected garden. There were drums of many shapes and sizes, ornate flutes and serpentine horns, and a variety of strings. Most of these pieces were wrought with minute workmanship, and some were studded with gems. One drum, the *mridanga*, was formed like a small barrel; both ends were covered with a parchment whose pitch was changed by tightening or loosening it with little leather thongs; one parchment head had been treated with manganese dust, boiled rice and tamarind juice in order to elicit from it a peculiar tone. The drummer used only his hands—sometimes the palm, sometimes the fingers, sometimes the merest finger-tips. Another player had a *tambura*, or lute, whose four long strings were sounded continuously as a deep and quiet background for the melody. One instrument, the *vina*, was especially sensitive and eloquent; its strings, stretched over a slender metal plate from a parchment-covered drum of wood at one end to a resounding hollow gourd at the other, were kept vibrating with a plectrum, while the player's left hand etched in the melody with fingers moving deftly from string to string. The visitor listened humbly, and understood nothing.

Music in India has a history of at least three thousand years. The Vedic hymns, like all Hindu poetry, were written to be sung; poetry and song, music and dance, were made one art in the ancient ritual. The Hindu dance, which, to the beam in the Occidental eye, seems as voluptuous and obscene as Western dancing seems to Hindus, has been, through the greater part of Indian history, a form of religious worship, a display of beauty in motion and rhythm for the honor and edification of the gods; only in modern times have the *devadasis* emerged from the temples in great number to entertain the secular and profane. To the Hindu these dances were no mere display of flesh; they were, in one aspect, an imitation of the rhythms and processes of the universe. Shiva himself was the god of the dance, and the dance of Shiva symbolized the very movement of the world.*

Musicians, singers and dancers, like all artists in India, belonged to the lowest castes. The Brahman might like to sing in private, and accompany himself on a *vina* or another stringed instrument; he might teach others to play, or sing, or dance; but he would never think of playing for hire, or of putting an instrument to his mouth. Public concerts were, until recently, a rarity in India; secular music was either the spontaneous singing or thrumming of the people, or it was performed, like the chamber music of Europe, before small gatherings in aristocratic homes. Akbar, himself skilled in music, had many musicians at his court; one of his singers, Tansen, became popular and wealthy, and died of drink at the age of thirty-four.[11] There were no amateurs, there were only professionals; music was not taught as a social accomplishment, and children were not beaten into Beethovens. The function of the public was not to play poorly, but to listen well.[12]

For listening to music, in India, is itself an art, and requires long training of ear and soul. The words may be no more intelligible to the Westerner than the words of the operas which he feels it his class duty to enjoy; they range, as everywhere, about the two subjects of religion and love; but the words are of little moment in Hindu music, and the singer, as in our most advanced literature, often replaces them with meaningless syllables. The music is written in scales more subtle and minute than ours. To our scale of twelve tones it adds ten "microtones," making a scale of twenty-two quarter-tones in all. Hindu music may be written in a notation composed of Sanskrit letters; usually it is neither written nor read, but is passed down "by ear" from generation to generation, or from composer to learner. It is not separated into bars, but glides in a continuous *legato* which frustrates a listener accustomed to regular emphases or beats. It has no chords, and does not deal in harmony; it confines itself to melody, with perhaps a background of undertones; in this sense it is much simpler and more primitive

---

* The secular Hindu dance has been revealed to Europe and America by the not quite orthodox art of Shankar, in which every movement of the body, the hands, the fingers and the eyes conveys a subtle and precise significance to the initiated spectator, and carries an undulating grace, and a precise and corporeal poetry, unknown in the Western dance since our democratic return to the African in art.

than European music, while it is more complex in scale and rhythm. The melodies are both limited and infinite: they must all derive from one or another of the thirty-six traditional modes or airs, but they may weave upon these themes an endless and seamless web of variation. Each of these themes, or *ragas*,* consists of five, six or seven notes, to one of which the musician constantly returns. Each *raga* is named from the mood that it wishes to suggest—"Dawn," "Spring," "Evening Beauty," "Intoxication," etc.—and is associated with a specific time of the day or the year. Hindu legend ascribes an occult power to these *ragas;* so it is said that a Bengal dancing-girl ended a drought by singing, as a kind of "Rain-drop Prelude," the *Megh mallar raga*, or rain-making theme.[13] Their antiquity has given the *ragas* a sacred character; he who plays them must observe them faithfully, as forms enacted by Shiva himself. One player, Narada, having performed them carelessly, was ushered into hell by Vishnu, and was shown men and women weeping over their broken limbs; these, said the god, were the *ragas* and *raginis* distorted and torn by Narada's reckless playing. Seeing which, we are told, Narada sought more humbly a greater perfection in his art.[14]

The Indian performer is not seriously hampered by the obligation to remain faithful to the *raga* that he has chosen for his program, any more than the Western composer of sonatas or symphonies is hampered by adhering to his theme; in either case what is lost in liberty is gained in access to coherence of structure and symmetry of form. The Hindu musician is like the Hindu philosopher; he starts with the finite and "sends his soul into the infinite"; he embroiders upon his theme until, through an undulating stream of rhythm and recurrence, even through a hypnotizing monotony of notes, he has created a kind of musical *Yoga*, a forgetfulness of will and individuality, of matter, space and time; the soul is lifted into an almost mystic union with something "deeply interfused," some profound, immense and quiet Being, some primordial and pervasive reality that smiles upon all striving wills, all change and death.

Probably we shall never care for Hindu music, and never comprehend it, until we have abandoned striving for being, progress for permanence, desire for acceptance, and motion for rest. This may come when Europe again is subject, and Asia again is master. But then Asia will have tired of being, permanence, acceptance and rest.

---

* More strictly speaking there are six *ragas*, or basic themes, each with five modifications called *ragini*. *Raga* means color, passion, mood; *ragini* is its feminine form.

III. PAINTING

Prehistoric — The frescoes of Ajanta — Rajput miniatures — The Mogul school—The painters—The theorists

A provincial is a man who judges the world in terms of his parish, and considers all unfamiliar things barbarous. It is told of the Emperor Jehangir—a man of taste and learning in the arts—that when he was shown a European painting he rejected it summarily; being "in oyle, he liked it not."[15] It is pleasant to know that even an emperor can be a provincial, and that it was as difficult for Jehangir to enjoy the oil-painting of Europe as it is for us to appreciate the minatures of India.

It is clear, from the drawings, in red pigment, of animals and a rhinoceros hunt in the prehistoric caves of Singanpur and Mirzapur, that Indian painting has had a history of many thousands of years. Palettes with ground colors ready for use abound among the remains of neolithic India.[16] Great gaps occur in the history of the art, because most of the early work was ruined by the climate, and much of the remainder was destroyed by Moslem "idol-breakers" from Mahmud to Aurangzeb.[17] The *Vinaya Pitaka* (ca. 300 B.C.) refers to King Pasenada's palace as containing picture galleries, and Fa-Hien and Yuan Chwang describe many buildings as famous for the excellence of their murals;[18] but no trace of these structures remains. One of the oldest frescoes in Tibet shows an artist painting a portrait of Buddha;[19] the later artist took it for granted that painting was an established art in Buddha's days.

The earliest dateable Indian painting is a group of Buddhist frescoes (ca. 100 B.C.) found on the walls of a cave in Sirguya, in the Central Provinces. From that time on the art of fresco painting—that is, painting upon freshly laid plaster before it dries—progressed step by step until on the walls of the caves at Ajanta* it reached a perfection never excelled even by Giotto or Leonardo. These temples were carved out of the rocky face of a mountain-side at various periods from the first to the seventh century A.D. For centuries they were lost to history and human memory after the decay of Buddhism; the jungle grew about them and almost buried them; bats, snakes and other beasts made their home there, and a thousand varieties of birds and insects fouled the paintings with their waste. In 1819 Europeans stumbled into the ruins, and were amazed to find on the walls frescoes that are now ranked among the masterpieces of the world's art.[20]

The temples have been called caves, for in most cases they are cut into the mountains. Cave No. XVI, for example, is an excavation sixty-five feet

---

* Near the village of Fardapur, in the native state of Hyderabad.

each way, upheld by twenty pillars; alongside the central hall are sixteen monastic cells; a porticoed veranda adorns the front, and a sanctuary hides in the back. Every wall is covered with frescoes. In 1879 sixteen of the twenty-nine temples contained paintings; by 1910 the frescoes in ten of these sixteen had been destroyed by exposure, and those in the remaining six had been mutilated by inept attempts at restoration.[21] Once these frescoes were brilliant with red, green, blue and purple pigments; nothing survives of the colors now except low-toned and blackened surfaces. Some of the paintings, thus obscured by time and ignorance, seem coarse and grotesque to us, who cannot read the Buddhist legends with Buddhist hearts; others are at once powerful and graceful, a revelation of the skill of craftsmen whose names perished long before their work.

Despite these depredations, Cave I is still rich in masterpieces. Here, on one wall, is (probably) a *Bodhisattwa*—a Buddhist saint entitled to *Nirvana*, but choosing, instead, repeated rebirths in order to minister to men. Never has the sadness of understanding been more profoundly portrayed;[22] one wonders which is finer or deeper—this, or Leonardo's kindred study of the head of Christ.* On another wall of the same temple is a study of Shiva and his wife Parvati, dressed in jewelry.[23] Nearby is a painting of four deer, tender with the Buddhist sympathy for animals; and on the ceiling is a design still alive with delicately drawn flowers and fowl.[24] On a wall of Cave XVII is a graceful representation, now half destroyed, of the god Vishnu, with his retinue, flying down from heaven to attend some event in the life of Buddha;[25] on another wall is a schematic but colorful portrait of a princess and her maids.[26] Mingled with these *chef-d'œuvres* are crowded frescoes of apparently poor workmanship, describing the youth, flight and temptation of Buddha.[27]

But we cannot judge these works in their original form from what survives of them today; and doubtless there are clues to their appreciation that are not revealed to alien souls. Even the Occidental, however, can admire the nobility of the subject, the majestic scope of the plan, the unity of the composition, the clearness, simplicity and decisiveness of the line, and—among many details—the astonishing perfection of that bane of all artists, the hands. Imagination can picture the artist-priests† who prayed in these cells and perhaps painted these walls and ceilings with fond and pious art while Europe lay buried in her early-medieval darkness. Here at Ajanta religious devotion fused architecture, sculpture and painting into a happy unity, and produced one of the sovereign monuments of Hindu art.

---

* Among his preliminary sketches for *The Last Supper*.
† A supposition. We do not know who painted these frescoes.

When their temples were closed or destroyed by Huns and Moslems the Hindus turned their pictorial skill to lesser forms. Among the Rajputs a school of painters arose who recorded in delicate miniatures the episodes of the *Mahabharata* and the *Ramayana*, and the heroic deeds of the Rajputana chieftains; often they were mere outlines, but always they were instinct with life, and perfect in design. There is, in the Museum of Fine Arts at Boston, a charming example of this style, symbolizing one of the *ragas* of music by means of graceful women, a stately tower, and a lowering sky.[29] Another example, in the Art Institute of Detroit, represents with unique delicacy a scene from the *Gita-Govinda*.[30] The human figures in these and other Hindu paintings were rarely drawn from models; the artist visualized them out of imagination and memory. He painted, usually, in brilliant *tempera* upon a paper surface; he used fine brushes made from the most delicate hairs that he could get from the squirrel, the camel, the goat or the mongoose;[31] and he achieved a refinement of line and decoration that delight even the foreign and inexpert eye.

Similar work was done in other parts of India, especially in the state of Kangra.[32] Another variety of the same *genre* developed under the Moguls at Delhi. Rising out of Persian calligraphy and the art of illuminating manuscripts, this style grew into a form of aristocratic portraiture corresponding, in its refinement and exclusiveness, to the chamber music that flourished at the court. Like the Rajput school, the Mogul painters strove for delicacy of line, sometimes using a brush made from a single hair; and they, too, rivaled one another in the skilful portrayal of the hand. But they put more color into their drawings, and less mysticism; they seldom touched religion or mythology; they confined themselves to the earth, and were as realistic as caution would permit. Their subjects were living men and women of imperial position and temper, not noted for humility; one after another these dignitaries sat for their portraits, until the picture galleries of that royal dilettante, Jehangir, were filled with the likenesses of every important ruler or courtier since the coming of Akbar to the throne. Akbar was the first of his dynasty to encourage painting; at the end of his reign, if we may believe Abu-l Fazl, there were a hundred masters in Delhi, and a thousand amateurs.[33] Jehangir's intelligent patronage developed the art, and widened its field from portraiture to the representation of hunting scenes and other natural backgrounds for the human figure—which still dominated the picture; one minature shows the Emperor himself almost in the claws of a lion that has clambered upon the rump of the imperial elephant and is reaching for the royal flesh, while an attendant realistically takes to his heels.[34] Under Shah Jehan the art reached its height, and began to decline; as in the case of Japanese prints, the widened popularity of the form gave it at once a wider audience and a less exacting taste.[35] Aurangzeb, by restoring the strict rule of Islam against images, completed the decay.

Through the intelligent beneficence of the Mogul kings Indian painters enjoyed at Delhi a prosperity that they had not known for many centuries. The guild of painters, which had kept itself alive from Buddhist times, renewed its youth, and some of its members escaped from the anonymity with which time's forgetfulness, and Hindu negligence of the individual, cover most Indian art. Out of seventeen artists considered preëminent in Akbar's reign, thirteen were Hindus.[36] The most favored of all the painters at the great Mogul's court was Dasvanth, whose lowly origin as the son of a palanquin-bearer aroused no prejudice against him in the eyes of the Emperor. The youth was eccentric, and insisted on drawing pictures wherever he went, and on whatever surface he found at hand. Akbar recognized his genius, and had his own drawing-master teach him. The boy became in time the greatest master of his age; but at the height of his fame he stabbed himself to death.[27]

Wherever men do things, other men will arise who will explain to them how things should be done. The Hindus, whose philosophy did not exalt logic, loved logic none the less, and delighted to formulate in the strictest and most rational rules the subtle procedure of every art. So, early in our era, the *Sandanga*, or "Six Limbs of Indian Painting," laid down, like a later and perhaps imitative Chinese,* six canons of excellence in pictorial art: (1) the knowledge of appearances; (2) correct perception, measure and structure; (3) the action of feelings on forms; (4) the infusion of grace, or artistic representation; (5) similitude; and (6) an artistic use of brush and colors. Later an elaborate esthetic code appeared, the *Shilpa-shastra*, in which the rules and traditions of each art were formulated for all time. The artist, we are told, should be learned in the *Vedas*, "delighting in the worship of God, faithful to his wife, avoiding strange women, and piously acquiring a knowledge of various sciences."[38]

We shall be helped in understanding Oriental painting if we remember, first, that it seeks to represent not things but feelings, and not to represent but to suggest; that it depends not on color but on line; that it aims to create esthetic and religious emotion rather than to reproduce reality; that it is interested in the "soul" or "spirit" of men and things, rather than in their material forms. Try as we will, however, we shall hardly find in Indian painting the technical development, or range and depth of significance, that characterize the pictorial art of China and Japan. Certain Hindus explain

---

* Hsieh Ho; cf. p. 752 below. The *Sandanga* is of uncertain date, being known to us through a thirteenth-century commentary.

this very fancifully: painting decayed among them, they tell us, because it was too easy, it was not a sufficiently laborious gift to offer to the gods.[39] Perhaps pictures, so mortally frail and transitory, did not quite satisfy the craving of the Hindu for some lasting embodiment of his chosen deity. Slowly, as Buddhism reconciled itself to imagery, and the Brahmanic shrines increased and multiplied, painting was replaced by statuary, color and line by lasting stone.

IV. SCULPTURE

Primitive—Buddhist—Gandhara—Gupta—"Colonial"—Estimate

We cannot trace the history of Indian sculpture from the statuettes of Mohenjo-daro to the age of Ashoka, but we may suspect that this is a gap in our knowledge rather than in the art. Perhaps India, temporarily impoverished by the Aryan invasions, reverted from stone to wood for its statuary; or perhaps the Aryans were too intent upon war to care for art. The oldest stone figures surviving in India go back only to Ashoka; but these show a skill so highly developed that we cannot doubt that the art had then behind it many centuries in growth.[40] Buddhism set up definite obstacles to both painting and statuary in its aversion to idolatry and secular imagery: Buddha forbade "imaginative drawings painted in figures of men and women";[41] and under this almost Mosaic prohibition pictorial and plastic art suffered in India as it had done in Judea and was to do in Islam. Gradually this Puritanism seems to have relaxed as Buddhism yielded its austerity and partook more and more of the Dravidian passion for symbol and myth. When the art of carving appears again (ca. 200 B.C.), in the stone bas-reliefs on the "rails" enclosing the Buddhist "stupas" or burial mounds at Bodh-gaya and Bharhut, it is as a component part of an architectural design rather than as an independent art; and to the end of its history Indian sculpture remained for the most part an accessory to architecture, and preferred relief to carving in the round.* In the Jain temples at Mathura, and the Buddhist shrines at Amaravati and Ajanta, this art of relief reached a high point of perfection. The rail at Amaravati, says a learned authority, "is the most voluptuous and the most delicate flower of Indian sculpture."[42]

Meanwhile, in the province of Gandhara in northwestern India, another type of sculpture was developing under the patronage of the Kushan kings. This mysterious dynasty, which came suddenly out of the north—probably

---

* An exception outweighing this generalization was the copper colossus of Buddha, eighty feet high, which Yuan Chwang saw at Pataliputra; through Yuan and other Far Eastern pilgrims to India this may have been one ancestor of the great Buddhas at Nara and Kamakura in Japan.

from Hellenized Bactria—brought with it a tendency to imitate Greek forms. The *Mahayana* Buddhism that captured the council of Kanishka opened the way by rescinding the prohibition of imagery. Under the tutelage of Greek instructors Hindu sculpture took on for a time a smooth Hellenistic face; Buddha was transformed into the likeness of Apollo, and became an aspirant to Olympus; drapery began to flow about Hindu deities and saints in the style of Pheidias' pediments, and pious *Bodhisattwas* rubbed elbows with jolly drunken Sileni.[43] Idealized and almost effeminate representations of the Master and his disciples were offset with horrible examples of decadent Greek realism, like the starving Buddha of Lahore, in which every rib and tendon is shown underneath a feminine face with ladylike coiffure and masculine beard.[44] This Greco-Buddhist art impressed Yuan Chwang, and through him and later pilgrims found its way into China, Korea and Japan;[45] but it had little influence upon the sculptural forms and methods of India itself. When, after some centuries of flourishing activity, the Gandhara school passed away, Indian art came to life again under Hindu rulers, took up the traditions left by the native artists of Bharhut, Amaravati and Mathura, and paid scant attention to the Greek interlude at Gandhara.

Sculpture, like nearly everything else in India, prospered under the Gupta line. Buddhism had now forgotten its hostility to images; and a reinvigorated Brahmanism encouraged symbolism and the adornment of religion with every art. The Mathura Museum holds a highly finished stone Buddha, with meditative eyes, sensual lips, too graceful a form, and clumsy Cubist feet. The Sarnath Museum has another stone Buddha, in the seated pose that was destined to dominate Buddhist sculpture; here the effect of peaceful contemplation and a pious kindliness is perfectly revealed. At Karachi is a small bronze Brahma, scandalously like Voltaire.[46]

Everywhere in India, in the millennium before the coming of the Moslems, the art of the sculptor, though limited as well as inspired by its subservience to architecture and religion, produced masterpieces. The pretty statue of Vishnu from Sultanpur,[47] the finely chiseled statue of Padmapani,[48] the gigantic three-faced Shiva (commonly called "*Trimurti*") carved in deep relief in the caves at Elephanta,[49] the almost Praxitelean stone statue worshiped at Nokkas as the goddess Rukmini,[50] the graceful dancing Shiva, or *Nataraja*, cast in bronze by the Chola artist-artisans of Tanjore,[51] the lovely stone deer of Mamallapuram,[52] and the handsome Shiva of Perur[53]—these are evidences of the spread of the carver's art into every province of India.

The same motives and methods crossed the frontiers of India proper, and produced masterpieces from Turkestan and Cambodia to Java and Ceylon. The student will find examples in the stone head, apparently of a boy, dug up from the sands of Khotan by Sir Aurel Stein's expedition;[54] the head of

Buddha from Siam;[55] the Egyptianly fine "Harihara" of Cambodia;[56] the magnificent bronzes of Java;[57] the Gandhara-like head of Shiva from Prambanam;[58] the supremely beautiful female figure ("Prajnaparamita") now in the Leyden Museum; the perfect *Bodhisattwa* in the Glyptothek at Copenhagen;[59] the calm and powerful Buddha,[60] and the finely chiseled Avalokiteshvara ("The Lord who looks down with pity upon all men"),[61] both from the great Javanese temple of Borobudur; or the massive primitive Buddha,[62] and the lovely "moonstone" doorstep,[63] of Anuradhapura in Ceylon. This dull list of works that must have cost the blood of many men in many centuries will suggest the influence of Hindu genius on the cultural colonies of India.

We find it hard to like this sculpture at first sight; only profound and modest minds can leave their environment behind them when they travel. We should have to be Hindus, or citizens of those countries that accepted the cultural leadership of India, to understand the symbolism of these statues, the complex functions and superhuman powers denoted by these multiple arms and legs, the terrible realism of these fanciful figures, expressing the Hindu sense of supernatural forces irrationally creative, irrationally fertile and irrationally destructive. It shocks us to find that everybody in Hindu villages is thin, and everybody in Hindu sculpture is fat; we forget that the statues are mostly of gods, who received the first fruits of the land. We are disconcerted on discovering that the Hindus colored their statuary, whereby we reveal our unawareness of the fact that the Greeks did likewise, and that something of the classic nobility of the Pheidian deities is due to the accidental disappearance of their paint. We are displeased at the comparative paucity of female figures in the Indian gallery; we mourn over the subjection of women which this seems to indicate, and never reflect that the cult of the nude female is not the indispensable basis of plastic art, that the profoundest beauty of woman may be more in motherhood than in youth, more in Demeter than in Aphrodite. Or we forget that the sculptor carved not what he dreamed of so much as what the priests laid down; that every art, in India, belonged to religion rather than to art, and was the handmaiden of theology. Or we take too seriously figures intended by the sculptor to be caricatures, or jests, or ogres designed to frighten away evil spirits; if we turn away from them in horror we merely attest the fulfilment of their aim.

Nevertheless, the sculpture of India never quite acquired the grace of her literature, or the sublimity of her architecture, or the depth of her philosophy; it mirrored chiefly the confused and uncertain insight of her religions. It excelled the sculpture of China and Japan, but it never equaled the cold perfection of Egyptian statuary, or the living and tempting beauty of Greek marble. To understand even its assumptions we should have to renew in our hearts the earnest and trusting piety of medieval days. In truth we ask too much of sculpture, as of painting, in India; we judge them as if they had been there, as here, independent arts, when in truth we have artificially isolated them for treatment according to our traditional rubrics and norms. If we could see them as the Hindu knows them, as integrated parts of the unsurpassed architecture of his country, we should have made some modest beginning towards understanding Indian art.

V. ARCHITECTURE

1. Hindu Architecture

Before Ashoka — Ashokan — Buddhist — Jain — The masterpieces of the north — Their destruction — The southern style— Monolithic temples — Structural temples

Nothing remains of Indian architecture before Ashoka's time. We have the brick ruins of Mohenjo-daro, but apparently the buildings of Vedic and Buddhist India were of wood, and Ashoka seems to have been the first to use stone for architectural purposes.[64] We hear, in the literature, of seven-storied structures,[65] and of palaces of some magnificence, but not a trace of them survives. Megasthenes describes the imperial residences of Chandragupta as superior to anything in Persia except Persepolis, on whose model they seem to have been designed.[66] This Persian influence persisted till Ashoka's time; it appears in the ground-plan of his palace, which corresponded with the "Hall of a Hundred Columns" at Persepolis;[67] and it shows again in the fine pillar of Ashoka at Lauriya, crowned with a lion-capital.

With the conversion of Ashoka to Buddhism, Indian architecture began to throw off this alien influence, and to take its inspiration and it symbols from the new religion. The transition is evident in the great capital which is all that now remains of another Ashokan pillar, at Sarnath;[68] here, in a composition of astonishing perfection, ranked by Sir John Marshall as equal to "anything of its kind in the ancient world,"[69] we have four powerful lions, standing back to back on guard, and thoroughly Persian in form and countenance; but beneath them is a frieze of well-carved figures including so Indian a favorite as the elephant, and so Indian a symbol as the Buddhist Wheel of the Law; and under the frieze is a great stone lotus, formerly mistaken for a Persian bell-capital, but now accepted as the most ancient, universal and characteristic of all the symbols in Indian art.[70] Represented upright, with the petals turned down and the pistil or seed-vessel showing, it stood for the womb of the world; or, as one of the fairest of nature's manifestations, it served as the throne of a god. The lotus or water-lily symbol migrated with Buddhism, and permeated the art of China and Japan. A like form, used as a design for windows and doors, became the "horseshoe arch" of Ashokan vaults and domes, originally derived from the "covered wagon" curvature of Bengali thatched roofs supported by rods of bent bamboo.[71]

The religious architecture of Buddhist days has left us a few ruined temples and a large number of "topes" and "rails." The "tope" or "stupa" was in early days a burial mound; under Buddhism it became a memorial shrine, usually housing the relics of a Buddhist saint. Most often the tope took the form of a dome of brick, crowned with a spire, and surrounded with a stone rail carved with bas-reliefs. One of the oldest topes is at Bharhut; but the reliefs there are primitively coarse. The most ornate of the extant rails is at Amaravati; here 17,000 square feet were covered with minute reliefs of a workmanship so excellent that Fergusson judged this rail to be "probably the most remarkable monument in India."[72] The best known of the *stupas* is the Sanchi tope, one of a group at Bhilsa in Bhopal. The stone gates apparently imitate ancient wooden forms, and anticipate the *pailus* or *toriis* that usually mark the approach to the temples of the Far East. Every foot of space on pillars, capitals, crosspieces and supports is cut into a wilderness of plant, animal, human and divine forms. On a pillar of the eastern gateway is a delicate carving of a perennial Buddhist symbol—the Bodhi-tree, scene of the Master's enlightenment; on the same gateway, gracefully spanning a bracket, is a sensuous goddess (a *Yakshi*) with heavy limbs, full hips, slim waist, and abounding breasts.[73]

While the dead saints slept in the topes, the living monks cut into the mountain rocks temples where they might live in isolation, sloth and peace, secure from the elements and from the glare and heat of the sun. We may judge the strength of the religious impulse in India by noting that over twelve hundred of these cave-temples remain of the many thousands that were built in the early centuries of our era, partly for Jains and Brahmans, but mostly for Buddhist communities. Often the entrance of these *viharas* (monasteries) was a simple portal in the form of a "horseshoe" or lotus arch; sometimes, as at Nasik, it was an ornate façade of strong columns, animal capitals, and patiently carved architrave; often it was adorned with pillars, stone screens or porticoes of admirable design.[74] The interior included a *chaitya* or assembly hall, with colonnades dividing nave from aisles, cells for the monks on either side, and an altar, bearing relics, at the inner end.* One of the oldest of these cave-temples, and perhaps the finest now surviving, is at Karle, between Poona and Bombay; here *Hinayana* Buddhism achieved its *chef-d'œuvre.*

---

* The correspondence of this interior with that of Christian churches has suggested a possible influence of Hindu styles upon early Christian architecture.[74a]

The caves at Ajanta, besides being the hiding-place of the greatest of Buddhist paintings, rank with Karle as examples of that composite art, half architecture and half sculpture, which characterizes the temples of India. Caves I and II have spacious assembly halls whose ceilings, cut and painted in sober yet elegant designs, are held up by powerful fluted pillars square at the base, round at the top, ornamented with flowery bands, and crowned with majestic capitals;[75] Cave XIX is distinguished by a façade richly decorated with adipose statuary and complex bas-reliefs;[76] in Cave XXVI gigantic columns rise to a frieze crowded with figures which only the greatest religious and artistic zeal could have carved in such detail.[77] Ajanta can hardly be refused the title of one of the major works in the history of art.

Of other Buddhist temples still existing in India the most impressive is the great tower at Bodh-gaya, significant for its thoroughly Gothic arches, and yet dating, apparently, back to the first century A.D.[78] All in all, the remains of Buddhist architecture are fragmentary, and their glory is more sculptural than structural; a lingering Puritanism, perhaps, kept them externally forbidding and bare. The Jains gave a more concentrated devotion to architecture, and during the eleventh and twelfth centuries their temples were the finest in India. They did not create a style of their own, being content to copy at first (as at Elura) the Buddhist plan of excavating temples in the mountain rocks, then the Vishnu or Shiva type of temples rising usually in a walled group upon a hill. These, too, were externally simple, but inwardly complex and rich—a happy symbol of the modest life. Piety placed statue after statue of Jain heroes in these shrines, until in the group at Shatrunjaya Fergusson counted 6449 figures.[79]

The Jain temple at Aihole is built almost in Greek style, with rectangular form, external colonnades, a portico, and a cell or central chamber within.[80] At Khajuraho Jains, Vaishnavites and Shivaites, as if to illustrate Hindu tolerance, built in close proximity some twenty-eight temples; among them the almost perfect Temple of Parshwanath[81] rises in cone upon cone to a majestic height, and shelters on its carved surfaces a veritable city of Jain saints. On Mt. Abu, lifted four thousand feet above the desert, the Jains built many temples, of which two survivors, the temples of Vimala and Tejahpala, are the greatest achievement of this sect in the field of art. The dome of the Tejahpala shrine is one of those overwhelming experiences which doom all writing about art to impotence and futility.[82] The Temple of Vimala, built entirely of white marble, is a maze of irregular pillars, joined with fanciful brackets to a more simple carved entablature; above is a marble dome too opulent in statuary, but carved into a stone lacework of moving magnificence, "finished," says Fergusson, "with a delicacy of detail and appropriateness of ornament which is probably unsurpassed by any similar example to be found anywhere else. Those introduced by the Gothic architects in Henry VII's Chapel at Westminster, or at Oxford, are coarse and clumsy in comparison."[83]

In these Jain temples, and their contemporaries, we see the transition from the circular form of the Buddhist shrine to the tower style of medieval India. The nave, or pillar-enclosed interior, of the assembly hall is taken outdoors, and made into a *mandapam* or porch; behind this is the cell; and above the cell rises, in successively receding levels, the carved and complicated tower. It was on this plan that the Hindu temples of the north were built. The most impressive of these is the group at Bhuvaneshwara, in the province of Orissa; and the finest of the group is the Rajarani Temple erected to Vishnu in the eleventh century A.D. It is a gigantic tower formed of juxtaposed semi-circular pillars covered with statuary and surmounted by receding layers of stone, the whole inward-curving tower ending in a great circular crown and a spire. Nearby is the Lingaraja Temple, larger than the Rajarani, but not so beautiful; nevertheless every inch of the surface has felt the sculptor's chisel, so that the cost of the carving has been reckoned at three times the cost of the structure.[84] The Hindu expressed his piety not merely by the imposing grandeur of his temples, but by their patiently worked detail; nothing was too good for the god.

It would be dull to list, without specific description and photographic representation, the other masterpieces of Hindu building in the north. And yet no record of Indian civilization could leave unnoticed the temples of Surya at Kanarak and Mudhera, the tower of Jagannath Puri, the lovely gateway at Vadnagar,[85] the massive temples of Sas-Bahu and Teli-ka-Mandir at Gwalior,[86] the palace of Rajah Man Sing, also at Gwalior,[87] and the Tower of Victory at Chitor.[88] Standing out from the mass are the Shivaite temples at Khajuraho, while in the same city the dome of the porch of the Khanwar Math Temple shows again the masculine strength of Indian architecture, and the richness and patience of Indian carving.[89] Even in its ruins the Temple of Shiva at Elephanta, with its massive fluted columns, its "mushroom" capitals, its unsurpassed reliefs, and its powerful statuary,[90] suggests to us an age of national vigor and artistic skill of which hardly the memory lives today.

We shall never be able to do justice to Indian art, for ignorance and fanaticism have destroyed its greatest achievements, and have half ruined the rest. At Elephanta the Portuguese certified their piety by smashing statuary and bas-reliefs in unrestrained barbarity; and almost everywhere in the north the Moslems brought to the ground those triumphs of Indian architecture, of the fifth and sixth centuries, which tradition ranks as far superior to the later works that arouse our wonder and admiration today. The Moslems decapitated statues, and tore them limb from limb; they appropriated for their mosques, and in great measure imitated, the graceful pillars of the Jain temples.[91] Time and fanaticism joined in the destruction, for the orthodox Hindus abandoned and neglected temples that had been profaned by the touch of alien hands.[92]

We may guess at the lost grandeur of north Indian architecture by the powerful edifices that still survive in the south, where Moslem rule entered only in minor degree, and after some habituation to India had softened Mohammedan hatred of Hindu ways. Further, the great age of temple architecture in the south came in the sixteenth and seventeenth centuries, after Akbar had tamed the Moslems and taught them some appreciation of Indian art. Consequently the south is rich in temples, usually superior to those that remain standing in the north, and more massive and impressive; Fergusson counted some thirty "Dravidian" or southern temples any one of which, in his estimate, must have cost as much as an English cathedral.[93] The south adapted the styles of the north by prefacing the *mandapam* or porch with a *gopuram* or gate, and supporting the porch with a lavish multiplicity of pillars. It played fondly with a hundred symbols, from the *swastika*,* emblem of the sun and the wheel of life, through a very menagerie of sacred animals. The snake, through its moulting, symbolized reincarnation; the bull was the enviable paragon of procreative power; the *linga*, or phallus, represented the generative excellence of Shiva, and often determined the form of the temple itself.

Three elements composed the structural plan of these southern temples: the gateway, the pillared porch, and the tower (*vimana*), which contained the main assembly hall or cell. With occasional exceptions like the palace of Tirumala Nayyak at Madura, all this south Indian architecture was ecclesiastical. Men did not bother to build magnificently for themselves, but gave their art to the priests and the gods; no circumstance could better show how spontaneously theocratic was the real government of India. Of the many buildings raised by the Chalukyan kings and their people, nothing remains but temples. Only a Hindu pietist rich in words could describe the lovely symmetry of the shrine at Ittagi, in Hydera-

* *Swastika* is a Sanskrit word, from *su*, well, and *asti*, being. This eternally recurring symbol appears among a great variety of peoples, primitive and modern, usually as a sign of well-being or good luck.

bad;[94][*] or the temple at Somnathpur in Mysore,[96] in which gigantic masses of stone are carved with the delicacy of lace; or the Hoyshaleshwara Temple at Halebid,[97] also in Mysore—"one of the buildings," says Fergusson, "on which the advocate of Hindu architecture would desire to take his stand." Here, he adds, "the artistic combination of horizontal with vertical lines, and the play of outline and of light and shade, far surpass anything in Gothic art. The effects are just what the medieval architects were often aiming at, but which they never attained so perfectly as was done at Halebid."[98]

If we marvel at the laborious piety that could carve eighteen hundred feet of frieze in the Halebid temple, and could portray in them two thousand elephants each different from all the rest,[99] what shall we say of the patience and courage that could undertake to cut a complete temple out of the solid rock? But this was a common achievement of the Hindu artisans. At Mamallapuram, on the east coast near Madras, they carved several *rathas* or pagodas, of which the fairest is the *Dharma-raja-ratha*, or monastery for the highest discipline. At Elura, a place of religious pilgrimage in Hyderabad, Buddhists, Jains and orthodox Hindus vied in excavating out of the mountain rock great monolithic temples of which the supreme example is the Hindu shrine of Kailasha[100]—named after Shiva's mythological paradise in the Himalayas. Here the tireless builders cut a hundred feet down into the stone to isolate the block—250 by 160 feet— that was to be the temple; then they carved the walls into powerful pillars, statues and bas-reliefs; then they chiseled out the interior, and lavished there the most amazing art: let the bold fresco of "The Lovers"[101] serve as a specimen. Finally, their architectural passion still unspent, they carved a series of chapels and monasteries deep into the rock on three sides of the quarry.[102] Some Hindus[103] consider the Kailasha Temple equal to any achievement in the history of art.

Such a structure, however, was a *tour de force*, like the Pyramids, and must have cost the sweat and blood of many men. Either the guilds or the masters never tired, for they scattered through every province of southern India gigantic shrines so numerous that the bewildered student or traveler loses their individual quality in the sum of their number and their power.

---

* Here, says Meadows Taylor, "the carving on some of the pillars, and of the lintels and architraves of the doors, is quite beyond description. No chased work in silver or gold could possibly be finer. By what tools this very hard, tough stone could have been wrought and polished as it is, is not at all intelligible at the present day."[95]

At Pattadakal Queen Lokamahadevi, one of the wives of the Chalukyan King Vikramaditya II, dedicated to Shiva the Virupaksha Temple, which ranks high among the great fanes of India.[104] At Tanjore, south of Madras, the Chola King Rajaraja the Great, after conquering all southern India and Ceylon, shared his spoils with Shiva by raising to him a stately temple designed to represent the generative symbol of the god.*[105] Near Trich-inopoly, west of Tanjore, the devotees of Vishnu erected on a lofty hill the Shri Rangam Temple, whose distinctive feature was a many-pillared *mandapam* in the form of a "Hall of a Thousand Columns," each column a single block of granite, elaborately carved; the Hindu artisans were yet at work completing the temple when they were scattered, and their labors ended, by the bullets of Frenchmen and Englishmen fighting for the pos-session of India.[106] Nearby, at Madura, the brothers Muttu and Tiruma-la Nayyak erected to Shiva a spacious shrine with another Hall of a Thousand Columns, a Sacred Tank, and ten *gopurams* or gateways, of which four rise to a great height and are carved into a wilderness of statuary. These structures form together one of the most impressive sights in India; we may judge from such fragmentary survivals the rich and spacious architecture of the Vijayanagar kings. Finally, at Ramesh-varam, amid the archipelago of isles that pave "Adam's Bridge" from India to Ceylon, the Brahmans of the south reared through five centuries (1200-1769 A.D.) a temple whose perimeter was graced with the most imposing of all corridors or porticoes—four thousand feet of double colonnades, exquisitely carved, and designed to give cool shade, and inspiring vistas of sun and sea, to the millions of pilgrims who to this day find their way from distant cities to lay their hopes and griefs upon the knees of the care-less gods.

2. "Colonial" Architecture
Ceylon—Java—Cambodia—The Khmers—Their religion—Angkor —Fall of the Khmers—Siam—Burma

Meanwhile Indian art had accompanied Indian religion across straits and frontiers into Ceylon, Java, Cambodia, Siam, Burma, Tibet, Khotan, Turkestan, Mongolia, China, Korea and Japan; "in Asia all roads lead

---

* The summit of the temple is a single block of stone twenty-five feet square, and weighing some eighty tons. According to Hindu tradition it was raised into place by be-ing drawn up an incline four miles long. Forced labor was probably employed in such works, instead of "man-enslaving" machinery.

from India."[107] Hindus from the Ganges valley settled Ceylon in the fifth century before Christ; Ashoka, two hundred years later, sent a son and a daughter to convert the population to Buddhism; and though the teeming island had to fight for fifteen centuries against Tamil invasions, it maintained a rich culture until it was taken over by the British in 1815.

Singhalese art began with *dagobas*—domed relic shrines like the *stupas* of the Buddhist north; it passed to great temples like that whose ruins mark the ancient capital, Anuradhapura; it produced some of the finest of the Buddha statues,[108] and a great variety of *objets d'art;* and it came to an end, for the time being, when the last great king of Ceylon, Kirti Shri Raja Singha, built the "Temple of the Tooth" at Kandy. The loss of independence has brought decadence to the upper classes, and the patronage and taste that provide a necessary stimulus and restraint for the artist have disappeared from Ceylon.[109]

Strange to say, the greatest of Buddhist temples—some students would call it the greatest of all temples anywhere[110]—is not in India but in Java. In the eighth century the Shailendra dynasty of Sumatra conquered Java, established Buddhism as the official religion, and financed the building of the massive fane of Borobudur (i.e., "Many Buddhas").[111] The temple proper is of moderate size, and of peculiar design—a small domical *stupa* surrounded by seventy-two smaller topes arranged about it in concentric circles. If this were all, Borobudur would be nothing; what constitutes the grandeur of the structure is the pedestal, four hundred feet square, an immense *mastaba* in seven receding stages. At every turn there are niches for statuary; 436 times the sculptors of Borobudur thought fit to carve the figure of Buddha. Still discontent, they cut into the walls of the stages three miles of bas-reliefs, depicting the legendary birth, youth and enlightenment of the Master, and with such skill that these reliefs are among the finest in Asia.[112] With this powerful Buddhist shrine, and the Brahmanical temples nearby at Prambanam, Javanese architecture reached its zenith, and quickly decayed. The island became for a time a maritime power, rose to wealth and luxury, and supported many poets. But in 1479 the Moslems began to people this tropical Paradise, and from that time it produced no art of consequence. The Dutch pounced upon it in 1595, and consumed it, province by province during the following century, until their control was complete.

Only one Hindu temple surpasses that of Borobudur, and it, too, is far from India—lost, indeed, in a distant jungle that covered it for centuries. In 1858 a French explorer, picking his way through the upper valley of the Mekong River, caught a glimpse, through trees and brush, of a sight that seemed to him miraculous: an enormous temple, incredibly majestic in design, stood amid the forest, intertwined and almost covered with shrubbery and foliage. That day he saw many temples, some of them already overgrown or split apart by trees; it seemed that he had arrived just in time to forestall the triumph of the wilderness over these works of men. Other Europeans had to come and corroborate his tale before Henri Mouhot was believed; then scientific expeditions descended upon the once silent retreat, and a whole school at Paris (*L'École de l'Extrême Orient*) devoted itself to charting and studying the find. Today Angkor Wat is one of the wonders of the world.*

At the beginning of the Christian era Indo-China, or Cambodia, was inhabited by a people essentially Chinese, partly Tibetan, called Khambujas or Khmers. When Kublai Khan's ambassador, Tcheou-ta-Kouan, visited the Khmer capital, Angkor Thom, he found a strong government ruling a nation that had drawn wealth out of its rice-paddies and its sweat. The king, Tcheou reported, had five wives: "one special, and four others for the cardinal points of the compass," with some four thousand concubines for more precise readings.[114] Gold and jewelry abounded; pleasure-boats dotted the lake; the streets of the capital were filled with chariots, curtained palanquins, elephants in rich caparison, and a population of almost a million souls. Hospitals were attached to the temples, and each had its corps of nurses and physicians.[115]

Though the people were Chinese, their culture was Hindu. Their religion was based upon a primitive worship of the serpent, Naga, whose fanlike head appears everywhere in Cambodian art; then the great gods of the Hindu triad—Brahma, Vishnu and Shiva—entered through Burma; almost at the same time Buddha came, and was joined with Vishnu and Shiva as a favorite divinity of the Khmers. Inscriptions tell of the enormous quantity of rice, butter and rare oils contributed daily by the people to the ministrants of the gods.[116]

To Shiva the Khmers, toward the end of the ninth century, dedicated the oldest of their surviving temples—the Bayon, now a forbidding ruin half overgrown with tenacious vegetation. The stones, laid without

---

* In 1604 a Portuguese missionary told of hunters reporting some ruins in the jungle, and another priest made a similar report in 1672; but no attention was paid to these statements.[113]

cement, have drawn apart in the course of a thousand years, stretching into ungodly grins the great faces of Brahma and Shiva which almost constitute the towers. Three centuries later the slaves and war-captives of the kings built Angkor Wat,[117] a masterpiece equal to the finest architectural achievements of the Egyptians, the Greeks, or the cathedral-builders of Europe. An enormous moat, twelve miles in length, surrounds the temple; over the moat runs a paved bridge guarded by dissuasive Nagas in stone; then an ornate enclosing wall; then spacious galleries, whose reliefs tell again the tales of the *Mahabharata* and the *Ramayana;* then the stately edifice itself, rising upon a broad base, by level after level of a terraced pyramid, to the sanctuary of the god, two hundred feet high. Here magnitude does not detract from beauty, but helps it to an imposing magnificence that startles the Western mind into some weak realization of the ancient grandeur once possessed by Oriental civilization. One sees in imagination the crowded population of the capital: the regimented slaves cutting, pulling and raising the heavy stones; the artisans carving reliefs and statuary as if time would never fail them; the priests deceiving and consoling the people; the *devadasis* (still pictured on the granite) deceiving the people and consoling the priests; the lordly aristocracy building palaces like the Phinean-Akas, with its spacious Terrace of Honor; and, raised above all by the labor of all, the powerful and ruthless kings.

The kings, needing many slaves, waged many wars. Often they won; but near the close of the thirteenth century—"in the middle of the way" of Dante's life—the armies of Siam defeated the Khmers, sacked their cities, and left their resplendent temples and palaces in ruins. Today a few tourists prowl among the loosened stones, and observe how patiently the trees have sunk their roots or insinuated their branches into the crevices of the rocks, slowly tearing them apart because stones cannot desire and grow. Tcheou-ta-Kouan speaks of the many books that were written by the people of Angkor, but not a page of this literature remains; like ourselves they wrote perishable thoughts upon perishable tissue, and all their immortals are dead. The marvelous reliefs show men and women wearing veils and nets to guard against mosquitoes and slimy, crawling things. The men and women are gone, surviving only on the stones. The mosquitoes and the lizards remain.

Nearby, in Siam, a people half Tibetan and half Chinese had gradually expelled the conquering Khmers, and had developed a civilization based upon

Hindu religion and art. After overcoming Cambodia the Siamese built a new capital, Ayuthia, on the site of an ancient city of the Khmers. From this seat they extended their sway until, about 1600, their empire included southern Burma, Cambodia, and the Malay Peninsula. Their trade reached to China on the east and to Europe on the west. Their artists made illuminated manuscripts, painted with lacquer on wood, fired porcelain in the Chinese style, embroidered beautiful silks, and occasionally carved statues of unique excellence.* Then, in the impartial rhythm of history, the Burmese captured Ayuthia, and destroyed it with all its art. In their new capital at Bangkok the Siamese built a great pagoda, whose excess of ornament cannot quite conceal the beauty of its design.

The Burmese were among the greatest builders in Asia. Coming down into these fertile fields from Mongolia and Tibet, they fell under Hindu influences, and from the fifth century onward produced an abundance of Buddhist, Vaishnavite and Shivaite statuary, and great *stupas* that culminated in the majestic temple of Ananda—one of the five thousand pagodas of their ancient capital, Pagan. Pagan was sacked by Kublai Khan, and for five hundred years the Burmese government vacillated from capital to capital. For a time Mandalay flourished as the center of Burma's life, and the home of artists who achieved beauty in many fields from embroidery and jewelry to the royal palace—which showed what they could do in the frail medium of wood.[118] The English, displeased with the treatment of their missionaries and their merchants, adopted Burma in 1886, and moved the capital to Rangoon, a city amenable to the disciplinary influence of the Imperial Navy. There the Burmese had built one of their finest shrines, the famous Shwe Dagon, that Golden Pagoda which draws to its spire millions upon millions of Burmese Buddhist pilgrims every year. For does not this temple contain the very hairs of Shakya-muni's head?

3. Moslem Architecture in India

The Afghan style — The Mogul style — Delhi—Agra — The Taj Mahal

The final triumph of Indian architecture came under the Moguls. The followers of Mohammed had proved themselves master builders wherever they had carried their arms—at Granada, at Cairo, at Jerusalem, at Baghdad; it was to be expected that this vigorous stock, after establishing itself securely in India, would raise upon the conquered soil mosques

---

* E.g., the lacquered stone Buddha in the Boston Museum of Fine Arts.

as resplendent as Omar's at Jerusalem, as massive as Hassan's at Cairo, and as delicate as the Alhambra. It is true that the "Afghan" dynasty used Hindu artisans, copied Hindu themes, and even appropriated the pillars of Hindu temples, for their architectural purposes, and that many mosques were merely Hindu temples rebuilt for Moslem prayer;[119] but this natural imitation passed quickly into a style so typically Moorish that one is surprised to find the Taj Mahal in India rather than in Persia, North Africa or Spain.

The beautiful Kutb-Minar* exemplifies the transition. It was part of a mosque begun at Old Delhi by Kutbu-d Din Aibak; it commemorated the victories of that bloody Sultan over the Hindus, and twenty-seven Hindu temples were dismembered to provide material for the mosque and the tower.[120] After withstanding the elements for seven centuries the great minaret—250 feet high, built of fine red sandstone, perfectly proportioned, and crowned on its topmost stages with white marble—is still one of the masterpieces of Indian technology and art. In general the Sultans of Delhi were too busy with killing to have much time for architecture, and such buildings as they have left us are mostly the tombs that they raised during their own lifetime as reminders that even they would die. The best example of these is the mausoleum of Sher Shah at Sasseram, in Bihar;[121] gigantic, solid, masculine, it was the last stage of the more virile Moorish manner before it softened into the architectural jewelry of the Mogul kings.

The tendency to unite the Mohammedan and the Hindu styles was fostered by the eclectic impartiality of Akbar; and the masterpieces that his artisans built for him wove Indian and Persian methods and *motifs* into an exquisite harmony symbolizing the frail merger of native and Moslem creeds in Akbar's synthetic faith. The first monument of his reign, the tomb erected by him near Delhi for his father Humayun, is already in a style of its own—simple in line, moderate in decoration, but foreshadowing in its grace the fairer edifices of Shah Jehan. At Fathpur-Sikri his artists built a city in which all the strength of the early Moguls merged with the refinement of the later emperors. A flight of steps leads up to an imposing portal in red sandstone, through whose lordly arch one passes into an enclosure filled with *chef-d'œuvres*. The

---

* I.e., minaret, from the Arabic *manarat*, a lamp or lighthouse.

just as well that native and European thieves coöperated in despoiling the tomb of its superabundant jewels, and of the golden railing, encrusted with precious stones, that once enclosed the sarcophagi of Jehan and his Queen. For Aurangzeb replaced the railing with an octagonal screen of almost transparent marble, carved into a miracle of alabaster lace; and it has seemed to some visitors that of all the minor and partial products of human art nothing has ever surpassed the beauty of this screen.

It is not the most sublime of all edifices, it is only the most beautiful. At any distance that hides its delicate details it is not imposing, but merely pleasing; only a nearer view reveals that its perfection has no proportion to its size. When in our hurried time we see enormous structures of a hundred stories raised in a year or two, and then consider how twenty-two thousand men toiled for twenty-two years on this little tomb, hardly a hundred feet high, we begin to sense the difference between industry and art. Perhaps the act of will involved in conceiving a building like the Taj Mahal was greater and profounder than the act of will of the greatest conqueror. If time were intelligent it would destroy everything else before the Taj, and would leave this evidence of man's alloyed nobility as the last man's consolation.

4. Indian Architecture and Civilization

Decay of Indian art—Hindu and Moslem architecture compared —General view of Indian civilization

Despite the screen, Aurangzeb was a misfortune for Mogul and Indian art. Dedicated fanatically to an exclusive religion, he saw in art nothing but idolatry and vanity. Already Shah Jehan had prohibited the erection of Hindu temples;[127] Aurangzeb not only continued the ban, but gave so economical a support to Moslem building that it, too, languished under his reign. Indian art followed him to the grave.

When we think of Indian architecture in summary and retrospect we find in it two themes, masculine and feminine, Hindu and Mohammedan, about which the structural symphony revolves. As, in the most famous of symphonies, the startling hammer-strokes of the opening bars are shortly followed by a strain of infinite delicacy, so in Indian architecture the over-powering monuments of the Hindu genius at Bodh-Gaya, Bhuvaneshwara, Madura and Tanjore are followed by the grace and melody of the Mogul style at Fathpur-Sikri, Delhi and Agra; and the two themes mingle in a confused elaboration to the end. It was said of the Moguls that they built like giants and finished liked jewelers; but this epigram might better have been applied to Indian architecture in general: the Hindus built like giants, and the Moguls ended like jewelers. Hindu architecture impresses us in its mass, Moorish architcture in its detail; the first had the sublimity of strength, the other had the perfection of beauty; the Hindus had passion and fertility, the Moors had taste and self-restraint. The Hindu covered his buildings with such exuberant statuary that one hesitates whether to class them as building or as sculpture; the Mohammedan abominated images, and confined himself to floral or geometrical decoration. The Hindus were the Gothic sculptor-architects of India's Middle Ages; the Moslems were the expatriated artists of the exotic Renaissance. All in all, the Hindu style reached greater heights, in proportion as sublimity excels loveliness; on second thought we perceive that Delhi Fort and the Taj Mahal, beside Angkor and Borobudur, are beautiful lyrics beside profound dramas—Petrarch beside Dante, Keats beside Shakespeare, Sappho beside Sophocles. One art is the graceful and partial expression of fortunate individuals, the other is the complete and powerful expression of a race.

Hence this little survey must conclude as it began, by confessing that none but a Hindu can quite appreciate the art of India, or write about it forgivably. To a European brought up on Greek and aristocratic canons of moderation and simplicity, this popular art of profuse ornament and wild complexity will seem at times almost primitive and barbarous. But that last word is the very adjective with which the classically-minded Goethe rejected Strasbourg's cathedral and the Gothic style; it is the reaction of reason to feeling, of rationalism to religion. Only a native believer can feel the majesty of the Hindu temples, for these were built to give not merely a form to beauty but a stimulus to piety and a pedestal to faith. Only our Middle Ages—only our Giottos and our Dantes—could understand India.

It is in these terms that we must view all Indian civilization—as the expression of a "medieval" people to whom religion is profounder than science, if only because religion accepts at the outset the eternity of human ignorance and the vanity of human power. In this piety lie the weakness and the strength of the Hindu: his superstition and his gentleness, his introversion and his insight, his backwardness and his depth, his weakness in war and his achievement in art. Doubtless his climate affected his religion, and coöperated with it to enfeeble him; therefore he yielded with fatalistic resignation to the Aryans, the Huns, the Moslems and the Europeans. History punished him for neglecting science; and when Clive's superior cannon slaughtered the native army at Plassey (1757), their roar announced the Industrial Revolution. In our time that Revolution will have its way with India, as it has written its will and character upon England, America, Germany, Russia and Japan; India, too, will have her capitalism and her socialism, her millionaires and her slums. The old civilization of India is finished. It began to die when the British came.

CHAPTER XXII

A Christian Epilogue

I. THE JOLLY BUCCANEERS

The arrival of the Europeans—The British Conquest—The Sepoy Mutiny—Advantages and disadvantages of British rule

IN many ways that civilization was already dead when Clive and Hastings discovered the riches of India. The long and disruptive reign of Aurangzeb, and the chaos and internal wars that followed it, left India ripe for reconquest; and the only question open to "manifest destiny" was as to which of the modernized powers of Europe should become its instrument. The French tried, and failed; they lost India, as well as Canada, at Rossbach and Waterloo. The English tried, and succeeded.

In 1498 Vasco da Gama, after a voyage of eleven months from Lisbon, anchored off Calicut. He was well received by the Hindu Raja of Malabar, who gave him a courteous letter to the King of Portugal: "Vasco da Gama, a nobleman of your household, has visited my kingdom, and has given me great pleasure. In my kingdom there is abundance of cinnamon, cloves, pepper, and precious stones. What I seek from your country is gold, silver, coral and scarlet." His Christian majesty answered by claiming India as a Portuguese colony, for reasons which the Raja was too backward to understand. To make matters clearer, Portugal sent a fleet to India, with instructions to spread Christianity and wage war. In the seventeenth century the Dutch arrived, and drove out the Portuguese; in the eighteenth the French and English came, and drove out the Dutch. Savage ordeals of battle decided which of them should civilize and tax the Hindus.

The East India Company had been founded in London in 1600 to buy cheap in India, and sell dear in Europe, the products of India and the East Indies.* As early as 1686 it announced its intention "to establish a large, well-grounded, sure English dominion in India for all time to come." It set up trading-posts at Madras, Calcutta and Bombay, fortified

---

* Goods bought for $2,000,000 in India were sold for $10,000,000 in England.[1] The stock of the Company rose to $32,000 a share.[2]

them, imported troops, fought battles, gave and took bribes, and exercised other functions of government. Clive gayly accepted "presents" amounting to $170,000 from Hindu rulers dependent upon his guns; pocketed from them, in addition, an annual tribute of $140,000; appointed Mir Jafar ruler of Bengal for $6,000,000; played one native prince against another, and gradually annexed their territories as the property of the East India Company; took to opium, was investigated and exonerated by Parliament, and killed himself (1774).' Warren Hastings, a man of courage, learning and ability, exacted contributions as high as a quarter of a million dollars from native princes to the coffers of the Company; accepted bribes to exact no more, exacted more, and annexed the states that could not pay; he occupied Oudh with his army, and sold the province to a prince for $2,500,000⁵—conquered and conqueror rivaled each other in venality. Such parts of India as were under the Company were subjected to a land tax of fifty per cent of the produce, and to other requisitions so numerous and severe that two-thirds of the population fled, while others sold their children to meet the rising rates.⁶ "Enormous fortunes," says Macaulay, "were rapidly accumulated at Calcutta, while thirty millions of human beings were reduced to the extremity of wretchedness. They had been accustomed to live under tyranny, but never under tyranny like this."⁷

By 1857 the crimes of the Company had so impoverished northeastern India that the natives broke out in desperate revolt. The British Government stepped in, suppressed the "mutiny," took over the captured territories as a colony of the Crown, paid the Company handsomely, and added the purchase price to the public debt of India.⁸ It was plain, blunt conquest, not to be judged, perhaps, by Commandments recited west of Suez, but to be understood in terms of Darwin and Nietzsche: a people that has lost the ability to govern itself, or to develop its natural resources, inevitably falls a prey to nations suffering from strength and greed.

The conquest brought certain advantages to India. Men like Bentinck, Canning, Munro, Elphinstone and Macaulay carried into the administration of the British provinces something of the generous liberalism that controlled England in 1832. Lord William Bentinck, with the aid and stimulus of native reformers like Ram Mohun Roy, put an end to suttee and thuggery. The English, after fighting 111 wars in India, with Indian money and troops,⁹ to complete the conquest of India, established peace throughout the peninsula, built railways, factories and schools, opened universities at Calcutta, Madras, Bombay, Lahore and Allahabad, brought the science and technology of England to India, inspired the East with the democratic ideals of the West, and played an important part in revealing to the world the cultural wealth of India's past. The price of these benefactions was a financial despotism by which a race of transient rulers drained India's wealth year by year as they returned to the reinvigorating north; an economic despotism that ruined India's industries, and threw her millions of artisans back upon an inadequate soil; and a political despotism that, coming so soon after the narrow tyranny of Aurangzeb, broke for a century the spirit of the Indian people.

II. LATTER-DAY SAINTS

Christianity in India—The "Brahma-Somaj"—Mohammedanism— Ramakrishna—Vivekananda

It was natural and characteristic that under these conditions India should seek consolation in religion. For a time she gave a cordial welcome to Christianity; she found in it many ethical ideals that she had honored for thousands of years; and "before the character and behavior of Europeans," says the blunt Abbé Dubois, "became well known to these people, it seemed possible that Christianity might take root among them."[10] Throughout the nineteenth century harassed missionaries tried to make the voice of Christ audible above the roar of the conquering cannon; they erected and equipped schools and hospitals, dispensed medicine and charity as well as theology, and brought to the Untouchables the first recognition of their humanity. But the contrast between Christian precept and the practice of Christians left the Hindus sceptical and satirical. They pointed out that the raising of Lazarus from the dead was unworthy of remark; their own religion had many more interesting and astonishing miracles than this; and any true *Yogi* could perform miracles today, while those of Christianity were apparently finished.[11] The Brahmans held their ground proudly, and offered against the orthodoxies of the West a system of thought quite as subtle, profound, and incredible. "The progress of Christianity in India," says Sir Charles Eliot, "has been insignificant."[12]

Nevertheless, the fascinating figure of Christ has had far more influence in India than may be measured by the fact that Christianity has converted six per cent of the population in three hundred years. The first signs of that influence appear in the *Bhagavad-Gita*;[13] the latest are evident in Gandhi and Tagore. The clearest instance is in the reform organization known as the *Brahma-Somaj*,* founded in 1828 by Ram Mohun Roy. No one could have approached the study of religion more conscientiously. Roy learned Sanskrit to read the *Vedas*, Pali to read the *Tripitaka* of Buddhism, Persian and Arabic to study Mohammedanism and the *Koran*, Hebrew to master the Old Testament and Greek to understand the New.[14] Then he took up English, and wrote it with such ease and grace that Jeremy Bentham wished that James Mill might profit from the example. In 1820 Roy published his *Precepts of Jesus: a Guide to Peace and Happiness*, and announced: "I have found the doctrines of Christ more conducive to moral principles, and better adapted for the use of rational beings, than any other which have come to my knowledge."[15] He proposed to his scandalized countrymen a new religion, which should abandon polytheism, polygamy, caste, child marriage, suttee and idolatry, and should worship one god—*Brahman*. Like Akbar he dreamed that all India might be united in so simple a faith; and like Akbar he underestimated the popularity of superstition. The *Brahma-Somaj*, after a hundred years of useful struggle, is now an extinct force in Indian life.†

The Moslems are the most powerful and interesting of the religious minorities of India; but the study of their religion belongs to a later volume. It is not astonishing that Mohammedanism, despite the zealous aid of Aurangzeb, failed to win India to Islam; the miracle is that Mohammedanism in India did not succumb to Hinduism. The survival of this simple and masculine monotheism amid a jungle of polytheism attests the virility of the Moslem mind; we need only recall the absorption of Buddhism by Brahmanism to realize the vigor of this resistance, and the measure of this achievement. Allah now has some 70,000,000 worshipers in India.

The Hindu has found little comfort in any alien faith; and the figures that have most inspired his religious consciousness in the nineteenth cen-

---

* Literally, the "Brahma Society"; known more fully as "The Society of the Believers in *Brahman*, the Supreme Spirit."

† It has today some 5,500 adherents.[16] Another reform organization, the *Arya-Somaj* (Aryan Society), founded by Swami Dyananda, and brilliantly carried forward by the late Lala Lajpat Rai, denounced caste, polytheism, superstition, idolatry and Christianity, and urged a return to the simpler religion of the *Vedas*. Its followers now number half a million.[17] A reverse influence, of Hinduism upon Christianity, appears in Theosophy—a mixture of Hindu mysticism and Christian morality, developed in India by two exotic women: Mme. Helena Blavatsky (1878) and Mrs. Annie Besant (1893).

tury were those that rooted their doctrine and practice in the ancient creeds of the people. Ramakrishna, a poor Brahman of Bengal, became for a time a Christian, and felt the lure of Christ;* he became at another time a Moslem, and joined in the austere ritual of Mohammedan prayer; but soon his pious heart brought him back to Hinduism, even to the terrible Kali whose priest he became, and whom he transformed into a Mother-Goddess overflowing with tenderness and affection. He rejected the ways of the intellect, and preached *Bhakti-yoga*—the discipline and union of love. "The knowledge of God," he said, "may be likened to a man, while love of God is like a woman. Knowledge has entry only to the outer rooms of God, and no one can enter into the inner mysteries of God save a lover."[18] Unlike Ram Mohun Roy, Ramakrishna took no trouble to educate himself; he learned no Sanskrit and no English; he wrote nothing, and shunned intellectual discourse. When a pompous logician asked him, "What are knowledge, knower, and the object known?" he answered, "Good man, I do not know all these niceties of scholastic learning. I know only my Mother Divine, and that I am her son."[19] All religions are good, he taught his followers; each is a way to God, or a stage on the way, adapted to the mind and heart of the seeker. To be converted from one religion to another is foolishness; one need only continue on his own way, and reach to the essence of his own faith. "All rivers flow to the ocean. Flow, and let others flow, too!"[20] He tolerated sympathetically the polytheism of the people, and accepted humbly the monism of the philosophers; but in his own living faith God was a spirit incarnated in all men, and the only true worship of God was the loving service of mankind.

Many fine souls, rich and poor, Brahman and Pariah, chose him as *Guru*, and formed an order and mission in his name. The most vivid of these followers was a proud young Kshatriya, Narendranath Dutt, who, full of Spencer and Darwin, first presented himself to Ramakrishna as an atheist unhappy in his atheism, but scornful of the myths and superstitions with which he identified religion. Conquered by Ramakrishna's patient kindliness, "Naren" became the young Master's most ardent disciple; he redefined God as "the totality of all souls,"[21] and called upon his fellow men to practise religion not through vain asceticism and meditation, but through absolute devotion to men.

* To the end of his life he accepted the divinity of Christ, but insisted that Buddha, Krishna and others were also incarnations of the one God. He himself, he assured Vivekananda, was a reincarnation of Rama and Krishna.[17a]

Leave to the next life the reading of the *Vedanta*, and the practice of meditation. Let this body which is here be put at the service of others! . . . The highest truth is this: God is present in all beings. They are His multiple forms. There is no other God to seek. He alone serves God who serves all other beings![22]

Changing his name to Vivekananda, he left India to seek funds abroad for the Ramakrishna Mission. In 1893 he found himself lost and penniless in Chicago. A day later he appeared in the Parliament of Religions at the World's Fair, addressed the meeting as a representative of Hinduism, and captured everyone by his magnificent presence, his gospel of the unity of all religions, and his simple ethics of human service as the best worship of God; atheism became a noble religion under the inspiration of his eloquence, and orthodox clergymen found themselves honoring a "heathen" who said that there was no other God than the souls of living things. Returning to India, he preached to his countrymen a more virile creed than any Hindu had offered them since Vedic days:

It is a man-making religion that we want. . . . Give up these weakening mysticisms, and be strong. . . . For the next fifty years . . . let all other, vain gods disappear from our minds. This is the only God that is awake, our own race, everywhere His hands, everywhere His feet, everywhere His ears; He covers everything. . . . The first of all worship is the worship of those all around us. . . . These are all our gods—men and animals; and the first gods we have to worship are our own countrymen.[23]

It was but a step from this to Gandhi.

III. TAGORE

Science and art—A family of geniuses—Youth of Rabindranath—His poetry—His politics—His school

Meanwhile, despite oppression, bitterness and poverty, India continued to create science, literature and art. Professor Jagadis Chandra Bose has won world-renown by his researches in electricity and the physiology of plants; and the work of Professor Chandrasekhara Raman in the physics of light has been crowned with the Nobel prize. In our own century a new school of painting has arisen in Bengal, which merges the richness of color in the Ajanta frescoes with the delicacy of line in the Rajput miniatures. The paintings of Abanindranath Tagore share modestly in the voluptuous mysticism and the delicate artistry that brought the poetry of his uncle to international fame.

The Tagores are one of the great families of history. Davendranath Tagore (Bengali *Thakur*) was one of the organizers, and later the head, of the *Brahma-Somaj*; a man of wealth, culture and sanctity, he became in his old age a heretic patriarch of Bengal. From him have descended the artists Abanindranath and Gogonendranath, the philosopher Dwijendranath, and the poet Rabindranath, Tagore—the last two being his sons.

Rabindranath was brought up in an atmosphere of comfort and refinement, in which music, poetry and high discourse were the very air that he breathed. He was a gentle spirit from birth, a Shelley who refused to die young or to grow old; so affectionate that squirrels climbed upon his knees, and birds perched upon his hands.[24] He was observant and receptive, and felt the eddying overtones of experience with a mystic sensitivity. Sometimes he would stand for hours on a balcony, noting with literary instinct the figure and features, the mannerisms and gait of each passer-by in the street; sometimes, on a sofa in an inner room, he would spend half a day silent with his memories and his dreams. He began to compose verses on a slate, happy in the thought that errors could be so easily wiped away.[25] Soon he was writing songs full of tenderness for India—for the beauty of her scenery, the loveliness of her women, and the sufferings of her people; and he composed the music for these songs himself. All India sang them, and the young poet thrilled to hear them on the lips of rough peasants as he traveled, unknown, through distant villages.[25] Here is one of them, translated from the Bengali by the author himself; who else has ever expressed with such sympathetic scepticism the divine nonsense of romantic love?

> Tell me if this be all true, my lover, tell me if this be true.
> When these eyes flash their lightning the dark clouds in your breast make stormy answer.
> Is it true that my lips are sweet like the opening bud of the first conscious love?
> Do the memories of vanished months of May linger in my limbs?
> Does the earth, like a harp, shiver into songs with the touch of my feet?

Is it then true that the dewdrops fall from the eyes of night when I
    am seen, and the morning light is glad when it wraps my body
    round?
Is it true, is it true, that your love traveled alone through ages and
    worlds in search of me?
That when you found me at last, your age-long desire found utter
    peace in my gentle speech and my eyes and lips and flowing hair?
Is it then true that the mystery of the Infinite is written on this
    little forehead of mine?
Tell me, my lover, if all this be true?[26]

There are many virtues in these poems*—an intense and yet sober
patriotism; a femininely subtle understanding of love and woman, nature
and man; a passionate penetration into the insight of India's philosophers;
and a Tennysonian delicacy of sentiment and phrase. If there is any fault
in them it is that they are too consistently beautiful, too monotonously
idealistic and tender. Every woman in them is lovely, and every man in
them is infatuated with woman, or death, or God; nature, though sometimes terrible, is always sublime, never bleak, or barren, or hideous.†
Perhaps the story of Chitra is Tagore's story: her lover Arjuna tires of her
in a year because she is completely and uninterruptedly beautiful; only
when she loses her beauty and, becoming strong, takes up the natural
labors of life, does the god love her again—a profound symbol of the
contented marriage.[28] Tagore confesses his limitations with captivating
grace:

My love, once upon a time your poet launched a great epic in his
    mind.
Alas, I was not careful, and it struck your ringing anklets and came
    to grief.
It broke up into scraps of songs, and lay scattered at your feet.[29]

Therefore he has sung lyrics to the end, and all the world except the
critics has heard him gladly. India was a little surprised when her poet

* The more important volumes are *Gitanjali* (1913), *Chitra* (1914), *The Post-Office*
(1914), *The Gardener* (1914), *Fruit-Gathering* (1916), and *Red Oleanders* (1925). The
poet's own *My Reminiscences* (1917) is a better guide to understanding him than E.
Thompson's *R. Tagore, Poet and Dramatist* (Oxford, 1926).

† Cf. his magnificent line: "When I go from hence let this be my parting word, that
what I have seen is unsurpassable."[27]

received the Nobel prize (1913); the Bengal reviewers had seen only his
faults, and the Calcutta professors had used his poems as examples of bad
Bengali.[30] The young Nationalists disliked him because his condemnation
of the abuses in India's moral life was stronger than his cry for political
freedom; and when he was knighted it seemed to them a betrayal of
India. He did not hold the honor long; for when, by a tragic misunderstanding, British soldiers fired into a religious gathering at Amritsar
(1919), Tagore returned his decorations to the Viceroy with a stinging
letter of renunciation. Today he is a solitary figure, perhaps the most impressive of all men now on the earth: a reformer who has had the courage to denounce the most basic of India's institutions—the caste system—
and the dearest of her beliefs—transmigration;[31] a Nationalist who longs
for India's liberty, but has dared to protest against the chauvinism and
self-seeking that play a part in the Nationalist movement; an educator who
has tired of oratory and politics, and has retreated to his *ashram* and
hermitage at Shantiniketan, to teach some of the new generation his gospel
of moral self-liberation; a poet broken-hearted by the premature death of
his wife, and by the humiliation of his country; a philosopher steeped in
the *Vedanta*,[32] a mystic hesitating, like Chandi Das, between woman and
God, and yet shorn of the ancestral faith by the extent of his learning;
a lover of Nature facing her messengers of death with no other consolation
than his unaging gift of song.

"Ah, poet, the evening draws near; your hair is turning grey.
Do you in your lonely musing hear the message of the hereafter?"

"It is evening," the poet said, "and I am listening because some one
    may call from the village, late though it be.
I watch if young straying hearts meet together, and two pairs of
    eager eyes beg for music to break their silence and speak for them.
Who is there to weave their passionate songs, if I sit on the shore
    of life and contemplate death and the beyond? . . .

It is a trifle that my hair is turning grey.
I am ever as young or as old as the youngest and the oldest of this
    village. . . .
They all have need for me, and I have no time to brood over the
    after-life.
I am of an age with each; what matter if my hair turns grey?"[33]

IV. EAST IS WEST

*Changing India—Economic changes—Social—The decaying caste
system — Castes and guilds — Untouchables — The
emergence of woman*

That a man unfamiliar with English till almost fifty should write
English so well is a sign of the ease with which some of the gaps can be
bridged between that East and that West whose mating another poet
has banned. For since the birth of Tagore the West has come to the
East in a hundred ways, and is changing every aspect of Oriental life.
Thirty thousand miles of railways have webbed the wastes and ghats of
India, and carried Western faces into every village; telegraph wires and
the printing press have brought to every student the news of a suggestively changing world; English schools have taught British history with
a view to making British citizens, and have unwittingly inculcated English
ideas of democracy and liberty. Even the East now justifies Heraclitus.

Reduced to poverty in the nineteenth century by the superior machinery of British looms and the higher calibre of British guns, India has
now turned her face reluctantly towards industrialization. Handicrafts
are dying, factories are growing. At Jamsetpur the Tata Iron and Steel
Company employs 45,000 men, and threatens the leadership of American
firms in the production of steel.[34] The coal production of India is mounting rapidly; within a generation China and India may overtake Europe
and America in lifting out of the soil the basic fuels and materials of
industry. Not only will these native resources meet native needs, they
may compete with the West for the markets of the world, and the
conquerors of Asia may suddenly find their markets gone, and the
standards of living of their people at home severely reduced, by the competition of low-wage labor in once docile and backward (i.e., agricultural) lands. In Bombay there are factories in mid-Victorian style, with
old-fashioned wages that bring tears of envy to the eyes of Occidental
Tories.* Hindu employers have replaced the British in many of these
industries, and exploit their fellow men with the rapacity of Europeans
bearing the white man's burden.

---

* In 1922 there were eighty-three cotton factories in Bombay, with 180,000 employees,
and an average wage-scale of thirty-three cents a day. Of 33,000,000 Indians engaged in
industry, 51% are women, 14% are children under fourteen.[35]

The economic basis of Indian society has not changed without affecting the social institutions and moral customs of the people. The caste system was conceived in terms of a static and agricultural society; it provided order, but gave no opening to unpedigreed genius, no purchase to ambition and hope, no stimulus to invention and enterprise; it was doomed when the Industrial Revolution reached India's shores. The machine does not respect persons: in most of the factories men work side by side without discrimination of caste, trains and trams give berth or standing-room to all who can pay, coöperative societies and political parties bring all grades together, and in the congestion of the urban theatre or street Brahman and Pariah rub elbows in unexpected fellowship. A raja announces that every caste and creed will find reception at his court; a Shudra becomes the enlightened ruler of Baroda; the *Brahma-Somaj* denounces caste, and the Bengal Provincial Congress of the National Congress advocates the abolition of all caste distinctions forthwith.[36] Slowly the machine lifts a new class to wealth and power, and brings the most ancient of living aristocracies to an end.

Already the caste terms are losing significance. The word *Vaisya* is used in books today, but has no application in actual life. Even the term *Shudra* has disappeared from the north, while in the south it is a loose designation for all non-Brahmans.[37] The lower castes of older days have in effect been replaced by over three thousand "castes" that are really guilds: bankers, merchants, manufacturers, farmers, professors, engineers, trackwalkers, college women, butchers, barbers, fishermen, actors, coal miners, washermen, cabmen, shop-girls, bootblacks—these are organized into occupational castes that differ from our trade-unions chiefly in the loose expectation that sons will follow the trades of their fathers.

The great tragedy of the caste system is that it has multiplied, from generation to generation, those Untouchables whose growing number and rebelliousness undermine the institution that created them. The Outcastes have received into their ranks all those who were enslaved by war or debt, all the children of marriages between Brahmans and Shudras, and all those unfortunates whose work, as scavengers, butchers, acrobats, conjurors or executioners was stamped as degrading by Brahmanical law;[38] and they have swollen their mass by the improvident fertility of those who have nothing to lose. Their bitter poverty has made cleanliness of body, clothing or food an impossible luxury for them; and their fellows shun them with every sense.* Therefore the laws of caste forbid an Untouchable to approach nearer than twenty-four feet to a Shudra, or seventy-four feet to a Brahman;[40] if the shadow of a Pariah falls upon a man of caste, the latter must remove the contamination by a purifying ablution. Whatever the Outcaste touches is thereby defiled.† In many parts of India he must not draw water from the public wells, or enter temples used by Brahmans, or send his children to the Hindu schools.[42] The British, whose policies have in some degree contributed to the impoverishment of the Outcastes, have brought them at least equality before the law, and equal access to all British-controlled colleges and schools. The Nationalist movement, under the inspiration of Gandhi, has done much to lessen the disabilities of the Untouchables. Perhaps another generation will see them externally and superficially free.

The coming of industry, and of Western ideas, is disturbing the ancient mastery of the Hindu male. Industrialization defers the age of marriage, and requires the "emancipation" of woman; that is to say, the woman cannot be lured into the factory unless she is persuaded that home is a prison, and is entitled by law to keep her earnings for herself. Many real reforms have come as incidents to this emancipation. Child marriage has been formally ended (1929) by raising the legal age of marriage to fourteen for girls and to eighteen for men;[43] suttee has disappeared, and the remarriage of widows grows daily;‡ polygamy is allowed, but few men practise it;[45] and tourists are disappointed to find that the temple dancers are almost extinct. In no other country is moral reform progressing so rapidly. Industrial city life is drawing women out of *purdah;* hardly six per cent of the women of India accept such seclusion today.[46] A number of lively periodicals for women discuss the most up-to-date questions; even a birth-control league has appeared,[47] and has faced bravely the gravest problem of India—indiscriminate fertility. In many of the provinces women vote and hold political office; twice women have been presi-

---

* "People who abstain entirely from animal food acquire such an acute sense of smell that they can perceive in a moment, from a person's breath, or from the exudation of the skin, whether that person has eaten meat or not; and that after a lapse of twenty-four hours."[39]

† In 1913 the child of a rich Hindu of Kohat fell into a fountain and was drowned. No one was at hand but its mother and a passing Outcaste. The latter offered to plunge into the water and rescue the child, but the mother refused; she preferred the death of her child to the defilement of the fountain.[41]

‡ In the year 1915 there were 15 remarriages of widows; in 1925 there were 2,263.[44]

dent of the Indian National Congress. Many of them have taken degrees at the universities, and have become doctors, lawyers, or professors.[48] Soon, no doubt, the tables will be turned, and women will rule. Must not some wild Western influence bear the guilt of this flaming appeal issued by a subaltern of Gandhi to the women of India?—

> Away with ancient *purdah!* Come out of the kitchens quick! Fling the pots and pans rattling into the corners! Tear the cloth from your eyes, and see the new world! Let your husbands and brothers cook for themselves. There is much work to be done to make India a nation![49]

V. THE NATIONALIST MOVEMENT

The westernized students — The secularization of heaven — The Indian National Congress

In 1923 there were over a thousand Hindus studying in England, presumably an equal number in America, perhaps an equal number elsewhere. They marveled at the privileges enjoyed by the lowliest citizens of western Europe and America; they studied the French and American Revolutions, and read the literature of reform and revolt; they gloated over the Bill of Rights, the Declaration of the Rights of Man, the Declaration of Independence, and the American Constitution; they went back to their countries as centers of infection for democratic ideas and the gospel of liberty. The industrial and scientific advances of the West, and the victory of the Allies in the War, gave to these ideas an irresistible prestige; soon every student was shouting the battle-cry of freedom. In the schools of England and America the Hindus learned to be free.

These Western-educated Orientals had not only taken on political ideals in the course of their education abroad, they had shed religious ideas; the two processes are usually associated, in biography and in history. They came to Europe as pious youths, wedded to Krishna, Shiva, Vishnu, Kali, Rama . . . ; they touched science, and their ancient faiths were shattered as by some sudden catalytic shock. Shorn of religious belief, which is the very spirit of India, the Westernized Hindus returned to their country disillusioned and sad; a thousand gods had dropped dead from the skies* Then, inevitably, Utopia filled the place of Heaven, democracy

---

* This does not apply to all. Some, in the significant phrase of Coomaraswamy, have "returned from Europe to India."

became a substitute for *Nirvana,* liberty replaced God. What had gone on in Europe in the second half of the eighteenth century now went on in the East.

Nevertheless the new ideas developed slowly. In 1885 a few Hindu leaders met at Bombay and founded the "Indian National Congress," but they do not seem to have dreamed then even of Home Rule. The effort of Lord Curzon to partition Bengal (that is, to destroy the unity and strength of the most powerful and politically conscious community in India) roused the Nationalists to a more rebel mood; and at the Congress of 1905 the uncompromising Tilak demanded *Swaraj.* He had created the word[50] out of Sanskrit roots still visible in its English translation—"self-rule." In that same eventful year Japan defeated Russia; and the East, which for a century had been fearful of the West, began to lay plans for the liberation of Asia. China followed Sun Yat Sen, took up the sword, and fell into the arms of Japan. India, weaponless, accepted as her leader one of the strangest figures in history, and gave to the world the unprecedented phenomenon of a revolution led by a saint, and waged without a gun.

VI. MAHATMA GANDHI

Portrait of a saint—The ascetic—The Christian—The education of Gandhi—In Africa—The Revolt of 1921—"I am the man"— Prison years—"Young India"—The revolution of the spinning-wheel—The achievements of Gandhi

Picture the ugliest, slightest, weakest man in Asia, with face and flesh of bronze, close-cropped gray head, high cheek-bones, kindly little brown eyes, a large and almost toothless mouth, larger ears, an enormous nose, thin arms and legs, clad in a loin cloth, standing before an English judge in India, on trial for preaching "non-coöperation" to his countrymen. Or picture him seated on a small carpet in a bare room at his *Satyagrahashram,* —School of Truth-Seekers—at Ahmedabad: his bony legs crossed under him in *yogi* fashion, soles upward, his hands busy at a spinning-wheel, his face lined with responsibility, his mind active with ready answers to every questioner of freedom. From 1920 to 1935 this naked weaver was both the spiritual and the political leader of 320,000,000 Indians. When he appeared in public, crowds gathered round him to touch his clothing or to kiss his feet.[51]

Four hours a day he spun the coarse *khaddar*, hoping by his example to persuade his countrymen to use this simple homespun instead of buying the product of those British looms that had ruined the textile industry of India. His only possessions were three rough cloths—two as his wardrobe and one as his bed. Once a rich lawyer, he had given all his property to the poor, and his wife, after some matronly hesitation, had followed his example. He slept on the bare floor, or on the earth. He lived on nuts, plantains, lemons, oranges, dates, rice, and goat's milk;[52] often for months together he took nothing but milk and fruit; once in his life he tasted meat; occasionally he ate nothing for weeks. "I can as well do without my eyes as without fasts. What the eyes are for the outer world, fasts are for the inner."[53] As the blood thins, he felt, the mind clears, irrelevancies fall away, and fundamental things—sometimes the very Soul of the World—rise out of *Maya* like Everest through the clouds.

At the same time that he fasted to see divinity he kept one toe on the earth, and advised his followers to take an enema daily when they fasted, lest they be poisoned with the acid products of the body's self-consumption just as they might be finding God.[54] When the Moslems and the Hindus killed one another in theological enthusiasm, and paid no heed to his pleas for peace, he went without food for three weeks to move them. He became so weak and frail through fasts and privations that when he addressed the great audiences that gathered to hear him, he spoke to them from an uplifted chair. He carried his asceticism into the field of sex, and wished, like Tolstoi, to limit all physical intercourse to deliberate reproduction. He too, in his youth, had indulged the flesh too much, and the news of his father's death had surprised him in the arms of love. Now he returned with passionate remorse to the *Brahmacharia* that had been preached to him in his boyhood—absolute abstention from all sensual desire. He persuaded his wife to live with him only as sister with brother; and "from that time," he tells us, "all dissension ceased."[55] When he realized that India's basic need was birth-control, he adopted not the methods of the West, but the theories of Malthus and Tolstoi.

Is it right for us, who know the situation, to bring forth children? We only multiply slaves and weaklings if we continue the process of procreation whilst we feel and remain helpless. . . . Not till India has become a free nation . . . have we the right to bring forth progeny. . . . I have not a shadow of doubt that married people, if

they wish well to the country and want to see India become a nation
of strong and handsome, well-formed men and women, would practice self-restraint and cease to procreate for the time being.[56]

Added to these elements in his character were qualities strangely like
those that, we are told, distinguished the Founder of Christianity. He did
not mouth the name of Christ, but he acted as if he accepted every word
of the Sermon on the Mount. Not since St. Francis of Assisi has any life
known to history been so marked by gentleness, disinterestedness, simplicity, and forgiveness of enemies. It was to the credit of his opponents,
but still more to his own, that his undiscourageable courtesy to them won
a fine courtesy from them in return; the Government sent him to jail
with profuse apologies. He never showed rancor or resentment. Thrice
he was attacked by mobs, and beaten almost to death; not once did he
retaliate; and when one of his assailants was arrested he refused to enter
a charge. Shortly after the worst of all riots between Moslems and Hindus,
when the Moplah Mohammedans butchered hundreds of unarmed Hindus
and offered their prepuces as a covenant to Allah, these same Moslems
were stricken with famine; Gandhi collected funds for them from all
India, and, with no regard for the best precedents, forwarded every *anna*,
without deduction for "overhead," to the starving enemy.[57]

Mohandas Karamchand Gandhi was born in 1869. His family belonged to the Vaisya caste, and to the Jain sect, and practised the *ahimsa*
principle of never injuring a living thing. His father was a capable administrator but an heretical financier; he lost place after place through honesty, gave nearly all his wealth to charity, and left the rest to his family.[58]
While still a boy Mohandas became an atheist, being displeased with the
adulterous gallantries of certain Hindu gods; and to make clear his everlasting scorn for religion, he ate meat. The meat disagreed with him, and
he returned to religion.

At eight he was engaged, and at twelve he was married, to Kasturbai,
who remained loyal to him through all his adventures, riches, poverty,
imprisonments, and *Brahmacharia*. At eighteen he passed examinations for
the university, and went to London to study law. In his first year there he
read eighty books on Christianity. The Sermon on the Mount "went
straight to my heart on the first reading."[59] He took the counsel to return
good for evil, and to love even one's enemies, as the highest expression of
all human idealism; and he resolved rather to fail with these than to succeed without them.

Returning to India in 1891, he practised law for a time in Bombay, refusing to prosecute for debt, and always reserving the right to abandon a case which he had come to think unjust. One case led him to South Africa; there he found his fellow-Hindus so maltreated that he forgot to return to India, but gave himself completely, without remuneration, to the cause of removing the disabilities of his countrymen in Africa. For twenty years he fought this issue out until the Government yielded. Only then did he return home.

Traveling through India he realized for the first time the complete destitution of his people. He was horrified by the skeletons whom he saw toiling in the fields, and the lowly Outcastes who did the menial work of the towns. It seemed to him that the discriminations against his countrymen abroad were merely one consequence of their poverty and subjection at home. Nevertheless he supported England loyally in the War; he even advocated the enlistment of Hindus who did not accept the principle of non-violence. He did not, at that time, agree with those who called for independence; he believed that British misgovernment in India was an exception, and that British government in general was good; that British government in India was bad just because it violated all the principles of British government at home; and that if the English people could be made to understand the case of the Hindus, it would soon accept them in full brotherhood into a commonwealth of free dominions.[60] He trusted that when the War was over, and Britain counted India's sacrifice for the Empire in men and wealth, it would no longer hesitate to give her liberty.

But at the close of the War the agitation for Home Rule was met by the Rowland Acts, which put an end to freedom of speech and press; by the establishment of the impotent legislature of the Montagu-Chelmsford reforms; and finally by the slaughter at Amritsar. Gandhi was shocked into decisive action. He returned to the Viceroy the decorations which he had received at various times from British governments; and he issued to India a call for active civil disobedience against the Government of India. The people responded not with peaceful resistance, as he had asked, but with bloodshed and violence; in Bombay, for example, they killed fifty-three unsympathetic Parsees.[61] Gandhi, vowed to *ahimsa*, sent out a second message, in which he called upon the people to postpone the campaign of civil disobedience, on the ground that it was degenerating into mob rule. Seldom in history had a man shown more courage in acting on principle, scorning expediency and popularity. The nation was astonished at his decision; it had supposed itself near to success, and it did not agree with Gandhi that the means might be as important as the end. The reputation of the *Mahatma* sank to the lowest ebb.

It was just at this point (in March, 1922) that the Government determined upon his arrest. He made no resistance, declined to engage a lawyer, and offered no defense. When the Prosecutor charged him with being responsible, through his publications, for the violence that had marked the outbreak of 1921, Gandhi replied in terms that lifted him at once to nobility.

> I wish to endorse all the blame that the learned Advocate-General has thrown on my shoulder in connection with the incidents in Bombay, Madras, and Chauri Chaura. Thinking over these deeply, and sleeping over them night after night, it is impossible for me to dissociate myself from these diabolical crimes. . . . The learned Advocate-General is quite right when he says that as a man of responsibility, a man having received a fair share of education, . . . I should have known the consequences of every one of my acts. I knew that I was playing with fire, I ran the risk, and if I was set free I would still do the same. I felt this morning that I would have failed in my duty if I did not say what I say here just now.
>
> I wanted to avoid violence. I want to avoid violence. Non-violence is the first article of my faith. It is also the last article of my creed. But I had to make my choice. I had either to submit to a system which I considered had done an irreparable harm to my country, or incur the risk of the mad fury of my people bursting forth when they understood the truth from my lips. I know that my people have sometimes gone mad. I am deeply sorry for it, and I am therefore here to submit not to a light penalty but to the highest penalty. I do not ask for mercy. I do not plead any extenuating act. I am here, therefore, to invite and cheerfully submit to the highest penalty that can be inflicted upon me for what in law is a deliberate crime and what appears to me to be the highest duty of a citizen.[62]

The Judge expressed his profound regret that he had to send to jail one whom millions of his countrymen considered "a great patriot and a great leader"; he admitted that even those who differed from Gandhi looked upon him "as a man of high ideals and of noble and even saintly life."[63] He sentenced him to prison for six years.

Gandhi was put under solitary confinement, but he did not complain. "I do not see any of the other prisoners," he wrote, "though I really do not see how my society could do them any harm." But "I feel happy. My nature likes loneliness. I love quietness. And now I have opportunity to engage in studies that I had to neglect in the outside world."[64] He instructed himself sedulously in the writings of Bacon, Carlyle, Ruskin, Emerson, Thoreau and Tolstoi, and solaced long hours with Ben Jonson and Walter Scott. He read and re-read the *Bhagavad-Gita*. He studied Sanskrit, Tamil and Urdu so that he might be able not only to write for scholars but to speak to the multitude. He drew up a detailed schedule of studies for the six years of his imprisonment, and pursued it faithfully till accident intervened. "I used to sit down to my books with the delight of a young man of twenty-four, and forgetting my four-and-fifty years and my poor health."[65]

Appendicitis secured his release, and Occidental medicine, which he had often denounced, secured his recovery. A vast crowd gathered at the prison gates to greet him on his exit, and many kissed his coarse garment as he passed. But he shunned politics and the public eye, pled his weakness and illness, and retired to his school at Ahmedabad, where he lived for many years in quiet isolation with his students. From that retreat, however, he sent forth weekly, through his mouthpiece *Young India*, editorials expounding his philosophy of revolution and life. He begged his followers to shun violence, not only because it would be suicidal, since India had no guns, but because it would only replace one despotism with another. "History," he told them, "teaches one that those who have, no doubt with honest motives, ousted the greedy by using brute force against them, have in their turn become a prey to the disease of the conquered. . . . My interest in India's freedom will cease if she adopts violent means. For their fruit will be not freedom, but slavery."[66]

The second element in his creed was the resolute rejection of modern industry, and a Rousseauian call for a return to the simple life of agriculture and domestic industry in the village. The confinement of men and women in factories, making with machines owned by others fractions of articles whose finished form they will never see, seemed to Gandhi a roundabout way of burying humanity under a pyramid of shoddy goods. Most machine products, he thought, are unnecessary; the labor saved in using them is consumed in making and repairing them; or if labor is really saved it is of no benefit to labor, but only to capital; labor is thrown by its own productivity into a panic of "technological unemployment."[67] So he renewed the *Swadeshi* movement announced in 1905 by Tilak; self-production was to be added to *Swaraj*, self-rule. Gandhi made the use of the *charka*, or spinning-wheel, a test of loyal adherence to the Nationalist movement; he asked that every Hindu, even the richest, should wear homespun, and boycott the alien and mechanical textiles of Britain, so that the homes of India might hum once more, through the dull winter, with the sound of the spinning-wheel.[68]

The response was not universal; it is difficult to stop history in its course. But India tried. Hindu students everywhere dressed in *khaddar*; highborn ladies abandoned their Japanese silk *saris* for coarse cloths woven by themselves; prostitutes in brothels and convicts in prison began to spin; and in many cities great Feasts of the Vanities were arranged, as in Savonarola's day, at which wealthy Hindus and merchants brought from their homes and warehouses all their imported cloth, and flung it into the fire. In one day at Bombay alone, 150,000 pieces were consumed by the flames.[69]

The movement away from industry failed, but it gave India for a decade a symbol of revolt, and helped to polarize her mute millions into a new unity of political consciousness. India doubted the means, but honored the purpose; and though it questioned Gandhi the statesman, it took to its heart Gandhi the saint, and for a moment became one in reverencing him. It was as Tagore said of him:

> He stopped at the thresholds of the huts of the thousands of dispossessed, dressed like one of their own. He spoke to them in their own language. Here was living truth at last, and not only quotations from books. For this reason the *Mahatma*, the name given to him by the people of India, is his real name. Who else has felt like him that all Indians are his own flesh and blood? . . . When love came to the door of India that door was opened wide. . . . At Gandhi's call India blossomed forth to new greatness, just as once before, in earlier times, when Buddha proclaimed the truth of fellow-feeling and compassion among all living creatures.[70]

It was Gandhi's task to unify India; and he accomplished it. Other tasks await other men.

VII. FAREWELL TO INDIA

One cannot conclude the history of India as one can conclude the history of Egypt, or Babylonia, or Assyria; for that history is still being made, that civilization is still creating. Culturally India has been reinvigorated by mental contact with the West, and her literature today is as fertile and noble as any. Spiritually she is still struggling with superstition and excess theological baggage, but there is no telling how quickly the acids of modern science will dissolve these supernumerary gods. Politically the last one hundred years have brought to India such unity as she has seldom had before: partly the unity of one alien government, partly the unity of one alien speech, but above all the unity of one welding aspiration to liberty. Economically India is passing, for better and for worse, out of medievalism into modern industry; her wealth and her trade will grow, and before the end of the century she will doubtless be among the powers of the earth.

We cannot claim for this civilization such direct gifts to our own as we have traced to Egypt and the Near East; for these last were the immediate ancestors of our own culture, while the history of India, China and Japan flowed in another stream, and is only now beginning to touch and influence the current of Occidental life. It is true that even across the Himalayan barrier India has sent to us such questionable gifts as grammar and logic, philosophy and fables, hypnotism and chess, and above all, our numerals and our decimal system. But these are not the essence of her spirit; they are trifles compared to what we may learn from her in the future. As invention, industry and trade bind the continents together, or as they fling us into conflict with Asia, we shall study its civilizations more closely, and shall absorb, even in enmity, some of its ways and thoughts. Perhaps, in return for conquest, arrogance and spoliation, India will teach us the tolerance and gentleness of the mature mind, the quiet content of the unacquisitive soul, the calm of the understanding spirit. and a unifying, pacifying love for all living things.

BOOK THREE

THE FAR EAST

A. CHINA

An emperor knows how to govern when poets are free to make verses, people to act plays, historians to tell the truth, ministers to give advice, the poor to grumble at taxes, students to learn lessons aloud, workmen to praise their skill and seek work, people to speak of anything, and old men to find fault with everything.

—*Address of the Duke of Shao to King Li-Wang, ca. 845 B.C.*[1]

CHRONOLOGY OF CHINESE CIVILIZATION*

2852-2205: *Legendary Rulers*:
2852-2737: Fu Hsi
2737-2697: Shen Nung
2697-2597: Huang Ti
2356-2255: Yao
2255-2205: Shun
2205-1766: *Hsia Dynasty*
2205-2197: Yü
1818-1766: Chieh Kuei
1766-1123: *Shang (and Yin) Dynasty*
1766-1753: T'ang
1198-1194: Wu Yih, the atheist emperor
1154-1123: Chou-Hsin, model of wickedness
1122-255: *Chou Dynasty*
1122-1115: Wu-Wang
Fl. 1123: Wen Wang, author (?) of the
Book of Changes
1115-1078: Cheng Wang
1115-1079: Chou Kung, author (?) of the
Chou-li, or *Laws of Chou*
770-255: The Feudal Age
683-640: Kuang Chung, prime minister of
Ts'i
604-517: Lao-tze (?)
551-478: Confucius
501: Confucius Chief Magistrate of
Chung-tu
498: Confucius Acting Supt. of Public Works in Duchy of Lu
497: Confucius Minister of Crime
496: Resignation of Confucius
496-483: Confucius' Wander-years
Fl. 450: Mo Ti, philosopher
403-221: Period of the Contending States

Fl. 390: Yang Chu, philosopher
372-289: Mencius, philosopher
B. 370: Chuang-tze, philosopher
D. 350: Ch'u P'ing, poet
B. 305: Hsün-tze, philosopher
D. 233: Han Fei, essayist
230-222: Conquest and unification of
China by Shih Huang-ti
255-206: *Ch'in Dynasty*
221-211: Shih Huang-ti, "First Emperor"
206 B.C.-221 A.D.: *Han Dynasty*
179-157 B.C.: Wen Ti
B. 145: Szuma Ch'ien, historian
140-87 B.C.: Wu Ti, reformer emperor
5-25 A.D.: Wang Mang, socialist emperor
67 A.D.: Coming of Buddhism to China
Ca. 100: First known manufacturer of
paper in China
200-400: Tartar invasions of China
221-264: Period of the Three Kingdoms
221-618: *The Minor Dynasties*
365-427: T'ao Ch'ien, poet
Fl. 364: Ku K'ai-chih, painter
490-640: Great Age of Buddhist Sculpture
618-905: *T'ang Dynasty*
618-627: Kao Tsu
627-650: T'ai Tsung
651-716: Li Ssu-hsün, painter
699-759: Wang Wei, painter
B. ca. 700: Wu Tao-tze, painter
705-762: Li Po, poet
712-770: Tu Fu, poet
713-756: Hsuan Tsung (Ming Huang)
755: Revolt of An Lu-shan

*All dates before 551 B.C. are approximate; all before 1800 A.D. are uncertain.

CHRONOLOGY OF CHINESE CIVILIZATION

A.D.

768-824: Han Yü, essayist
770: Oldest extant block prints
722-846: Po Chü-i, poet
868: Oldest extant printed book
907-960: *Five "Little Dynasties"*
932-953: Block printing of Chinese Classics
950: First appearance of paper money
960-1127: *Northern Sung Dynasty*
960-976: T'ai Tsu
970: First great Chinese encyclopedia
1069-1076: Administration of Wang An-shih, socialist prime minister
1040-1106: Li Lung-mien, painter
1041: Pi Sheng makes movable type
B. 1100: Kuo Hsi, painter
1101-1126: Hui Tsung, artist emperor
1126: Tatars sack Hui Tsung's capital, Pien Lang (K'aifeng); removal of capital to Lin-an (Hangchow)
1127-1279: *Southern Sung Dynasty*
1130-1200: Chu Hsi, philosopher
1161: First known use of gunpowder in war
1162-1227: Genghis Khan
1212: Genghis Khan invades China
1260-1368: *Yüan (Mongol) Dynasty*
1269-1295: Kublai Khan
1269: Marco Polo leaves Venice for China
1295: Marco Polo returns to Venice
1368-1644: *Ming Dynasty*
1368-1399: T'ai Tsu
1403-1425: Ch'eng Tsu (Yung Lo)
1517: Portugese at Canton
1571: Spanish take the Philippines

A.D.

1573-1620: Shen Tsung (Wan Li)
1637: English traders at Canton
1644-1912: *Ch'ing (Manchu) Dynasty*
1662-1722: K'ang Hsi
1736-1796: Ch'ien Lung
1795: First prohibition of opium trade
1800: Second prohibition of opium trade
1823-1901: Li Hung-chang, statesman
1834-1908: T'zu Hsi, "Dowager Empress"
1839-1842: First "Opium War"
1850-1864: T'ai-p'ing Rebellion
1856-1860: Second "Opium War"
1858-1860: Russia seizes Chinese territory north of the Amur River
1860: France seizes Indo-China
1866-1925: Sun Yat-sen
1875-1908: Kuang Hsu
1894: The Sino-Japanese War
1898: Germany takes Kiaochow; U. S. takes the Philippines
1898: The reform edicts of Kuang Hsu
1900: The Boxer Uprising
1905: Abolition of the examination system
1911: The Chinese Revolution
1912: (Jan.-Mar.): Sun Yat-sen Provisional President of the Chinese Republic
1912-1916: Yuan Shi-k'ai, President
1914: Japan takes Kiaochow
1915: The "Twenty-one Demands"
1920: *Pei-Hua* ("Plain Speech") adopted in the Chinese schools; height of the "New Tide"
1926: Chiang K'ai-shek and Borodin subdue the north
1927: The anti-communist reaction
1931: The Japanese occupy Manchuria

CHAPTER XXIII

The Age of the Philosophers

I. THE BEGINNINGS

1. Estimates of the Chinese

THE intellectual discovery of China was one of the achievements of the Enlightenment. "These peoples," Diderot wrote of the Chinese, "are superior to all other Asiatics in antiquity, art, intellect, wisdom, policy, and in their taste for philosophy; nay, in the judgment of certain authors, they dispute the palm in these matters with the most enlightened peoples of Europe."[a] "The body of this empire," said Voltaire, "has existed four thousand years, without having undergone any sensible alteration in its laws, customs, language, or even in its fashions of apparel. . . . The organization of this empire is in truth the best that the world has ever seen."[2] This respect of scholars has survived closer acquaintance, and in some contemporary observers it has reached the pitch of humble admiration. Count Keyserling, in one of the most instructive and imaginative books of our time, concludes that

> altogether the most perfect type of humanity as a normal phenomenon has been elaborated in ancient China . . . China has created the highest universal culture of being hitherto known . . . The greatness of China takes hold of and impresses me more and more . . . The great men of this country stand on a higher level of culture than ours do; . . . these gentlemen* . . . stand on an extraordinarily high level as types; especially their superiority impresses me. . . . How perfect the courtesy of the cultured Chinaman! . . . China's supremacy of form is unquestionable in all circumstances. . . . The Chinaman is perhaps the profoundest of all men.[3]

The Chinese do not trouble to deny this; and until the present century (there are now occasional exceptions) they were unanimous in regarding the inhabitants of Europe and America as barbarians.[4] It was the gentle

---

* The deposed Mandarins at Tsing-tao.

custom of the Chinese, in official documents before 1860, to employ the character for "barbarian" in rendering the term "foreigner"; and the barbarians had to stipulate by treaty that this translation should be improved.[5]* Like most other peoples of the earth, "the Chinese consider themselves the most polished and civilized of all nations."' Perhaps they are right, despite their political corruption and chaos, their backward science and sweated industry, their odorous cities and offal-strewn fields, their floods and famines, their apathy and cruelty, their poverty and superstition, their reckless breeding and suicidal wars, their slaughters and ignominious defeats. For behind this dark surface that now appears to the alien eye is one of the oldest and richest of living civilizations: a tradition of poetry reaching as far back as 1700 B.C.; a long record of philosophy idealistic and yet practical, profound and yet intelligible; a mastery of ceramics and painting unequaled in their kind; an easy perfection, rivaled only by the Japanese, in all the minor arts; the most effective morality to be found among the peoples of any time; a social organization that has held together more human beings, and has endured through more centuries, than any other known to history; a form of government which, until the Revolution destroyed it, was almost the ideal of philosophers; a society that was civilized when Greece was inhabited by barbarians, that saw the rise and fall of Babylonia and Assyria, Persia and Judea, Athens and Rome, Venice and Spain, and may yet survive when those Balkans called Europe have reverted to darkness and savagery. What is the secret of this durability of government, this artistry of hand, this poise and depth of soul?

2. The Middle Flowery Kingdom

Geography—Race—Prehistory

If we consider Russia as Asiatic—which it was till Peter, and may be again—then Europe becomes only a jagged promontory of Asia, the industrial projection of an agricultural hinterland, the tentative fingers or pseudopodia of a giant continent. Dominating that continent is China, as spacious as Europe, and as populous. Hemmed in, through most of its his-

---

* The Chinese scholar who helped Dr. Giles to translate some of the extracts in *Gems of Chinese Literature*, sent him, as a well-meant farewell, a poem in which occurred these gracious lines:

     From of old, literature has illumined the nation of nations;
     And now its influence has gone forth to regenerate a barbarian official.[6]

tory, by the largest ocean, the highest mountains, and one of the most extensive deserts in the world, China enjoyed an isolation that gave her comparative security and permanence, immutability and stagnation. Hence the Chinese called their country not *China* but *Tien-hua*—"Under the Heavens"—or *Sz-hai*—"Within the Four Seas"—or *Chung-kuo*—"Middle Kingdom"—or *Chung-hwa-kuo*—"Middle Flowery Kingdom"—or, by decree of the Revolution, *Chun-hwa-min-kuo*—"Middle Flowery People's Kingdom."[8] Flowers it has in abundance, and all the varied natural scenery that can come from sunshine and floating mists, perilous mountain crags, majestic rivers, deep gorges, and swift waterfalls amid rugged hills. Through the fertile south runs the Yang-tze River, three thousand miles in length; farther north the Hoang-ho, or Yellow River, descends from the western ranges amid plains of loess to carry its silt through vacillating estuaries once to the Yellow Sea, now to the Gulf of Pechili, tomorrow, possibly, to the Yellow Sea again. Along these and the Wei and other broad streams* Chinese civilization began, driving back the beast and the jungle, holding the surrounding barbarians at bay, clearing the soil of brush and bramble, ridding it of destructive insects and corrosive deposits like saltpetre, draining the marshes, fighting droughts and floods and devastating changes in the courses of the rivers, drawing the water patiently and wearily from these friendly enemies into a thousand canals, and building day by day through centuries—huts and houses, temples and schools, villages, cities and states. How long men have toiled to build the civilizations that men so readily destroy!

No one knows whence the Chinese came, or what was their race, or how old their civilization is. The remains of the "Peking Man"† suggest the great antiquity of the human ape in China; and the researches of Andrews have led him to conclude that Mongolia was thickly populated, as far back as 20,000 B.C., by a race whose tools corresponded to the "Azilian" development of mesolithic Europe, and whose descendants spread into Siberia and China as southern Mongolia dried up and became the Gobi Desert. The discoveries of Andersson and others in Honan and south Manchuria indicate a neolithic culture one or two thousand years later than similar stages in the prehistory of Egypt and Sumeria. Some of the stone tools found in these neolothic deposits resemble exactly, in shape

---

* The Yang-tze near Shanghai is three miles wide.
† Cf. p. 92 above.

and perforations, the iron knives now used in northern China to reap the sorghum crop; and this circumstance, small though it is, reveals the probability that Chinese culture has an impressive continuity of seven thousand years.[10]

We must not, through the blur of distance, exaggerate the homogeneity of this culture, or of the Chinese people. Some elements of their early art and industry appear to have come from Mesopotamia and Turkestan; for example, the neolithic pottery of Honan is almost identical with that of Anau and Susa.[11] The present "Mongolian" type is a highly complex mixture in which the primitive stock has been crossed and re-crossed by a hundred invading or immigrating stocks from Mongolia, southern Russia (the Scythians?), and central Asia.[12] China, like India, is to be compared with Europe as a whole rather than with any one nation of Europe; it is not the united home of one people, but a medley of human varieties different in origin, distinct in language, diverse in character and art, and often hostile to one another in customs, morals and government.

3. The Unknown Centuries

The Creation according to China—The coming of culture—Wine and chopsticks—The virtuous emperors—A royal atheist

China has been called "the paradise of historians." For centuries and millenniums it has had official historiographers who recorded everything that happened, and much besides. We cannot trust them further back than 776 B.C.; but if we lend them a ready ear they will explain in detail the history of China from 3000 B.C., and the more pious among them, like our own seers, will describe the creation of the world. P'an Ku, the first man (they tell us), after laboring on the task for eighteen thousand years, hammered the universe into shape about 2,229,000 B.C. As he worked his breath became the wind and the clouds, his voice became the thunder, his veins the rivers, his flesh the earth, his hair the grass and trees, his bones the metals, his sweat the rain; and the insects that clung to his body became the human race.[13] We have no evidence to disprove this ingenious cosmology.

The earliest kings, says Chinese legend, reigned eighteen thousand years each, and struggled hard to turn P'an Ku's lice into civilized men. Before the arrival of these "Celestial Emperors," we are told, "the people were like beasts, clothing themselves in skins, feeding on raw flesh, and knowing their mothers but not their fathers"—a limitation which Strindberg did not consider exclusively ancient or Chinese. Then came the emperor Fu Hsi, in precisely 2852 B.C.; with the help of his enlightened Queen he taught his people marriage, music, writing, painting, fishing with nets, the domestication of animals, and the feeding of silkworms for the secretion of silk. Dying, he appointed as his successor Shen Nung, who introduced agriculture, invented the wooden plough, established markets and trade, and developed the science of medicine from the curative values of plants. So legend, which loves personalities more than ideas, attributes to a few individuals the laborious advances of many generations. Then a vigorous soldier-emperor, Huang-ti, in a reign of a mere century, gave China the magnet and the wheel, appointed official historians, built the first brick structures in China, erected an observatory for the study of the stars, corrected the calendar, and redistributed the land. Yao ruled through another century, and so well that Confucius, writing of him eighteen hundred years later in what must have seemed a hectically "modern" age, mourned the degeneration of China. The old sage, who was not above the pious fraud of adorning a tale to point a moral, informs us that the Chinese people became virtuous by merely looking at Yao. As first aid to reformers, Yao placed outside his palace door a drum by which they might summon him to hear their grievances, and a tablet upon which they might write their advice to the government. "Now," says the famous *Book of History*,

> concerning the good Yao it is said that he ruled *Chung-kuo* for one hundred years, the years of his life being one hundred, ten and six. He was kind and benevolent as Heaven, wise and discerning as the gods. From afar his radiance was like a shining cloud, and approaching near him he was as brilliant as the sun. Rich was he without ostentation, and regal without luxuriousness. He wore a yellow cap and a dark tunic and rode in a red chariot drawn by white horses. The eaves of his thatch were not trimmed, and the rafters were unplaned, while the beams of his house had no ornamental ends. His principal food was soup, indifferently compounded, nor was he choice in selecting his grain. He drank his broth of lentils from a dish that was made of clay, using a wooden spoon. His person was not adorned with jewels, and his clothes were without embroidery, simple and without variety. He gave no attention to uncommon things and strange happenings, nor did he value those things that were rare and peculiar. He did not listen to songs of dalliance, his

chariot of state was not emblazoned. . . . In summer he wore his simple garb of cotton, and in winter he covered himself with skins of the deer. Yet was he the richest, the wisest, the longest-lived and most beloved of all that ever ruled *Chung-kuo*.[14]

The last of these "Five Rulers" was Shun, the model of filially devoted sons, the patient hero who fought the floods of the Hoang-ho, improved the calendar, standardized weights and measures, and endeared himself to scholastic posterity by reducing the size of the whip with which Chinese children were educated. In his old age Shun (Chinese tradition tells us) raised to a place beside himself on the throne the ablest of his aides, the great engineer Yü, who had controlled the floods of nine rivers by cutting through nine mountains and forming nine lakes; "but for Yü," say the Chinese, "we should all have been fishes."[15] In his reign, according to sacred legend, rice wine was discovered, and was presented to the Emperor; but Yü dashed it to the ground, predicting: "The day will come when this thing will cost some one a kingdom." He banished the discoverer and prohibited the new beverage; whereupon the Chinese, for the instruction of posterity, made wine the national beverage. Rejecting the principle of succession by royal appointment, Yü established the Hsia (i.e., "civilized") Dynasty by making the throne hereditary in his family, so that idiots alternated with mediocrities and geniuses in the government of China. The dynasty was brought to an end by the whimsical Emperor Chieh, who amused himself and his wife by compelling three thousand Chinese to jump to their euthanasy in a lake of wine.

We have no way of checking the accounts transmitted to us of the Hsia Dynasty by the early Chinese historians. Astronomers claim to have verified the solar eclipse mentioned by the records as occurring in the year 2165 B.C., but competent critics have challenged these calculations.[16] Bones found in Honan bear the names of rulers traditionally ascribed to the second or Shang Dynasty; and some bronze vessels of great antiquity are tentatively attributed to this period. For the rest we must rely on stories whose truth may not be proportioned to their charm. According to ancient tradition one of the Shang emperors, Wu Yi, was an atheist; he defied the gods, and blasphemed the Spirit of Heaven; he played chess with it, ordered a courtier to make its moves, and derided it when it lost; having dedicated to it a leathern bag, he filled the bag with blood, and amused himself by making it a target for his arrows. The historians, more virtuous than history, assure us that Wu Yi was struck dead with lightning.

Chou Hsin, royal inventor of chopsticks, brought the dynasty to an end by his incredible wickedness. "I have heard," he said, "that a man's heart has seven openings; I would fain make the experiment upon Pi Kan"—his minister. Chou's wife Ta-ki was a model of licentiousness and cruelty: at her court voluptuous dances were performed, and men and women gamboled naked in her gardens. When public criticism rose she sought to still it with novelties of torture: rebels were made to hold fiery metals in their hands, or to walk greased poles over a pit of live charcoal; when victims fell into the pit the Queen was much amused to see them roast.[17] Chou Hsin was overthrown by a conspiracy of rebels at home and invaders from the western state of Chou, who set up the Chou Dynasty, the most enduring of all the royal houses of China. The victorious leaders rewarded their aides by making them almost independent rulers of the many provinces into which the new realm was divided; in this way began that feudalism which proved so dangerous to government and yet so stimulating to Chinese letters and philosophy. The newcomers mingled their blood in marriage with the older stocks, and the mixture provided a slow biological prelude to the first historic civilization of the Far East.

4. The First Chinese Civilization

The Feudal Age in China—An able minister—The struggle between custom and law — Culture and anarchy — Love lyrics from the "Book of Odes"

The feudal states that now provided for almost a thousand years whatever political order China was to enjoy, were not the creation of the conquerors; they had grown out of the agricultural communities of primitive days through the absorption of the weaker by the stronger, or the merger of groups under a common chief for the defense of their fields against the encompassing barbarians. At one time there were over seventeen hundred of these principalities, ordinarily consisting of a walled town surrounded by cultivated land, with smaller walled suburbs constituting a protective circumference.[18] Slowly these provinces coalesced into fifty-five, covering what is now the district of Honan with neighboring portions of Shan-si, Shen-si and Shantung. Of these fifty-five the most important were Ts'i, which laid the bases of Chinese government, and Chin (or Tsin), which conquered all the rest, established a unified empire, and gave to China the name by which it is known to nearly all the world but itself.

The organizing genius of Ts'i was Kuan Chung, adviser to the Duke Huan. Kuan began his career in history by supporting Huan's brother against him in their competition for the control of Ts'i, and almost killed Huan in battle. Huan won, captured Kuan, and appointed him chief minister of the state. Kuan made his master powerful by replacing bronze with iron weapons and tools, and by establishing governmental monopoly or control of iron and salt. He taxed money, fish and salt, "in order to help the poor and reward wise and able men."[19] During his long ministry Ts'i became a well-ordered state, with a stabilized currency, an efficient administration, and a flourishing culture. Confucius, who praised politicians only by epitaph, said of Kuan: "Down to the present day the people enjoy the gifts which he conferred. But for Kuan Chung we should now be wearing our hair disheveled, and the lappets of our coats buttoning on the left side."*[20]

In the feudal courts was developed the characteristic courtesy of the Chinese gentleman. Gradually a code of manners, ceremonies and honor was established, which became so strict that it served as a substitute for religion among the upper classes of society. The foundations of law were laid, and a great struggle set in between the rule of custom as developed among the people and the rule of law as formulated by the state. Codes of law were issued by the duchies of Cheng and Chin (535, 512 B.C.), much to the horror of the peasantry, who predicted divine punishment for such outrages; and indeed the capital of Cheng was soon afterward destroyed by fire. The codes were partial to the aristocracy, who were exempted from the regulations on condition that they should discipline themselves; gentlemen murderers were allowed to commit suicide, and most of them did, in the fashion later so popular in *samurai* Japan. The people protested that they, too, could discipline themselves, and called for some Harmodius or Aristogiton to liberate them from this new tyranny of law. In the end the two hostile forces, custom and law, arrived at a wholesome compromise: the reach of law was narrowed to major or national issues, while the force of custom continued in all minor matters; and since human affairs are mostly minor matters, custom remained king.

As the organization of states proceeded, it found formulation in the *Chou-li*, or Law of Chou, a volume traditionally but incredibly ascribed to Chou-kung, uncle and prime minister of the second Duke of Chou. This legislation, suspiciously infused with the spirit of Confucius and Mencius, and therefore in all likelihood a product of the end rather than of the beginning of the Chou Dynasty, set for two thousand years the Chinese conception of government: an emperor ruling as the vicar and "Son of Heaven,"

---

* This is Confucius' gloomy way of indicating that but for Kuan the Chinese people would still be barbarians; for the barbarians habitually buttoned their coats on the left side.[21]

and holding power through the possession of virtue and piety; an aristocracy, partly of birth and partly of training, administering the offices of the state; a people dutifully tilling the soil, living in patriarchal families, enjoying civil rights but having no voice in public affairs; and a cabinet of six ministries controlling respectively the life and activities of the emperor, the welfare and early marriage of the people, the ceremonies and divinations of religion, the preparation and prosecution of war, the administration of justice, and the organization of public works.[22] It is an almost ideal code, more probably sprung from the mind of some anonymous and irresponsible Plato than from the practice of leaders sullied with actual power and dealing with actual men.

Since much deviltry can find room even in perfect constitutions, the political history of China during the Feudal Age was the usual mixture of persevering rascality with periodic reforms. As wealth increased, luxury and extravagance corrupted the aristocracy, while musicians and assassins, courtesans and philosophers mingled at the courts, and later in the capital at Lo-yang. Hardly a decade passed without some assault upon the new states by the hungry barbarians ever pressing upon the frontiers.[23] War became a necessity of defense, and soon a method of offense; it graduated from a game of the aristocracy to competitive slaughter among the people; heads were cut off by tens of thousands. Within a little more than two centuries, regicides disposed of thirty-six kings.[24] Anarchy grew, and the sages despaired.

Over these ancient obstacles life made its plodding way. The peasant sowed and reaped, occasionally for himself, usually for his feudal lord, to whom both he and the land belonged; not until the end of the dynasty did peasant proprietorship raise its head. The state—i.e., a loose association of feudal barons faintly acknowledging one ducal sovereign—conscripted labor for public works, and irrigated the fields with extensive canals; officials instructed the people in agriculture and arboriculture, and supervised the silk industry in all its details. Fishing and the mining of salt were in many provinces monopolized by the government.[25] Domestic trade flourished in the towns, and begot a small *bourgeoisie* possessed of almost modern comforts: they wore leather shoes, and dresses of homespun or silk; they rode in carts or chariots, or traveled on the rivers by boat; they lived in well-built houses, used tables and chairs, and ate their food from plates and dishes of ornamented pottery;[26] their standard of living was probably higher than that of their contemporaries in Solon's Greece, or Numa's Rome.

Amid conditions of disunity and apparent chaos the mental life of China showed a vitality disturbing to the generalizations of historians. For in this disorderly age were laid the bases of China's language, literature, philosophy and art; the combination of a life made newly secure by economic organization and provision, and a culture not yet forged into conformity by the tyranny of inescapable tradition and an imperial government, served as the social framework for the most creative period in the history of the Chinese mind. At every court, and in a thousand towns and villages, poets sang, potters turned their wheels, founders cast stately vessels, leisurely scribes formed into beauty the characters of the written language, sophists taught to eager students the tricks of the intellect, and philosophers pined over the imperfections of men and the decadence of states.

We shall study the art and language later, in their more complete and characteristic development; but the poetry and the philosophy belong specifically to this age, and constitute the classic period of Chinese thought. Most of the verse written before Confucius has disappeared; what remains of it is chiefly his own stern selection of the more respectable samples, gathered together in the *Shi-Ching*, or "Book of Odes," ranging over a thousand years from ancient compositions of the Shang Dynasty to highly modern poems as recent as Pythagoras. Its three hundred and five odes celebrate with untranslatable brevity and suggestive imagery the piety of religion, the hardships of war, and the solicitude of love. Hear the timeless lament of soldiers torn from their homes and dedicated to unintelligible death:

> How free are the wild geese on their wings,
> And the rest they find on the bushy Yu trees!
> But we, ceaseless toilers in the king's services,
> Cannot even plant our millet and rice.
>
> What will our parents have to rely on?
> O thou distant and azure Heaven!
> When shall all this end? . . .
> What leaves have not turned purple?
> What man is not torn from his wife?
> Mercy be on us soldiers:—
> Are we not also men?[27]

Though this age appears, to our ignorance, to have been almost the barbaric infancy of China, love poetry abounds in the *Odes*, and plays a gamut of many moods. In one of these poems, whispering to us across those buried centuries that seemed so model to Confucius, we hear the voice of eternally rebellious youth, as if to say that nothing is so old-fashioned as revolt:

I pray you, dear,
My little hamlet leave,
Nor break my willow-boughs;
'Tis not that I should grieve,
But I fear my sire to rouse.
Love pleads with passion disarrayed,—
"A sire's commands must be obeyed."

I pray you, dear,
Leap not across my wall,
Nor break my mulberry-boughs;
Not that I fear their fall,
But lest my brother's wrath should rouse,
Love pleads with passion disarrayed,—
"A brother's words must be obeyed."

I pray you, dear,
Steal not the garden down,
Nor break my sandal trees;
Not that I care for these,
But oh, I dread the talk of town.
Should lovers have their wilful way,
Whatever would the neighbors say?[28]

And another—the most nearly perfect, or the most excellently translated, of all—reveals to us the ageless antiquity of sentiment:

The morning glory climbs above my head,
Pale flowers of white and purple, blue and red.
    I am disquieted.

Down in the withered grasses something stirred;
I thought it was his footfall that I heard.
    Then a grasshopper chirred.

I climbed the hill just as the new moon showed,
I saw him coming on the southern road,
    My heart lays down its load.[29]

5. The Pre-Confucian Philosophers

*The "Book of Changes"—The "yang" and the "yin"—The Chinese
Enlightenment—Teng Shih, the Socrates of China*

The characteristic production of this epoch is philosophy. It is no
discredit to our species that in all ages its curiosity has outrun its wisdom,
and its ideals have set an impossible pace for its behavior. As far back
as 1250 B.C. we find Yu Tze sounding the keynote in a pithy fragment
then already stale, and now still fresh in counsel to laborious word-
mongers who do not know that all glory ends in bitterness: "He who
renounces fame has no sorrow"[30]—happy the man who has no history!
From that time until our own, China has produced philosophers.

As India is *par excellence* the land of metaphysics and religion, China
is by like preëminence the home of humanistic, or non-theological, philosophy. Almost the only important work of metaphysics in its literature
is the strange document with which the recorded history of Chinese
thought begins—the *I-Ching*, or "Book of Changes." Tradition insists
that it was written in prison by one of the founders of the Chou Dynasty,
Wen Wang, and that its simplest origin went back as far as Fu Hsi: this
legendary emperor, we are told, invented the eight *kua*, or mystic trigrams, which Chinese metaphysics identifies with the laws and elements
of nature. Each trigram consisted of three lines—some continuous and
representing the male principle or *yang*, some broken and representing
the female principle or *yin*. In this mystic dualism the *yang* represented
also the positive, active, productive and celestial principle of light, heat
and life, while the *yin* represented the negative, passive and earthly principle of darkness, cold and death. Wen Wang immortalized himself, and
racked the head of a billion Chinese, by doubling the number of strokes,
and thereby raising to sixty-four the number of possible combinations of
continuous and broken lines. To each of these arrangements some law
of nature corresponded. All science and history were contained in the
changeful interplay of the combinations; all wisdom lay hidden in the
sixty-four *hsiangs*, or ideas symbolically represented by the trigrams;
ultimately all reality could be reduced to the opposition and union of the
two basic factors in the universe—the male and the female principles, the
yang and the *yin*. The Chinese used the *Book of Changes* as a manual
of divination, and considered it the greatest of their classics; he who should

understand the combinations, we are told, would grasp all the laws of nature. Confucius, who edited the volume and adorned it with commentaries, ranked it above all other writings, and wished that he might be free to spend fifty years in its study.[31]

This strange volume, though congenial to the subtle occultism of the Chinese soul, is alien to the positive and practical spirit of Chinese philosophy. As far back as we can pry into the past of China we find philosophers; but of those who preceded Lao-tze time has preserved only an occasional fragment or an empty name. As in India, Persia, Judea and Greece, the sixth and fifth centuries saw, in China, a brilliant outburst of philosophical and literary genius; and as in Greece, it began with an epoch of rationalist "enlightenment." An age of war and chaos opened new roads to the advancement of unpedigreed talent, and established a demand, among the people of the towns, for instructors skilled in imparting the arts of the mind. These popular teachers soon discovered the uncertainty of theology, the relativity of morals and the imperfections of governments, and began to lay about them with Utopias; several of them were put to death by authorities who found it more difficult to answer than to kill. According to one Chinese tradition Confucius himself, during his tenure of office as Minister of Crime in the Duchy of Lu, condemned to death a seditious officer on the ground that "he was capable of gathering about him large crowds of men; that his arguments could easily appeal to the mob and make perversity respectable; and that his sophistry was sufficiently recalcitrant to take a stand against the accepted judgments of right."[32] Szuma-Ch'ien accepts the story; some other Chinese historians reject it;[33] let us hope that it is not true.

The most famous of these intellectual rebels was Teng Shih, who was executed by the Duke of Cheng during the youth of Confucius. Teng, says the Book of Lieh-tze, "taught the doctrines of the relativity of right and wrong, and employed inexhaustible arguments."[34] His enemies charged him with being willing to prove one thing one day and its opposite the next, if proper remuneration were forthcoming; he offered his services to those who were trying their cases in court, and allowed no prejudice to interfere with serviceability. A hostile Chinese historian tells a pretty story of him:

A wealthy man of Teng's native state was drowned in the Wei River, and his body was taken up by a man who demanded of the bereaved family a large sum of money for its redemption. The dead man's family sought Teng's counsel. "Wait," said the Sophist; "no other family will pay for the body." The advice was followed, and the man who held the corpse became anxious and also came to Teng Shih for advice. The Sophist gave the same counsel: "Wait; nowhere else can they obtain the body."[35]

Teng Shih composed a code of penology that proved too idealistic for the government of Cheng. Annoyed by pamphlets in which Teng criticized his policies, the prime minister prohibited the posting of pamphlets in public places. Teng thereupon delivered his pamphlets in person. The minister forbade the delivery of pamphlets. Teng smuggled them to his readers by concealing them in other articles. The government ended the argument by cutting off his head.[36]

6. The Old Master

Lao-tze—The "Tao"—On intellectuals in government—The foolishness of laws—A Rousseauian Utopia and a Christian ethic— Portrait of a wise man—The meeting of Lao-tze and Confucius

Lao-tze, greatest of the pre-Confucian philosophers, was wiser than Teng Shih; he knew the wisdom of silence, and lived, we may be sure, to a ripe old age—though we are not sure that he lived at all. The Chinese historian, Szuma Ch'ien, tells how Lao-tze, disgusted with the knavery of politicians and tired of his work as curator of the Royal Library of Chou, determined to leave China and seek some distant and secluded countryside. "On reaching the frontier the warden, Yin Hsi, said to him: 'So you are going into retirement. I beg you to write a book for me.' Thereupon Lao-tze wrote a book, in two parts, on *Tao* and *Te*, extending to over five thousand words. He then went away, and no one knows where he died."[37] Tradition, which knows everything, credits him with living eighty-seven years. All that remains of him is his name and his book, neither of which may have belonged to him. *Lao-tze* is a description, meaning "The Old Master"; his real name, we are told, was *Li*—that is to say, a plum. The book which is ascribed to him is of such doubtful authenticity that scholars quarrel learnedly about its origin.* But all are agreed that the *Tao-Te-Ching*—i.e., the "Book of the Way and of Virtue"—is the most important text of that Taoist philosophy which, in the opinion of Chinese students, existed long before Lao-tze, found many first-rate defenders after him, and became the religion of a considerable minority of the Chinese from his time to our own. The authorship of the *Tao-Te-Ching* is a secondary matter; but its ideas are among the most fascinating in the history of thought.

Tao means the Way: sometimes the Way of Nature, sometimes the Taoist Way of wise living; literally, a road. Basically, it is a way of thinking, or of refusing to think; for in the view of the Taoists thought is a superficial affair, good only for argument, and more harmful than beneficial to life; the Way is to be found by rejecting the intellect and all its wares, and leading a modest life of retirement, rusticity, and quiet contemplation of nature. Knowledge is not virtue; on the contrary, rascals have increased since education spread. Knowledge is not wisdom, for nothing is so far from a sage as an "intellectual." The worst conceivable government would be by philosophers; they botch every natural process with theory; their ability to make speeches and multiply ideas is precisely the sign of their incapacity for action.

> Those who are skilled do not dispute; the disputatious are not skilled. . . . When we renounce learning we have no troubles. . . . The sage constantly keeps men without knowledge and without desire, and where there are those who have knowledge, keeps them from presuming to act. . . . The ancients who showed their skill in practising the *Tao* did so not to enlighten the people, but to make them simple and ignorant. . . . The difficulty in governing the people arises from their having too much knowledge. He who tries to govern a state by his wisdom is a scourge to it, while he who does not do so is a blessing.⁴⁰

The intellectual man is a danger to the state because he thinks in terms of regulations and laws; he wishes to construct a society like geometry, and does not realize that such regulation destroys the living freedom and

---

* Professor Giles considers it a forgery composed after 200 B.C. by free pilfering from the works of the essayist and critic, Han Fei;³⁸ Dr. Legge holds that the frequent references to Lao (as "Lao Tan") in Chuang-tze and in Szuma Ch'ien warrant continued belief in the authenticity of the *Tao-Te-Ching*.³⁹

vigor of the parts. The simpler man, who knows from his own experience the pleasure and efficacy of work conceived and carried out in liberty, is less of a peril when he is in power, for he does not have to be told that a law is a dangerous thing, and may injure more than it may help." Such a ruler regulates men as little as possible; if he guides the nation it is away from all artifice and complexity towards a normal and artless simplicity, in which life would follow the wisely thoughtless routine of nature, and even writing would be put aside as an unnatural instrument of befuddlement and deviltry. Unhampered by regulations from the government, the spontaneous economic impulses of the people—their own lust for bread and love—would move the wheels of life in a simple and wholesome round. There would be few inventions, for these only add to the wealth of the rich and the power of the strong; there would be no books, no lawyers, no industries, and only village trade.

> In the kingdom the multiplication of prohibitions increases the poverty of the people. The more implements to add to their profit the people have, the greater disorder is there in the state and clan; the more acts of crafty dexterity men possess, the more do strange contrivances appear; the more display there is of legislation, the more thieves and robbers there are. Therefore a sage has said: "I will do nothing, and the people will be transformed of themselves; I will be fond of keeping still, and the people will of themselves be correct. I will take no trouble about it, and the people will of themselves become rich; I will manifest no ambition, and the people will of themselves attain to the primitive simplicity. . . .
> In a little state with a small population I would so order it that though there would be individuals in it with the abilities of ten or a hundred men, there should be no employment for them; I would make the people, while looking upon death as a grievous thing, yet not remove elsewhere (to avoid it). Though they had boats and carriages, they should have no occasion to ride in them; though they had buff coats and sharp weapons, they should have no occasion to don or use them. I would make the people return to the use of knotted cords.* They should think their (coarse) food sweet, their (plain) clothes beautiful, their (poor) dwellings places of rest, and their common ways sources of enjoyment. There should

---

* A form of communication that preceded writing. The word *make* is rather un-Laotzian.

be a neighboring state within sight, and the voices of the fowls and dogs should be heard all the way from it to us; but I would make the people to old age, even to death, not have any intercourse with it."⁴²

But what is this nature which Lao-tze wishes to accept as his guide? The Old Master draws as sharp a distinction between nature and civilization as Rousseau was to do in that gallery of echoes called "modern thought." Nature is natural activity, the silent flow of traditional events, the majestic order of the seasons and the sky; it is the *Tao*, or Way, exemplified and embodied in every brook and rock and star; it is that impartial, impersonal and yet rational law of things to which the law of conduct must conform if men desire to live in wisdom and peace. This law of things is the *Tao* or way of the universe, just as the law of conduct is the *Tao* or way of life; in truth, thinks Lao-tze, both *Taos* are one, and human life, in its essential and wholesome rhythm, is part of the rhythm of the world. In that cosmic *Tao* all the laws of nature are united and form together the Spinozistic *substance* of all reality; in it all natural forms and varieties find a proper place, and all apparent diversities and contradictions meet; it is the Absolute in which all particulars are resolved into one Hegelian unity.⁴³

In the ancient days, says Lao, nature made men and life simple and peaceful, and all the world was happy. But then men attained "knowledge," they complicated life with inventions, they lost all mental and moral innocence, they moved from the fields to the cities, and began to write books; hence all the misery of men, and the tears of the philosophers. The wise man will shun this urban complexity, this corrupting and enervating maze of law and civilization, and will hide himself in the lap of nature, far from any town, or books, or venal officials, or vain reformers. The secret of wisdom and of that quiet content which is the only lasting happiness that man can find, is a Stoic obedience to nature, an abandonment of all artifice and intellect, a trustful acceptance of nature's imperatives in instinct and feeling, a modest imitation of nature's silent ways. Perhaps there is no wiser passage in literature than this:

> All things in nature work silently. They come into being and possess nothing. They fulfil their function and make no claim. All things alike do their work, and then we see them subside. When they have reached their bloom each returns to its origin. Return-

ing to their origin means rest, or fulfilment of destiny. This re-
version is an eternal law. To know that law is wisdom."

Quiescence, a kind of philosophical inaction, a refusal to interfere with
the natural courses of things, is the mark of the wise man in every field.
If the state is in disorder, the proper thing to do is not to reform it, but to
make one's life an orderly performance of duty; if resistance is encoun-
tered, the wiser course is not to quarrel, fight, or make war, but to retire
silently, and to win, if at all, through yielding and patience; passivity has
its victories more often than action. Here Lao-tze talks almost with the
accents of Christ:

> If you do not quarrel, no one on earth will be able to quarrel with
> you. . . . Recompense injury with kindness. . . . To those who
> are good I am good, and to those who are not good I am also
> good; thus (all) get to be good. To those who are sincere I am sin-
> cere, and to those who are not sincere I am also sincere; and thus
> (all) get to be sincere. . . . The softest thing in the world dashes
> against and overcomes the hardest. . . . There is nothing in the
> world softer or weaker than water, and yet for attacking things
> that are firm and strong there is nothing that can take precedence
> of it.*[45]

All these doctrines culminate in Lao's conception of the sage. It is characteristic of Chinese thought that it speaks not of saints but of sages, not
so much of goodness as of wisdom; to the Chinese the ideal is not the pious
devotee but the mature and quiet mind, the man who, though fit to hold
high place in the world, retires to simplicity and silence. Silence is the
beginning of wisdom. Even of the *Tao* and wisdom the wise man does
not speak, for wisdom can be transmitted never by words, only by example and experience. "He who knows (the Way) does not speak about
it; he who speaks about it does not know it. He (who knows it) will keep
his mouth shut and close the portals of his nostrils."[47] The wise man is
modest, for at fifty† one should have discovered the relativity of knowledge and the frailty of wisdom; if the wise man knows more than other
men he tries to conceal it; "he will temper his brightness, and bring him-

---

* He adds, with reckless gallantry: "The female always overcomes the male by her
stillness."[46]

† The Chinese think of the sage as reaching the maturity of his powers about the age
of fifty, and living, through quietude and wisdom, to a century.[48]

self into agreement with the obscurity (of others);[49] he agrees with the simple rather than with the learned, and does not suffer from the novice's instinct of contradiction. He attaches no importance to riches or power, but reduces his desires to an almost Buddhist minimum:

> I have nothing that I value; I desire that my heart be completely subdued, emptied to emptiness. . . . The state of emptiness should be brought to the utmost degree, and that of stillness guarded with unwearying vigor. . . . Such a man cannot be treated familiarly or distantly; he is beyond all considerations of profit or injury, of nobility or meanness; he is the noblest man under heaven.[50]

It is unnecessary to point out the detailed correspondence of these ideas with those of Jean-Jacques Rousseau; the two men were coins of the same mould and mint, however different in date. It is a philosophy that periodically reappears, for in every generation many men weary of the struggle, cruelty, complexity and speed of city life, and write with more idealism than knowledge about the joys of rustic routine: one must have a long urban background in order to write rural poetry. "Nature" is a term that may lend itself to any ethic and any theology; it fits the science of Darwin and the unmorality of Nietzsche more snugly than the sweet reasonableness of Lao-tze and Christ. If one follows nature and acts naturally he is much more likely to murder and eat his enemies than to practise philosophy; there is small chance of his being humble, and less of his being silent. Even the painful tillage of the soil goes against the grain of a species primordially wont to hunt and kill; agriculture is as "unnatural" as industry.—And yet there is something medicinal in this philosophy; we suspect that we, too, when our fires begin to burn low, shall see wisdom in it, and shall want the healing peace of uncrowded mountains and spacious fields. Life oscillates between Voltaire and Rousseau, Confucius and Lao-tze, Socrates and Christ. After every idea has had its day with us and we have fought for it not wisely or too well, we in our turn shall tire of the battle, and pass on to the young our thinning fascicle of ideals. Then we shall take to the woods with Jacques, Jean-Jacques and Lao-tze; we shall make friends of the animals, and discourse more contentedly than Machiavelli with simple peasant minds; we shall leave the world to stew in its own deviltry, and shall take no further thought of its reform. Perhaps we shall burn every book but one behind us, and find a summary of wisdom in the *Tao-Te-Ching.*

We may imagine how irritating this philosophy must have been to Confucius, who, at the immature age of thirty-four, came up to Lo-yang, capital of Chou, and sought the Old Master's advice on some minutiæ of history.* Lao-tze, we are told, replied with harsh and cryptic brevity:

> Those about whom you inquire have moulded with their bones into dust. Nothing but their words remain. When the hour of the great man has struck he rises to leadership; but before his time has come he is hampered in all that he attempts. I have heard that the successful merchant carefully conceals his wealth, and acts as though he had nothing—that the great man, though abounding in achievements, is simple in his manners and appearance. Get rid of your pride and your many ambitions, your affectation and your extravagant aims. Your character gains nothing for all these. This is my advice to you.[61]

The Chinese historian relates that Confucius sensed at once the wisdom of these words, and took no offense from them; that on the contrary he said to his pupils, on his return from the dying sage: "I know how birds can fly, fishes swim, and animals run. But the runner may be snared, the swimmer hooked, and the flyer shot by the arrow. But there is the dragon—I cannot tell how he mounts on the wind through the clouds, and rises to heaven. Today I have seen Lao-tze, and can compare him only to the dragon."[62] Then the new master went forth to fulfil his own mission, and to become the most influential philosopher in history.

II. CONFUCIUS

1. The Sage in Search of a State

Birth and youth — Marriage and divorce — Pupils and methods — Appearance and character—The lady and the tiger—A definition of good government — Confucius in office — Wander-years—The consolations of old age

K'ung-fu-tze—K'ung the Master, as his pupils called K'ung Ch'iu—was born at Ch'ufu, in the then kingdom of Lu and the present province of Shantung, in the year 551 B.C. Chinese legend, not to be outdone by any

---

* The story is told by the greatest of Chinese historians, Szuma Ch'ien,[51] but it may be fiction. We are shocked to find Lao-tze in the busiest city of China in his eighty-seventh year.

rival lore, tells how apparitions announced his illegitimate birth[63] to his young mother, how dragons kept watch, and spirit-ladies perfumed the air, as she was delivered of him in a cave. He had, we are informed, the back of a dragon, the lips of an ox, and a mouth like the sea.[64] He came of the oldest family now in existence, for (the Chinese genealogists assure us) he was derived in direct line from the great emperor Huang-ti, and was destined to be the father of a long succession of K'ungs, unbroken to this day. His descendants numbered eleven thousand males a century ago; the town of his birth is still populated almost entirely by the fruit of his loins—or those of his only son; and one of his progeny is Finance Minister of the present Chinese Government at Nanking.[65]

His father was seventy years old when K'ung was born,[66] and died when the boy was three. Confucius worked after school to help support his mother, and took on in childhood, perhaps, that aged gravity which was to mark nearly every step of his history. Nevertheless he had time to become skilled in archery and music; to the latter he became so addicted that once, hearing an especially delectable performance, he was moved to the point of vegetarianism: for three months he did not eat meat.[67] He did not immediately agree with Nietzsche about a certain incompatibility between philosophy and marriage. He married at nineteen, divorced his wife at twenty-three, and does not seem to have married again.

At twenty-two' he began his career as a teacher, using his home as a schoolhouse, and charging whatever modest fee his pupils could pay. Three subjects formed the substance of his curriculum: history, poetry, and the rules of propriety. "A man's character," he said, "is formed by the Odes, developed by the Rites" (the rules of ceremony and courtesy), "and perfected by music."[68] Like Socrates he taught by word of mouth rather than by writing, and we know his views chiefly through the unreliable reports of his disciples. He gave to philosophers an example seldom heeded—to attack no other thinker, and waste no time in refutations. He taught no strict logical method, but he sharpened the wits of his students by gently exposing their fallacies, and making stern demands upon their alertness of mind. "When a man is not (in the habit of) saying, 'What shall I think of this? What shall I think of this?' I can indeed do nothing with him."[69] "I do not open up the truth to one who is not eager, nor help out any one who is not anxious to explain himself. When I have presented one corner of a subject to any one, and he cannot from it learn the other three, I do not repeat my lesson."[70] He was confident that only the wisest and the stupidest were beyond benefiting from instruction, and that no one could sincerely study humanistic philosophy without being improved in character as well as in mind. "It is not easy to find a man who has learned for three years without coming to be good."[71]

He had at first only a few pupils, but soon the news went about that behind the lips of an ox and the mouth like a sea there was a kindly heart and a well-furnished mind, and in the end he could boast that three thousand young men had studied under him, and had passed from his home to important positions in the world. Some of the students—once as many as seventy—lived with him like Hindu novices with their *guru*; and they developed an affection that often spoke out in their remonstrances against his exposure of his person to danger, or of his good name to calumny. Though always strict with them, he loved some of them more than his own son, and wept without measure when Hwuy died. "There was Yen Hwuy," he replied to Duke Gae, who had asked which of his pupils learned best; "*he* loved to learn. . . . I have not yet heard of any one who loves to learn (as he did). . . . Hwuy gave me no assistance; there was nothing that I said which did not give him delight. . . . He did not transfer his anger; he did not repeat a fault. Unfortunately, his appointed time was short, and he died; and now there is not (such another)."[72] Lazy students avoided him, or received short shrift from him; for he was not above instructing a sluggard with a blow of his staff, and sending him off with merciless verity. "Hard is the case of him who will stuff himself with food the whole day, without applying his mind to anything. . . . In youth not humble as befits a junior; in manhood doing nothing worthy of being handed down; and living on to an old age—this is to be a pest."[73]

He must have made a queer picture as he stood in his rooms, or, with nearly equal readiness, in the road, and taught his disciples history and poetry, manners and philosophy. The portraits that Chinese painters begot of him show him in his later years, with an almost hairless head gnarled and knotted with experience, and a face whose terrifying seriousness gave no inkling of the occasional humor and tenderness, and the keen esthetic sensitivity, that made him human despite his otherwise unbearable perfection. One of his music-teachers described him as he was in early middle age:

I have observed about Chung-ni many marks of a sage. He has river eyes and a dragon forehead—the very characteristics of Huang-ti. His arms are long, his back is like a tortoise, and he is nine (Chinese) feet six inches in height. . . . When he speaks he praises the ancient kings. He moves along the path of humility and' courtesy. He has heard of every subject, and retains with a strong memory. His knowledge of things seems inexhaustible. Have we not in him the rising of a sage?[74]

Legend assigns to his figure "forty-nine remarkable peculiarities." Once, when accident had separated him from his disciples during his wanderings, they located him at once by the report of a traveler that he had seen a monstrous-looking man with "the disconsolate appearance of a stray dog." When they repeated this description to Confucius he was much amused. "Capital!" he said, "capital!"[75]

He was an old-fashioned teacher, who believed that the maintenance of distance was indispensable to pedagogy. He was nothing if not formal, and the rules of etiquette and courtesy were his meat and drink. He tried to check and balance the natural epicureanism of the instincts with the puritanism and stoicism of his doctrine. At times he appears to have indulged himself in self-appreciation. "In a hamlet of ten families," he said, with some moderation, "there may be found one honorable and sincere as I am, but not so fond of learning."[76] "In letters I am perhaps equal to other men, but (the character of) the higher man, carrying out in his conduct what he professes, is what I have not yet attained to."[77] "If there were any of the princes who would employ me, in the course of twelve months I should have done something considerable. In three years (the government) would be perfected."[78] All in all, however, he bore his greatness with modesty. "There were four things," his disciples assure us, "from which the Master was entirely free. He had no foregone conclusions, no arbitrary predeterminations, no obstinacy, and no egoism."[79] He called himself "a transmitter and not a maker,"[80] and pretended that he was merely passing down what he had learned from the good emperors Yao and Shun. He strongly desired fame and place, but he would make no dishonorable compromises to secure or retain them; again and again he refused appointments to high office from men whose government seemed to him unjust. A man should say, he counseled his scholars, "I am not concerned that I have no place; I am concerned how I may fit myself for one. I am not concerned that I am not known; I seek to be worthy to be known."[81]

Among his pupils were the sons of Mang He, one of the ministers of the Duke of Lu. Through them Confucius was introduced to the Chou court at Lo-yang; but he kept a modest distance from the officials, preferring, as we have seen, to visit the dying sage Lao-tze. Returning to Lu, Confucius found his native province so disordered with civil strife that he removed to the neighboring state of T'si, accompanied by several of his pupils. Passing through rugged and deserted mountains on their way, they were surprised to find an old woman weeping beside a grave. Confucius sent Tsze-loo to inquire the cause of her grief. "My husband's father," she answered, "was killed here by a tiger, and my husband also; and now my son has met the same fate." When Confucius asked why she persisted in living in so dangerous a place, she replied: "There is no oppressive government here." "My children," said Confucius to his students, "remember this. Oppressive government is fiercer than a tiger."[82]

The Duke of Ts'i gave him audience, and was pleased with his answer to a question about good government. "There is good government when the prince is prince, and the minister is minister; when the father is father, and the son is son."[83] The Duke offered him for his support the revenues of the town of Lin-k'ew, but Confucius refused the gift, saying that he had done nothing to deserve such remuneration. The Duke was minded to insist on retaining him as an adviser, when his chief minister dissuaded him. "These scholars," said Gan Ying, "are impractical, and cannot be imitated. They are haughty and conceited of their own views, so that they will not be content in inferior positions. . . . This Mr. K'ung has a thousand peculiarities. It would take generations to exhaust all that he knows about the ceremonies of going up and going down."[84] Nothing came of it, and Confucius returned to Lu, to teach his pupils for fifteen years more before being called into public office.

His opportunity came when, at the turn of the century, he was made chief magistrate of the town of Chung-tu. According to Chinese tradition a veritable epidemic of honesty swept through the city; articles of value dropped in the street were left untouched, or returned to the owner.[85] Promoted by Duke Ting of Lu to be Acting Superintendent of Public Works, Confucius directed a survey of the lands of the state, and introduced many improvements in agriculture. Advanced again to be Minister of Crime, his appointment, we are told, sufficed of itself to put an end to crime. "Dishonesty and dissoluteness," say the Chinese records, "were ashamed, and hid their heads. Loyalty and good faith became the characteristics of the men, and chastity and docility those of the women. Strangers came in crowds from other states. Confucius became the idol of the people."[86]

This is too good to be true, and in any case proved too good to endure. Criminals put their hidden heads together, no doubt, and laid snares for the Master's feet. Neighboring states, say the historian, grew jealous of Lu, and fearful of its rising power. A wily minister of Ts'i suggested a stratagem to alienate the Duke of Lu from Confucius. The Duke of Ts'i sent to Ting a bevy of lovely "sing-song" girls, and one hundred and twenty still more beautiful horses. The Duke of Lu was captivated, ignored the disapproval of Confucius (who had taught him that the first principle of good government is good example), and scandalously neglected his ministers and the affairs of the state. "Master," said Tsze-loo, "it is time for you to be going." Reluctantly Confucius resigned, left Lu, and began thirteen years of homeless wandering. He remarked later that he had never "seen one who loves virtue as he loves beauty,"[87] and indeed, from some points of view, it is one of the most culpable oversights of nature that virtue and beauty so often come in separate packages.

The Master and a few faithful disciples, no longer welcome in his native state, passed now from province to province, receiving courtesies in some, undergoing dangers and privations in others. Twice they were attacked by ruffians, and once they were reduced almost to starvation, so that even Tsze-loo began to murmur that such a lot was hardly appropriate to the "higher man." The Duke of Wei offered Confucius the leadership of his government, but Confucius, disapproving of the Duke's principles, refused.[88] Once, as the little band was traveling through Ts'i, it came upon two old men who, in disgust with the corruption of the age, had retired like Lao-tze from public affairs and taken to a life of agricultural seclusion. One of them recognized Confucius, and reproached Tsze-loo for following him. "Disorder, like a swelling flood," said the recluse, "spreads over the whole empire; and who is he that will change it for you? Rather than follow one who withdraws from this state and that state, had you not better follow those who withdraw from the world altogether?"[89] Confucius gave much thought to this rebuke, but persisted in hoping that some state would again give him an opportunity to lead the way to reform and peace.

At last, in the sixty-ninth year of Confucius, Duke Gae succeeded to the throne of Lu, and sent three officers to the philosopher, bearing appropriate presents and an invitation to return to his native state. During the five years of life that remained to him Confucius lived in simplicity and honor, often consulted by the leaders of Lu, but wisely retiring to a literary seclusion, and devoting himself to the congenial work of editing the classics, and writing the history, of his people. When the Duke of Shi asked Tsze-loo about his master, and Tsze-loo did not answer him, Confucius, hearing of it, said: "Why did you not say to him?—He is simply a man who, in his eager pursuit of knowledge, forgets his food; who in the joy (of its attainment) forgets his sorrows; and who does not perceive that old age is coming on."[90] He consoled his solitude with poetry and philosophy, and rejoiced that his instincts now accorded with his reason. "At fifteen," he said, "I had my mind bent on learning. At thirty I stood firm. At forty I was free from doubt. At fifty I knew the decrees of Heaven. At sixty my ear was an obedient organ for the reception of truth. At seventy I could follow what my heart desired without transgressing what was right."[91]

He died at the age of seventy-two. Early one morning he was heard singing a mournful song:

> The great mountain must crumble,
> The strong beam must break,
> And the wise man wither away like a plant.

When his pupil Tsze-kung came to him he said: "No intelligent monarch arises; there is not one in the empire that will make me his master. My time is come to die."[92] He took to his couch, and after seven days he expired. His students buried him with pomp and ceremony befitting their affection for him; and building huts by his grave they lived there for three years, mourning for him as for a father. When all the others had gone Tsze-kung, who had loved him even beyond the rest, remained three years more, mourning alone by the Master's tomb.[93]

2. The Nine Classics

He left behind him five volumes apparently written or edited by his own hand, and therefore known to China as the "Five *Ching*," or Canonical Books. First, he edited the *Li-Chi*, or *Record of Rites*, believing that these ancient rules of propriety were subtle aides to the formation and mellowing of character, and the maintenance of social order and peace. Second, he wrote appendices and commentaries for the *I-Ching*, or *Book of Changes*, seeing in this the profoundest contribution yet made by China to that obscure realm of metaphysics which he himself had sedulously avoided in his philosophy. Third, he selected and arranged the *Shi-Ching*, or *Book of Odes*, in order to illustrate the nature of human life and the principles of morality. Fourth, he wrote the *Ch'un Ch'iu*, or *Spring and Autumn Annals*, to record with unadorned brevity the main events in the history of his own state of Lu. Fifth, and above all, he sought to inspire his pupils by gathering into a *Shu-Ching*, or *Book of History*, the most important and elevating events or legends of the early reigns, when China had been in some measure a unified empire, and its leaders, as Confucius thought, had been heroic and unselfish civilizers of the race. He did not think of his function, in these works, as that of an historian; rather he was a teacher, a moulder of youth; and he deliberately selected from the past such items as would rather inspire than disillusion his pupils; we should do him injustice if we turned to these volumes for an impartial and scientific account of Chinese history. He added to the record imaginary speeches and stories into which he poured as much as he could of his solicitude for morals and his admiration for wisdom. If he idealized the past of his country he did no more than we do with our own less ancient past; if already our earliest presidents have become sages and saints in hardly a century or two, surely to the historians of a thousand years hence they will seem as virtuous and perfect as Yao and Shun.

To these five *Ching* the Chinese add four *Shu*, or "Books" (of the Philosophers), to constitute the "Nine Classics." First and most important of these is the *Lun Yü*, or *Discourses and Dialogues*, known to the English world, through a whim of Legge's, as the "Analects"—i.e., the collected fragments—of Confucius. These pages are not from the Master's hand, but record, with exemplary clarity and brevity, his opinions and pronouncements as remembered by his followers. They were compiled within a few decades of Confucius' death, perhaps by the disciples of his disciples,[94] and are the least unreliable guide that we have to his philosophy. The most interesting and instructive of all statements in the Chinese Classics appears in the fourth and fifth paragraphs* of the second *Shu*—a work known to the Chinese as *Ta Hsüeh*, or *The Great Learning*. The Confucian philosopher and editor, Chu Hsi, attributed these paragraphs to Confucius, and the remainder of the treatise to Tseng Ts'an, one of the younger disciples; Kea Kwei, a scholar of the first century A.D., attributed the work to K'ung Chi, grandson of Confucius; the sceptical scholars of today agree that the au-

---

* Quoted on p. 668 below.

thorship is unknown.[95] All students concur in ascribing to this grandson the third philosophical classic of China, the *Chung Yung*, or *Doctrine of the Mean*. The last of the *Shu* is the *Book of Mencius*, of which we shall speak presently. With this volume ends the classic literature, but not the classic period, of Chinese thought. There were, as we shall see, rebels and heretics of every kind to protest against that masterpiece of conservatism, the philosophy of Confucius.

3. The Agnosticism of Confucius

A fragment of logic — The philosopher and the urchins — A formula of wisdom

Let us try to do justice to this doctrine; it is the view of life that we shall take when we round out our first half-century, and for all that we know it may be wiser than the poetry of our youth. If we ourselves are heretics and young, this is the philosophy that we must marry to our own in order that our half-truths may beget some understanding.

We shall not find here a *system* of philosophy—i.e., a consistent structure of logic, metaphysics, ethics and politics dominated by one idea (like the palaces of Nebuchadrezzar, which bore on every brick the name of the ruler). Confucius taught the art of reasoning not through rules or syllogisms, but by the perpetual play of his keen mind upon the opinions of his pupils; when they went out from his school they knew nothing about logic, but they could think clearly and to the point. Clarity and honesty of thought and expression were the first lessons of the Master. "The whole end of speech is to be understood"[96]—a lesson not always remembered by philosophy. "When you know a thing, to hold that you know it; and when you do not, to admit the fact—this is knowledge."[97] Obscurity of thought and insincere inaccuracy of speech seemed to him national calamities. If a prince who was not in actual fact and power a prince should cease to be called a prince, if a father who was not a fatherly father should cease to be called a father, if an unfilial son should cease to be called a son—then men might be stirred to reform abuses too often covered up with words. Hence when Tsze-loo told Confucius, "The prince of Wei has been waiting for you, in order with you to administer the government; what will you consider the first thing to be done?" he answered, to the astonishment of prince and pupil, "What is necessary is to rectify names."[98]

Since his dominating passion was the application of philosophy to conduct and government, Confucius avoided metaphysics, and tried to turn
the minds of his followers from all recondite or celestial concerns. Though
he made occasional mention of "Heaven" and prayer,[99] and counseled his
disciples to observe sedulously the traditional rites of ancestor worship
and national sacrifice,[100] he was so negative in his answers to theological
questions that modern commentators agree in calling him an agnostic.[101]
When Tsze-kung asked him, "Do the dead have knowledge, or are they
without knowledge?" Confucius refused to make any definite reply.[102]
When Ke Loo asked about "serving the spirits" (of the dead), the Master
responded: "While you are not able to serve men, how can you serve their
spirits?" Ke Loo asked: "I venture to ask about death?" and was answered: "While you do not know life, how can you know about death?"[103]
When Fan Ch'e inquired "what constituted wisdom?" Confucius said:
"To give one's self earnestly to the duties due to men, and, while respect-
ing spiritual beings, to keep aloof from them, may be called wisdom."[104]
His disciples tell us that "the subjects on which the Master did not talk
were extraordinary things, feats of strength, disorder, and spiritual
beings."[105] They were much disturbed by this philosophic modesty, and
doubtless wished that the Master would solve for them the mysteries of
heaven. The *Book of Lieh-tze* tells with glee the fable of the street-
urchins who ridiculed the Master when he confessed his inability to answer
their simple question—"Is the sun nearer to the earth at dawn, when it is
larger, or at noon, when it is hotter?"[106] The only metaphysics that Confucius would recognize was the search for unity in all phenomena, and the
effort to find some stabilizing harmony between the laws of right conduct
and the regularities of nature. "Tsze," he said to one of his favorites,
"you think, I suppose, that I am one who learns many things and keeps
them in his memory?" Tsze-kung replied, "Yes, but perhaps it is not so?"
"No," was the answer; "I seek unity, all-pervading."[107] This, after all, is
the essence of philosophy.

His master passion was for morality. The chaos of his time seemed to
him a moral chaos, caused perhaps by the weakening of the ancient faith
and the spread of Sophist scepticism as to right and wrong; it was to be
cured not by a return to the old beliefs, but by an earnest search for more
complete knowledge, and a moral regeneration based upon a soundly
regulated family life. The Confucian program is expressed pithily and
profoundly in the famous paragraphs of *The Great Learning*:

The ancients who wished to illustrate the highest virtue throughout the empire first ordered well their own states. Wishing to order
well their states, they first regulated their families. Wishing to regulate their families, they first cultivated their own selves. Wishing to
cultivate their own selves, they first rectified their hearts. Wishing to rectify their hearts, they first sought to be sincere in their
thoughts. Wishing to be sincere in their thoughts, they first extended to the utmost their knowledge. Such extension of knowledge lay in the investigation of things.

Things being investigated, knowledge became complete. Their
knowledge being complete, their thoughts were sincere. Their
thoughts being sincere, their hearts were then rectified. Their hearts
being rectified, their own selves were cultivated. Their own selves
being cultivated, their families were regulated. Their families being
regulated, their states were rightly governed. Their states being
rightly governed, the whole empire was made tranquil and happy.[108]

This is the keynote and substance of the Confucian philosophy; one
might forget all other words of the Master and his disciples, and yet carry
away with these "the essence of the matter," and a complete guide to life.
The world is at war, says Confucius, because its constituent states are improperly governed; these are improperly governed because no amount of
legislation can take the place of the natural social order provided by the
family; the family is in disorder, and fails to provide this natural social
order, because men forget that they cannot regulate their families if they
do not regulate themselves; they fail to regulate themselves because they
have not rectified their hearts—i.e., they have not cleansed their own souls
of disorderly desires; their hearts are not rectified because their thinking
is insincere, doing scant justice to reality and concealing rather than revealing their own natures; their thinking is insincere because they let
their wishes discolor the facts and determine their conclusions, instead of
seeking to extend their knowledge to the utmost by impartially investi-
gating the nature of things. Let men seek impartial knowledge, and their
thinking will become sincere; let their thoughts be sincere and their hearts
will be cleansed of disorderly desires; let their hearts be so cleansed, and
their own selves will be regulated; let their own selves be regulated, and
their families will automatically be regulated—not by virtuous sermonizing
or passionate punishments, but by the silent power of example itself; let
the family be so regulated with knowledge, sincerity and example, and it

will give forth such spontaneous social order that successful government will once more be a feasible thing; let the state maintain internal justice and tranquillity, and all the world will be peaceful and happy.—It is a counsel of perfection, and forgets that man is a beast of prey; but like Christianity it offers us a goal to strike at, and a ladder to climb. It is one of the golden texts of philosophy.

4. The Way of the Higher Man

Another portrait of the sage — Elements of character — The Golden Rule

Wisdom, therefore, begins at home, and the foundation of society is a disciplined individual in a disciplined family. Confucius agreed with Goethe that self-development is the root of social development; and when Tsze-loo asked him, "What constitutes the Higher Man?" he replied, "The cultivation of himself with reverential care."[109] Here and there, throughout the dialogues, we find him putting together, piece by piece, his picture of the ideal man—a union of philosopher and saint producing the sage. The Superman of Confucius is composed of three virtues severally selected as supreme by Socrates, Nietzsche and Christ: intelligence, courage, and good will. "The Higher Man is anxious lest he should not get truth; he is not anxious lest poverty should come upon him. . . . He is catholic, not partisan. . . . He requires that in what he says there should be nothing inaccurate."[110] But he is no mere intellect, not merely a scholar or a lover of knowledge; he has character as well as intelligence. "Where the solid qualities are in excess of accomplishments, we have rusticity; where the accomplishments are in excess of the solid qualities, we have the manners of a clerk. When the accomplishments and solid qualities are equally blended, we then have the man of complete virtue."[111] Intelligence is intellect with its feet on the earth.

The foundation of character is sincerity. "Is it not just an entire sincerity which marks the Higher Man?"[112] "He acts before he speaks, and afterwards speaks according to his actions."[113] "In archery we have something like the way of the Higher Man. When the archer misses the center of the target, he turns round and seeks for the cause of his failure in himself."[114] "What the Higher Man seeks is in himself; what the lower man seeks is in others. . . . The Higher Man is distressed by his want of ability, not . . . by men's not knowing him"; and yet "he dislikes the thought of his name not being mentioned after his death."[115] He "is modest in his speech, but exceeds in his actions. . . . He seldom speaks; when he does he is sure to hit the point. . . . That wherein the Higher Man cannot be equaled is simply this: his work, which other men cannot see."[116] He is moderate in word and deed; in everything "the Higher Man conforms with the path of the mean."[117] For "there is no end of things by which man is affected; and when his likings and dislikings are not subject to regulation, he is changed into the nature of things as they come before him."[118]* "The Higher Man moves so as to make his movements in all generations a universal path; he behaves so as to make his conduct in all generations a universal law; he speaks so as to make his words in all generations a universal norm."[120]† He accepts completely the Golden Rule, which is here laid down explicitly four centuries before Hillel and five centuries before Christ: "Chung-kung asked about perfect virtue. The Master said, . . . 'Not to do unto others as you would not wish done to yourself.' "[122] The principle is stated again and again, always negatively, and once in a single word. "Tsze-kung asked, 'Is there one word which may serve as a rule of practice for all one's life?' The Master said, 'Is not *reciprocity* such a word?' "[123] Nevertheless he did not wish, like Lao-tze, to return good for evil; and when one of his pupils asked him, "What do you say concerning the principle that injury should be recompensed with kindness?" he replied, more sharply than was his custom: "With what, then, will you recompense kindness? Recompense injury with justice, and recompense kindness with kindness."[124]

The very basis of the Higher Man's character is an overflowing sympathy towards all men. He is not angered by the excellences of other men; when he sees men of worth he thinks of equaling them; when he sees men of low worth he turns inward and examines himself;[124a] for there are few faults that we do not share with our neighbors. He pays no attention to slander or violent speech.[124b] He is courteous and affable to all, but he does not gush forth indiscriminate praise.[125] He treats his inferiors without contempt, and his superiors without seeking to court their favor.[126] He is grave in deportment, since men will not take seriously one who is not serious with them; he is slow in words and earnest in conduct; he is not quick with his tongue, or given to clever repartee; he is earnest because he has work to do—and this is the secret of his unaffected dignity.[127] He is courteous even to his familiars, but maintains his reserve towards all, even his son.[128] Confucius sums up the

---

* Cf. Spinoza: "We are tossed about by external causes in many ways, and like waves driven by contrary winds, we waver and are unconscious of the issue and our fate."[119]

† Cf. one of Kant's formulations of the "Categorical Imperative" of morals: "So to will that the maxim of thy conduct can become a universal law."[121]

qualities of his "Higher Man"—so similar to the *Megalopsychos*, or "Great-Minded Man," of Aristotle—in these words:

> The Higher Man has nine things which are subjects with him of thoughtful consideration. In regard to the use of his eyes he is anxious to see clearly. . . . In regard to his countenance he is anxious that it should be benign. In regard to his demeanor he is anxious that it should be respectful. In regard to his speech he is anxious that it should be sincere. In regard to his doing of business he is anxious that it should be reverently careful. In regard to what he doubts about, he is anxious to question others. When he is angry he thinks of the difficulties his anger may involve him in. When he sees gain to be got he thinks of righteousness.[129]

5. Confucian Politics

Popular sovereignty—Government by example—The decentralization of wealth — Music and manners — Socialism and revolution

None but such men, in the judgment of Confucius, could restore the family and redeem the state. Society rests upon the obedience of the children to their parents, and of the wife to her husband; when these go, chaos comes.[130] Only one thing is higher than this law of obedience, and that is the moral law. "In serving his parents (a son) may remonstrate with them, but gently; when he sees that they do not incline to follow (his advice), he shows an increased degree of reverence, but does not abandon (his purpose). . . . When the command is wrong, a son should resist his father, and a minister should resist his August Master."[131] Here was one root of Mencius' doctrine of the divine right of revolution.

There was not much of the revolutionist in Confucius; perhaps he suspected that the inheritors of a revolution are made of the same flesh as the men whom it deposed. But he wrote bravely enough in the *Book of Odes*: "Before the sovereigns of the Shang (Dynasty) had lost (the hearts of) the people, they were the mates of God. Take warning from the house of Shang. The great decree is not easily preserved."[132] The people are the actual and proper source of political sovereignty, for any government that does not retain their confidence sooner or later falls.

> Tsze-kung asked about government. The Master said, "(The requisites of government) are three: that there should be suffi-

ciency of food, sufficiency of military equipment, and the confidence of the people in their ruler." Tsze-kung said, "If it cannot be helped, and one of these must be dispensed with, which of the three should be foregone first?" "The military equipment," said the Master. Tsze-kung asked again, "If it cannot be helped, and one of the remaining two must be dispensed with, which of them should be foregone?" The Master answered, "Part with the food. From of old, death has been the lot of all men; but if the people have no faith (in their rulers) there is no standing (for the state)."[133]

The first principle of government, in the view of Confucius, is as the first principle of character—sincerity. Therefore the prime instrument of government is good example: the ruler must be an eminence of model behavior, from which, by prestige imitation, right conduct will pour down upon his people.

Ke K'ang asked Confucius about government, saying, "What do you say to killing the unprincipled for the good of the principled?" Confucius replied, "Sir, in carrying on your government, why should you use killing at all? Let your (evinced) desires be for what is good, and the people will be good. The relation between superiors and inferiors is like that between the wind and the grass. The grass must bend when the wind blows across it. . . . He who exercises government by means of his virtue may be compared to the north polar star, which keeps its place, and all the stars turn toward it. . . . Ke K'ang asked how to cause the people to reverence (their ruler), to be faithful to him, and to urge themselves to virtue. The Master said, "Let him preside over them with gravity—then they will reverence him. Let him be filial and kind to all—then they will be faithful to him. Let him advance the good and teach the incompetent—then they will eagerly seek to be virtuous."[134]

As good example is the first instrument of government, good appointments are the second. "Employ the upright and put aside the crooked; in this way the crooked can be made to be upright."[135] "The administration of government," says the *Doctrine of the Mean*, "lies in (getting proper) men. Such men are to be got by means of (the ruler's) own character."[136] What would not a ministry of Higher Men do, even in one generation, to cleanse the state and guide the people to a loftier level of civilization?[137] First of all, they would avoid foreign relations as much as possible, and seek to make their state so independent of outside supplies that it would never be tempted to war for them. They would reduce the luxury of courts, and seek a wide distribution of wealth, for "the centralization of wealth is the way to scatter the people, and letting it be scattered among them is the way to collect the people."[138] They would decrease punishments, and increase public instruction; for "there being instruction, there will be no distinction of classes."[139] The higher subjects would be forbidden to the mediocre, but music would be taught to all. "When one has mastered music completely, and regulates his heart and mind accordingly, the natural, correct, gentle and sincere heart is easily developed, and joy attends its development. . . . The best way to improve manners and customs is to . . . pay attention to the composition of the music played in the country.* . . . Manners and music should not for a moment be neglected by any one. . . . Benevolence is akin to music, and righteousness to good manners."[140]

Good manners, too, must be a care of the government, for when manners decay the nation decays with them. Imperceptibly the rules of propriety form at least the outward character,[141] and add to the sage the graciousness of the gentleman; we become what we do. Politically "the usages of propriety serve as dykes for the people against evil excesses"; and "he who thinks the old embankments useless, and destroys them, is sure to suffer from the desolation caused by overflowing water":[142] one almost hears the stern voice of the angry Master echoing those words today from that Hall of the Classics where once all his words were engraved in stone, and which revolution has left desecrated and forlorn.

And yet Confucius too had his Utopias and dreams, and might have sympathized at times with men who, convinced that the dynasty had lost "the great decree" or "mandate of Heaven," dragged down one system of order in the hope of rearing a better one on the ruins. In the end he became a socialist, and gave his fancy rein:

> When the Great Principle (of the Great Similarity) prevails, the whole world becomes a republic; they elect men of talents, virtue and ability; they talk about sincere agreement, and cultivate universal peace. Thus men do not regard as their parents only their

---

* "Let me write the songs of a nation," said Daniel O'Connell, "and I care not who makes its laws."

to its individuals, a dignity and profundity unequaled elsewhere in the world or in history. With the help of this philosophy China developed a harmonious community life, a zealous admiration for learning and wisdom, and a quiet and stable culture which made Chinese civilization strong enough to survive every invasion, and to remould every invader in its own image. Only in Christianity and in Buddhism can we find again so heroic an effort to transmute into decency the natural brutality of men. And today, as then, no better medicine could be prescribed for any people suffering from the disorder generated by an intellectualist education, a decadent moral code, and a weakened fibre of individual and national character, than the absorption of the Confucian philosophy by the nation's youth.

But that philosophy could not be a complete nourishment in itself. It was well fitted to a nation struggling out of chaos and weakness into order and strength, but it would prove a shackle upon a country compelled by international competition to change and grow. The rules of propriety, destined to form character and social order, became a strait-jacket forcing almost every vital action into a prescribed and unaltered mould. There was something prim and Puritan about Confucianism which checked too thoroughly the natural and vigorous impulses of mankind; its virtue was so complete as to bring sterility. No room was left in it for pleasure and adventure, and little for friendship and love. It helped to keep woman in supine debasement,[145] and its cold perfection froze the nation into a conservatism as hostile to progress as it was favorable to peace.

We must not blame all this upon Confucius; one cannot be expected to do the thinking of twenty centuries. We ask of a thinker only that, as the result of a lifetime of thought, he shall in some way illuminate our path to understanding. Few men have done this more certainly than Confucius. As we read him, and perceive how little of him must be erased today because of the growth of knowledge and the change of circumstance, how soundly he offers us guidance even in our contemporary world, we forget his platitudes and his unbearable perfection, and join his pious grandson, K'ung Chi in that superlative eulogy which began the deification of Confucius:

> Chung-ni (Confucius) handed down the doctrines of Yao and Shun as if they had been his ancestors, and elegantly displayed the

regulations of Wen and Wu, taking them as his model. Above he harmonized with the times of heaven, and below he was conformed to the water and land.

He may be compared to heaven and earth in their supporting and containing, their overshadowing and curtaining, all things. He may be compared to the four seasons in their alternating progress, and to the sun and moon in their successive shining. . . . ·

All-embracing and vast, he is like heaven. Deep and active as a fountain, he is like the abyss. He is seen, and the people all reverence him; he speaks, and the people all believe him; he acts, and the people are all pleased with him.

Therefore his fame overspreads the Middle Kingdom, and extends to all barbarous tribes. Wherever ships and carriages reach, wherever the strength of man penetrates, wherever the heavens overshadow and the earth sustains, wherever the sun and moon shine, wherever frosts and dews fall—all who have blood and breath unfeignedly honor and love him. Hence it is said: "He is the equal of Heaven."[146]

III. SOCIALISTS AND ANARCHISTS

The two hundred years that followed upon Confucius were centuries of lively controversy and raging heresy. Having discovered the pleasures of philosophy, some men, like Hui Sze and Kung Sun Lung, played with logic, and invented paradoxes of reasoning as varied and subtle as Zeno's.[147] Philosophers flocked to the city of Lo-yang as, in the same centuries, they were flocking to Benares and Athens; and they enjoyed in the Chinese capital all that freedom of speech and thought which made Athens the intellectual center of the Mediterranean world. Sophists called *Tsung-heng-kia*, or "Crisscross Philosophers," crowded the capital to teach all and sundry the art of persuading any man to anything.[148] To Lo-yang came Mencius, inheritor of the mantle of Confucius, Chuang-tze, greatest of Lao-tze's followers, Hsün-tze, the apostle of original evil, and Mo Ti, the prophet of universal love.

1. Mo Ti, Altruist

An early logician—Christian—and pacifist

"Mo Ti," said his enemy, Mencius, "loved all men, and would gladly wear out his whole being from head to heel for the benefit of mankind.[149]

He was a native of Lu, like Confucius, and flourished shortly after the passing of the sage. He condemned the impracticality of Confucius' thought, and offered to replace it by exhorting all men to love one another. He was among the earliest of Chinese logicians, and the worst of Chinese reasoners. He stated the problem of logic with great simplicity:

> These are what I call the Three Laws of Reasoning:
> 1. Where to find the foundation. Find it in the study of the experiences of the wisest men of the past.
> 2. How to take a general survey of it? Examine the facts of the actual experience of the people.
> 3. How to apply it? Put it into law and governmental policy, and see whether or not it is conducive to the welfare of the state and the people.[150]

On this basis Mo Ti proceeded to prove that ghosts and spirits are real, for many people have seen them. He objected strongly to Confucius' coldly impersonal view of heaven, and argued for the personality of God. Like Pascal, he thought religion a good wager: if the ancestors to whom we sacrifice hear us, we have made a good bargain; if they are quite dead, and unconscious of our offerings, the sacrifice gives us an opportunity to "gather our relatives and neighbors and participate in the enjoyment of the sacrificial victuals and drinks."[151]

In the same manner, reasons Mo Ti, universal love is the only solution of the social problem; for if it were applied there is no doubt that it would bring Utopia. "Men in general loving one another, the strong would not make prey of the weak, the many would not plunder the few, the rich would not insult the poor, the noble would not be insolent to the mean, and the deceitful would not impose upon the simple."[152] Selfishness is the source of all evil, from the acquisitiveness of the child to the conquest of an empire. Mo Ti marvels that a man who steals a pig is universally condemned and generally punished, while a man who invades and appropriates a kingdom is a hero to his people and a model to posterity.[153] From this pacifism Mo Ti advanced to such vigorous criticism of the state that his doctrine verged on anarchism, and frightened the authorities.[154] Once, his biographers assure us, when the State Engineer of the Kingdom of Chu was about to invade the state of Sung in order to test a new siege ladder which he had invented, Mo Ti dissuaded him by preaching to him his doctrine of universal love and peace. "Before I met you," said the

Engineer, "I had wanted to conquer the state of Sung. But since I have seen you I would not have it even if it were given to me without resistance but with no just cause." "If so," replied Mo Ti, "it is as if I had already given you the state of Sung. Do persist in your righteous course, and I will give you the whole world."[155]

The Confucian scholars, as well as the politicians of Lo-yang, met these amiable proposals with laughter.[156] Nevertheless Mo Ti had his followers, and for two centuries his views became the religion of a pacifistic sect. Two of his disciples, Sung Ping and Kung Sun Lung, waged active campaigns for disarmament.[157] Han Fei, the greatest critic of his age, attacked the movement from what we might call a Nietzchean standpoint, arguing that until men had actually sprouted the wings of universal love, war would continue to be the arbiter of nations. When Shih Huang-ti ordered his famous "burning of the books," the literature of Mohism was cast into the flames along with the volumes of Confucius; and unlike the writings and doctrines of the Master, the new religion did not survive the conflagration.[158]

2. Yang Chu, Egoist

An epicurean determinist—The case for wickedness

Meanwhile a precisely opposite doctrine had found vigorous expression among the Chinese. Yang Chu, of whom we know nothing except through the mouths of his enemies,[159] announced paradoxically that life is full of suffering, and that its chief purpose is pleasure. There is no god, said Yang, and no after-life; men are the helpless puppets of the blind natural forces that made them, and that gave them their unchosen ancestry and their inalienable character.[160] The wise man will accept this fate without complaint, but will not be fooled by all the nonsense of Confucius and Mo Ti about inherent virtue, universal love, and a good name: morality is a deception practised upon the simple by the clever; universal love is the delusion of children who do not know the universal enmity that forms the law of life; and a good name is a posthumous bauble which the fools who paid so dearly for it cannot enjoy. In life the good suffer like the bad, and the wicked seem to enjoy themselves more keenly than the good.[161] The wisest men of antiquity were not moralists and rulers, as Confucius supposed, but sensible sensualists who had the good fortune to antedate the legislators and the philosophers, and who enjoyed the pleasures of every impulse. It is true that the wicked sometimes leave a bad name behind them, but this is a matter that does not disturb their bones. Consider, says Yang Chu, the fate of the good and the evil:

All agree in considering Shun, Yü, Chou-kung and Confucius to have been the most admirable of men, and Chieh and Chou the most wicked.*

Now Shun had to plough the ground on the south of the Ho, and to play the potter by the Lei lake. His four limbs had not even a temporary rest; for his mouth and belly he could not even find pleasant food and warm clothing. No love of his parents rested upon him; no affection of his brothers and sisters. . . . When Yao at length resigned to him the throne, he was advanced in age; his wisdom was decayed; his son Shang-chun proved without ability; and he had finally to resign the throne to Yü. Sorrowfully came he to his death. Of all mortals never was one whose life was so worn out and empoisoned as his. . . .

All the energies of Yü were spent on his labors with the land; a child was born to him, but he could not foster it; he passed his door without entering; his body became bent and withered; the skin of his hands and feet became thick and callous. When at length Shun resigned to him the throne, he lived in a low mean house, though his sacrificial apron and cap were elegant. Sorrowfully came he to his death. Of all mortals never was one whose life was so saddened and embittered as his. . . .

Confucius understood the ways of the ancient sovereigns and kings. He responded to the invitations of the princes of his time. The tree was cut down over him in Sung; the traces of his footsteps were removed in Wei; he was reduced to extremity in Shang and Chou; he was surrounded in Ch'an and Ts'i; . . . he was disgraced by Yang Hu. Sorrowfully came he to his death. Of all mortals never was one whose life was so agitated and hurried as his.

These four sages, during their lives, had not a single day's joy. Since their death they have had a fame that will last through myriads of ages. But that fame is what no one who cares for what is real would chose. Celebrate them—they do not know it. Reward them—they do not know it. Their fame is no more to them than to the trunk of a tree, or a clod of earth.

(On the other hand) Chieh came into the accumulated wealth of

---

* For Shun and Yü cf. page 644 above; for Chieh and Chou (Hsin) cf. pp. 644-5.

many generations; to him belonged the honor of the royal seat; his wisdom was enough to enable him to set at defiance all below; his power was enough to shake the world. He indulged the pleasures to which his eyes and ears prompted him; he carried out whatever it came into his thoughts to do. Brightly came he to his death. Of all mortals never was one whose life was so luxurious and dissipated as his. Chou (Hsin) came into the accumulated wealth of many generations; to him belonged the honor of the royal seat; his power enabled him to do whatever he would; . . . he indulged his feelings in all his palaces; he gave the reins to his lusts through the long night; he never made himself bitter by the thought of propriety and righteousness. Brightly came he to his destruction. Of all mortals never was one whose life was as abandoned as his.

These two villains, during their lives, had the joy of gratifying their desires. Since their death, they have had the (evil) fame of folly and tyranny. But the reality (of enjoyment) is what no fame can give. Reproach them—they do not know it. Praise them—they do not know it. Their (ill) fame is no more to them than the trunk of a tree, or a clod of earth.[162]

How different all this is from Confucius! Again we suspect that time, who is a reactionary, has preserved for us the most respectable of Chinese thinkers, and has swallowed nearly all the rest in the limbo of forgotten souls. And perhaps time is right: humanity itself could not long survive if many were of Yan Chu's mind. The only answer to him is that society cannot exist if the individual does not coöperate with his followers in the give and take, the bear and forbear, of moral restraints; and the developed individual cannot exist without society; our life depends upon those very limitations that constrain us. Some historians have found in the spread of such egoist philosophies part cause of that disintegration which marked Chinese society in the fourth and third centuries before Christ.[163] No wonder that Mencius, the Dr. Johnson of his age, raised his voice in scandalized protest against the epicureanism of Yang Chu, as well as against the idealism of Mo Ti.

The words of Yang Chu and Mo Ti fill the world. If you listen to people's discourses about it, you will find that they have adopted the views of the one or the other. Now Yang's principle is, "Each for himself"—which does not acknowledge the claims of the sovereign. Mo's principle is, "To love all equally"—which does not acknowledge the peculiar affection due to a father. To acknowledge neither king nor father is to be in the state of a beast. If their principles are not stopped, and the principles of Confucius set forth, their perverse speaking will delude the people, and stop up the path of benevolence and righteousness.

I am alarmed by these things, and address myself to the defense of the doctrines of the former sages, and to oppose Yang and Mo. I drive away their licentious expressions, so that such perverse speakers may not be able to show themselves. When sages shall rise up again, they will not change my words.[164]

3. Mencius, Mentor of Princes

A model mother — A philosopher among kings — Are men by nature good?—Single tax—Mencius and the communists —The profit-motive—The right of revolution

Mencius, destined to be second in fame to Confucius alone in the rich annals of Chinese philosophy, belonged to the ancient family of Mang; his name Mang Ko was changed by an imperial decree to Mang-tze—i.e., Mang the Master or Philosopher; and the Latin-trained scholars of Europe transformed him into Mencius, as they had changed K'ung-fu-tze into Confucius.

We know the mother of Mencius almost as intimately as we know him; for Chinese historians, who have made her famous as a model of maternity, recount many pretty stories of her. Thrice, we are told, she changed her residence on his account: once because they lived near a cemetery, and the boy began to behave like an undertaker; another time because they lived near a slaughterhouse, and the boy imitated too well the cries of the slain animals; and again because they lived near a market place, and the boy began to act the part of a tradesman; finally she found a home near a school, and was satisfied. When the boy neglected his studies she cut through, in his presence, the thread of her shuttle; and when he asked why she did so destructive a thing, she explained that she was but imitating his own negligence, and the lack of continuity in his studies and his development. He became an assiduous student, married, resisted the temptation to divorce his wife, opened a school of philosophy, gathered a famous collection of students about him, and received invitations from various princes to come and discuss with them his theories of government. He hesitated to leave his mother in her old age, but she sent him off with a speech that endeared her to all Chinese males, and may have been composed by one of them.

> It does not belong to a woman to determine anything of herself, but she is subject to the rule of the three obediences. When young she has to obey her parents; when married she has to obey her husband; when a widow she has to obey her son. You are a man in your full maturity, and I am old. Do you act as your conviction of righteousness tells you you ought to do, and I will act according to the rule which belongs to me. Why should you be anxious about me?[165]

He went, for the itch to teach is a part of the itch to rule; scratch the one and find the other. Like Voltaire, Mencius preferred monarchy to democracy, on the ground that in democracy it is necessary to educate all if the government is to succeed, while under monarchy it is only required that the philosopher should bring one man—the king—to wisdom, in order to produce the perfect state. "Correct what is wrong in the prince's mind. Once rectify the prince, and the kingdom will be settled."[166] He went first to Ch'i, and tried to rectify its Prince Hsuan; he accepted an honorary office, but refused the salary that went with it; and soon finding that the Prince was not interested in philosophy, he withdrew to the small principality of T'ang, whose ruler became a sincere but ineffectual pupil. Mencius returned to Ch'i, and proved his growth in wisdom and understanding by accepting a lucrative office from Prince Hsuan. When, during these comfortable years, his mother died, he buried her with such pomp that his pupils were scandalized; he explained to them that it was only a sign of his filial devotion. Some years later Hsuan set out upon a war of conquest, and, resenting Mencius' untimely pacifism, terminated his employment. Hearing that the Prince of Sung had expressed his intention of ruling like a philosopher, Mencius journeyed to his court, but found that the report had been exaggerated. Like the men invited to an ancient wedding-feast, the various princes had many excuses for not being rectified. "I have an infirmity," said one of them; "I love valor." "I have an infirmity," said another; "I am fond of wealth."[167] Mencius retired from public life, and gave his declining years to the instruction of students and the composition of a work in which he described his conversations with the royalty of his time. We cannot tell to what extent these should be classed with those of Walter Savage Landor;

nor do we know whether this composition was the work of Mencius himself, or of his pupils, or of neither, or of both.[168] We can only say that the *Book of Mencius* is one of the most highly honored of China's philosophical classics.

His doctrine is as severely secular as that of Confucius. There is little here about logic, or epistemology, or metaphysics; the Confucians left such subtleties to the followers of Lao-tze, and confined themselves to moral and political speculation. What interests Mencius is the charting of the good life, and the establishment of government by good men. His basic claim is that men are by nature good,[169] and that the social problem arises not out of the nature of men but out of the wickedness of governments. Hence philosophers must become kings, or the kings of this world must become philosophers.

> "Now, if your Majesty will institute a government whose action will be benevolent, this will cause all the officers in the kingdom to wish to stand in your Majesty's court, and all the farmers to wish to plough in your Majesty's fields, and all the merchants to wish to store their goods in your Majesty's market-places, and all traveling strangers to wish to make their tours on your Majesty's roads, and all throughout the Kingdom who feel aggrieved by their rulers to wish to come and complain to your Majesty. And when they are so bent, who will be able to keep them back?"
>
> The King said, "I am stupid, and not able to advance to this."[170]

The good ruler would war not against other countries, but against the common enemy—poverty, for it is out of poverty and ignorance that crime and disorder come. To punish men for crimes committed as the result of a lack of opportunities offered them for employment is a dastardly trap to set for the people.[171] A government is responsible for the welfare of its people, and should regulate economic processes accordingly.[172] It should tax chiefly the ground itself, rather than what is built or done on it;[173] it should abolish all tariffs, and should develop universal and compulsory education as the soundest basis of a civilized development; "good laws are not equal to winning the people by good instruction."[174] "That whereby man differs from the lower animals is but small. Most people throw it away; only superior men preserve it."[175]

We perceive how old are the political problems, attitudes and solutions of our enlightened age when we learn that Mencius was rejected by the princes for his radicalism, and was scorned for his conservatism by the socialists and communists of his time. When the "shrike-tongued barbarian of the south," Hsu Hsing, raised the flag of the proletarian dictatorship, demanding that workingmen should be made the heads of the state ("The magistrates," said Hsu, "should be laboring men"), and many of "The Learned," then as now, flocked to the new standard, Mencius rejected the idea scornfully, and argued that government should be in the hands of educated men."[176] But he denounced the profit-motive in human society, and rebuked Sung K'ang for proposing to win the kings to pacifism by persuading them, in modern style, of the unprofitableness of war.

> Your aim is great, but your argument is not good. If you, starting from the point of profit, offer your persuasive counsels to the kings of Ch'in and Ch'i, and if those kings are pleased with the consideration of profit so as to stop the movements of their armies, then all belonging to those armies will rejoice in the cessation (of war), and will find their pleasures in (the pursuit of) profit. Ministers will serve the sovereign for the profit of which they cherish the thought; sons will serve their fathers, and younger brothers will serve their elder brothers, from the same consideration; and the issue will be that, abandoning benevolence and righteousness, sovereign and minister, father and son, younger brother and elder, will carry on all their intercourse with this thought of profit cherished in their breasts. But never has there been such a state (of society), without ruin being the result of it.[177]

He recognized the right of revolution, and preached it in the face of kings. He denounced war as a crime, and shocked the hero-worshipers of his time by writing: "There are men who say: 'I am skilful at marshaling troops, I am skilful at conducting a battle.' They are great criminals."[178] "There has never been a good war," he said.[179] He condemned the luxury of the courts, and sternly rebuked the king who fed his dogs and swine while famine was consuming his people.[180] When a king argued that he could not prevent famine, Mencius told him that he should resign.[181] "The people," he taught, "are the most important element (in a nation); . . . the sovereign is the lightest";[182] and the people have the right to depose their rulers, even, now and then, to kill them.

> The King Hsuan asked about the high ministers. . . . Mencius answered: "If the princes have great faults, they ought to remon-

strate with him; and if he do not listen to them after they have done so again and again, they ought to dethrone him." . . . Mencius proceeded: "Suppose that the chief criminal judge could not regulate the officers (under him), how would you deal with him?" The King said, "Dismiss him." Mencius again said: "If within the four borders (of your kingdom) there is not good government, what is to be done?" The King looked to the right and left, and spoke of other matters. . . . The King Hsuan asked, "Was it so that T'ang banished Chieh, and that King Wu smote Chou (Hsin)?" Mencius replied, "It is so in the records." The King said, "May a minister put his sovereign to death?" Mencius said: "He who outrages the benevolence (proper to his nature) is called a robber; he who outrages righteousness is called a ruffian. The robber and the ruffian we call a mere fellow. I have heard of the cutting off of the *fellow* Chou, but I have not heard of putting a *sovereign* to death."[183]

It was brave doctrine, and had much to do with the establishment of the principle, recognized by the kings as well as the people of China, that a ruler who arouses the enmity of his people has lost the "mandate of Heaven," and may be removed. It is not to be marveled at that Hung-wu, founder of the Ming Dynasty, having read with great indignation the conversations of Mencius with King Hsuan, ordered Mencius to be degraded from his place in the temple of Confucius, where a royal edict of 1084 had erected his tablet. But within a year the tablet was restored; and until the Revolution of 1911 Mencius remained one of the heroes of China, the second great name and influence in the history of Chinese orthodox philosophy. To him and to Chu Hsi* Confucius owed his intellectual leadership of China for more than two thousand years.

4. Hsün-tze, Realist

The evil nature of man—The necessity of law

There were many weaknesses in Mencius' philosophy, and his contemporaries exposed them with a fierce delight. Was it true that men were by nature good, and were led to evil only by wicked institutions?—or was human nature itself responsible for the ills of society? Here was an early formulation of a conflict that has raged for some eons between reformers and conservatives. Does education diminish crime, increase virtue,

---

* Cf. p. 731 below.

and lead men into Utopia? Are philosophers fit to govern states, or do their theories worse confound the confusion which they seek to cure?

The ablest and most hardheaded of Mencius' critics was a public official who seems to have died at the age of seventy about the year 235 B.C. As Mencius had believed human nature to be good in all men, so Hsün-tze believed it to be bad in all men; even Shun and Yao were savages at birth.[184] Hsün, in the fragment that remains of him, writes like another Hobbes:

> The nature of man is evil; the good which it shows is factitious.* There belongs to it, even at his birth, the love of gain; and as actions are in accordance with this, contentions and robberies grow up, and self-denial and yielding to others are not to be found (by nature); there belong to it envy and dislike, and as actions are in accordance with these, violence and injuries spring up, and self-devotedness and faith are not to be found; there belong to it the desires of the ears and the eyes, leading to the love of sounds and beauty, and as the actions are in accordance with these, lewdness and disorder spring up, and righteousness and propriety, with their various orderly displays, are not to be found. It thus appears that to follow man's nature and yield obedience to its feelings will assuredly conduct to contentions and robberies, to the violation of the duties belonging to every one's lot, and the confounding of all distinctions, till the issue will be a state of savagery; and that there must be the influence of teachers and laws, and the guidance of propriety and righteousness, from which will spring self-denial, yielding to others, and an observance of the well-ordered regulations of conduct, till the issue will be a state of good government. . . . The sage kings of antiquity, understanding that the nature of man was thus evil, . . . set up the principles of righteousness and propriety, and framed laws and regulations to straighten and ornament the feelings of that nature and correct them, . . . so that they might all go forth in the way of moral government and in agreement with reason.[185]

Hsün-tze concluded, like Turgeniev, that nature is not a temple but a workshop; she provides the raw material, but intelligence must do the rest. By proper training, he thought, these naturally evil men might be transformed even into saints, if that should be desirable.[186] Being also a poet, he put Francis Bacon into doggerel:

---

* I.e., the good in man is not born but made—by institutions and education.

You glorify Nature and meditate on her;
Why not domesticate her and regulate her?
You obey Nature and sing her praise;
Why not control her course and use it?
You look upon the seasons with reverence, and await them;
Why not respond to them by seasonly activities?
You depend on things and marvel at them;
Why not unfold your own ability and transform them?[197]

5. Chuang-tze, Idealist

*The Return to Nature—Governmentless society—The Way of
Nature—The limits of the intellect—The evolution of man—
The Button-Moulder—The influence of Chinese phi-
losophy in Europe*

The "return to Nature," however, could not be so readily discouraged; it found voice in this age as in every other, and by what might be called a natural accident its exponent was the most eloquent writer of his time. Chuang-tze, loving Nature as the only mistress who always welcomed him, whatever his infidelities or his age, poured into his philosophy the poetic sensitivity of a Rousseau, and yet sharpened it with the satiric wit of a Voltaire. Who could imagine Mencius so far forgetting himself as to describe a man as having "a large goitre like an earthenware jar?"[188] Chuang belongs to literature as well as to philosophy.

He was born in the province of Sung, and held minor office for a time in the city of Khi-yüan. He visited the same courts as Mencius, but neither, in his extant writings, mentions the other's name; perhaps they loved each other like contemporaries. Story has it that he refused high office twice. When the Duke of Wei offered him the prime ministry he dismissed the royal messengers with a curtness indicative of a writer's dreams: "Go away quickly, and do not soil me with your presence. I had rather amuse and enjoy myself in a filthy ditch than be subject to the rules and restrictions in the court of a sovereign."[189] While he was fishing two great officers brought him a message from the King of Khu: "I wish to trouble you with the charge of all my territories." Chuang, Chuang tells us, answered without turning away from his fishing:

"I have heard that in Khu there is a spirit-like tortoise-shell, the wearer of which died three thousand years ago, and which the king keeps, in his ancestral temple, in a hamper covered with a cloth. Was it better for the tortoise to die and leave its shell to be thus honored? Or would it have been better for it to live, and keep on dragging its tail after it over the mud?" The two officers said, "It would have been better for it to live, and draw its tail after it over the mud." "Go your ways," said Chuang; "I will keep on drawing my tail after me through the mud."[190]

His respect for governments equaled that of his spiritual ancestor, Lao-tze. He took delight in pointing out how many qualities kings and governors shared with thieves.[191] If, by some negligence on his part, a true philosopher should find himself in charge of a state, his proper course would be to do nothing, and allow men in freedom to build their own organs of self-government. "I have heard of letting the world be, and exercising forbearance; I have not heard of governing the world."[192] The Golden Age, which preceded the earliest kings, had no government; and Yao and Shun, instead of being so honored by China and Confucius, should be charged with having destroyed the primitive happiness of man-kind by introducing government. "In the age of perfect virtue men lived in common with birds and beasts, and were on terms of equality with all creatures, as forming one family: how could they know among them-selves the distinctions of superior men and small men?"[193]

The wise man, thinks Chuang, will take to his heels at the first sign of government, and will live as far as possible from both philosophers and kings. He will court the peace and silence of the woods (here was a theme that a thousand Chinese painters would seek to illustrate), and let his whole being, without any impediment of artifice or thought, follow the divine *Tao*—the law and flow of Nature's inexplicable life. He would be sparing of words, for words mislead as often as they guide, and the *Tao*—the Way and the Essence of Nature—can never be phrased in words or formed in thought; it can only be felt by the blood. He would reject the aid of machinery, preferring the older, more burdensome ways of simpler men; for machinery makes complexity, turbulence and inequality, and no man can live among machines and achieve peace.[194] He would avoid the ownership of property, and would find no use in his life for gold; like Timon he would let the gold lie hidden in the hills, and the pearls remain unsought in the deep. "His distinction is in understanding that all things belong to the one treasury, and that death and life should be viewed in the same way"[105]—as harmonious measures in the rhythm of Nature, waves of one sea.

The center of Chuang's thought, as of the thought of that half-legendary Lao-tze who seemed to him so much profounder than Confucius, was a mystic vision of an impersonal unity, so strangely akin to the doctrines of Buddha and the Upanishads that one is tempted to believe that Indian metaphysics had found its way into China long before the recorded coming of Buddhism four hundred years later. It is true that Chuang is an agnostic, a fatalist, a determinist and a pessimist; but this does not prevent him from being a kind of sceptical saint, a *Tao*-intoxicated man. He expresses his scepticism characteristically in a story:

> The Penumbra said to the Umbra:* "At one moment you move, at another you are at rest. At one moment you sit down, at another you get up. Why this instability of purpose?" "I depend," replied the Umbra, "upon something which causes me to do as I do; and that something depends upon something else which causes it to do as it does. . . . How can I tell why I do one thing or do not do another?" . . . When the body is decomposed, the mind will be decomposed along with it; must not the case be pronounced very deplorable? . . . The change—the rise and dissolution—of all things (continually) goes on, but we do not know who it is that maintains and continues the process. How do we know when any one begins? How do we know when he will end? We have simply to wait for it, and nothing more.[196]

These problems, Chuang suspects, are due less to the nature of things than to the limits of our thought; it is not to be wondered at that the effort of our imprisoned brains to understand the cosmos of which they are such minute particles should end in contradictions, "antinomies," and befuddlement. This attempt to explain the whole in terms of the part has been a gigantic immodesty, forgivable only on the ground of the amusement which it has caused; for humor, like philosophy, is a view of the part in terms of the whole, and neither is possible without the other. The intellect, says Chuang-tze, can never avail to understand ultimate things, or any profound thing, such as the growth of a child. "Disputation is a proof of not seeing clearly," and in order to understand the *Tao*, one "must

---

* In an eclipse the penumbra is the partly illuminated space between the umbra (the complete shadow) and the light. Perhaps, in Chuang's allegory, the complete shadow is the body, interrogated by the partly illuminated mind.

sternly suppress one's knowledge";[197] we have to forget our theories and feel the fact. Education is of no help towards such understanding; submersion in the flow of nature is all-important.

What is the *Tao* that the rare and favored mystic sees? It is inexpressible in words; weakly and with contradictions we describe it as the unity of all things, their quiet flow from origin to fulfilment, and the law that governs that flow. "Before there were heaven and earth, from of old it was, securely existing."[198] In that cosmic unity all contradictions are resolved, all distinctions fade, all opposites meet; within it and from its standpoint there is no good or bad, no white or black, no beautiful or ugly,* no great or small. "If one only knows that the universe is but (as small as) a tare seed, and the tip of a hair is as large as a mountain, then one may be said to have seen the relativity of things."[200] In that vague entirety no form is permanent, and none so unique that it cannot pass into another in the leisurely cycle of evolution.

> The seeds (of things) are multitudinous and minute. On the surface of the water they form a membranous texture. When they reach to where the land and water join they become the (lichens that form the) clothes of frogs and oysters. Coming to life on mounds and heights, they become the plantain; and receiving manure, appear as crows' feet. The roots of the crow's foot become grubs, and its leaves, butterflies. This butterfly is changed into an insect, and comes to life under a furnace. Then it has the form of a moth. The mother after a thousand days becomes a bird. . . . The *ying-hsi* uniting with a bamboo produces the *khing-ning;* this, the panther; the panther, the horse; and the horse the man. Man then enters into the great Machinery (of Evolution), from which all things come forth, and which they enter at death.[201]

It is not as clear as Darwin, but it will serve.

In this endless cycle man himself may pass into other forms; his present shape is transient, and from the viewpoint of eternity may be only superficially real—part of *Maya's* deceptive veil of difference.

> Once upon a time I, Chuang-tze, dreamt I was a butterfly, fluttering hither and thither, to all intents and purposes a butterfly. I was conscious only of following my fancies as a butterfly, and was

---

* "Hsi Shih was a beautiful woman; but when her features were reflected in the water the fish were frightened away."[199]

unconscious of my individuality as a man. Suddenly I awoke, and there I lay, myself again. Now I do not know whether I was then a man dreaming that I was a butterfly, or whether I am now a butterfly dreaming that I am a man.[202]

Death is therefore only a change of form, possibly for the better; it is, as Ibsen was to say, the great Button-Moulder who fuses us again in the furnace of change:

> Tze Lai fell ill and lay gasping at the point of death, while his wife and children stood around him weeping. Li went to ask for him, and said to them: "Hush! Get out of the way! Do not disturb him in his process of transformation." . . . Then, leaning against the door, he spoke to (the dying man). Tze Lai said: "A man's relations with the *Yin* and the *Yang* is more than that to his parents. If they are hastening my death, and I do not obey, I shall be considered unruly. There is the Great Mass (of Nature), that makes me carry this body, labor with this life, relax in old age, and rest in death. Therefore that which has taken care of my birth is that which will take care of my death. Here is a great founder casting his metal. If the metal, dancing up and down, should say, 'I must be made into a Mo Yeh' (a famous old sword), the great founder would surely consider this metal an evil one. So, if, merely because one has once assumed the human form, one insists on being a man, and a man only, the author of transformation will be sure to consider this one an evil being. Let us now regard heaven and earth as a great melting-pot, and the author of transformation as a great founder; and wherever we go, shall we not be at home? Quiet is our sleep, and calm is our awakening."[203]

When Chuang himself was about to die his disciples prepared for him a ceremonious funeral. But he bade them desist. "With heaven and earth for my coffin and shell, with the sun, moon and stars as my burial regalia, and with all creation to escort me to the grave—are not my funeral paraphernalia ready to hand?" The disciples protested that, unburied, he would be eaten by the carrion birds of the air. To which Chuang answered, with the smiling irony of all his words: "Above ground I shall be food for kites; below I shall be food for mole-crickets and ants. Why rob one to feed the other?"[204]

If we have spoken at such length of the ancient philosophers of China it is partly because the insoluble problems of human life and destiny irresistibly attract the inquisitive mind, and partly because the lore of her philosophers is the most precious portion of China's gift to the world. Long ago (in 1697) the cosmic-minded Leibnitz, after studying Chinese philosophy, appealed for the mingling and cross-fertilization of East and West. "The condition of affairs among ourselves," he wrote, in terms which have been useful to every generation, "is such that in view of the inordinate lengths to which the corruption of morals has advanced, I almost think it necessary that Chinese missionaries should be sent to us to teach us the aim and practice of national theology. . . . For I believe that if a wise man were to be appointed judge . . . of the goodness of peoples, he would award the golden apple to the Chinese."[205] He begged Peter the Great to build a land route to China, and he promoted the foundation of societies in Moscow and Berlin for the "opening up of China and the interchange of civilizations between China and Europe."[206] In 1721 Christian Wolff made an attempt in this direction by lecturing at Halle "On the Practical Philosophy of the Chinese." He was accused of atheism, and dismissed; but when Frederick mounted the throne he called him to Prussia, and restored him to honor.[207]

The Enlightenment took up Chinese philosophy at the same time that it carved out Chinese gardens and adorned its homes with *chinoiseries*. The Physiocrats seem to have been influenced by Lao-tze and Chuang-tze in their doctrine of *laissez-faire*;[208] and Rousseau at times talked so like the Old Master* that we at once correlate him with Lao-tze and Chuang, as we should correlate Voltaire with Confucius and Mencius, if these had been blessed with wit. "I have read the books of Confucius with attention," said Voltaire; "I have made extracts from them; I have found in them nothing but the purest morality, without the slightest tinge of charlatanism."[210] Goethe in 1770 recorded his resolution to read the philosophical classics of China; and when the guns of half the world resounded at Leipzig forty-three years later, the old sage paid no attention to them, being absorbed in Chinese literature.[211]

May this brief and superficial introduction lead the reader on to study the Chinese philosophers themselves, as Goethe studied them, and Voltaire, and Tolstoi.

---

* E.g.: "Luxury, dissoluteness and slavery have always been the chastisement of the ambitious efforts we have made to emerge from the happy ignorance in which Eternal Wisdom had placed us." Professor (now Senator) Elbert Thomas, who quotes this passage from the *Discourse on the Progress of the Sciences and Arts,* considers "Eternal Wisdom" an excellent translation of Lao-tze's "Eternal *Tao*."[209]

CHAPTER XXIV

The Age of the Poets

I. CHINA'S BISMARCK

The Period of Contending States — The suicide of Ch'u P'ing—
Shih Huang-ti unifies China—The Great Wall—The "Burn-
ing of the Books"—The failure of Shih Huang-ti

P RESUMABLY Confucius died an unhappy man, for philosophers love unity, and the nation that he had sought to unite under some powerful dynasty persisted in chaos, corruption and division. When the great unifier finally appeared, and succeeded, by his military and administrative genius, in welding the states of China into one, he ordered that all existing copies of Confucius' books should be burned.

We may judge the atmosphere of this "Period of the Contending States" from the story of Ch'u P'ing. Having risen to promise as a poet and to high place as an official, he found himself suddenly dismissed. He retired to the countryside, and contemplated life and death beside a quiet brook. Tell me, he asked an oracle,

> whether I should steadily pursue the path of truth and loyalty, or
> follow in the wake of a corrupt generation. Should I work in the
> fields with spade and hoe, or seek advancement in the retinue of a
> grandee? Should I court danger with outspoken words, or fawn
> in false tones upon the rich and great? Should I rest content in the
> cultivation of virtue, or practise the art of wheedling women in
> order to secure success? Should I be pure and clean-handed in my
> rectitude, or an oil-mouthed, slippery, time-serving sycophant?[1]

He dodged the dilemma by drowning himself (ca. 350 B.C.); and until our own day the Chinese people celebrated his fame annually in the Dragon-boat Festival, during which they searched for his body in every stream.

The man who unified China had the most disreputable origin that the Chinese historians could devise. Shih Huang-ti, we are informed, was the illegitimate son of the Queen of Ch'in (one of the western states) by the noble minister Lü, who was wont to hang a thousand pieces of gold at his gate as a reward to any man who should better his compositions by so much as a single word.[2] (His son did not inherit these literary tastes.) Shih, reports Szuma Ch'ien, forced his father to suicide, persecuted his mother, and ascended the ducal throne when he was twelve years of age. When he was twenty-five he began to conquer and annex the petty states into which China had so long been divided. In 230 B.C. he conquered Han; in 228, Chao; in 225, Wei; in 223, Ch'u; in 222, Yen; finally, in 221, the important state of Ch'i. For the first time in many centuries, perhaps for the first time in history, China was under one rule. The conqueror took the title of Shih Huang-ti, and turned to the task of giving the new empire a lasting constitution.

"A man with a very prominent nose, with large eyes, with the chest of a bird of prey, with the voice of a jackal, without beneficence, and with the heart of a tiger or a wolf"—this is the only description that the Chinese historians have left us of their favorite enemy.[3] He was a robust and obstinate soul, recognizing no god but himself, and pledged, like some Nietzschean Bismarck, to unify his country by blood and iron. Having forged and mounted the throne of China, one of his first acts was to protect the country from the barbarians on the north by piecing together and completing the walls already existing along the frontier; and he found the multitude of his domestic opponents a convenient source of recruits for this heroic symbol of Chinese grandeur and patience. The Great Wall, 1500 miles long, and adorned at intervals with massive gateways in the Assyrian style, is the largest structure ever reared by man; beside it, said Voltaire, "the pyramids of Egypt are only puerile and useless masses."[4] It took ten years and countless men; "it was the ruin of one generation," say the Chinese, "and the salvation of many." It did not quite keep out the barbarians, as we shall see; but it delayed and reduced their attacks. The Huns, barred for a time from Chinese soil, moved west into Europe and down into Italy; Rome fell because China built a wall.

Meanwhile Shih Huang-ti, like Napoleon, turned with pleasure from war to administration, and created the outlines of the future Chinese state. He accepted the advice of his Legalist prime minister, Li Ssü, and resolved to base Chinese society not, as heretofore, upon custom and local autonomy, but upon explicit law and a powerful central government. He broke the power of the feudal barons, replaced them with a nobility of functionaries appointed by the national ministry, placed in each district a military force independent of the civil governor, introduced uniform laws and regulations, simplified official ceremonies, issued a state coinage, divided most of the feudal estates, prepared for the prosperity of China by establishing peasant proprietorship of the soil, and paved the way for a completer unity by building great highways in every direction from his capital at Hien-yang. He embellished this city with many palaces, and persuaded the 120,000 richest and most powerful families of the empire to live under his observant eye. Traveling in disguise and unarmed, he made note of abuses and disorders, and then issued unmistakable orders for their correction. He encouraged science and discouraged letters.[5]

For the men of letters—the poets, the critics, the philosophers, above all the Confucian scholars—were his sworn foes. They fretted under his dictatorial authority, and saw in the establishment of one supreme government an end to that variety and liberty of thought and life which had made literature flourish amid the wars and divisions of the Chou Dynasty. When they protested to Shih Huang-ti against his ignoring of ancient ceremonies, he sent them curtly about their business.[6] A commission of mandarins, or official scholars, brought to him their unanimous suggestion that he should restore the feudal system by giving fiefs to his relatives; and they added: "For a person, in any matter, not to model himself on antiquity, and yet to achieve duration—that, to our knowledge, has never happened."[7] The prime minister, Li Ssü, who was at that time engaged in reforming the Chinese script, and establishing it approximately in the form which it retained till our own time, met these criticisms with an historic speech that did no service to Chinese letters:

> The Five Sovereigns did not repeat each other's actions, the Three Royal Dynasties did not imitate each other; . . . for the times had changed. Now your Majesty has for the first time accomplished a great work and has founded a glory which will last for ten thousand generations. The stupid mandarins are incapable of understanding this. . . . In ancient days China was divided up and troubled; there was no one who could unify her. That is why all the nobles flourished. In their discourses the mandarins all talk of the ancient days, in order to blacken the present. . . . They encourage the people to forge calumnies. This being so, if they are not opposed, among the upper classes the position of the sovereign will be depreciated, while among the lower classes associations will flourish. . . .

I suggest that the official histories, with the exception of the *Memoirs of Ch'in*, be all burnt, and that those who attempt to hide the *Shi-Ching*, the *Shu-Ching*,* and the *Discourses of the Hundred Schools*, be forced to bring them to the authorities to be burnt.[8]

The Emperor liked the idea considerably, and issued the order; the books of the historians were everywhere brought to the flames, so that the weight of the past should be removed from the present, and the history of China might begin with Shih Huang-ti. Scientific books, and the works of Mencius, seem to have been excepted from the conflagration, and many of the forbidden books were preserved in the Imperial Library, where they might be consulted by such students as had obtained official permission.[9] Since books were then written on strips of bamboo fastened with swivel pins, and a volume might be of some weight, the scholars who sought to evade the order were put to many difficulties. A number of them were detected; tradition says that many of them were sent to labor on the Great Wall, and that four hundred and sixty were put to death.[10] Nevertheless some of the *literati* memorized the complete works of Confucius, and passed them on by word of mouth to equal memories. Soon after the Emperor's death these volumes were freely circulated again, though many errors, presumably, had crept into their texts. The only permanent result was to lend an aroma of sanctity to the proscribed literature, and to make Shih Huang-ti unpopular with the Chinese historians. For generations the people expressed their judgment of him by befouling his grave.[11]

The destruction of powerful families, and of freedom in writing and speech, left Shih almost friendless in his declining years. Attempts were made to assassinate him; he discovered them in time, and slew the assailants with his own hand.[12] He sat on his throne with a sword across his knees, and let no man know in what room of his many palaces he would sleep.[13] Like Alexander he sought to strengthen his dynasty by spreading the notion that he was a god; but as the comparison limped, he, like Alexander, failed. He decreed that his dynastic successors should number themselves from him as "First Emperor," down to the ten thousandth of their line; but the line ended with his son. In his old age, if we credit the historians who hated him, he became superstitious, and went to much expense to find an elixir of immortality. When he died, his body was

---

* Cf. p. 665 below.

brought back secretly to his capital; and to conceal its smell it was con-
voyed by a caravan of decaying fish. Several hundred maidens (we are
told) were buried alive to keep him company; and his successor, grateful
for his death, lavished art and money upon the tomb. The roof was
studded with constellations, and a map of the empire was traced in quick-
silver on the floor of bronze. Machines were erected in the vault for the
automatic slaughter of intruders; and huge candles were lit in the hope
that they would for an indefinite period illuminate the doings of the dead
emperor and his queens. The workmen who brought the coffin into the
tomb were buried alive with their burden, lest they should live to reveal
the secret passage to the grave.[14]

II. EXPERIMENTS IN SOCIALISM

*Chaos and poverty—The Han Dynasty—The reforms of Wu Ti—
The income tax—The planned economy of Wang Mang
—Its overthrow—The Tatar invasion*

Disorder followed his death, as it has followed the passing of almost
every dictator in history; only an immortal can wisely take all power into
his hands. The people revolted against his son, killed him soon after he
had killed Li Ssü, and put an end to the Ch'in Dynasty within five years
after its founder's death. Rival princes established rival kingdoms, and
disorder ruled again. Then a clever *condottiere*, Kao-tsu, seized the throne
and founded the Han Dynasty, which, with some interruptions and a
change of capital,* lasted four hundred years. Wen Ti (179-57 B.C.)
restored freedom of speech and writing, revoked the edict by which Shih
Huang-ti had forbidden criticism of the government, pursued a policy
of peace, and inaugurated the Chinese custom of defeating a hostile general with gifts.[15]

The greatest of the Han emperors was Wu Ti. In a reign of over half
a century (140-87 B.C.) he pushed back the invading barbarians, and extended the rule of China over Korea, Manchuria, Annam, Indo-China and
Turkestan; now for the first time China acquired those vast dimensions
which we have been wont to associate with her name. Wu Ti experimented with socialism by establishing national ownership of natural re-

* The "Western Han" Dynasty, 206 B.C.—24 A.D., had its capital at Lo-yang, now Honan-
fu; the "Eastern Han" Dynasty, 24-221 A.D., had its capital at Ch'ang-an, now Sian-fu. The
Chinese still call themselves the "Sons of Han."

sources, to prevent private individuals from "reserving to their sole use the riches of the mountains and the sea in order to gain a fortune, and from putting the lower classes into subjection to themselves."[16] The production of salt and iron, and the manufacture and sale of fermented drinks, were made state monopolies. To break the power of middlemen and speculators—"those who buy on credit and make loans, those who buy to heap up in the towns, those who accumulate all sorts of commodities" as the contemporary historian, Szuma Ch'ien expressed it—Wu Ti established a national system of transport and exchange, and sought to control trade in such a way as to prevent sudden variations in price. State workingmen made all the means of transportation and delivery in the empire. The state stored surplus goods, selling them when prices were rising too rapidly, buying them when prices were falling; in this way, says Szuma Ch'ien, "the rich merchants and large shop-keepers would be prevented from making big profits, . . . and prices would be regulated throughout the empire."[17] All incomes had to be registered with the government, and had to pay an annual tax of five per cent. In order to facilitate the purchase and consumption of commodities the Emperor enlarged the supply of currency by issuing coins of silver alloyed with tin. Great public works were undertaken in order to provide employment for the millions whom private industry had failed to maintain; bridges were flung across China's streams, and innumerable canals were cut to bind the rivers and irrigate the fields.[18]*

For a time the new system flourished. Trade grew in amount, variety and extent, and bound China even with the distant nations of the Near East.[20] The capital, Lo-yang, increased in population and wealth, and the coffers of the government were swollen with revenue. Scholarship flourished, poetry abounded, and Chinese pottery began to be beautiful. In the Imperial Library there were 3,123 volumes on the classics, 2,705 on philosophy, 1,318 on poetry, 2,568 on mathematics, 868 on medicine, 790 on war.[21] Only those who had passed the state examinations were eligible

---

* "The situation," says Granet, ". . . was revolutionary. If the Emperor Wu had had some kindred spirit, he might have been able to profit by this and create, in a new order of society, the Chinese State. . . . But the Emperor only saw the most urgent needs. He seems only to have thought of using varied expedients from day to day—rejected when they had yielded sufficient to appear worn out—and new men—sacrificed as soon as they had succeeded well enough to assume a dangerous air of authority. The restlessness of the despot and the short vision of the imperial law-makers made China miss the rarest opportunity she had had to become a compact and organized state."[19]

to public office, and these examinations were open to all. China had never prospered so before.

A combination of natural misfortunes with human deviltry put an end to this brave experiment. Floods alternated with droughts, and raised prices beyond control. Harassed by the high cost of food and clothing, the people began to clamor for a return to the good old days of an idealized past, and proposed that the inventor of the new system should be boiled alive. Business men protested that state control had diminished healthy initiative and competition, and they objected to paying, for the support of these experiments, the high taxes levied upon them by the government.[22] Women entered the court, acquired a secret influence over important functionaries, and became an element in a wave of official corruption that spread far and wide after the death of the Emperor.[23] Counterfeiters imitated the new currency so successfully that it had to be withdrawn. The business of exploiting the weak was resumed under a new management, and for a century the reforms of Wu Ti were forgotten or reviled.

At the beginning of our era—eighty-four years after Wu Ti's death —another reformer ascended the throne of China, first as regent, and then as emperor. Wang Mang was of the highest type of Chinese gentleman.* Though rich, he lived temperately, even frugally, and scattered his income among his friends and the poor. Absorbed in the vital struggle to reörganize the economic and political life of his country, he found time nevertheless not only to patronize literature and scholarship, but to become an accomplished scholar himself. On his accession to power he surrounded himself not with the usual politicians, but with men trained in letters and philosophy; to these men his enemies attributed his failure, and his friends attributed his success.

Shocked by the development of slavery on the large estates of China, Wang Mang, at the very outset of his reign, abolished both the slavery and the estates by nationalizing the land. He divided the soil into equal tracts and distributed it among the peasants; and, to prevent the renewed concentration of wealth, he forbade the sale or purchase of land.[25] He continued the state monopolies of salt and iron, and added to them state ownership of mines and state control of the traffic in wine. Like Wu Ti he tried to protect the cultivator and the consumer against the merchant by fixing the prices of commodities. The state bought agricultural sur-

---

* Unless there is truth in the rumor circulated on the death of the boy emperor, in the year 5 A.D., that Wang Mang's family had poisoned him.[24]

pluses in time of plenty, and sold them in time of dearth. Loans were made by the government, at low rates of interest, for any productive enterprise.[26]

Wang had conceived his policies in economic terms, and had forgotten the nature of man. He worked long hours, day and night, to devise schemes that would make the nation rich and happy; and he was heart-broken to find that social disorder mounted during his reign. Natural calamities like drought and flood continued to disrupt his planned economy, and all the groups whose greed had been clipped by his reforms united to plot his fall. Revolts broke out, apparently among the people, but probably financed from above; and while Wang, bewildered by such ingratitude, struggled to control these insurrections, subject peoples weakened his prestige by throwing off the Chinese yoke, and the Hsiung-nu barbarians overran the northern provinces. The rich Liu family put itself at the head of a general rebellion, captured Chang-an, slew Wang Mang, and annulled his reforms. Everything was as before.

The Han line ended in a succession of weak emperors, and was followed by a chaos of petty dynasties and divided states. Despite the Great Wall the Tatars poured down into China, and conquered large areas of the north. And as the Huns broke down the organization of the Roman Empire, and helped to plunge Europe into a Dark Age for a hundred years, so the inroads of these kindred Tatars disordered the life of China, and put an end for a while to the growth of civilization. We may judge the strength of the Chinese stock, character and culture from the fact that this disturbance was much briefer and less profound than that which ruined Rome. After an interlude of war and chaos, and racial mixture with the invaders, Chinese civilization recovered, and enjoyed a brilliant resurrection. The very blood of the Tatars served, perhaps, to reinvigorate a nation already old. The Chinese accepted the conquerors, married them, civilized them, and advanced to the zenith of their history.

III. THE GLORY OF T'ANG

The new dynasty—T'ai Tsung's method of reducing crime—An age of prosperity—The "Brilliant Emperor"—The romance of Yang Kwei-fei—The rebellion of An Lu-shan

The great age of China owed its coming partly to this new biological mixture,* partly to the spiritual stimulation derived from the advent of

---

* Cf. Sir W. Flinders Petrie, *The Revolutions of Civilization*. London, n.d.

Buddhism, partly to the genius of one of China's greatest emperors, T'ai Tsung (627-50 A.D.) At the age of twenty-one he was raised to the throne by the abdication of his father, a second Kao-tsu, who had established the T'ang Dynasty nine years before. He began unprepossessingly by murdering the brothers who threatened to displace him; and then he exercised his military abilities by pushing back the invading barbarians into their native haunts, and reconquering those neighboring territories which had thrown off Chinese rule after the fall of the Han. Suddenly he grew tired of war, and returning to his capital, Ch'ang-an, gave himself to the ways of peace. He read and re-read the works of Confucius, and had them published in a resplendent format, saying: "By using a mirror of brass you may see to adjust your cap; by using antiquity as a mirror you may learn to foresee the rise and fall of empires." He refused all luxuries, and sent away the three thousand ladies who had been chosen to entertain him. When his ministers recommended severe laws for the repression of crime, he told them: "If I diminish expenses, lighten the taxes, employ only honest officials, so that the people have clothing enough, this will do more to abolish robbery than the employment of the severest punishments."[27]

One day he visited the jails of Ch'ang-an, and saw two hundred and ninety men who had been condemned to die. He sent them out to till the fields, relying solely on their word of honor that they would return. Every man came back; and T'ai Tsung was so well pleased that he set them all free. He laid it down then that no emperor should ratify a death sentence until he had fasted three days. He made his capital so beautiful that tourists flocked to it from India and Europe. Buddhist monks arrived in great numbers from India, and Chinese Buddhists, like Yuan Chwang, traveled freely to India to study the new religion of China at its source. Missionaries came to Ch'ang-an to preach Zoroastrianism and Nestorian Christianity; the Emperor, like Akbar, welcomed them, gave them protection and freedom, and exempted their temples from taxation, at a time when Europe was sunk in poverty, intellectual darkness, and theological strife. He himself remained, without dogma or prejudice, a simple Confucian. "When he died," says a brilliant historian, "the grief of the people knew no bounds, and even the foreign envoys cut themselves with knives and lancets and sprinkled the dead emperor's bier with their self-shed blood."[28]

He had paved the way for China's most creative age. Rich with fifty years of comparative peace and stable government, she began to export her surplus of rice, corn, silk, and spices, and spent her profits on unparalleled luxury. Her lakes were filled with carved and painted pleasure-boats; her rivers and canals were picturesque with commerce, and from her harbors ships sailed to distant ports on the Indian Ocean and the Persian Gulf. Never before had China known such wealth; never had she enjoyed such abundant food, such comfortable houses, such exquisite clothing.[29] While silk was selling in Europe for its weight in gold,[30] it was a routine article of dress for half the population of the larger cities of China, and fur coats were more frequent in eighth-century Ch'ang-an than in twentieth-century New York. One village near the capital had silk factories employing a hundred thousand men.[31] "What hospitality!" exclaimed Li Po, "what squandering of money! Red jade cups and rare dainty food on tables inlaid with green gems!"[32] Statues were carved out of rubies, and pretentious corpses were buried on beds of pearl.[33] The great race was suddenly enamored of beauty, and lavished honors on those who could create it. "At this age," says a Chinese critic, "whoever was a man was a poet."[34] Emperors promoted poets and painters to high office, and "Sir John Manville"* would have it that no one dared to address the Emperor save "it be mynstrelles that singen and tellen gestes."[35] In the eighteenth century of our era Manchu emperors ordered an anthology to be prepared of the T'ang poets; the result was thirty volumes, containing 48,900 poems by 2,300 poets; so much had survived the criticism of time. The Imperial Library had grown to 54,000 volumes. "At this time," says Murdoch, "China undoubtedly stood in the very forefront of civilization. She was then the most powerful, the most enlightened, the most progressive, and the best-governed, empire on the face of the globe.[36] "It was the most polished epoch that the world had ever seen."†

At the head and height of it was Ming Huang—i.e., "The Brilliant Emperor"—who ruled China, with certain intermissions, for some forty years (713-56 A.D.). He was a man full of human contradictions: he wrote poetry and made war upon distant lands, exacting tribute from Turkey,

---

* The assumed name of a French physician who in the fourteenth century composed a volume of travels, mostly imaginary, occasionally illuminating, always fascinating.

† Arthur Waley.[37] Cf. the *Encyclopedia Britannica* (14th ed., xviii, 361): "In the T'ang Dynasty. China was without doubt the greatest and most civilized power in the world."

Persia and Samarkand; he abolished capital punishment and reformed the administration of prisons and courts; he levied taxes mercilessly, suffered poets, artists and scholars gladly, and established a college of music in his "Pear Tree Garden." He began his reign like a Puritan, closing the silk factories and forbidding the ladies of the palace to wear jewelry or embroidery; he ended it like an epicurean, enjoying every art and every luxury, and at last sacrificing his throne for the smiles of Yang Kwei-fei.

When he met her he was sixty and she was twenty-seven; for ten years she had been the concubine of his eighteenth son. She was corpulent and wore false hair, but the Emperor loved her because she was obstinate, capricious, domineering and insolent. She accepted his admiration graciously, introduced him to five families of her relatives, and permitted him to find sinecures for them at the court. Ming called his lady "The Great Pure One," and learned from her the gentle art of dissipation. The Son of Heaven thought little now of the state and its affairs; he placed all the powers of government in the hands of the Pure One's brother, the corrupt and incapable Yang Kuo-chung; and while destruction gathered under him he reveled through the days and nights.

An Lu-shan, a Tatar courtier, also loved Yang Kwei-fei. He won the confidence of the Emperor, who promoted him to the post of provincial governor in the north, and placed under his command the finest armies in the realm. Suddenly An Lu-shan proclaimed himself emperor, and turned his armies toward Ch'ang-an. The long-neglected defenses fell, and Ming deserted his capital. The soldiers who escorted him rebelled, slew Yang Kuo-chung and all the five families, and, snatching Yang Kwei-fei from the monarch's hands, killed her before his eyes. Old and beaten, the Emperor abdicated. An Lu-shan's barbaric hordes sacked Ch'ang-an, and slaughtered the population indiscriminately.* Thirty-six million people are said to have lost their lives in the rebellion.[39] In the end it failed; An Lu-shan was killed by his son, who was killed by a general, who was killed by his son. By the year 762 A.D. the turmoil had worn itself out, and Ming Huang returned, heart-broken, to his ruined capital. There, a few months later, he died. In this framework of romance and tragedy the poetry of China flourished as never before.

- * "When the Tatars overthrew Ming Huang and sacked Chang-an," says Arthur Waley, "it was as if Turks had ravaged Versailles in the time of Louis XIV."[38]

IV. THE BANISHED ANGEL

An anecdote of Li Po—His youth, prowess and loves—On the imperial barge — The gospel of the grape — War — The Wanderings of Li Po—In prison—"Deathless Poetry"

One day, at the height of his reign, Ming Huang received ambassadors from Korea, who brought him important messages written in a dialect which none of his ministers could understand. "What!" exclaimed the Emperor, "among so many magistrates, so many scholars and warriors, cannot there be found a single one who knows enough to relieve us of vexation in this affair? If in three days no one is able to decipher this letter, every one of your appointments shall be suspended."

For a day the ministers consulted and fretted, fearing for their offices and their heads. Then Minister Ho Chi-chang approached the throne and said: "Your subject presumes to announce to your Majesty that there is a poet of great merit, called Li, at his house, who is profoundly acquainted with more than one science; command him to read this letter, for there is nothing of which he is not capable." The Emperor ordered Li to present himself at court immediately. But Li refused to come, saying that he could not possibly be worthy of the task assigned him, since his essay had been rejected by the mandarins at the last examination for public office. The Emperor soothed him by conferring upon him the title and robes of doctor of the first rank. Li came, found his examiners among the ministers, forced them to take off his boots, and then translated the document, which announced that Korea proposed to make war for the recovery of its freedom. Having read the message, Li dictated a learned and terrifying reply, which the Emperor signed without hesitation, almost believing what Ho whispered to him—that Li was an angel banished from heaven for some impish deviltry.* The Koreans sent apologies and tribute, and the Emperor sent part of the tribute to Li. Li gave it to the innkeeper, for he loved wine.

On the night of the poet's birth his mother—of the family of Li—had dreamed of Tai-po Hsing, the Great White Star, which in the West is called Venus. So the child was named Li, meaning plum, and surnamed Tai-po, which is to say, The White Star. At ten he had mastered all the books of Confucius, and was composing immortal poetry.

---

* It is a pretty tale, perhaps composed by Li Po.

At twelve he went to live like a philosopher in the mountains, and stayed there for many years. He grew in health and strength, practised swords-manship, and then announced his abilities to the world: "Though less than seven (Chinese) feet in height, I am strong enough to meet ten thousand men."[41] ("Ten thousand" is Chinese for many.) Then he wandered leis-urely about the earth, drinking the lore of love from varied lips. He sang a song to the "Maid of Wu":

> Wine of the grapes,
> Goblets of gold—
> And a pretty maid of Wu—
> She comes on pony-back; she is fifteen.
> Blue-painted eyebrows—
> Shoes of pink brocade—
> Inarticulate speech—
> But she sings bewitchingly well.
> So, feasting at the table,
> Inlaid with tortoise-shell,
> She gets drunk in my lap.
> Ah, child, what caresses
> Behind lily-broidered curtains![42]

He married, but earned so little money that his wife left him, taking the children with her. Was it to her, or to some less-wonted flame, that he wrote his wistful lines?—

> Fair one, when you were here, I filled the house with flowers.
> Fair one, now you are gone—only an empty couch is left.
> On the couch the embroidered quilt is rolled up; I cannot sleep.
> It is three years since you went. The perfume you left behind
>   haunts me still.
> The perfume strays about me forever; but where are you, Beloved?
> I sigh—the yellow leaves fall from the branch;
> I weep—the dew twinkles white on the green mosses.[43]

He consoled himself with wine, and became one of the "Six Idlers of the Bamboo Grove," who took life without haste, and let their songs and poems earn their uncertain bread. Hearing the wine of Niauchung highly commended, Li set out at once for that city, three hundred miles away.[44]

In his wanderings he met Tu Fu, who was to be his rival for China's poetic crown; they exchanged lyrics, went hand in hand like brothers, and slept under the same coverlet until fame divided them. Everybody loved them, for they were as harmless as saints, and spoke with the same pride and friendliness to paupers and kings. Finally they entered Ch'ang-an; and the jolly minister Ho loved Li's poetry so well that he sold gold ornaments to buy him drinks. Tu Fu describes him:

> As for Li Po, give him a jugful,
>   He will write one hundred poems.
> He dozes in a wine-shop
>   On a city-street of Chang-an;
> And though his Sovereign calls,
>
>   He will not board the Imperial barge.
> "Please, your Majesty," says he,
>   "I am a god of wine."

Those were merry days when the Emperor befriended him, and showered him with gifts for singing the praises of the Pure One, Yang Kwei-fei. Once Ming held a royal Feast of the Peonies in the Pavilion of Aloes, and sent for Li Po to come and make verses in honor of his mistress. Li came, but too drunk for poetry; court attendants threw cold water upon his amiable face, and soon the poet burst into song, celebrating the rivalry of the peonies with Lady Yang:

> The glory of trailing clouds is in her garments,
> And the radiance of a flower on her face.
> O heavenly apparition, found only far above
> On the top of the Mountain of Many Jewels,
> Or in the fairy Palace of Crystal when the moon is up!
> Yet I see her here in the earth's garden—
> The spring wind softly sweeps the balustrade,
> And the dew-drops glisten thickly. . . .
> Vanquished are the endless longings of love
> Borne into the heart on the winds of spring.[45]

Who would not have been pleased to be the object of such song? And yet the Lady Yang was persuaded that the poet had subtly satirized her; and from that moment she bred suspicion of him in the heart of the King.

He presented Li Po with a purse, and let him go. Once again the poet took to the open road, and consoled himself with wine. He joined those "Eight Immortals of the Wine Cup" whose drinkings were the talk of Ch'ang-an. He accepted the view of Liu Ling, who desired always to be followed by two servants, one with wine, the other with a spade to bury him where he fell; for, said Liu, "the affairs of this world are no more than duckweed in the river."⁴⁶ The poets of China were resolved to atone for the Puritanism of Chinese philosophy. "To wash and rinse our souls of their age-old sorrows," said Li Po, "we drained a hundred jugs of wine."⁴⁷ And he intones like Omar the gospel of the grape:

> The swift stream pours into the sea and returns never more.
> Do you not see high on yonder tower
> A white-haired one sorrowing before his bright mirror?
> In the morning those locks were like black silk,
> In the evening they are all like snow.
> Let us, while we may, taste the old delights,
> And leave not the golden cask of wine
> To stand alone in the moonlight. . . .
> I desire only the long ecstasy of wine,
> And desire not to awaken. . . .
>
> Now let you and me buy wine today!
> Why say we have not the price?
> My horse spotted with fine flowers,
> My fur coat worth a thousand pieces of gold,
> These I will take out, and call my boy
> To barter them for sweet wine,
> And with you twain, let me forget
> The sorrow of ten thousand ages!⁴⁸

What were these sorrows? The agony of despised love? Hardly; for though the Chinese take love as much to heart as we do, their poets do not so frequently intone its pains. It was war and exile, An Lu-shan and the taking of the capital, the flight of the Emperor and the death of Yang, the return of Ming Huang to his desolated halls, that gave Li the taste of human tragedy. "There is no end to war!" he mourns; and then his heart goes out to the women who have lost their husbands to Mars.

'Tis December. Lo, tne pensive maid of Yu-chow!
She will not sing, she will not smile; her moth eyebrows are di-
    sheveled.
She stands by the gate and watches the wayfarers pass,
Remembering him who snatched his sword and went to save the
    border-land,
Him who suffered bitterly in the cold beyond the Great Wall,
Him who fell in the battle, and will never come back.

In the tiger-striped gold case for her keeping
There remains a pair of white-feathered arrows
Amid the cobwebs and dust gathered of long years—
O empty dreams of love, too sad to look upon!
She takes them out and burns them to ashes.

By building a dam one may stop the flow of the Yellow River,
But who can assuage the grief of her heart when it snows, and
    the north wind blows?[49]

We picture him now wandering from city to city, from state to state, much as Tsui Tsung-chi described him: "A knapsack on your back filled with books, you go a thousand miles and more, a pilgrim. Under your sleeves there is a dagger, and in your pocket a collection of poems."[50] In these long wanderings his old friendship with nature gave him solace and an unnamable peace; and through his lines we see his land of flowers, and feel that urban civilization already lay heavy on the Chinese soul:

Why do I live among the green mountains?
I laugh and answer not, my soul is serene;
It dwells in another heaven and earth belonging to no man.
The peach trees are in flower, and the water flows on.[51]

Or again:

I saw the moonlight before my couch,
And wondered if it were not the frost on the ground.
I raised my head and looked out on the mountain-moon;
I bowed my head and thought of my far-off home.[52]

Now, as his hair grew white, his heart was flooded with longing for the scenes of his youth. How many times, in the artificial life of the capital, he had pined for the natural simplicity of parentage and home!

> In the land of Wu the mulberry leaves are green,
> And thrice the silkworms have gone to sleep.
> In East Luh, where my family stays,
> I wonder who is sowing those fields of ours.
> I cannot be back in time for the spring doings,
> Yet I can help nothing, traveling on the river.
>
> The south wind, blowing, wafts my homesick spirit
> And carries it up to the front of our familiar tavern.
> There I see a peach-tree on the east side of the house,
> With thick leaves and branches waving in the blue mist.
> It is the tree I planted before my parting three years ago.
> The peach-tree has grown now as tall as the tavern-roof,
> While I have wandered about without returning.
>
> Ping-yang, my pretty daughter, I see you stand
> By the peach-tree, and pluck a flowering branch.
> You pluck the flowers, but I am not there—
> How your tears flow like a stream of water!
> My little son, Po-chin, grown up to your sister's shoulders,
> You come out with her under the peach-tree;
> But who is there to pat you on the back?
>
> When I think of these things my senses fail,
> And a sharp pain cuts my heart every day.
> Now I tear off a piece of white silk to write this letter,
> And send it to you with my love a long way up the river.[53]

His last years were bitter, for he had never stooped to make money, and in the chaos of war and revolution he found no king to keep him from starvation. Gladly he accepted the offer of Li-ling, Prince of Yung, to join his staff; but Li-ling revolted against the successor of Ming Huang, and when the revolt was suppressed, Li Po found himself in jail, condemned to death as a traitor to the state. Then Kuo Tsi-i, the general who had put down the rebellion of An Lu-shan, begged that Li Po's life might be ransomed by the forfeit of his own rank and title. The Emperor commuted the sentence to perpetual banishment. Soon thereafter a general amnesty was declared, and the poet turned his faltering steps homeward. Three years later he sickened and died; and legend, discontent with an ordinary end for so rare a soul, told how he was drowned in a river while attempting, in hilarious intoxication, to embrace the water's reflection of the moon.

All in all, the thirty volumes of delicate and kindly verse which he left behind him warrant his reputation as the greatest poet of China. "He is the lofty peak of Tai," exclaims a Chinese critic, "towering above the thousand mountains and hills; he is the sun in whose presence a million stars of heaven lose their scintillating brilliance."[54] Ming Huang and Lady Yang are dead, but Li Po still sings.

> My ship is built of spice-wood and has a rudder of mulan;*
> Musicians sit at the two ends with jeweled bamboo flutes and pipes
>   of gold.
> What a pleasure it is, with a cask of sweet wine
> And singing girls beside me,
> To drift on the water hither and thither with the waves!
> I am happier than the fairy of the air,
> Who rode on his yellow crane,
> And free as the merman who followed the sea-gulls aimlessly.
> Now with the strokes of my inspired pen I shake the Five Mountains.
>
> My poem is done. I laugh, and my delight is vaster than the sea.
> O deathless poetry! The songs of Ch'u P'ing† are ever glorious as
>   the sun and moon,
> While the palaces and towers of the Chou kings have vanished from
>   the hills.[55]

V. SOME QUALITIES OF CHINESE POETRY

*"Free verse" — "Imagism" — "Every poem a picture and every
picture a poem" — Sentimentality — Perfection of form*

It is impossible to judge Chinese poetry from Li alone; to *feel* it (which is better than judging) one must surrender himself unhurriedly to many Chinese poets, and to the unique methods of their poetry. Certain subtle qualities of it are hidden from us in translation: we do not see the picturesque written characters, each a monosyllable, and yet expressing a

---

* A precious wood.
† Cf. p. 694 above.

complex idea; we do not see the lines, running from top to bottom and from right to left; we do not catch the meter and the rhyme, which adhere with proud rigidity to ancient precedents and laws; we do not hear the tones—the flats and sharps—that give a beat to Chinese verse; at least half the art of the Far Eastern poet is lost when he is read by what we should call a "foreigner." In the original a Chinese poem at its best is a form as polished and precious as a hawthorn vase; to us it is only a bit of deceptively "free" or "imagist" verse, half caught and weakly rendered by some earnest but alien mind.

What we do see is, above all, brevity. We are apt to think these poems too slight, and feel an unreal disappointment at missing the majesty and boredom of Milton and Homer. But the Chinese believe that all poetry must be brief; that a long poem is a contradiction in terms—since poetry, to them, is a moment's ecstasy, and dies when dragged out in epic reams. Its mission is to see and paint a picture with a stroke, and write a philosophy in a dozen lines; its ideal is infinite meaning in a little rhythm. Since pictures are of the essence of poetry, and the essence of Chinese writing is pictography, the written language of China is spontaneously poetic; it lends itself to writing in pictures, and shuns abstractions that cannot be phrased as things seen. Since abstractions multiply with civilization, the Chinese language, in its written form, has become a secret code of subtle suggestions; and in like manner, and perhaps for a like reason, Chinese poetry combines suggestion with concentration, and aims to reveal, through the picture it draws, some deeper thing invisible. It does not discuss, it intimates; it leaves out more than it says; and only an Oriental can fill it in. "The men of old," say the Chinese, "reckoned it the highest excellence in poetry that the meaning should be beyond the words, and that the reader should have to think it out for himself."[56] Like Chinese manners and art, Chinese poetry is a matter of infinite grace concealed in a placid simplicity. It foregoes metaphor, comparison and allusion, but relies on showing the thing itself, with a hint of its implications. It avoids exaggeration and passion, but appeals to the mature mind by understatement and restraint; it is seldom romantically excited in form, but knows how to express intense feeling in its own quietly classic way.

> Men pass their lives apart like stars that move but never meet.
> This eye, how blest it is that the same lamp gives light to both
>   of us!

Brief is youth's day.
Our temples already tell of waning life.
Even now half of those we know are spirits.
I am moved in the depths of my soul.

We may tire, at times, of a certain sentimentality in these poems, a vainly wistful mood of regret that time will not stop in its flight and let men and states be young forever. We perceive that the civilization of China was already old and weary in the days of Ming Huang, and that its poets, like the artists of the Orient in general, were fond of repeating old themes, and of spending their artistry on flawless form. But there is nothing quite like this poetry elsewhere, nothing to match it in delicacy of expression, in tenderness and yet moderation of feeling, in simplicity and brevity of phrase clothing the most considered thought. We are told that the poetry written under the T'ang emperors plays a large part in the training of every Chinese youth, and that one cannot meet an intelligent Chinese who does not know much of that poetry by heart. If this is so, then Li Po and Tu Fu are part of the answer that we must give to the question why almost every educated Chinese is an artist and a philosopher.

VI. TU FU

T'ao Ch'ien—Po Chü-i—Poems for malaria—Tu Fu and Li Po— A vision of war—Prosperous days—Destitution—Death

Li Po is the Keats of China, but there are other singers almost as fondly cherished by his countrymen. There is the simple and stoic T'ao Ch'ien, who left a government position because, as he said, he was unable any longer to "crook the hinges of his back for five pecks of rice a day"—that is, *kow-tow** for his salary. Like many another public man disgusted with the commercialism of official life, he went to live in the woods, seeking there "length of years and depth of wine," and finding the same solace and delight in the streams and mountains of China that her painters would later express on silk.

I pluck chrysanthemums under the eastern hedge,
Then gaze long at the distant summer hills.
The mountain air is fresh at the dawn of day;

---

* From the Chinese *K'o T'ou*—to knock the head on the ground in homage.

The flying birds two by two return.
In these things there lies a deep meaning;
Yet when we would express it, words suddenly fail us. . . .
What folly to spend one's life like a dropped leaf
Snared under the dust of streets!
But for thirteen years it was so I lived. . . .
For a long time I have lived in a cage;
Now I have returned.
For one must return
To fulfil one's nature.[57]

Po Chü-i took the other road, choosing public office and life in the capital; he rose from place to place until he was governor of the great city of Hangchow, and President of the Board of War. Nevertheless he lived to the age of seventy-two, wrote four thousand poems, and tasted Nature to his heart's content in interludes of exile.[58] He knew the secret of mingling solitude with crowds, and repose with an active life. He made not too many friends, being, as he said, of middling accomplishment in "calligraphy, painting, chess and gambling, which tend to bring men together in pleasurable intercourse."[59] He liked to talk with simple people, and story has it that he would read his poems to an old peasant woman, and simplify anything that she could not understand. Hence he became the best-loved of the Chinese poets among the common people; his poetry was inscribed everywhere, on the walls of schools and temples, and the cabins of ships. "You must not think," said a "sing-song" girl to a captain whom she was entertaining, "that I am an ordinary dancing girl; I can recite Master Po's 'Everlasting Wrong.'"[60]*

We have kept for the last the profound and lovable Tu Fu. "English writers on Chinese literature," says Arthur Waley, "are fond of announcing that Li T'ai-po is China's greatest poet; the Chinese themselves, however, award this place to Tu Fu."[61] We first hear of him at Chang-an; he had come up to take the examinations for office, and had failed. He was not dismayed, even though his failure had been specifically in the subject of poetry; he announced to the public that his poems were a good cure for malarial fever, and seems to have tried the cure himself.[62] Ming Huang read some of his verses, gave him, personally, another examination,

---

* The most famous of China's many renditions of the infatuation of Ming Huang with Yang Kwei-fei, her death in revolution, and Ming's misery in restoration. The poem is not quite everlasting, but too long for quotation here.

marked him successful, and appointed him secretary to General Tsoa. Emboldened, and forgetting for a moment his wife and children in their distant village, Tu Fu settled down in the capital, exchanged songs with Li Po, and studied the taverns, paying for his wine with poetry. He writes of Li:

> I love my Lord as younger brother loves elder brother,
> In autumn, exhilarated by wine, we sleep under a single quilt;
> Hand in hand, we daily walk together.[63]

Those were the days of the love of Ming for Yang Kwei-fei. Tu celebrated it like the other poets; but when revolution burst forth, and rival ambitions drenched China in blood, he turned his muse to sadder themes, and pictured the human side of war:

> Last night a government order came
> To enlist boys who had reached eighteen.
> They must help defend the capital. . . .
> *O Mother! O Children, do not weep so!*
> Shedding such tears will injure you.
> When tears stop flowing then bones come through,
> Nor Heaven nor Earth has compassion then. . . .
>
> Do you know that in Shantung there are two hundred counties
>   turned to the desert forlorn,
> Thousands of villages, farms, covered only with bushes, the thorn?
> Men are slain like dogs, women driven like hens along. . . .
>
> If I had only known how bad is the fate of boys
> I would have had my children all girls. . . .
> Boys are only born to be buried beneath tall grass.
> Still the bones of the war-dead of long ago are beside the Blue Sea
>   when you pass.
>
> They are wildly white and they lie exposed on the sand,
> Both the little young ghosts and the old ghosts gather here to cry
>   in a band.
> When the rains sweep down, and the autumn, and winds that chill,
> Their voices are loud, so loud that I learn how grief can kill. . . .

Birds make love in their dreams while they drift on the tide,
For the dusk's path the fireflies must make their own light.
Why should man kill man just in order to live?
In vain I sigh in the passing night.[64]

For two years, during the revolutionary interlude, he wandered about China, sharing his destitution with his wife and children, so poor that he begged for bread, and so humbled that he knelt to pray for blessings upon the man who took his family in and fed them for a while.[65] He was saved by the kindly general Yen Wu, who made him his secretary, put up with his moods and pranks, established him in a cottage by Washing Flower Stream, and required nothing more of him than that he should write poetry.* He was happy now, and sang blissfully of rain and flowers, mountains and the moon.

Of what use is a phrase or a fine stanza?
Before me but mountains, deep forests, too black.
I think I shall sell my art objects, my books,
And drink just of nature when pure at the source. . . .

When a place is so lovely
I walk slow. I long to let loveliness drown in my soul.
I like to touch bird-feathers.
I blow deep into them to find the soft hairs beneath.
I like to count stamens, too,
And even weigh their pollen-gold.
The grass is a delight to sit on.
I do not need wine here because the flowers intoxicate me so. . . .
To the deep of my bones I love old trees, and the jade-blue waves
    of the sea.[66]

The good general liked him so that he disturbed his peace, raising him to high office as a Censor in Ch'ang-an. Then suddenly the general died, war raged around the poet, and, left only with his genius, he soon found himself penniless again. His children, savage with hunger, sneered at him for his helplessness. He passed into a bitter and lonely old age, "an ugly thing now to the eye"; the roof of his cabin was torn away by the wind,

---

* A famous Chinese painting pictures "The Poet Tu Fu in the Thatched Cottage." It may be seen at the Metropolitan Museum of Art, New York.

and urchins robbed him of the straw of his bed while he looked on, too physically weak to resist.[67] Worst of all, he lost his taste for wine, and could no longer solve the problems of life in the fashion of Li Po. At last he turned to religion, and sought solace in Buddhism. Prematurely senile at fifty-nine, he made a pilgrimage to the Holy Huen Mountain to visit a famous temple. There he was discovered by a magistrate who had read his poetry. The official took the poet home, and ordered a banquet to be served in his honor; hot beef smoked, and sweet wine abounded; Tu Fu had not for many years seen such a feast. He ate hungrily. Then at his host's request, he tried to compose and sing; but he fell down exhausted. The next day he died.[68]

VII. PROSE

The abundance of Chinese literature — Romances — History — Szuma Ch'ien—Essays—Han Yü on the bone of Buddha

The T'ang poets are but a part of Chinese poetry, and poetry is a small part of China's literature. It is hard for us to realize the age and abundance of this literature, or its wide circulation among the people. Lack of copyright laws helped other factors to make printing cheap; and it was nothing unusual, before the advent of western ideas, to find bound sets of twenty volumes selling new at one dollar, encyclopedias in twenty volumes selling new at four dollars, and all the Chinese Classics together obtainable for two.[69] It is harder still for us to appreciate this literature, for the Chinese value form and style far above contents in judging a book, and form and style are betrayed by every translation. The Chinese pardonably consider their literature superior to any other than that of Greece; and perhaps the exception is due to Oriental courtesy.

Fiction, through which Occidental authors most readily rise to fame, is not ranked as literature by the Chinese. It hardly existed in China before the Mongols brought it in;[70] and even today the best of Chinese novels are classed by the *literati* as popular amusements unworthy of mention in a history of Chinese letters. The simple folk of the cities do not mind these distinctions, but turn without prejudice from the songs of Po Chü-i and Li Po to the anonymous interminable romances that, like the theatre, use the colloquial dialects of the people, and bring back to them vividly the dramatic events of their historic past. For almost all the famous novels of China take the form of historical fiction; few of them aim at realism, and fewer still attempt such psychological or social analysis as lift *The Brothers Karamazov*

and *The Magic Mountain, War and Peace* and *Les Miserables,* to the level
of great literature. One of the earliest Chinese novels is the *Shui Hu Chuan,*
or "Tale of the Water Margins," composed by a bevy of authors in the
fourteenth century;* one of the vastest is the *Hung Lou Men* (ca. 1650), a
twenty-four-volume "Dream of the Red Chamber"; one of the best is the
Liao Chai Chih I (ca. 1660), or "Strange Stories," much honored for the
beauty and terseness of its style; the most famous is the *San Kuo Chih Yen
I,* or "Romance of the Three Kingdoms," a twelve-hundred-page embellishment, by Lo Kuan-chung (1260-1341), of the wars and intrigues that followed the fall of the Han.† These expansive stories correspond to the
picaresque novels of eighteenth-century Europe; often (if one may report
mere hearsay in these matters) they combine the jolly portrayal of character
of *Tom Jones* with the lively narrative of *Gil Blas.* They are recommended
to the reader's leisurely old age.

The most respectable form of literature in China is history; and of all the
accepted forms it is also the most popular. No other nation has had so many
historians, certainly no other nation has written such extensive histories.
Even the early courts had their official scribes, who chronicled the achievements of their sovereigns and the portents of the time; and this office of
court historian, carried down to our own generation, has raised up in China
a mass of historical literature unequaled in length or dullness anywhere else
on the earth. The twenty-four official "Dynastic Histories" published in
1747 ran to 219 large volumes.[71] From the *Shu-Ching,* or "Book of History,"
so edifyingly bowdlerized by Confucius, and the *Tso-chuan,* a commentary
written a century later to illustrate and vivify the book of the Master, and
the *Annals of the Bamboo Books,* found in the tomb of a king of Wei, historiography advanced rapidly in China until, in the second century before
Christ, it produced a *chef-d'œuvre* in the *Historical Record* painstakingly
put together by Szuma Ch'ien.

Succeeding to his father as court astrologer, Szuma first reformed the
calendar, and then devoted his life to a task which his father had begun, of
narrating the history of China from the first mythical dynasty to his own
day. He had no *penchant* for beauty of style, but aimed merely to make
his record complete. He divided his book into five parts: (1) Annals of the
Emperors; (2) Chronological Tables; (3) Eight chapters on rites, music, the
pitch-pipes, the calendar, astrology, imperial sacrifices, water courses, and
political economy; (4) Annals of the Feudal Nobles; and (5) Biographies

---

* It has been well translated by Mrs. Pearl Buck under the title, *All Men Are Brothers,*
New York, 1933.
† Translated by C. H. Brewitt-Taylor, 2 vols., Shanghai, 1925.

of Eminent Men. The whole covered a period of nearly three thousand years, and took the form of 526,000 Chinese characters patiently scratched upon bamboo tablets with a style.[72] Then Szuma Ch'ien, having given his life to his book, sent his volumes to his emperor and the world with this modest preface:

> Your servant's physical strength is now relaxed; his eyes are short-sighted and dim; of his teeth but a few remain. His memory is so impaired that the events of the moment are forgotten as he turns away from them, his energies having been wholly exhausted in production of this book. He therefore hopes that your Majesty may pardon his vain attempt for the sake of his loyal intention, and in moments of leisure will deign to cast a sacred glance over this work, so as to learn from the rise and fall of former dynasties the secret of the successes and failures of the present hour. Then if such knowledge shall be applied for the advantage of the Empire, even though your servant may lay his bones in the Yellow Springs, the aim and ambition of his life will be fulfilled.[73]

We shall find none of the brilliance of Taine in the pages of Szuma Ch'ien, no charming gossip and anecdotes in the style of Herodotus, no sober concatenation of cause and effect as in Thucydides, no continental vision pictured in music as in Gibbon; for history seldom rises, in China, from an industry to an art. From Szuma Ch'ien to his namesake Szuma Kuang, who, eleven hundred years later, attempted again a universal history of China, the Chinese historians have labored to record faithfully—sometimes at the cost of their income or their lives—the events of a dynasty or a reign; they have spent their energies upon truth, and have left nothing for beauty. Perhaps they were right, and history should be a science rather than an art; perhaps the facts of the past are obscured when they come to us in the purple of Gibbon or the sermons of Carlyle. But we, too, have dull historians, and can match any nation in volumes dedicated to record—and gather—dust.

Livelier is the Chinese essay; for here art is not forbidden, and eloquence has loose rein. Famous beyond the rest in this field is the great Han Yü, whose books are so valued that tradition requires the reader to wash his hands in rose-water before touching them. Born among the humblest, Han Yü reached to the highest ranks in the service of the state, and fell from grace only because he protested too intelligibly against the imperial concessions to Buddhism. To Han the new religion was merely a Hindu superstition; and it offended him to his Confucian soul that the Emperor should lend his sanction to the intoxication of his people with this enervating dream.

Therefore he submitted (803 A.D.) a memorial to the Emperor, from which these lines may serve as an example of Chinese prose discolored even by honest translation:

Your servant has now heard that instructions have been issued to the priestly community to proceed to Feng-hsiang and receive a bone of Buddha, and that from a high tower your Majesty will view its introduction into the Imperial Palace; also that orders have been sent to the various temples, commanding that the relic be received with the proper ceremonies. Now, foolish though your servant may be, he is well aware that your Majesty does not do this in the vain hope of deriving advantages therefrom; but that in the fulness of our present plenty, and in the joy which reigns in the heart of all, there is a desire to fall in with the wishes of the people in the celebration at the capital of this delusive mummery. For how could the wisdom of your Majesty stoop to participate in such ridiculous beliefs? Still the people are slow of perception and easily beguiled; and should they behold your Majesty thus earnestly worshiping at the feet of Buddha, they would cry out, "See! the Son of Heaven, the All-Wise, is a fervent believer; who are we, his people, that we should spare our bodies?" Then would ensue a scorching of heads and burning of fingers; crowds would collect together, and tearing off their clothes and scattering their money, would spend their time from morn to eve in imitation of your Majesty's example. The result would be that by and by young and old, seized with the same enthusiasm, would totally neglect the business of their lives; and should your Majesty not prohibit it, they would be found flocking to the temples, ready to cut off an arm or slice their bodies as an offering to the god. Thus would our traditions and customs be seriously injured, and ourselves become a laughing-stock on the face of the earth. . . .

Therefore your servant, overwhelmed with shame for the Censors,* implores your Majesty that these bones be handed over for destruction by fire and water, whereby the root of this great evil may be exterminated for all time, and the people know how much the wisdom of your Majesty surpasses that of ordinary men. The glory of such a deed will be beyond all praise. And should the Lord Buddha have power to avenge this insult by the infliction of some misfortune, then let the vials of his wrath be poured out upon

---

* On the function of the Censors cf. p. 798 below. Not one of them, Han Yü implies, had protested against the plans of the Emperor Te Tsung to give his approval to Buddhism.

the person of your servant, who now calls Heaven to witness that
he will not repent him of his oath."[74]

In a conflict between superstition and philosophy one may safely wager
on the victory of superstition, for the world wisely prefers happiness to
wisdom. Han was exiled to a village in Kuang-tung, where the people were
still simple barbarians. He did not complain, but set himself, after the teaching of Confucius, to civilize them with his example; and he succeeded so
well that his picture today often bears the legend: "Wherever he passed,
he purified."[75] He was finally recalled to the capital, served his state well,
and died loaded with honors. His memorial tablet was placed in the Temple
of Confucius—a place usually reserved for the disciples or greatest exponents of the Master—because he had defended the doctrines of Confucianism so recklessly against the invasion of a once noble but now corrupted
faith.

VIII. THE STAGE

Its low repute in China — Origins — The play — The audience —
The actors—Music

It is difficult to classify Chinese drama, for it is not recognized by China
as either literature or art. Like many other elements of human life, its
repute is not proportioned to its popularity. The names of the dramatists
are seldom heard; and the actors, though they may give a lifetime to
preparation and accomplishment, and rise to a hectic fame, are looked
upon as members of an inferior order. Something of this odor, no doubt,
attached to actors in every civilization, above all in those medieval days
when drama was rebelliously differentiating itself from the religious pantomimes that had given it birth.

A similar origin is assigned to the Chinese theatre. Under the Chou
Dynasty religious ritual included certain dances performed with wands.
Tradition says that these dances were later forbidden, on the score that
they had become licentious; and it was apparently from this cleavage
that secular drama began.[76] Ming Huang, patron of so many arts, helped
the development of an independent drama by gathering about him a
company of male and female actors whom he called "The Young Folk of
the Pear Garden"; but it was not till the reign of Kublai Khan that the
Chinese theatre took on the scope of a national institution. In the year
1031 K'ung Tao-fu, a descendant of Confucius, was sent as Chinese envoy

to the Mongol Kitans, and was welcomed with a celebration that included a play. The buffoon, however, represented Confucius. K'ung Tao-fu walked out in a huff, but when he and other Chinese travelers among the Mongols returned to China they brought reports of a form of drama more advanced than any that China had yet known. When the Mongols conquered China they introduced to it both the novel and the theatre; and the classic examples of Chinese drama are still the plays that were written under the Mongol sway.[77]

The art developed slowly, for neither the church nor the state would support it. For the most part it was practised by strolling players, who set up a platform in some vacant field and performed before a village audience standing under the open sky. Occasionally mandarins engaged actors to perform at private dinner-parties, and sometimes a guild would produce a play. Theatres became more numerous during the nineteenth century, but even at its close there were only two in the large city of Nanking.[78] The drama was a mixture of history, poetry and music; usually some episode from an historical romance was the center of the plot; or scenes might be played from different dramas on the same evening. There was no limit to the length of the performance; it might be brief, or last several days; ordinarily it took six or seven hours, as with the best of con-temporary American plays. There was much swashbuckling and oratory, much violence of blood and speech; but the *dénouement* did its best to atone for reality by making virtue triumph in the end. The drama be-came an educational and ethical instrument, teaching the people some-thing about their history, and inculcating the Confucian virtues—above all, filial piety—with a demoralizing regularity.

The stage had little furnishing or scenery, and no exits; all the actors in the cast, along with their supernumeraries, sat on the stage throughout the play, rising when their rôles demanded; occasionally attendants served them tea. Other functionaries passed about among the audience selling to-bacco, tea and refreshments, and providing hot towels for the wiping of faces during summer evenings; drinking, eating and conversation were now and then interrupted by some exceptionally fine or loud acting on the stage. The actors had often to shout in order to be heard; and they wore masks in order that their rôles might be readily understood. As the result of Ch'ien Lung's prohibition of woman players, female parts were acted by men, and so well that when women were in our time again ad-mitted to the stage, they had to imitate their imitators in order to succeed. The actors were required to be experts in acrobatics and the dance, for their parts often called for skilful manipulation of the limbs, and almost every action had to be performed according to some ritual of grace in harmony with the music that accompanied the stage. Gestures were symbolic, and had to be precise and true to old conventions; in such accomplished actors as Mei Lan-fang the artistry of hands and body constituted half the poetry of the play. It was not completely theatre, not quite opera, not predominantly dance; it was a mixture almost medieval in quality, but as perfect in its kind as Palestrina's music, or stained glass.[79]

Music was seldom an independent art, but belonged as a handmaiden to religion and the stage. Tradition ascribed its origin, like so much else, to the legendary emperor Fu Hsi. The *Li-Chi*, or "Book of Rites," dating from before Confucius, contained or recorded several treatises on music; and the *Tso-chuan*, a century after Confucius, described eloquently the music to which the odes of Wei were sung. Already, by Kung-fu-tze's time, musical standards were ancient, and innovations were disturbing quiet souls; the sage complained of the lascivious airs that were in his day supplanting the supposedly moral tunes of the past.[80] Greco-Bactrian and Mongolian influences entered, and left their mark upon the simple Chinese scale. The Chinese knew of the division of the octave into twelve semi-tones, but they preferred to write their music in a pentatonic scale, corresponding roughly to our F, G, A, C, and D; to these whole tones they gave the names "Emperor," "Prime Minister," "Subject People," "State Affairs," and "Picture of the Universe." Harmony was understood, but was seldom used except for tuning instruments. The latter included such wind instruments as flutes, trumpets, oboes, whistles and gourds; such string instruments as viols and lutes; and such percussion instruments as tambourines and drums, bells and gongs, cymbals and castanets, and musical plates of agate or jade.[81] The effects were as weird and startling to an Occidental ear as the *Sonata Appassionata* might seem to the Chinese; nevertheless they lifted Confucius to a vegetarian ecstasy, and brought to many hearers that escape from the strife of wills and ideas which comes with the surrender to music well composed. The sages, said Han Yü, "taught man music in order to dissipate the melancholy of his soul."[82] They agreed with Nietzsche that life without music would be a mistake.

CHAPTER XXV

The Age of the Artists

I. THE SUNG RENAISSANCE

1. The Socialism of Wang An-shih

*The Sung Dynasty—A radical premier—His cure for unemploy-
ment—The regulation of industry—Codes of wages and prices
— The nationalization of commerce — State insurance
against unemployment, poverty and old age—Examinations for public office—The defeat of
Wang An-shih*

THE T'ang Dynasty never recovered from the revolution of An
Lu-shan. The emperors who followed Ming Huang were unable to
restore the imperial authority throughout the Empire; and after a century of senile debility the dynasty came to an end. Five dynasties followed in fifty-three years, but they were as feeble as they were brief.
As always in such cases a strong and brutal hand was needed to reëstablish
order. One soldier emerged above the chaos, and set up the Sung Dynasty,
with himself as its first emperor under the name of T'ai Tsu. The bureaucracy of Confucian officials was renewed, examinations for office
were resumed, and an attempt was made by an imperial councillor to
solve the problems of exploitation and poverty by an almost socialist control over the nation's economic life.

Wang An-shih (1021-86) is one of the many fascinating individuals
who enliven the lengthy annals of Chinese history. It is part of the bathos
of distance that our long removal from alien scenes obscures variety in
places and men, and submerges the most diverse personalities in a dull
uniformity of appearance and character. But even in the judgment of his
enemies—whose very number distinguished him—Wang stood out as a
man different from the rest, absorbed conscientiously in the enterprise of
government, devoted recklessly to the welfare of the people, leaving
himself no time for the care of his person or his clothes, rivaling the great

724

scholars of his age in learning and style, and fighting with mad courage the rich and powerful conservatives of his age. By a trick of chance the only great figure in the records of his country who resembled him was his namesake Wang Mang; already the turbid stream of history had traveled a thousand years since China's last outstanding experiment with socialist ideas.

On receiving the highest office in the command of the Emperor, Wang An-shih laid it down as a general principle that the government must hold itself responsible for the welfare of all its citizens. "The state," he said, "should take the entire management of commerce, industry and agriculture into its own hands, with a view to succoring the working classes and preventing them from being ground into the dust by the rich."[1] He began by abolishing the forced labor that had from time immemorial been exacted from the Chinese people by the government, and had often taken men from the fields at the very time when the sowing or the harvesting needed them; and nevertheless he carried out great engineering works for the prevention of floods. He rescued the peasants from the money-lenders who had enslaved them, and lent them, at what were then low rates of interest, funds for the planting of their crops. To the unemployed he gave free seed and other aid in setting up homesteads, on condition that they would repay the state out of the yield of their land. Boards were appointed in every district to regulate the wages of labor and the prices of the necessaries of life. Commerce was nationalized; the produce of each locality was bought by the government, part of it was stored for future local needs, and the rest was transported to be sold in state depots throughout the realm. A budget system was established, a budget commission submitted proposals and estimates of expenditure, and these estimates were so strictly adhered to in administration that the state was saved considerable sums which had previously fallen into those secret and spacious pockets that cross the path of every governmental dollar. Pensions were provided for the aged, the unemployed and the poor. Education and the examination system were reformed; the tests were devised to reveal acquaintance with facts rather than with words, and to shift the emphasis from literary style to the application of Confucian principles to current tasks; the rôle of formalism and rote memory in the training of children was reduced, and for a time, says a Chinese historian, "even the pupils at village schools threw away their text-books of rhetoric and began to study primers of history, geography, and political economy."[2]

Why did this noble experiment fail? First, perhaps, because of certain elements in it that were more practical than Utopian. Though most of the taxes were taken from the incomes of the rich, part of the heavy revenue needed for the enlarged expenses of the state was secured by appropriating a portion of the produce of every field. Soon the poor joined with the rich in complaining that taxes were too high; men are always readier to extend governmental functions than to pay for them. Further, Wang An-shih had reduced the standing army as a drain on the resources of the people, but had, as a means of replacing it, decreed the universal liability of every family of more than one male to provide a soldier in time of war. He had presented many families with horses and fodder, but on condition that the animals should be properly cared for, and be placed at the service of the government in its military need. When it turned out that invasion and revolution were multiplying the occasions of war, these measures brought Wang An-shih's popularity to a rapid end. Again, he had found it difficult to secure honest men to administer his measures; corruption spread throughout the mammoth bureaucracy, and China, like many nations since, saw itself faced with the ancient and bitter choice between private plunder and public "graft."

Conservatives, led by Wang's own brother and by the historian Szuma Kuang, denounced the experiment as inherently unsound; they argued that human corruptibility and incompetence made governmental control of industry impracticable, and that the best form of government was a *laissez-faire* which would rely on the natural economic impulses of men for the production of services and goods. The rich, stung by the high taxation of their fortunes and the monopoly of commerce by the government, poured out their resources in the resolve to discredit the measures of Wang An-shih, to obstruct their enforcement, and to bring them to a disgraceful end. The opposition, well organized, exerted pressure on the Emperor; and when a succession of floods and droughts was capped by the appearance of a terrifying comet in the sky, the Son of Heaven dismissed Wang from office, revoked his decrees, and called his enemies to power. Once again everything was as before.[3]

2. The Revival of Learning

The growth of scholarship—Paper and ink in China—Steps in the invention of printing — The oldest book — Paper money — Movable type—Anthologies, dictionaries, encyclopedias

Meanwhile, through all wars and revolutions, through all administrations and experiments, the life of the Chinese people flowed evenly on, not much disturbed by events too distant to be heard of until long since past. The Sung rule was overthrown in the north, but reëstablished itself in the south; the capital was moved from Pien Liang (now K'aifeng) to Lin-an (now Hangchow); in the new capital, as in the old, luxury and refinement grew, and traders came from many parts of the world to buy the unmatched products of Chinese industry and art. Emperor Hui Tsung (1101-25) set the fashion at Pien Liang by being an artist first and a ruler afterward: he painted pictures while the barbarians marched upon his capital, and founded an art academy that stimulated with exhibitions and prizes the arts that were to be the chief claim of the Sung era to the remembrance of mankind. Inspiring collections were made of Chinese bronzes, paintings, manuscripts and jades; great libraries were collected, and some of them survived the glories of war. Scholars and artists crowded the northern and southern capitals.

It was in this dynasty that printing entered like an imperceptibly completed revolution into the literary life of the Chinese. It had grown step by step through many centuries; now it was ready in both its phases— blocks to print whole pages, and movable type cast of metal in matrices— as a thoroughly Chinese invention,[4] the greatest, after writing, in the history of our race.

The first step in the development had to be the discovery of some more convenient writing material than the silk or bamboo that had contented the ancient Chinese. Silk was expensive, and bamboo was heavy; Mo Ti needed three carts to carry with him, in his travels, the bamboo books that were his chief possession; and Shih Huang-ti had to go over one hundred and twenty pounds of state documents every day.[5] About 105 A.D. one Ts'ai Lun informed the Emperor that he had invented a cheaper and lighter writing material, made of tree bark, hemp, rags and fish-nets. Ts'ai was given a high title and office by the Emperor, was involved in an intrigue with the Empress, was detected, "went home, took a bath, combed his hair, put on his best robes, and drank poison.'"⁶ The new art spread rapidly and far, for the oldest existing paper, found by Sir Aurel Stein in a spur of the Great Wall, is in the form of state documents pertaining to occurrences in the years 21-137 A.D., and apparently contemporary with the latest of those events; it is dated, therefore, about 150 A.D., only half a century after Ts'ai Lun's report of his invention.⁷ These early papers were of pure rag, essentially like the paper used in our own day when durability is desired. The Chinese developed paper almost to perfection by using a "sizing" of glue or gelatin, and a base of starchy paste, to strengthen the fibres and accelerate their absorption of ink. When the art was taught by the Chinese to the Arabs in the eighth century, and by the Arabs to Europe in the thirteenth, it was already complete.

Ink, too, came from the East; for though the Egyptian had made both ink and paper in what might be called the most ancient antiquity, it was from China that Europe learned the trick of mixing it out of lamp black; "India ink" was originally Chinese.⁸ Red ink, made of sulphide of mercury, had been used in China as far back as the Han Dynasty; black ink appeared there in the fourth century, and henceforth the use of red ink was made an imperial privilege. Black ink encouraged printing, for it was especially adapted for use on wooden blocks, and enjoyed almost complete indelibility. Blocks of paper have been found, in Central Asia, which had lain under water so long as to become petrified; but the writing, in ink, could still be clearly read.⁹

The use of seals in signatures was the unconscious origin of print; the Chinese word for print is still the same as the word for seal. At first these seals, as in the Near East, were impressed upon clay; about the fifth century they were moistened with ink. Meanwhile, in the second century, the text of the Classics had been cut in stone; and soon thereafter the custom arose of making inked rubbings from these inscriptions. In the sixth century we find large wooden seals used by the Taoists to print charms; a century later the Buddhist missionaries experimented with various methods of duplication, through seals, rubbings, stencils, and textile prints—the last an art of Indian derivation. The earliest extant block prints are a million charms printed in Japan about 770 A.D., in the Sanskrit language and the Chinese character— an excellent instance of cultural interaction in Asia. Many block prints were made during the T'ang Dynasty, but they were apparently destroyed or lost in the chaos of revolution that followed Ming Huang.¹⁰

In 1907 Sir Aurel Stein persuaded the Taoist priests of Chinese Turkestan to let him examine the "Caves of the Thousand Buddhas" at Tun-huang. In one of these chambers, which had apparently been walled up about the year 1035 A.D. and not opened again until 1900, lay 1130 bundles, each containing a dozen or more manuscript rolls; the whole formed a library of 15,000 books, written on paper, and as well preserved as if they had been inscribed the day before their modern discovery. It was among these manuscripts that the world's oldest printed book was found—the "Diamond Sutra" —a roll ending with these words: "Printed on (the equivalent of) May 11, 868, by Wang Chieh, for free general distribution, in order in deep reverence to perpetuate the memory of his parents."[11] Three other printed books were found in the mass of manuscripts; one of them marked a new development, for it was not a roll, like the "Diamond Sutra," but a tiny folded book, the first known of its now multitudinous kind. As in late medieval Europe and among primitive peoples in recent times, the first stimulus to printing came from religion, which sought to spread its doctrines by sight as well as sound, and to put its charms and prayers and legends into every hand. Almost as old as these pious forms of print, however, are playing cards—which appeared in China in 969 or sooner, and were introduced from China into Europe near the end of the fourteenth century.[12]

These early volumes had been printed with wooden blocks. In a Chinese letter written about 870 A.D. we find the oldest known mention of such work: "Once when I was in Szechuan I examined in a bookshop a school-book printed from wood."[13] Already, it seems, the art of printing had been developed; and it is interesting to observe that this development seems to have come first in western provinces like Szechuan and Turkestan, which had been prodded on to civilization by Buddhist missionaries from India, and had for a time enjoyed a culture independent of the eastern capitals. Block-printing was introduced to eastern China early in the tenth century when a prime minister, Feng Tao, persuaded the Emperor to provide funds for the printing of the Chinese Classics. The work took twenty years and filled one hundred and thirty volumes, for it included not only the texts but the most famous commentaries. When it was completed it gave the Classics a circulation that contributed vigorously to the revival of learning and the strengthening of Confucianism under the Sung kings.

One of the earliest forms of block printing was the manufacture of paper money. Appearing first in Szechuan in the tenth century, it became a favorite occupation of Chinese governments, and led within a century to experiments in inflation. In 1294 Persia imitated this new mode of creating wealth; in 1297 Marco Polo described with wonder the respect which the Chinese showed for these curious scraps of paper. It was not till 1656 that Europe learned the trick, and issued its first paper currency.[14]

Movable type was also a Chinese invention, but the absence of an alphabet, and the presence of 40,000 characters in written Chinese, made its use an impossible luxury in the Far East. Pi Sheng formed movable type of earthenware as early as 1041 A.D., but little use was found for the invention. In 1403 the Koreans produced the first metal type known to history: models were engraved in hard wood, moulds of porcelain paste were made from these models, and from these moulds, baked in an oven, the metal type was cast. The greatest of Korean emperors, T'ai Tsung, at once adopted the invention as an aid to government and the preservation of civilization. "Whoever is desirous of governing," said that enlightened monarch, "must have a wide acquaintance with the laws and the Classics. Then he will be able to act righteously without, and to maintain an upright character within, and thus to bring peace and order to the land. Our eastern country lies beyond the seas, and the number of books reaching us from China is small. The books printed from blocks are often imperfect, and moreover it is difficult to print in their entirety all the books that exist. I ordain therefore that characters be formed of bronze, and that everything without exception upon which I can lay my hands be printed, in order to pass on the tradition of what these works contain. That will be a blessing to us to all eternity. However, the costs shall not be taken from the people in taxes. I and my family, and those ministers who so wish, will privately bear the expense."[15]

From Korea the casting of movable type spread to Japan and back again to China, but not, apparently, until after Gutenberg's belated discovery in Europe. In Korea the use of movable type continued for two centuries and then decayed; in China its use was only occasional until merchants and missionaries from the West, as if returning an ancient gift, brought to the East the methods of European typography. From the days of Feng Tao to those of Li Hung-chang the Chinese clung to block-printing as the most feasible form for their language. Despite this limitation Chinese printers poured out a great mass of books upon the people. Dynastic histories in hundreds of volumes were issued between 994 and 1063; the entire Buddhist canon, in five thousand volumes, was completed by 972.[16] Writers found themselves armed with a weapon which they had never had before; their audience was widened from the aristocracy to the middle, even to part of the lower, classes; literature took on a more democratic tinge, and a more varied form. The art of block-printing was one of the sources of the Sung Renaissance.

Stimulated with this liberating invention, Chinese literature now became an unprecedented flood. All the glory of the Humanist revival in Italy was anticipated by two hundred years. The ancient classics were honored with a hundred editions and a thousand commentaries; the life of the past was captured by scholarly historians, and put down for millions of readers in the new marvel of type; vast anthologies of literature were collected, great dictionaries were compiled, and encyclopedias like mastodons made their way through the land. The first of any moment was that of Wu Shu (947-1002); for lack of an alphabet it was arranged under categories, covering chiefly the physical world. In 977 A.D. the Sung Emperor T'ai Tsung ordered the compilation of a larger encyclopedia; it ran to thirty-two volumes, and consisted for the most part of selections from 1,690 pre-existing books. Later, under the Ming Emperor Yung Lo (1403-25), an encyclopedia was written in ten thousand volumes, and proved too expensive to be printed; of the one copy handed down to posterity all but one hundred and sixty volumes were consumed by fire in the Boxer riots of 1900.[17] Never before had scholars so dominated a civilization.

3. The Rebirth of Philosophy

Chu Hsi—Wang Yang-ming—Beyond good and evil

These scholars were not all Confucians, for rival schools of thought had grown up in the course of fifteen centuries, and now the intellectual life of the exuberant race was stirred with much argument about it and about. The seepage of Buddhism into the Chinese soul had reached even the philosophers. Most of them now affected a habit of solitary meditation; some of them went so far as to scorn Confucius for scorning metaphysics, and to reject his method of approach to the problems of life and mind as too external and crude. Introspection became an accepted method of exploring the universe, and epistemology made its first appearance among the Chinese. Emperors took up Buddhism or Taoism as ways of promoting their popularity or of disciplining the people; and at times it seemed that the reign of Confucius over the Chinese mind was to end.

His saviour was Chu Hsi. Just as Shankara, in eighth-century India, had brought into an intellectual system the scattered insights of the Upanishads, and had made the *Vedanta* philosophy supreme; and just as Aquinas, in thirteenth-century Europe, was soon to weave Aristotle and St. Paul into the victorious Scholastic philosophy; so Chu Hsi, in twelfth-century China, took the loose apothegms of Confucius and built upon them a system of philosophy orderly enough to satisfy the taste of a scholarly age, and strong enough to preserve for seven centuries the leadership of the Confucians in the political and intellectual life of the Chinese.

The essential philosophic controversy of the time centered upon the interpretation of a passage in the *Great Learning*, attributed by both Chu Hsi and his opponents to Confucius.* What was meant by the astonishing demand that the ordering of states should be based upon the proper regulation of the family, that the regulation of the family should be based upon the regulation of one's self, that the regulation of one's self depended upon sincerity of thought, and that sincerity of thought arose from "the utmost extension of knowledge" through "the investigation of things"?

Chu Hsi answered that this meant just what it said; that philosophy, morals and statesmanship should begin with a modest study of realities. He accepted without protest the positivistic bent of the Master's mind; and though he labored over the problems of ontology at greater length than Confucius might have approved, he arrived at a strange combination of atheism and piety which might have interested the sage of Shantung. Like the *Book of Changes*, which has always dominated the metaphysics of the Chinese, Chu Hsi recognized a certain strident dualism in reality: everywhere the *Yang* and the *Yin*—activity and passivity, motion and rest —mingled like male and female principles, working on the five elements of water, fire, earth, metal and wood to produce the phenomena of creation; and everywhere *Li* and *Chi*—Law and Matter—equally external, coöperated to govern all things and give them form. But over all these forms, and combining them, was *T'ai chi*, the Absolute, the impersonal Law of Laws, or structure of the world. Chu Hsi identified this Absolute with the *T'ien* or Heaven of orthodox Confucianism; God, in his view, was a rational process without personality or figurable form. "Nature is nothing else than Law."[18]

This Law of the universe is also, said Chu, the law of morals and of politics. Morality is harmony with the laws of nature, and the highest statesmanship is the application of the laws of morality to the conduct of a state. Nature in every ultimate sense is good, and the nature of men is good; to follow nature is the secret of wisdom and peace. "Choi Mao Shu refrained from clearing away the grass from in front of his window, 'because,' he said, 'its impulse is just like my own.' "[19] One might conclude that the instincts are also good, and that one may follow them gayly; but Chu Hsi denounces them as the expression of matter *(Chi)*, and demands their subjection to reason and law *(Li)*.[20] It is difficult to be at once a moralist and a logician.

---

* The passage is quoted in full on page 668 above.

There were contradictions in this philosophy, but these did not disturb its leading opponent, the gentle and peculiar Wang Yang-ming. For Wang was a saint as well as a philosopher; the meditative spirit and habits of *Mahayana* Buddhism had sunk deeply into his soul. It seemed to him that the great error in Chu Hsi was not one of morals, but one of method; the investigation of things, he felt, should begin not with the examination of the external universe, but, as the Hindus had said, with the far profounder and more revealing world of the inner self. Not all the physical science of all the centuries would ever explain a bamboo shoot or a grain of rice.

> In former years I said to my friend Chien: "If, to be a sage or a virtuous man, one must investigate everything under heaven, how can at present any man possess such tremendous power?" Pointing to the bamboos in front of the pavilion, I asked him to investigate them and see. Both day and night Chien entered into an investigation of the principles of the bamboo. For three days he exhausted his mind and thought, until his mental energy was tired out and he took sick. At first I said that it was because his energy and strength were insufficient. Therefore I myself undertook to carry on the investigation. Day and night I was unable to understand the principles of the bamboo, until after seven days I also became ill because of having wearied and burdened my thoughts. In consequence we mutually sighed and said, "We cannot be either sages or virtuous men."[21]

So Wang Yang-ming put aside the examination of things, and put aside even the classics of antiquity; to read one's own heart and mind in solitary contemplation seemed to him to promise more wisdom than all objects and all books.[22] Exiled to a mountainous wilderness inhabited by barbarians and infested with poisonous snakes, he made friends and disciples of the criminals who had escaped to those parts; he taught them philosophy, cooked for them, and sang them songs. Once, at the midnight watch, he startled them by leaping from his cot and crying out ecstatically: "My nature, of course, is sufficient. I was wrong in looking for principles in things and affairs." His comrades were not sure that they followed him; but slowly he led them on to his idealistic conclusion: "The mind itself is the embodiment of natural law. Is there anything in the universe that exists independent of the mind? Is there any law apart from the mind?"[23]

He did not infer from this that God was a figment of the imagination; on the contrary he conceived of the Deity as a vague but omnipresent moral force, too great to be merely a person, and yet capable of feeling sympathy and anger toward men.[24]

From this idealistic starting-point he came to the same ethical principles as Chu Hsi. "Nature is the highest good," and the highest excellence lies in accepting the laws of Nature completely.[25] When it was pointed out to him that Nature seems to include snakes as well as philosophers, he replied, with a touch of Aquinas, Spinoza and Nietzsche, that "good" and "bad" are prejudices, terms applied to things according to their advantage or injury to one's self or mankind; Nature itself, he taught, is beyond good and evil, and ignores our egoistic terminology. A pupil reports, or invents, a dialogue which might have been entitled *Jenseits von Gut und Böse:*

> A little later he said: "This view of good and evil has its source in the body, and is probably mistaken." I was not able to comprehend. The Teacher said: "The purpose of heaven in bringing forth is even as in the instance of flowers and grass. In what way does it distinguish between good and evil? If you, my disciple, take delight in seeing the flowers, then you will consider flowers good and grass bad. If you desire to use the grass you will, in turn, consider the grass good. This type of good and evil has its source in the likes and dislikes of your mind. Therefore I know that you are mistaken."
>
> I said: "In that case there is neither good nor evil, is there?" The Teacher said: "The tranquillity resulting from the dominance of natural law is a state in which no discrimination is made between good and evil; while the stirring of the passion-nature is a state in which both good and evil are present. If there are no stirrings of the passion-nature, there is neither good nor evil, and this is what is called the highest good." . . .
>
> I said: "In that case good and evil are not at all present in things?" He said: "They are only in your mind."[26]

It was well that Wang and Buddhism sounded this subtle note of an idealist metaphysic in the halls of the correct and prim Confucians; for though these scholars had the justest view of human nature and government which philosophy had yet conceived, they were a trifle enamored of their wisdom, and had become an intellectual bureaucracy irksome and hostile to every free and creatively erring soul. If in the end the followers of Chu Hsi won the day, if his tablet was placed with high honors in the same hall with that of the Master himself, and his interpretations of the Classics became a law to all orthodox thought for seven hundred years, it was indeed a victory of sound and simple sense over the disturbing subtleties of the metaphysical mind. But a nation, like an individual, can be too sensible, too prosaically sane and unbearably right. It was partly because Chu Hsi and Confucianism triumphed so completely that China had to have her Revolution.

II. BRONZE, LACQUER AND JADE

The rôle of art in China—Textiles—Furniture—Jewelry—Fans—
The making of lacquer—The cutting of jade—Some master-
pieces in bronze—Chinese sculpture

The pursuit of wisdom and the passion for beauty are the two poles of the Chinese mind, and China might loosely be defined as philosophy and porcelain. As the pursuit of wisdom meant to China no airy metaphysic but a positive philosophy aiming at individual development and social order, so the passion for beauty was no esoteric estheticism, no dilettante concoction of art forms irrelevant to human affairs, but an earthly marriage of beauty and utility, a practical resolve to adorn the objects and implements of daily life. Until it began to yield its own ideals to Western influence, China refused to recognize any distinction between the artist and the artisan, or between the artisan and the worker; nearly all industry was *manu*facture, and all manufacture was handi*craft;* industry, like art, was the expression of personality in things. Hence China, while neglecting to provide its people, through large-scale industry, with conveniences common in the West, excelled every country in artistic taste and the multiplication of beautiful objects for daily use. From the characters in which he wrote to the dishes from which he ate, the comfortable Chinese demanded that everything about him should have some esthetic form, and evidence in its shape and texture the mature civilization of which it was a symbol and a part.

It was during the Sung Dynasty that this movement to beautify the person, the temple and the home reached its highest expression. It had been a part of the excellence of T'ang life, and would remain and spread under later dynasties; but now a long period of order and prosperity nourished every art, and gave to Chinese living a grace and adornment which it had never enjoyed before. In textiles and metalworking the craftsmen of China, during and after the Sung era, reached a degree of perfection never surpassed; in the cutting of jade and hard stones they went beyond all rivals anywhere; and in the carving of wood and ivory they were excelled only by their pupils in Japan.[27] Furniture was designed in a variety of unique and uncomfortable forms; cabinet-makers, living on a bowl of rice per day, sent forth one *objet de vertu*—one little piece of perfection—after another; and these minor products of a careful art, taking the place of expensive furniture and luxuries in homes, gave to their owners a pleasure which in the Occident only connoisseurs can know. Jewelry was not abundant, but it was admirably cut. Women and men cooled themselves with ornate fans of feathers or bamboo, of painted paper or silk; even beggars brandished elegant fans as they plied their ancient trade.

The art of lacquer began in China, and came to its fullest perfection in Japan. In the Far East lacquer is the natural product of a tree* indigenous to China, but now most sedulously cultivated by the Japanese. The sap is drawn from trunk and branches, strained, and heated to remove excess liquid; it is applied to thin wood, sometimes to metal or porcelain, and is dried by exposure to moisture.[28] Twenty or thirty coats, each slowly dried and painstakingly polished, are laid on, the applications varying in color and depth; then, in China, the finished lacquer is carved with a sharp V-shaped tool, each incision reaching to such a layer as to expose the color required by the design. The art grew slowly; it began as a form of writing upon bamboo strips; the material was used in the Chou Dynasty to decorate vessels, harness, carriages, etc.; in the second century A.D. it was applied to buildings and musical instruments; under the T'ang many lacquered articles were exported to Japan; under the Sung all branches of the industry took their definite form, and shipped their products to such distant ports as India and Arabia; under the Ming emperors the art was further perfected, and in some phases reached its zenith;[29] under the enlightened Manchu rulers K'ang-hsi and Ch'ien Lung great factories were built and maintained by imperial decree, and made such masterpieces as Ch'ien Lung's throne,[30] or the lacquered screen that K'ang-hsi presented to Leopold I, Emperor of the Holy Roman Empire.[31] The art continued at its height until the nineteenth century, when the

---

* The *Rhus vernicifera*. *Lacquer* is from the French *lacre*, resin, which in turn derives from the Latin *lac,* milk.

wars brought on by European merchants, and the poor taste of European importers and clients, caused the withdrawal of imperial support, lowered the standards, debased the designs, and left the leadership in lacquer to Japan.

Jade is as old as Chinese history, for it is found in the most ancient graves. The earliest records attribute its use as a "sound-stone" to 2500 B.C.: jade was cut in the form of a fish or elsewise, and suspended by a thong; when properly cut and struck it emitted a clear musical tone, astonishingly long sustained. The word was derived through the French *jade* from the Spanish *ijada* (Lat. *ilia*), meaning loins; the Spanish conquerors of America found that the Mexicans used the stone, powdered and mixed with water, as a cure for many internal disorders, and they brought this new prescription back to Europe along with American gold. The Chinese word for the stone is much more sensible; *jun* means soft like the dew.[32] Two minerals provide jade: jadeite and nephrite—silicates in the one case of aluminium and sodium, in the other of calcium and magnesium. Both are tough; the pressure of fifty tons is sometimes required to crush a one-inch cube; large pieces are usually broken by being subjected in quick succession first to extreme heat and then to cold water. The ingenuity of the Chinese artist is revealed in his ability to bring lustrous colors of green, brown, black and white out of these naturally colorless materials, and in the patient obstinacy with which he varies the forms, so that in all the world's collections of jade (barring buttons) no two pieces are alike. Examples begin to appear as far back as the Shang Dynasty, in the shape of a jade toad used in divine sacrifice;[33] and forms of great beauty were produced in the days of Confucius.[34] While various peoples used jadeite for axes, knives and other utensils, the Chinese held the stone in such reverence that they kept it almost exclusivly for art; they regarded it as more precious than silver or gold, or any jewelry;[35] they valued some small jades, like the thumb rings worn by the mandarins, at five thousand dollars, and some jade necklaces at $100,000; collectors spent years in search of a single piece. It has been estimated that an assemblage of all existing Chinese jades would form a collection unrivaled by any other material.[36]

Bronze is almost as old as jade in the art of China, and even more exalted in Chinese reverence. Legend tells how the ancient Emperor Yü, hero of the Chinese flood, cast the metals sent him as tribute by the nine provinces of his empire into the form of three nine-legged cauldrons, possessed of the magic power to ward off noxious influences, cause their contents to boil without fire, and generate spontaneously every delicacy. They became a sacred symbol of the imperial authority, were handed down carefully from dynasty to dynasty, but disappeared mysteriously on the fall of the Chou—a circumstance extremely injurious to the prestige of Shih Huang-ti. The casting and decoration of bronze became one of the fine arts of China, and produced collections that required forty-two volumes to catalogue them.[37] It made vessels for the religious ceremonies of the government and the home, and transformed a thousand varieties of utensils into works of art. Chinese bronzes are equaled only by the work of the Italian Renaissance, and there, perhaps, only by those "Gates of Paradise" which Ghiberti designed for the Baptistery of Florence.

The oldest existing pieces of Chinese bronze are sacrificial vessels recently discovered in Honan; Chinese scholars assign them to the Shang Dynasty, but European connoisseurs give them a later, though uncertain, date. The earliest dated remains are from the period of the Chou; an excellent example of these is the set of ceremonial vessels in the Metropolitan Museum of Art in New York. Most of the Chou bronzes were confiscated by Shih Huang-ti, lest the people melt them down and recast them as weapons. With the accumulated metal his artisans made twelve gigantic statues, each fifty feet high;[38] but not one foot of the fifty remains. Under the Han many fine vessels were made, often inlaid with gold. Artists trained in China cast several masterpieces for the Temple of Horiuji at Nara in Japan, the loveliest being three Amida-Buddhas seated in lotus-beds;[39] there is hardly anything finer than these figures in the history of bronze.* Under the Sung the art reached its height, if not of excellence, certainly of fertility; cauldrons, wine vessels, beakers, censers, weapons, mirrors, bells, drums, vases, plaques and figurines filled the shelves of connoisseurs and found some place in nearly every home. An attractive sample of Sung work is an incense burner in the form of a water buffalo mounted by Lao-tze, who bestrides it calmly in proof of the power of philosophy to tame the savage breast.[40] The casting is throughout of the thinness of paper, and the lapse of time has given the piece a patina or coating of mottled green that lends it the meretricious beauty of decay.† Under the Ming a slow deterioration

---

* Cf. p. 897 below.

† Patina (Latin for *dish*) is formed by the disintegration of the metal surface through contact with moisture or earth. It is the fashion today to value bronzes partly according to the green or black patina left on them by time—or by the acids used in the modern production of "ancient" art.

attacked the art; the size of the objects increased, the quality fell. Bronze, which had been a miraculous novelty in the Chalcolithic Age of the Emperor Yü, became a commonplace, and yielded its popularity to porcelain.

Sculpture was not one of the major arts, not even a fine art, to the Chinese.[41] By an act of rare modesty the Far East refused to class the human body under the rubric of beauty; its sculptors played a little with drapery, and used the figures of men—seldom of women—to study or represent certain types of consciousness; but they did not glorify the body. For the most part they confined their portraits of humanity to Buddhist saints and Taoist sages, ignoring the athletes and courtesans who gave such inspiration to the artists of Greece. In the sculpture of China animals were preferred even to philosophers and saints.

The earliest Chinese statues known to us are the twelve bronze colossi erected by Shih Huang-ti; they were melted by a Han ruler to make "small cash." A few little animals in bronze remain from the Han Dynasty; but nearly all the statuary of that epoch was destroyed by war or the negligence of time. The only important Han remains are the tomb-reliefs found in Shantung; here again the human figures are rare, the scenes being dominated by animals carved in thin relief. More akin to sculpture are the funerary statuettes of clay—mostly of animals, occasionally of servants or wives—which were buried with male corpses as a convenient substitute for suttee. Here and there animals in the round survive from this period, like the marble tiger, all muscle and watchfulness, that guarded the temple of Sniang-fu,[42] or the snarling bears in the Gardner collection at Boston, or the winged and goitrous lions of the Nanking tombs.[43] These animals, and the proud horses of the tomb-reliefs, show a mixture of Greco-Bactrian, Assyrian and Scythian influences; there is nothing about them distinctively Chinese.[44]

Meanwhile another influence was entering China, in the form of Buddhist theology and art. It made a home for itself first in Turkestan, and built there a civilization from which Stein and Pelliot have unearthed many tons of ruined statuary; some of it[45] seems equal to Hindu Buddhist art at its best. The Chinese took over those Buddhist forms without much alteration, and produced Buddhas as fair as any in Gandhara or India. The earliest of these appear in the Yün Kan cave temples of Shansi (ca. 490 A.D.); among the best are the figures in the Lung Men grottoes of Honan. Outside these grottoes stand several colossi, of which the most unique is a graceful *Bodhisattwa*, and the most imposing is the "Vairochana" Buddha (ca. 672 A.D.), destroyed at the base but still instructively serene.[46] Farther east, in Shantung, many cave temples have been found whose walls are carved with mythology in Hindu fashion, with here and there a powerful *Bodhisattwa* like that in the cave of Yun Men (ca. 600 A.D.).[47] The T'ang Dynasty continued the Buddhist tradition in sculpture, and carried it to perfection in the seated stone Buddha (ca. 639) found in the province of Shensi.[48] The later dynasties produced in clay some massive *Lohans*—disciples of the gentle Buddha who have the stern faces of financiers;* and some very beautiful figures of the *Mahayana* deity Kuan-yin, almost in the process of turning from a god into a goddess.[49]

After the T'ang Dynasty sculpture lost its religious inspiration, and took on a secular, occasionally a sensuous, character; moralists complained, as in Renaissance Italy, that the artists were making saints as graceful and supple as women; and Buddhist priests laid down severe iconographic rules forbidding the individualization of character or the accentuation of the body. Probably the strong moral bent of the Chinese impeded the development of sculpture; when the religious *motif* lost its impelling force, and the attractiveness of physical beauty was not allowed to take its place, sculpture in China decayed; religion destroyed what it could no longer inspire. Towards the end of the T'ang the fount of sculptural creation began to run dry. The Sung produced only a few extant pieces of distinction; the Mongols gave their energies to war; the Mings excelled for a passing moment in *bizarreries* and such colossi as the stone monsters that stand before the tombs of the Mings. Sculpture, choked by religious restrictions, gave up the ghost, and left the field of Chinese art to porcelain and painting.

III. PAGODAS AND PALACES

Chinese architecture—The Porcelain Tower of Nanking—The Jade
Pagoda of Peking—The Temple of Confucius—The Temple
and Altar of Heaven—The palaces of Kublai Khan—
A Chinese home—The interior—Color and form

Architecture, too, has been a minor art in China. Such master-builders as have labored there have hardly left a name behind them, and seem to have been less admired than the great potters. Large structures have been rare in China, even in honoring the gods; old buildings are seldom found, and only a few pagodas date back beyond the sixteenth century. Sung architects issued, in 1103 A.D., eight handsomely illustrated volumes on *The Method of Architecture;* but the masterpieces that they pictured

---

* There are some examples of this style in the Metropolitan Museum of Art.

were all of wood, and not a fragment of them survives. Drawings in the National Library at Paris, purporting to represent the dwellings and temples of Confucius' time, show that through its long history of over twenty-three centuries Chinese architecture has been content with the same designs, and the same modest proportions.[50] Perhaps the very sensitivity of the Chinese in matters of art and taste made them forego structures that might have seemed immodest and grandiose; and perhaps their superiority in intellect has somewhat hindered the scope of their imagination. Above all, Chinese architecture suffered from the absence of three institutions present in almost every other great nation of antiquity: an hereditary aristocracy, a powerful priesthood,[51] and a strong and wealthy central government. These are the forces that in the past have paid for the larger works of art—for the temples and palaces, the masses and operas, the great frescoes and sculptured tombs. And China was fortunate and unique: she had none of these institutions.

For a time the Buddhist faith captured the Chinese soul, and sufficient of China's income to build the great temples whose ruins have been so lately discovered in Turkestan.[52] Buddhist temples of a certain middling majesty survive throughout China, but they suffer severely when compared with the religious architecture of India. Pleasant natural approaches lead to them, usually up winding inclines marked by ornate gateways called *p'ai-lus*, and apparently derived from the "rails" of the Hindu topes; sometimes the entrance is spiritually barred by hideous images designed, in one sense or another, to frighten foreign devils away. One of the best of the Chinese Buddhist shrines is the Temple of the Sleeping Buddha, near the Summer Palace outside Peking; Fergusson called it "the finest architectural achievement in China."[53]

More characteristic of the Far East are the pagodas that dominate the landscape of almost every Chinese town.* Like the Buddhism that inspired them, these graceful edifices took over some of the superstitions of popular Taoism, and became centers not only of religious ceremony, but of geomantic divination—i.e., the discovery of the future by the study of lines and clefts in the earth. Communities erected pagodas in the belief that such structures could ward off wind and flood, propitiate evil spirits, and attract prosperity. Usually they took the form of octagonal brick towers rising on a stone foundation to five, seven, nine or thirteen stories, because even numbers

---

* Their origin, in name and fact, is in much dispute. The word may be taken from the Hindu-Persian term *but-kadah*—"house of idols"; the form may be indigenous to China, as some think,[54] or may be derived from the spire that crowned some Hindu topes.[55]

were unlucky.[56] The oldest standing pagoda is at Sung Yüeh Ssu, built in 523 A.D. on the sacred mountain of Sung Shan in Honan; one of the loveliest is the Pagoda of the Summer Palace; the most spectacular are the Jade Pagoda at Peking and the "Flask Pagoda" at Wu-tai-shan; the most famous was the Porcelain Tower of Nanking, built in 1412-31, distinguished by a facing of porcelain over its bricks, and destroyed by the T'ai-p'ing Rebellion in 1854.

The fairest temples of China are those dedicated to the official faith at Peking. The Temple of Confucius is guarded by a magnificent *p'ai-lu*, most delicately carved, but the temple itself is a monument to philosophy rather than to art. Built in the thirteenth century, it has been remodeled and restored many times since. On a wooden stand in an open niche is the "Tablet of the Soul of the Most Holy Ancestral Teacher Confucius;" and over the main altar is the dedication to "The Master and Model of Ten Thousand Generations." Near the South Tatar Wall of Peking stand the Temple of Heaven and the Altar of Heaven. The altar is an impressive series of marble stairs and terraces, whose number and arrangement had a magical significance; the temple is a modified pagoda of three stories, raised upon a marble platform, and built of unprepossessing brick and tile. Here, at three o'clock in the morning of the Chinese New Year, the Emperor prayed for the success of his dynasty and the prosperity of his people, and offered sacrifice to a neuter but, it was hoped, not neutral, Heaven. However, the temple was badly damaged by lightning in 1889.[57]

More attractive than these stolid shrines are the frail and ornate palaces that once housed princes and mandarins at Peking. A burst of architectural genius during the reign of Ch'eng Tsu (1403-25) reared the Great Hall at the tombs of the Ming Emperors, and raised a medley of royal residences in an enclosure destined to become known as the "Forbidden City," on the very site where Kublai Khan's palaces had amazed Marco Polo two centuries before. Ogrish lions stand watch at either side of the marble balustrades that lead to the marble terrace; hereon are official buildings with throne rooms, reception rooms, banquet rooms, and the other needs of royalty; and scattered about are the elaborate homes in which once lived the Imperial Family, their children and relatives, their servants and retainers, their eunuchs and concubines. The palaces hardly vary one from another; all have the same slender columns, the same pretty lattices, the same carved or lettered cornices, the same profusion of brilliant colors, the same upward-curving eaves of the same massively tiled roofs. And like these forbidden delicacies is the second Summer Palace, some miles away; perhaps more completely perfect of its kind, more gracefully proportioned and fastidiously carved, than the once royal homes of Peking.

If we try to express in brief compass the general characteristics of Chinese architecture, we find as a first feature the unpleasant wall that hides the main structures from the street. In the poorer sections these outer walls are continuous from home to home, and betray an ancient insecurity of life. Within the wall is a court, upon which open the doors and lattices of one or several homes. The houses of the poor are gloomy tenements, with narrow entrances and corridors, low ceilings, and floors of the good earth; in many families pigs, dogs, hens, men and women live in one room. The poorest of all live in rain-swept, wind-beaten huts of mud and straw. Those with slightly better incomes cover the floor with mats, or pave it with tiles. The well-to-do adorn the inner court with shrubs and flowers and pools, or surround their mansions with gardens in which nature's wild variety and playful sports find assiduous representation. Here are no primrose paths, no avenues of tulip-beds, no squares or circles or octagons of grass or flowers; instead, precarious footways wind casually through rock-laid gulleys over devious rivulets, and among trees whose trunks or limbs have been taught to take strange shapes to satisfy sophisticated souls. Here and there dainty pavilions, half hidden by the foliage, offer the wanderer rest.

The home itself is not an imposing affair, even when it is a palace. It is never more than one story in height; and if many rooms are needed, the tendency is to raise new edifices rather than to enlarge the old. Hence a palatial dwelling is seldom one united structure; it is a group of buildings of which the more important follow in a line from the entrance to the enclosure, while the secondary buildings are placed at either side. The favorite materials are wood and brick; stone rarely rises above the foundation terrace; brick is usually confined to the outer walls, earthen tiles provide the roof, and wood builds the decorative columns and the inner walls. Above the brightly colored walls an ornamental cornice runs. Neither the walls nor the columns support the roof; this, heavy though it is, rests only upon the posts that form part of the wooden frame. The roof is the major part of a Chinese temple or home. Built of glazed tiles—yellow if covering imperial heads, otherwise green, purple, red or blue—the roof makes a pretty picture in a natural surrounding, and even in the chaos of city streets. Perhaps the projecting bamboos of ancient tent-tops gave the Far Eastern roof its graceful upward curve at the eaves; but more probably this celebrated form arose merely from the desire of the Chinese builder to protect his structure from rain.[58] For there were few windows in China; Korean paper or pretty lattices took their place, and lattices would not keep out the rain.

The main doorway is not at the gable end, but on the southern façade; within the ornamented portal is usually a screen or wall, barring the visitor from an immediate view of the interior, and offering some discouragement to evil spirits, who must travel in a straight line. The hall and rooms are dim, for most of the daylight is kept out by the latticed openings and the projecting eaves. There are seldom any arrangements for ventilation, and the only heat supplied is from portable braziers, or brick beds built over a smoky fire; there are no chimneys and no flues.[59] Rich and poor suffer from cold, and go to bed fully clothed.[60] "Are you cold?" the traveler asks the Chinese; and the answer is often "Of course."[61] The ceiling may be hung with gaudy paper lanterns; the walls may be adorned with calligraphic scrolls, or ink sketches, or silk hangings skilfully embroidered and painted with rural scenes. The furniture is usually of heavy wood, stained to an ebony black, and luxuriantly carved; the lighter pieces may be of brilliant lacquer. The Chinese are the only Oriental nation that sits on chairs; and even they prefer to recline or squat. On a special table or shelf are the vessels used to offer sacrifice to the ancestral dead. In the rear are the apartments of the women. Separate rooms or detached buildings may house a library or a school.

The general impression left by Chinese architecture upon the foreign and untechnical observer is one of charming frailty. Color dominates form, and beauty here has to do without the aid of sublimity. The Chinese temple or palace seeks not to dominate nature, but to coöperate with it in that perfect harmony of the whole which depends upon the modesty of the parts. Those qualities that give a structure strength, security and permanence are absent here, as if the builders feared that earthquakes would stultify their pains. These buildings hardly belong to the same art as that which raised its monuments at Karnak and Persepolis, and on the Acropolis; they are not architecture as we of the Occident have known it, but rather the carving of wood, the glazing of pottery and the sculpture of stone; they harmonize better with porcelain and jade than with the ponderous edifices that a mixture of engineering and architecture gave to India, Mesopotamia or Rome. If we do not ask of them the grandeur and the solidity which their makers may never have cared to give them, if we accept them willingly as architectural cameos expressing the most delicate of tastes in the most fragile of structural forms, then they take their place as a natural and appropriate variety of Chinese art, and among the most gracious shapes ever fashioned by men.

IV. PAINTING

1. Masters of Chinese Painting

Ku K'ai-chhi, the "greatest painter, wit and fool"—Han Yü's miniature—The classic and the romantic schools—Wang Wei —Wu Tao-tze—Hui Tsung, the artist-emperor—Masters of the Sung age

The Occident has been forgivably slow in acquainting itself with Chinese painting, for almost every aspect and method of the art in the East differed from its practice in the West. First, the paintings of the Far East were never on canvas; occasionally they were wall frescoes, as in the period of Buddhist influence; sometimes, as in later days, they were on paper; but for the most part they were on silk, and the frailty of this material shortened the life of every masterpiece, and left the history of the art with mere memories and records of accomplishment. Further, the paintings had an air of thinness and slightness; most of them were in water-color, and lacked the full-bodied and sensuous tints of European pictures in oil. The Chinese tried oil-painting, but seem to have abandoned it as too coarse and heavy a method for their subtle purposes. To them painting, at least in its earliest forms, was a branch of calligraphy, or beautiful penmanship; the brush which they used for writing served them also for painting; and many of their *chef-d'œuvres* were drawn simply with brush and ink.* Finally, their greatest achievements were unconsciously hidden from Western travelers. For the Chinese do not flaunt their pictures on public or private walls; they roll them up and store them carefully away, and unfold them for occasional enjoyment as we take down and read a book. Such scroll paintings were arranged in sequence on a roll of paper or silk, and were "read" like a manuscript; smaller pictures were hung on a wall, but were seldom framed; sometimes a series

---

* Though writing is in its origin a form of drawing or painting, the Chinese classify painting as a form of writing, and consider calligraphy, or beautiful writing, as a major art. Specimens of fine writing are hung on the walls in Chinese and Japanese homes; and devotees of the art have pursued its masterpieces as modern collectors roam over continents to find a picture or a vase. The most famous of Chinese calligraphers was Wang Hsi-chih (ca. 400 A.D.); it was on the Chinese characters as formed by his graceful hand that the characters were cut when block-printing began. The great T'ang emperor, T'ai Tsung, resorted to theft to get from Pien-tsai a scroll written by Wang Hsi-chih. Thereupon Pien-tsai, we are told, lost appetite and died.[62]

of pictures was painted on a screen. By the time of the later Sung Dynasty the art of painting had already developed thirteen "branches,"[63] and innumerable forms.

Painting is mentioned in Chinese literature as an established art several centuries before Christ; and despite the interruptions of war it has continued in China to our own time. Tradition makes the first Chinese painter a woman, Lei, sister of the pious Emperor Shun; "alas," cried a disgusted critic, "that this divine art should have been invented by a woman!"[64] Nothing survives of Chou painting; but that the art was then already old appears from Confucius' report of how deeply he was affected by the frescoes in the Grand Temple at Lo-yang.[65] During the early years of the Han Dynasty a writer complained that a hero whom he admired had not been sufficiently painted: "Good artists are many; why does not one of them draw him?"[66] The story is told of an artist virtuoso of the time, Lieh-I, who could draw a perfectly straight line one thousand feet long, could etch a detailed map of China on a square inch of surface, and could fill his mouth with colored water and spit it out in the form of paintings; the phœnixes which he painted were so lifelike that people wondered why they did not fly away.[67] There are signs that Chinese painting reached one of its zeniths at the beginning of our era,[68] but war and time have destroyed the evidence. From the days when the Ch'in warriors sacked Lo-yang (ca. 249 B.C.), burning whatever they could not use, down to the Boxer Uprising (1900 A.D.), when the soldiers of Tung Cho employed the silk pictures of the Imperial Collection for wrapping purposes, the victories of art and war have alternated in their ancient conflict—destruction always certain, but creation never still.

As Christianity transformed Mediterranean culture and art in the third and fourth centuries after Christ, so Buddhism, in the same centuries, effected a theological and esthetic revolution in the life of China. While Confucianism retained its political power, Buddhism, mingling with Taoism, became the dominating force in art, and brought to the Chinese a stimulating contact with Hindu motives, symbols, methods and forms. The greatest genius of the Chinese Buddhist school of painting was Ku K'ai-chih, a man of such unique and positive personality that a web of anecdote or legend has meshed him in. He loved the girl next door, and offered her his hand; but she, not knowing how famous he was to be, refused him. He painted her form upon a wall, and stuck a thorn into the heart, whereupon the girl began to die. He approached her again, and she yielded; he removed the thorn from his picture, and forthwith the girl grew well. When the Buddhists tried to raise money to build a temple at Nanking he promised the fund one million "cash"; all China laughed at the offer, for Ku was as poor as an artist. "Give me the use of a wall," he asked. Having found a wall and secured privacy, he painted there the Buddhist saint Uimala-Kirti. When it was finished he sent for the priests, and explained to them how they might raise the million "cash." "On the first day you must charge 100,000 'cash' for admission" to see the picture; "on the second day, 50,000; on the third day let visitors subscribe what they please." They did as he told them, and took in a million "cash."[69] Ku painted a long series of Buddhist pictures, and many others, but nothing certainly his has come down to our day.* He wrote three treatises on painting, of which some fragments survive. Men, he said, were the most difficult things to paint; next came landscapes, then horses and gods.[72] He insisted on being a philosopher, too; under his portrait of the emperor he wrote: "In Nature there is nothing high which is not soon brought low. . . . When the sun has reached its noon, it begins to sink; when the moon is full it begins to wane. To rise to glory is as hard as to build a mountain out of grains of dust; to fall into calamity is as easy as the rebound of a tense spring."[73] His contemporaries ranked him as the outstanding man of his time in three lines: in painting, in wit, and in foolishness.[74]

Painting flourished at the T'ang court. "There are as many painters as morning stars," said Tu Fu, "but artists are few."[75] In the ninth century Chang Yen-yüan wrote a book called *Eminent Painters of All Ages*, in which he described the work of three hundred and seventy artists. A picture by a master, he tells us, brought in those days as much as twenty thousand ounces of silver. But he warns us against rating art in monetary terms; "good pictures," he writes, "are more priceless than gold or jade; bad ones are not worth a potsherd."[76] Of T'ang painters we still know the names of two hundred and twenty; of their work hardly anything remains, for the Tatar revolutionists who sacked Chang-an in 756 A.D. did not care for painting. We catch something of the art atmosphere that mingled with the poetry of the time, in the story of Han Yü, the famous

---

* The British Museum assigns to him a faded but lovely scroll of five pictures illustrating model family life;[70] the Temple of Confucius at Chü-fu contains a stone engraving purporting to follow a design of Ku; and the Freer Gallery at Washington contains two excellent copies of compositions attributed to him.[71]

"Prince of Literature." One day he won, from a fellow lodger at an inn, a precious miniature portraying, in the smallest compass, one hundred and twenty-three human figures, eighty-three horses, thirty other animals, three chariots, and two hundred and fifty-one articles. "I thought a great deal of it, for I could not believe that it was the work of a single man, uniting as it did in itself such a variety of excellences; and no sum would have tempted me to part from it. Next year I left the city, and went to Ho-yang; and there, one day, while discussing art with strangers, I produced the picture for them to see. Among them was a Mr. Chao, a Censor,* a highly cultivated man, who, when he saw it, seemed rather overcome, and at length said: 'That picture is a copy, made by me in my youth, of a work from the Imperial Gallery. I lost it twenty years ago while traveling in the province of Fukien.'" Han Yü at once presented the miniature to Mr. Chao.

Just as in Chinese religion two schools had taken shape, Confucian and Taoist-Buddhist—and just as two schools, led by Chu Hsi and Wang Yang-ming, were soon to develop in philosophy, representing respectively what we in the West would call the classic and the romantic types of mind; so in Chinese painting the northern artists accepted a stern tradition of classical sobriety and restraint, while the south gave color and form to feeling and imagination. The northern school set itself severely to secure correct modeling of figure and full clarity of line; the southern rebelled like Montmartre against such limitations, disdained a simple realism, and tried to use objects merely as elements in a spiritual experience, tones in a musical mood." Li Ssu-hsün, painting at the court of Ming Huang, found time, amid the fluctuations of political power and lonely exile, to establish the northern school. He painted some of the first Chinese landscapes, and achieved a degree of realism carried down in many a tale; the Emperor said he could hear, at night, the splash of the water that Li had painted upon an imperial screen; and a fish leaped to life out of another of his pictures and was later found in a pool—every nation tells such stories of its painters. The southern school sprouted out of the natural innovations of art, and the genius of Wang Wei; in his impressionist style a landscape became merely the symbol of a mood. A poet as well as a painter, Wang sought to bind the two arts by making the picture express a poem; it was of him that men first used the now trite phrase so applicable

* Cf. p. 798 below.

to nearly all Chinese poetry and painting: "Every poem is a picture, and every picture is a poem." (In many cases the poem is inscribed upon the picture, and is itself a calligraphic work of art.) Tung Ch'i-ch'ang, we are told, spent his whole life searching for a genuine Wang Wei.[78]*

The greatest painter of the T'ang epoch, and, by common consent, of all the Far East, rose above distinctions of school, and belonged rather to the Buddhist tradition of Chinese art. Wu Tao-tze deserved his name— Wu, Master of the *Tao* or Way, for all those impressions and formless thoughts which Lao-tze and Chuang-tze had found too subtle for words seemed to flow naturally into line and color under his brush. "A poverty-stricken orphan," a Chinese historian describes him, "but endowed with a divine nature, he had not assumed the cap of puberty ere he was already a master artist, and had flooded Lo-yang with his works." Chinese tradition has it that he was fond of wine and feats of strength, and thought like Poe that the spirit could work best under a little intoxication.[81] He excelled in every subject: men, gods, devils, Buddhas, birds, beasts, buildings, landscapes—all seemed to come naturally to his exuberant art. He painted with equal skill on silk, paper, and freshly-plastered walls; he made three hundred frescoes for Buddhist edifices, and one of these, containing more than a thousand figures, became as famous in China as "The Last Judgment" or "The Last Supper" in Europe. Ninety-three of his paintings were in the Imperial Gallery in the twelfth century, four hundred years after his death; but none remains anywhere today. His Buddhas, we are told, "fathomed the mysteries of life and death"; his picture of purgatory frightened some of the butchers and fishmongers of China into abandoning their scandalously ˙un-Buddhistic trades; his representation of Ming Huang's dream convinced the Emperor that Wu had had an identical vision.[82] When the monarch sent Wu to sketch the scenery along the Chia-ling River in Szechuan he was piqued to see the artist return without having sketched a line. "I have it all in my heart," said Wu; and isolating himself in a room of the palace, he threw off, we are assured, a hundred miles of landscape.[83]† When General Pei wished his portrait painted, Wu asked him not to pose, but to do a sword dance; after which the artist painted a picture that contemporaries felt constrained to ascribe to divine

---

* Only copies remain: chiefly a "Waterfall" in the Temple of Chisakuin at Kyoto,[79] and a roll (in both the British Museum and the Freer Gallery) entitled "Scenery of the Wang Ch'uan."[80]

† Cf. Croce's view that art lies in the conception rather than in the execution.[84]

inspiration. So great was his reputation that when he was finishing some Buddhist figures at the Hsing-shan Temple, "the whole of Chang-an" came to see him add the finishing touches. Surrounded by this assemblage, says a Chinese historian of the ninth century, "he executed the haloes with so violent a rush and swirl that it seemed as though a whirlwind possessed his hand, and all who saw it cried that some god was helping him":[85] the lazy will always attribute genius to some "inspiration" that comes for mere waiting. When Wu had lived long enough, says a pretty tale, he painted a vast landscape, stepped into the mouth of a cave pictured in it, and was never seen again.[86] Never had art known such mastery and delicacy of line.

Under the Sung emperors painting became a passion with the Chinese. Emancipating itself from subserviency to Buddhist themes, it poured forth an unprecedented number and variety of pictures. The Sung Emperor Hui Tsung was himself not the least of the eight hundred known painters of the day. In a roll which is one of the treasures of the Museum of Fine Arts in Boston he portrayed with astonishing simplicity and clarity the stages through which women carried the preparation of silk;[87] he founded an art museum richer in masterpieces than any collection that China has ever again known;[88] he elevated the Painting Academy from a mere department of the Literary College into an independent institution of the highest rank, substituted art tests for some of the literary exercises traditionally used in the examinations for political office, and raised men to the ministry for their excellence in art as often as for their skill in statesmanship.[89] The Tatars, hearing of all this, invaded China, deposed the Emperor, sacked the capital and destroyed nearly all of the paintings in the Imperial Museum, whose catalogue had filled twenty volumes.[90] The artist-emperor was carried away by the invaders, and died in captivity and disgrace.

Greater than this royal painter were Kuo Hsi and Li Lung-mien. "For tall pines, huge trees, swirling streams, beetling crags, steep precipices, mountain peaks, now lovely in the rising mist, now lost in an obscuring pall, with all their thousand ten thousand shapes—critics allow that Kuo Hsi strode across his generation."*[91] Li Lung-mien was an artist, a scholar, a successful official and a gentleman, honored by the Chinese as the perfect type of Chinese culture at its richest. He passed from the profession

---

* The Freer Gallery at Washington has a "Landscape on the Hoang-ho" uncertainly attributed to Kuo Hsi.[92]

of calligraphy to sketching and painting, and rarely used anything but ink; he gloried in the strict traditions of the Northern School, and spent himself upon accuracy and delicacy of line. He painted horses so well that when six that he had painted died, it was charged that his picture had stolen their vital principle from them. A Buddhist priest warned him that he would become a horse if he painted horses so often and so intently; he accepted the counsel of the monk, and painted five hundred *Lohans*. We may judge of his repute by the fact that Hui Tsung's imperial gallery, when it was sacked, contained one hundred and seven works by Li Lung-mien.

Other masters crowded the Sung scene: Mi Fei, an eccentric genius who was forever washing his hands or changing his clothes when he was not collecting old masters or transforming landscape painting with his "method of blobs"—daubs of ink laid on without the guidance of any contour line;* Hsia Kuei, whose long roll of scenes from the Yang-tze—its modest sources, its passage through loess and gorges, its gaping mouth filled with merchant ships and *sampans*—has led many students[93] to rank him at the head of all landscape painters of Orient and Occident; Ma Yuan, whose delicate landscapes and distant vistas adorn the Boston Museum of Fine Arts;† Liang K'ai, with his stately portrait of Li Po; Mu-ch'i, with his terrible tiger, his careless starling, and his morose but gentle Kuan-yin; and others whose names strike no familiar chords in Occidental memories, but are the tokens of a mind rich in the heritage of the East. "The Sung culture," says Fenollosa, "was the ripest expression of Chinese genius."[95]

When we try to estimate the quality of Chinese painting in the heyday of T'ang and Sung we are in the position of future historians who may try to write of the Italian Renaissance when all the works of Raphael, Leonardo and Michelangelo have been lost. After the ravages of barbaric hosts had destroyed the masterpieces of Chinese painting, and interrupted for centuries the continuity of Chinese development, painting seems to have lost heart; and though the later dynasties, native and alien, produced many artists of delicacy or power, none could rank with the men who had known paradise for a time at the courts of Ming Huang and Hui

---

* A landscape attributed to Mi Fei may be seen in Room E 11 of the Metropolitan Museum of Art.

† Particularly striking is "The Lady Ling-chao Standing in the Snow." The Lady (a Buddhist mystic of the eighth century) is quite still in meditation, like Socrates in the snow at Platæa. The world (the artist seems to say) is nothing except to a mind; and that mind can ignore it—for a while.

Tsung. When we think of the Chinese we must see them not merely as a people now stricken with poverty, weakened with corruption, torn with factions and disgraced with defeat, but as a nation that has had, in the long vista of its history, ages that could compare with those of Pericles, Augustus and the Medici, and may have such ages again.

2. Qualities of Chinese Painting

The rejection of perspective—Of realism—Line as nobler than color — Form as rhythm — Representation by suggestion — Conventions and restrictions—Sincerity of Chinese art

What is it that distinguishes Chinese painting, and makes it so completely different from every other school of painting in history except its own pupils in Japan? First, of course, its scroll or screen form. But this is an external matter; far more intrinsic and fundamental is the Chinese scorn of perspective and shadow. When two European painters accepted the invitation of the Emperor K'ang-hsi to come and paint decorations for his palaces, their work was rejected because they had made the farther columns in their pictures shorter than the nearer ones; nothing could be more false and artificial, argued the Chinese, than to represent distances where obviously there were none.[96] Neither party could understand the prejudice of the other, for the Europeans had been taught to look at a scene from a level with it, while the Chinese artists were accustomed to visualize it as seen from above.[97] Shadows, too, seemed to the Chinese to be out of place in a form of art which, as they understod it, aimed not to imitate reality, but to give pleasure, convey moods, and suggest ideas through the medium of perfect form.

The form was everything in these paintings, and it was sought not in warmth or splendor of color, but in rhythm and accuracy of line. In the early paintings color was sternly excluded, and in the masters it was rare; black ink and a brush were enough, for a color had nothing to do with form. Form, as the artist-theorist Hsieh Ho said, is rhythm: first in the sense that a Chinese painting is the visible record of a rhythmic gesture, a dance executed by the hand;[98] and again in the sense that a significant form reveals the "rhythm of the spirit," the essence and quiet movement of reality.[99] Finally, the body of rhythm is line—not as describing the actual contours of things, but as building forms that, through suggestion or symbol, express the soul. The skill of execution, as distinct from the power of perception, feeling and imagination, lies—in Chinese painting—almost entirely in accuracy and delicacy of line. The painter must observe with patient care, possess intense feeling under strict control, conceive his purpose clearly, and then, without the possibility of correction, transfer to the silk, with a few continuous and easeful strokes, his representative imagination. The art of line reached its apex in China and Japan, as the art of color touched its zenith in Venice and the Netherlands.

Chinese painting never cared for realism, but sought rather to suggest than to describe; it left "truth" to science, and gave itself to beauty. A branch emerging nowhence, and bearing a few leaves or blossoms against a clear sky, was sufficient subject for the greatest master; his handling and proportion of the empty background were tests of his courage and his skill. One of the subjects proposed to candidates for admission to Hui Tsung's Painting Academy may serve to illustrate the Chinese emphasis on indirect suggestion as against explicit representation: the contestants were asked to illustrate by paintings a line of poetry—"The hoof of his steed comes back heavily charged with the scent of the trampled flowers." The successful competitor was an artist who painted a rider with a cluster of butterflies following at the horse's heels.

As the form was everything, the subject might be anything. Men were rarely the center or essence of the picture; when they appeared they were almost always old, and nearly all alike. The Chinese painter, though he was never visibly a pessimist, seldom looked at the world through the eyes of youth. Portraits were painted, but indifferently well; the artist was not interested in individuals. He loved flowers and animals, apparently, far more than men, and spent himself upon them recklessly; Hui Tsung, with an empire at his command, gave half his life to painting birds and flowers. Sometimes the flowers or the animals were symbols, like the lotus or the dragon; but for the most part they were drawn for their own sake, because the charm and mystery of life appeared as completely in them as in a man. The horse was especially loved, and artists like Han Kan did hardly anything else but paint one form after another of that living embodiment of artistic line.

It is true that painting suffered in China, first from religious conventions, and then from academic restrictions; that the copying and imitation of old masters became a retarding fetich in the training of students, and that the artist was in many matters confined to a given number of permitted ways of fashioning his material.[100] "In my young days," said an eminent Sung critic, "I praised the master whose pictures I liked; but as my judgment matured I praised myself for liking what the masters had chosen to have me like."[101] It is astonishing how much vitality remained in this art despite its conventions and canons; it was here as Hume thought it had been with the censored writers of the French Enlightenment: the very limitations from which the artist suffered compelled him to be brilliant.

What saved the Chinese painters from stagnation was the sincerity of their feeling for nature. Taoism had taught it to them, and Buddhism had made it stronger by teaching them that man and nature are one in the flow and change and unity of life. As the poets found in nature a retreat from urban strife, and the philosophers sought in it a model of morals and a guide to life, so the painters brooded by solitary streams, and lost themselves in deeply wooded hills, feeling that in these speechless and lasting things the nameless spirit had expressed itself more clearly than in the turbulent career and thought of men.* Nature, which is so cruel in China, lavishing death with cold and flood, was accepted stoically as the supreme god of the Chinese, and received from them not merely religious sacrifice, but the worship of their philosophy, their literature and their art. Let it serve as an indication of the age and depth of culture in China that a thousand years before Claude Lorraine, Rousseau, Wordsworth and Chateaubriand the Chinese made nature a passion, and created a school of landscape painting whose work throughout the Far East became one of the sovereign expressions of mankind.

V. PORCELAIN

The ceramic art—The making of porcelain—Its early history— "Céladon" — Enamels — The skill of Hao Shih-chiu — "Cloisonné"—The age of K'ang-hsi—Of Ch'ien Lung

As we approach the most distinct art of China, in which her leadership of the world is least open to dispute, we find ourselves harassed by our tendency to class pottery as an industry. To us, accustomed to think of "china" in terms of the kitchen, a pottery is a place where "china" is made; it is a factory like any other, and its products do not arouse exalted associations. But to the Chinese, pottery was a major art; it pleased their practical and yet esthetic souls by combining beauty with use; it gave to their greatest national institution—the drinking of tea—utensils as lovely to the finger-tips as to the eye; and it adorned their homes with shapes so fair that even the poorest families might live in the presence of perfection. Pottery is the sculpture of the Chinese.

Pottery is, first, the industry that bakes clay into usable forms, second, the art that makes those forms beautiful, and third, the objects produced

---

* Landscape painting was called simply *shan-sui*—i.e., mountains and water.

by that industry and that art. Porcelain is vitrified pottery; that is, it is clay so mixed with minerals that when exposed to fire it melts or fuses into a translucent, but not transparent, substance resembling glass.* The Chinese made porcelain out of two minerals chiefly: kaolin—a pure white clay formed from decomposed felspar of granite, and *pe-tun-tse*—a fusible white quartz that gave the product its translucency. These materials were ground into a powder, worked up into a paste with water, moulded by hand or on the wheel, and subjected to high temperatures that fused the composition into a vitreous form, brilliant and durable. Sometimes the potters, not content with this simple white porcelain, covered the "paste"—i.e., the vessel formed but not yet fired—with a "glaze" or coating of fine glass, and then placed the vessel in the kiln; sometimes they applied the glaze after baking the paste into a "biscuit," and then placed the vessel over the fire again. Usually the glaze was colored; but in many cases the paste was painted in color before applying a transparent glaze, or colors were painted on the fired glaze and fused upon it by re-firing. These "over-glaze" colors, which we call enamels, were made of colored glass ground to powder and reduced to a liquid applicable with the painter's slender brush. Life-trained specialists painted the flowers, others the animals, others the landscapes, others the saints or sages who meditated among the mountains or rode upon strange beasts over the waves of the sea.

Chinese pottery is as old as the Stone Age; Professor Andersson has found pottery, in Honan and Kansu, which "can hardly be later in time than 3000 B.C.";[103] and the excellent form and finish of these vases assure us that even at this early date the industry had long since become an art. Some of the pieces resemble the pottery of Anau, and suggest a western origin for Chinese civilization. Far inferior to these neolithic products are the fragments of funerary pottery unearthed in Honan and ascribed to the declining years of the Shang Dynasty. No remains of artistic value appear again before the Han, when we find not only pottery, but the first known use of glass in the Far East.† Under the T'ang emperors the growing popularity of tea provided a creative stimulus for the ceramic art; genius or accident revealed, about the ninth century, the possibility of producing a vessel vitrified not only on the glazed surface (as under the Han and in other civilizations before this age) but throughout—i.e., true porcelain. In that century

---

* When porcelain was introduced into Europe it was named after the *porcellana*, or cowrie shell, which in turn derived its name from its supposed resemblance to the rounded back of a *porcella*, or little hog.[102]

† The Egyptians had glazed pottery unknown centuries before Christ. The decorations on the earliest glazed pottery of China indicate that China had learned the glazing process from the Near East.[104]

a Moslem traveler, Suleiman, reported to his countrymen: "They have in China a very fine clay with which they make vases as transparent as glass; water is seen through them." Excavations have recently discovered, on a ninth-century site at Samarra on the Tigris, pieces of porcelain of Chinese manufacture. The next recorded appearance of the substance outside of China was about 1171, when Saladin sent forty-one pieces of porcelain as a precious gift to the Sultan of Damascus.[105] The manufacture of porcelain is not known to have begun in Europe before 1470; it is mentioned then as an art which the Venetians had learned from the Arabs in the course of the Crusades.[106]

Sung was the classic period of Chinese porcelain. Ceramists ascribe to it both the oldest extant wares and the best; even the Ming potters of a later age, who sometimes equaled them, spoke of Sung pottery in reverential terms, and collectors treasured its masterpieces as beyond any price. The great factories at Ching-te-chen, founded in the sixth century near rich deposits of the minerals used for making and coloring earthenware, were officially recognized by the imperial court, and began to pour out upon China an unprecedented stream of porcelain plates, cups, bowls, vases, beakers, jars, bottles, ewers, boxes, chess-boards, candlesticks, maps, even enameled and gold-inlaid porcelain hat-racks.[107] Now for the first time appeared those jade-green pieces known as *céladon*,* which it has long been the highest ambition of the modern potter to produce, and of the collector to acquire.† Specimens of it were sent to Lorenzo de' Medici by the Sultan of Egypt in 1487. The Persians and the Turks valued it not only for its incredibly smooth texture and rich lustre, but as a detector of poisons; the vessels would change color, they believed, whenever poisonous substances were placed in them.[109] Pieces of *céladon* are handed down from generation to generation as priceless heirlooms in the families of connoisseurs.[110]

For almost three hundred years the workers of the Ming Dynasty labored to keep the art of porcelain on the high level to which the Sung potters had raised it, and they did not fall far short of success. Five hun-

---

* A term applied to them by the French of the seventeenth century from the name of the hero of d'Urfé's novel *l'Astrée*, who, in the dramatization of the story, was always dressed in green.[108]

† From the Occidental point of view the one is as hard as the other; for the Japanese, who have gathered in most of China's famous *céladon*, refuse to sell it at any price; and no later potter has been able to rival the perfection of Sung artistry in this field.

dred kilns burned at Ching-te-chen, and the imperial court alone used 96,000 pieces of chinaware to adorn its gardens, its tables and its rooms.[111] Now appeared the first good enamels—colors fired over the glaze. Yellow monochromes and "egg-shell" blue and white porcelains reached perfection; the blue and white silver-mounted cup named from the Emperor Wan-li (or Shen Tsung) is one of the world's masterpieces of the potter's art. Among the experts of the Wan-li age was Hao Shih-chiu, who could make wine-cups weighing less than one forty-eighth of an ounce. One day, says a Chinese historian, Hao called at the home of a high official and begged permission to examine a porcelain tripod owned by the statesman, and numbered among the choicest of Sung wares. Hao felt the tripod carefully with his hands, and secretly copied the form of its design on a paper concealed in his sleeve. Six months later he visited the official again, and said: "Your Excellency is the possessor of a tripod censer of white *Ting-yao.** Here is a similar one of mine." Tang, the official, compared the new tripod with his own, and could detect no difference; even the stand and cover of the tripod fitted Hao's completely. Hao smilingly admitted that his own piece was an imitation, and then sold it for sixty pieces of silver to Tang, who sold it for fifteen hundred.[112]

It was under the Mings that Chinese *cloisonné* attained its highest excellence. Both the word and the art came from outside: the word from the French *cloison* (partition), the art from the Near East of Byzantine days; the Chinese referred to its products occasionally as *Kuei kuo yao*—wares of the devils' country.[113] The art consists in cutting narrow strips of copper, silver or gold, soldering them edgewise upon the lines of a design previously drawn upon a metal object, filling the spaces between the *cloisons* (or wire lines) with appropriately colored enamel, exposing the vessel repeatedly to fire, grinding the hardened surface with pumice stone, polishing it with charcoal, and gilding the visible edges of the *cloisons*. The earliest known Chinese examples are some mirrors imported into Nara, Japan, about the middle of the eighth century. The oldest wares definitely marked belong to the end of the Mongol or Yüan Dynasty; the best, to the reign of the Ming Emperor Ching Ti. The last great period of Chinese *cloisonné* was under the great Manchu emperors of the eighteenth century.

The factories at Ching-te-chen were destroyed in the wars that ended the Ming Dynasty, and were not revived again until the accession of one

---

* The name given by the Chinese to an ivory-colored species of Sung porcelain.

of China's most enlightened rulers, K'ang-hsi, who, quite as much as his contemporary Louis XIV, was every inch a king. The factories at Ching-te-chen were rebuilt under his direction, and soon three thousand furnaces were in operation. Never had China, or any other country, seen such an abundance of elegant pottery. The Kang-hsi workers thought their wares inferior to those of Ming, but modern connoisseurs do not agree with them. Old forms were imitated perfectly, and new forms were developed in rich diversity. By coating a paste with a glaze of a different tempo of fusibility the Manchu potters produced the prickly surface of "crackle" ware; and by blowing bubbles of paint upon the glaze they turned out *soufflé* wares covered with little circles of color. They mastered the art of monochrome, and issued peach-bloom, coral, ruby, vermilion, *sang-de-bœuf* and Rose-du-Barry reds; cucumber, apple, peacock, grass and *céladon* greens; "Mazarin," azure, lilac and turquoise (or "kingfisher") blues; and yellows and whites of such velvet texture that one could only describe them as smoothness made visible. They created ornate styles distinguished by French collectors as *Famille Rose, Famille Verte, Famille Noir* and *Famille Jaune*—rose, green, black and yellow families.* In the field of polychromes they developed the difficult art of subjecting a vessel, in the kiln, to alternate draughts of clear and soot-laden air—the first providing, the second withdrawing, oxygen—in such ways that the green glaze was transformed into a flame of many colors, so that the French have called this variety *flambé*. They painted upon some of their wares high officials in flowing queue and robes, and created the "Mandarin" style. They painted flowers of the plum in white upon a blue (less often a black) background, and gave to the world the grace and delicacy of the hawthorn vase.

The last great age of Chinese porcelain came in the long and prosperous reign of Ch'ien Lung. Fertility was undiminished; and though the new forms had something less than the success of the K'ang-hsi innovations, the skill of the master-potters was still supreme. The *Famille Rose* attained its fullest perfection, and spread half the flowers and fruits of nature over the most brilliant glaze, while egg-shell porcelain provided costly lamp-shades for extravagant millionaires.[114] Then, through fifteen bloody years (1850-64), came the T'ai-p'ing Rebellion, ruining fifteen provinces, destroying six hundred cities, killing twenty million men and women, and

---

* Excellent specimens of the last two groups may be seen at the Metropolitan Museum of Art.

so impoverishing the Manchu Dynasty that it withdrew its support from the potteries, and allowed them to close their doors and scatter their craftsmen into a disordered world.

The art of porcelain, in China, has not recovered from that devastation, and perhaps it never will. For other factors have reinforced the destructiveness of war and the ending of imperial patronage. The growth of the export trade tempted the artists to design such pieces as best satisfied the taste of European buyers, and as that taste was not as fine as the Chinese, the bad pieces drove the good pieces out of circulation by a ceramic variation of Gresham's law. About the year 1840 English factories began to make inferior porcelain at Canton, exported it to Europe, and gave it the name of "chinaware"; factories at Sèvres in France, Meissen in Germany, and Burslem in England imitated the work of the Chinese, lowered the cost of production by installing machinery, and captured yearly more and more of China's foreign ceramic trade.

What survives is the memory of an art perhaps as completely lost as that of medieval stained glass; try as they will, the potters of Europe have been unable to equal the subtler forms of Chinese porcelain. Connoisseurs raise with every decade their monetary estimate of the masterpieces that survive; they ask five hundred dollars for a tea-cup, and receive $23,600 for a hawthorn vase; as far back as 1767 two "turquoise" porcelain "Dogs of Fo," at auction, brought five times as much as Guido Reni's "Infant Jesus," and thrice as much as Raphael's "Holy Family."[115] But any one who has felt, with eyes and fingers and every nerve, the loveliness of Chinese porcelain will resent these valuations, and count them as sacrilege; the world of beauty and the world of money never touch, even when beautiful things are sold. It is enough to say that Chinese porcelain is the summit and symbol of Chinese civilization, one of the noblest things that men have done to make their species forgivable on the earth.

CHAPTER XXVI

The People and the State

1. Marco Polo Visits Kublai Khan

The incredible travelers—Adventures of a Venetian in China—The elegance and prosperity of Hangchow — The palaces of Peking—The Mongol Conquest—Jenghiz Khan—Kublai Khan — His character and policy — His harem — "Marco Millions"

IN THE golden age of Venice, about the year 1295, two old men and a man of middle age, worn with hardship, laden with bundles, dressed in rags and covered with the dust of many roads, begged and then forced their way into the home from which, they claimed, they had set forth twenty-six years before. They had (they said) sailed many dangerous seas, scaled high mountains and plateaus, crossed bandit-ridden deserts, and passed four times through the Great Wall; they had stayed twenty years in Cathay,* and had served the mightiest monarch in the world. They told of an empire vaster, of cities more populous, and of a ruler far richer, than any known to Europe; of stones that were used for heating, of paper accepted in place of gold, and of nuts larger than a man's head; of nations where virginity was an impediment to marriage, and of others where strangers were entertained by the free use of the host's willing daughters and wives.[1] No man would believe them; and the people of Venice gave to the youngest and most garrulous of them the nickname "Marco Millions," because his tale was full of numbers large and marvelous.[2]

Mark and his father and uncle accepted this fate with good cheer, for they had brought back with them many precious stones from the distant capital, and these gave them such wealth as maintained them in high place in their city. When Venice went to war with Genoa in 1298, Marco

---

* An English form of the Russian name for China—*Kitai*, originally the name of a Mongolian tribe.

Polo received command of a galley; and when his ship was captured, and he was kept for a year in a Genoese jail, he consoled himself by dictating to an amenuensis the most famous travel-book in literature. He told with the charm of a simple and straightforward style how he, father Nicolo and uncle Maffeo had left Acre when Mark was but a boy of seventeen; how they had climbed over the Lebanon ranges and found their way through Mesopotamia to the Persian Gulf, and thence through Persia, Khorassan and Balkh to the Plateau of Pamir; how they had joined caravans that slowly marched to Kashgar and Khotan, and across the Gobi Desert to Tangut, and through the Wall to Shangtu, where the Great Khan received them as humble emissaries from the youthful West.*

They had not thought that they would stay in China beyond a year or two, but they found such lucrative service and commercial opportunities under Kublai that they remained almost a quarter of a century. Marco above all prospered, rising even to be governor of Hangchow. In fond memory he describes it as far ahead of any European city in the excellence of its building and bridges, the number of its public hospitals, the elegance of its villas, the profusion of facilities for pleasure and vice, the charm and beauty of its courtesans, the effective maintenance of public order, and the manners and refinement of its people. The city, he tells us, was a hundred miles in circuit.

> Its streets and canals are extensive, and of sufficient width to allow of boats on the one, and carriages on the other, to pass easily with articles necessary for the inhabitants. It is commonly said that the number of bridges, of all sizes, amounts to twelve thousand. Those which are thrown over the principal canals and are connected with the main streets, have arches so high, and built with so much skill, that vessels with their masts can pass under them. At the same time carts and horses can pass over, so well is the slope from the street graded to the height of the arch. . . . There are within the city ten principal squares or market-places, besides innumerable shops along the streets. Each side of these squares is half a mile in length, and in front of them is the main street, forty paces in width, and running in a direct line from one extremity of the city to the other. In a direction parallel to that of the main street . . . runs a very large canal, on the nearer bank of which capacious warehouses are

---

* "Shangtu" is Coleridge's "Xanadu." The central Asian regions described by Polo were not explored again by Europeans (with one forgotten exception) until 1838.

built of stone, for the accommodation of the merchants who arrive from India and other parts with their goods and effects. They are thus conveniently situated with respect to the market-places. In each of these, upon three days in every week, there is an assemblage of from forty to fifty thousand persons. . . .

The streets are all paved with stone and bricks. . . . The main street of the city is paved . . . to the width of ten paces on each side, the intermediate part being filled up with small gravel, and provided with arched drains for carrying off the rain-water that falls into the neighboring canals, so that it remains always dry. On this gravel carriages continually pass and repass. They are of a long shape, covered at the top, have curtains and cushions of silk, and are capable of holding six persons. Both men and women who feel disposed to take their pleasure are in the daily practice of hiring them for that purpose. . . .

There is an abundant quantity of game of all kinds. . . . From the sea, which is fifteen miles distant, there is daily brought up the river, to the city, a vast quantity of fish. . . . At the sight of such an importation of fish, you would think it impossible that it could be sold; and yet, in the course of a few hours, it is all taken off, so great is the number of inhabitants. . . . The streets connected with the market-squares are numerous, and in some of them are many cold baths, attended by servants of both sexes. The men and women who frequent them have from their childhood been accustomed at all times to wash in cold water, which they reckon conducive to health. At these bathing places, however, they have apartments provided with warm water, for the use of strangers, who cannot bear the shock of the cold. All are in the daily practice of washing their persons, and especially before their meals. . . .

In other streets are the quarters of the courtesans, who are here in such numbers as I dare not venture to report, . . . adorned with much finery, highly perfumed, occupying well-furnished houses, and attended by many female domestics. . . . In other streets are the dwellings of the physicians and the astrologers. . . . On each side of the principal street there are houses and mansions of great size. . . . The men as well as the women have fair complexions, and are handsome. The greater part of them are always clothed in silk. . . . The women have much beauty, and are brought up with delicate and languid habits. The costliness of their dresses, in silks and jewelry, can scarcely be imagined.[3]

Peking (or, as it was then called, Cambaluc) impressed Polo even more than Hangchow; his millions fail him in describing its wealth and population. The twelve suburbs were yet more beautiful than the city; for there the business class had built many handsome homes.⁴ In the city proper there were numerous hotels, and thousands of shops and booths. Food of all kinds abounded, and every day a thousand loads of raw silk entered the gates to be turned into clothing for the inhabitants. Though the Khan had residences at Hangchow, Shangtu and other places, the most extensive of his palaces was at Peking. A marble wall surrounded it, and marble steps led up to it; the main building was so large that "dinners could be served there to great multitudes of people." Marco admired the arrangement of the chambers, the delicate and transparent glazing of the windows, and the variety of colored tiles in the roof. He had never seen so opulent a city, or so magnificent a king.⁵

Doubtless the young Venetian learned to speak and read Chinese; and perhaps he learned from the official historians how Kublai and his Mongol ancestors had conquered China. The gradual drying up of the regions along the northwestern frontier into a desert land incapable of supporting its hardy population had sent the Mongols (i.e., "the brave") out on desperate raids to win new fields; and their success had left them with such a taste and aptitude for war that they never stopped until nearly all Asia, and parts of Europe, had fallen before their arms. Story had it that their fiery leader, Genghis Khan, had been born with a clot of blood in the palm of his hand. From the age of thirteen he began to weld the Mongol tribes into one, and terror was his instrument. He had prisoners nailed to a wooden ass, or chopped to pieces, or boiled in cauldrons, or flayed alive. When he received a letter from the Chinese Emperor Ning Tsung demanding his submission, he spat in the direction of the Dragon Throne and began at once his march across twelve hundred miles of the Gobi desert into the western provinces of China. Ninety Chinese cities were so completely destroyed that horsemen could ride over the devastated areas in the dark without stumbling. For five years the "Emperor of Mankind" laid north China waste. Then, frightened by an unfavorable conjunction of planets, he turned back towards his native village, and died of illness on the way.⁶

His successors, Ogodai, Mangu and Kublai, continued the campaign with barbaric energy; and the Chinese, who had for centuries given themselves to culture and neglected the arts of war, died with individual heroism and national ignominy. At Juining-fu a local Chinese ruler held out until all the aged and infirm had been killed and eaten by the beseiged, all the able-bodied men had fallen, and only women remained to guard the walls; then he set fire to the city and burned himself alive in his palace. The armies of Kublai swept down through China until they stood before the last retreat of the Sung Dynasty, Canton. Unable to resist, the Chinese general, Lu Hsiu-fu, took the boy emperor on his back, and leaped to a double death with him in the sea; and it is said that a hundred thousand Chinese drowned themselves rather than yield to the Mongol conqueror. Kublai gave the imperial corpse an honorable burial, and set himself to establish that Yüan ("Original") or Mongol Dynasty which was to rule China for less than a hundred years.

Kublai himself was no barbarian. The chief exception to this statement was not his treacherous diplomacy, which was in the manner of his time, but his treatment of the patriot and scholar, Wen T'ien-hsian, who, out of loyalty to the Sung Dynasty, refused to acknowledge Kublai's rule. He was imprisoned for three years, but would not yield. "My dungeon," he wrote, in one of the most famous passages in Chinese literature,

> is lighted by the will-o'-the-wisp alone; no breath of spring cheers the murky solitude in which I dwell. . . . Exposed to mist and dew, I had many times thought to die; and yet, through the seasons of two revolving years, disease hovered around me in vain. The dank, unhealthy soil to me became paradise itself. For there was that within me which misfortune could not steal away. And so I remained firm, gazing at the white clouds floating over my head, and bearing in my heart a sorrow boundless as the sky.

At length Kublai summoned him into the imperial presence. "What is it that you want?" asked the monarch. "By the grace of the Sung Emperor," answered Wen, "I became his Majesty's minister. I cannot serve two masters. I only ask to die." Kublai consented; and as Wen awaited the sword of the executioner upon his neck he made obeisance toward the south. as though the Sung emperor were still reigning in the southern capital, Nanking.[7]

Nevertheless, Kublai had the grace to recognize the civilized superiority of the Chinese, and to merge the customs of his own people into theirs.

Of necessity he abandoned the system of examinations for public office, since that system would have given him a completely Chinese bureaucracy; he restricted most higher offices to his Mongol followers, and tried for a time to introduce the Mongol alphabet. But for the greater part he and his people accepted the culture of China, and were soon transformed by it into Chinese. He tolerated the various religions philosophically, and flirted with Christianity as an instrument of pacification and rule. He reconstructed the Grand Canal between Tientsin and Hangchow, improved the highways, and provided a rapid postal service throughout a domain larger than any that has accepted the government of China since his day. He built great public granaries to store the surplus of good crops for public distribution in famine years, and remitted taxes to all peasants who had suffered from drought, storms, or insect depredations;* he organized a system of state care for aged scholars, orphans and the infirm; and he patronized munificently education, letters and the arts. Under him the calendar was revised, and the Imperial Academy was opened.[9] At Peking he reared a new capital, whose splendor and population were the marvel of visitors from other lands. Great palaces were built, and architecture flourished as never in China before.

"Now when all this happened," says Marco Polo, "Messer Polo was on the spot."[10] He became fairly intimate with the Khan, and describes his amusements in fond detail. Besides four wives called empresses, the Khan had many concubines, recruited from Ungut in Tatary, whose ladies seemed especially fair to the royal eye. Every second year, says Marco, officers of proved discrimination were sent to this region to enlist for his Majesty's service a hundred young women, according to specifications carefully laid down by the king.

> Upon their arrival in his presence, he causes a new examination to be made by a different set of inspectors, and from amongst them a further selection takes place, when thirty or forty are retained for his own chamber. . . . These are committed separately to the care of certain elderly ladies of the palace, whose duty it is to observe them attentively, during the course of the night, in order to ascertain that they have not any concealed imperfections, that they sleep

---

* "Not a day passes," writes Marco Polo, "in which there are not distributed, by the regular officers, twenty thousand vessels of rice, millet, and panicum. By reason of this admirable and astonishing liberality which the Great Khan exercises towards the poor, the people all adore him."[8]

tranquilly, do not snore, have sweet breath, and are free from unpleasant scent in any part of the body. Having undergone this rigorous scrutiny, they are divided into parties of five, each taking turn for three days and three nights in his Majesty's interior apartment, where they are to perform every service that is required of them, and he does with them as he likes. When this term is completed they are relieved by another party, and in this manner successively, until the whole number have taken their turn; when the first five recommence their attendance.[11]

After remaining in China for twenty years, Marco Polo, with his father and his uncle, took advantage of an embassy sent by the Khan to Persia, to return to their native city with a minimum of danger and expense. Kublai gave them a message to the Pope, and fitted them out with every comfort then known to travelers. The voyage around the Malay Peninsula to India and Persia, the overland journey to Trebizond on the Black Sea, and the final voyage to Venice, took them three years; and when they reached Europe they learned that both the Khan and the Pope were dead.* Marco himself, with characteristic obstinacy, lived to the age of seventy. On his deathbed his friends pleaded with him, for the salvation of his soul, to retract the obviously dishonest statements that he had made in his book; but he answered, stoutly: "I have not told half of what I saw." Soon after his death a new comic figure became popular at the Venetian carnivals. He was dressed like a clown, and amused the populace by his gross exaggerations. His name was Marco Millions.[13]

2. The Ming and the Ch'ing

Fall of the Mongols—The Ming Dynasty—The Manchu invasion —The Ch'ing Dynasty—An enlightened monarch—Ch'ien Lung rejects the Occident

Not for four centuries was China to know again so brilliant an age. The Yüan Dynasty quickly declined, for it was weakened by the collapse of the Mongol power in Europe and western Asia, and by the sinification (if so pedantic a convenience may be permitted for so repeated a phenomenon) of the Mongols in China itself. Only in an era of railroads, telegraph and print could so vast and artificial an empire, so divided by mountains,

---

* Kublai Khan had proved his conversion to civilization by developing gout.[12]

deserts and seas, be held permanently under one rule. The Mongols proved better warriors than administrators, and the successors of Kublai were forced to restore the examination system and to utilize Chinese capacity in government. The conquest produced in the end little change in native customs or ideas, except that it introduced, perhaps, such new forms as the novel and the drama into Chinese literature. Once more the Chinese married their conquerors, civilized them, and overthrew them. In 1368 an ex-Buddhist priest led a revolt, entered Peking in triumph, and proclaimed himself the first emperor of the Ming ("Brilliant") Dynasty. In the next generation an able monarch came to the throne, and under Yung Lo China again enjoyed prosperity and contributed to the arts. Nevertheless, the Brilliant Dynasty ended in a chaos of rebellion and invasion; at the very time when the country was divided into hostile factions, a new horde of conquerors poured through the Great Wall and laid seige to Peking.

The Manchus were a Tungusic people who had lived for many centuries in what is now Manchukuo (i.e., the Kingdom of the Manchus). Having extended their power northward to the Amur River, they turned back southward, and marched upon the Chinese capital. The last Ming emperor gathered his family about him, drank a toast to them, bade his wife kill herself,* and then hanged himself with his girdle after writing his last edict upon the lapel of his robe: "We, poor in virtue and of contemptible personality, have incurred the wrath of God on high. My ministers have deceived me. I am ashamed to meet my ancestors. Therefore I myself take off my crown, and with my hair covering my face await dismemberment at the hands of the rebels. Do not hurt a single one of my people."[15] The Manchus buried him with honor, and established the Ch'ing ("Unsullied") Dynasty that was to rule China until our own revolutionary age.

They, too, soon became Chinese, and the second ruler of the Dynasty, K'ang-hsi, gave China the most prosperous, peaceful and enlightened reign in the nation's history. Mounting the throne at the age of seven, K'ang-hsi took personal control, at the age of thirteen, of an empire that included not only China proper but Mongolia, Manchuria, Korea, Indo-China, Annam, Tibet and Turkestan; it was without doubt the largest, richest and most populous empire of its time. K'ang-hsi ruled it

---

* She obeyed, and story has it that many concubines followed her example.[14]

with a wisdom and justice that filled with envy the educated subjects of his contemporaries Aurangzeb and Louis XIV. He was a man energetic in body and active in mind; he found health in a vigorous outdoor life, and at the same time labored to make himself acquainted with the learning and arts of his time. He traveled throughout his realm, corrected abuses wherever he saw them, and reformed the penal code. He lived frugally, cut down the expenses of administration, and took pride in the welfare of the people.[16] Under his generous patronage and discriminating appreciation literature and scholarship flourished, and the art of porcelain reached one of the peaks of its career. He tolerated all the religions, studied Latin under the Jesuits, and put up patiently with the strange practices of European merchants in his ports. When he died, after a long and beneficent reign (1661-1722), he left these as his parting words: "There is cause for apprehension lest, in the centuries or millenniums to come, China may be endangered by collisions with the various nations of the West who come hither from beyond the seas."[17]

These problems, arising out of the increasing commerce and contacts of China with Europe came to the front again under another able emperor of the Manchu line—Ch'ien Lung. Ch'ien Lung wrote 34,000 poems; one of them, on "Tea," came to the attention of Voltaire, who sent his "compliments to the charming king of China."[18] French missionaries painted his portrait, and inscribed under it these indifferent verses:

> Occupé sans relâche à tous les soins divers
> D'un gouvernement qu'on admire,
> Le plus grand potentat qui soit dans l'univers
> Est le Meilleur lettré qui soit dans son Empire.*

He ruled China for two generations (1736-96), abdicated in his eighty-fifth year, and continued to dominate the government until his death (1799). During the last years of his reign an incident occurred which might have led the thoughtful to recall the forebodings of K'ang-hsi. England, which had aroused the Emperor's anger by importing opium into China, sent, in 1792, a commission under Lord Macartney to negotiate a commercial treaty with Ch'ien Lung. The commissioners explained

---

* "Occupied without rest in the diverse cares of a government which men admire, the greatest monarch in the world is also the most lettered man in his empire."

to him the advantages of trading with England, and added that the treaty which they sought would take for granted the equality of the British ruler with the Chinese emperor. Ch'ien Lung dictated this reply to George III:

> I set no value on objects strange and ingenious, and have no use for your country's manufactures. This, then, is my answer to your request to appoint a representative at my court, a request contrary to our dynastic usage, which could only result in inconvenience to yourself. I have expounded my views in detail and have commanded your tribute envoys to leave in peace on their homeward journeys. It behooves you, O King, to respect my sentiments and to display even greater devotion and loyalty in future, so that, by perpetual submission to our throne, you may secure peace and prosperity for your country hereafter.[19]

In these proud words China tried to stave off the Industrial Revolution. We shall see in the sequel how, nevertheless, that Revolution came. Meanwhile let us study the economic, political and moral elements of the unique and instructive civilization which that Revolution seems destined to destroy.

II. THE PEOPLE AND THEIR LANGUAGE*

*Population—Appearance—Dress—Peculiarities of Chinese speech—
Of Chinese writing*

The first element in the picture is number: there are many Chinese. Learned guessers calculate that the population of the Chinese states in 280 B.C. was around 14,000,000; in 200 A.D., 28,000,000; in 726, 41,500,000; in 1644, 89,000,000; in 1743, 150,000,000; in 1919, 330,000,000.[20] In the fourteenth century a European traveler counted in China "two hundred cities all greater than Venice."[21] The Chinese census is obtained through a registration law requiring every household to inscribe the names of its occupants upon a tablet at the entrance;[22] we do not know how accurate these tablets are, or the reports which purport to be based upon them. It is probable that China now harbors some 400,000,000 souls.

---

* The following description of Chinese society will apply chiefly to the nineteenth century; the changes brought on by contact with the West will be studied later. Every description must be taken with reserve, since a civilization is never quite the same over a long period of time or an extensive area of space.

The Chinese vary in stature, being shorter and weaker in the south, taller and stronger in the north; in general they are the most vigorous people in Asia. They show great physical stamina, magnificent courage in the bearing of hardships and pain, exceptional resistance to disease, and a climatic adaptability which has enabled them to prosper in almost every zone. Neither opium nor inbreeding nor syphilis has been able to impair their health, and the collapse of their social system has not been due to any visible deterioration in their biological or mental vitality.

The Chinese face is one of the most intelligent on earth, though not universally attractive. Some of the pauper class are incomparably ugly to our Western prejudice, and some criminals have an evil leer admirably suited to cinematic caricature; but the great majority have regular features calm with the physiological accident of low eyelids, and the social accumulation of centuries of civilization. The slant of the eyes is not so pronounced as one had been led to expect, and the yellow skin is often a pleasant suntanned brown. The women of the peasantry are almost as strong as the men; the ladies of the upper strata are delicate and pretty, starch themselves with powder, rouge their lips and cheeks, blacken their eyebrows, and train or thin them to resemble a willow leaf or the crescent moon.[23] The hair in both sexes is coarse and vigorous, and never curls. The women wear theirs in a tuft, usually adorned with flowers. Under the last dynasty the men, to please their rulers, adopted the Manchu custom of shaving the fore half of the head; in compensation they left the remainder uncut and gathered it into a long queue, which became in time an instrument of correction and a support of pride.[24] Beards were small, and were always shaved, though seldom by the owners thereof; barbers carried their shops about with them, and throve.

The head was ordinarily left bare; when men covered it they used in winter a cap of velvet or fur with a turned-up rim, and in summer a conical cap of finely woven filaments of bamboo, surmounted, in persons of any rank, by a colored ball and a silken fringe. Women, when they could afford it, clothed their heads with silk or cotton bands adorned with tinsel, trinkets or artificial flowers. Shoes were usually of warm cloth; since the floor was often of cold tile or earth, the Chinese carried a miniature carpet with him under each foot. By a custom begun at the court of the Emperor Li Hou-chu (ca. 970 A.D.), the feet of girls, at the age of seven, were compressed with tight bandages to prevent their further growth, so that the mature lady might walk with a mincing step erotically pleasing to the men. It was regarded as immodest to speak of a woman's foot, and as scandalous to look at one; in the presence of a lady even the word for shoe was tabu.[25] The practice spread to all ranks and groups except the Manchus and Tatars.

and became so rigid that a deception about the size of the bride's foot sufficed to annul an engagement or a marriage.[26] K'ang-hsi tried to stop the
custom, but failed; today it is one of the happier casualties of the Revolution.

Men covered their nakedness with trousers and tunics, almost always
blue. In winter the trousers were overlaid with leggings, and additional
tunics, sometimes to the number of thirteen, were put on. These were
kept on night and day throughout the winter, and were removed one by one
with the progress of spring.[27] The tunic fell variously to the loins, or the
knees, or the feet; it was buttoned closely up to the neck, and had immense
sleeves instead of pockets; China does not say that a man "pocketed" an
object, but that he "sleeved" it. Shirts and underwear were well-nigh unknown.[28] In the country women wore trousers like the men, since they were
accustomed to doing a man's work and more; in the towns they covered the
trousers with skirts. In the cities silk was almost as common as cotton.[29]
No belt compressed the waist, and no corsets held in the breasts. In general
the Chinese dress was more sensible, healthy and convenient than the garb of
the modern West. No tyranny of fashion harassed or exalted the life of the
Chinese woman; all urban classes dressed alike, and nearly all generations; the
quality of the garment might differ, but not the form; and all ranks might
be sure that the fashion would last as long as the gown.

The language of the Chinese differed from the rest of the world even
more distinctly than their dress. It had no alphabet, no spelling, no grammar, and no parts of speech; it is amazing how well and how long this
oldest and most populous nation on earth has managed without these
curses of Occidental youth. Perhaps in forgotten days there were inflections, declensions, conjugations, cases, numbers, tenses, moods; but the
language as far back as we can trace it shows none of them. Every word
in it may be a noun, a verb, an adjective or an adverb, according to its
context and its tone. Since the spoken dialects have only from four to
eight hundred monosyllabic word-sounds or vocables, and these must be
used to express the 40,000 characters of the written language, each vocable
has from four to nine "tones," so that its meaning is made to differ according to the manner in which it is sung. Gestures and context eke out these
tones, and make each sound serve many purposes; so the vocable *I* may
mean any one of sixty-nine things, *shi* may mean fifty-nine, *ku* twenty-
nine.[30] No other language has been at once so complex, so subtle and so
brief.

The written language was even more unique than the spoken. The objects exhumed in Honan, and tentatively dated back to the Shang Dynasty, bear writing in characters substantially like those in use until our own generation, so that—barring a few Copts who still speak ancient Egyptian—Chinese is both the oldest and the most widespread language spoken on the earth today. Originally, as we infer from a passage in Lao-tze, the Chinese used knotted cords to communicate messages. Probably the needs of priests in tracing magic formulas, and of potters in marking their vessels, led to the development of a pictorial script.[32] These primitive pictograms were the original form of the six hundred signs that are now the fundamental characters in Chinese writing. Some two hundred and fourteen of them have been named "radicals" because they enter as elements into nearly all the characters of the current language. The present characters are highly complex symbols, in which the primitive pictorial element has been overlaid with additions designed to define the term specifically, usually through some indication of its sound. Not only every word, but every idea, has its own separate sign; one sign represents a horse, another sign "a bay horse with a white belly," another "a horse with a white spot on his forehead." Some of the characters are still relatively simple: a curve over a straight line (i.e., the sun over the horizon) means "morning"; the sun and the moon together represent "light"; a mouth and a bird together mean "singing"; a woman beneath a roof means "peace"; a woman, a mouth and the sign for "crooked" constitute the character for "dangerous"; a man and a woman together mean "talkative"; "quarreling" is a woman with two mouths; "wife" is represented by signs for a woman, a broom and a storm.[33]

From some points of view this is a primitive language that has by supreme conservatism survived into "modern" times. Its difficulties are more obvious than its virtues. We are told that the Chinese takes from ten to fifty years to become acquainted with all the 40,000 characters in his language; but when we realize that these characters are not letters but ideas, and reflect on the length of time it would take us to master 40,000 ideas, or even a vocabulary of 40,000 words, we perceive that the terms of the comparison are unfair to the Chinese; what we should say is that it takes any one fifty years to master 40,000 ideas. In actual practice the average Chinese gets along quite well with three or four thousand signs, and learns these readily enough by finding their "radicals." The clearest advantage of such a language—expressing not sounds but ideas—is that it can be read by Koreans and Japanese as easily as by the Chinese, and provides the Far East with an international written language. Again it unites in one system of writing all the inhabitants of China, whose dialects differ to the point of mutual unintelligibility; the same character is read as different sounds or words in different localities. This advantage applies in time as well as in space; since the written language has remained essentially the same while the spoken language has diverged from it into a hundred dialects, the literature of China, written for two thousand years in these characters, can be read today by any literate Chinese, though we cannot tell how the ancient writers pronounced the words, or spoke the ideas, which the signs represent. This persistence of the same script amidst a flux and diversity of speech made for the preservation of Chinese thought and culture, and at the same time served as a powerful force for conservatism; old ideas held the stage and formed the mind of youth. The character of Chinese civilization is symbolized in this phenomenon of its unique script: its unity amid diversity and growth, its profound conservatism, and its unrivaled continuity. This system of writing was in every sense a high intellectual achievement; it classified the whole world—of objects, activities and qualities—under a few hundred root or "radical" signs, combined with these signs some fifteen hundred distinguishing marks, and made them represent, in their completed forms, all the ideas used in literature and life. We must not be too sure that our own diverse modes of writing down our thoughts are superior to this apparently primitive form. Leibnitz in the seventeenth century, and Sir Donald Ross in our time, dreamed of a system of written signs independent of spoken languages, free from their nationalist diversity and their variations in space and time, and capable, therefore, of expressing the ideas of different peoples in identical and mutually intelligible ways. But precisely such a sign language, uniting a hundred generations and a quarter of the earth's inhabitants, already exists in the Far East. The conclusion of the Oriental is logical and terrible: the rest of the world must learn to write Chinese.

III. THE PRACTICAL LIFE

1. In the Fields

The poverty of the peasant—Methods of husbandry—Crops—Tea
—Food—The stoicism of the village

All the varied literature of that language, all the subtleties of Chinese thought and the luxuries of Chinese life, rested in the last analysis on the fertility of the fields. Or rather on the toil of men—for fertile fields are not born but made. Through many centuries the early inhabitants of China must have fought against jungle and forest, beast and insect, drought and flood, saltpetre and frost to turn this vast wilderness into fruitful soil. And the victory had to be periodically rewon; a century of careless timber-cutting left a desert,* and a few years of neglect allowed the jungle to return. The struggle was bitter and perilous; at any moment the barbarians might rush in, and seize the slow growths of the cleared earth. Therefore the peasants, for their protection, lived not in isolated homesteads but in small communities, surrounded their villages with walls, went out together to plant and cultivate the soil, and often slept through the night on guard in their fields.

Their methods were simple, and yet they did not differ much from what they are today. Sometimes they used ploughs—first of wood, then of stone, then of iron; but more often they turned up their little plots patiently with the hoe. They helped the soil with any natural fertilizer they could find, and did not disdain to collect for this purpose the offal of dogs and men. From the earliest times they dug innumerable canals to bring the water of their many rivers to rice paddies or millet fields; deep channels were cut through miles of solid rock to tap some elusive stream, or to divert its course into a desiccated plain. Without rotation of crops or artificial manures, and often without draft animals of any kind, the Chinese have wrung two or three crops annually from at least half their soil, and have won more nourishment from the earth than any other people in history.[34]

The cereals they grew were chiefly millet and rice, with wheat and barley as lesser crops. The rice was turned into wine as well as food, but

---

* The denuded slopes and hills, unable to hold the rain-water that fell upon them, lost their top-soil, became arid, and offered no obstacle to the flooding of the valleys by the heavy rains.

the peasant never drank too much of it. His favorite drink, and next to rice his largest crop, was tea. Used first as a medicine, it grew in popularity until, in the days of the T'angs, it entered the realms of export and poetry. By the fifteenth century all the Far East was esthetically intoxicated with the ceremony of drinking tea; epicures searched for new varieties, and drinking tournaments were held to determine whose tea was the best.[35] Added to these products were delicious vegetables, sustaining legumes like the soy bean and its sprouts, doughty condiments like garlic and the onion, and a thousand varieties of berries and fruits.[36] Least of all products of rural toil was meat; now and then oxen and buffalos were used for ploughing, but stock-raising for food was confined to pigs and fowl.[37] A large part of the population lived by snaring fish from the streams and the sea.

Dry rice, macaroni, vermicelli, a few vegetables, and a little fish formed the diet of the poor; the well-to-do added pork and chicken, and the rich indulged a passion for duck; the most pretentious of Peking dinners consisted of a hundred courses of duck.[38] Cow's milk was rare and eggs were few and old, but the soy bean provided wholesome milk and cheese. Cooking was developed into a fine art, and made use of everything; grasses and seaweeds were plucked and birds' nests ravished to make tasty soups; dainty dishes were concocted out of sharks' fins and fish intestines, locusts and grasshoppers, grubs and silkworms, horses and mules, rats and watersnakes, cats and dogs.[40] The Chinese loved to eat; it was not unusual for a rich man's dinner to have forty courses, and to require three or four hours of gentlemanly absorption.

The poor man did not need so much time for his two meals a day. With all his toil the peasant, with exceptions here and there, was never secure from starvation until he was dead. The strong and clever accumulated large estates, and concentrated the wealth of the country into a few hands; occasionally, as under Shih Huang-ti, the soil was redivided among the population, but the natural inequality of men soon concentrated wealth again.[41] The majority of the peasants owned land, but as the population increased faster than the area under cultivation, the average holding became smaller with every century. The result was a poverty equaled only by destitute India: the typical family earned but $83 a year, many men lived on two cents a day, and millions died of hunger in each year.[42] For twenty centuries China has had an average of one famine annually;[43] partly because the peasant was exploited to the verge of subsistence, partly because reproduction outran the fertility of the soil, and partly because transport was so undeveloped that one region might starve while another had more than it required. Finally, flood might destroy what the landlord and the tax-collector had left; the Hoang-ho—which the people called "China's Sorrow"—might change its course, swamp a thousand villages, and leave another thousand with desiccated land.

The peasants bore these evils with stolid fortitude. "All that a man needs in this transitory life," said one of their proverbs, "is a hat and a bowl of rice."[44] They worked hard, but not fast; no complex machine hurried them, or racked their nerves with its noise, its danger and its speed. There were no weekends and no Sundays, but there were many holidays; periodically some festival, like the Feast of the New Year, or the Feast of the Lanterns, gave the worker some rest from his toil, and brightened with myth and drama the duller seasons of the year. When the winter turned away its scowling face, and the snow-nourished earth softened under the spring rains, the peasants went out once more to plant their narrow fields, and sang with good cheer the hopeful songs that had come down to them from the immemorial past.

2. In the Shops

Handicrafts—Silk—Factories—Guilds—Men of burden—Roads and canals—Merchants—Credit and coinage—Currency experiments—Printing-press inflation

Meanwhile industry flourished as nowhere else on earth before our eighteenth century. As far back as we can delve into Chinese history we find busy handicrafts in the home and thriving trade in the towns. The basic industries were the weaving of textiles and the breeding of worms for the secretion of silk; both were carried on by women in or near their cottages. Silk-weaving was a very ancient art, whose beginnings in China went back to the second millennium before Christ.*[45] The Chinese fed the worms on fresh-cut mulberry leaves, with startling results: on this diet a pound of (700,000) worms increased in weight to 9,500 pounds in forty-two days.[47] The adult worms were then placed in little tents of straw, around which

---

* The spinning of silk out of the cocoons of wild silkworms was known to the ancient classical world; but the breeding of the worms and the gathering and weaving of the silk as an industry were introduced into Europe from China by Nestorian monks about 552 A.D.[46] The art was brought from Constantinople to Sicily in the twelfth century, and to England in the fifteenth.

they wove their cocoons by emitting silk. The cocoons were dropped in hot water, the silk came away from its shell, was treated and woven, and was skilfully turned into a great variety of rich clothing, tapestries, embroideries and brocades for the upper classes of the world.* The raisers and weavers of silk wore cotton.

Even in the centuries before Christ this domestic industry had been supplemented with shops in the towns. As far back as 300 B.C. there had been an urban proletariat, organized with its masters into industrial guilds.[49] The growth of this shop industry filled the towns with a busy population, making the China of Kublai Khan quite the equal, industrially, of eighteenth-century Europe. "There are a thousand workshops for each craft," wrote Marco Polo, "and each furnishes employment for ten, fifteen, or twenty workmen, and in a few instances as many as forty. . . . The opulent masters in these shops do not labor with their own hands, but on the contrary assume airs of gentility and affect parade."[50] These guilds, like codified industries of our time, limited competition, and regulated wages, prices and hours; many of them restricted output in order to maintain the prices of their products; and perhaps their genial content with traditional ways must share some of the responsibility for retarding the growth of science in China, and obstructing the Industrial Revolution until all barriers and institutions are today being broken down by its flood.

The guilds undertook many of the functions which the once proud citizens of the West have surrendered to the state: they passed their own laws, and administered them fairly; they made strikes infrequent by arbitrating the disputes of employers and employees through mediation boards representing each side equally; they served in general as a self-governing and self-disciplining organization for industry, and provided an admirable escape from the modern dilemma between *laissez-faire* and the servile state. These guilds were formed not only by merchants, manufacturers and their workmen, but by such less exalted trades as barbers, coolies and cooks; even the beggars were united in a brotherhood that subjected its members to strict laws.[51] A small minority of town laborers were slaves, engaged for the most part in domestic service, and usually bonded to their masters for a period of years, or for life. In times of famine girls and orphans were exposed for sale at the price of a few "cash," and a father might at any time sell his daughters as bondservants. Such slavery, however, never reached the proportions that it attained in Greece and Rome; the majority of the workers were free agents or members of guilds, and the majority of the peasants

---

* It was not unusual for a Chinese host, when entertaining guests, to pass delicate fabrics around among them,[48] as another might exhibit porcelain or unravel his favorite paintings or calligraphic scrolls.

owned their land, and governed themselves in village communities largely independent of national control.[52]

The products of labor were carried on the backs of men; even human transport moved, for the most part, in sedan chairs raised upon the bruised but calloused shoulders of uncomplaining coolies.[*] Heavy buckets or enormous bundles were balanced on the ends of poles, and slung over the shoulder. Sometimes dray-carts were drawn by donkeys, but more often they were pulled by men. Muscle was so cheap that there was no encouragement to the development of animal or mechanical transport; and the primitiveness of transportation offered no stimulus to the improvement of roads. When European capital built the first Chinese railway (1876)—a ten-mile line between Shanghai and Woosung—the people protested that it would disturb and offend the spirit of the earth; and the opposition grew so vigorous that the government bought the railroad and heaved its rolling stock into the sea.[53] In the days of Shih Huang-ti and Kublai Khan imperial highways existed, paved with stone; but only their outlines now remain. The city streets were mere alleys eight feet wide, designed with a view to keeping out the sun. Bridges were numerous, and sometimes very beautiful, like the marble bridge at the Summer Palace. Commerce and travel used avenues of water almost as frequently as the land; 25,000 miles of canals served as a leisurely substitute for railways; and the Grand Canal between Hangchow and Tientsin, 650 miles long, begun about 300 A.D. and completed by Kublai Khan was surpassed only by the Great Wall in the modest list of China's engineering achievements. "Junks" and *sampans* plied the rivers busily, and provided not only cheap transportation for goods, but homes for millions of the poor.

The Chinese are natural merchants, and work many hours at the business of bargaining. Chinese philosophy and officialdom agreed in despising traders, and the Han emperors taxed them heavily, and forbade them to use carriages or silk. The educated classes displayed long nails as Western women wore French heels—to indicate their exemption from physical toil.[54] It was the custom to rank scholars, teachers and officials as the highest class, farmers as the next, artisans as the third, merchants as the lowest; for, said China, these last merely made profits by exchanging the fruits of other men's toil. Nevertheless they prospered, carried the products of Chinese fields and workshops to all corners of Asia, and became in the end the chief financial support of the government. Internal commerce was hindered by the *likin* tax, and foreign trade was made hazardous by robbers on land and pirates on the sea; but the merchants of China found a way, by sailing

---

[*] A word of Hindu origin, probably from the Tamil *kuli*, hired servant.

around the Malay Peninsula or plodding the caravan routes through Turkestan, to get their goods to India, Persia, Mesopotamia, at last even to
Rome.[55] Silk and tea, porcelain and paper, peaches and apricots, gunpowder
and playing cards, were the staple exports; in return for which the world
sent to China alfalfa and glass, carrots and peanuts, tobacco and opium.

Trade was facilitated by an ancient system of credit and coinage.
Merchants lent to one another at high rates of interest, averaging some
thirty-six per cent—though this was no higher than in Greece and Rome.[56]
Money-lenders took great risks, charged commensurate fees, and were
popular only at borrowing time; "wholesale robbers," said an old Chinese
proverb, "start a bank."[57] The oldest known currency of the country took
the form of shells, knives and silk; the first metal currency went back at
least to the fifth century B.C.[58] Under the Ch'in Dynasty gold was made
the standard of value by the government; but an alloy of copper and tin
served for the smaller coins, and gradually drove out the gold.* When
Wu Ti's experiment with a currency of silver alloyed with tin was ruined
by counterfeiters, the coins were replaced with leather strips a foot long,
which became the foster-parents of paper money. About the year 807, the
supply of copper having, like modern gold, become inadequate as compared with the rising abundance of goods, the Emperor Hsien Tsung
ordered that all copper currency should be deposited with the government, and issued in exchange for it certificates of indebtedness which received the name of "flying money" from the Chinese, who appear to have
taken their fiscal troubles as good-naturedly as the Americans of 1933.
The practice was discontinued after the passing of the emergency; but the
invention of block-printing tempted the government to apply the new
art to the making of money, and about 935 A.D. the semi-independent province of Szechuan, and in 970 the national government at Ch'ang-an, began the issuance of paper money. During the Sung Dynasty a fever of
printing-press inflation ruined many fortunes.[59] "The Emperor's Mint,"
wrote Polo of Kublai's treasury, "is in the city of Cambaluc (Peking);
and the way it is wrought is such that you might say that he hath the
Secret of Alchemy in perfection, and you would be right. For he makes
his money after this fashion"—and he proceeded to arouse the incredulous
scorn of his countrymen by describing the process by which the bark

---

* Copper is still the dominant currency, in the form of the "cash"—worth a third or a
half of a cent—and the "tael," which is worth a thousand "cash."

of the mulberry tree was pressed into bits of paper accepted by the people as the equivalent of gold.[60] Such were the sources of that flood of paper money which, ever since, has alternately accelerated and threatened the economic life of the world.

3. Invention and Science

Gunpowder, fireworks and war—The compass—Poverty of industrial invention—Geography—Mathematics—Physics—"Feng shui"—Astronomy—Medicine—Hygiene

The Chinese have been more facile in making inventions than in using them. Gunpowder appeared under the T'angs, but was very sensibly restricted to fireworks; not until the Sung Dynasty (1161 A.D.) was it formed into hand-grenades and employed in war. The Arabs became acquainted with saltpetre—the main constituent of gunpowder—in the course of their trade with China, and called it "Chinese snow"; they brought the secret of gunpowder westward, the Saracens turned it to military use, and Roger Bacon, the first European to mention it, may have learned of it through his study of Arab lore or his acquaintance with the central Asiatic traveler, De Rubruquis.[61]

The compass is of much greater antiquity. If we may believe Chinese historians, it was invented by the Duke of Chou in the reign of the Emperor Cheng Wang (1115-1078 B.C.) to guide certain foreign ambassadors back to their home lands; the Duke, we are told, presented the embassy with five chariots each equipped with a "south-pointing needle."[62] Very probably the magnetic properties of the lodestone were known to ancient China, but the use of it was confined to orienting temples. The magnetic needle was described in the *Sung-shu,* an historical work of the fifth century A.D., and was attributed by the author to the astronomer Chang Heng (d. 139 A.D.), who, however, had only rediscovered what China had known before. The oldest mention of the needle as useful for mariners occurs in a work of the early twelfth century, which ascribes this use of it to foreign—probably Arab—navigators plying between Sumatra and Canton.[63] About 1190 we find the first known European notice of the compass in a poem by Guyot de Provins.[64]

Despite the contribution of the compass and gunpowder, of paper and silk, of printing and porcelain, we cannot speak of the Chinese as an industrially inventive people. They were inventive in art, developing their own forms, and reaching a degree of sensitive perfection not surpassed in any other place or time; but before 1912 they were content with ancient economic ways, and had a perhaps prophetic scorn of labor-saving devices that hectically accelerate the pace of human toil and throw half the population out of work in order to enrich the rest. They were among the first to use coal for fuel, and mined it in small quantities as early as 122 B.C.;[65] but they developed no mechanisms to ease the slavery of mining, and left for the most part unexplored the mineral resources of their soil. Though they knew how to make glass they were satisfied to import it from the West. They made no watches or clocks or screws, and only the coarsest nails.[66] Through the two thousand years that intervened between the rise of the Han and the fall of the Manchus, industrial life remained substantially the same in China—as it remained substantially the same in Europe from Pericles to the Industrial Revolution.

In like manner China preferred the quiet and mannerly rule of tradition and scholarship to the exciting and disturbing growth of science and plutocracy. Of all the great civilizations it has been the poorest in contributions to the material technique of life. It produced excellent textbooks of agriculture and sericulture two centuries before Christ, and excelled in treatises on geography.[67] Its centenarian mathematician, Chang Ts'ang (d. 152 B.C.), left behind him a work on algebra and geometry, containing the first known mention of a negative quantity. Tsu Ch'ung-chih calculated the correct value of π to six decimal places, improved the magnet or "south-pointing vehicle," and is vaguely recorded to have experimented with a self-moving vessel.[68] Chang Heng invented a seismograph in 132 A.D.,* but for the most part Chinese physics lost itself in the occultism of *feng shui* and the metaphysics of the *yang* and the *yin*.† Chinese mathematicians apparently derived algebra from India, but developed geometry for themselves out of their need for measuring the land.[70] The astronomers of Confucius' time correctly calculated eclipses, and laid the bases of the Chinese calendar—twelve hours a day, and twelve months each beginning with the new moon; an extra month was added periodically to bring this lunar calendar in accord with the seasons and the sun.[71] Life on earth was lived in harmony with life in the sky; the

---

* His machine consisted of eight copper dragons placed on delicate springs around a bowl in whose center squatted a toad with open mouth. Each dragon held a copper ball in its mouth. When an earthquake occurred, the dragon nearest its source dropped its ball into the mouth of the toad. Once a dragon released its ball, though no shock had been felt by the inhabitants. Chang Heng was ridiculed as a charlatan, until a messenger arrived who told of an earthquake in a distant province.[69]

† *Feng shui* (wind and water) was the art, very widespread in China, of adapting the location of homes and graves to the currents of wind and water in the locality.

festivals of the year were regulated by sun and moon; the moral order of society itself was based upon the regularity of the planets and the stars.

Medicine in China was a characteristic mixture of empirical wisdom and popular superstition. It had its beginnings before recorded history, and produced great physicians long before Hippocrates. Already under the Chous the state held yearly examinations for admission to medical practice, and fixed the salaries of the successful applicants according to their showing in the tests. In the fourth century before Christ a Chinese governor ordered a careful dissection and anatomical study of forty beheaded criminals; but the results were lost in theoretical discussion, and dissection stopped. Chang Chung-ning, in the second century, wrote treatises on dietetics and fevers, which remained standard texts for a thousand years. In the third century Hua To wrote a volume on surgery, and made operations popular by inventing a wine which produced a general anesthesia; it is one of the stupidities of history that the formula for mixing this drink has been lost. About 300 A.D. Wang Shu-ho wrote a celebrated treatise on the pulse.[72] Towards the beginning of the sixth century T'ao Hung-ching composed an extensive description of the 730 drugs used in Chinese medicine; and a hundred years later Ch'ao Yuan-fang wrote a classic on the diseases of women and children. Medical encyclopedias were frequent under the T'angs, and specialist monographs under the Sungs.[73] A medical college was established in the Sung Dynasty, but most medical education was through apprenticeship. Drugs were abundant and various; one store, three centuries ago, sold a thousand dollars' worth every day.[74] Diagnosis was pedantically detailed; ten thousand varieties of fever were described, and twenty-four conditions of the pulse were distinguished. Inoculation—not vaccination—was used, probably in imitation of India, in the treatment of small-pox; and mercury was administered for syphilis. This disease seems to have appeared in China in the later years of the Ming Dynasty, to have run wild through the population, and to have left behind its course a comparative immunity to its more serious effects. Public sanitation, preventive medicine, hygiene and surgery made little progress in China; sewage and drainage systems were primitive, or hardly existed;[75] and some towns failed to solve the primary obligations of an organized society—to secure good water, and to dispose of waste.

Soap was a rare luxury, but lice and vermin were easily secured. The simpler Chinese learned to itch and scratch with Confucian equanimity. Medical science made no ascertainable progress from Shih Huang-ti to the Dowager; perhaps the same might be said of European medicine between Hippocrates and Pasteur. European medicine invaded China as an annex to Christianity; but the sick natives, until our own time, confined their use of it to surgery, and for the rest preferred their own physicians and their ancient herbs.

IV. RELIGION WITHOUT A CHURCH

Superstition and scepticism—Animism—The worship of Heaven—
Ancestor-worship—Confucianism—Taoism—The elixir of im-
mortality—Buddhism—Religious toleration and eclecti-
cism—Mohammedanism—Christianity—Causes of its
failure in China

Chinese society was built not on science but on a strange and unique mixture of religion, morals and philosophy. History has known no people more superstitious, and none more sceptical; no people more devoted to piety, and none more rationalistic and secular; no nation so free from clerical domination, and none but the Hindus so blessed and cursed with gods. How shall we explain these contradictions, except by ascribing to the philosophers of China a degree of influence unparalleled in history, and at the same time recognizing in the poverty of China an inexhausti-ble fountain of hopeful fantasy?

The religion of the primitive inhabitants was not unlike the faith of nature peoples generally: an animistic fear and worship of spirits lurking anywhere, a poetic reverence for the impressive forms and reproductive powers of the earth, and an awed adoration of a heaven whose energizing sunlight and fertilizing rains were part of the mystic *rapport* between ter-restrial life and the secret forces of the sky. Wind and thunder, trees and mountains, dragons and snakes were worshiped; but the greater fes-tivals celebrated above all the miracle of growth, and in the spring girls and young men danced and mated in the fields to give example of fertility to mother earth. Kings and priests were in those days near allied, and the early monarchs of China, in the edifying accounts which tendentious historians gave of them in later years, were statesmen-saints whose heroic deeds were always prefaced with prayers, and aided by the gods.[76]

In this primitive theology heaven and earth were bound together as two halves of a great cosmic unity, and were related very much as man and woman, lord and vassal, *yang* and *yin*. The order of the heavens and the moral behavior of mankind were kindred processes, parts of a uni-versal and necessary rhythm called *Tao*—the heavenly way; morality, like the law of the stars, was the coöperation of the part with the whole. The Supreme God was this mighty heaven itself, this moral order, this divine orderliness, that engulfed both men and things, dictating the right relationship of children to parents, of wives to husbands, of vassals to lords, of lords to the emperor, and of the emperor to God. It was a confused but noble conception, hovering between personality when the people prayed to *T'ien*—heaven as a deity—and impersonality when the philosophers spoke of *T'ien* as the just and beneficent, but hardly human or personal, sum of all those forces that ruled the sky, the earth, and men. Gradually, as philosophy developed, the personal conception of "Heaven" was confined to the masses of the people, and the impersonal conception was accepted by the educated classes and in the official religion of the state.⁷⁷

Out of these beginnings grew the two elements of the orthodox religion of China: the nation-wide worship of ancestors, and the Confucian worship of heaven and great men. Every day some modest offering—usually of food—was made to the departed, and prayers were sent up to their spirits; for the simple peasant or laborer believed that his parents and other forbears still lived in some ill-defined realm, and could bring him good or evil fortune. The educated Chinese offered similar sacrifice, but he looked upon the ritual not as worship so much as commemoration; it was wholesome for the soul and the race that these dead ones should be remembered and revered, for then the ancient ways which they had followed would also be revered, innovation would hesitate, and the empire would be at peace. There were some inconveniences in this religion, for it littered China with immense inviolable graves, impeding the construction of railroads and the tillage of the soil; but to the Chinese philosopher these were trivial difficulties when weighed in the balance against the political stability and spiritual continuity which ancestor worship gave to civilization. For through this profound institution the nation, which was shut out from physical and spatial unity by great distances and the poverty of transport, achieved a powerful spiritual unity in time; the generations were bound together with the tough web of tradition, and the individual life received an ennobling share and significance in a drama of timeless majesty and scope.

The religion adopted by the scholars and the state was at once a widening and a narrowing of this popular faith. Slowly, by increments of reverence from century to century, Confucius was lifted up, through imperial decrees, to a place second only to that of Heaven itself; every school raised a tablet, every city a temple, in his honor; and periodically the emperor and the officials offered incense and sacrifice to his spirit or his memory, as the greatest influence for good in all the rich memories of the race. He was not, in the understanding of the intelligent, a god; on the contrary he served for many Chinese as a substitute for a god; those who attended the services in his honor might be agnostics or atheists, and yet—if they honored him and their ancestors—they were accepted by their communities as pious and religious souls. Officially, however, the faith of the Confucians included a recognition of *Shang-ti*, the Supreme Ruling Force of the world; and every year the emperor offered ceremonious sacrifice, on the Altar of Heaven, to this impersonal divinity. Nothing was said, in this official faith, of immortality.[78] Heaven was not a place but the will of God, or the order of the world.

This simple and almost rationalistic religion never quite satisfied the people of China. Its doctrines gave too little room to the imagination of men, too little answer to their hopes and dreams, too little encouragement to the superstitions that enlivened their daily life. For the people, here as everywhere, brightened the prose of reality with the poetry of the supernatural; they felt a world of good or evil spirits hovering in the air about them and the earth beneath, and longed to appease the enmity or enlist the aid of these secret powers by magic incantation or prayer. They paid diviners to read the future for them in the lines of the *I-Ching*, or on the shells of tortoises, or in the movements of the stars; they hired magicians to orient their dwellings and graves to wind and water, and sorcerers to bring them sunshine or rain.[79] They exposed to death such children as were born to them on "unlucky" days,[80] and fervent daughters sometimes killed themselves to bring good or evil fortune to their parents.[81] In the south, particularly, the Chinese soul inclined to mysticism; it was repelled by the frigid rationalism of the Confucian faith, and hungered for a creed that would give China, like other nations, deathless consolations.

Therefore some popular theologians took the misty doctrine of Lao-tze and gradually transformed it into a religion. To the Old Master and to Chuang-tze the *Tao* had been a way of life for the attainment of individual peace on earth; they do not seem ever to have dreamed of it as a deity, much less as a price to be paid here for a life beyond the grave.[82] But in the second century of our era these doctrines were improved upon by men who claimed to have received, in direct line from Lao-tze, an elixir that would confer immortality. This drink became so popular that several emperors are said to have died from pious indulgence in it.[83] A mystagogue in Szechuan (ca. 148 A.D.) offered to cure all diseases with a simple talisman to be given in exchange for five packages of rice. Apparently miraculous cures were effected, and those who were not cured were told that their faith had been too weak.[84] The people flocked to the new religion, built temples for it, supported its priesthood generously, and poured into the new faith some part of their inexhaustible superstitious lore. Lao-tze was made a god, and was credited with a supernatural conception; he had been born, the faithful believed, already old and wise, having been in his mother's womb for eighty years.[85] They peopled the world with new devils and deities, frightened away the one with firecrackers exploding merrily in the temple courts, and with mighty gongs called the others out of slumber to hear their importunate prayers.

For a thousand years the Taoist faith had millions of adherents, converted many emperors, and fought long battles of intrigue to wrest from the Confucians the divine right to tax and spend. In the end it was broken down not by the logic of Confucius, but by the coming of a new religion even better suited than itself to inspire and console the common man. For the Buddhism that began its migration from India to China in the first century after Christ was not the hard and gloomy doctrine that the Enlightened One had preached five hundred years before; it was no ascetic creed, but a bright and happy faith in helping deities and a flowering paradise; it took the form, as time went on, of the Greater Vehicle, or *Mahayana*, which Kanishka's theologians had adapted to the emotional needs of simple men; it presented China with freshly personal and humane gods, like Amitabha, Ruler of Paradise, and Kuan-yin, god-then-goddess of mercy; it filled the Chinese pantheon with *Lohans* or *Arhats*—eighteen of the original disciples of Buddha—who stood ready at every turn to give of their merits to help a bewildered and suffering mankind. When, after the fall of the Han, China found itself torn with political chaos, and life seemed lost in a welter of insecurity and war, the harassed nation turned to Buddhism as the Roman world was at the same time turning to Christianity. Taoism opened its arms to take in the new faith, and in time became inextricably mingled with it in the Chinese soul. Emperors persecuted Buddhism, philosophers complained of its superstitions, statesmen were concerned over the fact that some of the best blood of China was being sterilized in monasteries; but in the end the government found again that religion is stronger than the state; the emperors made treaties of peace with the new gods; the Buddhist priests were allowed to collect alms and raise temples, and the bureaucracy of officials and scholars was per-force content to keep Confucianism as its own aristocratic creed. The new religion took possession of many old shrines, placed its monks and fanes along with those of the Taoists on the holy mountain Tai-shan, aroused the people to many pious pilgrimages, contributed powerfully to painting, sculpture, architecture, literature, and the development of print-ing, and brought a civilizing measure of gentleness into the Chinese soul. Then, it, too, like Taoism, fell into decay; its clergy became corrupt, its doctrine was permeated more and more by sinister deities and popular superstitions, and its political power, never strong, was practically de-stroyed by the renaissance of Confucianism under Chu Hsi. Today its temples are neglected, its resources are exhausted, and its only devotees are its impoverished priests.[86]

Nevertheless it has sunk into the national soul, and is still part of the complex but informal religion of the simpler Chinese. For religions in China are not mutually exclusive as in Europe and America, nor have they ever precipitated the country into religious wars. Normally they tol-erate one another not only in the state but in the same breast; and the average Chinese is at once an animist, a Taoist, a Buddhist and a Confu-cianist. He is a modest philosopher, and knows that nothing is certain; perhaps, after all, the theologian may be right, and there may be a para-dise; the best policy would be to humor all these creeds, and pay many diverse priests to say prayers over one's grave. While fortune smiles, however, the Chinese citizen does not pay much attention to the gods; he honors his ancestors, but lets the Taoist and the Buddhist temples get along with the attentions of the clergy and a few women. He is the most secular spirit ever produced, as a type, in known history; this life absorbs him; and when he prays he asks not for happiness in paradise, but for some profit here on earth.[87] If the god does not answer his prayers he may overwhelm him with abuse, and end by throwing him into the river. "No image-maker worships the gods," says a Chinese proverb; "he knows what stuff they are made of."[88]

Hence the average Chinese has not taken passionately to Mohamme-danism or Christianity; these offered him a heaven that Buddhism had already promised, but what he really wanted was a guarantee of happi-ness here. Most of the fifteen million Chinese Moslems are not really Chinese, but people of foreign origin or parentage.[89] Christianity entered China with the Nestorians about 636 A.D. The Emperor Tai Tsung gave it a sympathetic hearing, and protected its preachers from persecution. In 781 the Nestorians of China raised a monument on which they recorded their appreciation of this enlightened tolerance, and their hope that Christianity would soon win the whole land.[90] Since then Jesuit missionaries with heroic zeal and lofty learning, and Protestant missionaries backed with great American fortunes, have labored to realize the hope of the Nestorians. Today there are three million Christians in China; one per cent of the population has been converted in a thousand years.*

V. THE RULE OF MORALS

The high place of morals in Chinese society—The family—Children—Chastity—Prostitution—Premarital relations—Marriage and love—Monogamy and polygamy—Concubinage—Divorce—A Chinese empress—The patriarchal male—The subjection of woman—The Chinese character

Confucianism and ancestor worship survived so many rivals and so many attacks, during twenty centuries, because they were felt to be indispensable to that intense and exalted moral tradition upon which China had founded its life. As these were the religious sanctions, so the family was the great vehicle, of this ethical heritage. From parents to children the moral code was handed down across the generations, and became the invisible government of Chinese society; a code so stable and strong that that society maintained its order and discipline through nearly all the vicissitudes of the unsteady state. "What the Chinese," said Voltaire, "best know, cultivate the most, and have brought to the greatest perfection, is

---

* Christianity lost its opportunity early in the eighteenth century, when a quarrel arose between the Jesuits and other Roman Catholic orders in China. The Jesuits had, with characteristic statesmanship, found formulas by which the essential elements of Chinese piety—ancestor worship and the adoration of heaven—could be brought under Christian forms without disrupting deep-rooted institutions or endangering the moral stability of China; but the Dominicans and Franciscans demanded a stricter interpretation, and denounced all Chinese theology and ritual as inventions of the devil. The enlightened Emperor K'ang-hsi was highly sympathetic to Christianity; he entrusted his children to Jesuit tutors, and offered on certain conditions to become a Christian. When the Church officially adopted the rigid attitude of the Dominicans and the Franciscans, K'ang-hsi withdrew his support of Christianity, and his successors decided to oppose it actively.[91] In later days the greedy imperialism of the West weakened the persuasiveness of Christian preaching, and precipitated the passionate anti-Christianism of the revolutionary Chinese.

morality."⁹² "By building the house on a sound foundation," Confucius had said, "the world is made secure."⁹³

The Chinese proceeded on the assumption that the purpose of a moral code was to transform the chaos of sexual relations into an orderly institution for the rearing of children. The family's reason for being lay in the child. There could not, from the viewpoint of China, be too many children: a nation was always subject to attack, and needed defenders; the soil was rich, and could support many millions; even if there should be a bitter struggle for existence in large families and crowded communities, the weakest would be eliminated, and the ablest would survive and multiply to be a support and an honor to their aging parents, and to tend the ancestral graves religiously. Ancestor worship forged an endless chain of reproduction, and gave it a double strength; the husband must beget sons not only to sacrifice to him after his death, but to continue the sacrifices to his ancestors. "There are three things which are unfilial," said Mencius; "and the greatest of them is to have no posterity."⁹⁴

Sons were prayed for, and mothers were shamed forever if they had none; for sons could work better than girls in the fields, and could fight better in war; and a regulation not unconscious of this had long since decreed that only sons should be permitted to offer the ancestral sacrifice. Girls were a burden, for one had to rear them patiently only to see them go off, at maturity, to their husbands' homes, to labor there, and beget laborers, for another family. If too many daughters came, and times were very hard, the infant girl might without sin be left exposed in the furrows, to be killed by the night's frost or eaten by prowling swine.⁹⁵ Such progeny as survived the hazards and ailments of childhood were brought up with the tenderest affection; example took the place of blows in their education; and occasionally they were exchanged for a while for the children of kindred families, so that they might not be spoiled by an indulgent love.⁹⁶ The children were kept in the women's division of the home, and seldom mingled with the adult males until the age of seven. Then the boys, if the family could afford it, were sent to school, and were severely separated from the girls; from the age of ten they would be limited in their choice of associates to men and courtesans; and the frequency of homosexuality and male prostitution sometimes made this choice unreal.⁹⁷

Chastity was exalted and rigidly enforced in daughters, and was inculcated with such success that Chinese girls have been known to kill themselves because they believed that they had been dishonored by the accidental touch of a man.[98] But no effort was made to maintain chastity in the unmarried man; on the contrary, it was considered normal and legitimate that he should visit brothels; sex (in the male) was an appetite like hunger, and might be indulged in without any other disgrace than that which would in any case attach to immoderation.[99]* The supply of women to meet these demands had long since been an established institution in China; the famous premier of T'si, Kuan Chung, had provided a lupanar where traders from other states might leave their gains before departing for their homes.[101] Marco Polo described the courtesans of Kublai Khan's capital as incredibly numerous and ravishingly beautiful. They were licensed, regulated and segregated; and the most beautiful of them were supplied without charge to the members of foreign embassies.[102] In later times a special variety of charmers was developed, known as "sing-song girls," who, if that were preferred, would provide educated conversation for young men or for respectable husbands entertaining guests. Such girls were often versed in literature and philosophy, as well as skilled in music and the dance.[103]

Premarital relations were so free for men, and premarital association with men was so restricted for respectable women, that small opportunity was given for the growth of romantic love. A literature of such tender affection appeared under the T'angs, and some indication of the sentiment may be found as far back as the sixth century before Christ in the legend of Wei Sheng, who, having promised to meet a girl under a bridge, waited vainly for her there, though the water rose above his head and drowned him.[104] Doubtless Wei Sheng knew better than this, but it is significant that the poets thought that he might not. In general, however, love as a tender solicitude and attachment was more frequent between men than between the sexes; in this matter the Chinese agreed with the Greeks.[105]

Marriage had little to do with love; since its purpose was to bring healthy mates together for the rearing of abundant families, it could not, the Chinese thought, be left to the arbitrament of passion. Hence the sexes were kept apart while the parents sought eligible mates for their children. It was considered immoral for a man not to marry; celibacy was a crime against one's ancestors, the state and the race, and was never

---

* Men sometimes prepared themselves openly for a night in a brothel by pictures, aphrodisiacs and songs.[100] It should be added that this lenience towards marital deviations is disappearing today.

quite condoned even in the case of the clergy. In the ancient days a special official was appointed to see to it that every man was married by the age of thirty, and every woman by twenty.[106] With or without the help of professional intermediaries (*mei-ren*, "go-betweens"), parents arranged the betrothal of their children soon after puberty, sometimes before puberty, sometimes before birth.[107] Certain endogamic and exogamic limits were placed on the choice: the mate had to be of a family long known to the match-seeking parents, and yet sufficiently distant in relationship to be outside the clan. The father of the boy usually sent a substantial present to the father of the girl, but the girl in her turn was expected to bring a considerable dowry, chiefly in the form of goods, to her husband; and gifts of some value were ordinarily exchanged between the families at the marriage. The girl was kept in strict seclusion until the wedding. Her future mate could not see her except by stratagem—though that was often managed; in many cases he saw her for the first time when he removed her veil in the wedding cermony. This was a complex and symbolic ritual, in which the essential matter was that the bridegroom should be sufficiently wined to guard against the chance of a criminal bashfulness on his part;[108] as for the girl, she had been trained to be at once shy and obedient. After the marriage the bride lived with her husband in or near the house of his father; there she labored in servitude to her mate and his mother, until such time as the normal course of life and death liberated her from this slavery and left her ready to impose it upon the wives of her sons.

The poor were monogamous; but so eager was China for vigorous children that such men as could afford it were permitted by custom to take concubines, or "secondary wives." Polygamy was looked upon as eugenic, on the ground that those who could bear its expense would on the average be the abler men in their communities. If the first wife remained childless she would in most cases urge her husband to take an additional mate, and would often adopt as her own the child of the concubine. There were many instances in which wives, anxious to keep their husbands home, suggested that they should marry the courtesans to whom they were giving their attention and their substance, and should bring them home as secondary wives.[109] The wife of the Emperor Chuang-tchu was much praised in Chinese tradition because she was reported to have said: "I have never ceased to send people to all the neighboring towns to look for beautiful women in order that I might represent them as concubines to my lord.'"[110] Families rivaled one another in seeking the honor of providing a daughter for the royal harem. To guard the harem, and to attend to other duties at his court, the emperor was entitled to three thousand eunuchs. Most of these had been mutilated by their parents before the age of eight, in order to ensure their livelihood.[111]

In this paradise of the male the secondary wives were practically slaves, and the chief wife was merely the head of a reproductive establishment. Her prestige depended almost entirely on the number and sex of her children. Educated to accept her husband as a lord, she might win some modest happiness by falling quietly into the routine expected of her; and so adaptive is the human soul that the wife and husband, in these pre-arranged unions, seem to have lived in a peace no more violent than that which follows the happy endings of Western romantic love. The woman could be divorced for almost any cause, from barrenness to loquacity;[112] she herself could never divorce her husband, but she might leave him and return to her parents—though this was a matter of rare resort. Divorce in any case was infrequent; partly because the lot of the divorced woman was too unpleasant to be thought of, partly because the Chinese were natural philosophers, and took suffering as the order of the day.

Very probably, in pre-Confucian times, the family had centered around the mother as the source of its existence and its authority. In the earliest period, as we have seen, the people "knew their mothers but not their fathers"; and the character for a man's family name is still formed from the radical for "woman."[113] The word for "wife" meant "equal"; and the wife preserved her own name after marriage. As late as the third century of our era women held high administrative and executive positions in China, even to ruling the state;[114] the "Dowager Empress" merely followed in the steps of that Empress Lu who ruled China so severely from 195 to 180 B.C. Lu, "hard and inflexible," killed and poisoned her rivals and enemies with all the gusto of a Medicean; she chose and deposed kings, and had her husband's favorite concubine shorn of ears and eyes and thrown into a latrine.[115] Though hardly one in ten thousand Chinese were literate under the Manchus,[116] education was customary among the women of the upper classes in ancient days; many of them wrote poetry; and Pan Chao, the gifted sister of the historian P'an Ku (ca. 100 A.D.), completed his history after his death, and won high recognition from the emperor.[117]

Probably the establishment of the feudal system in China reduced the political and economic status of woman, and brought with it an especially rigorous form of the patriarchal family. Usually all the male descendants, and their wives and children, lived with the oldest male; and though the family owned its land in common, it acknowledged the complete authority of the patriarch over both the family and its property. By the time of Confucius the power of the father was almost absolute: he could sell his wife or his children into servitude, though he did so only under great need; and if he wished he could put his children to death with no other restraint than public opinion.[118] He ate his meals alone, not inviting either his wife or his children to table with him except on rare occasions. When he died his widow was expected to avoid remarriage; formerly she had been required to commit suttee in his honor, and cases of this occurred in China to the end of the nineteenth century.[119] He was courteous to his wife, as to everybody, but he maintained a severe distance, almost a separation of caste, between himself and his wife and children. The women lived in distinct quarters of the home, and seldom mingled with the men; social life was exclusively male, except for promiscuous women. The man thought of his wife as the mother of his children; he honored her not for her beauty or her culture, but for her fertility, her industry and her obedience. In a celebrated treatise the Lady Pan Ho-pan, from the same elevation of aristocracy, wrote with edifying humility of the proper condition of women:

> We occupy the last place in the human species, we are the weaker part of humanity; the basest functions are, and should be, our portion. . . . Rightly and justly does the Book of the Laws of the Sexes make use of these words: "If a woman has a husband after her own heart, it is for her whole life; if a woman has a husband against her heart, it is also for life."[120]

And Fu Hsüan sang:

> How sad it is to be a woman!
> Nothing on earth is held so cheap.
> Boys stand leaning at the door
> Like gods fallen out of heaven.
> Their hearts brave the Four Oceans,
> The wind and dust of a thousand miles.

No one is glad when a girl is born:
By her the family sets no store.
When she grows up she hides in her room,
Afraid to look a man in the face.
No one cries when she leaves her home—
Sudden as clouds when the rain stops.
She bows her head and composes her face,
Her teeth are pressed on her red lips:
She bows and kneels countless times.[121]

Perhaps such quotations do injustice to the Chinese home. There was rank subjection in it, and quarrels were frequent between man and woman, and among the children; but there were also much kindness and affection, much mutual helpfulness, and constant coöperation in the busy functioning of a natural home. Though economically subordinate the woman enjoyed the franchise of the tongue, and might scold her man into fright or flight in the best Occidental style. The patriarchal family could not be democratic, much less egalitarian, because the state left to the family the task of maintaining social order; the home was at once a nursery, a school, a workshop and a government. The relaxation of family discipline in America has been made possible only by the economic unimportance of the urban home, and the appropriation of family functions by the school, the factory and the state.

The type of character produced by these domestic institutions has won the highest praise of many travelers. Allowing for the many exceptions that weaken every social generalization, the average Chinese was a model of filial obedience and devotion, of wholesome respect and willing care for the old.* He accepted patiently the character-forming precepts of the *Li-chi* or Book of Ceremonies, carried easily its heavy burden of etiquette, regulated every phase of his life with its rules of passionless courtesy, and acquired under it an ease and excellence of manners, a poise and dignity of bearing, unknown to his compeers of the West—so that a coolie carrying dung through the streets might show better breeding, and more self-respect, than the alien merchant who sold him opium. The Chinese learned the art of compromise, and graciously "saved the face" of his worsted

---

* Chinese legend illustrates this with characteristic humor by the story of Hakuga, who was whipped daily by his mother, but never cried. One day, however, he cried as he was being beaten; and being asked the cause of this unusual disturbance he answered that he wept because his mother, now old and weak, was unable to hurt him with her blows.[122]

enemy. He was occasionally violent in speech and always loquacious, often unclean and not invariably sober, given to gambling and gluttony,* to petty peculation and courteous mendacity;[124] he worshiped the God of Wealth with too frank an idolatry,[125] and was as hungry for gold as a caricatured American; he was capable occasionally of cruelty and brutality, and accumulating injustices sometimes provoked him to mass outbreaks of pillage and slaughter. But in nearly all cases he was peaceable and kindly, ready to help his neighbors, disdainful of criminals and warriors, thrifty and industrious, leisurely but steady at his work, simple and unassuming in his mode of life, and comparatively honest in commerce and finance. He was silent and patient under the whip of adversity, and took good and evil fortune alike with a wise humility; he bore bereavement and agony with fatalistic self-control, and showed little sympathy for those who suffered them audibly; he mourned long and loyally for his departed relatives, and (when all his compromises had failed to elude it) faced his own death with philosophic calm. He was as sensitive to beauty as he was insensitive to pain; he brightened his cities with colorful decoration, and adorned his life with the maturest art.

If we wish to understand this civilization we must forget for a moment the bitter chaos and helplessness into which it has been thrown by its own internal weakness and by contact with the superior guns and machines of the West; we must see it at any of its many apogees—under the Chou princes, or Ming Huang, or Hui Tsung, or K'ang-hsi. For in those quiet and beauty-loving days the Chinese represented without doubt the highest civilization and the ripest culture that Asia, or perhaps any continent, had yet achieved.

VI. A GOVERNMENT PRAISED BY VOLTAIRE[126]

The submergence of the individual—Self-government—The village and the province—The laxity of the law—The severity of punishment—The Emperor—The Censor—Administrative boards— Education for public office—Nomination by education—The examination system—Its defects—Its virtues

The most impressive aspect of this civilization was its system of government. If the ideal state is a combination of democracy and aristocracy, the Chinese have had it for more than a thousand years; if the best gov-

---

* In many cities hucksters stood at the roadside with saucer, dice and cup in hand, ready for the casual gambler.[123]

ernment is that which governs least, then the Chinese have had the best. Never has a government governed so many people, or governed them so little, or so long.

Not that individualism, or individual liberty, flourished in China; on the contrary, the concept of the individual was weak, and lost him in the groups to which he belonged. He was, first of all, a member of a family and a passing unit in a stream of life between his ancestors and his posterity; by law and custom he was responsible for the acts of the others of his household, and they were responsible for his. Usually he belonged to some secret society, and, in the town, to a guild; these limited his rights to do as he pleased. A web of ancient custom bound him, and a powerful public opinion threatened him with ostracism if he seriously violated the morals or traditions of the group. It was precisely the strength of these popular organizations, rising naturally out of the needs and voluntary coöperation of the people, that made it possible for China to maintain itself in order and stability despite the weakness of law and the state.

But within the framework of these spontaneous institutions of self-government the Chinese remained politically and economically free. The great distances that separated one city from another, and all of them from the imperial capital, the dividing effect of mountains, deserts, and unbridged or unnavigable streams, the lack of transport and quick communication, and the difficulty of supporting an army large enough to enforce some central will upon four hundred million people, compelled the state to leave to each district an almost complete autonomy.

The unit of local administration was the village, loosely ruled by the family heads under the eye of a "headman" named by the government; a group of villages gathered about a town constituted a *hien,* or county, of which there were some thirteen hundred in China; two or more *hien,* ruled together from a city, constituted a *fu;* two or more *fu* formed a *tao,* or circuit; two or more *tao* made a *sheng,* or province; and eighteen provinces, under the Manchus, made the empire. The state appointed a magistrate to act as administrator, tax-collector and judge in each *hien;* a chief officer for each *fu* and each *tao;* and a judge, a treasurer, a governor, and sometimes a viceroy, for each province.[127] But these officials normally contented themselves with collecting taxes and "squeezes," judging such cases as voluntary arbitration had failed to settle, and, for the rest, leaving the maintenance of order to custom, the family, the clan and the guild. Each province was a semi-independent state, free from imperial interference or central legislation so long as it paid its tax-allotment and kept the peace. Lack of facilities for communication made the central government more an idea than a reality. The patriotic emotions of the people were spent upon their districts and provinces, and seldom extended to the empire as a whole.

In this loose structure law was weak, unpopular, and diverse. The people preferred to be ruled by custom, and to settle their disputes by face-saving compromises out of court. They expressed their view of litigation by such pithy proverbs as "Sue a flea and catch a bite," or "Win your lawsuit, lose your money." In many towns of several thousand population years passed without a case coming into the courts.[128] The laws had been codified under the T'ang emperors, but they dealt almost entirely with crime, and attempted no formulation of a civil code. Trials were simple, for no lawyer was allowed to argue a case in court, though licensed notaries might occasionally prepare, and read to the magistrate, a statement in behalf of a client.[129] There were no juries, and there was scant protection in the law against the sudden seizure and secret retention of a person by the officers of the state. Suspects were finger-printed,[130] and confessions were sometimes elicited by tortures slightly more physical than those now used for such purposes in the most enlightened cities. Punishment was severe, but hardly as barbarous as in most other countries of Asia; it began with cutting off the hair, and went on to flogging, banishment or death; if the criminal had exceptional merits or rank, he might be allowed to kill himself.[131] There were generous commutations of sentences, and capital punishment could in normal times be imposed only by the emperor. Theoretically, as with us, all persons were equal before the law. These laws never availed to prevent brigandage on the highways or corruption in office and the courts, but they coöperated modestly with custom and the family to give China a degree of social order and personal security not equaled by any other nation before our century.[132]

Poised precariously above these teeming millions sat the emperor. In theory he ruled by divine right; he was the "Son of Heaven," and represented the Supreme Being on earth.* By virtue of his godlike powers he ruled the seasons and commanded men to coördinate their lives with the divine order of the universe. His decrees were laws, and his judgments were

---

* Hence his realm was sometimes called *Tien-Chan*, the "heaven-ruled." Europeans translated this into the "Celestial Kingdom," and spoke of the Chinese learnedly as "Celestials."[133]

the final court; he administered the state and was the head of its religion; he appointed all officials, examined the highest contestants for office, and chose his successor to the throne. Actually his powers were wholesomely limited by custom and law. He was expected to rule without contravening the regulations that had come down from the sacred past; he might at any moment be rebuked by a strange dignitary known as the Censor; he was in effect imprisoned by a ring of counsellors and commissioners whose advice it was usually expedient for him to accept; and if he ruled very unjustly or unwell he lost, by common custom and consent, the "mandate of Heaven," and might be violently deposed without offense to religion or morality.

The Censor was head of a board whose function it was to inspect all officials in the administration of their duties; and the emperor was not exempt from this supervision. Several times in the course of history the Censor has reproved the emperor himself. For example, the Censor Sung respectfully suggested to the Emperor Chia Ch'ing (1796-1821 A.D.) a moderation in his attachment to actors and strong drink. Chia Ch'ing summoned Sung to his presence, and angrily asked him what punishment was proper for so insolent an official. Sung answered, "Death by the slicing process." Ordered to select a milder penalty, he answered, "Let me be beheaded." Ordered to select a milder penalty, he recommended that he be strangled. The Emperor, impressed by his courage and disturbed by his propinquity, made him governor of the province of Ili.[134]

The imperial government had come to be a highly complex administrative machine. Nearest to the throne was the Grand Council, composed of four "Great Ministers," usually headed by a prince of the royal blood; by custom it met daily, in the early hours of the morning, to determine the policies of the state. Superior in rank but inferior in influence was another group of advisers called the "Inner Cabinet." The work of administration was headed by "Six Boards": of Civil Office, of Revenue, of Ceremonies, of War, of Punishments, and of Works. There was a Colonial Office, for managing such distant territories as Mongolia, Sinkiang and Tibet; but there was no Foreign Office: China recognized no other nations as its equals, and made no provisions for dealing with them beyond arrangements for the reception of tribute-bearing embassies.

The weakness of the government lay in its limited revenues, its inadequate defenses, and its rejection of any instructive intercourse with the outside world. It taxed the land, monopolized the sale of salt, and impeded the development of commerce by levying, after 1852, a duty on the transit of goods along the main routes of the country; but the poverty of the people, the difficulty of collection, and the dishonesty of the collectors kept the national revenue at too low a point to finance the naval and military forces that might have saved China from invasion and shameful defeat.* Perhaps the basic defect was in the personnel of the government; the ability and honesty of its officials deteriorated throughout the nineteenth century, and left the nation essentially leaderless when half the wealth and power of the world were joining in an assault upon its independence, its resources and its institutions.

Nevertheless those officials had been chosen by the most unique, and all in all the most admirable, method ever developed for the selection of public servants. It was a method that would have interested Plato; and despite its failure and abandonment today it still endears China to the philosopher. Theoretically, the plan provided a perfect reconciliation of aristocracy and democracy: all men were to have an equal opportunity to make themselves fit for office, but office was to be open only to those who had made themselves fit. Practically, the method produced good results for a thousand years.

It began in the village schools—simple private institutions, often no more than a room in a cottage—where an individual teacher, out of his own meager remuneration, provided an elementary education for the sons of the prosperous; the poorer half of the population remained illiterate.[127] These schools were not financed by the state, nor were they conducted by the clergy; education, like marriage, remained, in China, independent of religion, except in so far as Confucianism was its creed. Hours were long and discipline was severe in these modest schoolhouses: the children reported to the teacher at sunrise, studied with him till ten, had breakfast, resumed their studies till five, and then were free for the day. Vacations were few and brief: there were no lessons after noon in the summer, but to atone for this leisure to work in the fields there were school sessions in the winter evenings. The chief instruments of instruction were the writings

---

* The imperial revenue towards the close of the last century averaged $75,000,000 a year; the revenues collected for local purposes amounted to an additional $175,000,000.[136] If these national receipts, essential to the maintenance of order, are compared with the $150,000,000 exacted of China by Japan in 1894, and the $300,000,000 indemnity asked by the Allies after the Boxer Rebellion, the collapse of China becomes a mere matter of bookkeeping.

of Confucius, the poetry of the T'ang, and a whip of clinging bamboo. The method was memory: day after day the young students learned by heart, and discussed with their teacher, the philosophy of K'ung the Master, until almost every word of it had sunk into their memories, and some of it into their hearts; China hoped that in this joyless and merciless way even a peasant lad might be turned into a philosopher and a gentleman. The graduate emerged with little information and much understanding, factually ignorant and mentally mature.*

It was on the basis of this education that China established—first tentatively under the Han, then definitely under the T'ang, dynasties—its system of examinations for public office. It is an evil for the people, said China, that its rulers should learn to rule by ruling; as far as possible they should learn to rule before ruling. It is an evil for the people that they should have no access to office, and that government should be the privilege of an hereditary few; but it is good for the people that office should be confined to those who have been prepared for it by ability and training. To offer to all men democratically an equal opportunity for such training, and to restrict office aristocratically to those who proved themselves best, was the solution that China proposed for the ancient and insoluble problem of government.

Therefore it periodically arranged, in each district, a public examination to which all males of any age were eligible. It tested the applicant in his memory and understanding of the writings of Confucius, in his knowledge of Chinese poetry and history, and in his capacity to write intelligently on the issues of moral and political life. Those who failed might study more and try again; those who succeeded received the degree of *Hsiu ts'ai*, entitling them to membership in the literary class, and to possible appointment to minor local offices; but more important than this, they became eligible—either at once or after further preparation—for the triennial provincial examinations, which offered similar but harder tests. Those who failed here might try again, and many did, so that some men passed these tests after eighty years of living and studying, and not a few died in the midst of the examinations. Those who succeeded were eligi-

---

* From these local schools the children might go on to one of the rare and poorly-equipped colleges of the empire; more frequently they studied with a tutor, or with a few precious books, at home. Needy students were often financed through such schooling by men of means, on the understanding that they would return the loan with interest on their appointment to office and their access to "squeeze."

ble for appointment to minor positions in the national service; and at the same time they were admitted to a final and especially severe examination at Peking. There in the Examination Hall were ten thousand cells, in which the contestants, cribbed and confined, lived with their own food and bedding for three separate days, while they wrote essays or theses on subjects announced to them after their imprisonment. The cells were unheated, uncomfortable, ill-lighted and unsanitary; only the spirit mattered! Typical tests were the composition of a poem on the theme: "The sound of the oars, and the green of the hills and water"; and the writing of an essay on this passage from the Confucian Classics: "Tsang Tsze said, 'To possess ability, and yet ask of those who do not; to know much, and yet inquire of those who know little; to possess, and yet appear not to possess; to be full, and yet appear empty.' " There was not a word in any of the tests about science, business or industry; the object was to reveal not knowledge but judgment and character. Those who survived the tests were at last eligible for the higher offices in the state.

The defects of the plan grew in the course of time. Though dishonesty in taking or judging the tests was sometimes punished with death, dishonesty found a way. The purchase of appointments became frequent and flagrant in the nineteenth century;[138] an inferior officer, for example, sold twenty thousand forged diplomas before he was exposed.[139] The form of the trial essay came to be a matter of custom, and students prepared themselves for it mechanically. The curriculum of studies tended to formalize culture and impede the progress of thought, for the ideas that circulated in it had been standardized for hundreds of years. The graduates became an official and intellectual bureaucracy, naturally arrogant and humanly selfish, occasionally despotic and often corrupt, and yet immune to public recall or control except through the desperate resort of the boycott or the strike. In short, the system had the faults that might be expected of any governmental structure conceived and operated by men. The faults of the system belonged to the men, not to the system; and no other had less.*

The merits of the system were abundant. Here were no manipulated nominations, no vulgar campaigns of misrepresentation and hypocrisy, no

---

* "Seldom," says Dr. Latourette, "has any large group of mankind been so prosperous and so nearly contented as were the Chinese under this governmental machinery when it was dominated by the ablest of the monarchs." This was likewise the opinion of the learned Capt. Brinkley.[140]

sham battles of twin parties, no noisy or corrupt elections, no ascent to office through a meretricious popularity. It was a democracy in the best sense of the term, as equality of opportunity for all in the competition for leadership and place; and it was an aristocracy in its finest form, as a government by the ablest men, democratically selected from every rank in every generation. By this system the national mind and ambition were turned in the direction of study, and the national heroes and models were men of culture rather than masters of wealth.* It was admirable that a society should make the experiment of being ruled, socially and politically, by men trained in philosophy and the humanities. It was an act of high tragedy when that system, and the entire civilization of which it formed the guiding part, were struck down and destroyed by the inexorable forces of evolution and history.

---

* "The Chinese," said Sir Robert Hart, "worship talent; they delight in literature, and everywhere they have their little clubs for learning, and for discussing each other's essays and verses."

CHAPTER XXVII

Revolution and Renewal

I. THE WHITE PERIL

*The conflict of Asia and Europe—The Portuguese—The Spanish—
The Dutch—The English—The opium trade—The Opium
Wars—The T'ai-p'ing Rebellion—The War with Japan
—The attempt to dismember China—The "Open
Door"—The Empress Dowager—The reforms
of Kuang Hsu—His removal from power
—The "Boxers"—The Indemnity*

THOSE forces took the form of the Industrial Revolution. A Europe vitalized and rejuvenated by the discovery of mechanical power and its application to ever-multiplying machinery, found itself capable of producing goods more cheaply than any nation or continent that still relied on handicrafts; it was unable to dispose of all these machine products to its own population, because it paid its workers somewhat less than the full value of their labor; it was forced to seek foreign markets for the surplus, and was driven, by imperialist necessity, to conquer the world. Under the compulsions of invention and circumstance the nineteenth century became a world-wide drama of conflict between the old, mature and fatigued civilizations of handicraft Asia, and the young, jejune, and invigorated civilizations of industrial Europe.

The Commercial Revolution of Columbus' time cleared the routes and prepared the way for the Industrial Revolution. Discoverers refound old lands, opened up new ports, and brought to the ancient cultures the novel products and ideas of the West. Early in the sixteenth century the adventurous Portuguese, having established themselves in India, captured Malacca, sailed around the Malay Peninsula, and arrived with their picturesque ships and terrible guns at Canton (1517). "Truculent and lawless, regarding all Eastern peoples as legitimate prey, they were little if any better than . . . pirates";[1] and the natives treated them as such. Their representatives were imprisoned, their demands for free trade were refused, and their settlements were periodically cleansed with massacres by the frightened and infuriated Chinese. But in return for their aid against other pirates, the Portuguese were rewarded in 1557 by receiving from Peking full liberty to settle in Macao, and to govern it as their own. There they built great opium factories, employing men, women and children; one factory alone paid to the Portuguese provincial government a revenue of $1,560,000 per year.[2]

Then came the Spanish, conquering the Philippines (1571), and setting themselves up in the Chinese island of Formosa; then the Dutch; then, in 1637, five English vessels sailed up the river to Canton, silenced with superior guns the batteries that opposed them, and disposed of their cargo.[3] The Portuguese taught the Chinese to smoke and buy tobacco, and, early in the eighteenth century, began the importation of opium from India into China. The Chinese Government forbade its use by the people, but the habit became so widespread that the annual consumption of the drug in China had raised its import to 4,000 chests by the year 1795.* The Government prohibited its importation in that year, and reiterated the prohibition in 1800, appealing to importers and population alike against the weakening of national vitality by this powerful opiate. The trade proceeded briskly despite these discouragements; the Chinese were as anxious to buy as the Europeans were eager to sell, and the local officials gratefully pocketed the bribes connected with the trade.

In 1838 the Peking Government ordered the strict enforcement of the edict against the importation of opium, and a vigorous official, Lin Tze-hsü, commanded the foreign importers at Canton to surrender such quantities as they held in their stores. When they refused he surrounded the foreign quarters, forced them to turn over to him 20,000 chests of the drug, and, in a kind of Canton Opium Party, destroyed the contents completely. The British withdrew to Hong Kong, and began the First "Opium War." They protested that it was not an opium war; that their anger was rather at the insolent pride with which the Chinese Government had received—or refused to receive—their representatives, and at the impediments, in the form of severe taxation and corrupt courts, which Chinese law and custom had raised against an orderly import trade. They bombarded those cities of China which they could reach from the coast, and compelled peace by capturing control, at Chinkiang, of the Grand Canal. The Treaty

* The meaning of this may be felt by recalling that a vest-pocket package of opium costs $30.[4]

of Nanking avoided all mention of opium, ceded the island of Hong Kong to the British, forced Chinese tariffs down to five per cent, opened five "treaty ports" (Canton, Amoy, Foochow, Ningpo and Shanghai) to foreign trade, levied upon China an indemnity to cover the cost of the war and the destroyed opium, and stipulated that British citizens in China, when accused of violating laws, should be tried and judged only by British courts.[5] Other countries, including the United States and France, asked and obtained the application of these "extra-territorial rights" to their traders and nationals in China.

This war was the beginning of the disintegration of the ancient regime. The Government had lost "face" in its dealings with Europeans; it had first scorned, then defied, then yielded; and no courtly phrases could conceal the facts from educated natives or gloating foreigners. At once the authority of the Government was weakened wherever the news of its defeat penetrated, and forces that might have held their peace broke out now in open rebellion against Peking. In 1843 an enthusiast named Hung Hsiu-ch'üan, after a brief acquaintance with Protestantism, and some visions, came to the conclusion that he had been chosen by God to rid China of idolatry and convert it to Christianity. Beginning with this modest purpose, Hung finally led a movement to overthrow the Manchus and establish a new dynasty—the *T'ai P'ing*, or Great Peace. His followers, actuated partly by religious fanaticism, partly by desire to reform China on Western lines, fought valiantly, smashed idols, slaughtered Chinese, destroyed many old libraries and academies and the porcelain works at Ching-te-chen, captured Nanking, held it for twelve years (1853-65), marched on Peking while their leader wallowed in luxury and safety behind them, broke into disorder because of incompetent generalship, were defeated, and fell back into the indiscriminate ocean of Chinese humanity.[6]

In the midst of this dangerous T'ai-p'ing Rebellion the Government was called upon to defend itself against Europe in the Second "Opium War" (1856-60). Great Britain, supported in varying degrees by France and the United States, demanded the legalization of the opium traffic (which had continued, despite prohibitions, between the wars), access to more cities, and the honorable admission of Western envoys to the court at Peking. When the Chinese refused, the French and English captured Canton, sent its Viceroy in chains to India, took the forts at Tientsin, advanced upon the capital, and destroyed the Summer Palace in revenge for the torture and execution of Allied emissaries in Peking. The victors forced upon the defeated a treaty that opened ten new ports and the Yangtze River to foreign trade, arranged for the reception of European and American ministers and ambassadors on terms of equality with China, guaranteed toleration of missionaries and traders in every part of the country, removed missionaries from the jurisdiction of Chinese officials, further freed Western nationals from the operation of Chinese laws, ceded to Great Britain a strip of the mainland opposite Hong Kong, legalized the importation of opium, and charged China with an indemnity to pay for the cost of her tuition in Occidental ways.

Encouraged by their easy victories, the European nations proceeded to help themselves to one piece of China after another. Russia took the territory north of the Amur and east of the Ussuri River (1860); the French revenged the death of a missionary by appropriating Indo-China (1885); Japan pounced upon her neighbor and civilizer in a sudden war (1894), defeated her in a year, took Formosa, liberated Korea from China for later (1910) absorption by Japan, and charged China an indemnity of $170,-000,000 for causing so much trouble.' On condition that China pay an additional indemnity to Japan, Russia prevented Japan from also taking the Liaotung Peninsula, which three years later Russia took over and fortified as her own. The murder of two missionaries by Chinese enabled Germany to seize the peninsula of Shantung (1898). The realm of the once powerful government was divided into "spheres of influence," in which one or another European power secured special privileges for mining and trade. Alarmed by the prospects of an actual partition, Japan, foreseeing her own later need of China, joined with America in a demand for an "Open Door": that is, that while certain "spheres of interest" might be recognized, all nations should be allowed to trade in China on equal terms —tariffs and transport charges to be the same for all. To put herself in a proper position for bargaining in these matters, the United States took over the Philippines (1898), and declared by this act her intention to share in the struggle for Chinese trade.

Meanwhile another and simultaneous act of the drama was being played behind palace walls in Peking. When the Allies entered the capital in triumph at the close of the Second "Opium War" (1860), the young emperor, Hsien Feng, fled to Jehol; there, a year later, he died, leaving the throne to his five-year-old son. The secondary wife who had been the mother of this boy took the reins of empire in her own hands, and as Tz'u

Hsi—known to the world as the "Dowager Empress"*—governed China ruthlessly, cynically and well for a generation. In her youth she had ruled by beauty; now she ruled by her wits and her will. When the son conveniently died on approaching his majority (1875), the Empress, careless of precedent and objection, placed another minor—Kuang Hsu—on the throne, and continued to rule. For a generation, with the help of clever statesmen like Li Hung-chang, the doughty Empress kept China at peace and won for it a certain respect from the predatory Powers. But the sudden invasion of China by Japan, and the rapid series of renewed spoliations by Europe after the triumph of the Japanese, caused a strong movement to rise in the capital in favor of imitating Japan's imitation of the West—i.e., for organizing a large army, building railroads and factories, and striving to acquire the industrial wealth with which Japan and Europe had financed their victories. The Empress and her advisers opposed this tendency with all their influence, but it secretly won the adherence of Kuang Hsu, who had now been permitted to ascend the throne as emperor in his own right. Suddenly Kuang, without consulting "Old Buddha" (as her court called the Empress), issued to the Chinese people (1898) a series of astonishing decrees which, if they could have been accepted and enforced, would have advanced China vigorously and yet peaceably on the road to Westernization, and might have averted the fall of the dynasty and the collapse of the nation into chaos and misery. The young emperor ordered the establishment of a new system of schools, to teach not only the old Confucian Classics, but the scientific culture of the West; the translation into Chinese of all the important works of Occidental science, literature and technology; the encouragement of railroad building; and the reform of the army and the navy with a definite view to meeting the "crisis," as he put it, "where we are beset on all sides by powerful neighbors who craftily seek advantage from us, and who are trying to combine together in overpowering us." The Dowager Empress, shocked by what seemed to her the precipitate radicalism of these edicts, imprisoned Kuang Hsu in one of the imperial palaces, annulled his decrees, and made herself again the government of China.

A reaction now set in against all Western ideas, and the subtle Dowager diverted it amiably to her purposes. An organization known as the *I Ho Ch'uan*—literally "Righteous Harmony Fists," historically the "Box-

---

* A dowager is a widow endowed—usually with a title coming down to her from her dead husband.

ers"—had been formed by some rebels who wished to overthrow the Empress and her dynasty. She persuaded its leaders to turn the fury of their movement against invading foreigners rather than against herself. The Boxers accepted the mission, called for the expulsion of all aliens from China, and, in a frenzy of patriotic virtue, began to kill Christians indiscriminately in many sections of the country (1900). Allied soldiers again marched on Peking, this time to protect their nationals hiding in terror in the narrow quarters of the foreign Legations. The Empress and her court fled to Hsianfu, and the troops of England, France, Russia, Germany, Japan and the United States sacked the city, killed many Chinese in revenge, and looted or ruined valuable property.* The Allies imposed upon the broken Leviathan an indemnity of $330,000,000, to be collected by European control of Chinese import customs and the salt monopoly. Considerable portions of this indemnity were later remitted to China by the United States, Great Britain, Russia and Japan, usually with the stipulation that the remitted sums be spent in educating students from China in the universities of the remitting nation. It was a gesture of generosity, which proved more effective in the undoing of old China than almost any other single factor in this historic and tragic conflict of East and West.

II. THE DEATH OF A CIVILIZATION

The Indemnity students—Their Westernization—Their disintegrative effect in China—The rôle of the missionary—Sun Yat-sen, the Christian—His youthful adventures—His meeting with Li Hungchang—His plans for a revolution—Their success—Yuan Shik'ai—The death of Sun Yat-sen—Chaos and pillage—Communism—"The north pacified"—Chiang Kai-shek—Japan in Manchuria—At Shanghai

These "indemnity students" and thousands of others now left China to explore the civilization of its conquerors. Many went to England, more to Germany, more to America, more to Japan; every year hundreds of them were graduated from the universities of America alone. They came

---

* Captain Brinkley writes: "It sends a thrill of horror through every white man's bosom to learn that forty missionary women and twenty-five little children were butchered by the Boxers. But in T'ungchow alone, a city where the Chinese made no resistance, and where there was no fighting, five hundred and seventy-three Chinese women of the upper classes committed suicide rather than survive the indignities they had suffered."⁹

at an early and impressionable age, before they had matured to the point of understanding the depth and values of their own national culture. They drank in with gratitude and admiration the novel education given in the science, methods, history and ideas of the West; they were amazed at the comforts and vigorous life they saw about them, the freedom of the Western individual, and the enfranchisement of the people. They studied Western philosophy, lost faith in the religion of their fathers, and enjoyed the position of respectable radicals encouraged by their educators and their new environment in their rebellion against all the elements in the civilization of their native land. Year by year thousands of such deracinated youths returned to China, fretted against the slow tempo and material backwardness of their country, and sowed in every city the seeds of inquiry and revolt.

An endless chain of circumstances helped them. For two generations the merchants and missionaries who had conquered China from the West had acted, willingly or not, as centers of foreign infection; they had lived in a style, and with such comforts and conveniences, as made the young Chinese about them anxious to adopt so promising a civilization; they had undermined, in an active minority, the religious faith that had supported the old moral code; they had set one generation against another by advocating the abandonment of ancestor worship; and though they preached a gentle Jesus meek and mild, they were protected in emergencies by guns whose size and efficacy offered the dominating lesson of Europe to the Orient. Christianity, which had been in its origin an uprising of the oppressed, became once more, in these Chinese converts, a ferment of revolution.

Among the converts was the leader of the Revolution. In 1866 a tenant farmer near Canton fathered a troublesome boy whom the world, with no conscious sarcasm, was to christen Sun Yat-sen — i.e., Sun, the Fairy of Tranquillity.[10] Sun became so Christian that he defaced the images of the gods in the temple of his native village. An older brother, who had migrated to Hawaii, brought the boy to Honolulu and placed him in a school conducted by an Anglican bishop and offering a thoroughly Occidental education.[11] Returning to China, Sun entered the British Medical College, and became its first Chinese graduate. Largely as a result of these studies he lost all religious faith;[12] and at the same time the indignities to which he found himself and his fellow Chinese subjected at the foreign-controlled customs offices and in the foreign quarters of the treaty ports turned his thoughts to revolution. The inability of a corrupt and reactionary government to prevent the defeat of great China by little Japan, or the commercial partition of the country by European powers, filled him with humiliation and resentment, and made him feel that the first step in the liberation of China must be the overthrow of the Manchu dynasty.

His first move was characteristic of his self-confidence, his idealism, and his simplicity. He boarded a steamer and traveled sixteen hundred miles north, at his own expense, to lay before Li Hung-chang, vice-regent of the Empress Dowager, his plans for reforming the country and restoring its prestige. Refused a hearing, Sun began a lifetime of adventure and wandering in the quest of funds for a Chinese revolution. He won the support of many mercantile guilds and powerful secret societies, whose leaders were envious of the imperial aristocracy, and longed for a government in which the new manufacturing and trading classes would play a rôle commensurate with their rising wealth. Then he traveled overseas to America and Europe, gathering modest sums from a million laundrymen and a thousand Chinese merchants. In London the Chinese Legation illegally arrested him, and was about to send him secretly to China in chains as a traitor to his government, when a missionary who had taught him in his youth aroused the British Government to rescue him. For fifteen years more he passed from city to city over the world, collecting all in all two and a half million dollars for the Revolution; and apparently he spent almost none of this money on himself. Suddenly, in the midst of his travels, a message informed him that the revolutionary forces had won the south, were winning the north, and had chosen him as Provisional President of the Chinese Republic. A few weeks later he landed in triumph at Hong Kong, where, twenty years back, he had been humiliated by the British officials of the port.

The Empress Dowager had died in 1908, having arranged the death of the imprisoned emperor Kuang Hsu the day before. She was succeeded by Kuang's nephew, P'u Yi, now Emperor of Manchukuo. In the last years of the great Dowager and the first of her infant heir, many reforms in the direction of modernizing China were effected by the Government: railways were built, chiefly with foreign capital and under foreign management; examinations for public office were abandoned; a new system of schools was established, a National Assembly was called for 1910, and a nine-year program was laid down for the gradual establishment of a constitutional monarchy, culminating in universal suffrage growing step by step with universal education. The decree announcing

this program added: "Any impetuosity shown in introducing these reforms will, in the end, be so much labor lost."[13] But the Revolution could
not be halted by this deathbed repentance of an ailing dynasty. On
February 12, 1912, the young Emperor, faced by revolt on every side and
finding no army willing to defend him, abdicated; and the Regent, Prince
Ch'un, issued one of the most characteristic edicts in Chinese history:

> Today the people of the whole Empire have their minds bent
> upon a Republic.... The will of Providence is clear, and the people's
> wishes are plain. How could I, for the sake of the glory and the
> honor of one family, thwart the desire of teeming millions? Where-
> fore I, with the Emperor, decide that the form of government in
> China shall be a constitutional republic, to comfort the longing of all
> within the Empire, and to act in harmony with the ancient sages,
> who regarded the throne as a public heritage."[14]

The Revolutionists behaved magnanimously to P'u Yi: they gave him
his life, a comfortable palace, an ample annuity, and a concubine. The
Manchus had come in like lions, and had gone out like lambs.

The new republic paid for its peaceful birth with a stormy life. Yüan
Shi-kai, a diplomat of the old school, possessed an army that might have
impeded the Revolution. He demanded the presidency as the price of his
support; and Sun Yat-sen, only beginning to enjoy his office, yielded and
retired magnificently to private life. Yuan, encouraged by strong financial
groups native and foreign, plotted to make himself emperor and to found
a new dynasty, on the ground that only in this way could the incipient
break-up of China be stayed. Sun Yat-sen branded him as a traitor, and
called upon his followers to renew the Revolution; but before the issue
could come to battle Yuan took sick and died.

China has not known order or unity since. Sun Yat-sen proved too
idealistic, too good an orator and too poor a statesman, to take the reins
and guide his nation to peace. He passed from one plan and theory to another, offended his middle-class supporters by his apparent acceptance of
communism, and retired to Canton to teach and inspire its youth and occasionally to rule its people.* China, left without a government that all
sections would recognize, deprived of the unifying symbol of the monarchy, broken of its habit of obedience to custom and law, and weak
in the patriotism that attaches the soul not to a district but to the country

---

* He died at Peking in 1925, at the most opportune moment for his conservative enemies.

as a whole, fell into an intermittent war of north against south, of section against section, of property against hunger, of old against young.
Adventurers organized armies, ruled as *tuchuns* over isolated provinces,
levied their own taxes, raised their own opium,[15] and sallied forth occasionally to annex new victims to their subject population. Industry and
trade, taxed by one victorious general after another, fell into disorder
and despair; bandits exacted tribute, stole and killed, and no organized
force could control them. Men became soldiers or thieves lest they should
starve, and ravaged the fields of men who, so despoiled, became soldiers or
thieves lest they should starve. The savings of a lifetime or the modest
stores of a thrifty family were, as often as not, appropriated by a general
or looted by a robber band. In the province of Honan alone, in 1931, there
were 400,000 bandits.[16]

In the midst of this chaos (1922) Russia sent two of its ablest diplomats, Karakhan and Joffe, with orders to bring China into the circle of
the Communist Revolution. Karakhan prepared the way by surrendering
Russia's claims to "extra-territoriality," and by signing a treaty that recognized the full authority and international status of the revolutionary
government. The subtle Joffe found little difficulty in converting Sun
Yat-sen to sympathy with communism, for Sun had been rebuffed by
every other power. In an incredibly short time, with the help of seventy
Soviet officers, a new Nationalist army was formed and trained. Under
command of Sun's former secretary Chiang Kai-shek, but guided largely
by a Russian adviser, Michael Borodin, this army marched northward
from Canton, conquered one city after another, and finally established its
power in Peking.* In the moment of victory the victors divided; Chiang
Kai-shek attacked the communist movement in Oriental style, and established a military dictatorship realistically responsive to the will of business
and finance.

It is as difficult for a nation as for an individual to take no comfort from
a neighbor's misfortune. Japan, which in the plans of Sun Yat-sen, was to
be the friend and ally of China against the West, and which had stimulated the Chinese revolt by her swift and successful imitation of Europe
in industry, diplomacy and war, saw in the disorder and weakness of her

---

* From that time on the city, whose name had meant "northern capital," was renamed
Peiping, i.e., "the north pacified"; while the Nationalist Government, in order to be near
its financial sources at Shanghai, maintained its headquarters at the "southern capital,"
Nanking.

ancient teacher an opportunity for solving the problems that had arisen out of her very success. For Japan could not discourage the growth of her population without endangering her capacity for self-defense against obviously possible aggression; she could not support an increasing population unless she developed industry and trade; she could not develop industry without importing iron, coal and other resources in which her own soil was deficient, nor could she develop trade profitably unless she had a large share in the only great market left free by the European colonization of the globe. But China was supposedly rich in iron and coal, and offered, at Japan's door, potentially the greatest market in the world. What nation, faced with the apparent choice between returning to agriculture and subjection, or advancing to industrial imperialism and conquest, could have resisted the temptation to snatch the prizes of prostrate China while the other imperial vultures were tearing one another's throats on the fields of France?

So Japan, soon after the outbreak of the Great War, declared herself at war with Germany, and pounced upon the Kiaochow territory which Germany had "leased" from China sixteen years before. Then she presented to the government of Yuan Shi-kai "Twenty-One Demands" which would have made China a political and economic colony of Japan; and only the protest of the United States and the boycott of Japanese goods in China under the leadership of its enraged students prevented these commands from being enforced. Students wept in the streets, or killed themselves, in shame at the humiliation of their country." The Japanese listened with cynical humor to the moral indignation of a Europe that had been gnawing at China for half a century, and waited patiently for another opportunity. It came when Europe and America were engulfed in the debacle of an imperialist industry that had depended upon foreign markets for the absorption of "surplus" products unpurchasable by their producers at home. Japan marched into Manchuria, set up the former emperor of China, P'u Yi, first as president, then as emperor, of the new state of Manchukuo, and by political alliance, economic penetration and military control, placed herself in a favored position for the exploitation of Manchuria's natural resources, employable population and commercial possibilities. The European world, which had proposed a moratorium on robbery after it had gathered in all available spoils, joined America feebly in protests against this candid plunder, but prepared, as always, to accept victory as justification in the end.

The final humiliation came at Shanghai. Angered by the successful boycott of her goods, Japan landed her undefeated troops at the richest port in China, occupied and destroyed the district of Chapei, and demanded the restraint of the boycott associations by the Chinese Government. The Chinese defended themselves with a new heroism, and the Nineteenth Route Army from Canton, almost unaided, held the well-equipped forces of Japan at bay for two months. The Nanking Government offered a compromise, Japan withdrew from Shanghai, and China, nursing its wounds, resolved to build from the bottom a new and more vigorous civilization, capable of preserving and defending itself against a rapacious world.

III. BEGINNINGS OF A NEW ORDER

Change in the village—In the town—The factories—Commerce—Labor unions—Wages—The new government—Nationalism vs. Westernization —The dethronement of Confucius—The reaction against religion—The new morality—Marriage in transition—Birth control—Co-education— The "New Tide" in literature and philosophy—The new language of literature—Hu Shih—Elements of destruction—Elements of renewal

Once everything changed except the East; now there is nothing in the East that does not change. The most conservative nation in history has suddenly become, after Russia, the most radical, and is destroying with a will customs and institutions once held inviolate. It is not merely the end of a dynasty, as in 1644; it is the moulting of a civilization.

Change comes last and least to the village, for the slow sobriety of the soil does not encourage innovation; even the new generation must plant in order to reap. But now seven thousand miles of railroad traverse the countryside; and though a decade of chaos and native management has left them in bad repair, and war has conscripted them too often for its purposes, yet they bind the eastern villages with the cities of the coast, and daily bear their trickle of Western novelties into a million peasant homes. Here one may find such foreign-devilish importations as kerosene, kerosene lamps, matches, cigarettes, even American wheat; for sometimes, so poor is transport, it costs more to carry goods from the Chinese interior to the marine provinces than it does to bring them to these from Australia or the United States.[18] It becomes clear that the economic growth of a civilization depends upon transportation. Twenty thousand miles of dirt roads have been built, over which, with Oriental irregularity, six thousand buses travel, always full. When the gasoline engine has bound these innumerable villages together it will have accomplished one of the greatest changes in Chinese history—the end of famine.

In the towns the triumph of the West goes on more rapidly. Handicrafts are dying under the competition of cheaply-transported machine-made goods from abroad; millions of artisans flounder about in unemployment, and are drawn into the jaws of the factories that foreign and domestic capital is building along the coast. The hand loom, still spinning in the village, is silent in the city; imported cotton and cotton cloths flood the country, and textile factories rise to induct impoverished Chinese into the novel serfdom of the mill. Great blast-furnaces burn at Hankow, as weird and horrible as any in the West. Canneries, bakeries, cement works, chemical works, breweries, distilleries, power works, glass works, shoe factories, paper mills, soap and candle factories, sugar refineries—all of them have now been planted on Chinese soil, and slowly transform the domestic artisan into a factory hand. The development of the new industries is retarded because investment hesitates in a world disordered by permanent revolution; it is obstructed further by the difficulty and costliness of transport, by the inadequacy of local raw materials, and by that amiable Chinese habit which places the family above every other loyalty, and turns every native office and factory into a nest of genial nepotism and incompetence.[19] Commerce, too, is impeded by inland tariffs and coastal customs, and the universal demand for bribes or "squeeze";[20] but it is growing more rapidly than industry, and plays the central rôle in the economic transformation of China.*

The new industries have destroyed the guilds, and have thrown into chaos the relations of employer and employee. The guilds had lived by regulating wages and prices through agreements between owners and workers whose products had no rivals in local trade; but as transport and commerce increased, and brought distant goods to compete in every town with the handiwork of the guilds, it was found impossible to control prices or to regulate wages without surrendering to the dictates of foreign

---

* Once Great Britain dominated the import trade; now it accounts for 14%, the United States for 17%, Japan for 27%;[21] and the Japanese leadership in this field mounts with every year. Between 1910 and 1930 Chinese trade increased 600% to approximately one and a half billion dollars.[22]

competitors and capital. The guilds have therefore disintegrated and divided into chambers of commerce on the one side and labor unions on the other. The chambers discuss order, loyalty and economic liberty, and the workers discuss starvation. Strikes and boycotts are frequent, but they have been more successful in compelling foreign concessions to the Chinese Government than in raising the remuneration of labor. In 1928 the Department of Social Affairs of the Chinese Municipality of Shanghai computed the average weekly wage of the textile-mill workers as varying from $1.73 to $2.76 for men, and from $1.10 to $1.78 for women. In flour mills the male weekly average pay was $1.96; in cement mills $1.72; in glass works $1.84; in match-factories $2.11; among the skilled workers of the electric power plants, $3.10; in the machine shops, $3.24; among the printers, $4.55.[23] The wealth enjoyed by the printers was doubtless due to their better organization, and the cost of suddenly replacing them. The first unions were formed in 1919; they grew in number and power until, in the days of Borodin, they proposed to take over the management of China; they were repressed ruthlessly after Chiang Kai-shek's break with Russia; today the laws against them are severe, but they multiply nevertheless as the sole refuge of the workers against an industrial system that has only begun to pass labor legislation, and has not yet begun to enforce it.[24] The bitter destitution of the city proletaires, working twelve hours a day, hovering on the margin of subsistence, and facing starvation if employment should fail, is worse than the ancient poverty of the village, where the poor could not see the rich, and accepted their lot as the natural and immemorial fate of mankind.

Perhaps some of these evils might have been avoided if the political transformation of eastern China had not been so rapid and complete. The mandarin aristocracy, though it had lost vitality and was dishonored with corruption, might have held the new industrial forces in check until China could accept them without chaos or slavery; and then the growth of industry would have generated year by year a new class that might have stepped peaceably into political power, as the manufacturers had displaced the landed aristocracy of England. But the new government found itself without an army, without experienced leaders, and without funds; the *Kuomintang*, or People's Party, established to liberate a nation, found that it must stand by while foreign and domestic capital subjugated it; conceived in democracy and baptized with the blood of communism, it became dependent upon Shanghai bankers, abandoned democracy for dictatorship, and tried to destroy the unions.* For the Party depends upon the army, and the army upon money, and money upon loans; until the Army is strong enough to conquer China the Government cannot tax China; and until it can tax China the Government must take advice where it takes its funds. Even so it has accomplished much. It has brought back to China full control over her tariffs and —within the internationalism of finance—over her industries; it has organized, trained and equipped an Army which may some day be used against others than Chinese; it has enlarged the area that acknowledges its authority, and has reduced, in that area, the banditry that was stifling the nation's economic life. It takes a day to make a revolution, and a generation to make a government.

The disunity of China reflects and follows from the division that lies in the Chinese soul. The most powerful feeling in China today is hatred of foreigners; the most powerful process in China today is imitation of foreigners. China knows that the West does not deserve this flattery, but China is forced by the very spirit and impetus of the times to give it, for the age offers to all nations the choice of industrialism or vassalage. So the Chinese of the eastern cities pass from fields to factories, from robes to trousers, from the simple melodies of the past to the saxophone symphonies of the West; they surrender their own fine taste in dress and furniture and art, adorn their walls with European paintings, and erect office buildings in the least attractive of American styles. Their women have ceased to compress their feet from north to south, and begin, in the superior manner of the Occident, to compress them from east to west.† Their philosophers abandon the unobtrusive and mannerly rationalism of Confucius, and take up with Renaissance enthusiasm the pugnacious rationalism of Moscow, London, Berlin, Paris and New York.

The dethronement of Confucius has something of the character of both the Renaissance and the Enlightenment; it is at once the overthrow of the Chinese Aristotle, and the rejection of the racial gods. For a time the new state persecuted Buddhism and the monastic orders; like the Revolutionists of France, the Chinese rebels were freethinkers without concealment, openly hostile to religion, and worshiping only reason. Confucianism tolerated the popular faiths on the assumption, presumably, that

---

* In 1927 alone many thousands of workers were executed for belonging to labor unions.[25]

† Some Chinese women pad their shoes to conceal the fact that their feet were bound.[26]

as long as there is poverty there will be gods; the Revolution, fondly believing that poverty can be destroyed, had no need of gods. Confucianism
took agriculture and the family for granted, and formulated an ethic designed to maintain order and content within the circle of the home and
the field; the Revolution is bound for industry, and needs a new morality
to accord with urban and individual life. Confucianism endured because
access to political office and scholarly occupations demanded a knowledge
and acceptance of it; but the examinations are gone, and science takes the
place of ethical and political philosophy in the schools; man is now to be
moulded not to government but to industry. Confucianism was conservative, and checked the ideals of youth with the caution of old age;
the Revolution is made of youth, and will have none of these ancient
restraints; it smiles at the old sage's warning that "he who thinks the old
embankments useless and destroys them is sure to suffer from the desolation caused by overflowing water."*[27]

The Revolution has, of course, put an end to official religion, and no
sacrifice mounts any longer from the Altar of Heaven to the impersonal
and silent T'ien. Ancestor worship is tolerated, but visibly decays; more
and more the men tend to leave it to the women, who were once thought
unfit to officiate at these sacred rites. Half of the Revolutionary leaders
were educated in Christian schools; but the Revolution, despite the Meth-
odism of Chiang Kai-shek, is unfavorable to any supernatural faith, and
gives to its schoolbooks an atheistic tint.[29] The new religion, which tries
to fill the emotional void left by the departure of the gods, is nationalism,
as in Russia it is communism. Meanwhile this creed does not satisfy all;
many proletaires seek in the adventure of oracles and mediums a refuge
from the prose of their daily toil; and the people of the village still find
some solace from their poverty in the mystic quiet of the ancient shrines.

Shorn of its sanctions in government, religion and economic life, the
traditional moral code, which seemed a generation ago unchangeable,
disintegrates with geometrical acceleration. Next to the invasion of industry the most striking change in the China of today is the destruction
of the old family system, and its replacement with an individualism that
leaves every man free and alone to face the world. Loyalty to the family, on which the old order was founded, is superseded in theory by
loyalty to the state; and as the novel loyalty has not yet graduated from

* P. 673 above. Latterly the "New Life" movement, let by Chiang Kai-shek, has attempted, with some success, to restore Confucianism.

theory into practice, the new society lacks a moral base. Agriculture favors the family because, before the coming of machinery, the land could most economically be tilled by a group united by blood and paternal authority; industry disrupts the family, because it offers its places and rewards to individuals rather than to groups, does not always offer them these rewards in the same place, and recognizes no obligation to aid the weak out of the resources of the strong; the natural communism of the family finds no support in the bitter competition of industry and trade. The younger generation, always irked by the authority of the old, takes with a will to the anonymity of the city and the individualism of the "job." Perhaps the omnipotence of the father helped to precipitate the Revolution; the reactionary is always to blame for the excesses of the radical. So China has cut itself off from all roots, and no one knows whether it can sink new roots in time to save its cultural life.

The old marriage forms disappear with the authority of the family. The majority of marriages are still arranged by the parents, but in the city marriage by free choice of the young tends more and more to prevail. The individual considers himself free not only to mate as he pleases, but to make experiments in marriage which might shock the West. Nietzsche thought Asia right about women, and considered their subjection the only alternative to their unchecked ascendancy; but Asia is choosing Europe's way, not Nietzsche's. Polygamy diminishes, for the modern wife objects to a concubine. Divorce is uncommon, but the road to it is wider than ever before.* Co-education is the rule in the universities, and the free mingling of the sexes is usual in the cities. Women have established their own law and medical schools, even their own bank.[31] Those of them that are members of the Party have received the franchise, and places have been found for them on the highest committees of both the Party and the Government.[32] They have turned their backs upon infanticide, and are beginning to practise birth control.† Population has not

---

* The Revolution grants it where both parties ask for it; but where the husband is under thirty, or the wife is under twenty-five, the consent of the parents is required for a divorce. The old causes for which the husband may divorce his wife remain in force—barrenness, infidelity, neglect of duty, loquacity, thievishness, jealousy, or serious disease; but these are not allowed to apply if the wife has mourned three years for her husband's parents, or has no family to return to, or has been faithful to her husband during his rise from poverty to wealth.[30]

† The frank display of contraceptive devices in Chinese drug-stores may suggest to the West a convenient escape from the "Yellow Peril."

noticeably increased since the Revolution; perhaps the vast tide of Chinese humanity has begun to ebb.[33]

Nevertheless fifty thousand new Chinese are born every day.[34] They are destined to be new in every way: new in the cut of their clothes and their hair, new in education and occupation, in habits and manners, in religion and philosophy. The queue is gone, and so are the graceful manners of the older time; the hatreds of revolution have coarsened the spirit, and radicals find it hard to be courteous to conservatives.[35] The phlegmatic quality of the ancient race is being changed by the speed of industry into something more expressive and volatile; these stolid faces conceal active and excitable souls. The love of peace that came to China after centuries of war is being broken down by the contemplation of national dismemberment and defeat; the schools are drilling every student into a soldier, and the general is a hero once more.

The whole world of education has been transformed. The schools have thrown Confucius out of the window, and taken science in. The rejection was not quite necessary for the admission, since the doctrine of Confucius accorded well with the spirit of science; but the conquest of the logical by the psychological is the warp and woof of history. Mathematics and mechanics are popular, for these can make machines; machines can make wealth and guns, and guns may preserve liberty. Medical education is progressing, largely as the result of the cosmopolitan beneficence of the Rockefeller fortune.* Despite the impoverishment of the country, new schools, high schools and colleges have multiplied rapidly, and the hope of Young China is that soon every child will receive a free education, and that democracy may be widened as education grows.

A revolution akin to that of the Renaissance has come to Chinese literature and philosophy. The importation of Western texts has had the fertilizing influence that Greek manuscripts had upon the Italian mind. And just as Italy, in her awakening, abandoned Latin to write in the vernacular, so China, under the leadership of the brilliant Hu Shih, has turned the popular "Mandarin" dialect into a literary language, the *Pai Hua*. Hu

---

* In 1932 the Union Medical College, a five-million dollar gift of John D. Rockefeller, Jr., was opened to medical students of either sex. The China Medical Board, financed by the Rockefeller Foundation, maintains nineteen hospitals, three medical schools, and sixty-five scholarships.[36]

Shih took his literary fate in his hands by writing in this "plain language" a *History of Chinese Philosophy* (1919). His courage carried the day; half a thousand periodicals adopted *Pai Hua,* and it was made the official written language of the schools. Meanwhile the "Thousand Character Movement" sought to reduce the 40,000 characters of the scholars to some 1300 characters for common use. In these ways the Mandarin speech is being rapidly spread throughout the provinces; and perhaps within the century China will have one language, and be near to cultural unity again.

Under the stimulus of a popular language and an eager people, literature flourishes. Novels, poems, histories and plays become almost as numerous as the population. Newspapers and periodicals cover the land. The literature of the West is being translated *en masse,* and American motion pictures, expounded by a Chinese interpreter at the side of the screen, are delighting the profound and simple Chinese soul. Philosophy has returned to the great heretics of the past, has given them a new hearing and exposition, and has taken on all the vigor and radicalism of European thought in the sixteenth century. And as Italy, newly freed from ecclesiastical leading-strings, admired the secularism of the Greek mind, so the new China listens with especial eagerness to Western thinkers like John Dewey and Bertrand Russell, whose independence of all theology and respect for experience and experiment as the only logic, accord completely with the mood of a nation that is trying to have its Reformation, Renaissance, Enlightenment and Revolution in one generation.* Hu Shih scorns our praise of the "spiritual values" of Asia, and finds more spiritual worth in the reorganization of industry and government for the elimination of poverty than in all the "wisdom of the East."[37] He describes Confucius as "a very old man," and suggests that a better perspective of Chinese thought would appear if the heretical schools of the fifth, fourth and third centuries B.C. were given their due place in Chinese history.[38] Nevertheless, in the midst of the swirling "New Tide" of which he has been one of the most active leaders, he has kept suffi-

---

* Latterly, under the influence of Chiang Kai-skek's New Life movement, the acceptance of Western models in mind and morals has abated; China and Japan are beginning to make their own motion-pictures; radicalism is giving way before a renewed conservatism; and China is tending to join with Japan in a revolt against European and American ideas and ways.

cient sanity to see the value even of old men, and he has formulated the problem of his country perfectly:

> It would surely be a great loss to mankind at large if the acceptance of this new civilization should take the form of abrupt displacement instead of organic assimilation, thereby causing the disappearance of the old civilization. The real problem, therefore, may be restated thus: How can we best assimilate modern civilization in such a manner as to make it congenial and congruous and continuous with the civilization of our own making?[39]

All the surface conditions of China today tempt the observer to conclude that China will not solve the problem. When one contemplates the desolation of China's fields, blighted with drought or ruined with floods, the waste of her timber, the stupor of her exhausted peasants, the high mortality of her children, the unnerving toil of her factory-slaves, the disease-ridden slums and tax-ridden homes of her cities, her bribe-infested commerce and her foreign-dominated industry, the corruption of her government, the weakness of her defenses and the bitter factionalism of her people, one wonders for a moment whether China can ever be great again, whether she can once more consume her conquerors and live her own creative life. But under the surface, if we care to look, we may see the factors of convalescence and renewal. This soil, so vast in extent and so varied in form, is rich in the minerals that make a country industrially great; not as rich as Richtofen supposed, but almost certainly richer than the tentative surveys of our day have revealed; as industry moves inland it will come upon ores and fuels as unsuspected now as the mineral and fuel wealth of America was undreamed of a century ago. This nation, after three thousand years of grandeur and decay, of repeated deaths and resurrections, exhibits today all the physical and mental vitality that we find in its most creative periods; there is no people in the world more vigorous or more intelligent, no other people so adaptable to circumstance, so resistant to disease, so resilient after disaster and suffering, so trained by history to calm endurance and patient recovery. Imagination cannot describe the possibilities of a civilization mingling the physical, labor and mental resources of such a people with the technological equipment of modern industry. Very probably such wealth will be produced in China as even America has never known, and once again, as so often in the past, China will lead the world in luxury and the art of life.

No victory of arms, or tyranny of alien finance, can long suppress a nation so rich in resources and vitality. The invader will lose funds or patience before the loins of China will lose virility; within a century China will have absorbed and civilized her conquerors, and will have learned all the technique of what transiently bears the name of modern industry; roads and communications will give her unity, economy and thrift will give her funds, and a strong government will give her order and peace. Every chaos is a transition. In the end disorder cures and balances itself with dictatorship; old obstacles are roughly cleared away, and fresh growth is free. Revolution, like death and style, is the removal of rubbish, the surgery of the superfluous; it comes only when there are many things ready to die. China has died many times before; and many times she has been reborn.

B. JAPAN

Great Yamato (Japan) is a divine country. It is only our land whose foundations were first laid by the Divine Ancestor. It alone has been transmitted by the Sun Goddess to a long line of her descendants. There is nothing of this kind in foreign countries. Therefore it is called the Divine Land.

—*Chikafusa Kitabatake,* 1334, *in Murdoch,*
History of Japan, i, 571.

CHRONOLOGY OF JAPANESE CIVILIZATION*

I. THE HISTORICAL BACKGROUND

1. *Primitive Japan*:

Ca. 660 B.C.: Entrance of the Mongols
Ca. 660-585 B.C.: Jimmu, Emperor (?)
412-53 A.D.: Inkyo, Emperor
522 A.D.: Buddhism enters Japan
592-621: Shotoku Taishi, Regent
593-628: Suiko, Empress
645: The Great Reform

2. *Imperial Japan*:

668-71: Tenchi Tenno, Emperor
690-702: Jito, Empress
697-707: Mommu, Emperor
702: The Taiho Code of Laws
710-94: The *Heijo* Epoch: Nara the capital
724-56: Shomu, Emperor
749-59, 765-70: Koken, Empress
794-1192: The *Heian* Epoch: Kyoto the
    capital
877-949: Yozei, Emperor
898-930: Daigo, Emperor
901-22: The Period of *Engi*

3. *Feudal Japan*:

1186-99: Yoritomo
1203-19: Minamoto Sanetomo
1200-1333: *The Kamakura Bakufu*
1199-1333: The Hojo Regency

1222-82: Nichiren, founder of the Lotus
    Sect
1291: Kublai Khan invades Japan
1318-39: Go Daigo, Emperor
1335-1573: *The Ashikaga Shogunate*
1387-95: Yoshimitsu
1436-80: Yoshimasa
1573-82: Nobunaga
1581-98: Hideyoshi
1592: Hideyoshi fails to conquer Korea
1597: Hideyoshi expels the priests
1600: Battle of Sekigahara
1603-1867: *The Tokugawa Shogunate*
1603-16: Iyeyasu
1605: Siege of Osaka
1614: Iyeyasu's anti-Christian edict
1605-23: Hidetada
1623-51: Iyemitsu
1657: The great fire of Tokyo
1680-1709: Tsunayoshi
1688-1703: The period of *Genroku*
1709-12: Iyenobu
1716-45: Yoshimune
1721: Yoshimune codifies Japanese law
1787-1836: Iyenari
1853-8: Iyesada
1858-66: Iyemochi
1866-8: Keiki

II. LITERATURE

845-903: Sugawara Michizane, Patron Saint
    of Letters

1. *Poetry:*

665-731: Tahito
D. 737: Hitomaro
724-56: Akahito
750: The *Manyoshu*
883-946: Tsurayaki
905: The *Kokinshu*
1118-90: Saigyo Hoshi
1234: The *Hyaku-nin-isshu*
1643-94: Matsura Basho
1703-75: Lady Kaga no-Chiyo

2. *Drama:*

1350-1650: The *No* plays
1653-1724: Chikamatsu Monzayemon

3. *Fiction:*

978-1031?: Lady Murasaki no-Shikibu
1001-4: The *Genji Monogatari*
1761-1816: Santo Kioden
1767-1848: Kyokutei Bakin
D. 1831: Jippensha Ikku

4. *History and Scholarship*:

712: The *Kojiki*
720: The *Nihongi*
1334: Kitabatake's *Jintoshotoki*
1622-1704: Mitsu-kuni
1630: Hayashi Razan founds University of
    Tokyo
1657-1725: Arai Hakuseki
1697-1769: Mabuchi
1730-1801: Moto-ori Norinaga

---

* Dates of rulers are of their accession and their death. Several abdicated, or were assassinated or deposed.

5. *The Essay:*
Ca. 1000: Lady Sei Shonagon
1154-1216: Kamo no-Chomei

6. *Philosophy:*
1560-1619: Fujiwara Seigwa
1583-1657: Hayashi Razan

1608-48: Nakaye Toju
1630-1714: Kaibara Ekken
1619-91: Kumazawa Banzan
1627-1705: Ito Jinsai
1666-1728: Ogyu Sorai
1670-1736: Ito Togai

III. ART

1. *Architecture:*
Ca. 616: The temples of Horiuji
Ca. 1400: The palaces of Yoshimitsu
1543-90: Kano Yeitoku
Ca. 1630: The Mausoleum of Iyeyasu

2. *Sculpture:*
747: The Nara *Daibutsu*
774-835: Kobo Daishi
1180-1220: Unkei
1252: The Kamakura *Daibutsu*
1594-1634: Hidari Jingaro

3. *Pottery:*
Ca. 1229: Shirozemon
Ca. 1650: Kakiemon
Ca. 1655: Ninsei
1663-1743: Kenzan
Ca. 1664: Goto Saijiro
D. 1855: Zengoro Hozen

4. *Painting:*
Ca. 950: Kose no-Kanaoka
Ca. 1010: Takayoshi

Ca. 1017: Yeishin Sozu
1053-1140: Toba Sojo
1146-1205: Fujiwara Takanobu
Ca. 1250: Keion (?)
Ca. 1250: Tosa Gon-no-kumi
1351-1427: Cho Densu
Ca. 1400: Shubun
1420-1506: Sesshiu
D. 1490: Kano Masanobu
1476-1559: Kano Motonobu
Ca. 1600: Koyetsu
1578-1650: Iwasa Matabei
1602-74: Kano Tanyu
1618-94: Hishikawa Moronobu
1661-1716: Korin
1718-70: Harunobu
1733-95: Maruyami Okyo
1742-1814: Kiyonaga
1747-1821: Mori Zozen
1753-1806: Utamaro
Ca. 1790: Sharaku
1760-1849: Hokusai
1797-1858: Hiroshige

IV. THE NEW JAPAN

1853: Admiral Perry enters Uraga Bay
1854: Admiral Perry's second visit
1854: Treaty of Kanagawa
1862: The Richardson Affair
1862: The bombardment of Kagoshima
1863: Ito and Inouye visit Europe
1868: Restoration of the imperial power
1868-1912: Meiji, Emperor
1870: Tokyo becomes the imperial capital
1871: Abolition of feudalism
1872: First Japanese railway
1877: The Satsuma Rebellion
1889: The new Constitution
1894: The War with China
1895: The annexation of Formosa
1902-22: The Anglo-Japanese Alliance

1904: The War with Russia
1910: The annexation of Korea
1912: End of the *Meiji* Era
1912-25: Taisho, Emperor
1914: Capture of Tsingtao
1915: The Twenty-one Demands
1917: The Lansing-Ishii Agreement
1922: The Washington Conference
1924: The restriction of Japanese immigration into America
1925: Hirohito, Emperor
1931: The invasion of Manchuria
1932: The attack at Shanghai
1935: Notice given to terminate Washington Agreement in 1936

CHAPTER XXVIII

The Makers of Japan

THE history of Japan is an unfinished drama in which three acts have been played. The first—barring the primitive and legendary centuries —is classical Buddhist Japan (522-1603 A.D.), suddenly civilized by China and Korea, refined and softened by religion, and creating the historic masterpieces of Japanese literature and art. The second is the feudal and peaceful Japan of the Tokugawa Shogunate (1603-1868), isolated and self-contained, seeking no alien territory and no external trade, content with agriculture and wedded to art and philosophy. The third act is modern Japan, opened up in 1853 by an American fleet, forced by conditions within and without into trade and industry, seeking foreign materials and markets, fighting wars of irrepressible expansion, imitating the imperialistic ardor and methods of the West, and threatening both the ascendancy of the white race and the peace of the world. By every historical precedent the next act will be war.

The Japanese have studied our civilization carefully, in order to absorb its values and surpass it. Perhaps we should be wise to study their civilization as patiently as they have studied ours, so that when the crisis comes that must issue either in war or understanding, we may be capable of understanding.

I. THE CHILDREN OF THE GODS

How Japan was created—The rôle of earthquakes

In the beginning, says the oldest of Japanese histories,[1] were the gods. Male and female they were born, and died, until at last two of them, Izanagi and Izanami, brother and sister, were commanded by the elder deities to create Japan. So they stood on the floating bridge of heaven, thrust down into the ocean a jeweled spear, and held it aloft in the sky. The drops that fell from the spear became the Sacred Islands. By watching the tadpoles in the water the gods learned the secret of copulation; Izanagi and Izanami mated, and gave birth to the Japanese race. From Izanagi's left eye was born Amaterasu, Goddess of the Sun, and from her grandson Ninigi sprang in divine and unbroken lineage all the emperors of *Dai Nippon*. From that day until this there has been but one imperial dynasty in Japan.*

There were 4,223 drops from the jeweled spear, for there are that number of islands in the archipelago called Japan.† Six hundred of them are inhabited, but only five are of any considerable size. The largest—Hondo or Honshu—is 1,130 miles long, averages some 73 miles in width, and contains in its 81,000 square miles half the area of the islands. Their situation, like their recent history, resembles that of England: the surrounding seas have protected them from conquest, while their 13,000 miles of seacoast have made them a seafaring people, destined by geographical encouragement and commercial necessity to a widespread mastery of the seas. Warm winds and currents from the south mingle with the cool air of the mountain-tops to give Japan an English climate, rich in rain and cloudy days,⁴ nourishing to short but rapid-running rivers, and propitious to vegetation and scenery. Here, outside the cities and the slums, half the land is an Eden in blossom-time; and the mountains are no tumbled heaps of rock and dirt, but artistic forms designed, like Fuji, in almost perfect lines.‡

Doubtless these isles were born of earthquakes rather than from dripping spears.⁰ No other land—except, perhaps, South America—has suffered so bitterly from convulsions of the soil. In the year 599 the earth shook and swallowed villages in its laughter; meteors fell and comets flashed, and snow whitened the streets in mid-July; drought and famine followed, and millions of Japanese died. In 1703 an earthquake killed 32,000 in Tokyo alone. In 1885 the capital was wrecked again; great clefts opened in the earth, and engulfed thousands; the dead were carried away in cartloads and buried *en masse*. In 1923 earthquake, tidal wave and fire took 100,000 lives in Tokyo, and 37,000 in Yokohama and near-

---

* If this account be questioned as improbable, the objection has long since been answered by the most influential of Japanese critics, Moto-ori: "The very inconsistency is the proof of the authenticity of the record; for who would have gone out of his way to invent a story apparently so ridiculous and incredible?"²

† The name *Japan* is probably a corruption of the Malay word for the islands—*Japang* or *Japun;* this is a rendering of the Japanese term *Nippon*, which in turn is a corruption of the Chinese name for "the place the sun comes from"—*Jih-pen*. The Japanese usually prefix to *Nippon* the adjective *Dai*, meaning "Great."³

‡ Fuji-san (less classically Fuji-yama), idol of artists and priests, approximates to a gently sloping cone. Many thousands of pilgrims ascend its 12,365 feet in any year. Fuji (Ainu for "fire") erupted last in 1707.⁵

by; Kamakura, so kind to Buddha, was almost totally destroyed,[7] while the benign colossus of the Hindu saint survived shaken but unperturbed amid the ruins, as if to illustrate the chief lesson of history—that the gods can be silent in many languages. The people were for a moment puzzled by this abundance of disaster in a land divinely created and ruled; at last they explained the agitations as due to a large subterranean fish, which wriggled when its slumber was disturbed.[8] They do not seem to have thought of abandoning this adventurous habitat; on the day after the last great quake the school-children used bits of broken plaster for pencils, and the tiles of their shattered homes for slates.[9] The nation bore patiently these lashings of circumstance, and emerged from repeated ruin undiscourageably industrious, and ominously brave.

II. PRIMITIVE JAPAN

Racial components — Early civilization — Religion — "Shinto"— Buddhism—The beginnings of art—The "Great Reform"

Japanese origins, like all others, are lost in the cosmic nebula of theory. Three elements appear to be mingled in the race: a primitive white strain through the "Ainus" who seem to have entered Japan from the region of the Amur River in neolithic times; a yellow, Mongol strain coming from or through Korea about the seventh century before Christ; and a brown-black, Malay and Indonesian strain filtering in from the islands of the south. Here, as elsewhere, a mingling of diverse stocks preceded by many hundreds of years the establishment of a new racial type speaking with a new voice and creating a new civilization. That the mixture is not yet complete may be seen in the contrast between the tall, slim, long-headed aristocrat and the short, stout, broad-headed common man.

Chinese annals of the fourth century describe the Japanese as "dwarfs," and add that "they have neither oxen nor wild beasts; they tattoo their faces in patterns varying with their rank; they wear garments woven in one piece; they have spears, bows and arrows tipped with stone or iron. They wear no shoes, are law-abiding and polygamous, addicted to strong drink and long-lived. . . . The women smear their bodies with pink and scarlet" paint.[11] "There is no theft," these records state, "and litigation is infrequent";[12] civilization had hardly begun. Lafcadio Hearn, with uxorious clairvoyance, painted this early age as an Eden unsullied with exploitation or poverty; and Fenollosa pictured the peasantry as composed of independent soldier-gentlemen.[13] Handicrafts came over from Korea in the third century A.D., and were soon organized into guilds.[14] Beneath these free artisans was a considerable slave class, recruited from prisons and battlefields.[15] Social organization was partly feudal, partly tribal; some peasants tilled the soil as vassals of landed barons, and each clan had its well-nigh sovereign head.[16] Government was primitively loose and weak.

Animism and totemism, ancestor worship and sex worship[17] satisfied the religious needs of the early Japanese. Spirits were everywhere—in the planets and stars of the sky, in the plants and insects of the field, in trees and beasts and men.[18] Deities innumerable hovered over the home and its inmates, and danced in the flame and glow of the lamp.[19] Divination was practised by burning the bones of a deer or the shell of a tortoise, and studying with expert aid the marks and lines produced by the fire; by this means, say the ancient Chinese chronicles, "they ascertain good and bad luck, and whether or not to undertake journeys and voyages."[20] The dead were feared and worshiped, for their ill will might generate much mischief in the world; to placate them precious objects were placed in their graves—for example, a sword in the case of a man, a mirror in the case of a woman; and prayers and delicacies were offered before their ancestral tablets every day.[21] Human sacrifices were resorted to now and then to stop excessive rain or to ensure the stability of a building or a wall; and the retainers of a dead lord were occasionally buried with him to defend him in his epilogue.[22]

Out of ancestor worship came the oldest living religion of Japan. *Shinto*, the Way of the Gods, took three forms: the domestic cult of family ancestors, the communal cult of clan ancestors, and the state cult of the imperial ancestors and the founding gods. The divine progenitor of the imperial line was addressed with humble petitions, seven times a year, by the emperor or his representatives; and special prayers were offered up to him when the nation was embarking upon some particularly holy cause, like the taking of Shantung (1914).[23] *Shinto* required no creed, no elaborate ritual, no moral code; it had no special priesthood, and no consoling doctrine of immortality and heaven; all that it asked of its devotees was an occasional pilgrimage, and pious reverence for one's ancestors, the emperor, and the past. It was for a time superseded because it was too modest in its rewards and its demands.

In 522 Buddhism, which had entered China five hundred years before, passed over from the continent, and began a rapid conquest of Japan. Two elements met to give it victory: the religious needs of the people, and the political needs of the state. For it was not Buddha's Buddhism that came, agnostic, pessimistic and puritan, dreaming of blissful extinction; it was the *Mahayana* Buddhism of gentle gods like Amida and Kwannon, of cheerful ceremonial, saving *Bodhisattwas,* and personal immortality. Better still, it inculcated, with irresistible grace, all those virtues of piety, peacefulness and obedience which make a people amenable to government; it gave to the oppressed such hopes and consolations as might reconcile them to content with their simple lot; it redeemed the prose and routine of a laborious life with the poetry of myth and prayer and the drama of colorful festival; and it offered to the people that unity of feeling and belief which statesmen have always welcomed as a source of social order and a pillar of national strength.

We do not know whether it was statesmanship or piety that brought victory to Buddhism in Japan. When, in 586 A.D., the Emperor Yomei died, the succession was contested in arms by two rival families, both of them politically devoted to the new creed. Prince Shotoku Taishi, who had been born, we are told, with a holy relic clasped in his infant hand, led the Buddhist faction to victory, established the Empress Suiko on the throne, and for twenty-nine years (592-621) ruled the Sacred Islands as Prince Imperial and Regent. He lavished funds upon Buddhist temples, encouraged and supported the Buddhist clergy, promulgated the Buddhist ethic in national decrees, and became in general the Ashoka of Japanese Buddhism. He patronized the arts and sciences, imported artists and artisans from Korea and China, wrote history, painted pictures, and supervised the building of the Horiuji Temple, the oldest extant masterpiece in the art history of Japan.

Despite the work of this versatile civilizer, and all the virtues inculcated or preached by Buddhism, another violent crisis came to Japan within a generation after Shotoku's death. An ambitious aristocrat, Kamatari, arranged with Prince Naka a palace revolution that marked so definite a change in the political history of Nippon that native historians refer to it enthusiastically as the "Great Reform" (645). The heir-apparent was assassinated, a senile puppet was placed upon the throne, and Kamatari as chief minister, through Prince Naka as heir-apparent and then as Emperor Tenchi, reconstructed the Japanese government into an autocratic imperial power. The sovereign was elevated from the leadership of the principal clan to paramount authority over every official in Japan; all governors were to be appointed by him, all taxes paid directly to him, all the land of the realm was declared his. Japan graduated rapidly from a loose association of clans and semi-feudal chieftains into a closely-knit monarchical state.

III. THE IMPERIAL AGE

*The emperors—The aristocracy—The influence of China—The
Golden Age of Kyoto—Decadence*

From that time onward the emperor enjoyed impressive titles. Sometimes he was called *Tenshi*, or "Son of Heaven"; usually *Tenno*, or "Heavenly King"; rarely *Mikado*, or "August Gateway." He had the distinction of receiving a new appellation after his death, and of being known in history by an individual name quite different from that which he bore during his life. To ensure the continuity of the imperial line, the emperor was allowed to have as many wives or consorts as he desired; and the succession went not necessarily to his first son, but to any of his progeny who seemed to him, or to the Warwicks of the time, most likely to prove strongest, or weakest, on the throne. In the early days of the Kyoto period the emperors inclined to piety; some of them abdicated to become Buddhist monks, and one of them forbade fishing as an insult to Buddha.[25] Yozei was a troublesome exception who illustrated the perils of active monarchy: he made people climb trees, and then shot them down with bow and arrow; he seized maidens in the street, tied them up with lute strings, and cast them into ponds; it pleased His Majesty to ride through the capital and to belabor the citizens with his whip; at last his subjects deposed him in an outbreak of political impiety rare in the history of Japan.[26] In 794 the headquarters of the government were removed from Nara to Nagaoka, and shortly thereafter to Kyoto ("Capital of Peace"); this remained the capital during those four centuries (794-1192) which most historians agree in calling the Golden Age of Japan. By 1190 Kyoto had a population of half a million, more than any European city of the time except Constantinople and Cordova.[27] One part of the town was given over to the cottages and hovels of the populace, which seems to have lived cheerfully in its humble poverty; another part, discreetly secluded, contained the gardens and palaces of the aristocracy and the Imperial Family. The people of the court were appropriately called "Dwellers above the Clouds."[28] For here as elsewhere the progress of civilization and technology had brought an increase in social distinctions; the rough equality of pioneer days had given way to the inequality that comes inevitably when increasing wealth is distributed among men according to their diverse capacity, character, and privilege. Great families arose like the Fujiwara, the Taira, the Minamoto and the Sugawara, who made and unmade emperors, and fought with one another in the lusty manner of the Italian Renaissance. Sugawara Michizane endeared himself to Japan by his patronage of literature, and is now worshiped as the God of Letters, in whose honor a school holiday is declared on the twenty-fifth day of every month; and the young *Shogun* Minamoto Sanetomo distinguished himself by composing on the morning before his assassination this simple stanza, in the chastest Japanese style:

> If I should come no more,
> Plum-tree beside my door,
> Forget not thou the spring,
> Faithfully blossoming.[29]

Under the enlightened Daigo (898-930), greatest of the emperors set up by the Fujiwara clan, Japan continued to absorb, and began to rival, the culture and luxury of China, then flourishing at its height under the T'ang. Having taken their religion from the Middle Kingdom, the Japanese proceeded to take from the same source their dress and their sports, their cooking and their writing, their poetry and their administrative methods, their music and their arts, their gardens and their architecture; even their handsome capitals, Nara and Kyoto, were laid out in imitation of Ch'ang-an.[30] Japan imported Chinese culture a thousand years ago as it imported Europe and America in our own day: first with haste, then with discrimination; jealously maintaining its own spirit and character, zealously adapting the new ways to ancient and native ends.

Stimulated by its great neighbor, and protected by orderly and continuous government, Japan now entered that *Engi* period (901-922) which is accounted the acme of the Golden Age.* Wealth accumulated, and was centered in a fashionable life of luxury, refinement and culture hardly equaled again until the courts of the Medici and the *salons* of the French Enlightenment. Kyoto became the Paris and Versailles of France, elegant in poetry and dress, practised in manners and arts, and setting for all the nation the standards of learning and taste. Every appetite was full

---

* "This period named 'Engi,'" says the enthusiastic Fenollosa, "must doubtless be reckoned the high-water mark of Japanese civilization, as Ming Huang's had been that of China. Never again would either China or Japan be quite so rich, splendid, and full of free genius. . . . In general culture and luxurious refinement of a life which equally ministered to mind and body, not only not in Japan, but perhaps not in the world was there ever again anything quite so exquisite."[31]

and free; the *cuisine* invented novelties for the palate and heaped up feasts for *gourmands* and *gourmets;* and fornication or adultery was winked at as a very venial sin.[32] Silks of fine texture clothed every lord and lady, and harmonies of color wavered on every sleeve. Music and the dance adorned the life of temple and court, and graced aristocratic homes attractively landscaped without, and luxuriously finished with interiors of bronze or pearl, ivory or gold, or wood most delicately carved.[33] Literature flourished, and morals decayed.

Such epochs of glittering refinement tend to be brief, for they rest insecurely upon concentrated wealth that may at any moment be destroyed by the fluctuations of trade, the impatience of the exploited, or the fortunes of war. The extravagance of the court finally ruined the solvency of the state; the exaltation of culture above ability filled administrative posts with incompetent poetasters, under whose scented noses corruption multiplied unnoticed; at last offices were sold to the highest bidder.[34] Crime rose among the poor as luxury mounted among the rich; brigands and pirates infested the roads and the seas, and preyed impartially upon the people and the emperor; tax-gatherers were robbed as they brought their revenues to the court. Gangs of bandits were organized in the provinces, and even in the capital itself; for a time Japan's most notorious criminal, like ours, lived in open splendor, too powerful to be arrested or annoyed.[35] The neglect of martial habits and virtues, or military organization and defense, left the government exposed to assault from any ruthless buccaneer. The great families raised their own armies, and began an epoch of civil war in which they contended chaotically for the right to name the emperor. The emperor himself was every day more helpless, while the heads of the clans became again almost independent lords. Once more history moved in its ancient oscillation between a powerful central government and a feudal decentralized regime.

IV. THE DICTATORS

The "shoguns"—The Kamakura "Bakufu"—The Hojo Regency—
Kublai Khan's invasion — The Ashikaga Shogunate — The
three buccaneers

Tempted by this situation, a class of military dictators arose, who assumed full authority over various sections of the archipelago, and recognized the emperor merely as the divine façade of Japan, to be maintained at a minimum of expense. The peasants, no longer protected from bandits by imperial armies or police, paid taxes to the *shoguns*, or generals, instead of to the emperor, for only the *shoguns* were able to safeguard them from robbery.[36] The feudal system triumphed in Japan for the same reason that it had triumphed in Europe: local sources of authority grew in power as a central and distant government failed to maintain security and order.

About the year 1192 a member of the Minamoto clan, Yoritomo, gathered about him an army of soldiers and vassals, and established an independent authority which, from its seat, acquired the name of the "Kamakura *Bakufu*." The very word *bakufu* meant a military office, and indicated bluntly the nature of the new regime. The great Yoritomo died suddenly in 1198,* and was succeeded by his weakling sons; for, says a Japanese proverb, "the great man has no seed."[38] A rival family set up in 1199 the "Hojo Regency," which for 134 years ruled the *shoguns* who ruled the emperors. Kublai Khan took advantage of this trinitarian government to attempt the conquest of Japan, for clever Koreans, fearful of it, had described it to him as desirably rich. Kublai ordered from his ship-builders so vast a fleet that Chinese poets represented the hills as mourning for their denuded forests.[39] The Japanese, in heroic retrospect, reckoned the vessels at 70,000, but less patriotic historians are content with 3,500 ships and 100,000 men. This gigantic armada appeared off the coast of Japan late in the year 1291. The brave islanders sailed out to meet it in an improvised and comparatively tiny fleet; but, as in the case of a smaller but more famous Armada,† a "Great Wind," renowned in thankful memory, arose, smashed the ships of the mighty Khan upon the rocks, drowned 70,000 of his sailors, and saved the others for a life of slavery in Japan.

The turn of the Hojos came in 1333. For they, too, had been poisoned by power, and hereditary rule had passed in time from scoundrels and geniuses to cowards and fools. Takatoki, last of the line, had a passion for dogs; he accepted them in lieu of taxes, and collected from four to five thousand of them; he kept them in kennels with gold and silver decorations, fed them on fish and fowl, and had them carried in palan-

---

* Both rider and horse, we are told, were thrown into a panic by seeing the ghost of the brother whom Yoritomo had murdered; the horse stumbled, the rider fell, and Yoritomo died some months later, at the age of fifty-three.[37] The story is vouched for by his enemies.

† The Spanish Armada of 1588, on its arrival in the English Channel, had some 120 ships, with 24,000 men.[38a]

quins to take the air. The contemporary emperor, Go Daigo, saw in the degeneration of his keepers an opportunity to reassert the imperial power. The Minamoto and Ashikaga clans rallied to him, and led his forces, after many defeats, to victory over the Regency. Takatoki and 870 of his vassals and generals retired to a temple, drank a last cup of *sake,* and committed *hara-kiri.* "This," said one of them as he pulled out his intestines with his own hand, "gives a fine relish to the wine."[40]

Ashikaga Takauji turned against the Emperor whom he had helped to restore, fought with successful stratagem and treachery the armies sent to subdue him, replaced Go Daigo with the puppet emperor Kogon, and set up at Kyoto that Ashikaga Shogunate which was to rule Japan through 250 years of chaos and intermittent civil war. It must be admitted that part of this disorder was due to the nobler side of the Ashikaga dictators —their love and patronage of art. Yoshimitsu, tired of strife, turned his hand to painting, and became not the least artist of his time; Yoshimasa befriended many painters, subsidized a dozen arts, and grew into so refined a connoisseur that the pieces selected by him and his associates are the most coveted prizes of collectors today.[41] Meanwhile, however, the prosaic tasks of organization were neglected, and neither the rich *shoguns* nor the impoverished emperors seemed able to maintain public security or peace.

It was this very chaos and looseness of life, and the call of the nation for leaders who would give it order, that produced a trio of buccaneers famous in Japanese history. In their youth, says tradition, Nobunaga, Hideyoshi and Iyeyasu resolved together to restore unity to their country, and each took a solemn oath that he would obey as vassal whichever of the others should win the imperial consent to administer Japan.[42] Nobunaga tried first, and failed; Hideyoshi tried second, and died just short of success; Iyeyasu bided his time, tried last of all, founded the Tokugawa Shogunate, and inaugurated one of the longest periods of peace, and one of the richest epochs of art, in human history.

V. GREAT MONKEY-FACE

The rise of Hideyoshi—The attack upon Korea—The conflict with Christianity

Queen Elizabeth and Akbar, as the Japanese would instructively put it, were contemporaries of the great Hideyoshi. He was a peasant's son, known to his friends, and later to his subjects, as *Sarumen Kanja*—"Monkey-Face"; for not even Confucius could rival him in ugliness. Unable to discipline him, his parents sent him to a monastic school; but Hideyoshi made such fun of the Buddhist priests, and raised such turmoil and insurrections, that he was expelled. He was apprenticed to various trades, and was discharged thirty-seven times;[42] he became a bandit, decided that more could be stolen by law than against it, joined the service of a *Samurai* (i.e., a "sword-bearing man"), saved his master's life, and was thereafter allowed to carry a sword. He joined Nobunaga, helped him with brains as well as courage, and, when Nobunaga died (1582), took the lead of the lawless rebels who had set out to conquer their native land. Within three years Hideyoshi had made himself ruler of half the empire, had won the admiration of the impotent emperor, and felt strong enough to digest Korea and China. "With Korean troops," he modestly announced to the Son of Heaven, "aided by your illustrious influence, I intend to bring the whole of China under my sway. When that is effected, the three countries (China, Korea and Japan) will be one. I shall do it as easily as a man rolls up a piece of matting and carries it away under his arm."[44] He tried hard; but a villainous Korean invented a metal war-boat—a pre-plagiarism of the *Monitor* and the *Merrimac*—and destroyed one after another of the troop-laden ships that Hideyoshi had dispatched to Korea (1592). Seventy-two vessels were sunk in one day, and the very sea ran blood; forty-eight other vessels were beached and deserted by the Japanese, and burned to the water by the victors. After an indecisive alternation of successes and defeats the attempt to conquer Korea and China was postponed until the twentieth century. Hideyoshi, said the Korean king, had tried to "measure the ocean in a cockle-shell."[45]

Meanwhile Hideyoshi had settled down to enjoy and administer the Regency that he had established. He provided himself with three hundred concubines, but he bestowed a substantial sum upon the peasant wife whom he had long ago divorced. He looked up one of his old employers, and returned to him with interest the money that he had stolen from him in apprentice days. He did not dare ask the Emperor's consent to his assumption of the title of *Shogun;* but his contemporaries gave him, in compensation, the name of *Taiko*, or "Great Sovereign," which, by one of those strange verbal Odysseys that characterize philology, is now entering our language as *tycoon*. "Cunning and crafty beyond belief," as a missionary described him,[46] he subtly disarmed the people by order-

ing all metal weapons to be contributed as material for a colossal statue
—the *Daibutsu,* or Great Buddha, of Kyoto. He appears to have had
no religious beliefs, but he was not above making use of religion for the
purposes of ambition or statesmanship.

Christianity had come to Japan in 1549 in the person of one of the
first and noblest of Jesuits, St. Francis Xavier. The little community
which he established grew so rapidly that within a generation after his
coming there were seventy Jesuits and 150,000 converts in the empire.[47]
They were so numerous in Nagasaki that they made that trading port a
Christian city, and persuaded its local ruler, Omura, to use direct action
in spreading the new faith.[48] "Within Nagasaki territory," says Lafcadio
Hearn, "Buddhism was totally suppressed—its priests being persecuted
and driven away."[49] Alarmed at this spiritual invasion, and suspecting
it of political designs, Hideyoshi sent a messenger to the Vice-Provincial
of the Jesuits in Japan, armed with five peremptory questions:

> 1. Why, and by what authority, he (the Vice-Provincial) and his
> *religieux* (members of religious orders) constrained Hideyoshi's sub-
> jects to become Christians?
> 2. Why they induced their disciples and their sectaries to over-
> throw temples?
> 3. Why they persecuted the Buddhist priests?
> 4. Why they and the other Portuguese ate animals useful to man,
> such as oxen and cows?
> 5. Why he allowed the merchants of his nation to buy Japanese
> and make slaves of them in the Indies?[50]

Not satisfied with the replies, Hideyoshi issued, in 1587, the following edict:

> Having learned from our faithful councillors that foreign *religieux*
> have come into our realm, where they preach a law contrary to that
> of Japan, and that they have even had the audacity to destroy temples
> dedicated to our (native gods) Kami and Hotoke; although this out-
> rage merits the severest punishment, wishing nevertheless to show
> them mercy, we order them under pain of death to quit Japan
> within twenty days. During that space no harm or hurt will come
> to them. But at the expiration of that term, we order that if any of
> them be found in our States, they shall be seized and punished as the
> greatest criminals.[51]

Amid all these alarms the great buccaneer found time to encourage artists, to take part in *No* plays, and to support Rikyu in making the tea ceremony a stimulant to Japanese pottery and an essential adornment of Japanese life. He died in 1598, having exacted from Iyeyasu a promise to build a new capital at Yedo (now Tokyo), and to recognize Hideyoshi's son Hideyori as heir to the Regency in Japan.

VI. THE GREAT SHOGUN

The accession of Iyeyasu—His philosophy—Iyeyasu and Christianity—Death of Iyeyasu—The Tokugawa Shogunate

Hideyoshi being dead, Iyeyasu pointed out that he had drawn the blood for his oath not from his finger or his gums, as the code of the *Samurai* required, but from a scratch behind his ear; hence the oath was not binding.[52] He overwhelmed the forces of certain rival leaders at Sekigahara in a battle that left 40,000 dead. He tolerated Hideyori till his coming of age made him dangerous, and then suggested to him the wisdom of submission. Rebuked, he besieged the gigantic Castle of Osaka where Hideyori was established, captured it while the youth committed *hara-kiri*, and ensured his hold upon power by killing all of Hideyori's children, legitimate and illegitimate. Then Iyeyasu organized peace as ably and ruthlessly as he had organized war, and administered Japan so well that it was content to be ruled by his posterity and his principles for eight generations.

He was a man of his own ideas, and made his morals as he went along. When a very presentable woman came to him with the complaint that one of his officials had killed her husband in order to possess her, Iyeyasu ordered the official to disembowel himself, and made the lady his concubine.[53] Like Socrates he ranked wisdom as the only virtue, and charted some of its paths in that strange "Legacy," or intellectual testament, which he bequeathed to his family at his death.

> Life is like unto a long journey with a heavy burden. Let thy step be slow and steady, that thou stumble not. Persuade thyself that imperfection and inconvenience is the natural lot of mortals, and there will be no room for discontent, neither for despair. When ambitious desires arise in thy heart, recall the days of extremity thou hast passed through. Forbearance is the root of quietness and assurance

forever. Look upon wrath as thy enemy. If thou knowest only what it is to conquer, and knowest not what it is to be defeated, woe unto thee; it will fare ill with thee. Find fault with thyself rather than with others.[54]

Having captured power by arms, he decided that Japan had no need of further war, and devoted himself to furthering the ways and virtues of peace. To win the *Samurai* from the habits of the sword he encouraged them to study literature and philosophy, and to contribute to the arts; and under the rule which he established, culture flourished in Japan and militarism decayed. "The people," he wrote, "are the foundation of the Empire,"[55] and he invoked the "special commiseration" of his successors for the "widower, the widowed, the orphaned and the lonely." But he had no democratic predispositions: the greatest of all crimes, he thought, was insubordination; a "fellow" who stepped out of his rank was to be cut down on the spot; and the entire family of a rebel should be put to death.[56] The feudal order, in his judgment, was the best that could be devised for actual human beings; it provided a rational balance between central and local power, it established a natural and hereditary system of social and economic organization, and it preserved the continuity of a society without subjecting it to despotic authority. It must be admitted that Iyeyasu organized the most perfect form of feudal government ever known.[57]

Like most statesmen he thought of religion chiefly as an organ of social discipline, and regretted that the variety of human beliefs canceled half this good by the disorder of hostile creeds. To his completely political mind the traditional faith of the Japanese people—a careless mixture of Shintoism and Buddhism—was an invaluable bond cementing the race into spiritual unity, moral order and patriotic devotion; and though at first he approached Christianity with the lenient eye and broad intelligence of Akbar, and refrained from enforcing against it the angry edicts of Hideyoshi, he was disturbed by its intolerance, its bitter denunciation of the native faith as idolatry, and the discord which its passionate dogmatism aroused not only between the converts and the nation, but among the neophytes themselves. Finally his resentment was stirred by the discovery that missionaries sometimes allowed themselves to be used as vanguards for conquerors, and were, here and there, conspiring against the

Japanese state.⁵⁸* In 1614 he forbade the practice or preaching of the Christian religion in Japan, and ordered all converts either to depart from the country or to renounce their new beliefs. Many priests evaded the decree, and some of them were arrested. None was executed during the lifetime of Iyeyasu; but after his death the fury of the bureaucrats was turned against the Christians, and a violent and brutal persecution ensued which practically stamped Christianity out of Japan. In 1638 the remaining Christians gathered to the number of 37,000 on the peninsula of Shimabara, fortified it, and made a last stand for the freedom of worship. Iyemitsu, grandson of Iyeyasu, sent a large armed force to subdue them. When, after a three months' siege, their stronghold was taken, all but one hundred and five of the survivors were massacred in the streets.

Iyeyasu and Shakespeare were contemporaries in death. The doughty *Shogun* left his power to his son Hidetada, with a simple admonition: "Take care of the people. Strive to be virtuous. Never neglect to protect the country." And to the nobles who stood at his deathbed he left advice in the best tradition of Confucius and Mencius: "My son has now come of age. I feel no anxiety for the future of the state. But should my successor commit any grave fault in his administration, do you administer affairs yourselves. The country is not the country of one man, but the country of the nation. If my descendants lose their power because of their misdeeds, I shall not regret it."⁶⁰

His descendants conducted themselves much better than monarchs can usually be expected to behave over a great length of time. Hidetada was a harmless mediocrity; Iyemitsu represented a stronger mood of the stock, and sternly suppressed a movement to restore to actual power the still reigning but not ruling emperors. Tsunayoshi lavished patronage upon men of letters, and on the great rival schools of painting, Kano and Tosa, that embellished the *Genroku* age (1688-1703). Yoshimune set himself

---

* In 1596 a Spanish galleon was forced into a Japanese harbor by Japanese boats, was purposely driven by them upon a reef that broke it in two, and then was pillaged by the local governor on the ground that Japanese law permitted the authorities to appropriate all vessels stranded on their shores. The outraged pilot, Landecho, protested to Hideyoshi's Minister of Works, Masuda. Masuda asked how it was that the Christian Church had won so many lands to be subject to one man; and Landecho, being a seaman rather than a diplomat, answered: "Our kings begin by sending, into the countries they wish to conquer, *religieux* who induce the people to embrace our religion; and when they have made considerable progress, troops are sent who combine with the new Christians; and then our kings have not much trouble in accomplishing the rest."⁵⁹

to the ever-recurrent purpose of abolishing poverty, at the very time when his treasury faced an unusual deficit. He borrowed extensively from the merchant class, attacked the extravagance of the rich, and stoically reduced the expenditures of his government, even to the extent of dismissing the fifty fairest ladies of the court. He dressed in cotton cloth, slept on a peasant's pallet, and dined on the simplest fare. He had a complaint box placed before the palace of the Supreme Court, and invited the people to submit criticisms of any governmental policy or official. When one Yamashita sent in a caustic indictment of his whole administration Yoshimune had the document read aloud in public, and rewarded the author for his candor with a substantial gift.[61]

It was the judgment of Lafcadio Hearn that "the Tokugawa period was the happiest in the long life of the nation."[62] History, though it can never quite know the past, inclines tentatively to the same conclusion. How could one, seeing Japan today, suspect that on those now excited islands, only a century ago, lived a people poor but content, enjoying a long epoch of peace under the rule of a military class, and pursuing in quiet isolation the highest aims of literature and art?

CHAPTER XXIX

The Political and Moral Foundations

A tentative approach

IF, NOW, we try to picture the Japan that died in 1853, we should
remember that it may be as hard to understand, as it might be to fight,
a people five thousand miles distant, and differing from us in color and
language, government and religion, manners and morals, character and
ideals, literature and art. Hearn was more intimate with Japan than any
other Western writer of his time, and yet he spoke of "the immense difficulty of perceiving and comprehending what underlies the surface of Japanese life."¹ "Your information about us," a genial Japanese essayist reminds the Occident, "is based on the meagre translations of our immense
literature, if not on the unreliable anecdotes of passing travelers. . . . We
Asiatics are often appalled by the curious web of facts and fancies which
has been woven concerning us. We are pictured as living on the perfume
of the lotus, if not on mice and cockroaches."² What follows, therefore, is
a tentative approach—based upon the briefest direct acquaintance—to Japanese civilization and character; each student must correct it by long and
personal experience. The first lesson of philosophy is that we may all be
mistaken.

I. THE SAMURAI

*The powerless emperor—The powers of the "shogun"—The sword
of the "Samurai"—The code of the "Samurai"—"Hara-kiri"—
The Forty-seven "Ronin"—A commuted sentence*

Theoretically at the head of the nation was the divine emperor. The
actually ruling house—the hereditary shogunate—allowed the emperor and
his court $25,000 a year for maintaining the impressive and useful fiction
of uninterrupted rule.* Many people of the court practised some domestic
handicraft to sustain themselves: some made umbrellas, others made chop-

---

* This sum, however, was probably equivalent to a quarter of a million dollars in
current American money.

845

sticks, or toothpicks, or playing cards. The Tokugawa *shoguns* made it a principle to leave the emperor no authority whatever, to seclude him from the people, to surround him with women, and to weaken him with effeminacy and idleness. The imperial family yielded its powers gracefully, and contented itself with dictating the fashions of aristocratic dress.[3]

Meanwhile the *shogun* luxuriated in the slowly growing wealth of Japan, and assumed prerogatives normally belonging to the emperor. When he was borne through the streets in his ox-carriage or palanquin the police required every house along the route, and all the shutters of upper windows, to be closed; all fires were to be extinguished, all dogs and cats were to be locked up, and the people themselves were to kneel by the roadside with their heads upon their hands and their hands upon the ground.[4] The *shogun* had a large personal retinue, including four jesters, and eight cultured ladies dedicated to entertain him without reserve.[5] He was advised by a cabinet of twelve members: a "Great Senior," five "Seniors" or ministers, and six "Sub-Elders" who formed a junior council. As in China, a Board of Censors supervised all administrative offices, and kept watch upon the feudal lords. These lords, or *Daimyo* ("Great Name"), formally acknowledged allegiance only to the emperor; and some of them, like the Shimadzu family that ruled Satsuma, successfully limited the *shogun's* authority, and finally overthrew it.

Below the lords were the baronets, and below these the squires; and serving the lords were a million or more *Samurai*—sword-bearing guardsmen. The basic principle of Japanese feudal society was that every gentleman was a soldier, and every soldier a gentleman;[6] here lay the sharpest difference between Japan and that pacific China which thought that every gentleman should be a scholar rather than a warrior. Though they loved, and partly formed themselves on, such swashbuckling novels as the Chinese *Romance of the Three Kingdoms*, the *Samurai* scorned mere learning, and called the literary *savant* a book-smelling sot.[7] They had many privileges: they were exempt from taxation, received a regular stipend of rice from the baron whom they served, and performed no labor except occasionally to die for their country. They looked down upon love as a graceful game, and preferred Greek friendship; they made a business of gambling and brawling, and kept their swords in condition by paying the executioner to let them cut off condemned heads.[8] His sword, in Iyeyasu's famous phrase, was "the soul of the *Samurai*," and found remarkably frequent expression despite prolonged national peace. He had the right, according to Iyeyasu,* to cut down at once any member of the lower classes who offended him; and when his steel was new and he wished to make trial of it, he was as likely to try it on a beggar as on a dog.[10] "A famous swordsman having obtained a new sword," says Longford, "took up his place by the Nihon Bashi (the central bridge of Yedo) to await a chance of testing it. By and by a fat peasant came along, merrily drunk, and the swordsman dealt him the *Nashi-wari* (pear-splitter) so effectively that he cut him right through from the top of his head down to the fork. The peasant continued on his way, not knowing that anything had happened to him, till he stumbled against a coolie, and fell in two neatly severed pieces."[11] Of such trivial consequence is the difference, so troublesome to philosophers, between the One and the Many.

The *Samurai* had other graces than this jolly despatch with which they transformed time into eternity. They accepted a stern code of honor—*Bushido*,* or the Way of the Knight—whose central theory was its definition of virtue: "the power of deciding upon a certain course of conduct in accordance with reason, without wavering; to die when it is right to die, to strike when it is right to strike."[12] They were tried by their own code, but it was more severe than the common law.[13] They despised all material enterprise and gain, and refused to lend, borrow or count money; they seldom broke a promise, and they risked their lives readily for anyone who appealed to them for just aid. They made a principle of hard and frugal living; they limited themselves to one meal a day, and accustomed themselves to eat any food that came to hand, and to hold it. They bore all suffering silently, and suppressed every display of emotion; their women were taught to rejoice when informed that their husbands had been killed on the battlefield.[14] They recognized no obligation except that of loyalty to their superiors; this was, in their code, a higher law than parental or filial love. It was a common thing for a *Samurai* to disembowel himself on the death of his lord, in order to serve and protect him in the other world. When the *Shogun* Iyemitsu was dying in 1651 he reminded his prime minister, Hotto, of this duty of *junshi*, or "following in death"; Hotto killed himself without a word, and several subordinates imitated him.[15] When the Emperor Mutsuhito went to his ancestors in 1912 General Nogi and his wife committed suicide in loyalty to him.[16] Not even the traditions of Rome's finest soldiers bred greater courage, asceticism and self-control than were demanded by the code of the *Samurai*.

* A word coined by the late Inazo Nitobe.

The final law of *Bushido* was *hara-kiri*—suicide by disembowelment. The occasions when this would be expected of a *Samurai* were almost beyond count, and the practice of it so frequent that little notice was taken of it. If a man of rank had been condemned to death he was allowed, as an expression of the emperor's esteem, to cut through his abdomen from left to right and then down to the pelvis with the small sword which he always carried for this purpose. If he had been defeated in battle, or had been compelled to surrender, he was as like as not to rip open his belly. (*Hara-kiri* means belly-cutting; it is a vulgar word seldom used by the Japanese, who prefer to call it *seppuku*.) When, in 1895, Japan yielded to European pressure and abandoned Liaotung, forty military men committed *hara-kiri* in protest. During the war of 1905 many officers and men in the Japanese navy killed themselves rather than be captured by the Russians. If his superior did something offensive to him, the good *Samurai* might gash himself to death at his master's gate. The art of *seppuku*—the precise ritual of ripping—was one of the first items in the education of *Samurai* youth; and the last tribute of affection that could be paid to a friend was to stand by him and cut off his head as soon as he had carved his paunch.[17] Out of this training, and the traditions bound up with it, has come some part of the Japanese soldier's comparative fearlessness of death.*

Murder, like suicide, was allowed occasionally to replace the law. Feudal Japan economized on policemen not only by having many *bonzes*, but by allowing the son or brother of a murdered man to take the law into his own hand; and this recognition of the right of revenge, though it begot half the novels and plays of Japanese literature, intercepted many crimes. The *Samurai*, however, usually felt called upon to commit *hara-kiri* after exercising this privilege of personal revenge. When the famous Forty-seven *Ronin* ("Wave Men"—i.e., unattached *Samurai*), to avenge a death, had cut off the head of Kotsuké no Suké with supreme courtesy and the most refined apologies, they retired in dignity to estates named by the *Shogun*, and neatly killed themselves (1703). Priests returned Kotsuké's head to his retainers, who gave them this simple receipt:

---

* *Hara-kiri* was forbidden to women and plebeians; but women were allowed to commit *jigaki*—i.e., they were permitted, as a protest against an offense, to pierce the throat with a dagger, and to sever the arteries by a single thrust. Every woman of quality received technical training in the art of cutting her throat, and was taught to bind her lower limbs together before killing herself, lest her corpse should be found in an immodest position.[18]

Memorandum:

Item: One head.

Item: One paper parcel.

The above articles are acknowledged to have been received.

    (Signed)   Sayada Mogobai

          Saito Kunai

This is probably the most famous and typical event in the history of Japan, and one of the most significant for the understanding of Japanese character. Its protagonists are still, in the popular view, heroes and saints; to this day pious hands deck their graves, and incense never ceases to rise before their resting place.[19]

Towards the end of Iyeyasu's regency two brothers, Sakon and Naiki, twenty-four and seventeen years of age respectively, tried to kill him because of wrongs which they felt that he had inflicted upon their father. They were caught as they entered the camp, and were sentenced to death. Iyeyasu was so moved by their courage that he commuted their sentences to self-disembowelment; and in accord with the customs of the time he included their younger brother, the eight-year-old Hachimaro, in this merciful decree. The physician who attended the boys has left us a description of the scene:

> When they were all seated in a row for final despatch, Sakon turned to the youngest and said—"Go thou first, for I wish to be sure that thou doest it right." Upon the little one's replying that, as he had never seen *seppuku* performed, he would like to see his brothers do it, and then he could follow them, the older brothers smiled between their tears:—"Well said, little fellow. So canst thou well boast of being our father's child." When they had placed him between them, Sakon thrust the dagger into the left side of his abdomen and said—"Look, brother! Dost understand now? Only, don't push the dagger too far, lest thou fall back. Lean forward, rather, and keep thy knees well composed." Naiki did likewise, and said to the boy—"Keep thine eyes open, or else thou mayst look like a dying woman. If thy dagger feels anything within and thy strength fails, take courage, and double thy effort to cut across." The child looked from one to the other, and when both had expired, he calmly half denuded himself and followed the example set him on either hand.[20]

II. THE LAW

The first code—Group responsibility—Punishments

The legal system of Japan was a vigorous supplement to private assassination and revenge. It had its origins partly in the ancient usages of the people, partly in the Chinese codes of the seventh century; law accompanied religion in the migration of culture from China to Japan.[21] Tenchi Tenno began the formulation of a system of laws which was completed and promulgated under the boy Emperor Mommu in 702. In the feudal epoch this and other codes of the imperial age fell into disuse, and each fief legislated independently; the *Samurai* recognized no law beyond the will and decrees of his *Daimyo*.[22]

Until 1721 it was the custom of Japan to hold the entire family responsible for the good behavior of each member, and, in most localities, to charge each family in a group of five with responsibility for all. The grown sons of an adult who had been condemned to be crucified or burned were executed with him, and his younger sons, on coming of age, were banished.[23] Ordeal was used in medieval trials, and torture remained popular, in its milder forms, till modern times. The Japanese used the rack on some Christians, in vengeful imitation of the Inquisition; but more often their subtle minds were content to bind a man with ropes into a constrained position that became more agonizing with every minute.[24] Whippings for trifling offenses were frequent, and death could be earned by any one of a great variety of crimes. The Emperor Shomu (724-56) abolished capital punishment and made compassion the rule of government; but crime increased after his death, and the Emperor Konin (770-81) not only restored the death penalty, but decreed that thieves should be publicly scourged until they died.[25] Capital punishment also took the form of strangling, beheading, crucifixion, quartering, burning, or boiling in oil.[26] Iyeyasu put an end to the old custom of pulling a condemned man in two between oxen, or binding him to a public post and inviting each passer-by to take a turn in cutting through him, from shoulder to crotch, with a saw.[27] Iyeyasu laid it down that the frequent resort to severe punishments proved not the criminality of the people so much as the corruption and incompetence of the officials.[28] Yoshimune was disgusted to find that the prisons of his time had no sanitary arrangements, and that among the prisoners were several whose trials, though begun sixteen years back, were still unfinished, so that the accusations against them were forgotten, and the witnesses were dead.[29] This most enlightened of the *shoguns* reformed the prisons, improved and accelerated judicial procedure, abolished family responsibility, and labored sedulously for years to formulate the first unified code of Japanese feudal law (1721).

III. THE TOILERS

Castes—An experiment in the nationalization of land—State fixing of wages—A famine—Handicrafts—Artisans and guilds

In the imperial age society had been divided into eight *sei* or castes; in the feudal epoch these were softened into four classes: *Samurai*, artisans, peasants, and merchants—the last being also, in social ranking, least. Beneath these classes was a large body of slaves, numbering some five per cent of the population, and composed of criminals, war-captives, or children seized and sold by kidnappers, or children sold into slavery by their parents.[*][30] Lower even than these slaves was a caste of pariahs known as *Eta*, considered despicable and unclean by Buddhist Japan because they acted as butchers, tanners and scavengers.[32]

The great bulk of the population (which numbered in Yoshimune's days some thirty millions), was composed of peasant proprietors, intensively cultivating that one-eighth of Japan's mountainous soil which lends itself to tillage.[†] In the Nara period the state nationalized the land, and rented it to the peasant for six years or, at most, till death; but the government discovered that men did not care to improve or properly care for land that might in a short time be assigned to others; and the experiment ended in a restoration of private ownership, with state provision of funds in the spring to finance the planting and reaping of the crops.[33] Despite this aid, the life of the peasant was not one of degenerative ease. His farm was a tiny tract, for even in feudal days one square mile had to support two thousand men.[34] He had to contribute annually to the state thirty days of forced labor, during which death by a spear-thrust might be the penalty of a moment's idleness.[‡][35] The government took from him, in

---

* This practice was forbidden in 1699.[31]
† The arable exceptions were—and are—fertilized with human waste.
‡ During the months of July and August a *siesta* was permitted from noon till four o'clock. Sick workers were fed by the state, and free coffins were provided for those who died during the *corvée*.[36]

taxes and levies of many kinds, 6% of his product in the seventh century, 72% in the twelfth, and 40% in the nineteenth.[37] His tools were of the simplest sort; his clothing was poor and slight in the winter, and usually nothing at all in the summer; his furniture was a rice-pot, a few bowls, and some chopsticks; his home was a hut so flimsy that half a week sufficed to build it.[38] Every now and then earthquakes leveled his cottage, or famine emptied his frame. If he worked for another man his wages, like all wages in Tokugawa Japan, were fixed by the government;[39] but this did not prevent them from being cruelly low. In one of the most famous works of Japanese literature — Kamo Chomei's *Hojoki* — the author describes, as crowded into the eight years between 1177 and 1185, an earthquake, a famine, and a fire that almost destroyed Kyoto.* His eyewitness account of the famine of 1181 is one of the classic examples of Japanese prose:

> In all the provinces people left their lands and sought other parts, or, forgetting their homes, went to live among the hills. All kinds of prayers were begun, and even religious practices which were unusual in ordinary times were revived, but to no purpose whatever. . . . The inhabitants of the capital offered to sacrifice their valuables of all kinds, one after another (for food), but nobody cared to look at them. . . . Beggars swarmed by the roadsides, and our ears were filled with the sound of their lamentations. . . . Everybody was dying of hunger; and as time went on our condition became as desperate as that of the fish in the small pool of the story. At last even respectable-looking people wearing hats, and with their feet covered, might be seen begging importunately from door to door. Sometimes, while you wondered how such utterly wretched creatures could walk at all, they fell down before your eyes. By garden walls or on the roadsides countless persons died of famine, and as their bodies were not removed, the world was filled with evil odors. As their bodies changed there were many sights which the eyes could not endure to see. . . . People who had no means pulled down their houses and sold the materials in the market. It was said that a load for one man was not enough to provide him with sustenance for a single day. It was strange to see, among this firewood, pieces adorned in places with vermilion, or silver, or gold leaf. . . . Another very pitiable thing was that when there were a man and a woman

---

* The worst of the many fires in Japanese history was that which completely wiped out Yedo (Tokyo) in 1657, with the loss of 100,000 lives.

who were strongly attached to each other, the one whose love was the greater, and whose devotion was the more profound, always died first. The reason was that they put themselves last, and, whether man or woman, gave up to the dearly beloved one anything which they might chance to have begged. As a matter of course, parents died before their children. Again, infants might be seen clinging to the breast of their mother, not knowing that she was already dead. . . . The number of those who died in central Kyoto during the fourth and fifth months alone was 42,300.[40]

Contrast with this brutal interlude in the growth of the soil Kaempfer's bright picture of Japanese handicrafts as he saw them in the Kyoto of 1691:

Kyoto is the great magazine of all Japanese manufactures and commodities, and the chief mercantile town in the Empire. There is scarce a house in this large capital where there is not something made or sold. Here they refine copper, coin money, print books, weave the richest stuffs with gold and silver flowers. The best and scarcest dyes, the most artful carvings, all sorts of musical instruments, pictures, japanned cabinets, all sorts of things wrought in gold and other metals, particularly in steel, as the best tempered blades and other arms, are made here in the utmost perfection, as are also the richest dresses, and after the best fashion; all sorts of toys, puppets moving their heads of themselves, and numberless other things too numerous to be mentioned here. In short, there is nothing that can be thought of but what may be found at Kyoto, and nothing, though ever so neatly wrought, can be imported from abroad but what some artist or other in this capital will undertake to imitate. . . . There are but few houses in all the chief streets where there is not something to be sold, and for my part I could not help admiring whence they can have customers enough for such an immense quantity of goods.[41]

All the arts and industries of China had long since been imported into Japan; and as today Japan begins to excel her Western instructors in economy and efficiency of mechanical production,[42] so during the Tokugawa Shogunate her handicraftsmen began to rival, and sometimes to excel, the Chinese and Koreans from whom they had learned their art. Most of the work, in the manner of medieval Europe, was done in the home by families who passed down their occupation and their skill from father to son, and often took the name of their craft; and, again as in our Middle Ages, great guilds were formed, not so much of simple workers as of masters who mercilessly exploited the artisans, and zealously restricted the admission of new members to the guilds.⁴³ One of the most powerful of the guilds was that of the money-changers, who accepted deposits, issued vouchers and promissory notes, made loans to commerce, industry and government, and (by 1636) performed all the major functions of finance.⁴⁴ Rich merchants and financiers rose to prominence in the cities, and began to look with jealous eye upon the exclusive political power of a feudal aristocracy that angered them by scorning the pursuit of gold. Slowly, throughout the Tokugawa era, the mercantile wealth of the nation grew, until at last it was ready to coöperate with American gifts and European guns in bursting the shell of the old Japan.

IV. THE PEOPLE

Stature—Cosmetics—Costume—Diet—Etiquette—"Sake"—The tea ceremony—The flower ceremony—Love of nature—Gardens—Homes

This most important people in the contemporary political world is modest in stature, averaging five feet three-and-a-half inches for the men, four feet ten-and-a-half inches for the women. One of their great warriors, Tamura Maro, was described as "a man of very fine figure, . . . five feet five inches tall."⁴⁵ Some dieticians believe that this brevity is due to insufficiency of lime in the Japanese diet, due in turn to lack of milk, and this to the expensiveness of grazing areas in so crowded a land;⁴⁶ but such a theory, like everything in dietetics, must be looked upon as highly hypothetical. The women seem fragile and weak, but probably their energy, like that of the men, is one of nervous courage rather than of physical strength, and cannot be seen outside of emergencies. Their beauty is a matter of expression and carriage as well as of feature; their dainty grace is a typical product of Japanese art.

Cosmetics are popular and ancient in Japan as elsewhere; even in the early days of Kyoto's leadership every male of quality rouged his cheeks, powdered his face, sprinkled his clothes with perfume, and carried a mirror with him wherever he went. ⁴⁷ Powder has been for centuries the female complexion of Japan; the Lady Sei Shonagon, in her *Pillow Sketches* (ca. 991 A.D.), says demurely: "I bent my head down and hid my face with my sleeve at the risk of brushing off my powder and appearing with a spotted face."[48] Fashionable ladies rouged their cheeks, colored their nails, and occasionally gilded the lower lip; to complete their toilette sixteen articles were required in the seventeenth century, and twenty in the eighteenth. They recognized fifteen styles of front hair and twelve styles of back hair; they shaved their eyebrows, painted "crescent moons" or other forms in their place, or substituted for them two little black spots high up on the forehead, to match their artificially blackened teeth. To construct the architecture of a woman's hair was a task that took from two to six hours of expert labor. In the Heian epoch the majority of the men shaved the crown of the head, gathered the rest in a queue, and laid the queue athwart the crown so as to divide it into equal halves. Beards, though sparse, were a necessity; those who had none by nature wore false ones, and a pair of tweezers for the care of the beard was furnished to every guest at any fashionable house.[49]

Japanese costume, in the Nara age, imitated the Chinese, with tunic and trousers covered by a tight robe. In the Kyoto period the robe became looser and multiple; men as well as women wore from two to twenty superimposed robes, whose colors were determined by the rank of the wearer, and provided many prismatic displays at the edges of the sleeves. At one time the lady's sleeves reached below her knees, and bore, each of them, a little bell that tinkled as she walked. On days when the streets were wet from rain or snow they walked on wooden slippers raised by wooden cleats an inch or so above the earth. In the Tokugawa era dress became so extravagant that the *shoguns*, careless of history, tried to check it by sumptuary laws; silk-lined and embroidered breeches and socks were outlawed, beards were forbidden, certain ways of wearing the hair were proscribed, and at times the police were instructed to arrest anyone wearing fine garments in the street. Occasionally these laws were obeyed; for the most part they were circumvented by the ingenuity of human folly.[50] In time the rage for plural robes abated, and the Japanese became one of the most simply, modestly and tastefully dressed of peoples.

Nor did they yield to any other nation in habits of cleanliness. Among those who could afford it clothes were changed three times a day; and poor as well as rich bathed the body daily.[51]* In the villages the people bathed in tubs outside their doors in summer, while gossiping industriously with their neighbors.[52] Hot baths at 110 degrees Fahrenheit were used as a method of keeping warm in winter. Diet was simple and wholesome until luxury came;

---

* In 1905 Tokyo had 1100 public baths, in which 500,000 persons bathed daily for 1¼ cents.[53]

the early Chinese descriptions of the Japanese noted that "they are a long-lived race, and persons who have reached one hundred years are very common."[54] The staple food of the people was rice, to which were added fish, vegetables, sea-weed, fruit and meat according to income. Meat was a rare dish except among the aristocracy and the soldiery. On a regimen of rice, a little fish and no meat, the coolie developed good lungs and tough muscles, and could run from fifty to eighty miles in twenty-four hours without distress; when he added meat he lost this capacity.[55]* The emperors of the Kyoto period made pious efforts to enforce Buddhist dietary laws by forbidding the slaughter or eating of animals; but when the people found that the priests themselves clandestinely violated these laws, they took to meat as a delicacy, and used it to excess whenever their means permitted.[57]

To the Japanese, as to the Chinese and the French, fine cooking was an essential grace of civilization. Its practitioners, like artists and philosophers, divided into warring schools, and fought one another with recipes. Table manners became at least as important as religion; elaborate enactments prescribed the order and quantity of bites, and the posture of the body at each stage of the meal. Ladies were forbidden to make a sound while eating or drinking; but men were expected to indicate their appreciation of a host's generosity by a little grateful belching.[58] The diners sat on one or two heels on mats, at a table raised but a few inches above the floor; or the food might be laid upon the mat, without any table at all. Usually the meal was begun with a hot drink of rice-wine; for had not the poet Tahito declared, far back in the seventh century, that *sake* was the one solution for all the problems of life?

> That which the seven sages sought,
> Those men of olden times,
> Was *sake*, beyond all doubt.
>
> Instead of holding forth
> Wisely, with grave mien,
> How much better to drink *sake*,
> To get drunk, and to shout aloud.
>
> Since it is true
> That death comes at last for all,
> Let us be joyful
> While we are alive.

---

* On the other hand those Japanese who have adopted a non-physical life while continuing to eat large quantities of rice are succumbing to digestive disorders.[56]

Even the jewel that sparkles in the night
Is less to us than the uplifting of the heart
Which comes by drinking *sake*.[59]

More sacred than *sake*, to the aristocracy, was tea. This gracious remedy for the tastelessness of boiled water was introduced from China into Japan, unsuccessfully in 805, successfully in 1191. At first the people shunned the leaf as a poison, and would have nothing to do with it; but when a few cups of the outlandish beverage quickly cleared the head of a *shogun* who had drunk too much *sake* the night before, the Japanese recognized the utility of tea. Its costliness added to its charm: tiny jars of it were given as precious gifts, even to reward warriors for mighty deeds of valor, and the fortunate possessors gathered their friends about them to share the royal drink. The Japanese made a graceful and complex ceremony out of tea-drinking, and Rikyu established for it six inviolable rules that raised it to a cult. The signal bidding the guests to enter the tea pavilion, said Rikyu, must be given by wooden clappers; the ablution bowl must be kept constantly filled with pure water; any guest conscious of inadequacy or inelegance in the furniture or the surroundings must leave at once, and as quietly as possible; no trivial gossip was to be indulged in, but only matters of noble and serious import were to be discussed; no word of deceit or flattery should pass any lip; and the affair should not last beyond four hours. No tea-pot was used at such *Cha-no-yu* ("hot water for tea") reunions; powdered tea was placed in a cup of choice design, hot water was added, and the cup was passed from guest to guest, each wiping its rim carefully with a napkin. When the last drinker had consumed the last drop the cup was passed around again, to be critically examined as a work of ceramic art.[60] In this way the tea-ceremony stimulated the potters to produce ever lovelier cups and bowls, and helped to form the manners of the Japanese into tranquillity, courtesy and charm.*

Flowers, too, became a cult in Japan, and the same Rikyu who formulated the ritual of tea valued his flowers as much as his cups. When he heard that Hideyoshi was coming to see his famous collection of chrysanthemums, Rikyu destroyed all the blossoms in his garden but one, so that

---

* The tea-crop, of course, is now one of the important products of Japan. The Dutch East India Co. appears to have brought Europe its first tea in 1610, and to have sold it at some $4.00 a pound. Jonas Hanway, in 1756, argued that European men were losing their stature, and women their beauty, through the drinking of tea; and reformers denounced the custom as a filthy barbarism.[61]

this might shine unrivaled before the terrible *shogun.**[62] The art of flower-arrangement grew step by step with "Teaism" in the fifteenth and six-teenth centuries, and became in the seventeenth an independent devotion. "Flower-masters" arose who taught men and women how flowers should be grown in the garden and placed in the home; it was not enough, they said, to admire the blossoms, but one must learn to see as much loveliness in the leaf, the bough or the stalk as in the flower, as much beauty in one flower as in a thousand; and one must arrange them with a view not merely to color but to grouping and line.[64] Tea, flowers, poetry, and the dance became requisites of womanhood among the aristocracy of Japan.

Flowers are the religion of the Japanese; they worship them with sacrificial fervor and national accord. They watch for the blossoms appropriate to each season; and when, for a week or two in early April, the cherry-tree blooms, all Japan seems to leave its work to gaze at it, or even to make pilgrimages to places where the miracle is most abundant and complete.† The cherry-tree is cultivated not for any fruit but for its blossom—the emblem of the faithful warrior ready to die for his country at the moment of his fullest life.[65] Criminals *en route* to execution will sometimes ask for a flower.[66] The Lady Chiyo, in a famous poem, tells of a girl who came to draw water from a well, but, finding bucket and rope entwined with con-volvuli, went elsewhere for water rather than break the tendrils.[67] "The heart of man," says Tsurayuki, "can never be understood; but in my native village the flowers give forth their perfume as before."[68] These simple lines are among the greatest of Japanese poems, for they express in perfect and irreducible form a profound characteristic of a race, and one of the rare conclusions of philosophy. Never has another people shown such love of nature as one finds in Japan; nowhere else have men and women accepted so completely all natural moods of earth, sky and sea; nowhere else have men so carefully cultivated gardens, or nourished plants in their growth, or tended them in the home. Japan did not have to wait for a Rousseau or a Wordsworth to tell it that mountains were sublime, or that lakes might be beautiful. There is hardly a dwelling in Japan without a vase of flowers in it, and hardly a poem in Japanese literature without a landscape in its lines. As Oscar Wilde thought that England should

---

* The *Taiko* and the Tea-Master loved each other like geniuses. The first accused the other of dishonesty, and was accused in turn of seducing Rikyu's daughter. In the end Rikyu committed *hara-kiri.*[63]

† Similar pilgrimages are made to see the maple leaves turning in the fall.

not fight France because the French wrote perfect prose, so America might seek peace to the end with a nation that thirsts for beauty almost as passionately as it hungers for power.

The art of gardening was imported from China along with Buddhism and tea; but here again the Japanese transformed creatively what they had absorbed through imitation. They found an esthetic value in asymmetry, a new charm in the surprises of unhackneyed forms; they dwarfed trees and shrubs by confining their roots in pots, and with impish humor and tyrannical affection trained them into shapes that might within a garden wall represent the wind-twisted trees of stormy Japan; they searched the craters of their volcanoes and the most precipitous shores of their seas to find rocks fused into metal by hidden fires, or moulded by patient breakers into quaint and gnarled forms; they dug little lakes, channeled roving rivulets, and crossed them with bridges that seemed to spring from the natural growth of the woods; and through all these varied formations they wore, with imperceptible design, footpaths that would lead now to startling novelties and now to cool and silent retreats.

Where space and means allowed they attached their homes to their gardens rather than their gardens to their homes. Their houses were frail but pretty; earthquakes made tall buildings dangerous, but the carpenter and woodworker knew how to bind eaves, gables and lattices into a dwelling ascetically simple, esthetically perfect, and architecturally unique. Here were no curtains, sofas, beds, tables or chairs, no obtrusive display of the dweller's wealth and luxury, no museum of pictures, statuary or bric-a-brac; but in some alcove a blossoming branch, on the wall a silk or paper painting or specimen of calligraphy, on the matted floor a cushion fronted by a lectern and flanked by a bookcase on one side and an arm-rest on the other, and, hidden in a cupboard, mattresses and coverings to be spread on the floor when the time should come to sleep. Within such modest quarters, or in the peasant's fragile hut, the Japanese family lived, and through all storms of war and revolution, of political corruption and religious strife, carried on the life and civilization of the Sacred Isles.

V. THE FAMILY

The paternal autocrat—The status of woman—Children—Sexual morality—The "geisha"—Love

For the real source of social order, in the Orient even more than in the West, was the family; and the omnipotence of the father, in Japan as throughout the East, expressed not a backward condition of society but a preference for familial rather than political government. The individual was less important in the East than in the Occident because the state was weaker, and required a strongly organized and disciplined family to take the place of a far-reaching and pervasive central authority. Freedom was conceived in terms of the family rather than of the individual; for (the family being the economic unit of production as well as the social unit of order) success or failure, survival or death, came not to the separate person but to the family. The power of the father was tyrannical, but it had the painless grace of seeming natural, necessary, and human. He could dismiss a son-in-law or a daughter-in-law from the patriarchal household, while keeping the grandchildren with him; he could kill a child convicted of unchastity or a serious crime; he could sell his children into slavery or prostitution;* and he could divorce his wife with a word.[70] If he was a simple commoner he was expected to be monogamous; but if he belonged to the higher classes he was entitled to keep concubines, and no notice was to be taken of his occasional infidelities.[71] When Christianity entered Japan, native writers complained that it disturbed the peace of families by insinuating that concubinage and adultery were sins.[72]

As in China, the position of woman was higher in the earlier than in the later stages of the civilization. Six empresses appear among the rulers of the imperial age; and at Kyoto women played an important, indeed a leading, rôle in the social and literary life of the nation. In that heyday of Japanese culture, if we may hazard hypotheses in such esoteric fields, the wives outstripped their husbands in adultery, and sold their virtue for an epigram.[73] The Lady Sei Shonagon describes a youth about to send a love-note to his mistress, but interrupting it to make love to a passing girl; and this amiable essayist adds: "I wonder if, when this lover sent his letter, tied with a dewy spray of *hagi* flower, his messenger hesitated to present it to the lady because she also had a guest?"[74] Under the influence of feudal militarism, and in the natural and historical alternation of laxity and re-

---

* This was done only in the lower classes, and in extreme need.[69]

straint, the Chinese theory of the subjection of woman to man won a wide influence, "society" became predominantly male, and women were dedicated to the "Three Obediences"—to father, husband and son. Education, except in etiquette, was rarely wasted upon them, and fidelity was exacted on penalty of death. If a husband caught his wife in adultery he was authorized to kill her and her paramour at once; to which the subtle Iyeyasu added that if he killed the woman but spared the man he was himself to be put to death.[76] The philosopher Ekken advised the husband to divorce his wife if she talked too loudly or too long; but if the husband happened to be dissolute and brutal, said Ekken, the wife should treat him with doubled kindness and gentleness. Under this rigorous and long-continued training the Japanese woman became the most industrious, faithful and obedient of wives, and harassed travelers began to wonder whether a system that had produced such gracious results should not be adopted in the West.[77]

Contrary to the most ancient and sacred customs of Oriental society, fertility was not encouraged in *Samurai* Japan. As the population grew the little islands felt themselves crowded, and it became a matter of good repute in a *Samurai* not to marry before thirty, and not to have more children than two.[78] Nevertheless every man was expected to marry and beget children. If his wife proved barren he could divorce her; and if she gave him only daughters he was admonished to adopt a son, lest his name and property perish; for daughters could not inherit.[79] Children were trained in the Chinese virtues and literature of filial piety, for on this, as the source of family order, rested the discipline and security of the state. The Empress Koken, in the eighth century, ordered every Japanese household to provide itself with a copy of the "Classic of Filial Piety," and every student in the provincial schools or the universities was required to become a master of it. Except for the *Samurai*, whose loyalty to his lord was his highest obligation, filial piety was the basic and supreme virtue of the Japanese; even his relation to the emperor was to be one of filial affection and obedience. Until the West came, with its disruptive ideas of individual freedom, this cardinal virtue constituted nearly all the moral code of the commoner in Japan. The conversion of the islands to Christianity was made almost impossible by the Biblical command that a man should leave his father and his mother and cleave to his wife.[80]

Other virtues than obedience and loyalty were less emphasized than in contemporary Europe. Chastity was desirable, and some higher-class women killed themselves when their virginity was threatened;[81] but a single lapse was not synonymous with ruin. The most famous of Japanese novels, the *Genji Monogatari*, is an epic of aristocratic seduction; and the most famous of Japanese essays, the *Pillow Sketches* of the Lady Sei Shonagon, reads in places like a treatise on the etiquette of sin.[82] The desires of the flesh were looked upon as natural, like hunger and thirst, and thousands of men, many of them respectable husbands, crowded, at night, the *Yoshiwara*, or "Flower District," of Tokyo. There, in the most orderly disorderly houses in the world, fifteen thousand trained and licensed courtesans sat of an evening behind their lattices, gorgeously attired and powder-white, ready to provide song, dance and venery for unmated or ill-mated men.[83]

The best educated of the courtesans were the *geisha* girls, whose very name indicated that they were persons (*sha*) capable of an artistic performance (*gei*). Like the *hetairai* of Greece they affected literature as well as love, and seasoned their promiscuity with poetry. The *Shogun* Iyenari (1787-1836), who had already (1791) forbidden mixed bathing as occasionally encouraging immorality,[84] issued a rigorous edict against the *geisha* in 1822, describing her as "a female singer who, magnificently appareled, hires herself out to amuse guests at restaurants, ostensibly by dancing and singing, but really by practices of a very different character."[85] These women were henceforth to be classed as prostitutes, along with those "numberless wenches" who, in Kaempfer's day, filled every tea-shop in the village and every inn on the road.[86] Nevertheless, parties and families continued to invite the *geisha* to provide entertainment at social affairs; finishing schools were established where older *geisha* trained young apprentices in their varied arts; and periodically, at the *Kaburenjo*, teachers and pupils served ceremonial tea, and gave a public performance of their more presentable accomplishments. Parents hard put to support their daughters sometimes, with their manipulated "consent," apprenticed them to the *geisha* for a consideration; and a thousand Japanese novels have told tales of girls who sold themselves to the trade to save their families from starvation.[87]

These customs, however startling, do not differ essentially from the habits and institutions of the Occident, except perhaps in candor, refinement and grace. The vast majority of Japanese girls, we are assured, remained as chaste as the virgins of the West.[88] Despite such frank arrangements the Japanese managed to live lives of comparative order and decency, and though they did not often allow love to determine marriage for life, they were capable of the tenderest affection for the objects of their desire. Instances are frequent, in the current history as well as in the imaginative literature of Japan, where young men and women have killed themselves in the hope of enjoying in eternity the unity forbidden them by their parents on earth.[89] Love is not the major theme of Japanese poetry, but here and there its note is struck with unmatched simplicity, sincerity and depth.

> Oh! that the white waves far out
> On the Sea of Ise
> Were but flowers,
> That I might gather them
> And bring them as a gift to my love.[90]

And, again with characteristic mingling of nature and feeling, the great Tsurayuki tells in four lines the story of his rejected love:

> Naught is so fleeting as the cherry-flower,
> You say . . . yet I remember well the hour
> When life's bloom withered at one spoken word—
> And not a breath of wind had stirred.[91]

VI. THE SAINTS

Religion in Japan — The transformation of Buddhism — The priests — Sceptics

That same devotion which speaks in patriotism and love, in affection for parents, children, mate and fatherland, inevitably sought in the universe as a whole some central power to which it might attach itself in loyalty, and through which it might derive some value and significance larger than one person, and more lasting than one life. The Japanese are only a moderately religious people—not profoundly and overwhelmingly religious like the Hindus, nor passionately and fanatically religious like the tortured saints of medieval Catholicism or the warring saints of the Reformation; and yet they are distinctly more given to piety and prayer, and a happy-ending philosophy, than their sceptical cousins across the Yellow Sea.

Buddhism came from its founder a cloud of pessimistic exhortation, inviting men to death; but under the skies of Japan it was soon transformed into a cult of protecting deities, pleasant ceremonies, joyful festivals, Rousseauian pilgrimages, and a consoling paradise. It is true that there were hells too in Japanese Buddhism—indeed, one hundred and twenty-eight of them, designed for every purpose and enemy. There was a world of demons as well as of saints, and a personal Devil (*Oni*) with horns, flat nose, claws and fangs; he lived in some dark, northeastern realm, to which he would, now and then, lure women to give him pleasure, or men to provide him with proteins.[92] But on the other hand there were *Bodhisattwas* ready to transfer to human beings a portion of the grace they had accumulated by many incarnations of virtuous living; and there were gracious deities, like Our Lady Kwannon and the Christlike Jizo, who were the very essence of divine tenderness. Worship was only partly by prayer at the household altars and the temple shrines; a large part of it consisted of merry processions in which religion was subordinated to gayety, and piety took the form of feminine fashion-displays and masculine revelry. The more serious devotee might cleanse his spirit by praying for a quarter of an hour under a waterfall in the depth of winter; or he might go on pilgrimages from shrine to shrine of his sect, meanwhile feasting his soul on the beauty of his native land. For the Japanese could choose among many varieties of Buddhism: he might seek self-realization and bliss through the quiet practices of *Zen* ("meditation"); he might follow the fiery Nichiren into the Lotus Sect, and find salvation through learning the "Lotus Law"; he might join the Spirit Sect, and fast and pray until Buddha appeared to him in the flesh; he might be comforted by the Sect of the Pure Land, and be saved by faith alone; or he might find his way in patient pilgrimage to the monastery of Koyasan, and attain paradise by being buried in ground made holy by the bones of Kobo Daishi, the great scholar, saint and artist who, in the ninth century, had founded *Shingon*, the Sect of the True Word.

All in all, Japanese Buddhism was one of the pleasantest of man's myths. It conquered Japan peacefully, and complaisantly found room, within its theology and its pantheon, for the doctrines and deities of *Shinto*: Buddha was amalgamated with Amaterasu, and a modest place was set apart, in Buddhist temples, for a *Shinto* shrine. The Buddhist priests of the earlier centuries were men of devotion, learning and kindliness, who profoundly influenced and advanced Japanese letters and arts; some of them were great painters or sculptors, and some were scholars whose painstaking translation of Buddhist and Chinese literature proved a fertile stimulus to the cultural development of Japan. Success, however, ruined the later priests; many became lazy and greedy (note the jolly caricatures so often made of them by Japanese carvers in ivory or wood); and some traveled so far from Buddha as to organize their own armies for the establishment or maintenance of political power.[93] Since they were providing the first necessity of life—a consolatory hope—their industry flourished even when others decayed; their wealth grew from century to century, while the poverty of the people remained.[94] The priests assured the faithful that a man of forty could purchase another decade of life by paying forty temples to say masses in his name; at fifty he could buy ten years more by engaging fifty temples; at sixty years sixty temples—and so till, through insufficient piety, he died.*[95] Under the Tokugawa regime the monks drank bibulously, kept mistresses candidly, practised pederasty,† and sold the cozier places in the hierarchy to the highest bidders.[96]

During the eighteenth century Buddhism seems to have lost its hold upon the nation; the *shoguns* went over to Confucianism, Mabuchi and Moto-ori led a movement for the restoration of *Shinto*, and scholars like Ichikawa and Arai Hakuseki attempted a rationalist critique of religious belief. Ichikawa argued boldly that verbal tradition could never be quite as trustworthy as written record; that writing had not come to Japan until almost a thousand years after the supposed origin of the islands and their inhabitants from the spear-drops and loins of the gods; that the claim of the imperial family to divine origin was merely a political device; and that if the ancestors of men were not human beings they were much more likely to have been animals than gods.[99] The civilization of the old Japan, like so many others, had begun with religion and was ending with philosophy.

---

* "It was mainly in seasons when people were starving," says Murdoch, "or dying in tens of thousands from pestilence, that the monks in the great Kyoto and Nara monasteries fared most sumptuously; for it was in times like these that believers were most lavish in their gifts and benefactions."[96]

† "In 1454 . . . boys were often sold to the priests, who shaved their eyebrows, powdered their faces, dressed them in female garb, and put them to the vilest of uses; for since the days of Yoshimitsu, who had set an evil example in this as in so many other matters, the practice of pederasty had become very common, especially in the monasteries, although it was by no means confined to them."[97]

VII. THE THINKERS

*Confucius reaches Japan—A critic of religion—The religion of
scholarship—Kaibara Ekken—On education—On pleasure—
The rival schools — A Japanese Spinoza — Ito Jinsai—
Ito Togai—Ogyu Sorai—The war of the scholars—
Mabuchi—Moto-ori*

Philosophy, like religion, came to Japan from China. And as Buddhism
had reached Nippon six hundred years after its entrance into the Middle
Flowery People's Kingdom, so philosophy, in the form of Sung Confucianism, awoke to consciousness in Japan almost four hundred years
after China had given it a second birth. About the middle of the sixteenth
century a scion of Japan's most famous family, Fujiwara Seigwa, discontent with the knowledge that he had received as a monk, and having heard
of great sages in China, resolved to go and study there. Intercourse with
China having been forbidden in 1552, the young priest made plans to cross
the water in a smuggling vessel. While waiting in an inn at the port he
overheard a student reading aloud, in Japanese, from a Chinese volume on
Confucius. Seigwa was overjoyed to find that the book was Chu Hsi's
commentary on "The Great Learning." "This," he exclaimed, "is what I
have so long desired." By sedulous searching he obtained a copy of this
and other products of Sung philosophy, and became so absorbed in their
discussions that he forgot to go to China. Within a few years he had gathered about him a group of young scholars, who looked upon the Chinese
philosophers as the revelation of a brave new world of secular thought.
Iyeyasu heard of these developments, and asked Seigwa to come and expound to him the Confucian classics; but the proud priest, preferring the
quiet of his study, sent a brilliant pupil in his place. Nevertheless the more
active-minded youths of his time made a pathway to his door, and his lectures attracted so much attention that the Buddhist monks of Kyoto complained, saying it was an outrage that anyone but an orthodox and practising priest should deliver public lectures or teach the people.[100] The matter
was simplified by Seigwa's sudden death (1619).

The pupil whom he had sent to Iyeyasu soon outranked him in fame and
influence. The first Tokugawa *shoguns* took a fancy to Hayashi Razan,
and made him their counsellor and the formulator of their public pronouncements. Iyemitsu set a fashion for the nobility by attending

Hayashi's lectures in 1630; and soon the young Confucian had so filled his hearers with enthusiasm for Chinese philosophy that he had no trouble in winning them from both Buddhism and Christianity to the simple moral creed bequeathed to the Far East by the sage of Shantung. Christian theology, he told them, was a medley of incredible fancies, while Buddhism was a degenerate doctrine that threatened to weaken the fibre and morale of the Japanese nation. "You priests," said Razan, "maintain that this world is impermanent and ephemeral. By your enchantments you cause people to forget the social relations; you make an end of all the duties and all the proprieties. Then you proclaim: 'Man's path is full of sins; leave your father and mother, leave your master, leave your children, and seek for salvation.' Now I tell you that I have studied much; but I have nowhere found that there was a path for a man apart from loyalty to one's lord, and of filial piety towards one's parents."[101] Hayashi was enjoying an old age of quiet renown when the great fire of Tokyo, in 1657, included him among its hundred thousand casualties. His disciples ran to warn him of the danger, but he merely nodded his head, and turned back to his book. When the flames were actually around him he ordered a palanquin, and was carried away in it while still reading his book. Like countless others, he passed that night under the stars; and three days later he died of the cold that he had caught during the conflagration.

Nature sought to atone for his death by giving Japan, in the following year, one of the most enthusiastic of Confucians. Muro Kyuso chose as his patron deity the God of Learning. Before Michizane's shrine he spent, in his youth, an entire night in prayer; and then he dedicated himself to knowledge with youthful resolutions strangely akin to those of his contemporary, Spinoza.*

> I will arise every morning at six o'clock and retire each evening at twelve o'clock.
> Except when prevented by guests, sickness or other unavoidable circumstances, I will not be idle. . . .
> I will not speak falsehoods.
> I will avoid useless words, even with inferiors.
> I will be temperate in eating and drinking.
> If lustful desires arise I will destroy them at once, without nourishing them at all.

---

* Cf. the opening pages of *De Intellectus Emendatione*.

Wandering thought destroys the value of reading. I will be careful to guard against lack of concentration, and over-haste.

I will seek self-culture, not allowing my mind to be disturbed by
the desire for fame or gain.

Engraving these rules on my heart I will attempt to follow them.
The gods be my witness.[102]

Nevertheless, Kyuso did not preach a scholastic seclusion, but with the
broad-mindedness of a Goethe directed character into the stream of the
world:

Seclusion is one method, and is good; but a superior man rejoices
when his friends come. A man polishes himself by association with
others. Every man who desires learning should seek to be polished
in this way. But if he shuts himself away from everything and
everybody, he is guilty of violating the great way. . . . The Way of
the Sages is not sundered from matters of everyday life. . . . Though
the Buddhists withdraw themselves from human relations, cutting
out the relation of master and subject, parent and child, they are
not able to cut out love from themselves. . . . It is selfishness to seek
happiness in the future world. . . . Think not that God is something
distant, but seek for him in your own hearts; for the heart is the
abode of God.[103]

The most attractive of these early Japanese Confucians is not usually
classed among the philosophers, for like Goethe and Emerson he had the
skill to phrase his wisdom gracefully, and jealous literature claims him for
her own. Like Aristotle Kaibara Ekken was the son of a physician, and
passed from medicine to a cautious empirical philosophy. Despite a busy
public career, including many official posts, he found time to become the
greatest scholar of his day. His books numbered more than a hundred,
and made him known throughout Japan; for they were written not in Chinese (then the language of his fellow philosophers) but in such simple
Japanese that any literate person might understand them. Despite his learning and renown he had, along with the vanity of every writer, the humility
of every sage. Once, says tradition, a passenger on a vessel plying along
the Japanese coast undertook to lecture to his fellow travelers on the ethics
of Confucius. At first every one attended with typical Japanese curiosity
and eagerness to learn; but as the speaker went on his audience, finding
him a bore who had no nose for distinguishing a live fact from a dead one,

melted swiftly away, until only one listener remained. This solitary auditor, however, followed the discourse with such devout concentration that the lecturer, having finished, inquired his name. "Kaibara Ekken," was the quiet reply. The orator was abashed to discover that for an hour or more he had been attempting to instruct in Confucianism the most celebrated Confucian master of the age.[104]

Ekken's philosophy was as free from theology as K'ung's, and clung agnostically to the earth. "Foolish men, while doing crooked things, offer their prayers to questionable gods, striving to obtain happiness."[105] With him philosophy was an effort to unify experience into wisdom, and desire into character; and it seemed to him more pressing and important to unify character than to unify knowledge. He speaks with strangely contemporary pertinence:

> The aim of learning is not merely to widen knowledge but to form character. Its object is to make us true men, rather than learned men. . . . The moral teaching which was regarded as the trunk of all learning in the schools of the olden days is hardly studied in our schools today, because of the numerous branches of study required. No longer do men deem it worth while to listen to the teachings of the hoary sages of the past. Consequently the amiable relations between master and servant, superior and inferior, older and younger are sacrificed on the altar of the god called "Individual Right." . . . The chief reason why the teachings of the sages are not more appreciated by the people is because scholars endeavor to show off their learning, rather than to make it their endeavor to live up to the teachings of the sages.[106]

The young men of his time seem to have reproved him for his conservatism, for he flings at them a lesson which every vigorous generation has to relearn.

> Children, you may think an old man's words wearisome; yet, when your father or grandfather teaches, do not turn your head away, but listen. Though you may think the tradition of your family stupid, do not break it into pieces, for it is the embodiment of the wisdom of your fathers.[107]

Perhaps he deserved reproof, for the most famous of his books, the *Onna Daikaku*, or "The Great Learning for Women," had a strong reactionary influence on the position of women in Japan. But he was no gloomy preacher intent on finding sin in every delight; he knew that one task of the educator is to teach us how to enjoy our environment, as well as (if we can) to understand and control it.

Do not let a day slip by without enjoyment. . . . Do not allow yourself to be tormented by the stupidity of others. . . . Remember that from its earliest beginnings the world has never been free from fools. . . . Let us not then distress ourselves, nor lose our pleasure, even though our own children, brothers and relations, happen to be selfish, ignoring our best efforts to make them otherwise. . . . *Sake* is the beautiful gift of Heaven. Drunk in small quantities it expands the heart, lifts the downcast spirit, drowns cares, and improves the health. Thus it helps a man and also his friends to enjoy pleasures. But he who drinks too much loses his respectability, becomes over-talkative, and utters abusive words like a madman. . . . Enjoy *sake* by drinking just enough to give you a slight exhilaration, and thus enjoy seeing flowers when they are just bursting into bloom. To drink too much and spoil this great gift of Heaven is foolish.[108]

Like most philosophers, he found the last refuge of his happiness in nature.

If we make our heart the fountain-head of pleasure, our eyes and ears the gates of pleasure, and keep away base desires, then our pleasure shall be plentiful; for we can then become the master of mountains, water, moon and flowers. We do not need to ask any man for them, neither, to obtain them, need we pay a single *sen;* they have no specified owner. Those who can enjoy the beauty in the Heaven above and the Earth beneath need not envy the luxury of the rich, for they are richer than the richest. . . . The scenery is constantly changing. No two mornings or two evenings are quite alike. . . . At this moment one feels as if all the beauty of the world had gone. But then the snow begins to fall, and one awakens the next morning to find the village and the mountains transformed into silver, while the once bare trees seem alive with flowers. . . . Winter resembles the night's sleep, which restores our strength and energy. . . .
Loving flowers, I rise early;
Loving the moon, I retire late. . . .
Men come and go like passing streams;
But the moon remains throughout the ages.[109]

In Japan, even more than in China, the influence of Confucius on philosophic thought overwhelmed all the resistance of unplaced rebels on the one hand, and mystic idealists on the other. The *Shushi* school of Seigwa, Razan and Ekken took its name from Chu Hsi, and followed his orthodox and conservative interpretation of the Chinese classics. For a time it was opposed by the *Oyomei* school, which took its lead from Wang Yangming,* known to Nippon as Oyomei. Like Wang, the Japanese philosophers of *Oyomei* sought to deduce right and wrong from the conscience of the individual rather than from the traditions of society and the teachings of the ancient sages. "I had for many years been a devout believer in *Shushi*," says Nakaye Toju (1608-48), "when, by the mercy of Heaven, the collected works of Oyomei were brought for the first time to Japan. Had it not been for the aid of their teaching, my life would have been empty and barren."[110] So Nakaye devoted himself to expounding an idealist monism, in which the world was a unity of *ki* and *ri*—of things (or "modes") and reason or law. God and this unity were one; the world of things was his body, the universal law was his soul.[111] Like Spinoza, Wang Yang-ming and the Scholastics of Europe, Nakaye accepted this universal law with a kind of *amor dei intellectualis*, and accounted good and evil as human terms and prejudices describing no objective entities; and, again strangely like Spinoza, he found a certain immortality in the contemplative union of the individual spirit with the timeless laws or reason of the world.

> Man's mind is the mind of the sensible world, but we have another mind which is called conscience. This is reason itself, and does not belong to form (or "mode"). It is infinite and eternal. As our conscience is one with (the divine or universal) reason, it has no beginning or end. If we act in accord with (such) reason or conscience, we are ourselves the incarnations of the infinite and eternal, and have eternal life.[112]

Nakaye was a man of saintly sincerity, but his philosophy pleased neither the people nor the government. The Shogunate trembled at the notion that every man might judge for himself what was right and what was wrong. When another exponent of *Oyomei*, Kumazawa Banzan, passed from metaphysics to politics, and criticized the ignorance and idleness of the *Samurai*, an order was sent out for his arrest. Kumazawa, recognizing

---

* Cf. page 733 above.

the importance of the heels as especially philosophical organs, fled to the mountains, and passed most of his remaining years in sylvan obscurity.¹¹³ In 1795 an edict went forth against the further teaching of the *Oyomei* philosophy; and so docile was the mind of Japan that from that time on *Oyomei* concealed itself within the phrases of Confucianism, or entered as a modest component into that military *Zen* which, by a typical paradox of history, transformed the pacific faith of Buddha into the inspiration of patriotic warriors.

As Japanese scholarship developed, and became directly acquainted with the writings of Confucius rather than merely with his Sung interpreters, men like Ito Jinsai and Ogyu Sorai established the Classical School of Japanese thought, which insisted on going over the heads of all commentators to the great K'ung himself. Ito Jinsai's family did not agree with him about the value of Confucius; they taunted him with the impracticability of his studies, and predicted that he would die in poverty. "Scholarship," they told him, "belongs to the Chinese. It is useless in Japan. Even though you obtain it you cannot sell it. Far better become a physician and make money." The young student listened without hearing; he forgot the rank and wealth of his family, put aside all material ambition, gave his house and property to a younger brother, and went to live in solitude so that he might study without distraction. He was handsome, and was sometimes mistaken for a prince; but he dressed like a peasant and shunned the public eye. "Jinsai," says a Japanese historian,

> was very poor, so poor that at the end of the year he could not make New Year's rice cakes; but he was very calm about it. His wife came, and kneeling down before him said: "I will do the housework under any circumstances; but there is one thing that is unbearable. Our boy Genso does not understand the meaning of our poverty; he envies the neighbor's children their rice cakes. I scold him, but my heart is torn in two." Jinsai continued to pore over his books without making any reply. Then, taking off his garnet ring, he handed it to his wife, as much as to say, "Sell this, and buy some rice cakes."¹¹⁴

At Kyoto Jinsai opened a private school, and lectured there for forty years, training, all in all, some three thousand students in philosophy. He spoke occasionally of metaphysics, and described the universe as a living organism in which life always overrode death; but like Confucius he had a warm prejudice in favor of the terrestrial practical.

That which is useless in governing the state, or in walking in the way of human relations, is useless. . . . Learning must be active and living; learning must not be mere dead theory or speculation. . . . Those who know the way seek it in their daily life. . . . If apart from human relations we hope to find the way, it is like trying to catch the wind. . . . The ordinary way is excellent; there is no more excellent in the world.[115]

After the death of Jinsai his school and work were carried on by his son, Ito Togai. Togai laughed at fame, and said: "How can you help calling a man, whose name is forgotten as soon as he dies, an animal or sand? But is it not a mistake for man to be eager to make books, or construct sentences, in order that his name may be admired, and may not be forgotten?"[116] He wrote two hundred and forty-two volumes; but for the rest he lived a life of modesty and wisdom. The critics complained that these books were strong in what Molière called *virtus dormitiva;* nevertheless Togai's pupils pointed out that he had written two hundred and forty-two books without saying an unkind word of any other philosopher. When he died they placed this enviable epitaph upon his tomb:

He did not talk about the faults of others. . . .
He cared for nothing but books.
His life was uneventful.[117]

The greatest of these later Confucians was Ogyu Sorai; as he himself put the matter, "From the time of Jimmu, the first emperor of Japan, how few scholars have been my equal!" Unlike Togai he enjoyed controversy, and spoke his mind violently about philosophers living or dead. When an inquiring young man asked him, "What do you like besides reading?" he answered, "There is nothing better than eating burnt beans and criticizing the great men of Japan." "Sorai," said Namikawa Tenjin, "is a very great man, but he thinks that he knows all that there is to be known. This is a bad habit."[118] Ogyu could be modest when he wished: all the Japanese, he said, explicitly including himself, were barbarians; only the Chinese were civilized; and "if there is anything that ought to be said, it has already been said by the ancient kings or Confucius."[119] The *Samurai* and the scholars raged at him, but the reformer *shogun,* Yoshimune, enjoyed his courage, and protected him against the intellectual mob. Sorai set up his rostrum at Yedo, and like Hsün-tze denouncing the sentimentality of Mo Ti, or

Hobbes refuting Rousseau before Rousseau's birth, flung his laughing logic at Jinsai, who had announced that man is naturally good. On the contrary, said Sorai, man is a natural villain, and grasps whatever he can reach; only artificial morals and laws, and merciless education, turn him into a tolerable citizen.

> As soon as men are born, desires spring up. When we cannot realize our desires, which are unlimited, struggle arises; when struggle arises, confusion follows. As the ancient kings hated confusion, they founded propriety and righteousness, and with these governed the desires of the people. . . . Morality is nothing but the necessary means for controlling the subjects of the Empire. It did not originate with nature, nor with the impulses of man's heart, but it was devised by the superior intelligence of certain sages, and authority was given to it by the state.[120]

As if to confirm the pessimism of Sorai, Japanese thought in the century that followed him fell even from the modest level to which its imitation of Confucius had raised it, and lost itself in a bitter ink-shedding war between the idolaters of China and the worshipers of Japan. In this battle of the ancients against the moderns the moderns won by their superior admiration of antiquity. The *Kangakusha*, or (pro-)Chinese scholars, called their own country barbarous, argued that all wisdom was Chinese, and contented themselves with translating and commenting upon Chinese literature and philosophy. The *Wagakusha*, or (pro-)Japanese scholars, denounced this attitude as obscurantist and unpatriotic, and called upon the nation to turn its back upon China and renew its strength at the sources of its own poetry and history. Mabuchi attacked the Chinese as an inherently vicious people, exalted the Japanese as naturally good, and attributed the lack of early or native Japanese literature and philosophy to the fact that the Japanese did not need instruction in virtue or intelligence.*

Inspired by a visit to Mabuchi, a young physician by the name of Motoori Norinaga devoted thirty-four years to writing a forty-four-volume commentary on the *Kojiki*, or "Records of Ancient Events"—the classical

---

* From Sir E. Satow's *paraphrase* of Mabuchi's teaching: "In ancient times, when men's dispositions were straightforward, a complicated system of morals was unnecessary . . . . In those days it was unnecessary to have a doctrine of right and wrong. But the Chinese, being bad at heart . . . were only good on the outside, and their bad acts became of such magnitude that society was thrown into disorder. The Japanese, being straightforward, could do without teaching.[121]

repository of Japanese, especially of *Shinto*, legends. This commentary, the *Kojiki-den*, was a virorous assault upon everything Chinese, in or out of Japan. It boldly upheld the literal truth of the primitive stories that recounted the divine origin of the Japanese islands, emperors and people; and under the very eyes of the Tokugawa regents it stimulated among the intellectuals of Japan that movement back to their own language, ways and traditions which was ultimately to revive *Shinto* as against Buddhism, and restore the supremacy of the emperors over the *shoguns*. "Japan," wrote Moto-ori, "is the country which gave birth to the Goddess of the Sun, Amaterasu; and this fact proves its superiority over all other countries."[122] His pupil Hirata carried on the argument after Moto-ori's death:

> It is most lamentable that so much ignorance should prevail as to the evidences of the two fundamental doctrines that Japan is the country of the gods, and her inhabitants the descendants of the gods. Between the Japanese people and the Chinese, Hindus, Russians, Dutch, Siamese, Cambodians, and other nations of the world, there is a difference of kind rather than of degree. It was not out of vainglory that the inhabitants of this country called it the land of the gods. The gods who created all countries belonged, without exception, to the Divine Age, and were all born in Japan, so that Japan is their native country, and all the world acknowledges the appropriateness of the title. The Koreans were the first to become acquainted with this truth, and from them it was gradually diffused through the globe, and accepted by everyone. . . . Foreign countries were of course produced by the power of the creator gods, but they were not begotten by Izanagi and Izanami, nor did they give birth to the Goddess of the Sun, which is the cause of their inferiority.[123]

Such were the men and the opinions that established the *Sonno Jo-i* movement to "honor the Emperor and expel the foreign barbarians." In the nineteenth century that movement inspired the Japanese people to overthrow the Shogunate and reëstablish the supremacy of the Divine House. In the twentieth it plays a living rôle in nourishing that fiery patriotism which will not be content until the Son of Heaven rules all the fertile millions of the resurrected East.

CHAPTER XXX

The Mind and Art of Old Japan

I. LANGUAGE AND EDUCATION

The language—Writing—Education

MEANWHILE the Japanese had borrowed their systems of writing and education from the barbarian Chinese. Their language was peculiarly their own, presumably Mongolian and akin to the Korean, but not demonstrably derived from this or any other known tongue. It differed especially from the Chinese in being polysyllabic and agglutinative, and yet simple; it had few aspirates, no gutturals, no compound or final consonants (except *n*); and almost every vowel was melodiously long. The grammar, too, was a natural and easy system; it dispensed with number and gender in its nouns, with degrees of comparison in its adjectives, and with personal inflections in its verbs; it had few personal pronouns, and no relative pronouns at all. On the other hand there were inflections of negation and mood in adjectives and verbs; troublesome "postpositions"—modifying suffixes—were used instead of prepositions; and complex honorifics like "Your humble servant" and "Your Excellency" took the place of the first and second personal pronouns.

The language dispensed even with writing, apparently, until Koreans and Chinese brought the art to Japan in the early centuries of our era; and then the Japanese were content for hundreds of years to express their Italianly beautiful speech in the ideographs of the Middle Kingdom. Since a complete Chinese character had to be used for each syllable of a Japanese word, Japanese writing, in the Nara age, was very nearly the most laborious ever known. During the ninth century that law of economy which determines so much of philology brought to the relief of Japan two simplified forms of writing. In each of them a Chinese character, shortened into cursive form, was used to represent one of the forty-seven syllables that constitute the spoken speech of Japan; and this syllabary of forty-seven characters served instead of an alphabet.* Since a large part of Japanese literature is in Chinese, and most of the remainder is written not in the popular syllabary but in a combination of Chinese characters and native alphabets, few Western scholars

---

* The *katakana* script reduced these syllabic symbols to straight lines—as in the "tabloid" press, the larger billboards, and the illuminated signs of modern Japan.[1]

have been able to master it in the original. Our knowledge of Japanese literature is consequently fragmentary and deceptive, and our judgments of it can
be of little worth. The Jesuits, harassed with these linguistic barriers, reported
that the language of the islands had been invented by the Devil to prevent the
preaching of the Gospel to the Japanese.*²

Writing remained for a long time a luxury of the higher classes; until the
latter part of the nineteenth century no pretense was made of spreading the
art among the people. In the Kyoto age the rich families maintained schools
for their children; and the emperors Tenchi and Mommu, at the beginning of
the eighth century, established at Kyoto the first Japanese university. Gradually a system of provincial schools was developed under governmental control; their graduates were eligible to enter the university, and those graduates
of the university who passed the required tests became eligible for public
office. The civil wars of the early feudal period broke down this educational progress, and Japan neglected the arts of the mind until the Tokugawa
Shogunate reorganized peace and encouraged learning and literature. Iyeyasu
was scandalized to find that ninety per cent of the *Samurai* could not read or
write.⁵ In 1630 Hayashi Razan established at Yedo a training-school in public
administration and Confucian philosophy, which later developed into the
University of Tokyo; and Kumazawa, in 1666, founded at Shizutani the first
provincial college. By allowing teachers to wear the sword and boast the
rank of the *Samurai*, the government induced students, doctors and priests to
set up private schools in homes or temples for the provision of elementary
education; in 1750 there were eight hundred such schools, with some forty
thousand students. All these institutions were for the sons of the *Samurai*;
merchants and peasants had to be content with popular lecturers, and only
prosperous women received any formal education. Universal education, in
Japan as in Europe, had to wait for the needs and compulsions of an industrial
life.⁶

---

* Printing, like writing, came from China as part of Buddhist lore; the oldest extant
examples of printing in the world are some Buddhist charms block-printed at the command of the Empress Shotoku in the year 770 A.D.³ Movable type entered from Korea
about 1596, but the expense involved in printing a language still composed of thousands
of characters kept its use from spreading until the Restoration of 1858 opened the doors
to European influence. Even today a Japanese newspaper requires a font of several
thousand characters.⁴ Japanese typography, despite these difficulties, is one of the most
attractive forms of printing in our time.

II. POETRY

*The "Manyoshu"—The "Kokinshu"—Characteristics of Japanese
poetry—Examples—The game of poetry—
The "hokka"-gamblers*

The earliest Japanese literature that has come down to us is poetry, and the earliest Japanese poetry is by native scholars accounted the best. One of the oldest and most famous of Japanese books is the *Manyoshu*, or "Book of Ten Thousand Leaves," in which two editors collected into twenty volumes some 4,500 poems composed during the preceding four centuries. Here in particular appeared the work of Hitomaro and Akahito, the chief poetic glories of the Nara age. When his beloved died, and the smoke from the funeral pyre ascended into the hills, Hitomaro wrote an elegy briefer than *In Memoriam:*

> Oh, is it my beloved, the cloud that wanders
> In the ravine
> Of the deep secluded Hatsuse Mountain?[7]

A further effort to preserve Japanese poetry from time's mortality was made by the Emperor Daigo, who brought together eleven hundred poems of the preceding one hundred and fifty years into an anthology known as the *Kokinshu*—"Poems Ancient and Modern." His chief aide was the poet-scholar Tsurayuki whose preface seems more interesting to us today than the fragments which the book has brought down to us from his laconic muse:

> The poetry of Japan, as a seed, springs from the heart of man creating countless leaves of language. . . . In a world full of things man strives to find words to express the impression left on his heart by sight and sound. . . . And so the heart of man came to find expression in words for his joy in the beauty of blossoms, his wonder at the song of birds, and his tender welcome of the mists that bathe the landscapes, as well as his mournful sympathy with the evanescent morning dew. . . . To verse the poets were moved when they saw the ground white with snowy showers of fallen cherry blossoms on spring mornings, or heard on autumn evenings the rustle of falling leaves; or year after year gazed upon the mirror's doleful reflections of the ravages of time, . . . or trembled as they watched the ephemeral dewdrop quivering on the beaded grass.[8]

Tsurayuki well expressed the recurrent theme of Japanese poetry—the moods and phases, the blossoming and decay, of nature in isles made scenic by volcanoes, and verdant with abundant rain. The poets of Japan delight in the less hackneyed aspects of field and woods and sea—trout splashing in mountain brooks, frogs leaping suddenly into noiseless pools, shores without tides, hills cut with motionless mists, or a drop of rain nestling like a gem in a folded blade of grass. Often they interweave a song of love with their worship of the growing world, or mourn elegiacally the brevity of flowers, love and life. Seldom, however, does this nation of warriors sing of war, and only now and then does its poetry lift the heart in hymns. After the Nara period the great majority of the poems were brief; out of eleven hundred in the *Kokinshu* all but five were in the pithy *tanka* form— five lines of five, seven, five, seven and seven syllables. In these poems there is no rhyme, for the almost invariable vowel ending of Japanese words would have left too narrow a variety for the poet's choice; nor is there any accent, tone or quantity. There are strange tricks of speech: "pillow words," or meaningless prefixes added for the sake of euphony; "prefaces," or sentences prefixed to a poem to round out its form rather than to develop its ideas; and "pivot words" used punningly in startling diversities of sense to bind one sentence with the next. These, to the Japanese, are devices sanctified by time, like alliteration or rhyme to the English; and their popular appeal does not draw the poet into vulgarity. On the contrary these classic poems are essentially aristocratic in thought and form. Born in a courtly atmosphere, they are fashioned with an almost haughty restraint; they seek perfection of modeling rather than novelty of meaning; they suppress rather than express emotion; and they are too proud to be anything but brief. Nowhere else have writers been so expressively reticent; it is as if the poets of Japan had had a mind to atone by their modesty for the braggadocio of her historians. To write three pages about the west wind, say the Japanese, is to show a plebeian verbosity; the real artist must not so much think for the reader as lure him into active thought; he must seek and find one fresh perception that will arouse in him all the ideas and all the feelings which the Occidental poet insists on working out in self-centered and monopolistic detail. Each poem, to the Japanese, must be the quiet record of one moment's inspiration.

So we shall be misled if we seek in these anthologies, or in that *Golden Treasury* of Japan, the *Hyaku-nin-isshu*—"Single Verses by a Hundred People"—any heroic or epic strain, any sustained or lyric flight; these poets, like the rash wits of the Mermaid Tavern, were willing to hang their lives on a line. So when Saigyo Hoshi, having lost his dearest friend, became a monk, and mystically found in the shrines at Ise the solace he was seeking, he wrote no *Adonaîs*, nor even a *Lycidas*, but these simple lines:

> What it is
> That dwelleth here
> I know not;
> Yet my heart is full of gratitude,
> And the tears trickle down.[9]

And when the Lady Kaga no Chiyo lost her husband she wrote, merely:

> All things that seem
> Are but
> One dreamer's dream....
> I sleep.... I wake....
> How wide
> The bed with none beside.[10]

Then, having lost also her child, she added two lines:

> Today, how far may he have wandered,
> The brave hunter of dragon-flies![11]

In the imperial circles at Nara and Kyoto the composition of *tankas* became an aristocratic sport; female chastity, which in ancient India had required an elephant as its price, was often satisfied, at these courts, with thirty-one syllables of poetry cleverly turned.[12] It was a usual thing for the emperor to entertain his guests by handing them words with which to fashion a poem;[13] and the literature of the time refers casually to people conversing with one another in acrostic poetry, or reciting *tankas* as they walked in the streets.[14] Periodically, at the height of the Heian age, the emperor arranged a poetry contest or tournament, in which as many as fifteen hundred candidates competed before learned judges in the making of *tanka* epigrams. In 951 a special Poetry Bureau was established for the management of these jousts, and the winning pieces in each contest were deposited in the archives of the institution.

In the sixteenth century Japanese poetry felt guilty of long-windedness, and decided to shorten the *tanka*—originally the completion, by one person, of a poem begun by another—into the *hokku*—a "single utterance" of three lines, boasting of five, seven and five syllables, or seventeen in all. In the *Genroku* age (1688-1704) the composition of these *hokku* became first a fashion, then a craze; for the Japanese people resembles the American in an emotional-intellectual sensitivity that makes for the rapid rise and fall of mental styles. Men and women, merchants and warriors, artisans and peasants neglected the affairs of life to match *hokku* epigrams, constructed at a moment's warning. The Japanese, with whom gambling is a favorite passion, wagered so much money in *hokku*-composing contests that some enterprising souls made a business of conducting them, fleecing thousands of devotees daily, until at last the government was forced to raid these poetical resorts and prohibit this new mercenary art.[15] The most distinguished master of the *hokku* was Matsura Basho (1643-94), whose birth, it seemed to Yone Noguchi, "was the greatest happening in our Japanese annals."[16] Basho, a young *Samurai*, was so deeply moved by the death of his lord and teacher that he abandoned the life of the court, renounced all physical pleasures, gave himself to wandering, meditation and teaching, and expressed his quiet philosophy in fragments of nature poetry highly revered by Japanese *literati* as perfect examples of concentrated suggestion:

> The old pond,
> Aye, and the sound of a frog leaping into the water.

Or

> A stem of grass, whereon
> A dragon-fly essayed to light.[17]

III. PROSE

1. Fiction

Lady Murasaki—The "Tale of Genji"—Its excellence—Later Japanese fiction—A humorist

If Japanese poems are too brief for the taste of the Western mind, we may console ourselves with the Japanese novel, whose masterpieces run into twenty, sometimes thirty, volumes.[18] The most highly regarded of them is the *Genji Monogatari* (literally and undeniably "Gossip about

Genji"), which in one edition fills 4,234 pages.[19] This delightful romance was composed about the year 1001 A.D. by the Lady Murasaki no-Shikibu. A Fujiwara of ancient blood, she married another Fujiwara in 997, but was left a widow four years later. She dulled her sorrow by writing an historical novel in fifty-four books. After filling all the paper she could find, she laid sacrilegious hands upon the sacred *sutras* of a Buddhist temple, and used them for manuscript;[20] even paper was once a luxury.

The hero of the tale is the son of an emperor by his favorite concubine Kiritsubo, who is so beautiful that all the other concubines are jealous of her, and actually tease her to death. Murasaki, perhaps exaggerating the male's capacity for devotion, represents the Emperor as inconsolable.

> As the years went by, the Emperor did not forget his lost lady; and though many women were brought to the palace in the hope that he might take pleasure in them, he turned from them all, believing that there was not anyone in the world like her whom he had lost. . . . Continually he pined that fate should not have allowed them to fulfil the vow which morning and evening was ever talked of between them, the vow that their lives should be as the twin birds that share a wing, the twin trees that share a bough.[21]

Genji grows up to be a dashing prince, with more looks than morals; he passes from one mistress to another with the versatility of Tom Jones, and outmodes that conventional hero by his indifference to gender. He is a woman's idea of a man—all sentiment and seduction, always brooding and languishing over one woman or the next. Occasionally, "in great unhappiness he returned to his wife's house."[22] The Lady Murasaki retails his adventures gaily, and excuses him and herself with irresistible grace:

> The young Prince would be thought to be positively neglecting his duty if he did not indulge in a few escapades; and every one would regard his conduct as perfectly natural and proper even when it was such as they would not have dreamed of permitting to ordinary people. . . . I should indeed be very loath to recount in all their detail matters which he took so much trouble to conceal, did I not know that if you found that I had omitted anything you would at once ask why, just because he was supposed to be an emperor's son, I must needs put a favorable showing on his conduct by leaving out

all his indiscretions; and you would soon be saying that this was no
history but a mere made-up tale designed to influence the judgment
of posterity. As it is, I shall be called a scandal-monger; but that I
cannot help.[23]

In the course of his amours Genji falls ill, repents him of his adventures,
and visits a monastery for pious converse with a priest. But there he sees a
lovely princess (modestly named Murasaki), and thoughts of her distract
him as the priest rebukes him for his sins.

> The priest began to tell stories about the uncertainty of this life
> and the retributions of the life to come. Genji was appalled to think
> how heavy his own sins had already been. It was bad enough to
> think that he would have them on his conscience for the rest of his
> present life. But then there was also the life to come. What terrible
> punishments he had to look forward to! And all the while the priest
> was speaking Genji thought of his own wickedness. What a good
> idea it would be to turn hermit, and live in some such place! . . .
> But immediately his thoughts strayed to the lovely face which he
> had seen that afternoon; and longing to know more of her he asked,
> "Who lives with you here?"[24]

By the coöperation of the author Genji's first wife dies in childbirth, and
he is left free to give first place in his home to his new princess, Murasaki.*
It may be that the excellence of the translation gives this book an ex-
traneous advantage over other Japanese masterpieces that have been
rendered into English; perhaps Mr. Waley, like Fitzgerald, has improved
upon his original. If, for the occasion, we can forget our own moral code,
and fall in with one that permits men and women, as Wordsworth said of
those in *Wilhelm Meister*, to "mate like flies in the air," we shall derive
from this *Tale of Genji* the most attractive glimpse yet opened to us of the
beauties hidden in Japanese literature. Murasaki writes with a naturalness
and ease that soon turn her pages into the charming gossip of a cultured
friend. The men and women, above all the children, who move through
her leisurely pages are ingratiatingly real; and the world which she de-

---

* The present writer regrets that the brevity of life has prevented his reading more
than the first of the four volumes into which Arthur Waley has so perfectly translated
Murasaki's tale.

scribes, though it is confined for the most part to imperial palaces and palatial homes, has all the color of a life actually lived or seen.* It is an aristocratic life, not much concerned with the cost of bread and love; but within that limitation it is described without sensational resort to exceptional characters or events. As Lady Murasaki makes Uma no-Kami say of certain realistic painters:

> Ordinary hills and rivers, just as they are, houses such as you may see everywhere, with all their real beauty of harmony and form— quietly to draw such scenes as this, or to show what lies behind some intimate hedge that is folded away far from the world, and thick trees upon some unheroic hill, and all this with befitting care for composition, proportion and the life—such works demand the highest master's utmost skill, and must needs draw the common craftsman into a thousand blunders.[26]

No later Japanese novel has reached the excellence of *Genji*, or has had so profound an influence upon the literary development of the language.[27] During the eighteenth century fiction had another zenith, and various novelists succeeded in surpassing the Lady Murasaki in the length of their tales, or the freedom of their pornography.[28] Santo Kioden published in 1791 an *Edifying Story Book*, but it proved so little to its purpose that the authorities, under the law prohibiting indecency, sentenced him to be handcuffed for fifty days in his own home. Santo was a vendor of tobacco-pouches and quack medicines; he married a harlot, and made his first reputation by a volume on the brothels of Tokyo. He gradually reformed the morals of his pen, but could not unteach his public the habit of buying great quantities of his books. Encouraged, he violated all precedents in the history of Japanese fiction by demanding payment from the men who published his works; his predecessors, it seemed, had been content with an in-

---

* Even into the ordinary home our Lady enters with understanding, and makes Uma no-Kami express, about the year 1000, a modernistic plea for feminine education: "Then there is the zealous housewife, who, regardless of her appearance, twists her hair behind her ears, and devotes herself entirely to the details of our domestic welfare. The husband, in his comings and goings about the world, is certain to see and hear many things which he cannot discuss with strangers, but would gladly talk over with an intimate who could listen with sympathy and understanding, some one who could laugh with him or weep, as need be. It often happens, too, that some political event will greatly perturb or amuse him, and he sits apart longing to tell some one about it. But the wife only says, lightly, 'What is the matter?' and shows no interest. This is apt to be very trying."[25]

vitation to dinner. Most of the fiction writers were poor Bohemians, whom the people classed with actors among the lowest ranks of society." Less sensational and more ably written than Kioden's were the novels of Kyokutei Bakin (1767-1848), who, like Scott and Dumas, transformed history into vivid romance. His readers grew so fond of him that he unwound one of his stories into a hundred volumes. Hokusai illustrated some of Bakin's novels until, being geniuses, they quarreled and parted.

The jolliest of these later novelists was Jippensha Ikku (d. 1831), the Le Sage and Dickens of Japan. Ikku began his adult life with three marriages, of which two were quickly ended by fathers-in-law who could not understand his literary habits. He accepted poverty with good humor, and, having no furniture, hung his bare walls with paintings of the furniture he might have had. On holidays he sacrificed to the gods with pictures of excellent offerings. Being presented with a bathtub in the common interest, he carried it home inverted on his head, and overthrew with ready wit the pedestrians who fell in his way. When his publisher came to see him he invited him to take a bath; and while his invitation was being accepted he decked himself in the publisher's clothes, and paid his New Year's Day calls in proper ceremonial costume. His masterpiece, the *Hizakurige*, was published in twelve parts between 1802 and 1822, and told a rollicking tale in the vein of *The Posthumous Papers of the Pickwick Club*—Aston calls it "the most humorous and entertaining book in the Japanese language."" On his deathbed Ikku enjoined his pupils to place upon his corpse, before the cremation then usual in Japan, certain packets which he solemnly entrusted to them. At his funeral, prayers having been said, the pyre was lighted, whereupon it turned out that the packets were full of firecrackers, which exploded merrily. Ikku had kept his youthful promise that his life would be full of surprises, even after his death.

2. History

The historians—Arai Hakuseki

We shall not find Japanese historiography so interesting as its fiction, though we may have some difficulty in distinguishing them. The oldest surviving work in Japanese literature is the *Kojiki*, or "Record of Ancient Things," written in Chinese characters by Yasumaro in 712; here legend so often takes the place of fact that the highest *Shinto* loyalty would be needed to accept it as history." After the Great Reform of 645 the government thought it advisable to transform the past again; and about 720 a new history appeared, the *Nihongi*, or "Record of Nippon," written in the Chinese language, and adorned with passages bravely stolen from Chinese works and sometimes placed, without any fetishism of chronology, in the mouths of ancient Japanese. Nevertheless the book was a more serious attempt to record the facts than the *Kojiki* had been, and it provided the foundation for most later histories of early Japan. From that time to this there have been many histories of the country, each more patriotic than the last. In 1334 Kitabatake wrote a "History of the True Succession of the Divine Monarchs"—the *Jintoshotoki*—on this modest and now familiar note:

> Great Yamato (Japan) is a divine country. It is only our land whose foundations were first laid by the Divine Ancestor. It alone has been transmitted by the Sun Goddess to a long line of her descendants. There is nothing of this kind in foreign countries. Therefore it is called the Divine Land.[32]

First printed in 1649, this work began that movement for the restoration of the ancient faith and state which culminated in the passionate polemics of Moto-ori. The very grandson of Iyeyasu, Mitsu-kuni, by his *Dai Nihonshi* ("The Great History of Japan," 1851)—a 240-volume picture of the imperial and feudal past—played a posthumous part in preparing his countrymen to overthrow the Tokugawa Shogunate.

Perhaps the most scholarly and impartial of Japanese historians was Arai Hakuseki, whose learning dominated the intellectual life of Yedo in the second half of the seventeenth century. Arai smiled at the theology of the orthodox Christian missionaries as "very childish,"[33] but he was bold enough to ridicule also some of the legends which his own people mistook for history.[34] His greatest work, the *Hankampu*, a thirty-volume history of the *Daimyo*, is one of the marvels of literature; for though it must have required much research, it appears to have been composed within a few months.[35] Arai derived something of his learning and judgment from his study of the Chinese philosophers. When he lectured on the Confucian classics the *Shogun* Iyenobu, we are told, listened with rapt and reverent attention, in summer refraining from brushing the mosquitoes from his head, in winter turning his head away from the speaker before wiping his running nose.[36] In his autobiography Arai paints a devout picture of his father, and shows the Japanese citizen at his simplest and best:

> Ever since I came to understand the heart of things, my memory is that the daily routine of his life was exactly the same. He never failed to get up an hour before daybreak. He then had a cold bath,

and did his hair himself. In cold weather the woman who was my mother would propose to order hot water for him, but this he would not allow, as he wished to avoid giving the servants trouble. When he was over seventy, and my mother also was advanced in years, sometimes, when the cold weather was unendurable, a lighted brazier was brought in, and they lay down to sleep with their feet against it. Beside the fire was placed a kettle with hot water, which my father drank when he got up. Both of them honored the way of Buddha. My father, when he had arranged his hair and adjusted his clothing, never neglected to make obeisance to Buddha. . . . After he was dressed he waited quietly for the dawn, and then went out to his official duty. . . . He was never known to betray anger, nor do I remember that, even when he laughed, he gave way to boisterous mirth. Much less did he ever descend to violent language when he had occasion to reprimand anyone. In his conversation he used as few words as possible. His demeanor was grave. I have never seen him startled, flurried, or impatient. . . . The room he usually occupied he kept cleanly swept, had an old picture hung on the wall, and a few flowers which were in season were set out in a vase. He would spend the day looking at them. He painted a little in black and white, not being fond of colors. When in good health he never troubled the servant, but did everything for himself.[37]

3.   The Essay

The Lady Sei Shonagon—Kamo no-Chomei

Arai was an essayist as well as an historian, and made brilliant contributions to what is perhaps the most delightful department of Japanese literature. Here, as in fiction, a woman stands at the top; for Lady Sei Shonagon's "Pillow Sketches" (*Makura Zoshi*) is usually accorded the highest as well as the earliest place in this field. Brought up in the same court and generation as Lady Murasaki, she chose to describe the refined and scandalous life about her in casual sketches whose excellence in the original can only be guessed at by us from the charm that survives in translation. Born a Fujiwara, she rose to be a lady in waiting to the Empress. On the latter's death Lady Sei retired, some say to a convent, others say to poverty. Her book shows no touch of either. She takes the easy morals of her time according to the easy judgment of her time, and does not think too highly of spoil-sport ecclesiastics.

A preacher ought to be a good-looking man. It is then easier to
keep your eyes fixed on his face, without which it is impossible to
benefit by his discourse. Otherwise the eyes wander and you forget
to listen. Ugly preachers have therefore a grave responsibility. . . .
If preachers were of a more suitable age I should have pleasure in
giving a more favorable judgment. As matters actually stand, their
sins are too fearful to think of.[38]

She adds little lists of her likes and dislikes:

Cheerful things:
    Coming home from an excursion with the carriages full to over-
        flowing;
    To have lots of footmen who make the oxen and the carriages
        speed along;
    A river-boat going down stream;
    Teeth nicely blackened. . . .
Dreary things:
    A nursery where a child has died;
    A brazier with the fire gone out;
    A coachman who is hated by his ox;
    The birth of a succession of female children in the house of a
        scholar.
Detestable things:
    People who, when you are telling a story, break in with "Oh,
        I know," and give quite a different version from your
        own. . . .
    While on friendly terms with a man, to hear him sound the
        praises of a woman whom he has known. . . .
    A visitor who tells a long story when you are in a hurry. . . .
    The snoring of a man whom you are trying to conceal, and
        who has gone to sleep in a place where he has no busi-
        ness. . . .
    Fleas.[39]

The Lady's only rival for the highest place in the Japanese essay is Kamo
no-Chomei. Being refused the succession to his father as the superior
guardian of the *Shinto* shrine of Kamo at Kyoto, Chomei became a Buddhist monk, and at fifty retired to a contemplative life in a mountain hermitage. There he wrote his farewell to the busy world under the title of

Hojoki (1212)— i.e., "The Record of Ten Feet Square." After describing the difficulties and annoyances of city life, and the great famine of 1181,* he tells how he built himself a hut ten feet square and seven feet high, and settled down contentedly to undisturbed philosophy and a quiet comradeship with natural things. An American, reading him, hears the voice of Thoreau in thirteenth-century Japan. Apparently every generation has had its Walden Pond.

IV. THE DRAMA

The "No" plays — Their character — The popular stage — The Japanese Shakespeare—Summary judgment

Last of all, and hardest to understand, is the Japanese drama. Brought up in our English tradition of the theatre, from *Henry IV* to *Mary of Scotland*, how shall we ever attune ourselves to tolerate what must seem to us the fustian and pantomime of the No plays of Japan? We must forget Shakespeare and go back to *Everyman*, and even farther to the religious origins of Greek and modern European drama; then we shall be oriented to watch the development of the ancient *Shinto* pantomime, the ecclesiastical *kagura* dance, into that illumination of pantomime by dialogue which constitutes the No (or lyrical) form of Japanese play. About the fourteenth century Buddhist priests added choral songs to their processional pantomimes; then they added individual characters, contrived a plot to give them action as well as speech, and the drama was born.⁴⁰

These plays, like the Greek, were performed in trilogies; and occasionally *Kyogen*, or farces ("mad words"), were acted in the intervals, to relieve and facilitate the tension of emotion and thought. The first part of the trilogy was devoted to propitiating the gods, and was hardly more than a religious pantomime; the second was performed in full armor, and was designed to frighten all evil spirits away; the third was of a milder mood, and sought to portray some charming aspect of nature, or some delightful phase of Japanese life.⁴¹ The lines were written for the most part in blank verse of twelve syllables. The actors were men of standing, even among the aristocracy; a playbill survives which indicates that Nobunaga, Hideyoshi and Iyeyasu all participated as actors in a No play about 1580.⁴² Each actor wore a mask, carved out of wood with an artistry that makes such masks a prize for the art collector of today. Scenery was

---

* His description of this has been quoted above, p. 852.

meagre; the passionate imagination of the audience could be relied upon
to create the background of the action. The stories were of the simplest,
and did not matter much: one of the most popular told of the impoverished *Samurai* who, to warm a wandering monk, cut down his most cherished plants to make a fire; whereupon the monk turned out to be the
Regent, and gave the knight a goodly reward. But as we in the West may
go again and again to hear an opera whose story is old and perhaps ridiculous, so the Japanese, even today, weep over this oft-told tale,[43] because the
excellence of the acting renews on each occasion the power and significance of the play. To the hasty and businesslike visitor such performances as he may find of these dramatized lyrics are rather amusing than impressive; nevertheless a Japanese poet says of them: "Oh, what a tragedy
and beauty in the *No* stage! I always think that it would certainly be a
great thing if the *No* drama could be properly introduced into the West.
The result would be no small protest against the Western stage. It would
mean a revelation."[44] Japan itself, however, has not composed such plays
since the seventeenth century, though it acts them devotedly today.

The history of the drama, in most countries, is a gradual change from
the predominance of the chorus to the supremacy of some individual rôle
—at which point, in most such sequences, development ends. As the his-
trionic art advanced in tradition and excellence in Japan it created popular
personalities who subordinated the play to themselves. Finally pantomime and religion sank to a subordinate rôle, and the drama became a
war of individuals, full of violence and romance. So was born the *kabuki
shibai*, or popular theatre, of Japan. The first such theatre was established
about the year 1600 by a nun who, tired of convent walls, set up a stage at
Osaka, and practised dancing for a livelihood.[45] As in England and France,
the presence of women on the stage seemed revolting and was forbidden;
and since the upper classes (except in safe disguise) shunned these performances, the actors became almost a pariah caste, with no social incentive to keep their profession from immorality and corruption. Men per-
force took the parts of women, and carried their imitation to such a point as
to deceive not only their audiences but themselves; many of these actors of
female rôles remained women off the stage.[46] Perhaps because lighting was
poor, the actors painted their faces with vivid colors, and wore robes of
gorgeous designs to indicate and dignify their rôles. Back of the stage and
about it, usually, were choral and individual reciters, who sometimes carried on the vocal parts while the actors confined themselves to pantomime.
The audience sat on the matted floor, or in tiers of boxes at either side.[47]

The most famous name in the popular drama of Japan is Chikamatsu Monzayemon (1653-1724). His countrymen compare him with Shakespeare; English critics, resenting the comparison, accuse Chikamatsu of violence, extravagance, bombast, and improbable plots, while granting him "a certain barbaric vigor and luxuriance";⁴⁸ apparently the similarity is complete. Such foreign plays seem mere melodrama to us, because either the meaning or the nuances of the language are concealed from us; but this would probably be the effect of a Shakespearean play upon one unable to appreciate its language or follow its thought. Chikamatsu seems to have made undue use of lovers' suicides to cap his climaxes, in the style of *Romeo and Juliet*; but perhaps with this excuse, that suicide was almost as popular in Japanese life as on the stage.

A foreign historian, in these matters, can only report, but cannot judge. Japanese acting, to a transient observer, seems less complex and mature, but more vigorous and exalting than the European; Japanese plays seem more plebeianly melodramatic, but less emasculated with superficial intellectualism, than the plays of France, England and America today. So, reversely, Japanese poetry seems slight and bloodless, and too aristocratically refined, to us whose appetite has taken in lyrics of almost epic length (like *Maud*), and epics of such dulness that doubtless Homer himself would nod if he were compelled to read the accumulated *Iliad*. The Japanese novel seems sensational and sentimental; and yet two of the supreme masterpieces of English fiction—*Tom Jones* and *Pickwick Papers*—have apparently their equal counterparts in the *Genji Monogatari* and the *Hizakurige*, and perhaps Lady Murasaki excels in subtlety, grace and understanding even the great Fielding himself. All things are dull that are remote and obscure; and things Japanese will remain obscure to us until we can completely forget our Western heritage and completely absorb Japan's.

V. THE ART OF LITTLE THINGS

*Creative imitation—Music and the dance—"Inro" and "netsuke"—
Hidari Jingaro—Lacquer*

The outward forms of Japanese art, like almost every external feature of Japanese life, came from China; the inner force and spirit, like everything essential in Japan, came from the people themselves. It is true that the wave of ideas and immigration that brought Buddhism to Japan in the seventh century brought also, from China and Korea, art forms and impulses bound up with that faith, and no more original with China and Korea than with Japan; it is true, even, that cultural elements entered not only from China and India, but from Assyria and Greece—the features of the Kamakura *Buddha*, for example, are more Greco-Bactrian than Japanese. But such foreign stimuli were used creatively in Japan; its people learned quickly to distinguish beauty from ugliness; its rich men sometimes prized objects of art more than land or gold,* and its artists labored with self-effacing devotion. These men, though arduously trained through a long apprenticeship, seldom received more than an artisan's wage; if for a moment wealth came to them they gave it away with Bohemian recklessness, and soon relapsed into a natural and comfortable poverty.[50] But only the artist-artisans of ancient Egypt and Greece, or of medieval China, could rival their industry, taste and skill.

The very life of the people was instinct with art—in the neatness of their homes, the beauty of their clothing, the refinements of their ornaments, and their spontaneous addiction to song and dance. For music, like life, had come to Japan from the gods themselves; had not Izanagi and Izanami sung in choruses at the creation of the earth? A thousand years later the Emperor Inkyo, we read, played on a *wagon* (a kind of zither), and his Empress danced, at an imperial banquet given in 419 to signalize the opening of a new palace. When Inkyo died a Korean king sent eighty musicians to attend the funeral; and these players taught the Japanese new instruments and new modes—some from Korea, some from China, some from India. When the *Daibutsu* was installed in the temple of Todaiji at Nara (752), music from T'ang Chinese masters was played in the ceremony; and the *Shoso-in*, or Imperial Treasure-house, at Nara still shows the varied instruments used in those ancient days. Singing and recitative, court music and monastic dance music, formed the classical modes, while popular airs were strummed on the *biwa*—a lute—or the *samisen*—a three-stringed banjo.[51] The Japanese had no great composers, and wrote no books about music; their simple compositions, played in five notes of the harmonic minor scale, had no harmony, and no distinction of major and minor keys; but almost every Japanese could play some one of the twenty instruments which had come over from the continent; and any one of these, when properly played, said the Japanese, would make the very dust on the ceil-

* Hideyoshi's generals, after successful campaigns, seem to have been content—occasionally—to be rewarded not with new areas and revenues, but with rare pieces of pottery or porcelain.[49]

ing dance.[52] The dance itself enjoyed "a vogue unparalleled in any other country"[53]—not so much as an appendage to love as in the service of religious or communal ceremony; sometimes a whole village turned out in costume to celebrate a joyful occasion with a universal dance. Professional dancers entertained great audiences with their skill; and men as well as women, even in the highest circles, gave much time to the art. When Prince Genji, says the Lady Murasaki, danced the "Waves of the Blue Sea" with his friend To no-Chujo, everyone was moved. "Never had the onlookers seen feet tread so delicately, nor heads so exquisitely poised. . . . So moving and beautiful was this dance that at the end of it the Emperor's eyes were wet, and all the princes and great gentlemen wept aloud."[54]

Meanwhile all who could afford it adorned their persons not only with fine brocades and painted silks, but with delicate objects characteristic, almost definitive, of the old Japan. Shrinking ladies flirted from behind fans of alluring loveliness, while men flaunted *netsuke, inro* and expensively carved swords. The *inro* was a little box attached to the belt by a cord; it was usually composed of several infolding cases carefully carved in ivory or wood, and contained tobacco, coins, writing materials, or other casual necessities. To keep the cord from slipping under the belt, it was bound at the other end to a tiny toggle or *netsuke* (from *ne*, end, and *tsuke*, to fasten), upon whose cramped surface some artist had fashioned, with lavish care, the forms of deities or demons, philosophers or fairies, birds or reptiles, fishes or insects, flowers or leaves, or scenes from the life of the people. Here that impish humor in which Japanese art so far excels all others found free and yet modest play. Only the most careful examination can reveal the full subtlety and significance of these representations; but even a glance at this microcosm of fat women and priests, of agile monkeys and delightful bugs, cut upon less than a cubic inch of ivory or wood, brings home to the student the unique and passionately artistic quality of the Japanese people.*

Hidari (i.e., "left-handed") Jingaro was the most famous of Japanese sculptors in wood. Legend told how he had lost an arm and gotten a name: when an offended conqueror demanded of Jingaro's *Daimyo* the life of his daughter, Jingaro carved a severed head so realistically that the conqueror ordered the artist's right hand to be cut off as punishment for killing the daughter of his lord.[55] It was Jingaro whose chisel formed the

---

* The author is indebted to Mr. Adolf Kroch of Chicago for permission to examine his fine collection of *netsuke* and *inro*.

elephants and the sleeping cat at the shrine of Iyeyasu at Nikko, and the "Gate of the Imperial Envoy" at the Nishi-Hongwan Temple in Kyoto. On the inner panels of this gate the artist told the story of the Chinese sage who washed his ear because it had been contaminated by a proposal that he should accept the throne of his country, and the austere cowherd who quarreled with the sage for thus defiling the river.[56] But Jingaro was merely the most characterful of the now nameless artists who adorned a thousand structures with lovingly carved or lacquered wood. The lacquer tree found in the islands a peculiarly congenial habitat, and was nourished with skilful care. The artisans sometimes covered with successive coats of lacquer, cotton and lacquer a form chiseled in wood; but more often they went to the pains of modeling a statue in clay, making from this a hollow mould, and then pouring into the mould several layers of lacquer, each thicker than before.[57] The Japanese carver lifted wood to a full equality with marble as a material for art, and filled shrines, mausolea and palaces with the fairest wood-decoration known in Asia.

VI. ARCHITECTURE

Temples—Palaces—The shrine of Iyeyasu—Homes

In the year 594 the Empress Suiko, being convinced of the truth or utility of Buddhism, ordered the building of Buddhist temples throughout her realm. Prince Shotoku, who was entrusted with carrying out this edict, brought in from Korea priests, architects, wood-carvers, bronze founders, clay modelers, masons, gilders, tile-makers, weavers, and other skilled artisans.[58] This vast cultural importation was almost the beginning of art in Japan, for *Shinto* had frowned upon ornate edifices and had countenanced no figures to misrepresent the gods. From that moment Buddhist shrines and statuary filled the land. The temples were essentially like those of China, but more richly ornamented and more delicately carved. Here, too, majestic *torii*, or gateways, marked the ascent or approach to the sacred retreat; bright colors adorned the wooden walls, great beams held up a tiled roof gleaming under the sun, and minor structures—a drum-tower, e. g., or a pagoda—mediated between the central sanctuary and the surrounding trees. The greatest achievements of the foreign artists was the group of temples at Horiuji, raised under the guidance of Prince Shotoku near Nara about the year 616. It stands to the credit of the most living of building materials that one of these wooden edifices has survived unnumbered earthquakes and outlasted a hundred thousand temples of stone; and it stands to the glory of the builders that nothing erected in later Japan has surpassed the simple majesty of this oldest shrine. Perhaps as beautiful, and only slightly younger, are the temples of Nara itself, above all the perfectly proportioned Golden Hall of the Todaiji Temple there; Nara, says Ralph Adams Cram, contains "the most precious architecture in all Asia."[59]

The next zenith of building in Japan came under the Ashikaga Shogunate. Yoshimitsu, resolved to make Kyoto the fairest capital on earth, built for the gods a pagoda 360 feet high; for his mother the Takakura Palace, of which a single door cost 20,000 pieces of gold ($150,000); for himself a Flower Palace, that consumed $5,000,000; and the Golden Pavilion of Kinkakuji for the glory of all.[60] Hideyoshi too tried to rival Kublai Khan, and built at Momoyama a "Palace of Pleasure" which his whim tore down again a few years after its completion; we may judge its magnificence from the "day long portal" removed from it to adorn the temple of Nishi-Hongwan; all day long, said its admirers, one might gaze at that carved portal without exhausting its excellence. Kano Yeitoku played Ictinus and Pheidias to Hideyoshi, but adorned his buildings with Venetian splendor rather than with Attic restraint; never had Japan, or Asia, seen such abounding decoration before. Under Hideyoshi, too, the gloomy Castle of Osaka took form, to dominate the Pittsburgh of Japan, and become the death-place of his son.

Iyeyasu inclined rather to philosophy and letters than to art; but after his death his grandson, Iyemitsu, content himself with a wooden shanty for his palace, lavished the resources of Japanese wealth and art to build around the ashes of Iyeyasu at Nikko the fairest memorial ever raised to any individual in the Far East. Here, ninety miles from Tokyo, on a quiet hill reached by a shaded avenue of stately cryptomerias, the architects of the *Shogun* laid down first a series of spacious and gradual approaches, then an ornate but lovely Yo-mei-mon Gate, then, by a brook crossed with a sacred and untouchable bridge, a series of mausolea and temples in lacquered wood, femininely beautiful and frail. The decoration is extravagant, the construction is weak, the omnipresent red paint flares like a hectic rouge amid the modest green of the trees; and yet a country incarnadined with blossoms every spring may need brighter colors to express its spirit than those that might serve and please a less impassioned race.

We cannot quite call this architecture great, for the demon of earthquake has willed that Japan should build on a timid scale, and not pile stones into the sky to crash destructively when the planet wrinkles its skin. Hence the homes are of wood and seldom rise beyond a story or two; only the repeated experience of fire and the reiterated commands of the government prevailed upon the citizens of the cities, when they could afford it, to cover their wooden cottages and palaces with roofs of tile. The aristocracy, unable to raise their mansions into the clouds, spread them spaciously over the earth, despite an imperial edict limiting the size of a dwelling to 240 yards square. A palace, was rarely one building; usually it was a main structure connected by covered walks with subordinate edifices for various groups in the family. There was no distinction of dining-room, living-room or bedroom; the same chamber could serve any purpose, for at a moment's notice a table might be laid down upon the matted floor, or the rolled up bedding might be taken from its hiding-place and spread out for the night. Sliding panels or removable partitions separated or united the rooms, and even the latticed or windowed walls were easily folded up to give full play to the sun, or the cooling evening air. Pretty blinds of split bamboo offered shade and privacy. Windows were a luxury; in the poorer homes the summer light found many openings, which in winter were blocked up with oiled paper to keep out the cold. Japanese architecture gives the appearance of having been born in the tropics, and of having been transported too recklesssly into islands that stretch up their necks to shivering Kamchatka. In the more southern towns these fragile and simple homes have a style and beauty of their own, and offer appropriate dwellings for the once gay children of the sun.

VII. METALS AND STATUES

Swords—Mirrors—The Trinity of Horiuji—Colossi—Religion and sculpture

The sword of the *Samurai* was stronger than his dwelling, for the metal-workers of Japan spent themselves on making blades superior to those of Damascus or Toledo,[a] sharp enough to sever a man from shoulder to thigh at a blow, and ornamented with guards and handles so highly decorated, or so heavily inlaid with gems, that they were not always perfectly adapted to homicide. Other workers in metal made bronze mirrors so brilliant that legends arose to commemorate their perfection. So a peasant, having bought a mirror for the first time, thought that he recognized in it the face of his dead father; he hid it as a great treasure, but so often consulted it that his suspicious wife ferreted it out, and was horrified to find in it the picture of a woman about her own age, who was apparently her husband's mistress.[62] Still other artisans cast tremendous bells, like the forty-nine-ton monster at Nara (732 A.D.), and brought from them a sweeter tone than our clanging metal clappers elicit in the West, by striking a boss on the outer surface of the bell with a swinging beam of wood.

The sculptors used wood or metal rather than stone, since their soil was poor in granite and marble; and yet, despite all difficulties of material, they came to surpass their Chinese and Korean teachers in this most definitive of all the arts—for every other art secretly emulates sculpture's patient removal of the inappropriate. Almost the earliest, and perhaps the greatest, masterpiece of sculpture in Japan is the bronze Trinity at Horiuji —a Buddha seated on a lotus bud between two *Bodhisattwas*, before a screen and halo of bronze only less beautiful than the stone lacery of Aurangzeb's screen in the Taj Mahal. We do not know whose hands reared these temples and built this statuary; we may admit Korean teachers, Chinese examples, Indian motives, even Greek influences coming down from far Ionia across a thousand years; but we are sure that this Trinity is among the most signal accomplishments in the history of art.*

Possibly because their stature was short, and their bodies could hardly contain all the ambitions and capacities of their souls, the Japanese took pleasure in building colossi, and had better success in this questionable art than even the Egyptians. In the year 747, an epidemic of smallpox having broken out in Japan, the Emperor Shomu commissioned Kimimaro to cast a gigantic Buddha in propitiation of the gods. For this purpose Kimimaro used 437 tons of bronze, 288 pounds of gold, 165 pounds of

---

* Perhaps the great Shotoku Taishi, statesman and artist, had something to do with this achievement, for we know that he plied the chisel, and cut many statues in wood.[63] Kobo Daishi (ca. 816) was a sculptor as well as a painter, a scholar and a saint; Hokusai, to suggest his versatility, pictured him wielding five brushes at once, with hands and feet and mouth.[64] Unkei (1180-1220) made characterful portrait-busts of himself and many priests, and carved delightfully terrible figures of Hell's Supreme Court, and those snarling gods whose function it was to frighten away, with the ugliness of their faces, all spirits of evil. His father Kokei, his son Jokei, and his pupil Jokaku helped him to make the Japanese supreme in the art of sculpturing wood.

mercury, seven tons of vegetable wax, and several tons of charcoal. Two years and seven attempts were required for the work. The head was cast in a single mould, but the body was formed of several metal plates soldered together and thickly covered with gold. More impressive to the foreign eye than this saturnine countenance at Nara is the *Daibutsu* of Kamakura, cast of bronze in 1252 by Ono Goroyemon; here, perhaps because the colossus sits on an elevation in the open air, within a pleasant entourage of trees, the size seems to accord with the purpose, and the artist has expressed with remarkable simplicity the spirit of Buddhist contemplation and peace. Once a temple housed the figure, as still is the case at Nara; but in 1495 a great tidal wave destroyed both the temple and the town, leaving the bronze philosopher serene amid widespread destruction, suffering and death. Hideyoshi too built a colossus at Kyoto; for five years fifty thousand men labored at this Buddha, and the great *Taiko* himself, clad in the garb of a common laborer, sometimes helped them conspicuously at their task. But hardly had it been erected when, in 1596, an earthquake threw it down, and scattered the wreckage of its sheltering sanctuary about its head. Hideyoshi, says Japanese story, shot an arrow at the fallen idol, saying, scornfully, "I placed you here at great expense, and you cannot even defend your own temple."[65]

From such colossi to dangling *netsuke* Japanese sculpture ran the range of every figure and every size. Sometimes its masters, like Takamura today, gave years of labor to figures hardly a foot tall, and took delight in representing gnarled octogenarians, jolly gourmands and philosophic friars. It was good that humor sustained them, for most of the gains that came from their toil went to their subtle employers rather than to themselves, and in their larger works they were much harassed by conventions of subject and treatment laid upon them by the priests. The priests wanted gods, not courtesans, from the sculptors; they wished to inspire the people to piety, or to fashion their virtues with fear, rather than to arouse in them the sense and ecstasy of beauty. Bound hand and soul to religion, sculpture decayed when faith lost its warmth and power; and, as in Egypt, the stiffness of conventions, when piety had fled, became the rigor of death.

VIII. POTTERY

The Chinese stimulus—The potters of Hizen—Pottery and tea—
How Goto Saijiro brought the art of porcelain from Hizen
to Kaga—The nineteenth century

In a sense it is not quite just to Japan to speak of her importing civilization from Korea and China, except in the sense in which northwestern
Europe took its civilization from Greece and Rome. We might also view all
the peoples of the Far East as one ethnic and cultural unity, in which each
part, like the provinces of one country, produced in its time and place an art
and culture akin to and dependent upon the art and culture of the rest. So
Japanese pottery is a part and phase of Far Eastern ceramics, fundamentally
like the Chinese, and yet stamped with the characteristic delicacy and fineness
of all Japanese work. Until the coming of the Korean artisans in the seventh
century, Japanese pottery was merely an industry, moulding crude materials
for common use; there was, apparently, no glazed pottery in the Far East before the eighth century, much less any porcelain.[66] The industry became an
art largely as a result of the entrance of tea in the thirteenth century. Chinese
tea-cups of Sung design came in with tea, and aroused the admiration of the
Japanese. In the year 1223 Kato Shirozemon, a Japanese potter, made his
way perilously to China, studied ceramics there for six years, returned to set
up his own factory at Seto, and so far surpassed all preceding pottery in the
islands that *Seto-mono*, or *Seto-ware*, became a generic name for all Japanese
pottery, just as *chinaware*, in the seventeenth century, became the English
term for porcelain. The *Shogun* Yoritomo made Shirozemon's future by
setting the fashion of rewarding minor services with presents of Shirozemon's
tea-jars, filled with the new marvel of powdered tea. Today the surviving
specimens of this *Toshiro-yaki** are accounted almost beyond price; they are
swathed in costly brocade, and kept in boxes of the finest lacquer, while their
owners are spoken of with bated breath as the aristocracy of connoisseurs.[67]

Three hundred years later another Japanese, Shonzui, was lured to China to
study its famous potteries. On his return he established a factory at Arita,
in the province of Hizen. He was harassed, however, by the difficulty of
finding in the soil of his country minerals as well adapted as those of China
to make a fine *pâte;* and it was said of his products that one of their main
ingredients was the bones of his artisans. Nevertheless Shonzui's wares of
Mohammedan blue were so excellent that the Chinese potters of the eighteenth century did their best to imitate them for export under his counter-

---

* Toshiro was another name for Shirozemon; *yaki* means ware.

feited name; and the extant examples of his work are now as highly valued as the rarest paintings of Japan's greatest masters of the brush.⁶⁸ About 1605 a Korean, Risampei, discovered at Izumi-yama, in the Arita district, immense deposits of porcelain stone; and from that moment Hizen became the center of the ceramic industry in Japan. In Arita, too, labored the famous Kakiemon, who, after learning the art of enameling from a Chinese ship-master, made his name almost synonymous with delicately decorated enameled porcelain. Dutch merchants shipped large quantities of Hizen products to Europe from the port of Arita at Imari; 44,943 pieces went to Holland alone in the year 1664. This brilliant *Imari-yaki* became the rage in Europe, and inspired Aebregt de Keiser to inaugurate the golden age of Dutch ceramics in his factories at Delft.

Meanwhile the rise of the tea ceremony had stimulated a further development in Japan. In 1578 Nobunaga, at the suggestion of the tea-master Rikyu, gave a large order for cups and other tea utensils to a family of Korean potters at Kyoto. A few years later Hideyoshi rewarded the family with a gold seal, and made its wares, the *Raku-yaki*, almost *de rigueur* for the ritual of drinking tea. Hideyoshi's generals returned from their unsuccessful invasion of Korea with numerous captives, among whom, by a discrimination unusual in warriors, were many artists. In 1596 Shimazu Yoshihiro brought to Satsuma a hundred skilled Koreans, including seventeen potters; and these men, with their successors, established throughout the world the high reputation of Satsuma for that richly colored glazed ware to which an Italian town has given our name of *faïence*. But the greatest Japanese master in this branch of the art was the Kyoto potter Ninsei. Not only did he originate enameled *faïence*, but he gave to his products a grace and proud restraint that have made them precious to collectors ever since, so that his mark has been more often counterfeited than that of any other artist in Japan.⁶⁹ Because of his work, decorated *faïence* mounted to the intensity of a craze in the capital, and in some quarters of Kyoto every second house was turned into a miniature pottery.⁷⁰ Only less famous than Ninsei was Kenzan, older brother of the painter Korin.

The romance that so often lurks behind ceramics appears in the story of how Goto Saijiro brought the art of porcelain from Hizen to Kaga. An excellent bed of potter's stone having been discovered near the village of Kutani, the feudal lord of the province resolved to establish a porcelain industry there; and Goto was sent to Hizen to study its methods of firing and design. But the secrets of the potters were so carefully concealed from outsiders that Goto for a while was baffled. Finally he disguised himself as a servant, and accepted a menial place in the household of a potter. After three years his master admitted him to a pottery, and there Goto worked for four years more. Then he deserted the wife whom he had married at Hizen and the children whom she had borne to him, and fled to Kaga, where he gave his lord a full report of the methods he had learned. From that time on (1664) the potters of Kutani became masters, and *Kutani-yaki* rivaled the best wares of Japan.[71]

The Hizen potteries retained their leadership throughout the eighteenth century, largely as a result of the benevolent care which the feudal lord of Hirado lavished upon the workmen in his factories; for a century (1750-1843) the blue Michawaki wares of Hirado stood at the head of Japanese porcelains. In the nineteenth century Zengoro Hozen brought the leadership to Kyoto by clever imitations that often surpassed his models, so that sometimes it became impossible to decide which was the original and which was the copy. In the final quarter of the century Japan developed *cloisonné* enameling from the crude condition in which it had remained since its entry from China, and took the lead of the world in this field of ceramics.[72] Other branches deteriorated during the same period, for the rising demand of Europe for Japanese pottery led to a style of exaggerated decoration alien to the native taste, and the habits engendered in meeting these foreign orders affected the skill and weakened the traditions of the art. Here, as everywhere, the coming of industry has been for a while a blight; mass production has taken the place of quality, and mass consumption has replaced discriminating taste. Perhaps, after invention has run its fertile course, and social organization and experience have spread the gift of leisure and taught its creative use, the curse may be turned into a blessing; industry may lavish comforts upon the majority of men, while the worker, after paying his lowered tribute of hours to the machine, may once again become an artisan, and turn the mechanical product, by loving individual treatment, into a work of personality and art.

IX. PAINTING

Difficulties of the subject—Methods and materials—Forms and ideals—Korean origins and Buddhist inspiration—The Tosa School—The return to China—Sesshiu—The Kano School —Koyetsu and Korin—The Realistic School

Japanese painting, even more than the other topics that have demanded a place in these pages, is a subject that only specialists should touch; and if it is included here, along with other esoteric realms wherein angels have feared to tread, it is in the hope that through this veil of errors some glimpse may come, to the reader, of the fulness and quality of Japanese civilization. The masterpieces of Japanese painting cover a period of twelve hundred years, are divided amongst a complex multiplicity of schools, have been lost or injured in the flow of time, and are nearly all hidden away in private collections in Japan.* Those few *chef-d'œuvres* that are open to alien study are so different in form, method, style and material from Western pictures that no competent judgment can be passed upon them by the Occidental mind.

First of all, like their models in China, the paintings of Japan were once made with the same brush that was used in writing, and, as in Greece, the word for writing and for painting was originally one; painting was a graphic art. This initial fact has determined half the characteristics of Far Eastern painting, from the materials used to the subordination of color to line. The materials are simple: ink or water-colors, a brush, and absorbent paper or silk. The labor is difficult: the artist works not erect but on his knees, bending over the silk or paper on the floor; and he must learn to control his stroke so as to make seventy-one different degrees or styles of touch.[73] In the earlier centuries, when Buddhism ruled the art of Japan, frescoes were painted, much in the manner of Ajanta or Turkestan; but nearly all the extant works of high repute take the form either of *makimono* (scrolls), *kakemono* (hangings), or screens. These pictures were made not to be arranged indigestibly in picture galleries—for there are no such galleries in Japan—but to be viewed in private by the owner and his friends, or to form a part of some decorative scheme in a temple, a palace or a home. They were very seldom portraits of specific personalities; usually they were glimpses of nature, or scenes of martial action, or strokes of humorous or satirical observation of the ways of animals, women and men.

They were poems of feeling rather than representations of things, and were closer to philosophy than to photography. The Japanese artist let realism alone, and rarely tried to imitate the external form of reality. He scornfully left out shadows as irrelevant to essences, preferring to paint in *plein air,* with no modeling play of light and shade; and he smiled at Western insistence on the perspective reduction of distant things. "In Japanese painting," said Hokusai, with philosophic tolerance, "form and color are represented without any attempt at relief, but in European methods relief and illusion are sought for."[74] The Japanese artist wished to convey a feel-

---

* Perhaps the best of all collections of the Kano School—Mr. Beppu's at Tokyo—was almost completely destroyed by the earthquake of 1923.

ing rather than an object, to suggest rather than to represent; it was unnecessary, in his judgment, to show more than a few significant elements in a scene; as in a Japanese poem, only so much should be shown as would arouse the appreciative mind to contribute to the esthetic result by its own imagination. The painter too was a poet, and valued the rhythm of line and the music of forms infinitely more than the haphazard shape and structure of things. And like the poet he felt that if he were true to his own feeling it would be realism enough.

It was probably Korea that brought painting to the restless empire that now has conquered her. Korean artists, presumably, painted the flowing and colorful frescoes of the Horiuji Temple, for there is nothing in the known history of Japan before the seventh century that could explain the sudden native achievement of such faultless excellence. The next stimulus came directly from China, through the studies there of the Japanese priests Kobo Daishi and Dengyo Daishi; on his return to Japan in 806 Kobo Daishi gave himself to painting as well as to sculpture, literature and piety, and some of the oldest masterpieces are from his many-sided brush. Buddhism stimulated art in Japan, as it had done in China; the *Zen* practice of meditation lent itself to brooding creativeness in color and form almost as readily as in philosophy and poetry; and visions of Amida Buddha became as frequent in Japanese art as Annunciations and Crucifixions on the walls and canvases of the Renaissance. The priest Yeishin Sozu (d. 1017) was the Fra Angelico and El Greco of this age, whose risings and descendings of Amida made him the greatest religious painter in the history of Japan. By this time, however, Kose no-Kanaoka (fl. ca. 950) had begun the secularization of Japanese painting; birds, flowers and animals began to rival gods and saints on the scrolls.

But Kose's brush still thought in Chinese terms, and moved along Chinese lines. It was not till the suspension of intercourse with China in the ninth century had given Japan the first of five centuries of isolation that she began to paint her own scenery and subjects in her own way. About 1150, under the patronage of imperial and aristocratic circles at Kyoto, a national school of painting arose which protested against imported motives and styles, and set itself to decorate the luxurious homes of the capital with the flowers and landscapes of Japan. The school had almost as many names as it had masters: *Yamato-riu*, or Japanese Style; *Waga-riu*, again meaning Japanese Style; *Kasuga*, after its reputed founder; and finally the Tosa School, after its principal representative in the thirteenth century, Tosa Gon-no-kumi; thereafter to the end of its history the name Tosa was borne by all the artists of the line. They deserved their nationalist name, for there is nothing in Chinese art that corresponds to the ardor and dash, the variety and humor, of the narrative scrolls of love and war which came from the brushes of this group. Takayoshi, about 1010, painted in colors gorgeous illustrations of the seductive tale of Genji; Toba Sojo amused himself by drawing lively satires of the priestly and other scoundrels of his time, under the guise of monkeys and frogs; Fujiwara Takanobu, towards the end of the twelfth century, finding his high lineage worthless in terms of rice and *sake*, turned to the brush for a living, and drew great portraits of Yoritomo and others, quite unlike anything yet done in China; his son Fujiwara Nobuzane patiently painted the portraits of thirty-six poets; and in the thirteenth century Kasuga's son, Keion, or someone else, drew those animated scrolls which are among the world's most brilliant achievements in the field of draughtsmanship.

Slowly these native sources of inspiration seemed to dry up into conventional forms and styles, and Japanese art turned once more for nourishment to the new schools of painting that had arisen in the China of the Sung Renaissance. The impulse to imitation was for a time uncontrolled; Japanese artists who had never seen the Middle Kingdom spent their lives in painting Chinese characters and scenes. Cho Densu painted sixteen *Rakan (Lohans, Arhats,* Buddhist saints), now among the treasures of the Freer Gallery in Washington; Shubun took the precaution of being born and reared in China, so that, on coming to live in Japan, he could paint Chinese landscapes from memory as well as from imagination.

It was during this second Chinese mood of Japanese painting that the greatest figure in all the pictorial art of Japan appeared. Sesshiu was a Zen priest at Sokokuji, one of the several art schools established by Yoshimitsu, the Ashikaga *Shogun.* Even as a youth he astonished his townsmen with his draughtsmanship; and legend, not knowing how to express its awe, told how, when he was tied to a post for misbehavior, he had drawn with his toes such realistic mice that they came to life and bit through the cords that bound him.[75] Hungry to know the masters of Ming China at first hand, he secured credentials from his religious superiors as well as from the *Shogun,* and sailed across the sea. He was disappointed to find that Chinese painting was in decay, but he consoled himself with the varied life and culture of the great kingdom, and went back to his own land filled and inspired with a thousand ideas. The artists and nobles of China, says a pretty tale, accompanied him to the vessel which was to take him back to Japan, and showered white paper upon him with requests that he should paint a few strokes, if no more, upon them and send them back; hence, according to this story, his pen name Sesshiu, meaning "Ship of Snow.""" Arrived in Japan, he seems to have been welcomed as a prince, and to have been offered many emoluments by the *Shogun* Yoshimasa; but (if we may believe what we read) he refused these favors, and retired to his country parish in Choshu. Now he threw off, as if each were a moment's trifle, one masterpiece after another, until nearly every phase of Chinese scenery and life had taken lasting form under his brush. Seldom had China, never had Japan, seen paintings so various in scope, so vigorous in conception and execution, so decisive in line. In his old age the artists of Japan made a path to his door and honored him, even before his death, as a supreme artist. Today a picture of Sesshiu is to a Japanese collector what a Leonardo is to a European; and legend, which transforms intangible opinions into pretty tales, tells how one possessor of a Sesshiu, finding himself caught in a conflagration beyond possibility of escape, slashed open his body with his sword, and plunged into his abdomen the priceless scroll—which was later found unharmed within his half-consumed corpse."

The ascendancy of Chinese influence continued among the many artists patronized by the feudal lords of the Ashikaga and Tokugawa Shogunates. Each baronial court had its official painter, who was commissioned to train hundreds of young artists who might be turned, at a moment's notice, to the decoration of a palace. The temples now were almost ignored, for art was being secularized in proportion as wealth increased. Towards the end of the fifteenth century Kano Masanobu established at Kyoto, under Ashikaga patronage, a school of secular painters known from his first name, and devoted to upholding the severely classical and Chinese traditions in Japanese art. His son, Kano Motonobu, reached in this direction a mastery second only to that of Sesshiu himself. A story told of him illustrates admirably the concentration of mind and purpose that constitutes the greater part of genius. Having been commissioned to paint a series of cranes, Motonobu was discovered, evening after evening, walking and behaving like a crane. It turned out that he imitated, each night, the crane that he planned to paint the following day. A man must go to bed with his purpose in order to wake up to fame. Motonobu's grandson, Kano Yeitoku, though a scion of the Kano line, developed under the protection of Hideyoshi an ornate style all the world away from the restrained classicism of his progenitors. Tanyu transferred the seat of the school from Kyoto to Yedo, took service under the Tokugawas, and helped to decorate the mausoleum of Iyeyasu at Nikko. Gradually, despite these adaptations to the spirit of the times, the Kano dynasty exhausted its impetus, and Japan turned to other masters for fresh beginnings.

About 1660 a new group of painters arrived on the scene, named, from its leaders, the Koyetsu-Korin School. In the natural oscillation of philosophies and styles, the Chinese manners and subjects of Sesshiu and Kano seemed now conservative and worn out; and the new artists turned to domestic scenes and motives for their subject-matter and inspiration. Koyetsu was a man of such diverse talents as bring to mind Carlyle's jealous claim that he had never known any great man who could not have been any sort of a great man; for he was distinguished as a calligrapher, a painter, and a designer in metal, lacquer and wood. Like William Morris he inaugurated a revival of fine printing, and supervised a village in which his craftsmen pursued their varied arts under his direction.[78] His only rival for the first place among the painters of the Tokugawa age was Korin, that astonishing master of trees and flowers, who, his contemporaries tell us, could with one stroke of his brush place a leaf of iris upon the silk and make it live.[79] No other painter has been so purely and completely Japanese, or so typically Japanese in the taste and delicacy of his work.*

The last of the historic schools of Japanese painting in the strictest sense was founded at Kyoto in the eighteenth century by Maruyami Okyo. A man of the people, Okyo, stimulated by some knowledge of European painting, resolved to abandon the now thinned-out idealism and impressionism of the older style, and to attempt a realistic description of simple scenes from everyday life. He became especially fond of drawing animals, and kept many species of them about him as objects of his brush. Having painted a wild boar, he showed his work to hunters, and was disappointed to find that they thought his pictured boar was dead. He tried again and again, until at last they admitted that the boar might not be dead but merely asleep.[81] Since the aristocracy at Kyoto was penniless, Okyo had to sell his pictures to the middle classes; and this economic compulsion had much to do with turning him to popular subjects, even to the painting of some Kyoto belles. The older artists were horrified, but Okyo persisted in his unconventional ways. Mori Sosen accepted Okyo's naturalistic lead, turned and lived with the animals in order to portray them faithfully, and became Japan's greatest painter of monkeys and deer. By the time Okyo died (1795) the realists had won all along the line, and a completely popular school had captured the attention not only of Japan but of the world.

---

* The Metropolitan Museum of Art in New York has acquired a Korin "Wave-Screen," which Ledoux pronounced to be "one of the greatest works of this type that has ever been permitted to leave Japan."[80]

X. PRINTS

The "Ukiyoye" School — Its founders — Its masters — Hokusai
—Hiroshige

It is another jest of history that Japanese art should be most widely
known and influential in the West through that one of all its forms which
is least honored in Japan. About the middle of the eighteenth century the
art of engraving, which had come to Japan in the luggage of Buddhism
half a millennium before, was turned to the illustration of books and the life
of the people. The old subjects and methods had lost the tang of novelty
and interest; men were surfeited with Buddhist saints, Chinese philosophers, meditative animals and immaculate flowers; the new classes that
were slowly rising to prominence looked to art for some reflection of their
own affairs, and began to produce artists willing to meet these demands.
Since painting required leisure and expense, and produced but one picture
at a time, the new artists adapted engraving to their purposes, cut their
pictures into wood, and made as many cheap prints from the blocks as
their democratic purchasers required. These prints were at first colored
by hand. Then, about 1740, three blocks were made: one uncolored,
another partly colored rose-red, the third colored here and there in green;
and the paper was impressed upon each block in turn. Finally, in 1764,
Harunobu made the first polychrome prints, and paved the way for those
vivid sketches, by Hokusai and Hiroshige, which proved so suggestive
and stimulating to culture-weary Europeans thirsting for novelty. So was
born the *Ukiyoye* School of "Pictures of the Passing World."

Its painters were not the first who had taken the untitled man as the
object of their art. Iwasa Matabei, early in the seventeenth century, had
shocked the *Samurai* by depicting, on a six-panel screen, men, women and
children in the unrestrained attitudes of common life; in 1900 this screen
(the *Hikone Biobu*) was chosen by the Japanese Government for exhibition in Paris, and was insured on its voyage for 30,000 yen ($15,000).[82]
About 1660 Hishikawa Moronobu, a designer of Kyoto dress patterns,
made the earliest block prints, first for the illustration of books, then as
broadsheets scattered among the people, almost like picture postcards
among ourselves today. About 1687 Toru Kujomoto, designer of posters
for the Osaka theatres, moved to Yedo, and taught the *Ukiyoye* School
(which belonged entirely to the capital) how profitable it might be to

make prints of the famous actors of the day. From the stage the new artists passed to the brothels of the Yoshiwara, and gave to many a fragile beauty a taste of immortality. Bare breasts and gleaming limbs entered with disarming coyness into the once religious and philosophical sanctuaries of Japanese painting.

The masters of the developed art appeared towards the middle of the eighteenth century. Harunobu made prints of twelve or even fifteen colors from as many blocks, and, remorseful over his early pictures for the stage, painted with typical Japanese delicacy the graceful world of happy youth. Kiyonaga reached the first zenith of artistry in this school, and wove color and line into the swaying and yet erect figures of aristocratic women. Sharaku seems to have given only two years of his life to designing prints; but in this short time he lifted himself to the top of his tribe by his portraits of the Forty-seven *Ronin,* and his savagely ironic pictures of the stage's shooting "stars." Utamaro, rich in versatility and genius, master of line and design, etched the whole range of life from insects to courtesans; he spent half his career in the Yoshiwara, exhausted himself in pleasure and work, and earned a year in jail (1804) by picturing Hideyoshi with five concubines.[88] Wearied of normal people in normal attitudes, Utamaro portrayed his refined and complaisant ladies in almost spiritual slenderness, with tilted heads, elongated and slanting eyes, lengthened faces, and mysterious figures wrapped in flowing and multitudinous robes. A degenerating taste exalted this style into a bizarre mannerism, and was bringing the *Ukiyoye* School close to corruption and decay, when its two most famous masters arose to give it another half-century of life.

"The Old Man Mad with Painting," as Hokusai called himself, lived almost four-score years and ten, but mourned the tardiness of perfection and the brevity of life.

From my sixth year onwards a peculiar mania for drawing all sorts of things took possession of me. At my fiftieth year I had published quite a number of works of every possible description, but none were to my satisfaction. Real work began with me only in my seventieth year. Now at seventy-five the real appreciation of nature awakens within me. I therefore hope that at eighty I may have arrived at a certain power of intuition which will develop further to my ninetieth year, so that at the age of a hundred I can probably assert that my intuition is thoroughly artistic. And should it be granted to me to live a hundred and ten years, I hope that a vital and true comprehension of nature may radiate from every one of my lines and dots. . . . I invite those who are going to live as long as I to convince themselves whether I shall keep my word. Written at the age of seventy-five years by me, formerly Hokusai, now called the Old Man Mad with Painting."[84]

Like most of the *Ukiyoye* artists he was born of the artisan class, the son of a mirror-maker. Apprenticed to the artist Shunso, he was expelled for originality, and went back to his family to live in poverty and hardship throughout his long life. Unable to live by painting, he peddled food and almanacs. When his house burned down he merely composed a *hokka*:

It has burned down;
How serene the flowers in their falling![85]

When, at the age of eighty-nine, he was discovered by death, he surrendered reluctantly, saying: "If the gods had given me only ten years more I could have become a really great painter."[86]

He left behind him five hundred volumes of thirty thousand drawings. Intoxicated with the unconscious artistry of natural forms, he pictured in loving and varied repetition mountains, rocks, rivers, bridges, waterfalls and the sea. Having issued a book of "Thirty-six Views of Fuji," he went back, like the fascinated priest of Buddhist legend,* to sit at the foot of the sacred mount again, and draw "One Hundred Views of Fuji." In a series named "The Imagery of the Poets" he returned to the loftier subjects of Japanese art, and showed, among others, the great Li Po beside the chasm and cascade of Lu. In 1812 he issued the first of fifteen volumes called *Mangwa*—a series of realistic drawings of the homeliest details of common life, piquant with humor and scandalous with burlesque. These he flung off without care or effort, a dozen a day, until he had illustrated every nook and cranny of plebeian Japan. Never had the nation seen such fertility, such swift and penetrating conception, such reckless vitality of execution. As American critics looked down upon Whitman, so Japanese critics and art circles looked down upon Hokusai, seeing only the turbulence of his brush and the occasional vulgarity of his mind. But

* Who, having been exiled from Japan, sailed every day across the sea to gaze upon the Holy Mountain.

when he died his neighbors—who had not known that Whistler, in a modest moment, would rank him as the greatest painter since Velasquez[87]—marveled to see so long a funeral issue from so simple a home.

Less famous in the West but more respected in the East was the last great figure of the *Ukiyoye* School—Hiroshige (1796-1858). The hundred thousand distinct prints that claim his parentage picture the landscapes of his country more faithfully than Hokusai's, and with an art that has earned Hiroshige rank as probably the greatest landscape painter of Japan. Hokusai, standing before nature, drew not the scene but some airy fantasy suggested by it to his imagination; Hiroshige loved the world itself in all its forms, and drew these so loyally that the traveler may still recognize the objects and contours that inspired him. About 1830 he set out along the *Tokaido* or post road from Tokyo to Kyoto, and, like a true poet, thought less of his goal than of the diverting and significant scenes which he met on his way. When at last his trip was finished, he gathered his impressions together in his most famous work—"The Fifty-three Stations of the *Tokaido*" (1834). He liked to picture rain and the night in all their mystic forms, and the only man who surpassed him in this—Whistler—modeled his nocturnes upon Hiroshige's.[88] He too loved Fuji, and made "Thirty-six Views" of the mountain; but also he loved his native Tokyo, and made "One Hundred Views of Yedo" shortly before he died. He lived less years than Hokusai, but yielded up the torch with more content:

> I leave my brush at Azuma
> And go on the journey to the Holy West,
> To visit the famous scenery there.[*89]

XI. JAPANESE ART AND CIVILIZATION

A retrospect—Contrasts—An estimate—The doom of the old Japan

The Japanese print was almost the last phase of that subtle and delicate civilization which crumbled under the impact of Occidental industry, just as the cynical pessimism of the Western mind today may be the final aspect of a civilization doomed to die under the heel of Oriental industry. Because that medieval Japan which survived till 1853 was harmless to us,

---

* An excellent collection of Hiroshige's prints may be seen in the Boston Museum.

we can appreciate its beauty patronizingly; and it will be hard to find in a Japan of competing factories and threatening guns the charm that lures us in the selected loveliness of the past. We know, in our prosaic moments, that there was much cruelty in that old Japan, that peasants were poor and workers were oppressed, that women were slaves there, and might in hard times be sold into promiscuity, that life was cheap, and that in the end there was no law for the common man but the sword of the *Samurai*. But in Europe too men were cruel and women were a subject class, peasants were poor and workers were oppressed, life was hard and thought was dangerous, and in the end there was no law but the will of the lord or the king.

And as we can feel some affection for that old Europe because, in the midst of poverty, exploitation and bigotry, men built cathedrals in which every stone was carved in beauty, or martyred themselves to earn for their successors the right to think, or fought for justice until they created those civil liberties which are the most precious and precarious portion of our inheritance, so behind the bluster of the *Samurai* we honor the bravery that still gives to Japan a power above its numbers and its wealth; behind the lazy monks we sense the poetry of Buddhism, and acknowledge its endless incentives to poetry and art; behind the sharp blow of cruelty, and the seeming rudeness of the strong to the weak, we recognize the courtliest manners, the most pleasant ceremonies, and an unrivaled devotion to nature's beauty in all her forms. Behind the enslavement of women we see their beauty, their tenderness, and their incomparable grace; and amid the despotism of the family we hear the happiness of children playing in the garden of the East.

We are not much moved today by the restrained brevity and untranslatable suggestiveness of Japanese poetry; and yet it was this poetry, as well as the Chinese, that suggested the "free verse" and "imagism" of our time. There is scant originality in Japan's philosophers, and in her historians a dearth of the high impartiality that we expect of those whose books are not an annex to their country's armed or diplomatic force. But these were minor things in the life of Japan; she gave herself wisely to the creation of beauty rather than to the pursuit of truth. The soil she lived on was too treacherous to encourage sublime architecture, and yet the houses she built "are, from the esthetic point of view, the most perfect ever designed."[90] No country in modern times has rivaled her in the grace and loveliness of little things—the clothing of the women, the artistry of fans and parasols, of cups and toys, of *inro* and *netsuke*, the splendor of lacquer and the exquisite carving of wood. No other modern people has quite equaled the Japanese in restraint and delicacy of decoration, or in widespread refinement and sureness of taste. It is true that Japanese porcelain is less highly valued, even by the Japanese, than that of Sung and Ming; but if only the Chinese product surpasses it, the work of the Japanese potter still ranks above that of the modern European. And though Japanese painting lacks the strength and depth of Chinese, and Japanese prints are mere poster art at their worst, and at their best the transient redemption of hurried trivialities with a national perfection of grace and line, nevertheless it was Japanese rather than Chinese painting, and Japanese prints rather than Japanese water-colors, that revolutionized pictorial art in the nineteenth century, and gave the stimulus to a hundred experiments in fresh creative forms. These prints, sweeping into Europe in the wake of reopened trade after 1860, profoundly affected Monet, Manet, Degas and Whistler; they put an end to the "brown sauce" that had been served with almost every European painting from Leonardo to Millet; they filled the canvases of Europe with sunshine, and encouraged the painter to be a poet rather than a photographer. "The story of the beautiful," said Whistler, with the swagger that made all but his contemporaries love him, "is already complete—hewn in the marbles of the Parthenon, and broidered, with the birds, upon the fan of Hokusai—at the foot of Fuji-yama."[92]

We hope that this is not quite true; but it was unconsciously true for the old Japan. She died four years after Hokusai. In the comfort and peace of her isolation she had forgotten that a nation must keep abreast of the world if it does not wish to be enslaved. While Japan carved her *inro* and flourished her fans, Europe was establishing a science that was almost entirely unknown to the East; and that science, built up year by year in laboratories apparently far removed from the stream of the world's affairs, at last gave Europe the mechanized industries that enabled her to make the goods of life more cheaply—however less beautifully—than Asia's skilful artisans could turn them out by hand. Sooner or later those cheaper goods would win the markets of Asia, ruining the economic and changing the political life of countries pleasantly becalmed in the handicraft stage. Worse than that, science made explosives, battleships and guns that could kill a little more completely than the sword of the most heroic *Samurai;*

of what use was the bravery of a knight against the dastardly anonymity of a shell?

There is no more amazing or portentous phenomenon in modern history than the way in which sleeping Japan, roughly awakened by the cannon of the West, leaped to the lesson, bettered the instruction, accepted science, industry and war, defeated all her competitors either in battle or in trade, and became, within two generations, the most aggressive nation in the contemporary world.

CHAPTER XXXI

The New Japan

I. THE POLITICAL REVOLUTION

*The decay of the Shogunate—America knocks at the door—The
Restoration—The Westernization of Japan—Political recon-
struction — The new constitution — Law — The army —
The war with Russia—Its political results*

THE death of a civilization seldom comes from without; internal decay
must weaken the fibre of a society before external influences or attacks can change its essential structure, or bring it to an end. A ruling family rarely contains within itself that persistent vitality and subtle adaptability
which enduring domination requires; the founder exhausts half the strength
of the stock, and leaves to mediocrity the burdens that only genius could
bear. The Tokugawas after Iyeyasu governed moderately well, but, barring Yoshimune, they numbered no positive personalities in their line.
Within eight generations after Iyeyasu's death the feudal barons were
disturbing the Shogunate with sporadic revolts; taxes were delayed or
withheld, and the Yedo treasury, despite desperate economies, became
inadequate to finance national security or defense.[1] Two centuries and
more of peace had softened the *Samurāi*, and had disaccustomed the people
to the hardships and sacrifices of war; epicurean habits had displaced the
stoic simplicity of Hideyoshi's days, and the country, suddenly called upon
to protect its sovereignty, found itself physically and morally unarmed.
The Japanese intellect fretted under the exclusion of foreign intercourse,
and heard with restless curiosity of the rising wealth and varied civilization
of Europe and America; it studied Mabuchi and Moto-ori, and secretly
branded the *shoguns* as usurpers who had violated the continuity of the
Imperial dynasty; it could not reconcile the divine descent of the Emperor with the impotent poverty to which the Tokugawas had condemned
him. From their hiding-places in the Yoshiwara and elsewhere, subterranean pamphleteers began to flood the cities with passionate appeals for
the overthrow of the Shogunate, and the restoration of the Imperial power.

914

Upon this harassed and resourceless Government the news burst in 1853 that an American fleet, ignoring Japanese prohibitions, had entered Uraga Bay, and that its commander insisted upon seeing the supreme authority in Japan. Commodore Perry had four ships of war and 560 men; but instead of making a display of even this modest force, he sent a courteous note to the *Shogun* Iyeyoshi, assuring him that the American Government asked nothing more than the opening of a few Japanese ports to American trade, and some arrangements for the protection of such American seamen as might be shipwrecked on Japanese shores. The T'ai-p'ing Rebellion called Perry back to his base in Chinese waters; but in 1854 he returned to Japan armed with a larger squadron and a persuasive variety of gifts—perfumes, clocks, stoves, whiskey . . . —for the Emperor, the Empresses, and the princes of the blood. The new *Shogun*, Iyesada, neglected to transmit these presents to the royal family, but consented to sign the Treaty of Kanagawa, which conceded in effect all the American demands. Perry praised the courtesy of the islanders, and announced, with imperfect foresight, that "if the Japanese came to the United States they would find the navigable waters of the country free to them, and that they would not be debarred even from the gold-fields of California."[2] By this and later treaties the major ports of Japan were open to commerce from abroad, tariffs were specified and limited, and Japan agreed that Europeans and Americans accused of crime in the islands should be tried by their own consular courts. Stipulations were made and accepted that all persecution of Christianity should cease in the Empire; and at the same time the United States offered to sell to Japan such arms and battleships as she might need, and to lend officers and craftsmen for the instruction of this absurdly pacific nation in the arts of war.[3]

The Japanese people suffered keenly from the humiliation of these treaties, though later they acknowledged them as the impartial instruments of evolution and destiny. Some of them wished to fight the foreigners at any cost, to expel them all, and restore a self-contained agricultural and feudal regime. Others saw the necessity of imitating rather than expelling the West; the only course by which Japan could avoid the repeated defeats and the economic subjection which Europe was then imposing upon China was by learning as rapidly as possible the methods of Western industry, and the technique of modern war. With astonishing finesse the Westernizing leaders used the baronial lords as aides in overthrowing the Shogunate and restoring the Emperor, and then used the Imperial authority to overthrow feudalism and introduce Occidental industry. So in 1867 the feudal lords persuaded the last of the *shoguns*, Keiki, to abdicate. "Almost all the acts of the administration," said Keiki, "are far from perfect, and I confess it with shame that the present unsatisfactory condition of affairs is due to my shortcomings and incompetence. Now that foreign intercourse becomes daily more extensive, unless the government is directed from one central authority, the foundations of the state will fall to pieces.'" The Emperor Meiji replied tersely that "Tokugawa Keiki's proposal to restore the administrative authority to the Imperial Court is accepted"; and on January 1, 1868 the new "Era of Meiji" was officially begun. The old religion of *Shinto* was revised, and an intensive propaganda convinced the people that the restored emperor was divine in lineage and wisdom, and that his decrees were to be accepted as the edicts of the gods.

Armed with this new power, the Westernizers achieved almost a miracle in the rapid transformation of their country. Ito and Inouye braved their way through every prohibition and obstacle to Europe, studied its industries and institutions, marveled at the railroad, the steamship, the telegraph and the battleship, and came back inflamed with a patriotic resolve to Europeanize Japan. Englishmen were brought in to superintend the construction of railways, the erection of telegraphs, and the building of a navy; Frenchmen were commissioned to recast the laws and train the army; Germans were assigned to the organization of medicine and public health; Americans were engaged to establish a system of universal education; and to make matters complete, Italians were imported to instruct the Japanese in sculpture and painting.⁵ There were temporary, even bloody, reactions, and at times the spirit of Japan rebelled against this hectic and artificial metamorphosis; but in the end the machine had its way, and the Industrial Revolution added Japan to its realm.

Of necessity that Revolution (the only real revolution in modern history) lifted to wealth and economic power a new class of men—manufacturers, merchants and financiers—who in the old Japan had been ranked at the very bottom of the social scale. This rising *bourgeoisie* quietly used its means and influence first to destroy feudalism, and then to reduce to an imposing pretense the restored authority of the throne. In 1871 the Government persuaded the barons to surrender their ancient privileges, and consoled them with government bonds in exchange for

their lands.* Bound by ties of interest to the new society, the old aristocracy gave its services loyally to the Government, and enabled it to effect with bloodless ease the transition from a medieval to a modern state.
Ito Hirobumi, recently returned from a second visit to Europe, created,
in imitation of Germany, a new nobility of five orders—princes, marquises,
counts, viscounts and barons; but these men were the rewarded servants,
not the feudal enemies, of the industrial regime.

Modestly and tirelessly Ito labored to give his country a form of government that would avoid what seemed to him the excesses of democracy,
and yet enlist and encourage the talent of every class for a rapid economic
development.   Under his leadership Japan promulgated, in 1889, its first
constitution. At the top of the legal structure was the emperor, technically supreme, owning all land in fee simple, commander of an army and
a navy responsible to him alone, and giving to the Empire the strength
of unity, continuity, and regal prestige. Graciously he consented to delegate his law-making power, so long as it pleased him, to a Diet of two
chambers—a House of Peers and a House of Representatives; but the ministers of state were to be appointed by him, and to be accountable to him
rather than to the Diet. Underneath was a small electorate of some 460,-
000 voters, severely limited by a property qualification; successive liberal-
izations of the franchise raised the number of voters to 13,000,000 by 1928.
Corruption in office has kept pace with the extension of democracy.*

Along with these political developments went a new system of law
(1881), based largely upon the Napoleonic Code, and representing a
courageous advance on the medieval legislation of the feudal age. Civil
rights were liberally granted—freedom of speech, press, assembly and worship, inviolability of correspondence and domicile, and security from arrest
or punishment except by due process of law.† Torture and ordeal were
abolished, the *Eta* were freed from their caste disabilities, and all classes
were made theoretically equal before the law. Prisons were improved,
prisoners were paid for their work, and on their liberation they were
equipped with some modest capital to set them up in agriculture or trade.
Despite the lenience of the code, crime remained rare;[7] and if an orderly

---

* This process corresponded essentially to the abolition of feudalism, serfdom or slavery
in France in 1789, in Russia in 1862, and in the United States in 1863.

† These rights have been narrowly restricted by the war fever of the Manchurian adventure.

acceptance of law is a mark of civilization, Japan (allowing for a few assassinations) must stand in the first rank of modern states.

Perhaps the most significant feature of the new Constitution was the exemption of the army and the navy from any superior except the Emperor. Never forgetting the humiliation of 1853, Japan resolved to build an armed force that would make her master of her own destiny, and ultimately lord of the East. Not only did she establish conscription; she made every school in the land a military training camp and a nursery of nationalist ardor. With an amazing aptitude for organization and discipline, she soon brought her armed power to a point where she could speak to the "foreign barbarians" on equal terms, and might undertake that gradual absorption of China which Europe had contemplated but never achieved. In 1894, resenting the despatch of Chinese troops to put down an insurrection in Korea, and China's persistent reference to Korea as a tributary state under Chinese suzerainty, Japan declared war upon her ancient tutor, surprised the world with the speed of her victory, and exacted from China the acknowledgment of Korea's independence, the cession of Formosa and Port Arthur (at the tip of the Liaotung Peninsula), and an indemnity of 200,000,000 taels. Germany and France supported Russia in "advising" Japan to withdraw from Port Arthur on condition of receiving an additional indemnity of 30,000,000 taels (from China). Japan yielded, but kept the rebuff in bitter memory while she waited for revenge.

From that hour Japan prepared herself grimly for that conflict with Russia which imperialistic expansion in both empires made apparently inevitable. Availing herself of England's fear that Russia might advance into India, Japan concluded with the mistress of the seas an alliance (1902-22) by which each party contracted to come to the aid of its ally in case either should go to war with a third power, and another power should intervene. Seldom had England's diplomats signed away so much of England's liberty. When, in 1904, the war with Russia began, English and American bankers lent Japan huge sums to finance her victories against the Tsar.[8] Nogi captured Port Arthur, and moved his army north in time to turn the scales in the slaughter of Mukden—the bloodiest battle in history before our own incomparable Great War. Germany and France seem to have contemplated coming to the aid of Russia by diplomacy or arms; but President Roosevelt made it known that in such case he would "promptly side with Japan."[9] Meanwhile a Russian squadron of twenty-nine ships had gallantly sailed around the Cape of Good Hope, in the longest war-voyage ever made by a modern fleet, to face the Japanese in their own waters. Admiral Togo, making the first known naval use of radio, kept himself informed of the Russian flotilla's course, and pounced upon it in the Straits of Tsushima on May 27, 1905. To all his commanders Togo flashed a characteristic message: "The rise or fall of the Empire depends on this battle."[10] The Japanese lost 116 killed and 538 wounded; the Russians lost 4000 dead and 7000 prisoners, and all but three of their ships were captured or sunk.

The "Battle of the Sea of Japan" was a turning point in modern history. Not only did it end the expansion of Russia into Chinese territory; it ended also the rule of Europe in the East, and began that resurrection of Asia which promises to be the central political process of our century. All Asia took heart at the sight of the little island empire defeating the most populous power in Europe; China plotted her revolution, and India began to dream of freedom. As for Japan, it thought not of extending liberty but of capturing power. It secured from Russsia an acknowledgment of Japan's paramount position in Korea, and then, in 1910, formally annexed that ancient and once highly civilized kingdom. When the Emperor Meiji died, in 1912, after a long and benevolent career as ruler, artist and poet, he could take to the progenitor gods of Japan the message that the nation which they had created, and which at the outset of his reign had been a plaything in the hands of the impious West, was now supreme in the Orient, and was well on its way to becoming the pivot of history.

II. THE INDUSTRIAL REVOLUTION

Industrialization—Factories—Wages—Strikes—Poverty—The Japanese point of view

Meanwhile, in the course of half a century, Japan had changed every aspect of its life. The peasant, though poor, was free; he could own a modest parcel of land by paying an annual tax or rental to the state; and no lord could hinder him if he chose to leave the fields and seek his fortune in the cities. For there were great cities now along the coast: Tokyo (i.e., the "Eastern Capital"), with its royal and aristocratic palaces, its spacious parks and crowded baths, and a population second only to that of London and New York; Osaka, once a fishing village and a castle, now a dark abyss of hovels, factories and skyscrapers, the center of the industries of Japan; and Yokohama and Kobe, from whose gigantic wharves, equipped with every modern mechanism, those industries despatched to a thousand ports the second largest merchant marine in the world.*

The leap from feudalism to capitalism was eased by an unprecedented use of every aid. Foreign experts were brought in, and Japanese assistants obeyed their instructions eagerly; within fifteen years the clever learners had made such progress that the foreign specialists were paid off and courteously sent home. Following the lead of Germany the Government took over posts, railroads, telegraphs and telephones; but at the same time it made generous loans to private industries, and protected them with high tariffs from the competition of factories abroad. The indemnity paid by the Chinese after the war of 1894 financed and stimulated the industrialization of Japan precisely as the French indemnity of 1871 had accelerated the industrialization of Germany. Japan, like the Germany of a generation before, was able to begin with modern equipment and feudal discipline, while their long-established competitors struggled with obsolescent machinery and rebellious workingmen. Power was cheap in Japan, and wages were low; laborers were loyally submissive to their chiefs; factory laws came late, and were leniently enforced.[12] In 1933 the new Osaka spindles needed one girl for twenty-five machines; the old Lancashire spindles required one man for six.[13]

The number of factories doubled from 1908 to 1918, and again from 1918 to 1924; by 1931 they had increased by fifty per cent more,[14] while industry in the West plumbed the depths of depression. In 1933 Japan took first place as an exporter of textile products, sending out two of the five-and-a-half billion yards of cotton goods consumed in that year by the world.[15] By abandoning the gold standard in 1931, and allowing the *yen* to fall to forty per cent of its former value in international exchange, Japan increased her foreign sales fifty per cent from 1932 to 1933.[16] Domestic as well as foreign commerce flourished, and great merchant families, like the Mitsui and the Mitsubishi, amassed such fortunes that the military joined the wage-earning classes in meditating governmental absorption or control of industry and trade.†

---

* By the last official census Yokohama had 620,000 population, Kobe 787,000, Osaka 2,114,804, and Greater Tokyo 5,311,000.

† Transport by land did not grow as rapidly as marine trade, for the mountainous backbone of the islands made commerce prefer the sea. Roads remained poor by comparison with the West; and automobiles have only recently begun to be a peril in Japan.

While the growth of commerce generated a new and prosperous middle class, the manual workers bore the brunt of the low production costs through which Japan undersold her competitors in the markets of the world. The average wage of the men in 1931 was $1.17 a day; of the women, 48 cents a day; 51 per cent of the industrial workers were women, and twelve per cent were under sixteen years of age.[19]* Strikes were frequent and communism was growing when the war spirit of 1931 turned the nation to patriotic coöperation and conformity; "dangerous thoughts" were made illegal, and labor unions, never strong in Japan, were subjected to severe restrictions.[20] Great slums developed in Osaka, Kobe and Tokyo; in those of Tokyo a family of five occupied an average room space of from eight to ten feet square—a trifle more than the area covered by a double bed; in those of Kobe twenty thousand paupers, criminals, defectives and prostitutes lived in such filth that each year epidemics decimated them, and infant mortality rose to four times its average for the remainder of Japan.[21] Communists like Katayama and Christian Socialists like Kagawa fought violently or peaceably against these conditions, until at last the Government undertook the greatest slum-clearing project in history.

A generation ago Lafcadio Hearn expressed a bitter judgment upon the modern regime in Japan:

> Under the new order of things forms of social misery never before known in the history of the race are being developed. Some idea of this misery may be obtained from the fact that the number of poor people in Tokyo unable to pay their residence tax is upward of 50,000; yet the amount of the tax is only about twenty *sen*, or ten cents in American money. Prior to the accumulation of wealth in the hands of the minority there was never any such want in any part of Japan—except, of course, as a temporary consequence of war.[22]

Already, however, the *jinricksha*, or "man-power-vehicle," traditionally ascribed to an inventive American missionary in the early eighties,[17] is disappearing before American and domestic motor cars and 200,000 miles of highway have been paved. Tokyo has a subway which compares favorably with those of Europe and America. The first Japanese railway was built in 1872, over a brave stretch of eighteen miles; by 1932 the narrow islands had 13,734 miles of iron roads. The new express from Dairen (near Port Arthur) to Hsinking (formerly Changchun), the capital of Manchuria, makes the 700 kilometers at the rate of 120 kilometers (approximately 75 miles) per hour.[18]

* The low remuneration of women is partly due to the expensively high turn-over among the women workers, who usually leave industry when they have amassed a marriage dowry.

The "accumulation of wealth in the hands of the minority" is, no doubt, a universal and apparently unfailing concomitant of civilization. Japanese employers believe that the wages which they pay are not too low in relation to the comparative inefficiency of Japanese labor, and the low cost of living in Japan.[33] Low wages, thinks Japan, are necessary for low costs; low costs are necessary for the capture of foreign markets; foreign markets are necessary for an industry dependent upon imported fuels and minerals; industry is necessary for the support of a growing population in islands only twelve per cent of whose soil permits cultivation; and industry is necessary to that wealth and armament without which Japan could not defend herself against the rapacious West.

III. THE CULTURAL REVOLUTION

Changes in dress—In manners—The Japanese character—Morals and marriage in transition — Religion — Science — Japanese medicine — Art and taste — Language and education — Naturalistic fiction—New forms of poetry

Have the people themselves been changed by their Industrial Revolution? Certain external innovations catch the eye: the lugubrious bifurcate costume of the European man has captured and enclosed most urban males; but the women continue to clothe themselves in loose and colorful robes, bound at the waist with brocaded bands that meet in a spacious bow at the back.* Shoes are replacing wooden clogs as roads improve; but a large proportion of both sexes still move about in bare and undeformed feet. In the greater cities one may find every variation and combination of native and European dress, as if to symbolize a transformation hurried and incomplete.

Manners are still a model of diplomatic courtesy, though men adhere to their ancient custom of preceding women in entering or leaving a room or in walking along the street. Language is deviously polite, and rarely profane; a formal humility clothes a fierce self-respect, and etiquette graces the most sincere hostility. The Japanese character, like that of man everywhere, is a mosaic of contradictions; for life offers us diverse situations at divers times, and demands of us alternately force and gentleness, levity and gravity, patience and courage, modesty and pride. Therefore we must not be prejudiced against the Japanese because they are senti-

---

* Women engaged in teaching or industry wear uniforms of Occidental cut. Both sexes, after working hours, relax into the traditional costumes.

mental and realistic, sensitive and stoical, expressive and reticent, excitable and restrained; aboundingly cheerful, humorous and pleasure-loving, and inclined to picturesque suicide; lovingly kind—often to animals, sometimes to women—and occasionally cruel to animals and men.* The typical Japanese has all the qualities of the warrior—pugnacity and courage, and an unrivaled readiness to die; and yet, very often, he has the soul of an artist—sensuous, impressionable, and almost instinctively possessed of taste. He is sober and unostentatious, frugal and industrious, curious and studious, loyal and patient, with an heroic capacity for details; he is cunning and supple, like most physically small persons; he has a nimble intelligence, not highly creative in the field of thought, but capable of quick comprehension, adaptation, and practical achievement. The spirit and vanity of a Frenchman, the courage and narrowness of a Briton, the hot temper and artistry of an Italian, the energy and commercialism of an American, the sensitiveness and shrewdness of a Jew—all these have come together to make the Japanese.

Contact and conflict with the West have altered in some ways the moral life of Japan. The traditional honesty of its people† largely continues; but the extension of the franchise and the keen competition of modern trade have brought to Japan a proportionate share of democratic venality, industrial ruthlessness and financial legerdemain. *Bushido* survives here and there among the higher soldiery, and offers a mild aristocratic check to commercial and political deviltry. Despite the law-abiding patience of the common people assassination is frequent—not as a corrective of reactionary despotism but usually as an encouragement to aggressive patriotism. The Black Dragon Society, led by the apparently untouchable Toyama, has dedicated itself for over forty years to promoting among Japanese officials a policy of conquest in Korea and Manchuria;‡ and in the pursuit of this purpose it has given assassination a popular rôle in the political machinery of Japan.[26]

---

* During the chaos that followed the earthquake of 1923 the Japanese of Yokohama, while being fed by American relief ships, took advantage of the turmoil to slaughter hundreds (some say thousands) of unarmed radicals and Koreans in the streets.[24] Some passionate patriot, it seems, had aroused the Japanese by announcing that the Koreans (who were a mere handful) were planning to overthrow the Government and kill the Emperor.

† "I have lived," said Lafcadio Hearn, "in districts where no case of theft had occurred for hundreds of years—where the newly-built prisons of Meiji remained empty and useless."[25]

‡ *Black Dragon* is the Chinese name for the Amur River, which separates Manchuria from Siberia. The Japanese look upon assassination as merely a dignified substitute for exile.

The Far East has paralleled the West in that moral disturbance which accompanies every profound change in the economic basis of life. The eternal war of the generations—the revolt of over-eager youth against over-cautious age—has been intensified by the growth of individualist industry, and the weakening of religious faith. The transit from country to city, and the replacement of the family by the individual as the legal and responsible unit of economic and political society, has undermined parental authority, and subjected the customs and morals of centuries to the hasty judgment of adolescence. In the larger centers the young rebel against marriages parentally arranged; and the new couples, instead of taking up their residence in the establishment of the bridegroom's father, tend increasingly to set up separate and independent homes—or apartments. The rapid industrialization of women has necessitated a loosening of the bonds that held them to domestic subserviency. Divorce is as common as in America, and more convenient; it may be had by signing a registration book and paying a fee of ten cents.[27] Concubinage has been made illegal, but in practice it is still permitted to those who can afford to ignore the law.[28]

In Japan as elsewhere the machine is the enemy of the priest. Spencer and Stuart Mill were imported along with English technology, and the reign of Confucius in Japanese philosophy came to a sudden end. "The generation now at school," said Chamberlain in 1905, "is distinctly Voltairean."[29] By the same token—through its modern alliance with the machine—science prospered, and won a characteristic devotion, in Japan, from some of the most brilliant investigators of our time.* Japanese medicine, though dependent in most stages upon China or Korea, has made swift progress under European—especially German—example and stimulus. The work of Takamine in the discovery of adrenalin and the study of vitamins; of Kitasato in tetanus and pneumonia, and in the development of an anti-toxin for diphtheria; and, most famous and brilliant of all, of Noguchi in syphilis and yellow fever— these achievements indicate the rapidity with which the Japanese have ceased to be pupils, and have become teachers, of the world.

Hideyo Noguchi was born in 1876 in one of the lesser islands, and in a family so poor that his father deserted on learning that another child was due. The neglected boy fell into a brazier; his left hand was burned to a stump, and his right hand was injured almost to the point of uselessness.

---

* Such science as existed in Japan before 1853 was mostly an importation from the parental mainland. The Japanese calendar, previously based upon the phases of the moon, was readjusted to the solar year by a Korean priest about 604 A.D. In 680 A.D. Chinese modifications were introduced, and Japan took over (and still retains) the Chinese method of reckoning events by reference to the name and year of the reigning emperor. The Gregorian calendar was adopted by Japan in 1873.

Shunned at school because of his scars and deformities, he was planning to kill himself when a surgeon came to the village, treated the right hand successfully, and so won Noguchi's gratitude that the lad there and then dedicated himself to medicine. "I will be a Napoleon to save instead of to kill," he announced; "I can already get along on four hours of sleep at night."[30] Penniless, he worked in a pharmacy until he had persuaded its owner to advance him funds for the study of medicine. After graduating he came to the United States, and offered his services to the Medical Corps of the Army at Washington in return for his expenses. The Rockefeller Foundation for Medical Research gave him a laboratory, and Noguchi, literally single-handed, entered upon a fruitful career of experiment and research. He produced the first pure culture of the syphilitic germ, discovered the syphilitic nature of general paralysis and locomotor ataxia, and finally (1918) isolated the yellow fever parasite. Made famous and momentarily affluent, he went back to Japan, honored his old mother, and knelt in gratitude to the kindly pharmacist who had paid for his medical education. Then he went to Africa to study the yellow fever that was raging along the Gold Coast, was himself infected with it, and died (1928) at the pitifully early age of fifty-two.

The development of science, in Japan as in the West, has been accompanied by a decay of the traditional arts. The overthrow of the old aristocracy destroyed a nursery of taste, and left each generation to develop its own norms of excellence anew. The influx of foreign money seeking native wares led to rapid quantitative production, and debased the standards of Japanese design. When the buyers turned to the quest for ancient works, the artisans became forgers, and the manufacture of antiques became in Japan, as in China, one of the most flourishing of modern arts. *Cloisonné* is probably the only branch of ceramics that has progressed in Japan since the coming of the West. The chaotic passage from handicraft to machinery, and the sudden irruption of foreign tastes and ways clothed in the gaudy prestige of victory and wealth, have unsettled the esthetic sense of Japan, and weakened the sureness of her taste. Perhaps, now that Japan has chosen the sword, she is destined to repeat the history of Rome—imitative in art, but masterly in administration and war.*

A flattery of Occidental modes has marked for a generation the intellectual life of the new empire. European words crowded into the language, news-

---

* The current fever of nationalism has brought with it a revival of native *motifs* and styles.

papers were organized in Western style, and a system of public schools was established after American exemplars. Japan heroically resolved to make itself the most literate nation on earth, and it succeeded; in 1925 99.4 per cent of all Japanese children attended school,[31] and in 1927, 93 per cent of the people could read.[32] Students took religiously to the new secular learning; hundreds of them lost their health in their eagerness for knowledge,[33] and the Government was obliged to take active measures for the encouragement of athletics, gymnastics and games of every kind from *ju-jitsu* to baseball. Education was removed from religious auspices, and became more thoroughly secularized in Japan than in most European nations. Five imperial universities were supported, and forty-one other universities, only less imperial, gathered in thousands of zealous students. By 1931 the Imperial University of Tokyo had 8,064 students, and the University of Kyoto had 5,552.[34]

Japanese literature, in the last quarter of the century, lost itself in a series of imitative fashions. English liberalism, Russian realism, Nietzschean individualism and American pragmatism swept the intelligentsia in turn, until the spirit of nationalism reasserted itself, and Japanese writers began to explore their native material in their native ways. A young woman, Ichi-yo, before dying in 1896 at the age of twenty-four, inaugurated a naturalistic movement in fiction by presenting vividly the misery and subjection of women in Japan.[35] In 1906 the poet Toson brought this movement to its height with a long novel—*Hakai* or "The Breaking of the Pledge"—which told in poetic prose the story of a teacher who, having promised his father never to reveal the fact that he was of *Eta* or slave origin, worked his way by ability and education to a high position, fell in love with a girl of refinement and social standing, and then, in a burst of honesty, confessed his origin, surrendered his sweetheart and his place, and left Japan forever. This novel contributed powerfully to the agitation that finally ended the historic disabilities of the *Eta* class.

The *tanka* and the *hokka* were the last forms of Japanese culture to yield to the influence of the West. For forty years after the Restoration they continued to be the required modes of Japanese verse, and the poetic spirit lost itself in miracles of ingenuity and artifice. Then, in 1897, Toson, a young teacher of Sendai, sold to a publisher, for fifteen dollars, a volume of poems whose individual length constituted a revolution almost as startling as any that had shaken the fabric of the state. The public, tired of elegant epigrams, responded gratefully, and made the publisher rich. Other poets followed the path that Toson had explored, and the *tanka* and *hokka* surrendered at last their thousand-year-old domination.[36]

Despite the new forms the old Imperial Poetry Contest still continues. Every year the Emperor announces a theme, and sets an example by inditing an ode to it; the Empress follows him; and then twenty-five thousand Japanese, of every sort and condition, send in their compositions to the Poetry Bureau at the Imperial Palace, to be judged by the highest bards of the land. The ten poems accounted best are read to the Emperor and the Empress, and are printed in the New Year's issue of the Japanese press.[37] It is an admirable custom, fit to turn the soul for a moment from commercialism and war, and proving that Japanese literature is still a vital part in the life of the most vital nation in the contemporary world.

IV. THE NEW EMPIRE

The precarious bases of the new civilization—Causes of Japanese imperialism—The Twenty-one Demands—The Washington Conference—The Immigration Act of 1924—The invasion of Manchuria—The new kingdom—Japan and Russia—Japan and Europe—Must America fight Japan?

Despite its rapid growth in wealth and power the new Japan rested upon precarious foundations. Its population had mounted from 3,000,-000 in the days of Shotoku Taishi to some 17,000,000 under Hideyoshi, some 30,000,000 under Yoshimune, and over 55,000,000 at the end of Meiji's reign (1912).* It had doubled in a century, and the mountain-ribbed islands, so sparsely arable, contained with difficulty their multiplying millions. An insular population half as great as that of the United States had to support itself on an area one-twentieth as large.[38] It could maintain itself only by manufactures; and yet Japan was tragically poor in the fuels and minerals indispensable to industry. Hydro-electric power

---

* In 1934 the population of the Japanese Empire (i.e., Japan, Korea, Formosa and some minor possessions) totaled eighty millions. Should Japan succeed in reconciling the inhabitants of Manchuria to Japanese rule, it will control, for industry and war, 110,000,000 people. As the population of Japan alone increases by a million a year, and that of the United States is rapidly approaching a stationary condition, the two systems may soon confront each other with approximately equal populations.

lurked in the streams that flowed from the mountains to the sea, but the full development of this resource would add only one-third to the power already used,[39] and could not be relied upon for the expanding needs of the future. Coal was found here and there, in almost inaccessible veins, in the islands of Kyushu and Hokkaido, and oil could be secured from Sakhalin; but iron, the very bone and sinew of industry, was almost completely absent from Japanese soil.[40] Finally, the low standard of living to which the nature of the strong and the costliness of materials and power had condemned the masses of Japan made consumption lag more and more behind production; every year, from factories ever better equipped, there poured forth a mounting surplus of goods unpurchasable at home and crying out for markets abroad.

Out of such conditions imperialism is born—that is, the effort of an economic system to exercise control, through its agent the government, over foreign regions upon which it is believed to depend for fuels, markets, materials or dividends. Where could Japan find those opportunities and those materials? She could not look to Indo-China, or India, or Australia, or the Philippines; for these had been preëmpted by Western powers, and their tariff walls favored their white masters against Japan. Clearly China had been placed at Nippon's door as a providentially designed market for Japanese goods; and Manchuria—rich in coal and iron, rich in the wheat that the islands could not profitably grow, rich in human resources for industry, taxation and war—Manchuria belonged by manifest destiny to Japan. By what right? By the same right whereby England had taken India and Australia, France Indo-China, Germany Shantung, Russia Port Arthur, and America the Philippines—the right of the need of the strong. In the long run no excuses would be necessary; all that was needed was power and an opportunity. In the eyes of a Darwinian world success would sanction every means.

Opportunity came generously—first with the Great War, then with the breakdown of European and American economic life. The War did not merely accelerate production in Japan (as in America) by giving to industry an ideal foreign market—a continent at war; at the same time it absorbed and weakened Europe, and left Japan with almost a free hand in the East. Therefore she invaded Shantung in 1914; and a year later she presented to China those "Twenty-one Demands" which, if they had been enforced, would have made all China a gigantic colony of little Japan.

Group I of the Demands asked Chinese recognition of Japanese suzerainty in Shantung; Group II asked certain industrial privileges, and an acknowledgment of Japan's special rights, in Manchuria and Eastern Mongolia; Group III proposed that the greatest of mining companies on the mainland should become a joint concern of China and Japan; Group IV (aimed at America's request for a coaling station near Foochow) stipulated that "no island, port or harbor along the coast shall be ceded to any third Power." Group V modestly suggested that the Chinese should hereafter employ Japanese advisers in their political, economic and military affairs; that the police authority in the major cities of China should be jointly administered by Chinese and Japanese; that China should purchase at least fifty per cent of all her munitions from Japan; that Japan should be allowed to build three important railways in China; and that Japan should have the right freely to establish railways, mines and harbors in the Province of Fukien.⁴¹

The United States protested that some of these Demands violated the territorial integrity of China, and the principle of the Open Door. Japan withdrew Group V, modified the remaining Demands, and presented them to China with an ultimatum on May 7, 1915. China accepted them on the following day. A Chinese boycott of Japanese goods ensued; but Japan proceeded on the historically correct assumption that boycotts are sooner or later frustrated by the tendency of trade to follow the line of lowest costs. In 1917 the suave Viscount Ishii explained the Japanese position to the American people, and persuaded Secretary of State Lansing to sign an agreement recognizing "that Japan has special interests in China, particularly in the part to which her possessions are contiguous." In 1922, at the Washington Conference, Secretary of State Hughes prevailed upon the Japanese to acknowledge the principle of the "Open Door" in China, and to be content with a navy sixty per cent as large as England's or America's.* At the close of the Conference Japan agreed to return to China that part of Shantung (Tsingtao) which she had taken from Germany during the War. The Anglo-Japanese Alliance died a silent death, and America dreamed cozily of eternal peace.

Out of this youthful confidence in the future came one of the gravest failures of American diplomacy. Finding the people of the Pacific Coast troubled by the influx of Japanese into California, President Theodore Roosevelt in 1907, with the good sense that hid behind his popular bluster. quietly negotiated with the Japanese Government a "Gentlemen's Agree-

---

* The ratio of 5-5-3 was based upon the greater extent of coast-lines or possessions requiring English or American defense, as compared with the limited and protected territory of Japan.

ment" by which Japan promised to forbid the emigration of her laborers to the United States. But the high birth rate of those already admitted continued to disturb the western states, and several of them enacted laws preventing aliens from acquiring land. When, in 1924, the American Congress decided to restrict immigration, it refused to apply to the races of Asia that principle of quotas on which the reduced immigration of European peoples was to be allowed;* instead it forbade the entrance of Asiatics altogether. Approximately the same result would have been se-cured by applying the quota to all races, without discrimination or name; and Secretary Hughes protested "that the legislation would seem to be quite unnecessary even for the purpose for which it is devised."[42] But hot-heads interpreted as a threat the warning uttered by the Japanese Am-bassador of the "grave consequences" that might come from the act; and in a fever of resentment the Immigration Bill was passed.

All Japan flared up at what appeared to be a deliberate insult. Meetings were held, speeches were made, and a patriot committed *hara-kiri* at the door of Viscount Inouye's home in order to express the national sense of shame. The Japanese leaders, knowing that the country had been weak-ened by the earthquake of 1923, held their peace and bided their time. In the natural course of events America and Europe would some day be weakened in turn; and then Japan would seize her second opportunity, and take her delayed revenge.

When the greatest of all wars was followed by almost the greatest of all depressions, Japan saw a long-awaited chance to establish her mastery in the Far East. Announcing that her businessmen had been maltreated by the Chinese authorities in Manchuria, and secretly fearful that her rail-way and other investments there were threatened with ruin by the compe-tition of the Chinese, Japan, in September, 1931, allowed her army, of its own initiative, to advance into Manchuria. China, disordered with revolu-tion, provincial separatism and purchasable politicians, could make no uni-fied resistance except to resort again to the boycott of Japanese goods; and when Japan, in alleged protest against boycott propaganda, invaded Shang-hai (1932), only a fraction of China rose to repel the invasion. The ob-jections of the United States were cautiously approved of "in principle" by European powers too absorbed in their individual commercial interests

---

* By this principle the number of immigrants from any country was to bear the same ratio to the total of permitted annual immigration as persons of that nationality had borne to the total population of America in 1890.

to take decisive and united action against this dramatic termination of the white man's brief authority in the distant East. The League of Nations appointed a commission under the Earl of Lytton, which made an apparently thorough and impartial investigation and report; but Japan withdrew from the League on the same ground on which America, in 1935, refused to join in the World Court—that she did not care to be judged by a court of her enemies. The boycott reduced Japanese imports into China by forty-seven per cent between August, 1932, and May, 1933; but meanwhile Japanese trade was ousting Chinese commerce in the Philippines, the Malay States and South Seas, and, so soon as 1934, Japanese diplomats, with the aid of Chinese statesmen, persuaded China to write a tariff law favoring Japanese products as against those of the Western powers.[43]

In March, 1932, Japanese authority installed Henry P'u Yi, inheritor of the Manchu throne in China, as Chief Executive of the new state of Manchukuo; and two years later it made him Emperor under the name of Kang Teh. The officials were either Japanese or complaisant Chinese; but behind every Chinese official was a Japanese adviser.[44] While the "Open Door" was technically maintained, ways were found to place Manchukuoan trade and resources in Japanese hands.[45] Immigration from Japan failed to develop, but Japanese capital poured in abundantly. Railways were built for commercial and military purposes, highways were rapidly improved, and negotiations were begun for the purchase of the Chinese Eastern Railway from the Soviet. The Japanese army, victorious and competent, not only organized the new state, but dictated the policy of the Government at Tokyo. It conquered the province of Jehol for Pu-yi, advanced almost to Peiping, retreated magnanimously, and bided its time.

Meanwhile Japanese representatives at Nanking strain every *yen* to win from the Chinese Government an acceptance of Japanese leadership in every economic and political aspect of Chinese life. When China has been won, by conquest or by loans, Japan will be ready to deal with her ancient enemy—once the Empire of all the Russias, now the Union of Soviet Socialist Republics. Up along Mongolia's caravan route through Kalgan and Urga, or across the Manchukuoan border into Chita, or at any one of a hundred vulnerable points where the Trans-Siberian Railway, still for the most part single-tracked in the Far East, coils itself about the new state, the Japanese army may strike and cut the spinal cord that binds China, Vladivostok and Trans-Baikalia with the Russian capital. Feverishly, heroically,

Russia prepares for the irrepressible conflict. At Kuznetzk and Magneto-gorsk she develops great coal mines and steel factories, capable of being transformed into giant munition plants; while at Vladivostok a host of submarines arranges to entertain a Japanese fleet, and hundreds of bomb-ing planes have their eyes on Japan's centers of production and transport, and her cities of flimsy wood.

Behind this ominous foreground stand the tamed and frustrated Western powers: America chafing at the loss of Chinese markets, France wonder-ing how long she can hold Indo-China, England disturbed about Australia and India, and harassed by Japanese competition not only in China but throughout her empire in the East. Nevertheless France prefers to help finance Japan rather than to antagonize her; and canny Britain waits in unprecedented patience, hoping that each of her great competitors in Asiatic trade will destroy the other and leave the world to England again. Every day the conflict of interest becomes more acute, and approaches nearer to open strife. Japan insists that foreign companies selling oil to Japan shall maintain on her soil a reserve of oil sufficient to supply the islands for half a year in case of emergency. Manchukuo is closing her doors to non-Japanese oil. Japan, over the protests of Americans, and over the veto of the Uruguayan President, has won permission from the legislature of Uruguay to build on the River Plate a free port for the duti-less entry or manufacture of Japanese goods. From that strategic center the commercial and financial penetration of Latin America will proceed at a rate unequaled since Germany's rapid conquest of South American trade helped to bring on the Great War, and America's participation in it. As the memory of that war begins to fade, preparations for another be-come the order of the day.

Must America fight Japan? Our economic system gives to the investing class so generous a share of the wealth created by science, management and labor that too little is left to the mass of producers to enable them to buy back as much as they produce; a surplus of goods is created which cries out for the conquest of foreign markets as the only alternative to inter-rupting production—or spreading the power of consumption—at home. But this is even truer of the Japanese economic system than of our own; it too must conquer foreign markets, not only to maintain its centralized wealth, but to secure the fuels and raw materials indispensable to her in-dustries. By the sardonic irony of history that same Japan which America awoke from peaceful agriculture in 1853, and prodded into industry and trade, now turns all her power and subtlety to winning by underselling, and to controlling by conquest or diplomacy, precisely those Asiatic markets upon which America has fixed her hopes as potentially the richest outlet for her surplus goods. Usually in history, when two nations have contested for the same markets, the nation that has lost in the economic competition, if it is stronger in resources and armament, has made war upon its enemy.*

* Written in 1934.

Envoi

OUR ORIENTAL HERITAGE

We have passed in unwilling haste through four thousand years of history, and over the richest civilizations of the largest continent. It is impossible that we have understood these civilizations, or done them justice; for how can one mind, in one lifetime, comprehend or appraise the heritage of a race? The institutions, customs, arts and morals of a people represent the natural selection of its countless trial-and-error experiments, the accumulated and unformulable wisdom of all its generations; and neither the intelligence of a philosopher nor the intellect of a sophomore can suffice to compass them understandingly, much less to judge them with justice. Europe and America are the spoiled child and grandchild of Asia, and have never quite realized the wealth of their pre-classical inheritance. But if, now, we sum up those arts and ways which the West has derived from the East, or which, to our current and limited knowledge, appear first in the Orient, we shall find ourselves drawing up unconsciously an outline of civilization.

The first element of civilization is labor—tillage, industry, transport and trade. In Egypt and Asia we meet with the oldest known cultivation of the soil,* the oldest irrigation systems, and the first† production of those encouraging beverages without which, apparently, modern civilization could hardly exist—beer and wine and tea. Handicrafts and engineering were as highly developed in Egypt before Moses as in Europe before Voltaire; building with bricks has a history at least as old as Sargon I; the potter's wheel and the wagon wheel appear first in Elam, linen and glass in Egypt, silk and gunpowder in China. The horse rides out of Central Asia into Mesopotamia, Egypt and Europe; Phœnician vessels circumnavigate Africa before the age of Pericles; the compass comes from China and produces a commercial revolution in Europe. Sumeria shows us the first business contracts, the first credit system, the first use of gold and

---

* It is possible that agriculture and the domestication of animals are as ancient in neolithic Europe as in neolithic Asia; but it seems more likely that the New Stone Age cultures of Europe were younger than those of Africa and Asia. Cf. Chapter VI above.

† In this and subsequent statements the word *known* is to be understood.

934

silver as standards of value; and China first accomplishes the miracle of having paper accepted in place of silver or gold.

The second element of civilization is government—the organization and protection of life and society through the clan and the family, law and the state. The village community appears in India, and the city-state in Sumeria and Assyria. Egypt takes a census, levies an income tax, and maintains internal peace through many centuries with a model minimum of force. Ur-Engur and Hammurabi formulate great codes of law, and Darius organizes, with imperial army and post, one of the best administered empires in the annals of government.

The third element of civilization is morality—customs and manners, conscience and charity; a law built into the spirit, and generating at last that sense of right and wrong, that order and discipline of desire, without which a society disintegrates into individuals, and falls forfeit to some coherent state. Courtesy came out of the ancient courts of Egypt, Mesopotamia and Persia; even today the Far East might teach manners and dignity to the brusque and impatient West. Monogamy appeared in Egypt, and began a long struggle to prove itself and survive in competition with the inequitable but eugenic polygamy of Asia. Out of Egypt came the first cry for social justice; out of Judea the first plea for human brotherhood, the first formulation of the moral consciousness of mankind.

The fourth element of civilization is religion—the use of man's supernatural beliefs for the consolation of suffering, the elevation of character, and the strengthening of social instincts and order. From Sumeria, Babylonia and Judea the most cherished myths and traditions of Europe were derived; in the soil of the Orient grew the stories of the Creation and the Flood, the Fall and Redemption of man; and out of many mother goddesses came at last "the fairest flower of all poesy," as Heine called Mary, the Mother of God. Out of Palestine came monotheism, and the fairest songs of love and praise in literature, and the loneliest, lowliest, and most impressive figure in history.

The fifth element in civilization is science—clear seeing, exact recording, impartial testing, and the slow accumulation of a knowledge objective enough to generate prediction and control. Egypt develops arithmetic and geometry, and establishes the calendar; Egyptian priests and physicians practise medicine, explore diseases enematically, perform a hundred varieties of surgical operation, and anticipate something of the Hippocratic oath. Babylonia studies the stars, charts the zodiac, and gives us our division of the month into four weeks, of the clock into twelve hours, of the hour into sixty minutes, of the minute into sixty seconds. India transmits through the Arabs her simple numerals and magical decimals, and teaches Europe the subtleties of hypnotism and the technique of vaccination.

The sixth element of civilization is philosophy—the attempt of man to capture something of that total perspective which in his modest intervals he knows that only Infinity can possess; the brave and hopeless inquiry into the first causes of things, and their final significance; the consideration of truth and beauty, of virtue and justice, of ideal men and states. All this appears in the Orient a little sooner than in Europe: the Egyptians and the Babylonians ponder human nature and destiny, and the Jews write immortal comments on life and death, while Europe tarries in barbarism; the Hindus play with logic and epistemology at least as early as Parmenides and Zeno of Elea; the Upanishads delve into metaphysics, and Buddha propounds a very modern psychology some centuries before Socrates is born. And if India drowns philosophy in religion, and fails to emancipate reason from hope, China resolutely secularizes her thought, and produces, again before Socrates, a thinker whose sober wisdom needs hardly any change to be a guide to our contemporary life, and an inspiration to those who would honorably govern states.

The seventh element of civilization is letters—the transmission of language, the education of youth, the development of writing, the creation of poetry and drama, the stimulus of romance, and the written remembrance of things past. The oldest schools known to us are those of Egypt and Mesopotamia; even the oldest schools of government are Egyptian. Out of Asia, apparently, came writing; out of Egypt the alphabet, paper and ink; out of China, print. The Babylonians seem to have compiled the oldest grammars and dictionaries, and to have collected the first libraries; and it may well be that the universities of India preceded Plato's Academy. The Assyrians polished chronicles into history, the Egyptians puffed up history into the epic, and the Far East gave to the modern world those delicate forms of poetry that rest all their excellence on subtle insights phrased in a moment's imagery. Nabonidus and Ashurbanipal, whose relics are exhumed by archeologists, were archeologists; and some of the fables that amuse our children go back to ancient India.

The eighth element of civilization is art—the embellishment of life with pleasing color, rhythm and form. In its simplest aspect—the adornment of the body—we find elegant clothing, exquisite jewelry and scandalous cosmetics in the early ages of Egyptian, Sumerian and Indian civilization. Fine furniture, graceful pottery, and excellent carving in ivory and wood fill the Egyptian tombs. Surely the Greeks must have learned something of their skill in sculpture and architecture, in painting and bas-relief, not only from Asia and Crete, but from the masterpieces that in their day still gleamed in the mirror of the Nile. From Egypt and Mesopotamia Greece took the models for her Doric and Ionic columns; from those same lands came to us not merely the column but the arch, the vault, the clerestory and the dome; and the *ziggurats* of the ancient Near East have had some share in moulding the architecture of America today. Chinese painting and Japanese prints changed the tone and current of nineteenth century European art; and Chinese porcelain raised a new perfection for Europe to emulate. The sombre splendor of the Gregorian chant goes back age by age to the plaintive songs of exiled Jews gathering timidly in scattered synagogues.

These are some of the elements of civilization, and a part of the legacy of the East to the West.

Nevertheless much was left for the classic world to add to this rich inheritance. Crete would build a civilization almost as ancient as Egypt's, and would serve as a bridge to bind the cultures of Asia, Africa and Greece. Greece would transform art by seeking not size but perfection; it would marry a feminine delicacy of form and finish to the masculine architecture and statuary of Egypt, and would provide the scene for the greatest age in the history of art. It would apply to all the realms of literature the creative exuberance of the free mind; it would contribute meandering epics, profound tragedies, hilarious comedies and fascinating histories to the store of European letters. It would organize universities, and establish for a brilliant interlude the secular independence of thought; it would develop beyond any precedent the mathematics and astronomy, the physics and medicine, bequeathed it by Egypt and the East; it would originate the sciences of life, and the naturalistic view of man; it would bring philosophy to consciousness and order, and would consider with unaided rationality all the problems of our life; it would emancipate the educated classes from ecclesiasticism and superstition, and would attempt a morality independent of supernatural aid. It would conceive man as a citizen rather than as a subject; it would give him political liberty, civil rights, and an unparalleled measure of mental and moral freedom; it would create democracy and invent the individual.

Rome would take over this abounding culture, spread it throughout the Mediterranean world, protect it for half a millennium from barbarian assault, and then transmit it, through Roman literature and the Latin languages, to northern Europe; it would lift woman to a power and splendor, and a mental emancipation, which perhaps she had never known before; it would give Europe a new calendar, and teach it the principles of political organization and social security; it would establish the rights of the individual in an orderly system of laws that would help to hold the continent together through centuries of poverty, chaos and superstition.

Meanwhile the Near East and Egypt would blossom again under the stimulus of Greek and Roman trade and thought. Carthage would revive all the wealth and luxury of Sidon and Tyre; the *Talmud* would accumulate in the hands of dispersed but loyal Jews; science and philosophy would flourish at Alexandria, and out of the mixture of European and Oriental cultures would come a religion destined in part to destroy, in part to preserve and augment, the civilization of Greece and Rome. Everything was ready to produce the culminating epochs of classical antiquity: Athens under Pericles, Rome under Augustus, and Jerusalem in the age of Herod. The stage was set for the three-fold drama of Plato, Cæsar, and Christ.

AMOUNT
20.78

SEE BACK OF STATEMENT FOR IMPORTANT INFORMATION

DESCRIPTION

* LINEN DEPT

DEPT.
151

REFERENCE NUMBER
82

DATE
11/23/9

STORE 4

ALL OF US AT STEKETEE'S WISH YOU AND YOURS
A HAPPY HOLIDAY SEASON

PURCHASE, PAYMENTS & CREDITS SHOWN ABOVE FOR ACCOUNT NO. 50-521-443 ARE A DETAILED LIST FOR THE MONTH ENDING 11/25/79

PREVIOUS BALANCE
.00

PAYMENTS
.00

CREDITS RETURNS
.00

FINANCE CHG. COMPUTED ON THIS BALANCE
.00

FINANCE CHARGE
.00

CHARGES
20.78

NEW BALANCE
20.78

MINIMUM PAYMENT
5.00

To avoid FINANCE CHARGES at the (ANNUAL PERCENTAGE RATE OF 18%), pay your new balance in full by the 25TH of next month. Transactions made after billing date shown will appear on your next statement. Thank you. PAUL STEKETEE & SONS.

...fined in the text

God.

...sixteenth of a rupee, or about

figures upon a background.

East.

middle classes.

...hastity.

with cement.

Coup a etat (F)—a violent but merely political revolution.
Coup d'œil (F)—a glance of the eye.
Credat qui vult (F)—let who will believe it.
Cuisine (F)—kitchen; cooking.

*A=Arabic; C=Chinese; E=Egyptian; F=French; G=German; Gr=Greek; He=Hebrew; H=one of the Hindu languages; I=Italian; J=Japanese; L=Latin; S=Sumerian; Sp=Spanish.

Daibutsu (J)—Great Buddha; usually applied to the colossi of Buddha.
Daimyo (J)—lord.
De fontibus non disputandum (L)—there is no use disputing about origins.
Dénouement (F)—issue; conclusion.
De rigueur (F)—rigorously required by convention.
Devadasi (H)—literally, a servant of the gods; usually, a temple courtesan in India.
Dharana (H)—the sixth stage of *Yoga*.
Dharma (H)—duty.
Dhyana (H)—the seventh stage of *Yoga*.
Djinn (A)—spirits.
Dolce far niente (I)—(it is) sweet to do nothing.
Dramatis personae (L)—persons of the drama.
Dreckapothek (G)—treatment by excrementitious drugs.

En masse (F)—in a mass.
Esprit (F)—spirit.
Ex tempore (L)—on the spur of the moment.

Faïence (F)—richly colored glazed earthenware, named from the Italian town of Faënza, formerly famed for such pottery.
Faux pas (F)—a false step.
Fellaheen (A)—peasants.
Fête des Fous (F)—Feast of Fools.
Fiacre (F)—an open cab.
Flagrante delicto (L)—literally, while the crime is blazing; in the very act.
Flambé (F)—blazed.

Geisha (J)—an educated courtesan.
Genre (F)—class, kind.
Ghat (H)—a mountain-pass; a landing-place; steps leading down to water.
Glaucopis Athene (Gr)—owl-eyed Athene.
Gopuram (H)—gateway.
Gotra (H)—group.
Gunas (H)—active qualities.
Guru (H)—teacher.

Hara-kiri (J)—self-disembowelment.
Here boöpis (Gr)—cow-eyed Here (Juno).
Hetairai (Gr)—the educated courtesans of Greece.

Ibid. (L)—in the same place.
Id. (L)—the same person or author.
Inro (J)—boxes worn at the girdle.

Jenseits von Gut und Böse (G)—beyond good and evil.

Jinricksha (J)—a man-drawn open cab.

Ju jitsu (J)—literally, the soft art; a Japanese method of self-defense without weapons, by a variety of skilful physical artifices.

Junshi (J)—following in death; the suicide of a subordinate to serve his dead lord in the other world.

Jus primæ noctis (L)—the right of (possessing the bride on) the first night.

Kadamba (H)—an Indian flower.

Kakemono (J)—a pictorial or calligraphic hanging.

Karma (H)—deed; the law that every deed receives its reward or punishment in this life or in a reincarnation.

Khaddar (H)—Indian homespun.

Kusha (H)—an Indian grass.

Kutaja (H)—an Indian flower.

Labia minora (L)—the smaller folds of the vulva.

Laissez-faire (F)—literally, let it be; the theory or practice of leaving the economic life of a society free from governmental control.

Lapis lazuli (L)—a stone of rich azure blue.

La politique n'a pas d'entrailles (F)—politics has no bowels (of mercy).

La seule morale (F)—the only morality.

Le chanson de Roland (F)—the Song of Roland.

L'École de l'Extrême Orient—School of the Far East.

Legato (I)—smoothly; without breaks.

Les savants ne sont pas curieux (F)—scholars have no curiosity (Anatole France).

Lex talionis (L)—the law of retaliation.

Lingua franca (L)—a common tongue.

Lohan (C)—one who has earned *Nirvana*.

Mahatma (H)—great soul.

Manas (H)—mind.

Mandapam (H)—porch.

Mardi Gras (F)—literally, fat Tuesday, the last day of carnival before *Mercredi Maigre*, Lean (fasting) Wednesday and the beginning of Lent.

Mastaba (A)—an oblong sloping tomb.

Mater dolorosa (L)—the sorrowful Mother.

Mina (L from Gr. from He)—a coin of the ancient Near East, worth (in Babylonia) sixty shekels.

Mise-en scène (F)—the scenic situation.

Moksha (H)—deliverance.

Motif (F)—a characteristic feature or theme.

Mullah (A)—a Moslem scholar.

Muni (H)—saint.

Naga (H)—snake.
Nandi (H)—the benediction introducing a Hindu drama.
Nautch (H)—a Hindu temple dancer.
Netsuke (J)—carved knobs for holding a tassel.
Nishka (H)—a coin often used as an ornament.
Nom de plume (F)—a pen-name.
Nyama (H)—the second stage of *Yoga*.

Odium literarium (L)—a mutual dislike occasionally noticeable among authors.
Objets d'art (L)—art objects.

Pace (L)—with peace; with all respect to.
Pankha (H)—a fan.
Parvenu (F)—one recently arrived at wealth or place.
Passim (L)—here and there.
Pâte (F)—the potter's vessel in its paste form.
Patesi (S)—the priest-magistrate of an early Mesopotamian state.
Penchant (F)—inclination.
Petite marmite (F)—a small pot.
Pièce de résistance (F)—the main item.
Pishachas (H)—ghosts; goblins.
Plein air (F)—full air; a theory and school of painting which emphasized the representation of scenes in the open air, as against studio painting.
Prakriti (H)—producer.
Pranayama (H)—the fourth stage of *Yoga*.
Pratyahara (H)—the fifth stage of *Yoga*.
Protégé (F)—a person protected and aided by another.
Pro tempore (L)—for the time.
Purdah (A)—a screen or curtain; the seclusion of women.
Purusha (H)—person, spirit.

Qui vive (F)—who lives; who goes there?; alert.

Raconteurs (F)—story-tellers.
Raga (H)—a musical *motif* or melody.
Raja (H)—king; *Maharaja*—great king.
Raksha (H)—a nocturnal demon.
Ramadan (A)—the ninth month of the Moslem year, during which no food must be taken between sunrise and sunset.
Rapport (F)—intimate relation.
Religieux (F)—members of religious orders.
Rig (H)—a hymn.
Rishi (H)—a wise man.
Ronin (J)—an unattached *Samurai*.
Rupee (H)—an Indian coin worth about 32 cents.

Sake (J)—rice wine.

Salonnière (F)—a frequenter of a *salon;* usually referring to the French *salons* or drawing-room receptions of the seventeenth or eighteenth centuries.

Samadhi (H)—the eighth stage of *Yoga.*

Samaj (H)—assembly; society.

Samhita (H)—collection.

Samohini (H)—a drug.

Sang-de-bœuf (F)—(color of) bull's blood.

Sannyasi (H)—a hermit saint.

Sari (H)—a silk robe.

Sati (H)—suttee; devoted wife; the burial of a widow with her husband.

Savant (F)—scholar.

Sei (J)—caste.

Sen (J)—a Japanese coin, worth one-hundredth of a *yen.*

Se non è vero è ben trovato (I)—if it is not true it is well invented.

Seppuku (J)—ritual self-disembowelment.

Sesquipedalia verba (L)—words a foot and a half long.

Shaduf (A)—a bucket swung on a pole to lift water.

Shakhti (H)—the female energy of a god.

Shaman (H)—a magician, or miracle-working priest.

Shastra (H)—a text-book.

Shastra (H)—treatise.

Shekel (He)—a coin of the Near East, of varying value.

Shinto (J)—the Way of the Gods; the worship of the national deities and the emperor in Japan.

Shloka (H)—couplet.

Shogun (J)—general; military governor.

Siesta (Sp)—a short sleep or rest.

Silindhra (H)—an Indian flower.

Sine qua non (L)—an indispensable condition.

Soufflé (F)—blown.

Swadeshi (H)—economic nationalism; the exclusive use of native products.

Swaraj (H)—self-rule.

Tantra (H)—rule or ritual.

Tattwa (H)—reality.

Tempera (I)—distemper; painting in which the pigments are mixed or "tempered" with an emulsion of egg, usually with the addition of "size" (diluted glue) to secure adhesion.

Terra cotta (I)—baked clay, coated with glaze.

Torii (J)—gateways.

Tour de force (F)—an act of sudden ability.

Uræus (L)—a serpent image symbolizing wisdom and life; usually worn by the Egyptian kings.

Virtus dormitiva (L)—soporific power.

Yaki (J)—wares.
Yen (J)—a Japanese coin, normally worth about fifty cents.

Ziggurat (Assyrian-Babylonian)—a tower of superimposed and diminishing
stories, usually surrounded by external stairs.

Bibliography*

of books referred to in the text

ALLEN, GRANT: Evolution of the Idea of God. New York, 1897.
ANDREWS, ROY C.: On the Trail of Ancient Man. New York, 1930.
ARMSTRONG, R. C.: Light from the East: Studies in Japanese Confucianism. University of Toronto Press, 1914.
ARNOLD, SIR EDWIN: The Song Celestial, or *Bhagavad-Gita*. London, 1925.
ARRIAN: Anabasis of Alexander, and Indica. London, 1893.
ASTON, W. G.: History of Japanese Literature. New York, 1899.
AYSCOUGH, FLORENCE: Tu Fu: The Autobiography of a Chinese Poet. Boston, 1929.

BABUR: The Babur-nama in English. Tr. by Annette Beveridge. London, 1922.
BAIKIE, REV. JAS.: The Amarna Age. New York, 1926.
BARNES, JOS., ed.: Empire in the East. New York, 1934.
BARNETT, L. D.: Antiquities of India. New York, 1914.
BARNETT, L. D.: The Heart of India. London, 1924.
BEBEL, AUGUST: Woman under Socialism. New York, 1923.
BESANT, ANNIE: India. Madras, 1923.
BINYON, LAURENCE: Flight of the Dragon. London, 1927.
BISLAND, ELIZABETH (Mrs. E. B. Wetmore): Three Wise Men of the East. Chapel Hill, N. C., 1930.
BOAS, FRANZ: Anthropology and Modern Life. New York, 1928.
BORCHARDT UND RICKE: Egypt. Berlin, 1929.
BOULGER, D. C.: History of China. 4v. London, 1881.
BREASTED, JAS. H.: Ancient Records of Egypt. 5v. Chicago, 1906.
*BREASTED, JAS. H.: Ancient Times. Boston, 1916.
*BREASTED, JAS. H.: The Conquest of Civilization. New York, 1926. (A revision of *Ancient Times*. The best single-volume history of the ancient Mediterranean world.)
BREASTED, JAS. H.: The Dawn of Conscience. New York, 1933.
*BREASTED, JAS. H.: The Development of Religion and Thought in Ancient Egypt. New York, 1912.
BREASTED, JAS. H.: A History of Egypt. New York, 1912.
BREASTED, JAS. H.: The Oriental Institute. Chicago, 1933.
BRIFFAULT, ROBERT: The Mothers. 3v. New York, 1927.
BRINKLEY, CAPT. F.: China: Its History, Arts and Literature. 10v. Boston, 1902.

---

*Books starred are recommended for further study.

945

BRINKLEY, CAPT. F.: Japan: Its History, Arts and Literature. 8v. Boston
          and Tokyo.
BROWN, BRIAN: The Story of Confucius. Philadelphia, 1927.
BROWN, BRIAN: Wisdom of the Egyptians. New York, 1923.
BROWN, BRIAN: Wisdom of the Hebrews. New York, 1925.
BROWN, BRIAN: Wisdom of the Hindus. New York, 1921.
BROWN, PERCY: Indian Painting. Calcutta, 1927.
BRYAN, J. J.: The Literature of Japan. London, 1929.
BÜCHER, KARL: Industrial Evolution. New York, 1901.
BUCK, PEARL, tr.: All Men Are Brothers. 2v. New York, 1933.
*BUCKLE, H. T.: Introduction to the History of Civilization in England. 4v.
          New York, 1913.
BULLEY, MARGARET: Ancient and Medieval Art. New York, 1914.
BUXTON, L. H. DUDLEY: The Peoples of Asia. New York, 1925.

CAMBRIDGE ANCIENT HISTORY. Vols. i-vi. New York, 1924. (Referred to as
          CAH.)
CANDEE, HELEN: Angkor the Magnificent. New York, 1924.
CAPART, JEAN: Lectures on Egyptian Art. Univ. of N. C. Press, 1928.
*CAPART, JEAN: Thebes. London, 1926.
CARLYLE, THOS.: Complete Works, Vol. I, Heroes and Hero Worship.
CARPENTER, EDWARD: Pagan and Christian Creeds. New York, 1920.
CHAMBERLAIN, B. H.: Things Japanese. London, 1905.
CHAMBERLAIN, W. H.: Soviet Russia. Boston, 1930.
CHATTERJI, JAGADISH C.: The Hindu Realism. Allahabad, 1912.
CHATTERJI, JAGADISH C.: India's Outlook on Life. New York, 1930.
CHILDE, V. GORDON: The Dawn of European Civilization. New York, 1925.
CHILDE, V. GORDON: The Most Ancient East. London, 1928.
CHIROL, SIR VALENTINE: India. London, 1926.
CHU HSI: The Philosophy of Human Nature. London, 1922.
CHURCHWARD, JAS.: The Children of Mu. New York, 1931.
CHURCHWARD, JAS.: The Lost Continent of Mu. New York, 1932.
*CLOSE, UPTON (Josef Washington Hall): Challenge: Behind the Face of
          Japan. New York, 1934.
CLOSE, UPTON: The Revolt of Asia. New York, 1928.
*CONFUCIUS: Analects, in Legge, Jas.: The Chinese Classics; Vol. I: The Life
          and Teachings of Confucius. London, 1895.
CONFUCIUS: The Book of History; rendered and compiled by W. G. Old.
          London, 1918.
COOK'S GUIDE TO PEKING. Peking, 1924.
*COOMARASWAMY, ANANDA K.: The Dance of Siva. New York, 1924.
COOMARASWAMY, ANANDA K.: History of Indian and Indonesian Art. New
          York, 1927.
COTTERILL, H. B.: A History of Art. 2v. New York, 1922.
COWAN, A. R.: A Guide to World History. London, 1923.
COWAN, A. R.: Master Clues in World History. London, 1914.

CRANMER-BYNG, L.: The Book of Odes. London, 1927.
CRAWLEY, E.: The Mystic Rose. 2v. New York, 1927.
CROCE, BENEDETTO: Esthetic. London, 1922.
CURTIS, W. E.: Modern India. New York, 1909.

DARMESTETER, JAS., ed. and tr.: The Zend-Avesta. 2v. Oxford, 1895.
DARWIN, CHARLES: Descent of Man. New York, A. L. Burt, no date.
DARWIN, CHARLES: Journal of Researches into the Geology and Natural History of the Various Countries Visited during the Voyage of H.M.S. *Beagle* round the World. London, 1910.
DAS GUPTA, SURENDRANATH: A History of Indian Philosophy. Cambridge U. P., 1922.
DAS GUPTA, SURENDRANATH: Yoga as Philosophy and Religion. London, 1924.
DAVIDS, T. W. RHYS: Buddhist India. New York, 1903.
*DAVIDS, T. W. RHYS: Dialogues of the Buddha; being vols. ii-iv of Sacred Books of the Buddhists. Oxford, 1923.
*DAWSON, MILES: Ethics of Confucius. New York, 1915.
DAWSON, MILES: The Ethical Religion of Zoroaster. New York, 1931.
DAY, CLIVE: A History of Commerce. London, 1926.
DELAPORTE, L.: Mesopotamia. London, 1925.
DE MORGAN, JACQUES: Prehistoric Man. New York, 1925.
DEUSSEN, PAUL: The Philosophy of the Upanishads. Edinburgh, 1919.
DEUSSEN, PAUL: System of the Vedanta. Chicago, 1912.
DHALLA, M. N.: Zoroastrian Civilization. New York, 1922.
*DICKINSON, G. LOWES: An Essay on the Civilization of India, China and Japan. New York, 1926.
DIODORUS SICULUS: Library of History. Loeb Classical Library. Vol. i, New York, 1933.
DOANE, T. W.: Bible Myths, and Their Parallels in Other Religions. New York, 1882.
DOWNING, DR. J. G.: "Cosmetics, Past and Present," in Journal of the American Medical Society, June 23, 1934.
DUBOIS, ABBÉ J. A.: Hindu Manners, Customs and Ceremonies. Oxford, 1928.
DURCKHEIM, EMILE: The Elementary Forms of the Religious Life. New York, 1915.
DUTT, R. C.: The Civilization of India. Dent, London, n.d.
DUTT, R. C.: The Economic History of India: 1757-1837. 5th ed. Kegan Paul, London, n.d.
DUTT, R. C.: The Economic History of India in the Victorian Age. 5th ed. London, n.d.
*DUTT, R. C., tr.: The Ramayana and Mahabharata. Everyman Library.

EDDY, SHERWOOD: The Challenge of the East. New York, 1931.
EDMUNDS, A. J.: Buddhist and Christian Gospels. 2v. Philadelphia, 1908.
EKKEN, KAIBARA: The Way of Contentment. Tr. Hoshino. London, 1913.
ELIOT, SIR CHARLES: Hinduism and Buddhism. 3v. London, 1921.

ELLIS, HAVELOCK: Man and Woman. New York, 1900.
ELLIS, HAVELOCK: Studies in the Psychology of Sex. 6v. Philadelphia, 1910-11.
ELPHINSTONE, MOUNTSTUART: History of India. London, 1916.
ENCYCLOPEDIA BRITANNICA. 14th edition, unless otherwise specified.
*ERMAN, ADOLF: Life in Ancient Egypt. London, 1894.
ERMAN, ADOLF: Literature of the Ancient Egyptians. London, 1927.

FARNELL, L. R.: Greece and Babylon. Edinburgh, 1911.
*FAURE, ELIE: History of Art. 4v. New York, 1921.
FEBVRE, LUCIEN: Geographical Introduction to History. New York, 1925.
FENOLLOSA, E. F.: Epochs of Chinese and Japanese Art. 2v. New York, 1921.
FERGUSON, J. C.: Outlines of Chinese Art. University of Chicago, 1919.
FERGUSSON, JAS.: History of Indian and Eastern Architecture, 2v. London, 1910.
FERGUSSON, JAS.: History of Architecture in All Countries. 2v. London, 1874.
FICKE, A. D.: Chats on Japanese Prints. London, 1915.
FIRISHTAH, MUHAMMAD QASIM: History of Hindostan. Tr. Alex. Dow. 3v. London, 1803.
FISCHER, OTTO: Die Kunst Indiens, Chinas und Japans. Berlin, 1928.
FRAZER, SIR J. G.: Adonis, Attis, Osiris. London, 1907.
*FRAZER, SIR J. G.: The Golden Bough. One-volume ed. New York, 1930.
FRAZER, R. W.: Literary History of India. London, 1920.
FREUD, S.: Totem and Taboo. Leipzig, 1913.
FRY, R. E., ed.: Chinese Art. New York, 1925.
FÜLOP-MILLER, RENÉ: Lenin and Gandhi. London, 1927.

*GANDHI, M. K.: His Own Story. Ed. by C. F. Andrews. New York, 1930.
GANDHI, M. K.: Young India, 1924-6. New York, 1927.
GANGOLY, O. C.: Art of Java. Calcutta, n.d.
GANGOLY, O. C.: Indian Architecture. Calcutta, n.d.
GARBE, RICHARD, ed.: The Samkhya-Pravacana-Bhasya, or Commentary on the Exposition of the Sankhya Philosophy by Vijnanabhikshu. Harvard University, 1895.
GARRISON, F. H.: History of Medicine. Phila., 1929
GATENBY, E. V.: The Cloud-Men of Yamato. London, 1929.
GEORG, EUGEN: The Adventure of Mankind. New York, 1931.
GILES, H. A.: Gems of Chinese Literature: Prose. Shanghai, 1923.
GILES, H. A.: History of Chinese Literature. New York, 1928.
GILES, H. A.: Introduction to the History of Chinese Pictorial Art. Shanghai, 1918.
GILES, H. A.: Quips from a Chinese Jest-Book. Shanghai, 1925.
GOLDENWEISER, A. A.: History, Psychology and Culture. New York, 1933.
GOUR, SIR HARI SINGH: The Spirit of Buddhism. Calcutta, 1929.
GOWEN, H. H.: History of Indian Literature. New York, 1931.

*GOWEN, H. H.: Outline History of Japan. New York, 1927.
*GOWEN, H. H. and HALL, JOSEF W. ("Upton Close"): Outline History of China. New York, 1927.
GRAETZ, H.: Popular History of the Jews. 8v. New York, 1919.
GRANET, MARCEL: Chinese Civilization. New York, 1930.
GRAY, R. M. and PAREKH, M. C.: Mahatma Gandhi. Calcutta, 1928.
GROSSE, ERNST: Beginnings of Art. New York, 1897.
GUÉNON, RENÉ: Man and His Becoming according to the Vedanta, London, 1928.
GULLAND, W. G.: Chinese Porcelain, 2v. London, 1911.

*HALL, JOSEF W.: Eminent Asians. New York, 1929.
HALL, MANLY P.: Encyclopedic Outline of Masonic, Hermetic, Qabbalistic and Rosicrucian Symbolical Philosophy. San Francisco, 1928.
HALLAM, H.: View of the State of Europe during the Middle Ages. New York, 1845.
HARDIE, J. KEIR: India: Impressions and Suggestions. London, 1909.
HARDING, T. SWANN: Fads, Frauds and Physicians. New York, 1930.
HARPER, R. F., ed.: Assyrian and Babylonian Literature. New York, 1904.
HARPER, R. F., ed.: The Code of Hammurabi. University of Chicago, 1904.
HAVELL, E. B.: Ancient and Medieval Architecture of India. London, 1915.
HAVELL, E. B.: Ideals of Indian Art. New York, 1920.
HAVELL, E. B.: History of Aryan Rule in India. Harrap, London, n.d.
HAYES, E. C.: Introduction to the Study of Sociology. New York, 1918.
HEARN, LAFCADIO: Japan: an Interpretation. New York, 1928.
HERACLITUS: Fragments, tr. by G. T. W. Patrick. Baltimore, 1889.
*HERODOTUS: Histories, tr. by Cary. London, 1901. References are to book and chapter (section).
HIMES, NORMAN: Medical History of Contraception. In MS.
HIPPOCRATES: Works, tr. Jones. Loeb Classical Library. London, 1923.
HIRTH, FRIEDRICH: Ancient History of China. New York, 1923.
HOBHOUSE, L. T.: Morals in Evolution. New York, 1916.
HOBSON, R. L.: Chinese Art. New York, 1927.
HOERNLÉ, R. F. A.: Studies in Contemporary Metaphysics. New York, 1920.
HOLLAND, CLIVE: Things Seen in Japan. Seeley, Service & Co., London, n.d.
*HOLY BIBLE; Revised Version. American Bible Society, New York, 1914.
HOWARD, CLIFFORD: Sex Worship. Chicago, 1909.
HUART, CLEMENT: Ancient Persian and Iranian Civilization. New York, 1927.
HU SHIH: Development of the Logical Method in Ancient China. Shanghai, 1922.
*HUME, R. E., ed.: The Thirteen Principal Upanishads. Oxford U. P., 1921.
HUNTINGDON, E.: Civilization and Climate. Yale U. P., 1905.
HUNTINGDON, E.: The Pulse of Asia. Boston, 1907.

INDIAN YEAR BOOK, 1929. Bombay, 1929.

JASTROW, MORRIS, JR.: The Book of Job. Phila., 1920.
JASTROW, MORRIS, JR.: The Civilization of Babylonia and Assyria. Phila., 1915.
JASTROW, MORRIS, JR.: A Gentle Cynic. Phila., 1919.
JEWISH ENCYCLOPEDIA. 12v. New York, 1901.
JOSEPHUS, F.: Works, tr. Whiston. 2v. Boston, 1811.
JUNG, C. G.: Psychology of the Unconscious. New York, 1916.

*KABIR: Songs, tr. Tagore. New York, 1915.
*KALIDASA: Sakuntala. Prepared for the English Stage by Kedar nath Das
        Gupta and Laurence Binyon. London, 1920.
KALLEN, H. M.: The Book of Job as a Greek Tragedy. New York, 1918.
KAPILA: Aphorisms of the Sankhya Philosophy. Allahabad, 1852.
KEYSERLING, COUNT HERMANN, ed.: The Book of Marriage. New York, 1926.
KEYSERLING, COUNT HERMANN: Creative Understanding. New York, 1929.
*KEYSERLING, COUNT HERMANN: Travel Diary of a Philosopher. 2v. New
        York, 1925.
KÖHLER, KARL: History of Costume. New York, 1928.
KOHN, HANS: History of Nationalism in the East. New York, 1929.
*KROPOTKIN, PETER: Mutual Aid. New York, 1902.

LACROIX, PAUL: History of Prostitution. 2v. New York, 1931.
LAJPAT RAI, L.: England's Debt to India. New York, 1917.
LAJPAT RAI, L.: Unhappy India. Calcutta, 1928.
LANGDON, S.: Babylonian Wisdom. London, 1923.
*LATOURETTE, K. S.: The Chinese: Their History and Culture. 2v. New
        York, 1934.
LAYARD, A. H.: Nineveh and Its Remains. 2v. London, 1850.
LEDOUX, L. V.: The Art of Japan. New York, 1927.
LEGENDRE, DR. A. F.: Modern Chinese Civilization. London, 1929.
*LEGGE, JAS.: The Chinese Classics translated into English. Vol. I: The Life
        and Teachings of Confucius. London, 1895.
*LEGGE, JAS.: The Sacred Books of China:.The Texts of Taoism. 2v. Oxford
        U. P., 1927.
*LEONARD, W. E.: Gilgamesh, a Rendering in Free Rhythm. New York, 1934.
LETOURNEAU, C. F.: Evolution of Marriage and the Family. New York, 1891.
LILLIE, ARTHUR: Rama and Homer. London, 1912.
*LI PO: Works, done into English verse by Shigeyoshi Obata. New York,
        1928.
LIPPERT, JULIUS: Evolution of Culture. New York, 1931.
LO KUAN-CHUNG: Romance of the Three Kingdoms. Tr. C. H. Brewitt-
        Taylor. 2v. Shanghai, 1925.
LORENZ, D. E.: The 'Round the World Traveler. New York, 1927.
LOTI, PIERRE: India. London, 1929.

Lowie, R. H.: Are We Civilized? New York, 1929.
Lowie, R. H.: Primitive Religion. New York, 1924.
Lubbock, Sir John: The Origin of Civilization. London, 1912.
Lull, R. S., ed.: The Evolution of Man. Yale U. P., 1922.

*Macaulay, T. B.: Critical and Historical Essays. Everyman Library. 2v.
Macdonell, A. A.: History of Sanskrit Literature. New York, 1900.
Macdonell, A. A.: India's Past. Oxford, 1927.
Maine, Sir Henry: Ancient Law. Everyman Library.
Mallock, W.: Lucretius on Life and Death. Phila., 1878.
Marshall, Sir John: Prehistoric Civilization of the Indus. Illustrated London News, Jan. 7, 1928.
Mason, O. T.: Origins of Invention. New York, 1899.
Mason, W. A.: History of the Art of Writing. New York, 1920.
*Maspero, G.: Art in Egypt. New York, 1922.
*Maspero, G.: The Dawn of Civilization: Egypt and Chaldæa. London, 1897.
*Maspero, G.: The Struggle of the Nations: Egypt, Syria and Assyria. London, 1896.
*Maspero, G.: The Passing of the Empires. London, 1900.
McCabe, Jos.: The Story of Religious Controversy. Boston, 1929.
McCrindle, J. W.: Ancient India as described by Megasthenes and Arrian. Calcutta, 1877.
Melamed, S. M.: Spinoza and Buddha. Chicago, 1933.
Mencius: Works, tr. Legge. 2v. Oxford, 1895.
Mencken, H. L.: Treatise on the Gods. New York, 1930.
Minney, R. J.: Shiva, or the Future of India. London, 1929.
Monier-Williams, Sir M.: Indian Wisdom. London, 1893.
Moon, P. T.: Imperialism and World Politics. New York, 1930.
Moret, A. and Davy, G.: From Tribe to Empire. New York, 1926.
Mukerji, D. G.: A Son of Mother India Answers. New York, 1928.
Mukerji, D. G.: Visit India with Me. New York, 1929.
Müller-Lyer, F.: Evolution of Modern Marriage. New York, 1930.
Müller-Lyer, F.: The Family. New York, 1931.
Müller-Lyer, F.: History of Social Development. New York, 1921.
*Müller, Max: Lectures on the Science of Language. 2v. New York, 1866.
Müller, Max: Six Systems of Indian Philosophy. London, 1919.
Müller, Max: India: What Can It Teach Us? London, 1919.
*Murasaki, Lady: The Tale of Genji, tr. Arthur Waley. London, 1927.
Murdoch, Jas.: History of Japan. 3v. London, 1925.
Murray, G.: Aristophanes and the War Party. London, 1919.
Muthu, D. C.: The Antiquity of Hindu Medicine and Civilization. London, 1930.

Nag, Kalidas: Greater India. Calcutta, 1926.
Naidu, Sarojini: The Sceptred Flute: Songs of India. New York, 1928.

NIETZSCHE, F.: Genealogy of Morals. London, 1913.

NITOBÉ, INAZO: Bushido: The Soul of Japan. New York, 1905.

NIVEDITA, SISTER (Margaret E. Noble): The Web of Indian Life. London, 1918.

NOGUCHI, YONE: The Spirit of Japanese Poetry. London, 1914.

NORTON, H. K.: China and the Powers. New York, 1927.

OKAKURA-KAKUSO: The Book of Tea. New York, 1912.

OLMSTEAD, A. T.: History of Assyria. New York, 1923.

OPPENHEIMER, FRANZ: The State. Indianapolis, 1914.

OSBORN, H. F.: Men of the Old Stone Age. New York, 1915.

OTTO, RUDOLF: Mysticism, East and West. New York, 1932.

PARK, NO YONG: Making a New China. Boston, 1929.

PARMELEE, M.: Oriental and Occidental Culture. New York, 1928.

PEFFER, N.: China: The Collapse of a Civilization. New York, 1930.

PELLIOT, P.: Les grottes de Touen-Houang. 6v. Paris, 1914-29.

PERROT, G. and CHIPIEZ, C.: History of Art in Chaldea and Assyria. 2v. London, 1884.

PETRIE, SIR W. FLINDERS: Egypt and Israel. London, 1925.

PETRIE, SIR W. FLINDERS: The Formation of the Alphabet. London, 1912.

*PETRIE, SIR W. FLINDERS: The Revolutions of Civilization. London, 1911.

PIJOAN, JOS.: History of Art. 3v. New York, 1927.

PITKIN, W. B.: A Short Introduction to the History of Human Stupidity. New York, 1932.

PITTARD, E.: Race and History. New York, 1926.

PLATO: Dialogues. Tr. Jowett. 4v. New York, n.d.

PLUTARCH: Lives. 3v. Everyman Library.

*POLO, MARCO: Travels, ed. Manuel Komroff. New York, 1926.

POTTER, CHARLES F.: The Story of Religion. New York, 1929.

*POWYS, J. C.: The Meaning of Culture. New York, 1929.

PRATT, W. S.: The History of Music. New York, 1927.

QUINTUS CURTIUS: Works, tr. Knight. Cambridge, England, 1882.

RADAKRISHNAN, S.: The Hindu View of Life. London, 1928.

RADAKRISHNAN, S.: Indian Philosophy. 2vo. Macmillan, New York, n.d.

RATZEL, F.: History of Mankind. 2v. London, 1896.

RAWLINSON, GEO.: Five Great Monarchies of the Ancient Eastern World. 3v. New York, 1887.

RAWLINSON, GEO., ed.: Herodotus. 4v. London, 1862.

REDESDALE, LORD: Tales of Old Japan. London, 1928.

REICHWIN, A.: China and Europe: Intellectual and Artistic Contacts in the Eighteenth Century. New York, 1925.

*REINACH, S.: Orpheus: A History of Religions. New York, 1909 and 1930.

RENAN, E.: History of the People of Israel. 5v. New York, 1888.

RENARD, G.: Life and Work in Prehistoric Times. New York, 1929.

REPORT OF THE INDIAN CENTRAL COMMITTEE. Calcutta, 1929.

RICKARD, T. A.: Man and Metals. 2v. New York, 1932.

RIVERS, W. H. PITT: Instinct and the Unconscious. Cambridge U. P., 1920.

RIVERS, W. H. PITT: Social Organization. New York, 1924.

ROBIE, W. F.: The Art of Love. Boston, 1921.

*ROBINSON, J. H.: article "Civilization" in Encyclopedia Britannica, 14th ed.

ROLLAND, ROMAIN: Mahatma Gandhi. New York, 1924.

ROLLAND, ROMAIN: Prophets of the New India. New York, 1930.

ROSS, E. A.: The Changing Chinese. New York, 1911.

ROSS, E. A.: Foundations of Sociology. New York, 1905.

ROSS, E. A.: Social Control. New York, 1906.

ROSTOVTZEFF, M.: A History of the Ancient World. 2v. Oxford, 1930.

RUSSELL, BERTRAND: Marriage and Morals. New York, 1929.

SANGER, WM.: History of Prostitution. New York, 1910.

SANSUM, DR. W. D.: The Normal Diet. St. Louis, 1930.

SARKAR, B. K.: Hindu Achievements in Exact Science. New York, 1918.

SARRE, F.: Die Kunst des alten Persien. Berlin, 1925.

SARTON, GEO.: Introduction to the History of Science. Vol. I. Baltimore, 1930.

SCHÄFER, H. and ANDRAE, W.: Die Kunst des alten Orients. Berlin, 1925.

SCHNEIDER, HERMANN: History of World Civilization. Tr. Green. 2v. New York, 1931.

SCHOPENHAUER, A.: The World as Will and Idea. Tr. Haldane and Kemp. 3v. London, 1883.

SEDGWICK, W. and TYLER, H.: Short History of Science. New York, 1927.

SEWELL, ROBERT: A Forgotten Empire, Vijayanagar. London, 1900.

SHAW, G. B.: Man and Superman. New York, 1914.

SHELLEY, P. B.: Complete Works. London, 1888.

*SHONAGON, LADY SEI: Sketch Book; tr. N. Kobayashi. London, 1930.

SHOTWELL, JAS. T.: The Religious Revolution of To-day. Boston, 1913.

SIDHANTA, N. K.: The Heroic Age of India. New York, 1930.

SIMON, SIR JOHN, Chairman: Report of the Indian Statutory Commission. 2v. London, 1930.

SIRÉN, OSVALD: Chinese Paintings in American Collections. 5v. Paris, 1927.

SKEAT, W. W.: Etymological Dictionary of the English Language. Oxford, 1893.

SMITH, A. H.: Chinese Characteristics. New York, 1894.

SMITH, G. ELLIOT: The Ancient Egyptians and the Origin of Civilization. London, 1923.

SMITH, G. ELLIOT: Human History. New York, 1929.

SMITH, W. ROBERTSON: The Religion of the Semites. New York, 1889.

*SMITH, V. A.: Akbar. Oxford, 1919.

SMITH, V. A.: Asoka. Oxford, 1920.

SMITH, V. A.: Oxford History of India. Oxford, 1923.

SOLLAS, W. J.: Ancient Hunters. New York, 1924.

SPEARING, H. G.: Childhood of Art. New York, 1913.

SPENCER, HERBERT: Principles of Sociology. 3v. New York, 1910.

*SPENGLER, OSWALD: Decline of the West. 2v. New York, 1926-8.

SPINOZA, B.: Ethic, tr. W. H. White. New York, 1883.

SPRENGLING, M.: The Alphabet: Its Rise and Development from the Sinai
        Inscriptions. Oriental Institute Publications. Chicago,
        1931.

STEIN, SIR M. AUREL: Innermost Asia. 4v. Oxford, 1928.

STRABO: Geography. 8v. Loeb Classical Library. New York, 1917-32.

*SUMNER, W. G.: Folkways. Boston, 1906.

SUMNER, W. G. and KELLER, A. G.: Science of Society. 3v. New Haven, 1928.

SUNDERLAND, J. T.: India in Bondage. New York, 1929.

SUTHERLAND, A.: Origin and Growth of the Moral Instincts. 2v. London,
        1898.

SUTHERLAND, G. A., ed.: A System of Diet and Dietetics. New York, 1925.

SUZUKI, A. T.: Brief History of Early Chinese Philosophy. London, 1914.

SYKES, SIR PERCY: Persia. Oxford, 1922.

TABOUIS, G. R.: Nebuchadnezzar. New York, 1931.

TACITUS: Histories. Tr. Murphy. London, 1930.

*TAGORE, R.: Chitra. London, 1924.

*TAGORE, R.: The Gardener. Leipzig, 1921.

TAGORE, R.: Gitanjali and Fruit-Gathering. New York, 1918.

TAGORE, R.: My Reminiscences. New York, 1917.

TAGORE, R.: Personality. London, 1926.

TAGORE, R.: Sadhana: The Realization of Life. Leipzig, 1921.

TARDE, G.: The Laws of Imitation. New York, 1903.

*THOMAS, E. D.: Chinese Political Thought. New York, 1927.

THOMAS, E. J.: Life of Buddha. New York, 1927.

THOMAS, W. I.: Source Book for Social Origins. Boston, 1909.

THOMSON, E. J.: Rabindranath Tagore. Calcutta, 1921.

THOREAU, H. D.: Walden. Everyman Library.

*THORNDIKE, LYNN: Short History of Civilization. New York, 1926.

*TIETJENS, EUNICE, ed.: Poetry of the Orient. New York, 1928.

TOD, LT.-COL. JAS.: Annals and Antiquities of Rajasthan. 2v. Calcutta, 1894.

TSURUMI, Y.: Present Day Japan. New York, 1926.

*TU FU: Poems, tr. Edna Worthley Underwood and Chi Hwang Chu. Port-
        land, Me., 1929.

TYLOR, E. B.: Anthropology. New York, 1906.

TYLOR, E. B.: Primitive Culture. 2v. New York, 1889.

TYRRELL, C. A.: The Royal Road to Health. New York, 1912.

UNDERWOOD, A. C.: Contemporary Thought of India. New York, 1931.

*VAN DOREN, MARK: Anthology of World Poetry. New York, 1928.
VENKATESWARA, S. V.: Indian Culture through the Ages. Vol. I: Education
           and the Propagation of Culture. London, 1928.
VINOGRADOFF, SIR P.: Outlines of Historical Jurisprudence. 2v. Oxford, 1922.
*VOLTAIRE, F. M. A. DE: Works. 32v. New York, 1927.

WALEY, ARTHUR: Introduction to the Study of Chinese Painting. London,
           1923.
*WALEY, ARTHUR: 170 Chinese Poems. New York, 1923.
WALSH, CLARA A.: The Master-Singers of Japan. London, 1914.
WANG YANG-MING: The Philosophy of, tr. by F. G. Henke. London and
           Chicago, 1916.
WARD, C. O.: The Ancient Lowly. 2v. Chicago, 1907.
WATTERS, T.: On Yuan Chuang's Travels in India. 2v. London, 1904.
WEIGALL, ARTHUR: Life and Times of Akhnaton. New York, 1923.
WEIGALL, ARTHUR: Life and Times of Cleopatra. New York, 1924.
WESTERMARCK, E.: History of Human Marriage. 2v. London, 1921.
WESTERMARCK, E.: Origin and Development of the Moral Ideas. 2v. Lon-
           don, 1917-24.
WESTERMARCK, E.: Short History of Marriage. New York, 1926.
WHITE, E. M.: Woman in World History. Jenkins, London, n.d.
WHITE, W. A.: Mechanisms of Character Formation. New York, 1916.
WHITMAN, WALT: Leaves of Grass. Phila., 1900.
WILHELM, R.: Short History of Chinese Civilization. New York, 1929.
WILHELM, R.: The Soul of China. New York, 1928.
WILLIAMS, E. T.: China Yesterday and Today. New York, 1927.
WILLIAMS, H. S.: History of Science. 5v. New York, 1904.
WILLIAMS, S. WELLS: The Middle Kingdom. 2v. New York, 1895.
WILLIS, R.: Benedict de Spinoza. London, 1870.
WINTERNITZ, M.: History of Indian Literature. Vol. I. Calcutta, 1927.
WOOD, ERNEST: An Englishman Defends Mother India. Madras, 1929.
WOOLLEY, C. LEONARD: The Sumerians. Oxford, 1928.
WORLD ALMANAC, 1935. New York, 1935.
WU, CHAO-CHU: The Nationalist Program for China. Yale U. P., 1929.

XENOPHON: Anabasis. Loeb Classical Library.
XENOPHON: Cyropædia. Loeb Classical Library.

YANG CHU: Garden of Pleasure. London, 1912.

ZIMAND, SAVEL: Living India. New York, 1928.

Notes[*]

1. Supplement to *Essai sur les mœurs;* quoted by Buckle, H. T., *History of Civilization,* i, 581.

CHAPTER I

2. Robinson, J. H., art. Civilization, *Encyclopedia Britannica,* 14th ed.

CHAPTER II

1. Spengler, O., *The Decline of the West; The Hour of Decision.*
2. Hayes, *Sociology,* 494.
3. Lippert, J., *Evolution of Culture,* 38.
4. Spencer, H., *Principles of Sociology,* i, 60.
5. Sumner and Keller, *Science of Society,* i, 51; Sumner, W. G., *Folkways,* 119-22; Renard, G., *Life and Work in Prehistoric Times,* 36; Mason, O. T., *Origins of Invention,* 298.
6. Ibid., 316.
7. Sumner and Keller, i, 132.
8. Roth, H. L., in Thomas, W. I., *Source Book for Social Origins,* 111.
9. Ibid.; Mason, O. T., 190; Lippert, 165.
10. Renard, 123.
11. Briffault, *The Mothers,* ii, 460.
12. Renard, 35.
13. Sutherland, G. A., ed., *A System of Diet and Dietetics,* 45.
14. Ibid., 33-4; Ratzel, F., *History of Mankind,* i, 90.
15. Sutherland, G. A., 43, 45; Müller-Lyer, F., *History of Social Development,* 70.
16. Ibid., 86.
17. Sumner, *Folkways,* 329; Ratzel, 129; Renard, 40-2; Westermarck, E., *Origin and Development of the Moral Ideas,* i, 553-62.
18. Sumner and Keller, ii, 1234.
19. Sumner, *Folkways,* 329.
20. Renard, 40-2.
21. Sumner and Keller, ii, 1230.
22. Briffault, ii, 399.
23. Sumner and Keller, ii, 1234.
24. Cowan, A. R., *Master Clues in World History,* 10.
25. Renard, 39.
26. Mason, O. T., 23.
27. Briffault, i, 461-5.
28. Mason, O. T., 224f.
29. Müller-Lyer, *Social Development,* 102.
30. Ibid., 144-6.
30a. Ibid., 167; Ratzel, 87.
31. Thomas, W. I., 113-7; Renard, 154-5; Müller-Lyer, 306; Sumner and Keller, i, 150-3.
32. Sumner, *Folkways,* 142.
33. Mason, O. T., 71.
34. Müller-Lyer, *Social Development,* 238-9; Renard, 158.
35. Sumner and Keller, i, 268-72, 300, 320; Lubbock, Sir J., *Origin of Civilization,* 373-5; Campbell, Bishop R., in New York *Times,* 1-11-33.
36. Bücher, K., Industrial Evolution, 57.
37. Kropotkin, Prince P., *Mutual Aid,* 90.
38. Mason, O. T., 27.
39. Sumner and Keller, i, 270-2.
40. Briffault, ii, 494-7.
41. Sumner and Keller, i, 328f.
42. In Lippert, 39.
43. *A Naturalist's Voyage Around the World,* 242, in Briffault, ii, 494.
43a. Westermarck, *Moral Ideas,* i, 35-42.
44. Hobhouse, L. T., *Morals in Evolution,* 244-5; Cowan, A. R., *Guide to World History,* 22; Sumner and Keller, i, 58.
45. Hobhouse, 272.

[*] The full title of a book is given only on its first occurrence in these Notes; abbreviated later references may be filled out by consulting the foregoing *Bibliographical Guide to Books Referred to in the Text.*

CHAPTER III

1. Sumner and Keller, i, 16, 418, 461; Westermarck, *Moral Ideas,* i, 195-8.
2. Sumner and Keller, i, 461.
3. Rivers, W. H. R., *Social Organization,* 166.
4. Briffault, ii, 364, 494; Ratzel, 133; Sumner and Keller, 470-3.
5. Ibid., 463, 473.
6. Ibid., 370, 358.
7. Renard, 149; Westmarck, *Moral Ideas,* ii, 836-9; Ratzel, 130; Hobhouse, 239; Sumner and Keller, i, 18, 372, 366, 392, 394, 713.
8. Nietzsche, *Genealogy of Morals,* 103.
9. American *Journal of Sociology,* March, 1905.
10. Oppenheimer, Franz, *The State,* 16.
11. In Ross, E. A., *Social Control,* 50.
12. In Sumner and Keller, i, 704.
13. Ibid., 709.
14. Cowan, *Guide to World History,* 18f.
15. Sumner and Keller, i, 486.
16. Spencer, *Sociology,* iii, 316.
17. Ibid, i, 66.
18. Melville, *Typee,* 222, in Briffault, ii, 356.
19. Briffault, ibid.
20. Sumner and Keller, i, 687.
21. Lubbock, 330.
22. Hobhouse, 73-101; Kropotkin, *Mutual Aid,* 131; Thomas, W. I., 301.
23. Sumner and Keller, i, 682-7.
24. For examples cf. Westermarck, *Moral Ideas,* i, 14-5, 20.
25. Lubbock, 363-7; Sumner and Keller, i, 454; Briffault, ii, 499; Maine, Sir H., *Ancient Law,* 109; Boas, Franz, *Anthropology and Modern Life,* 221.
26. Sutherland, A., *Origin and Growth of the Moral Instincts,* i, 4-5.
27. Sumner and Keller, iii, 1498; Lippert, 75, 659.
28. Sumner and Keller, iii, 1501.
29. Ibid., 1500; Renard, 198; Briffault, ii, 518, 434.
30. Vinogradoff, Sir P., *Outlines of Historical Jurisprudence,* i, 212; Briffault, i, 503, 513.
31. Sumner, *Folkways,* 364.
32. Briffault, i, 508-9; Sumner and Keller, i, 540; iii, 1949; Rivers, *Social Organization,* 12.
33. Moret and Davy, *From Tribe to Empire,* 40; Briffault, i, 308; Müller-Lyer, *The Family,* 1 24-7; Sumner and Keller, iii, 1939.
34. White, E. M., *Woman in World History,* 35; Briffault, i, 309; Lippert, 223; Sumner and Keller, iii, 1990.
35. Hobhouse, 170.
36. Müller-Lyer, *Family,* 118.
37. Ibid., 232.
38. Sumner and Keller, iii, 1733.
39. Lubbock, 5.
40. Müller-Lyer, *Evolution of Modern Marriage,* 112.
41. Briffault, i, 460; Renard, 101.
42. Briffault, i, 466, 478, 484, 509.
43. Ellis, H., *Man and Woman,* 316; Sumner and Keller, i, 128.
44. Ibid., iii, 1763, 1843; Ratzel, 134; Westermarck, *Moral Ideas,* i, 235.
45. Lubbock, 67.
46. Lubbock in Thomas, W. I., 108.
47. Westermarck, *Moral Ideas,* ii, 420, 629.
48. Crawley, E., *The Mystic Rose,* in Thomas, W. I., 515-7, 525.
49. Westermarck, *Moral Ideas,* ii, 638-45; Sumner and Keller, iii, 1737.
50. Ibid., 1753.
51. Vinogradoff, i, 197; Müller-Lyer, *Social Development,* 208.

CHAPTER IV

1. Darwin, C., *Descent of Man,* 110.
2. Ellis, H., *Studies in the Psychology of Sex,* vi, 422.
3. Westermarck, E., *History of Human Marriage,* i, 32, 35.
4. Briffault, ii, 154.
5. Sumner and Keller, iii, 1547f. Further examples of sexual communism may be found in Briffault, i, 645; ii, 2-13; Lubbock, 68-9.
6. Müller-Lyer, *Family,* 55.
6a. *Encyclopedia Britannica,* xiii, 206.
7. Sumner and Keller, iii, 1548.
8. Briffault, ii, 81.
9. Lubbock, 69.
10. Lippert, 67.

11. Polo, Marco, *Travels*, 70.
12. Letourneau, *Marriage*, in Sumner and Keller, iii, 1521.
13. Westermarck, *Short History of Human Marriage*, 265; Müller-Lyer, *Family*, 49; Sumner and Keller, iii, 1563; Briffault, i, 629f.
14. Ibid., 649.
15. Sumner and Keller, iii, 1565.
16. Examples in Briffault, i, 767n; Sumner and Keller iii, 1901; Lippert, 670.
17. Examples in Briffault, i, 641f, 663; Vinogradoff, i, 173.
    Vinogradoff, i, 173.
18. Westermarck, *Moral Ideas*, i, 387.
19. Briffault, ii, 315; Hobhouse, 140.
20. Müller-Lyer, *Modern Marriage*, 34.
21. Spencer, *Sociology*, i, 722; Westermarck, *Moral Ideas*, i, 388; Sumner, *Folkways*, 265, 351; Sumner and Keller, i, 22; iii, 1863; Briffault, ii, 261, 267, 271.
22. Lowie, R. H., *Are We Civilized?*, 128.
23. Sumner and Keller, iii, 1534, 1540; Westermarck, *Moral Ideas*, i, 399.
24. Gen., xxix. Similar customs existed in Africa, India and Australia; cf. Müller-Lyer, *Modern Marriage*, 123.
25. Sumner and Keller, iii, 1625-6; Vinogradoff, 209; further examples in Lubbock, 91; Müller-Lyer, *Family*, 86; Westermarck, *Moral Ideas*, i, 435.
26. Briffault, i, 244f.
26a. Lippert, 295; Müller-Lyer, *Social Development*, 270.
27. Sumner and Keller, iii, 1631. Briffault interprets this wedding custom as a reminiscence of the transition from matrilocal to patriarchal marriage—i, 240-50.
28. Hobhouse, 158.
29. Sumner and Keller, iii, 1629.
30. Briffault, ii, 244.
31. Müller-Lyer, *Modern Marriage*, 125.
32. Hobhouse, 151; Westermarck, *Moral Ideas*, i, 383; Sumner and Keller, 1650.
33. Ibid., 1648.
34. Ibid., 1649. Herodotus (I, 196) reported a similar custom in the fifth century B.C., and Burckhardt found it in Arabia in the nineteenth century (Müller-Lyer, *Modern Marriage*, 127).
35. Briffault, i, 219-21.
36. Lowie, *Are We Civilized?*, 125.
37. Briffault, ii, 215.
38. Sumner and Keller, iii, 1658.
39. In Lubbock, 53.
40. Ibid., 54-7; Sumner and Keller, iii, 1503-8; Briffault, ii, 141-3.
41. Müller-Lyer, *Modern Marriage*, 51.
43. Briffault, ii, 70f.
44. Briffault, ii, 2-13, 67, 70-2. Briffault has gathered into a ten-page footnote the evidence for the wide spread of pre-marital sexual freedom in the primitive world. Cf. also Lowie, *Are We Civilized?*, 123; and Sumner and Keller, iii, 1553-7.
45. Ibid., 1556; Briffault, ii, 65; Westermarck, i, 441.
46. Lowie, 127.
47. Briffault, iii, 313; Müller-Lyer, *Modern Marriage*, 32.
48. Briffault, ii, 222-3; Westermarck, *Short History*, 13.
49. Sumner and Keller, iii, 1682; Sumner, *Folkways*, 358.
50. Ibid., 361; Sumner and Keller, iii, 1674.
51. Ibid., 1554; Briffault, iii, 344.
52. S & K, iii, 1682.
52a. For examples cf. Westermarck, *Human Marriage*, i, 530-45; or Müller-Lyer, *Modern Marriage*, 39-41.
53. Müller-Lyer, *Social Development*, 132-3; Sumner, *Folkways*, 439.
54. Briffault, iii, 260f.
55. Ibid, 307; Ratzel, 93.
56. Sumner, *Folkways*, 450.
57. Reinach, *Orpheus*, 74.
58. cf. Briffault, ii, 112-7; Vinogradoff, 173.
59. S. & K., iii, 1528.
60. Ibid., 1771.
61. Ibid., 1677-8.
62. Ibid., 1831.
63. Quoted in Briffault, ii, 76.
64. Ibid., S & K, iii, 1831.
65. Müller-Lyer, *Family*, 102.
66. S & K, iii, 1890.
67. Ibid.; Sumner, *Folkways*, 314; Briffault, ii, 71; Westermarck, *Moral Ideas*, ii, 413; E. A. Rout, "Sex Hygiene of the New Zealand Maori," in *The Medical Journal and Record*, Nov. 17, 1926; *The Birth Control Review*, April, 1932, p. 112.
68. Westermarck, *Moral Ideas*, ii, 394-401.
69. Lowie, *Are We Civilized?*, 138.
70. Müller-Lyer, *Family*, 104.
71. S & K, i, 54.
72. Briffault, ii, 391.
73. Renard, 135.

74. Westermarck, *Moral Ideas*, ii, 383.
75. Ibid., i, 290; Spencer, *Sociology*, i, 46.
76. Westermarck, *Moral Ideas*, i, 88; S & K, i, 336.
77. Kropotkin, 90.
78. Lowie, *Are We Civilized?*, 141.
79. Instances in Thomas, W. I., 108; White, E. M., 40; Briffault, i, 453; Ratzel, 135.
80. Westermarck, *Moral Ideas*, ii, 422, 678.
81. Hobhouse, 79; Briffault, ii, 353.
82. Ibid., 185.
83. Thomas, W. I., 154.
84. Examples in S & K, i, 641-3.
85. Briffault, ii, 143-4.
86. Ibid., 500-1; Kropotkin, 101, 105; Westermarck, *Moral Ideas*, ii, 539-40; Lowie, 141.
87. Hobhouse, 29; Spencer, *Sociology*, i, 69; Kropotkin, 90-1.
88. Müller-Lyer, *Modern Marriage*, 26; Briffault, i, 636.
89. Ibid., 640.
90. Müller-Lyer, 31.
91. Lowie, 164.
92. Westermarck, *Moral Ideas*, i, 150-1; Sumner, *Folkways*, 460.
93. Ibid, 454.
94. Ibid., 13; S & K, i, 358.
95. Kropotkin, 112-3; Briffault, ii, 357, 490; S & K, i, 659; Westermarck, ii, 556.
96. Strabo, *Geography*, I, 2, 8.
96a. S & K, ii, 1419.
96b. Ibid.
96c. Briffault, ii, 510.
96d. Lippert, 6.
96e. Briffault, ii, 503.
97. Williams, H. S., *History of Science*, i, 15.
98. Briffault, ii, 645.
99. Ibid., 657.
100. S & K, ii, 859; Lippert, 115.
101. *Brihadaranyaka Upanishad*, iv., 3; Davids, T. W. Rhys, *Buddhist India*, 252; Deussen, Paul, *The Philosophy of the Upanishads*, 302.
102. Carpenter, Edward, *Pagan and Christian Creeds*, 80.
103. Powys, John Cowper, *The Meaning of Culture*, 180.
104. Briffault, ii, 577, 583-92, 632.
105. Ibid., 147; Carpenter, 48.
106. Jung, C. G., *Psychology of the Unconscious*, 173.
107. Allen, G., *Evolution of the Idea of God*, 237.
108. Briffault, ii, 508-9.
109. Frazer, Sir J. G., *The Golden Bough*, 1-v ed., 112, 115.
110. De Morgan, Jacques, *Prehistoric Man*, 249.
111. Frazer, *Golden Bough*, 165-7.
112. Jung, 173.
113. Briffault, iii, 117.
114. Ibid., ii, 592.
115. Ibid., 481.
116. Reinach, 19.
117. Freud, S., *Totem and Taboo*. For a criticism of the theory cf. Goldenweiser, A. A., *History, Psychology and Culture*, 201-8.
118. Durckheim, E., *Elementary Forms of the Religious Life*.
119. Briffault, ii, 468.
120. Reinach, *Orpheus*, 1909 ed., 76, 81; Tarde, G., *Laws of Imitation*, 273-5; Murray, G., *Aristophanes and the War Party*, 23, 37.
121. Spencer, *Sociology*, i, 406; Frazer, *Golden Bough*, vii.
122. Reinach, 1909 ed., 80.
123. Allen, 30.
124. Examples in Lippert, 103.
125. Smith, W. Robertson, *The Religion of the Semites*, 42.
126. Hoernle, R. F. A., *Studies in Contemporary Metaphysics*, 181.
127. Reinach (1909), 111.
128. Frazer, *Golden Bough*, 13.
129. Frazer, *Adonis, Attis, Osiris*, 356.
130. Briffault, iii, 196.
131. Ibid., 199.
132. Frazer, *Golden Bough*, 337, 432; Allen, 246.
133. Georg, E., *The Adventure of Mankind*, 202.
134. S & K, ii, 1252.
135. Ibid.
136. Sumner, *Folkways*, 336-9, 553-5.
137. Ibid., 337; Frazer, *Golden Bough*, 489.
138. Westermarck, *Moral Ideas*, ii, 373, 376, 563.
139. Ratzel, 45.
140. Reinach, 1930 ed., 23.
141. Ratzel, 133.
142. 2 Sam. vi, 4-7.
143. Diodorus Siculus, *Library of History*, I, lxxxiv.
144. Briffault, ii, 366, 387.
145. Sumner, *Folkways*, 511.

CHAPTER V

1. Ratzel, 34; Müller-Lyer, *Social Development*, 50-3, 61.
2. Ibid., 46-9, 54; Renard, 57; Robinson, J. H., 735, 740; France, A., *M. Bergeret a Paris*.
3. Lubbock, 227, 339, 342f.
4. Müller, Max, *Lectures on the Science of Language*, i, 360.
5. Tylor, E. B., *Anthropology*, 125.
6. Müller, *Science of Language*, i, 265, 303n; ii, 39.
7. Venkateswara, S. V., *Indian Culture through the Ages*, Vol. I., *Education and the Propagation of Culture*, 6; Ratzel, 31.
8. White, W. A., *Mechanisms of Character Formation*, 83.
9. Lubbock, 353-4.
10. Briffault, i, 106.
11. Ibid., 107; Russell, B., *Marriage and Morals*, 243.
12. S & K, i, 554.
13. Briffault, ii, 190.
14. Ibid., 192-3.
15. Lubbock, 35.
16. Maspero, G., *Dawn of Civilization*, quoted in Mason, W. A., *History of the Art of Writing*, 39.
17. Lubbock, 299.
18. Mason, W. A., ch. ii; Lubbock, 35.
19. Mason, W. A., 146-54.
20. Briffault, i, 18.
21. Spencer, *Sociology*, iii, 218-26.
22. Mason, W. A., 149; further examples in Lowie, 202.
23. Spencer, *Sociology*, iii, 247f.
24. Tylor, *Primitive Culture*, i, 243-8, 261, 266; Lubbock, 299.
25. Thoreau, H. D., *Walden*.
26. Briffault, ii, 601.
27. Mason, O. T., in Thomas, *Source Book*, 366.
28. Briffault, i, 485.
29. Examples in Lowie, *Are We Civilized?*, 250.
29a. Matt., viii, 28.

30. Lowie, 250; S & K, ii, 979; Spencer, *Sociology*, iii, 194; Garrison, F. H., *History of Medicine*, 22, 33; Harding, T. Swann, *Fads, Frauds and Physicians*, 148.
31. Garrison, 26.
32. Marett, H. R., *Hibbert Journal*, Oct., 1918; Carpenter, *Pagan and Christian Creeds*, 176.
33. Lowie, 247.
34. In Garrison, 45.
35. Briffault, ii, 157-8, 162-3.
36. Darwin, *Descent of Man*, 660.
37. Briffault, ii, 176.
38. Spencer, i, 65; Ratzel, 95.
39. Grosse, E., *The Beginnings of Art*, 55-63; Pijoan, J., *History of Art*, i, 4.
40. Grosse, 58.
41. Renard, 91.
42. Lubbock, 45.
43. Ratzel, 105.
44. Lubbock, 51; Grosse, 80.
45. In Thomas, *Source Book*, 555.
46. Grosse, 70; Lubbock, 46-50.
47. Georg, 104.
48. Grosse, 81.
49. Briffault, ii, 161.
50. Grosse, 83.
51. Ratzel, 95.
52. Müller-Lyer, *Social Development*, 142.
53. Grosse, 53.
54. Ibid.
55. Briffault, ii, 297.
56. Ratzel in Thomas, *Source Book*, 557.
57. Lowie, 80.
58. Sumner, *Folkways*, 187.
59. *Enc. Brit.*, xviii, 373.
60. Mason, O. T., 156, 164.
61. Ibid., 52.
62. Pijoan, i, 12.
63. Ibid., 8.
64. Spencer, iii, 294-304; Ratzel, 47.
65. Renard, 56.
66. Pratt, W. S., *The History of Music*, 26-31.
67. Grosse, E., in Thomas, *Source Book*, 586.

CHAPTER VI

2. Osborn, H. F., *Men of the Old Stone Age*, 23.
3. N. Y. *Times*, July 31 and Nov. 5, 1931.
4. Lull, *The Evolution of Man*, 26.
5. Sollas, W. J., *Ancient Hunters*, 438-42.
6. Keith, Sir A., N. Y. *Times*, Oct. 12, 1930.
7. De Morgan, J., *Prehistoric Man*, 57-8.
8. Pittard, Eugene, *Race and History*, 70.
9. Keith, *l.c.*
10. Pittard, 311; Childe, V. G., *The Most Ancient East*, 26.
11. Andrews, R. C., *On the Trail of Ancient Man*, 309-12.
12. Skeat, W. M., *An Etymological Dictionary of the English Language*, 252; Lippert, 166.
14. Osborn, 270-1.
15. Lippert, 133.
16. Lowie, *Are We Civilized?*, 51.
17. Müller-Lyer, *Social Development*, 99; Lippert, 130; S & K, i, 191.
18. Bulley, M., *Ancient and Medieval Art*, 14.
19. De Morgan, 197.
20. Spearing, H. G., *The Childhood of Art*, 92; Bulley, 12.
21. Osborn, fig. 166.
22. N. Y. *Times*, Jan. 22, 1934.
23. Bulley, 17.
24. Spearing, 45.
26. Renard, 86.
27. Rickard, T. A., *Man and Metals*, i, 67.
28. De Morgan, x.
29. Ibid., 169; Renard, 27.
30. De Morgan, 172, fig. 94.
31. Pitkin, W. B., *A Short Introduction to the History of Human Stupidity*, 53.
32. Carpenter, E., *Pagan and Christian Creeds*, 74; Lowie, 58; Ratzel in Thomas, *Source Book*, 93.
33. Lowie, 60.
34. Febvre, L., *A Geographical Introduction to History*, 261.
35. Rickard, i, 81; Schneider, H., *The History of World Civilization*, i, 20.
36. Breasted, J. H., *Ancient Times*, 29.
37. Renard, 102.
38. De Morgan, 187.
39. Mason, O. T., *Origins of Invention*, 154.

40. E.g., De Morgan, 226, fig. 135.
41. Renard, 79.
42. Lowie, 114; De Morgan, 269.
43. Renard, 112; Rickard, i, 77.
44. Georg, 105.
45. De Morgan, 235, 240; Renard, 27; Childe, V. G., *The Dawn of European Civilization*, 129-38; Georg, 89.
46. Schneider, H., i, 23-9.
47. Ibid, 30-1.
48. Garrison, *History of Medicine*, 28; Renard, 190.
49. Rickard, i, 84.
50. Ibid., 109, 141.
51. Ibid., 114.
52. Ibid., 118.
53. Rostovtzeff, M., in Coomaraswamy, A. K., *History of Indian and Indonesian Art*, 3.
54. *Cambridge Ancient History*, i, 103.
55. De Morgan, 126.
56. Rickard, i, 169-70; De Morgan, 91.
57. Rickard, i, 85-6.
58. Ibid., 86.
59. Ibid., 141-8; Renard, 29-30.
60. Mason, W. A., *History of Writing*, 313.
60a. CAH (*Cambridge Ancient History*), i, 376.
61. Petrie, Sir W. F., *The Formation of the Alphabet*, in Mason, W. A., 329.
62. *Encyc. Brit.*, i, 680.
63. Tylor, *Anthropology*, 168.
64. De Morgan, 257.
65. Breasted, *Ancient Times*, 42; Mason, W. A., 210, 321.
66. Ibid., 331.
67. *Encyc. Brit.*, i, 681.
68. Plato, *Timaeus*, 25; *Critias*, 113.
69. Georg, 223.
70. Childe, *The Most Ancient East*, 21-6.
71. Georg, 51.
72. Keith, Sir A., N. Y. *Times*, Oct. 12, 1930; Buxton, L. H. D., *The Peoples of Asia*, 83.
73. CAH, i, 579.
74. Ibid., 86, 90-1, 362.
75. Keith, l.c.; Briffault, ii, 507; CAH, i, 362; Coomaraswamy, *History*, 3.
76. CAH, i, 85-6.

CHAPTER VII

1. CAH, i, 86, 361; Childe, *The Most Ancient East*, 126; Keith in N. Y. *Times*, April 3, 1932.
2. Breasted, J. H., *Oriental Institute*, 8.
3. Childe, 128, 146.
4. De Morgan, 208; CAH, i, 362, 578.
5. Moret, 199; CAH, i, 361, 579.
6. Woolley, C. L., *The Sumerians*, 189.
7. Jastrow, Morris, *The Civilization of Babylonia and Assyria*, 101.
8. CAH, i, 127.
9. Pijoan, i, 104; Ball, C. J., in Parmelee, M., *Oriental and Occidental Culture*, 18.
10. Childe, 160, 173; Maspero, G., *Dawn of Civilization*, 718-20; CAH, i, 364; Woolley, 13.
11. CAH, i, 456.
12. Berosus in CAH, i, 150.
13. Maspero, *Struggle of the Nations*, iv.
14. Woolley, 69; CAH, i, 387.
15. Ibid., 388.
16. Woolley, 73; CAH, i, 403.
17. Harper, R. F., ed., *Assyrian and Babylonian Literature*, 1.
18. CAH, i, 405.
19. Woolley, 140; Maspero, *Dawn*, 637; CAH, i, 427.
20. Ibid., i, 435.
21. Ibid., i, 472.
23. Jastrow, 7; Maspero, *Dawn*, 554; Childe, *Ancient East*, 124; CAH, i, 463.
24. Woolley, 112-4.
25. Childe, 170.
26. Woolley, 13.
27. Delaporte, L., *Mesopotamia*, 112.
28. Woolley, 13; Delaporte, 172; CAH, i, 507; N. Y. *Times*, Aug. 2, 1932.
29. Childe, 147.
30. Ibid., 169; *Encyc. Brit.*, ii, 845; Delaporte, 106.
31. Ibid.; Woolley, 117-8; CAH, i, 427.
32. Woolley, 92; Delaporte, 101.
33. Woolley, 126; CAH, i, 461.
34. Maspero, *Dawn*, 709f.
35. Ibid., 606-7, 722; Woolley, 79; CAH, i, 540.
36. Maspero, *Dawn*, 721-3.
37. CAH, i, 461.
38. Woolley, 93.
39. Maspero, 655.
40. CAH, i, 443-4, 448.
41. Jastrow, 277.
42. Woolley, 126.
43. Jastrow, 130.
44. Woolley, 13.
45. Ibid., 120.
46. CAH, i, 400.
47. Langdon, S., *Babylonian Wisdom*, 18-21.
48. Woolley, 108-9.
49. Ibid., 13.
50. Jastrow, 466.
51. Woolley, 106.
52. CAH, i, 370-1; Woolley, 40, 43, 54.
53. Ibid., 92, 101.
54. CAH, i, 376.
55. Maspero, *Dawn*, 723-8; CAH, i, 371-2.
56. Maspero, *Struggle*, iv.
57. CAH, i, 550; iii, 226.
58. Woolley, 37.
59. Delaporte, 172.
60. Woolley, 37, 191.
61. Maspero, *Dawn*, 709-18.
62. Jastrow, 106; Woolley, 40, 144; Maspero, 630.
63. Ibid., 601.
64. Schäfer, H., and Andrae, W., *Die Kunst des Alten Orients*, 469; Woolley, 66.
65. CAH, i, 400.
66. Woolley, 46; N. Y. *Times*, April 13, 1934.
67. Schäfer, 482.
68. Ibid., 485.
69. Woolley, 188; CAH, i, 463.
70. Moret, 164; Childe, *Ancient East*, 216.
71. Hall, H. R., in *Encyc. Brit.*, viii, 45.
72. Maspero, *Dawn*, 46; CAH, i, 255.
73. Ibid., 372.
74. Ibid., 255, 263, 581; De Morgan, 102; Hall, H. R., l.c.
75. Ibid., CAH, i; 579.
76. CAH, i, 263, 581.
77. CAH, i, 252, 581; Hall, l.c., 44-5.
78. De Morgan, 102.
79. Hall, l.c.; CAH, i, 581.
80. Such objects are pictured for comparison in De Morgan, 102.
81. Woolley, 187; Hall, l.c., 45.
82. Smith, G. Elliot, *The Ancient Egyptians and the Origin of Civilization*, xii.

CHAPTER VIII

1. Strabo, *Geography*, I, iii, 4.
2. Maspero, *Dawn*, 24.
3. Erman, A., *Life in Ancient Egypt*, 13; CAH, i, 317.
4. Erman, 29.
5. Diodorus Siculus, I, lxiv, 3. The face value of the talent in the time of Diodorus was $1,000 in gold, worth in purchasing power some $10,000 today.
6. *Encyc. Brit.*, viii, 42.
7. In Capart, J., *Thebes*, 40.
8. The Harris Papyrus in Capart, 237.
9. Capart, 27; Breasted, J. H., *Ancient Records of Egypt*, ii, 131.
10. CAH, i, 116; ii, 100.
11. Breasted, *Ancient Times*, 97, 455; CAH, i, 117.
12. Ibid., 116.
13. De Morgan, 25; CAH, i, 33-6; Keith in N. Y. *Times*, Oct. 12, 1930; Moret, 117f.
14. Breasted in CAH, i, 86.
15. *Encyc. Brit.*, viii, 42; Moret, 119; De Morgan, 92.
16. Moret, 119; CAH, i, 270-1.
17. Smith, G. Elliot, *Human History*, 264; Childe, *Ancient East*, 38.
18. Pittard, 419; CAH, i, 270-1; Smith, G. Elliot, *Ancient Egyptians*, 50.
19. CAH, i, 372, 255, 263; De Morgan, 102.
20. Maspero, *Dawn*, 45; CAH, i, 244-5, 254-6; Pittard, 413; Moret, 158; Smith, *Ancient Egyptians*, 24.
21. Maspero, *Passing of the Empires*, viii; De Morgan, 101.
22. Diodorus, I, xciv, 2. Diodorus adds, by way of comparison: "Among the Jews Moyses referred his laws to the god who is invoked as Iao."
23. Ibid., I, xlv, 1.
24. *Encyc. Brit.*, viii, 45.
25. Schäfer, 209.
26. Ibid., 247.
27. Ibid., 211.
28. Ibid., 228-9.
29. Herodotus, II, 124.
30. Capart, J., *Lectures on Egyptian Art*, 98.
31. CAH, i, 335.
32. Maspero, *Art in Egypt*, 15.
33. Schäfer, 248.
34. Herodotus, II, 86.
35. In Cotterill, *History of Art*, i, 10.
36. Breasted, J. H., *Development of Religion and Thought in Ancient Egypt*, 203.
37. CAH, i, 308.
38. Breasted, J. H., *History of Egypt*, 266-7.
39. Breasted, *Ancient Records*, ii, 78-121; Maspero, *The Struggle of the Nations*, 236-7.
40. Ibid., 237-9; Breasted, *History*, 273; White, E. M., 49.
41. CAH, ii, 65.
42. Ibid., ch. iv.
43. Ibid., 79.
43a. Breasted, *History*, 320.
44. Weigall, A., *Life and Times of Akhnaton*, 8.
45. Erman, 20.
46. So a stele of Amenhotep III expresses it in Capart, *Thebes*, 182.
47. Ibid., 182, 197.
48. Diodorus, I, xxxi, 8.
49. Herodotus, II, 14.
50. Erman, 199.
51. Herodotus, II, 95.
52. Maspero, *Dawn*, 330.
53. Genesis, xlvii, 26.
54. Erman, 441.
55. Erman, A., *Literature of the Ancient Egyptians*, 187.
56. Maspero, *Dawn*, 65; Lippert, 197.
57. Maspero, *Dawn*, 331-2.
58. Moret, 357.
59. Rickard, T. A., i, 192-203; De Morgan, 114.
60. Diodorus, III, xii, tr. by Rickard, i, 209-10.
61. Erman, *Life*, 451-5.
62. Breasted, *Ancient Times*, 64; Maspero, *Struggle*, 739.
63. Müller-Lyer, *Social Development*, 105.
64. Diodorus, I, lxxiv, 6.
65. Ibid.
66. Hobhouse, *Morals in Evolution*, 283.
67. Erman, *Life*, 124-5.
68. Maspero, *Struggle*, 441.
69. Diodorus, I, lii; Rickard, i, 183.
70. N. Y. *Times*, April 16, 1933.
71. Herodotus, II, 124; Wilkinson in Rawlinson's Herodotus, ii, 200n.
72. Capart, *Thebes*, 32.

73. Erman, *Life*, 488-93; Borchardt and Ricke, *Egypt*. p. v.
74. CAH, ii, 423.
75. Erman, *Life*, 494.
76. Maspero, *Struggle*, 109.
77. Ibid., 285, 289, 407, 582; CAH, ii, 79.
78. Maspero, *Dawn*, 330; Schneider, H., i, 86.
79. CAH, ii, 212.
80. Diodorus, I, lxxvii, 2.
81. Diodorus, I, lxxv, 3.
82. Sumner, *Folkways*, 236.
83. Diodorus, I, lxxviii, 3.
84. Hobhouse, 108; Maspero, *Dawn*, 337, 479-80; Erman, *Life*, 141.
85. Maspero, *Dawn*, 337.
86. Capart, *Thebes*, 161.
87. Breasted, J. H., *Dawn of Conscience*, 208-10.
88. Erman, *Life*, 67; Diodorus, I, lxx.
89. Erman, *Life*, 121.
90. Moret, 124.
91. Erman, *Literature*, 27.
92. Maspero, *Dawn*, 278.
93. Breasted, *History*, 75.
94. Erman, *Life*, 153, Sumner, *Folkways*, 485.
95. Maspero, *Dawn*, 51.
96. Erman, *Life*, 76.
97. In Briffault, i, 384.
98. In White, E. M., 46.
99. Petrie, Sir W. F., *Egypt and Israel*, 23.
100. Hobhouse, 187.
101. Ibid., 185.
102. Ibid., 186; Erman, *Life*, 185.
103. Petrie, 23.
104. Frazer, *Adonis*, 397.
105. Briffault, i, 384.
106. Diodorus, I, lxxvii, 7; lxxx, 3.
107. Maspero, *Struggle*, 272.
108. Briffault, ii, 174.
109. Ibid., 383.
110. Maspero, *Struggle*, 503; Erman, *Life*, 155.
111. Ibid.; Sanger, W. W., *History of Prostitution*, 40-1; Georg, 172.
112. Erman, *Life*, 247f.
113. Sumner, *Folkways*, 541; Maspero, *Struggle*, 536.
114. Erman, *Life*, 387.
115. In Breasted, *Dawn of Conscience*, 324; cf. Proverbs, xv, 16-7. For further correspondence between the Egyptian and the Jewish authors cf. Breasted, 372-7.

116. Hobhouse, 247; Maspero, *Dawn*, 269; *Struggle*, 228.
117. Strabo, XVII, i, 53.
118. Erman, *Literature*, xxix; 47.
119. Maspero, *Dawn*, 195; *Encyc. Brit.*, vii, 329.
120. Spearing, 230.
121. Maspero, *Dawn*, 47-8, 271.
122. CAH, ii, 422.
123. Breasted, *History*, 27; Erman, *Life*, 229f; Downing, Dr. J. G., *Cosmetics, Past and Present*, 2088f.
124. CAH, ii, 421.
125. Maspero, *Struggle*, 504; Erman, *Life*, 212.
126. Schäfer, 235.
127. Sumner, *Folkways*, 191; Maspero, *Struggle*, 494; CAH, ii, 421.
128. Maspero, *Dawn*, 57, 491f.
129. CAH, ii, 421.
130. Diodorus, I, lxxxi; Mencken, H. L., *Treatise on the Gods*, 117.
131. Spencer, *Sociology*, iii, 278.
132. Erman, *Life*, 328, 384.
133. Ibid., 256; Erman, *Literature*, xliii.
134. Ibid., 185.
135. Erman, *Life*, 256, 328.
136. Schneider, H., i, 94.
137. Erman, *Life*, 447; Breasted, *History*, 97.
138. Erman, *Literature*, xxxvii, xlii.
139. Maspero, *Dawn*, 46.
140. Erman, *Literature*, xxxvi-vii; Erman, *Life*, 333f Breasted *Ancient Times*, 42; Maspero, *Dawn*, 221-3; De Morgan, 256.
141. Father Batin, address at Oriental Institute, Chicago, March 29, 1932; CAH, i, 189; Sprengling, M., *The Alphabet*, passim.
141a. N. Y. *Times*, Oct. 18, 1934.
142. Maspero, *Dawn*, 398.
143. CAH, i, 121; Erman, *Literature*, 1; Breasted, *Development*, 178.
144. Breasted, J. H., *Oriental Institute*, 149f.
145. Erman, *Life*, 370.
146. Erman, *Literature*, 30-1.
147. Ibid., 22-8.
148. Maspero, *Dawn*, 438.
149. Maspero, *Struggle*, 499.
150. Maspero, *Dawn*, 497.
151. Breasted, *Dawn of Conscience*, 71.
152. Erman, *Literature*, 35-6.
153. CAH, ii, 225.
154. Exs. in Erman, *Literature*, xxx-xxxiv.

155. Erman, *Life*, 389.
156. Schneider, H., i, 81.
157. Breasted, *Ancient Records*, i, 51.
158. Schneider, H., i, 91-2.
159. Erman, *Literature*, 109.
160. Erman, *Literature*, xxv-vii; Maspero, *Struggle*, 494f.
161. Maspero, *Dawn*, 204.
162. Hall, M. P., *An Encyclopedic Outline of Masonic, Hermetic, Qabbalistic and Rosicrucian Symbolic Philosophy*, 37.
163. Sedgwick, W. T., and Tyler, H. W., *A Short History of Science*, 312.
164. Maspero, *Dawn*, 328.
165. Sedgwick and Tyler, 29.
166. Schneider, H., i, 85-6.
167. CAH, ii, 216; *Encyc. Brit.*, viii, 57.
168. Sedgwick and Tyler, 30.
169. Ibid., 89; Breasted, J. H., *Conquest of Civilization*, 88.
170. Williams, H. S., *History of Science*, i, 41.
171. Ibid., i, 34.
172. Spencer, *Sociology*, iii, 251.
173. Tabouis, G. R., *Nebuchadnezzar*, 318; Breasted, *Ancient Times*, 91.
174. Strabo, XVII, i, 46; Diodorus, I, l, 2.
175. Herodotus, II, 4; CAH, i, 248; Breasted, *History*, 14, 33; *Ancient Times*, 45; Erman, *Life*, 10; Childe, *Ancient East*, 5; Williams, H. S., i, 38f; Maspero, *Dawn*, 16-7, 205-9; Moret, 134; Schneider, H., i, 85; Sedgwick and Tyler, 33; Frazer, *Adonis*, 280, 286-9; *Encyc. Brit.*, iv, 576; v, 654.
176. Ebers Papyrus, 99, 1f, in Erman, *Life*, 357-8.
177. Ibid., 353.
178. Garrison, 57.
179. Herodotus, II, 84; III, 1.
180. Erman, *Life*, 362.
181. Garrison, 55-9; Maspero, *Dawn*, 217; Breasted, *Conquest of Civilization*, 88.
182. Smith, G. Elliot, *The Ancient Egyptians*, 57.
182a. Himes, Norman, *Medical History of Contraception*, Chap. II, §1. The suppositories contained chemicals identical with those now used in contraceptive jellies. The matter, however, is not beyond doubt.
183. Erman, *Life*, 360; Maspero, *Dawn*, 219-20; Harding, T. Swann, *Fads*, 328.
184. Garrison, 53.

185. Smith, G. E., *Ancient Egyptians*, 62; Diodorus, I, xxviii, 3.
186. Breasted, *Dawn of Conscience*, 353n.
187. Diodorus, I, lxxxii, 1-2.
188. Pliny, *Historia Naturalis*, VIII, in Tyrrell, Dr. C. A., *Royal Road to Health*, 57.
189. Herodotus, II, 77.
190. Erman, *Life*, 167-96; Capart, *Thebes*, figs. 4 and 107-9.
191. Maspero, *Art*, 132.
192. Pijoan, i, 101; Fergusson, Jas., *History of Architecture in All Countries*, i, 22; Breasted, *History*, 100.
193. E.g., Maspero, *Struggle*, xi.
194. At Beni-Hasan, Lisht, etc.
195. At Medinet-Habu.
196. Maspero, *Art*. 84.
197. Schäfel, *Tafel* VI; Breasted, *Dawn*, 218.
198. Fry, R. E., *Chinese Art*, 13.
199. Schäfer, 358; Capart, *Lectures*, fig. 176.
200. Maspero, *Art*, 174.
201. Schäfer, 343; CAH, ii, 103.
202. Baikie, Jas., *Amarna Age*, 241, 256. All three are in the State Museum at Berlin.
203. Cairo Museum; Maspero, *Art*, fig. 461; Schäfer, 433.
204. Athens Museum; Maspero, *Struggle*, 535.
205. Schäfer, 445.
206. Louvre; Schäfer, 190.
207. Cairo Museum; Schäfer, 246-7.
208. Cairo Museum; Schäfer, 254.
209. Capart, *Thebes*, 173f.
210. Cairo Museum; Breasted, *History*, fig. 55; Maspero, *Art*, fig. 92.
211. Ibid., fig. 194.
212. Schäfer, *Tafel* IX.
213. E.g., Schäfer, 305, 418.
214. Maspero, *Art*, fig. 287.
215. Schäfer, 367.
216. Ibid., *Tafel* XVI.
217. Maspero, *Art*, 67.
218. Erman, *Life*, 448; CAH, ii, 422.
219. CAH, ii, 105; Erman, 250-1.
220. Breasted, *Ancient Records*, ii, 147.
221. Spencer, *Sociology*, iii, 299.
222. Cf. Plato, *Timæus*, 22B.
223. Maspero, *Dawn*, 399.
224. Brown, B., *Wisdom of the Egyptians*, 96-116; Breasted, *Dawn*, 136f.
225. Ibid., 198.

226. Breasted, *Development*, 215.
227. Ibid., 188; *Dawn of Conscience*, 168.
228. Breasted, *Development*, 182.
229. Maspero, *Dawn*, 639.
230. Ibid., 86.
231. Ibid., 95, 92.
232. Ibid., 156-8.
233. Ibid., 120-1.
234. Renard, 121.
235. Capart, *Thebes*, 66; Maspero, *Dawn*, 119; *Struggle*, 536.
236. Maspero, *Dawn*, 102-3.
237. Briffault, iii, 187.
238. Hommel in Maspero, *Dawn*, 45.
239. Howard, Clifford, *Sex Worship*, 98.
240. Diodorus, I, lxxxviii, 1-3; Howard, C., 79; Tod, Lt.-Col. Jas., *Annals and Antiquities of Rajasthan*, 570; Briffault, iii, 205.
241. Carpenter, *Pagan and Christian Creeds*, 183.
242. Maspero, *Dawn*, 110-1.
243. Breasted, *Development*, 24-33; Frazer, *Adonis*, 269-75; 383.
244. Diodorus, I, xiv, 1.
245. Frazer, *Adonis*, 346-50; Maspero, *Dawn*, 131-2; Macrobius, *Saturnalia*, I, 18, in McCabe, Jos., *Story of Religious Controversy*, 169.
246. *Encyc. Brit.*, 11th ed., ix, 52.
247. Moret, 5; Maspero, *Dawn*, 265.
248. Herodotus, II, 37.
249. Breasted, *Dawn of Conscience*, 46, 83.
250. Breasted, *Development*, 293; Brown, B., *Wisdom of the Egyptians*, 178; Maspero, *Dawn*, 199.

251. Translation by Robert Hillyer, in Van Doren, Mark, *Anthology of World Poetry*, 237.
252. In Maspero, *Dawn*, 189-90.
253. Breasted, *Development*, 291.
254. Erman, *Life*, 353; exs. in Erman, *Literature*, 39-43.
255. Maspero, *Dawn*, 282; Briffault, ii, 510.
256. Erman, *Life*, 352.
257. Herodotus, II, 82.
258. Breasted, *Development*, 296, 308.
258a. Capart, *Thebes*, 95.
259. Ibid, 76.
260. In Weigall, *Akhnaton*, 86.
261. Breasted, *Development*, 315.
262. E.g., Breasted, *Ancient Records*, ii, 369.
263. Breasted, *Development*, 324f.
264. The parallelisms are listed in Weigall, *Akhnaton*, 134-6, and in Breasted, *Dawn of Conscience*, 182f.
265. Breasted, *Development*, 314.
266. Weigall, 102, 105.
267. Capart, *Lectures*, fig. 104.
268. Weigall, 103.
269. Petrie in Weigall, 178; Breasted, *History*, 378.
270. Weigall, 116; Baikie, 284.
272. Baikie, 435.
273. CAH, ii, 154; Breasted, *History*, 446.
274. Ibid., 491.
275. Capart, *Thebes*, 69.
276. Erman, *Life*, 129.
277. Weigall, A., *Life and Times of Cleopatra*.
278. Faure, Elie, *History of Art*, i, p. xlvii.

CHAPTER IX

1. Maspero, *Passing of the Empires*, 783.
2. CAH, i, 399.
3. The quotations are from Heraclitus, *Fragments*, and Mallock, W., *Lucretius on Life and Death*.
4. Harper, R. F., *Code of Hammurabi*, 3-7.
5. Jastrow, M., *Civilization of Babylonia and Assyria*, 283-4.
6. Sumner, *Folkways*, 504.
7. CAH, iii, 250.
8. Harper, *Code*, 99-100.
9. CAH, i, 489; Maspero, *Struggle*, 43-4.
10. Maspero, *Dawn*, 759; Rawlinson, *Five Great Monarchies of the Ancient Eastern World*, iii, 22-3; McCabe, 141-2; Delaporte, 194-6.
11. CAH, ii, 429; iii, 101.
12. Harper, *Assyrian and Babylonian Literature*, 220.
13. Maspero, *Passing*, 567.
14. Jastrow, 466.
15. Daniel, iv, 30.
16. Rawlinson, ii, 510.
17. Herodotus, I, 178. Strabo, to prove his moderation, says 44 (XVI, i, 5).
18. Tabouis, 306.
19. Rawlinson, ii, 514; Herodotus, I, 180.
20. Diodorus, II, ix, 2.
21. Tabouis, 307.

22. Herodotus, I, 181.
23. CAH., i, 503.
24. Diodorus, II, x, 6; Strabo, XVI, i, 5; Maspero, *Passing*, 564, 782; CAH, i, 506-8; Rawlinson, ii, 517.
25. Maspero, *Dawn*, 761.
26. CAH., i, 541.
27. Berosus in Tabouis, 307.
28. Maspero, *Dawn*, 763-4; Delaporte, 107.
29. Maspero, *Dawn*, 556.
30. Strabo, XVI, i, 15. Attendants extinguished the flames with torrents of water.
31. Layard, A. H., *Ninevah and its Remains*, ii, 413.
32. *Code of Hammurabi*, sections 187-9; Delaporte, 113.
33. Lowie, *Are We Civilized?*, 119; CAH, i, 501.
34. Lowie, 60; Maspero, *Dawn*, 769; CAH, i, 107, 501; ii, 227.
35. East India House Inscription in Tabouis, 287.
36. Xenophon, Cyropædia, V, iv, 33. The probable invention of this letter by Xenophon hardly lessens its pertinence.
37. Tabouis, 210.
38. Maspero, *Dawn*, 751-2.
38a. Jastrow, 292n.
39. Ibid., 326; CAH, i, 545; Maspero *Dawn*, 749, 761; Delaporte, 118, 126, 231; Tabouis, 241.
40. Cf. e.g., Harper, *Assyrian and Babylonian Literature*, xlviii-ix.
41. *Encyc. Brit.*, ii, 863.
42. *Code*, 48.
43. CAH, i, 526; Maspero, *Dawn*, 760; Delaporte, 110; Jastrow, 299.
44. Delaporte, 122; Maspero, *Dawn*, 720.
45. CAH, i, 520-1; Maspero, *Dawn*, 742-4; Jastrow, 326.
46. Maspero, 735.
47. Ibid., 708.
48. Olmstead, A. T., *History of Assyria*, 525-8.
49. *Code*, 2, 132.
50. Delaporte, 134.
51. *Code*, 196.
52. 210.
53. 198.
54. Ibid.
55. 202-4.
56. 195.
57. 218.

58. 194.
59. 143.
60. CAH., i, 517-8.
61. *Code*, 228f.
62. Jastrow, 305, 362; Maspero, *Dawn*, 748; CAH, i, 526.
63. Harper, *Code*, p. 11.
64. Jastrow, 488; CAH, i, 513.
65. CAH, iii, 237.
66. Maspero, *Dawn*, 679, 750; CAH, i, 535.
67. Delaporte, 133-4.
68. Maspero, 636.
69. CAH, i, 529-32.
70. Maspero, 645-6.
71. Ibid., 644.
72. Ibid., 643, 650; Jastrow, 193.
73. Briffault, iii, 169.
74. CAH, i, 208, 530.
75. Ibid., 500.
76. Briffault, iii, 88.
77. Maspero, 537.
78. Cf. Langdon, *Babylonian Wisdom*, 18-21.
79. Maspero, 546.
80. Ibid., 566-72.
81. Jastrow, 453-9; Frazer, *Adonis*, 6-7; Briffault, iii, 90; CAH, i, 461; iii, 232.
82. Briffault, iii, 90; Harper, *Assyrian and Babylonian Literature*, liii.
83. Cf. e.g., Harper, 420-1.
84. Tabouis, 387.
85. Jastrow, 280; Maspero, 691-2.
86. Ibid, 687.
87. Ibid., 684-6.
88. Ibid., 689; Jastrow, 381; CAH, i, 531.
89. Jastrow, 249.
90. Maspero, 692.
91. Tabouis, 159, 165, 351.
92. Briffault, iii, 94.
93. Woolley, 125.
94. CAH, iii, 216-7.
95. Harper, *Literature*, 433-9.
96. Maspero, 682.
97. Jastrow, 253-4; Maspero, 643; Harper, lix.
98. Jastrow, 241-9.
99. Ibid., 267; Tabouis, 343-4, 374.
100. Williams, H. S., i, 74.
101. Tabouis, 365.
102. Herodotus, I, 199; Strabo, XVI, i, 20.
103. "This view is now generally discredited."—Briffault, iii, 203.
104. So Farnell thinks—Sumner, *Folkways*, 541. Frazer (Adonis, 50) rejects this interpretation.

105. Frazer, 53.
106. Briffault, iii, 203.
107. Amos, ii, 7; Sumner and Keller, ii, 1273.
108. Frazer, 52; Lacroix, Paul, *History of Prostitution*, i, 21-4, 109.
109. Briffault, iii, 220.
110. Jastrow, 309.
111. Maspero, 738-9.
112. Schneider, H., i, 155.
113. CAH, i, 547.
114. Ibid., 522-3; Hobhouse, 180; Maspero, 734.
115. Ibid.
116. Herodotus, I, 196. Several writers, however, described the custom as flourishing 400 years after Herodotus; cf. Rawlinson's *Herodotus*, i, 271.
117. Maspero, 737.
118. Section 132.
119. Sumner, *Folkways*, 378.
120. 141-2; Jastrow, 302-3.
121. 143.
122. CAH, i, 524; Maspero, 735-7; *Code*, 142.
123. *Encyc. Brit.*, ii, 863.
124. Maspero, 739.
125. Harper, *Literature*, xlviii; CAH, i, 520.
126. Woolley, 118; White, E. M., 71-5.
127. Maspero, 739.
128. Ibid., 735-8.
129. III, 159.
130. Layard, ii, 411; Sanger, 42.
131. Herodotus, I, 196.
132. V, l, in Tabouis, 366.
133. Delaporte, 199.
134. Jastrow, 31, 69-97; Mason, W. A., 266; CAH, i, 124-5.
135. Jastrow, 275-6; Delaporte, 198; Schneider, H., i, 181; Breasted, *Conquest of Civilization*, 152.
136. Schneider, i, 168.
137. Maspero, 564; CAH, i, 150.
138. Leonard, W. E., *Gilgamesh*, 3.
139. Ibid., 8.
140. Maspero, 570f.
141. Delaporte, ix.
142. Jastrow, 415.
143. Pratt, *History of Music*, 45; Rawlinson, iii, 20; Schneider, i, 168; Tabouis, 354; CAH, i, 533.
144. Perrot and Chipiez, *History of Art in Chaldea and Assyria*, ii, 292.
145. Cf. "The Lion of Babylon," Jastrow Plate XVIII, a work of glazed tile from the reign of Nebuchadrezzar II.
146. Herodotus, I, 180.
147. Tabouis, 313.
148. Jastrow, 10; Maspero, 624-7.
149. Jastrow, 258, 261, 492; Maspero, 778-80; Strabo, XVI, i, 6; Rawlinson, ñ, 580.
150. Sarton, Geo., *Introduction to the History of Science*, 71.
151. Rawlinson, ii, 575; Schneider, i, 171-5; Lowie, 268; Sedgwick and Tyler, 29; CAH, iii, 238f.
152. Tabouis, 47, 317.
153. Schneider, i, 171-5.
154. Maspero, 545.
155. Tabouis, 204, 366.
156. New Orleans *States*, Feb. 24, 1932.
157. *Code*, 215-7.
158. 218.
159. Maspero, 780f; Jastrow, 250f.
160. Ibid.; Tabouis, 294, 393.
161. Herodotus, I, 197; Strabo, XVI, i, 20.
162. Schneider, i, 166.
163. Jastrow, 475-83; Langdon, lf, 35-6.
164. Ibid., 1.
165. Jastrow, 461-3.
166. Tabouis, 254, 382.
167. Daniel, iv, 33.
168. Tabouis, 230, 264, 383.
169. Maspero, *Passing*, 626.
170. CAH, iii, 208. Jastrow, 184, believes that it was the priestly party which, disgusted with the heresies of Nabonidus, admitted Alexander.
171. Jastrow, 185; CAH, i, 568.

CHAPTER X

1. CAH, i, 468.
2. New York *Times*, Dec. 26, 1932.
3. CAH, ii, 429.
4. Olmstead, 16; CAH, i, 126.
4a. N. Y. *Times*, Feb. 24, 1933; Mar. 20, 1934.
5. CAH, ii, 248.
6. Harper, *Literature*, 16-7.
7. Jastrow, 166-7; Maspero, *Struggle*, 663-4.
8. Ibid., 50-2; Maspero, *Passing*, 27, 50.
9. Ibid., 85, 94-5; CAH, iii, 25.
10. Diodorus, II, vi-xx; Maspero, *Struggle*, 617; CAH, iii, 27.

11. Maspero, *Passing*, 243.
12. Olmstead, 309.
13. Maspero, *Passing*, 275-6.
14. Ibid., 345; CAH, iii, 79.
15. Harper, *Literature*, 94-127.
16. Delaporte, 343-4.
17. Maspero, *Passing*, 412f.
18. Olmstead, 488, 494; CAH, iii, 88, 127; Jastrow, 182; Delaporte, 223.
19. Diodorus, II, xxiii, 1-2.
20. Olmstead, 519, 525-8, 531; Maspero, *Passing*, 401-2.
21. Rawlinson, ii, 235.
22. CAH, iii, 100.
23. Maspero, *Passing*, 7.
24. Ibid., 9-10.
25. Rawlinson, i, 474.
26. Ibid., 467.
27. Maspero, *Struggle*, 627-38.
28. CAH, iii, 104-7; Rawlinson, i, 477-9.
29. CAH, l.c.
30. *Encyc. Brit.*, ii, 865.
31. Ibid., 863.
32. Maspero, *Passing*, 422-3.
33. Olmstead, 510, 531.
34. Ibid., 522-3, 558.
35. CAH, iii, 186.
35a. Olmstead, 331.
36. Rawlinson, i, 405.
37. Olmstead, 537.
38. Ibid., 518; Maspero, *Passing*, 317-9; CAH, iii, 76, 96-7; Delaporte, 353; Rawlinson, i, 401-2.
39. CAH, iii, 107.
40. Ibid.; Delaporte, 285, 352.
40a. Olmstead, 624.
41. Maspero, *Passing*, 269.
42. Delaporte, 282; CAH, iii, 104-7.
43. Maspero, *Passing*, 91, 262.
44. Olmstead, 87.
45. CAH, iii, 13.
46. Delaporte, vii.
47. Faure, i, 90.

48. Maspero, 545-6.
49. CAH, iii, 90-1.
50. Ibid., 89-90.
51. Delaporte, 354.
52. CAH, iii, 102, 241, 249.
53. Breasted, *Ancient Times*, 161; Jastrow, 21.
54. Maspero, 461-3.
55. *Encyc. Brit.*, ii, 851.
56. Rawlinson, i, 277; Delaporte, 338; Jastrow, 407; CAH, iii, 109.
57. Schäfer, 555; now in the British Museum.
58. Schäfer, 531.
59. Ibid., 546; in the British Museum.
60. Oriental Institute, Chicago.
61. British Museum.
62. Schäfer, *Tafel* XXXIV.
63. Ibid., 537, 558-9; Jastrow, f. p. 24.
64. Faure, i, 91; Br. Mus.
65. Rawlinson, i, 509.
66. Schäfer, 656.
67. E.g., Baikie, f. p. 213; and Pijoan, i, figs. 175-6.
68. Fergusson, *History of Architecture*, i. 35, 174-6, 205.
69. Rawlinson, i, 299.
70. Layard, ii, 262f.
71. Jastrow, 374; translation slightly improved.
72. Br. Mus.
73. Rawlinson, i, 284.
74. CAH, iii, 16, 75-7; Maspero, *Passing*, 45, 260-8, 310-4, 376; Pijoan, i, 121, 111-8; Jastrow, 415; Schäfer, 542-3.
75. Maspero, *Passing*, 460.
76. Harper, *Literature*, 125-6.
77. CAH, iii, 127.
78. Diodorus, ii, xxiii, 3.
79. Preserved in Diodorus, II, xxvii, 2. Cf. Maspero, *Passing*, 448.
80. Nahum, iii, 1.

CHAPTER XI

1. Cowan, A. R., *Master-clues in World-History*, 311; Petrie, *Egypt and Israel*, 26.
2. Breasted, *Conquest of Civilization*, 192n.
3. *Encyc. Brit.*, xi, 600-1.
4. Hrozný, F., *ibid.*, 603.
4a. New York *World-Telegram*, Mar. 16, 1935.

5. Ibid., 606. Certain archeologists (e.g., Hrozný) have been especially moved by the lenience of the Hittite code with sexual perversions.
6. CAH, iii, 200.
7. Herodotus, IV, 64.
8. Maspero, *Passing*, 479f; Hippocrates, *Airs, Waters, Places*, xvii-xxii.

9. Ibid., xvii.
10. Frazer, *Adonis*, 219f.
11. Ibid.; Maspero, *Passing*, 333.
12. Frazer, 34, 219-24; Hall, M. P., *An Encyclopedic Outline of Masonic Philosophy*, 36.
13. Herodotus, I, 93.
14. Ibid., I, 87.
15. Febvre, L., *Geographical Introduction to History*, 322.
16. Moret, 350.
17. Herodotus, II, 44.
18. Strabo, XVI, ii, 23.
19. Diodorus Siculus V, xxxv; Rickard, i, 276.
20. *Decline and Fall of the Roman Empire*, ed. 1903, i, 296, in Rickard, i, 278.
21. Maspero, *Struggle*, 192f, 203, 585; Day, Clive, *A History of Commerce*, 12-14; Briffault, i, 463; Sedgwick and Tyler, 14.
22. Rickard, i, 283.
23. Herodotus, IV, 42.
24. Maspero, *Struggle*, 199, 740-1.
25. Arrian, II, xv.
26. Ibid., VI, 220.
27. Zechariah, ix, 3.
28. XV, ii, 23.

29. Frazer, *Adonis*, 183-4; Maspero, *Struggle*, 174-9; Bebel, A., *Woman under Socialism*, 39; Briffault, iii, 220; Sanger, *The History of Prostitution*, 42.
30. Sedgwick and Tyler, 15; Doane, T. W., *Bible Myths*, 41.
31. E.g., Herodotus, V, 58.
32. Dussaud, in Venkateswara, 328.
33. CAH, i, 189.
34. Maspero, *Struggle*, 572f.
35. *Proceedings of the Oriental Institute*, Chicago, March 29, 1932.
36. New York *Times*, Aug. 8, 1930.
37. Ward, C. O., *The Ancient Lowly*, ii, 83, 85.
38. CAH, ii, 328-9.
39. Frazer, *Adonis*, 32-5.
40. Ibid., 225-7; Maspero, *Struggle*, 154-9.
41. Ibid., 160-1.
42. Deut., xviii, 10; 2 Kings, xxiii, 10; Sumner, *Folkways*, 554.
43. Frazer, 84; Maspero, *Passing*, 80; CAH, iii. 372.
44. Mason, W. A., *History of the Art of Writing*, 306; Maspero, *Passing*, 35; Rivers, W. H., *Instinct and the Unconscious*, 132.

CHAPTER XII

1. Exod. iii, 8; Numb. xiv, 8; Deut. xxvi, 15, etc.
2. Quoted in Huntingdon, E., *The Pulse of Asia*, 368.
3. New York *Times*, Jan. 20, 1932; May 17, 1932.
4. CAH, ii, 719n; *Encyc. Brit.*, xiii, 42.
5. Gen. xi, 31.
6. Petrie, *Egypt and Israel*, 17.
7. CAH, ii, 356.
8. Breasted, *Dawn of Conscience*, 349.
9. Maspero, *Struggle*, 70-1, 442-3.
10. Exod. xii, 40; Petrie, 38.
11. Exod. i; Deut. x, 22.
12. Exod. i, 12.
13. Josephus, *Works*, ii, 466; *Contra Apion*, i.
14. Strabo, XVI, ii, 35; Tacitus, *Histories*, V, iii, tr'n Murphy, London, 1930, 498.
15. Exod, v, 4-5; Ward, *Ancient Lowly*, ii, 76.
16. Schneider, i, 285.
17. United Press Dispatch from London, Jan. 25, 1932.

18. New York *Times*, April 18, 1932.
19. Numb. xxxi, 1-18; Deut. vii, 16, xx, 13-17; Joshua viii, 26, x, 24f, xii.
20. Ibid., xi, 23; Judges v, 31.
21. CAH, iii, 363; Maspero, *Passing*, 127; *Struggle*, 752; Buxton, *Peoples of Asia*, 97.
22. Renan, *History of the People of Israel*, i, 86.
23. Schneider, i, 300; Mason, *Art of Writing*, 289.
23a. N. Y. *Times*, Oct. 18, 1934.
24. Maspero, *Struggle*, 684.
25. Judges xvii, 6.
26. 1 Sam. viii, 10-20; cf. Deut. xvii, 14-20.
27. Judges xiii-xvi; xv, 15.
28. 2 Sam. vi, 14.
29. 1 Kings ii, 9.
30. 2 Sam. xi.
31. 2 Sam. xviii, 33.
32. 1 Kings iii, 12.
33. 1 Kings iv, 32.
34. 1 Kings ix, 26-8.
35. Ibid.

36. 1 Kings x.
37. Ibid., x, 14.
38. *Jewish Encyclopedia*, ix, 350; Graetz, H., *Popular History of the Jews*, i, 271.
39. Renan, ii, 100.
40. 2 Chron. ix, 21.
41. Maspero, *Struggle*, 737-40.
42. Josephus, *Antiquities*, VIII, 7.
43. 1 Kings iii, 2.
44. 1 Chron. xxix, 2-8.
45. CAH, iii, 347.
46. Ibid.
47. 2 Chron. iii, 4-7; iv, *passim*.
48. 2 Chron. ii, 7-10, 16; 1 Kings v, 6.
49. 2 Chron. ii, 17-18.
50. Cf. 1 Kings vi, 1, with vii, 2.
51. Fergusson, *History of Architecture*, i, 209-11.
52. Shotwell, J., *The Religious Revolution of Today*, 30.
53. Josephus, VIII, 13.
54. CAH, iii, 428.
55. Numb. xxi, 8-9; 2 Kings xviii, 4.
56. Allen, G., *Evolution of the Idea of God*, 192f; Howard, C., *Sex Worship*, 154-5.
57. Smith, W. Robertson, *Religion of the Ancient Semites*, 101.
58. Reinach, *History of Religions* (1930), 176-7.
59. Exod. vii.
60. New York *Times*, May 9, 1931.
61. Exod. xii, 7, 13.
62. Exod. xxxiii, 19.
63. Gen. xxxi, 11-12.
64. Exod. xxxiii, 23.
65. 1 Kings xx, 23.
66. Exod. xv, 3.
67. 2 Sam. xxii, 35.
68. Exod. xxiii, 27-30.
69. Lev. xxv, 23.
70. Exod. xiv, 18.
71. Numb. xxv, 4.
72. Exod. xx, 5-6.
73. Ibid., xxxii, 11-14.
74. Numb. xiv, 13-18.
75. Gen. xviii.
76. Deut. xxviii, 16-28, 61. Cf. the formula of excommunication in the case of Spinoza, in Willis, *Benedict de Spinoza*, 34.
77. Exod. xx, 5; xxxiv, 14; xxiii, 24.
78. Ruth i, 15; Judges xi, 24.

79. Exod, xv, 11; xviii, 11.
80. 2 Chron. ii, 5.
81. Ezek. viii, 14.
82. Jer. ii, 28; xxxii, 35.
83. 2 Kings v, 15.
84. 2 Sam. vi, 7; 1 Chron. xiii, 10.
85. Sumner, *Folkways*, 554.
86. CAH, iii, 451f.
87. Numb. xviii, 23.
88. Ezra vii, 24.
90. Numb. xviii, 9f.
91. Isaiah xxviii, 7; Judges viii, 33; ix, 27; 2 Kings xvii, 9-12, 16-17; xxiii, 10-13; Lamentations ii, 7.
92. Ezek. xvi, 21; xxiii, 37; Isaiah, lvii, 5.
93. Amos ii, 6.
94. CAH, iii, 458-9; Frazer, *Adonis*, 66.
95. Jer. xxix, 26.
96. Maspero, *Passing*, 783.
97. Applied by G. B. Shaw to Christ in "The Revolutionist's Handbook," appended to *Man and Superman*.
98. CAH, vi, 188.
99. Like Isaiah xl-lxvi.
100. CAH, iii, 462.
101. Amos v-vi.
102. Ibid., iii, 12, 15.
103. New York *Times*, Jan. 7, 1934.
104. Hosea viii, 6-7.
105. 2 Kings xviii, 27; Isaiah xxxv, 12.
106. Maspero, *Passing*, 290; CAH, iii, 390.
107. Sarton, 58.
108. Isaiah vii, 8.
109. Ibid., xvi, 7.
110. III, 14-15; v, 8; x, 1f.
111. I, 11f.
112. Amos ix, 14-15.
113. Isaiah vii, 14; ix, 6; xi, 1-6; ii, 4. The final passage is repeated in Micah iv, 3.
114. Hosea xii, 7.
115. 2 Kings xxii, 8; xxiii, 2; 2 Chron. xxxiv, 15, 31-2.
116. Sarton, 63; CAH, iii, 482.
117. 2 Kings xxiii, 2, 4, 10, 13.
118. 2 Kings xxv, 7.
119. Psalm CXXXVII.
120. Jer. xxvii, 6-8.
121. XV, 10; xx, 14.
122. V, 1.
123. V, 8.
124. XXXIV, 8f.
125. VII, 22-3.
126. XXIII, 11; v, 31; iv, 4; ix, 26.
127. XVIII, 23.

128. IV, 20-31; v, 19; ix, 1.
128a. Arguments for doubting Jeremiah's authorship of *Lamentations* may be found in the *Jew. Encyc.*, vii, 598.
129. Lam. i, 12; iii, 38f; Jer. xii, 1.
130. Ezek. xvi, xxiii.
131. Ibid., xxii, xxxviii, 2.
132. Ibid., xxxvi.
132a. CAH, vi, 183; *Enc. Brit.*, iii, 503.
133. Isaiah lxi, 1.
134. Ibid., xl, 3, 10-11; liii, 3-6.
134a. CAH, iii, 498.
135. LXV, 25.
136. XLV, 5.
137. XL, 12, 15, 17, 18, 22, 26.
138. Ezra i, 7-11; Maspero, *Struggle*, 638f; *Passing*, 784.
139. Nehemiah x, 29.
140. 2 Kings xxii, 10; xxiii, 2; Nehem. viii, 18.
141. CAH, vi, 175.
142. *Enc. Brit.*, iii, 502.
142a. *Jew. Encyc.*, v, 322.
143. Ibid.; Sarton, 108; Maspero, *Passing*, 131-2.
144. CAH, iii, 481.
145. Doane, *Bible Myths*, chapter i, *passim*.
146. Ibid., 10.
147. Ibid., ch. i.
148. Cf. Doane, 18-48.
149. Sarton, 63.
150. Renan, iv, 163.
151. Reinach (1930), 19; Frazer, Sir J. G., *The Golden Bough*, 472.
152. Exod. xxi-ii; Lev. xviii.
153. Spencer, *Sociology*, iii, 189.
154. Garrison, *History of Medicine*, 67.
155. Ibid.
156. Ibid.
157. Briffault, iii, 331.
158. Renan, i, 105.
159. Diodorus Siculus I, xciv, 1-2; Doane, 59-61.
160. Diodorus, ibid.
161. Lev. xxiv, 11-16; Deut. vii, xiii, xvii, 2-5.
163. Petrie, *Egypt and Israel*, 60-1; CAH, iii, 427-8.
164. Ezra i, 7-11.
165. 2 Chron. v, 13.
166. 2 Sam. vi, 6.
167. *Enc. Brit.*, 11th ed., xv, 311; *Jew. Encyc.*, vii, 88.

168. Briffault, ii, 433; Sumner and Keller, ii, 1113.
168a. Reinach (1930), 195; *Jew. Encyc.*, v. 377.
169. Gen. xxiv, 58; Judges i, 12.
170. Howard, 58.
172. Judges iv, 4.
173. 2 Kings xxii, 14.
174. Briffault, iii, 362; Howard, 49; Dubois, 212; Sumner, *Folkways*, 316, 321.
175. Gen. xxx, 1.
176. Cf. Maspero, *Struggle*, 733, 776;CAH, ii, 373.
177. Maspero, ibid.
178. Cf. 2 Kings iii, 18-19; Joshua vi, 21, 24.
179. 1 Kings xx, 29.
180. Deut. vii, 6; xiv, 2; 2 Sam. vii, 23, etc.
181. Sanger, *History of Prostitution*, 36.
182. Ibid., 35; Gen. xix, 24-5.
183. Sanger, 37-9.
184. Gen. xxix, 20.
185. Deut. xxi, 10-14.
186. Judges xxi, 20-1.
187. Gen. xxxi, 15; Ruth iv, 10; Hobhouse, *Morals in Evolution*, 197f; Briffault, ii, 212; Lippert, 310.
187a. Westermarck, *Moral Ideas*, ii, 609; White, E. M., *Woman in World History*, 169f.
188. Gen. xxx.
189. Deut. xxv, 5.
190. Lev. xx, 10; Deut. xxii, 22.
191. Westermarck, i, 427.
193. Deut. xxiv, 1; Westermarck, ii, 649; Hobhouse, 197f.
194. Gen. xxiv, 67.
195. Lev. xxv, 23.
196. Renard, 160; CAH, i, 201.
197. Deut. xv, 6; xxviii, 12.
198. Sumner, *Folkways*, 276.
199. 2 Kings iv, 1; Matt. xviii, 25.
200. Lev. xxv, 14, 17.
201. Exod. xxi, 2; Deut. xv, 12-14.
202. Lev. xxv, 10.
203. Deut. xv, 7-8; Lev. xxv, 36.
204. Exod. xxi, 10; Deut. xxiv, 19-20.
205. Gen. xxiv, 2-3.
206. Graetz, i, 173.
207. Deut. xvii, 8-12.
208. Numb. v, 27-9.
209. Ibid., 6-8.
210. Exod. xxi, 15-21; xxii, 19.
211. Exod. xxii, 18.

212. Numb. xxxv, 19.
213. Deut. xix.
214. Exod. xxi, 23-5; Lev. xxiv, 9-20.
215. Exod. xx, 17.
216. Renan, ii, 307.
217. *Jew Encyc.*, vii, 381; Graetz, i, 224.
218. *Enc. Brit.*, iii, 504. The *Psalms* seem to have been collected in their present form ca. 150 B.C.—Ibid., xxii, 539.
219. In the poem entitled "Walt Whitman," sect. 44; *Leaves of Grass*, 84-5.
219a. The *Jew Encyc.*, xi, 467, assigns its composition to 200-100 B.C.
220. Song of Solomon i, 13-16; ii, 1, 5, 7, 16, 17; vii, 11, 12.
221. Prov. vii, 26; vi, 32; xxx, 18-19.
222. Ibid., v, 18-19; xv, 17.
223. Ibid., vi, 6, 9.
224. XXII, 29.
225. I, 32; xxviii, 20.
226. XIV, 23; xxviii, 11, xvii, 28.
227. XVI, 22; iii., 13-17.
228. *Enc. Brit.*, iii, 504.
229. Jastrow, M., *Book of Job*, 121.
230. Kallen, H., *Book of Job as a Greek Tragedy*, Introduction.
230a. Carlyle, Thos., *Complete Works*, Vol. i, *Heroes and Hero-Worship*, p. 280, Lect. II.
231. Job vii, 9-10; xiv, 12.
232. Psalm LXXIII, 12.
233. Psalms XLII, XLIII, 23; LXXIV, 22; LXXXIX, 46; CXV, 2.

234. Job xii, 2-3, 6; xiii, i, 4-5.
235. XXXI, 35.
236. Renan, v, 148; Jastrow, *Job*, 180.
237. Job xxxviii, 1—xl, 2. It has been argued that these chapters are an independent "nature-poem," artificially attached to the *Book of Job*.
238. Job xlii, 7-8.
239. Sarton, 180.
240. Eccles. i, 1.
241. Ibid., vii, 15; iv, 1; v, 8.
242. IX, 11.
243. V, 10, 12.
244. V, 11.
245. VII, 10.
246. I, 9-10.
247. I, 11.
248. I, 2-7; iv, 2-3; vii, 1.
250. VIII, 15; ii, 24; v, 18; ii, 1.
251. VII, 28, 26.
252. IX, 8.
253. XII, 12.
254. VII, 11, 16.
255. Exod. xxxiii, 20.
256. Eccles. i, 13-18.
257. III, 19, 22; viii, 10. For the Talmudic interpretation of the final chapter of *Ecclesiastes*, cf. Jastrow, M., *A Gentle Cynic*, 189f.
258. Josephus, *Antiquities, XI*, 8; *Works*, i, 417. The account is questioned by some critics—cf. *Jew. Encyc.*, i, 342.

CHAPTER XIII

1. Huart, C., *Ancient Persian and Iranian Civilization*, 25-6.
2. Maspero, *Passing*, 452.
3. Herodotus, I, 99.
4. Ibid., i, 74.
5. Rawlinson, ii, 370.
6. Daniel, vi, 8.
7. Rawlinson, ii, 316-7.
8. Huart, 27.
9. Herodotus, I, 119.
10. *Encyc. Brit.*, xvii, 571.
11. Rawlinson, iii, 389.
12. Maspero, 668-71.
13. Rawlinson, iii, 398.
14. Herodotus, III, 134.
15. Sykes, Sir P., *Persia*, 6.
16. XV, iii, 10.
17. The population estimates are those of Rawlinson, iii, 422, 241.

18. Strabo, XV, ii, 8; Rawlinson, ii, 306; iii, 164; Maspero, 452.
19. Dhalla, M. N., *Zoroastrian Civilization*, 211, 222, 259; Rawlinson, iii, 202-4; Köhler, Carl, *History of Costume*, 75-6.
20. Rawlinson, iii, 211, 243.
21. Adapted from Rawlinson, iii, 250-1.
22. Huart, 22.
23. Schneider, i, 350.
24. Mason, W. A., 264.
25. Dhalla, 141-2.
26. Herodotus, I, 126.
27. Strabo, XV, iii, 20; Herodotus, I, 133.
28. Dhalla, 187-8.
29. Herodotus, V, 52.
30. CAH, iv, 200.
31. Dhalla, 218.

32. Ibid., 144, 257; Müller, Max, *India: What Can It Teach Us?*, 19.
33. Rawlinson, iii, 427.
34. CAH, iv, 185-6.
35. Rawlinson, iii, 245.
36. Ibid., 171-2.
37. Ibid., 228; Plutarch, *Life of Artaxerxes*, chs. 5-17.
38. Rawlinson, iii, 221.
39. Dhalla, 237.
40. Ibid., 89.
41. Rawlinson, iii, 241.
42. Herodotus, VII, 39. But perhaps Herodotus had been listening to old wives' tales.
43. Dhalla, 95-9.
44. Ibid., 106.
45. Herodotus, V, 25.
46. Darmesteter, J., *The Zend-Avesta*, i, p. lxxxiiif.
47. Ibid.
48. Huart, 78; Darmesteter, lxxxvii; Rawlinson, iii, 246.
49. Ibid.; Sumner, *Folkways*, 236.
50. Plutarch, *Artaxerxes*, in *Lives*, iii, 464.
51. Rawlinson, iii, 427; Herodotus, III, 95; Maspero, Passing, 690f; CAH, iv, 198f.
53. Maspero, 572f.
54. Vendidad, XIX, vi, 45.
55. Darmesteter, i, xxxvii; *Encyc. Brit.*, xxiii, 987.
56. Dawson, M. M., *Ethical Religion of Zoroaster*, xiv.
57. Rawlinson, ii, 323.
58. Edouard Meyer dates Zarathustra about 1000 B.C.; so also Duncker and Hummel (*Encyc. Brit.*, xxiii, 987; Dawson, xv); A. V. W. Jackson places him about 660-583 B.C. (Sarton, 61).
59. Briffault, iii, 191.
60. Dhalla, 72.
61. Schneider, i, 333; CAH, iv, 210f; Rawlinson, ii, 323.
62. *Encyc. Brit.*, xxiii, 942-3; Rawlinson, ii, 322; Dhalla, 38f.
63. Ibid., 40-2; *Encyc. Brit.*, xxiii, 942-3; Maspero, *Passing*, 575-6; Huart, xviii; CAH, iv, 207.
64. *Encyc. Brit.*, l.c.
65. Darmesteter, xxvii, Gour, Sir Hari Singh, *Spirit of Buddhism*, 12.
66. Vend. II, 4, 29, 41.
67. Ibid., 22-43.
68. Darmesteter, lxiii-iv.
69. Yasna, xliv, 4.
70. Darmesteter, lv, lxv.
71. Dawson, 52f.
72. *Encyc. Brit.*, xxiii, 988.
73. Dawson, 46.
74. Maspero, *Passing*, 583-4; Schneider, i, 336; Rawlinson, ii, 340.
75. Dawson, 125.
76. *Shayast-la-Shayast*, XX, 6, in Dawson, 131.
77. Vend. IV, 1.
78. Ibid., XVI, iii, 18.
79. Herdotous, I, 134.
80. *Shayast-la-Shayast*, VII, 6, 7, 1, in Dawson, 36-7.
81. Westermarck, *Morals*, ii, 434; Herodotus, VII, 114; Rawlinson, iii, 350n.
82. Strabo, XV, iii, 13; Maspero, 592-4.
83. Reinach (1930), 73; Rawlinson, ii, 338.
84. The "Ormuzd" Yast, in Darmesteter, ii, 21.
85. Nask VIII, 58-73, in Darmesteter, i, 380-1.
86. Vend., XIX, v, 27-34; Yast 22; Yasna LI, 15; Maspero, 590.
87. Yasna XLV, 7.
88. Dawson, 246-7.
89. Ibid., 256f.
90. Ibid., 250-3.
91. CAH, iv, 211.
92. Cf., e.g., Darmesteter, i, pp. lxxii-iii.
93. CAH, iv, 209.
94. Dhalla, 201, 218; Maspero, 595.
95. Harper, *Literature*, 181.
96. Dhalla, 250-1.
97. Herodotus, IX, 109; Rawlinson, iii, 170.
98. Ibid., iii, 518, 524.
99. Ibid., 170.
100. Strabo, XV, iii, 20.
101. Dhalla, 221.
102. Herodotus, I, 80; Xenophon, *Cyropaedia*, I, ii, 8; VIII, viii, 9; Strabo, XV, iii, 18; Rawlinson, iii, 236.
103. Dhalla, 155; Dawson, 36-7.
104. Dhalla, 119, 190-1.
105. E.g., Vend. IX.
106. Darmesteter, i, p. lxxviii.
107. Vend. VIII, 61-5.
108. I, 4.
109. I, 135.
110. Vend. VIII, v, 32; vi, 27.
111. Strabo, XV, iii, 17; Vend. IV, iii, 47.
112. Ibid., iii, 1.
113. XV, ii, 20f.

114. XX, i, 4; XV, iv, 50-1.
115. XXI, i, 1.
116. Maspero, 588. These cases were apparently confined to the Magi.
117. Herodotus, VII, 83; IX, 76; Rawlinson, iii, 238.
118. Esther, ii, 14; Rawlinson, iii, 219.
119. Dhalla, 74-6, 219; Rawlinson, iii, 222, 237.
119a. Plutarch, Artaxerxes, *Lives*, iii, 463-6.
120. Dhalla, 70-1.
121. Herodotus, I, 139; Dhalla, 219.
122. Vend. XV, 9-12; XVI, 1-2.
123. Bundahis, XVI, 1, 2, in Dawson, 156.
124. Venkateswara, 177; Dhalla, 225.
125. Ibid., 83-5; Dawson, 151.
126. Herodotus, I, 136.
127. Strabo, XV, iii, 18.
128. Darmesteter, i, p. lxxx.
129. Vend. VII, vii, 41f.
130. Ibid., 36-40.
131. Rawlinson, iii, 235.
132. N. Y. *Times*, Jan. 6, 1931.

133. Dhalla, 176, 195, 256; Rawlinson, iii, 234.
134. N. Y. *Times*, Jan. 23, 1933.
135. Dhalla, 253-4.
136. Rawlinson, iii, 278.
137. N. Y. *Times*, July 28, 1932.
138. Fergusson, *History of Architecture*, i, 198-9; Rawlinson, iii, 298.
139. Breasted in N. Y. *Times*, March 9, 1932.
140. CAH, iv, 204.
140a. Dhalla, 260-1.
140b. Rawlinson, iii, 244, 400.
141. Maspero, 715.
142. Arrian, *Anabasis of Alexander*, I, 15.
143. Josephus, *Antiquities*, XI, viii, 3.
144. Arrian, I, 16.
145. Quintus Curtius, III, 17.
146. Arrian, II, 11, 13; Plutarch, *Life of Alexander*, ch. 20.
147. Quintus Curtius, X, 17; CAH, vi, 369.
148. Plutarch, *Alexander*, ch. 31; Arrian, III, 8.

CHAPTER XIV

1. In Rolland, R., *Prophets of the New India*, 395, 449-50.
1a. Winternitz, M., *A History of Indian Literature*, i, 8.
2. Ibid., 18-21.
3. Keyserling, Count H., *Travel Diary of a Philosopher*, 265.
4. Chirol, Sir Valentine, *India*, 4.
5. Dubois, Abbé J. A., *Hindu Manners, Customs and Ceremonies*, 95, 321.
6. Smith, Vincent, *Oxford History of India*, 2; Childe, V. G., *The Most Ancient East*, 202; Pittard, *Race and History*, 388; Coomaraswamy, *History of Indian and Indonesian Art*, 6; Parmelee, M., *Oriental and Occidental Culture*, 23-4.
7. Marshall, Sir John, *The Prehistoric Civilization of the Indus*, *Illustrated London News*, Jan. 7, 1928, 1.
8. Childe, 209.
9. In Muthu, D. C., *The Antiquity of Hindu Medicine*, 2.
10. Sir John Marshall in *The Modern Review*, Calcutta, April 1932, 367.
11. Coomaraswamy in *Encyclopedia Britannica*, xii, 211-12.
12. New York *Times*, Aug. 2, 1932.

13. Macdonell, A. A., *India's Past*, 9.
14. Ibid.
15. Childe, 211.
16. Woolley, 8.
17. Childe, 202.
18. Ibid, 220, 211.
19. New York *Times*, April 8, 1932.
20. Gour, *Spirit of Buddhism*, 524; Radhakrishnan, S., *Indian Philosophy*, 75.
21. Smith, *Oxford History*, 14.
22. Davids, T. W. Rhys, *Dialogues of the Buddha*, being vols. ii-iv of *Sacred Books of the Buddhists*, ii, 97; Venkateswara, 10.
23. Monier-Williams, Sir M., *Indian Wisdom*, 227.
24. Winternitz, 304.
25. Jastrow, 85.
26. Winternitz, 64.
27. Westermarck, *Moral Ideas*, i, 216, 222; Havell, E. B., *History of Aryan Rule in India*, 35; Davids, *Buddhist India*, 51; *Dialogues of the Buddha*, iii, 79.
28. Buxton, *The Peoples of Asia*, 121.
29. Davids, *Buddhist India*, 56, 62; Smith, *Oxford History*, 37.

30. Sidhanta, N. K., *The Heroic Age of India*, 206; *Mahabharata*, IX, v, 30.
31. Havell, 33.
32. Dutt, R. C., tr., *The Ramayana and Mahabharata*, Everyman Library, 189.
33. Davids, *Buddhist India*, 60.
34. Davids, *Dialogues*, ii, 114, 128.
35. Dutt, R. C., *The Civilization of India*, 21; Davids, *Buddhist India*, 55.
36. Macdonell, *India's Past*, 39.
37. Gray, R. M. and Parekh, M. C., *Mahatma Gandhi*, 37.
38. *Buddhist India*, 46, 51, 101-2; Winternitz, 64.
39. *Buddhist India*, 90, 96, 70, 101.
40. Ibid., 70, 98; Winternitz, 65; Havell, *History*, 129; Muthu, 11.
41. Winternitz, 212.
42. *Buddhist India*, 100-1.
43. Ibid., 72.
44. Dutt, *Ramayana*, 231.
45. Arrian, quoted in Sunderland, Jabez T., *India in Bondage*, 178; Strabo, XV, i, 53.
46. Winternitz, 66-7.
47. Venkateswara, 140.
48. Sidhanta, 149; Tagore in Keyserling, *The Book of Marriage*, 108.
49. Sidhanta, 153.
50. Dutt, *Ramayana*, 192.
51. Smith, Oxford History, 7; Barnett, L. D., *Antiquities of India*, 116.
52. Havell, *History*, 14; Barnett, 109.
53. Monier-Williams, 439; Winternitz, 66.
54. Lajpat Rai, L., *Unhappy India*, 151, 176.
55. *Mahabharata*, III, xxxiii, 82; Sidhanta, 160.
56. Sidhanta, 165, 168; Barnett, 119; Briffault, i, 346.
57. Radhakrishnan, i, 119; Eliot, Sir Charles, *Hinduism and Buddhism*, i, 6; *Buddhist India*, 226; Smith, 70; Das Gupta, Surendranath, *A History of Indian Philosophy*, 25.
58. *Buddhist India*, 220-4; Radhakrishnan, i, 483.
59. Ibid., 117.
60. Winternitz, 140.
61. Hume, R. E., *The Thirteen Principal Upanishads*, 169.
62. Das Gupta, 6.
63. Radhakrishnan, i, 76.
64. Eliot, i, 58; Macdonell, 32-3.
65. Eliot, i, 62; Winternitz, 76.
66. Eliot, i, 59.
67. Radhakrishnan, i, 105.
68. Ibid., 78.
69. *Brihadaranyaka Upanishad*, i, 4; Hume 81.
70. Radhakrishnan, i, 114-5.
71. *Katha Upanishad*, i, 8; Radhakrishnan, i, 250; Müller, Max, *Six Systems of Hindu Philosophy*, 131.
72. Eliot, i, xv; *Buddhist India*, 241; Radhakrishnan, i, 108.
73. Ibid., 107; Winternitz, 215; Gour, 5.
74. Frazer, R. W., *A Literary History of India*, 243.
75. Dutt, *Ramayana*, 318; Briffault, i, 346, iii, 188.
76. Ibid.
77. Macdonell, 24.
78. Winternitz, 208; Das Gupta 21.
79. Buddhist India, 241.
80. Winternitz, 207.
81. Dutt, *Civilization of India*, 33.
82. Müller, Max, *Lectures on the Science of Language*, ii, 234-7, 276; Skeat, W. W., *Etymological Dictionary of the English Language*, 729f.
83. In Elphinstone, M., *History of India*, 161.
84. *Buddhist India*, 153; Winternitz 41-4.
85. Ibid., 31-2; Macdonell, 7; *Buddhist India*, 114.
86. Ibid, 120.
87. Müller, Max, *India: What Can It Teach Us?*, London, 1919, 206; Wintnitz, 32.
89. Dubois, 425.
90. Radhakrishnan, i, 67; Eliot, i, 51.
91. Ibid., i, 53.
92. Winternitz, 69, 79; Müller, *India*, 97; Macdonell, 35.
93. Tr. by Macdonell in Tietjens, Eunice, *Poetry of the Orient*, 248.
94. Tr. by Max Müller in Smith, *Oxford History*, 20.
95. In Müller, *India*, 254.
96. Winternitz, 243; Radhakrishnan, i, 137; Deussen, Paul, *The Philosophy of the Upanishads*, 13.
97. Eliot, i, 51; Radhakrishnan, i, 141.
98. Cf., e.g., a passage in Chatterji, J. C., *India's Outlook on Life*, 42.
99. E.g., *Chandogya Upanishad*, v, 2; Hume 229.

100. They are listed in Radhakrishnan, 143.
101. Eliot, i, 93.
102. Hume, 144.
103. *Shvetashvatara Upanishad*, i, 1; Radhakrishnan, i, 150.
104. Hume, 4:2.
105. *Katha Upanishad*, ii, 23; *Brihadaranyaka Upanishad*, iii, 5, iv, 4; Radhakrishnan, i, 177.
106. *Katha Upan.*, iv, 1; Radhakrishnan, i, 145.
107. *Katha Upan.*, ii, 24.

108. *Chandogya Upan.*, vi, 7.
109. Radhakrishnan, i, 151.
110. *Brih. Upan.*, ii, 2, iv, 4.
111. Ibid., iii, 9.
112. *Chand. Upan.*, vi, 12.
113. Radhakrishnan, i, 94, 96.
117. Radhakrishnan, i, 249-51; Macdonell, 48.
118. *Brih. Upan.*, iv, 4.
119. Radhakrishnan, i, 239.
120. *Mundaka Upan.*, iii, 2; Radhakrishnan, i, 236.

CHAPTER XV

1. *Chand. Upan.*, i, 12; Radhakrishnan, 1. 149.
2. Ibid., 278.
3. In Hume, 65.
4. Davids, *Dialogues of the Buddha*, ii, 73-5; Radhakrishnan, i, 274.
5. Dutt, *Ramayana*, 60-1.
6. Müller, *Six Systems*, 17; Radhak., i, 278.
7. Eliot, i, xix; Müller, *Six Systems*, 23; Davids, *Buddhist India*, 141.
8. Radhak., i, 278.
9. Monier-Williams, 120-2.
10. Das Gupta, 78; Radhak., i, 279.
11. Ibid., 281.
12. Das Gupta, 79.
13. Monier-Williams, 120; Müller, *Six Systems*, 100.
14. Radhak., i, 280.
15. Ibid., 281-2.
16. Ibid., 287; Smith, *Oxford History*, 50.
17. Radhak., i, 301.
18. Ibid., 329; Eliot, i, 106.
19. Ibid.
20. Radhak, i, 331, 293.
21. Ibid., 327; Eliot, i, 110, 113, 115; Smith, *Oxford History*, 53; Smith, Vincent, *Akbar*, 167; Dubois, 521.
22. Smith, *Oxford History*, 210.
23. Eliot., i, 112.
24. Ibid., 115.
25. Thomas, E. J., *The Life of Buddha as Legend and History*, 20.
26. Eliot, i, 244n.
27. Gour, introd.; Davids, *Dialogues*, ii, 117; Radhak., i, 347, 351; Eliot, i, 133, 173.
28. Thomas, E. J., 31-3.

29. Eliot, i, 131; Venkateswara, 169; Havell, *History*, 49.
30. Thomas, 50-1.
31. Ibid., 54.
32. Ibid., 55.
33. Ibid., 65.
34. Radhak., i, 343-5.
35. Eliot, i, 129.
36. *Dialogues*, ii, 5.
37. Gour, 405.
38. *Dialogues*, iii, 102.
39. Thomas, 87.
40. Radhak., i, 363.
41. Eliot, i, 203.
42. Ibid., 250.
43. Dutt, *Civilization of India*, 44.
44. Radhak., i, 475.
45. *Dialogues*, iii, 154.
46. Radhak., i, 421.
47. *Dialogues*, ii, 35.
48. Ibid., 186.
49. Ibid., 254.
50. Ibid., 280-2.
51. Ibid., 37.
52. Radhak., i, 356; Gour, 10.
53. Radhak., i, 438, 475; *Dialogues*, ii, 123; Eliot, i, xxii.
54. Radhak., i, 354.
55. Ibid., 424; Gour, 10; Eliot, i, 247.
56. Gour, 542; Radhak., i, 465.
57. Eliot, i, xcv.
58. Gour, 280-4.
59. Eliot, i, xxii.
60. Gour, 392-4; Radhak., i, 355.
61. Thomas, 208.
62. Radhak, i, 456.
63. Ibid., 375.
64. Ibid., 369, 385, 392; *Buddhist India*, 188, 257; Thomas, 88.

65. Das Gupta, 240; Gour, 335.
66. Eliot, i, 191; *Dialogues*, ii, 188.
67. Eliot, i, 210; *Dialogues*, ii, 71.
68. Eliot, i, 227; Radhak, i, 389.
69. Thomas, 189.
70. Macdonell, 48; Radhak., i, 444; Eliot, i, xxi.
71. Gour, 312-4, 333.
73. *Dialogues*, ii, 190.
74. Eliot, i, 224; Müller, *Six Systems*, 373; Thomas, 187.
75. Radhak., i, 446.
76. Eliot, i, 224.

77. Ibid., i, 227; Thomas, 145.
80. *Dialogues*, ii, 55, iii, 94; Watters, Thos. *On Yuan Chwang's Travels in India*, i, 374.
81. Thomas, 134.
82. *Buddhist India*, 300; Radhak, i, 351.
83. Thomas, 100.
84. Ibid., 100-2.
85. *Dialogues*, ii, 1-26.
86. Eliot, i, 160.
87. *Dialogues*, iii, 87.
88. Ibid., 108.
89. Thomas, 153.

CHAPTER XVI

1. Arrian, *Anabasis of Alexander*, V, 19, VI, 2.
2. Smith, *Oxford History*, 66.
3. Kohn, H., *History of Natonalism in the East*, 350.
4. Arrian, *Indica*, X.
5. In Dutt, *Civilization of India*, 50.
6. Arrian, *Anabasis*, VI, 2.
7. Ibid., V, 8; Strabo, XV, i, 28.
8. *Enc. Brit.*, xii, 212.
9. Smith, *Oxford History*, 62.
10. Arrian, *Indica*, X.
11. Havell, 75.
12. Smith, *Oxford History*, 77.
13. Ibid., 114.
14. Ibid., 79.
15. Havell, *History*, 82-3.
16. It is of uncertain authenticity. Sarton (147) accepts it as Kautilya's, but Macdonell (*India's Past*, 170) considers it the work of a later writer.
17. In Smith, *Oxford History*, 84.
18. Smith, *Akbar*, 396.
19. Smith, *Oxford History*, 76, 87.
20. Ibid., 311.
21. Strabo, XV, i, 40.
22. Havell, 82.
23. Barnett, 99-100; Havell, 82.
24. Ibid., 69, 80.
25. Ibid., 74.
26. Ibid., 71f; Barnett, 107.
27. Davids, *Buddhist India*, 264; Havell, ibid.
28. Strabo, XV, i, 51.
28a. Havell, 78.
28b. Smith, *Oxford History*, 87.
29. *Candide*.
30. Havell, 88.

31. Ibid., 91-2; Smith, *Oxford History*, 101.
32. Smith, V., *Asoka*, 67; Davids, *Buddhist India*, 297.
33. Smith, *Asoka*, 92.
34. Ibid., 60.
35. Provincial Edict I; Havell, 93.
36. Havell, 100; Smith, *Asoka*, 67.
37. Watters, ii, 91.
38. Muthu, 35.
39. Rock Edict XIII.
40. Havell, 100; Smith, *Oxford History*, 135; Melamed, S. M., *Spinoza and Buddha*, 302-3, 308.
41. Rock Edict VI.
42. Pillar Edict V.
43. Watters, 99.
44. Davids, *Buddhist India*, 308; Smith, *Oxford History*, 126.
45. Ibid., 155.
46. Nag, Kalidas, *Greater India*, 27.
47. Besant, Annie, *India*, 15.
48. Smith, *Ox. H.*, 154.
49. Tr. by James Legge, in Gowen, *Indian Literature*, 336.
50. Havell, 158.
51. Nag, 25.
52. Havell, E. B., *The Ancient and Medieval Architecture of India*, xxv.
53. Ibid., 207.
54. Watters, i, 344.
55. Havell, *History*, 204.
56. Watters, ii, 348-9; Havell, 203-4.
57. Fenollosa, E. F., *Epochs of Chinese and Japanese Art*, i, 85.
58. Arrian, *Anabasis*, V, 4.
59. Tod, Lt.-Col. James, *Annals and Antiquities of Rajasthan*, ii, 115.

60. Tod, i, 209.
61. Keyserling, *Travel Diary*, i, 184.
62. Tod, i, 244f.
63. Smith, *Ox. H.*, 311.
64. Ibid., 304.
65. Ibid., 309.
66. Ibid., 308; Havell, *History*, 402.
67. Smith, *Ox. H.*, 308-10.
68. Ibid., 312-13.
69. Ibid., 314.
70. Ibid., 309.
71. Sewell, Robert, *A Forgotten Empire, Vijayanagar*, in Smith, *Ox. H.*, 306.
72. From an ancient Moslem chronicle, *Tabakat-i-Nasiri*, in Smith, *Ox. H.*, 192.
73. Havell, *History*, 286.
74. Elphinstone, Mountstuart, *History of India*, 333, 337-8.
75. *Tabakat-i-Nasiri*, in Smith, *Ox. H.*, 222-3.
76. Smith, 226, 232, 245.
77. Ibn Batuta, in Smith, 240.
78. Smith, 303.
80. In Smith, 234.
81. Ibid.
82. *Queen Mab*.
83. Havell, *History*, 368.
84. Ibid.; Smith, 252.
85. Elphinstone, 415; Smith, *Akbar*, 10.
86. Smith, *Ox. H.*, 321.
87. Firishtah, Muhammad Qasim, *History of Hindustan*, ii, 188.
88. Elphinstone, 430.
89. Babur, *Memoirs*, 1.
90. Smith, *Akbar*, 98, 148, 358; Havell, *History*, 479.
91. Smith, *Akbar*, 226, 379, 383; Besant, 23.

92. Smith, *Akbar*, 333.
93. Firishtah, 399.
94. Smith, *Akbar*, 333-6, 65, 77, 343, 115, 160, 108; Smith, *Ox. H.*, 311; Besant, *India*, 23.
95. Havell, *History*, 478.
96. Smith, *Akbar*, 406.
97. Ibid., 424-5.
98. Ibid., 235-7.
99. In Frazer, *History of Indian Literature*, 358.
100. Havell, *History*, 499.
101. Brown, Percy, *Indian Painting*, 49; Smith, *Akbar*, 421-2.
102. Ibid., 350; Havell, *History*, 493-4.
103. Ibid., 494.
104. Ibid., 493.
105. Frazer, 357.
106. Smith, *Akbar*, 133, 176, 181, 257, 350; Havell, *History*, 493, 510.
107. Smith, *Akbar*, 212.
108. Ibid., 216-21.
109. Smith, *Akbar*, 301, 323, 325.
110. Smith, *Ox. H.*, 387.
111. Elphinstone, 540.
112. Lorenz, D. E., *'Round the World Traveler*, 373.
113. Smith, *Ox. H.*, 395.
114. Ibid., 393.
115. Elphinstone, 586.
116. Ibid., 577; Smith, *Ox. H.*, 445-7.
117. Ibid., 439.
118. Fergusson, Jas., *History of Indian and Eastern Architecture*, ii, 88.
119. Tod, i, 349.
120. Smith, *Ox. H.*, 448.
121. Ibid., 446.

CHAPTER XVII

1. Smith, *Akbar*, 401; *Indian Year Book*, Bombay, 1929, 563; Minney, R. J., *Shiva: or The Future of India*, 50.
2. Havell, *History*, 160; Eliot, ii, 171; Dubois, 190.
3. Parmelee, 148n.
4. Smith, *Ox. H.*, 315.
5. Havell, 80, 261.
6. Strabo, XV, i, 40; Siddhanta, 180; Dubois, 57.
7. Barnett, 107; Havell, *Ancient and Medieval Architecture*, 208; Tod, i, 362.
8. Sarkar, B. K., *Hindu Achievements in Exact Science*, 68.

9. III, 102.
10. In Strabo, XV, i, 44.
11. Sarkar, 68; Lajpat Rai, L., *England's Debt to India*, 176.
12. Havell, *Architecture*, 129; Fergusson, *Indian Architecture*, ii, 208.
13. Lajpat Rai, *England's Debt*, ibid.
14. Moon, P. T., *Imperialism and World Politics*, 292.
15. Lajpat Rai, *England's Debt*, 121.
16. III, 106.
17. Sarton, 535.
18. Lajpat Rai, *England's Debt*, 123.
19. Ibid.

20. Polo, *Travels*, 307.
21. Muthu, 100.
22. Venkateswara, 11; Smith, *Ox. H.*, 15.
23. Lajpat Rai, *England's Debt*, 162-3.
24. Havell, *History*, 75, 130.
25. Ibid., 140.
26. Lajpat Rai, *England's Debt*, 165.
27. Barnett, 211-15.
28. Macdonell, 265-70.
29. Smith, *Akbar*, 157.
30. Fragment XXVII B in McCrindle, J. W., *Ancient India as Described by Megasthenes and Arrian*, 73.
31. Monier-Williams, 263; Minney, 75.
32. Barnett, 130; Monier-Williams, 264.
33. Dubois, 657.
34. Sidhanta, 178; Havell, *History*, 234; Smith, *Ox. H.*, 312.
35. Besant, 23; Dutt, *Civilization of India*, 121.
36. Dubois, 81-7.
37. Lajpat Rai, *England's Debt*, 12.
38. Smith, *Akbar*, 389-91.
39. Ibid., 393.
40. Ibid., 392.
41. Watters, i, 340.
42. Elphinstone, 329; cf. Smith, *Ox. H.*, 257.
43. Elphinstone, 477.
44. Smith, *Ox. H.*, 392.
45. Smith, *Akbar*, 395.
46. Ibid., 108.
47. Lajpat Rai, *Unhappy India*, 315.
48. Minney, 72.
49. Lajpat Rai, *England's Debt*, 25.
50. Macaulay, T. B., Essay on Clive, in *Critical and Historical Essays*, i, 544.
51. Havell, *History*, 235; Havell, *Architecture*, xxvi. This liberty, of course, was at its minimum under Chandragupta Maurya.
52. Laws of Manu, vii, 15, 20-4, 218, in Monier-Williams, 256, 285.
53. Smith, *Ox. H.*, 229.
54. Ibid., 266.
55. Barnett, 124; Dubois, 654; Smith, *Ox. H.*, 109.
56. Dubois, 654.
57. Smith, *Ox. H.*, 249.
58. Ibid., 249, 313; Barnett, 122.
59. Monier-Williams, 204-6.
60. Max Müller, *India*, 12.
62. Dubois, 722; cf. also 661 and 717.
63. Monier-Williams, 203, 233, 268.
64. Simon, Sir John, Chairman, *Report of the Indian Statutory Commission*, i, 35.
65. Davids, *Buddhist India*, 150.
66. Tod, i, 479; Hallam, Henry, *View of the State of Europe during the Middle Ages*, ch. vii, p. 263.
66a. Barnett, 106; Dubois, 177.
67. Manu xix, 313; Monier-Williams, 234.
68. Maine, *Ancient Law*, 165; Monier-Williams, 266.
69. Barnett, 112.
70. Lubbock, *Origin of Civilization*, 379.
71. Winternitz, 147; Radhak., i, 356; Monier-Williams, 236.
72. Dubois, 590-2.
73. Barnett, 123; Davids, *Dialogues*, ii, 285.
75. Havell, *History*, 50.
76. Monier-Williams, 233.
77. Dubois, 98, 169.
78. Manu, i, 100; Monier-Williams, 237.
79. Dubois, 176.
80. Manu, iii, 100.
81. Barnett, 114.
82. Dubois, 593.
83. Manu, viii, 380-1.
85. Manu, xi, 206.
86. Barnett, 123.
87. Ibid., 121; Winternitz, 198.
88. Eliot, i, 37; Simon, i, 35.
89. Manu, iv, 147.
90. Ibid., ii, 87.
91. XI, 261.
92. IV, 27-8.
93. Dubois, 165, 237, 249.
94. Ibid., 187.
95. Manu, ii, 177-8.
96. VIII, 336-8.
97. II, 179.
98. Book xviii; Arnold, Sir Edwin, *The Song Celestial*, 107.
99. Tagore, R., *Sadhana*, 127.
100. Smith, *Ox. H.*, 42.
101. Ibid., 34.
102. IX, 45.
103. Barnett, 117.
104. Sumner, *Folkways*, 315.
105. Tod, i, 602; Smith, *Ox. H.*, 690.
106. Wood, Ernest, *An Englishman Defends Mother India*, 103.
107. Dubois, 205; Havell, E. B., *The Ideals of Indian Art*, 93.
108. Tagore in Keyserling, *The Book of Marriage*, 104, 108

109. Hall, Josef ("Upton Close"), *Eminent Asians*, 505.
110. Lajpat Rai, *Unhappy India*, 186.
111. Dubois, 231; *Census of India*, 1921, i, 151; Mukerji, D. G., *A Son of Mother India Answers*, 19.
112. Barnett, 115.
113. Lajpat Rai, *Unhappy India*, 159.
114. Robie, W. F., *The Art of Love*, 18f; Macdonell, 174.
115. Robie, 36.
116. Ibid., 32.
117. Frazer, *Adonis*, 54-5; Curtis, W. E., *Modern India*, 284-5.
118. Dubois, 585.
119. Cf., e.g., the "Fifty Stanzas" of Bilhana, in Tietjens, 303-6.
120. Coomaraswamy, A. K., *Dance of Shiva*, 103, 108.
121. Monier-Williams, 244.
122. Dubois, 214.
123. Strabo, I, i, 62.
124. Manu, III, 12-15, ix, 45, 85, 101; Monier-Williams, 243.
125. Tod, i, 284n.
126. Nivedita, Sister (Margaret E. Noble), *The Web of Indian Life*, 40.
127. Barnett, 109.
128. XV, i, 62.
129. Havell, Ideals, 91.
130. In Bebel, *Woman under Socialism*, 52.
131. In Tod, i, 604.
132. Barnett, 109.
133. Dubois, 339-40.
134. Manu, iv, 43; Barnett, 110.
135. Manu, v, 154-6.
136. Westermarck, *Moral Ideas*, ii, 650.
137. Dubois, 337.
138. Tagore, R., *Chitra*, 45.
139. Manu, ix, 18.
140. III, 33, 82; Sidhanta, 160.
141. Frazer, R. W., 179.
142. VIII, 416.
143. Monier-Williams, 267; Tod, i, 605.
144. Barnett, 116; Westermarck, ii, 650.
145. Manu, ix, 2, 12, iii, 57, 60-3.
146. Tod, i, 604.
147. II, 145; Wood, 27.
148. Tod, i, 590n; Zimand, S., *Living India*, 124-5.
149. Dubois, 313.
150. Herodotus, IV, 71, V, 5.
151. *Enc. Brit.*, xxi, 624.
152. *Rig-veda*, x, 18; Sidhanta, 165n.

153. I, 125, xv, 33, xvi, 7, xii, 149; Sidhanta, 165.
154. Smith, *Ox. H.*, 309.
155. XV, i, 30, 62.
156. *Enc. Brit.*, xxi, 625.
157. Tod, i, 604; Smith, *Ox. H.*, 233.
158. Coomaraswamy, *Dance of Shiva*, 93.
159. Smith, *Ox. H.*, 309.
160. Manu, v, 162, ix, 47, 65; Parmelee, 114.
161. Lajpat Rai, *Unhappy India*, 198.
162. Ibid., 192, 196.
163. Tod, i, 575.
164. Dubois, 331.
165. Ibid., 78, 337, 355, 587; Sumner, *Folkways*, 457.
166. Dubois, 340; Coomaraswamy, *Dance*, 94.
167. Bebel, 52; Sumner, 457.
168. IV, 203.
169. Wood, 292, 195.
170. Lajpat Rai, *Unhappy India*, 284.
171. Ibid., 280.
172. Watters, i, 152.
173. Dubois, 184, 248; Wood, 196.
174. Sumner, 457.
175. Dubois, 708-10.
176. The scatophilic student will find these matters piously detailed by the Abbè Dubois, 237f.
177. Sumner, 457; Wood, 343.
178. Wood, 286.
179. Dubois, 325.
180. Ibid., 78.
181. Ibid., 341; Coomaraswamy, *History*, 210.
182. Dubois, 324.
183. Loti, Pierre, *India*, 113; Parmelee, 138.
184. Loti, 210.
185. Dubois, 662.
186. Westermarck, i, 89.
187. Macaulay, *Essays*, i, 562.
188. Manu, viii, 103-4; Monier-Williams, 273.
189. Watters, i, 171.
190. Müller, *India*, 57.
191. Hardie, J. Keir, *India*, 60.
192. Mukerji, *A Son*, 43.
193. Smith, *Ox. H.*, 666f.
194. Dubois, 120.
195. Examples of the latter quality will be found in Dubois, 660, or in almost any account of the recent revolts.
196. Frazer, R. W., 163; Dubois, 509.
197. Simon, i, 48.

198. Müller, *India*, 41.
199. Davids, *Dialogues*, ii, 9-11.
200. Skeat, *s.v. check; Enc. Brit.*, art, "Chess."
201. Dubois, 670.
202. *Enc. Brit.*, viii, 175.
203. Havell, *History*, 477.

204. Nivedita, 11f.
205. Dubois, 595.
206. Briffault, iii, 198.
207. Gandhi, M. K., *His Own Story*, 45.
208. Davids, *Buddhist India*, 78.
209. Watters, i, 175.
210. Westermarck, i, 244-6.

CHAPTER XVIII

1. Davids, *Dialogues*, iii, 184.
2. Winternitz, 562.
3. Fergusson, i, 174.
4. Edmunds, A. J., *Buddhistic and Christian Gospels*, Philadelphia, 1908, 2v.
5. Havell, *History*, 101; Eliot, i, 147.
6. Eliot, ii, 110.
7. Ibid., i, xciii; Simon, i, 79.
8. Sarton, 367, 428; Smith, *Ox. H.*, 174; Fenollosa, ii, 213; i, 82; Nag, 34-5.
9. Fergusson, i, 292.
10. Monier-Williams, 429.
11. Dubois, 626; Doane, *Bible Myths*, 278f; Carpenter, Edward, *Pagan and Christian Creeds*, 24.
12. Indian Year Book, 1929, 21.
13. Eliot, ii, 222.
14. Lorenz, 335; Dubois, 112.
15. *Modern Review*, Calcutta, April, 1932, p. 367; Childe, *The Most Ancient East*, 209.
16. Rawlinson, *Five Great Monarchies*, ii, 335n.
17. Eliot, ii, 288; Kohn, 380.
18. Eliot, ii, 287.
19. *Modern Review*, June, 1931, p. 713.
20. Eliot, ii, 282.
21. Ibid., 145.
22. Dubois, 571, 641.
23. Ibid.; Coomaraswamy, *History*, 68, 181.
24. Lorenz, 333.
25. Wood, 204; Dubois, 43, 182, 638-9.
26. Zimand, 132.
27. Wood, 208.
28. Eliot, i, 211.
29. Havell, *Architecture*, xxxv.
30. Winternitz, 529.
31. *Vishnupurana*, z, 16, in Otto, Rudolf, *Mysticism, East and West*, 55-6.
32. Dubois, 545; Eliot, i, 46.
33. Monier-Williams, 178, 331; Dubois, 415; Eliot, i, lxviii, 46.
34. Eliot, i, lxvi; Fülop-Miller, R., *Lenin and Gandhi*, 248.

35. Manu, xii, 62; Monier-Williams, 55, 276; Radhak., i, 250.
36. Watters, i, 281.
37. Dubois, 562.
38. Ibid., 248.
39. Eliot, i, lxxvii; Monier-Williams, 55; *Mahabharata*, XII, 2798; Manu, iv, 88-90, xii, 75-77, iv, 182, 260, vi, 32, ii, 244.
40. Dubois, 565.
41. Eliot, i, lxvi.
42. Quoted by Winternitz, 7.
43. Article on "The Failure of Every Philosophical Attempt in Theodicy," 1791, in Radhak., i, 364.
44. From the *Mahabharata*; reference lost.
45. In Brown, Brian, *Wisdom of the Hindus*, 32.
46. *Ramayana*, etc., 152.
47. Brown, B., *Hindus*, 222f.
48. Rolland, R., *Prophets of the New India*, 49.
50. Dubois, 379f.
51. Briffault, ii, 451.
52. Davids, *Buddhist India*, 216; Dubois, 149, 329, 382f.
53. Sumner, *Folkways*, 547; Eliot, ii, 143; Dubois, 629; Monier-Williams, 522-3.
54. Dubois, 541, 631.
55. Murray's *India*, London, 1905, 434.
56. Eliot, ii, 173.
57. Dubois, 595.
58. Vivekananda in Wood, 156.
59. Havell, *Architecture*, 107; Eliot, ii, 225.
60. In Wood, 154.
61. Simon, i, 24; Lorenz, 332; Eliot, ii, 173; Dubois, 296.
62. Monier-Williams, 430.
63. Dubois, 647.
64. Winternitz, 565; Smith, *Ox. H.*, 690.
65. Dubois, 597.
66. *Enc. Brit.*, xiii, 175.
67. Smith, *Ox. H.*, 155, 315.
68. Dubois, 110.
69. Ibid., 180-1.

70. Eliot, iii, 422.
71. Dubois, 43; Wood, 205.
72. Dubois, 43.
73. Watters, i, 319.
74. Dubois, 500-9, 523f.
75. Ibid., 206.
76. Eliot, ii, 322.
77. Radhak., i, 345.
78. Ibid., 484.

79. Arnold, *The Song Celestial*, 94.
80. Brown, B., *Hindus*, 218-20; Barnett, *The Heart of India*, 112.
81. Elphinstone, 476; Loti, 34; Eliot, i, xxxvii, 40-1; Radhak., i, 27; Dubois, 119n.
82. Kohn, 352.
83. Smith, *Ox. H.*, x.
84. Gour, 9.

CHAPTER XIX

1. Spencer, *Sociology*, iii, 248.
3. Sarton, 378.
4. Ibid., 409, 428; Sedgwick and Tyler, 160.
5. Barnett, 188-90.
6. Muthu, 97.
7. De Morgan in Sarkar, 8.
8. Reference lost.
8a. *Journal of the American Oriental Society*, Vol. 51, No. 1, p. 51.
9. Sarton, 601.
10. Monier-Williams, 174; Sedgwick 159; Sarkar, 12.
11. Ibid.
12. Muthu, 92; Sedgwick, 157f.
13. Ibid.; Lowie, R. H., *Are We Civilized?*, 269; Sarkar, 14.
14. Muthu, 92; Sarkar, 14-15.
15. Monier-Williams, 183-4.
16. Sedgwick, 157.
17. Sarkar, 17.
18. Sedgwick, 157; Muthu, 94; Sarkar, 23-4.
19. Muthu, 97; Radhak., i, 317-8.
20. Sarkar, 36f.
21. Ibid., 37-8.
22. Muthu, 104; Sarkar, 39-46.
22a. Ibid., 45.
23. Garrison, 71; Sarkar, 56.
24. Sarkar, 57-9.
25. Ibid., 63.
26. Lajpat Rai, *Unhappy India*, 163-4.
27. Sarkar, 63.
28. Ibid., 65.
29. Muthu, 14.
30. Sarton, 77; Garrison, 71.
31. Barnett, 220.
32. Muthu, 50.
33. Ibid., 39; Barnett, 221; Sarton, 480.
34. Sarton, 77; Garrison, 72.
35. Muthu, 26; Macdonell, 180.
36. Garrison, 29.
37. Muthu, 26.

38. Ibid., 27.
39. Garrison, 70.
40. Ibid., 71.
41. Macdonell, 179.
42. Harding, T. Swann, *Fads, Frauds and Physicians*, 147.
43. Watters, i, 174; Venkateswara, 193.
44. Barnett, 224; Garrison, 71.
45. Ibid.; Muthu, 33.
46. Garrison, 71; Lajpat Rai, *Unhappy India*, 286.
47. Eliot, i, lxxxix; Lajpat Rai, 285.
48. Muthu, 44.
49. Garrison, 73.
50. Ibid., 72.
51. Macdonell, 180.
52. Havell, *History*, 255.
53. Lajpat Rai, 287.
54. Radhak, i, 55.
56. Müller, *Six Systems*, 11; Havell, *History*, 412.
57. Das Gupta, 406.
58. Havell, *History*, 208.
59. Coomaraswamy, *Dance*, f. p. 130.
60. Davids, *Dialogues*, ii, 26f; Müller, *Six Systems*, 17; Radhak, i, 483.
61. Keyserling, *Travel Diary*, i, 106; ii, 157.
62. Müller, *Six Systems*, 219, 235; Radhak., i, 57, 276, ii, 23; Das Gupta, 8.
63. Radhak., ii, 36, 43.
64. Ibid., 34, 127, 173; Müller, 427.
65. Radhak., i, 281, ii, 42, 134.
66. Gowen, *Indian Literature*, 127; Radhak, ii, 29, 197, 202, 227; Dutt, *Civilization of India*, 35; Müller, 438; Chatterji, J. C., *The Hindu Realism*, 20, 22.
67. Radhak., ii, 249.
68. Ibid.
69. Gowen, 128.
70. Ibid., 30; Monier-Williams, 78; Müller, 84, 219f.
70a. E.g., XII, 13703.

70b. Radhak., ii, 249.
71. Macdonell, 93.
72. Müller, x.
73. Kapila, *The Aphorisms of the Sankhya Philosophy*, Aph. 79.
74. Gour, 23.
75. Eliot, ii, 302; Monier-Williams, 88.
76. Kapila, Aph. 98.
77. Monier-Williams, 84.
78. Müller, xi.
79. Kapila, Aph. 100; Monier-Williams, 88.
80. Kapila, p. 75, Aph. 67.
81. Radhak., i, 279.
82. In Brown, B., *Hindus*, 212.
83. Eliot, ii, 301.
84. Kapila in Brown, B., *Hindus*, 213.
85. Kapila, Aph. 56.
86. Ibid., Aphs. 83-4.
87. In Brown, B., 211.
88. Monier-Williams, 90-1.
89. Ibid., 92.
90. *Rig-veda* x, 136.3; Radhak., i, 111.
91. Eliot, i, 303.
92. Arrian, *Anabasis*, VII, 3.
93. Some authorities, however, attribute the *Yoga-sutra* to the fourth century A.D.—Radhak., ii, 340.
94. Watters, i, 148.
95. Polo, 300.
96. Lorenz, 356.
97. Chatterji, *India's Outlook on Life*, 61n; Radhak., i, 337.
98. Müller, *Six Systems*, 324-5.
99. Coomaraswamy, *Dance*, 50; Radhak., ii, 344; Das Gupta, S., *Yoga as Philosophy and Religion*, vii; Parmelee, 64; Eliot, i, 303-4; Davids, *Buddhist India*, 242.
100. Chatterji, *India's Outlook*, 65.
101. Müller, *Six Systems*, 349.
102. *The World as Will and Idea*, tr. Haldane and Kemp, iii, 254; Eliot, i, 309.
103. Radhak., ii, 360.
104. Vyasa in Radhak., ii, 362.

105. Eliot, i, 305; Radhak., ii, 371; Müller, 308-10, 324-5.
106. Chatterji, *Realism*, 6; Dubois, 98.
107. Patanjali in Brown, B., *Hindus*, 183; Radhak., i, 366.
108. Das Gupta, *Yoga*, 157; Eliot, i, 319; Chatterji, *India's Outlook*, 40.
109. Dubois, 529, 601.
110. Eliot, ii, 295.
111. Radhak., ii, 494; Das Gupta, *History*, 434.
112. Radhak., i, 45-6.
113. Radhak., ii, 528-31, 565-87; Deussen, Paul, *System of the Vedanta*, 241-4; Macdonell, 47; Radhakrishnan, S., *The Hindu View of Life*, 65-6; Otto, 3.
114. Eliot, i, xlii-iii; Deussen, *Vedanta*, 272, 458.
115. Radhak., ii, 544f.
115a. Guénon, René, *Man and His Becoming*, 259.
116. Deussen, 39, 126, 139, 212.
117. Coomaraswamy, *Dance*, 113.
118. Müller, *Six Systems*, 194.
119. Eliot, ii, 312; Deussen, 255, 300, 477; Radhak., ii, 633, 643.
120. Deussen, 402-10, 457.
121. Eliot, ii, 40.
122. In Deussen, 106.
123. Ibid., 286.
124. Radhak., ii, 448.
125. In Müller, *Six Systems*, 181.
126. Radhak., ii, 771.
127. Dickinson, G. Lowes, *An Essay on the Civilizations of India, China and Japan*, 33.
128. Keyserling, *Travel Diary*, i, 257.
129. *Isavasya Upanishad*, in Brown, B., *Hindus*, 159.
130. Ibid.
131. *De Intellectus Emendatione*.
132. Cf. Otto, 219-32. Melamed, S. M., in *Spinoza and Buddha*, has tried to trace the influence of Hindu pantheism upon the great Jew of Amsterdam.

CHAPTER XX

1. Das Gupta, *Yoga*, 16; Radhak., ii, 570.
2. Macdonell, 61; Winternitz, 46-7.
3. *Mahabharata*, II, 5; Davids, *Buddhist India*, 108. Rhys Davids dates the oldest extant Indian (bark) MS. about the beginning of the Christian era. (*Ibid.*, 124.)

4. Ibid., 118.
5. Indian Year Book, 1929, 633.
6. Winternitz, 33, 35.
7. Lajpat Rai, *Unhappy India*, 18, 27.
8. Venkateswara, 83; Max Müller in Hardie, 5.
9. Smith, *Ox. H.*, 114.

10. Venkateswara, 83; Havell, *History*, 409.
11. Venkateswara, 85, 100, 239.
12. Ibid., 114, 84; Frazer, R. W., 161.
13. Venkateswara, 148.
14. Havell, *History*, Plate XLI.
15. Venkateswara, 231-2; Smith, *Ox. H.*, 61; Havell, *History*, 140; Muthu, 32, 74; *Modern Review*, March, 1915, 334.
16. Watters, ii, 164-5.
17. Venkateswara, 239, 140, 121, 82; Muthu, 77.
18. Tod, i, 348n.
19. Ibid.
20. *Ramayana*, etc., 324.
21. Eliot, i, xc.
22. Tietjens, 246.
23. VI, 13, 50.
23a. *Ramayana*, etc., 303-7.
24. V, 1517; Monier-Williams, 448.
25. In Brown, B., *Hindus*, 41.
26. In Winternitz, 441.
27. In Brown, B., 27.
28. Eliot, ii, 200.
29. Radhak., i, 519; Winternitz, 17.
30. Professor Bhandakar in Radhak., i, 524.
31. Richard Garbe, *ibid.*
32. Arnold, *The Song Celestial*, 4-5.
33. Ibid., 9.
34. Ibid., 41, 31.
35. Macdonell, 91.
36. Gowen, 251; Müller, *India*, 81.
37. Arthur Lillie, in *Rama and Homer*, has tried to show that Homer borrowed both his subjects from the Indian epics; but there seems hardly any question that the latter are younger than the *Iliad* and the *Odyssey*.
38. Dutt, *Ramayana*, etc., 1-2.
39. Ibid., 77.
40. Ibid., 10.
41. Ibid., 34.
42. Ibid., 36.

43. Ibid., 47, 75.
44. Ibid., 145.
45. Gowen, *Indian Literature*, 203.
46. Ibid., 219.
47. Macdonell, 97-106.
48. In Gowen, 361.
49. Ibid., 363.
50. Monier-Williams, 476-94.
51. Gowen, 358-9.
52. Coomaraswamy, *Dance*, 33.
53. Kalidasa, *Shakuntala*, 101-3.
54. Ibid., 139-40.
55. Tr. by Monier-Williams, in Gowen, 317.
56. Frazer, R. W., 288.
57. Kalidasa, xiii.
58. Macdonell, 123-9.
59. Macdonell in Tietjens, 24-5.
60. In Gowen, 407-8.
61. Ibid., 504.
62. Ibid., 437-42.
63. Tietjens, 301; Gowen, 411-13; Barnett, *Hart of India*, 121.
64. Frazer, R. W., 365; Gowen, 487.
64a. Coomaraswamy, *Dance*, 105; Rolland, *Prophets*, 6n.
65. Barnett, *Heart*, 54.
66. Sir George Grierson in Smith, *Akbar*, 420.
67. Macdonell, 226; Winternitz, 476; Gandhi, *His Own Story*, 71.
68. Barnett, *Heart*, 63.
69. Venkateswara, 246, 249; Havell, *History*, 237.
70. Frazer, R. W., 318n.
71. Ibid., 345.
72. Eliot, ii, 263; Gowen, 491; Dutt, 101.
73. Tr. by Tagore.
74. Kabir, *Songs of Kabir*, tr. by R. Tagore, 91, 69.
75. Eliot, ii, 262.
76. Ibid., 265.

CHAPTER XXI

1. Coomaraswamy, *History*, 4.
2. Ibid., Plate II, 2.
3. Fergusson, i, 4.
4. Smith, *Akbar*, 412.
5. Coomaraswamy, fig. 381.
6. Ibid., 134.
7. Ibid., figs. 368-78.
8. Ibid., 139.
9. Ibid., 137.

10. Ibid., 138.
11. Smith, *Akbar*, 422.
12. Coomaraswamy, *Dance*, 73.
13. Program of dances by Shankar, New York, 1933.
14. Coomaraswamy, *Dance*, 75, 78.
15. Brown, Percy, *Indian Painting*, 121.
16. Childe, *Ancient East*, 37; Brown, P., 15, 111.

17. Havell, *Ideals,* 132; Brown, P., 17.
18. Ibid., 38.
19. Ibid., 20.
20. E.g., by Faure, *History of Art,* ii, 26; and Havell, *Architecture,* 150.
21. Brown, P., 29-30.
22. Havell, *Architecture,* Plate XLIV; Fischer, Otto, *Die Kunst Indiens, Chinas und Japans,* 200.
23. Havell, *Architecture,* 149.
24. Coomaraswamy, *History,* figs. 7 and 185.
25. Havell, *Architecture,* Pl. XLV.
26. Fischer, *Tafel* VI.
27. Ibid., 188-94.
29. Coomaraswamy, *Dance,* Pl. XVIII.
30. Coomaraswamy, *History,* fig. 269.
31. Brown, P., 120.
32. Cf. a charming example in Fischer, 273.
33. Brown, P., 8, 47, 50, 100; Smith, *Ox. H.,* 128; Smith, *Akbar,* 428-30.
34. Brown, P., 85.
35. Ibid., 96.
36. Ibid., 89; Smith, *Akbar,* 429.
37. Ibid., 226.
38. Coomaraswamy, *Dance,* 26.
39. Havell, *Ideals,* 46.
40. Fenollosa, i, 30; Fergusson, i, 52; Smith, *Ox. H.,* 111.
41. Gour, 530; Havell, *History,* 111.
42. Coomaraswamy, *History,* 70.
43. Fenollosa, i, 4, 81; Thomas, E. J., 221; Coomaraswamy, *Dance,* 52; Eliot, i, xxxi; Smith, *Ox. H.,* 67.
44. Fischer, 168; Central Museum, Lahore.
45. Fenollosa, i, 81.
46. Coomaraswamy, *History,* fig. 168.
47. Ca. 950 A.D.; Coomaraswamy, *History,* fig. 222; Lucknow Museum.
48. Ca. 1050 A.D.; Coomaraswamy, *History,* fig. 223; Lucknow Museum.
49. Ca. 750 A.D.; Havell, *History,* f. p. 204.
50. Ca. 950 A.D.; Coomaraswamy, *History,* Pl. LXX.
51. Ca. 700; Havell, *History,* f. 244; a variant, in copper, from the 17th century, is in the British Museum.
52. Ca. 750; Coomaraswamy, *Dance,* p. 26.
53. Ca. 1650; Coomaraswamy, *History,* fig. 248.
54. Fenollosa, i, f. 84.
55. Fischer, *Tafel* XVI; Coomaraswamy, *History,* cvi; Boston Museum of Fine Arts.
56. Coomaraswamy, fig. 333.
57. Gangoly, O. C., *Indian Architecture,* xxxiv-viii.
58. Ibid., frontispiece.
59. Havell, *Ideals,* f. 168.
60. Metropolitan Museum of Art, New York City; Coomaraswamy, *History,* fig. 101.
61. Havell, *Ideals,* f. 34.
62. Ca. 100 A.D.; Coomaraswamy, XCVIII.
63. Ibid., xcv.
64. Havell, *History,* 104; Fergusson, i, 51.
65. Davids, *Buddhist India,* 70.
66. Havell, *Architecture,* 2; Smith, *Ox. H.,* 111; Eliot, iii, 450; Coomaraswamy, *History,* 22.
67. Spooner, D. B., in Gowen, 270.
68. Fischer, 144-5.
69. In Smith, *Ox. H.,* 112.
70. Havell, *History,* 106; Coomaraswamy, *History,* 17.
71. Havell, *Architecture,* 55.
72. Fergusson, i, 119.
73. Coomaraswamy, *History,* fig. 54.
74. Ibid., fig. 31.
74a. Fergusson, i, 55; Coomaraswamy, 19.
75. Fischer, 186.
76. Ibid., *Tafel* IV.
77. Ibid., 175.
78. Havell, *Architecture,* 98, and Pl. XXV.
79. Fergusson, ii, 26.
80. Havell, *Architecture,* Pl. XIV.
81. Fergusson, ii, frontispiece.
82. Coomaraswamy, LXVIII.
83. Fergusson, ii, 41 and Pl. XX.
84. Ibid., 101.
85. Fergusson, ii, Pl. XXIV.
86. Ibid., 138-9.
87. Coomaraswamy, *History,* fig. 252.
88. Havell, *History,* f. p. 344.
89. Havell, *Architecture,* Plates LXXIV-VI.
90. Fischer, 214-5.
91. Loti, 168; Fergusson, ii, 7, 32, 87.
92. E.g., the temple at Baroli, Fergusson, ii, 133.
93. Fergusson, i, 352.
94. Ibid., Pl. XII, p. 424.
95. Ibid.
96. Gangoly, Pl. LXXIV.
97. Coomaraswamy, *History,* fig. 211; Fischer, 251.
98. Fergusson, i, 448.
99. Macdonell, 83.

100. Coomaraswamy, *History*, fig. 192; Fischer, 221.
101. Ibid., 222.
102. Havell, *Architecture*, 195; Fergusson, i, 327, 342, 348.
103. E.g., Mukerji, D. G., *Visit India with Me*, New York, 1929, 12.
104. Coomaraswamy, *History*, 95, Pl. LII.
105. Fischer, 248-9; Fergusson, i, 362-6.
106. Ibid., 368-72.
107. Dr. Coomaraswamy.
108. Coomaraswamy, *History*, XCVI.
109. Ibid., 169.
110. Gangoly, 29.
111. Coomaraswamy, *History*, fig. 349; Gangoly, xi.
112. Exs. in Gangoly, xii-xv.
113. Candee, Helen C., *Angkor the Magnificent*, 302.
114. Ibid., 186.
115. 131, 257, 294.
116. 258.
117. Fischer, 280.
118. Coomaraswamy, *History*, 173.
119. Havell, *History*, 327, 296, 376; *Architecture*, 207; Fergusson, ii, 87, 7.
120. Smith, *Ox. H.*, 223; Frazer, R. W., 363.
121. Smith, f. 329.
122. Fergusson, ii, 309.
123. Ibid., 308n.
124. Lorenz, 376.
125. Chirol, *India*, 54.
126. Lorenz, 379.
127. Smith, *Ox. H.*, 421.

CHAPTER XXII

1. Zimand, 31.
2. Smith, *Ox. H.*, 502.
3. In Zimand, 32.
4. Ibid., 31-4; Smith, 505; Macauley, i, 504, 580; Dutt, R. C., *The Economic History of India in the Victorian Age*, 18-23, 32-3.
5. Macaulay, i, 568-70, 603.
6. Dutt, *Economic History*, 67, 76, 375; Macaulay, i, 529.
7. Ibid., 528.
8. Dutt, xiii, 399, 417.
9. Sunderland, 135; Lajpat Rai, *Unhappy India*, 343.
10. Dubois, 300.
11. Ibid., 607.
12. Eliot, iii, 409.
13. Monier-Williams, 126.
14. Frazer, R. W., 397.
15. Ibid., 395.
16. Eliot, i, xlvi.
17. Rolland, *Prophets*, 119; Zimand, 85-6; Wood, 327; Eliot, i, xlviii; Underwood, A. C., *Contemporary Thought of India*, 137f.
17a. Rolland, 61, 260.
18. Ibid., xxvi; Eliot, ii, 162.
19. Brown, B., *Hindus*, 269.
20. Rolland, 160, 243; Brown, B., 264-5.
21. Rolland, 427.
22. Ibid., 251, 293, 449-50.
23. Ibid., 395.
24. Tagore, R., *Gitanjali*, New York, 1928, xvii; *My Reminiscences*, 15, 201, 215.
25. Thompson, E. J., *Rabindranath Tagore*, 82.
26. Tagore, R., *The Gardener*, 74-5.
27. Tagore, *Gitanjali*, 88.
28. Tagore, *Chitra*, esp. pp. 57-8.
29. Tagore, *The Gardener*, 84.
30. Thompson, E. J., 43.
31. Ibid., 94, 99; Fülop-Miller, 246; Underwood, A. C., 152.
32. Tagore, R., *Sadhana*, 25, 64.
33. *The Gardener*, 13-15.
34. Kohn, 105.
35. Zimand, 181; Lorenz, 402; Indian Year Book, 1929, 29.
36. "Close, Upton" (Josef Washington Hall), *The Revolt of Asia*, 235; Sunderland, 204; Underwood, 153.
37. Smith, *Ox. H.*, 35.
38. Simon, i, 37; Dubois, 73.
39. Ibid., 190.
40. Havell, *History*, 165; Lorenz, 327.
41. Kohn, 426.
42. Simon, i, 38.
43. Lajpat Rai, *Unhappy India*, lviii, 191; Mukerji, *A Son*, 27; Sunderland, 247; New York *Times*, Sept. 24, 1929, Dec. 31, 1931.
44. Wood, 111; Sunderland, 248.
45. Indian Year Book, 23.
46. Wood, 117.
47. Kohn, 425.
48. Prof. Sudhindra Bose, in *The Nation*, New York, June 19, 1929.
49. New York *Times*, June 16, 1930.

50. Hall, J. W., 427; Fülop-Miller, 272.
51. Ibid., 171.
52. Ibid., 174-6.
53. Gandhi, M. K., *Young India*, 123.
54. Ibid., 133.
55. Hall, 408.
56. Fülop-Miller, 202-3.
57. Ganadhi, *Young India*, 21.
58. Rolland, *Mahatma Gandhi*, 7.
59. Ibid., 40; Hall, 400.
60. Gray and Parekh, *Mahatma Gandhi*, 27; Parmelee, 302.

61. Simon, i, 249.
62. Fülop-Miller, 299; Rolland, *Gandhi*, 220; Kohn, 410-12.
63. Fülop-Miller, 177.
64. Ibid., 315.
65. Ibid., 186.
66. Gandhi, *Young India*, 869, 2.
67. Hall, 506; Fülop-Miller, 227.
68. Zimand, 220.
69. Fülop-Miller, 171-2.
70. Ibid., 207, 162.

CHAPTER XXIII

1. I am indebted for this quotation from the *Book of Rites* to Upton Close. Cf. Gowen and Hall, *Outline History of China*, 50; Hirth, F., *Ancient History of China*, 155.
1a. Reichwein, A., China and Europe: *Intellectual and Artistic Contacts in the Eighteenth Century*, 92.
2. Ibid., 89f.; Voltaire, Works, New York, 1927, xiii, 19.
3. Keyserling, *Creative Understanding*, 122, 203; *Travel Diary*, ii, 67, 58, 50, 57, 48, 68.
4. Lippert, 91; Keyserling, Travel Diary, ii, 53.
5. Smith, A. H., *Chinese Characteristics*, 98.
6. Giles, H. A., *Gems of Chinese Literature: Prose*, 119.
7. Williams, S. Wells, *Middle Kinigdom*, i, 5; Brinkley, Capt. F., *China: Its History, Arts and Literature*, x, 3.
8. Ibid., 2; Hall, J. W., *Eminent Asians*, 41.
10. Pittard, 397; Buxton, 153; Granet, *Chinese Civilization*, New York, 1930, 63; Latourette, K. S., *The Chinese: Their History and Culture*, 35-6; New York Times, Feb. 15, 1933.
11. Lowie, 182; Fergusson, J., *History of Indian and Eastern Architecture*, ii, 468; Legendre, A. F., *Modern Chinese Civilization*, 234; Granet, 64.
12. Ibid., 215, 230.
13. Gowen and Hall, 26-7.
14. Confucius (?), *Book of History*, rendered and compiled by W. G. Old, 20-1.
15. Giles, *Gems*, 72.

16. Hirth, 40.
17. Ibid., 53-7.
18. Wilhelm, R., *Short History of Chinese Civilization*; 124; Granet, 86.
19. Ibid., 87.
20. Confucius, *Analects*, XIV, xviii, 2, in Legge, Jas., *Chinese Classics, Vol. I: Life and Teachings of Confucius*.
21. Legge, 213n.
22. Hirth, 107-8; Latourette, i, 57; Gowen and Hall, 64; Schneider, H., ii, 796-8.
23. Granet, 78.
24. Ibid., 32-3; Hu Shih, *Development of the Logical Method in Ancient China*, 22; Latourette, i, 52.
25. Ibid., 58-9; Granet, 87-8; Hirth, 110.
26. Giles, H. A., *History of Chinese Literature*, 5.
27. *Book of Odes*, I, x, 8, and xii, 10, in Hu Shih, Pt. I, p. 4.
28. Cranmer-Byng, L., *The Book of Odes*, 51.
29. Tr. by Helen Waddell in Van Doren, *Anthology of World Poetry*, 1.
30. In Yang Chu's *Garden of Pleasure*, 64.
31. Fenollosa, E. F., *Epochs of Chinese and Japanese Art*, 14; Hirth, 59-62; Hu Shih, 28f; Suzuki, D. T., *Brief History of Early Chinese Philosophy*, 14; Murdoch, Jas., *History of Japan*, iii, 108.
32. Hu Shih, 12.
33. Legge, 75n.
34. In Hu Shih, 12.
35. Ibid., 13.
36. Ibid., 12.
37. Giles, *History*, 57; Legge, Jas., *The Texts of Taoism*, i, 4-5.
38. Giles, *History*, 57; Giles, *Gems*, 55.
39. Legge, *Texts of Taoism*, i, 4f.

40. II, lxxxi, 3; I, lxv, 1-2.
41. In Suzuki, 81.
42. II, lvii, 2-3; lxxx. Parenthetical passages, in this and other quotations, are usually explanatory interpolations, nearly always of the translator.
43. Yang Chu, 16, 19; Schneider, ii, 810; Hu Shih, 14; Wilhelm, *Short History*, 247.
44. I, xvi, 1-2.
45. I, xliii, 1; xlix, 2; lxi, 2; lxiii, 1; lxxviii, 1; lxxxi, 1; Giles, *History*, 73.
46. II, lxi, 2.
47. II, lvi, 1-2.
48. Granet, 55.
49. II, lvi, 2.
50. I, xvi, 1; II, lvi, 3; Parmelee, 43.
51. Legge, *Texts of Taoism*, 34; *Life and Teachings of Confucius*, 64.
61. Legge, *Texts*, 34.
62. Ibid.
63. Szuma Ch'ien in Legge, *Life*, 58n.
64. Ibid.
65. Legge, *Life*, 55-8; Wilhelm, R., *Soul of China*, 104.
66. Hirth, 229.
67. *Analects*, VII, xiii.
68. VIII, viii.
69. XV, xv.
70. VII, viii.
71. VII, xii.
72. VI, ii, XI, iii.
73. XVII, xxii; XIV; xlvi.
74. Legge, *Life*, 65.
75. Ibid., 79.
76. V, xxvii.
77. VII, xxxii.
78. XIII, x.
79. IX, iv.
80. VII, i.
81. IV, xiv.
82. Legge, *Life*, 67.
83. XII, xi.
84. Legge, *Life*, 68.
85. Ibid., 72.
86. Ibid., 75.
87. IX, xvii.
88. Legge, 83.
89. Ibid., 82.
90. XV, xviii.
91. II, iv.
92. Legge, 82.
93. Mencius, *Works of*, tr. by Legge, III, ʒ, iv, 13.

94. Wilhelm, *Short History*, 143; Legge, *Life*, 16.
95. Ibid., 267, 27; Hu Shih, 4.
96. XV, 40.
97. II, xvii.
98. XIII, iii.
99. III, xiii, 2.
100. IX, xv.
101. Legge, *Life*, 101; Giles, *History*, 33; Suzuki, 20.
102. Legge, 101.
103. XI, xi.
104. VI, 20.
105. VII, 20.
106. Giles, *History*, 69.
107. XV, ii.
108. *Great Learning*, I, 4-5, in Legge, *Life*, 266. I have ventured to change "illustrate illustrious virtue" in Legge's translation, to "illustrate the highest virtue"; and the words "own selves" have been substitiued for "persons," since "the cultivation of the person" has now a misleading connotation.
109. XIV, xlv.
110. XV, xxxi; II, xiv; XIII, iii, 7.
111. VI, xvi.
112. *Doctrine of the Mean*, XII, 4, in Legge.
113. *Analects*, II, xiii.
114. *Doctrine of the Mean*, XIV, 5.
115. XV, xviii-xx.
116. XIV, xxix; XI, xiii, 3; *D. of M.*, XXXIII, 2.
117. Ibid., XI, 3.
118. *Li-chi*, XVII, i, 11-2.
119. Spinoza, *Ethics*, Bk. III, Prop. 59.
120. *D. of M.*, XXIX, tr. by Suzuki, 64.
121. Suzuki, 63.
122. *Analects*, XII, ii; V, xvi.
123. XV, xxiii.
124. XIV, xxxvi, 1-2.
124a. IV, xvii.
124b. XII, vi.
125. XIII, xxiii.
126. *D. of M.*, XIV, 3.
127. IV, xxiv; V, iii, 2; XVII, vi; XV, xxi.
128. V, xvi; XVI, xiii, 5.
129. XVI, 10.
130. I, ii, 2; Legge, *Life*, 106.
131. IV, xviii; *Li-chi*, XII, i, 15; Brown, B., *Story of Confucius*, 183.
132. *Great Learning*, X, 5.
133. *Analects*, XII, vii.
134. XII, xix; II, ii, xx.

135. XII, xxiii, 3.
136. *D. of M.*, XX, 4.
137. *Analects*, XIII, x-xii.
138. *Great Learning*, X, 9.
139. *Analects*, XII, xix; XV, xxxviii.
140. *Li-chi*, XVII, i, 28; iii, 23; Brown, *Story of Confucius*, 181.
141. *Analects*, XX, iii, 3.
142. *Li-chi*, XXVII, 33; XXIII, 7-8.
143. Ibid., VII. i, 2-3, quoted in Dawson, *Ethics of Confucius*, 299, from Chen Huang-chang, *The Economic Principles of Confucius and His School.*
144. Latourette, i, 80-1.
145. Legge, *Life*, 106.
146. *D. of M.*, XXX-XXXI.
147. Hu Shih, 109f.
148. Hirth, 307.
149. Mencus, VII, i, 26, in Hu Shih, 58.
150. Hu Shih, 72.
151. Ibid., 57, 75; Latourette, i, 78.
152. In Hirth, 281.
153. Hu Shih, 69-70.
154. Thomas, E. D., *Chinese Political Thought*, 29-30.
155. Hu Shih, 58.
156. Mencius, Introd., 111.
157. Wilhelm, *Short History*, 150; Hu Shih 110.
158. Hu Shih, 62.
159. Mencius, Introd., 93.
160. Yang Chu, 10, 51; Latourette, i, 80.
161. Mencius, Introd., 96; Yang Chu, 57.
162. Mencius, Introd., 96-7.
163. Hirth, 27-9.
164. Mencius, III, ii, 9.
165. Mencius, Introd., 14-18.
166. Ibid., 42.
167. Ibid., I, ii, 3; ii, 5; pp. 156, 162.
168. Ibid., 12.
169. VI, i, 2.
170. I, i, 7.

171. III, i, 3.
172. I, i, 3.
173. II, i, 5.
174. Thomas, E. D., 37; Williams, S. Wells, i, 670.
175. IV, ii, 19.
176. Mencius, Introd., 30-1.
177. VI, ii, 4.
178. VII, ii, 4.
179. Quoted in Thomas, E. D., 37.
180. I, i, 3.
181. II, ii, 4.
182. VII, ii, 14.
183. V, ii, 9; I, ii, 6-8.
184. Mencius., Introd., 84.
185. Ibid., 79-80.
186. Ibid., 86.
187. In Hu Shih, 152.
188. Legge, Texts of Taoism, V, 5.
189. Ibid., Introd., 37.
190. XVII, 11.
191. In Thomas, E. D., 100.
192. XI, 1.
193. XVI, 2; IX, 2.
194. XII, 11.
195. XII, 2.
196. II, 2; XX, 7; Giles, *Gems*, 32.
197. II, 7; XXII, 5.
198. VI, 7.
199. In Suzuki, 36.
200. XVII, 4; Hu Shih, 146.
201. XVIII, 6.
202. II, 11; tr. by Giles, *History*, 63.
203. VI, 10; tr. by Suzuki, 181-2.
204. In Giles, *History*, 68.
205. In Reichwein, 79f.
206. Ibid.
207. Ibid., 84.
208. Wilhelm, *Soul of China*, 233.
209. Thomas, E. D., 25.
210. Voltaire, *Works*, iv, 82.
211. Reichwein, 131; Hirth, vii.

CHAPTER XXIV

1 Giles, *Gems*, 33.
2. Granet, 37; Gowen and Hall, 84; Giles, *History*, 78.
3. Granet, 41.
4. Voltaire, *Works*. iv, 82.
5. Granet, 37, 97-8, 101-3; Boulger, D. C., *History of China*, i, 68-70; Wilhelm, *Short History*, 157.
6. Boulger, i, 71.
7. Granet, 38.
8. Ibid.

9. Ibid., 103; Schneider, ii, 790; Wilhelm, *Short History*, 160-1; Lautourette, i, 96.
10. Gowen and Hall, 84f; Giles, *History*, 78.
11. Hall, J. W., *Eminent Asians*, 6.
12. Boulger, i, 64.
13. Ibid., 62; Latourette, i, 99.
14. Granet, 38-40; Boulger, i, 77; Giles in G(owen) & H(all), 92.
15. Boulger, i, 106; Granet, 44.
16. Szuma Ch'ien in Granet, 113.

17. Ibid.
18. Granet, 112-3.
19. Ibid., 118.
20. Fenollosa, i, 77.
21. Waley, Arthur, *Introduction to the Study of Chinese Painting*, 27; G & H, 102.
22. Granet, 113-5.
23. Wilhelm, *Short History*, 186, 194.
24. Lautourette, i, 121.
25. Ibid., 120-2.
26. Ibid., 122.
27. G & H, 118.
28. Ibid., 117-21.
29. Fenollosa, i, 117.
30. Voltaire, *Works*, xiii, 26.
31. Tu Fu, *Poems*, tr. by Edna W. Underwood, xli.
32. Li-Po, *Works*, done into English Verse by Shigeyoshi Obata, 91.
33. Tu Fu, xlviii.
34. In Li-Po, 1.
35. In Tu Fu, xli.
36. Murdoch, *History of Japan*, i, 146.
37. Waley, *Chinese Painting*, 142.
38. Ibid., 97.
39. Wilhelm, *Short History*, 224.
40. Williams, S. Wells, i, 696f.
41. Li-Po, 20.
42. Ibid., 95.
43. Ibid., 30.
44. Williams, S. Wells, i, 697.
45. Li-Po, 31.
46. G & H, 113.
47. Li-Po, 100.
48. Ibid., 84.
49. 138.
50. 191.
51. 71.

52. 55.
53. 97.
54. Ibid., ii.
55. Ibid., 25.
56. Giles, *History*, 50.
57. Translations by Arthur Waley, Amy Lowell and Florence Ayscough, in Van Doren, *Anthology*, 18-20.
58. Waley, Arthur, 170 *Chinese Poems*, 106-8.
59. Ibid., 162.
60. Ibid., 168.
61. In Van Doren, 24.
62. Giles, *History*, 156; Ayscough, Florence, *Tu Fu: The Autobiography of a Chinese Poet*, 105.
63. Ibid., 75.
64. Tu Fu, *Poems*, 118, 184, 154.
65. Ibid., 95.
66. 30, 7, 132.
67. 137.
68. 72, 133, and introd.
69. Williams, S. Wells, i, 602.
70. Giles, *History*, 276.
71. Ibid., 102.
72. Ibid.
73. Thomas, E. D., 5.
74. Giles, *History*, 200-3.
75. Ibid., 160.
76. G & H, 156.
77. Wilhelm, *Short History*, 255; Giles, *History*, 258.
78. Williams, S. Wells, i, 820; Latourette, ii, 220.
79. Ibid., 221.
80. Wilhelm, 141.
81. Pratt, *History of Music*, 32-5.
82. Giles, *Gems*, 117.

CHAPTER XXV

1. G & H, 142.
2. Ibid., 141.
3. Ibid., 140-3; Latourette, i, 252-7; Wilhelm, 237-8; Murdoch, iii, 106f; Fenollosa, ii, 33, 57.
4. G & H, 133, quoting Walter T. Swingle, Librarian of the U. S. Dept. of Agriculture.
5. Carter, *Invention of Printing* 2.
6. Ibid., 3.
7. Ibid., 96.
8. Sarton, 369.
9. Carter, 25.
10. Ibid., 145; Sarton, 512.

11. Carter, 41.
12. Ibid., 43, 183.
13. G & H, 133.
14. Carter, 250.
15. Ibid., 178, 171.
16. Ibid., 177-8; Sarton, 663.
17. Ibid.; G & H, 164; Giles, *History*, 296.
18. Chu Hsi, *Philosophy of Human Nature*, 75; Bryan, J. J., *Literature of Japan*, 122; Latourette, i, 262-3; Williams, S. Wells, i, 683; Wilhelm, *Short History*, 249-50; Aston, W. G., *History of Japanese Literature*, 226-7.

19. Chu Hsi, 68.
20. Wilhelm, 249-50.
21. Wang Yang-ming, *Philosophy*, tr. by Fredk. G. Henke, 177-8.
22. Armstrong, R. C., *Light from the East: Studies in Japanese Confucianism*, 121; Brinkley, Capt. F., *Japan: Its History, Arts and Literature*, iv, 125.
23. Wang Yang-Ming, 8, 12, 50, 59.
24. Brinkley, *Japan*, iv, 125.
25. Wang Yang-ming, 106, 52.
26. Ibid., 115-6.
27. Hobson, R. L., *Chinese Art*, 14.
28. *Encyc. Brit.*, xiii, 575.
29. Cf. the imperial marriage-table in Hobson, R. L., Pl. LXXXIII.
30. Ibid., XCI.
31. Illustrated in *Encyc. Brit.*, xiii, f. p. 576.
32. Ferguson, J. C., *Outlines of Chinese Art*, 67.
33. Hobson, R. L., LXXVIII.
34. Ibid., LXXVII, 1.
35. Lorenz, *'Round the World Traveler*, 197.
36. *Encyc. Brit.*, xii, 864.
37. Fry, R. E., *Chinese Art*, 31; Granet, 37, *Encyc. Brit.*, iv, 245.
38. *Chinese Art*, 33.
39. Fischer, Otto, 374.
40. *Encyc. Brit.*, Pl. XIV, f. p. 246; collection of Mr. Warren E. Cox.
41. *Chinese Art*, 47.
42. Faure, *History of Art*, ii, 55.
43. *Encyc. Brit.*, v, f. p. 581.
44. Siren, O., in *Encyc. Brit.*, v, 581; *Chinese Art*, 48.
45. Stein, Sir Aurel, *Innermost Asia*, Vol. i, Plates VIII, XI, XIX and XXIV.
46. *Encyc. Brit.*, v. f. p. 586, Plate X, 2; Fischer, 366.
47. *Encyc. Brit.*, v. f. p. 584, Pl. VII, 4.
48. Ibid., f. p. 585, Pl. VIII, 2.
49. Ibid., f. p. 586, Pl. XI, 2 and 3.
50. Fergusson, Jas., *History of Indian and Eastern Architecture*, ii, 454.
51. Fergusson, Jas., in Williams, S. Wells, i, 727.
52. Cf. the decorative design reproduced in Stein, Sir A., *Innermost Asia*, Vol. iii, Pl. XXV; and the patiently carved and ornamental ceiling shown in Pelliot, Vol. iv, Pl. CCXXV.
53. Fergusson, op. cit., ii, 464.
54. Coomaraswamy, *History*, 152.
55. Williams, S. Wells, i, 744.
56. Lorenz, 203.
57. Cook's, *Guide to Peking*, 28, 30.
58. Fergusson, ii, 481.
59. Legendre, 79.
60. Ibid., 156.
61. Smith, *Chinese Characteristics*, 134.
62. Waley, *Chinese Painting*, 69-70.
63. Siren, Osvald, *Chinese Paintings in American Collections*, i, 36.
64. Giles, H. A., *Introduction to the History of Chinese Pictorial Art*, 2.
65. Wilhelm, *Short History*, 38.
66. Giles, *Pictorial Art*, 3.
67. Ibid.; Waley, *Chinese Painting*, 32.
68. Fenollosa, ii, p. xxx.
69. Waley, *Chinese Painting*, 45.
70. *Encyc. Brit.*, art. on "Chinese Painting," Pl. II, 6.
71. Fischer, 325-31.
72. Waley, 49.
73. Ibid., 51.
74. Giles, *Pictorial Art*, 21.
75. Tu Fu, 97; cf. 175 and 187.
76. Giles, *Pictorial Art*, 79.
77. Wilhelm, 244.
78. Waley, 183.
79. Fenollosa, i. f. p. 120; Fischer, 490.
80. Ibid., 424.
81. Giles, 47-8.
82. Ibid., 50; Binyon, L., *Flight of the Dragon*, 43.
83. Giles, 47.
84. Croce, Benedetto, *Esthetic*, 50.
85. In Waley, 117.
86. Binyon, 111.
87. Siren, i, Plates 5-8; *Encyc. Brit.*, "Chinese Painting," Pl. II, 4.
88. Fenollosa, ii, 27.
89. Waley, 177.
90. G & H, 146.
91. A Chinese writer in Giles, *Pictorial Art*, 115.
92. Fischer, 492.
93. E.g., Fenollosa, ii, 42.
95. Ibid., 62.
96. Gulland, W. G., *Chinese Porcelain*, i, 16.
97. *Chinese Art*, 11.
98. Ibid., 2.
99. Hsieh Ho in Coomaraswamy, *Dance of Siva*, 43.
100. Binyon. 65-8; *Chinese Art*, 47.

101. In Okakura-Kakuso, *The Book of Tea*, 108.
102. Gulland, i, 3.
103. *Encyc. Brit.*, xviii, 361.
104. Ibid.; Legendre, 233.
105. *Encyc. Brit.*, xviii, 362; Carter, 93.
106. Ibid., l.c.
107. Brinkley, *China*, ix, 229.

108. Ibid., 62.
109. Ibid., 87; Gulland, 139.
110. Brinkley, 75.
111. G & H, 165.
112. Brinkley, *China*, ix, 256.
113. *Encyc. Brit.*, viii, 419.
114. Brinkley, *China*, ix, 210, 215.
115. Ibid., 376, 554; *Encyc. Brit.*, art. "Ceramics."

CHAPTER XXVI

1. Polo, Travels, 78, 188.
2. Ibid., v-vii; a perfect introduction, to which the present account is much indebted.
3. Polo, 232-40.
4. 152.
5. 129.
6. G & H, 135f.
7. Giles, *History*, 248-9.
8. Polo, 172.
9. Giles, 247.
10. Polo, 158.
11. Ibid., 125.
12. 149.
13. P. xxiv of Komroff's Introduction.
14. G & H, 172.
15. Ibid.
16. Latourette, i, 330; Wilhelm, *Short History*, 260; G & H, 195; Giles, *History*, 291; Gulland, W. G., ii, 288.
17. G & H, 209.
18. Ibid., 227.
19. Quoted in Parmelee, 218, and in Bisland, Elizabeth, *Three Wise Men of the East*, 125.
20. Wilhelm, 204; Latourette, i, 203; G & H, 186; Brinkley, *China*, x, 4.
21. Latourette, i, 289.
22. Brinkley, l.c., 12.
23. Williams, S. Wells, i, 770.
24. Ibid., 762.
25. Wilhelm in Keyserling, *Book of Marriage*, 133; Waley, *Chinese Painting*, 165.
26. Legendre, 23.
27. Ibid., 75; Park, No Yong, *Making a New China*, 122.
28. Smith, *Chinese Characteristics*, 127.
29. Polo, 236.
30. Pitkin, *Short Introduction*, 182.
32. Wilhelm, *Short History*, 64.
33. Mason, *Art of Writing*, 154-79.
34. Legendre, 67, 113.

35. Okakura, 3, 36.
36. Granet, 144-5.
37. Legendre, 114.
38. Wilhelm, *Soul of China*, 339.
40. Smith, *Characteristics*, 21; Park, No Yong, 123; Legendre, 86; Williams, S. Wells, i, 775-80.
41. Latourette, i, 225.
42. Park, 121; Smith, *Characteristics*, 19.
43. Eddy, Sherwood, *Challenge of the East*, 81.
44. Giles, *Gems*, 285.
45. Murdoch, iii, 262.
46. Sarton, 452.
47. National Geographic Magazine, April, 1932, p. 511.
48. Sumner and Keller, iii, 2095.
49. Wilhelm, *Short History*, 134; Wilhelm, *Soul of China*, 361-2; G & H, 59.
50. Polo, 236.
51. Peffer, N., *China: the Collapse of a Civilization*, 25-32; Parmelee, 101; Legendre, 57.
52. Williams, S. Wells, i, 413; Wilhelm, *Short History*, 11.
53. Park, 85; G & H, 290.
54. Park, 67.
55. Latourette, ii, 206; G & H, 2-3.
56. Renard, 161.
57. Park, 92.
58. Sumner, *Folkways*, 153; Latourette, i, 63.
59. Ibid., 252.
60. Polo, 159; Carter, 77.
61. Carter, 92.
62. Hirth, 126f.
63. Ibid.
64. Carter, 93.
65. Polo, 170n.
66. Legendre, 107-10.
67. Sarton, 371, 676; Schneider, ii, 860.
68. Sarton, 183, 410.
69. Waley, *Chinese Painting*, 30.

70. Schneider, ii, 837.
71. Voltaire, *Works*, iv, 82; Hirth, 119; Wilhelm, *Soul*, 306.
72. Garrison, 73; Schneider, ii, 859; Sarton, 310, 325, 342.
73. Ibid., 436, 481; Garrison, 73.
74. Latourette, 313; Garrison, 75.
75. Williams, S. Wells, i, 738; Legendre, 56.
76. Wilhelm, *Short History*, 79, 81; Smith, *Characteristics*, 290, 297; Spengler, O., *Decline of the West*, ii, 286; Granet, 163; Latourette, ii, 163-5.
77. Smith, *Characteristics*, 292; Suzuki, 47, 112, 139; Wilhelm, *Short History*, 69.
78. Hirth, 81.
79. Ibid., 118; Smith, 164, 331.
80. Granet, 321.
81. Wilhelm, *Soul*, 125.
82. Legge, *Texts of Taoism*, i, 41.
83. Suzuki, 72; Wilhelm, *Short History*, 248.
84. Waley, *Chinese Painting*, 28.
85. Potter, Chas. F., *Story of Religion*, 198.
86. Wilhelm, *Soul*, 357; Murdoch, iii, 104; Waley, 33-4, 79; Sarton, 470, 552; Carter, 32; Gulland, 27; Latourette, i, 171, 214; ii, 154-5; G & H, 104; Schneider, ii, 803.
87. Smith, *Characteristics*, 89; Latourette, ii, 129; Parmelee, 81.
88. Smith, 304; Legendre, 197.
89. Wilhelm, *Short History*, 224; Lorenz, 202.
90. G & H, 118, 527.
91. Fenollosa, ii, 149.
92. Voltaire, *Works*, xiii, 29.
93. Quoted by Wilhelm in Keyserling, *Book of Marriage*, 137.
94. Mencius, IV, i, 26.
95. Latourette, ii, 197; Granet, 321; Williams, S. Wells, i, 836; Legendre, 26.
96. Wilhelm in Keyserling, 137; Wilhelm, *Soul*, 22; Wilhelm, *Short Hstory*, 104; Smith, 213.
97. Granet, 345; Williams, S. Wells, i, 836; Westermarck, *Moral Ideas*, i, 462; Ellis, H., *Studies in the Psychology of Sex*, vol. ii, *Sexual Inversion*, 6f.
98. Briffault, iii, 346.
99. Ibid.; Wilhelm in Keyserling, 126.

100. Williams, S. Wells, i, 834.
101. Brinkley, *China*, x, 101.
102. Polo, 134, 152, 235.
103. Parmelee, 182; Briffault, ii, 333.
104. Li-Po, 152.
105. Walev, 170 *Chinese Poems*, 19; Keyserling, *Travel Diary*, ii, 97.
106. Hirth, 116.
107. Williams, S. Wells, 785.
108. Ibid., 787-90.
109. Wilhelm, in Keyserling, *Book of Marriage*, 134.
110. Briffault, ii, 263.
111. Williams, S. Wells, i, 407-8.
112. Park, 133.
113. Wilhelm, *Short History*, 59; Wilhelm, in Keyserling, 123; Briffault, i, 362f.
114. Thomas, E. D., 134; Briffault, i, 368.
115. Granet, 43.
116. Briffault, ii, 331.
117. Cranmer-Byng, *The Book of Odes*, 11; Giles, *History*, 108, 274.
118. Smith, 194; Sumner and Keller, iii, 1754; Legendre, 18.
119. *Li-chi*, IX, iii, 7; Smith, 215; Sumner and Keller, iii, 1844.
120. In Briffault, ii, 331.
121. Waley, 170 *Chinese Poems*, 94.
122. Armstrong, 56.
123. Williams, S. Wells, i, 825.
124. Westermarck, *Moral Ideas*, i, 89; Keyserling, *Travel Diary*, ii, 65; Smith, 192; Legendre, 122.
125. Wilhelm, *Soul*, 309.
126. Voltaire, *Works*, xiii, 19.
127. Brinkley, *China*, x, 37, 44, 49.
128. Smith, 225.
129. Thomas, E. D., 236; Williams, S. Wells, i, 504; Latourette, ii, 46.
130. Garrison, 75.
131. Williams, i, 391-2; Latourette, ii, 46.
132. Williams, ii, 512; Hirth, 123; Wilhelm, *Soul*, 19.
133. Brinkley, l.c., 3.
134. Ibid., 78.
136. Ibid., 92.
137. Williams, i, 544.
138. Legendre, 158; Hall, J. W., *Eminent Asians*, 35.
139. Williams, i, 569.
140. Latourette, ii, 21; Brinkley, *China*, x, 86.

CHAPTER XXVII

1. Latourette, i, 313.
2. Lorenz, 248.
3. Latourette, i, 314.
4. Lorenz, 248; G & H, 238.
5. Norton, H. K., *China and the Powers*, 55; Latourette, i, 367; Peffer, 57.
6. Latourette, i, 376, 385; Norton, 56.
7. Park, 149.
8. Peffer, 88f; Latourette, i, 413.
9. G & H, 306.
10. Hall, *Eminent Asians*, 17; Peffer, 151.
11. Latourette, i, 411.
12. Hall, 33.
13. Peffer, 93.
14. G & H, 314.
15. N. Y. *Times*, Feb. 11, 1934.
16. Eddy, *Challenge of the East*, 73.
18. Park, 86.
19. Latourette, ii, 93-6.
20. Eddy, 74.
21. Park, 89.
22. Eddy, 89.
23. Peffer, 241.
24. Peffer, 251.
25. *Modern Review*, Calcutta, May 1, 1931.
26. Peffer, 185.
27. Latourette, ii 174.
29. Ibid. 176.
30. Parmelee 94.
31. Park, 135; Lorenz, 192.
32. Wu, Chao-chu, *The Nationalist Program for China*, 28.
33. Legendre, 240.
34. Park, 114.
35. Close, Upton, *Revolt of Asia*, 245.
36. Lorenz, 250.
38. Hu Shih, 8.
39. Ibid., 7.

CHAPTER XXVIII

1. The *Kojiki* (681-711), in Murdoch, i, 59f, and Gowen, H. H., *Outline History of Japan*, 37f.
2. Murdoch, iii, 483.
3. Gowen, *Japan*, 13; Chamberlain, B. H., *Things Japanese*, 249.
4. Gowen, 25, reports three days of rain or snow in the average week.
5. Gowen, 17, 21; Chamberlain, B. H., 195; Redesdale, Lord, *Tales of Old Japan*, 2.
6. Chamberlain, B. H., 127.
7. Gowen, 99; Murdoch, iii, 211, 395-7; Chamberlain, 130.
8. Ibid., 128.
9. Hearn, Lafcadio, Japan: *An Interpretation*, 455.
11. Gowen, 61; Murdoch, i, 38.
12. Ibid.
13. Hearn, 448; Fenollosa, ii, 159.
14. Fenollosa, i, 64; Murdoch, i, 98-9.
15. Gowen, 64.
16. Murdoch, i, 94, 97.
17. Armstrong, 5, 18.
18. Ibid., 2.
19. Hearn, 53.
20. Murdoch, i, 39.
21. Brinkley, Capt. F., *Japan: Its History, Arts and Literature*, v, 118· Hearn, 45, 51.
22. Gowen, 67.
23. Ibid., 65.
25. Ibid., 118.
26. Murdoch, i, 240-1.
27. Ibid., i, 377-8; Gowen, 116.
28. Murasaki, Lady, *Tale of Genji*, 27.
29. Tietjens, 156; tr. Curtis Hidden Page, Some authors attribute the poem to Michizane (Gowen, 119).
30. Close, Upton, *Challenge: Behind the Face of Japan*, 28; Gowen, 105; Latourette, i, 226.
31. Fenollosa, i, 149.
32. Brinkley *Japan* iv, 148.
33. Fenollosa i, 153.
34. Murdoch, i, 279.
35. Brinkley, i, 230.
36. Murdoch, i, 228-30.
37. Gowen, 147.
38. Murdoch, ii 711.
38a. Close, *Challenge*, 54.
39. Gowen, 156.
40. Ibid., 161-2; Murdoch, i, 545; Brinkley, ii, 190.
41. Ibid., ii, 108; viii, 17.
42. Close, 33.
43. Ibid., 34.
44. Murdoch, ii, 305.
45. Ibid., ii, 311.
46. Froez in Murdoch, ii, 369.

47. Gowen, 191.
48. Murdoch, ii, 89, 90, 238; Hearn, 365; Gowen, 191.
49. Hearn, 365.
50. Murdoch, ii, 241.
51. Ibid., 243.
52. Close, 44.
53. Brinkley, ii, 219.
54. Armstrong, 35.

55. Close, 56.
56. Ibid., 57-8.
57. Aston, 218-9; Bryan, 117.
58. Murdoch, ii, 492f.
59. Ibid., ii, 288.
60. Brinkley, ii, 205.
61. Murdoch, iii, 315-30.
62. Hearn, 390.

CHAPTER XXIX

1. Hearn, 3.
2. Okakura, 10, 8.
3. Brinkley, iv, 6-7, 134; Murdoch, iii, 171.
4. Brinkley, ii, 115; iv, 172.
5. Ibid., iv, 36.
6. Chamberlain, B. H., 415.
7. Nitobe, Inazo, Bushido, the Soul of Japan, 18.
8. Brinkley, iv, 147, 217; Redesdale, 40.
9. Section 45 of Iyeyasu's "Legacy," in Hearn, 193; Murdoch, iii, 40.
10. Ibid.
11. J. H. Longford, in Murdoch, iii, 40n. Longford adds, Se non è vero è ben trovato.
12. Nitobe, 23.
13. Brinkley, iv, 56.
14. Ibid., 142, 109.
15. Hearn, 313; Gowen, 251.
16. Ibid., 364.
17. Murdoch, iii, 221; Aston, 231; Chamberlain, Things Japanese, 220-1; Hearn, 318.
18. Close, 59; Nitobe, 141.
19. Redesdale, 13, 16-7, 272; Aston, 230; Murdoch, iii, 235.
20. Nitobe, 121.
21. Murdoch, i, 188-9.
22. Brinkley, Japan, iv, 53; Hearn 328.
23. Brinkley, iv, 55, 92; Close, 58.
24. Brinkley, iv, 61.
25. Ibid., 63.
26. Hearn, 195.
27. Close, 58.
28. Hearn, 378.
29. Murdoch, iii. 336; Brinkley, iv, 67.
30. Hearn, 260, 255; Murdoch, i, 172; Brinkley, i, 238, 241; iv, 111.
31. Gowen, 97.
32. Chamberlain, 150; Redesdale, 116; Armstrong, 19.

33. Brinkley, i, 133.
34. Murdoch, i, 17.
35. Brinkley, v, 195; ii, 118.
36. Gowen, 98.
37. Brinkley, ii, 118; v, 1; Murdoch, i, 603.
38. Ibid.
39. Close, 341.
40. In Aston, 149-50.
41. History of Japan, iii, 21, in Murdoch, iii, 171.
42. Cf. Close, 369.
43. Murdoch, iii, 446-50.
44. Encyc. Brit., viii, 910.
45. Gowen, 115.
46. Sansum, W. D., M.D., Normal Diet, 76.
47. Brinkley, i, 209, 213.
48. Shonagon, Lady Sei, Sketch Book, 29.
49. Brinkley, iv, 176-81; ii, 92, 104; Hearn, 257; Holland, Clive, Things Seen in Japan, 172.
50. Brinkley, i, 139, 209-10; iv, 160, 175, 180.
51. Brinkley, iv, 176.
52. Chamberlain, 60.
53. Ibid.
54. Murdoch, i, 40.
55. Brinkley, iv, 164.
56. Ibid.
57. Ibid., i, 146; ii, 106.
58. Ibid., ii, 111-2.
59. Gatenby, E. V., Cloud Men of Yamato, 35-6.
60. Brinkley, ii, 258-66.
61. Okakura, 15.
62. Gowen, 213.
63. Ibid.
64. Okakura, 139; Brinkley, iii, 9.
65. Walsh, Clara, Master-Singers of Japan, 108.
66. Gowen, 23.
67. Binyon, 30.

68. Gatenby, 25.
69. Hearn, 85.
70. Ibid., 75, 80-1, 89; Murdoch, iii, 75.
71. Aston, 232; Hearn, 78; Redesdale, 92; Brinkley, i, 149.
72. Armstrong, 55.
73. Brinkley, i, 188.
74. Shonagon, 50.
76. Brinkley, iv, 142; Close, 62; Chamberlain, 504.
77. Ibid., 501; Keyserling, *Travel Diary*, ii, 171.
78. Close, 61.
79. Hearn, 68, 83.
80. Genesis, ii, 24; Chamberlain, 166.
81. Nitobe, 141.
82. Cf., e.g., the passage quoted· in Bryan, 88.
83. Redesdale, 37; Ficke, A. D., *Chats on Japanese Prints*, 210; Chamberlain, 525; Keyserling, *Travel Diary*, ii, 200.
84. Brinkley, iv., 116.
85. Ibid., 120.
86. Murdoch, iii, 216.
87. Brinkley, ii, 49.
88. Redesdale, 34.
89. Brinkley, v, 257.
90. By Prince Aki, 740 A.D., in Gatenby, 33.
91. Tr. by Curtis Hidden Page, in Tietjens, 144.
92. Brinkley, v, 207; Murdock, iii, 112.
93. Ibid., ii, 18-9.
94. Ibid., ii, 18; Brinkley, i, 181.
95. Ibid., i, 182.
96. Murdoch, i, 489.
97. Ibid., 603.
98. Ibid., 605; Armstrong, 171.
99. Brinkley, v, 254.
100. Murdoch, iii, 101, 113.
101. Ibid., 115-9.
102. Armstrong, 65f.
103. Ibid., 76, 78; Aston, 263-4.
104. Ekken, Kaibara, *Way of Contentment*, tr. by K. Hoshino, 7f.
105. Ibid., 90.
106. 24, 17.
107. 24.
108. 33, 39, 43.
109. 35, 44, 59, 61, 49, 54. I have ventured to print the last two lines as poetry, though the text gives them as prose.
110. Murdoch, iii, 127.
111. Armstrong, 133.
112. Ibid.
113. Murdoch, iii, 129f.
114. In Armstrong, 222.
115. Ibid., 236f, 226.
116. 263-4.
117. 261.
118. 241f.
119. 255; Murdoch, iii, 481.
120. Ibid., iii, 343-4.
121. Ibid. 474.
122. Ibid., 476f, 485; Aston, 319-32.
123. Murdoch, iii, 491-2.

CHAPTER XXX

1. Close, 28.
2. Bryan, 13-15; Aston, 56-7; Gowen, 125.
3. Carter, 35.
4. Ibid., 178.
5. Close, 77.
6. Brinkley, i, 229; iv, 136.
7. Gatenby, 27.
8. Bryan, 54, 74.
9. Aston, 263.
10. Tr. by Curtis Hidden Page, in Tietjens, 162.
11. Tietjens, 163.
12. Murdoch, i, 515,
13. Murasaki, Lady, 239.
14. Ibid., 149, 235; Shonagon, 51.
15. Murdoch, iii, 326.
16. Noguchi, Yone, *Spirit of Japanese Poetry*, 11.
17. Gatenby, 97-102; Tietjens, 159.
18. Holland, 157.
19. Murdoch, iii, 470.
20. Gowen, 128.
21. Murasaki, 33, 29.
22. Ibid., 75.
23. 98, 134.
24. 144.
25. 46.
26. 50.
27. Bryan, 65; Gowen, 128.
28. Holland, 137; Aston, 56.
29. Ibid., 346-8, 391.
30. Ibid., 269-71.
31. Ibid., 392.
32. Murdoch, i, 571.
33. Aston, 255.
34. Brinkley, v, 112.

35. Aston, 249.
36. Gowen, 268.
37. Murdoch, iii, 240.
38. Aston, 116.
39. Ibid., 114f. I have changed the order of the last five items.
40. Aston, 197-9; Bryan, 100.
41. Redesdale, 84.
42. Close, 65.
43. Okakura, 132.
44. Noguchi, 11.
45. Bryan, 136.
46. Brinkley, iv, 110.
47. Ibid., vi, 113-5.
48. Aston, 279.
49. Okakura, 112; Brinkley, viii, 29.
50. Brinkley, vii, 319.
51. *Encyc. Brit.*, vii, 960.
52. Brinkley, i, 219; iv, 156; Chamberlain, 340-3.
53. Brinkley, iv, 78.
54. Murasaki, 212.
55. Chamberlain, 84.
56. Brinkley, vii, 157.
57. Ibid., vii, 84.
58. Fenollosa, i, 56.
59. Gowen, 105.
60. Murdoch, i, 593.
61. Ledoux, L. V., *Art of Japan,* 62.
62. Armstrong, 9.
63. Brinkley, vii, 77.
64. Gowen, 124.
65. Ibid., 213.
66. Brinkley, viii, 11.
67. Ibid., 265.
68. 25.
69. 180.
70. 185.
71. 236.
72. Brinkley, vii, 339.
73. Ibid., 9.
74. Binyon, 53.
75. Ibid., 20.
76. Fenollosa, ii, 81.
77. Okakura, 113.
78. *Encyc. Brit.*, vii, 964.
79. Ledoux, 26.
80. Ibid., 28.
81. Gowen, 284.
82. Fenollosa, ii, 183. It should be added that in the opinion of some critics Matabei is a mythical personage.
83. Ficke, 282-94.
84. Gowen, 285; Ficke, 363.
85. Noguchi, 27.
86. Ficke, 363.
87. Gowen, 284.
88. Fenollosa, ii, 204.
89. Gowen, 286.
90. Dickinson, G. Lowes, 65.
91. *Ten O'Clock, sub fine.*

CHAPTER XXXI

1. Murdoch, iii, 456; Gowen, 287.
2. Ibid., 298-9.
3. 300.
4. 312.
5. Brinkley, iv, 217.
6. Ibid., 81, 256.
7. Close, 325.
8. Ibid., 165.
9. Gowen, 349.
10. Close, 149.
12. Gowen, 376.
13. Close, 372.
14. *World Almanac*, 1935, p. 667.
15. Close, 395.
16. *Almanac*, 668; Close, 391; N. Y. *Times*, April 15, 1934.
17. Gowen, 341.
18. Close, 289.
19. Eddy, 119; Park, 250; Holland, 148-52; Barnes, Jos., ed., *Empire in the East,* 70.
20. Eddy, 124f.
21. Ibid., 118, 136.
22. Hearn, 488.
23. Barnes, 69; Close, 373. The Maurette Report, of June 1, 1934, to the International Labor Office, accepts this explanation of the low wage-level in Japan.
24. Close, 344.
25. Hearn, 17.
26. Close, 134-42.
27. Chamberlain, 314; Close, 302.
28. Ibid., 198.
29. Chamberlain, 447.
30. Close, 177f.
31. Eddy, 127.
32. *Almanac*, 669.
33. Brinkley, v, 83.
34. *Almanac*, 669.
35. Tsurumi, Y., *Present-Day Japan,* 68f.
36. Walsh, 116; Bryan, 40, 194.

37. Tsurumi, 59.
38. Gowen, 416.
39. Barnes, 51.
40. Ibid., 48-50, 197.
41. Gowen, 369-70.

42. Ibid., 402.
43. Barnes, 75; Close, 377.
44. *Almanac*, 674.
45. Barnes, 62.

Index

I am indebted for this index to the careful and scholarly work of Mr. Wallace Brockway. Dates are given where obtainable, except in the case of living persons who are only incidentally mentioned in the text. The pronunciation of Oriental words is indicated by the system of diacritical marks used in the Merriam-Webster Dictionary, but here considerably simplified.* The Indian pronunciations have been supplied by Dr. A. K. Coomaraswamy; Chinese words follow for the most part the pronunciations given in Gowen and Hall's *Outline History of China*. Japanese words, and most Chinese words, have no accent. In the case of ancient Egyptian and Near Eastern words there is no agreement among the learned; and the pronunciations here offered are merely the present writer's unauthoritative suggestions. **W. D.**

---

* The diacritical marks used in this index will indicate that the letters so marked are to be sounded approximately like the italicized letters in the following words: āle, câre, ădd, ärm, sōfȧ (ȧ like ŭ in *nut*); *ch*air; ēve, ĕvĕnts, makēr; go; īce, ĭll; ᴋ like *ch* in German *Ich*; ôrb, ŏdd; fōōd; fŏŏt; oȋl, *out*; ūnite, ŭp, menü; short ŭ, when italicized, will be as in *circus*.

1001

A

Aaron (ā'ron), 12, 302*, 309

Abacus, 79

Abbeville, 90

Abdu-r Razzak (äbd-ēr-räz-zäk'), Persian traveler (1413-1475?), 457, 458

Abhidhamma (à-bĭ-dàm'-mà), 428*

Abipones, 50, 56

Abortion, in primitive societies, 49-50; in Assyria, 275; in Judea, 334; in Persia, 376; in India, 489

Abraham, 66, 173, 179, 297, 300, 311

Absalom (äb'-sa-lŭm), son of Solomon (ca. 950 B.C.), 305

Abu (à-boo'), 127

Abu Shahrein (ä'-boo shärīn') *see* Eridu

Abu Simbel (ä'-boo-sĭmbl), 1.º8, 213, 214

Abu-l Fazl (äb'-ool-fáz-l), Indian statesman and historian (ca. 1550-1600), 471, 579, 580, 591

Abusir (äb'-oo-sēr), 189

Abydos (à-bĭ'-dŏs), 152, 189, 395†

Abyssinians, 27, 46, 62

Achæans, 215, 397

Achæmenid (à-kĕm'-ĕ-nĭd) Dynasty, 352, 385

Acheulean (à-shû'-lĕ-àn) Culture, 93

Achilles, 570

Acre (ä'-kēr), 154*, 761

Adam, 310, 329

Adam's Bridge, 393, 602

Adapa (ä'-dà-pà), 128

Aden (ä'-den), 291

Admonitions of Ipuwer (ĭ'-pū-wēr), 194-195

Adonai (ä-dō-nī'), 332

Adonaïs (ă-dō-nä'-ĭs), 880

Adoni (ä-dō'-nī), 295, 297

Adonis, 120, 206

Adultery, in primitive societies, 48; in Sumeria, 130; in Egypt, 164; in Babylonia, 246, 247; in Assyria, 275, 276; in Judea, 335, 336; in India, 490; in China, 788; in Japan, 861

Advaita (äd-vĭ'-tà), 513, 549*

Ægean Sea, 104, 215, 286, 355

Æschylus, Greek dramatist (525-456 B.C.), 95

Æsop, Greek fabulist (619-564 B.C.), 175

Afghanistan (äf-găn-ĭs-tän'), 116, 355, 356, 358, 392, 441, 446, 459, 460

Africa, circumnavigation of, 293

Agade (ă'-gà-dé), 118, 121

Agamemnon, 297

Agni (àg'-nĭ), 402, 403

Agra (ä'-grà), 393, 467, 468, 473, 474, 481, 501, 580, 608, 609, 610.

Agriculture, 135, 934; in primitive societies, 8-9, 24, 33; in prehistoric cultures, 99; in Sumeria, 124, 135, 136*; in Egypt, 135, 136*, 145-146, 156-157; in Babylonia, 226; in Assyria, 274; in Persia, 357; in India, 399-400, 477-478; in China, 774; in Japan, 851

Ahab (ä'-hăb), King of Israel (ca. 875-850 B.C.), 309*, 314, 317*

Ahasuerus (à-hăz-ū-ē'-rŭs), the Wandering Jew, 349

Ahaz (ä'-hăz), King of Judah (ca. 700 B.C.), 317

Ahimsa (à-hĭm'-zà), 421, 520, 543, 628, 629

Ahmad Shah (äк'-màd shäh), Sultan of Delhi (1422-1435), 461

Ahmadnagar (äк-màd-nà'-gàr), 458

Ahmasi (äh'-mà-sī), Egyptian queen (ca. 1500 B.C.), 153

Ahmedabad (äк'-mĕd-ä-bäd'), 393, 626, 631

Ahmes (äh'-mēz), Papyrus, 180

Ahriman (äh'-rĭ-män), 351, 366, 367, 368, 369

Ahura-Mazda (ä'-hoo-rà-mäz'-dà), 60, 331, 351, 357, 361, 364, 365, 366-367, 368, 369-370, 371, 372, 373, 374, 379

Aihole (ī-hōl'), 598

Ain-i Akbari (ī-nī àk'-bàrī), 579

Ainus (ī-noōz), 831

Ajanta (à-jàn'-tä), 452, 456, 557, 589-590, 593, 597, 619, 902

Ajita Kasakambalin (à'-jĭ-tà kà-sà-kàm'-bà-lĭn), Indian sceptic, 417

Ajmer (àj'-mār), 393

Ajur-veda (a'-yoōr-vā'-dà), 530

Akahito (ä-kä-hē-tō), Japanese poet (724-756), 878

Akbar (àk'-bàr), Mogul emperor (1560-1605), 206, 222* 391, 443, 446-450, 451, 454, 465-472, 473, 477, 479, 480, 482, 483, 495, 501, 503, 579, 591, 600, 607-608, 702, 838, 842

Akbar Nama, 579

Akerblad, Johan David, Baron, Swedish Orientalist and diplomat (1760-1819), 145*

Akhetaton (äk'-à-tä'-tŏn), 210

Akkad, (äk'-äd), 118, 121, 124, 126, 127, 135, 218, 219, 249, 265, 266

Alasani-Peddana (à-là-sà-nĭ-pĕd'-dä-nà), Indian poet (fl. 1520), 458

Alau-d-din (à-lä'-oo-dēn'), Sultan of Delhi (1296-1315), 455-456, 461, 462

Alberuni (äl-bä-roō'-nī), Arabian scholar (997-1030), 462, 579

Aleutian Islands, 13, 26, 32

Alexander the Great, King of Macedon (336-323 B.C.), 104, 120, 137, 142, 215-216, 244, 263, 270, 271, 288*, 294, 341, 349, 352, 353, 362, 363, 365*, 378, 382-385, 401, 440, 441, 450, 495, 529, 532, 542, 554, 560, 571, 697
Alexandria, 137, 181, 216, 294, 341, 343, 479
Algebra, 527-528, 781
Algiers (ăl-jērz'), 94
Algonquin Indians, 43, 77
Alhambra, 606
Alighieri, Dante, Italian poet (1265-1321), 174, 178, 518, 605, 611
All Men Are Brothers, 718*
Allahabad (ăl'-lä-hä-bàd'), 614
Allat (äl-lät'), 240
Allenby, Edmund Henry, Viscount, British general (1861-   ), 154
Alphabets, 105, 106, 172, 295-296, 357
Alps, 91
Altamira, 94, 96
Amadai (ă'-mà-dī), see Medes
Amara (à-mä'-rà), 117
Amaravati (à-mà-rä'-và-tē), 593, 594, 597
Amarna (à-mär'-nà) Letters, 222, 300, 305§
Amarpal (à-mär'-päl), father of Hammurabi (ca. 2150 B.C.), 301
Amaterasu (ä-mä-tē-rä-soō), 829, 864, 875
Amber (ăm'-bär), 454, 475
Amboyna (ăm-boi'-nà), 60
Amenemhet (ä'-měn-ĕm'-hĕt) I, King of Egypt (2212-2192 B.C.), 151-152, 174
Amenemhet III, King of Egypt (2061-2013 B.C.). 152, 187
Amenhotep (ä'-měn-hō'tĕp), Egyptian sculptor (ca. 1400 B.C.), 192
Amenhotep II, King of Egypt (1447-1420 B.C.), 155
Amenhotep III, King of Egypt (1412-1376 B.C.), 141, 142, 155, 164, 185, 188, 191, 192, 205, 206, 223, 235
Amenhotep IV, King of Egypt (1380-1362 B.C.), 128, 164, 168, 178, 179, 188, 192, 205-212, 213, 223, 340, 370, 449
Ameni (ä'-mä-nē), 190
Amida (ä-mĭ-dà), 504, 738, 838, 903; see Buddha
Amitabha (ä-mē-tä-bä), 786
Ammon (city), 312
Ammon (oasis), 353
Ammonites, 285, 299
Amon (ä'-mŏn), 142, 153, 155, 167, 199, 201, 206, 210, 214
Amon-Ra (ä-mon-rä'), 206*

Amorites (ă'-môr-ītz), 123, 285, 298
Amos (ä'-mŏs), Hebrew prophet (fl. 800 B.C.), 262, 301, 315, 316-317, 319, 320, 365
Amoy (à-moi') River, 767, 806
Ampthill, Odo William Leopold Russell, Baron, British statesman (1829-1884), 532
Amraphael, see Amarpal
Amritsar (àm'-rĭt-sàr), 621
Amur (ä-moōr'), River, 831, 923‡
Amurru (à-moō'-roō), 298
An Lu-shan (än loo-shän'), Chinese rebel (fl. 755), 704, 708, 710, 714
Anacharsis, Scythian philosopher (6th century B.C.), 47
Anacreon, Greek poet (560-475 B.C.), 341
Anaita (à-nà-ē'-tà), 365, 371-372
Analects, 665
Ananda (ä'-nàn-dà), the St. John of Buddhism (ca. 500 B.C.), 398, 431, 438, 439
Ananda, 550, 606
Anatomy, in Egypt, 181-182; in India, 529; in China, 782
Anau (ăn'-ou), 108, 117*, 642, 755
Anaxagoras, Greek philosopher (500-428 B.C.), 59, 533
Anaximander, Greek philosopher (ca. 610-546 B.C.), 533
Anaximenes, Greek philosopher, (fl. 500 B.C.), 533
Ancestor worship, 63, 64; in Persia, 365; in China, 63, 784; in Japan, 63, 832
Ancyra (ăn-sī'-rà), 286†
Andaman Islands, 45, 87
Andersson, Johan, 641, 755
Andrews, Roy Chapman, 94, 641
Angelico (Giovanni da Fiesole), Fra, Italian painter (1387-1455), 903
Angkor Thom (ăng'-kor tôm), 604
Angkor Wat (wät), 90, 603-604, 605, 611
Anglo-Japanese Alliance, 929
Angola (ăn-gō'-lä), 40
Angora (ăng-gôr'-ä), 286†
Angro-Mainyus, see Ahriman
Animal worship, 61; in Egypt, 198-199; in Judea, 314; in Persia, 365; in India, 509-510; in Japan, 832
Animism, 58-59, 67
Annals of the Bamboo Books, 718
Annals of Rajasthan, Tod's, 455
Annam (ăn'-năm), 697, 757
Anquetil-Duperron, Abraham Hyacinthe, French Orientalist (1731-1805), 365* 391*, 481
Anshan (än-shän'), 352

Antigone, 31
Antiochus I Soter (an-tī'-o-kŭs sō'-tar), King of Syria and Babylonia (280-261 B.C.), 446
Antonines, 3, 364
Anu (ăn-ōō), 234
Anubis (à-nū'-bĭs), 201
Anupu (ăn-ū'-pōō) 175-176
Anuradhapura (à-nōō'-räd-hà-pōō'-rà), 506 595, 603
Aphrodite, 60, 127, 235, 372, 595
Apis (ā'-pĭs), 353
Apollo Belvedere, 280
Apollonius of Perga, Greek geometer (fl. 222-205 B.C.), 527
Apsu, 236
Aqueducts, 274
Aquinas, St. Thomas, Italian Scholastic (1225-1274), 547, 731, 734
Arabia, 109, 135, 140, 158, 228, 290, 291, 306, 400, 736
Arabian Nights' Entertainments, 578†
Arabs, 24*, 47, 139, 169, 216, 218, 298, 460, 479, 505, 527, 529, 532, 756, 780
Aralu (ä'-rä-lōō), 238, 239, 240
Aramæans, 298, 299
Aramaic alphabet, 106, 357
Aranyaka (à-ràn'-yá-kà), 407
Arapaho Indians, 73
Ararat (är'-ä-răt), 287; see Armenia
Araru (ä'-rà-rōō), 251
Araxes (à-răx'-ēz) River, 356*
Arbela (är-bē'-là), 265, 385*
Archimedes, Greek scientist (287-212 B.C.), 527
Architecture, 136; in primitive societies, 14, 87; in prehistoric cultures, 101, 102; in Sumeria, 124, 132-133; in Egypt, 136, 184-185; in Babylonia, 136, 224-225, 227, 255-256; in Assyria, 280-282; in Judea, 307-308; in Persia, 378-381; in India, 596-612; in China, 740-744; in Japan, 894-896
Argistis II, King of Armenia (ca. 708 B.C.), 287
Arhats (är'-hàts), 421, 435, 450
Ariana (ä-rē-ä'-nà), 356
Ariège, 97
Aristobulus, Greek historian (fl. 330 B.C.), 492*
Aristogiton, Athenian patriot (ca. 525 B.C.), 646
Aristotle, Greek philosopher (384-322 B.C.), 20, 107, 529, 532, 535, 536, 539, 560, 671, 731, 868
Arita (är-ē-tä), 900

Arjuna (àr'-jōō-nà), 508, 565, 566, 620
Ark of the Covenant, 69, 307, 313
Armada, Invincible, 837
Armageddon, 154
Armenia, 119, 266, 269, 270, 286, 354, 355, 363
Armies, Sumerian, 126; Assyrian, 270-271; Persian, 360; Indian, 443, 465-466; Japanese, see Samurai
Arnold, Sir Edwin, English poet and Orientalist (1832-1904), 423*, 541†
Arnold, Matthew, English poet and critic (1822-1888), 368
Arran, 356
Arrian (Flavius Arrianus), Greek historian, 441†, 442, 445*, 455*
Arsacid (är-săs'-ĭd) Dynasty, 365*
Arses (är'-sēz), King of Persia, (339-336 B.C.), 382
Arsinöe, 164
Art, 83, 936-937; in Sumeria, 132-134; in Egypt, 184-193; in Babylonia, 254-256; in Assyria, 278-281; in Persia, 377-381; in India, 584-612; in China, 724-759; in Japan, 893-913
Artabhaga (är-tà-bhä'-gà), 533
Artaxerxes I (är-tà-zērx'-ēz), King of Persia (464-423 B.C.), 380, 382
Artaxerxes II, King of Persia (404-359 B.C.), 362, 372, 373, 375*, 377, 378*, 380
Artaxerxes III Ochus, King of Persia (359-338 B.C.), 382
Arthashastra (àr-tà-shäs'-tra), 443
Arthur, semi-fabulous British prince (ca. 500), 455
Aryabhata (ä-ryà-bhá'-tà), Indian mathematician (ca. 499), 452, 526, 527, 528
Aryans, 73*, 116, 286*, 287, 356, 363, 394, 396, 397, 398, 399-400
Arya-Somaj (ä'-ryà-sō-mäj'), 616†
Asana (ä'-sà-nà), 543
Ashikaga (ä-shē-kä-gä) Shogunate, 838, 895, 905
Ashikaga Takauji (tà-kou-jē), Japanese statesman and shogun (fl. 1340), 838
Ashkanians, 285
Ashoka (à-shō'-kà), Indian religious teacher (273-232 B.C.), 391, 407, 446-450, 451, 453, 456, 484, 503, 505, 506, 571, 593, 596, 603, 833
Ashramas (ä'-shrà-màz), 522
Ashtoreth (äsh'-tô-rĕth), 235
Ashur (ä'-shōōr) (city), 119, 135, 265, 272, 278, 311
Ashur (god), 265, 268, 276, 277

Ashurbanipal (ä'-shōōr-băn'-ê-päl), King of Assyria (669-626 B.C.), 117, 237*, 243, 249, 250, 266, 268-269, 270, 272, 275, 277, 278, 279, 281-283, 311

Ashurnasirpal (ä'-shōōr-nä'-zēr-päl') II, King of Assyria (884-859 B.C.), 267, 271, 278, 279, 280

Ashurnirari (ä'-shōōr-nē-rä'-rē), King of Assyria (753-746 B.C.), 266*

Ashvaghosha (àsh-và-gō'-shà), Indian religion teacher (ca. 120), 450, 571-572, 579

Ashvamedha (àsh-và-mā'-dà), 405

Asia Minor, 227, 264, 286, 287, 299, 352, 363

Assam (ăs-săm'), 32, 45, 451, 454

Assuan (ăs-swän), 185

Assumption (El Greco), 97

Assyria, 24*, 61, 117, 123, 124, 135, 215, 223, 226, 237*, 248, 265-284, 285, 287, 288, 289, 290, 296, 299, 302, 307, 317, 318, 324, 350, 351, 352, 354, 355, 363, 380, 633, 892

Astarte (ăs-tär'-tē), 235, 294-295, 296-297, 314, 321

Astika (äs'-tĕ-kà) philosophies, 534

Aston, W. G., 885

Astrology, 79; in Babylonia, 257, 276; in Assyria, 276; in India, 518, 526; in modern times, 80*

Astronomy, origins of, 79-80; in Egypt, 180-181; in Babylonia, 256-257, 276; in Assyria, 276; in India, 526-527; in China, 644, 781-782

Astruc (ä-strük') Jean, French medical writer (1684-1766), 329*

Astyages (ăs-tī'-à-jēz), King of the Medes (ca. 560 B.C.), 351-352

Asvala (àsh'-và-là), 533

Atar, 369

Atharva-veda (à-tàr'-và vä'-dà), 402, 407, 495, 530

Atheism, in primitive societies, 56-57

Athene, 62

Athens, 1, 167, 355, 381, 395†, 640, 677

Atlantis, 107

Atman (ät'-màn), 412-413, 414, 418, 546, 548, 550, 566

Aton (ä'-tŏn), 206-210, 211, 212, 213

Atossa (à-tŏs'-sà), wife of Darius I (ca. 500 B.C.), 355

Atossa, daughter and wife of Artaxerxes II (ca. 375 B.C.), 375*

Atreya (à-trā'-yà), Indian physiologist (ca. 500 B.C.), 530, 532

Attila, King of the Huns (ca. 400-454), 452

Atys (ā-tĭs), 288

Augustine, St., Bishop of Hippo, Latin writer and Father of the Church (354-430), 475

Augustus (Caius Caesar Julius Octavianus), Roman emperor (31 B.C.-14 A.D.), 752

Aurangzeb (ō'-ràng-zāb), Mogul emperor (1658-1707), 391*, 466, 474-476, 482, 558, 589, 592, 610, 613, 615, 616, 768, 897

Aurelius Antoninus, Marcus, Roman emperor (161-180), 449

Aurignacian Culture, 93, 94, 97

Australians, 6, 7, 8, 21, 32, 43, 52, 62, 74, 84, 88-89, 103, 245

Auta (ou'-tà), Egyptian artist (about 1370 B.C.), 211

Avalokiteshvara (à'-và-lō'-kĕ-tāsh'-và-rà), 507, 595

Avidya (à-vēd'-yà), 548, 549

Ayodhya (à-yō'-dyà), 451, 567, 568, 569, 570

Ayuthia (à-yōō'-tĭ-yà), 606

Azilian Culture, 641

Aztecs, 9

B

Baal (bā'-äl), 294, 297, 309, 312, 314, 321; also see Bel

Baalzebub (bā'-äl-zē-bŭb), 312

Babar (bä'-bàr) Archipelago, 64

Babel (bā'-bl), Tower of, 225*; also see Babylon

Babur (bä'-bēr), Mogul emperor (1483-1530), 464, 465, 472, 579

Babur-nama, 579

Babylon, 1, 2, 14, 37, 104, 118, 120, 135, 215, 219, 221-222, 223, 224-225, 227, 228, 232, 235, 248, 250, 263, 266, 267, 268, 272, 283, 295, 296, 303, 306, 307, 312, 314, 318, 323, 324, 326, 327, 332, 343, 352, 354, 376, 384, 479, 633; Hanging Gardens, 218, 225; Kasr, 225; Ishtar Gate, 225; Sacred Way, 225; Temple of Marduk, 225; Tower of Babel, 224, 225

Babylonia, 61, 116, 117, 119*, 120, 123, 124, 131, 132, 135, 136, 152, 171, 176, 215, 218-264, 265, 266, 267-268, 270, 272, 274, 275, 276, 278, 283, 285, 286, 289, 291, 299, 301, 321, 322, 323, 329, 352, 354, 355, 359*, 363, 380, 393, 395, 397, 534, 640

Bacchus (băk-ŭs), 65

Bacon, Francis, Viscount St. Albans, English philosopher and statesman (1561-1626), 107, 631, 687, 780

Bactra, 108

Bactria, 355, 397†, 593

Badaoni (bà-dä'-ō-nē), Indian historian (fl. 1600), 469
Badarayana (bä-dä-rà'-yà-nà), *Vedanta* philosopher (ca. 200 B.C.), 546
Badarians, 103, 145
Baganda (bà-gän'-dà), 25
Baghdad (bǎg-dǎd' or bàg-däd'), 395*, 527, 532, 606
Bagoas (bà-gō'-às), Persian eunuch and general (executed 336 B.C.), 382
Baila (bī'-là), 38
Bakin, Kyokutei (bä-kǐn, kyō-kōō-tä), Japanese novelist (1767-1848), 885
Bakufu (bä-kōō-fōō), 837
Balawat (bä'-là-wät'), 278, 280
Balban-Gheias-ed-din (bäl'-bän-gī'-às-ěd-dēn'), Sultan of Delhi (1265-1286), 461
Bali (bä'-lē), 47
Balkh (bälk), 761
Balonda, Queen of the, 46
Balta-atrua (bäl'-trà-ä'-trōō-à), 259, 260
Baluchistan (bà-lōō'-chǐ-stän'), 355, 395†, 440, 446
Bana (bä'-nà), Indian historian (ca. 650), 749
Banerji (bǎn-ēr-jē), R. D., 394
Bangerangs, 50
Bangkok (bǎng-kǒk'), 606
Bantus (bǎn'-tōōz), 65, 67
Baroda (bà-rō'-dà), 623
Baronga, 87
Bartoli, Daniele, Italian Jesuit, traveler, and writer (1608-1685), 471
Baruch (bär'-ŭk), Hebrew minor prophet (ca. 600 B.C.), 322
Bas-relief, in Sumeria, 133; in Egypt, 189-190; in Babylonia, 254-255; in Assyria, 278-279; in Persia, 379-380; in India, 593; in China, 739
Bathsheba (bǎth-shē'-bà), 303*, 305
Bau (bou), 129
Bayon (bä'-yǒn), 604-605
Beaumarchais, Pierre Auguste Caron de, French dramatist (1732-1799), 45
Beautiful Joyous Songs, etc., 176-177
Bedouins (běd'-ōō-ǐnz), 2, 229, 291, 303, 309
Beersheba (bēr-shē'-bà), 299
Begouën, Louis, French archeologist, 97
Behistun (bā-hǐs-tōōn'), 249, 373
Bek (běk), Egyptian sculptor (ca. 1370 B.C.), 192, 211
Bel (bāl), 232, 234
Belgium, 92
Belit (bā'-lǐt), 277

Bel-Marduk (bāl-mär'-dōŏk), 235
Benares (běn-är'-ěs), 393, 428, 437, 465, 490, 521, 543, 547, 557, 582, 583, 677
Benares, University of, 530, 547
Bengal (běn-gôl'), 29, 393, 420, 451, 461, 479, 481, 509, 581, 614, 621
Bengal, Bay of, 393
Bengal Provincial Council of the National Congress, 623
Beni-Hasan (bē'-nē-hä'-sàn), 185, 190
Benjamin, son of Jacob, 336, 340
Bentham, Jeremy, English political economist (1748-1832), 616
Bentinck, Lord William Charles Cavenish, Governor General of India (1774-1839), 609*†, 614
Beppu Collection, Tokyo, 902*
Berar (bā-rär'), 576
Bergson, Henri, French philosopher (1859-), 434, 554*
Berlin, 286†, 693, 817
Berlin Museum, 181, 189
Bernier, François, French traveler and physician (1625-1688), 479, 559
Berosus (bē-rō'-sōōs), Babylonian historian (4th century B.C.), 118*, 250, 364
Besant, Annie, English theosophist (1847-1933), 616†
Bhakti-yoga (bàk'-tǐ-yō'-gà), 522, 617
Bharata (bà'-rà-tà), 561, 576
Bharhut (bär'-hōŏt), 593, 594, 597
Bhartri-hari (bàr'-trī-hä-rǐ), Indian sage (ca. 650), 517, 556, 580
Bhasa (bä'-sà), Indian dramatist (ca. 350), 572
Bhaskara (bàs'-kà-rà), Indian mathematician (fl. 1114), 528
Bhava Misra (bàv'-à mēs'-rà), Indian medical encyclopedist (ca. 1550), 530-531
Bhavabhuti (bà'-và-bōō'-tǐ), Indian dramatist (ca. 500), 576
Bhavagad-Gita (bà'-gà-vàd-gē'-tä), 488, 523, 541†, 547, 561, 564-567, 616, 631
Bhikkhus (bǐk'-kōōz), 437
Bhilsa (bēl'-sä'), 597
Bhimnagar (bēm'nà-gàr), 460
Bhishma (bēsh'-mà), 562, 564
Bhopal (bō-päl'), 597
Bhuvaneshwara (bōō'-vàn-āsh-wà-rà), 599, 610
Bible, 294, 299, 301*, 305, 320, 328, 339-349, 565
Bibliothèque Nationale, Paris, 741
Bidar (bǐ-där'). 458

Bihar (bǐ-här'), 419, 607
Bijapur (bē'-jä-pōōr), 458
Bikaner (bǐ-kà-när'), 454
Bill of Rights, 625
Bindusara (bǐn-dōō-sä'-rà), Indian king (298-273 B.C.), 446
Birbal (bēr-bäl'), Indian poet (fl. 1600), 468
Birth control, 71*
Bismarck-Schönhausen, Otto Eduard Leopold, Prince von, Prussian statesman (1815-1904), 554, 695
Bithynians, 285, 358
Bitiu (bǐ-tū'), 175-176
Black Death, 3
Black Dragon Society, 923
Black Sea, 116, 215, 226, 286, 287, 292, 766
Blake, William, English artist and poet (1757-1828), 550*
Blavatsky, Helena Petrovna, Russian mystic (1831-1891), 616†
Boaz, 336
Boccaccio, Giovanni, Italian novelist (1313-1375), 555
Bodh-gaya (bōd-gà-yä'), 427*, 431, 593, 597, 610
Bodhi tree, 402, 427†, 506
Bodhisattwas (bō-dē-sàt'-wàz), 423, 450, 504, 739, 833, 864
Boëthius, Anicius Manlius Severinus, Roman philosopher and statesman (475-525), 340
Boghaz Keui (bō-gäz' kù'-é), 286
Bokhara (bō-kä'-rà), 350
Bombay, 393, 394, 486, 597, 613, 614, 629, 662, 630, 632
Bombay Presidency, 394
Bonaparte, Napoleon, see Napoleon I
Bond Street, 395
Bondei, 50
Bongos, 85
Bonwick, J., 84
Book of Ceremonies, 646, 659, 794
Book of Changes, 650-651, 665, 732
"Book of the Covenant," 321, 328
Book of the Dead, 203-204, 371
Book of History, 643, 665, 718
"Book of the Law of Moses," 328
Book of Lieh-tze (lē'-ŭ-dzŭ), 651, 667
Book of Mencius (měn'-shǐ-ŭs), 666, 682
Book of Odes, 648-649, 659, 665, 671
Book of Rites, 664
Book of a Thousand Leaves, 878
Book of the Way and of Virtue, 653
Borneo, 8, 37, 46, 64, 99*
Borobudur (bô-rō'-bōō-dōōr'), 595, 603, 611

Borodin, Mikhail, Russian Soviet general, 812, 816
Bororos, 81
Borsippa (bōr-sǐp'-pà), 249, 255
Bose, Sir Jagadis Chandra (bōs, jà-gà-dēsh' chàn'-drà), Indian physicist and biologist (1858-   ), 618-619
Bosporus (bŏs'-pôr-ŭs), 286, 355
Bossuet, Jacques Bénigne, Bishop of Meaux, French preacher (1627-1704), 199, 340
Boston Museum of Fine Arts, 591, 606*, 750, 751
Boswell, James, Scotch biographer (1740-1795), 2*
Botany, in Assyria, 276; in India, 530
Botocudos, 38, 85
Boucher de Perthes, Jacques, French archeologist (1788-1868), 90
Boulak (bōō'-läk) Papyrus, 165
Boxer Rebellion, 731, 746, 799*, 807-808
Brahma (bràk'-mä), 403*, 408, 409*, 413*, 507, 508, 509, 511, 594, 604, 605
Brahma (poem), 415
"Brahma script," 406
Brahmachari (bràk-mà-chä'-rē), 522
Brahmacharia (bràk-mà-chä'-rē-à), 541†, 543, 627, 628
Brahmagupta (bràk-mà-gōōp'-tà), Indian astronomer (598-660), 452, 526, 527, 528
Brahman (bràk'-màn), 411, 412, 413, 414, 416, 517, 544-545, 546, 547, 548-549, 550, 551, 553, 616
Brahmanas (bràk'-mà-nàz), 405, 407
Brahmans, 28, 398, 399, 405, 419, 447, 449, 452, 480, 483-488, 490, 495, 502, 508, 509*, 510, 511, 518, 520, 522, 523, 524, 535, 552, 561, 564, 581, 582, 597, 602, 623, 624
Brahma-Somaj (bràk-mà-sō-mäj'), 615, 623
Brahma-sutra, 546
Braid, James, English surgeon and psychologist (1795-1861) 532
Brazil, 50, 73, 79, 81, 98
Breaking of the Pledge, 926
Breasted, James H., 117*, 136*, 143, 174*, 205, 218, 378†
Breuil, Abbé Henri Édouard Prosper, 92
Brewitt-Taylor, C. H., 718†
Briffault, Robert, 42*, 84, 331
Brihadaranyaka Upanishad (brǐ-hàd-ä-ràn'-yà-kà ōō-pàn'-ǐ-shàd'), 402*
Brihadratha (brǐ-hàd-rà'-tà), King of Magadha (d. 185 B.C.), 449-450
Brihaspati (brǐ-hàs'-pà-tǐ), Indian sceptic, 4:8

Brihatkatha (brĭ-hát'-kȧ-tȧ), Indian poet (1st century), 579

Brinkley, Frank, 801*, 808*

Brinton, Daniel Garrison, American ethnologist (1837-1899), 26

British Guiana, 70

British Medical College, Hong Hong, 809

British Museum, 145*, 155, 159, 161, 167, 188, 206*, 279, 747*, 749*

Bronze Age, 103-104

Brothers Karamazov, 717

Bruno, Giordano, Italian philosopher (1550-1600), 469

Buck, Pearl, 718*, 754

Buckle, Henry Thomas, English historian (1822-1862), 299

Buddha (bŏŏd'-dȧ), Indian religious teacher 563-483 B.C.), 193, 325, 398, 399, 400, 415, 416, 417, 422-439, 449, 480, 501, 503, 504-505, 506, 516, 522, 534, 535, 536, 541, 542, 546, 547, 578, 579, 589, 590, 593*, 594, 595, 603, 604, 617*, 690, 720, 830, 834, 864, 886, 887, 892, 897-898

Buddha-charita (bŏŏd-dȧ-chȧ'-rĕ-tȧ), 579

Buddhism, 419, 428-439, 447-450, 453, 454, 458, 459, 484, 503-507, 508*, 520, 534, 554, 589, 593, 596, 603, 657, 675, 676, 701-702, 719-720, 731, 733, 734-735, 739-740, 741, 746, 748, 750, 786, 818, 829, 832-833, 834, 842, 856, 859, 864-865, 866, 872, 891, 894, 911

Bundahish (bŏŏn'-dȧ-hĭsh), 365‡, 376

Burial, in Sumeria, 128; in Egypt, 148-150; in Babylonia, 240; in Persia, 372; in India, 501-502

Burma (bûr'-mȧ), 32, 45, 46, 393, 479, 506, 602, 606

Burnouf, Eugène, French Orientalist (1801-1852), 391*

Burraburiash (bŏŏ-rȧ-bŏŏ'-rĕ-äsh) II, King of Karduniash (ca. 1400 B.C.), 223*

Burslem, 759

Bushido (bŏŏ-shē-dō'), 847-848, 923

Bushmen, 6, 14, 21, 45

Byblos (bĭb'-lŏs), 106, 294, 295

Byron, George Gordon Noel, Baron, English poet (1788-1824), 269, 283

C

Cadiz, 239

Cæsar, Caius Julius, Roman general, statesman and historian (100-44 B.C.), 39, 137, 139, 181, 216, 246, 271, 305, 398, 467, 585

Cæsars, 216*

Caillé, René, French traveler (1799-1838), 43

Cairo, 138-139, 140, 145, 216, 606

Cairo Museum, 148, 152, 186, 187, 188

Cajori, Florian, 528*

Calanus (kȧ-lä'-nŭs), Indian philosopher (ca. 542-543)

Calculus, 79

Calcutta, 393, 394, 500, 613, 614, 621

Calendar, origins of, 79-80; in Sumeria, 125; in Egypt, 180-181; in Babylonia, 258; in India, 527; in China, 781

Calicut, 478, 613

California, 915, 929

California Indians, 48

Cambaluc (kȧm'-bȧ-lŏŏk), 763, 779; also *see* Peking

Cambodia, 391, 506, 507, 594, 595, 602, 603-605, 606

Cambridge Ancient History, 181*

Cambyses (kam-bī'-sēz), King of Persia 529-522 B.C.), 215, 353-354, 361

Cameroons, 56, 65

Canaan (kā-'nȧn), 285, 298, 300, 301, 302, 310

Canada, 94, 613

Canals, 358, 765

Canneh (kȧn'-nā), 291

Cannibalism, in primitive societies, 10-11; in later ages, 10

Canning, Charles John, Viscount, Governor General of India (1812-1862), 614

Canton (kȧn'-tŏn), 759, 764, 780, 803, 804, 805, 809, 811, 814

Canton Opium Party, 804

Capart, Jean, 143

Cappadocia, 285, 355

Carchemish (kär'-kĕ-mĭsh), 153, 224, 227, 287, 290, 321

Carians, 285

Caribs, 54

Carlyle, Thomas, British essayist, historian, and philosopher (1795-1881), 343, 631, 719, 906

Caroline Islands, 77

Carter, Howard, English archeologist (1873-), 143

Carthage, 1, 66, 90, 215, 293, 295, 353

Cartier, Jacques, French explorer (1494-1536), 81

Caruso, Enrico, Italian operatic tenor (1868-1921), 192

Carver, T. N., 17

Casanova de Seingalt, Giovanni Giacomo, Italian adventurer (1725-1803), 62

Caspian Sea, 286*, 350, 353, 394, 397†
Castes, origins of, 20; in Sumeria, 125; in Egypt, 159; in Assyria, 274-275; in India, 398, 484-489, 623-624; in Japan, 851
Cathay, 760
Caucasus, 119, 266, 283, 286, 355
Cave of a Thousand Buddhas, 728-729
Celestial Kingdom, 797*
Censorinus, Latin grammarian (fl. 238), 181
Censors, 798
Central America, 42, 54
Century of Love, 580
Ceramics, in primitive societies, 87; in prehistoric cultures, 101; Sumerian, 117, 133-134; Egyptian, 191; Babylonian, 227; Assyrian, 278; Indian, 585; Chinese, 754-759; Japanese, 899-901
Ceres, 60, 200
Ceylon (sē-lŏn'), 14, 21, 56, 391, 392, 393, 394, 401, 449, 450, 451, 456, 503, 506, 531*, 594, 595, 602, 603
Chaco, Gran, 50
Chaldæa (kăl-dē'-à), 179. Also see Mesopotamia, Babylonia
Châlons-sur-Marne, 72
Chalukya (chä-lōok-yà), 456, 600
Chamberlain, B. H., 924
Champollion, Jean-François, French archeologist (1790-1832), 91, 142, 144-145
Ch'an (chän) (state), 680
Chand Bardei (chànd bàr-dī'), Indian poet, 580
Chandalas (chàn-dä'-làz), 399, 452, 487
Chandi Das (chàn'-dē-däs'), Indian poet (ca. 1400), 491, 580-581, 621
Chandogya Upanishad (chän-dŏ'-gya ōo-pàn'-ĭ-shàd'), 416
Chandragupta Maurya (chàn'-drà-gōop'-tà maw'-rē-yà), King of Magadha (322-298 B.C.), 441-445, 477, 478, 481, 493, 596
Chandragupta I, King of Magadha (320-330), 451
Chang Heng (jäng hŭng), Chinese astronomer (fl. 139), 780, 781
Chang Ts'ang (jäng tsäng), Chinese mathematician (died 152 B.C.), 781
Chang Yen-yüan (jäng yăn-ü-wän'), Chinese historian of art (9th century), 747
Ch'ang-an (chäng-än), 453, 454, 698*, 701, 702, 703, 704, 707, 708, 714, 747, 779, 835
Changchun (jäng-jōon), 920†
Chanson de Roland, 455
Chao (jou) (state), 695
Chapei (jä-pā), 814

Charaka (chà'-rà-kà), Indian physician, (fl. 120), 450, 530, 531, 532
Charlemagne, see Charles I
Charles I, King of France and Emperor of the West (742-814), 151, 391*, 455
Charon, 202
Chartres, 307
Charvakas (chär'-vä-kàz), 418-419, 522, 534
Chastity, in primitive society, 45-46
Chateaubriand, François Auguste, Viscount de, Frenchman of letters (1768-1848), 754
Chatterjee, Bankim Chandra (chàt-ēr-jē', bän'-kĭm chàn'-drà), Indian novelist (1838-1894), 555
Chaucer, Geoffrey, English poet (1328-1400), 178
Chauna (chou'-nà) Buddha's charioteer, 426
Chauri Chaura (chou'-rē chou'-rà), 630
Chehil Minar (chä-hĭl mē-när'), 379-380
Chellean Culture, 93
Chelmsford, Frederick John Napier Thesiger, Viscount (1863-1933), 621
Chemistry, 529
Chemosh (kē'-mŏsh), national god of the Moabites, 312, 321
Cheng (jŭng) (duchy), 646
Ch'eng Wang (chŭng wäng), Chinese emperor (1115-1078 B.C.), 780
Cheops (kē'-ŏps) see Khufu
Chephren (kĕ'-frĕn), see Khafre
Cherokee Indians, 49
Chess, 500
Cheyenne Indians, 49
Chi (jē), Duke of (ca. 480 B.C.), 664
Ch'i (chē) (state), 645, 646, 662, 663, 680, 683, 685, 790
Ch'i, Duke of (ca. 520 B.C.), 662, 663
Chia Ch'ing (jē-äh' ching), Chinese emperor (1796-1821), 798
Chia-ling (jē-äh'-lĭng) River, 749
Chiang Kai-shek (jē-äng' kĭ-shĕk'), Chinese dictator (1888-   ), 812, 816, 818
Chibchas, 15
Chicago, 618
Chicago, University of, Iraq Expedition, 274*
Chieh Kuei (jē'-ŭ gwä), Chinese emperor (1818-1766 B.C.), 644, 680-681, 686
Ch'ien Lung (chē-än' lōong), Chinese emperor (1736-1796), 722, 736, 758, 768-769
Chikamatsu Monzayemon (chĭk-ä-mät-sōo mōn-zä-yä-mōn), Japanese dramatist (1653-1724), 891
Childe, V. Gordon, 395†

Childhood, in primitive societies, 50-51
Ch'in (chĭn) (province), 645-6, 685, 694
Ch'in (chĭn) Dynasty, 779
Ch'in, Queen of, mother of Shih Huang-ti (ca. 250 B.C.), 694
China, 13, 42, 60, 93, 94, 108, 144, 162, 191, 222*, 312*, 422, 449, 451, 453, 464, 479, 501, 504, 506, 527, 594, 595, 596, 602, 606, 622, 626, 628, 633, 639-823, 829, 833, 835, 839, 846, 853, 857, 859, 860, 861, 866, 872, 874, 875, 876, 877*, 891, 892, 903, 912, 918, 919, 920, 924, 925, 928-929, 930, 931, 932
China Medical Board, 820*
Chinese Eastern Railroad, 931
Chinese Revolution, 641, 642, 686, 810-811, 818, 819
Ching (jĭng), Five, 664-665
Ching Ti (jĭng dē), Chinese emperor (1450-1457), 757
Ch'ing (chĭng) Dynasty, 767; also see Manchu Dynasty
Ching-te-chen (jĭng-dā-jŭn'), 757, 758, 805
Chinkiang (jĭn-jē-äng'), 804
Chippewa Indians, 33
Chita (chḗ-tä'), 931
Chitaldrug (chĭt-àl-drŏŏg'), 396*
Chitor (chĭ-tōr'), 393, 455-456, 461, 475
Chitra (chĭ'-trà), 620*
Chittagong (chĭt'-à-gŏng) Hill tribes, 16
Choctaw Indians, 74
Cholas (chō-làz), 456, 490
Choshu (chō-shŏŏ), 905
Chota Nagpur (chō'-tä näg'-pŏŏr), 501
Chou (jō) (state), 645, 652, 658, 662, 680
Chou, Duke of, 646, 780
Chou Dynasty, 645, 650, 696, 721, 736, 738, 782
Chou Hsin (jō sĭn), Chinese Nero (1154-1123 B.C.), 645, 680, 681, 686
Chou Kou Tien (jō gō tē-ăn'), 90, 92
Chou-kung (jō-gŏŏng), Chinese statesman and legislator (1115-1079 B.C.), 646, 680
Chou-li (jō-lē), 646
Christ, 305, 310, 317, 318, 319, 320, 323, 325, 333†, 337, 349, 428, 429, 431, 449, 565, 590, 614, 617, 656, 657, 669, 670
Christianity, 62, 201, 202, 240, 319, 367, 368, 469, 470, 471, 504, 505, 508*, 524, 613, 615, 676, 746, 787-788, 840, 842-843, 861
Christians, Early, 242
Christian Science, 544*
Christmas, 372
Chrysostom, St. John, Greek Christian Father (347?-407), 17

Ch'u (chŏŏ) (kingdom), 678, 695
Chu Hsi (jŏŏ shē), Confucian philosopher (1130-1200), 665, 686, 731-732, 735, 748, 787, 866, 871
Ch'u Ping (chŏŏ bĭng), Chinese poet (died ca. 350 B.C.), 694
Chuang-tze (jwäng-dzŭ), Chinese philosopher (born 370 B.C.), 653*, 677, 688-692, 693, 785
Chü-fu (chü-fŏŏ), 658, 747
Chung-hwa-min-kuo (jŏŏng-whä-mĭn-gwō), China's name for China, 641
Chung-kung (jŏŏng-gŏŏng), Confucian disciple (ca. 500 B.C.), 670
Chung-kuo, or Middle Kingdom, 643-644
Chung-tu (jŏŏng-dŏŏ), 662
Cicero, Marcus Tullius, Roman orator and man of letters (106-43 B.C.), 27*
Cilicia, 355
Cilicians, 285
Cimbri, 86
Cimmerians, 267, 273, 285
Cincinnatus, Lucius Quinctius, Roman dictator (ca. 520-440 B.C.), 568
Cinderella, 175
Circumcision, 313, 331
Circus Maximus, 275
City of the Dead, 141
Civil service examinations, 800-802
Civilization, a young word, 2*; defined, 1, 5*
Clan, 21-22, 29
Classes, see caste system
Classic of Filial Piety, 861
Clay Cart, 572-574, 576
Cleopatra, Queen of Egypt (51-30 B.C.), 140, 144, 165, 216
Clive, Robert, Baron, English general and statesman (1725-1774), 481-482, 612, 613, 614
Clothing, in primitive societies, 47, 85-86
Code Napoléon, 917
"Coffin Texts," 174
Colebrooke, Henry Thomas, English Orientalist (1765-1837), 391*
Coleridge, Samuel Taylor, English poet and critic (1772-1834), 761*
Colombia, 15
Colonisation, 293
Colosseum, 479
Columbus, Christopher, Italian explorer (1451-1506), 104, 391*, 479, 803
Combarelles, 97*
Compass, 780
Complete System of Natural Astrology, 526

Concubinage, 41
Confucius (kŏn-fū-shǐ-ŭs), Chinese philosopher (551-479 B.C.), 193, 325, 422, 643, 646, 648, 649, 651, 657, 658-677, 678, 679, 680, 681, 682, 684, 686, 689, 690, 693, 694, 697, 702, 705, 718, 721, 722, 723, 731, 732, 737, 747*, 784-785, 786, 789, 793, 800, 817, 818, 820, 821, 839, 866, 867, 868-869, 870, 872, 873, 924
Congo, 10, 65, 75
Congo River, 86
Conquistadores, 9
Constantine the Great, Roman emperor (306-337), 246
Constantinople, 776*, 834
Constitution of the United States, 625
Conti, Niccolò, Italian traveler (fl. 1419-1444), 457, 481, 495
Cook, Captain James, English circumnavigator (1728-1779), 84, 86, 104
Cooking, in primitive societies, 9-10; in prehistoric cultures, 95; Babylonian, 226; Indian, 477; Chinese, 775; Japanese, 836, 856
Coomaraswamy (kōōm-à-rà-swäm'-ê), Ananda K., 625*
Copenhagen, Glyptothek at, 595
Copper, 102-103, 136
Copts, 772
Cordova, 834
Corsica, 293
Cosmetics, in primitive societies, 84-85; in Sumeria, 130; in Egypt, 168-169; in Babylonia, 248; in Judea, 303; in Persia, 356; in India, 499; in China, 770; in Japan, 854-855
Cosmos (Von Humboldt), 462
Costume, Sumerian, 119; Egyptian, 169; Babylonian, 222; in Judea, 303; Persian, 356; Indian, 498; Chinese, 770-771; Japanese, 836, 855, 922
Counting, 78-79
Coup-de-poing, 93, 95
Courts, in primitive societies, 28
Cousin, Victor, French philosopher (1792-1867), 53
Cram, Ralph Adams, 895
Creation, in Sumerian legend, 134; in Babylonian legend, 236, 237*; in the Old Testament, 329-330; in the Vedas, 409
Crespigny, C. de, 37
Cretans, 217
Crete, 97, 106, 107, 116, 141, 160, 215, 218, 254, 286-287, 293, 295, 331‡, 397, 578†
Crime, in primitive societies, 52-53

Critique of Pure Reason, 547
Croce, Benedetto, 749†
Croesus (krē'-zōōs), King of Lydia (570-546 B.C.), 289-290, 353, 354
Cro-Magnons, 92, 93, 94, 95, 96, 97
Croo, 42
Crusaders, 120
Crusades, 479, 756
Crux ansata, 199
Ctesias, Greek historian and physician (fl. 400 B.C.), 283
Culture, defined, 5*
Cultures, primitive, see under Acheulean Culture, Aurignacian Culture, etc.
Cunaxa (kū-năx'-à), 362*, 382
Curzon, George Nathaniel, Marquess Curzon of Kedleston, Viceroy of India (1859-1925), 626
Custom, 26-27
Cyaxares (sī-ăx'-à-rēz), King of the Medes (640-584 B.C.), 225, 283, 351
Cybele (sïb'-ê-lē), 60, 200, 288, 296
Cyprus, 245, 292, 293, 295
Cyril, St., Archbishop of Alexandria (376?-444), 216
Cyropædia, 352
Cyrus the Great, King of the Medes and the Persians (555-529 B.C.), 120, 182, 227, 263, 287, 290, 325*, 326, 327, 352-353, 357, 359, 378, 380, 381
Cyrus the Younger, Persian prince (424?-401 B.C.), 362*
Czechoslovakia, 94, 97

D

Đaevas, 367
Daibutsu (dī-bōō-tsōō), 840, 897-898
Daigo (dī-gō), Emperor of Japan (898-930), 835, 878
Daimyo (dī-myō), 846, 850, 886, 893
Dairen (dī-rĕn'), 920†
Dalai Lama (dä-lī lä-mä), 507
Damaras, 38, 79
Damascus, 267, 296, 303, 317, 337, 756, 896
"Damascus" steel, 529
Damayanti (dà-mà-yàn-tē'), 491, 564
Dan, 299
Dananu (dä'-nä-nōō), Elamite general (ca. 650 B.C.), 269
Dance, origins of, 88; in Egypt, 166; in India, 586-587; in China, 721, 723; in Japan, 893
Danes, 10
Daniel, 223, 263, 340, 346, 351

Daniyal (dàn'-ĕ-yál), son of Akbar (ca. 1600), 495
Dante, *see* Alighieri
Danube River, 355
Daric, 358*
Darius (dà-rī'-ŭs) I Hystaspes, King of Persia (521-485 B.C.), 31, 249, 291, 327, 354-355, 356, 358, 359-360, 362, 364, 365, 371, 373, 375, 378-379, 381
Darius II Ochus, King of Persia (423-404 B.C.), 382
Darius III Codomannus, King of Persia (338-330 B.C.), 363, 382-385
Darmesteter, James, French critic (1849-1894), 367*
Darwin, Charles Robert, English naturalist (1809-1882), 17, 84, 86, 95, 617, 657, 691
Dasa-ratha (dà-shà-rà'-tà), 567, 568, 570
Daulatabad (dou-là-tä'-bäd), 461
David, King of the Jews (1010-974 B.C.), 241, 259, 304-305, 306, 310, 312, 332, 339, 340, 374, 581
Davids, T. W. Rhys, English Orientalist (1843-1922), 391*, 428*
Dawn Man, *see* Piltdown Man
Dawson, Charles, 92
Dawson, Christopher, 222*
De Intellectus Emendatione, 867*
Deborah (dĕb'ô-rà), Hebrew prophetess (13th century B.C.), 333, 340
Deccan (dĕk'-kän), 394, 396, 456, 473, 475, 555, 581
Decimal system, 180, 527, 781
Declaration of Independence, 625
Declaration of the Rights of Man, 625
Degas, Edgar, French painter (1834-1917), 912
Deioces (dī'-ō-sēz), King of the Medes (fl. 709 B.C.), 340
Delaware Indians, 22
Delft, 900
Delhi (dĕl'ĭ), 2, 393, 394, 460-461, 463, 464, 465, 468, 469, 478, 484, 591, 592, 607, 608, 610
Delhi Sultanate, 460-464
Delilah (dĕ-lī'-là), 340
Delphic oracle, 77
Delta of the Nile, 137-138, 287
Demeter, 60, 127, 200, 235, 238, 595
Democritus, Greek philosopher (400?-357? B.C.), 529, 536, 552
De Morgan, Jacques, French archeologist 1857-1924), 94, 117*, 122
Denderah (dĕn'-dēr-ä), 185

Dengyo Daishi (dĕn-gyō dī-shē), Japanese painter (10th century), 903
Denmark, 98
Der-el-Bahri (dàr-ĕl-bä'-rē), 154, 185, 188, 189
Description de l'Égypte, 144
Desmoulins, Camille, French revolutionary (1762-1794), 24
Detroit Museum of Fine Arts, 591
Deuteronomy, 321-329
Devadasis (dā-và-dä'-sēz), 490-491, 496, 586
Devadatta (dā-và-dàt'-tà), 436
Dewey, John, 535, 821
Dhanamjaya (dà'-nàm-jà-yà'), Indian dramatic theorist (ca. 1000), 574*
Dhanwantari (dàn-wàn-tà-rē'), Indian physician (ca. 525 B.C.), 530, 532
Dharana (dàr'-à-nà), 544
Dharma (dàr'-mà), 484, 487, 488
Dharma-shastras (dàr'-mà-shäs'-tràz), 483-484
Dhrita-rashtra (drĭ'-tà-räsh'-trà), 562, 570
Dhyana (dyä'-nà), 544
Dialogue of a Misanthrope, 195-196
"Diamond Sutra," 729
Dickens, Charles, English novelist (1812-1870), 885
Dicta, Mt., 391‡
Diderot, Denis, French encyclopedist (1713-1784), 639
Dingiraddamu (dĭn-gĕ-räd'-dà-noō), Sumerian poet (ca. 2800 B.C.), 121
Din Ilahi (dĭn ĭ-lä'-hĭ), 470-471
Dinkard, 365
Dinkas, 60, 86
Diodorus Siculus, Greek historian (1st century B.C.), 69, 139*, 147, 158, 159*, 165, 166, 183, 224*, 267, 269, 283*, 331‡, 384*
Diogenes, Greek cynic philosopher (ca. 413-323 B.C.), 542
Diomedes, 16
Dionysus, 331‡, 403
Diophantus, Greek mathematician (fl. 360), 528*
Discourse on the Progress of the Sciences and Arts, 693*
Discourses and Dialogues, 665
Dishonesty, in primitive societies, 52
Divorce, in primitive societies, 49; in Sumeria, 130; in Egypt, 166; in Babylonia, 247; in Judea, 336; in India, 494; in China, 792; in Japan, 924
Doctrine of the Mean, 666, 672
Dog Island, 104
"Dogs of Fo," 759

Domestication of animals, 135; in primitive
societies, 8; in prehistoric cultures, 99-100;
in Sumeria, 125, 135; in Egypt, 135; in
China, 774
Dominicans, 788*
Dordogne, 92
Dorians, 215, 397
"Double standard," origins of, 34-35
Doukhobors, 498
Dowager Empress, *see* T'zu Hsi
Drama, in India, 571-577; in China, 721-723;
in Japan, 889-891
Draupadi (drou'-pà-dē), 401, 561, 570
Dravidians, 61-62, 396, 397, 398, 406, 479,
485*, 593, 600
Dream of the Red Chamber, 718
Dreams, 57-58
Druids, 60
Dryden, John, English poet and dramatist
(1631-1700), 391*
Dubois, Jean Antoine, French missionary
(1765-1848), 199*, 480, 484*, 486*, 491,
496, 499, 515*, 521*, 522*, 545*, 615
Duel, in primitive societies, 28
Dumas, Alexandre, *père*, French novelist
(1803-1870), 885
Dungi (dōōn'-gē), King of Ur (ca. 2400
B.C.), 123, 127, 135
Duodecimal system, 79
Durga (dōōr-gä'), 509; also *see* Kali
Durga-Puja (dōōr-gä'-pōō-jä'), 501
Durkheim, Emile, 62*
Dur-Sharrukin (dōōr-shär'-rōōk-ĭn), *see*
Khorsabad
Duryodhan, *i.e.*, Duryodhana (dōōr-yō'-dà-
nà), 562
Dushyanti (dōōsh'-yàn-tē), 575, 576
Düsseldorf, 94
Dutch, 603, 613, 804
Dutch East India Company, 857*
Dutt, Narendranath (dŭt, nä-rĕn'-drà-nàt),
see Vivekananda
Dyaks (dĭ'-ăkz), 15, 22, 53, 54, 64
Dyananda, Sarasvaty (dä-yä'-nàn-dà, sà-
ràs'-và-té), Indian reformer (1824-1883),
616†
Dyaus pitar (dyous pĭ-tär'), 60, 401

E

Ea (ē'-à), 128, 237, 238
Eannatum (ē-ăn'-nà-tōōm), King of Lagash
(ca. 2800 B.C.), 133
Earth worship, 60-61
East India Company, 479, 613-614

Easter, 79
Easter Island, 77, 78, 107
Eastern Archipelago, 77, 78, 87
Eastern Han Dynasty, 698*
Ebers Papyrus, 182, 183
Ecbatana (ĕk-băt'-à-nà), 227, 350, 352, 362,
379, 442
Ecclesiastes, 259, 261. 262*, 329, 345, 346-
349, 523
École de l'extrème Orient, 604
Eden, 61, 219
Edifying Story Book, 884
Edmunds, J. A., 504†
Edomites, 285, 298, 299
Education in primitive societies, 74-75; in
Sumeria, 129; in Egypt, 170-171; in Persia,
376; in India, 485, 556-560; in China, 661-
662, 799-800, 819-820; in Japan, 877, 926
Egypt, 24*, 47, 61, 68, 94, 97, 103, 104, 105,
106, 107, 108, 109, 116, 117, 119, 125, 133,
135, 136, 137-217, 218, 222, 223-224, 226,
227, 228, 247, 248, 254, 263, 265, 266, 267,
268, 270, 285, 288, 289, 293, 295, 296, 298,
300, 301, 306, 307, 310, 313, 318, 321, 324,
329, 331‡, 353, 354, 362, 363, 370, 379, 384,
393, 395, 400, 449, 479, 532, 578†, 633, 641,
728, 755†, 892
Egypt and Israel, 300*
"Eight Immortals of the Wine Cup," 708
Eighteenth Dynasty, 152, 160, 170
Eightfold Way, 430, 447
Ekken, Kaibara (kī-bä-rà ĕk-kĕn), Japanese
philosopher (1630-1714), 861, 868-870, 871
Ekron (ĕk-rôn), 312
El (ĕl), 294, 297
Elam (ē-lăm), 102, 105, 106, 108, 117, 121,
123, 126, 133, 219, 252, 265, 268, 270, 362
Elamites, 117, 123
Elegy Written in a Country Churchyard,
223
Elephanta (ĕ-lĕ-făn'-tà), 594, 599
Elephantine (ĕl-ê-făn-tī'né), 185
Eleventh Dynasty (Egypt), 183
Elihu (é-lī'-ū), 345
Elijah (é-lī'-jä), the Tishbite, Hebrew
prophet translated to heaven (ca. 895
B.C.), 313, 314, 315
Eliot, Sir Charles, 428*, 434*, 544†, 561, 615
Elisha (é-lī'-shà), Hebrew prophet (ca. 890-
840 B.C.), 312*, 314
Elizabeth, Queen of England (1558-1603),
469, 838
Elliotson, John, English physician (1791-
1868), 532

Elohim (ĕ-lō'-hĭm), 297, 329
Elphinstone, Mountstuart, British Colonial administrator (1779-1859), 474, 481, 614
Elura (ĕ-lōō'-rä), 598, 601
Elysian Fields, 202
Emerson, Ralph Waldo, American philosopher and poet (1803-1882), 352, 415, 631
Eminent Painters of All Ages, 747
Empedocles, Greek philosopher (fl. 500 B.C.), 533
Empire (Egypt), 151*, 154, 169, 170, 190, 191
Encyclopedia Britannica (14th edition), 703†
Engi (ĕn-gē) Period (in Japan), 835
Engidu (ĕn'-gĭ-dōō), 251-254
Engineering, in Sumeria, 124, 133; in Egypt, 159-160; in Babylonia, 224†, 225, 226; in Assyria, 274; in Persia, 358; in India, 478, 601; in China, 695, 696, 774, 778
England, 3, 24*, 247, 292, 293, 323, 393, 409, 554, 576, 606, 612, 613, 629, 804, 808, 810, 815*, 817, 830, 890, 891, 918, 928, 932
English (language), 406, 622
English (race), 500
Enlil (ĕn'-lĭl), 127
Enlil-nadin-apli (ĕn'-lĭl-nä-dēn'-ä-plē), King of Babylonia (1122-1116 B.C.), 223*
Enoch (ē'-nŭk), 313, 346
Enquiries into Religion and Culture, 222*
Entemenu (ĕn-tĕ-mĕ'-mōō), 134*
Eoanthropus, see Piltdown Man
Ephraim (ē'-frä-ĭm) (kingdom), 315, 317, 329
Epicureanism, 195
Epicurus, Greek philosopher (340-270 B.C.), 56, 421
Erech (ē'-rĕk), *see* Uruk
Ereshkigal (ĕ-rĕsh'-kĕ-gäl), 238
Eridu (ĕr'-ĭ-dōō), 118, 119, 128, 133
Esarhaddon (ē-sär-hăd'-dŏn), King of Assyria (681-699 B.C.), 268, 278, 281
Eschatology, Sumerian, 128-129; Egyptian, 148, 149, 150, 202-204; Babylonian, 240; Persian, 370-371; Indian, 413-414, 514-517; Chinese, 784, 785; Japanese, 864
Escorial, 604
Esdaile, James, British psychologist (1808-1859), 532
Eskimos, 6, 13, 17, 22, 32, 52, 53, 54, 57, 88
Essai sur le Pali, 391*
Essays, Chinese, 719-721; Japanese, 887-889
Esther, 303*, 333, 340
Eta (ē-tà), 851, 926

Ethiopia, 269, 318
Ethiopians, 24*, 146, 215
Euclid, Greek geometer (fl. 300 B.C.), 240
Euler, Leonard, Swiss mathematician (1707-1783), 528
Euphrates River, 118, 119, 123, 124, 136, 154-160, 218, 219*, 221, 226, 227, 228, 268, 299, 358, 394
Euripides, Greek dramatist (480-406 B.C.), 341*, 577
Eve, 330
Everyman, 889
Exodus, the, 214, 301*, 302
Exogamy, 41-42
Ezekiel (ē-zē'-kyĕl), (ca. 580 B.C.), 312, 324-325
Ezra (ĕz'-rà), Hebrew scribe and reformer (fl. 444 B.C.), 328, 329

F

Fables, Egyptian, 175; Babylonian, 250; Indian, 578
Fa-Hien (fä-hē'-àn), Chinese traveler (fl. 399-414), 451-452, 589
Fakir (fà-kēr'), 545*
Family, 29-35; in Sumeria, 130; in Egypt, 164-166; in Babylonia, 247; in Assyria, 275; in Judea, 303, 333-334, 335-337; in Persia, 374, 375; in India, 492; in China, 789, 791, 792, 793, 794, 819; in Japan, 860-861
Fardapur (fär-dà-pōōr'), 589*
Farghana (fär-gä'-nà), 464
Fars (färz), 356, 372
Farsistan (fär-sĭs-tän'), *see* Fars
Father, the, in primitive societies, 30-32, 34
Fathpur-Sikri (fàt-pōōr-sĭk'-rē), 467, 468, 471, 481, 607-608, 610
Faure, Élie, 217
Faust (Goethe), 574
Fayum (fä-yōōm'), 94, 159
Fellatah (fĕl'-à-tà), 85
Feng Tao (fŭng dou), Chinese statesman and patron of printing (ca. 932), 729, 730
Fenollosa, Ernest, 751, 831, 853*
Fergusson, James, Scotch architect and historian of architecture (1808-1886), 504†, 597, 598-599, 600, 601, 741
Fête des fous, 66
Fetishism, 67
Fichte, Johann Gottlieb, German philosopher (1762-1810), 554
Fiction, Egyptian, 175; Hebrew, 340; Indian, 579-580; Chinese, 717-718; Japanese, 881-885, 926

Fielding, Henry, English novelist (1707-1754), 891
Fifth Dynasty (Egypt), 161, 189
Fiji, 34, 35, 77
Fijians, 10, 27, 60
Finance, in Sumeria, 125, 126; in Egypt, 160-161; in Babylonia, 228-229; in Assyria, 274; in Lydia, 289; in Phoenicia, 295; in Persia, 358; in India, 395, 400-401, 480; in China, 779-780; in Japan, 934
Fines, in primitive societies, 27-28; in Babylonia, 230-232; in India, 487
Finland, 103
Fire, in primitive societies, 10, 11-12; in prehistoric cultures, 95-96
Firishta, Muhammad Qasim (fé-rēsh'-tà, moo-häm'-màt kä'-zĭm), Moslem historian (ca. 1610), 467, 579
Firoz Shah (fé-rōz' shä), Sultan of Delhi (1351-1388), 458, 461, 483
Fishing, in primitive societies, 6-7; in Egypt, 156; in Babylonia, 226-227; in China, 647
FitzGerald, Edward, English poet (1809-1883), 883
Five Ching (jĭng), 664-665
"Five Rulers," 643-644
Flood, 330; in Sumerian legend, 119-120, 134; in the Bible, 330
Florence, 1, 3, 738
"Flower District," Tokyo, 862
Flowers, see gardens
Font de Gaume, 97*
Foochow (foo-chou), 805, 929
Food, in primitive societies, 5-11; in Sumeria, 128; in Egypt, 156; in Babylonia, 226-227; in Assyria, 274*; in Judea, 330; in Persia, 357; in India, 497; in China, 774-775; in Japan, 855-856
"Forbidden City," 742
Formosa (fôr-mō'-sà), 804, 806, 918, 927*
Fort Sargon, see Khorsabad
Fouché, Joseph, Duke of Otranto, French statesman (1763-1820), 151
Four Shu (shoo), 665-666
Fourth Dynasty (Egypt), 135, 140, 147, 173, 181
France, 19*, 24, 92, 93, 94, 96, 97, 98, 99*, 613, 695, 805, 806, 808, 813, 890, 891, 917*, 918, 920, 928, 932
France, Anatole (Jacques Thibault) French author (1844-1924), 47, 497
Francis of Assisi, St., Italian mystic (1182-1230), 628
Franciscans, 788*

Frankfort, Henri, 395*
Franklin, Benjamin, American author and statesman (1706-1790), 12, 83
Frazer, Sir James George, 96, 330*
Frederick II the Great, King of Prussia (1712-1786), 219, 693
Freer Art Gallery, Washington, D. C., 747*, 750*
French Academy, 144, 581
French Revolution, 24
Freud, Sigmund, 62*, 88
Freya, 60
Fruit-Gathering, 620*
Fu Hsi (foo-shē), Chinese semi-mythical emperor (2852-2737 B.C.), 643, 650, 723
Fu Hsüan (foo shwän), Chinese poet, 793, 794
Fuegians, 10, 18, 21, 53, 86
Fuji-san (foo-jē-sän), 830‡ see Fuji-yama
Fujiwara (foo-jē-wä-rà) family, 835, 882, 887
Fujiwara Seigwa (sīg-wä), Japanese philosopher (1560-1619), 866, 871
Fujiwara Takanobu (tä-kä-nō-boo), Japanese painter (1146-1205), 904
Fuji-yama (foo-jē-yä-mä), 830, 909, 910, 912
Fukien (foo-jē-än'), 748, 929
Furniture, in Sumeria, 133; in Egypt, 184, 191; in Babylonia, 254; in Assyria, 278; in Persia, 378; in China, 736; in Japan, 859
Futuna, 37, 53

G

Gae (gā), Duke of Lu (loo) (fl. 480 B.C.), 660, 663-664
Gæa (gē'-à), 58
Gadarene swine, 80
Galilee, Sea of, 92, 300
Gallas, 62, 86
Galton, Sir Francis, English scientist (1822-1911), 38
Gama, Vasco da, Portuguese navigator 1469-1524), 293, 391*, 613
Games, in Egypt, 168; in Persia, 359; in India, 400, 444, 500-501
Gan Ying (gän yĭng), Chinese statesman (ca. 500 B.C.), 662
Gandhara (gän-dä'-rà), 392, 593-594, 739
Gandhari (gän'-dä-rē), 562, 570
Gandhi, Mohandas Karamchand (gän'-de, mō'-hàn-däs kä-ràm-chänd'), Indian reformer (1869-   ), 391, 415, 421-422, 489*, 517, 519, 565, 581, 618, 624, 626-632

Ganesha (gà-nä′-shà), 509, 511
Ganges (găn′-jēz) River, 393, 397, 436, 453, 464, 501, 502, 521, 603
Garbe, Richard, 536
Gardener, The, 620*
Gardens, in Egypt, 184; in Babylonia, 225; in Persia, 378; in India, 481; in China, 641; in Japan, 857-858, 859
Gardner Collection, Boston, 739
Gargi (gär′-gĭ), 401, 410, 533
Garrison, F. H., 531, 532
Garstang, John, 300, 302*
Gasur (gä-sōōr′), 258*
"Gates of Paradise," 738
Gaudapada (gou′-dà-pä-dà), Indian religious commentator (ca. 780), 546
Gaugamela (gou-gà-mē′-là), 385
Gauls, 60, 152
Gautama (gou′-tà-mà), *see* Buddha
Gautama (clan), 422
Gautier, Théophile, French critic and man of letters (1810-1872), 85, 96, 192
Gaza (gä′-zà), 154, 160
Gebel-el-Arak (gä′-bĕl-ĕl-à-räk′), 136, 146
Gedrosia (gĕ-drō′-zĕ-à), 440
Geisha (gä-shà), 490, 862
Genesis, 219*, 300*, 301, 328, 329, 339-340
Geneva, 323
Genghis Khan (jĕn′-gĭz kän′), Tartar conqueror (1164-1227), 463, 464, 465, 763
Genji (gĕn-jē), *Tale of,* 862, 881-884, 891, 893
Genoa, 479, 760, 761
Genroku (gĕn-rō-kōō) Period (in Japan), 843, 881
Geography, in Babylonia, 258*; in China, 781
Geometry, in Egypt, 179; in Babylonia, 256; in India, 528; in China, 781
Georg, Eugen, 85
George III, King of Great Britain (1760-1820), 769
George IV, King of Great Britain (1820-1830), 609*
Gerar (jĕ-rär′), 104
Germans, 58
Germany, 24, 92, 397, 806, 808, 809, 813, 917, 918, 920, 928
Ghazni (gŭz′-nĕ), 460
Ghiberti, Lorenzo, Italian sculptor (1378-1455), 738
Ghiyosu-d-din (gĕ-yō′-sōōd-dēn′), Sultan of Delhi (murdered 1501), 483*
Ghost worship, 63

Ghuri (gōō′-rē), 460-461
Gibbon, Edward, English historian (1737-1794), 292*, 578, 719
Gibraltar, 293, 358
Gideon, Judge of Israel (died ca. 1236 B.C.), 302
Gil Blas, 718
Gileah (gĭl′-é-à), 304
Giles, H. A., English Sinologist (1846-1935), 640*, 653*
Gilgamesh (gĭl′-gà-mĕsh), 120, 235, 250-254, 261
Gilgamesh, epic of, 120, 132, 250-254, 261
Giotto (nickname of Angiolotto di Bondone), Italian painter (1276-1336), 589, 611
Gippsland, 85
Gita-Govinda (gē′-tä-gō′-vĭn-dà), 580, 591
Gitanjali (gĕ-tän′-jà-lĕ), 620*
Gizeh (gē′-zĕ), 140, 147
Gnosticism, 553
Go Daigo (gō dī-gō), Emperor of Japan (1318-1339), 838
Goa (gō′-à), 393, 469, 524
Gobi (gō′-bĕ) Desert, 641, 761
God the Father, 64
Gods, multiplicity of, 59-64
Goethe, Johann Wolfgang von, German poet (1749-1832), 141, 391*, 574, 577, 611, 669, 693, 868
Gold Coast, 43, 83, 925
Golden Calf, 309, 311
Golden Rule, 564, 670
Goliath (gō-lī′-äth), 305
Golkonda (gŏl-kŏn′-dà), 458
Gomorrah (gō-mä′-rà), 311, 335
Good Hope, Cape of, 293, 919
"Good Mind," 367
"Gordian knot," 288*
Gordios, 288
Gorki, Maxim (pen name of Aleksei Maximovich Pyeshkov), Russian novelist (1868-), 310
Gothic architecture, 599
Goto Saijiro (gō-tō sī-jē-rō), Japanese potter (ca. 1664), 900-901
Göttingen, 249
Government, origins of, 21-23, 69; in Sumeria, 126-127; in Egypt, 161-164; in Babylonia, 230; in Assyria, 270-274; in Judea, 306; in Persia, 359-364; in India, 443-445, 465-466; in China, 672-674, 684, 689, 695-697, 698-699, 700-701, 724-726, 795-802, 817; in Japan, 842, 846, 917-918, 935

Governor General of India, 487
Govinda (gō'-vĭn-dà), Indian religious commentator (ca. 800), 546
Gracchi, 19*
Grammar, 250, 556, 578
Granada, 606
Grand Canal (Tientsin-Hangchow), 765, 778
Granet, Marcel, 699*
Granicus (grå-nĭ'-cŭs), battle of the (334 B.C.), 373*, 383
Gray, Thomas, English poet (1716-1771), 223
Great Britain, 1, 391
Great Learning, 665, 667-668, 732, 866
Great Learning for Women, 869-870
Great Mother, 60, 288
Great Reform (in Japan), 833, 885
Great Spirit, 54
Great Wall, 695, 697, 701, 760, 761, 767, 778
Greater Vehicle, see Mahayana Buddhism
Greco, El (Domenico Theotocopuli), Greek painter (1548-1625), 97, 903
Greco-Buddhist art, 593-594
Greece, 24*, 33, 61, 116, 117, 136, 137, 140, 141, 144, 152, 172, 185, 190, 197, 200, 215, 218, 226, 227, 264, 265, 288, 290, 293, 295, 299, 312, 329, 340, 349, 355, 362, 376, 379, 380, 383, 391*, 394, 400, 422, 449, 480, 532, 571, 647, 651, 739, 777, 892, 899
Greed, in primitive societies, 51-52
Greek (language), 406
Greeks, 47, 58, 60, 63, 64, 70, 85, 97, 106, 118*, 128, 159, 166, 179, 183, 193, 217, 218, 225, 240, 245*, 248, 256, 263, 269, 276, 279, 280, 287, 288, 293, 295, 358, 364, 365*, 366, 373, 380, 383, 384, 441, 450, 526, 527, 554, 561, 574
Greenland, 54, 85, 93
Gregorian calendar, 181
Gregory XIII (Ugo Buoncompagni), Pope (1572-1585), 181
Gresham's law, 759
Grihastha (grĭ-hàs'-tà), 522
Grimm's Law, 406*
Grotefend, Georg Friedrich, German scholar (1775-1853), 249
Guaranis, 79
Guayaquil Indians, 66
Guaycurus, 50
Gubarrru (gōō-bär'-rōō), Babylonian hero, 262
Gudea (gōō-dā'-ä), King of Lagash (ca. 2600 B.C.), 122, 128, 131, 134, 291

Guilds, in Assyria, 274; in Syria, 296; in Persia, 377; in China, 777, 816; in Japan, 854
Gujarat (gōō'-jà-ràt'), 478-479
Gumplowicz, Ludwik, Polish sociologist (1838-1909), 23-24
Gunadhya (gōō-nä'-dyà), Indian poet (1st century), 579
Gunavarman (gōō-nà-vàr'-màn), Indian scientist, 452
Gupta (gōōp'-tà) Dynasty, 450, 451, 452, 454, 481, 484, 487, 529, 575
Guru (gōō'-rōō), 522, 557, 660
Gutenberg, Johann, German "inventor" of printing (1400?-1468), 730
Gwalior (gwä'-lyàr), 393, 599
Gyges (gī'-gēz), King of Lydia (ca. 652 B.C.), 289

H

Habiru (hä-bē'-rōō), 300; also see Jews
Hachimaro (hä-chē-mä'-rō), youthful Japanese hero (ca 1615), 849
Hadrian (Hadrianus Publius Ælius), Roman emperor (117-138), 364
Haifa (hī'-fà), 300
Hakai (hä-kī), 926
Hakuga (hä-kōō-gä), 794*
Hakuseki Arai (hä-kōō-zä-kē ä-rī), Japanese scholar and historian (1657-1725), 865, 886-887
Halebid (hä'-lä-bēd), 601
Halle, University of, 693
Hallstatt, 104
Halo, 59
Halys (hăl-ĭs) River, 286†
Hamadan (hä-mä-dän'), 350*
Hammer of Folly, 551
Hammurabi (hä-mōōr-ä'-bē), King of Babylonia (2123-2081 B.C.), 27, 28, 104, 120, 127, 219, 220, 221, 227, 228, 230, 232, 233, 246, 258, 270, 291, 301
Hammurabi, Code of, 27, 28, 127, 135, 219-221, 230-232, 246-247, 264, 272, 286, 331‡, 338, 377
Han (hän) (state), 695
Han Dynasty, 675, 698, 702, 728, 738, 739, 746, 755, 781, 786, 800
Han Fei (hän fä), Chinese critic and essayist (died 233 B.C.), 653*, 679
Han Kan (hän kän), Chinese artist (ca. 730), 753
Han Yü (hän yü), Chinese essayist (768-824), 719-721, 723, 747-748

Hananiah (hăn-à-nī′-à), Hebrew prophet ca. 600 B.C.), 323

Hangchow (hăng-chou′), 727, 761-762, 763, 765, 778, 815

Hanging Gardens, see Babylon

Hankampu (hän-käm-pōō), 886

Hanuman (hà′-nōō-màn), 402

Hanway, Jonas, English traveler (1712-1786), 857*

Hao Shih-chiu (hou shĭ-jē-ōō′), Chinese ceramic artist (ca. 1600), 757

Haoma (hŏ′-mà), 364

Hapuseneb (hä-pōō′-sĕ-nĕb), Egyptian architect (ca. 1500 B.C.), 192

Hara-kiri (hä-rä-kē-rē), 53, 502, 848-849

Harappa (hà-ràp′-pä), 394

Hardie, James Keir, Scotch labor leader (1856-1915), 499

Harem, in Egypt, 164†; in Babylonia, 225; in Assyria, 275; in Judea, 300; in Persia, 374, 375; in India, 467, 472, 494; in China, 792

Har-Megiddo (här-mĕ-gĭd′-dō), 154, 321

Harmhab (härm′-häb), King of Egypt (1346-1322 B.C.), 213

Harmodius, Athenian patriot (ca. 525 B.C.), 646

Haroun-al-Rashid (hä-rōōn-är-rà-shēd), Caliph of Bagdhad (786-809), 467, 532

Harpagus (här′-pa-gŭs), Median general (ca. 555 B.C.), 352

Harri (hä′-rē), 286*

Harris Papyrus, 177

Harsha-charita (här′-sha-chàr′-ĭ-tà), 579

Harsha-Vardhana (hàr′-shà-vàr′-dà-nà), Indian king (606-648), 452-453, 454, 503, 576

Hart, Sir Robert, Irish statesman in China 1835-1911), 802*

Harunobu Suzuki (hä-rōō-nŏ-bōō sōō-zōō-kē), Japanese engraver (1718-1770), 907, 908

Harvard Library Expedition, 317*

Harvest festivals, 65-66

Harvey, William, English anatomist (1578-1657), 182, 531

Hassan (häs-sän′), mosque of, Cairo, 607

Hastings, Warren, Governor General of India (1732-1818), 609*, 613, 614

Hathor (hăth′-ôr), 185, 198 199

Hatshepsut (hà-chĕp′-sŭt), Queen of Egypt (1501-1479 B.C.), 140, 141, 143, 153-154, 165, 185, 188, 189-190, 300, 302*

Havell, E. B., 415, 452

Hawaii, 37, 38, 809

Hayashi Razan (hä-yà-shē rä-zän), Japanese essayist (1583-1657), 866-867, 871, 877

Hearn, Lafcadio, Irish author and educator (1850-1904), 831, 840, 844, 845, 921, 923†

Hebrew language, 73

Hebrews, 300; see Jews

Hedin, Sven Anders, 506

Hegel, Georg Wilhelm Friedrich, German philosopher (1770-1831), 410

Heian (hā′yăn) Epoch (in Japan), 834, 855

Heidelberg, 92

Heine, Heinrich, German poet (1799-1856), 339, 516*

Helen of Troy, 570

Heliopolis, 152, 162, 203*

Hellespont, 286, 358, 383

Henotheism, 312

Henry IV, 889

Henry VII's Chapel, Westminster Abbey, 599

Henry VIII, King of England (1509-1547), 457

Hepat (hā-pät′), 286†

Heraclitus, Greek philosopher (576-480 B.C.), 434, 533, 622

Herat (hĕr-ät′), 227

Hercules, 294

Herder, Johann Gottfried von, German philosopher and man of letters (1744-1803), 391*

Herding, in primitive societies, 8, 24, 34; in Egypt, 156; in India, 399

Here, 62

Hermes, 179*, 277*

Hermes Trismegistus, 179*; see Thoth

Herodotus, Greek historian (ca. 484-425 B.C.), 118*, 138, 139, 147-148, 150, 160, 184, 201-202, 204-205, 224, 244-245, 246, 248, 289-290, 292, 293, 350, 352, 353, 358, 369, 374, 478, 494, 578, 719

Hesiod, Greek poet (ca. 800 B.C.), 329‡

Hesiré (hĕ-zī′-rà), Egyptian prince, 189

Hetairai, 490, 862

Hezekiah (hĕ-zĕ-kī′-à), King of Judah (ca. 720 B.C.), 309, 317

Hidari Jingaro (hē-dä-rĕ jĭng-ä-rō), Japanese sculptor (1594-1634), 893-894

Hidetada (hē-dä-tä-dä), Japanese shogun (1605-1623), 843

Hideyori (hē-dĕ-yôr-ē), Japanese shogun (ca. 1600), 841

Hideyoshi (hī-dĕ-yŏ-shē), Japanese shogun (1581-1598), 838-841, 889, 895, 898, 908, 914, 927

Hien-yang (hē-an-yäng'), 696
Hierapolis (hĭ-ēr-ăp'-ō-lĭs), 297
Hieroglyphics, 144-145, 172-173
Highways, in Egypt, 160; in Babylonia, 227, 228; in Persia, 358; in India, 444-445, 480, 778
Hilkiah (hĭl-kī'-à), Hebrew religious teacher (ca. 620 B.C.), 320
Hillel (hĭl'-ĕl), Jewish Rabbi and Talmudist (ca. 110 B.C.), 310, 670
Himalayas (hĭ-mä'-là-yàz), 91, 392, 393, 454, 551, 576
Hinayana (hē-nà-yä'-nà) Buddhism, 503, 504, 597
Hincks, Edward, Irish Egyptologist (1791-1866), 118*
Hindi (hĭn'dē), 555
Hindu, meaning of, 392*
Hindu Kush (hĭn'-doo koosh'), 392, 440
Hindu Manners, Customs, and Ceremonies, 199*
Hinduism, 507-525
Hindus, 193, 286*, 365, 366, 391-633
Hindustan (hĭn-doo-stän'), meaning of, 393
Hippocrates, Greek physician (460-357 B.C.), 287*, 782
Hippocratic oath, 182
Hirado (hē-rä-dō), 901
Hiram, King of Tyre (fl. 950 B.C.), 294, 295, 306
Hirata (hē-rä-tä), Japanese scholar (ca. 1810), 875
Hiroshige (hē-rō-shē-gé), Japanese engraver 1797-1858), 907, 910
Hishikawa Moronobu (hē-shē-kä-wä mō-rō-nō-boo), Japanese painter (1618-1694), 907
Historical Record, 718
History, in Sumeria, 132; in Egypt, 178; in Babylonia, 250; in Assyria, 277; in Judea, 339-340; in India, 578-579; in China, 718-719; in Japan, 885-887
History of Chinese Philosophy, 821
History of India, 579
History of the True Succession of the Divine Monarchs, 886
Hitomaro (hē-tō-mä-rō), Japanese poet (died 737), 878
Hitopadesha (hĭ-tō-pà-dā'-shà), 578
Hittites, 158, 212, 266, 286-287, 288, 310, 397†
Hiung-nu, *see* Hsiung-nu
Hivites, 310
Hizakurige (hē-zä-koo-ré-gē), 885, 891
Hizen (hē-zĕn), 900, 901
Ho Chi-chang (hō jē-jäng), Chinese statesman (fl. 725), 705

Hoang-ho (hwäng-hō) River, 641, 776
Hobbes, Thomas, English philosopher (1588-1679), 544*, 687, 874
Hojo (hō-jō) Regency (in Japan), 837-838
Hojoki (hō-jō-kē), 852-889
Hokkaido (hŏk-kī-dō), 928
Hokku (hŏk-koo), 880, 881, 926
Hokusai, Katsuhika (hŏk-oo-sä-é, kät-soo-hē-kä), Japanese engraver (1760-1849), 885, 902, 907, 908-910, 912
Holi (hō'-lē), 501
Holmes, Oliver Wendell, M.D., American writer (1809-1894), 81
Holy Family (Raphael), 759
Holy Sepulchre, 120
Homer, 16, 62, 106, 391, 400, 410, 712
Honan (hō-nän), 641, 642, 645, 698, 738, 739, 755, 772
Hongkong (hŏng-kŏng), 804, 805, 806, 809, 810
Honjo (hŏn-jō), 830
Honolulu, 809
Hor, Egyptian architect (ca. 1400 B.C.), 206*
Horiuji (hôr-ē-oo-jē), 738, 833, 894-895, 897, 903
Horus (hôr-ŭs), 198, 200-201
Hosea (hō-zē'-à or hō-zā'-à), Hebrew prophet (ca. 785-725 B.C.), 317, 336
Hospitality, in primitive societies, 54
Hôtel-Dieu (Paris), 81
Hotoke (hō-tō-kä), 840
Hottentots, 6, 42, 43, 52, 65, 85
Hotto (hŏt-tō), Japanese statesman (died 1651), 847
Hoyshaleshwara (hoi-shàl-äsh'-wà-rà) Temple, 601
Hrozný, Frederic, 286
Hsia (shē-äh') Dynasty, 644
Hsia Kuei (shē-äh' gway), Chinese artist (1180-1230), 751
Hsianfu (shē-än'-foo), 808
Hsieh Ho (shē-ä-hō), art theorist (6th century), 592*, 752
Hsien Feng (shē-än fūng), Chinese emperor (1851-1862), 806
Hsien Tsung (shē-än dzoong), Chinese emperor (806-821), 779
Hsing-shan (shĭng-shän) Temple, 750
Hsinking (shĭn-jĭng), 920†
Hsiung-nu (shē-oong-noo), 701
Hsu Hsing (shoo shĭng), Chinese radical (ca. 300 B.C.), 685
Hsuan (shwän), King of Ch'i, 683, 685-686

Hsuan Tsung (shwän dzōong), *see* Ming Huang

Hsün-tze (shün-dzŭ), apostle of evil (ca. 305-235 B.C.), 687-688

Hu Shih (hōo-shǐ), Chinese literary reformer (1891-   ), 821-822

Hua To (hwä dō), Chinese medical writer (3rd century,) 782

Huan (hwän), Duke of Ch'i (685-643 B.C.), 645-646

Huang Ti (hwäng dē), Chinese emperor (2697-2597 B.C.), 643, 659, 660-661

Huber, Sir William, British judge in India (early 19th century), 497

Huen (hwän) Mountain, 717

Hughes, Charles Evans, American statesman and jurist (1862-   ), 929, 930

Hui Sze (whä-dzŭ), Chinese philosopher (3rd century), 677

Hui Tsung (whä dzōong), Chinese emperor (1101-1125), 727, 750, 751, 752, 753, 795

Huldah (hōol'-dà), Hebrew prophetess (ca. 625 B.C.), 333

Human sacrifice, 66-67; in Sumeria, 128; in Assyria, 272; in Phoenicia, 295; in Syria, 297; in Judea, 311, 315

Humanism, 730

Humayun (hōo-mä-yōon'), Mogul emperor (1530-1542; 1555-1556), 464, 468, 472, 607

Humboldt, Friedrich Heinrich Alexander, Baron von, German scholar and traveler (1769-1859), 462

Humboldt, Karl Wilhelm, Baron von, German statesman and philologist (1767-1835), 565

Hume, David, Scotch philosopher and historian (1711-1776), 418, 434

Hung Hsiu-ch'üan (hōong sē-ōo chwǎn), T'ai-p'ing leader (died 1864), 805

Hung Wu (hōong wōo), Chinese emperor (1386-1399), 686

Huns, 152, 452, 454, 459, 591, 695, 701

Hunting, in primitive societies, 6-7, 24, 30, 33; in Babylonia, 226; in Assyria, 226, 229, 278, 279; in Persia, 378; in India, 477

Hyaku-nin-isshu (hyä-kōo-nǐn-ǐsh-ōo), 879-880

Hydaspes (hī-dăs'-pēz) River, 440

Hyderabad (hī'-dēr-ä bäd), (city), 393

Hyderabad (state), 589, 600-601

Hygiene, in Egypt, 183-184; in Judea, 331; in Persia, 373-374; in India, 497, 498, 521; in China, 782, 855

Hyksos (hĭk'-sōs), the, 24*, 152, 154, 160, 166, 177, 223, 227, 300, 301

Hymn to the Sun, 178, 206-210

Hypatia, Greek philosopher and mathematician (?-415), 216

Hypnotism, 532

Hystaspes (hĭs-täs'-pēz), father of Darius I (ca. 550 B.C.), 364, 365*

I

Iamblichus (ī-ăm'-blĭ-kŭs), Syrian philosopher (fl. 325), 179*

Iberians, 10

Ibrahim (ĭb'-rà-hēm') II, Sultan of Delhi (1517-1526), 464

Ibsen, Henrik, Norwegian poet and dramatist (1828-1906), 58, 692

Ice Age, 91*

Iceland, 107

Ichikawa (ēch-ē-kä-wä), Japanese philosopher (17th century), 865

I-Ching (ē-jǐng), 650-651, 665, 785

Ictinus, Greek architect (fl. 450 B.C.), 141, 895

Igorots, 45

Ikhnaton (ĭk'-nä-tŏn), *see* Amenhotep IV

Ili (ē-lē), 798

Iliad, 250, 310, 561, 564, 891

Imari-yaki (e-mä-rē-yä-kē), 900

Imhotep (ĭm-hō'-těp), Egyptian physician, architect, and statesman (ca. 3150 B.C.), 147, 192

Imitation of Christ, 570

In Memoriam, 878

Inana-yoga (ĭn-ä'-nà-yō'-gà), 522

Inazo Nitobe (i-nä-tsō nē-tō-bē), Japanese publicist (died 1933), 847*

Incas, 41

Incest, in Egypt, 164; in Babylonia, 231; in India, 401

India, 34, 47, 60, 61, 93, 94, 99*, 103, 104, 108, 116, 117, 125, 144, 159, 199*, 206, 222*, 227, 247, 274*, 286, 292, 312*, 329, 353, 355, 358, 359*, 363, 372, 385, 391-633, 642, 651, 736, 744, 779, 786, 804, 805, 875, 892, 928

Indian, meaning of, 392*

Indian National Congress, 623, 625, 626

Indian Ocean, 703

Indians, American, 2, 5-6, 8, 9, 13, 14, 15, 16, 17, 18, 22, 23, 27, 32, 33, 35, 41, 42, 45, 48, 49, 53, 54, 56, 60, 61, 73, 77, 83

Indo-China, 604, 698, 767, 806, 928

Indo-Europeans, 285, 286*, 291, 350, 397‡

Indra (ĭn'-drà), 285, 397†, 402, 403, 507

Indus (ĭn'-dŭs) River, 355, 393, 397‡, 440, 463

Industrial Revolution, 20*, 70, 94, 96, 159, 274, 333, 478, 480, 516, 612, 623, 769, 803, 916-922

Industry, 11-16, 934; in Sumeria, 124-125; in Egypt, 157-161; in Babylonia, 227; in Assyria, 274; in Persia, 357-358; in India, 400, 479; in China, 776-778, 815; in Japan, 919-920

Ineni (ĭ-nä-nē), Egyptian architect (ca. 1530 B.C.), 192

Infant Jesus (Reni), 759

Infanticide, in primitive societies, 50

Initiation rites, 75

Ink, 171

Inkyo (ĭn'-kyō), Emperor of Japan (412-453), 892

Innini (ĭn'-nĭn-ē), 127

Inouye, Marquis Kaoru (ĭn-ōō-yé, kä-ō-rōō), Japanese statesman (1839-1915), 916, 930

Inquisition, Holy, 469, 524

Inro (ĭn-ro), 893

Instructions of Ptah-hotep, 193-194

Interglacial Stages, 91*

International Exposition of Persian Art, London (1931), 378*

Ionia, 264, 290, 355

Ionians, 479

Iphigenia, 66, 297

Ipuwer (ĭp'-ū-wēr), 194, 195

Iran (é-rän'), 356; see Persia

Iranian Plateau, 117

Iraq (é-räk') 117

Iraq Expedition of the University of Chicago, 274*

Iraq Museum, Baghdad, 134*

Ireland, 58

Irish, 10

Iron Age, 104

Iroquois Indians, 14, 22, 32, 62

Isaac, Hebrew patriarch, 66, 297, 337

Isaiah (ī-zā'-à), Hebrew prophet (fl. 720 B.C.), 210, 235, 262, 301, 312, 317-320, 324, 325-327, 334*, 341, 365, 422*

Ise (ī-sē), 880

Ishii, Viscount Kikujiro (ē-shé-ē, kē-kōō-jē-rō), Japanese statesman (1866-   ), 929

Ishtar (ĭsh'-tär), 60, 123, 127, 200, 234, 235-236, 238-239, 247, 251, 253, 256, 266, 294-295, 341

Ishvara (ēsh'-và-rà), 548, 550

Ishvara Krishna (ēsh'-và-rà krĭsh'-nà), Indian religious teacher (5th century), 536*

Isin (ē'-zĭn), 123

Isis (ī'-sĭs), 185, 200-201

Islam (ĭs-läm'), 35, 39, 247, 463, 469-470, 524

Israel (ĭz'-rà-ĕl), 315*; also see Jews

Issus (ĭs-sŭs), 373*, 383

Italians, 279, 397

Italy, 92, 97, 99*, 108, 152, 215, 293, 555, 695, 730, 821

Ito, Marquis Hirobumi (ē-tō, nē-rō-bōō-mē), Japanese statesman (1840-1909), 916, 917

Ito Jinsai (ē-tō jĭn-sī), Japanese philosopher (1627-1705), 872-873

Ito Togai (ē-tō tō-gī), Japanese philosopher (1670-1736), 873

Ittagi (ĭt-tä-gē), 600-601

Ius primæ noctis (yŭs prē'-mī nŏk'-tĭs), 38, 245, 486*

Iwasa Matabei (ē-wä-sä mä-tä-bä), Japanese painter (1578-1650), 907

Iyemitsu (é-yé-mĭt-sōō), Japanese *shogun* (1623-1651), 843, 847, 895

Iyenari (é-yé-nä-rē), Japanese *shogun* (1787-1836), 862

Iyenobu (é-yé-nō-bōō), Japanese *shogun* (1709-1712), 886

Iyesada (é-yé-sä-dä), Japanese *shogun* (1853-1858), 915

Iyeyasu (é-yé-yä-sōō), Japanese *shogun* (1603-1616), 838, 841-843, 846-847, 849, 850, 866, 877, 886, 889, 894, 895, 905, 914

Iyeyoshi (é-yé-yŏsh-ē), Japanese *shogun* (1837-1852), 915

Izanagi (ē-zä-nä-gé), 829, 875, 892

Izanami (ē-zä-nä-mē), 829, 875, 892

J

Jabali (jà'-bà-lē), 461

Jacob, Hebrew patriarch, 41, 310, 314*, 334, 336, 340

Jacobi, H., 419*

Jacobins, 19*

Jade, 737

Jagannath Puri (jà'-gàn-nät-pōōr'ĭ), 599

Jahanara (jä-hà-när'-à), daughter of Shah Jehan (ca. 1658), 474

Jaimini (jī'-mĭn-ĭ), Indian religious teacher (4th century, B.C. ?), 545-546

Jainism (jīn'-ism), 419, 420-422, 459, 469, 471, 508*, 520, 529, 534, 597, 598, 599, 600, 601, 626

Jaipur (jī'-pōōr), 393, 585

James I, King of England and VI of Scotland (1567[S], 1603[E]-1625), 317

James, William, American psychologist (1842-1910), 535

Jamsetpur (jäm-shĕd-pōōr'), 622

Janak(a) (jä'-nà-kà), 414, 567-568

Japan, 3, 42, 98, 103, 162, 166, 184, 192, 312*, 449, 450, 501, 504, 506, 577, 594, 595, 596, 602, 626, 633, 646, 730, 736, 738, 752, 753, 757, 773, 799*, 806, 807, 808, 809, 810, 813, 814, 815*, 829-933

Japan, Emperor of, 59

Japanese, 53, 640

Jastrow, Morris, 343*

Jataka (jä'-tà-kà) books, 423, 578

Java, 65, 92, 391, 451, 594, 595, 602, 603

Jaxartes (jäx-är'-tez) River, 353

Jayadeva (jä-yà-dā'-và), Indian poet 491, 580

Jefferson, Thomas, President of the United States (1743-1826), 304

Jehangir (jà-hän'-gēr), Mogul emperor (1605-1627), 471-473, 480, 483*, 579, 591, 608, 609

Jehoiakim (jĕ-hoi'-à-kim), King of Judah (608-597 B.C.), 321

Jehol (rĕh-hō[l]), 806, 931

Jehovah (jĕ-hō'-và), see Yahveh

Jenghiz Khan, see Genghis Khan

Jeremiah, Hebrew prophet (fl. 600), 312, 315, 322-324, 422*

Jericho, 300, 302*

Jerusalem, 267, 298, 305-306, 307, 314, 315, 316, 317, 321, 323, 324, 325, 326, 327-328, 334*, 348, 384, 606

Jesuits, 94, 469, 768, 788, 840, 877

Jewelry, in primitive societies, 86; in Sumeria, 119, 130; in Egypt, 169-170, 191-192; in Babylonia, 254; in Assyria, 265, 278; in Persia, 378; in India, 499, 585; in China, 736, 737

Jewish Encyclopedia, 306*

Jews, 62, 117, 118, 213, 217, 218, 234, 235, 236, 242, 245, 263, 267, 268, 284, 287, 297, 298, 299-349, 358, 367, 469, 508*

Jezebel (jĕz'-ĕ-bĕl), wife of King Ahab, (ca. 875-850 B.C.), 317*

Jimmu (jĭm-mōō), emperor of Japan (660-585 B.C.), 873

Jinas (jĭ'-nàs), 420

Jintoshotoki (jĭn-tō-shō-tō-kē), 886

Jippensha Ikku (jĕp-pĕn-shà ĭk-ōō), Japanese novelist (died 1831), 885

Jizo (jĕ-zō), 864

Job (jōb), 259, 261, 343-346, 367

Joffe (yŏf-fä), A., Russian diplomat (died ca. 1928), 812

Johnson, Samuel, English author and lexicographer (1709-1784), 2*, 681

Johur (jō'-hōōr), 456, 495

Jojaku (jō-kä-kōō), Japanese woodcarver (13th century), 897*

Jokai (jō-kī), Japanese woodcarver (13th century), 897*

Jonathan, son of King Saul (ca. 1010 B.C.), 304-305

Jones, Sir William, English Orientalist (1746-1794), 391*, 406, 574, 578*

Jonson, Ben, English poet and dramatist (1574-1637), 631

Jordan River, 298

Joseph, Hebrew patriarch (ca. 1900 B.C.), 340

Josephine, Empress of the French (1763-1814), 246

Josephus, Flavius, Jewish historian (37-96?), 179, 299, 301†, 307, 383

Joshua (jōsh'-ū-à), Hebrew leader (died ca. 1425 B.C.), 302

Josiah (jō-sī'-à), King of the Jews (641-610 B.C.), 203*, 320-321, 328, 333, 364

Juangs, 8

Jubilee, 337-338

Judah (kingdom), 315, 317, 321, 322, 323, 329

Judea, 68, 218, 299-349, 422*, 640, 651

Judges (of Israel), 304

Juggernaut, 520*

Julian calendar, 181

Juma Masjid (jä'-mĕ màs'-jĕd), 608

Jumna (jŭm'-nà) River, 393, 460, 474, 479, 521

Jupiter, 402

K

Ka (kä), 148, 149, 150, 202

Kaapiru (kä'-pē-rōō), Egyptian official, 186; also see Sheik-el-Beled

Kabir (kà-bēr'), Indian poet (1440-1518), 470, 523, 582-583

Kabuki Shibai (kä-bōō-kē shē-bī), 890-891

Kabul (kä'-bōōl), 227, 392, 450, 464

Kadesh (kä'-dĕsh), 213

Kaempfer, Engelbrecht, German botanist and traveler (1651-1716), 853, 862

Kaffirs, 35, 42, 45, 53, 64, 65, 75

Kaga (kä-gà), 900, 901

Kaga no-Chiyo (kä-gà nō-chē-yō), Lady, Japanese poet (1703-1775), 858, 880

Kagawa, Toyohiko (kä-gà-wä tō-yō-hē-kō), Japanese socialist, 921

K'aifeng (kī-fŭng), 727

Kaikeyi (kī′-kā-ē), 568
Kailasha (kī-läsh′-à) Temple, 601
Kakiemon (kä-kē-yā-mŏn), Japanese potter (ca. 1650), 900
Kala-at-Sherghat (kà-lät′-shâr′-gàt), see Ashur (city)
Kalakh (kà-läkh′), 265, 266, 278, 279, 280
Kalgan (kàl-gän), 931
Kalhana (kàl′-hà-nà), Indian historian, 579
Kali (kä′-lē), 200, 499, 501, 509, 511, 519, 520, 617, 625
Kalidasa (kä-lē-dä′-sà), Indian poet (ca. 400), 391*, 451, 452, 572, 574-576, 578
Kalingas (kä′-lĭn-gàz), 446
Kali-yuga (kä′-lē-yōō′-gà), 513
Kallen, Horace M., 343*
Kalpa (kàl′-pà), 513
Kamakura (kä-mà-kōō-rà), 450, 830, 837, 892, 894, 895, 898, 905
Kamakura Bakufu, 837
Kamasutra (kä-mà-sōō′-trà), 490
Kamatari (kä-mà-tä-rē), Japanese statesman (fl. 645), 833
Kambinana, 57
Kamchadals (kăm′-chà-dălz), 45, 50
Kamchatka (kàm-chàt′-kà), 896
Kami (kä-mē), 840
Kamo no-Chomei (kä-mö nō-chō-mā), Japanese essayist (1154-1216), 852, 888-889
Kamo (kä-mō) Temple, 888
Kanada (kà′-nà-dà), Indian philosopher (date unknown), 528, 529, 536, 546
Kanarak (kà-när′-àk), 599
Kanarese (kă′-nà-rēz), 555
Kanauj (kà-nouj′), 452, 453
Kandahar (kàn′-dà-här), 392
Kandy (kän′-dē), 450, 506, 585, 603
Kang Teh (käng dä), 931; also see P′u Yi
Kangakusha (kän-gà-kōō′-shà) scholars, 874
K′ang-hsi (käng-shē), Chinese emperor (1662-1722), 736, 752, 758, 767-768, 771, 788*, 795
Kangra (käng-rà), 591
Kanishka (kàn′-ĭsh-kà), King of the Kushans (ca. 120), 450-451, 504, 506, 571, 594, 786
Kano Masanobu (kä-nō mä-sà-nō-bōō), Japanese painter (died 1490), 905
Kano Motonobu (kä-nō mō-tō-nō-bōō), Japanese painter (1476-1559), 905
Kano School (of Japanese painting), 843, 902*, 905-906
Kano Tanyu (tän-yōō), Japanese painter 1602-1674), 905
Kano Yeitoku (yā-tō-koo), Japanese architect (1543-1590), 905

Kansu (gän-sōō), 755
Kant, Immanuel, German philosopher (1724-1804), 346, 410, 510, 516*, 538, 547, 549, 551*, 552, 670
Kantara (kän′-tà-rà), 154
Kanthaka (kàn′-tà-kà), 426
Kao Tsu (gou dzoo), Chinese emperor (206-194 B.C.), 698
Kao Tsu, Chinese Emperor (618-627), 702
Kapila (kà′-pĭ-là), Indian Sankhya philosopher (ca. 500 B.C.), 536-541, 546, 547
Kapilavastu (kà′-pĭ-là-vàs′-tōō), 422, 423, 436
Karachi (kà-rä′-chē), 393, 594
Karakhan (kä-rà-kän′), Leo, Russian diplomat, 812
Karduniash (kär-dōō′-nế-äsh), 223*
Karle (kär′-lế), 597, 598
Karma (kàr′-mà), 427, 435, 509, 514-516, 550, 553
Karma-yoga (kàr′-mà yō′-gà), 522
Karnak (kär′-nàk), 140, 142-143, 144, 145, 152, 153, 185, 189, 191, 206, 214, 379, 744; buildings at: Festival Hall of Thutmose III, 143, 145; Hypostyle Hall, 143, 213; obelisks of Queen Hatshepsut, 143, 153; Promenade of Thutmose III, 143, 155; Temple of Amon, 142; Temple of Ptah, 143
Kartikeya (kär-tĭ-kā′-yà), 507
Kashgar (käsh′-gär′), 761
Kashmir (käsh′-mēr′), 392, 479, 585
Kassites (kăs′-sīts), 152, 222, 223, 227, 248, 257, 266, 397
Kasturbai (kàs-tōōr′-bī), wife of M. K. Gandhi, 628
Katakana (kä-tà-kä-nà) script, 876*
Katayama, Sen (kä-tä-yä-mä, sĕn), Japanese communist (died 1933), 921
Katha Upanishad (kà-tä′ ōō-pàn′-ĭ-shàd), 405
Kathæi (kà-tē′-ī), 495
Kathasaritzagara (kà-tä′-sà-rĭt-sà′-gà-rà), 579
Kaushitaki (kou′-shī-tà-kĭ) Upanishad, 518
Kautilya Chanakya (kou′-tĭl-yà chä-nàk′-yà), Indian statesman (ca. 322-298 B.C.), 441, 443
Ke K′ang (kä käng), Confucian disciple (ca. 500 B.C.), 672
Ke Loo (kä lōō), Confucian disciple (ca. 500 B.C.), 667
Kea Kwei (kä-yà kwă), Chinese scholar (1st century), 665
Keats, John, English poet (1795-1821), 611, 713

Keiki (kā-kē), last of the Tokugawa *shoguns* (1866-1868), 916

Keion (kĭ-ŏn), Japanese painter, (ca. 1250), 904

Keiser, Aabregt de, Dutch ceramic artist (17th century), 900

Keith, Sir Arthur, 99

Kenzan (kĕn-zän), Japanese potter (1663-1743), 900

Kepler, Johann, German astronomer (1571-1630), 60

Keriya (kā'-rĕ-yà), *see* Peyn

Ket (kĕt), 201

Keyserling, Count Hermann, 455†, 534, 554*, 639

Khafre (kă'-frā), King of Egypt (3067-3011 B.C.), 148, 150, 186, 187

Kharosthi (kà-rōsh'-tē) script, 556

Khekheperre-Sonbu (kē-kē-pâr'-rĕ sŏn-bōō), Egyptian scholar (ca. 2150 B.C.), 178

Khi-yüan (kē-ē-ăn), 688

Khmers (kmârz), 604-605, 606

Khnum (knōōm), 185

Khnumhotep (knōōm-hō'-tĕp), King of Egypt (ca. 2180 B.C.), 185, 190

Khorassan (kō-ràs-sän'), 761

Khordah Avesta (kôr'-dä à-vĕs'-tà), 365‡

Khorsabad (kôr-sà-bäd'), 266*, 279, 280

Khotan (kō-tän'), 594, 602, 761

Khu (kōō), 688-9

Khosrou (kŏs-rōō') II, King of Persia (590-628), 456

Khufu (kōō'-fōō), King of Egypt (3098-3075 B.C.), 147, 149, 150, 291, 395

Khusru (kŭs-rōō), son of Jehangir (ca. 1620), 472

Kiaochow (jyou-jō'), 806

Kimimaro (kē-mē-mä-rō), Japanese sculptor (fl. 747), 897-898

King James Version, 317, 341

Kings (book), 339

Kingship, 22; in Sumeria, 126; in Egypt, 163-164; in Babylonia, 230, 232-233, 234; in Assyria, 266, 273; in Persia, 360-361; in India, 442-443, 482-483; in China, 797-798; in Japan, 834

Kiritsubo (kē-rĕt-sōō-bō), 882

Kirti Shri Raja Singha (kĕr'-tĭ shrē rä'-jä sĭng'-hā), King of Ceylon (18th century), 603

Kish (kĭsh), 118, 120, 125, 127, 221, 395*

Kitabatake (kĭt-à-bä-tà-kā), Japanese scholar and historian (fl. 1334), 886

Kitans (kĕ-tänz'), 721-722, 760*

Kitasato, Baron Shibasaburo (kĭt-à-sä-tō, shē-bà-sä-bōō-rō), Japanese scientist (1856-   ), 924

Kitchen middens, 98, 101

Kiyonaga (kē-yō-nä-gà), Japanese engraver (1742-1814), 908

Knemhotep (knĕm-hō'-tĕp), Egyptian dwarf, 187

Kobe (kō-bä), 920, 921

Kobo Daishi (kō-bō dī-shē), Japanese saint and artist, founder of Shintoism (9th century), 864, 897*, 903

Kohat (kō-hät'), 624†

Koheleth (kō-hĕl'-ĕth), 346*

Kohl, 169

Kojiki (kō-jē-kē), 874-875, 885

Kokei (kō-kā), Japanese woodcarver (12th century), 897*

Koken (kō-kĕn), Empress of Japan (749-759; 765-770), 861

Kokinshu (kō-kĭn-shōō), 878†, 879

Kolben, Peter, German naturalist (1675-1726), 52

Konin (kō-nĭn), Emperor of Japan (770-781), 850

Koran (kôr-än'), 463, 469, 470, 474, 476, 565, 609, 616

Korea (kôr-ē'-à), 506, 594, 602, 698, 705, 730, 767, 773, 806, 829, 831, 832, 833, 839, 853, 875, 877*, 892, 894, 899, 903, 918, 919, 923, 924, 927*

Korin, Ogata (kō-rĭn ō-gä-tà), Japanese painter (1661-1716), 900, 906

Korvouva, 57

Kosala (kō'-sà-là), 567, 568, 569; also *see* Oudh

Kose no-Kanaoka (kō-sä nō-kä-nà-ō-kà), Japanese painter (ca. 950), 903

Kotsuke no Suké (kŏt-sōō-kä nō sōō-kà), Japanese noble (died 1703), 848-849

Kow-tow, 713

Koyetsu (kō-yĕt-sōō), Japanese painter (ca. 1600), 906

Koyetsu-Korin School (of Japanese painting), 906

Koyosan (kō-yō-sän), 864

Krishna (krĭsh'-nà) (god), 403, 507-508, 511, 552, 564, 565-566, 570, 580, 617*, 625

Krishna (tribe), 403

Krishna deva Raya (krĭsh'-nà dä'-và rä'-yà), King of Vijayanagar (1509-1529), 457, 458

Kroch, Adolf, 893*

Kshatriyas (kshà'-trĭ-yàz), 359*, 398, 399, 419, 424, 455, 487, 565, 567

Kuan Ching (gwän jĭng), Prime Minister of Ts'i (fl. 683-640 B.C.), 645-646, 790
Kuang Hsu (gwäng shōō), Chinese emperor (1875-1908), 807, 810
Kuan-yin (gwän-yĭn), 740, 751, 786
Kublai Khan (kōō' blī khän), Chinese emperor (1269-1295), 604, 606, 721, 742, 761, 763-766, 767, 777, 778, 779, 790, 837, 895
Kubus, 21
Kukis, 67
Kumara (kōō-mä'-rà), King of Assam (ca. 630), 454
Kumazawa Banzan (kōō-mà-zä-wà bän-zän), Japanese philosopher (1619-1691), 871-872, 877
K'ung (kōōng) (family), 659
K'ung Chi (kōōng jē), Chinese sage, grandson of Confucius (ca. 470 B.C.), 665-666, 676-677
K'ung Ch'iu (kōōng chē-ōō'), see Confucius
Kung Sun Lung (gōōng sōōn lōōng), Chinese sage (ca. 425 B.C.), 677, 679
K'ung Tao-fu (kōōng dou foo), Chinese diplomat (fl. 1031), 721-722
K'ung-fu-tze (kōōng-fōō-dzŭ), see Confucius
Kuo Hsi (gwō-shē), Chinese painter (born 1100), 750
Kuo K'ai-chih (gwō-kī-jĭh), Chinese painter (fl. 364), 746-747
Kuo Tsi-i (gwō dzē-é), Chinese general (fl. 755), 710
Kuomintang (gwō-mĭn-däng), 817
Kurdistan (kōōr-dĭ-stän'), 350
Kurds (kōōrdz), 266
Kurna (kōōr'-nà), 118
Kurral (kōōr'-räl), 581-582
Kurus (kōō'-rōōz), 561-562, 565
Kushans (kōō'-shänz), 450, 504
Kutani (kōō-tä-nē), 900, 901
Kutb-d Din Aibak (kōōt'-ōōb-ōōd dēn ī'bàk), Sultan of Delhi (1206-1210), 461, 607
Kutb-Minar (kōōt'-ōōb mĭ-när'), 607
Kuyunjik (kōō-yōōn'-jĭk), see Nineveh
Kuznetzk (kōōz-nyĕtsk'), 932
Kwannon (kwän-nŏn), 833, 864
Kyogen (kyō-gĕn), 889
Kyoto (kyō-tō), 749*, 834, 835, 840, 852-853, 855, 860, 865*, 866, 872, 877, 880, 888, 894, 895, 898, 900, 902, 903, 905, 906, 910
Kyoto, University of, 926
Kyushu (kyōō-shōō), 928

L

La Fontaine (lä fŏn-tĕn), Jean de, French fabulist (1621-1695), 175
La Tène, 104
Laban (lā'-bàn), Jacob's father-in-law, 41, 310
Lacquer, 736-737, 894
Lagash (lä'-gäsh), 118, 120, 121, 122, 127, 129
Lahore (lä-hor'), 392, 472, 594, 614
Lake dwellers, the, 98-99, 101, 103
Lake of the Deeds of Rama, 581
Lakshman (làksh'-màn), 569
Lakshmi (làksh-mē'), 509
Lalitavistara (lä'-lē-tä-vĭs'-tà-rà), 423*
Lamarck, Jean Baptiste de Monet, Chevalier de, French naturalist (1744-1829), 538
Lamentations, 324
Lancashire, 920
Landecho, Spanish sailor (fl. 1596), 843*
Lander, Richard, English traveler (1804-1835), 43
Landor, Walter Savage, English man of letters (1775-1864), 683-684
Language, 72-73; in primitive societies, 74; in Sumeria, 118*; in Egypt, 145, 172-173; in Babylonia, 249-250; in Assyria, 266; in Judea, 303; in Persia, 356-357; in India, 391*, 405-406, 555-556; in China, 74, 771-773; in Japan, 876-877
Lansing, Robert, American statesman (1864-1928), 929
Lao-tse (lou'-dzŭ), Chinese sage (604-517 B.C.), 77, 422*, 429, 651, 652-658, 662, 663, 670, 677, 684, 689, 690-693, 772, 785, 786
Laplace, Pierre Simon, French astronomer and mathematician (1749-1827), 527, 538
Larsa (lär'-sà), 118, 123, 234
Last Judgment (Michelangelo), 749
Last Supper (Da Vinci), 97, 590*, 749
Latin (language), 406*
Latourette, K. S., 801*
Lauriya (lôr'-ē-yà), 596
Laussel, 97
Law, 135; in primitive societies, 25-29; in Sumeria, 120-121, 127; in Egypt, 161-162; in Babylonia, 135, 219, 220-221, 230-232; in Assyria, 272; in the Hittite Empire, 287; in Judea, 328-339; in Persia, 361, 374; in India, 444, 483-488, 494, 495; in China, 646-647, 797
Lazarus, 614
Le Sage, Alain René, French novelist and dramatist (1668-1747), 885

League of Nations, 22, 931

League of the Iroquois, 22

Leah (lē′-à), one of Jacob's wives, 41, 336

Lebanon (lĕb′-à-nŭn), 154, 292, 296, 761

Ledoux, L. V., 906*

Legalists, 674-675

Legge, James, British orientalist (1815-1897), 653*, 665

Leibnitz, Gottfried Wilhelm, Baron von, German philosopher and mathematician (1646-1716), 345, 516*, 536, 693, 773

Leipzig, 693

Lemnos, 95

Lenguas, 50

Lenin *nom de guerre* of Vladimir Ulyanov, Russian Soviet leader (1870-1924), 314

Leonardo, *see* Vinci, Leonardo da

Leopold I, Holy Roman Emperor (1658-1705), 736

Lepsius, Karl Richard, German philologist (1813-1884), 203*

Les Eyzies, 97*

Lesser Vehicle, see *Hinayana* Buddhism

Letourneau, C., 38

Levi (lē′-vī), Hebrew patriarch (ca. 1700 B.C.), 314

Levirate, 39

Levites, 309, 314, 328

Leviticus, 330, 331*

Lex talionis (lĕx tă-lē-ō′-nĭs), 27, 230-231, 338

Leyden Museum, 157, 595

Lhasa (lä′-sà), 506, 507

Li (lē), Lao-tze's real name, 652

Li and *Chi* (lē, jē), 732

Li Hou-chu (lē-hō-jōō), Chinese emperor (ca. 970), 770

Li Hung-chang (lē hoong jäng), Chinese statesman (1823-1901), 730, 807, 810

Li Lung-mien (lē lōong mē-ăn′), Chinese painter (1040-1106), 750-751

Li Po (lē bō), Chinese poet (705-762), 703, 705-711, 713, 714, 717, 751, 909

Li Ssu (lē sü), Chinese statesman (fl. 215 B.C.), 695, 696

Li Ssu-hsün (lē sōō-shün), Chinese painter (651-716), 748

Liang K'ai (lē-äng′ kī), Chinese painter (ca. 750), 751

Liao Chai Chih I (lyou jī jē ē), 718

Liaotung (lyou′-dōong), 806, 848, 918

Liberia, 16

Libraries, in Sumeria, 131-132; in Egypt, 174; in Babylonia, 249; in Assyria, 237*, 243, 249, 250, 266*, 269, 277; in India, 468, 556; in China, 697, 699, 727

Libya, 215

Libyans, 184, 215

Lichchavi (lĭch′-chà-vē), 419

Li-Chi (lē jē), 664, 723, 794

Lieh-I (lē′-ŭ-ē), Chinese painter (1st century), 746

Light of Asia, 423*

Li-ling (lē-lĭng), Prince of Yung (ca. 756), 710

Lin Tze-hsü (lĭn dzŭ-shü), Chinese statesman (ca. 1838), 804

Lin-an (lē-nän′), 727

Linga (lĭn-gà), 519, 520

Lingaraja (ĭn-gà-rä′-jà) Temple, 599

Lingayats (lĭn′-gä-yàts), 519

Ling-chao (lĭng jou), Lady, Chinese Buddhist mystic (8th century), 751†

Lin-k'ew (lĭn-chḗ-ōō′), 662

Lippert, Julius, German sociologist (1859-1909), 42*

Literature, 936; Sumerian, 132; Egyptian, 173-179; Babylonian, 176-178, 241-243, 250-254; Assyrian, 277; Hebrew, 316, 318, 320, 322, 324, 325-327, 329-330, 339-349 (also see Prophets, Bible, Old Testament, New Testament, etc.); Persian, *see Zend-Avesta;* Indian, 407-409, 458, 555-583; Chinese, 648-649, 664-666, 705-723, 821; Japanese, 878-891, 926-927

Liturgy, in Babylonia, 242-243

Liu Ling (lē-ōō′ lĭng), Chinese poet (third century), 708

Lives of the Saints, 570

Locke, John, English philosopher (1632-1704), 552

Loire River, 226

Lokamahadevi (lō′-kà-mà-hä-dā′-vē), wife of Vikramaditya Chalukya (ca. 1100), 602

Lombards, 397

London, 2, 17, 481, 613, 810, 817

Longfellow, Henry Wadsworth, American poet (1807-1882), 491

Longford, J., 847

Lorraine, Claude (nickname of Claude Gelée), French painter (1600-1682), 754

Los Angeles, 393, 543

Loti, Pierre (Julien Viaud), French author 1850-1923), 499

Lotus Sect, 864

Louis XIV, King of France (1643-1715), 163, 704*, 758, 768

Louvre, 122, 134, 161, 186, 188, 219†, 289, 295

Lower California Indians, 27

Lo-yang (lō-yäng'), 647, 658, 662, 677, 679, 698*, 699, 746, 750

Lu (loō), Chinese empress (195-180 B.C.), 792

Lu (state), 651, 658, 662, 663, 664, 678, 909

Lü (lü), father of Shih Huang-ti (ca. 222 B.C.), 695

Lu Hsiu-fu (loō shé-oō'-foō), Chinese hero (died 1260), 764

Lubari, 60

Lucretius Carus, Titus, Roman poet (95-53 B.C.), 57

Lucullus, Lucius Lincinius, Roman general (110-56? B.C.), 226

Lugal-zaggisi (loō-gäl-zà-gē'-zé), Sumerian king, 121

Lun Yü (lwĕn ü), 665

Lung Men (loŏng mŭn), 739

Luther, Martin, German religious reformer (1483-1546), 504-505

Luxor (lŭk'-sôr), 140, 142, 144, 178, 214

Lycaonians (lĭ-kā-ō'-nē-ånz), 285

Lycians (lĭs-yånz), 285

Lycidas, 880

Lydia (lĭd'-yà), 245, 288, 289-290, 352, 355, 358, 362, 380

Lytton Report, 931

M

Ma (mä), Phrygian goddess, 288

Ma Yuan (mä yoō-ăn'), Chinese painter (ca. 1200), 751

Mabuchi (mä-boō-chē), Japanese Shintoist leader (1697-1769), 865, 874, 914

Macao (mä-kow), 804

Macartney, George, Earl of, British statesman (1737-1806), 768

Macartney mission, 768-769

Macaulay, Thomas Babington, Lord, English man of letters and statesman (1800-1859), 499, 614

Maccabees (măc'-à-bēz), 331†, 335

Macdonell, A. A., 395†

Macedon, 216, 284, 385

Machiavelli, Nicolò, Italian statesman and author (1469-1527), 443

Macusis, 70

Madagascans, 8, 50

Madai (mä'-dī), 350; see Medes

Madras (mà-dräs'), 393, 394, 456, 581, 586, 600, 601, 602, 613, 615, 630

Madras Presidency, 393, 457

Madrid, 608

Madura (mä'-doō-rà), 393, 456, 581, 600, 602, 610

Mæonians (mē-), 285

Mafuie, 60

Magadha (mä'-gà-dà), 441, 449, 451, 505

Magdalenian Culture, 94, 96, 97

Magi, 365, 372

Magic, 64-65, 67-68, 77; in Sumeria, 125; in Egypt, 204-205; in Babylonia, 243-244; in Assyria, 276; in Judea, 309; in India, 518

Magic Mountain, 718

Magnesia, 296

Magnetogorsk, 932

Magog (mà-gŏg'), 324

Mahabharata (mà-hà-bhä'-rà-tà), 398, 452, 468, 469, 491, 493, 495, 515, 517, 523, 524-536*, 541, 542, 561-564, 571, 576, 605

Mahavira (mà-hä'-vē'-rà), founder of Jainism (599-527 B.C.), 419-420, 422*

Mahayana (mà-hä'-yä'-nà) Buddhism, 450, 454, 504, 594, 733, 786, 833

Mahmud (mä-moōd'), Sultan of Ghazni (gŭz'-né), (997-1030), 460, 462, 589

Mahmud Tughlak (toōgh'-làk), Sultan of Delhi (ca. 1398), 463

Mahrati (mà-rä'-tē) (language), 581

Maison Dieu, Paris, 451*

Maitreyi (mī-trā'-yē), 410-411

Maitri Upanishad (mĭ'-trē oō-pàn'-ĭ-shàd'), 411

Makura Zoshi (mä-koō-rà zō-shē), 887

Malabar, 45, 613

Malacca, 38, 803

Malay Peninsula, 506, 606, 766, 779, 803

Malay States, 931

Malayan (language), 555

Malinowski, B., 31

Malta, 293

Malthus, Robert Thomas, English political economist (1766-1834), 347, 627

Malwa (mäl-wä'), 452

Mamallapuram (mä'-mà-là-poōr'-àm), 594, 601

Mamelukes, 186

Man, Age of, 102

Manava (mä'-nà-và) Brahmans, 484

Manchu (măn'-choō) Dynasty, 675, 736, 759, 768, 781, 792, 796, 805, 811

Manchukuo (män-jō-gwō'), 767, 811, 931-932; see Manchuria

Manchuria (măn-chōōr′-ĭ-à), 98, 108, 641, 698, 767, 770, 813, 917†, 920†, 923, 927*, 928, 929, 930, 931, 932

Mandalay, 393, 606

Mandarin dialect, 821

"Mandeville, Sir John," French physician and traveler (14th century), 703

Manet, Edouard, French painter (1832-1883), 912

Manetho (măn′-ê-thō), Egyptian author and priest (ca. 300-250 B.C.), 179*, 301†

Mang (mäng) family, 682

Mang He (mäng hä), Chinese statesman (ca. 500 B.C.), 662

Mangu (măn′-gōō), Grand Khan of the Mongols (1250-1259), 763

Mangwa (män-gwä), 909

Manish-tusu (mä-nĭsh′-tōō-sōō?), King of Akkad, 126

Mantras (màn′-tràz), 407, 518, 610

Manu (mà′-nōō), semi-historical Indian lawgiver, 484

Manu, Code of, 28*, 482, 484, 485-488, 489, 491-492, 493, 494, 495, 496-497, 499, 530, 541, 564

Manuel I, King of Portugal (1495-1521), 613

Manufacture, in Sumeria, 124; in Egypt, 158-159; in Babylonia, 227; in Assyria, 274; in India, 479; in China, 735, 777; in Japan, 853-854

Manyoshu (män-yō-shōō), 878

Maoris (mä′-ô-rēz), 42, 50

Mara (mä′-rà), 426

Maracaibo, Lake, 99*

Marathon, 355, 360, 381

"Marco Millions," 760, 766; *see* Polo, Marco

Mardi Gras, 37, 66

Marduk (mär′-dŏŏk), 221, 223, 225, 233, 235, 237, 240, 241, 256, 261, 268, 278

Marquesas (mär-kä′-zàs) Islanders, 26

Marriage, in primitive societies, 36-44, 48; in Sumeria, 129-130; in Egypt, 164; in Babylonia, 246-247; in Assyria, 275; in Judea, 335-337; in Persia, 374-375; in India, 401, 489-490, 491-492; in China, 790-792, 819; in Japan, 924

Marseilles, 293

Marshall, Sir John, 394-395, 396, 442*, 508, 596

Marston, Sir Charles, 173*

Marston Expedition of the University of Liverpool, 302*

Maruyami Okyo (mä-rōō-yä-mē ō-kyō), Japanese painter (1733-1795), 906

Marwar (mär-wär′), 454

Mary, mother of Jesus, 247, 511

Mary of Scotland, 889

Mas-d'Azil, 98

Maskarin Gosala (mäs′-kà-rĭn gō′-sä-là), Indian sceptic, 417

Mason, William A., 76-77

Maspero, Gaston, French Egyptologist (1846-1916), 143, 145, 186-187, 188

Mass (ritual), 62

Massagetæ (măs-sà-gē′-tē), 353, 355

Masuda (mä-sōō-dà), Japanese statesman (fl. 1596), 843*

Mathematics, in primitive societies, 78-79; in Sumeria, 124; in Egypt, 179-180; in Babylonia, 256; in India, 527-528; in China, 781

Mathura (ma′-tōō-rà), 450, 460, 477, 593, 594

Matsura Basho (mät-sōō-rà bä-shō), Japanese poet (1643-1694), 881

Maud, 891

Maurya (môr′-yà) Dynasty, 441, 454

May Day, 65, 66

May King and Queen, 65

Maya (mä′-yä), 540, 548, 549, 550, 551, 552, 553

Maya, Buddha's mother (died 563 B.C.), 423, 424, 425*

Mayas, 527*

Mazzoth (mät′-sàt), 332

Measurement, standards of, 80

Mecca, 471

Medes, 223, 283, 286*, 287, 350-352, 356, 363, 365, 397†

Media (mē′-dyà), 269, 270, 350-352, 353, 354, 355

Medici, 155, 751, 835

Medici, Lorenzo de', Florentine statesman and poet (1448-1492), 216, 756

Medicine, origins of, 80-81; in Sumeria, 125; in Egypt, 182-184; in Babylonia, 258-259; in Assyria, 276; in Persia, 377; in India, 530-532; in China, 782; in Japan, 924

Medinet-Habu (mē-dē′-nĕt-hä′bōō), 185

Mediterranean Signary, the, 105

Mediums of exchange, in primitive societies, 15-16; in Sumeria, 125; in Egypt, 160-161; in Babylonia, 228; in Assyria, 274; in Lydia, 289; in Judea, 306, 337; in Persia, 358; in India, 400, 480, 481; in China, 779-780; in Japan, 854, 920

Medum (mē-dōōm′), 190

Megasthenes (mĕ-găs'-thĕ-nēz), Greek geographer (ca. 300 B.C.), 391*, 441, 443, 445, 478, 480, 493, 596
Mei Lan-fang (mā län-fäng'), Chinese actor (20th century), 723
Meiji (mā-jē), see Mutsuhito
Meiji Era (in Japan), 916
Meissen, 759
Melanesians, 11, 16, 31, 42, 81, 84
Melkarth (mĕl-kärth), 294
Melos, 293
Melville, Herman, American novelist (1819-1891), 26
Memnon, colossi of, 141, 188
Memphis, 2, 140, 147, 151, 216, 248, 268, 353
Menander, King of Bacteria (ca. 100 B.C.), 523
Mencius (mĕn-shĭ-ŭs), Chinese philosopher (372-289 B.C.), 646, 674, 677, 681, 682-686, 687, 688, 693, 697, 789, 843
Mendes, 199
Menes (mē'-nēz), possibly Egypt's first king (ca. 3500 B.C.), 140, 147
Menkaure (mĕn-kou'-rē), King of Egypt (3011-2988 B.C.), 150, 186
Menstruation, 70
Mephibosheth (mĕ-fĭb'-ō-shĕth), Jewish pretender (ca. 900 B.C.), 305
Mercury, 179*, 277*
Mermaid Tavern, 880
Merneptah (mĕr-nĕp'-tä), King of Egypt 1233-1223 B.C.), 301
Mesha (mā'-shà), King of Moab (ca. 840 B.C.), 295, 297
Mesopotamia, 103, 105, 108, 109, 118, 119, 121, 124, 131, 133, 135, 136, 138, 179, 218-264, 295, 298, 299, 380, 395, 400, 578†, 641, 744, 779
Messiah, 319, 320, 325-326
Messianism, 195
Metals, Age of, 102-104
Metalwork, Sumerian, 133-134; Egyptian, 191, 192; Babylonian, 227, 254; Assyrian, 278; Lydian, 289; Indian, 585; Chinese, 737-739; Japanese, 896
Method of Architecture, 740-741
Metropolitan Museum of Art, New York, 143*, 150*, 188, 190*, 479*, 716*, 738, 740†, 758*, 906
Mewar (mā-wär'), 454, 455, 465
Mexico, 9, 66, 93, 292*, 329, 737
Mi Fei (mē fā), Chinese painter (1051-1107), 751

Michelangelo (Buanarotti), Italian artist (1474-1564), 751
Micronesia, 32
Midas (mī'-dàs), 288
Middle Flowery Kingdom, 641
Middle Flowery People's Kingdom, 641
Middle Kingdom (China), 643-644
Middle Kingdom (Egypt), 151*, 152, 169, 174*, 176, 178, 190, 191, 195
Mihiragula (mĭ-hĭ-rà'-gōo-là), Hunnish king (502-542), 452
Mikado (mĭ-kä'-dō), 834
Milan cathedral, 379
Milcom (mĭl'-kŏm), god of the Ammonites, 312, 321
Miletus, 218
Milinda, 523; see Menander
Mill, James, British historian and political economist (1773-1836), 616
Mill, John Stuart, English philosopher and economist (1806-1873), 924
Millet, Jean-François, French painter (1815-1875), 912
Milton, John, English poet (1608-1684), 712
Minamoto (mē-nä-mō-tō) family, 835, 837, 838
Minamoto Sanetomo (sä-nä-tō-mō), Japanese shogun (1203-1219), 835
Ming Dynasty, 686, 724, 736, 738-739, 740, 742, 757, 758, 767, 782, 904, 912
Ming Huang (mĭng hwäng), Chinese emperor (713-756), 703-704, 705, 707-708, 711, 713, 714-715, 721, 728, 749, 795, 835*
Mining, in primitive cultures, 100, 103-104; in Egypt, 157-158; in Babylonia, 227; in Assyria, 274; in the Hittite Empire, 286; in Armenia, 287; in India, 444, 478; in China, 647, 781
Minos, 90, 331‡
Mir Jafar (mēr jà'-fàr), Nawab of Bengal (1757-1760; 1763-1765), 614
Miriam, sister of Moses, 333
Mirzapur (mēr-zà-pōor'), 589
Miserables, Les, 718
Mississippi River, 99
Mitanni (mĭ-tăn'-nĕ), 266, 285-286†
Mithra (mĭth'-rà), 285, 365, 370, 371-372
Mithridates (mĭth-rĭ-dā'-tēz), Persian soldier (ca. 400 B.C.), 362*
Mitra (mē'-trà), Hindu deity, 397†, 403
Mitsubishi (mĭt-sōo-bē-shē) family, 920
Mitsui (mĭt-sōo-ē) family, 920
Mitsu-kuni (mĭt-sōo-kōo-nē), Japanese scholar and historian (1622-1704), 886

Mo Ti (mō dē), philosopher of universal love (ca. 450 B.C.), 677-679, 681, 682, 873

Moab (mō'-ăb), 295, 297, 311, 318, 324

Moabites, 285, 298, 299, 303, 312

Modesty, in primitive societies, 46-48

Moeris (mē'-rĭs) Lake, 159-160

Moguls (mō'-gŭlz), 391, 442, 464, 476, 480, 591, 611

Mohammed (mō-hăm'-ĕd), Arabian religious leader (571-632), 39, 291

Mohamudgara (mō-hä'-mŏod-gä-rà), 551

Mohenjo-daro (mō-hän'-jō-dä'-rō), 90, 289*, 391, 394-396, 478, 508, 584, 593, 596

Mohism, 678-679

Molière (assumed name of Jean-Baptiste Poquelin), French dramatist (1622-1673), 873

Moloch (mō'-lŏk), 66, 295, 312, 321

Molucca Islands, 60

Mommu (mō-mōō), Emperor of Japan (697-707), 850, 877

Momoyama (mō-mō-yä-mà), 895

Mona Lisa, 186

Monaco, 400

Monet, Claude, French painter (1840-1926), 912

Money, see Mediums of exchange

Mongol Dynasty, 757, 764, 766

Mongolia, 94, 140, 449, 504, 602, 606, 641, 767.

Mongols, 60, 119, 152, 763, 764-766, 798, 831

Monier-Williams, Sir Monier, English Orientalist (1819-1899), 397*

Monitor and Merrimac, 839

Montaigne, Michel Eyquem de, French essayist and philosopher (1533-1592), 11

Montesquieu, Charles de Secondat, Baron de, French man of letters (1689-1755), 299

Montmartre, 748

Moon worship, 59, 60; in Egypt, 198

Moors, 216

Montagu-Chelmsford reforms, 629

Moplah (mō'-plà), 628

Morality, 935; defined, 47; in primitive societies, 44-56; in Sumeria, 129-130; in Egypt, 166-167; in Babylonia, 244-248; in Assyria, 275; in Judea, 331-339; in Persia, 374; in India, 401, 488-497; in China, 788-795; in Japan, 923, 924

Morbihan, 102

Morgan, John Pierpont, 479*

Morgan, Lewis Henry, American ethnologist (1818-1881), 73

Mori Zozen (môr-ē zō-zĕn), Japanese painter (1747-1821), 906

Morocco, 140

Morris, William, English poet and artist (1834-1896), 906

Mosaic Code, 219, 220*, 330-339, 374

Moscow, 693, 817

Moses, 12, 28, 219, 300, 301, 302, 303, 309, 310, 311, 312, 313, 321, 340, 348, 374

Moslems, 392, 453, 455, 456, 458, 460, 463, 471, 508*, 584, 599-600, 603

Mosul, (mō-sōōl'), 265, 478

Mother, the, in primitive societies, 30-32

Mother of God, 200, 201, 235

Moti Masjid (mō'-tḗ màs'-jēd), 608, 609

Moto-ori Noringa (mō-tō-ō-rē nō-rē-nä-gà), (1730-1801), Japanese historian of Shinto legends, 830*, 865, 874-875, 914

Mouhot, Henri, French Orientalist (ca. 1858), 604

Mound Builders, 99, 103, 104

Mount Abu (ä'-bōo), 598-599

Mousterian Culture, 93, 94, 300

Mridanga (mrĭ-dàn'-gà), 586

Mu-ch'i (mōo-chĭ), Chinese painter (10th century), 751

Mudhera (mōo-dä'-rà), 599

Muhammad bin Tughlak (mōo-hàm' màd bĭn tōōgh'-làk), Sultan of Delhi (1325-1351), 461

Mukden (mōok'-dĕn), 918

Müller, Friedrich Max, English philologist (1823-1900), 164, 312, 391*

Multan (mōōl-tän'), 459, 465

Mummification, 150

Mumtaz Mahal (mŏom'-tàz mà-hàl'), Shah Jehan's wife (died 1631), 473, 474, 609

Münchausen, Hieronymus Karl Friedrich, Baron, German teller of tale tales (1720-1797), 294

Munro, Sir Thomas, British general and Colonial administrator (1761-1827), 614

Murasaki no-Shikibu (mōo-rä-sä-kē nō-shĭk-ĭ-bōo), Lady, Japanese novelist (978-1031?), 882, 883, 884, 891

Murdoch, James, 703, 865*

Muro Kyuso (mōo-rō kū-zō), Japanese philosopher (fl. 1700), 867-868

Murray Islands, 45

Murray River tribes, 33

Murshidabad (mōor-shĕd'-à-bäd), 481

Musa, Ibn (mōo'-zà, ĭb-n), Arabian mathematician (died ca. 850 B.C.), 527

Music, origins of, 88; in Egypt, 192; in Babylonia, 254; in Persia, 378; in India, 586-588; in China, 723; in Japan, 892-893

Mussolini, Benito, Italian statesman (1883-), 69

Mutsuhito (mōōt-sōō-hē-tō), Emperor of Japan (1868-1912), 846, 916, 919, 923, 927

Muttu Virappa Nayyak (mōōt'-tōō vē-ràp'-pa nä'-yäk), Prince of Madura (early 17th century), 602

My Reminiscences (Tagore), 620*

Mycerinus (mǐs-ēr-ǐ'-ǔs), *see* Menkaure

Mylitta (mǐ-lǐt'-tà), 37, 245*, 295; *see* Ishtar

Mysians, 285

Mysore (mī-sôr') (city), 393, 456

Mysore (state), 396, 457, 510, 601

N

Nabonidus (nǎb-ō-nī'-dǔs), King of Babylon (556-539 B.C.), 263

Nabopolassar (nǎb-ō-pō-lǎs'ēr), King of Babylonia (ca. 625-605 B.C.), 223, 224, 283

Nabu (nä'-bōō), 256, 277

Nadir Shah (nä'-dēr shä), Persian conqueror and ruler (1734-1747), 473*

Naga (nä'-gà) (dragon god), 395,* 402, 604, 605

Nagaoka (nä-gà-ō'-kà), 834

Nagarjuna (nä'-gär-jōō'-nà), Indian scientist (2nd century B.C.), 450, 529

Nagas (nä'-gàz) (tribe), 396, 398

Nagasaki (nä-gà-sä-kē), 840

Nagasena (nä-gà-sā'-nà), Indian sage (ca. 100 B.C.), 523

Naharina (nä-hä-rē'-nà), 164

Naiki (nī-kē), Japanese hero (ca. 1615), 849

Nakaye Toju (nä-kī-yě tō-jōō), Japanese philosopher (1608-1648), 871

Naksh-i-Rustam (näk'-shě-rōōs-täm'), 356, 378

Nala (nà'-là), 491, 564

Nalanda (nä'-làn-dà), 454, 557-558

Nambudri (näm-bōō'-drǐ) Brahmans, 486*

Namikawa Tenjin (nä-mě-kä-wä těn-jēn), Japanese philosopher (ca. 1700), 873

Nana, 288†

Nanak (nä'-nàk), founder of the Sikhs (ca. 1468-1539), 583

Nanda (nàn'-dà) (family), 441

Nanda, Magadhan prince (ca. 523 B.C.), 437

Nandi (nàn'-dē), 402

Nanking (nǎn'-king, nän-jǐng), 659, 722, 739, 742, 747, 764, 805

Nanking, Treaty of, 804-805

Nanking Government, 812*, 814

Nannar (nàn'-när), 133, 234

Naomi (nä'-ō-mě, nä-ō'-mě), 312

Napoleon I, Emperor of the French (1804-1815), 69, 91, 139, 141, 144, 145, 154*, 163, 164, 246, 270, 353, 466, 467, 695

Nara (nä-rà), 738, 757, 834, 835, 851, 855, 865*, 876, 878, 879, 880, 892, 897-898

Narada (nä'-rà-dà), 588

Naram-sin (när'-äm-sǐn'), King of Sumeria and Akkad (2795-2739 B.C.), 122, 133, 255

Narbada (nàr-bà-dä') River, 397‡

Nasik (nä'-sǐk), 597

Nasiru-d-din (nä'-sēr-ōōd-dēn'), Sultan of Delhi (fl. 1510), 483*

Nastika (näs'-tǐ-kà), philodophies, 534

Nastiks, 416-417

Nationalists (Indian), 621, 626, 629-630, 632

Naucratis (nô'-krà-tǐs), 138

Nautch (nôch) girls, 490

Neanderthal Man, 92, 93, 94, 95, 300

Near East, 93, 105, 116, 118*, 120, 132, 134-135, 154-160, 174, 181, 212, 215, 223, 224, 226, 227, 255, 263, 265, 268, 270, 271, 273, 281, 284, 285, 288, 290, 292, 293, 295, 298, 303, 306, 326, 329, 335, 337, 339, 353, 356, 357, 362, 478, 728, 755†

Nebo (nē'-bō), 235

Nebraska, 94

Neb-sent (něb'-sěnt), Egyptian lady (ca. 3100 B.C.), 165

Nebuchadrezzar (něb'-ūk-àd-rěz'-ēr) II, King of Babylon (605-562 B.C.), 223-224, 225, 227, 228, 229, 233, 241, 257, 262, 285, 298, 321, 322, 324, 327, 666

Necho (nē-kō), *see* Niku II

Negroes, American, 6

Neo-Confucianism, 675

Neolithic man, 98-102, 106, 117

Neo-Platonism, 553

Nepal (ně-pôl'), 451, 506

Nephthys(něf'-thǐs), 201

Nergal (nēr'-gäl), 240, 256

Nero, Lucius Domitius, Roman emperor 54-68), 269

Nestorianism, 702, 787-788

Netherlands, 753

Netsuke (nět-sōō-kä), 893, 898

New Britain, 10, 46, 49, 57, 84

New Caledonia, 35, 77, 84

New Georgia, 45

New Guinea, 15, 32, 34, 42, 43, 45, 84, 99*

New Hanover, 84

New Hebrides, 34

New Holland, 79
"New Life" movement, 818*
New Mexico, 94
New South Wales, 14
New Testament, 415, 416, 616
"New Tide" movement, 821-822
New York, 133*, 393, 703
New Zealand, 29, 84
Newton, Sir Isaac, English scientist (1642-1727), 529
Nichiren (nĭ-chē-rĕn), founder of the Lotus Sect (1222-1282), 864
Nietzsche, Friedrich Wilhelm, German philosopher (1844-1900), 23, 177, 376, 457*, 539*, 554, 657, 659, 723, 734, 819
Nigeria, 45, 75
Nihongi (nyē-hōng-gĭ), 886
Nikko (nyĭk-kō), 894
Nikon Bashi (nyĭk-ōn bä-shē) (Tokyo bridge), 847
Niku (nē'-kōo) II, King of Egypt (609-593 B.C.), 321
Nile River, 94*, 109, 135, 137, 138, 140, 141, 142, 144, 145, 146, 152, 156, 160, 161, 179, 180, 181, 183, 185, 190, 197, 200, 202, 214, 218, 299, 300, 358, 396
Nimrud (nim'-rōod), see Kalakh
Nina (nē'-na), 266
Nineveh (nĭn'-ĕ-vĕ), 1, 14, 117, 135, 218, 223, 237*, 256, 265, 266, 268, 269, 274, 276, 278, 279, 281-282, 283, 284, 290, 303, 306, 307, 317, 321, 351, 380
Ning Tsung (nĭng dzŏong), Emperor of China (ca. 1212), 763
Ningirsu (nĭn-gēr'-sōo), 117
Ningpo (nĭng-po), 805
Ninigi (nĭn-ĭ-jĭ), 830
Ninil (nĭn'-ĭl), 256
Ninkarsag (nĭn-kär'-säg), 127
Ninlil (nĭn'-lĭl), 127
Ninsei (nĭn'-sā), Japanese potter (ca. 1655), 900
Nippon (nĭp-pŏn'), 830†; see Japan
Nippur (nĭp-pōor'), 118, 120, 121, 123, 127, 132
Nirvana (nēr-vä'-nà), 394, 428, 435-436, 504, 517, 518, 535, 541, 549, 564
Nishi-Hongwan (nĭsh-ē hŏng-wän) Temple, 894, 895
Nisin (nē-zĭn), 118
Niyama (nē-yä-mä), 543
No plays, 841, 889-890
Noah, 290*, 330
Nobel prizes, 391, 619, 621

Nobunaga (nō-bōo-nä-gà), Japanese shogun (1573-1582), 838, 839, 889, 900
Nofretete (nō-frä-tā'-tä), wife of Amenhotep IV (fl. 1380-1362 B.C.), 118, 212
Nofrit (nō'-frĭt), wife of Rahotep, 187
Nogi, Count Maresuke (nō-gĕ, mä-rä-sōo-kä), Japanese general (1849-1912), 846, 918
Noguchi, Hideyo (hē-dä-yō nō-gōo-chē), Japanese scientist (1876-1928), 924-925
Noguchi, Yone (yō-nä), Japanese poet, 881
Nomarchs, 146
Nomes, 146-147
North America, 99*, 103, 108, 391
North Star, 293
Nubia (nū'-bĭ-à), 46, 140, 158, 213
Numa Pompilius, 647
Nur Jehan (noor jà-hän'), Jehangir's wife (ca. 1625), 472-473, 609
Nut (nōot), 198, 201
Nutmose (nōot'-mōz), Egyptian artist (ca. 1370 B. C.), 211
Nyaya (nyä'-yà) philosophy, 535-536
Nyaya Sutra (sōo'-trà), 533

O

Oannes (ō-ăn'-ās), 118*, 237
Ocean of Music, 529*
Oceania, 14, 87, 104; also see Melanesians, Polynesians
Ochus (ō'-kŭs), see Artaxerxes III Ochus
O'Connell, Daniel, Irish orator and politician (1775-1847), 673*
Odyssey, 561, 564, 567
Ogodai (ō-gō-dī), Grand Khan of the Mongols (1229-1241), 763
Ogyu Sorai (ōg-yōo sō-rī), Japanese philosopher (1666-1728), 872, 873-874
Ojeda, Alonso de, Spanish explorer (ca. 1470-1508), 99*
Ojibwa Indians, 61
Oklahoma, 94
Old Kingdom (Egypt), 142, 150*, 169, 176, 178, 184, 187, 189, 190, 194
Old Persian, 249, 356-357
Old Testament, 313, 318, 328, 329, 334, 339, 341, 510, 616
Omaha Indians, 16, 22, 75
Omar (ō'-mär), mosque of, Jerusalem, 607
Omura (ō-mōo-rà), Lord of Nagasaki (16th century), 840
Onan (ō'-năn), biblical character, 39
Onna Daikaku (ōn-nà dī-kà-kōo), 869-870

Ono Goroyemon (ō-nō gō-rō-yā-mŏn), Japanese sculptor (ca. 1252), 898
Onomatopœia, 73
"Open Door," 806, 929
Open Door to the Hidden Heathendom, 391*
Ophelia, 518
Ophir (ō'-fēr), 306
Opium War, first, 804, 805
Opium War, second, 805
Oppenheim, Baron von, 286†
Oppenheimer, Franz, 23
Oppert, Julius, German Orientalist (1825-1905), 118*-119*
Orang Sakai, 38
Ordeal, in primitive societies, 28
Oriental Museum (University of Chicago) Expedition, 378†
Orinoco Indians, 42, 86
Orion, 198
Orissa (ō-rǐs'-sà), 599
Orphism, 553
Osaka (ō-sä-kä), 841, 890, 895, 919-920, 921
Osiris (ō-sī'-rǐs), 178, 199, 200, 202
Oudh (oud), 567, 614
Ouranos, 58
Outcastes, 399, 477, 489, 520, 623, 624
Ovid (Publius Ovidius Naso), Roman poet (43 B.C.-A.D. 18), 62
Oxford, 211, 595
Oxford Field Expedition, 125
Oyomei (ō-yō-mā), 871; *see* Wang Yang-ming
Oyomei philosophy, 871-872

P

Pactolus (păc-tō'-lŭs) River, 285
Padmapani (pàd-mà-pä'-nē), 594
Paes, Domingos, Portuguese missionary (fl. 1522), 457
Pahlavi (pä'-là-vē), 357
Painting, origins of, 87, 94, 96-97; Sumerian, 132; Egyptian, 190-191; Babylonian, 255; Assyrian, 278; Persian, 380; Indian, 589-593; Chinese, 745-754; Japanese, 901-906
Paleolithic man, 90-98
Palestine, 94, 104, 109, 137, 152, 173, 224, 227, 248, 270, 298, 299, 300, 301, 305*, 307, 321, 333, 355, 363, 371
Palestrina, Giovanni Pierluigi da, Italian composer (1524-1594), 723
Pali (pä'-lē), 555
Pallavas (pàl'-là-vàz), 456
Pamirs (pä-mērz'), 392, 393

Pamphylians (păm-fǐl'-yànz), 285
Pan, 58
P'an Chao (pän jō), Chinese female scholar (ca. 100), 792
Pan Ho-pan (pän hō-pän), Lady, Chinese bluestocking, 793
P'an Ku (pän gōō), the Chinese Adam, 642
P'an Ku, Chinese historian (ca. 100), 792
Panchagavia (pàn-chà-gà'-vyà), 521
Panchatantra (pàn-chà-tàn'-trà), 578
Pandavas (pän'-dà-vàz), 561-562, 565
Pandora, 330
Pandyas (pën'-dyàz), 456
Panini (pä'-nǐ-nǐ), Indian grammarian (7th century B.C.), 556
Panipat (pän'-ǐ-pät), 464
Paper, 171
Paphos (Cyprus), 293
Papuans, 32, 43, 45, 48, 49, 50
Paraguay, 50
Parchesi, 501
Parganait (pär'-gà-nīt) (caste of peasants), 501
Pariahs (pà-rī'-àz), *see* Outcastes
Paribbajaka (pà-rǐ-bä'-jà-kà), 417
Paris, 442, 604, 817, 835
Parjanya, 402
Park, Mungo, Scotch explorer (1771-1805), 83
Parmenides, Greek philosopher (5th century B.C.), 533, 551*, 553
Parmenio, Macedonian general (400-330 B.C.), 384
Parsees, 372, 508*, 629
Parshwanath (pär'-shwà-nàt), 598
Parthenon, 307, 912
Parthia, 479
Parvati (pär'-và-tē) (an aspect of Kali), 509, 590
Parysatis (pà-rǐs'-à-tǐs), mother of Artaxerxes II (ca. 400 B.C.), 375*
Pasargadæ (pà-sär'-gà-dē), 362, 378
Pascal, Blaise, French mathematician and philosopher (1623-1662), 678
Paschal Lamb, 333*
Pasenada or Pasenadi (pà-sä'-nà-dǐ), 589
Pasteur, Louis, French scientist (1822-1895), 782
Patanjali (pà-tàn'-jà-lē), Indian *Yoga* teacher (ca. 150 B.C.), 504, 508†, 543, 544, 556
Patesis (pà-tā'-zēz), 126, 233, 266
Pataliputra (pä'-tà-lǐ-pōō'-trà), 422, 441, 442, 444, 445, 449, 451, 593*
Patna (pàt'-nà), 441* *see* Pataliputra

Pattadakal (pȧt'-ȧ-dȧ-kȧl), 602
Paul, St., Apostle of the Gentiles (martyred A.D. 67), 20, 342, 731
Paulists, 469
Pawnee Indians, 66
Peacock Throne, 473, 608
"Pear Tree Garden," 704
Peary, Robert Edwin, American arctic explorer (1856-1920), 6
Pechili (bā-jē'-lé), Gulf of, 641
Pei (bā), Chinese general (ca. 700), 749
Pei, W. C., 92
Peiping (bā-bǐng), 2, 92, 94, 152, 812†; also see Peking
Peking (bā-jǐng), 741, 742, 763, 767, 775, 779, 804, 805, 806, 812, 931
Peking Man, 92, 102, 641, 765
Pelew Islands, 32
Pelliot, P., 506, 739
Pelusium (pḗ-lū'-shǐ-ŭm), 227, 267*
Penelope, 570
Penguin Island, 47
Pennsylvania, University of, 119*
Penology, see Punishment
Pentateuch, 299, 301, 310, 328, 340
Pentecost, 332
Pepi (pā'-pḗ) II, King of Egypt (2738-2644 B.C.), 151
Pericles, Athenian statesman (499-429 B.C.), 123, 139, 141, 751, 781
Persephone, 238
Persepolis (pḗr-sĕp-ō-lǐs), 90, 128, 362, 365*, 378, 379-380, 381, 384, 385, 596, 744
Persia, 24*, 60, 108, 109, 117, 182, 189, 215, 222*, 226, 248, 249, 263, 270, 272, 278, 280, 284, 285, 286, 287, 290, 294, 299, 313, 326, 328, 329, 349, 350-385, 392, 397, 405, 422*, 440, 450, 464, 473*, 478, 480, 501, 529, 596, 607, 640, 651, 703, 729, 766, 779
Persian Gulf, 117, 118, 119, 121, 221, 224, 228, 267, 290, 292, 356, 479, 703, 761
Peru, 2, 16, 292*
Perur (pā'-rōor), 594
Peruvian Indians, 65, 77, 81
Pesach (pā-sȧк), 332-333
Peschel, Oskar Ferdinand, German geographer (1826-1875), 159
Peshawar (pā-shä'-wär), 392, 450
Peter the Great, Czar of Russia (1682-1725), 314, 640, 693
Petrarch (Francesco Petrarca), Italian poet (1304-1374), 555, 611
Petrie, Sir William Flinders, 104, 105, 143, 145, 166, 211, 212*, 296, 300*, 301, 701*

Petronius Arbiter, Roman author (died A.D. 66), 155
Peyn (pān), 38
Phallic worship, 61; in Egypt, 199; in Judea, 309; in India, 501, 518-520
Pharaohs, 41, 142, 148, 151, 156, 160, 162, 163-164, 178, 192, 201, 228
Pharos (fā'-rŏs), at Alexandria, 137
Pheidias, Greek sculptor (ca. 490-432 B.C.), 895
Philae (fī'-lḗ), 185
Philistines (fǐ-lǐs'-tǐnz), 267, 285, 298, 299, 300, 304, 315
Philippine (fǐl'-ǐ-pēn) Islands, 45, 46, 53, 804, 806, 928, 931
Philo Judaeus (fī'-lō jōō-dē'-ŭs), Greek Jewish philosopher (20 B.C.-A.D. 50), 367*
Philosophy, 936; Egyptian, 193-197; Babylonian, 259-263; Hebrew, 339, 343-349; Indian, 410-415, 416-419, 513-517, 533-554; Chinese, 650-651, 653-658, 659-660, 661, 666-674, 675, 676, 677-682, 684-693, 731-735, 783-788, 821; Japanese, 866-876
Phoenicia (fḗ-nǐsh'-ǐ-ȧ), 66, 105, 106, 160, 172, 245, 250, 265, 270, 291-296, 298, 303, 306, 308, 355, 363
Phoenician Star, 293
Phoenicians, 215, 217
Phrygia (frǐj'-ǐ-ȧ), 245, 286†, 288-289, 296, 355
Physics, in India, 528-529; in China, 781
Physiocrats, 693
Physiology, in Egypt, 181-182; in India, 529-530; in China, 782
Pi Kan (bē gän), Chinese official (ca. 1140 B.C.), 645
Pi Sheng (bē shŭng), Chinese printer (fl. 1041), 729-730
Pickwick Papers, 885, 891
Picts, 10
Pien Liang (byǎn lē-äng'), 727
Pien-tsai (byǎn-dzī), Chinese connoisseur (ca. 640), 745*
Pillow Sketches, 854, 862, 887-888
Piltdown Man, 92
Pisidians, 285
Pitakas (pǐ'-tȧ-kȧz), 428*
Pittsburgh, 895
Plassey (pläs'-sḗ), 584, 612
Plataea, 360, 381, 751
Plate River, 932
Plato, Greek philosopher (427-347 B.C.), 107, 167, 329, 428*, 533, 553, 799
Playboy of the Western World, 53*

Pleistocene Epochs, 92, 93

Pliny the Elder (Caius Plinius Secundus), Roman naturalist and encyclopedist (23-79), 183, 462, 479

Plutarch, Greek historian (46?-120?), 199, 362*, 373, 384*, 578

Po Chü-i (bō jü-ē), Chinese poet and statesman (722-846), 714, 717

Poe, Edgar Allan, American man of letters (1809-1849), 749

Poems Ancient and Modern, 878

Poetry, in primitive societies, 77-78; in Sumeria, 121-132; in Egypt, 176-178; in Babylonia, 120, 132, 235-236, 241-243, 250-254; in Judea, 340-342; in Persia, 377; in India, 408-409, 561-571, 579-583, 619-621; in China, 648-649, 705-717; in Japan, 878-881, 926-927

Poetry Bureau (Japanese), 880, 927

Poland, 94

Polo, 501

Polo, Marco, Venetian traveler (1254-1324), 38, 391*, 478-479, 543, 729, 742, 760, 761, 763, 765, 766, 777, 779, 790

Polybius, Greek historian (ca. 206-128 B.C.), 379

Polygamy, in primitive societies, 39-41; in Judea, 336; in Persia, 374; in India, 492; in China, 791, 819

Polygyny, 39

Polynesians, 6, 10, 16, 45, 69, 77, 79-80, 103, 107, 329

Pompey the Great (Cneius Pompeius Magnus), Roman general (106-48 B.C.), 137

Pondicherry (pŏn-dĭ-chěr'-ê), 393

Poo See (bōō sā), 330

Poona (pōō'-nà), 393, 597

Popes, 331, 535

Population, of Egypt, 214; of India, 391; of China, 769; of Japan, 851, 920*, 927

Porcelain, *see* Ceramics

Port Arthur, 918, 920†, 928

Portugal, 98, 599, 613, 803, 804

Porus (pôr'-ŭs), Indian king (ca. 325 B.C.), 440, 529

Poseidon, 58

Postal service, in Egypt, 160

Postglacial Stage, 91*

Post-Office, 620*

Potala (pō'-tà-là), 507

Potter's wheel, 117

Pottery, *see* ceramics

Prajapati (prà-jä'-pà-tê), 403, 404, 416, 513

Prakrit (prä'-krĭt), 555, 574

Prakriti (prà'-krĭ-tê), 537, 539, 541

Pranayama (prä'-nä-yà-mà), 543

Prambanam (pràm-bä'-nàm), 603

Pratyahara (prà'-tyà-hä'-rà), 543

Praxiteles, Greek sculptor (fl. 360 B.C.), 186

Precepts of Jesus, 616

Premarital relations, in primitive societies, 44-45

Prexaspes (prex-ăs'-pēz), son of Cambyses (ca. 525 B.C.), 354

Priam, 90

Priests, 68; in Sumeria, 126, 128, 129; in Egypt, 201, 202, 214-215; in Babylonia, 230, 232-234; in Assyria, 271-272; in Judea, 313-314, 338; in Persia, 361, 377; in India, 399, 484-488 (also *see* Brahmans); in Japan, 864-865

Prince, 443

Printing, in India, 468, 556†, 585†; in China, 728-730; in Japan, 877*

Prints, 907-910

Prithivi (prĭ-tĭ-wē), 402

Prometheus, 95

Property, private, in primitive societies, 18-20; in Egypt, 161; in Babylonia, 232; in Judea, 337-338; in India, 483, 484

Prophets, 314-328, 340

Prostitution, in primitive societies, 45; in Sumeria, 129; in Egypt, 166; in Babylonia, 37, 244-246; in Assyria, 275; in Lydia, 289; in Judea, 335; in India, 444, 458, 490-491, 496; in China, 790; in Japan, 862

Protagoras, Greek philosopher (fl. 440 B.C.), 422

Proverbs, 167, 334, 342-343, 349

Provins, Guyot de, medieval poet (ca. 1190), 780

Psalms, 210*, 242, 340-341, 343, 408, 581

Psamtik (psäm'-tĭk) I, King of Egypt, Prince of Saïs (663-609 B.C.), 215

Ptah (ptä), 143, 201

Ptah-hotep (ptä-hō'-těp), Egyptian official (ca. 2880 B.C.), 165, 193, 194

Ptolemies, 41, 137, 142, 160, 166, 190, 216*

P'u Yi (pōō yē), now Kang Teh (käng dä), Emperor of Manchukuo, last Chinese emperor (born 1906), 810, 811, 813, 931

Pudmini (pŭd'-mĭ-nê), Rajput princess (ca. 1303?), 455-456

Pueblo Indians, 87

Puget Sound, 1

Pulakeshin (pōō-là-kä'-shĭn) II, Chalukyan king (608-642), 456

Pumpelly, Raphael, American geologist (1837-1923), 108, 117*

Punishment, in primitive societies, 28-29; in Egypt, 162; in Babylonia, 231; in Assyria, 272; in Judea, 338; in Persia, 361-362; in India, 483, 486; in China, 797; in Japan, 850

Punjab (pàn-jäb'), 392, 393, 394, 450, 459, 495

Punt (poont), 153, 189-190

Purana Kashyapa (poo-rä'-nà kä'-shyà-pà), Indian sceptic, 417

Puranas, 504*, 511-513, 516, 541

Purbach, Georg, German astronomer (1423-1461), 528

Purdah (pàr'-dà), 46, 286, 287, 375, 401, 494, 625

Pure Land, Sect of the, 864

Puritans, 242, 313

Purusha (poo'-roo-shà), 411, 538, 539, 541, 566

Puruvaras (poo-roo'-rà-vàz), 511

Purva-Mimansa (poor'-và mē-män'-sà) philosophy, 545-546

Pushtimargiya (poosh'-tĭ-märg'-yà) Brahmans, 486*

Puymre (pwĭm'-rĕ), Egyptian architect (ca. 1500 B.C.), 192

Pygmies, 21, 37, 56

"Pyramid Texts," 174

Pyramids, 138, 139, 140, 144, 147, 148-149, 150, 151, 177, 179, 180, 181, 185, 191, 203*, 216, 308, 395

Pyrenees, 91

Pythagoras, Greek philosopher (6th century B.C.), 533, 536*, 553, 648

"Pythagorean Law," 529

Q

Questions of King Milinda, 523

Quintus Curtius Rufus, Roman historian (fl. 41-54), 248, 383, 384*

R

Ra or Re (rä or rā), 198, 199, 201

Rabindranath Tagore (rà-bĭnd'-rà-nàt tä-gôr'): Poet and Dramatist (E. J. Thompson), 620*

Rachel, Jacob's favorite wife, 41, 303*, 333, 334, 336, 340

Radha (rä'-dà), 580

Ragas (rä'-gàz), 588

Rahotep (rä-hŏ'-tĕp), Egyptian prince (ca. 3100 B.C.?), 149, 187

Rahula (rä'-hoo-là), Buddha's son (ca. 523 B.C.), 425, 437

Rai, Lajpat (rī làj'-pàt), Indian reformer, 497, 616*

Raj Sing (räj sĭng), Rana of Mewar (fl. 1661), 478

Rajaraja, Chola king (fl. 1000), 490

Rajarani (rä-jà-rä'-nē) Temple, 599

Rajasthan (rä-jà-stän'), 495; see Rajputana

Rajatarangini (rä-jà-tà-ràn'-gĭ-nĭ), 579

Rajmahal (räj-mà-hàl') Hills, 501

Rajputana (räj-poo-tä'-nà), 454, 579

Rajputs (räj'-poots), 393, 454-456, 467, 487, 492†, 498, 502, 591

Ram Mohun Roy (räm mō'-hŭn roi), Indian reformer and scholar (1772-1833), 614, 616, 617

Rama (rä'-mà), 417, 451, 511, 552, 561, 567-570, 581, 617*, 625

Rama Raja, Regent of Vijayanagar (fl. 1542-1565), 459

Rama-charita-manasa (rä'-mà-chà'-rĭ-tà-mä'-nà-sà), 581

Ramadan (räm-à-dän'), 471

Ramakrishna (rä'-mà-krĭsh'-nà), Indian religious leader (1836-1886), 617

Ramakrishna Mission, 618

Raman, Chandrasekhara (rä'-màn, chàn'-drà-shä'-kà-rà), Indian physicist (1888-   ), 391, 619

Ramananda (rä-mä'-nàn-dà), Indian preacher (ca. 1460), 582

Ramanuja (rä-mà-noo'-jà), Indian saint and sage (ca. 1050), 552

Ramayana (rä-mä'-yà-nà), 398, 402, 417, 517, 524, 567-571, 605

Rameses (räm'-ĕ-sēz) II, King of Egypt (1300-1233 B.C.), 104, 141, 142, 178, 185, 188, 189, 213-214, 286, 306

Rameses III, King of Egypt (1204-1172 B.C.), 159, 214

Rameses IV, King of Egypt (1172-1166 B.C.), 178

Rameshvaram (räm-äsh'-và-ràm), 393, 519, 602

Ramesseum (räm-ĕ-sē'-ŭm), 170, 185, 214

Rangoon (răn-goon'), 393, 606

Ranofer (rän'-ō-fĕr), Egyptian high priest (ca. 3040 B.C.), 169

Raphael Sanzio, Italian painter (1483-1520), 751, 759

Ratzenhofer, 23

Ravan(a) (rä'-vàn-[à]), 569

Ravenna, 2

Rawalpindi (rä'-wȧl-pĭn'-dĭ), 440, 441-442
Rawlinson, Sir Henry Creswicke, English
    Orientalist and official (1810-1895), 119*,
    249
Rayas (rä'-yȧz), 458
Re, see Ra
Rebecca, wife of Isaac, 303*, 337
Record of Nippon, 886
Record of Ten Feet Square, 889
Records of Ancient Events, 874-875, 885
Red Oleanders (Tagore), 620*
Red Sea, 135, 152, 160, 190, 214, 306, 358
Reichard, 83
Reinach, Salomon, French scholar (1858-
    1932), 96, 390*
Rekh-mara (rĕkh-mä'-rȧ), Egyptian official
    (ca. 1500 B.C.), 103
Religion, as an agent of morality, 55-56, 69-
    71; sources of, 59; its objects of worship,
    59-64; its methods, 64-68; in primitive so-
    cieties, 56-71; in Sumeria, 127-129, 135; in
    Egypt, 197-205, 206, 210; in Babylonia, 135,
    232-244; in Assyria, 275; in Phrygia, 288;
    in Phoenicia, 294-295; in Syria, 296-297;
    in Judea, 308-314, 319, 320, 321, 322, 323,
    325, 326, 327; in Persia, 364-372; in India,
    402-405, 420-422, 428-439, 469-472, 503-525;
    in China, 783-788, 818; in Japan, 832-833,
    840-841, 842-843, 863-865, 898
Re'mery-Ptah (rä'-měr-ê ptä), Egyptian
    singer, 192
Renan, Joseph Ernest, French scholar (1823-
    1892), 73, 303, 330, 345*
Reni, Guido, Italian painter (1575-1642), 759
Reszke, Edouard de, Polish operatic tenor
    (1856-1917), 192
Revelation, 376
Revenge, in primitive societies, 27
Revolutions of Civilization, 701*
Rhodes, 293
Rhodesia, 66, 94, 104
Richtofen, Ferdinand, Baron von, German
    geologist and Asiatic traveler (1833-1905),
    822
Rig-veda (rĭg-vā'-dȧ), 366, 401, 407, 408-409,
    413*, 436, 495, 508†, 530
Rikyu (rĭk-ū), tea master (ca. 1590), 841,
    857-858, 900
Risampei (rê-säm'-pā), Korean ceramic art-
    ist (fl. 1605), 900
Rishis (rĭsh'ēz), 545
Rita (rĭ'-tȧ), 404
Rivers, W. H. R., 16
Robenhausen, 102

Robinson Crusoe, 174
Rock Edicts, 447-448, 527
Rockefeller, John D., Jr., 820*
Rockefeller Foundation for Medical Re-
    search, 820*, 925
Roger, Abraham, Dutch missionary (fl.
    1651), 391*
Roman Catholic Church, 242, 469, 504-505
Romance of the Three Kingdoms, 718, 846
Romans, 16, 118*, 159, 179, 183, 217, 288,
    377, 397, 478
Rome, 3, 19*, 24*, 61, 76, 116, 117, 136, 140,
    152, 172, 185, 200, 216, 218, 226, 227, 247,
    265, 272, 275, 284, 299, 315, 340, 354, 362,
    363, 381-382, 451, 479, 529, 554, 640, 647,
    695, 701, 744, 777, 778, 847, 899, 925
Rome (city), 155, 294, 457
Romeo and Juliet, 891
Ronin (rō'-nĭn), Forty-seven, 848-849, 908
Roosevelt, Theodore, President of the
    United States (1858-1919), 918, 929-930
Rosetta (rō'-zĕt'-tȧ) Stone, the, 145
Rosh-ha-shanah (rōsh hä-shä'-nȧ), 332
Ross, Sir Donald, 773
Rossbach, 613
Rousseau, Jean-Jacques, French philosopher
    (1712-1778), 655, 657, 688, 693, 754, 858,
    873, 874
Rowland Acts, 629
Rowley, H., 65
Roxana (rŏx-ȧn'-ȧ), wife and sister of Cam-
    byses (ca. 525 B.C.), 354
Royal Asiatic Society, 249
Rubruquis, Guillaume de, medieval traveler
    and missionary (fl. 1253), 780
Rudra (rŏŏ'-drȧ), 402
Rukmini (rŏŏk-mĭ-nĭ), 594
Ruskin, John, English critic (1819-1900),
    188, 631
Russell, Bertrand, Earl, 821
Russia, 19*, 26, 35, 37, 42, 99*, 103, 116, 355,
    356, 392, 506, 626, 640, 642, 806, 808, 812,
    814, 848, 875, 917*, 918-919, 928, 931, 932,
    933
Ruth, 312, 336

S

Sabitu (sä'-bĭ-too), 253, 261
Sacia (sä'-shȧ), 354
Sacramento River Valley, 8
"Sacred Books of the East," 391*
Sahu (sä'-hŏŏ), 198
Saigyo Hoshi (sī-gyō hō-shé), Japanese
    poet (1118-1190), 880

Saint Peter's, Basilica of, Rome, 609
Saïs (sä-ĭs), 138
Saïte (sä'-ĭt) Age (Egypt), 151*, 179, 188
Sake (sä-kē), 856-857
Sakhalin (säĸ'-à-lēn'), 928
Sakkarah (sà-kä'-rà), 147, 186, 189
Sakon (sä-kōn), Japanese hero (ca. 1615), 849
Saladin (säl'-à-dĭn), Sultan of Egypt and Syria (1137-1193), 756
Salamis, 381, 383
Salim Chisti (sä'-lĭm chĭs'-tê), Indian statesman and sage (ca. 1590), 468, 608
Samadhi (sà-mä'-dĭ), 544
Samaria (sà-mä'-rĭ-à), 267, 298, 315, 317, 324, 329
Samarkand (säm-är-kănd'), 350, 453, 463, 464, 703
Samarra (sà-mär'-rà), 135, 756
Sama-veda (sä'-mà-vä'-dà), 407
Samgita-ratnakara (sàn-gē'-tà-ràt-nä'-kà-rà), 529*
Sammuramat (sà-mōōr'-à-mät), Queen of Assyria (811-808 B.C.), 267
Samoa, 16, 17, 22, 49, 60, 107
Samoyeds, 32
Samson, Hebrew prophet and judge (ca. 1130 B.C.), 250, 305*, 340
Samudragupta (sà-mōōd-rà-gōōp'-tà), King of Magadha (330-380), 451
Samuel, Hebrew judge (ca. 1025 B.C.), 339
Samurais (sä'-mōō-rīz), 839, 841, 842, 846-849, 850, 861, 871, 873, 877, 911
San Bartolomeo, Fra Paolino da, Austrian monk (18th century), 391*
San Kuo Chih Yen I (sän-gwo-jē-yăn-ē), 718
Sandanga (sän-däng'-à), 592
Sangaya (sàn'-gä-yà), Indian agnostic, 416-417
Sangha (sàn'-gà), 438, 505
Sankhya (sän'-kyà) philosophy, 534, 536-541, 546, 564, 566
Sankhya-karika (sän'-kyà-kä'-rĭ-kà), 536*
Sankhya-sutras (sōō'-tràz), 536*
Sannyasi (sàn-nyä'-sē), 522
Sanskrit, 356, 391*, 405-406, 452, 458, 520, 550
Santo Kioden (sän-to kyō-děn), Japanese novelist (1761-1816), 884-885
Sappho, Greek poet (7th century B.C.), 611
Saracens, 120, 780
Sarah, wife of Abraham, 333, 336
Sardanapalus (sär'-dà-nà-pä'-lŭs), see Ashurbanipal

Sardinia, 98, 293
Sardis, 218, 227, 289, 290, 351, 352, 353, 358
Sargon I, King of Akkad and Sumeria (2872-2817 B.C.), 120, 121-122, 250, 257
Sargon II, King of Assyria (722-705 B.C.), 266*, 272, 278, 279, 280-281, 298
Sarnath (sär'-nàt), 428, 447, 594, 596
Sarton, George, 330, 346*
Sarzac, Ernest de, 131
Sas-Bahu (shàsh-bä'-hōō), 599
Sassanid (sàs'-sà-nĭd) Dynasty, 372
Sasseram (sàs'-sēr-äm), 607
Satan, 344, 367
Satapatha (shà'-tà-pà-tà) Upanishad, 414*
Satow, Sir Ernest Mason, British diplomat and publicist (1843-1929), 874*
Satrapies, 355, 362-363
Satraps (sä'-träps), 359*
Satsuma (sät-sōō-mà), 846, 900
Saturnalia, 37, 65-66
Saul, King of the Jews (1025-1010 B.C.), 304-305, 310, 339
Sautuola, Marcelino de (sou-tōō-ō'-là, mär-thěl-ē'-nō dŭ), Spanish archeologist, 96
Savage, T. S., 37
Savitar (sà'-vĭ-tàr), 403
Savitri (sà'-vĭ-trē), 564
Savonarola, Girolamo, Italian monk and reformer (1452-1498), 632
Scarification, 85
Schelling, Friedrich Wilhelm von, German philosopher (1775-1854), 391*, 554
Schlegel, August Wilhelm von, German philologist (1767-1845), 391*
Schlegel, Friedrich, German philosopher and critic (1772-1829), 391*
Schliemann, Heinrich, German acheologist (1822-1890), 91, 107
Schneider, Hermann, 102
Scholarship, in Babylonia, 248, 250; in China, 727-731; in Japan, 874
Scholastics, 871
Schoolcraft, Henry Rowe, American ethnologist (1793-1864), 49
Schopenhauer, Arthur, German philosopher (1788-1860), 194-195, 391*, 410, 411, 415, 427†, 516*, 544†, 554
Schweinfurth, Georg August, German-Russian traveler (1836-   ), 135
Science, origins of, 67, 68, 78; in Sumeria, 125; in Egypt, 179-184; in Babylonia, 256-259; in Assyria, 276; in Persia, 377; in India, 462, 526-532, 618-619; in China, 780-782; in Japan, 924, 925, 935-936

Scotland, 99*, 323
Scott, Sir Walter, Scotch novelist and poet (1771-1832), 631, 885
Scribe (statue), 186, 187
Scribes, in Egypt, 161, 186, 187; in Babylonia, 248; in Assyria, 271; in India, 556; In China, 745*
Sculpture, origins of, 87; classical, 97; Egyptian, 186-190; Babylonian, 255, 256; Assyrian, 135, 279-280; Hebrew, 332; Persian, 378, 380; Indian, 593-596; Chinese, 739-740; Japanese, 97, 897-898
Scythians (sĭ'-thĭ-ȧnz), 273, 283, 287, 355, 450, 454, 459, 494, 642
Sea of Japan, battle of the, 919
Sebek (sĕb'-ĕk), 199
Sei Shonagon (sā shō-nȧ-gôn), Lady, Japanese essayist (ca. 1000), 854, 860, 862, 887-888
Selene, 58
Seleucus Nicator (sĕ-lū'-cŭs nĕ-kā'-tôr), King of Syria (312-280 B.C.), 441
Semiramis (sĕ-mĭr'-ȧ-mĭs), see Sammuramat
Semites, 66, 118, 120, 127, 290-298
Seneca Indians, 32
Senart, 436
Sendai (sĕn-dī), 926
Senegalese, 43
Senkereh (sĕn'-kĕr-ā), see Larsa
Senmut (sĕn-mōot), Egyptian architect (ca. 1500 B.C.), 192
Sennacherib (sĕn-ăk'-ĕr-ĭb), King of Assyria (705-681 B.C.), 223, 267, 268, 273, 274, 275, 278, 279, 289*, 317
Senusret (sĕn'-ōos-rĕt) I, King of Egypt (2192-2157 B.C.), 152, 188
Senusret II, King of Egypt (2115-2099 B.C.), 178
Senusret III, King of Egypt (2099-2061 B.C.), 152, 159-160, 187-188
Sepoy (sĕ'-poi) Mutiny, 608*
Seppuku, 848; see hara-kiri
Serabit-el-khadim (sĕr-ä'-bĭt-el-kä-dēm'), 296
Serbia, 42
Sermon on the Mount, 628
Sesostris (sĕ-sŏs'-trĭs), see Senusret I
Sesshiu (sĕs-shū), Japanese painter (1420-1506), 904-905
Set (sĕt), 178, 200
Seti (sā'-tĕ) I, King of Egypt (1321-1300 B.C.), 185, 189, 213
Seti II, King of Egypt (1214-1210 B.C.), Seto (sā-tō), 899
Seton-Karr, W. H., 94
Seven Wonders of the World, 225

Sèvres, 759
Shabattu (shä'-bät-tōo), 332
Shabuoth (shä'-vōo'-ōth), 332
Shadufs (shä'-dōofs), 226, 274
Shah (shä), 359*
Shah Jehan (jä-hän'), Mogul emperor (1628-1658), 468, 473-474, 475, 476, 481, 560, 591, 607, 608, 609-610
Shakespeare, William (1564-1616), 173, 184, 340, 581, 843, 889, 891
Shakti (shȧk'-tĕ) sects, 505, 509, 519
Shakuntala (shȧ-kōon'-tȧ-lȧ), 391*, 561, 574-576, 577
Shakuntala, 561, 575-576
Shakya-muni (shä'-kyȧ-mōo-nĭ), 423‡; see Buddha
Shakyas (shä'-kyȧz), 422
Shalmaneser (shăl-mȧ-nē'-sēr) I, King of Assyria (fl. 1267 B.C.), 266
Shalmaneser III, King of Assyria (859-824 B.C.), 267
Shamans (shä'-mȧnz), 77, 542
Shamash (shä'-mäsh), 123, 127, 219, 234, 256, 272, 331‡
Shamash-napishtim (shä'-mäsh-nä-pĭsh'-tĭm), 237, 250, 253, 330
Shamashnazir (shä'-mäsh-nä-zēr'), Babylonian daughter-merchant, 246
Shamash-shum-ukin (shōom-ōo'-kĭn), brother of Ashurbanipal (ca. 650 B.C.), 272
Shamsi-Adad (shäm'-sē-ȧ-däd) VII, King of Assyria (824-811 B.C.), 278
Shang (shäng) Dynasty, 644, 648, 671, 737, 738, 755, 772
Shang (state), 680
Shanghai, 641*, 728, 805, 812*, 814, 816, 930
Shangtu (shäng-dōo), 761
Shankar (shȧn'-kȧr), Indian dancer, 587*
Shankara (shȧn'-kȧ-rȧ), Indian philosopher (788-820), 505, 533, 541, 546-551, 552, 554, 731
Shansi (shän-sē), 645, 739
Shantiniketan (shän'-tĭ-nĭ-kā'-tȧn), 621
Shantung (shän tōong'; Chinese shän dōong), 645, 739-740, 832, 928, 929
Sharaku (shä-rȧ-kōo), Japanese engraver (ca. 1790), 908
Sharamgadeva (shärȧm-gȧ-dā'-vȧ), Indian musical theorist (1210-1247), 529*
Shat-Azalla (shät-ȧ-zäl'-la), 258*
Shatrunjaya (shȧ-trōon'-jä-yȧ), 598
Sheba (shĕ'-bȧ), Queen of, 306
Sheik-el-Beled (shäk-ĕl-bä'-lĕd), 168, 186, 187

Shelley, Percy Bysshe, English poet (1792-1822), 205, 211, 463

Shem, 290*

Shen Nung (shŭn nōōng), Chinese emperor (2737-2697 B.C.), 643

Shen Tsung (shŭn dzōōng), Chinese emperor (1573-1620), 757

Shensi (shän-se; differs only in tone from Shansi), 645

Sheol (shē'-ōl), 313

Shepherd Kings, see Hyksos

Sher Shah (shär shä), Mogul emperor (1542-1545), 464, 480, 607

Sheshonk (shä'-shŏnk) I, King of Egypt (947-925 B.C.), 315

Shi-Ching (shĭ-jĭng), 648-649, 665

Shih Huang-ti (shĭ hwäng-dē), Chinese emperor (221-211 B.C.), 675, 679, 694-698, 727, 738, 739, 775, 778, 782

Shiloh (shĭ'-lō), 336

Shimabara (shĭm-à-bä-rà), 843

Shimadzu (shĭm-äd-zōō) family, 846

Shimazu Yoshihiro (shĭm-äd-zōō yō-shĭ-hē-rō), Japanese ceramic artist (fl. 1596), 900

Shimel (shĭm'-ĕl), Hebrew warrior (died ca. 974 B.C.), 305

Shimla (shĭm'-là), 392

Shilpa-shastra (shĭl'-pà-shäs'-trà), 592

Shingon (shĭn-gôn), 864; see Shintoism

Shintoism (shĭn'-tō-ĭzm), 832, 864, 865, 875, 885, 889, 892, 894

Shippurla (shĭp-pōōr'-là), see Lagash

Ships and shipbuilding, in Egypt, 160; in Babylonia, 221-222, 228; in Phoenicia, 293; in Persia, 358; in India, 400, 479; in China, 778

Shirozemon (shē-rō-zä-mŏn), Japanese potter (ca. 1229,) 899

Shiva (shĭ'-và), 413*, 453, 507, 508-509, 511, 519, 524, 587, 590, 594, 598, 599, 602, 604, 605, 625

Shivaites (shē'-và-ītz), 508, 519, 598, 606

Shizutani (shē-zōō-tä-nē), 877

Shoguns (shō-gōōnz), 837, 839, 846

Shomu (shō-mōō), Emperor of Japan (724-756), 850, 897

Shonzui (shŏn-zōō-é), Japanese ceramic artist (16th century), 899-900

Shotoku (shō-tō-kōō), Empress of Japan (ca. 770), 877*

Shotuku Taishi (tī-shē), Regent of Japan (592-621), 833, 894, 927

Shri Rangam (shrē ràng'-àm) Temple, 602

Shu (shōō), 201

Shub-ad (shōōb'-ăd), Sumerian queen (ca. 3500 B.C.), 130, 133

Shubun (shōō-bōōn), Japanese painter (ca. 1400), 904

Shu-Ching (shoo jĭng), 643, 665, 718

Shuddhodhana (shōōd'-ō-dà-nà), Buddha's father (6th century B.C.), 422, 423, 424, 437

Shudraka (shōō'-drà-kà), 572

Shudras (shoo'-dràz), 399, 480, 485-487, 498, 520, 623, 624

Shui Hu Chuan (shwē hōō jwän), 718

Shun (shwĭn), Chinese emperor (2255-2205 B.C.), 644, 661, 676, 680, 687, 689, 746

Shushan (shōō-shän'), 117

Shushi (shōō-shē), 871; Japanese form of Chu Hsi, q.v.

Shushi philosophers, 871

Shwasanved Upanishad (shwä-sän'-vàd ōō-pàn'-ĭ-shàd), 416, 523

Shwe Dagon (shwä dä-gōn'), 606

Siam, 46, 595, 602, 605-606

Sian-fu (sē-än-fōō), 698*

Siberia, 38, 45, 94, 923‡

Sibu (sē'-boo), 198

Sicily, 293, 776*

Siddhantas (sĭd-dän'-tàz), 526, 527

Siddhartha (sĭd-där'-tà), 423‡; see Buddha

Sidon (sī'-dŏn), 106, 227, 294, 306, 308, 337

Sikhs (sēx), 496, 508*

Sin (sĭn), Mesopotamian deity, 127-128, 256

Sinai (sī'-nī), 140, 173, 302

Sinbad the Sailor, 174

Sind (sĭnd), 394, 396, 479

Singanpur (sĭn'-gän-pōōr'), 589

Single Verses by a Hundred People, 879-880

Sirguya (sēr-gōō'-yà), 589

Sinkiang (sĭn-jē-äng'), 798

Sinuhe (sĭn-ōō-é), Egyptian official and traveler (ca. 2180 B.C.), 174, 175

Sirius, 181

Sissa (sĭs'-sà), Brahman, reputed inventor of chess (ca. 500), 500*

Sit, see Set

Sita (sē'-tä), 402, 403, 517, 568-570

"Six Idlers of the Bamboo Grove," 706

Sixth Dynasty (Egypt), 292

Skeat, Walter William, English philologist (1835-1912), 73

Sky worship, in Egypt, 197-198; in Babylonia, 234; in India, 402, 403

Slavery, in primitive societies, 19-20; in Sumeria, 125; in Egypt, 159; in Babylonia, 229; in Assyria, 275; in Phoenicia, 292-293; in Judea, 337-338; in India, 466, 480
Slavs, 42
Sleeping Buddha Temple, 741
Smerdis (smâr-dĭs), brother of Cambyses (ca. 525 B.C.), 353
"Smerdis," pretender to Persian throne (521 B.C.), 354, 360
Smith, Sir Andrew, 84
Smith, Edwin, discoverer of the Edwin Smith Papyrus (1822-1906), 182
Smith, Sir G. Elliot, 92, 136*
Smith, Vincent, 442*, 445, 481, 499-500
Smith, William Robertson, Scotch Orientalist (1846-1894), 330*
Smith Papyrus, 182
Snefrunofr (snĕf'-rōō-nō'-fĕr), Egyptian singer, 192
Socrates, Greek philosopher (469-399 B.C.), 193, 352, 428, 657, 659, 669, 751†, 841
Sodum (sŏd'-ŭm), 311, 355
Sogdiana (sŏg-dē-ā'-nà), 355
Sogdians, 397†
Sokokuji (sō-kō-kōō-jē), 904
Solomon, King of the Jews (974-937 B.C.), 304, 305-308, 309*, 312, 314, 315, 332, 335, 337, 339, 342, 346*, 348, 479
Solomon Islands, 10, 34
Solon, Athenian lawgiver (640-558 B.C.), 290, 647
Solutrian Culture, 94
Soma (sō'-ma), 403, 405
Soma, Hindu god, 403, 404
Somadeva (sō-mà-dā'và), Indian poet (11th century), 579
Somaliland, 46, 94, 189
Somalis, 42-43, 78
Somme River, 90
Somnath (sōm'-nàt), 460
Somnathpur (sōm-nàt-pōōr'), 601
"Son of Heaven," 797-798
Sonata Appassionata, 723
Song Celestial, 541†
Song of Solomon, 341-342, 580
Sonno Jo-i (sôn-nō-jō-ē), 875
Sopdit (sōp'-dĭt), 198
Sophocles, Greek dramatic poet (495-406 B.C.), 611
Sostratus, Greek architect (fl. 300 B.C.), 137
Sothic (sō'-thĭk) cycle, 181*
Sothis (sō'-thĭs), see Sirius
South Africa, 38, 94, 103, 104, 629

South America, 830
South Pole, 107
South Sea Islanders, 16; also see Melanesians, Polynesians
Soyots (sō-yōtz), 45
Spain, 92, 97, 105, 108, 215, 292, 293, 469, 607, 640, 737, 804
Sparta, 355
Spencer, Herbert, English philosopher (1820-1903), 25, 78, 88, 538, 617, 924
Sphinx, 139, 172, 186
Spinoza, Baruch, Dutch Jewish philosopher (1632-1677), 311, 412, 553*, 655, 670*, 734, 867, 871
Spirit Sect, 864
Spring and Autumn Annals, 665
Srong-tsan Gampo (srŏng'-tsän gäm'-pō?), King of Tibet (629-50), 506
State, origins of, 23-25
Statira (stà-tī'-rà), wife of Artaxerxes II (ca. 380 B.C.), 375*
Stein, Sir M. Aurel, 506, 594, 728-729, 739
Still Bay Culture, 94
Stoicism, 195, 524
Stone Age, 102, 104; Old, 91, 93, 94, 104; New, 91, 99, 100, 101, 104
Stonehenge, 102
Story of Sinuhe, 174-175
Story of the Shipwrecked Sailor, 174
Strabo, Greek geographer (63? B.C.-A.D. 24?), 137*, 227, 357†, 294, 356, 357*, 442, 492*, 495
Strange Stories, 718
Strasbourg cathedral, 611
Stream of Kings, 579
Strindberg, August, Swedish dramatist and man of letters (1849-1912), 643
Subhadda (sōō-bàd'-dà), Buddhist radical (ca. 480 B.C.), 503
Suez, 109, 135, 214, 315
Sugawara (sōō-gä-wä-rà) family, 835
Sugawara Michizane (mĭch-ĭ-zä-nĕ'), patron saint of Japanese literature (845-903), 835, 867
Suicide, in primitive societies, 53; in India, 502; in China, 646; in Japan, 53, 848-849
Suiko (sōō-ē-kō), Empress of Japan (593-628), 833, 899
Sukkoth (sōōk'-kōth), 332
Suleiman (sōō'-là-män'), Moslem traveler (9th century), 756
Sultanpur (sōōl-tän'-pōōr'), 589
Sumatra (sōō-mä'-trà), 21, 64, 99*, 603, 780

Sumeria (soo mē'-rĕ-à), 104-105, 106, 107, 108, 116-136, 218, 226, 237*, 249, 250, 254, 255, 261, 262, 265, 270, 272, 300, 395, 479, 509, 532, 584, 641

Summer Palace, 741, 742, 778, 805

Sumner, William Graham, 17-18, 24

Sun worship, 59, 60; in Egypt, 198, 206-210, 212; in Babylonia, 234; in Persia, 365, 366, 369-370, 371 (also see Zoroastrianism); in India, 402, 403

Sun Yat-sen (soon'-yăt'-sĕn'; Chinese swŭn yŭn), President of China (1866-1925), 626, 809-812, 813

Sung (soong), Chinese censor (ca. 1800), 798

Sung (state), 678-679, 680, 688

Sung, Prince of (ca. 310 B.C.), 683

Sung Dynasty, 675, 724, 727, 735, 736, 740, 746, 751, 755, 756, 764, 779, 780, 782, 866, 872, 899, 904, 912

Sung K'ang (soong käng), Chinese pacifist (ca. 320 B.C.), 685

Sung Ping (bǐng), Chinese philosopher (ca. 425 B.C.), 679

Sung Shan (shän) (mountain), 742

Sung Yüeh Ssu (ē'-ŭ-soo), 742

Sung-shu (shoo), 780

Superior, Lake, 105

Sur Das (soor däs), Indian poet (1483-1573), 580

Surat (soo-rät') 393

Surgery, origins of, 81; in Egypt, 182; in Babylonia, 258; in Judea, 331; in India, 531; in China, 782

Surpa-nakha (soor'-pà-nà-kà), 569

Surya (soor'-yà), 403, 599

Surya Siddhana, 528

Susa (soo'-sà), 105, 108, 117, 119, 121, 122, 219, 283, 356*, 358, 362, 380, 384, 440, 442, 642

Sushruta (soosh'-roo-tà), Indian physician (ca. 500 B.C.), 530, 531, 532

Susiana (soo-sĕ-ä'-nà), 354

Suti (soo'-tē), Egyptian architect (ca. 1400 B.C.), 206*

Sutras (soot-ràz), 407*, 418, 428, 534

Sutta, Pali form of sutra, q.v.

Suttee (sŭt-tē), 48, 149, 402, 494-496, 793

Swadeshi (swà-dā'-shĕ), 632

Swaraj (swà-räj'), 555, 626, 632

Swastika (swä'-stĭ-kà), 600

Swift, Jonathan, Irish satirist and churchman (1667-1745), 11

Swinburne, Algernon Charles, English poet (1837-1909), 195

Switzerland, 92, 98, 99, 104

Synge, John Millington, Irish dramatist (1871-1909), 53*

Syria, 94, 153, 154, 155, 160, 188, 191, 206, 212, 214, 215, 222, 224, 245, 269, 286, 292, 296-297, 299, 300, 317, 318, 321, 355, 447, 450

Syrians, 217, 267

Systema Brahmanicum (sĭs-tā'-mà brämän'-ĭ-cŭm), 391*

Szechuan (sŭ-chwän') province, 729, 749, 779, 786

Szuma Ch'ien (soo'-mä chē-än'), Chinese historian (born 145 B.C.), 651, 652, 653*, 658*, 695, 699, 718-719

Szuma Kuang (gwäng), Chinese historian (fl. 1076), 719, 726

T

Ta Hsüeh (dä shü'-ûh), 665

Tabi-utul-Enlil (tä'-bĕ-oo'-tool-ĕn'-lĭl), King of Nippur, 260-261

Tabus (tà-booz'), 69-70

Tacitus, Caius Cornelius, Roman historian (fl. 55-120), 578

Tagore, Abanindranath (tä-gôr', ä-bä-nĭn'-drà-nàt), Indian artist, 619

Tagore, Davendranath (dä-vĕn'-drà-nàt), Indian reformer, 619

Tagore, Dwijendranath (dwē-jĕn'-drà-nàt), Indian philosopher, 619

Tagore, Gogonendranath (gō-gō-nĕn'-drà-nàt), Indian artist, 619

Tagore, Rabindranath (rä-bĭn'-drà-nàt), Indian poet (1861-   ), 391, 415, 493, 582†, 619-621, 622

Tagtug, 129

Tahiti, 6, 10, 32, 38, 45, 77, 107

Tahito (tä-hē-tō), Japanese poet (665-731), 856

T'ai Tsu (tī dzoo), Chinese emperor (960-976), 724

T'ai Tsung (tī dzoong), Chinese emperor 627-650), 675, 702, 782

T'ai Tsung, Chinese emperor (976-998), 731

T'ai Tsung, Korean emperor (15th century), 730

Taiko (tī-kō), 839

Taine, Hippolyte Adolphe (1828-1893), French critic, 199, 719

T'ai-p'ing (tī-pǐng) Rebellion, 742, 758-759, 805, 915

Taira (tī-rà) family, 835

Tai-shan (tī-shän) (mountain), 787

Taj Mahal (taj' mà-hál'), 473, 609-610, 611, 897
Takamine (tä-kà-mē-nĕ), Japanese scientist, 924
Takayoshi (tä-kä-yō-shē), Japanese painter (ca. 1010), 904
Ta-ki (tä-kĕ), wife of Chou Hsin (ca. 1135 B.C.), 645
Tale of the Water Margins, 718
Talent (money), 306*, 358*
Talikota (tä'-lĭ-kō'-tà), 457, 459
Talleyrand-Périgord, Charles Maurice de, Prince of Benevento, French statesman and wit (1754-1838), 151
Talmud (täl'-mōod), 329, 519
Tambura (tàm-bōo'-ra), 586
Tamerlane (tăm'-ēr-lāne), 463; see Timur-i-lang
Tamil (tà'-mĭl) language, 555, 581
Tamils, 446, 490
Tammuz ((täm'-mōoz), 120, 127, 238-239, 241*, 295, 312, 341
Tamura Maro (tä'-mōo-rà mä-rō), Japanese general (ca. 800), 854
T'ang (täng) Dynasty, 675, 702, 703, 724, 728, 735, 736, 740, 745*, 749, 751, 755, 775, 780, 782, 790, 797, 800, 835
T'ang (state), 683
Tangut (tän'-gōot), 761
Tanjore (tăn-jôr'), 393, 490, 585, 594, 602, 610
Tanka (tän-kà), 880, 926
Tantras (tàn'-tràs), 518, 519, 541
Tao (dou), 653, 689, 783
T'ao Ch'ien (dow chē-ăn'), Chinese poet (365-427), 713-714
T'ao Hung-ching (dou hōong jǐng), Chinese writer (6th century), 782
Taoism (dou'-ĭs-m) 653-658, 675, 728, 731, 741, 746, 748, 754, 786-787
Tao-Te-Ching (dou-dä-jing), 653, 657
Tarahumaras, 7
Tashkent (tàsh-kĕnt'), 453
Tasmanians, 14, 21, 74, 79
Tata (tä-tä) Iron and Steel Company, 622
Tatars (tä'-tĕrz), 701, 750, 770
Tattooing, 85
Tattwas (tàt' twàz), 537-538, 539
Taxation, in Sumeria, 126; in Egypt, 160, 214; in Judea, 308; in Persia, 363; in India, 480; in China, 699; in Japan, 851-852
Taxila (tä'-ksĭ-là), 440, 441-442, 450, 492*, 557
Taylor, Meadows, 601*

Tcheou-ta-Kouan (chē-ōō'-tä-gwän), Chinese diplomat (ca. 1275), 604, 605
Tecunas, 73
Tefnut (tĕf-nōot'), 201
Tejahpala (tä'-jà-pä'-là) Temple, 598
Tekoschet (tä'-kō-shĕt), 189
Tell-Asmar (tĕl-às-mär'), 395*
Tell-el-Amarna (tĕl-ĕl-à-mär'-nà), 188, 205, 211, 212*
Tell-el-Ubaid (tĕl-ĕl-ōōb'-à-ĭd), 133
Tell Halaf (tĕl-hà-läf'), 286
Tello (tĕl'lō), 131
Telugu (tĕl'-ōō-gōō) (dialect), 458, 555
Telugus (tribe), 495
Temple, 307-308, 309, 314, 315, 318, 321, 323, 324, 326, 327, 332, 333, 335, 337
Ten Commandments, 312, 331-339, 374
Ten Thousand (Xenophon's), 284
Tenchi (tĕn-chē), 834
Tenchi Tenno (tĕn-nō), Emperor of Japan (668-671), 833, 850, 877
Teng Shih (tŭng shī), Chinese radical (ca. 530 B.C.), 651-652
Tengri, 60
Tennyson, Alfred, Baron, English poet (1809-1892), 491, 550*, 620
Tepe Gawra (tä'-pä-gôr'-à), 265
Thaïs, Athenian courtesan (4th century B.C.), 82
Thales, Greek philosopher and scientist (640-546 B.C.), 533, 552
Thamos (thä'-mŏs), King of Egypt (mythical), 76
Thanatopsis, 408
Thapsacus (thăp'-sà-kŭs), 228
Thebes, 140, 151, 153, 154, 155, 167, 190, 191, 210, 213, 217*, 248, 307, 314, 449
Théodut, Father, 13
Theosophy, 554*, 616†
Third Dynasty (Egypt), 140, 147, 165
Thirteen, as an unlucky number, 79
Thomas, Elbert, 693*
Thoreau, Henry David, American writer (1817-1862), 79, 631, 889
Thoth (thōth), 76, 147, 179, 199, 203*, 277*, 331‡
Thracians, 494
Thucydides, Greek historian (ca. 471-399 B.C.), 578, 719
Thugs, 499-500
Thutmose (thŭt'-mōz), Egyptian artist (ca. 1370 B.C.), 188, 192
Thutmose I, King of Egypt (1545-1514 B.C.), 153, 154, 185

Thutmose II, King of Egypt (1514-1501), 153

Thutmose III, King of Egypt (1479-1447 B.C.), 111, 142, 143, 153, 154-155, 160, 178, 181, 184, 185, 188, 189, 205, 210, 222, 270, 300, 302*

Thutmose IV, King of Egypt (1420-1412 B.C.), 155

Ti, 60

Tiamat (tyä'-màt), 236-237, 278

Tiberius Claudius Nero Cæsar, Roman emperor (14-37), 381

Tibet (tĭ-bĕt), 38, 39, 45, 140, 329, 391, 401, 449, 501, 504, 506-507, 589, 602, 606, 767, 798

Tientsin (tĭnt'-sĭn), 765, 778, 805

Tiglath-Pileser (tĭg'làth-pĭ-lē'-zēr) I, King of Assyria (1115-1102 B.C.), 266-267, 280

Tiglath-Pileser III, King of Assyria (745-727 B.C.), 267, 270

Tigris (tī'-grĭs) River, 117, 118, 119, 124, 135, 136, 218, 221, 265, 286†, 299, 756

Tilak (tĭ'-làk), Bal Gangadhar, Indian Nationalist leader (1856-1920), 626, 632

Timbuktu, 3

Timon of Athens, 175, 689

Timur-i-lang (tĭ-mōōr'-ĭ-lang'), Turkish conqueror (1336-1405), 463, 464, 465

Ting (dĭng), Duke of Lu (ca. 500 B.C.), 662, 663

Tinnevelly (tĭn'-nē-vēl'-lĭ), 456

Tirumalai Nayyak (tĭ'-rōō-mà-lī nä'-yàk), Prince of Madura (1623-1659), 600, 602

Tiruvallaver (tĭ'-rōō-vàl'-lōō-vàr), Indian poet (ca. 950), 581-582

Tiy (tē-ḗ) mother of Amenhotep IV (ca. 1400 B.C.), 168

Tlingits, 6

To no-Chujo (tō-nō-chōō-jō), 893

Toba Sojo (tō-bà sō-jō), Japanese painter (1053-1140), 904

Tod, James, British army officer and Orientalist (1782-1835), 455, 492†, 496*

Todaiji (tō-dī-jē) Temple, 892, 895

Todas, 39

Togo, Count Heihachiro (tō-gō, hà-hà-chē-rō), Japanese naval hero (1847-1934), 919

Togos, 42

Tokugawa (tō-kōō-gä-wà) Shogunate, 829, 838, 844, 846, 852, 853, 855, 865, 866, 871, 875, 877, 886, 905, 906, 914

Tokyo (tō-kyō), 830, 841, 847, 852*, 862, 867, 873, 877, 884, 886, 895, 905, 910, 914, 919, 920*, 921, 931

Tokyo, University of, 877, 926

Toledo, Spain, 896

Tolstoy, Count Leo Nikolaiëvitch, Russian writer and reformer (1828-1910), 627, 631, 693

Tom Jones, 718, 882, 891

Tom Sawyer, 410

Tomb of Nakht, 191

Tools, in primitive societies, 12-13; in prehistoric cultures, 93-95, 100-101, 103, 104; in Sumeria, 124; in Egypt, 145; in Babylonia, 227; in India, 395, 601*

Topheth (tō'-fĕt), 321

Torah (tō'-rà), 328

Toramana (tō-rà-mä'-nà), Hunnish King (500-502), 452

Torres Straits, 85

Torture, in Egypt, 162; in Assyria, 272, 275-276; in Persia, 361-362, 373; in India, 483; in China, 797; in Japan, 850

Toru Kojomoto (tō-rōō kō-jō-mō-tō), Japanese engraver (fl. 1687), 907-908

Tosa Gon-no-kumi (tō-sà gŏn-nō-kōō-mē), Japanese painter (ca. 1250), 903

Tosa School (of Japanese painting), 843, 903-904

Toson (tō-sŏn), Japanese novelist and poet, 926-927

Totemism, 61-62, 76-77, 332

Tours, 460

"Towers of Silence," 372

Toyama, Mitsuru, Japanese nationalist leader (1855-   ), 923

Trade, in primitive societies, 15-16; in prehistoric cultures, 101; in Sumeria, 125, 131, 135; in Egypt, 135, 160-161; in Babylonia, 228; in Assyria, 274; in Phoenicia, 292-293; in Judea, 306; in Persia, 358; in India, 400, 479; in China, 778-779, 815; in Japan, 932

Trajan, Marcus Ulpius, Roman emperor (98-117), 364

Trans-Baikalia, 932

Transport, in primitive societies, 14-15; in prehistoric cultures, 101; in Sumeria, 125; in Egypt, 160; in Babylonia, 227; in Phoenicia, 292-293; in Persia, 358; in India, 400, 444-445, 479; in China, 778; in Japan, 920†, 934

Trans-Siberian Railroad, 931

Travancore (trà'-vàn-kôr'), 456

Trebizond (trĕb'-ĭ-zŏnd'), 766

Tribe, the, 22

Trichinopoly (trĭ'-chĭ-nŏp'-ō-lĭ), 393, 602

Trobriand Islanders, 31, 54

Troubadours, 177

Troy, 91, 107, 215
Ts'ai Lun (tsī lōōn), inventor of paper (ca. 105), 727-728
Tseng Ts'an (dzŭng tsän), Confucian disciple (ca. 490 B.C.), 665
Ts'i (state), see Ch'i (state)
Ts'i, Duke of, see Ch'i, Duke of
Tsin, see Chin
Tsing-tao (chĭng dow), 639*, 929
Tsoa (tsō-à), Chinese general (ca. 740), 715
Tso-chuan (dzō jwăn), 718, 723
Tsu Ch'ung-chih (dzōō chōōng-jĕ), Chinese mathematician (430-501), 781
Tsunayoshi (tsōō-nà-yŏsh-ĕ), Japanese shogun (1680-1709), 843
Tsurayaki (tsōō-rŭ-yä-kĕ), Japanese poet (883-946), 858, 863, 878-879
Tsushima (tsōō-shē-mà), 919
Tsze-kung (tsŭ-kōōng), Confucian disciple (ca. 500 B.C.), 664, 666, 670, 671-672
Tsze-loo (tsŭ-lōō), Confucian disciple (ca. 500 B.C.), 662, 663, 664, 666, 669
Tuaregs, 46, 47
Tu Fu (dōō fōō), Chinese poet (712-770), 707, 713, 714-717, 747
Tukaram (tōō-kà-räm'), Indian poet (1608-1649), 581
Tulsi Das (tōōl'-sē däs), Indian poet (1532-1624), 581
Tung Cho (tōōng jō), Boxer general, 746
Tungabadra (tōōn'-gà-bà'-drà) River, 457
T'ungchow (tōōng-jō), 808*
Tungus, 21
Tun-huang (tōōn hwäng,) 728
Tunis, 94
Turgeniev, Ivan, Russian novelist and dramatist (1818-1883), 687
Turin Musuem, 188
Turkestan, 108, 140, 506, 571, 594, 606, 642, 728, 729, 739, 741, 767, 779, 902
Turkey, 703
Turks, 24*, 154, 286†, 362, 450, 459, 464*, 756
Tutenkhamon (tōōt'-ängk-ä'-měn), King of Egypt (1360-1350 B.C.), 141, 155, 191, 213
Tutenkhaton (tōōt-ěn-khä'-tŏn), see Tutenkhamon
Twelfth Dynasty (Egypt), 151, 185, 187
Twenty-one Demands, 813, 928-929
Twenty-second Dynasty (Egypt,) 185
Twoshtri (twàsh'-trĭ), 492
Tycoon, 839
Tyre (tīr), 106, 227, 228, 292, 294, 295, 303, 306, 308, 317, 318, 324, 337, 384

T'zu Hsi (tzŭ shē), Chinese dowager empress (1834-1908), 782, 806-808, 810

U

Udaipur (ōō-dī'-pōōr), 393, 475
Udayana (ōō-dä'-yà-nà), Indian scientist (ca. 975), 529
Uganda, 45
Uimala-Kirti (ōō-ē'-mà-là-kēr-tĕ), Buddhist saint, 747
Ujjain (ōōj-jīn'), 451, 557, 575
Ukiyoye (ōō-kǐ-yŏ-yē) engravers, 907, 908, 910
Ulysses, 570
Uma (ōō'-mä), aspect of Kali, 509
Uma no-Kami (ōō-mä-nō-kä-mē), 884
Ungut (ōōn'-gōōt), 765
United Provinces, 486†
United States, 93, 391, 444-445, 737, 805, 806, 808, 809, 813, 815, 829, 835, 891, 915, 917*, 918, 928, 929-930, 931, 932-933
United States Army Medical Corps, 925
United States Bureau of Standards, 400
Unkei (ōōn-kā), Japanese woodcarver (1180-1220), 897*
Untouchables, see Outcastes
Upanishads (ōō-pän'-ĭ-shàdz), 58, 391, 404, 407, 409, 410-415, 416, 417, 419, 470, 542, 545, 546, 547, 551*, 554, 564, 566, 571, 690
Ur (ōōr) 103, 118, 119, 120, 122-123, 132, 133-134, 136, 179, 215-234, 300, 395
Urartu (ōō-rär'-tōō), 287; see Armenia
Urdu (ōōr'-dōō), 555
Ur-engur (oor-ěn'-gōōr), King of Ur (ca. 2450 B.C.), 122-123, 127, 135
Urfé, Honoré d', French novelist (1568-1626), 756*
Urga (ōōr'-gä), 931
Uriah (ū-rī'-à), Hittite general (ca. 900 B.C.), 305
Ur-nina (ōōr-nē'-nà), King of Lagash (3100 B.C.), 133
Uruguay, 932
Uruk (ōōr'-ōōk), 118, 119, 120, 123, 127, 234, 250, 251, 252, 253
Urukagina (ōō-rōō-ōōk-ä-jē'-nà?), King of Lagash (ca. 2900 B.C.), 120-121, 128, 129
Uruvela (ōōr-ōō-vä'-là), 426
Urvashi (ōōr-vàsh'-ē), 511
Ushas (ōō'-shàz), 403
Ussher, James, Archbishop of Armagh and biblical chronologer (1581-1656), 300
Ussuri (ōōs-sōōr'-ē) River, 806

Utamaro (ōō-tả-mä-rō), Japanese engraver (1753-1806), 908

Uzzah (ŭz'-zả), 69, 313

V

Vaccination, 531-5

Vachaspati (vä'-chảs-pả'-tǐ), Indian scientist (850), 529

Vadnagar (vảd-nả'-gảr), 599

Vaghbata (väg'-bhả-tả), Indian medical writer (ca. 625), 530

Vaishali (vī'-shả-lě), 419, 422

Vaisheshika (vī-shä'-shǐ-kả) philosophy, 528, 536

Vaishnavites (vīsh'-nả-vītz), 508, 598, 606

Vaisyas (vī'-shyảs), 399, 487, 623, 678

Vajjians (vä'-jě-ảns), 398

Valley of the Kings, 154

Valmiki (väl'-mē-kǐ), Indian poet (ca. 100 B.C.), 567, 570

Vanaprastha (vả-nả-prảs'-tả), 522

Vandamme, Dominique-René, French general (1770-1830), 466

Varahamihira (va-rä'-hả-mǐ'-hǐ-rả), Indian astronomer (505-587), 452, 526

Varuna (vả'-rōō-nả), 285, 397†, 402, 403-404

Vasanti (vả-sản'-tē), 501

Vashubandu (vảsh-ōō-bảnd'-ōō), Buddhist commentator (ca. 320-380), 452

Vatsyayana (vảt-syä'-yả-nả), 490

Vayu (vä'-yōō), 402

Vedanta (vả-dän'-tả) philosophy, 541, 546-551, 552, 554, 618, 621, 731

Vedas (vä'-dảz), 365*, 366, 398, 401, 403, 406-409, 416, 419, 420, 433, 485, 486, 493, 505, 507, 511, 523, 534, 535, 542, 546, 553, 557, 562*, 565, 571, 572, 596, 616

Veddahs (věd'-dảz), 14, 21, 56

Vedic (věd'-ǐk) Age, 397-398, 399, 401, 406, 493, 494, 495, 524, 530, 618

Vegetation rites, 65

Velasquez de Silva, Diego Rodriguez, Spanish painter (1599-1660,) 910

Vemana (vě-mä'-nả), Indian poet (17th century), 523-524

Vendidad (věn'-dǐ-dảd), 365‡

Venezuela, 99*

Venice, 2, 479, 640, 753, 760, 766, 769, 776

Venus, 60, 235, 238, 255

Venus (planet), 257

Versailles, 704*, 835

Victoria (Australia), 50

Victoria Institute, Madras, 585

Vidarbha (vǐ'-dảr'-bả), 557

Videhas (vǐ-dä'-hảz), 533, 567

Vijayanagar (vē'-jả-yả-nả'-gảr) (city), 456, 457-458, 459

Vijayanagar (state), 456-459, 477†, 495, 602

Vikramaditya Chalukya (vǐ-krảm-ä'-dǐt-yả chä'-lōōk-yả), King of Magadha (1076-1126), 457*, 602

Vikramaditya Gupta (vǐ-kram-ä'-dǐt-ya gōōp'-tả), King of Magadha (380-413), 451, 478, 576

Vimala (vǐ'-mả-lả) Temple, 598-599

Vina (vē-nä'), 586

Vinaya (vǐ'-nả-yả), 428*

Vinaya Pitaka, 589

Vinci, Leonardo da, Italian artist (1452-1519), 97, 182, 589, 590, 751, 905, 912

Virginity, in primitive societies, 45-46

Virocana (vē-rō-kä'-nả), 416

Virupaksha (vǐ-rōō'-päk-shả) Temple, 602

Vishnu (vǐsh'-nōō), 402, 413*, 458, 506, 507, 508, 511, 523, 524, 552, 565, 588, 590, 594, 598, 602, 604, 625

Vishnupurana, 511-513

Vishtaspa (vǐsh-tảs'-pả), 364; *see* Hystaspes

Vispered (vǐs'-pēr-ěd), 365‡

Vivasvat (vǐ-vảs'-vảt), 403

Vivekananda, Swami (vē-vả-kän'-ản-dả, swä'-mě) (Narendranath Dutt), Indian philosopher (1863-1902), 617*, 618

Vizierate, in Egypt, 162-163

Vladivostok (vlả-dǐ-vǒs-tǒk'), 932

Volga River, 355

Vologesus (vǒl-ō-jē'-zus) V, King of Parthia (209-222) 365‡

Voltaire (François Marie Arouet de), French writer (1694-1778), 348, 445, 511, 550, 578, 594, 639, 657, 683, 688, 693, 695, 768, 788-789

Vorderasiatisches Museum, Berlin, 225†

Vyasa (vyả'-sả), the Indian Homer, 511, 561

W

Wabunias, Queen of the, 86

Wagakusha (wä-gả-kōō-shả) scholars, 874

Wages, in Egypt, 159, 214; in Babylonia, 231; in Persia, 363; in India, 481; in China, 816; in Japan, 852, 921

Wagner, Richard, German composer (1813-1883), 58

Wagon-wheel, 14, 117

Wales, 92

Waley, Arthur, 703†, 704*, 714, 883

Wallace, Alfred Russel, English biologist and naturalist (1822-1913), 25-26

Wang An-shih (wäng än-shǐ), Chinese so-
cialist statesman (fl. 1070), 724-726
Wang Chieh (wäng jē'-ŭh), Chinese printer
(fl. 868), 729
Wang Hsi-chih (wäng shē-jǐ), Chinese cal-
ligrapher (ca. 400), 745*
Wang Mang (wäng mäng), Chinese em-
peror (5-25), 700-701
Wang Shu-ho (wäng shŏō-hō), Chinese
medical writer (ca. 300), 782
Wang Wei (wäng wā), Chinese painter
(699-759), 748-749
Wang Yang-ming (wäng yäng-mǐng), Chi-
nese philosopher (1472-1528), 733-735, 748,
871
Wan-li (wän-lē), see Shen Tsing
War, in primitive societies, 22-23
War and Peace, 718
Ward, C. O., 302
Ward, Lester Frank, American sociologist
(1841-1913), 23
Warfare, Sumerian, 126; Assyrian, 270-271,
272-273; Persian, 360; Indian, 443; Chinese,
647; Japanese, 918 (see, also, Samurai)
Warka, see Uruk
Warwick, Richard Neville, Earl of ("The
King-Maker"), 834
Washington Conference (1922), 929
Waterloo, 613
Wealth, of Egypt, 214, 215; of Babylonia,
229; of Phoenicia, 294; of Judea, 306; of
Persia, 363; of India, 481-482; of China,
703, 763; of Japan, 920
Weaving, in primitive societies, 13; in pre-
historic cultures, 100-101; in Egypt, 191;
in Babylonia, 227; in India, 478-479, 585;
in China, 776-777
Wei (wā) (state), 663, 680, 695
Wei, Dukes of, 663, 666, 688
Wei River, 641, 651
Wei Sheng (wā shŭng), 790
Weigall, Arthur, British Egyptologist (1880-
1934), 134
Weismann, August, German zoölogist (1834-
1914), 529
Wen Ti (wŭn dē), Chinese emperor (179-
157 B.C.), 698
Wen T'ien-hsian (wŭn tē-än'shē-äng), Chi-
nese patriot and scholar (ca. 1260), 764
Wen Wang (wŭn wäng), Chinese emperor
(fl. 1123 B.C.), 650
Westermarck, Edward, 499

Western Han Dynasty, 698*
Westminster Abbey (Henry VII's Chapel),
599
Whistler, James Abbott MacNeill, Ameri-
can etcher and painter (1834-1903), 909,
910, 912
Whitman, Walt, American poet (1819-
1892), 341*, 516, 909
Whitsuntide, 65
Wilde, Oscar O'Flahertie Fingal Wills,
Irish poet and dramatist (1856-1900), 858-
859
Wilhelm Meister, 883
Wilson, Thomas Woodrow, President of
the United States (1856-1924), 467
Winckler, Hugo, German Assyriologist
(died 1913), 286
Winter Palace Hotel, at Luxor, 140
Winternitz, M., 536*, 579
Wisdom of Amenope, 167
Wolff, Christian, German philosopher and
mathematician (1679-1754), 693
Woman, position of, in primitive societies,
30-35, 69-70; in Sumeria, 129-130; in
Egypt, 164-167; in Babylonia, 247-248; in
Assyria, 275; in Judea, 333, 334, 339; in
Persia, 375; in India, 400-401, 493-496; in
China, 792, 819-820; in Japan, 860-861
Woodward, Sir Arthur Smith, 92
Woolley, C. Leonard, 119, 130, 395†
Woosung (wŏō'-sŏōng), 778
Wordsworth, William, English poet (1770-
1850), 754, 858, 883
Works and Days, 329‡
World Court, 931
World's Columbian Expedition, 618
Writing, 135; origins of, 14, 76-77, 104-106;
in Sumeria, 118*, 130-131, 135; in Egypt,
131, 135, 144-145, 171-173; in Babylonia,
119*, 131, 248-249; in the Hittite Empire,
286-287; in Phoenicia, 295-296, 298; in
Persia, 357; in India, 406-407; in China,
76, 745*, 772-773; in Japan, 76, 877
Wu Shu (wŏō shŏō), Chinese encyclopedist
(947-1002), 731
Wu Tao-tze (wŏō dow-dzŭ), Chinese
painter (born ca. 700), 749-750
Wu Ti (wŏō dē), Chinese emperor (140-
87 B.C.), 675, 698-700, 779
Wu Wang, Chinese emperor (1122-1115
B.C.), 686
Wu Yi (wŏō yē), Chinese emperor (1198-
1194 B.C.), 644, 677
Wu-tai-shan (wŏō-dī-shän), 742

X

"Xanadu" (kän'-á-dōō), 761*
Xanthippe, Greek, wife of Socrates (ca. 470-400 B.C.), 165
Xavier, St. Francis, Apostle of the Indies (1506-1552), 469-471
Xenophon, Greek historian and general (445-355 B.C.), 284, 352
Xerxes (zêrx'-ēz) I, King of Persia (485-464 B.C.), 222*, 249, 294, 358, 360, 373, 378, 379, 381-382, 383, 384
Xerxes II, King of Persia (425 B.C.), 382

Y

Yahu (yä'-hōō), 310; see Yahveh
Yahveh (yä'-vä), 210, 211, 302, 305, 307, 309, 310-313, 318, 320, 321, 323, 324, 325, 326, 329, 332, 333, 335, 336, 338, 340, 344, 345, 346, 348, 349, 370
Yajnavalkya (yäj'-nà-vàl-kyà), 410-411, 413, 414-415, 533
Yajur-veda (yàj'-ōōr-vä'-dà), 407
Yakuts, 38, 52
Yama (yä'-mà), 405, 408-409, 516, 543
Yami (yä'-mē), 408-409
Yang and yin (yäng, yĭn), 650, 732, 783
Yang Chu (yäng jōō), Chinese Epicurean philosopher (fl. 390 B.C.), 679-682
Yang Kwei-fei (gwä-fä) (died 755), 704, 707, 708, 714*, 715
Yang-tze (yäng-dzŭ) River, 641*, 806
Yano Yeitoku (yä-nō yä-tō-kōō), Japanese sculptor (ca. 1590), 895
Yao (you), Chinese emperor (2356-2255 B.C.), 643, 661, 676, 687, 689
Yariba, 43
Yashts (yäsh-t-s), 365‡
Yasna (yäs'-nà), 365‡, 367
Yasumaro (yä-sōō-mä-rō), Japanese historian (ca. 712), 885
Yedo (yä-dō), 841; see Tokyo
Yeishin Sozu (yä-shĭn sō-zōō), Japanese painter (ca. 1017), 903
Yellow River, see Hoang-ho
Yellow Sea, 641, 863
Yemen (yĕm'-ĕn), 135
Yen Hwuy (yän hwē), Confucian disciple (ca. 500 B.C.), 660
Yoga (yō'-gà), 504, 541-545, 564
Yoga-sutras, 543
Yogis (yō'-gēz), 541-542, 545, 614
Yokohama (yō-kō-hä-mà), 830, 920

Yomei (yō-mä), Emperor of Japan (died 586), 833
Yoni (yō'-nĭ), 519, 520
Yoritomo (yôr-ĭ-tō-mō), Japanese dictator (1186-1199), 837
Yoritomo, Japanese shogun (13th century), 899
Yoshimasa (yōsh-ĭ-mä-zà), Japanese shogun (1436-1480), 838, 905
Yoshimitsu (yōsh-ĭ-mĭt-sōō), Japanese shogun (1387-1395), 838, 865†, 895, 904
Yoshimune (yōsh-ĭ-mōō-nế), Japanese shogun (1716-1745), 843-844, 850-851, 873, 914, 927
Yoshiwara (yōsh-ĭ-wä-rà), 862
"Young Folk of the Pear Garden," 721
Young India, 631
Young, Thomas, English philosopher and scholar (1773-1829), 145*
Yozei (yō-zä), Emperor of Japan (877-949), 834
Yü (ü), Chinese emperor (2205-2197 B.C.), 644, 680, 737-738, 739
Yu Tze (yōō-dzŭ), Chinese philosopher (ca. 1250 B.C.), 650
Yuan Chwang (yōō-än' chwäng'), Chinese traveler in India (7th century), 421, 446, 449, 453-454, 456, 481, 497, 499, 501, 521, 531, 557, 589, 593*, 594, 702
Yuan (yōō-än') Dynasty, 757; see Mongol Dynasty
Yuan Shi-kai (yōō-än' shĭ-kī), President of China (1848-1916), 811
Yucatan, 2, 90, 107
Yudishthira (yōō-dĭsh-tē'-rà), 516, 561, 570
Yuga (yōō'-gà), 513
Yün Kan (ün kän), 739
Yun Men (yōōn mŭn), 740
Yung Lo (yōōng lō), Chinese emperor 1403-1425), 731, 742, 767

Z

Zagros (zä-grōs) Mountains, 122
Zapouna (zä-pōō'-nà), 296
Zarathustra (zä-rà-thŭs'-trà), Median sage (660-583 B.C.), 331‡, 364-368, 370, 371, 372, 374, 375*, 422*
Zechariah (zĕk-à-rī'-à), Hebrew prophet (ca. 520 B.C.), 294
Zedekiah (zĕd-ế-kĩ'-à), King of Judah 597-586 B.C.), 321-322, 323, 324
Zen (zĕn), 864, 872, 903
Zend (language), 357, 397†

Zend-Avesta (zĕnd-à-vĕs'-tà), 350, 357, 364, 365-366, 369, 370, 374, 376, 406

Zengoro Hozen (zĕn-gō-rō hō-zĕn), Japanese potter (died 1855), 901

Zeno, Greek philosopher (ca. 342-270 B.C.), 553

Zephaniah (zĕf-à-nĭ'-à), Hebrew prophet (ca. 630 B.C.), 345*

Zerubbabel (zĕr-ŭb'-à-bĕl), Hebrew prince (fl. 520 B.C.), 327

Zeus, 60, 402

Ziggurats (zĭg'-gŏŏ-rătz), 133

Zophar (zō'-fär), 344

Zoroaster (zō'-rō-ăs'-tĕr), *see* Zarathustra

Zoroastrianism, 351, 354, 364-372, 374, 405, 469, 471, 508*

Zoser (zō'-sĕr), King of Egypt (ca. 3150 B.C.), 147, 186, 189

Zulus, 48, 57

About the Authors

WILL DURANT was born in North Adams, Massachusetts, in 1885. He was educated in the Catholic parochial schools there and in Kearny, New Jersey, and thereafter in St. Peter's (Jesuit) College, Jersey City, New Jersey, and Columbia University, New York. For a summer he served as a cub reporter on the New York *Journal*, in 1907, but finding the work too strenuous for his temperament, he settled down at Seton Hall College, South Orange, New Jersey, to teach Latin, French, English, and geometry (1907–11). He entered the seminary at Seton Hall in 1909, but withdrew in 1911 for reasons which he has described in his book *Transition*. He passed from this quiet seminary to the most radical circles in New York, and became (1911–13) the teacher of the Ferrer Modern School, an experiment in libertarian education. In 1912 he toured Europe at the invitation and expense of Alden Freeman, who had befriended him and now undertook to broaden his borders.

Returning to the Ferrer School, he fell in love with one of his pupils, resigned his position, and married her (1913). For four years he took graduate work at Columbia University, specializing in biology under Morgan and Calkins and in philosophy under Woodbridge and Dewey. He received the doctorate in philosophy in 1917, and taught philosophy at Columbia University for one year. In 1914, in a Presbyterian church in New York, he began those lectures on history, literature, and philosophy which, continuing twice weekly for thirteen years, provided the initial material for his later works.

The unexpected success of *The Story of Philosophy* (1926) enabled him to retire from teaching in 1927. Thenceforth, except for some incidental essays, Mr. and Mrs. Durant gave nearly all their working hours (eight to fourteen daily) to *The Story of Civilization*. To better prepare themselves they toured Europe in 1927, went around the world in 1930 to study Egypt, the Near East, India, China, and Japan, and toured the globe again in 1932 to visit Japan, Manchuria, Siberia, Russia, and Poland. These travels provided the background for *Our Oriental Heritage* (1935) as the first volume in *The Story of Civilization*. Several further visits to Europe prepared for Volume II, *The Life of Greece* (1939) and Volume III, *Caesar and Christ* (1944). In 1948, six months in Turkey, Iraq, Iran, Egypt, and Europe provided perspective for Volume IV, *The Age of Faith* (1950). In 1951 Mr. and Mrs. Durant returned to Italy to add to a lifetime of gleanings for Volume V, *The Renaissance* (1953); and in 1954 further studies in Italy, Switzerland, Germany, France, and England opened new vistas for Volume VI, *The Reformation* (1957).

Mrs. Durant's share in the preparation of these volumes became more and more substantial with each year, until in the case of Volume VII, *The Age of Reason Begins* (1961), it was so pervasive that justice required the union of both names on the title page. The name Ariel was first applied to his wife by Mr. Durant in his novel *Transition* (1927) and in his *Mansions of Philosophy* (1929) —now reissued as *The Pleasures of Philosophy*.

With the publication of Volume X, *Rousseau and Revolution*, the Durants have concluded over four decades of work.

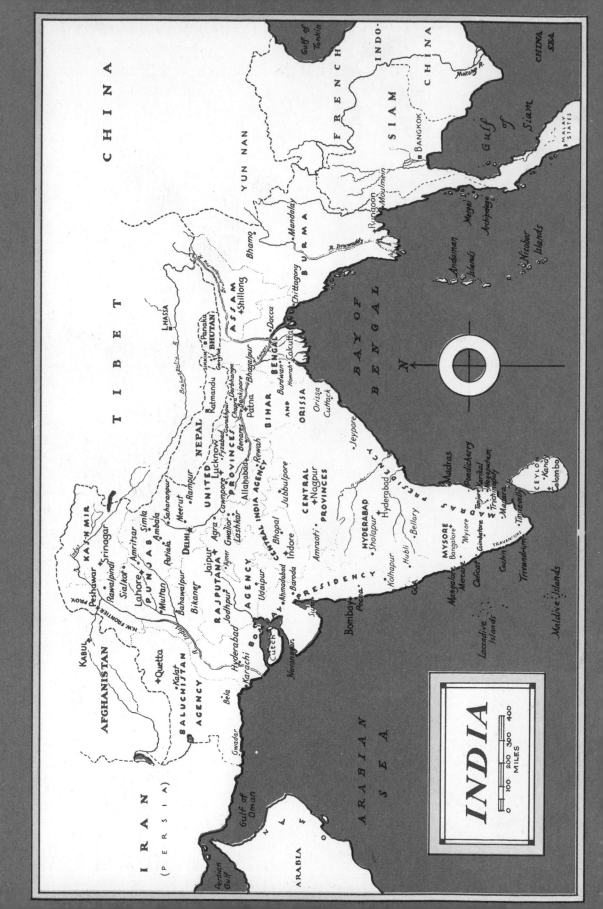